International Directory of
COMPANY
HISTORIES

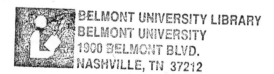

International Directory of
COMPANY HISTORIES

VOLUME 57

Editor

Jay P. Pederson

ST. JAMES PRESS®

Detroit • New York • San Diego • San Francisco • Cleveland • New Haven, Conn. • Waterville, Maine • London • Munich

THOMSON

GALE

International Directory of Company Histories, Volume 57

Jay P. Pederson, Editor

Project Editor
Miranda H. Ferrara

Editorial
Erin Bealmear, Joann Cerrito, Jim Craddock, Stephen Cusack, Peter M. Gareffa, Kristin Hart, Melissa Hill, Margaret Mazurkiewicz, Carol A. Schwartz, Christine Tomassini, Michael J. Tyrkus

Imaging and Multimedia
Randy Bassett, Lezlie Light

Manufacturing
Rhonda Williams

LIBRARY OF CONGRESS CATALOG NUMBER 89-190943

ISBN: 1-55862-493-7

BRITISH LIBRARY CATALOGUING IN PUBLICATION DATA

International directory of company histories. Vol. 57
I. Jay P. Pederson
33.87409

Printed in the United States of America
10 9 8 7 6 5 4 3 2 1

86941

CONTENTS _____

Company Histories

PREFACE

The St. James Press series *The International Directory of Company Histories (IDCH)* is intended for reference use by students, business people, librarians, historians, economists, investors, job candidates, and others who seek to learn more about the historical development of the world's most important companies. To date, *IDCH* has covered over 6,150 companies in 57 volumes.

Inclusion Criteria

Most companies chosen for inclusion in *IDCH* have achieved a minimum of US$25 million in annual sales and are leading influences in their industries or geographical locations. Companies may be publicly held, private, or nonprofit. State-owned companies that are important in their industries and that may operate much like public or private companies also are included. Wholly owned subsidiaries and divisions are profiled if they meet the requirements for inclusion. Entries on companies that have had major changes since they were last profiled may be selected for updating.

The *IDCH* series highlights 10% private and nonprofit companies, and features updated entries on approximately 45 companies per volume.

Entry Format

Each entry begins with the company's legal name, the address of its headquarters, its telephone, toll-free, and fax numbers, and its web site. A statement of public, private, state, or parent ownership follows. A company with a legal name in both English and the language of its headquarters country is listed by the English name, with the native-language name in parentheses.

The company's founding or earliest incorporation date, the number of employees, and the most recent available sales figures follow. Sales figures are given in local currencies with equivalents in U.S. dollars. For some private companies, sales figures are estimates and indicated by the abbreviation *est.* The entry lists the exchanges on which a company's stock is traded and its ticker symbol, as well as the company's NAIC codes.

Entries generally contain a *Company Perspectives* box which provides a short summary of the company's mission, goals, and ideals, a *Key Dates* box highlighting milestones in the company's history, lists of *Principal Subsidiaries, Principal Divisions, Principal Operating Units, Principal Competitors,* and articles for *Further Reading.*

American spelling is used throughout *IDCH*, and the word ''billion'' is used in its U.S. sense of one thousand million.

Sources

Entries have been compiled from publicly accessible sources both in print and on the Internet such as general and academic periodicals, books, annual reports, and material supplied by the companies themselves.

Cumulative Indexes

IDCH contains three indexes: the **Index to Companies**, which provides an alphabetical index to companies discussed in the text as well as to companies profiled, the **Index to Industries**, which allows researchers to locate companies by their principal industry, and the **Geographic Index**, which lists companies alphabetically by the country of their headquarters. The indexes are cumulative and specific instructions for using them are found immediately preceding each index.

Suggestions Welcome

Comments and suggestions from users of *IDCH* on any aspect of the product as well as suggestions for companies to be included or updated are cordially invited. Please write:

The Editor
International Directory of Company Histories
St. James Press
27500 Drake Rd.
Farmington Hills, Michigan 48331-3535

AB	Aktiebolag (Finland, Sweden)
AB Oy	Aktiebolag Osakeyhtiot (Finland)
A.E.	Anonimos Eteria (Greece)
AG	Aktiengesellschaft (Austria, Germany, Switzerland, Liechtenstein)
A.O.	Anonim Ortaklari/Ortakligi (Turkey)
ApS	Amparteselskab (Denmark)
A.Š.	Anonim Širketi (Turkey)
A/S	Aksjeselskap (Norway); Aktieselskab (Denmark, Sweden)
Ay	Avoinyhtio (Finland)
B.A.	Buttengewone Aansprakeiijkheid (The Netherlands)
Bhd.	Berhad (Malaysia, Brunei)
B.V.	Besloten Vennootschap (Belgium, The Netherlands)
C.A.	Compania Anonima (Ecuador, Venezuela)
C. de R.L.	Compania de Responsabilidad Limitada (Spain)
Co.	Company
Corp.	Corporation
CRL	Companhia a Responsabilidao Limitida (Portugal, Spain)
C.V.	Commanditaire Vennootschap (The Netherlands, Belgium)
G.I.E.	Groupement d'Interet Economique (France)
GmbH	Gesellschaft mit beschraenkter Haftung (Austria, Germany, Switzerland)
Inc.	Incorporated (United States, Canada)
I/S	Interessentselskab (Denmark); Interesentselskap (Norway)
KG/KGaA	Kommanditgesellschaft/Kommanditgesellschaft auf Aktien (Austria, Germany, Switzerland)
KK	Kabushiki Kaisha (Japan)
K/S	Kommanditselskab (Denmark); Kommandittselskap (Norway)
Lda.	Limitada (Spain)
L.L.C.	Limited Liability Company (United States)
Ltd.	Limited (Various)
Ltda.	Limitada (Brazil, Portugal)
Ltee.	Limitee (Canada, France)
mbH	mit beschraenkter Haftung (Austria, Germany)
N.V.	Naamloze Vennootschap (Belgium, The Netherlands)
OAO	Otkrytoe Aktsionernoe Obshchestve (Russia)
OOO	Obschestvo s Ogranichennoi Otvetstvennostiu (Russia)
Oy	Osakeyhtiö (Finland)
PLC	Public Limited Co. (United Kingdom, Ireland)
Pty.	Proprietary (Australia, South Africa, United Kingdom)
S.A.	Société Anonyme (Belgium, France, Greece, Luxembourg, Switzerland, Arab speaking countries); Sociedad Anónima (Latin America [except Brazil], Spain, Mexico); Sociedades Anônimas (Brazil, Portugal)
SAA	Societe Anonyme Arabienne
S.A.R.L.	Sociedade Anonima de Responsabilidade Limitada (Brazil, Portugal); Société à Responsabilité Limitée (France, Belgium, Luxembourg)
S.A.S.	Societá in Accomandita Semplice (Italy); Societe Anonyme Syrienne (Arab speaking countries)
Sdn. Bhd.	Sendirian Berhad (Malaysia)
S.p.A.	Società per Azioni (Italy)
Sp. z.o.o.	Spólka z ograniczona odpowiedzialnoscia (Poland)
S.R.L.	Società a Responsabilità Limitata (Italy); Sociedad de Responsabilidad Limitada (Spain, Mexico, Latin America [except Brazil])
S.R.O.	Spolecnost s Rucenim Omezenym (Czechoslovakia
Ste.	Societe (France, Belgium, Luxembourg, Switzerland)
VAG	Verein der Arbeitgeber (Austria, Germany)
YK	Yugen Kaisha (Japan)
ZAO	Zakrytoe Aktsionernoe Obshchestve (Russia)

$	United States dollar	K	Zambian kwacha
£	United Kingdom pound	KD	Kuwaiti dinar
¥	Japanese yen	L	Italian lira
A$	Australian dollar	LuxFr	Luxembourgian franc
AED	United Arab Emirates dirham	M$	Malaysian ringgit
B	Thai baht	N	Nigerian naira
B	Venezuelan bolivar	Nfl	Netherlands florin
BD	Bahraini dinar	NIS	Israeli new shekel
BFr	Belgian franc	NKr	Norwegian krone
C$	Canadian dollar	NT$	Taiwanese dollar
CHF	Switzerland franc	NZ$	New Zealand dollar
COL	Colombian peso	P	Philippine peso
Cr	Brazilian cruzado	PLN	Polish zloty
CZK	Czech Republic koruny	PkR	Pakistan Rupee
DA	Algerian dinar	Pta	Spanish peseta
Dfl	Netherlands florin	R	Brazilian real
DKr	Danish krone	R	South African rand
DM	German mark	RMB	Chinese renminbi
E£	Egyptian pound	RO	Omani rial
Esc	Portuguese escudo	Rp	Indonesian rupiah
EUR	Euro dollars	Rs	Indian rupee
FFr	French franc	Ru	Russian ruble
Fmk	Finnish markka	S$	Singapore dollar
GRD	Greek drachma	Sch	Austrian schilling
HK$	Hong Kong dollar	SFr	Swiss franc
HUF	Hungarian forint	SKr	Swedish krona
IR£	Irish pound	SRls	Saudi Arabian riyal
ISK	Icelandic króna	TD	Tunisian dinar
J$	Jamaican dollar	W	Korean won

International Directory of

COMPANY
HISTORIES

A.P. Møller - Maersk A/S

Esplanaden 50
DK-1098 Copenhagen K
Denmark
Telephone: (+45) 3363-3363
Fax: (+45) 3363-3501
Web site: http://www.apmoller.com

Public Company
Incorporated: 1904 as Aktieselskabet
   Dampskibsselskabet Svendborg
Employees: 60,000
Sales: $21.38 billion (2002)
Stock Exchanges: Copenhagen
Ticker Symbol: MAERSKA
NAIC: 483111 Deep Sea Freight Transportation; 481111
   Scheduled Passenger Air Transportation; 484110
   General Freight Trucking, Local; 484121 General
   Freight Trucking, Long-Distance, Truckload; 551112
   Offices of Other Holding Companies

A.P. Møller - Maersk A/S (A.P. Møller), known throughout the world for its Maersk shipping line, is a diversified conglomerate operating in the shipping, oil and gas, shipbuilding, retail, IT, and other industries. The company's Maersk Sealand shipping operation is the world's leading container shipper, with 250 vessels in its fleet and a deadweight capacity of more than 12 million tons. Maersk Tankers is one of the world's largest tanker operators, with a fleet of 100 vessels and deadweight capacity of more than 17 million tons. The company also operates a fleet of 45 semi-refrigerated and five fully refrigerated gas carriers under subsidiary Maersk Gas Carriers. The company's Shipping division also offers brokering, logistics, and supply services, and includes South African subsidiary Safmarine, Dutch-Swedish subsidiary Svitzer Wijsmuller, and cargo logistics and ferry operator Norfolkline. In its Oil and Gas division, A.P. Møller controls the concession for the exploration and production of oil and gas in Denmark, in partnership with Shell and Texaco. Together, Møller's Shipping and Oil and Gas—brought together in a complicated ownership structure under two publicly listed

companies, Aktieselskabet Dampskibsselskabet Svendborg and Dampskibsselskabet af 1912, Aktieselskab—contributed more than DKr 89 billion ($10 billion) of A.P. Møller's approximately DKr 144 billion ($18.9 billion) in sales. The remainder is provided through four additional divisions: Industrial, Retail, Air Transport, and IT. Industrial includes Odensk Steel Shipyard, one of the world's leading shipbuilders; Maersk Container Industri, a manufacturer of containers; A/S Roulunds Fabriker Group, a manufacturer of components, such as belts and hoses, for the automotive industry; Maersk Medical, a leading global manufacturer of sterile, single-use medical equipment and supplies. Under Retail, A.P. Møller is Denmark's second largest supermarket operator, through subsidiary Dansk Supermarked A/S, which operates under the Fotex, Netto, Bilko, A-Z, Toj og Sko, and Bugatti retail names in Denmark, England, Germany, Poland, and Sweden. A.P. Møller's Air Transport division is composed of Maersk Air, the leading privately owned airline in Denmark, operating both domestic and international passenger and cargo flights. Last, A.P. Møller's IT division is a leading provider of IT services to the Danish and other markets, including the United States, Japan, Sweden, India, and England. A.P. Møller, which is traded on the Copenhagen stock exchange, remains controlled by the founding Møller family, through Chairman Mærsk McKinney Møller. Since the early 1990s, however, the company's day-to-day operations have been guided by CEO Jess Søderberg.

Founding a Global Shipping Giant at the End of the 19th Century

A.P. Møller's origins trace back to Denmark's shipping industry at the end of the 19th century. In 1886, Peter Maersk Møller was named captain of his first vessel, called the *Laura,* on the funnel of which was placed the emblem of a seven-pointed star—which was later to become known throughout the world as part of the Maersk logo. In 1904 Møller and his son, Arnold Peter Møller, went into the shipping business on their own, founding a new company, Aktieselskabet Dampskibsselskabet Svendborg, or the Steamship Company of Svendborg, based in that Danish town. The Møllers bought their first ship, a used steamship with a deadweight capacity of 2,200 tons. This vessel was given the name *Svendborg* and it, too, sported a

Company Perspectives:

Values and Philosophy: Shipowner A.P. Møller's old saying about "Constant Care" is still an important part of the values in the A.P. Møller Group. An example is the goal-oriented theoretical and practical training of new, young employees which ensures an efficient and resourceful team of personnel. Each staff member, in his or her own individual fashion, is expected to contribute to the reinforcement of the A.P. Møller Group's worldwide position and the continuation and further development of the process which began in Svendborg in 1904.

In the further development of the A.P. Møller Group the keywords will continue to be: Quality, service and reliability.

seven-pointed star, now painted against the blue background that was to remain an integral part of the Maersk logo.

By the end of their first decade in business, the Møllers had built up a fleet of six vessels and had founded a second company, Dampskibsselskabet af 1912, Aktieselskab (The Steamship Company of 1912), which was based in Copenhagen. This company and its ships also adopted the seven-pointed star for their funnels and flags. Over the following decade, the Møllers expanded their shipping business into new directions, adding brokering services in 1914—and becoming one of the world's leading ship brokers over the course of the century—then founding their own shipyard, at Odensk, in 1917. The Odensk Steel Shipyard, with a capacity for building vessels up to 40,000 tons, quickly became an important asset for the company, which saw its fleet top 18 vessels and nearly 30,000 tons of deadweight capacity in 1918.

A.P. Møller formally adopted the Maersk name for its shipping operations in 1928, when it launched a new passenger and cargo liner service operating between the United States and Asia. The name "Maersk" had been Peter Møller's mother's maiden name, and itself was thought to stem from the Danish word "marsk" (marsh). Maersk now set sail to conquer the world's oceans, establishing itself as a major shipping name. At this time, the company added its first tanker operations, with five tankers joining the company's 35-vessel fleet. At the beginning of the 1930s, Møller's total deadweight capacity had topped 160,000 tons. By the end of that decade, the company's fleet had swelled to 46 vessels.

The next generation of the Møller family joined the company in 1940 when Maersk McKinney Møller, the son of A.P. Møller, then aged 26, was named a company partner. Yet the younger Møller's career was nearly cut short before it even began. When the Nazis occupied Denmark in 1940, Maersk Møller left the country, traveling to the United States. A.P. Møller remained behind but refused to allow his company to serve the Nazi occupier and instead placed control of the company's operations under Maersk Møller in the United States. In that way, A.P. Møller's fleet was placed at the disposal of the Allied forces. By the war's end the Maersk fleet had lost more than half of its ships, with deadweight capacity dropping back to 120,000 tons.

With the rest of the European shipping and shipbuilding industries in disarray, A.P. Møller grew strongly in the postwar era. Maersk Møller, as well as the company's headquarters, returned to Denmark in 1947. Yet the company's wartime exile had left its mark, as the company's operations became more and more international in scope, starting with the establishment of a new ship brokering operation, Maersk Company, in the United Kingdom in 1951.

A.P. Møller's shipbuilding arm received a boost in the mid-1950s when it was awarded the contract to build a number of 50,000-ton tankers for the California Shipping Company. Yet the Odensk yard was too small to accommodate tankers of this size, and in 1957 the company started construction of a new yard, in Lindo, which, when it was completed in 1959, gave the company shipbuilding capacity up to 200,000 tons.

Diversifying in the 1960s

While shipping, grouped under the Aktieselskabet Dampskibsselskabet Svendborg and Dampskibsselskabet af 1912, Aktieselskab subsidiaries, remained the core of A.P. Møller's operation, in the 1960s the company began to diversify its holdings. One of the first of the company's expansion efforts came in 1961, when A.P. Møller acquired automotive parts supplier Roulunds Fabriker. That company's history dated back to 1736 and its founding as a ropewalk—where ropes were made. In 1872, Roulunds began production of power transmission belts, an activity that led it to begin supplying components for the nascent automotive industry, including brake linings, added in 1926. In the 1930s, Roulunds' production expanded to include conveyor belts, but by the time of its takeover by Møller, Roulunds had turned its specialty to the automotive market, particularly the original equipment market, winning such contracts as supplying disc brakes for the Volvo I40 in 1966 and fan belts for Ford's European branch in 1967.

A still more significant development for A.P. Møller came in 1962 when the company was awarded the exclusive concession for the exploration and production of oil and gas in Denmark. The company founded a new subsidiary, Maersk Olie og Gas, which formed a joint venture with Texaco and Shell called the Dansk Undergrunds Consortium (DUC). By 1972 DUC had succeeded in starting up production, and production levels later topped 500,000 barrels per day, with gas production reaching one billion cubic meters per day. Olie og Gas also started up operations in Qatar and Algeria.

In 1964, A.P. Møller struck out into yet a new direction when it acquired supermarket group F. Salling A/S. Founded in 1906 as Salling Stormagasin, the division was renamed Dansk Supermarked and grew to become the second largest retail group in Denmark, before spreading out to include stores, under the Netto banner, in Germany, Poland, Sweden, and England.

The death of A.P. Møller in 1965 brought a close to more than 60 years in business, which had seen the company grow from a single vessel to a fleet of nearly 90 vessels and the creation of an internationally operating and diversified business. Maersk McKinney Møller took over control of the company that year and continued the diversification effort begun by his father. The younger Møller proved to have inherited his father's

---

Key Dates:

1904: Peter Maersk Møller and Arnold Peter Møller buy a used steamship and found Aktieselskabet Dampskibsselskabet Svendborg (The Steamship Company of Svendborg).

1912: The Møllers establish a second shipping company, Dampskibsselskabet af 1912, Aktieselskab (Shipping Company of 1912) based in Copenhagen.

1917: The company establishes Odensk shipyards in order to build ships for its own and other fleets.

1928: The company launches liner service between the United States and Asia and establishes the Maersk name for its shipping operations.

1959: A new shipyard at Lindo is completed in order to construct larger vessels.

1961: The company acquires Roulunds Fabriker, the first of a long series of acquisitions that diversifies A.P. Møller beyond shipping.

1962: The company receives exclusive concession for the exploration and production of Denmark's oil and gas reserves and forms DUC partnership with Texaco and Shell.

1969: The company extends Lindo shipyard with a new dry-dock capable of building vessels up to 650,000 tons.

1970: The company founds Maersk Air and takes over Odense-Copenhagen and other flight routes.

1972: DUC begins oil and gas production, and Møller launches its first gas carrier.

1982: A.P. Møller goes public by listing its two shipping companies, Aktieselskabet Dampskibsselskabet Svendborg and Dampskibsselskabet af 1912, Aktieselskab, on the Copenhagen stock exchange.

1985: The company acquires Norfolkline.

1988: The first Panamax container ship is delivered.

1991: Maersk Container Industri is launched to manufacture containers.

1995: The company forms a global cooperation alliance with Sealand Containers.

1999: The company acquires Sealand from CSX, forming Maersk Sealand, and Safmarine, based in South Africa.

2002: The company announces its intention to sell off Roulunds and its medical products subsidiary, Maersk Medical; the company acquires West African liner business from Torm, of Denmark.

---

business acumen, and over the next 30 years was responsible for transforming A.P. Møller into one of the world's leading shipping companies.

The company's next diversification move came in 1968, when it acquired Phama-Plast. That company had been founded just four years earlier as one of the first in Denmark to produce single-use and disposable medical products from plastic. That subsidiary was renamed Maersk Medical. Two years later, A.P. Møller took to the air with the founding of Maersk Air, which assumed the Odense-Funen and Odense-Copenhagen flight routes from Falk Air. Maersk Air began operations in 1970 with a fleet of three new Fokker F-27 Friendships; in 1973 it added to its fleet with five used Boeing 707-720B aircraft. That same year saw the launch of the company's IT services division, which later became an internationally operating subsidiary under the name Maersk IT. The company extended its interest in plastics with the acquisition of Rosti A/S in 1971, which manufactured among other items bottles, themoplastic packing foam, and flowerpots.

The company's oil and gas activities had led it to diversify in other areas as well, such as the formation of Maersk Supply Service, in 1967, providing transportation and other support services for offshore operations. In 1972, the company added the operation of drilling rigs and related oil and gas production units to its list of activities. The beginning of gas production by DUC in 1972 also led the company to found a fleet of dedicated gas tankers, with the reception of the company's first gas tanker that same year. A year later, Maersk became an early entrant into a promising new shipping category—that of the container ship. The company's first container ship was dubbed the *Svendborg Maersk*, a fitting start for what was shaping up as a revolution in international shipping. Indeed, the adoption of containers, which enabled ships to carry larger, yet segmented

loads, enabled the shipping industry to counter the growing competition from the air freight industry.

The adoption of container ships on the one hand, and of the new "supertankers"—vessels with dryweight capacity of more than 200,000 tons introduced at the end of the 1960s—on the other stretched the company's Lindo shipyard to its limit. In 1969 the company began construction of a new drydock capable of building ships with capacities ranging up to 650,000 tons, and by 1973 the company had completed construction of a 330,000-ton vessel. At the same time, the transition of the shipping industry to container ships created a demand for new services, such as the brokerage and consolidation of container cargoes. A.P. Møller entered this market at the end of the 1970s with the formation of the company's Mercantile office, which operated in Taiwan, Hong Kong, and Singapore. That business later became a full-fledged subsidiary, under the name of Maersk Logistics.

Shipping Leader in the 21st Century

A.P. Møller went public in 1982, listing its two operating companies, Aktieselskabet Dampskibsselskabet Svendborg and Dampskibsselskabet af 1912, Aktieselskab, on the Copenhagen stock exchange, while A.P. Møller itself remained a family-controlled partnership and in firm control of its diversified business empire. The company continued to grow strongly through the 1980s. In 1985, for example, A.P. Møller added to its shipping business with the acquisition of Norfolkline. Established in 1960, Norfolkline operated door-to-door logistics services, with an emphasis on frozen products, in Europe, and also operated ferry lines between the United Kingdom and the continent.

The rising importance of container transport led Møller's Odensk operation to begin construction of the new "Panamax" containers—so-called because they reached the maximum width able to pass through the Panama Canal—in 1988. The company's own use of containers led it to extend its industrial operations in 1991 with the formation of Maersk Container Industri, a manufacturer of containers for Maersk and other shippers.

Maersk McKinney Møller retired in 1993 to the position of chairman, tapping Jess Soderberg for the position of CEO. The company continued to develop its shipping wing throughout the world, including acquiring East Asiatic Co., a liner shipping specialist, and forming a vessel-sharing cooperation agreement with the United States' Sealand, a subsidiary of CSX Corporation, in 1991. That agreement was extended into a global alliance in 1995. Then, in 1999, the partners announced that Maersk had acquired Sealand, creating a new world shipping leader, Maersk Sealand, with a fleet of more than 250 vessels. That same year, Maersk had already boosted its container shipping business with the acquisition of South Africa's Safmarine Container Lines.

By then, Maersk had expanded its oil and gas operation as well, beginning oil production in Qatar in 1994. Maersk's shipbuilding continued to make headlines, launching the world's largest container ship in 1996—then topping that vessel again the following year. The Odensk shipbuilding business expanded beyond Denmark at the end of the 1990s, acquiring the Baltija shipyard in Lithuania in 1997 and the Stralsund, Germany-based Volkswerft Stralsund yard in 1998. The Sealand acquisition also had boosted the company's logistics business, which was renamed Maersk Logistics in 2000, and which went on an acquisition drive at the beginning of the new century, acquiring O'Neill & Whitaker of the United States, O'Farrells International in Australia, D'Click in France, and OY Arealog in Finland, all in 2001.

The downturn in the global shipping market in 2001, with a reduction in shipments coupled with an oversupply of containers contributing to slashing rates, brought A.P. Møller into difficulty by 2002. The company announced its intention to shed a number of its noncore operations, including its Roulunds automotive business and the Maersk Medical subsidiary. Meanwhile, the company continued to add to its shipping business, acquiring the West African liner business from fellow Danish shipper Torm in 2002. A.P. Møller also faced pressure from the stock market—in the wake of the Enron scandal, the company

now faced pressure to adopt a greater transparency to its financial statements. Perhaps then A.P. Møller would reveal just how far it had sailed in its first 100 years.

Principal Subsidiaries

A.P. Møller Finance S.A. (Switzerland); A.P. Møller Singapore Pte. Ltd.; A/S Em. Z. Svitzer Group; A/S Roulunds Fabriker Group; Danbor Service A/S Group; Dansk Industri Syndikat A/S; Dansk Supermarked Group; Maersk Air A/S Group; Maersk A/S Group; Maersk Company Canada Ltd.; Maersk Company Limited; Maersk Data A/S Group; Maersk Gulf Ltd.; Maersk Hong Kong Ltd; Maersk Inc. Group; Maersk Medical A/S Group; Maersk Olie og Gas AS Group; Maersk Sealand; Maersk Singapore Pte. Ltd; Maersk South America Ltd.; Norfolkline B.V.; Odense Staalskibsvaerft A/S Group; Rosti A/S Group.

Principal Divisions

Shipping; Oil; Gas; Industrial; Retail; Air Transport; IT.

Principal Competitors

Sumitomo Corporation; TUI AG; FedEx Corporation; Canadian Pacific Ltd.; ThyssenKrupp Materials und Services AG; Tank- og Ruteskibe I/S; Nippon Express Company Ltd.; Exel plc; Danzas Group; Koninklijke Vopak NV; Kuhne und Nagel AG und Co; SCHENKER AG; Kawasaki Kisen Kaisha Ltd.

Further Reading

"A.P. Møller Buys Torm West Africa Service," *Journal of Commerce Week,* September 16, 2002, p. 10.

Cottrill, Ken, "Business As Usual?," *Traffic World,* August 2, 1999, p. 31.

"Denmark Company: Maersk Sealand Expects Loss in '02," *Journal of Commerce,* August 29, 2002

Hahn-Pedersen, Morten, *AP Møller and the Danish Oil,* Copenhagen: JH Schultz Information.

Hornby, Ove, *With Constant Care,* Copehagen: JH Schultz Information.

Porter, Janet, "Recovery Fails to Lift AP Møller's Forecast Loss," *Australasian Business Intelligence,* April 15, 2002.

"Pressure on AP Møller to Be Open," *Australasian Business Intelligence,* April 23, 2002.

—M. L. Cohen

Abatix Corp.

8201 Eastpoint Drive, Suite 500
Dallas, Texas 75227
U.S.A.
Telephone: (214) 381-1146
Toll Free: (800) 426-3983
Fax: (214) 388-0443
Web site: http://www.abatix.com

Public Company
Incorporated: 1984 as T&T Supply Company
Employees: 130
Sales: $59.8 million (2002)
Stock Exchanges: NASDAQ
Ticker Symbol: ABIX
NAIC: 421450 Medical, Dental, and Hospital Equipment
and Supplies Wholesalers

Dallas, Texas-based Abatix Corp. is a publicly traded, regional supplier of more than 30,000 personal protection and safety products to some 6,000 customers involved in the environmental, industrial safety, and construction industries. The company's wholly owned subsidiary International Enviroguard Systems, Inc. (IESI) also sells disposable protective clothing. Abatix operates seven distribution centers located in the states of Arizona, California, Nevada, Texas, and Washington. Chief Executive Officer and founder Terry W. Shaver owns nearly one-third of the company.

Launching the Company in 1983

Shaver founded the predecessor to Abatix, T&T Supply Company, Inc., in May 1983. He gained previous experience in the industrial safety equipment and supply business by working as a sales representative for Dallas distributor Global Safety Resources, Inc. from 1979 to 1983. Before that he worked as a sales rep for Continental Industrial Supply Corp., a Texas company, which distributed industrial equipment and supplies. Shaver also spent a year and a half representing Dallas-based Briggs-Weaver, Inc., another industrial equipment and supply distributor. Shaver enjoyed a successful start with T&T, turning a profit in his first year. The business was officially incorporated in Texas in March 1984. In February 1985 Shaver hired Gary L. Cox, who would become the chief operating officer and an instrumental player in the growth of Abatix. Before coming to T&T Cox served as a vice-president for a Dallas real estate and construction firm, Diamond Built, Inc. Prior to that position, he spent ten years at W.R. Cox Electric, Inc., a Dallas electrical contracting company, where he ultimately served as president from 1980 until 1984.

In 1986, T&T generated revenues in excess of $1 million. At this time the company also became a supplier to the fast-growing asbestos abatement industry. For the first several decades of the 20th century asbestos had been a common fireproofing material used in about 20 percent of all residential, industrial, commercial, and governmental buildings in the United States. Researchers came to realize, however, that the asbestos was brittle, creating a dust that could be breathed in and potentially lead to such diseases as mesothelioma, asbestosis, and lung cancer. As public concern mounted with the release of corroborating studies, Congress in 1984 made $800 million available to the Environmental Protection Agency to launch an asbestos abatement program for schools. Congress then passed further legislation in 1986, the Asbestos School Hazard Abatement Act, while local and state governments enacted similar legislation. For asbestos removal contractors, and suppliers like T&T, the asbestos abatement business held great potential. By some estimates, the asbestos abatement was a $3.5 billion industry by the end of the 1980s, of which the kind of equipment and supplies sold by Abatix accounted for nearly $400 million. By 1988 T&T was well established in its new line of endeavor, prompting management to rename the company Abatix Environmental Corp., which was more in keeping with its new focus, as it worked to become a one-stop supplier for asbestos abatement companies. The company sold one-time purchase items, such as machines that circulated the air in an asbestos containment area, as well as disposable items such as suits and gloves, and polyethylene sheets. In order to better serve its customers, who were often pressed for time, Abatix also carried general hardware items: flashlights, hammers, stapleguns, mops, buckets, and even shampoo and soap for workers who needed to shower after a shift in an asbestos containment area. Another service provided to contractors was a 24-hour hotline.

In December 1988 Abatix opened its second office, located in Hayward, California, a community near Oakland that management believed was underserviced and ripe for its contractor-friendly approach. In March 1989 Abatix went public, selling 300,000 shares in an initial offering that netted $1.1 million. Abatix stock then began trading on the NASDAQ exchange. It was a small cap company that for the year topped $8 million in revenues. Much of the money was earmarked for expanding inventories and the launching of new distribution centers. The company shied away from major markets, leary of cutthroat competition that would trim even closer the industry's small margins. Overall, Abatix was content to grow at a steady, sustainable rate.

Seeking Diversification in the 1990s

By 1990, asbestos abatement accounted for 85 percent of Abatix's annual revenues. Management, worried that it was too committed to this sector, initiated a diversification effort, with the intent of lowering that number to the 50 percent range. Much of this caution was the result of recent debates in academic circles and within the industry about the effects of asbestos cleanup, with many suggesting that cleanup activity might actually cause more contamination than simply leaving the sites alone. Although Abatix and other industry voices were highly critical of this view, the company took steps to beef up its involvement in supplying companies that handled other hazardous materials. At the same time, however, Abatix continued to expand its asbestos operations. In February 1990 it opened an office and distribution operation in Houston and also doubled the size of its Hayward facility to keep up with strong asbestos abatement activity in California, which had been one of the most aggressive states in pursuing removal programs. To better serve this key territory, in 1991 Abatix opened a southern California office in Santa Fe Springs.

Abatix continued to expand in the early 1990s, becoming involved in the construction supply industry in 1992. It also grew via external means for the first time. In October of that year it acquired International Enviroguard Systems, Inc. for 250,000 shares of stock. The Corpus Christi, Texas-based company manufactured sorbents, hydrocarbon-cleanup products, which were mostly used in the hazardous materials industry. Expansion efforts on the asbestos side of the business continued in early 1993 with the opening of distribution centers in Phoenix and Denver. As a result of these moves, Abatix saw its sales grow from $11.4 million in 1992 to more than $19 million in 1993. The company opened an asbestos abatement supply cen-

ter in Seattle in January 1994 and several months later launched an operation in Corpus Christi, in order to better take advantage of its IESI facilities. It was also during 1994 that IESI began to import products that Abatix and other companies distributed in the U.S. market. IESI's original sorbent business, on the other hand, was losing money, and in December 1994 management, believing that there was little chance for recovery, opted to sell these manufacturing assets. Several months later, the Corpus Christi site was sold because the market was simply too small to support the business and all operations were integrated with the Houston office, which served the central and south Texas region. IESI, in the meantime, continued its import business.

In 1994 Abatix recorded revenues of nearly $26 million and posted net income of $217,000. The company took steps the following year to grow its distribution services to the construction tools supply industry. It expanded its Phoenix operation to serve that sector and in December 1995 launched a Las Vegas, Nevada, operation, which concentrated on the construction tool business although it also carried the entire Abatix product line. Revenues grew at a modest rate in 1995, totaling $27.6 million, but the company enjoyed its most profitable year, netting $813,000.

In addition to the asbestos abatement sector Abatix also served contractors involved in lead abatement. Lead-based paints had been known for many years to be hazardous to health, but legal requirements for cleanup had been scant, resulting in modest growth in this area for companies like Abatix. In 1996, however, both the EPA and the Department of Housing and Urban Development instituted new rules concerning lead-based paint in residential properties, whereby home buyers had the right to test for lead-based paint before signing a contract and sellers were required to disclose any known lead hazards. As a consequence the lead abatement business picked up and more asbestos cleanup companies began to enter the field. Abatix also looked to take advantage of this potentially high-growth area.

Abatix in 1996 aggressively pursued the construction and industrial supply industries, as the company topped $33 million in revenues. That number grew to nearly $35 million in 1997, with profits reaching $841,000. A year later, as Abatix focused on growing the construction supply side of the business, it topped 100 in headcount. The company also exceeded $1 million in profits for the first time, $1.17 million on revenues of nearly $38 million.

Acquisitions Due to 1998 Strategy Shift

Also in 1998 the company hired Banc One Capital Corporation to serve as a strategic advisor, to assist management in determining the best way to maintain growth. By November an analysis was complete and the board of directors agreed to pursue a plan to expand via merger and acquisition. Only a few weeks later, in January 1999, this strategy was implemented when Abatix completed the acquisition of Keliher Hardware Company in a $975,000 transaction. The Los Angeles-based industrial supply distributor was well established in the southern California market, with 80 years in business. For Abatix the deal bolstered its presence in this important market and also broadened its product lines. The merged businesses now operated out of Santa Fe Springs, Los Angeles, and Long Beach.

Key Dates:

1983: Terry Shaver launches T&T Supply.
1986: The company begins to supply the asbestos abatement industry.
1988: The company name changes to Abatix Environmental Corp.
1989: The company goes public.
1999: Keliher Hardware Company and North State Supply Co. are acquired; the company's name is changed to Abatix Corp.
2002: The company supplies the domestic preparedness industry.

In early 1999 Abatix completed a comprehensive marketing study that led it to restructure its management team to take advantage of the company's strengths and focus on three strategic areas in order to expand both its range of products and its customer base. Abatix planned, first, to take advantage of the Internet and e-commerce technologies to help customers procure products in a timely and cost-effective manner. In keeping with its approach from the outset of the business, Abatix also was dedicated to creating the first comprehensive supply-chain model in the construction industry, thus bringing the "one-stop shopping" idea to a new level. Finally, Abatix sought to take better advantage of its knowledgeable personnel. More than just selling a broad range of products and providing solid service to customers, Abatix wanted to offer its industry expertise to further assist customers in growing their own businesses.

Abatix also was committed to achieving diversification in its business mix and thus become less dependent on the asbestos abatement industry. In April 1999 the company closed its Denver asbestos operation, which had been experiencing declining sales. Abatix also took further steps to achieve diversification through external means. In May 1999 Abatix announced the $2.8 million acquisition of Phoenix-based North State Supply Company. Abatix paid $2.1 million in cash and assumed $785,000 in debt. North State was an eight-year-old construction tool supply distributor with two locations in the Phoenix market. The business was founded by Dan Birnley, who had more than 20 years of experience in the contractor/industrial supply business. Birnley agreed to stay on to run the Phoenix operation for Abatix. As with the Keliher acquisition, this deal helped Abatix to lessen its dependence on the asbestos abatement supply market. By the end of 1999 asbestos would account for just 35 percent of total sales, a significant decrease from the 48 percent share the previous year. In keeping with its shift in focus, the company also decided at this time to shorten its name from Abatix Environmental Corp. to the more neutral-sounding Abatix Corp. In 1999, revenues grew to $44.6 million, although profits receded somewhat, totaling $461,000.

Abatix devoted much of 2000 to absorbing its acquisitions. It incorporated the new product lines into the company's previous operations. It also devoted time and resources to develop its e-commerce site, in keeping with management's new strategic vision. The company's business was impacted by a black mold scare that occurred late in 2000, which spurred business in 2001. When Tropical Storm Allison struck Houston in June 2001 and caused widespread water damage that could have led to mold problems, Abatix sold an even greater volume of cleanup products. Revenues that improved modestly in 2000 over the previous year, totaling $48 million, soared in 2001, reaching more than $54.7 million. In addition, net income grew from $598,000 in 2000 to a record $1.2 million in 2001. These results were especially impressive given the poor state of the national economy.

In 2001 Abatix launched its e-commerce initiative, but perhaps of more importance to the future growth of the company were the terrorist attacks that took place on September 11, 2001. Government agencies at all levels began to prepare for future attacks. In 2002 Abatix took steps to enter the domestic preparedness industry. Supplies needed by first responders were identified and a special catalog was assembled to sell the line. In 2002 Abatix posted sales of nearly $60 million. Of that amount, about 55 percent came from environmental contractors, 17 percent from the construction industry, 16 percent from industrial safety companies, and 13 percent from other firms. Although the company expected that most of its sales would continue to come from environmental contractors, with the domestic preparedness market expected to grow in coming years, Abatix was likely to achieve a more balanced slate of customers than it had ever achieved in the past.

Principal Subsidiaries

International Enviroguard Systems, Inc.

Principal Competitors

Specialty Products & Insulation Co; Strategic Distribution, Inc.; Vallen Corporation.

Further Reading

"Abatix Environmental Corp.," *Wall Street Transcript,* December 26, 1994.
Smith, Frank, "Asbestos Concerns Boost Business for Abatix," *Dallas Business Journal,* January 8, 1990, p. 8.
——, "Asbestos Dispute Spurs Abatix to Diversify," *Dallas Business Journal,* July 23, 1990, p. 6.
——, "Institutional Investors Grab Stake in Abatix Environmental," *Dallas Business Journal,* May 7, 1990, p. 4.
Vonder Haar, Steven, "Asbestos Removal Material Supplier Plans Public Offering for Expansion," *Dallas Business Journal,* February 13, 1989, p. 6.

—Ed Dinger

Advance Auto Parts, Inc.

5673 Airport Road
Roanoke, Virginia 24012
U.S.A.
Telephone: (540) 362-4911
Fax: (540) 561-1448
Web site: http://www.advance-auto.com

Public Company
Founded: 1932 as Advance Stores
Employees: 30,464
Sales: $3.3 billion (2002)
Stock Exchanges: New York
Ticker Symbol: AAP
NAIC: 441310 Automotive Parts and Accessories Stores

Advance Auto Parts, Inc. is the second largest auto parts and accessories retailer in the United States, trailing only AutoZone. The Roanoke, Virginia-based company operates more than 2,400 stores located in 38 states, Puerto Rico, and the Virgin Islands, serving both the ''do-it-yourself'' customer as well as commercial accounts. Further, it is a partner in PartsAmerica .com, an online auto parts retailing venture. A public company traded on the New York Stock Exchange, Advance became a member of the *Fortune* 500 in 2003.

Founding the Company in 1932

The Advance chain was founded by Arthur Taubman, the son of Austro-Hungarian immigrants. Born in 1901 in Astoria, New York, he grew up in Manhattan's impoverished Lower East Side. As he later joked, he grew up forever hungry and food became a prime motivation for achieving success. At the age of 13 he dropped out of school to take a job in a department store, where he gained valuable retailing experience. Still a teenager, he served in the Navy during World War I. When he returned from his stint in the service, he became partners with one of his brothers in a small retail chain called Taubman's, selling both auto parts and household goods. The business, based in Pittsburgh, prospered through the 1920s and spread as far north as Boston and as far south as Washington, D.C., but it could not

survive the onset of the Great Depression and ultimately failed. Living in Baltimore in 1932, Taubman learned of a struggling, three-store, Roanoke-based auto parts business called Advance Stores that was for sale. It had two stores in Roanoke and another in Lynchburg, Virginia. In order to help him raise the down payment to buy the chain, his wife Grace offered her wedding ring, which he then pawned along with his own Masonic ring. Taubman quickly succeeded in turning around the retail chain, despite having no more than a grade school education; his business knowledge was the result of reading books and practical experience. According to company lore he ran Advance by following a four-point philosophy: provide value to customers; earn a reputation for honesty and integrity; ensure repeat business by providing quality merchandise and good customer service; and treat employees like family.

The difficult economic conditions of the 1930s helped to spur Advance's early growth. To put people to work the federal government funded major road paving projects, prompting motorists to drive their cars, which at the time required far more maintenance than contemporary models. For instance, oil required changing after only 500 miles, while brakes lasted little more than 10,000 miles and tires were only good for approximately 7,000 miles. Moreover, the poor economy caused more people to hold onto their cars longer, resulting in greater business for auto parts retailers like Advance. After a decade of owning Advance, Taubman had grown the chain to 21 stores. With the United States' entry into World War II, however, Advance was forced to adjust, due to a shortage of raw materials like rubber that limited the amount of auto parts that could be produced, as well as gas rationing that dramatically cut back on car usage and the need for maintenance. As a result, Advance Stores began to stock a wide variety of housewares and appliances, items it would continue to sell even after the war was over. It was also during World War II that Arthur Taubman made his mark in another way. He used his position as a successful businessman to help some 500 Jews escape the Holocaust of Nazi Germany by signing immigration papers, claiming that they were cousins and promising financial support (which never became necessary). When asked by government officials about his unusually high number of cousins, Taubman reportedly commented, ''Every Jew who is in danger is my first cousin.'' Taubman would later become a key player in the racial integration of Roanoke, and a major philanthropist in the community.

Advance Stores added to its mix of products in the 25 years that followed World War II. Not only did the chain sell auto parts, it installed items such as tires, batteries, and seatcovers at service bays that became part of the stores. According to the *Roanoke Times,* "At a store opening in Roanoke in 1961, the company touted its sales of lawn mowers, picnic equipment, lawn and garden tools, radios and phonographs, television and appliances, sporting goods, fishing tackle hardware, bicycles and accessories. . . . During Christmas, shoppers could buy toys." By the time Taubman was ready to retire and turn over control of the company to his son, Nicholas, the Advance chain totaled 54 stores.

Focusing on Auto Parts in the 1970s

Nicholas Taubman was 34 years old and a vice-president of the company when his father gave up control. Unlike his father, he had the opportunity to receive an excellent education. He attended a private prep school in Mercersburg, Pennsylvania, and later the Wharton School of Finance and Commerce at The University of Pennsylvania. He told the press at the time he took over for his father that he expected the chain to one day be 100 units strong in its market, which now included Virginia, the Carolinas, and a western section of Tennessee. For the next few years Taubman pursued this modest goal, then began to take a hard look at the business. As reported by the *Roanoke Times,* "One day in the mid-1970s, Nicholas Taubman said he took a critical look at one of the company's North Carolina stores. On display out front were garbage cans, a kid's gym set, a tiller and housewares. He tried to think of how customers viewed Advance Stores. He couldn't think of the company's niche. 'Everything I'm looking at I can buy (somewhere else) with more service, more variety and cheaper,' Taubman said to himself. So he began eliminating items that didn't sell well. During the transition, the company tried various products and brands— stoves, refrigerators, furniture. 'There were far more failures than successes,' Taubman said."

In 1978 the company changed its name from Advance Stores to Advance Auto and took other steps to become a high-volume retailer of auto parts. Aside from discontinuing consumer products and closing down its credit department, Advance also eliminated its service department. To better serve its new core market, the do-it-yourself car repairman, the company in 1982 introduced its PDQ (Parts Delivered Quickly) system, which promised delivery of some 25,000 auto parts within 24 hours. (Today it includes more than 250,000 items.) When the transi-

tion to auto parts was complete the company changed its name again, in 1985 becoming Advance Auto Parts.

In 1985 Taubman reached his original goal of 100 stores, but by now he began to envision the creation of a much larger company. To help him lead Advance he named longtime employee Garnett Smith, who had risen through the ranks, as president of the business, while he took on the title of chief executive officer. Together they launched an aggressive expansion program, so that by 1991 the chain included 211 stores, making it the country's eighth largest auto parts retailer. By the end of 1993 the chain included 352 stores located in eight states, and was now one of the fastest growing auto parts retailers in the country. A year later the company's founder, Arthur Taubman, died in Boca Raton, Florida, while the chain continued to expand at an accelerated clip. Although the clear preference was to build new stores, in early 1995 Advance grew by external means, buying 30 Georgia stores of Columbus, Ohio-based Nationwise Auto Parts, bringing the total number of Advance units to more than 500. By the middle of 1996 Advance owned 660 stores, generating an estimated $808 million in annual revenues. At the time it was ranked as the second largest auto parts chain, trailing only AutoZone with its 1,300 stores and $1.8 billion in sales. However, with the industry rapidly consolidating, the rankings behind AutoZone would fluctuate over the next several years.

In addition to managing a far-flung chain, Taubman faced the question of family succession. Neither of his two children, daughter Lara or son Marc, were apparently interested in running the family business. Marc, who had been working for the company, quit and moved to New Mexico to run a ranch he owned. In February 1997 Taubman retained Goldman Sachs to either sell the company or arrange to take it public, but by May the business was taken off the block. In September 1997 Taubman stepped down as CEO in favor of Smith, although he stayed on as chairman of the board. A deal to sell Advance was finally reached in April 1998, one that would ensure the business would stay in Roanoke, an important consideration to Taubman. The private investment firm of Freeman Spogli & Co. agreed to pay $351 million for an 86 percent stake in the company, with the Taubman family retaining the balance. Taubman also stayed on as chairman and Smith continued to manage the day-to-day affairs of the business. Taubman told the press at the time, "If I were 50, I wouldn't have sold it. You see yourself running out of time. There are some other things you want to do besides working seven days a week."

Acquiring Western Auto in 1998

In August 1998 Advance took its first major step under its new ownership arrangement when it acquired Western Auto from Sears, Roebuck & Co., paying $175 million in cash and a 40 percent stake in Advance. Of the 590 Western Auto stores acquired, 98 were closed because they were either unprofitable or their markets overlapped with Advance outlets. As a result of the acquisition, sales for 1998 totaled $1.22 billion, but Advance posted a loss of $2.2 million, the first loss since Arthur Taubman pawned his wife's ring to launch the business. The industry continued to consolidate rapidly, with sales in the do-it-yourself market remaining flat and essentially forcing

Key Dates:

1932: Arthur Taubman acquires a three-store chain to launch the business.
1969: Arthur Taubman retires and son Nicholas Taubman assumes control.
1978: Advance Stores changes its name to Advance Auto.
1985: Advance Auto focuses on auto parts exclusively, becoming Advance Auto Parts.
1998: The company is sold to Freeman Spogli & Co.
2001: Discount Auto Parts is acquired.
2003: Advance makes the *Fortune* 500 list.

the majors to fight for even more of a market share in order to achieve acceptable margins.

At the end of 1999 Smith retired after 43 years with Advance, citing a desire to spend more time with his ailing wife, although he remained on the company's board of directors. He was soon replaced as CEO by Lawrence P. Castellani, who had a wealth of executive experience, but in groceries, not auto parts. Having started out as a stock boy for a Tops Markets supermarket in 1962, he helped to build the small grocery chain into a large regional player that in 1991 was bought by Dutch giant Ahold, which named him CEO. He took over Advance in the midst of digesting the Western Auto acquisition. At the same time, the chain was launching an Internet business called PartsAmerica, a joint venture with CSK Auto, a major force in auto parts in the western United States, and Sequoia Capital. The business plan called for the two retailers to use their combined 2,500 stores, 3,000 delivery trucks, and dozens of distribution centers to offer same-day delivery of parts to all 50 states, Puerto Rico, and the Virgin Islands.

The Advance balance sheet returned to the black in 2000, and by 2001 was again positioned to grow the chain through acquisition. In April of that year it bought Carport Auto Parts, a 51-store regional chain located in Alabama and Mississippi. A more important deal was struck in November 2001 when Advance acquired Discount Auto Parts, Inc., a southeastern chain operating 577 stores with some $660 million in annual revenues. Advance paid approximately $520 million in cash and stock and assumed debt of approximately $267 million in the transaction. As a result, Advance now owned more than 2,400 stores located in 38 states, a business capable of generating more than $3 billion in annual sales. Moreover, by buying Discount, Advance's holding company, Advance Holding Corp., became a public company, which began trading on the New York Stock Exchange in November 2001. Once again, however, Advance faced the challenge of assimilating a significant acquisition without losing momentum in a highly competitive industry. The transition proceeded smoothly enough so that by the summer of 2002 Advance was able to make yet another acquisition, albeit on a much smaller scale. It bought 55 stores

of the Maryland-based Auto Trak Parts chain, which had lapsed into bankruptcy. By paying $16 million for inventory and fixtures and assuming existing leases, Advance was able to pick the bones of the chain, which numbered 196 stores a year earlier when the company filed Chapter 11 bankruptcy and had since dropped to just 78 stores. For a modest cost Advance increased its presence in the key market of Washington, D.C.

In November 2002 Sears announced that it planned to sell the 8.4 million shares it received in Advance for the Western Auto chain. A few weeks later a secondary offering was held in order to sell the Sears stake in the company, which now amounted to 24 percent, as well as to raise additional cash for Advance to be used to pay off some of the debt it had accumulated in its rapid ascent in the industry.

By the start of 2003 it appeared that Advance had successfully digested the Discount acquisition. The company closed 130 of the stores, which overlapped with Advance outlets. Of the ones that remained, 164 Discount stores were converted to the Advance Auto banner, while in Florida, where the Discount name retained a strong resonance with consumers, some 400 stores adopted the name Advance Discount Auto Parts. Also at the start of 2003, Advance launched a test program selling insurance at several stores, with the possibility of expanding the program if it proved to be successful after a six-month trial. Later in the spring, the company reached a significant milestone when it was announced that it made the *Fortune* 500 list, placing at number 466 with sales of $3.3 billion in 2002. (AutoZone in the meantime ranked 314 on the strength of $5.4 billion in sales.) It was a fitting sendoff for Nicholas Taubman and Garnett Smith, who had earlier in the year resigned from the company's board of directors after decades of devotion that built a small, obscure auto parts and household goods chain into the second largest auto parts retailer in the United States.

Principal Subsidiaries

Advance Stores Company, Incorporated.

Principal Competitors

AutoZone, Inc.; Genuine Parts Company; The Pep Boys—Manny, Moe & Jack; Wal-Mart Stores, Inc.

Further Reading

Edwards, Greg, ''Advance Notice,'' *Virginia Business Magazine,* June 1997.
Silvey, Larry, ''Advance Is the Right Name for This Company,'' *Aftermarket Business,* December 2002, p. 10.
Stewart, Keisha, ''Roanoke County, Va.-Based Auto Parts Firm Takes Risks to Gain Success,'' *Roanoke Times,* January 20, 2003.
Telfer, George F.W., ''Advance Auto Sells Majority Stake to Private Investment Firm,'' *Roanoke Times,* March 13, 1998.

—Ed Dinger

Advanstar Communications, Inc.

---

545 Boylston St.
Boston, Massachusetts 02116
U.S.A.
Telephone: (617) 267-6500
Fax: (617) 267-6900
Web site: http://www.advanstar.com

Wholly Owned Subsidiary of DLJ Merchant Banking
  Partners
Incorporated: 1987 as Edgell Communications, Inc.
Employees: 1,300
Sales: $307.18 million (2002)
NAIC: 561920 Convention and Trade Show Organizers;
  511120 Periodical Publishers

Advanstar Communications, Inc. publishes more than 100 business journals and directories and operates about 80 trade shows and professional conferences. The company's publications, which are typically distributed free of charge, include such titles as *Motor Age, Travel Agent,* and *Cosmetic Surgery News,* and cover a broad range of subject areas including healthcare, pharmaceuticals, manufacturing, telecommunications, digital media, beauty, e-learning, call center management, art, and marketing. The firm is also the leading operator of fashion industry trade shows in the United States, with such major events as the twice-yearly MAGIC shows in Las Vegas, and it also runs many similar expositions that are linked to the periodicals it publishes. Advanstar operates primarily in the United States, but also does business in Europe, Latin America, and Asia.

Beginnings

The roots of Advanstar Communications stretch back to 1939 and the founding of Davidson Publishing Company. Davidson was formed to publish trade papers, publications that covered the news of a specific industry and offered suppliers the opportunity to advertise to potential customers. Its first publication was called *Paper Sales,* and over the next two decades Davidson expanded to more than ten publications in the paper, stationery, food, and fur industries. The company, which moved

several times before it settled in Duluth, Minnesota, also operated its own printing plant.

Meanwhile, in 1945, a recent graduate of Michigan State University named Robert Edgell got a job publishing a magazine called *Export Trade and Shipper* in New York. After just six months he decided to found his own publishing company, which he named Edgell and Associates. His first title covered the hearing aid industry, and the company later found success with other periodicals, including *Drive-In Management.*

In 1961 Edgell joined with a number of other parties to found a firm called Ojibway Press, headquartered in Duluth, Minnesota. It absorbed Davidson Publishing as part of a joint venture, and soon acquired another company called Knit Goods Publishing, owners of *Lingerie Merchandising* and *Hosiery and Underwear Review.* Over the next few years Ojibway built up its list of titles to 21, including such publications as *Meat* and *Industrial Gas.* In 1968 it was sold for $5.5 million in stock to Harcourt, Brace & World (later known as Harcourt Brace Jovanovich, or HBJ). Ojibway would form the backbone of Harbrace Publications, Inc., which was also made up of Byrum Publications, Brookhill Publishing Co., and several titles purchased from Haire Publishing Corp.

At this time Robert Edgell left to pursue other ventures, but in 1970 he was lured back to run Harbrace, and over the next decade and a half he built it into one of the largest professional magazine publishers in the United States. In 1984 Edgell formed a trade show business, Harcourt Expositions and Conferences, and the following year completed the acquisition of school supply distributor Beckley-Cardy, Inc., which had been founded in 1907 and was the leader in its field. By now the company was known as HBJ Publications, Inc., and was having success with such titles as *Modern Medicine, Physician Management, American Salon,* and *Food Management.* About 55 were business periodicals, while the rest were directories and trade show publications.

1987: Leveraged Buyout

In 1987 Harcourt Brace Jovanovich was forced to seek a large infusion of cash to cover the cost of fighting off a hostile

Company Perspectives:

Our mission is to be the leading provider of information and communications products to targeted business and professional markets.

takeover bid, and it made the decision to sell the successful HBJ Publications division, in part because as a standalone unit it was easily divested. In December 1987 a group led by Edgell, several other managers, and investment firm Kidder, Peabody & Co. agreed to pay $334.1 million for HBJ Publications, which included the expositions and school supply businesses.

The spinoff unit was renamed Edgell Communications, Inc., and headquartered in Cleveland, Ohio. It was officially owned by a new holding company called New Century Communications, Inc. At this time Edgell had approximately 1,800 employees, with annual revenues of $189 million and operating income of $21 million. The deal, which was structured as a leveraged buyout, had been negotiated during a stock market boom, though it was finalized just after the stock crash of October 1987. The resultant $330 million debt load would require annual interest payments of $36 million, $15 million more than the publishing division had ever made in profits. Despite this ominous gap, company executives expressed confidence that the business would grow rapidly enough to cover the difference. However, in the months after the deal was struck the publishing industry entered a slump which saw ad revenues drop by as much as 20 percent, and it became apparent that Edgell would not earn the amount needed to service its debt.

In mid-1989 Robert Edgell negotiated a deal to sell the firm to a British publisher, but the price was rejected by the company's board. Edgell Communications was now in full belt-tightening mode, and it sold a trade show and a publication and folded another title, and then moved its Expositions unit from Connecticut to Cleveland.

In March 1990 Robert Edgell stepped down as CEO, reportedly under pressure from Kidder, Peabody. In April Richard Swank, a former information industry executive with experience in financial matters, was named to replace Edgell, and he quickly began work on restructuring the firm's debt. The company's employment ranks shrank to 1,400, and in July Edgell defaulted on an interest payment of $7 million, which led Standard & Poor's to downgrade its credit rating to "D," the lowest level. In October the company dissolved its sales promotion department and put seven magazines up for sale.

On New Year's Day, 1991, former CEO Robert Edgell jumped to his death from the seventh-floor balcony of his retirement home in Florida. He was apparently despondent over the company's financial problems and their impact on his family and former coworkers, who owned a large amount of now worthless stock. Edgell's post-CEO job as consultant to the firm that still bore his name had ended the day before his death.

The year 1991 saw the company sell most of the publications that had been put on the block, reorganize senior management, and lay off 100 more employees. Late in the year a restructuring

plan was reached with a majority of the firm's lenders and bond holders, after an earlier proposal by Kidder, Peabody had been rejected. After a so-called "prepackaged" Chapter 11 filing, much of Edgell's debt would be converted to common stock, making the company's new majority owner Goldman, Sachs & Co. of New York, which had been quietly buying up the firm's bonds. General Electric Capital Corp., the parent of Kidder, Peabody which now owned most of its stake, would halve its interest rates, and afterwards would control only a small portion of the firm. The deal reduced the company's debt from $368 million to $192 million.

1992: Edgell Becomes Advanstar

By the spring of 1992 the firm, now renamed Advanstar Communications, Inc., was out of bankruptcy protection and moving forward. The company had reduced its payroll to 1,200 and its list of titles to 44. Advanstar soon announced plans to spend as much as $80 million on acquisitions, focusing on such emerging fields as hazardous-materials management and telecommunications. The company's centralized power structure had been replaced with five publishing groups, each of which held six to nine magazines worth $20 million in revenues. A new $2 million electronic publishing system was also purchased to cut costs and give editors more control over design of the magazines.

During 1992 the company's layoffs continued, and it also put the Beckley-Cardy and Davidson Printing subsidiaries up for sale. The former unit, which employed 400 and had sales of $76.5 million, accounted for more than a third of the firm's $187.5 million in revenues for 1991. The year saw Advanstar make a number of acquisitions, including *Art Business News, Voice Processing Magazine,* Infotext Publishing Inc., and The Tower Companies, publisher of *Hazmat World* and *Motion Control.* The two latter companies had estimated revenues of $7 million each, and produced a number of trade shows that complemented their publications. Eight Advanstar titles were simultaneously put up for sale as the firm sought to tighten its focus and concentrate on rapidly growing fields.

In January 1993 the acquisitions continued with the purchase of Aster Publishing Corp. of Eugene, Oregon, for an estimated $25 million. Aster, which had revenues of more than $24 million, published 14 trade magazines including *Pharmaceutical Technology* and *Managed Healthcare,* and ran a number of related events. Owner Edward Aster received a 10 percent stake in Advanstar and was named its president. By this time the company had also sold the Beckley-Cardy and Davidson Printing subsidiaries and related real estate, as well as seven of the magazines it had put up for sale. The eighth, *Food & Drug Packaging,* was folded.

Under Aster Advanstar began to expand its trade show business, which heretofore had accounted for about 10 percent of revenues. In May 1993 the firm also closed its Denver offices and moved the plastics-oriented titles published there to Eugene, Oregon. The move backfired, however, when only one of the 40 employees involved elected to relocate, and the remainder began publishing their own competing magazines. In October Advanstar sold the recently acquired *Motion Control* and bought *High Color,* which was later renamed *PC Graphics*

& Video. A short time later the firm bought ShowBiz Expo, operator of movie production trade shows in Los Angeles and New York, and a Hong Kong-based firm that organized financial and telecommunications conferences. Advanstar now owned a total of 80 trade shows and conferences.

At the end of 1993 CEO Richard Swank left the firm and Aster added his duties to the job of president. Advanstar reported revenues of $140.1 million for the year and suffered what it termed a "paper loss" of $40.8 million, an improvement over the $110 million revenues and $77 million loss of 1992.

In the spring of 1994 the company formed a new subsidiary called Advanstar Millennium to develop multimedia information products and make foreign licensing deals, and folded its *Candy Marketer* and *Advanced Composites* magazines. In August Edward Aster, who had been described by some as "abrasive," abruptly resigned and was replaced by Richard Swank on an interim basis. Six months later Gary Ingersoll was named to the top post. He had an extensive background in the publishing and exposition industries, having worked for such firms as The Chilton Company and PEMCO.

At this time Advanstar was again close to defaulting on its loans, which were once more being renegotiated. Among several other problems the company's medical and plastics magazines were doing poorly, with the three that made up the latter category now on the block. Following the Aster-initiated move to Oregon ad revenues had dropped from $7 million to $2 million.

In January 1995 Advanstar successfully completed the restructuring of its debt and took the plastics titles off the block after a deal fell through at the 11th hour. During the year the firm started new magazines called *America's Network* (for telecommunications professionals) and *ITS World* (which covered "intelligent transportation systems"), and created three new quarterly buyers' guides for different specialty fields. The company also acquired *Commicaciones* magazine, a Spanish-language publication for public and private network providers and folded *Enterprise Communications,* formerly known as *Voice Processing.* Advanstar had now acquired 23 new titles and launched four since it had emerged from Chapter 11.

Sale to Hellman & Friedman in 1996

In early 1996 the revitalized Advanstar was put up for sale, and in May it was sold to Hellman & Friedman Capital Partners III, L.P. of San Francisco for $237 million. The deal would also pay off the firm's senior debt. Following the sale Robert Krakoff was installed as chairman and CEO to replace Gary Ingersoll, who had suffered a brain hemorrhage. Krakoff, 60, had recently served as the head of Cahners Publishing.

During the latter half of 1996 Advanstar purchased Hospitality Resources Worldwide, publisher of the *Deals Digest* and the *Luxury Digest,* and bought two California-based beauty products expositions and two call center trade shows. The firm was also busy preparing for the launch of *Cosmetic Surgery Times.* In early 1997 Advanstar added 18 more trade shows through the purchase of Expocon Management Associates of Connecticut and Haircolor USA. New publications acquired included *TurfGrass Trends* and several Latin American telecommunications titles. In the summer, the company was again restructured into five separate industry-focused units headed by executive vice-presidents.

The end of 1997 saw the startup of two new publications, *Mining Engineering & Technology* and *Premier Hotels & Resorts,* and the purchase of a stake in *Telecom Asia* magazine. In early 1998 the acquisitions continued with the purchase of H&T Feiras e Congressos Ltda., the leading Latin American telecommunications industry trade show sponsor, *TelEvolution Magazine* of Canada and its related trade show, and Tele-Professional, Inc. of Iowa, which published three magazines and organized two trade shows. The company also formed 50/50 joint ventures to produce medical device, video software, and consumer electronics trade shows.

In April 1998 Advanstar announced its largest acquisition ever, the $234 million purchase of MAGIC International, Inc., operator of the biggest apparel expositions in the United States. MAGIC, which had revenues of $40 million, put on shows in Las Vegas twice yearly under the names "MAGIC," "WWDMAGIC," and "MAGIC Kids." After this, nearly 50 percent of Advanstar's revenues would come from trade shows, which had proven more profitable than magazine publishing. Other activities, which accounted for about 5 percent of the firm's income, included direct mail and database products and services.

Other acquisitions during the year included *Applied Business Telecommunications* and *Travel Agent* magazine, the largest title in its category in the United States. Advanstar also partnered with MM Editions, a French firm, to produce a call center show and related directory publication in that country, and sold *ITS World.* The company was now preparing to launch another new magazine, *DCC* (Digital Content Creation), which would complement a Canadian trade show it had acquired.

For 1998 Advanstar reported revenues of $259.8 million and a loss of $28.4 million, mainly attributed to the MAGIC purchase. The firm now had 1,300 employees and had moved its official headquarters to Boston, where CEO Krakoff was based, though many operations remained in Cleveland and in other cities where the firm's publications were edited. Advanstar now published 110 magazines and directories, organized 107 trade shows and conferences, and operated more than 100 related web sites.

During 1999 the company continued acquiring trade shows including London-based Digital Media World and Customer Relationship Management Solutions, and also started *Web Merchant,* a quarterly Internet business-to-business retail publication. In May the firm increased its fashion industry offerings substantially with the $133 million acquisition of the Larkin Group of Massachusetts, which put on 16 fashion and fabric trade shows and also published *Accent,* a monthly magazine. The deal made Advanstar the largest fashion industry trade show producer in the United States. Plans were also being laid for an initial public offering, but this was abandoned in the summer. Company officials cited the low valuation levels of similar firms in announcing the cancellation. Late in the year the firm bought a German information technology publisher and trade show organizer, and partnered with PurchasePro to start 20 online communities that would be tied to Advanstar's largest trade show and publishing sectors, including pharmaceuticals and telecommunications. A new sister company was created to run the web sites, Advanstar.com, which later became known as Hive4.com.

Purchase of Advanstar by DLJ: 2000

In April 2000 Hellman & Friedman put Advanstar up for sale for a reported $1 billion. A deal was reached in August for the firm to be acquired by DLJ Merchant Banking Partners, an affiliate of New York-based Donaldson Lufkin & Jenrette & Co. The price was estimated at more than $900 million in cash and securities, plus assumption of $520 million in debt. DLJ's deep pockets held some $750 million more for Advanstar to make new acquisitions.

The company continued to roll out new publications during this period, including *Medical Design World,* which debuted in the fall. In the spring of 2001 Advanstar spent an estimated $15–$20 million to buy three automotive-related titles from Cahners Business Information, including *Motor Age.* At the same time the firm was trimming its Internet operations and reducing staff in that area. During the latter half of 2001 more trade shows and conferences were launched, including TechLearn, an e-learning expo done in conjunction with The Masie Center of Florida. Revenues for the year grew to $347 million, with a loss of $33.6 million. The red ink was tagged to the cost of acquisitions, reduced advertising revenues, and the

poor response to several conferences that had been held in the wake of the September 11 terrorist attacks on the United States.

In 2002 the firm sold its Global Cosmetic Industry show and made more acquisitions including First Global Media Group of London, which published six auto-related magazines and held a trade show. In the fall Advanstar bought *HT--the Magazine for Healthcare Travel Professionals, Salon News,* and the *Look Book,* and announced the launch of *Modern Healthcare for Women,* which was designed for patients sitting in doctor's offices. The company recorded sales of $307.2 million for 2002, a decline of 11.5 percent. Losses hit $124.3 million, this time attributed to the adoption of new accounting standards and the writeoff of $37.2 million owed by the firm's affiliated dot.com unit. The company's trade show income had also dropped almost 15 percent, to $159 million, while earnings from publications slid to $131 million, a decrease of 8 percent. Advanstar had cut another 286 jobs since January 2001.

During the first half of 2003 the company launched a new division to develop conferences and trade shows for the pharmaceutical industry and created new events in the healthcare, art, beauty, and e-learning markets. In August Advanstar closed on a private placement of $360 million to pay down debt, and then reached an agreement to buy the Medical Economics Communications Group, Dental Products Report Group, and Veterinary Healthcare Communications Group of Thomson Healthcare for $135 million. The acquisition would add 15 magazines including *Medical Economics* and *RN Magazine,* along with a trade show and a number of continuing education programs.

Advanstar Communications, Inc. had established itself as a leader in the business publication and trade show fields. Though it was still far from profitable, the company's business was well-established and its deep-pocketed owners appeared committed to seeing it through.

Principal Divisions

International Art and Beauty Group; Pharmaceutical Group; Science Group; Healthcare Group; Post Group; Powersports Group; Video Group; Automotive Group; Advanstar Technology Communities; MAGIC International (Fashion and Apparel Group).

Principal Competitors

The McGraw-Hill Companies, Inc.; Primedia, Inc.; Reed Elsevier Group plc; Advance Publications, Inc.; Penton Media.

Further Reading

"Advanstar Communications Sold to Hellman & Friedman Capital Partners," *Business Publisher,* April 16, 1996.
"Advanstar Purchases 'HT-The Magazine for Healthcare Travel Professionals'," *Business Publisher,* October 17, 2002, p. 1.
"Advanstar Purchases The Larkin Group and 'Sensors' Magazine," *Business Publisher,* July 31, 1999, p. 1.
Ashyk, Lori, "Edgell Pinching Pennies, Working Itself Out of Debt," *Crain's Cleveland Business,* July 31, 1989, p. 1.
——, "HBJ Units' Publisher Already Plans to Grow," *Crain's Cleveland Business,* November 23, 1987, p. 1.

Brandt, John R., "Is There Life After Debt?," *Corporate Cleveland,* June 1, 1992, p. 21.

Dixon, Teresa, "Advanstar Agrees to Sell to N.Y. Investment Firm," *Cleveland Plain Dealer,* August 16, 2000, p. 1C.

Dougherty, Philip H., "A New Problem—Name All the Magazines," *New York Times,* January 19, 1969, p. F19.

Gleisser, Marcus, "Advanstar Communications Buys Apparel Show Producer," *Cleveland Plain Dealer,* April 9, 1998, p. 2C.

Greene, Jay, "Edgell Communications Zips Out of Bankruptcy," *Cleveland Plain Dealer,* January 24, 1992.

"Harcourt Agrees to Sell Business Publications, School Supplies Units," *Associated Press,* November 16, 1987.

"Harcourt Seeking Buyer for Magazine Division," *Houston Chronicle,* August 21, 1987, p. 2.

Harrison, Kimberly P., "Advanstar Chief Hitches Star to Trade Shows," *Crain's Cleveland Business,* May 10, 1993, p. 1.

Hochwald, Lambeth, "The Death & Life of Advanstar," *Folio,* April 1, 1993, p. 60.

Kelly, Keith J., "Ingersoll Tackles Troubled Advanstar," *Advertising Age,* December 5, 1994.

Masterton, John, "Edgell: What Went Wrong?," *Folio,* May 1, 1990, p. 23.

Mooney, Barbara, "GE Seen Tightening Its Grip on Edgell," *Crain's Cleveland Business,* April 9, 1990, p. 1.

Mooney, Barbara, and Ken Myers, "CEO Swank Sees Edgell Sidestepping Ch. 11 Risk," *Crain's Cleveland Business,* August 27, 1990, p. 1.

Myers, Ken, "Edgell's New CEO Confident He'll Fit In," *Crain's Cleveland Business,* April 16, 1990, p. 3.

Pae, Terence P., "The Magician's Last Trick (Robert Edgell of Edgell Communications)," *Fortune,* May 20, 1991, p. 92.

Palagano, Teresa, "Fashionably Acquisitive," *Folio,* August 1, 2001, p. 28.

Silber, Tony, "More Challenges Await Advanstar," *Folio,* September 1, 1994, p. 21.

Yerak, Rebecca, "Edgell Defaults on Debt Payment," *Cleveland Plain Dealer,* July 17, 1990.

—Frank Uhle

Allianz

Allianz AG

Königinstrasse 28
D-80802 Munich
Germany
Telephone: +49-89-38-00-00
Fax: +49-89-34-99-41
Web site: http://www.allianz.com

Public Company
Incorporated: 1890 as Allianz Versicherungs-Aktien-
 Gesellschaft
Employees: 179,146
Total Assets: EUR 852.1 billion ($895 billion) (2002)
Stock Exchanges: New York
Ticker Symbol: AZ
NAIC: 524113 Direct Life Insurance Carriers; 524130
 Reinsurance Carriers (pt); 524114 Direct Health and
 Medical Insurance Carriers (pt); 524126 Direct
 Property and Casualty Insurance Carriers (pt); 524210
 Insurance Agencies and Brokerages; 551112 Offices
 of Other Holding Companies; 522110 Commercial
 Banking (pt); 523110 Investment Banking and
 Securities Dealing

Once known primarily as a German insurance company, Allianz AG has grown to become one of the world's leading financial services providers. Structured as a holding company of approximately 700 companies in over 70 countries, Allianz AG operates in three core business areas: property and casualty insurance, life and health insurance, and asset management and banking. In its property and casualty insurance sector, which is overseen by Munich-based Allianz Versicherungs-AG, Allianz is the leading insurance provider in Germany and one of the largest providers of corporate insurance in the world. The company is also the top life insurance provider in Germany, and recent acquisitions outside Germany have made Allianz an international leader in this, its second business segment. Under the auspices of Allianz Dresdner Asset Management, Allianz AG has over EUR 1.1 trillion under management in its newest sector—asset management and banking.

Early Years: 1890–1919

The company was founded as Allianz Versicherungs-Aktien-Gesellschaft in 1890 by Carl Thieme, director of the Munich Reinsurance Company, and the private banker Wilhelm Finck, at the time when the German economy had gotten back into its stride after a long depression and was entering the second phase of its industrial revolution. Taking advantage of the rapid spread of mechanization in the workplace and the steeply rising number of industrial and traffic accidents, Thieme and Finck began by concentrating on accident and liability insurance. From the 1890s until World War I, however, Allianz grew and prospered mainly through freight insurance, which with reinsurance has been fundamental to the Allianz story from its beginning. In the view of leading experts of the time, the freight insurance market was very overcrowded, but Paul von der Nahmer, Allianz's second company chairman who led the firm from 1894 with Carl Thieme and from 1904 alone, spotted the great possibilities offered by the rapid expansion in the volume of German trade. In 1913, when Allianz had already become by far the largest German freight insurer, this division produced almost 45 percent of the firm's premium income.

Before World War I, Allianz had already begun to extend its scope, although it was still far from offering a full composite range. In 1900 it received the first German license to sell plant insurance, and in 1911 it was also licensed to insure against mechanical breakdowns, a service available exclusively from Allianz until 1924. For three decades the role played in the firm's business by these two classes of insurance did not increase, but Allianz's expertise in this area due to its early involvement is one reason for the firm's present undisputed position as market leader in the field of engineering—that is, mechanical, plant, and equipment—insurance. In 1905 Allianz included direct fire insurance in its list of benefits.

Growth in the 1920s

Allianz's advance from medium size to the rank of largest insurance group in Germany took place within a few years, between the end of World War I and the mid-1920s. Before the war the Berlin-based firm had drawn only about 20 percent of its premium income from abroad. Afterward, like all German insurers, it was cut off from international markets almost completely but later, in a rise unparalleled in the history of German insurance, it came to dominate the whole industry. The foundation for this achievement had been laid by Paul von der Nahmer with his sound and farsighted financial strategy. As one of the few people to assess accurately the effects that war would have on the future of Germany's currency and its insurance industry, he had taken early steps to provide Allianz with substantial foreign currency reserves that helped it to achieve an almost proverbial stability amidst the chaos of inflation. After his death in 1921 his successor, Dr. Kurt Schmitt, used these financial reserves to enable Allianz to establish the highest turnover of all German insurers.

In 1917, at the age of 31, Schmitt was made executive managing director. His innovations were to lead the company to the top of the German insurance industry and to a major global presence. He attempted to establish a foothold in all markets, to expand into all classes of insurance, and to extend the company's international activities. The conditions of the Treaty of Versailles had stood in the way of the latter aim, but his efforts to make the firm active in all classes of insurance were therefore all the more successful. In 1918 he established the motor insurance company Kraft-Versicherungs-AG (Motor Insurance AG), the first large company in Germany to specialize in motor vehicle risks. Immediately after the war ended he also sought collaboration with large life insurance companies. When these negotiations unexpectedly broke down early in 1922, Schmitt, by then chairman of the board of Allianz, founded within the space of ten days the Allianz Lebensversicherungsbank-AG (Allianz Life-Assurance Bank AG), which by 1927 had grown into the largest life insurance company in Europe.

During the hyperinflation of 1922–23, numerous mergers speeded the firm on its way to the top. Specialist insurance companies were finding it particularly hard to survive, and the German insurance market was hit by a wave of mergers. Allianz concentrated on absorbing only those companies that would fill existing gaps in its own range, both of services and of regions served.

In the years of rapid currency depreciation, Allianz's merger policy differed markedly from that of other companies. It suc-ceeded because it was directed towards maximum rationalization. Whereas in other groups mergers tended to result in little more than a hodgepodge of individual companies, the Berlin group immediately welded all its member companies into an organic whole, created a new overall structure, and finally undertook radical rationalization at home and abroad. The latter task was achieved principally by Hans Hess, who had joined Allianz in 1918.

Until the early 1920s Allianz, in common with all other German insurance companies, employed outdated administration and organization techniques. The Allianz board was the first to realize that combating the effects of inflation and employee rationalization would have to be top priorities. Hess succeeded in introducing the basic principles of scientific management into the insurance business. By means of an assortment of technical and, even more importantly, organizational improvements, he managed a significant increase in productivity and a reduction in costs. He spread a network of branch offices across Germany and ensured that the latest equipment was installed. He replaced the old, strongly independent insurance agents, each working for several companies covering the most varied types of insurance, with agents trained in composite insurance and working solely for Allianz. He also set up a system of incentive schemes for employees, run with an element of sporting competition. Alongside this initiative came the extension of the social installations and services provided for staff. These measures gave the firm great stability in periods of crisis. Even during the world depression Allianz was able to maintain its volume of premiums and considerably increase the number of personnel.

Whereas during the inflation period the firm had concentrated on broadening its scope, after the stabilization of the currency in 1923–24 it set its sights on growth in volume. It was engaged in a major expansion of its capacities when in the mid-1920s a new wave of amalgamation policies hit German industry, and large groups formed for chemicals manufacture, electrical engineering, and heavy industry gave rise to a significant increase in risk potential.

In 1927 the group surprised the public by announcing a merger with the famous Stuttgarter Verein Versicherungs-AG, the market leader in accident and liability insurance. It was the largest merger to date in the history of German insurance. When in the summer of 1929 the Frankfurter Allgemeine Versicherungs-AG, the second largest insurance group in Germany, collapsed as the result of illegal, loss-making noninsurance deals, Allianz decided within 24 hours to meet all of the Frankfurter's obligations to its clients. With Münchener Rückver-sicherungs-AG, Allianz immediately founded the Neue Frankfurter Allgemeine Versicherungs-AG to assume the Frankfurter's liabilities. This dramatic rescue operation saved the whole insurance industry from a serious loss of public confidence and from state intervention in its affairs.

Prewar Germany and World War II

The industry could not, however, escape government interference after Adolf Hitler came to power in 1933 and enlisted savers and insurance policy holders in his secret financial preparations for war. From 1935 onwards the regime obliged insur-

Key Dates:

1890: Carl Thieme and Wilhelm Finck found Allianz Versicherungs-Aktien-Gesellschaft.
1917: Dr. Kurt Schmitt becomes company's executive managing director.
1922: Allianz creates Allianz Lebensversicherungsbank-AG (Allianz Life-Assurance Bank AG).
1927: Allianz merges with Stuttgarter Verein Versicherungs-AG.
1943: Allianz's headquarters in Berlin are destroyed.
1975: Allianz establishes the Allianz International Insurance Company Ltd. in London.
1977: Allianz enters the American market with creation of the Allianz International Insurance Company Ltd.
1985: Company reorganizes its operations; Allianz AG is established as a holding company.
1990: Allianz acquires the state insurance company of the former German Democratic Republic (East Germany).
1991: Allianz acquires Fireman's Fund Insurance Company.
1997: Allianz acquires Assurances Générales de France (AGF).
2000: Allianz purchases PIMCO Advisors.
2001: Allianz takes over Dresdner Bank.

ance companies to increase their subscriptions to government loans; from the summer of 1942 three-quarters of their investment capital was affected in this way.

It was in an attempt to protect the industry from this sort of encroachment that in 1933, after much hesitation, Kurt Schmitt agreed to become trade minister in Hitler's second cabinet. He was convinced he would be able to restrain National Socialism and lead it in the direction he wished it to go. A few weeks were enough to make him regret his action; he gave up the attempt, and after a year took the first opportunity to withdraw from politics. In 1935 he became chairman of the supervisory board of Allianz Lebensversicherungs-AG and in 1938 he was made chairman of the board of directors of Münchener Rück. In 1933 he had been succeeded as chairman of Allianz Versicherungs-AG by his former deputy, Hans Hess, who during the whole of the Third Reich made no secret—even in public—of his profound dislike of Naziism and took part in the resistance movement against Hitler.

During the 1920s and 1930s Allianz expanded its range, venturing into completely new areas of insurance. Its innovations in the field of engineering insurance were particularly forward-looking. It was the first in Germany to offer installation and guarantee insurance, in 1923, and construction and civil engineering insurance, in 1934. While other insurers still saw their role purely and simply in terms of providing financial compensation for loss, Allianz built up an independent technical-advice and loss-prevention service. In 1920, using special engineers, it carried out the first regular inspection of power plants. From 1924 it also published *Der Maschinen-Schaden* (Mechanical Breakdown), a periodical that today continues to combine the utmost

practicality with high scientific standards. In 1932 Allianz set up its first materials- and equipment-testing installation, which swiftly became a highly reputed center for loss research. The firm completed its activities in this area in 1938 with the introduction of a fire damage prevention service. Political conditions in the interwar years, however, meant that it could only scratch the surface of its international aspirations.

World War II hit Allianz hard. The head office in Berlin was completely demolished, and since it was situated in the eastern part of the city there could be no question of rebuilding it. The partition of Germany after the war also meant the loss of a large part of its marketing area, together with several of its most successful branch offices. At the end of the war the various specialized sections of the company were scattered all over Germany in various locations. There was no longer any headquarters. With the difficulty of communications between the western zone of Germany and West Berlin, particularly after the Berlin blockade of 1948, it became clear that in the interest of the company as a whole, Berlin must now be ruled out as a future base. The seat of the central management was therefore moved to Munich, and that of Allianz Lebensversicherungs-AG to Stuttgart.

Growth in the Postwar Era

In October 1948 Hess relinquished the chairmanship of the board of management. He was succeeded by Hans Goudefroy, who made it his business to preserve the assets of the Allianz group and its internal stability even after the currency reform of 1948. In the mid-1950s, under his leadership, Allianz completed its second phase of rationalization. The adoption of electronic data processing—in 1956 the board of directors started using one of Europe's earliest computers—is a striking example of the many innovations embraced since then by Allianz. At the same time, by a rapid expansion of its foreign business network, the group regained its leading position in the German insurance market. Such dramatic growth was without precedent in Europe. Outstripping all other insurers, Allianz acquired a presence in every part of the Federal Republic of Germany, and owing to its new slogan, "... höffentlich Allianz versichert!'' (I hope you're insured with Allianz!). Created in the mid-1950s, it became known to virtually everybody.

During the 1950s and 1960s Allianz concentrated almost exclusively on the home market, with the emphasis on private insurance, though it did make some advances in the large-risk industrial sector, particularly in the area of engineering insurance. In February 1962, following the premature death of Goudefroy at the end of the preceding year, the chairmanship of the board of management was taken over by Alfred Haase, previously organization manager of the Allianz group. In a smooth transition, Haase carried on the work of his predecessor, further expanding the network of agents, developing the domestic private insurance business, and continuing internal rationalization. During his term of office the Allianz Allgemeine Rechtsschutzversicherungs-AG (Allianz General Patent Insurance A.G.) was founded; it commenced trading in 1970. Haase also presided over further developments in loss prevention. In 1969 the old testing installation was renamed the Allianz Center for Technology and in 1971 it was enlarged by the creation of the Institute of Motor Vehicle Technology.

New Leadership in the 1970s

At the turn of the 1970s the German insurance industry was faced with new problems, most notably a cost explosion due to steep wage rises throughout the whole economy. In addition a sharp increase in the accident rate had taken the motor insurance sector into the red. Competition throughout the industry was becoming much fiercer, too. Although Allianz's turnover continued to climb, net yield began to fall. Into this very difficult situation stepped Wolfgang Schieren, who in 1971 came to the group as managing director. As had happened half a century before under Kurt Schmitt, there began a new phase in the firm's history. Schieren began by ordering a halt to staff recruitment and instigating a radical cost reduction program. While competitors' staff numbers continued to rise, the Munich group was already economizing in order to invest for the future.

A second consequence of Schieren's appointment was that Allianz ceased concentrating its acquisition activities primarily on private insurance and gave equal consideration to large-risk industrial and commercial business. Within a few years the firm became the foremost German concern in this increasingly important sector, in certain areas of which, such as engineering insurance, it became a world leader. Restructuring of the organization of industrial insurance formed part of this new orientation. In 1987 an operation began that was to extend over several years, aimed at simplifying the hitherto complicated classifications of large-risk industrial insurance.

Finally, under Wolfgang Schieren, Allianz evolved from a domestically focused business to an internationally oriented insurer. In 1970 the group's premium income was DM 4 billion, only 3.2 percent derived from abroad; by 1989, out of a total income of DM 31.8 billion, 40 percent came from foreign premiums. Allianz reacted promptly to the increasing internationalism of German industry as West Germany developed, from the beginning of the 1970s, from being a mere exporter to being a foreign investor. As Allianz expanded its services to industry, it wanted to offer its clients insurance coverage for their foreign investments, too. It was realized early on at Allianz's Munich headquarters that dramatic changes were taking place in industry and that an insurer who was active only at a national level could no longer meet the needs of increasingly multinational enterprises.

During the first phase of these foreign activities Allianz tried to gain a foothold in foreign markets mainly by setting up new companies. The Allianz International Insurance Company Ltd. began trading in London in 1975, and similar companies were established in Spain and the Netherlands. In France the Paris board of directors was enlarged. In 1977 the firm ventured into the U.S. market for the first time, setting up the Allianz Insurance Company to deal in property insurance in Los Angeles. This development ended the first phase of Allianz's foreign expansion.

In 1974, constrained by the legal upper limit set for foreign investors, Allianz had bought a 30 percent share in a Brazilian insurance company, which from then on traded under the name of Allianz Ultramar. In 1977 the group acquired from Commercial Union of London the Anglo-Elementar-Versicherungs-AG with headquarters in Vienna, and two years later, in the United States, the North American Life and Casualty Company, based in Minneapolis, Minnesota, as well as the Fidelity Union Life Insurance Company of Dallas. In the same period Allianz established a foothold in Australia, and in 1981 it moved into Chile.

The creation of this world network went almost unnoticed by the public until the beginning of the 1980s when Allianz, in a dramatic takeover attempt, tried to obtain a majority holding in the British Eagle Star Insurance Company. By June 1981 the German group had acquired almost 30 percent of Eagle Star's shares. At the end of 1983 there was a battle between Allianz and the conglomerate BAT Industries for the remaining shares. BAT emerged the victor, though Allianz made a profit of £156.5 million by selling off the Eagle Star shares bought in 1981.

In 1986 Allianz did succeed in establishing itself in the United Kingdom, however, when it acquired from BTR plc the Cornhill Insurance Company, founded in 1905. Cornhill's foreign interests afforded, among other advantages, an entry into the developing east Asian market. In 1984 Allianz had already taken a further step towards internationalism with the acquisition of a majority holding in the Riunione Adriatica di Sicurtá (RAS), the second largest insurance company in Italy. Through RAS's wide foreign network Allianz gained entry into several countries in which it previously had had little or no representation.

International Expansion in the 1980s

Interests were acquired in Argentina, Spain, and Greece, and a new company was formed in Indonesia. In collaboration with local banks, life insurance companies were set up in Spain and Greece. In 1985 Allianz reorganized as Allianz Aktiengesellschaft Holding, to reflect its size and diversity. In September 1989, in the fight for control of the French insurance group VIA/Rhin et Moselle, Allianz acquired—within the space of a few days—first 50 percent, then 65 percent of the shares as the previous owner, the conglomerate Compagnie de Navigation Mixte, with the help of Allianz managed to fend off a takeover attempt by the state insurance company AGF and the bank Paribas. Another sensational acquisition, this time in Budapest at the end of 1989, was that of a 49 percent interest in Hungary's former state insurance company Hungária Biztositó, which had come into being three years earlier when the state monopoly company was split into two parts. Allianz thus demonstrated its interest in any East European market willing to adapt to the free market economy. Finally, Allianz made a considerable stir at home by buying a 51 percent interest in Deutsche Versicherungs-AG, which was founded on July 1, 1990, to take over the business of the former East German state insurance service. Other German insurers raised objections, to no avail, about the monopolistic nature of the takeover, and about the fire sale price paid—DM 270 million ($162 million). As part of the takeover, Allianz also obtained the right to purchase the other 49 percent of the firm, which Allianz later proceeded to do.

The crowning achievement among all these foreign activities was undoubtedly the $1.1 billion acquisition of the Firemen's Fund Insurance Company of Novato, California, a U.S. property and casualty insurance group whose 1989 premiums of $3.4 billion made it the 14th largest insurer in the country. By this one move—which took place in Allianz's centennial year, 1990—the Allianz group almost quadrupled its premium income in the United States. Another significant move came in 1991 when Allianz received a license to sell insurance in Japan, the first German insurer to obtain such permission. With this spate of activity, Allianz became the most internationally active insurer in the world.

This unprecedented expansion would not have been possible without group restructuring. The company's erstwhile structure, with Allianz Versicherungs-AG functioning in dual roles as both a primary insurance company operating in Germany as well as a holding company, impeded the company's expansion of its international activities and industrial involvement, as well as the growth of its intergroup reinsurance company. To rectify the situation, Schieren engineered the transfer of Allianz's direct German property insurance business to a fully owned subsidiary named Allianz Versicherungs-AG (Allianz Insurance AG) in 1985. The interest in Allianz Lebensversicherungs-AG (Allianz Life Insurance AG) and the foreign subsidiaries remained under the holding company now trading as Allianz AG, which had also taken over the reinsurance business passed on by the Allianz companies.

Schieren would score one further coup on the eve of his retirement, which came in October 2001, when Allianz took over Dresdner Bank. Anticipating the coming elimination of barriers in the banking and insurance markets in Europe, Schieren wished to build a Europe-wide network of banks and insurance offices that would send clients to each other. The move was also seen as a challenge to German financial giant Deutsche Bank, Germany's largest bank and a competitor to Allianz in the insurance industry.

Links between German companies, such as the ones between Allianz and Dresdner, became stronger in the early 1990s. For example, both Dresdner Bank and Deutsche Bank each owned 10 percent of Allianz. The power of Allianz, however, was shown by its $230 billion in investments, including an average 10 percent stake in every public company in Germany. Most of these investments were credited to Schieren, who upon his retirement was succeeded by Dr. Henning Schulter-Noelle, former chairman of Allianz Lebensversicherungs.

Schulter-Noelle's first challenge was to stem the hemorrhaging of Allianz's newly acquired East German subsidiary, Deutsche Versicherungs. Thanks in large part to the difficulty of integrating the East German offices into the Allianz network, Allianz suffered its first underwriting loss in two decades, posting a DM 1.78 billion ($1.17 billion) loss in 1992. In response, Allianz reorganized its German operations and cut its East German workforce in half. In 1993 the company took further action by forcing its industrial policyholders to either pay higher premiums, improve risk management, or retain more risk. Through such moves the underwriting losses were reduced to DM 1.19 billion in 1993 and to DM 348 million in 1994. At the same time, operating results at Deutsche Versicherungs were steadily improving, from a loss of more than DM 550 million in 1991 to a loss of just DM 3 million in 1994.

In 1994 Allianz increased its capital base more than 6 percent through a share offering. The cash was to be used for further expansion, this time focusing on small and medium-sized insurance firms in Europe that did not feel they would be able to deal with the coming deregulation of the European market. The first such acquisition occurred later that year when Allianz purchased the direct insurance units of Swiss Reinsurance Company. In the purchase, Allianz gained the Swiss-based Elvia group, which propelled Allianz to the number five position in Swiss insurance; Lloyd Adriatico, an Italian insurer particularly strong in automobile insurance, which solidified Allianz's number two position in insurance in Italy; and Vereinte, a German insurance company which Allianz was forced to divest because of antitrust regulations.

In the United States, Allianz's Fireman's Fund acquisition was suffering from a property and casualty market that continued to be depressed. Although premium volume increased a modest 6.6 percent in 1994, earnings were greatly affected by catastrophic losses totaling $116 million, more than $57 million of which resulted from the January earthquake in Northridge, California, alone. In 1995 Fireman's Fund increased its reserve for environmental claims by $800 million as a provision against liability damages it might incur as a result of Superfund lawsuits.

Since the company continued to be nettled by underwriting losses, Allianz Versicherungs announced in mid-1995 that for large risks it would no longer abide by the quasi cartel rating system that held sway in Germany. Allianz's new system would be based on the individual risk of the policyholder, leading to reduced premiums for good risks, increased premiums for poor risks, and eliminated policies for the poorest risks.

Additional Expansion in the 1990s

The late 1990s were a period of further expansion for Allianz. In particular, the company set its sights on developing its insurance business in Asia. After the Asian economic crisis of 1997, many countries in the region were more receptive to foreign investment than ever before. With such investments, Allianz stood to gain considerably if the wounded economies regained their strength. In 1997 Allianz announced its formal entry into the Chinese life insurance market with the establishment of a joint venture with the Chinese insurer Dazhong. This new entity, named Allianz Dazhong, began operations in 1998, and initially focused on selling life insurance through 300 agents to both mainland Chinese and foreigners living in China, though Allianz made no secret of its plans to expand into offering liability insurance services to large Chinese manufacturers.

Allianz also moved into Korea during this period. In 1999, the company took over the country's fourth largest life insurer and renamed it Allianz First Life. The following year, Allianz gained a controlling 12.5 percent share of Hana Bank, the country's fourth largest financial institution. Initially, Allianz concentrated on leveraging Hana's distribution channels by installing agents from Allianz First Life at Hana's 280 branches. But Allianz soon launched a 50/50 joint venture with Hana, named Hana Allianz Investment Management, to move Allianz into a new business area in Korea—asset management. The joint venture managed assets from Allianz First Life and Hana Bank at the same time that it offered equity and bond products and mutual funds and developed new financial services products.

Allianz sought to make key acquisitions elsewhere in the world as well. Significant among these was Allianz's 1997 purchase of the French-based insurer Assurances Générales de France (AGF) for $10.42 billion. To complete the deal, Allianz waged a long battle with the Italian company Assicuriazioni Generali SpA (Generali), which was engaged in an attempted hostile takeover of AGF. Despite its complex nature—which ultimately involved Allianz giving control of AMB, Germany's third largest insurance group, to Generali in order to reach a compromise—the AGF purchase offered Allianz clear advantages. As an analyst told the *Wall Street Journal Europe*, "[t]he acquisition will push Allianz toward the front of the European insurance sector."

The company did not limit its sights to the insurance sector, however. Allianz's entry into the asset management sector in Korea presaged a broader move into financial services worldwide. In 1998, Allianz established asset management as a core business activity through the creation of a new Munich-based division, Alliance Asset Management. Two years later, Allianz made this new focus clearer when it acquired a 70 percent stake in PIMCO Advisors Holding from the California-based Pacific Life Insurance Co. for about $3.3 billion. With over $256 billion in assets under management, PIMCO was one of the largest investment management companies in the United States. Allianz gained control of Oppenheimer Capital as part of the PIMCO deal as well, further expanding its market share.

The company was not ready to rest on its laurels, though. Hard on the heels of the PIMCO deal, Allianz bought the California money management firm Nicholas-Applegate Capital Management for about $2.2 billion. Although two years earlier, in 1998, Allianz had virtually no money management presence, the Nicholas-Applegate purchase made Allianz a dominant force in this sector with $604 billion in assets under management.

It took another year, though, for Allianz to fully realize its goal to become a full-fledged *global* financial services player. It did so with its high-profile 2001 takeover of Dresdner Bank A.G., Germany's third largest bank. The cash-and-stock deal was valued at about EUR 22 billion ($20 billion). Although Allianz was already Dresdner's biggest shareholder, the purchase gave Allianz full control of the bank, and in the process, created a finance group with a full range of insurance and banking products. As the *Globe and Mail* reported, the Dresdner deal went a "long way toward fulfilling Allianz's vision of becoming a European financial powerhouse with tentacles in insurance, asset management, and retail banking. With [this] deal, Allianz could stake a claim to be one of the top five global financial companies offering a panoply of services in the style of U.S. financial giant Citigroup, Inc."

New Challenges: 2001 and Beyond

Allianz's acquisitions and diversification made the company significantly larger and more powerful, but were not sufficient to immunize it from the vicissitudes of the market and world events. The terrorist attacks in New York and Washington, D.C. on September 11, 2001, had a catastrophic impact on Allianz, and the insurance industry as a whole. The day's damage was estimated between $30 billion and $80 billion—the most severe loss ever incurred by the insurance industry. The downturn of the world's financial markets after September 11 had an even more adverse impact on Allianz. Just as the company moved into asset

management and financial services in a big way, stock markets plummeted and investors lost confidence. Allianz's share price lost more than half its value as a result.

To counter these trends, Allianz boss Schulte-Noelle announced that 2002 would be a "year of consolidation," in which the company would cut costs, integrate Dresdner Bank, streamline operations in its insurance business, and boost performance in asset management. However, it made little progress on these goals, and with a reported net loss of $1.2 billion, 2002 proved to be one of Allianz's worst years ever. Schulte-Noelle stepped down and was succeeded in 2003 by Michael Diekmann, a 15-year Allianz veteran who had headed its insurance business in North and South America. In July 2003, Diekmann announced that he intended to slow the pace of Allianz's expansion. Reaching profitability—not expanding its operations—would become the company's primary objective.

Principal Subsidiaries

Adriatica de Seguros C.A. (Venezuela); AGF Allianz Argentina Compania de Seguros Generales S.A.; AGF Brasil Seguros S.A.; Allianz Compania de Seguros S.A. (Chile); Allianz Cornhill Insurance (Far East) Ltd. (Hong Kong); Allianz Elementar Versicherung-AG (Austria); Allianz Fire and Marine Insurance Japan Ltd.; Allianz First Life Insurance Co. Ltd. (South Korea); Allianz Globus Marine Versicherungs-AG; Allianz Insurance Company (U.S.A.); Allianz Insurance Company of Canada; Allianz Insurance Ltd. (South Africa); Allianz Insurance of Namibia Ltd.; Allianz Insurance (Singapore) Pte. Ltd.; Allianz Irish Life Holdings; Allianz Lebensversicherungs-AG; Allianz Life Insurance Company of North America (U.S.A.); Allianz Mexico S.A. Compania de Seguros; Allianz Nederland N.V.; Allianz poist'ovna, a.s. (Slovakia); Allianz pojist'ovna, a.s. (Czech Republic); Allianz Subalpina Societa di Assicurazioni e Riassicurazioni S.p.A. (Italy); Allianz Tiriac Insurance (Romania); Allianz Versicherung (Schweiz) AG (Switzerland); Assurances Generales de France (65%); Assurances Generales de Laos; P.T. Asuransi Allianz Utama Indonesia Banque AGF (France); Bayerische Versicherungsbank AG (90%); Cornhill Insurance PLC (U.K.); Deutsche Lebensversicherungs-AG; Domus-Forsikringsaktieselskabet (Denmark); Dresdner Bank A.G.; ELVIA Assurances S.A. (Belgium); ELVIA Reiseversicherungen (Switzerland); Fireman's Fund Insurance Company (U.S.A.); France Life (South Korea); Frankfurter Versicherungs-AG; Hungaria Biztosito Rt (Hungary); International Reinsurance Company S.A. (Luxembourg); Jefferson Insurance Company (U.S.A.); Koc Allianz Hayat Sigorta T.A.S. (Turkey); Les Assurances Federales IARD (France); Malaysian British Assurance Berhad; Manufacturers' Mutual Insurance Group (Australia); Monticello Insurance Company; Munchener Ruckversicherungs-Gesellschaft AG (Munich Re) (22%); National Insurance Company Berhad (Brunei); Ost-West Allianz Insurance Company (Russia); Portugal Previdente Companhia de Seguros S.A.; Rhin et Moselle Assurances Françaises Compagnie d'Assurances sur la Vie (France); Royal Nederland Schade; T.U. Allianz BGZ Polska Zycie S.A. (Poland); Zwolsche Algemeene Levensverzekering N.V. (Netherlands).

Principal Competitors

Mitsui Sumitomo Insurance Co., Ltd.; Müncher Rückversicherungs-Gesellschaft Aktiengesellschaft; New York

Life Insurance Company; Nippon Life Insurance Company; Prudential Financial, Inc.; Prudential plc; Royal & Sun Alliance Group plc; State Farm Insurance Companies.

Further Reading

"Allianz, the First of the Few," *Economist,* August 11, 1990, pp. 79–80.

"Allianz to Hike Rates: Policyholders Drafted into War on Underwriting Losses," *Business Insurance,* November 8, 1993, pp. 25, 27.

Arps, Ludwig, *Wechselvolle Zeiten: 75 Jahre Allianz Versicherung 1890–1965,* Munich: Allianz-Versicherungs-AG, 1975.

Borscheid, Peter, *100 Jahre Allianz 1890–1990,* Munich: Allianz Aktiengesellschaft Holding, 1990.

Collings, Richard, "Allianz Is Buying Nicholas-Applegate," *Investment Management Weekly,* October 23, 2000.

Fisher, Andrew, and Ralph Atkins, "Deceptive Image of Anonymity," *Financial Times,* December 15, 1994, p. 25.

Fuhrmans, Vanessa, "Allianz Gets Started on Major Shuffle of Industrial Assets," *Wall Street Journal Europe,* February 11, 2000.

"Hana Bank, Allianz to Form Strategic Partnership," *Korea Times,* March 6, 2000.

Kirk, Don Lewis, "Allianz Goes Own Way in Setting Rates," *Business Insurance,* June 5, 1995, pp. 39–40.

Raghavan, Anita, and Marcus Walker, "Insurer Allianz in Talks to Acquire Dresdner Bank," *Globe and Mail,* March 29, 2001.

Rhoads, Christopher, and Marcus Walker, "Insurer Allianz Nears Deal to Acquire Dresdner," *Wall Street Journal,* March 30, 2001.

Steinborn, Deborah, "Allianz Shares Poised to Rise on AGF Bid," *Wall Street Journal Europe,* November 20, 1997.

Steinmetz, Greg, "Bigger or Better? Allianz Wants Both," *Wall Street Journal,* May 30, 1995, p. A11.

Templeman, John, et al., "A Challenger for Germany's Heavyweight Banking Title," *Business Week,* August 12, 1991, pp. 36–37.

"Underwriting Loss Triggers Fall in Allianz Stock," *Business Insurance,* August 24, 1992, pp. 23, 25.

"A Wholly German Empire," *Economist,* November 2, 1991, pp. 77–78.

—Peter Borscheid (translated from the German by Olive Classe)
—updates: David E. Salamie; Rebecca Stanfel

AMB Property Corporation

Pier 1, Bay 1
San Francisco, California 94111
U.S.A.
Telephone: (415) 394-9000
Toll Free: (877) 285-3111
Fax: (415) 394-9001
Web site: http://www.amb.com

Public Company
Incorporated: 1997
Employees: 184
Sales: $624.7 million (2002)
Stock Exchanges: New York
Ticker Symbol: AMB
NAIC: 525930 Real Estate Investment Trusts

Operating out of San Francisco, AMB Property Corporation is a real estate investment trust (REIT) concentrating on industrial properties. AMB's portfolio includes approximately 1,000 buildings, encompassing some 96.5 million square feet, located in 30 markets in North America, Europe, and Asia. The REIT concentrates on distribution facilities near ports, airports, and highways. In addition, subsidiary AMB Capital Partners, LLC provides real estate investment and management services for outside investors. AMB is one of the few REITs seeking to grow aggressively overseas.

Company Origins

The letters AMB represent the initials of the last names of the company's three founders: Douglas D. Abbey, Hamid R. Moghadam, and T. Robert Burke. Of the three, Moghadam was particularly influential in the establishment and growth of the business. Moghadam was born the only son and youngest child of a wealthy family in Iran before the overthrow of the shah in 1979. His father not only ran a successful construction and residential development business in Tehran, he also was involved in a number of other businesses, including banking and oil exploration. Moghadam went to Switzerland as a teenager to attend a British academy, where he became fluent in English. A gifted student, he graduated at the age of 16, the same year that his father died. As the only son he was expected to take over the family business. In order to be better prepared he came to the United States to further his studies at the Massachusetts Institute of Technology. In just four and one half years he earned a bachelor's degree and a master's degree in civil engineering and construction management, graduating in January 1978. He returned home to Iran to join the family business but he was still considered too young and so returned to the United States, this time to attend Stanford Business School. It was while he was at Stanford that the shah was deposed and the hostage crisis at the American embassy in Tehran unfolded. The new Islamic-led government nationalized the assets of the family business. Given the political climate in Iran, Moghadam decided to remain in the United States.

Moghadam completed his M.B.A. at Stanford in 1980, graduating near the top of his class, yet despite his academic credentials he discovered that at the height of American hostility toward Iran, no company wanted to hire him. Moghadam told the *Wall Street Journal* in a 2000 article, "I can't say it was discrimination, but it certainly looked that way to me. People at that time had negative reactions to anything that had to do with Iran." He received 80 rejection letters, and years later he quipped, "I actually got more rejections than interviews." The best he could find was a temporary position with Homestake Mining Co. in San Francisco. Moghadam was then hired by one of his former Stanford professors, John McMahan, to do real estate advisory work. McMahan described Moghadam to the *San Francisco Business Times*, as "one of the brightest people I've ever known." Moghadam soon teamed up with Douglas Abbey, a colleague from McMahan's office, to form Abbey, Moghadam & Company to continue their work in the real estate advisory business. A year later, in 1984, they were joined by Robert Burke and the three men established AMB Institutional Realty Advisors.

Initially, AMB was an investment management firm that provided real estate investment advisory services to major pension funds, endowments, and foundations. It began investing and managing on behalf of these institutions, focusing on office, industrial, and community shopping centers. In 1987 AMB decided to exit the office area and over the next two years sold off the office properties. In the 15 years the company operated before converting to a public REIT, AMB developed a disciplined approach to investing. Acquisitions started with a thorough evaluation of a property by an acquisitions officer. The deal was then vetted by a regional manager before going to the firm's Investment Committee, which following a due diligence process rendered final judgment on the deal. In addition, AMB created proprietary systems and procedures that it used to manage acquisitions as well as monitor important market data.

Because of AMB's focus on private and institutional clients, it did not join the rush of real estate firms that converted to REIT ownership in 1993 and 1994. REITs had been created by Congress in 1960 as a way for small investors to become involved in real estate in a manner similar to mutual funds. REITs could be taken public and their shares traded just like stock. They were also subject to regulation by the Securities and Exchange Commission. Unlike other stocks, however, REITs were required by law to pay out at least 95 percent of their taxable income to shareholders each year, a provision that severely limited the ability of REITs to retain internally generated funds. During the first 25 years of existence, REITs were only allowed to own real estate, a situation that hindered their growth. Third parties had to be contracted to manage the properties. Not until the Tax Reform Act of 1986 changed the nature of real estate investment did REITs begin to be truly viable. Limited partnership tax shelter schemes that had competed for potential investments were shut down by the act: Interest and depreciation deductions were greatly reduced so that taxpayers could not generate paper losses in order to lower their tax liabilities. Separately, the act also permitted REITs to provide customary services for property, in effect allowing the trusts to operate and manage the properties they owned. Despite these major changes in law, the REIT was still not a fully utilized structure. In the latter half of the 1980s, banks, insurance companies, pension funds, and foreign investors (in particular, the Japanese) provided the lion's share of real estate investment funds. The resulting glutted marketplace led to a shakeout that hampered real estate firms less disciplined than AMB. With real estate available at distressed prices in the early 1990s, REITs finally became an attractive mainstream investment option and many real estate firms went public starting in 1993.

Avoiding Conversion to REIT Status in the Early 1990s

While dozens of newly formed REITs expanded aggressively in the mid-1990s, AMB stayed focused on its client business, managing the properties in which it often held less than a 20

percent stake. Approximately two-thirds of the portfolio was dedicated to industrial properties, and the rest to strip malls. Major pension funds and foundations that owned the majority of the properties included the World Bank pension plan, the Ford Foundation, and Stanford University. The most significant expansion in AMB's activities during this time occurred in 1995, when it opened an East Coast acquisition/asset management office in Boston. But increasingly institutional investors were looking for the more liquid form of ownership that publicly traded shares provided. It was becoming clear that AMB's advisory-based approach to real estate was being superseded by the REIT model. Merging AMB's managed assets into a REIT was not an easy task, however, as outlined in a 1997 *Wall Street Journal* article: "Several advisory companies ... have attempted to 'roll-up' the assets they manage into IPOs but met resistance. 'With poor performance you can't use a roll-up to solve your liquidity problems,' says Nori Gerardo Lietz of Pension Consulting Alliance. 'The Clients won't buy into management a second time.' ... Analysts say AMB is succeeding where other advisers stumbled largely because its clients are satisfied. AMB's properties have outperformed an average of private real-estate portfolios by about 4.5 percent a year for the past 10 years, according to a filing made with the Securities and Exchange Commission."

After AMB convinced its clients to form a REIT, AMB Property Corporation was formed in 1997, representing the merged assets of AMB Institutional Realty Advisors in exchange for shares of common stock. On November 20, 1997, the REIT completed its initial public offering (IPO), netting around $300 million. With more than $2 billion in assets, AMB, listed on the New York Stock Exchange, became one of the largest publicly traded real estate companies in the United States. Although now a REIT, AMB differed in fundamental ways from other trusts, which had been created by former developers who opted to perform a number of tasks, from leasing and property management to pursuing acquisition strategies. Because AMB had been a research-based investment manager, it preferred to outsource property management and development. AMB also opted to retain its advisory function, which would result in much needed private funding in the future when capital became tight. Unlike other REITs, of course, AMB had longstanding and successful relationships with private institutions that made tapping into this source a viable alternative.

AMB wasted little time in acquiring new properties, pursuing a strategy of assembling a national network of warehouse sites in key locations, including transportation hubs San Francisco, Chicago, and northern New Jersey, essentially creating an AMB brand, so that companies could house inventory in AMB warehouses and know delivery was within a day's truck drive. The *San Francisco Chronicle* explained in a 1998 article: "AMB shuns hot, faddish investments such as office buildings, hotels, and apartments. Those properties are cyclical and can turn suddenly cold," says Hamid Moghadam. ... 'Warehouses are very stable; the demand for them is fairly constant,' Moghadam says. 'No matter what happens to the economy, you have to distribute tires, toilet paper and cereal. It's the same with shopping centers. People have to buy groceries.' "

In December 1997, only days after its IPO, AMB picked up another 5.5 million square feet of rentable industrial properties, located in 11 U.S. markets, including Reno, Nevada; Dallas, Texas; and Albany, New York. During the first three months of 1998 it acquired another 790,000 square feet of industrial property and 730,000 square feet of retail property. AMB in 1999 took a major gamble when it decided to sell off shopping center assets and focus on developing distribution facilities for e-commerce companies. In its largest transaction, AMB sold $560 million of its shopping centers to Burnham Pacific Properties. By the time the selloff was complete in 2000, AMB had shed around $1 billion in retail assets. The goal was to devote resources to high throughput distribution properties located near airports, seaports, and trucking centers to serve customers with time-sensitive warehousing needs. The company even trademarked the term ''eSpace,'' which stood for ''expedited space'' to describe the concept. In this regard AMB established a strategic alliance with Internet grocer Webvan, investing $5 million in the company and leasing more than one million square feet in three cities to the start-up. When the dot-com bubble burst in 2001, however, Webvan went out of business and AMB lost its investment. But the warehouse space used by Webvan was soon rented at high rates to credit-worthy tenants. Although dissuaded from future investments in its tenants, AMB continued to pursue a strategy of targeting industrial properties located in transportation hub markets, catering to logistics and freight-forwarding customers that needed to ship products on an expedited basis. As a result, AMB was able to command higher rents and enjoy strong tenant retention and occupancy rates.

Tapping Private Equity in 1999

AMB was successful in 1999 in drawing on relationships established during its days as a private investment manager to tap into private equity funds to fuel further growth. Through the creation of the AMB Institutional Alliance Fund I, the REIT was able to raise $300 million. AMB would co-invest at least 20 percent in the fund and also receive management fees and incentives for meeting predetermined performance hurdles for managing the properties purchased by the fund. Through these additional fees, AMB could earn an enhanced return on its 20 percent equity interest while building a larger operating platform. It also held an edge over many REITs that, because of depressed stock prices, were unable to raise additional cash through the public market. A significant portion of the Alliance Fund was used in 2000 when AMB paid $730 million to acquire 145 industrial buildings, which housed approximately 10.5 mil-

lion square feet. AMB also succeeded in forming partnerships with other companies to develop new warehousing facilities. It established an especially fruitful relationship with Dallas-based Trammell Crow Co., with the two companies joining forces to develop on-tarmac facilities in airports to better serve the high-speed shipping requirements of many customers.

AMB continued its pattern of growth in 2001, although a deteriorating economy forced the company to cut back somewhat on its investments. In 2002 AMB took yet another risk when it decided to embark on what the *San Francisco Business Times* called ''a risky international expansion.'' The REIT began to sell off properties in 16 U.S. markets in order to focus on 11 domestic transportation hubs as well as key international locations. Moghadam told the *San Francisco Business Times,* ''Our strategy is tied to global trade, and this forces us to look at international markets and redeploy cash overseas. Our customers are pushing us to help them with their global problems. There are few reliable warehouse sources that are up to international standards and companies want to simplify the business relying on a few vendors.'' Some of those customers included such major transportation companies as FedEx, UPS, DHL, and APL, which required highly secure warehouses in parts of the world where there was a severe shortage of modern facilities. The first international development project was an 800,000-square-foot facility in Mexico City for a major multinational consumer goods company. In addition, AMB targeted expansion into Europe and Asia. It opened an Amsterdam office in order to develop projects in or close to airports located in the key cities of Amsterdam, London, Paris, Frankfurt, and Madrid. The company made its first European investments in Paris and in Asia. AMB also invested in Singapore and announced development plans for a large industrial park in Tokyo. Although well financed and well managed, the success of the company's new international strategy remained to be seen.

Principal Subsidiaries

AMB Property, L.P.; AMB Property II, L.P.; Long Gatem L.L.C.

Principal Competitors

CenterPoint Properties Trust; Duke Realty Corporation; Kilroy Realty Corporation.

Further Reading

Ginsberg, Steve, ''Real Estate CEO Rolls Dice Again in New Foreign Gambit,'' *San Francisco Business Times,* August 30, 2002.

Kirkpatrick, David D., ''Performance Lets AMB Go Where Others Fail,'' *Wall Street Journal,* October 1, 1997, p. B14.

Louis, Arthur M., ''Slow, Steady Wins the Race,'' *San Francisco Chronicle,* March 27, 1998, p. C1.

Robson, Douglas, ''Man of Vision,'' *San Francisco Business Times,* November 5, 1999, p. 23.

Smith, Ray A., ''At AMB, Warehouse Meet the New Economy,'' *Wall Street Journal,* November 29, 2000, p. B12.

—Ed Dinger

Amec Spie S.A.

Parc Saint-Christophe,
10, avenue de l'Entreprise
95800 Cergy Saint-Christophe Cedex
France
Telephone: +33 1-34-24-30-00
Fax: +33 1-34-24-33-20
Web site: http://www.spie.fr

Subsidiary of AMEC plc
Incorporated: 1900 as Société Parisienne pour l'Industrie
    des Chemins de Fer et des Tramways Electriques
Employees: 24,700
Sales: EUR 3.41 billion ($3.1 billion) (2002)
NAIC: 237990 Other Heavy and Civil Engineering
    Construction; 236210 Industrial Building
    Construction; 237110 Water and Sewer Line and
    Related Structures Construction; 237310 Highway,
    Street, and Bridge Construction

Amec Spie S.A.—known simply as Spie until March 2003—is one of Europe's leading providers of engineering and project management services for both the public sector and private industry, with an emphasis on the electrical engineering, telecommunications, and IT sectors. A series of acquisitions starting in 2001, including VDH in Belgium, Export Telecom Services (ETS), DCCS, and a controlling stake in Matra Nortel Communications Distribution, creating Spie Communications, has transformed Amec Spie into a world-leading communications and network infrastructure support provider. Elsewhere, Amec Spie delivers design and consulting services, as well as turnkey project design and management for manufacturing, rail, and other construction projects—Spie was part of the consortium that built the Channel Tunnel. Following its acquisition by the United Kingdom's AMEC plc, begun in 1997 and completed in 2003, Spie has been restructured into three primary, independently operating subsidiaries: Amec Spie S.A. has become the main holding company for subsidiaries Spie Trindel, Spie Communications, and Spie Energie Services. The former Spie railroad engineering and construction operations have be-

come Amec's continental European rail group, Amec Spie Rail. Lastly, Spie's construction unit has kept its name—one of the oldest in the French construction industry—Spie Batignolles. Amec has indicated its interest in selling off Spie Batignolles as it reorients itself as an engineering services specialist. Amec Spie reported revenues of EUR 3.4 billion ($3 billion) in 2002, more than 90 percent of which were generated in Europe (and 70 percent from within France). The addition of Spie will raise AMEC's revenues to £5.5 billion (more than $9 billion).

Building France in the 19th Century

Spie had long played a central role in the construction of France's—and later the world's—infrastructure. The earliest member of the later Spie was founded in 1846 by Ernest Gouin. With financial backing from, among others, James de Rothschild, Gouin, an engineer who had been working for the Paris Saint-Germain railroad, founded his own workshop in Batignolles. The company, Ernest Gouin et Cie, started out to build steam locomotives for another railroad, Compagnie des Chemins de Fer du Nord, which had been founded the year before.

The economic downturn of 1847, which cut off orders for Gouin's steam locomotives, forced the company to look elsewhere for business. In that year, Gouin turned its metal-working expertise to the public works market, and became the first in France to begin constructing steel bridges. Gouin completed its first bridge in 1852, at Asnières.

Gouin's success at Asnières led the company to expand its operations over the next decade to provide complete bridge construction services, from the design and engineering to laying the foundations, performing brick and stonework, and then constructing the access ramps as well. In 1862, Gouin's growing operations started railroad construction as well. By the end of the 1860s, Gouin was able to provide turnkey construction projects, including ground preparation and draining.

Gouin changed its name to Société de Construction de Batignolles (SCB) in 1871, becoming a public company. Railroad operations became increasingly important for the company, as it became one of France's leaders in that sector. At the same time, SCB continued to manufacture locomotives, exiting that area only in 1928. SCB nonetheless maintained an interest in that area through a subsidiary, Compagnie Générale de Construction de Locomotives Batignolles-Châtillon, set up in 1917. SCB gained expertise building tunnels—the company participated in a first attempt to build a tunnel across the English Channel in 1882—and that expertise, coupled with its bridge-building experience, led the company to expand its railroad construction operations worldwide.

International Infrastructures Giant in the 1970s

The turn of the 20th century saw the rise of a number of other great French enterprises, including Schneider and Empain, both of which were to play an important role in forming the later Spie Batignolles. Groupe Empain had been founded in the late 19th century by Edouard Empain, of Belgium. From humble origins, Empain had become an important early figure in building Belgium's railroads—yet when the Belgian government took control of the country's railroad system, Empain turned to France for his future projects.

In 1881, Empain, later made a baron, founded his own bank in order to provide funding for his industrial interests. Empain's specialty was the construction of electric tramways and other electricity-driven urban mass transportation systems. In the 1890s, Empain's group of companies became one of the world's leaders in that area, building transportation systems throughout Europe and Russia, and as far away as China, Cairo, and the Belgian Congo.

In 1898, Empain became part of the group in building the Paris Metro—considered the company's masterpiece. As part of that project, Empain created a new company in 1900, the Société Parisienne pour l'Industrie des Chemins de Fer et des Tramways Electriques. While its operations also including track laying and other construction services, the company already specialized in the design, engineering, and construction of the electrical infrastructure needed for the electric-powered rail systems.

The Paris-based business soon expanded into other infrastructure projects—in 1923, it built the first high-pressure gas pipeline in France. By 1946, the company had simplified its name, to Société Parisienne pour l'Industrie Electrique (SPIE). The destruction of large parts of France's infrastructure during World War II, coupled with the rapid growth of the country's economy during the 1950s and 1960s, enabled SPIE to grow rapidly into a major presence in the country's electrical engineering sector. Yet SPIE had also entered the larger infrastructure market, gaining expertise in oil and gas pipeline construc-

tion. By the mid-1960s, the company had entered the general industrial construction market as well. In 1966, as France launched a large-scale drive to install a national grid of nuclear power generation facilities, SPIE joined in a consortium to establish Thermatome, dedicated to the engineering and installation of electric systems for the nuclear power industry.

Empain, which had regrouped its international railroad operations under the holding company Electrorail in the 1930s, had lost much of those businesses in the decolonization movement of the postwar era. The loss of these operations, which boosted SPIE's importance with the Empain group, led Empain to seek new expansion. In 1960, Empain acquired a 25 percent stake in another ailing French institution, Schneider & Co.

Schneider, founded in 1836 by brothers Adolphe and Eugène Schneider, had become one of France's leading industrial conglomerates, with a major presence in the shipbuilding industry. In the 1950s, Schneider had restructured its vast holdings into three primary businesses: CITRA (Compagnie Industrial de Travaux), which took over Schneider's construction and public works operations in 1949; SFAC, which became Creusot-Loire in 1970, grouping Schneider's steel works and related businesses; and the mining concern Droitaumont-Bruville.

The accidental death of Charles Schneider, the last of the Schneider family to hold an active role in the company's direction, threw Schneider into disarray. With its main businesses slumping, Schneider gradually came under the control of the Empain group. By the end of the decade, the two companies were merged, forming Empain-Schneider.

During that decade, Schneider had acquired a stake in SCB. In 1968, Empain-Schneider decided to merge SCB with SPIE, forming a new, internationally operating infrastructure and construction concern, Spie Batignolles. Then, in 1972, Spie Batignolles became a major force in the worldwide infrastructure market with the absorption of Empain-Schneider's CITRA unit.

Acquiring Size in the 1980s

The oil crisis of the 1970s and the resulting recession cut into Spie Batignolles' market in Europe. On the other hand, the rise in prominence of the oil-producing nations presented a new international opportunity for the company, and Spie Batignolles became a leading force in pipeline engineering and construction. In 1977, Spie Batignolles' pipeline business took on still greater prominence within the group, following the acquisition of pipeline specialist CAPAG. Founded in 1938, Capag had established itself as one of the sector's leaders, both in France and abroad.

Spie Batignolles' strong growth through the 1970s was not mirrored by Empain-Schneider. By the beginning of the 1980s, the conglomerate was struggling beneath the weight of an ill-considered diversification program, which had brought the industrial giant into such unrelated sectors as magazine publishing, ski manufacturing, and even fashion design. In 1981, the company was restructured, and the Empain family lost control of the company, which became known as Schneider. The beginning of a new crisis in the steel industry at the time encouraged Schneider in its vast restructuring, which saw it streamline itself through the 1980s and into the 1990s as an electrical sector specialist.

Key Dates:

1836: Eugène and Adolphe Schneider found Schneider & Co.
1846: Ernest Gouin founds Ernest Gouin et Cie in Batignolles, France; begins building steam locomotives.
1847: Gouin diversifies into metal bridge construction.
1871: Gouin goes public and changes name to Société de Construction de Batignolles (SCB).
1900: Edouard Empain founds Société Parisienne pour l'Industrie des Chemins de Fer et des Tramways Electriques (SPIE), which begins working on Paris Metro project.
1923: SPIE expands into other infrastructure projects, building France's first high-pressure gas pipeline; Travaux Industriels pour l'Electricité (Trindel) is founded.
1946: SPIE changes name to Société Parisienne pour l'Industrie Electrique.
1949: CITRA (Compagnie Industrial de Travaux) is created as part of Schneider's reorganization.
1960: Empain acquires a stake in Schneider, leading to a takeover of Schneider and the formation of Empain-Schneider.
1968: SPIE and SCB merge to form Spie Batignolles.
1972: Spie Batignolles absorbs CITRA.
1997: Schneider sells Spie Batignolles to management buyout group and AMEC plc.
1998: Company changes name to Spie S.A.
2003: AMEC plc acquires 100 percent control of Spie, which is regrouped into three independent companies, Amec Spie, Amec Spie Rail, and Spie Batignolles.

Spie Batignolles itself continued to expand its engineering and infrastructure activities, boosting its electrical contracting wing with the acquisition of a stake in Trindel in 1982. That company had been founded in 1923 as Travaux Industriels pour l'Electricité, as the Lorraine agency for the company Force et Lumière Electriques. Founded in 1898, that company, later known as FORCLUM, became responsible for installing a major part of France's high-tension electrical network. Trindel meanwhile diversified into other areas following World War II, adding expertise in the steel, chemicals, and petrochemicals markets, as well as in the construction of hydroelectric plants. In the 1970s, Trindel had entered the international arena, active particularly in the Middle East and Africa. Spie Batignolles acquired full control of Trindel in 1984, changing the new subsidiary's name to Spie Trindel. Over the next decade, Spie Trindel became one of Spie Batignolles' largest operations, accounting for nearly one-third of its revenues.

As its oil pipelines operations slowed at the end of the 1980s, Spie Batignolles continued to emphasize its other components, including electrical engineering and construction. In 1987, the company purchased Paris-based construction specialist Société de Construction Générale et de Produits Manufacturés. Another acquisition, in 1989, of Tondella, further consolidated Spie Batignolles' position as a leader in France's construction sector.

By then, Spie Batignolles had moved to expand its electrical engineering business into the rest of Europe with the 1988 purchase of Belgium's Abay TS.

The company also returned to its roots, acquiring in 1989 the track-laying specialist Drouard, a move that helped launch Spie Batignolles into the fast-expanding high-speed train market. Spie-Drouard then became a primary component of Spie Batignolles' rail subsidiary, Spie Rail. That year, also, Spie Batignolles won a concession for the new English Channel Tunnel, supplying the electromechanical and power supply systems for the project.

By the end of the 1980s, Spie Batignolles had succeeded in refocusing its operations, as electrical engineering now accounted for roughly half of its revenues, which topped Fr 24 billion (approximately $4.5 billion). The company had also succeeded in expanding its international operations, which provided some one-third of its sales that year. The company boosted its electrical engineering operations again in 1993, when it acquired two Portugal-based companies, OELE and EVALE.

New Ownership for the New Century

Yet, with the disruptions caused by the Persian Gulf War and the plunge into a new recession at the beginning of the 1990s, Spie Batignolles began posting losses. Schneider, which was completing its reorganization as an electrical products company, began to seek to divest Spie Batignolles. Schneider attracted a number of acquisition offers, which were rejected as too low. Then in 1996, Jean Monville, then CEO of Spie Batignolles, approached the head of Schneider with the idea of a management buyout of Spie Batignolles. The buyout offer, however, extended beyond Spie Batignolles' management to include the company's entire workforce. In the end, more than 80 percent of Spie Batignolles' employees joined in the buyout, raising EUR 281 million under a new holding company, Finanicière Spie SCA.

The Spie buyout group gained a partner at the end of 1996 when it was joined by the United Kingdom's AMEC plc. Amec put up EUR 192 million for a 46 percent stake in Spie Batignolles, raising the total buyout price to EUR 350 million. The stake in Spie Batignolles fit in with AMEC's own dual strategy of gaining international scale while reorienting itself from a construction specialty to a larger engineering services group. As part of AMEC's participation agreement, AMEC gained the option to acquire 100 percent of Spie Batignolles by 2003. The buyout was completed in 1997.

Throughout the end of the 1990s and into the new decade, Spie Batignolles and AMEC tightened their relationship. Spie Batignolles itself began to focus more and more on building up its electrical engineering component to match AMEC's own push into the engineering services sector. In 1997, Spie Batignolles acquired Melotte, based in the Netherlands, strengthening its position in that country's electrical engineering market. As part of its refocusing effort, Spie Batignolles changed its name to Spie S.A., grouping its operations under three primary subsidiaries, Spie-Trindel; Spie Enertrans, for its energy and transportation sector operations; and the construction group Spie Batignolles.

Spie acquired a controlling stake in Laurent Bouillet, France's leading HVAC (heating, ventilation, and air-conditioning) specialist in 1999. That year, also, Spie turned to expanding its range of electrical engineering services, targeting the telecommunications and IT networking markets at the turn of the century, acquiring Elona, based in France, and EDS, based in Germany.

Spie's electrical engineering business continued to grow by acquisition in 2000, with the purchase of Electron, based in Breda, in the Netherlands, the second largest electrical engineering firm in that country; and two Portuguese companies, Cisec and Sometin. These acquisitions, like the Lauren Bouillet acquisition, completed in 2000, were part of Spie's reorientation as an engineering services firm.

In 2001, Spie continued to build up its telecom and IT services, acquiring Matra Nortel Communications Distribution, VDH, based in Belgium, and Export Telecom Services, which became part of a new unit, Spie Communications. Spie's acquisition drive continued into 2002, with purchases including oil industry services provider Foraid; Maintel, which specialized in providing telecommunications services to the offshore and onshore oil and gas industry, and Osiris, a provider of engineering services for the nuclear power industry.

By then, AMEC had revealed its intention to exercise its option to gain 100 percent control of Spie, a move completed in March 2003. Following the acquisition, AMEC announced a reorganization of its European holdings, creating three independently operating subsidiaries, Amec Spie, for engineering services; Amec Rail, for its railroad operations; and Spie Batignolles, which retained Spie's construction business. At that time, AMEC announced its interest in selling off Spie Batignolles, as it completed its transition into a world-leading engineering ser-

vices group. Amec Spie, inheriting more than a century as a leader in the European market, promised to play a central role in AMEC's future growth.

Principal Subsidiaries

Spie Trindel; Spie Communications; Spie Energie Services; Amec Spie Rail; Spie Batignolles.

Principal Competitors

Halliburton Co.; Sumitomo Corp.; Mitsubishi Heavy Industries Ltd.; Nippon Steel Corp.; Bouygues SA; Skanska AB; VINCI SA; Taisei Corp.; Shimizu Corp.; Hochtief AG; Obayashi Corp.; Kawasaki Steel Corp.; Nippon Express Company Ltd.; AREVA; mg technologies ag; Ishikawajima-Harima Heavy Industries Company Ltd.; Colas SA; Kumagai Gumi Company Ltd.; HBG, Hollandsche Beton Groep nv; Eurovia SA; Grupo Dragados SA; Fomento de Construcciones y Contratas SA; NCC AB; Technip-Coflexip SA; Babcock Borsig AG; Balfour Beatty PLC.

Further Reading

Jacquin, Jean-Baptiste, "Spie-Batignolles, l'entreprise aux 12 000 salariés-capitalistes," *L'Expansion*, March 6, 1997, p. 66.

"Spie accelere sa sortie du BTP avant de rejoindre Amec, *Les Echos*, September 4, 2002, p. 4.

"Spie souhaite accelerer sur la criossance dans les services," *Les Echos*, March 16, 2000, p. 22.

Taylor, Andrew, "Amec Set for Stake in French Group," *Financial Times*, October 19, 1996, p. 18.

Withers, Malcolm, "French Stake Mop-up to Cost AMEC £172 million," *Evening Standard*, August 29, 2002, p. 37.

—M.L. Cohen

Anteon Corporation

3211 Jermantown Road, Suite 700
Fairfax, Virginia 22030
U.S.A.
Telephone: (703) 246-0200
Fax: (703) 246-0294
Web site: http://www.anteon.com

Public Company
Incorporated: 1996
Employees: 7,200
Sales: $825.82 million (2002)
Stock Exchanges: New York
Ticker Symbol: ANT
NAIC: 541512 Computer Systems Design Services;
541330 Engineering Services; 511210 Software
Publishers

Anteon Corporation provides information technology solutions and engineering services to government clients. Anteon designs, integrates, and maintains advance systems for national defense, intelligence, emergency response, and other government missions. The company contracts with virtually all military services, including the U.S. Army, Navy, and Marine Corps, as well as dozens of other civilian and defense organizations within the federal government.

Origins

Although Anteon traces its origins to the 1970s, the true core of the company was created in 1996 through an acquisition—an appropriate beginning for an enterprise whose greatest successes were on the acquisitive front. The company began as the professional services division of Ogden Corporation, a conglomerate whose core businesses were involved in providing concessions at sports venues and on-the-tarmac service to airlines at airports across the nation. Ogden Corporation purchased the professional services assets in the 1980s, forming what would become known as Ogden Professional Services. By the mid-1990s, Ogden Professional Services employed 1,200 pro-

grammers, engineers, and technical analysts who oversaw more than 200 computer contracts awarded by the federal government. The combination seemed an odd mix; a technically oriented, federal government-supported business owned by a company that sold beer and hot dogs. Ogden Professional Services was not Ogden Corporation's only asset to appear out of place, however. Among other companies, Ogden Corporation also owned W.J. Schafer Associates, a firm that provided scientific support to government agencies, including the Pentagon's ballistic missile defense organization. The anomalies were the result of Ogden Corp's strategic diversification, but by the mid-1990s the company had decided to shelve its strategy and focus on its core businesses. Ogden Professional Services, W.J. Schafer Associates, and other assets that diverted the company's attention were put up for sale.

There were a number of different suitors interested in Ogden Professional Services, and each submitted a bid. In January 1996, the winner was announced, a New York-based investment firm named Caxton Corp. A hedge-fund operator, Caxton paid $40 million for the Ogden division, which at the time was generating $109 million in annual revenue, a sum collected from serving 60 federal agencies. Caxton renamed its acquisition Anteon Corporation and announced ambitious plans for its new property. Caxton executives declared their intention to invest in Anteon's growth by acquiring competitors, hoping to triple the company's size within the next few years. The professional services firm was considered to be too small to survive in the government contracting market, a market that analysts predicted would be dominated by large companies able to reap the benefits of efficiencies of scale and scope. The objective was aggressive growth, and to realize their goal Caxton officials appointed Joseph M. Kampf as Anteon's new chief executive officer.

No individual had a greater influence on the strident growth achieved from 1996 forward than Kampf. Kampf received a B.A. in economics from the University of North Carolina, which he used to secure several operational and financial management positions in the United States and South America. After garnering praise in his early professional career, Kampf was hired as an executive by The Penn Central Corporation. First, Kampf served as senior vice-president of the company's

6,500-employee federal systems group. Next, he was named executive vice-president of a Penn Central subsidiary named Vitro Corp., a company that earned most of its income serving as a contractor for the U.S. Navy. From Vitro Corp, Kampf joined Anteon, where his experience and contacts as a senior executive for a Navy contractor would leave an indelible imprint on the newly formed Anteon.

The purchase of Ogden Professional Services by Caxton was completed in April 1996, marking the beginning of the company's bid to become a major player in the defense contracting industry. One month after being recast as Anteon, the company announced it had secured a $32 million contract to provide technical and managerial services to the Navy. In the years ahead, Anteon achieved the bulk of its growth through acquisitions, but the value of adding business such as the $32 million Navy contract was not to be underestimated. Anteon recorded impressive growth through internal means as well, averaging 15 percent annual growth during the late 1990s and early 21st century—a rate of growth calculated without the one-time surge in sales provided by an acquisition. The company's ability to achieve steady growth through internal, or organic, means spoke highly of the Kampf-led management team, whose expertise provided a sturdy foundation to support the acquisitions that soon would be absorbed into the company's operations.

Anteon's acquisition campaign followed a methodical, calculated course. The process of identifying competitors to acquire involved screening hundreds of candidates, from which the company pared down the list to no more than a half-dozen targets. Although the company's revenue volume swelled considerably on an annual basis following the appointment of Kampf, it did so by rarely acquiring more than one company in a single calendar year. The first year of the Kampf era ended without any acquisitions completed, but Kampf hailed the first year of new ownership as "a dynamic year, highlighted by a 30 percent growth in revenue," according to an April 24, 1997 company press release. Kampf used the occasion to explain his bold plans for the future, which he described as "aggressive but achievable," in the Anteon press release. Largely through acquisitions, Kampf planned to reach the $500 million-in-sales mark in 36 months. Kampf planned to hit his financial target by branching out into new technological fields and by broadening the company's customer base to include more federal clients.

Acquisitions Beginning in 1997

The first addition to the company arrived more than a year after the Caxton-led buyout. In late August 1997, Anteon paid

$19 million to acquire Vector Data Systems, Inc., a $35 million-in-sales supplier of information systems and services for the collection, analysis, and distribution of military intelligence data. Next, in May 1998, the company paid $45.9 million to acquire Techmatics, Inc., a $56.7 million-in-sales company based in the same community as Anteon, Fairfax, Virginia. Founded in 1982, Techmatics recorded robust growth during the 1990s, increasing its sales at an annual rate of 20 percent to become one of the fastest growing technology companies in the federal service industry. Techmatics' largest customer was the Department of Defense, for which the company provided engineering services for numerous programs. Techmatics engineering and program management services were used in large-scale military system development, such as the Navy's surface ship fleet, on-ship combat systems, and missile defense programs. With the addition of Vector Data and Techmatics, Anteon's workforce eclipsed 2,300 employees, having roughly doubled in size within two years. Sales for the year fell just shy of $250 million, halfway towards Kampf's target of $500 million by 2000.

Anteon acquired its third company a little more than a year after purchasing Techmatics. In June 1999, the company purchased Analysis & Technology, Inc., the largest acquisition in the first seven years of Anteon's existence. Analysis & Technology, which generated $170.4 million in sales before its acquisition, provided a full range of engineering and information technology services to federal and commercial customers, relying heavily, like Techmatics, on business with the Department of Defense. Anteon paid $155.6 million to complete the deal, gaining 1,700 Analysis & Technology employees and a number of offices scattered across the country. As Anteon exited the 1990s, its payroll comprised more than 4,000 employees in 70 offices. Sales in 1999 inched past $400 million.

As Anteon grew, both through external and internal means, its stature within the industry increased as well. In 1999, *Defense News* published its list of the "World's Top 100 Defense Firms." On the list was Anteon, earning 85th place in the rankings, which were derived using data from survey responses submitted by companies throughout the world. *Defense News* was not the only publication to acknowledge Anteon's resolute rise within the industry. *Federal Computer Week*, among other independent sources, recognized the company as a leading information technology integrator, giving Kampf and his executives further incentive to actualize their expansion plan. By this point, with the half-billion-dollar goal in reach, Kampf was setting his sights higher, making reference to Anteon becoming a multibillion-dollar company. The company's progress in the next several years suggested that Kampf's objective was not far-fetched, as the company continued to perform admirably, both in its efficient absorption of other companies and in its ability to record strong organic growth.

After the acquisition of Analysis & Technology, nearly a year-and-a-half passed before Anteon completed another acquisition. In October 2000, the company acquired Chantilly, Virginia-based Sherikon, Inc., paying roughly $35 million for the $65 million-in-sales company. Privately held Sherikon, with 750 employees and 14 offices, provided technology services to federal, state, and local clients. Founded in 1984, the company operated in 21 states and internationally as well, with offices in Puerto Rico, Germany, and Italy.

In 2000, Kampf easily reached the sales goal he set three years earlier. Anteon generated $542.8 million in sales for the year, and dramatically increased its industry ranking. When *Defense News* published its annual list of rankings, Anteon occupied the 58th position, leaping into the mid-tier of defense contractors worldwide. In the months leading up to the company's next acquisition, internal growth drove it forward, as Anteon registered an organic growth rate of more than 20 percent during the first six months of 2001. "The acquisitions get the headlines," Kampf explained in an August 7, 2001 company press release, "but it is the organic growth that demonstrates a company's ability to win new business and provide high quality services to its customers."

Anteon's fifth acquisition was the smallest of the company's purchases, but its addition added meaningfully to the breadth of its services. In July 2001, Anteon acquired the training systems division of SIGCOM, Inc. Referred to as SIGCOM Training, the $12.5 million-in-sales division was acquired for $11 million. SIGCOM Training provided advanced simulations systems for military and government organizations such as the U.S. Army, U.S. Marine Corps, U.S. Navy Seals, the Federal Bureau of Investigation, the British Special Forces, and North Atlantic Treaty Organization troops. SIGCOM Training's specialty was in simulating combat conditions in urban areas.

Initial Public Offering of Stock in 2002

When Caxton acquired Ogden Professional Services, the consensus among analysts was that the hedge-fund firm would either sell the company or take it public. The latter option was the course taken, ending Anteon's existence as a privately held concern. In March 2002, the company completed its initial public offering (IPO) of stock, raising $270 million that was used to pay down the company's debt. Anteon ended the year with $825 million in sales, and a contract backlog of $4.3 billion.

As Anteon embarked on a new era as a publicly traded concern, it exuded considerable strength, holding sway as a company of far greater stature than the professional services division inherited by Kampf and his executive team. Its debt significantly reduced by the proceeds of the IPO, the company enjoyed the financial freedom to continue its aggressive rise as a defense contractor. In May 2003, the company grabbed the business press headlines again, completing the sixth acquisition since Kampf was appointed chief executive officer. The acquisition of Information Spectrum Inc. (ISI), a maker of optical security cards for the U.S. State Department, was driven, in part, by the business created in the aftermath of the attacks on September 11, 2001. Seeking to bolster its ability to secure business from the Homeland Security Department, Anteon significantly increased its chances to secure a contract with the potential to be worth hundreds of millions of dollars by purchasing ISI. Anteon's executive vice-president for corporate development explained the reasoning behind the acquisition in an April 24, 2003 interview with *Knight Ridder/Tribune Business News*. "ISI is unique in that it is the only company making optical cards for the U.S. government," he said. "We're hoping to combine those technologies with our own integrated-circuits technology to win the contract."

The addition of ISI added $130.5 million in sales, 1,200 employees, and 27 U.S.-based offices to Anteon's ever expanding operations. In the years ahead, the company promised to figure prominently in the billions of dollars being awarded by a host of federal agencies. With Kampf leading the company's charge, Anteon promised to be a prominent player in the defense contracting market for years to come.

Principal Subsidiaries

Vector Data Systems, Inc.; Techmatics, Inc.; Analysis & Technology, Inc.; Sherikon, Inc.; Information Spectrum, Inc.

Principal Competitors

Booz Allen Hamilton Inc.; Electronic Data Systems Corporation; Raytheon Company.

Further Reading

"Anteon Awarded Major Contract to Support Army Units," *EDP Weekly's IT Monitor,* March 31, 2003, p. 8.
"Anteon Looks to Bank on Federal Spending," *IPO Reporter,* January 7, 2002.
Bonasia, J., "Defense Contractor Anteon Timed Its IPO Just Right," *Investor's Business Daily,* March 13, 2002, p. A06.
"Fairfax's Anteon to Buy Annandale's ISI; $90.7 Million Acquisition to Help Bigger Firm Get Homeland-Security Business," *Washington Times,* April 24, 2003, p. C14.
Higgins, Marguerite, "Fairfax, Va.-Based Firm Anteon Aims to Ramp Up Homeland-Security Business," *Knight Ridder/Tribune Business News,* April 24, 2003.
Pearlstein, Steven, "Surviving the Sale at Ogden, Panic Turns to Promise at a Divested Division," *Washington Post,* May 6, 1996, p. F19.
Woodard, Christopher, "Anteon Corp.," *Investor's Business Daily,* June 28, 2002, p. A06.

—Jeffrey L. Covell

AOL Time Warner

AOL Time Warner Inc.

75 Rockefeller Plaza
New York, New York 10019
U.S.A.
Telephone: (212) 484-8000
Fax: (212) 489-6183
Web site: http://www.aoltimewarner.com

Public Company
Incorporated: 2001
Employees: 88,500
Sales: $40.96 billion (2002)
Stock Exchanges: New York
Ticker Symbol: AOL
NAIC: 514191 On-Line Information Services; 541519
   Other Computer Related Services; 512110 Motion
   Picture and Video Production; 512120 Motion Picture
   and Video Distribution (pt); 511120 Periodical
   Publishers (pt); 511130 Book Publishers; 513210
   Cable Networks; 513120 Television Broadcasting;
   334612 Prerecorded Compact Disc (Except Software),
   Tape, and Record Reproducing (pt); 711211 Sports
   Teams and Clubs

Global media powerhouse AOL Time Warner Inc. represents one of the most ambitious corporate mergers in U.S. history, combining the vast entertainment, network, and publishing interests of the Time Warner group with the world's largest online service, AOL. Yet the merger, which when completed in 2001 promised a new era of media content and delivery, quickly ran into snags—not the least of which was the sagging and possibly outmoded fortunes of AOL itself. Affected by downturns in the high-technology industry and in advertising spending, AOL Time Warner (AOL TW) has seen its value plummet from nearly $285 billion at the time of the merger to as low as $61 billion just two years later. The company's revenues, which rose to nearly $41 billion, nonetheless produced losses of almost $98 billion in 2002—the largest loss in U.S. corporate history. Much of that can be blamed on the perennial money-loser America Online, which in 2002 saw

its subscriber base shrink for the first time due to AOL's late entry into the high-speed Internet market. Yet AOL TW remains the industry heavyweight, with operations grouped under two main business units: Media & Communications Group; and Entertainment & Networks. The former gathers such AOL TW companies as America Online, the AOL TW Book Group; AOL TW Interactive Video; the magazine publishing group Time Inc.; and Time Warner Cable, the number two cable network in the United States. Under Entertainment & Networks, AOL TW groups its Home Box Office and Turner Broadcasting System cable and satellite networks, including CNN, TNT, the Cartoon Network and other television holdings; cinema, including Warner Bros., New Line Cinema and Castle Rock Entertainment; and music, centered on Warner Bros. Music and including Atlantic and Elektra companies. Films, including such 2000s blockbusters as the *Harry Potter* series and the *Lord of the Rings,* produce 23 percent of sales. AOL is the next largest unit, at 20 percent of sales, followed by Networks (18 percent), Cable Television (16 percent), Publishing (13 percent) and Music (10 percent). Nearly 80 percent of the company's revenues are produced in the United States. Richard Parsons took over as company chairman in 2002 and has been leading the company on a streamlining effort designed to pay down debt and restore investor confidence in the company. The company was forced to abandon plans to sell off the AOL TW Book Group in 2003 when it could not find a suitable purchase offer. Meanwhile, AOL TW pressed ahead with plans to spin off its TW Cable holdings as a public company, possibly for late 2003.

Cinema Pioneers

The merger of AOL and Time Warner in 2001 brought together four of the United States' most important media pioneers of the 20th century, grouping Warner Bros. (cinema), Time (publishing), TBS (cable television), and AOL (online services). Each of the these companies had been instrumental in establishing and defining the industries in which they came to become dominant players.

The Warner brothers—Harry, the oldest, born in 1881, Albert, Jack, and Sam—were the sons of Polish-Jewish immigrants who settled in Youngstown, Ohio. The Warners tried

Company Perspectives:

Our Mission is to become the world's most respected and valued company by connecting, informing and entertaining people everywhere in innovative ways that will enrich their lives.

their hand at a variety of occupations, until Sam Warner discovered the Edison Kinetoscope and began working as a projectionist. The Warners soon pooled their savings, some $1,000, to buy their own projector and launched their own traveling picture show—their first showing, in a mortuary, generated $300 in a single week.

By 1903, the Warners had opened their own theater in Newcastle, Pennsylvania, with the entire family chipping in, including baby Jack Warner who provided in-between show entertainment. The following year, the Warners established their own distribution company, Duquesne Amusement & Supply Co., which was driven out of business in 1909 by the Edison Trust monopoly which was intent on stamping out patent infringements. Instead, the Warners bought a new projector and once again went on the road. As part of their new business, Sam and Jack Warner produced their first film, called *Peril of the Plains,* in 1911.

In 1915, the brothers split up, with Sam and Jack Warner moving to California in order to make films—the weather there permitted a year-round filmmaking schedule—while Harry and Albert opened an office in New York in order to handle distribution. Warner Bros.' first hit came in 1918 with the film *My Four Years in Germany,* which grossed $1.5 million and permitted the company to open its own studios in Los Angeles that year. Warner Bros. quickly released a stream of slapstick comedies; its first big star, however, was a dog—Rin Tin Tin—that appeared in a string of films in the 1920s.

Warner Bros. made movie history in that decade. In 1925, Sam Warner went east (leaving Jack Warner in charge of the production studios). The company had acquired Brooklyn-based Vitagraph Studios, and Sam Warner now formed a partnership with Western Electric & Telegraph, called Vitaphone, to work on means of synchronizing sound with film. The invention was to lead to the release of *The Jazz Singer* in 1927, considered to be the first successful "talkie." Sam Warner died the night before the film's showing. Yet *The Jazz Singer* represented no mere success. Instead, it revolutionized the film industry, ushering in an a new era in entertainment.

Founding a Media Empire in the 1920s

In the meantime, another company was fast placing its imprint on the U.S. media markets. Briton Hadden and Henry Luce met as students at the Hotchkiss School in Connecticut, where Hadden served as editor-in-chief at the school newspaper, while Luce held the same position for the school's *Hotchkiss Literary Monthly.* Hadden and Luce became friends and enrolled in Yale University together, where they became chairman and editor, respectively, of the *Yale Daily News.* While serving in the officers' training school during World War I,

Luce and Hadden came up with an idea for a new type of newspaper.

Luce and Hadden parted ways briefly, but by 1921 had come back together, now as reporters for the *Baltimore News.* The pair returned to their idea for a new style of newspaper, and in 1922 resigned their positions, founding what was to become the Time Inc. publishing empire. By 1923, Hadden and Luce had succeeded in raising some $86,000, and the first issue of *Time* was launched in March of that year. Hadden took the role of editor, while Luce became the magazine's business manager. Under their leadership, *Time* quickly established new journalistic standards, including a requirement that everything printed in the magazine be attributed to a source.

By 1924, *Time* already boasted a paid subscriber base of 30,000. In that year, the pair launched a second magazine title, the *Saturday Review of Literature.* The following year, the company moved its headquarters to Cleveland, Ohio, in a move to cut costs. In 1928, however, the company split its operations in two, with its printing handled by R.R. Donnelley in Chicago, and its editorial offices returned to New York City. Meanwhile, under Hadden's editorial direction the company launched a second title, *Tide,* geared toward the advertising industry, in 1927.

Hadden died in 1929 at the age of 31, leaving Luce alone to handle the company's growing success. Luce now took over sole leadership of the company, placing his imprint on the company's editorial direction. The following year, after selling off *Tide,* Luce proposed a new magazine, to be called *Fortune,* catering specifically to the country's business world. *Fortune* enjoyed quick success, despite—or perhaps because of—the country's plunge into the Depression Era.

Time made a tentative entry into radio, with its own "March of Time" show in 1931. Yet the company remained focused on its growing magazine empire. In 1932, Luce, whose span of interests included architecture, led the company to acquire 75 percent of *Architectural Forum,* taking full control of the title the following year. Over the course of the following decade, Luce transformed that magazine into an industry leader, boosting its circulation from 5,000 to more than 40,000. Nonetheless, the title remained a money-loser.

Luce's next foray came in 1936, with the launch of a new type of magazine based on photographic essays. The new weekly title, called, simply enough, *Life,* debuted in November of that year and became an instant success. Expensive to produce, *Life* lost money in its early years, despite its soaring circulation. At the same time, the new title drained off a number of existing *Time* readers. Nonetheless, *Life* turned its first profit in 1939—and, with the outbreak of World War II, began its glory years as arguably the United States' most influential magazine. By 1941, *Life* boasted a circulation of more than 3.3 million. *Time,* meanwhile, had boosted its readership to nearly one million—including some 200,000 subscribers that transferred to the title after Time Inc. acquired the *Literary Digest* in 1938.

By then, Time had established a new corporate structure, with its three primary titles, *Time, Life,* and *Fortune,* each becoming a separate division within the company, with their own publishers, editors, and advertising directors. Meanwhile, Luce stepped down from his position as president and CEO of

Key Dates:

1903: The Warner brothers open their own movie theater in Newcastle, Pennsylvania.

1911: The Warners produce their first film, *Perils of the Plains.*

1915: Sam and Jack Warner move to Los Angeles, setting up film production studios, while Harry and Albert Warner set up distribution company in New York.

1923: Briton Hadden and Henry Robinson Luce publish the first issue of *Time* magazine.

1924: Hadden and Luce launch their second publication, the *Saturday Review of Literature.*

1925: Warner Bros. acquires Vitagraph Studios in New York, launches Vitaphone joint venture.

1927: Warner Bros. releases *The Jazz Singer* and revolutionizes film history by introducing the "talkie."

1929: Warner Bros. acquires Stanley-Crandall movie theater network

1930: Time Inc. publishes the first issue of *Fortune.*

1936: Company publishes the first issue of *Life.*

1949: Warner Bros. is forced to sell off its movie theater network.

1954: Company launches *Sports Illustrated.*

1961: Company forms Time-Life Books, a book publishing subsidiary.

1966: Jack Warner sells Warner Bros. to Seven Arts.

1969: Kinney National Services acquires Warner Bros. (and renames itself Warner Communications in 1971).

1970: Ted Turner acquires first television station in Atlanta, forming future Turner Broadcasting System.

1972: Time ceases publication of *Life*; launches Home Box Office (HBO) cable TV network and *Money* magazine.

1974: Company publishes first issue of *People.*

1976: Turner renames his television station as Superstation TBS and begins supplying programming to cable television operators.

1980: Time launches Cinemax cable TV network; TBS launches CNN.

1985: Steve Case forms Quantum Computer Services, Inc. to provide online service for Commodore computer users.

1988: Quantum introduces an online service for owners of IBM computers.

1989: Quantum begins offering an online service for Apple computer users; introduces "America Online," a new nationwide network for computer owners.

1990: Time Inc. acquires Warner Communications, forming Time Warner Inc.

1991: Quantum Computer Services changes its name to America Online.

1992: Time Warner forms Time Warner Entertainment subsidiary to house its cable companies; America Online (AOL) makes an initial public offering, announces an alliance with Apple Computer.

1993: AOL introduces an online service designed specifically for Windows users.

1996: Time Warner acquires Turner Broadcasting System.

1998: America Online acquires Internet service provider Compuserve.

1999: AOL acquires Netscape, as well as MovieFone, Spinner, and NullSoft.

2001: AOL acquires Time Warner in a $106 billion mega-merger.

2003: Company proposes dropping "AOL" from its name.

Time Inc. in order to concentrate on his role as editor-in-chief of the company's growing magazine empire. Roy Larsen, who had been chairman of the company, took over the president and CEO positions as well in 1939. Toward the end of the war years, a new generation of leaders began their rise in the company, including C.D. Jackson, who organized the company's international pool of reporters; James A. Linen, who took over as publisher and the editorial force behind *Time*; and Edward Thompson, who became managing editor of *Life* in 1949. Under this new generation, Time Inc. prepared to enter its glory days as one of the United States' dominant publishers.

Coming of Age in the 1970s

By the 1950s, Warner Bros. had emerged as one of the five major players in the U.S. film industry. In 1929, using the proceeds from *The Jazz Singer,* the company bought up the sprawling Burbank, California studios of First National Pictures. That purchase gave the company room to expand production—and became the site of a large swatch of filmmaking history. The company was also enjoying its standing as co-owner of the Vitaphone patent, which had become required technology for the industry. At the same time, Warner Bros. shrewdly bought up the Stanley-Crandall movie theater network

in 1929, giving its control of nearly 25 percent of the United States' movie theater circuit by the 1930s.

Warner Bros. turned a profit of $14 million in 1929. By 1933, however, its losses, the product of slouching audiences, had topped more than $100 million. Yet Warner Bros. was already entering a new era, with the arrival of the legendary Darryl Zanuck, originally hired as a writer for the *Rin Tin Tin* series, as the studio's head of production. Under Zanuck, Warner Bros. turned to producing so-called urban melodramas, including *Little Caesar,* which singlehandedly launched the gangster film genre and the career of acting great Edward G. Robinson. Warner Bros. quickly discovered a number of other stars in the 1930s, including James Cagney, who starred in 1931's *Public Enemy.* Another hit commodity for the studio was Errol Flynn, who brought T*he Adventures of Robin Hood* to life. At the same time, Warner Bros. became known for its cartoon shorts featuring such characters as Bugs Bunny, and for lighter musicals, including the Busby Berkeley series.

While Warner Bros. adopted the "factory" approach to filmmaking of its competitors, it nonetheless carved a reputation for itself as a maker of "films that mattered." By the 1940s, the studio had been responsible for the careers of such stars as

Humphrey Bogart, Bette Davis, Lauren Bacall, Doris Day, and directing greats Frank Capra, John Huston, and Ernst Lubitsch. By 1942, Warner Bros. appeared at its peak, with the release of the unequaled *Casablanca.*

That film was also to represent the company's heyday, however. The company's support for the U.S. war effort had resulted in a wash of mediocre, if highly patriotic films. In 1946, the government, seeking to strike at the monopoly on the film industry held by the top film companies, passed legislation requiring the studios to exit at least one of the three areas of operations in the industry, production, distribution, and exhibition. In 1949, Warner Bros. chose to sell off its theater network—in the process shedding its guaranteed movie venues.

The next hit to Warner Bros. was the arrival of television. Still led by production head Jack Warner and distribution head Harry Warner, the company turned its back on the new medium, except to sell off broadcasting rights to the company's film catalog at cut-rate prices. Very quickly, the company found itself in nightly face-to-face competition with its own and greatest films.

With the end of the factory production system in the 1950s, Warner Bros. appeared to be settling in for a slow fadeout. Despite a few notable successes—such as the discovery of Marlon Brando and James Dean in the 1950s, and the 1960s successes of *Who's Afraid of Virginia Woolf?*, the Jack Warner-produced Oscar Winner *My Fair Lady*, and the Arthur Penn masterpiece *Bonnie and Clyde*—the Warner Bros. era seemed at an end. Harry Warner had died in 1958, and Albert Warner, in 1967. By then, Jack Warner had sold the company to Seven Arts Production Ltd. for $32 million. He died in 1978.

Renamed Warner Brothers-Seven Arts, the company under its new owners became more interested in the money to be made by selling broadcasting rights to the Warner Bros.' film library, rather than in making new movies. Instead, Warner Brothers branched out in 1969, paying $17 million for Atlantic Records, which had been founded by Ahmet Ertegun in the 1950s, pioneering the rhythm and blues market, and which had become one of the industry's seminal record companies. Atlantic soon began building its own stable of labels, adding another industry pioneer, Elektra Records, in 1970.

By then, Warner Brothers was being brought back to life. In 1969, the company was acquired by Kinney National Services, a diversified conglomerate built up by Steven Ross in the 1950s and 1960s. Ross quickly divested most of Kinney's operations, retaining its media holdings, which were renamed Warner Communications in 1971.

Warner claimed new success over the next decade. Its movie production studios quickly began turning out hits, including *Woodstock, All the President's Men*, and *The Exorcist*. By the end of the decade the company string of successes included *Superman* and the Clint Eastwood vehicle *Every Which Way But Loose*. The company's music businesses were also growing strongly, especially with the rise in prominence of FM radio. Warner Communications also diversified into the wider media market, acquiring holdings in the nascent cable television market, publishing operations, a magazine distribution business, and, in 1976, video game producer Atari, for which it paid just

$26 million. By 1980, Warner Communications had seen its revenues soar to $2 billion.

Throughout this period, Time Inc. itself was emerging into a media powerhouse. In 1954, the company had a new success when it launched *Sports Illustrated,* a pioneer in the relatively young professional sports market. Although that title remained unprofitable for some time, it continued to grow, later becoming one of the company's most important magazine franchises.

Time had also begun to diversify by the 1950s, adding book publishing to its successful magazine publishing holdings. In 1952, it established subsidiary Time-Life Broadcast, which acquired a 50 percent stake in the KOB radio and television stations in Albuquerque, New Mexico. The company bought majority control of Intermountain Broadcasting Television Corporation in Utah, then, in 1954, bought full control of Colorado's KLZ radio and television stations. Time's broadcast stable grew to include the acquisition of a group of stations held by Bitner, for $16 million, giving it a presence in Michigan, Indiana, and Minnesota. By the end of the decade, the company sold off its stakes in Utah and Minneapolis, and instead bought up stations in San Diego and Bakersfield, California.

A new generation took over at Time at the beginning of the 1960s, which oversaw the creation of a new and successful unit, Time-Life Books, in 1961, and extended the company into textbook publishing with the purchase of Silver Burdett Co., for $6 million in 1962. The company's book publishing operation took a step forward in 1968, when it paid $17 million in stock to acquire Little, Brown and Company, based in Boston.

Time's magazine empire, and especially *Life,* faced new competition in the 1960s from titles including *Look* and *The Saturday Evening Post*. Although these titles quickly faded, Time, which had seen its production costs soar, while both circulation and advertising revenues dwindled, was forced to pull the plug on *Life*, which had once again slipped into losses. After losing more than $30 million, *Life* ceased publication in 1972. Instead, that year, Time launched a new title, *Money*, to capture the growing consumer interest in personal finance. Two years later, the company produced a new success, the extremely popular *People* magazine.

In the meantime, Time's diversification had taken it beyond publishing and media, into paper production, through the East Texas Pulp and Paper Company joint venture with Houston Oil Company, and the $128 million merger-acquisition of Temple Industries, a maker of lumber and other wood products, in 1973. By 1978, the company had even entered the packaging industry, paying $272 million for Inland Container Corporation. Yet media remained the company's major focus, and by 1983, Inland and Temple were merged together and spun off to Time Inc.'s shareholders.

Instead, Time turned its focus on a young and hot property—HBO. At the beginning of the 1970s, Time had sold off its broadcasting operations with the intention of concentrating its interests in the newly developing cable television industry. The company formed its own pay-TV service, Home Box Office, through a subsidiary, under the direction of J. Richard Munro—who later became company chairman and CEO. HBO began broadcasting in 1972, in Wilkes-Barre, Pennsylvania, with an initial subscriber base of just 365. By the beginning of the 1980s, HBO had established itself as one of the largest and most successful pay-TV stations. In 1980, Time had a new cable television hit with the launch of Cinemax. By then, too, Time had gained a majority stake in American Television and Communications Corporation, one of the country's largest cable television systems.

Time continued growing strongly through the 1980s, boosting its publishing wing with the purchase of Scott Foresman in 1985, and adding a number of new magazine titles, including *Progressive Farmer*, with the 1985 purchase of Southern Progress Corp. By 1988, the company published 24 magazines. The following year, it reached an agreement to merge with Warner Communications, creating the world's largest media company.

Media Mega-Mergers in the 1990s

Warner had hit a bump in the early 1980s. As the owner of Atari, Warner had become vulnerable to the sudden collapse of the video game industry, which sent Warner's stock price plummeting. Warner, still led by Steven Ross, was forced to fend off a hostile takeover attempt from Rupert Murdoch, by bringing in "white knight" Herbert Siegel as a major shareholder and director. Ross and Siegel eventually began what became a public feud.

The company sold off Atari in 1984, as its losses mounted to more than $1 billion. The company began a restructuring program, and by 1986, its revenues were once again building strongly, topping $2.8 billion. Warner had booked a number of cinema successes, including such hits as *The Color Purple* and *Pale Rider*. Meanwhile, Warner Records had risen to become the United States' top record label, with such stars as Madonna, Prince, Genesis, Van Halen, and others ensuring brisk CD sales.

Warner was finding success in the cable television market as well. In 1985, the company reached a five-year licensing agreement with HBO, giving it exclusive rights to new Warner films. In 1986, Warner, which had formed its own cable television service with American Expression, bought out its partner, paying $393 million for full control of Warner Amex Cable. Two years later, the deregulation of the cable industry unleashed Warner Cable's value—which soared in some estimates to as high as $3 billion.

Deregulation also marked the beginning of a new era of media consolidation. Warner joined in, buying up Lorimar Telepictures in a stock swap deal worth $600 million. The purchase gave Warner control of the companies behind such hit television series as *Dallas* and *The Waltons*. Yet just two months later, Warner approached Time with the proposition that the two companies merge.

Originally designed as a stock-swap agreement, the companies' plans were nearly derailed by a sudden hostile takeover offer for Time from Paramount Communications, which bid nearly $11 million. Rejecting the offer, Time instead launched a $14 billion acquisition of Warner Communications. Paramount's attempt to block that deal was ultimately struck down in court, and a new media giant appeared on the global scene.

Time Warner started out with leadership positions in most of its markets, including the second largest cable television operation in the United States, the leading pay-television service, and top-performing magazine, book publishing, music, and film businesses as well. The company worked quickly to integrate its businesses, selling of Scott Foresman for $455 million at the end of 1989, combining its publishing operations into a new Time Warner Publishing unit. The pairing also seemed to produce immediate synergies, such as the launch of the new *Entertainment Weekly*, combining Time's publishing competence with Warner's media interests.

The company also began making acquisitions, including that of *Sunset* magazine publisher Lane Publishing Company, for $225 million, in 1989. Yet the company's growth—and share price—was burdened by its $11.2 billion in debt. In 1991, the company took a first step toward reducing its debt by launching a controversial rights offering which hinged share prices on the number of participants; after objections from the SEC, the company went ahead with a more standard offering, which raised $2.6 billion. In October of that same year, Time Warner brought in two new investors, Toshiba and C. Itoh & Co. (later ITOCHU), which each paid $500 million in exchange for a 6.5 percent stake in the company. As part of that deal, Time Warner spun off a number of its assets, including its publishing, journalism, and music operations, including Home Box Office, Warner Bros. Pictures, and Time Warner Cable, into a new, separately listed company, Time Warner Entertainment, which began business with a market value of $20 billion.

Time Warner sought new growth areas into the 1990s, launching Time Warner Communications in 1991 in an attempt to gain a spot in the coming new market for telephony applications. In that year, the company debuted its own interactive television service, Quantum, which, like other interactive TV efforts of the time failed to attract enthusiasm from customers. Instead, in 1993, TWC set its sights on the local telephone market, beginning a $1 billion investment program to install its own fiber optic networks and switching equipment in a number of markets where it already had a cable television presence. In order to provide funding for the effort, Time Warner sold a stake of 25 percent of its Time Warner Cable unit to US West (later called MediaOne Group) for $2.5 billion—heralded as the latest "mega-deal" in an era of rapid media industry consolidation. Yet, TWC's effort to impose itself on the local telephone market ultimately failed.

More successful moves by the company included its acquisition of CPP/Belwin in 1994, making the company the world's largest publisher of printed music. The company also acquired a 50 percent stake in Columbia House, the music and video distributor. In 1994, Time Warner flirted with the idea of acquiring small but fast-growing online service America Online. Instead, the company decided to go directly to the Internet, launching its own pay-for-content "portal," called Pathfinder. That service remained a perennial money-loser, however, and was at last shut down in 1999. These moves were expanded with the launch of such titles as *Time for Kids* in 1995, *People en Español* in 1996, and *Teen People* in 1998.

Time Warner launched its own television network in 1995, called WB TV. In that year, also, the company stepped up its cable television holdings with the purchase of Houston Industries' cable television network for $2.3 billion. The company was later one of the first to offer high-speed Internet access—Roadrunner based on the popular cartoon character from the Warner Bros. portfolio—through its cable network. By then, Time Warner had a new chairman, Gerald Levin, appointed after Steven Ross died of cancer in 1993. Levin had started out with Time Inc., helping to found HBO in 1972, before rising to become the man behind the Time Warner merger.

At the mid-1990s, however, Levin and Time Warner remained dogged by criticism from the investment community for its ballooning debt load, four straight years of losses, and a slumping share price. The company also faced skepticism about its ability to bring ''synergy''—the buzzword for such media megamergers—to its operations; indeed, the various pieces of the Time Warner empire were rarely required to cooperate, and often seemed to work against one another. For example, the company's WB network often had to turn to competing cable operators for space on the dial after being rebuffed by Time Warner Cable operators, a move that thwarted Time Warner's ambition to expand its range of television channels.

The company began a new round of restructuring in the mid-1990s, including renegotiating parts of its debt. Levin also brought in Richard Parsons, who had recently rescued Dime Savings Bank from bankruptcy, as president of Time Warner in 1995. By then, Time Warner's debt had ballooned to $16 billion. Nonetheless, the company, which had made no secret of its interest in building or buying its own network (and had been a contender for the NBC network in the early 1990s), chose to go deeper in debt, announcing its acquisition of Turner Broadcasting System.

Like Time and Warner, TBS had itself been a pioneer in the U.S. media market. TBS had been built up by flamboyant Robert Edward ''Ted'' Turner, who, at the end of the 1960s, transformed a small Atlanta-based billboard advertising company founded by his father into a television broadcaster by merging into the Rice Broadcasting Company in 1970. A public company, Rice owned its own UHF television station broadcasting to the Atlanta region—Turner renamed the company Turner Communications Corporation.

Through the 1970s, Turner began acquiring rights to broadcast Atlanta-based sports events—and then began buying the teams themselves. Meanwhile, Turner had recognized the potential represented in the new cable television services being set up around the company, and particularly their need for stations. In 1976, Turner transformed his station into Superstation WTBS and began signing up cable operators around the country to carry the station. Showing primarily reruns and the company-owned teams, which included the Atlanta Hawks basketball and Atlanta Braves baseball teams, TBS slowly but surely gained a market, and the confidence of advertisers.

TBS extended its television offering in 1980 with the creation of the Cable News Network, or CNN, the first live, 24-hour, all-news broadcast. That station was followed in 1981 by an affiliated station, Headline News, which soon became ubiquitous in hotel rooms around the world. In 1982, TBS extended the CNN format to the radio, with the launch of CNN Radio. The company also began to make tentative moves into production, notably through its creation of the Goodwill Games, which debuted in 1985.

Turner showed even greater ambitions in the mid-1980s, when TBS launched a takeover attempt of national television network CBS in 1985. CBS fought back however, and Turner was forced to withdraw the bid. Instead, TBS began acquisition talks with MGM/UA Entertainment and its main shareholder, Kirk Kerkorian. In 1986, the two sides agreed to allow TBS to pay $1.4 billion to acquire MGM/UA, as well as take on $700 million in MGM-related debt, then sell back the UA portion to Kerkorian for $480 million. Following the heavily criticized deal, Turner was forced to sell off most of MGM's assets—keeping only its film library—to pay off short-term notes. Many of those assets went to Kerkorian and UA. Another provision of the deal, which set required dividend limits, also threatened Turner's control of the newly enlarged company.

In 1987, Turner responded to that threat by selling off a 37 percent stake of TBS to a consortium of 31 cable operators, headed by Telecommunications Inc., in a deal that secured Turner's control of the company's voting rights. The following year, TBS debuted a new television channel, Turner Network Television, based on the company's control of the vast MGM film library. By 1990, Turner's investment in CNN had paid off, when, with the outbreak of the Persian Gulf War, that new station became the primary source of information for news watchers worldwide.

In the 1990s, Turner moved into film production, acquiring New Line Cinema and Castle Rock Studios, and continued to build up its array of television stations. In 1991, TBS paid $320 million to acquire Hanna-Barbera Productions, giving the company access to some 3,000 hours of television programs, and, especially cartoons such as *Yogi Bear, The Flintstones,* and *The Jetsons.* The following year, TBS launched a new television station, The Cartoon Network. That station soon began broadcasting to more than 100 countries. Backed by an investment from Time Warner, which acquired 18 percent of TBS, Turner now turned his attention to acquiring a network. Turner set his sights on NBC—coming head-to-head with his major shareholder, which blocked Turner's effort.

Yet Turner and Time Warner quickly found new common ground in the face of the fast-rising success of the Fox Network, backed by Rupert Murdoch. By 1995 Time Warner and Turner had begun negotiations to merge their two companies. Talks dragged on for more than a year, but in the end resulted in a merger worth $7.6 billion. Gerald Levin remained chairman of the enlarged company, while Ted Turner, the group's largest individual shareholder, was named vice-chairman, leading Time Warner on a broad cost-cutting and restructuring effort. At the same time, Turner used Time Warner's clout to boost the stature of TBS and the other Turner stations, particularly by pursuing first-run broadcasting rights to a number of hit films.

By the late 1990s, Time Warner appeared to have turned the corner. Sales were rising, and by the end of 1998, the company was once again profitable. These gains helped provide a boost to the company's stock price, which tripled by the middle of 1999. Yet by then, Time Warner appeared old-fashioned as a new spate of high-technology companies captured the imagination of the business world—and the stock market. Among the top-rated new companies was America Online, or AOL as it came to be called.

Pioneering the Online Market in the 1980s

AOL's origins lay in the nascent online community of the early 1980s. Although Compuserve had launched an online service targeting business customers in the late 1960s, the first consumer-oriented system, called The Source, began in 1978. An early user was Steve Case, who signed on in 1982. Case went to work for another company, Control Video Corporation (CVC), which began work on a system to connect Atari and Commodore users online and deliver video game content. That system failed to attract interest, however.

Instead, Case, and partners Marc Seriff and Jim Kimsey, convinced Commodore to launch its own online service. CVC changed its name to Quantum Computers Services and in 1985 debuted Q-link, which enabled users to download software, access information, play games, and, importantly, chat online. By 1986, Q-link had attracted some 10,000 users. Quantum quickly sought to extend its technology to other computer platforms, forming a similar service, Applelink, in partnership with Apple Computers, in 1987, and, in 1988, entering the PC market with PC-link. Apple's displeasure at this latest development led the companies to part ways—Apple paid Quantum $2.5 million to give up their license to the Apple logo. Faced with the need to find a new name for their service, Case and partners decided on America Online.

The new America Online debuted in 1989—featuring a number of voice messages (such as ''You've Got Mail'' and ''Welcome'') that were to play an important part in the service's success. At first dedicated to the Apple computer community (which featured sound; the majority of PCs remained mute at the end of the 1980s), Quantum began work on a PC version of their service. Yet the company nearly sold itself to Compuserve, which had offered $50 million for Quantum in 1991. Instead, AOL launched the first DOS version of America Online in February of that year. By the end of the year, the company had changed its name to America Online Inc.

Early on, Virginia-based AOL recognized the need for partnerships in order to extend its reach across the United States. One of the first of these was a deal with the Tribune Company, publisher of the *Chicago Tribune,* to create a local version of AOL based on news and information from the newspaper, in exchange for a $5 million contribution from Tribune (which gave it a 9.5 percent stake in AOL). The service was a quick success, attracting a large number of users. The company also entered an agreement with SeniorNet, an organization which encouraged senior citizens to adopt computer technology, to encourage SeniorNet members to join AOL. The company began providing specialized content for the senior citizen market, and paid SeniorNet for each new membership. These moves became part of an overall strategy of targeting niche markets and special interest groups, rather than the general public, as the company expanded its network.

AOL went public in 1992, listing on the NASDAQ exchange. That year, the company met with Microsoft's Bill Gates (fellow Microsoft executive Paul Allen had already announced his own plans to buy AOL), to discuss the possibility of AOL designing an online service for Microsoft. Instead, Microsoft decided to launch its own service, which became known as MSN. AOL decided to go it alone, and in January 1993 released the latest version of AOL, now capable of running on the Windows operating system.

AOL began to grow quickly, topping 300,000 subscribers by mid-1993, generating revenues of more than $40 million. In July of that year, the company stepped up its marketing campaign, beginning a strategy of sending out computer diskettes offering membership kits, AOL software, and free connection time. The diskettes quickly became ubiquitous, found in magazines, mailboxes, and pre-installed on a growing number of new computers. New users flooded in, and by 1994 the company had swelled to 400,000 users. In return, AOL stepped up its content offerings, bringing online content from a wide variety of sources, including National Public Radio, Matra Hachette, the *San Jose Mercury News,* and many others.

America Online was not the only online service—Compuserve and Prodigy, backed by Sears and IBM, had both grown strongly—but it was the fastest growing. Until 1994, these services represented the quickest way for the average consumer to get online, yet confined the user to the service's own proprietary network. By then, however, the Internet was coming of age for consumer use, backed by new graphics technology enabling what became known as the World Wide Web. A new breed of Internet Service Providers came into being, offering unlimited access to the Internet at fixed rates. In response, AOL was forced to change its own pricing policy. The company also began offering access to the Internet through its own network.

Many observers considered AOL's days numbered as the Internet caught on in the mid-1990s. Yet AOL quickly proved its critics wrong. Indeed, the company garnered a reputation among consumers as the easiest means of gaining access to the Internet. For many other consumers, AOL represented a ''safe'' alternative to the unruly and often unnavigable World Wide Web. By the end of 1994, AOL's membership had topped one million subscribers. The company also moved to increase its technology capacity, buying multimedia developer Redgate Communications; Navisoft, a designer of web-publishing tools; and Booklink Technologies, which had been developing Internet browser software. The following year, AOL added WAIS and Medior, and began offering web-page publishing services to its customers. In another acquisition, AOL bought Global Network Navigator, gaining control of the then popular web search tool WebCrawler. AOL also bought its own Internet service provider, ANS, that year.

By the end of 1995, AOL had signed on more than 4.5 million users. Yet the rapid advances of the Internet and the increasing ease by which consumers were able to set up their own Internet connections had begun to lure away increasing numbers of AOL subscribers. To counter the outflow—and rival MSN's recently announced unlimited access offer—AOL launched its own single monthly fee offering unlimited access. Yet the surge in online use that resulted nearly snapped AOL's already struggling infrastructure. After a series of system overloads, crashes, and increasing difficulties of customers simply connecting to the network, AOL agreed to provide refunds to its customers. AOL also stepped up its infrastructure spending, earmarking some $700 million to enhance its capacity.

AOL meanwhile remained highly unprofitable. For a time, the company had managed to show marketing costs—the company spent as much as $375 for each new customer—as capital expenses, but had ended the accounting practice in 1996. Instead, AOL went commercial, adopting a new policy of selling exclusives to its content providers. Barnes & Noble, as an example, paid $40 million to become the sole bookseller within the AOL network. In another, often bemoaned move, AOL began selling advertising space within its online space, and particularly in its extremely popular chat rooms. The company's growing community—more than eight million by the end of 1997—enabled the company to charge premium advertising rates.

The resulting rise in profitability enabled AOL's share price to skyrocket, as shares reached $80 per share in 1998—and then split two for one. Meanwhile, AOL had launched a new and ambitious round of acquisitions. In 1997, the company agreed to trade its ANS Internet service in exchange for Compuserve, then owned by WorldCom. The addition of Compuserve, which AOL pledged to maintain as a separate service, added another 2.6 million customers to AOL's ranks. That acquisition was followed by the purchase of ICQ, a highly popular service enabling users to send so-called "Instant Messages" across the Internet. Incorporated into the AOL software, the service quickly became one of the most widely used features of AOL.

In November 1998, AOL launched an even larger acquisition, paying $4.2 billion to acquire software developer Netscape Communications, in a deal that also included a strategic agreement with sworn Microsoft enemy Sun Microsystems. That company had been based on the originators of the World Wide Web concept and had long dominated the Internet browser market. Even so, Microsoft's entry into that software segment, Internet Explorer, and especially the software giant's decision to offer its browser software for free, had cut deeply into Netscape's hold on the browser market. Netscape attempted to fight back by giving away its software as well; yet the software was plagued by incompatibility issues (with Microsoft's Windows software, notably) and soon after the AOL acquisition, Netscape announced that it would end future development of Netscape Navigator.

Throughout this time, AOL's membership continued to swell, topping 15 million subscribers by decade's end. A growing part of this user base had come from the company's moves overseas, as it set up subsidiaries and joint-venture partnerships in order to enter France, the United Kingdom, and Canada in 1996; Japan in 1997; and Australia in 1998. The following year, AOL entered Brazil and Hong Kong. In the new decade, the company's worldwide expansion continued, and by 2001, AOL was by far the world's largest online service, counting some 26 million subscribers.

Steve Case's ambitions moved beyond mere online access—he now sought to transform AOL on the one hand, into a content provider, and on the other, into a cross-platform provider. To this end, the company began a new round of acquisitions at the end of the 1990s and the beginning of the next decade, acquiring the MovieFone electronic ticketing service; Spinner Networks, which provided an online music service; Nullsoft, which produced the highly popular online and desktop music software, Winamp; and Internet-based map provider MapQuest, the latter

at a cost of $1.1 billion. Other acquisitions at the time included iAmaze and Quack.com.

At the same time, the company launched a number of initiatives as part of its "AOL Anywhere" program designed to place the company into a variety of new markets, including handheld devices and mobile telephones. As part of that effort the company formed alliances with the AT&T and Japan's mobile phone leader NTT DoCoMo. Then in December 2000, it acquired Tegic Communications, a maker of software for the wireless market. In the meantime, the company also attempted to crack the television market, launching the interactive television service, AOLTV. Yet AOLTV stumbled from the outset.

Merging Technologies in the 21st Century

AOL had the online service, but found it impossible to achieve the depth of content it would need in what many observers promised was to become a new era of the convergence of media and technology. Time Warner, for its part, had the content—but had given up its attempt to crack the online market. In 1999, the two sides began talks about merging the two companies. By the beginning of 2000, Case and Levin had hammered out the outlines of the deal, which involved AOL acquiring Time Warner in a stock swap worth some $166 billion. AOL was to control 55 percent of the resulting combined operation.

The deal faced the scrutiny of both the U.S. and European Community regulators, which required the companies to shed a number of its European partnerships, and open up its U.S. cable network to third-party Internet providers. The merger was finally completed in January 2001, creating a new corporation, AOL Time Warner Inc., with a share value of a staggering $364 billion. Steve Case took the position of company chairman, while Gerald Levin claimed the CEO spot. The AOL team, it became clear, intended to lead the newly enlarged company.

Yet this latest mega-merger appeared doomed from the start. Soon after the creation of AOL Time Warner, the technology market went into a nosedive, and the newly enlarged company saw its own share price go into a long downward spiral. The September 11, 2001 attacks further crippled the company, as advertising revenues dwindled. Despite continued growth in AOL customers—reaching 33 million by the end of 2001 and topping 35 million by the middle of the next year—AOL had seen its costs for attracting and retaining its members skyrocket.

Indeed, AOL found itself more and more threatened by the advent of new high-speed Internet technology—while it still relied almost entirely on its now outmoded dial-up service. Then, in 2002, AOL Time Warner faced even more troubles when the SEC placed the company under investigation for accounting irregularities committed by AOL before the merger—specifically, that AOL had overstated its advertising revenues, which in turn inflated its profits.

Struggling under a debt load of more than $26 billion, AOL Time Warner limped through 2002 to post a record loss of $98.7 billion—the largest loss in corporate history. Much of that loss came through AOL, as the company fought to retain its membership. By the beginning of 2003, the online service recorded its first net subscriber losses for the first time in its history. A bright spot for AOL Time Warner as a whole was its rising revenues, which topped $40 billion for the first time in 2002.

Meanwhile, heads began to roll at AOL Time Warner. After Steve Case attempted to oust Gerald Levin at the end of 2002, Case found himself under pressure to resign—which he did, in January 2003. Shareholder confidence was further eroded when Ted Turner, who remained the company's largest shareholder, announced that he was selling off half of his holding (Turner's stock was said to have lost as much as $7 billion in value). Levin then announced his intention to turn over the reins of the company to his longtime number two man, Richard Parsons.

Parsons immediately set to work reassuring investors—as AOL Time Warner's share price dropped below $10, valuing the company at just $61 billion. Parsons was committed to streamlining the company and to driving down its huge debt burden. As part of that effort, Parsons planned to shed a number of assets, including the company's CD production unit, its Atlanta-area sports teams, as well as its book publishing arm, AOL Time Warner Book Group. Yet by June 2003, the company was forced to retreat from the book group sale, after it proved unable to find a buyer willing to offer a suitable price. Another streamlining project, that of the spinoff Time Warner Cable as a separate, publicly listed company, was postponed. That move was expected to occur by the end of the year, however.

AOL attempted to strike back at its own sagging fortunes by launching a new service, dubbed AOL for Broadband, which gave access to AOL's service through its own or third-parties' high-speed Internet networks. The service, priced at $14.95 per month, was already being criticized as too little, too late, as observers began to question AOL's continued viability, and even suggest that AOL Time Warner sell off AOL altogether. Fueling the speculation was the announcement which came in late summer 2003 that the business was planning to drop "AOL" from its name. Yet Parsons announced that the company, now under control of the Time Warner faction, remained committed to its online segment and expected its fortunes to turn around by 2004.

AOL Time Warner hoped to meet the challenges of merging its operations and achieving the potential synergies offered by its diversified holdings. With its array of world-beating content spanning the publishing, music, television, and film industries, and delivery platforms touching into nearly every consumer segment, AOL Time Warner remained one of the most ambitious milestones in U.S. corporate history.

Principal Subsidiaries

America Online, Inc.; American Television and Communications Corporation; AOLTV, Inc.; AOL Asia Limited; AOL GP Holdings LLC (Australia); AOL Europe SA; AOL Technologies Ireland Limited; Asiaweek Limited; Atlanta Hockey Club, Inc.; Atlanta National League Baseball Club, Inc.; Atlantic Recording Corporation; Book-of-the-Month Club, Inc.; Cable News International, Inc.; Cable News Network LP, LLLP; The Cartoon Network LP, LLLP; Castle Rock Entertainment, Inc.; Century Venture Corporation (50%); The Columbia House Company (50%); Comedy Partners, L.P. (50%); CompuServe Interactive Services, Inc.; Courtroom Television Network LLC (50%); CNN America, Inc.; CNN Investment Company, Inc.; CNN Newsource Sales, Inc.; DC Comics (50%); Digital City, Inc.; Digital Marketing Services, Inc.; DoCoMo AOL Inc. (40%); E.C. Publications, Inc.; Elektra Entertainment Group Inc.; Embleton Ltd.; Entertainment Weekly, Inc.; Erie Telecommunications Inc. (54%); Goodwill Games, Inc.; Hanna-Barbera Entertainment Co., Inc.; Hawks Basketball, Inc.; HB Holding Co.; ICQ Limited; Ivy Hill Corporation; Kansas City Cable Partners (50%); Little, Brown and Company Inc.; London Records 90 Limited; London-Sire Records Inc.; MapQuest.com, Inc.; MovieFone, Inc.; Netscape Communications Corporation; New Chappell Inc.; New Line Cinema Corporation; The Parenting Group Inc.; Quack.com, Inc.; Rhino Entertainment Company; Southern Progress Corporation; Spinner Networks, Inc.; Summit Communications Group, Inc.; Sunset Publishing Corporation; Superstation, Inc.; Tegic Communications Corporation; TEN Investment Company, Inc.; Texas Cable Partners L.P. (50%); Time Distribution Services, Inc.; Time Inc.; Time Inc. Ventures; Time International Inc.; Time Life Inc.; Time Publishing Ventures, Inc.; Time Warner Companies, Inc.; Time Warner Entertainment-Advance/Newhouse Partnership (64%); Time Warner Inc.; Time Warner Trade Publishing Inc.; Times Mirror Magazines, Inc.; Turner Broadcasting Sales, Inc.; Turner Broadcasting System, Inc.; Turner Broadcasting System Asia Pacific, Inc.; Turner Broadcasting System (Holdings) Europe Ltd.; Turner Classic Movies LP, LLLP; Turner Entertainment Group, Inc.; Turner Entertainment Networks, Inc.; Turner Entertainment Networks Asia, Inc.; Turner Home Entertainment, Inc.; Turner Home Satellite, Inc.; Turner International, Inc.; Turner Network Television LP, LLLP; Turner Pictures Group, Inc.; Turner Sports, Inc.; TWI Cable Inc.; Warner Books, Inc.; Warner Bros. Music International Inc.; Warner Bros. Publications U.S. Inc.; Warner Bros. Records Inc.; Warner Communications Inc.; Warner Music Canada Ltd.; Warner Music Group Inc.; Warner Music Newco Limited; Warner Publisher Services Inc.; Warner Special Products Inc.; Warner/Chappell Music, Inc.; Warner-Elektra-Atlantic Corporation; Warner-Tamerlane Publishing Corp.; WB Music Corp.; WCI Record Club Inc.; WEA International Inc.; WEA Manufacturing Inc.

Principal Competitors

AT&T Broadband; Comcast Corporation; DIRECTV, Inc.; Dow Jones & Company, Inc.; Earthlink, Inc.; Lagardère SCA; McGraw-Hill Companies, Inc.; Microsoft Corporation; National Broadcasting Company, Inc.; Pearson plc; Prodigy Communications Corporation; The Walt Disney Company; Tribune Company; Viacom Inc.; Virgin Group Ltd.; Yahoo! Inc.

Further Reading

Barakat, Michael, "America Online's Goal Is 'AOL Anywhere,'" *St. Louis Post-Dispatch,* October 11, 2000, p. B8.

Bianco, Anthony, and Tom Lowry, "Can Dick Parsons Rescue AOL Time Warner?," *Business Week,* May 19, 2003.

Brown, Rich, "Viacom, Time Warner Bury the Hatchet," *Broadcasting,* August 24, 1992.

Bruck, Connie, *Master of the Game: Steve Ross and the Creation of Time Warner,* New York: Viking Penguin, 1995.

Elson, Robert T., *Time Inc.: The Intimate History of a Publishing Enterprise—1923–1941,* New York: Atheneum, 1968.

——, *The World of Time Inc.: The Intimate History of a Publishing Enterprise—1941–1960,* New York: Athenaeum, 1973.

Eng, Paul M., "America Online Is Hooked Up for Growth," *Business Week,* June 21, 1993.

Fabrikant, Geraldine, "Time Warner Shows Gains As It Shrinks Merger's Debt," *New York Times,* February 9, 1993.

Fass, Allison, "AOL Time Over?," *Forbes,* June 23, 2003, p. 49.

Gunther, Marc, "The Internet Is Mr. Case's Neighborhood," *Fortune,* March 30, 1998, pp. 68–77.

Higgins, John M., "Black Ink, Slow Growth at Time Warner," *Multichannel News,* April 27, 1992.

"Internet Riders," *Economist,* November 28, 1998, pp. 63–64.

Loomis, Carol J., "Why AOL's Accounting Problems Keep Popping Up," *Fortune,* April 28, 2003, p. 85.

Miller, Michael W., "Tycoon Is Tapping into Online Service," *Wall Street Journal,* May 24, 1993.

Prendergast, Curtis, and Geoffrey Colvin, *The World of Time Inc.: The Intimate History of a Changing Enterprise—1960–1980,* New York: Athenaeum, 1986.

Ramo, Joshua Cooper, John Greenwald, and Michael Krantz, "How AOL Lost the Battles but Won the War," *Time,* September 22, 1997, pp. 46–54.

Schwartz, Evan I., "For America Online, Nothing Is As Nice As a Niche," *Business Week,* September 14, 1992.

Shook, David, "Will Cable Be AOL's Lifeline?," *Business Week,* March 10, 2003.

Siklos, Richard, et al., "Welcome to the 21st Century: With One Stunning Stroke, AOL and Time Warner Create a Colossus and Redefine the Future," *Business Week,* January 24, 2000, p. 36.

Swisher, Kara, *AOL.com: How Steve Case Beat Bill Gates, Nailed the Netheads, and Made Millions in the War for the Web,* New York: Crown Publishing Group, 1999.

"Time Warner Refinances $6.2B Debt," *Multichannel News,* May 18, 1992.

Wooten, Terry, *Planet AOL: From "Anywhere" to "Everywhere" with Time Warner and Beyond,* New York: Prentice Hall Press, 2001.

Yang, Catherine, et al., "Richard Parsons Leaps the First Hurdle," *Business Week,* May 19, 2003.

——, "Show Time for AOL Time Warner," *Business Week,* January 15, 2001, p. 56.

—M.L. Cohen

ARACRUZ

Aracruz Celulose S.A.

Rua Lauro Müller, 116, 40° andar
22299-900 Rio de Janeiro
Brazil
Telephone: +55-21-3820-8111
Fax: +55-21-3820-8202
Web site: http://www.aracruz.com.br

Public Company
Incorporated: 1972
Employees: 1,601
Sales: $669.0 million (2002)
Stock Exchanges: Sao Paulo New York
*Ticker Symbol*s: BOVESPA; ARA
NAIC: 322110 Pulp Mills; 113110 Timber Tract
Operations; 113210 Forest Nurseries and Gathering of
Forest Products; 115310 Support Activities for
Forestry

Brazil-based Aracruz Celulose S.A. is the world's leading producer of bleached eucalyptus pulp for the paper industry and one of the world's largest wood pulp producers. The company has an annual production capacity of 2.4 million tons, through two mill sites. Barra do Riacho, the company's main site located in Espirito Santo, produces two million tons of pulp with three full-scale production units, including boilers, digesters, and bleach and drying lines. The company also operates its own private port, Portocel, in Espirito Santo. Aracruz's other site, Riocell, was acquired in 2003; located in Rio Grande do Sul, it produces 400,000 tons of bleach eucalyptus pulp each year. The company is also constructing a third site, through its 50/50 Veracel Celulose joint-venture with Stora Enso, at Eunapolis, in Bahia, which will have a production capacity of 900,000 tons upon completion in 2005. Aracruz produces its own wood through its management of nearly 190,000 hectares of planted eucalyptus—a fast-growing hardwood not native to Brazil. The company has played an active role in developing new genetic varieties of eucalyptus to meet its production needs. As part of its longstanding commitment to sustainable development, the company's eucalyptus plantations are interspersed by native tree species. The company's eco-friendly policies extend to its production facilities, which are outfitted with chemical recovery systems, water treatment facilities, and biomass power generating systems making use of the company's own waste production. In addition to pulp, Aracruz has diversified, launching its own line of hardwood products. Aracruz is led by Luiz Kaufmann. Founder Erling Lorentzen and family remain major shareholders in the company.

Planting a Wood Pulp Giant in the 1960s

Born in 1923, Erling Lorentzen had been forced to flee his native Norway after that country was occupied by the Nazis during World War II. Lorentzen, part of a shipping family with interests in Brazil, joined the Norwegian resistance and was sent to Great Britain, where he received military training. Lorentzen then returned to Norway, and, undercover as a farmer, took command of some 800 resistance fighters.

Following the war, Lorentzen, who had not been able to complete high school, was granted the right to enroll in the M.B.A. program at Harvard University. Returning to Norway, Lorentzen began working for his father's shipping company, acting as a representative in Brazil. Lorentzen also found a wife—Princess Ragnhild Alexandra, daughter of then King Olaf V and sister of the future King Haakon. The marriage marked the first time a member of European royalty had married a commoner.

Yet Erling Lorentzen proved no common businessman. The Lorentzens moved to Brazil during the 1950s and set up a gas distribution business in conjunction with the family's holdings. By then, interest was beginning to grow in developing a wood pulp industry in Brazil. The country offered a number of natural advantages, including plenty of space and low wages. But most importantly, Brazil boasted a climate of year-round sun and warm weather. Whereas the planting-to-pulping time span of trees planted for pulp production in northern climates ranged from 15 years to as much as 50 years in northern Europe, Brazil's climate offered the possibility to grow trees with a five-year turnaround rate.

Initial attempts by another company to begin wood pulp production failed, however, due to the poor choice of tree—although eucalyptus had been introduced to Brazil in the early part of the 20th century, Jari had chosen a different species, imported from Indonesia, that did not react well to Brazil's soil. In the meantime, Brazil's forest continued to be devastated. With no coal deposits of its own, the country cut down its trees in order to produce charcoal. The situation was particularly dire in the northern coastal state of Espirito Santo, where most of the forests had been destroyed, sinking the population further into poverty.

Lorentzen began gathering funding from private investors and government sources and began buying up land in Espirito Santo with the intention of developing new eucalyptus plantations. Lorentzen quickly decided on using a variety of eucalyptus, in part for its quick growth cycle of just seven years in Brazil's climate. Eucalyptus presented other advantages, particularly in that a tree will grow back from the stump after it has been cut down, enabling the same tree to be harvested up to three times, lowering the investment and reducing the length of the growth cycle.

By 1967, Lorentzen had formed Aracruz Florestal S.A. and begun planting its first eucalyptus forests using seed produced in Brazil. Because these trees were not genetically developed, the initial planting presented a number of difficulties, including a susceptibility to trunk rot and irregular growth and shape patterns. Nonetheless, by 1972, the company began its first harvest and began eyeing the start-up of pulp production. As part of that development, Lorentzen formed a new company, Aracruz Celulose, which absorbed the original Aracruz company as its subsidiary. Aracruz Forestal was fully merged into its parent in 1993.

Yet Aracruz was not satisfied with the quality of its eucalyptus forests. In 1973, the company launched a research and development program in order to enhance the quality of its forests by developing varieties of eucalyptus adapted to Brazil's soil and climate conditions. In particular the company sought to develop fast-growing, disease-resistant species with uniform growing cycles, straight trunks, and few side branches—which would allow more dense planting.

From the start, however, Aracruz emphasized the need for environmentally friendly plantation policies, including the interspersing of its eucalyptus plantations with significant acreage set aside for native species. This move not only protected native plant species in the area, it also helped limit the effects of insect and disease on Aracruz's eucalyptus forests. The company also began seeking financing for construction of its own pulp mill, a difficult task in the slumping market of the mid-1970s.

Aracruz launched actual production of wood pulp only in 1978. The company's production unit at Barra do Riacho, in Espirito Santo, initially had capacity of 400,000 tons per year.

Aracruz's timing proved fortunate: soon after it launched production, worldwide pulp prices began to rise again, and by the mid-1980s had paid off its debts. Aracruz quickly developed into one of the world's lowest-cost producers of wood pulp, with per-tonnage prices as much as one-third or more that of competing world markets.

Aracruz continued developing its own eucalyptus species, producing seeds for its own plantations. In the early 1980s, however, its seeds began attracting outside interest, and the company began selling seeds to third parties as well. As the company perfected its seed stock, it began developing its own cloning program for commercial development. By selecting superior seeds for its cloned trees, the company was able to make significant strides in improving not only growth rates, but also in uniformity and quality, helping it to reduce its own costs still further. Cloning presented its own disadvantages, such as a greater vulnerability to certain diseases, requiring the development of special planting techniques, including interspersing with native tree species.

Aracruz found other ways to reduce its costs, including locating its production close to its forests. The company also used waste byproducts, and especially wood bark, as fuel, providing nearly 90 percent of its own energy needs. In 1985, Aracruz built its own private port, called Portocel, in order to service its production unit, a move that helped it reduce its production costs still more.

Erling Lorentzen stepped down from a day to day role with the company in 1987, becoming company chairman. By then, Aracruz had grown into the nation's number two pulp producer, trailing Industrias Klabian de Papel a Celulose, which weighed in at twice the size of Aracruz. Yet Aracruz turned out high profits—in 1988, the company posted net profits of $147 million on revenues of $227 million.

Drive for Growth in the 1990s

Aracruz's strong profits and low debt rate encouraged it to begin building for the future. Kaufmann had become convinced of a coming boom in pulp demand, particularly from the rapidly growing Asian and South American markets, and sought to position Aracruz as a major producer to meet that demand. The company began construction on a second pulp mill to boost its total production capacity to more than one million tons per year. That facility, in Espirito Santo, came online in 1991. The total cost of the project, at $1.2 billion, also included an investment of more than $170 million on expanding Aracruz's forest holdings.

The slumping worldwide economy and falling pulp prices caught up with Aracruz in the early 1990s, however. The company was forced to restructure, slashing a number of jobs in a wide cost-cutting effort. Nonetheless, the company went ahead with a public listing, becoming the first Brazilian company to place its shares on the New York Stock Exchange in 1992. The following year, the company brought in a new CEO, Luiz Kaufmann.

Under Kaufmann, Aracruz continued its drive to increase profitability, aided by a new surge in world pulp prices. By the end of 1994, Aracruz was once again producing profits. Nonetheless, Kaufmann had become convinced of the need to diver-

Key Dates:

1967: Erling Lorentzen establishes Aracruz Florestal S.A. and begins planting eucalyptus trees for pulp production.

1972: Aracruz Celulose is formed, regrouping Aracruz Florestal as its subsidiary.

1978: Company begins production of wood pulp.

1985: Company constructs private port, Portocel.

1988: Aracruz begins construction of second pulp mill, which comes on line in 1991.

1992: Company lists shares on New York Stock Exchange as ADRs.

1997: Company forms Tecflor joint venture with U.S.-based Gutchess.

1998: Company adds 200,000 tons production capacity.

2000: Aracruz launches construction of new $930 million pulp mill to expand production to 1.3 million tons; acquires 45 percent stake in Veracel joint venture.

2001: Company joins with Votorantim Celulose e Papel, the number four pulp producer in Brazil, to acquire majority control of the number two company, Celulose Nipo-Brasileira, also known as Cenibra, for $670 million.

2003: Company forms joint venture with Stora Enso to build new production facility at Veracel; acquires Riocel pulp production unit from Klabin.

sify the company beyond its pulp business. In 1997, Aracruz teamed up with the United States' Gutchess International Group in order to launch a joint venture company, Tecflor Industrial, and build a $45 million sawmill in Posto da Mata, in Brazil's Bahia. The joint venture, held at 60 percent by Aracruz, brought the company into the production of lumber products, under the brand name Lyptus.

Meantime, Aracruz continued to expand its own production facilities, adding 200,000 tons per year capacity in 1998, bringing its total to 1.3 million tons annually. In 1999, the company extended its diversification effort, renaming subsidiary Tecflor as Aracruz Produtos de Madeira, and beginning production of hardwood products for the flooring and furniture industries.

In 2000, the company launched a new expansion effort, with an extension of its Espirito Santo operations, including construction of a third production unit. Built at a cost of $923 million, the new pulp mill added 700,000 tons of capacity per year to the company. Aracruz also added to its own tree stand as well, earmarking some $220 million to expand its land holdings and tree plantations. It also paid $83 million to acquire a 45 percent stake in Veracel, a pulp mill joint venture between Stora Enso and Odebrecht.

Aracruz's third unit allowed it to claim the spot as the world's leading producer of eucalyptus wood pulp, with production totals of more than two million tons per year. Mean-

while, the company played a key role in the consolidation of Brazil's pulp industry. In 2001, the company joined with Votorantim Celulose e Papel, the number four pulp producer in Brazil, to acquire majority control of the number two company, Celulose Nipo-Brasileira, also known as Cenibra, for $670 million. That acquisition gave Aracruz a stake in Cenibra's production capacity of some 800,000 tons per year.

With the launch of production at its new C unit in 2002, Aracruz topped 1.65 million tons of production for the year, with full capacity expected to be reached in 2003. In that year, however, Aracruz stepped up its expansion effort, starting with the launch of a joint venture project with Veracel partner Stora Enso to build one of the world's largest pulp production plants, in Bahia. The plant, to be built at a cost of $870 million, was expected to start production in 2005 and reach a capacity of 900,000 tons per year.

One month after the agreement with Stora Enso, Aracruz struck again, reaching an agreement to acquire longtime rival Klabin's pulp production unit, Riocell S.A., for $610 million. Aracruz was expected to continue Riocell's $500 million expansion program, started under Klabin. The completion of that project, as well as the addition of the new Veracel plant, was expected to push Aracruz's total production beyond 3.5 million tons per year. The company also expected its revenues to top $1 billion in 2003. A pioneer in Brazil's eucalyptus pulp industry, Aracruz now took a place among the industry's global giants.

Principal Subsidiaries

Aracruz (Europe) S.A.; Aracruz Celulose (U.S.A.), Inc.; Aracruz Empreendimentos Sociedade Civil Ltda.; Aracruz Nordeste S.A.; Aracruz Produtos de Madeira S.A.; Aracruz Trading S.A.; Mucuri Agroflorestal S.A.; Portocel Terminal Especializado de Barra do Riacho S.A. (51%); Terra Plana Agropecuária Ltda.; Veracel Celulose S.A. (45%).

Principal Competitors

Companhia Suzano de Papel e Celulose; Industrias Klabin de Papel e Celulose S.A.; Votorantim Celulose e Papel S.A.; Bahia Sul Celulose S.A.; Ripasa S.A. Celulose e Papel; Igaras Papeis e Embalagens S.A.; Inpacel Industria De Papel Arapoti S.A.; Jari Celulose S.A.; Celucat S.A.

Further Reading

"A Forestry Giant Spreads Its Branches," *BusinessWeek*, September 2, 1996.

Griffith, Victoria, "Reversal of Fortune," *LatinFinance*, October 1994, p. 61.

Kepp, Michael, "Brazil Pulp Giant Buys Rival," *Daily Deal,* June 3, 2003.

——, "Brazil's Aracruz, Votorantim Buy Rival Cenibra," *Daily Deal*, June 5, 2001.

"New Pulp Mill for Stora Enso and Aracruz Celulose," *Print Week*, May 16, 2003, p. 14.

—M.L. Cohen

Ariba, Inc.

807 11th Avenue
Sunnyvale, California 94089
U.S.A.
Telephone: (650) 390-1000
Fax: (650) 390-1100
Web site: http://www.ariba.com

Public Company
Incorporated: 1996
Employees: 836
Sales: $229.8 million (2002)
Stock Exchanges: NASDAQ
Ticker Symbol: ARBA
NAIC: 511210 Software Publishers

Ariba, Inc. is a Sunnyvale, California company that provides software and network services to help corporations manage "spend," defined as all nonpayroll expenses associated with the running of a business. Ariba's suite of spend management software applications are accessed by customers via the Internet, offering them real-time data. These applications can then be used in conjunction with the Ariba Supplier Network in order to purchase goods and services. More than 34,000 suppliers worldwide are connected to the network. Ariba also offers technical support services, implementation, training, and consulting. Customers include 40 of the *Fortune* 100, and the company estimates that Ariba software is found on nearly four million desktops around the world.

Forming Ariba in 1996

Of the seven men who founded Ariba in 1996, Steve Krach was the most influential. He was born in Rocky River, Ohio, the son of John "Butch" Krach, who owned Litco Industries, a steel fabricator where Keith landed his first job cleaning bathrooms, then later graduated to spray painting. He went to Purdue University to study industrial engineering and at the end of his sophomore year he won a scholarship and summer job with General Motors, working in the Cadillac division in down-

town Detroit. It proved to be a learning experience in a number of ways. He realized the importance of establishing good interpersonal relationships, a crucial factor in his first job at Cadillac serving as the night product foreman on the chassis line. According to Krach he quickly discovered that discipline was poor and that the top priorities of the 30 men who operated the line were "drugs and prostitution." As a result, Krach told the *Financial Times* in October 2000, "I made friends with the biggest guy on the chassis line." Another aspect of the plant that would directly influence the creation of Ariba was restrictive, paperwork-intensive procedures, including procurement. As Krach described it, "It was a total nightmare. Guys would pull out these thick books all the time, they could not act without a manual." After graduating from Purdue, Krach earned an M.B.A. from Harvard University, paid for by GM. He then returned to GM, a rising star in the organization, becoming the company's youngest vice-president at the age of 26. He now learned even more about the frustrations of procurement at a large organization: "At GM I had to fill out so much paperwork to buy a new PC and software that I would go to the store myself, pay the 35 percent retail mark-up, put it on my expense form, and then beg for forgiveness." When he was not skirting the bureaucracy, Krach was successfully launching GM's robotics division in 1982. In just five years he created from scratch a market leader generating annual sales of $200 million.

Krach's involvement in robotics brought him into contact with California's Silicon Valley, where he ultimately concluded that his future resided. In 1987 he decided to leave GM, teaming up with a Harvard friend and some IBM research scientists to found a start-up company to develop computer-aided design software for mechanical engineers. The business was named Rasna Corp., and over the next nine years Krach served as the chief operating officer, playing an instrumental role in the company's rapid rise. In 1995 Parametric Technology Corp. bought Rasna for $200 million, creating 31 Rasna millionaires. For his part, Krach walked away with $10 million at just 40 years of age.

Although rich enough to retire, Krach looked for a new business opportunity. He could have easily secured financing

Company Perspectives:

Ariba offers a powerful suite of solutions to help companies manage "spend" so that expenses fall faster than revenues in down times, and grow more slowly than revenues in up time. Ariba Spend Management Solutions significantly improves the bottom line results of a business.

for a new venture or taken a well-paying CEO position at an existing start-up. Instead in early 1996 he became a $150,000-a-year "entrepreneur in residence" for Benchmark Capital, a venture capital (VC) firm. He was brought in by Benchmark partner Bob Kagle, who had met Krach when both men worked for GM. They had kept in contact by meeting for breakfast a few times each year. *Fortune* summarized Krach's new position: "From an office at Benchmark's digs on Sand Hill Road, a strip of land in Menlo Park, Calif., so crowded with moneymen that it is to Silicon Valley what Wall Street once was to the robber barons, Krach would spend his days playing venture capitalist—meeting with industry leaders and other VCs, attending Benchmark's Monday-morning partners' meetings, listening to pitches from eager entrepreneurs looking for funding, and generally ruminating on the future of technology. Eventually, if he felt like it, he could form his own company and Benchmark would fund it." Moreover, Krach was under no obligation to Benchmark and could strike a financing deal with another VC firm. But for Benchmark it was a risk worth taking. *Fortune* explained that funding an entrepreneur in residence was "hardly some kind of VC-subsidized welfare. Venture firms often get better returns from companies created by EIRs than they get by buying equity in existing startups."

Although promised plenty of time to decide on a new venture, Krach, soon after joining the Benchmark program, almost became involved in what Kagle called "one of those hot, new sexy Internet things." Kagle talked him out of the project, and Krach continued to attend the Monday morning partners meetings, schmoozed at the Friday night beer bashes, and took part in a plethora of breakfast and luncheon meetings at the trendiest eateries Silicon Valley had to offer. After three months of the EIR grind, he decided to team up with a new Benchmark entrepreneur in residence, Paul Hegarty, a close associate of Apple Computer's Steve Jobs and former vice-president of engineering at Jobs's Next Software Inc., which later became part of Apple.

Krach and Hegarty brainstormed and came up with the idea of automating the purchase of common supplies and services, the attraction of which Krach knew from his days at GM. Krach brought in some former Rasna executives to found the business: Rob DeSantis, who became the head of sales at Ariba; Edward Kinsey, who became CFO; and Paul Tuow, who was put in charge of business development. They soon learned, however, that others were pursuing a similar idea. John Mumford, the cofounder and chairman of what would become Office Depot and managing partner of the Woodside, California, VC firm of Crosspoint Venture Partners was also interested in automating the purchasing process for companies and had already enlisted

the support of two Crosspoint entrepreneurs in residence: Bobby Lent, a former executive at Inmac, a computer accessory and supplies company; and Boris Putanec, a veteran from the Internet Shopping Network. Mumford's group was in need of a leader and when he learned about the venture taking shape at Benchmark he contacted Krach, on whom he had received a glowing report. Krach and the Crosspoint EIRs hit it off and they agreed to join forces. Lent became vice-president of strategy, and Putanec the head of development.

In September 1996 the four EIRs and three former Rasna executives incorporated Ariba, the name drawn from the Spanish word for "up," "arriba." (The first idea for a name was ProcureSoft, but the founders soon changed their minds.) Krach became president and CEO of the enterprise. In the beginning the strategy was to focus on the buyers in the procurement process, in the belief that the suppliers would quickly come on board in an effort to follow the money. The first round of funding was completed later in the month. Benchmark paid $3 million to acquire a 19 percent stake in the business and Crosspoint invested $2.5 million for a 16 percent share. Because of the difficulty in finding suitable real estate in the area, the company's dozen employees worked out of four Benchmark offices for the first three months. The first blueprint of the product architecture was done in crayon on a paper tablecloth during a lunch at Quadrus Café in Menlo Park. In these early months the company operated in what Krach called stealth mode, keeping a low profile while it met with some prospective customers, 60 *Fortune* 500 companies, asking them what would be the ideal solution to their cumbersome, paper-based procurement process. Krach told *Upside* in a 2001 interview, "The answer was: 'It would have a walk-up user interface. It could parametrically change business models. It could integrate to our financial systems. It would hook right up to the supplies. It would run on this new thing called the Internet.' "

After three months Ariba had a prototype product and DeSantis began to approach major corporations, his sales pitch bolstered by research from Killen Associates in Palo Alto, which maintained that a 5 percent decrease in the cost of procurements could result in as much as a 20 percent increase in profits. Even before the product was ready Ariba was able to sign up software licensing deals with three major customers: Cisco Systems, Advanced Micro Devices, and Octel Communications. The company shipped its first product (now known as Ariba Buyer) in May 1997. Krach quickly moved to take advantage of the company's momentum and sought a second round of investment, which would normally remain in the realm of venture capital firms. Instead, he looked for money from investors that generally came in on later rounds, asking six times the price paid in the initial round. The gambit worked, so that Ariba's valuation increased from $16 million to $113 million in just nine months. "In fact," according to *Fortune,* "there had been so much investor interest in Ariba that the company actually turned down an even higher price, fearing the effect of an unrealistic valuation." As it was, Ariba accepted far more money than it had planned, $13.2 million instead of $6 million. Although involved in the pedestrian business of buying supplies, Ariba was sexy enough for savvy investors.

```
┌─────────────────────────────────────────────┐
│              Key Dates:                      │
│                                              │
│ 1996:  Ariba is incorporated.                │
│ 1997:  The first product is shipped.         │
│ 1999:  The company makes its initial public  │
│        offering.                             │
│ 2001:  Steve Krach steps down as CEO.        │
└─────────────────────────────────────────────┘
```

Ariba devoted much of 1998 to recruiting top-notch personnel, while Ariba Buyer underwent several revisions within a year. Hiring was such a top priority at this stage that Krach estimated he devoted about 40 percent of his time to the task. To help retain staff and create a productive team, Ariba also began to establish its own company culture, creating a climate of what would be called ''scary fun.'' Employees were encouraged to take risks, and to reinforce the concept on the recreational side Ariba sponsored such activities as a rafting trip and a go-cart race at a Malibu course. Also key to staff retention was a rigorous, three-stage interview process.

In April 1999 the company began to operate a supplier network, entering the business-to-business marketplace, as Ariba began to take the next step in its strategy for becoming a leader in what Krach called the global electronic trade revolution. The endeavor was aided in its ambition by establishing strategic alliances with other companies. IBM, in addition to being a customer, agreed to resell Ariba products around the world; e-payment service arrangements were made with American Express and Bank of America; and Descartes provided logistics commerce services, an area in which the Canadian company was a leader. In June 1999 Ariba went public at $23 per share. On its first day of trading it reached $90 and for the next several months continued to climb. By the end of the year Ariba stock reached $259 per share, then split two for one. It was a stunning success for a three-year-old company that was still losing money, as evidenced by the fact that Krach's stake in the business, which was gaudy enough when it was valued at $473 million after the first day of trading, exceeded $1.5 billion when the post-split share price proceeded to hit $150 in December 1999.

Nevertheless, Ariba was not ensured a position as one of the winners when the global electronic revolution was finally sorted out. The company faced formidable challenges from emerging e-marketplace web sites that provided a place where corporate buyers and sellers could conduct business. In order to attain crucial technology needed for online business auctions, in December 1999 Ariba agreed to pay $465 million in stock to acquire TradingDynamics, Inc.—a hefty price for the business in light of its $4 million in sales. TradingDynamics' CEO then suggested to Krach that Ariba should consider acquiring Tradex Technologies, Inc., which could fill in another gap, software for building online communities of buyers and sellers. In March 2000 Ariba closed on a deal to buy Tradex for $1.4 billion in stock. As a result of these transactions, Ariba shipped two new products in 2000, Ariba Dynamic Trade and Ariba Marketplace. Later in 2000 Ariba made yet another significant acquisition, paying more than $600 million in stock for SupplierMarket .com, which led to the launching of Ariba Sourcing.

In the autumn of 2000 the prospects for Ariba appeared quite bright, with Krach announcing that the company planned to turn a profit by the end of the year. In September 2000 the price of Ariba stock reached $168.75, which would prove to be a high-water mark. The company did in fact post a $10 million profit in the December quarter but was about to enter a difficult period, as did many in the technology sector when a faltering economy forced corporations to retrench and cut back on investments. In just nine months Ariba stock lost 95 percent of its value. Nevertheless the company started out 2001 in growth mode, and even negotiated a $2.55 billion stock swap purchase of Agile Software, developer of collaborative e-commerce supply chain software. Within a matter of weeks, however, the deal was off, following the reporting of a severe drop in revenues at Ariba. Moreover, the excitement about online marketplaces evaporated, as companies decided to manage their spending in-house, and the company was forced to take a $1.4 billion write-down on its purchase of Tradex. With the future of the economy uncertain, Ariba took drastic cost-cutting measures, slashing its payroll and laying off 700 workers, or about a third of its staff.

In May 2001 Krach stepped down as CEO, remaining on as chairman, and promoting President and COO Larry Mueller to replace him. Mueller's time at the helm would be brief, less than three months, but it would have long-term repercussions. According to press reports Mueller resigned suddenly, ''amid internal criticism of his management style.'' Krach returned to the CEO post on an interim basis while a replacement was recruited. In October 2002 CFO Robert Caleroni, a recent hire, assumed the position and set about the task of refocusing the company on its spend management capabilities. He cut another 350 jobs and instituted other cost-saving measures, such as eliminating holiday parties and free bottled water.

In early 2003 Ariba received unwelcomed publicity when it was forced to restate financial results for fiscal 2001 due to an unusual $10 million payment made to Mueller by Krach. Two weeks later the company announced that it was expanding its restatement to cover ten quarters after an internal investigation revealed that millions of dollars in items listed as company expenses should have been considered compensation for Mueller, including $1.2 million in chartered jet service. Calderoni, in the meantime, flew coach as he traveled the country trying to drum up business for the company's original Ariba Buyer. Procurement software was staging a comeback in the marketplace, but whether the new CEO would be successful in reviving the fortunes of Ariba was very much in doubt. ''I thought I was joining a small, fast-growing organization,'' Calderoni told *Forbes* in March 2003, ''I only got the 'small.' ''

Principal Subsidiaries

Ariba Canada, Inc.; Ariba Latin America, Inc.; Ariba Deutschland GmbH (Germany); Ariba U.K. Limited.

Principal Competitors

FreeMarkets, Inc.; Oracle Corporation; PeopleSoft, Inc.

Further Reading

Dempsey, Michael, "View from the Top: Keith Krach of Ariba," *Financial Times,* October 18, 2000, p. 3.

Fonseca, Natalie, "An E-commerce Rising Star," *Upside,* June 1999, pp. 113–17.

Gomes, Lee, "Ariba Faces Earnings Shortfall, Layoffs," *Wall Street Journal,* April 3, 2001.

"How Ariba Got Airborne," *Business Week,* September 18, 2000, p. 126.

Littman, Jonathan, "Supplies-Side Economics," *Upside,* July 1998, pp. 64–65.

Melvin, Chuck, "Ariba Has Arrived," *Plain Dealer,* December 26, 1999, p. 1E.

Murphy, Victoria, "The Thrifty Boss," *Forbes,* March 3, 2003, p. 89.

Warner, Melanie, "The New Way to Start Up in Silicon Valley," *Fortune,* March 2, 1998, pp. 168–74.

—Ed Dinger

ASICS Corporation

1-1, Minatojima-Nakamachi 7-chrome, Chuo-ku
Kobe, 650-8555
Japan
Telephone: +81-78-303-2231
Fax: +81-78-303-2241
Web site: http://www.asics.co.jp

Public Company
Incorporated: 1949 as Onitsuka Co., Ltd.
Employees: 4,109
Sales: ¥128,901 million ($969 million) (2002)
Stock Exchanges: Tokyo
NAIC: 316211 Rubber and Plastics Footwear
   Manufacturing; 315228 Men's and Boys' Cut and
   Sew Other Outerwear Manufacturing; 315999 Other
   Apparel Accessories and Other Apparel Manufactur-
   ing; 316219 Other Footwear Manufacturing; 339920
   Sporting and Athletic Good Manufacturing

ASICS Corporation is one of Japan's top makers of sport shoes and other equipment. The company takes its name from the Latin phrase *anima sana in corpore sano,* "a sound mind in a sound body." In the United States, ASICS is best known for its running shoes; it also produces footwear and accessories for a number of other sports, including basketball, volleyball, and wrestling. It dominates the Japanese market for basketball shoes. ASICS has a formidable presence in the international running community. It sponsors the New York City Marathon, where 40 percent of recent competitors wore the company's shoes. The company has subsidiaries in Australia, Brazil, China, Europe, and Korea in addition to its Irvine, California-based ASICS Tiger Corporation unit.

Origins

Kihachiro Onitsuka formed the predecessor of ASICS Corp., Onitsuka Co., Ltd., in Kobe, Japan, in 1949. He was motivated by the use of sports as a means to rehabilitate juveniles there after World War II.

Onitsuka lacked experience in making shoes, but he threw himself enthusiastically into researching their physiology. He also drew ideas from other areas of life. The suction cups of an octopus in his salad inspired the design of basketball shoe soles. In fact, the company claimed Japan's first basketball shoes, nicknamed "Bashu," which featured a tiger face on the sole. This would become a company trademark.

Onitsuka displayed a commitment to innovation from the start. The company's first volleyball shoes, introduced in 1951, had vulcanized rubber soles. The Tiger Marathon Tabi incorporated a number of technical innovations. Vinylon, a synthetic fiber, was used in the uppers. A band along the side of the shoe helped support the arch. Onitsuka continued to upgrade its offerings for long-distance runners throughout the mid-1950s. The durable Ekiden Marup was its first marathon shoe with a rounded toe.

One of Onitsuka's offerings even attracted the great barefoot marathon champion Abebe Bikila, who began wearing the company's Magic Runner shoes. This model, introduced in 1959, used a number of vent holes to cool the sole of the foot. Onitsuka had developed the Magic Runner as a means to avoid the corns he had seen on other marathoners' feet. Japanese marathoner Kenji Kimihara used the Magic Runner shoes to win a silver medal at the 1968 Mexico Olympics.

Olympic Prominence in the 1960s and 1970s

The company's products were becoming more common at the Olympics and other world-class sporting events. A number of top athletes from countries other than Japan were wearing Onitsuka shoes; they won silver and bronze medals at the 1964 Tokyo Olympics. A 1966 market survey found nearly two-thirds of athletes at the Boston Marathon wearing them.

Product development continued to keep pace. A variety of new technologies were introduced in training, basketball, and tennis shoes in the early 1960s. Onitsuka reportedly was the first to employ synthetic leather in shoe manufacture. The company also introduced a new line of shoes for soccer, which was being introduced into the elementary school curriculum.

The 1960s also saw Onitsuka's development of the first track shoes with interchangeable spikes in its "Run Spark" line. This allowed sprinters to modify them for specific events and track conditions while extending the life of the shoes.

Onitsuka launched its "Olympic Line" after years of gathering suggestions from top athletes. This series marked the introduction of the ASICS trademark design of two vertical lines intersecting a pair of lines emanating from the heel of the shoe. These lines were said to provide reinforcement as well as decoration. The first shoes to feature the Tiger Stripes were the Mexico 66 model, introduced two years before the 1968 Olympic Games in Mexico City.

One version of the shoes so popular with competitive runners found an unexpected new audience in the late 1960s. The blue nylon "Marup Nylon SP" became the unofficial school footwear of a generation of Japanese youth. More than 400,000 pairs were sold after their introduction in 1967.

The Corsair line of jogging shoes was unveiled in 1969. These were designed for cushioning and comfort. A derivative of the Corsair called the Cortes was one of sports giant Nike's first products.

The reasonably priced "Bomber" line of soccer shoes capitalized on soccer's popularity in Japan in the early 1970s. Onitsuka began to invest in overseas markets. The company set up a U.S. subsidiary in Irvine, California, in 1973. Two years later, a West German unit was established in Dusseldorf.

Technical innovations continued. Onitsuka developed the first shoe designed for the new all-weather, synthetic surface tracks that were being introduced in the 1970s. The Tiger Paw DS-5700 debuted in 1974. Onitsuka was an earlier user of the cushioning material EVA (ethylene vinyl acetate), which would become ubiquitous in all manner of sports shoes around the world. It appeared in Onitsuka's Limber-Up XL trainers in 1975.

Formation of ASICS: 1977

ASICS was created by the merger of Onitsuka Co., Ltd. with fishing and sporting goods company GTO and athletic uniform maker JELENK in 1977. Onitsuka was named president of the new company.

ASICS claimed another innovation with its Rota series of volleyball shoes introduced in 1978. These were said to be the first in which the outsole was designed to absorb shock. The California, a descendant of the Corsair jogger, came out the same year. Among other features, it had a reflective surface to alert drivers in low visibility. ASICS Tiger, the U.S. affiliate, began marketing the Montreal III jogger, which featured a "Cush-Hole" air vent in the heel.

ASICS developed shoes for Japan's Olympic teams to wear to the 1980 Olympic Games in Moscow. However, Japan joined the U.S.-led boycott in protest of the Soviet invasion of Afghanistan, and the shoes were not worn. (They would become part of ASICS' spring 2004 "retro" line-up, however.)

By the early 1980s, ASICS was exporting to 80 countries, including some behind the Iron Curtain. In order to mitigate exchange rate fluctuations and import restrictions, the company began licensing production overseas to the United States (jogging shoes), followed by Israel (training shoes), and Greece and Australia (training apparel).

The company's sales units in the United States and West Germany initially had difficulty breaking into Western markets; together they lost ¥1.2 billion ($5.1 million) in 1981. The dominance of Adidas AG and a lack of effective salespeople limited ASICS in Western Europe.

The U.S. subsidiary was recapitalized and reorganized into the new ASICS Tiger Corporation in August 1981. After problems with excessive inventory, the U.S. unit cut out its distributor in favor of direct sales to retailers. The company began a marketing arrangement with Second Sole Co., a California sporting goods store, during the lead-up to the 1984 Los Angeles Olympic Games. Parent company ASICS Corporation's sales rose 19 percent to ¥73 billion in 1981/82, while pretax profits more than doubled to ¥6 billion. U.S. sales were $30 million.

A joint venture with Cambuci, S.A. began making and selling ASICS brand shoes in Brazil in mid-1984. ASICS also set up subsidiaries in Taiwan and South Korea. Licensed production of ASICS wrestling shoes began in mainland China in early 1988. ASICS began to shift production from South Korea to Indonesia in 1990 due to rising labor costs and frequent strikes.

ASICS designers focused on the problem of minimizing runners' energy loss in the Task XL-1, which came out in 1985. The outsole of these shoes featured a studded "Cactus Plate" reinforced with "Whisker" crystallized fiber material.

Success Gels in the Late 1980s

Shock-absorbing gels began appearing in ASICS shoes with the appearance of the Freaks jogging shoe and the Fable Radick basketball shoe in 1987. The gel allowed for lighter shoes than those cushioned by EVA sponge; it helped make the brand a favorite among competitive runners.

ASICS began building a new ¥4 billion ($27 million) sports engineering lab in Kobe in 1987. Several months later, ASICS Corp. became the Japanese marketing agent for French ski manufacturer Dynamic S.A. ASICS had already been marketing Atomic brand skis in Japan since 1979.

Key Dates:

1949: Onitsuka Co., Ltd. is founded in Kobe, Japan.
1963: Precursor to Nike, Inc. imports 200 pairs of Onitsuka Tiger shoes to the United States.
1966: Mexico 66 running shoes are first with Tiger Stripe trademark.
1967: Marup Nylon SP covers feet of a generation of Japanese schoolchildren.
1973: U.S. subsidiary is established.
1975: European unit is established in West Germany.
1977: ASICS is formed by the merger of Onitsuka with GTO and JELENK.
1984: Brazilian venture is established.
1992: ASICS supplies staff, torchbearers at Barcelona Olympics.
2000: Naoko Takahashi wins women's marathon at Sydney Olympics wearing ASICS.
2004: Retro ASICS footwear is brought back in "Onitsuka Tiger" line.

Some of ASICS' efforts were dedicated more towards fashion than performance. It introduced a line of pastel women's sneakers in 1988, and took over distribution for LA Gear sneakers in Japan in 1990.

ASICS Corp. ended the 1980s with international sales approaching $1 billion. The U.S. unit, which was strong in running, volleyball, and wrestling markets, had sales of $110 million in 1989. By belatedly focusing more attention on marketing and advertising in the hype-driven U.S. market, ASICS would see sales growth exceeding 20 percent a year there for the next five years.

New Challenges in the 1990s

In 1990, ASICS recapitalized its subsidiaries in the United States, West Germany (ASICS Tiger GmbH), and Australia (ASICS Tiger Oceania). ASICS Corporation posted its first net loss (¥1.13 billion) since its founding, in the fiscal year ended January 1991. A computer business had racked up significant debt while ASICS closed a Taiwan subsidiary. The company remained committed to raising its international profile. As official shoe supplier for the 1992 Barcelona Olympics, ASICS supplied shoes for 20,000 Olympic staff and 60,000 torchbearers.

ASICS introduced a line of lightweight, durable shoes exclusively for professional athletes in 1990. Marathon Sortie EX featured a proprietary blend of synthetic leather and urethane, allowing for lighter soles. The TARTHER 195 a, a consumer version with thicker midsoles, was introduced the next year.

A unique offering for ASICS Corp. was its President shoes, lightweight dress shoes with static-resistant soles. Aimed at Japanese executives, they sold for up to ¥46,000 ($350) a pair. In the mid-1990s, ASICS brought out a sandal inspired by a medieval Japanese design.

After a return to profitability, sales fell 9 percent to ¥94.62 billion in 1994–95, producing a loss of ¥1.13 billion. The

company's U.S. operations were reorganized in 1995; by this time, ASICS Tiger had sales in the range of $250 million a year.

ASICS and other Japanese shoemakers had to deal with the incursion of American brands Nike, New Balance, and Converse on their home turf. To counter, ASICS released a line of shoes without its trademark stripes in April 1997. At the same time, it had taken over Japanese distribution of a hip line of American footwear and snowboard gear for Altoona, Pennsylvania-based Airwalk Footwear.

ASICS benefited from the popularity of niche brands of running shoes in the United States in the late 1990s. The company extended its brand into a series of walking shoes, following the trend of walking as a form of physical fitness.

ASICS remained committed to competitive track and field. It continued to develop new shoes for the ultra-competitive field of sprinting, where success was measured in 1/100ths of a second. The Tiger Paw Cyberzero of 1996 featured a molded heel protector and "holding belts" or straps for support and fit.

ASICS introduced a couple of new sports shoes for young children in 1999 and 2000. The first, called SUKU2, featured straps instead of laces and offered plenty of toe room. The second, the "G.D." series, was named after American physician Glenn Doman, who had studied the effect of exercise on development of children's brains. "G.D." shoes were designed to simulate the feeling of being barefoot, with plenty of cushioning, flexibility, and breathability.

Looking Back, Looking Forward: 2000 and Beyond

The Sydney Olympics in 2000 represented another special achievement for the company. Naoko Takahashi won the women's marathon using customized shoes specially developed for her. One of her legs was a few millimeters shorter than the other. Hitoshi Mimura, ASICS' master craftsman who first joined the company in 1967, fashioned these shoes and ones for other top athletes.

Southeast Asia was another important market for ASICS, providing revenues of ¥200 million in 2001. The company aimed to more than double that figure by 2008 as it built three sales networks focusing on South Korea, greater China, and the rest of the region. Revenues were ¥128.9 billion ($969 million) in the fiscal year ended March 31, 2002. ASICS and its subsidiaries supplied outerwear for Japanese, Dutch, and Italian teams at the 2002 Winter Olympics in Salt Lake City.

The trend toward retro-styled sneakers led to some legal battles for ASICS. It sued discount retailers Target and Fred's and shoemakers Reebok and Harkham Industries, for allegedly infringing upon its trademark stripe design.

ASICS Tiger recalled a number of vintage designs from 1966 to 1983 for its Onitsuka Tiger line-up for spring 2004, as well as a retro-inspired line called SportStyle. ASICS Corporation was projected to have sales of ¥73.5 billion ($622.3 million) for the fiscal year ending March 31, 2004, with net income of ¥1.4 billion.

Principal Subsidiaries

ASICS Europe B.V. (The Netherlands); ASICS Sports Corporation (South Korea); ASICS Tiger Corporation (U.S.A.); ASICS Tiger do Brasil Ltda. (Brazil); ASICS Tiger Oceana Pty. (Australia).

Principal Competitors

Adidas-Salomon AG; Mizuno Corporation; New Balance Athletic Shoe Inc.; Nike, Inc.; Reebok International Ltd.; Saucony Inc.

Further Reading

"Adidas America and Other Athletic Footwear Companies Will Participate in Winter Olympics, Albeit in Non-Traditional Categories," *FN*, February 4, 2002, p. 96.

"Airwalk Raises Japan Profile; Will Distribute Airwalk Footwear and Snowboarding Goods in Japan," *Footwear News*, March 3, 1997, p. 7.

"ASICS Boosting Production Capacity, Marketing Effort," *Japan Economic Journal*, November 11, 1989, p. 20.

"ASICS Will Extend Know-How on Sports Shoes to Foreign Nations," *Japan Economic Journal*, April 14, 1981, p. 18.

Carlson, Scott, "Japanese Shoemaker Sues Target, Alleging Sneaker Violates Trademark Protection," *St. Paul Pioneer Press*, June 24, 2003.

"Japanese Sporting Goods Makers Not Doing Well Abroad," *Jiji Press Ticker Service*, March 20, 1982.

Magiera, Marcy, "Smaller Rivals 'Do It' to Nike; ASICS, Puma Ape Theme," *Advertising Age*, May 15, 1989, p. 42.

Mori, Kazuo, "Sporting Goods Mogul Pursues World Peace," *Nikkei Weekly* (Japan), October 19, 1991, p. 7.

Mouchard, Andre, "ASICS Gets Ads Up, Running; OC-Based Athletic-Shoe Maker Decides to Take on the Big Boys," *Orange County Register*, April 9, 1993, p. C1.

"Multi-Strap Shoes Allow Wearer to Step Back in Time," *Nikkei Weekly* (Japan), December 25, 1995, p. 13.

Rechtin, Mark, "ASICS Challenges Nike, L.A. Gear Without Big Names," *Orange County Business Journal*, May 14, 1990, p. 1.

Reidy, Chris, "Niche Brands Gain Larger Share of Athletic-Shoe Market," *Boston Globe*, April 12, 2000.

"Rivals Step Carefully in Nike's Wake," *Nikkei Weekly* (Japan), September 1, 1997, p. 7.

Rourke, Elizabeth, Maura Troester, and David E. Salamie, "NIKE, Inc.," *International Directory of Company Histories, Vol. 36*, Farmington Hills, Mich.: St. James Press, 2001.

Solo, Sally, "Developing U.S. Market Is ASICS' Top Priority," *Footwear News*, October 12, 1987, p. 28.

"Sporting Goods Companies Vie for Olympic Business," *Japan Economic Journal*, March 8, 1983.

Takagi, Shinji, "Executives Slip on Repellent Shoes," *Japan Economic Journal*, March 16, 1991, p. 21.

—Frederick C. Ingram

Atlantic Premium Brands, Ltd.

1033 Skokie Boulevard, Suite 600
Northbrook, Illinois 60062
U.S.A.
Telephone: (847) 412-6200
Fax: (847) 412-9766
Web site: http://www.atlanticpremiumbrands.com

Public Company
Incorporated: 1991 as Maryland Beverage Company
Employees: 485
Sales: $122.3 million (2002)
Stock Exchanges: voluntarily delisted from AMEX
Ticker Symbol: ABR
NAIC: 422470 Meat and Meat Product Wholesalers

Operating out of the Chicago suburb of Northbrook, Illinois, Atlantic Premium Brands, Ltd. (APB) owns several premium meat brands, distributed to a contiguous 12-state region comprised mostly of midwestern and southwestern states. Through its Texas-based Carlton Foods Corporation subsidiary, ABP produces smoked sausage products, primarily sold in Texas. Subsidiary Prefco Corporation markets and distributes APB branded meat, as well as unbranded meat, and frozen entrees to grocery stores. The company's Blue Ribbon brand includes sausage and bacon products, as well as home meal replacement items that include Texas-style, fully cooked barbecue entrees. J.C. Potter Sausage Company is an Oklahoma business that makes and sells premium, branded smoked sausages, breakfast sausage, and breakfast entrees, and also conducts a private-label program. Richard's Cajun Foods Corporation, the last of the APB main subsidiaries, is a Louisiana business that produces and distributes Cajun-style frozen entrees as well as smoked sausages, boudin, pork and turkey tasso, pork hocks, and head cheese.

Origins in the Mid-1980s As a Beverage Company

APB was originally the Maryland Beverage Company, established in Maryland in 1986 by William Albright, Jr., and his wife Stephanie. Albright grew up immersed in the beverage industry. His father owned Albright Wholesale Co., one of the largest beer distributorships in the state of Maryland. Albright went to work for the company in 1980 and was instrumental in Albright Wholesale's move to distribute Soho Natural Sodas, a trendy product in the mid-1980s. Recognizing the potential of such alternative beverages, Albright decided to form a separate company to focus on the business. In 1986, Albright, who was 28, and his wife, who was 23, scraped together $20,000—$10,000 from savings and a $10,000 loan—and launched a start-up they dubbed Maryland Beverage Company. In addition to Soho, the product line grew to include Elliott's Amazing Juice, Deer Creek Spring Water, Snapple, Mystic, and Orangina. With Bill providing his expertise in distribution and Stephanie handling the marketing, by 1991 the Albrights had built a company generating $22 million in yearly sales. At this point they decided to cash in.

In September 1991 a Chicago-based private equity firm, Sterling Capital Partners, bought Maryland Beverage for more than $4 million and subsequently incorporated the business. Sterling Capital was established in 1983, concentrating on real estate, venture capital, and buyouts. Acquiring Maryland Beverage was part of an initial strategy to assemble a slate of similar alternative beverage distributors throughout the United States and create a national network. To achieve this end Maryland Beverage was readied to be taken public and the name was changed to reflect a less provincial scope. In September 1993 the company was reincorporated in Delaware as Atlantic Beverage Company. Assuming the chairmanship of Atlantic Beverage was one of Sterling's cofounders, Eric D. Becker. One of the directors was Merrick M. Elfman, the company's current chairman. An initial public offering (IPO) of stock was completed in November 1993, with nearly 1.2 million shares of common stock sold at $6.50 per share. The IPO netted more than $6 million, of which $4.2 million was used to pay down debt and the balance set aside for future acquisitions.

Several months after going public, Atlantic Beverage took a step that its chairman thought was going to be the cornerstone of the company's national ambitions—acquiring certain assets of Flying Fruit Fantasy, USA, Inc. for $580,000 in cash plus stock. Atlantic Beverage gained the worldwide marketing and distribution rights to fruitshakes dispensed from automated machines using vacuum-packed ingredients. Flying Fruit was well known in the Baltimore and Washington, D.C. markets; the business had been launched 14 years earlier by Robert Groth, a former part-owner/bartender of a Washington suburb restaurant. He experimented with fruit juices and ice to develop exotic drinks for his customers, eventually coming up with a fruitshake that he decided to test outside of the bar. He set up a stand at an outdoor fair on Capitol Hill and was so pleased with the results that he fixed up an old milk truck to sell his fruitshakes at other weekend fairs. Groth built up a cult following, with many of his customers sporting T-shirts with the company's colorful logo. He continued to operate out of a truck until he was finally able to obtain a coveted spot in a mall. Fortunately for Groth, Baltimore's Harborplace was on the verge of opening and on the lookout for unique tenants. The mall's developer saw the Flying Fruit truck at a crafts fair and signed up the young company as a tenant when Harborplace opened in the summer of 1980. With that toehold in the market, Groth was able to grow the business over the next decade, expanding to some 30 locations in the Baltimore-Washington, D.C. corridor. The company also began establishing carts in airports in Salt Lake City, Detroit, and New York, as well as selling franchises.

Becker and Atlantic Beverage were convinced that in the early 1990s Flying Fruit had not yet reached its full potential. In a statement released at the time, Becker maintained, "This nutritious product can be sold through a wide variety of distribution channels, and we see an opportunity to introduce Automated Fruitshake Centers to a number of Atlantic Beverages' existing customers. Once a dispensing machine is installed, a 'razor and blade' effect comes into play as retailers begin placing repeat orders for fruitshake concentrate." Within three years Atlantic Beverage planned to install as many as 1,000 machines in new locations.

Long before three years were over, however, Atlantic Beverage decided to ground its Flying Fruit business. Coupled with new competition from other drink sellers that cut into revenues and start-up costs incurred in launching its Flying Fruit endeavor, Atlantic Beverage experienced a sharp downturn in its fortunes. Moreover, the company endured three consecutive profitless years after being acquired by Sterling Capital, resulting in the company being dropped from the NASDAQ National Market list of stocks and relegated to the Small Cap Market.

In January 1996 Atlantic Beverage closed down the company's frozen beverage division, which only contributed about 2 percent of the company's $25 million in annual revenues. It had been clear for some time that Becker's hopes for Flying Fruit had been misplaced and already there was a plan being put into place to reposition Atlantic Beverage and diversify into food products so that the company would be less dependent on

beverages. This strategy was being orchestrated at Sterling's Chicago offices by Alan F. Sussna, who came to the project from Bain & Company, a well-known consulting firm that specialized in turning around companies. The acquisition strategy called for Atlantic Beverage to target small, already successful premium meat brands.

Beginning Diversification in the Mid-1990s

The first step in the diversification effort took place in February 1996 when Atlantic Beverage agreed to pay approximately $11 million to acquire Prefco Corporation, which included the Blue Ribbon brand, and Carlton Foods. In 1995 the two companies together generated revenues of $117 million. Prefco was a spinoff of Blue Ribbon Packing Company, founded in Houston in 1948 by German immigrants Hans and Erna Pauly. They used old German recipes to make smoked sausages and were so successful that they were able to evolve into a full-service meat packing company, with a slaughtering operation and rendering company. With the death of Hans Pauly in 1963, the eldest son, Fred J. Pauly, assumed control, and over the next 25 years he transformed Blue Ribbon into a major Southwest packing business. In 1986 a son-in-law of the founders, Franklin M. Roth, became president of the firm and established Prefco to serve independent grocery stores and small supermarket chains. He also extended the Blue Ribbon brand of sausage and bacon products throughout Texas. Carlton Foods, founded in Houston in 1941, also had a long history producing smoked sausage in the Texas market. Through the 1972 acquisition of a processing company in New Braunfels it expanded into the central Texas market. Carlton launched a private-label manufacturing program in 1985.

Atlantic continued its acquisition spree when later in 1996 it bought Richard's Cajun Country Food Processors in a deal worth nearly $3.5 million. The company's founder was Lonnie Richard, who drew on his grandmother's family recipes for smoked sausage and boudin, which he learned while working at her small southwestern Louisiana grocery store. He launched the business in 1981 and then retired 15 years later. He was succeeded as president of the company, just before it was purchased by Atlantic Beverage, by a childhood friend, banker Ronnie Doucet. In October 1996 Atlantic Beverage completed yet another acquisition, paying approximately $3.3 million in cash and stock for Kentucky-based Grogan's Sausage, Inc. and Grogan's Farm. Finally, in November 1996 Atlantic Beverage, through its Grogan's subsidiary, bought Partin's Sausage for $400,000 in cash.

Also in 1996 Atlantic Beverage underwent personnel changes in the top ranks. Sussna was named president and chief executive officer in March, and Becker was replaced as chairman by Elfman in July. Because Sussna was so instrumental in the company's sudden rise, company headquarters was moved to the Chicago area to accommodate him. To reflect its new business mix, the company then changed its name again, this time to Atlantic Premium Brands, Ltd., effective June 1, 1997.

APB completed another acquisition in March 1998, paying nearly $12 million in cash for J.C. Potter Sausage Company, a Durant, Oklahoma-based maker of breakfast sausage. The company was founded in 1949 by J.C. Potter, a veteran of World

War II who returned home after his stint in the service to work as a butcher in a grocery store. He, too, relied on a family recipe for making sausage and ultimately established the J.C. Potter product as the leading brand in Oklahoma.

Sussna next tried to maximize the potential of the companies APB acquired. Up-to-date management tools were brought to bear to make the operations more efficient, including the use of production planning systems, budgeting models, consumer research, marketing plans, and advanced financial reporting systems. Sussna also looked to create synergy between the APB subsidiaries, which now began to cross-market each other's products, and in some cases manufacture products for one another to round off product lines. In addition, Sussna instituted a strategy of creating value-added products that would help insulate the company from commodity price swings. Another major reason for this approach was the state of breakfast sausage sales, which grew stagnant nationwide in the late 1990s. In response, Grogan created home-cooked frozen country meals, such as chicken and dumplings, and country ham and white beans, ready to eat in 20 minutes. Blue Ribbon brought out a line of microwaveable, refrigerated barbecue entrees, including sliced beef brisket, brisket and sausage combo, pork spareribs, babyback ribs, shredded beef, and half chicken mesquite, all relying on a proprietary barbecue sauce. Richard's, for its part, introduced a line of frozen Cajun entrées that began with crawfish étouffée, chicken and sausage jambalaya, seafood gumbo, pork and sausage jambalaya, chicken and sausage piquante, red beans and sausage, and meatball stew. These items soon were followed by crawfish and corn macque choix, chicken fricassee, and Cajun corn soup.

Sussna's strategy was working well for APB, as revenues approached $200 million in 1999, with a net profit of nearly $1.2 million. The company's original beverage business now contributed less than 10 percent of its sales. Starting in late 1998 and culminating in January 1999, APB disposed of its beverage assets, casting its lot entirely with its meat products.

Struggling in the Early 2000s

The promising launch of Sussna's diversification strategy would start to experience problems, however, due in large part to the company dependence on one very large customer, Sam's Club, which decided to establish its own distribution operation. Sam's accounted for 43 percent of APB's net sales in 1999 and 30 percent in 2000. As a result, revenues fell to $177 million in 2000, and then plunged to $134 million in 2001 and $122.3 million in 2002.

In January 2003 Sussna resigned and APB's chief operating officer, Thomas M. Dalton, took over as president. A few months later, in May 2003, the company took the unusual step of voluntarily delisting its shares from trading on the American Stock Exchange. Management felt that delisting was in the best interests of the company due to a number of reasons: there were few shareholders, primarily company officers; the costs associated with reporting hurt profits; there was not enough trading activity to make the stock a viable source of financing; and no analysts covered the company. APB hoped to make its shares available through broker "pink sheets," but clearly management had more pressing concerns as it attempted to revitalize its struggling business.

Principal Subsidiaries

Carlton Foods Corporation; Grogan's Farm, Inc.; J.C. Potter Sausage Company; Prefco Corporation; Richard's Cajun Foods Corporation; Texas Traditions, Inc.

Principal Competitors

ConAgra Foods, Inc.; Hormel Foods Corporation; Sara Lee Corporation.

Further Reading

Cheshire, Mark, "Atlantic Beverage's Corporate Relocation Reflects Bid to Move Beyond MD. Market," *Daily Record,* November 16, 1996, p. 7A.
Galosich, Allison, "Enterprising Tactics," *National Provisioner,* November 1998, p. 53.
Hinden, Stan, "Atlantic Beverage Hopes to Quench a Thirst," *Washington Post,* October 11, 1993, p. F31.
Johnson, Tom, "Atlantic Beverage Fattens Profits with Acquisitions of Meatpackers," *Daily Record,* August 6, 1996, p. 3A.

—Ed Dinger

Bailey Nurseries, Inc.

1325 Bailey Road
St. Paul, Minnesota 55119
U.S.A.
Telephone: (651) 459 9744
Toll Free: (800) 829-8898
Fax: (651) 459-5100
Web site: http://www.baileynursery.com

Private Company
Incorporated: 1905
Employees: 500
Sales: $65 million (2002 est.)
NAIC: 424930 Flower, Nursery Stock, and Florists
  Supplies Wholesalers

Bailey Nurseries, Inc. is a family owned and operated wholesale nursery and ranks consistently among the top ten U.S. nurseries. Bailey's corporate headquarters is in Newport, Minnesota, in the suburbs of St. Paul. The company conducts business in 47 states and has a small international presence with sales to Canada and China. In addition to its Minnesota operations, Bailey has growing facilities in Oregon and Washington state.

The First Generation, a Labor of Love: 1800s to 1943

The Bailey family tradition of working the soil dates back many generations, and the Bailey Nurseries story itself encompasses four generations of Bailey family members who have devoted their careers to cultivating trees, shrubs, and plants.

The genesis of the company came at the end of the 19th century, when a young Minnesota farmer's son, John Vincent (J.V.) Bailey, realized his passion for the land and sought out a modern education in agriculture. Bailey enrolled at the St. Paul campus of the University of Minnesota's Agricultural School in 1892. Students at the school were taught the most recent agricultural and technological innovations of the day. J.V. Bailey was a conscientious student who committed himself to his study of all manner of agricultural science. Bailey worked his way through school by staffing the entomology laboratory on campus and graduated from the University of Minnesota in 1896.

Though Bailey was well educated, his financial reserves were limited and he found himself with very little money for acquiring land on which to practice his newfound knowledge. Challenged but not despondent, Bailey took what was left of his life's savings, a mere $10, and invested it in some agricultural rental land his first year out of school. The venture on the rented land proved unsuccessful and Bailey failed to turn a profit.

Bailey remained undaunted and leased land a second season. This time his prospecting paid off. Bailey had planted a melon crop on a rocky hillside near Newport, Minnesota, land for which conventional farmers of the time saw little use. In a remarkable turn of luck, Bailey realized a $3,000 profit.

In order to accomplish his bountiful harvest, Bailey had enriched the soil using additives to make the rocky soil adequate for planting; next he built miniature cold-frame greenhouses out of recycled glass photo negatives and lumber. The combination of hard work and innovation paid off and left Bailey with enough money to purchase 80 acres of land and begin his farm in earnest.

Several important factors contributed to Bailey's fortune in the early years. The St. Paul Farmer's Market was a newly created Minnesota enterprise which afforded J.V. Bailey a convenient place to sell his produce, and Bailey was willing to work hard to achieve his goals.

The market supplied city dwellers and restaurateurs fresh farm products at reasonable prices, and became an instant success. With his wagonload of produce, Bailey was one of the market's principal vendors, and as such earned a citywide reputation for high-quality goods.

In the first decade, the St. Paul Farmer's Market had several hundred growers represented in individual stands. The industrious Bailey was determined to get to market early and set up his wares in one of the choicest positions on the market floor. This was not an easy accomplishment when one considers that the trip to St. Paul by wagon took Bailey two and a half hours

---

Company Perspectives:

Bailey Nurseries, Inc. is widely recognized as one of the United States' largest wholesale nurseries, serving customers throughout the U.S., several Canadian provinces and beyond. Our products are distributed by more than 4,500 nursery retailers, landscapers, and garden center operations and can be found as far away as Beijing, China. Through its 95 years, Bailey has earned a reputation as a leader in the nursery industry with inventive techniques, high-quality plants and active involvement in industry organizations. The integrity and innovation on which the company was built remain its hallmarks today. Still a family-owned business, the fourth generation of the Bailey family is now actively involved in all facets of the nursery's daily operations.

---

from his farmstead. The route was a little more than eight miles by horse and cart, with a heavy load to pull on bumpy and dusty dirt roads that made the trip arduous.

With the initial triumph of the market, a bank known as the Produce Exchange Bank was begun, with J.V. Bailey as one of the bank's founders. In other market lore, Bailey was immortalized as the first vendor to arrive at market by motorized vehicle. The primitive automobile was a kind of makeshift truck. Bailey had attached a large crate for produce on the back of an automobile and his creation helped improve his business considerably. The rudimentary pickup allowed Bailey to arrive at the market in less time and enabled him to make several trips back and forth to his farm to restock his supply. More sales meant more revenue, and revenue for Bailey translated into additional land holdings.

In 1911 Bailey saw a need to diversify his product offerings and began to introduce nursery products to his goods at market. Flowers, ornamental shrubs, and evergreens were sold at the Bailey stand with immediate success. In a short time Bailey began to catalogue his nursery stock and increased demand led to his hiring his first employees.

While the company flourished in the beginning of the 20th century, Bailey married and bought more land, but like most businesses the hard times of the 1930s caused a rapid decline.

During the Great Depression, Bailey Nurseries suffered some minor setbacks. The Baileys mortgaged some of their land holdings in order to support the family. The family's fruit trees, especially their apples, proved to be an important cash crop during these lean years. The family and business weathered the Depression and by 1933 the company held over 300 acres, and housed a modern office and plant storage facilities. It was at this time that the second generation of Baileys began to manage the company. Vincent Bailey was hired as superintendent of production and Gordon Bailey took over the administrative duties of the company. J.V.'s daughter, Beth, partnered with Gordon in the offices in her role as secretary and bookkeeper.

When war broke out in the 1940s, Bailey Nurseries faced challenges on several fronts. The workforce that the company had relied on to work its land—predominantly young, male,

blue-collar workers—had joined the military ranks and left a tremendous labor shortage on the homefront. To keep up with production, the company relied on migrant laborers, mainly Mexican nationals, to fill the gap.

New Generation at the Helm: 1943–80s

In 1943 company founder John Vincent Bailey passed away from heart problems, leaving the business fully to his offspring. In 1950 Bailey Nurseries hired its first full-time salesman, who traveled the countryside searching out vendors interested in stocking Bailey trees, shrubs, and container grown nursery plants. Many of the small roadside nurseries that exist in small towns along rural Minnesota routes got their start selling Bailey Nurseries' products.

In 1955 Bailey Nurseries became the first business of its kind to institute a profit-sharing plan for its full-time permanent employees. The profit-sharing standard Bailey set did not reproduce industrywide for many years to come. Under the second generation, an important directional decision took place. In 1956, with a growing wholesale operation, the Bailey brothers decided to eliminate the retail division and focus solely on expanding the company's wholesale services. Retail facilities were converted to growing space, and the company readied itself for large-scale expansion.

By 1962 Bailey Nurseries had over 600 acres of land and maintained 450 acres of trees, shrubs, and nursery plants. The company had been rapidly expanding and concentrating its resources on further refining the operation.

To improve upon its plant stock the company invested in its storage facilities throughout its operation. Beginning in the late 1960s Bailey installed automatic humidity and refrigeration controls to provide a safe climate-controlled environment for its bareroot stock. These state-of-the-art facilities contributed greatly to the production of high-quality nursery stock. The dormant storage areas maintained temperature levels by means of a mechanized ventilation system, refrigeration, and rapid humidity controls produced when compressed air is circulated over water. By the time representatives of the third generation of Baileys—Gordon, Jr., and Rod—became chairman and president, respectively, those family members that had maintained an active role in the company bought out other relatives who had inherited equity in the company.

In 1977 Bailey Nurseries expanded its facilities by establishing business sites in the Pacific Northwest. It opened farms in Yamhill and Sauvie Island, Oregon, and in Sunnyside, Washington.

In 1980 Margaret and Gordon Bailey, Sr., established a faculty chair in environmental horticulture at the University of Minnesota. Gordon, Sr., was honored for his substantial work in the nursery industry by being inducted into the American Nurserymen's Hall of Fame. Bailey's father, J.V., had helped organize the Association and served as its first president.

In 1981 the nursery instituted a central propagation center in Cottage Grove, Minnesota. The facility, known as Nord Farm, served as the seeding operation for over 4.6 million trees and shrubs each year.

Key Dates:

1905: John Vincent and Elizabeth Bailey establish Bailey Nurseries.

1911: Bailey Nurseries diversifies to sell flowers, shrubs, evergreens, and cattle; Bailey establishes catalogue.

1926: J.V. Bailey becomes first president of the Minnesota Nurserymen's Association.

1933: Bailey holdings include over 300 acres, an office, and ventilated storage facilities.

1943: John Vincent Bailey dies of heart problems.

1950: Bailey Nurseries hires its first full-time salesperson.

1956: Gordon and Vincent Bailey, sons of the founder, decide to only pursue wholesale business.

1989: Bailey Nurseries begins producing container grown trees.

1991: Rose hybridization program is begun at Yamhill, Oregon.

2002: Bailey's Love and Peace rose wins national rose award.

Nord Farm seasonally shifted its production from bedding plants (perennials and annual flowers as well as vegetables and herbs) to soft wood plant seedlings in summer. Bailey grew over 175,000 flats of annual plants and over 40,000 hanging flower baskets for the home gardener.

The decades of the 1980s and 1990s saw a significant increase in hobby gardening. Spurred on by television celebrities such as Martha Stewart and Rebecca Kolls, shows including the *Victory Garden,* and the HGTV network, landscape centers and do-it-yourself home centers grew exponentially. In 1996 Bailey Nurseries became home to the nationally syndicated show *Rebecca's Garden,* with local master gardener Rebecca Kolls. Bailey Nurseries as a wholesale supplier did not miss out on these boom times and grew with the nation's renewed interest in home landscaping.

Blooming with Roses: 1990s–2000s

In 1991 Bailey Nurseries began its rose breeding program. Based at the nursery's Yamhill, Oregon site, the company produced a vast variety of high quality rose stock for its retailers. The rose program resulted in over 35,000 rose variety crosses each year. The 250,000 seeds that were produced through the hybridization were then evaluated for several important qualities that produced a good rose.

In 1992 Bailey Nurseries hired a professional rose hybrider named Ping Lim to oversee the cultivation of new roses. The company focused its production on hardy shrub roses that could tolerate tougher climates with good disease resistance. A rose catalogue was made available to retailers to keep current with the new varieties Bailey had developed. By 2003 roses had become one of Bailey Nurseries' largest selling products, with over 800,000 roses planted each year. The company produced its first All-American Rose Selections award-winning rose "Love and Peace" in 2002.

According to the company web site, by 2003 Bailey Nurseries had over 5,000 acres in active cultivation. The company maintained over five million cubic feet of cold storage space dedicated to housing over 7.5 million dormant plants. The company planted 2.7 million fruit and shade trees and more than six million shrubs and vines.

In 1998 Bailey Nurseries had bought land in Hastings, Minnesota, to serve primarily as a tree farm for container tree production. The company produced over 100,000 container grown trees each year. Tree sizes and prices varied greatly with container sizes ranging from five to 25 gallons.

In 1999, Chairman Gordon Bailey, Jr., continued the family philanthropic tradition by taking part in a cross-country bike trip to raise money for the Horticultural Research Institute. Bailey logged over 2,100 miles for an endowment fund at the Institute.

Industry consolidation had not been an enormous factor in the nursery industry as of the 2000s, but predictions were being made that such consolidations were coming. Bailey's diversification, large size, and strong name recognition placed it in a solid position to remain one of the industry's leaders.

Principal Competitors

Ball Horticultural Company; Shermin Nurseries; Celebrity Inc.; Florimex Worldwide Inc.

Further Reading

Broede, Jim, "Woodbury, Minnesota, Eyes 100 Acres for a Business Campus," *St. Paul Pioneer Press,* May 3, 1998.

Egerstrom, Lee, "*Newport, Minnesota-Area Nursery Shows Classic Challenges of Family Business,*" June 10, 2002.

"Flexibility Helps in Adjusting to Tight Labor Market," *Employee Benefit News,* May 1, 1998.

Solberg, Carla, "Gordon Bailey: Chairman, Bailey Nurseries," *Corporate Report Minnesota,* August 1999, p. 8.

—Susan B. Culligan

Baker Hughes Incorporated

3900 Essex Lane, Suite 1200
Post Office Box 4740
Houston, Texas 77210-4740
U.S.A.
Telephone: (713) 439-8600
Toll Free: (800) 229-7447
Fax: (713) 439-8699
Web site: http://www.bakerhughes.com

Public Company
Incorporated: 1987
Employees: 26,500
Sales: $5.02 billion (2002)
Stock Exchanges: New York Pacific Swiss
Ticker Symbol: BHI
NAIC: 213111 Drilling Oil and Gas Wells; 213112
Support Activities for Oil and Gas Operations;
333132 Oil and Gas Field Machinery and Equipment
Manufacturing; 325998 All Other Miscellaneous
Chemical Product and Preparation Manufacturing

Baker Hughes Incorporated is the product of the 1987 merger of two oilfield-services companies with surprisingly similar histories, Baker Oil Tools and Hughes Tool Company. Both were founded shortly before World War I by aggressive entrepreneurs who won valuable patents and earned gushing royalties on early oil-extraction devices. Both continued as domestic powerhouses until, at slightly different cues, they embarked on massive worldwide expansion and diversification projects. Baker and Hughes became public companies within ten years of each other as the influence of their founding families diminished. The two rivals experienced the fluctuations of an unpredictable world oil market jarred by political and economic events. Finally, the companies suffered financial slumps in the lean years of the 1980s, leading to their turbulent but successful consolidation.

There were differences, however, between Baker Oil Tools—later Baker International Corporation—and Hughes Tool. Hughes became the neglected plaything of Howard Hughes, Jr., the founder's famous billionaire son, who used the oil company's constant wellspring of cash to finance ventures in airplanes, real estate, and motion pictures. Baker, on the other hand, built a reputation, through careful yet ambitious expansion, as one of the industry's best-run firms, largely on the efforts of E.H. Clark, an executive whose tenure spanned 40 years. In the early 2000s, Baker Hughes, the offspring, ranked as a leading provider of products and services to the world petroleum and continuous process industries. Its size and influence was not solely a result of the merger, but of a number of key post-1987 acquisitions, the largest of which was the $3.3 billion purchase of Western Atlas, Inc., completed in 1998.

History of Hughes Tool Company

The invention of the first rotary drill bit, used to drill oil wells through rock, led to the creation of Sharp-Hughes Tool Company in 1909. Howard Hughes, Sr., and Walter Sharp developed and manufactured the rotary drill bit, an invention so important to the fledgling oil industry of 1909 that variations of the same bit are used today. When Sharp died in 1912, Hughes bought Sharp's share of the business. Hughes incorporated the business the following year, and in 1915 dropped Sharp's name from the company. Armed with the exclusive patent to an essential product, Hughes brought his Houston-based company unrivaled market dominance for decades. Even after many key patents expired, during the 1930s and 1940s Hughes Tool was able to dominate the drill-bit business. During World War I Hughes developed a boring machine that could drill into enemy trenches. Explosives then could be dropped into the trenches. Although the secretary of war personally thanked Hughes for his contribution, the machine was never used because of the sudden shift, toward the end of the war, from trench warfare to active warfare.

If the market dominance of Hughes Tool was secured by the elder Howard Hughes before World War I, its tenor as an undiversified, closely held giant was set by the founder's son and namesake. The 19-year-old Howard Hughes, Jr., inherited the company in 1924 following the death of his father. Under Hughes, Jr., the oilfield-product company became a massive enterprise that he used largely to fund his various avocations.

During World War II Hughes operated a gun plant and a strut-making facility for aircraft, in Dickinson, Texas.

Howard Hughes—who founded Hughes Aircraft Company, purchased over 78 percent of TransWorld Airlines' stock and held a substantial investment in RKO Pictures—remained the sole owner of Hughes Tool until 1972, when he put the company on the market. Hughes Tool became a publicly owned company, in a transaction reportedly valued at $150 million. Although successful, despite a general slump in the drilling industry from 1958 to 1972, Hughes Tool had remained undiversified, primarily because Howard Hughes wanted it that way. "Mr. Hughes, of course, felt he was personally diversified, so he never really considered diversifying the tool company," Raymond Holliday, a former Hughes chairman, told *Business Week* in October 1980. With public stockholders and a booming oil economy, especially after the Organization of Petroleum Exporting Countries (OPEC) oil embargo of the early 1970s, Hughes Tool made up for lost time, bringing on worldwide acquisitions and start-up projects.

Under the leadership of chairman James Lesch the firm purchased the Byron Jackson oilfield-equipment division of Borg-Warner in 1974, for $46 million. In 1978 Hughes bought Brown Oil Tools, another family-owned business, whose founder had underutilized his 377 lucrative patents. With its massive expansion and the favorable oil-industry climate, Hughes Tool surged. By 1981—a peak year in the industry—new business activities, which largely meant non-drill-bit products and services, accounted for 55 percent of the company's sales.

When the bottom fell out of the market in 1982, Hughes found itself a bloated, overextended, and debt-ridden concern. Under the guidance of President William Kistler, an engineer who came up through the core drill-bit division, the company retrenched to its roots, concentrating on bits and shying away from services. For example, the company shut down 30 foreign offices and streamlined 11 divisions into one. In 1983 Hughes hired outside consultants Bain & Company to trim fat, laying off 36 percent of its workforce. The company still had one weapon neither world markets nor competitors could take away: a patented O-ring rock-bit seal. In 1986 Hughes won a $227 million patent-infringement judgment from Smith International,

Inc., a California concern that had copied Hughes's drill seal too closely. In 1985 Hughes had been awarded $122 million from Dresser Industries, Inc. for patent violation. One rival that had innovated around Hughes's patent rather than copying it was Baker International.

Hughes Tool floundered through the mid-1980s. For the three years beginning in 1983, Hughes lost $200 million. Often cited as a potential takeover target, the company was faced with an offer it could not refuse when approached for a merger with Baker.

History of Baker International Corporation

Like Hughes Tool, Baker grew out of a single invention—the Baker Casing Shoe—a device to ensure the uninterrupted flow of oil through a well, developed in 1907 by Californian Reuben C. "Carl" Baker. Baker licensed his patents and incorporated the Baker Casing Shoe Company in 1913, mainly to protect his numerous patents on products that would soon become the industry standard. During World War I Baker was a member of the local draft board, although his company did not devote any of its production to goods to support the war effort. Baker lived off his royalties until the 1920s when he began manufacturing his own tools. In 1928, after successfully manufacturing tools in Huntington Park, California, for several years, Baker called the company Baker Oil Tools, Inc., a name it would carry for 40 years.

The Great Depression hit Baker hard, causing it to lay off numerous workers, but the late 1930s and 1940s were years of solid growth. During this period the company started offices in many states, including Texas, Wyoming, Illinois, Missouri, and Louisiana. During World War II Baker retooled to produce gun-recoil mechanisms. Following the war Baker prospered. In the ten years after 1948 it opened 50 new offices in 16 states. In 1956 Carl Baker retired at age 85, leaving the company in the hands of Theodore Sutter, an executive who had joined the company in the early 1920s. Carl Baker died shortly after his retirement. Under Sutter the company began to expand globally, and it went public in 1961.

When E.H. "Hubie" Clark, Jr., assumed control of Baker in 1965, the company developed into a global powerhouse. Clark, who had joined the company as a recent mechanical-engineering graduate from the California Institute of Technology in 1947, led Baker, now based in Orange, California, to new heights. Although Baker remained based in California, in 1965 the company's Houston operation was as large as the California operation. Clark acquired some 20 companies, the largest of which was Reed Tool Company, a drill-bit manufacturer purchased in 1975. Clark worked hard to predict trends in oil supply and demand. Baker operations were begun in Peru, Nigeria, Libya, Iran, and Australia, among other countries, and in 1976 the company changed its name to Baker International Corporation.

The company's reputation for quality and Clark's renown as a manager put Baker into the 1980s in solid shape. Even Baker could not avoid the downturn of petroleum-related business after 1981. Clark and Baker President James D. Woods sought to improve efficiency in the slow-growing industry. The even-

Key Dates:

1907: Reuben C. "Carl" Baker develops the Baker Casing Shoe, a device to ensure the uninterrupted flow of oil through a well.

1909: Invention of the first rotary drill bit leads to the creation of Sharp-Hughes Tool Company, led by Howard Hughes, Sr., and Walter Sharp.

1912: Sharp dies, and Hughes buys Sharp's share of the business.

1913: Baker organizes Baker Casing Shoe Company to hold and license his patents.

1915: Hughes renames his company Hughes Tool Company.

1924: Upon Hughes's death, ownership of Hughes Tool passes to Howard Hughes, Jr., who over the next several decades uses the firm's steady inflow of cash to fund his various avocations.

1928: Having expanded into the manufacturing of his own tools, Baker changes the name of his company to Baker Oil Tools, Inc.

1961: Baker Oil Tools goes public.

1972: Hughes Tool is taken public.

1975: Hughes acquires drill-bit maker Reed Tool Company.

1976: Baker Oil Tools changes its name to Baker International Corporation.

1987: Hughes Tool and Baker International merge to form Baker Hughes Incorporated.

1990: Eastman Christensen Company, maker of directional and horizontal drilling equipment, is acquired.

1991: Company spins off its pumping service unit, BJ Services, to the public.

1992: Eastman Christensen is merged with Hughes Tool Company to form a new division, Hughes Christensen Company; Teleco Oilfield Services Inc. is acquired; Teleco and four other Baker Hughes drilling systems companies are combined into a new division, Baker Hughes INTEQ.

1997: Petrolite is acquired, augmenting the firm's specialty chemical division, which is renamed Baker Petrolite; Drilex International Inc., provider of directional drilling services, is purchased and merged into Baker Hughes INTEQ.

1998: Baker Hughes acquires Western Atlas Inc., resulting in the creation of two new divisions: Western Geophysical (seismic data services) and Baker Atlas (down-hole services).

1999: Discovery of accounting irregularities at INTEQ division lead to a restatement of prior years' earnings.

2000: Baker Hughes contributes Western Geophysical to a joint venture with Schlumberger called Western GECO, 30 percent owned by Baker Hughes.

---

tual answer was to merge with its Houston-based competitor, Hughes Tool. Both companies had been losing money, and they hoped to eliminate overproduction by merging.

Merger of Baker and Hughes in 1987

"This industry is plagued with overcapacity," said one Baker official, as he announced on October 22, 1986, that the two oil-services firms would merge. Wall Street immediately applauded the move, a complex stock swap that favored Baker stockholders by giving them one share of the new company for each share they owned, compared with an eight-tenths-of-a-share deal for Hughes shareholders. Reflecting the greater general strength of Baker, its executives were to be given the top posts: Clark was to be the new chairman and Woods the new president and chief executive officer, while William A. Kistler, Hughes's chairman, would be named the merged company's vice-chairman. The new company's home would be Houston, where Hughes was based, and where Baker already had extensive operations. Baker's Orange, California, headquarters housed relatively few employees.

Wall Street showed its excitement over the merger by trading up the stock prices of both companies following the merger announcement, but the federal government frowned on the potential antitrust ramifications of combining two such powerful outfits. Indeed, the U.S. Justice Department announced on January 25, 1987, that it would attempt to block the merger, citing reduced competition in markets for some oil-exploration machinery. As top executives worked out a consent agreement with the Justice Department, Hughes executives attempted to

pull out of the merger. Baker responded in strong terms: it would sue Hughes for $1 billion if it failed to carry through with the agreement. After several delays Hughes capitulated. On April 3, 1987, Hughes agreed to the terms of the consent decree—which included the divestiture of the domestic operations of Reed Tool Company and some other units—and the merger was completed, creating an oil-services company second in size only to Schlumberger Limited.

Post-Merger Years Marked by Restructuring, Divestments, and Acquisitions

The consolidated company did not stop charging forward after the merger. Baker Hughes Incorporated outpaced its competition in the late 1980s. Part of its success was in realignment: Woods slashed 6,000 jobs, closed several plants, and took a $1 billion write-off for restructuring expenses. The result was $90 million less in annual costs and impressive sales. The company was already profitable by fiscal 1988. Woods added the chairmanship of Baker Hughes to his title in 1989.

Throughout the late 1980s and early 1990s, Baker Hughes did not hesitate to divest itself of unprofitable and/or noncore operations and to bolster the company through acquisition. In May 1989 its longtime money-losing mining equipment operation was sold to Tampella Ltd. of Finland for $155 million. In April 1990 Baker Hughes added the world's leading maker of directional and horizontal drilling equipment, Eastman Christensen Company, in a $550 million deal with Norton Co. The U.S. Department of Justice approved the deal, but only after Baker Hughes agreed to divest its own diamond drill business.

In 1992 Eastman Christensen was merged with Hughes Tool Company to form a new division called Hughes Christensen Company.

In 1991 Baker Hughes divested Baker Hughes Tubular Services and also spun off to the public its profitable but lawsuit-plagued BJ Services Inc. pumping service unit. Parker & Parsley Petroleum Co. had filed suit against Baker Hughes and Dresser Industries—the two of which had originally jointly owned the predecessor of BJ Services—alleging that BJ Services had shortchanged Parker & Parsley on materials used to stimulate wells. A 1990 jury verdict awarding Parker & Parsley $185 million was later overturned, but in 1993 the three parties settled out of court for $115 million, with Baker Hughes and Dresser each responsible for half, or $57.5 million.

In 1992 Baker Hughes spent $350 million to buy Teleco Oilfield Services Inc. from Sonat Inc. Teleco was a pioneer in services for both directional and horizontal drilling. Later that year, Teleco and four other Baker Hughes companies specializing in drilling systems—Milpark Drilling Fluids, Baker Sand Control, Develco, and EXLOG—were combined into a new Baker Hughes INTEQ division, which enabled the company to offer comprehensive solutions for all phases of drilling projects.

Divestments continued in 1994 with the sales of EnviroTech Pumpsystems to the Weir Group of Scotland for $210 million and of EnviroTech Measurements & Controls to Thermo Electron Corp. for $134 million. In October 1995 Max L. Lukens, who had been with the company since 1981, was named president and chief operating officer, with Woods remaining chairman and CEO.

After enjoying its best post-merger year to date in fiscal 1996 (with $3.03 billion in revenues and profits of $176.4 million), Baker Hughes was busy in 1997 making acquisitions, three of which closed in July. Drilex International Inc., a provider of directional drilling services, was acquired for $108.8 million and was subsequently folded into Baker Hughes INTEQ. The company paid $751.2 million for Petrolite Corporation, thus augmenting its specialty chemical division which was soon renamed Baker Petrolite and which became the leading provider to the oilfield chemical market. In the third July purchase, the Environmental Technology Division of German machinery maker Deutz AG was bought for $53 million; the division specialized in centrifuges and dryers and added to the existing centrifuge and filter product lines of the Baker Hughes Process Equipment Company. Then in October a $31.5 million deal to purchase Oil Dynamics, Inc. from Franklin Electric Co., Inc. was completed. Oil Dynamics was a manufacturer of electric submersible pumps used to lift crude oil and it was added to the company's Centrilift division. The year 1997 was also noteworthy for the retirement of Woods, who had not only made the Baker Hughes merger happen but had also focused and bolstered the company's product and service lines through more than 30 separate divestments and acquisitions. Woods was succeeded by Lukens.

The 1998 Western Atlas Merger and Succeeding Years

Consolidation in the oil-services industry continued in 1998, with the largest deal being the acquisition of Dresser Industries by Halliburton Company. Baker Hughes kept pace with its industry rivals, and maintained its number three position among oil-service firms (behind Halliburton and Schlumberger), by acquiring Western Atlas Inc. in August 1998 for $3.3 billion in stock and the assumption of $1.3 billion in debt. Western Atlas, which had been spun off from Litton Industries Inc. in 1994, was the industry's leading geoscience firm, specializing in seismic exploration, reservoir description, and field development services, as well as down-hole data services. The acquired operations were placed within two new Baker Hughes divisions: Western Geophysical for the seismic services and Baker Atlas for the down-hole services. Baker Hughes could now offer a full range of oilfield services, or ''life-of-the-field'' packages, from seismic surveys to drilling to production management. Following the merger, Lukens remained in charge of Baker Hughes as chairman and CEO.

As it was completing the Western Atlas merger, Baker Hughes began to feel the effects of another severe industry downturn. Demand for oilfield services declined sharply during the second half of 1998 as a result of the combined effects of the Asian economic crisis, tropical storms, and slumping oil prices. The company went into cost-cutting mode, slashing about 10,000 jobs from the payroll by the end of 1999 (about one-fourth of the total workforce), consolidating manufacturing facilities and field offices, and achieving nearly $1 billion in cost savings. Charges for merger-related costs and restructuring expenses totaled more than $800 million for 1998, resulting in a net loss for the year of nearly $300 million. Baker Hughes also sold off some real estate to raise money to reduce its enlarged debt load, upgraded its information technology systems to improve the tracking of inventory and equipment, and created a new financial performance system in which a manager's performance would be tied to profits in the person's area.

Despite the new initiatives and restructuring efforts, as well as higher oil prices in the later months of the year, Baker Hughes's financial performance continued to suffer during 1999. In November the company warned that its fourth-quarter earnings would trail analysts' estimates. One month later the company announced that it had uncovered accounting irregularities at its INTEQ division amounting to $31 million; the firm was subsequently forced to restate its earnings for the previous three years. In the wake of this debacle, INTEQ's president was replaced, and in February 2000 Lukens resigned under pressure. Joe B. Foster, a Baker Hughes outside director and head of Newfield Exploration Company, was named interim chairman and CEO. Wall Street was growing increasingly skeptical about the prospects for a turnaround, with Warburg Dillon Read analyst Byron Dunn telling the *Wall Street Journal* that the accounting snafu was ''a symptom of a broader dysfunctional corporate culture.''

To further reduce the still-burdensome debt load, Baker Hughes announced in February 2000 that it would sell its process systems unit, which had little relation to the core oil-services operations. Unable to sell it as a whole, the company divided the unit into three entities in 2001: BIRD Machine, EIMCO Process Equipment, and a newly formed joint venture, Petreco International, which was 49 percent owned by Baker Hughes. EIMCO was subsequently sold to Groupe Laperriere & Verreault, Inc. for about $50 million in November 2002.

In the meantime, Baker Hughes and Schlumberger reached an agreement in June 2000 to combine their seismic units, Western Geophysical and Geco-Prakla, respectively, into a new joint venture firm called Western GECO. Schlumberger paid Baker Hughes about $500 million to take a 70 percent stake in the venture, while Baker Hughes took the remaining 30 percent. Upon completion of the deal in November 2000, Baker Hughes used the proceeds to further reduce its debt.

In August 2000 Michael E. Wiley was hired to be the new chairman, president, and CEO of Baker Hughes. Wiley had been the president and COO of Atlantic Richfield Company from 1997 until May 2000, when that firm was acquired by BP Amoco. Baker Hughes continued to trim its operations under the new leader, announcing in October 2000 its intention to exit from the oil and gas exploration and production business. By early 2003 this exit had been completed through the sale of a 40 percent stake in a Nigerian oil field.

Although the company's financial performance improved in 2001 and 2002, concerns about the corporate culture at Baker Hughes once more came into the foreground. The Securities and Exchange Commission (SEC) charged that two high-ranking company officers, the CFO and the controller, authorized the payment of a $75,000 bribe to an Indonesian government official in March 1999. (The two officers both resigned later in 1999.) The bribe was made to induce the official to reduce the company's tax liability from $3.2 million to $270,000. This was a violation of the Foreign Corrupt Practices Act. The SEC further alleged that similar payoffs had been made in India and Brazil. In September 2001 Baker Hughes reached a settlement with the SEC regarding these charges, without the firm admitting or denying the charges and without a fine being levied. Then in March 2002 a former Baker Hughes employee filed a civil lawsuit claiming that he had been fired in October 2001 for refusing to pay a bribe to a Nigerian oil official in order to secure a large drilling contract. Both the SEC and the Justice Department soon launched investigations into the matter.

Principal Subsidiaries

Western Atlas Inc.; Baker Hughes GmbH (Austria); Baker Hughes (Deutschland) GmbH (Germany); Baker Hughes INTEQ GmbH (Germany); Baker Hughes Limited (U.K.); Baker Hughes Canada Company; Baker Hughes Espana, S.L. (Spain); Baker Hughes SRL (Venezuela).

Principal Divisions

Baker Atlas; Baker Oil Tools; Baker Petrolite Corporation; Centrilift; Hughes Christensen Company; INTEQ; BIRD Machine.

Principal Competitors

Schlumberger Limited; Halliburton Company; Smith International, Inc.; Weatherford International Ltd.; BJ Services Company; Precision Drilling Corporation; Petroleum Geo-Services ASA; John Wood Group PLC; GE Betz; Ondeo Nalco Energy Services, L.P.; Grant Prideco, Inc.; Sandvik Smith AB; Compagnie Générale de Géophysique, S.A.; Veritas DGC Inc.

Further Reading

Antosh, Nelson, ''Baker Says Accounting Woes Over,'' *Houston Chronicle,* February 18, 2001, Sec. 3, p. 1.

''Baker Hughes, Western Atlas Agree to Merge,'' *Oil and Gas Journal,* May 18, 1998, p. 30.

The Baker Story, Houston: Baker International Inc., 1979.

Byrne, Harlan S., ''Baker Hughes: It Shifts Operations to Exploit Overseas Drilling Activity,'' *Barron's,* April 6, 1992, pp. 47–48.

Goldberg, Laura, ''SEC, Justice Probe Baker Hughes,'' *Houston Chronicle,* March 30, 2002, Sec. 3, p. 1.

Grabarek, Brooke H., ''Baker Hughes: Oil and Gas, or Hot Air?,'' *Financial World,* October 25, 1994, pp. 18, 20.

Greer, Jim, ''Lawsuits Gush in Baker Hughes,'' *Houston Business Journal,* January 7, 2000, p. 1.

Ivey, Mark, ''Baker Hughes: It Pays to Be a Big Spender,'' *Business Week,* March 12, 1990, p. 81.

Miller, William H., ''A Merger That's Worked: Jim Woods Is Piloting Baker Hughes Inc. to Profit,'' *Industry Week,* April 15, 1991, pp. 21–23.

Norman, James R., ''Black Gold or Black Hole?,'' *Forbes,* November 26, 1990, p. 10.

——, ''Cloud over Baker,'' *Forbes,* May 11, 1992, p. 220.

——, ''Hot Potato?,'' *Forbes,* July 9, 1990, pp. 38–39.

Palmeri, Christopher, ''Drilling Home a Message,'' *Forbes,* August 9, 1999, p. 82.

''Schlumberger, Baker Hughes Combine Seismic Units,'' *Oil and Gas Journal,* June 12, 2000, p. 28.

Tejada, Carlos, ''Baker Hughes Has Accord to Acquire Western Atlas for $5.5 Billion in Stock,'' *Wall Street Journal,* May 11, 1998, p. A3.

——, ''Baker Hughes Inc. to Buy Petrolite in a Stock Deal,'' *Wall Street Journal,* February 27, 1997, p. C6.

——, ''Baker Hughes Names Foster Interim CEO,'' *Wall Street Journal,* February 1, 2000, p. A3.

——, ''Baker Hughes Says Accounting Glitches May Require $50 Million in Charges,'' *Wall Street Journal,* December 10, 1999, p. A4.

——, ''Oil-Services Firm Tries to Find Footing, Calm Holders,'' *Wall Street Journal,* October 14, 1999, p. B4.

Vogel, Todd, ''Baker Hughes Lops Off a Weak Limb,'' *Business Week,* May 29, 1989, p. 34.

Yip, Pamela, ''Baker Hughes to Cut Another 2,450 Workers,'' *Houston Chronicle,* February 2, 1999, Sec. 3, p. 1.

—Adam Lashinsky
—update: David E. Salamie

Brasil Telecom Participaçoes S.A.

SIA Sul
ASP, Lote D, Bloco B
71215-000 Brasília, D.F.
Brazil
Telephone: +55-61-415-1414
Fax: +55-61-415-1315
Web site: http://www.brasiltelecom.net.br

Public Company
Incorporated: 1998
Employees: 5,565
Sales: R 7.07 billion ($1.99 billion) (2002)
Stock Exchanges: Sao Paulo New York
Ticker Symbol: BRP
NAIC: 517212 Cellular and Other Wireless
  Telecommunications; 517110 Wired
  Telecommunications Carriers

Brasil Telecom Participaçoes S.A. is the holding company for Brasil Telecom S.A. Born from the breakup of Brazil's state-owned Telebras telephone monopoly, Brasil Telecom, or BrT, is one of the rising stars on the Latin American telecommunications scene, providing fixed-line services to Brazil's southern regions, including the states of Acre, Rondônia, Mato Grosso, Mato Grosso do Sul, Tocantins, Goiás, Santa Catarina, Paraná, and Rio Grande do Sul. The company also provides telecommunications services to Brazil's Federal District. In all, BrT's concession area encompasses more than 41 million people, or nearly 25 percent of the country's total population. The company has been rapidly adding new connections—inheriting Telebras's mostly dilapidated and highly inefficient network—and in 2003 already boasted more than 10.5 million subscriber lines. As this figure represented only 23 percent of its coverage area's total population, BrT can look forward to years of fixed-line growth. On top of its local and interregional telephone services (Brazil's national and international long-distance services are governed by Embratel), BrT has been pushing its Internet access and, especially, broadband services, and a launch into the mobile telecommunications market. Both of

these activities are expected to enable BrT to expand its telecommunications services nationwide. As part of that effort, BrT began making acquisitions, including the purchase of Globenet, which owns a fiber optic cable linking Brazil with the United States, a 20 percent stake in Internet access provider MetroRed, and the long-distance carrier Intelig, formerly owned by Sprint, France Telecom, and the National Grid of the United Kingdom. Listed on both the Sao Paulo and New York stock exchanges, BrT is controlled by Telecom Italia and the Brazilian investment company Banco Opportunity. Carla Cico, an Italian native, is the company's CEO.

Imperial Interest in the 19th Century

Brazil began installing its own electric telegraph network in 1851, and inaugurated its first public network in Rio de Janeiro the following year. The telegraph developed rapidly in the country, and by 1855 the network reached more than 20,000 kilometers. The first long-distance connection opened in 1856, connecting Rio de Janeiro with Porto Alegre, more than 1,000 kilometers to the south. In 1874, the country laid its first underwater cable, which connected cities along the country's northern coast.

Yet the telegraph faced new competition that decade—the telephone. Brazil played an offhand, although important, role in the telephone's development. Some years earlier, the country's Emperor Pedro II had traveled to the United States and met with Alexander Graham Bell at the Boston School for the Deaf. Pedro II had returned to the United States for the Centennial Exhibition of 1876, which Bell had set up as a small and overlooked exhibit for his invention, the telephone. Pedro II had come along just in time, as Bell's invention underwent scrutiny from the exhibition's judges, who took notice when the Brazilian emperor tried the telephone and famously cried out: "Dios! It works!"

Emperor Pedro II had a telephone line installed in his palace that same year, marking the start of telephone history in Brazil. Early development of the telephone in the country went quickly, with much of the growing installed network centered on the then-capital of Rio de Janeiro. Over the following decades, states and local authorities claimed the right to grant licenses for building telephone networks, a situation that led to the development of a highly fragmented telephone system in the country. Indeed, by 1940, Brazil counted more than 800 separate companies servicing the country's cities—while the poor rural areas remained unconnected.

By the 1960s, the number of companies operating in Brazil had swelled to more than 1,000. Among them was Telecomunicaçoes do Paraná, or Telepar, set up in 1963, which became the most direct predecessor of the later Brasil Telecom. Yet development of the country's network had stagnated over the previous decades. This was due in large part to the widespread policy among competing telecommunications companies to maintain unrealistically low subscriber rates. With high line connection fees and low revenues from rates, the generally small-scale companies lacked the funds for technological and other investments.

In the mid-1960s, Brazil's growing population remained vastly underserved by its telephone companies, with a density rate of just 1.6 per 100, nearly three times less than the world average. Nonetheless, the Brazilian market had moved in the direction toward more consolidated, large-scale companies, much of which had come under foreign control. Such was the case with Companhia Telefonica Brasileira, held by Canada-based Brazilian Traction Light and Power, which had gained control of nearly 70 percent of the country's telephone lines. Yet there remained little coordination among the various telephone systems, which also used a variety of incompatible technologies, and completing a long-distance call at the time could require as much as two to three days of waiting.

The Brazilian government had recognized the strategic importance of the telephone system and began making moves to take control of the sector. In 1962, the government passed a new Telecommunications Code that gave the government the monopoly control over the operation and regulation of the country's telephone system. The same legislation created a National Telecommunications Council, which had as its objective the drafting of a National Telecommunications Plan for consolidating and upgrading the country's telephone network, including converting operations to a single technology.

Another feature of the legislation called for the creation of more realistic rates, as well as a surtax on telephone calls. The tax, which stood at 20 percent for local calls and 30 percent for international calls, went into a National Telecommunications Fund (FNT) to be used for upgrading technology and subsidizing new telephone lines. Finally, the new code created the Brazilian Telecommunications Enterprise, or Embratel, which ultimately became responsible for long-distance and international telephone transmissions.

The military coup of 1964 disrupted the timing of these plans, and the formation of Embratel, owned by the government

in conjunction with a number of major corporate customers, was postponed until 1965. Financed by the FNT, Embratel took over domestic and international trunk operations, began working on connecting the underserved Amazon region in the country's north, and also started work on integrating the various technologies in operation around the country.

In 1967, the government created a new regulatory body, the Ministry of Communications, also known as Minicom, which began the process of rationalizing the country's telephone system. In 1968, Minicom took a big step toward streamlining the sector when it took over Companhia Telefonica Brasileira. A change in the country's constitution, which stipulated that only state-owned authorities were permitted to offer telecommunications services, aided in consolidating the fragmented sector.

The next step in reforming Brazil's telecommunications system came in 1972 with the creation of a new, state-controlled body, Telecomunicaçoes Brasileiras S.A., or Telebras. The new company, owned at 80 percent by the Brazilian government, took over Embratel and began acquiring most of the country's telecommunications companies. For this Telebras set up a network of operating subsidiaries, initially 37, then later reduced to just 27—one for each Brazilian state—as well as Embratel. By 1980, the number of private telecommunications companies had dropped to just 150, which operated only some 250,000 telephones among them.

Although Telebras gained majority control of most of these new, larger companies, management of many, if not most, remained under the scrutiny of the states themselves. As before, the system lacked coordination on a national level and ultimately led to inefficiencies and slow technological investment and development. Nonetheless, into the mid-1970s, the new system appeared to be working, as the number of telephone connections jumped to five million by the end of the decade.

This growth was due in part to the adoption of a unique financing scheme, in which potential subscribers were required to pay up front for the new line—in 1992, this figure was worth about $4,000, at the turn of the century some $2,500—in exchange for stock in Telebras. This scheme ultimately reduced the government's stake in Telebras to just 52 percent, yet reinforced the great disparity in telephone service, effectively blocking the country's large poor population from access to the public telephone network.

In the meantime, the network's growth had more or less come to a standstill after the first of a series of economic crises in the late 1970s. The addition of new subscriber lines slowed to a crawl through the 1980s and reached only ten million lines at the beginning of the decade. Meanwhile, the government began dipping into Telebras' coffers in order to fill mounting state deficits, cutting short new technological and infrastructure developments.

The situation only worsened in the late 1980s with the rise to power of the Sarney government, which replaced the last of Telebras' professional management with political appointees. Corruption became a rule as Brazil's telephone system deteriorated rapidly, and waiting lists for new lines stretched into years. In the meantime, Telebras' rates once again sank to

Key Dates:

1876: The first telephone line is installed in the palace of Emperor Pedro II.

1963: Telepar (predecessor to Brasil Telecom) is founded.

1965: Empratel, which takes over control of Brazil's national and international long-distance services, is created.

1967: The Ministry of Communications (Minicom) is created.

1972: Telebras is created and the takeover of regional telecom companies, including Telepar, occurs.

1995: The Brazilian government announces plans to privatize the telecommunications industry.

1997: The General Telecommunications Law is passed.

1998: Telebras breaks up; Telepar is reformed as Tele Centro Sul and purchased by Telecom Italia and Banco Opportunity.

2000: Tele Centro Sul changes its name to Brasil Telecom; CRT is acquired from Telefonica.

2001: The company announces an R 4 billion ($2 billion) investment program.

2002: Lokau.com, GlobeNet Communications, and iBest Company are acquired; the company purchases a mobile telephone license.

2003: The company acquires MetroRed and Intelig and begins national expansion.

unreasonably low levels; adjusted for inflation, the nation's phone rates dropped by some 80 percent during the decade.

The 1980s were not entirely without a bright spot for the country's telecommunications sector. The successful launch of the country's first telecommunications-capable satellite, BrasilSat-I in 1985, followed by BrasilSat-II the next year, enabled the extension of telecommunications services to the entire country.

Forming a Telecom Powerhouse in the New Century

The 1980s and 1990s marked the start of a wave of deregulation and privatization of many of the world's state-owned or controlled telecommunications systems, including much of Latin America. In the early 1990s, the new Brazilian government began plans to privatize Telebras as well, a move that required a change in the country's constitution. Yet political infighting doomed that effort; at the same time government intervention prevented the company from raising capital for a much needed modernization program.

Despite its difficulties, Telebras was able to introduce cellular telephone services to the country in the mid-1990s. By then, the company's revenues neared $15 billion, with more than 21 million customers sharing some 13 million phone lines. Yet there were another 15 million on waiting lists to receive fixed-line phone services, and another five million waiting for cellular phone services. In addition, half of the country's businesses had no phone service at all.

Reform of the country's telecommunications sector finally got underway in 1995, leading to the adoption of new legislation, the General Communications Law, in 1997. The law created a new regulation body, Anatel, an autonomous body reporting to Minicom and the Brazilian government. The law also paved the way for the breakup of Telebras.

That momentous event began in January 1998, when Telebras' mobile telephone operations were spun off into eight separate and independent companies. By May 1998, Telebras completed its breakup, creating 12 new holding companies— eight for the mobile telephone operations, one for Embratel, and three companies created as regional fixed-line operators providing local and interregional long-distance telephone services. Among this later group was Telepar, placed under the holding company Tele Centro Sul, which took over the eight fixed-line companies operating in the country's western, central, and southern regions. Telepar itself was renamed Brasil Telecom.

A partnership between Banco Opportunity and Telecom Italia paid the Brazilian government $1.7 billion to acquire Tele Centro Sul in 1998. Like its counterparts, Tele Centro Sul was given strict targets and a tight deadline for the upgrade and expansion of its fixed-line operations in its region. Completion of the government's requirement would then gain the company permission to expand its services beyond its core region. Tele Centro Sul began a massive investment program, boosting its number of fixed lines past 8,000 by the year 2000. At that time, the company changed its name to underscore its national ambitions, to Brasil Telecom S.A., while its holding company became known as Brasil Telecom Participaçoes. At the end of 2000, the company acquired CRT—previously held by Telefonica—which provided fixed-line services in Rio Grande do Sul.

Brasil Telecom announced a R 4.2 billion ($2 billion) investment effort in 2001, with the goal of meeting its targets and receiving permission to expand beyond its core regional base in 2002. Leading the charge was new CEO Carla Cico, an Italian native who had previously worked in the Chinese telecommunications market. Cico led a restructuring of the company, including slashing its payroll in half (although most of these employees were given new jobs in a call center subsidiary), and then cut a further 1,000 jobs the following year. The company also centralized its management at its Brasilia headquarters.

At the end of 2001, at which time the company was forced into a partial opening of its network to outside competitors, Brasil Telecom began targeting growth in the Internet sector, buying iBest Company and Lokau.com. In January 2002, the company began offering free e-mail accounts as well, and by the middle of the year had begun negotiations to acquire three more companies—MetroRed, Intelig, and Globenet. These purchases, completed by 2003 for the most part, gave the company operations beyond its core region, including in Sao Paulo, Rio de Janeiro, and Belo Horizonte.

Brasil Telecom met its government-imposed target in early 2003—ahead of its initial December 2003 predictions—with more than ten million installed lines. This enabled the company to begin planning its national expansion in earnest. As part of that drive, the company bid for and won a mobile telephone license for the country's Personal Communication System, paying R $191 million. The company then began plans to roll out its own mobile telephone service. In August 2003, Cico announced the company's intention to invest some $300 million in the initial launch; though awaiting Anatel approval, the anticipated roll-out meant more than one million new customers over the next year. Brazil's telecommunications sector finally appeared to have come of age—and Brasil Telecom was poised to establish itself as a national industry powerhouse.

Principal Subsidiaries

Brasil Telecom S.A.; BrT Serviços de Internet S.A.; Brasil Telecom Celular S.A.

Principal Competitors

TeleComunicacoes de Minas; Embratel Participacoes S.A; Tele Norte Leste Participacoes S.A.; Nextel Telecomunicacoes Ltda; Vesper; Nokia Do Brasil Tecnologia Ltda.; Bse S.A.; Tele Centro Oeste Celular Participacoes S.A.; Quadrata Comunicacoes Empresariais Ltda.; Sercom S.A.; Telerj Celular S.A.; Picolli Service Com E Prest De Servicos Ltda.

Further Reading

Baker, Mark, "Telebras: The Biggest Show on Earth," *Privatisation International*, May 1998, p. 4.

"Brasil Telecom Achieves Goals Earlier Than Expected," *Latin America Telecom*, January 2003, p. 3.

"Brasil Telecom: An Italian CEO Brings New Style to Brazil's Telecommunications Sector," *Institutional Investor*, September 2002, p. SS13.

"Brasil Telecom Gets Acquisitive," *LatinFinance*, October 2002, p. 6.

"Brasil Telecom to Spend $300 Mln on Mobile Launch," *Reuters*, August 6, 2003.

"Brasil Telecom to Take Over Other Companies," *South American Business Information*, August 13, 2002.

Epstein, Jack, "Unbundling Telebras," *Time*, August 10, 1998.

Padgett, Time, "Carla Cico: CEO and President of Brasil Telecom," *Time*, December 2, 2002, p. 54.

Romero, Simon, "Brasil Telecom Gains Advantage from the Problems of Others on Its Home Turf," *New York Times*, September 23, 2002, p. C5.

Sherwood, Sonja, "Brasil Telecom's Cultural Iconoclast: Career Path Less Traveled," *Chief Executive*, February 2002, p. 6.

—M.L. Cohen

Command Security Corporation

Route 55 Lexington Park
P.O. Box 340
Lagrangeville, New York 12540
U.S.A.
Telephone: (845) 454-3703
Fax: (845) 454-0075
Web site: http://www.commandsecurity.com

Public Company
Incorporated: 1980
Employees: 3,027
Sales: $94.31 million (2003)
Stock Exchanges: NASDAQ
Ticker Symbol: CMMD
NAIC: 561612 Security Guards and Patrol Services

Command Security Corporation provides a variety of security services in several states (New York, New Jersey, California, Illinois, Connecticut, Pennsylvania, and Florida). It also performs back-office operations for a number of other security companies across the United States. The company's main markets are New York, Los Angeles, Miami, and Chicago. The Guard Services division accounted for about 32 percent of revenues in fiscal 2003; Aviation Services accounted for nearly all of the remainder (Support Services accounted for less than 1 percent). Command's security guards are deployed at locations such as hospitals, offices, and industrial sites. The company has aggressively sought to make up for business lost due to federalization of pre-board screening through other airport security assignments.

Collegiate Beginnings

Command Security Corporation's origins can be traced to the early 1980s. It was incorporated under New York law on May 9, 1980. *Equities* reported it was started with only a $200 loan. Company Chairman William C. Vassell started the business while a student at Western Connecticut State College. Condominiums were his original market, followed later by banks and hospitals. Vassell became president, chairman, and CEO of Command Security after attaining a 100 percent equity interest in the company in 1983. He had previously owned half of the company.

Command acquired two Connecticut firms, Garvey Security and Shamrock Security, in 1987. Each had revenues of more than $1 million a year. In the late 1980s, the security industry was booming due to increased attention to loss prevention and more outsourcing of security functions. By the end of the decade, Command was billing about $15 million a year, and had expanded to south Florida.

Public in 1990

Command went public in 1990, when revenues were $14.8 million. A new, lucrative line of business was started when Command began providing computerized accounting services to other security companies.

Command's proprietary Comguard computer system went online in June 1990. Comguard kept track of scheduling, qualifications, and other variables in real time, as well as kept track of billing and payroll. Command's fee for these services was 4 to 6 percent of the client firm's revenues, reported *Equities*. This business also kept Command apprised of potential acquisition candidates.

Revenues were about $38 million in 1991, when Command Security was the 21st largest security company in the United States, accounting to the *Security Letter*. In April 1992, Command merged its New York City security operations with that of its back-office client, Madison Detective Bureau Inc. The Madison name, which dated back to 1932, was retained. Madison had revenues of $8 million a year at the time. Command acquired Madison in November 1993 for $2.2 million in canceled and assumed debt. Action Protective Systems, a New York area firm, was acquired from its French parent ECCO Securité in September 1992.

In 1993, Command accelerated its acquisition drive, acquiring seven security companies in a year and a half. By the end of this drive, Command had added offices in New Jersey, California, Illinois, and Massachusetts to its three key hubs in New York, Connecticut, and southern Florida.

National Kinney Systems was acquired from ISS International Service System, Inc. in October 1993. It had revenues of more than $20 million a year, and was active in Los Angeles, Chicago, and especially New York, where it had been in business since the late 1960s.

Big Business in the Mid-1990s

The bombing of the World Trade Center in 1993 brought new attention to the importance of security for public facilities. In addition, a recession was prompting some corporations to outsource their security operations. Command was taking in over $65 million a year by 1994. It had eight branches and employed 3,000 security guards.

The security business, a $6.5 billion industry in the United States, had 6,500 small companies competing in the mid-1990s. However, four national security companies (Pinkerton's, Inc. (later owned by Securitas AB), Burns International Security Services, Inc., The Wackenhut Corporation, and Wells Fargo Corporation) dominated the industry. Command was about the same size as three dozen other regional companies.

Command expanded its guard business by acquiring Miami's General Security Corp. in October 1994. United Security Group Inc., a New York company with annual revenues of $25 million, was acquired on February 24, 1995, for $4 million in cash and $1 million in assumed debt. Command bought Chicago-based National Security Ltd. the next month. National Security had revenues of about $2.6 million a year.

After United Security was acquired, John B. Goldsborough, formerly its president and CEO, took the top spots at Command Security, succeeding William Vassell, who remained chairman. Goldsborough resigned as president and CEO of Command in May 1995.

In 1996, Command Security employed 3,800 guards, some of them hired out to other security companies. Supervisors, dispatchers, and managers added another 150 employees. In addition to guard services, Command was also offering detective and related consulting services. Uniquely, Command soon began applying its back-office expertise to manage the off-duty security work of police officers employed by the Stamford, Connecticut police department.

Revenue (apart from service company revenue) for fiscal 1996 was $55 million. After three years of net losses, the company showed net income of $511,000. (Back-office services for other security companies were not included in Command's

profit and loss statements. These amounted to roughly $20 million.) By this time, Command had relocated its headquarters from New York City to Lagrangeville, New York, saving the company $100,000 a year. Command also sold off a Boston office during the year.

Reliance Security Group PLC acquired a 37.3 percent shareholding in Command for about $6 million in the fall of 2000. Command had revenues of $71 million a year at the time. Reliance obtained its shareholding by buying out a group of Command's dissident shareholders at a hefty premium. The dissidents had halted Command's rapid progress with a 1997 lawsuit.

Vassell was already aiming to build Command Security into a $1 billion company. It recently added Miami International to its roster of airport clients including LAX and JFK. According to *Equities*, Vassell at the same time was focusing the company on higher margin areas of the security business, such as protecting ATM service personnel (on behalf of NCR and Diebold) and providing security for international airlines. The ATM business was begun in 1998; Command signed up 290 independent affiliates to create national coverage. Command remained involved in traditional services such as access control, patrolling, and crowd control; this division accounted for about 60 percent of revenues. Aviation Services was the next largest division, with around a 40 percent share of revenues. Command also handled a number of different types of detective work, ranging from due diligence to surveillance and arson investigations.

Changes After 9/11

Security screening at the nation's airports was federalized following the September 11, 2001 terrorist attacks on the United States. Thus, Command lost all of its pre-board screening contracts in November 2002. However, the company was able to replace some of this business with other services, such as verifying documents and screening baggage. It also added three new airports to its client list—San Jose, Baltimore-Washington, and Portland.

Command had built up a significant business there through its Aviation Safeguards Inc. subsidiary, which had 1,500 employees nationwide. Aviation Safeguards accounted for about 35 percent of Command's $72 million in annual revenue before the federalization; half of Aviation Safeguards' revenue was from airport screening.

Command did experience an increased demand for security guards from owners of commercial buildings in the immediate aftermath of 9/11. Command Chairman William Vassell reported that customers were taking security more seriously. Revenues for fiscal 2003 rose to $94.3 million from the previous year's $84.2 million.

In October 2001, Aviation Safeguards took over screening at the Philadelphia airport from Argenbright Security Inc., which was facing federal charges over using unqualified personnel.

The war in Iraq, the SARS epidemic, and several airline bankruptcies cut into Command's business. (This trend had started even before 9/11, with Tower Air, Inc.'s bankruptcy in fiscal 2000. Two years earlier, GFM Bayview, a back-office

Key Dates:

1980: Command Security is incorporated in New York.
1983: William Vassell acquires 100 percent control of company.
1987: Two Connecticut security firms are acquired.
1990: Command goes public, offers back-office services to other companies.
1993: National Kinney Systems and Madison Detective Bureau are acquired.
1994: General Security acquisition brings Command to Miami.
2000: Reliance Security acquires 37 percent shareholding.
2002: Pre-board screening at U.S. airports is federalized.
2003: Reliance divests its holding in Command.

client to whom Command had extended a significant amount of credit, had folded.) Command achieved a net income of $2.4 million on record revenues of $83.9 million in fiscal 2002.

Reliance divested its holding in Command in 2003. Being part-owned by a foreign (British) company had begun to interfere with Command's U.S. government business; the screeners who had let the 9/11 hijackers through security checkpoints had been employed by three foreign-owned companies.

Some areas of airport security were not federalized, including cargo security. In addition, five airports retained private security in a pilot program. On the down side, a few of Command's airline clients filed for bankruptcy in 2002 and 2003.

After 9/11, organizations were more willing to pay a premium for experienced, well-trained security personnel in addition to advanced access control technologies. Airports and nuclear facilities were obviously targets for terrorists; religious institutions, especially synagogues, also provided a demand for more comprehensive security.

Principal Divisions

Aviation Services; Guard Services; Support Services.

Principal Competitors

Securicor PLC; Securitas AB; The Wackenhut Corporation.

Further Reading

Arroyo, Arnaldo, "Command Security Rides the New National Trend," *Equities,* July/August 2002, pp. 16–19.

Brooks, George, "Crime Can Pay," *Equities,* March/April 1998, pp. 17+.

——, "The Dream Continues," *Equities,* May/June 2001, p. 22.

——, "New Beginning for Command Security," *Equities,* November/December 2000, pp. 56+.

——, "Progress Report on Command Security," *Equities,* June 1997, pp. 24+.

Brooks, George, and Robert J. Flaherty, "Command Security Makes Crime Pay," *Equities,* December 1996, pp. 20+.

"CEO Interview: Command Security Corp. (CMMD)," *Wall Street Transcript,* February 14, 1994.

Flaherty, Robert J., and Arnaldo Arroyo, "Command Security Corporation," *Equities: Special Situations,* October 2000, pp. 2+.

Foss, Brad, "Airline Security Experts: Security Often Dictated by Profit Motives," *Associated Press Newswires,* September 12, 2001.

—— "Federal Takeover of Airport Screening Does Not Spell Disaster for Large Security Companies," *Associated Press Newswires,* November 20, 2001.

Gelbart, Marcia, "Atlanta-Based Security Company Will No Longer Cover Philadelphia Airport," *Philadelphia Inquirer,* October 5, 2001.

——, "Federal Air Security Legislation Means Changes for Private Aviation Firms," *Philadelphia Inquirer,* November 20, 2001.

Goo, Sara Kehaulani, "Airports Favor Private-Sector Screeners," *Washington Post,* May 30, 2003, p. E1.

Mastandrea, John, "Security Industry Booming As Crime-Awareness Grows," *Fairfield County Business Journal,* July 4, 1988, p. 11.

Nemes, Judith, "Owners Tighten Security with Technology; Install Turnstiles, TVs, Sensors," *Crain's New York Business,* January 14, 2002, p. 45.

Scaglione, Fred, "Follow Up: Command's Opportunity in Turmoil," *Equities,* January-June 2003, p. 38.

Stewart, James, "Reliance Takes £6.6M Write-Down," *Independent* (London), June 27, 2003, p. 21.

Vassell, William C., Edward A. Ramsdell, and David O. Tharp, "Bringing Contract Services On-Line," *Security Management,* December 1, 1993, p. 40.

—Frederick C. Ingram

AmBev

Companhia de Bebidas das Américas

Rua Renato Paes de Barros, 1017, 4th Floor
04530-001 Sao Paulo
Brazil
Telephone: +55-11-2122-1200
Fax: +55-11-3741-1856
Web site: http://www.ambev.com.br

Public Company
Incorporated: 2000
Employees: 18,136
Sales: R 7.33 billion ($2.51 billion) (2002)
Stock Exchanges: Sao Paulo New York
Ticker Symbol: AMBV
NAIC: 551112 Offices of Other Holding Companies;
    312111 Soft Drink Manufacturing; 312120 Breweries

AmBev, more formally known as Companhia de Bebidas das Américas, is the world's fifth largest brewer. Formed from the 2000 merger of Brazilian beer titans Companhia Cerveceria Brahma and Grupo Antarctica Paulista, AmBev controls nearly 70 percent of Brazil's beer market—one of the world's largest and most dynamic—through its three core brands: Skol, Brahma, and Antarctica. These brands represented the world's 3rd, 9th, and 19th of the global top-selling beers. The company is also a leading player in the country's soft drinks market, through its Guarana fruit-flavored soda and its Pepsi bottling franchise. Yet the rationale behind the AmBev merger was to create a regional and international beverages powerhouse, and as such AmBev has been pursuing expansion into other South American markets. In 2003, for example, the company gained a dominant position in the Argentinean beer market through its purchase of a stake in that country's Quilmes. AmBev also has targeted Venezuela, Uruguay, Paraguay, Peru, and the Central American region for its near-term growth. Nonetheless, international beer sales made up only 5 percent of the company's total sales, which topped R 7.3 billion ($2.5 billion) in 2002. Domestic beer sales remain the company's largest revenue generator, at 76 percent of total sales. Soft drinks provide another 15 percent of sales. AmBev's operations are based on a network of 33 beverage

plants in Brazil, as well as six additional international plants. Listed on the Sao Paulo and New York stock exchanges, AmBev is led by CEO Magim Rodriguez Junio and cochairmen Mercel Herrmann Telles and Victorio Carlos de Marchi.

Brazilian Beer Pioneers in the 19th Century

Companhia de Bebidas das Américas, or AmBev (for the American Beverage Company), combined longtime rivals Companhia Cerveceria Brahma and Grupo Antarctica Paulista into one of Brazil's largest corporations and the number five brewery and beverage company in the world. Both companies had long dominated the Brazilian beer market, and both had their roots in the late 19th century.

Beer arrived in Brazil at the beginning of the 19th century, when it was imported by the Portuguese royal family into the country. For most of the first half of the century, beer remained reserved only for the privileged few who could afford to pay for the imported beverage. Although rudimentary efforts to brew beers in Brazil already had produced a native specialty, Cerveja Barbante (named after the twine used to keep the cork from popping out of the bottle), the first native brewery was constructed only in 1853 in Petropolis, in Rio De Janeiro, and began producing Bohemia branded beer. The first native Brazilian beer brands appeared soon after.

The 1880s proved a turning point for Brazilian beer production. In 1885, a new business, Companhia Antarctica Paulista, was established by a group of friends including Antonio Zerrener and Adam Ditrik in the Agua Branca district of Sao Paulo. Although that company initially supplied ice and prepared foods, it soon switched over to brewing beer. By 1890, Antarctica had grown to more than 200 employees and was producing more than 40,000 hectoliters per year. The company officially incorporated the following year as Sociedade Anônima da Antarctica in 1891. Antarctica later grew into one of the country's largest brewers and leading brands.

By then, Brazil had seen the start of another major brewer, when Joseph Villiger, an immigrant from Switzerland, decided to begin brewing the European-style beer he missed from home. In 1888, Villiger set up Villiger & Cie and began producing his

74

own Brahma branded beer. Named after the Hindu god, Brahma beer grew from an initial output of 12,000 liters per day to become Brazil's "other" leading brand.

Both the Antarctica and Brahma breweries changed hands in the 1890s. Two of Antarctica's founding partners formed a new partnership, Zerrener, Bulow & Cia, to take a majority share of the company in 1893. A year later, Georg Maschke & Cie bought the Brahma brewery, changing the company's name to Georg Maschke & Cia Cervejaria Brahma. Villiger had not abandoned beer production, however, and in 1899 bought up Cervejaria Bavaria, launching his own brand, Franzkiskaner-Brau.

Five years later, Villiger sold that brewery as well, to fast-growing Antarctica. Brahma, too, had been expanding steadily, acquiring Preiss Hausler & Cie and its production of Tetuonia branded beer. With its beer production now topping six million liters, the Brahma brewery went public that year, officially changing its name from Villiger & Cie to Manufatura de Cerveja Brahma Villiger & Companhia.

Rivals in the 20th Century

For the most part, Antarctica and Brahma had grown strongly but within their separate regions. In the early 20th century, however, the two companies began to expand their distribution and production into other Brazilian states and regions. Both companies also began expanding their brands portfolios, adding a variety of beer types, including the popular "Chopp" (the Brazilian term for draft) beers. At the same time, the company began adding to its production capacity. Antarctica launched its second production unit in Ribeirao, in the state of Sao Paulo, in 1911.

Brahma rolled out its Malzbier in 1914, then turned its attention to external growth. In 1921, the company acquired the sales and distribution license for the Germania brand, later known as Guanabara, which had been one of the earliest of the Brazilian beer brands. In 1934, the company had a new hit on its hands with the introduction of its bottled draft beer, Brahma Chopp. That beer quickly became a Brazilian bestseller, lifting the company to the top of the country's brewing industry.

Antarctica, too, boasted strong brand growth in the first half of the century, as it diversified beyond beer production. In 1921, the company introduced a soft drink based on the Guarana berry—which contained a natural stimulant said to be three times stronger than that of coffee. That drink became a national favorite, rivaled only by the entry of Coca-Cola into the Brazilian market. Brahma, not to be outdone, introduced its own guarana-based soft drink in 1927.

By the 1950s, Brahma and Antarctica had emerged as the chief rivals for the Brazilian beer and soft drinks markets. Both companies had expanded strongly, with Brahma's production base reaching six breweries and a malting plant by the early 1950s. In 1954, Antarctica established its own malting plant in Sao Paulo. Two years later the company formed a beverage marketing and distribution subsidiary, Dubar S.A.

Brahma entered enemy territory in 1960 when it acquired Sao Paulo-based Companhia Paulista de Cerveja Vienense. Antarctica responded the following year by purchasing control of the Bohemian brewery, adding that pioneering beer brand to its stable of brands.

The 1970s and 1980s were a period of further consolidation of the Brazilian beer industry, led by Antarctica and Brahma. The latter expanded its coverage to Brazil's north and northeast when it acquired Astra SA in 1971. That acquisition not only gave the company additional production facilities in the region, but also access to a regional distribution network. In 1980, Brahma made a still more significant acquisition when it acquired Cervejarias Reunidas Skol Caracu S.A., giving it control not only of the 100-year-old Caracu brand, but also the fast-growing Skol brand (which, on an international level, grew to become the world's number three-selling beer by the dawn of the next century). The addition of the Skol brand enabled Brahma to join the world's top ten beer producers by the middle of the decade. By the beginning of the next decade, it had climbed into the number six position.

Antarctica, too, had been growing through acquisitions which expanded its own national coverage; these included Cervejaria Perola and Companhia Itacolomy in 1973 and Cervejaria Serramalte and Companhia Alterosa de Cervejas in 1980. At the same time, Antarctica had been expanding its domestic production park, building plants in Goiânia, Montenegro, Rio de Janeiro, and Viana, in 1973, then in Rio Grande do Sul in 1975 and in Teresina in 1976. The company also began franchising soft drink brands, and opened a new production plant for that operation in Rio de Janeiro in 1978. The following year, Antarctica ventured into the international market, beginning exports to the United States, Europe, and Asia.

International Brewing Powerhouse in the New Century

Both Brahma and Antarctica continued opening new production plants through the 1980s and into the 1990s. In 1990, however, Brahma underwent a sea of change when it found itself with a new majority shareholder, Banco Garantia. Under its new owners, Brahma received a new CEO, Marcel Telles, who led the company on a drastic restructuring. Among other features of that effort, Telles introduced U.S.-styled incentive programs, including stock options to boost production. Telles also slashed the company's payroll in half and introduced new production and distribution technology. Telles' leadership paid off, and by the

Key Dates:

1885: Companhia Antarctica Paulista is established by a group of friends including Antonio Zerrener and Adam Ditrik in the Agua Branca district of Sao Paulo.

1888: Joseph Villiger, a Swiss native, sets up Villiger & Cie and begins brewing European-style beer under the Brahma brand.

1904: Villiger & Cie goes public, changing its name to Cerveja Brahma Villiger & Companhia.

1934: Brahma releases bottled Brahma Chopp, which quickly becomes one of Brazil's best-selling beers.

1960: Brahma acquires Sao Paulo-based Companhia Paulista de Cerveja Vienense.

1961: Antarctica acquires Brazil's oldest brewery and beer brand, Cervejaria Bohemia.

1971: Brahma acquires Astra, extending its reach to north of Brazil.

1972: Antarctica acquires Cervejaria Polar and Cervejaria de Manaus.

1979: Antarctica begins beer exports to the United States, Europe, and Asia.

1980: Brahma acquires Cervejarias Reunidas Skol Caracu S.A.

1990: Brahma is acquired by Banco Garantia; new management leads the company on profit-boosting restructuring as Brahma becomes the world's number six beer producer.

1992: Brahma begins exports of Brahma Chopp to Argentina.

1994: Antarctica acquires Venezuela's Cervecera Nacional.

1996: Brahma opens a new production plant in Rio de Janeiro with production capacity of 12 million hectoliters.

1999: Brahma and Antarctica agree to merge to form a dominant Brazilian beverage group.

2000: AmBev merger is approved as the company becomes the world's fifth largest brewer; the company joins with France's Danone to acquire 57 percent of the Salus brewing group, based in Uruguay and that country's second largest brewer.

2001: The company acquires Cerveceria y Malteria Paysandu, in Uruguay, gaining 45 percent of that market; Cerveceria Internacional in Paraguay is acquired.

2003: The company acquires Quilmes of Argentina, gaining a 70 percent share of the Argentina market; the company begins construction on its first brewery in Peru.

end of the 1990s, Brahma's per-employee production had been multiplied by five, while earnings had grown nearly tenfold.

Brahma also had begun an aggressive international expansion, targeting its neighboring South American markets ahead of the Mercosur agreement, which lifted trade barriers in 1995. The large Argentina market became a primary target, and the company went head to head in competition with Argentinean beer leader Quilmes, slashing prices on its popular Brahma Chopp in order to undersell Quilmes' own brands. In October 1992, Brahma began construction on a new $40 million plant to cement its growing sales in Argentina.

Antarctica meantime turned to the Venezuelan market, buying up that country's Cervecera Nacional in 1994. By then, U.S. and other foreign beer producers had begun attempting to break into the South American beer markets, and especially into Brazil, which by then was among the world's top five beer producers. In 1995, Brahma formed an agreement with the United States' Miller Brewing Company to distribute that company's Miller Genuine Draft in Brazil. The following year, Antarctica found a U.S. partner as well, forming Budweiser Brasil with Anheuser-Busch. In that year, Skol began its own partnership, with Denmark's Carlsberg.

Yet these brands presented little competition to Brahma, Antarctica, and Skol, which together dominated nearly 70 percent of the Brazilian market. Brahma had further emphasized its clout in 1996 when it opened a new plant in Rio de Janeiro. With a production capacity of 12 million hectoliters per year, the plant was then the largest and most modern on the continent.

By the end of the 1990s, Brahma and Antarctica continued to duke it out for Brazil's top spot. Meanwhile, in the rest of the

world, the beverages industry was undergoing a rapid consolidation, and new, global powerhouses had begun to emerge. At the end of the 1990s, Antarctica became the target of interest for partner Anheuser-Busch, which proposed a takeover of the Brazilian company. Antarctica rejected the offer, however.

Instead, Brahma Chairman Jorge Paul Lemann approached Antarctica with the proposition of creating a Brazilian megabrewer, one capable of competing beyond Brazil on the broader international market. This time Antarctica gave in, and at the end of 1999 the two parties announced the creation of Companhia de Bebidas das Américas, or, less formally, AmBev.

AmBev immediately claimed the number five spot among the world's beverage makers—and the number four spot among the world's top breweries. The combined entity—forced to sell off its Bavaria brewery holdings to Molson for $98 million in order to satisfy monopolies commission requirements—now controlled 70 percent of Brazil's beer market, and began plans to expand throughout South America.

The new AmBev was listed on the Sao Paulo and New York stock exchanges in September 2000 and immediately hit the acquisition trail, joining with France's Danone to acquire 57 percent of the Salus brewing group, based in Uruguay and that country's second largest brewer. That acquisition gave AmBev control of some 25 percent of the country's beer market. Uruguay remained an AmBev target in 2001, when it bought nearly 100 percent control of Cervecería y Malteria Paysandú. That company added such brands as Norteña and Prinz, boosting AmBev's share of the market to 45 percent, as well as malting facilities and mineral water bottling operations.

From Uruguay, AmBev turned to Paraguay, paying $12 million to acquire Cerveceria Internacional. The company, which through Brahma had been involved in distribution partnerships with PepsiCo since the early 1980s, strengthened that relationship, as Pepsi took over international distribution of AmBev's Guarana soft drinks, introducing them to Europe— starting in Lisbon—in that year. In exchange, AmBev acquired the Brazilian production and distribution license to PepsiCo's Gatorade, and then, the following year, Mountain Dew and Pepsi Twist as well.

AmBev meanwhile continued its assault on the Argentinean market, once again slashing prices to undercut its main Quilmes rival there. By May 2002, however, AmBev had succeeded in wearing Quilmes down, as the two sides agreed to integrate aspects of their operations in Argentina. By the beginning of 2003, however, that agreement turned into a full-scale takeover, as Quilmes merged into AmBev in a deal worth some $600 million.

The newly enlarged AmBev now added Quilmes' control of 70 percent of Argentina's beer market, together with 80 percent of Paraguay and 55 percent of Uruguay. Yet AmBev had no intention of slowing down, announcing that its next targets were to be Peru and Central America. By May 2003, the company had begun to make good on its word, announcing its intention to build a $38 million brewery in Peru in order to go head to head with that country's dominant player, Bavaria, of Colombia. Yet few observers expected AmBev's future ambitions to remain with Latin America as it continued to assert itself as one of the global beverage industry's heavyweights in the new century.

Principal Subsidiaries

ANEP – Antarctica Empreendimentos e Participaçoes Ltda.; Indústria de Bebidas Antarctica do Sudeste S.A.; CRBS S.A.; Cervejaria Astra S.A. (96.7%); Indústria de Bebidas Antarctica Polar S.A. (96.9%); Jalua Spain S.A.; Monthiers S.A.; C.A. Cervecera Nacional S.A. (Venezuela; 50.2%).

Principal Competitors

Altria Group Inc.; Philip Morris USA; Anheuser-Busch Companies Inc.; Madhvani Group; Groupe Danone; Kirin Brewery Company Ltd.; Asahi Breweries Ltd.; Interbrew SA/NV; Carlsberg A/S; Orkla ASA; Allied Domecq PLC; Dr. August Oetker KG; Fomento Economico Mexicano S.A. de CV; Sapporo Breweries Ltd.

Further Reading

"AmBev Building on Combined Strengths," *Institutional Investor,* July 2001, p. 1.
"Andean Venture," *Latin Trade,* May 2003, p. 16.
"Brazil, Argentine Brewers Join Forces," *United Press International,* January 14, 2003.
Downe, Andrew, "Expansion on Tap," *Latin Trade,* April 2001, p. 28.
Kirkman, Alexandra, "Thirsty," *Forbes,* October 1, 2001, p. 74.

—M.L. Cohen

Creative Technology Ltd.

31 International Business Park
Creative Resource 609921
Singapore
Telephone: (+65) 6895-4000
Fax: (+65) 6895-4999
Web site: http://www.creative.com

Public Company
Incorporated: 1981
Sales: $805.9 million (2002)
Stock Exchanges: Singapore
Ticker Symbol: CREAF
NAIC: 334119 Other Computer Peripheral Equipment
 Manufacturing

Creative Technology Ltd. is a living legend in the global computer industry. The creator of the famed Soundblaster series of sound cards—one of the pioneer products of the multimedia revolution—Creative has maintained its dominance of that market segment with the success of the Audigy series of sound cards, launched in 2001. Yet Creative has expanded its focus beyond the PC world to embrace what it calls the Lifestyle Digital Entertainment market (LDE), launching a range of products including the Nomad line of MP3 players; computer speaker systems, under its own brand name as well as under higher-end subsidiary brand Cambridge Soundworks; digital cameras; and, in 2003, the Prodikeys, which combines a computer keyboard with a 37-key music keyboard. These efforts have helped reduce the company's reliance on its core sound card business (the company is also the leading supplier of OEM sound chips and cards to the computer industry), which nonetheless generate 44 percent of total sales, which slipped to $805 million in 2002 (from $1.2 billion the year before). Nearly half of the company's sales are generated in the United States and elsewhere in the Americas; Europe represents 32 percent of sales, with Asia making up the remainder. The company also produces Chinese-language and bilingual software for the Singapore market. Other subsidiaries include E-mu Systems, a leading maker of sound synthesis products. In late 2002, Creative Technology, which had pioneered the 3D graphics market in the mid-1990s, acquired U.S.-based 3Dlabs and launched

its first new graphics card, the Wildcat VP, under the 3Dlabs name. Cofounder Sim Wong Hoo remains the company's chairman and CEO.

Blasting to Success in the 1980s

Creative Technology was founded in 1981 with an investment of $6,000 between childhood friends Sim Wong Hoo and Ng Kai Wa. Both Sim and Ng, who had formed a 30-person harmonica orchestra in college, had backgrounds in engineering. Following graduation, Sim held a number of jobs, including a stint on an offshore oil platform, and along the way taught himself how to program computers. An early project consisted of attaching speakers to a microcomputer and writing software that enabled the computer to produce sound.

Creative Technology started out in a small store in a shopping mall in Singapore, at first selling computers and providing computer training services, particularly for the Apple II computer system. Creative decided to enter the computer business itself, and began designing its own computer based on the Apple II design. In 1984, Creative Technology released its first computer, the Cubic 99, which, based on a dual processor system, was compatible with both the Apple and CP/M operating systems—that computer, which featured its own sound chip that enabled voice synthesis and playback, became known as the "Talking Computer."

Sim and Ng were joined by Chay Kwong Soon in 1986. By then, Creative had invested some $500,000 into the development of a new, IBM-PC compatible computer, dubbed the Cubic CT. Specifically developed for the Singapore market, that computer featured a Chinese-language operating system capable of translating documents from and to English and Chinese. The Cubic CT also provided color graphics—a rarity at the time—and, especially, a board designed by Creative that enabled true audio reproduction, a first in the computer industry. Yet the Cubic CT proved complicated and not entirely reliable, and nearly forced the company to fold. As Sim later acknowledged: "I had hoped that a multilingual society like Singapore would need a multilingual computer. I was wrong. Also, I realized by looking only at Singapore, we were just like a frog looking at the sky from the bottom of the well."

Despite the failure of the computer system, Creative Technology continued to develop its sound card, shifting its focus from language reproduction to music. The resulting sound card was called the Creative Music System. The company also recognized that the U.S. market, which already dominated the world computer market in terms of sales, was its likeliest route to success. In 1988, Sim moved to California, establishing a subsidiary, Creative Labs, and vowing not to return to Singapore until the company was successful. As Ng revealed to *Businessweek,* "He told everybody that he would not come back unless he made $1 million selling 20,000 of our music soundcards. Everybody thought that he was crazy."

Yet Sim recognized the potential of the small, but growing, market for computer games. In 1988 Creative brought out a new version of its sound card, called the Game Blaster. Sim signed a number of game developers to create games making use of the sound card's features. The Game Blaster, which provided stereo sound to PC-compatible computers, was an instant success. By the end of 1989, Sim had more than met his goal, as the company's sales neared $5.5 million.

By then, however, Creative had created computer history. In November 1989 the company launched its newest sound card, the Soundblaster. That board, which provided 11-voice FM synthesis, recording capability, and a MIDI-compatible joystick port, revolutionized the PC market, almost singlehandedly launching the multimedia era. The success of the Soundblaster was aided by the release of Intel's 386 processor and the graphics-based Microsoft Windows 3.0 operating system. By the end of 1990, the Soundblaster was the number one-selling computer add-on product. The following year, the company's position in the PC industry was consecrated when the new-generation Soundblaster Pro sound card was adopted as the industry's multimedia standard. From then on, all games and sound cards were required to be "Soundblaster-compatible."

Creative had continued to develop other products, including PJS, a Chinese operating system, accompanied by Views, a word processing and desktop publishing application supported by a base of 70,000 Chinese characters, both released in 1989. The success of the Soundblaster series, however, led the company to expand its multimedia product line. At the time, computers were generally sold as bare bones systems—users seeking sound and other multimedia support were required to install add-on devices. Creative took the initiative, launching the first in a line of Multimedia Upgrade Kits, which added sound cards, CD-ROM drives, and multimedia software to PCs.

Creative quickly found itself confronted by a number of competitors—and even playing catch-up, as others released the first 16-bit sound cards at the end of 1991. Creative launched its own 16-bit card, the Soundblaster 16, which also emulated full-duplex (simultaneous recording and playback) in 1992. The strength of the Soundblaster name enabled it to retain its dominance of the sound card market. Into the mid-1990s, as more and more games—and software in general—were released on CD-ROM, sales of the company's upgrade kits swelled.

Searching for a Successor in the 1990s

Creative went public in 1992, becoming the first company from Singapore to list on the NASDAQ exchange. The listing enabled the company to acquire the technology it needed to continue to enhance its core sound card line. In 1992, Creative teamed with E-mu Systems, which had been developing a new generation of wavetable synthesis technology—enabling the truer reproduction of instrument sounds as well as the creation of unique sounds. The partnership resulted in the release of the Wave Blaster add-on board for the Sound Blaster16 series.

Creative acquired E-mu Systems itself in March 1993, paying nearly $54 million. The growth of Sound Blaster sales worldwide prompted Creative to form Creative Pacific Pty in Australia in a joint venture with that country's Compumart. The company launched another joint venture for the Japanese market that year, Creative Media KK, in partnership with I-O Data Device. In Europe, meanwhile, Creative acquired computer products distributor Westpoint Creative, which was renamed Creative Labs (UK) Ltd. The following year, the company opened manufacturing facilities in Dublin, Ireland, through subsidiary Creative Labs (Ireland).

Creative's success was remarkable. By 1994, the company's revenues had topped $650 million. In that year, Creative listed its stock on the Singapore stock exchange as well. A year later, the company's sales had soared past $1.2 billion. Yet Sim and Ng had recognized their increasing vulnerability as a one-product company. The rise of multimedia had brought a swarm of often lower-priced competitors. At the same time, PC manufacturers were moving to adopt multimedia features, including CD-ROM drives and sound chips, as standard equipment on new PCs. Creative was able to impose itself as the market leader in the supply of OEM sound chips and cards, yet these products sold for far lower than its premium-priced retail line.

Creative's search for a successor for its sound card success led it in a variety of directions. The company began manufacturing its own CD-ROM drives. When it could not keep up with the rapid developments in drive technology, however, it was forced to abandon the effort, dumping its inventory and taking a loss of more than $30 million in 1995. At the same time, its share price had slumped by some 75 percent.

Other diversification efforts proved equally fruitless. In 1993, the company had acquired ShareVision Technology Inc., releasing a line of desktop videoconferencing products in 1994. That year, the company purchased modem maker Digicom Systems Inc., and released the Phone Blaster line in 1995. Yet Creative was unable to impose itself in either market.

Creative saw more success with its entry into the video card market, launching what it claimed was the first 3D-capable graphics card for video games, the 3D Blaster in 1995. The following year, the company added a second line of add-on video accelerators, the Graphics Blaster. Yet the company was unable to replicate its sound card success, and its share of the graphics market, in the face of rivals such as 3dfx, Matrox, ATI, and Nvidia, remained rather low. Nonetheless, the company ranked as a key player until the end of the 1990s, and the graphics card came to represent more than 20 percent of its sales. Creative's losses and its difficulties finding a new direction led to disagreements among its cofounders, and in 1995, Ng and Chay both left the company, leaving Sim alone at the helm.

Lifestyle Digital Entertainment Company in the 2000s

Yet Creative had misjudged the strength of its brand name in its core sound card market, as its fears of losing market share proved unfounded. Indeed the Sound Blaster line continued to dominate the audio market through the end of the decade, particularly with the huge success of the Sound Blaster AWE 64

line, released in 1996. That success was followed by the even more successful Sound Blaster Live line in 1998. By then, the company had extended its Upgrade Kit line to include DVD-ROMs, sound and graphics cards capable of enabling DVD playback through the computer.

The continued success of the Sound Blaster line led the company to refocus itself as a sound company—despite a foray into the Internet and e-commerce market in the late 1990s and early 2000s, which met with limited success. Instead, Creative began developing its own line of speaker systems to match its sound cards, a move that was enhanced in 1997 when it acquired noted speaker manufacturer Cambridge Soundworks.

Creative also was preparing a leap into another audio market with high potential—that of MP3 players. As part of that effort, the company acquired Opti Systems Inc. in 1997 and Silicon Engineering in 1998. Then in 1999, the company debuted its first portable MP3 player, the Nomad. The company also released its own line of popular "webcams," which led it to develop a line of digital cameras in the early 2000s.

The slump in the Internet and high technology led Creative to shut down most of its Internet ventures and reorganize its operations again. The company refocused on extending its core product line—which now included its newest generation of sound cards, the Audigy line launched in 2001—into what it called the "Lifestyle Digital Entertainment" (LDE) market. As personal computers were increasingly moving out of the home office and becoming the heart of home entertainment systems, Creative's strategy called for it to leverage its world-renowned brand name beyond the PC market, taking the company into head-to-head competition with the world's giant home entertainment appliance manufacturers.

By 2003, Creative had prepared a line of some 20 LDE products, including speaker systems, cameras, MP3 players, and sound cards. The company also had acquired graphics card maker 3Dlabs in 2002, reentering the graphics card market—by then dominated by ATI and Nvidia—with the launch of the Wildcat VP. Despite a slump in sales that year, from $1.2 billion in 2001 to just $805 million in 2002, Creative Technology and leader Sim Wong Hoo remained one of the rare survivors among computer industry pioneers.

Principal Subsidiaries

Broadxent, Inc. (U.S.A.); Cambridge Soundworks (U.S.A.); Creative Advanced Technology Center (U.S.A.); Creative Future Computer Co., Ltd. (China); Creative Labs (Portugal); Creative Labs A/S (Denmark); Creative Labs GmbH (Germany); Creative Labs (HK) Limited (Hong Kong); Creative Labs, Inc. (Canada); Creative Labs, Inc. (U.S.A.); Creative Labs (Ireland) Ltd.; Creative Labs NV (Belgium); Creative Labs Pty Ltd. (Australia); Creative Labs (Pty) Ltd. (South Africa); Creative Labs SA (France); Creative Labs Sdn Bhd (Malaysia); Creative Labs SL (Spain); Creative Labs Srl (Italy); Creative Labs Taiwan Co., Ltd; Creative Media KK (Japan); Creative Technologies Scandinavia AB (Sweden); Cubic Electronics Sdn Bhd (Malaysia); Data Stream KK (Japan); E-mu Systems, Inc. (U.S.A.); hifi.com (U.S.A.).

Principal Competitors

Logitech SA; ATI Technologies, Inc.; Guillemot Corporation; Elsa AG; Matrox Graphics; Trust SA.

Further Reading

"Creative's Genius," *AsiaWeek,* October 2, 2000.

Gain, Bruce, "Creative Technology to Use 3Dlabs Buyout to Re-enter Graphics IC Market," *EBN,* March 18, 2002, p. 24.

Hamm, Steve, "Singapore's No. 1 Slinger," *PC Week,* November 4, 1996, p. A6.

Pinaroc, Joel D., "Creative Does Home Entertainment," *Philippine Daily Inquirer,* May 5, 2003.

"The Sweet Sound of Success for Creative Technology," *BusinessWeek,* September 8, 1997.

—M.L. Cohen

CREMONINI

Cremonini S.p.A.

Via Modena, 53
41014 Castelvetro, Modena
Italy
Telephone: (+39) 059-754611
Fax: (+39) 059-754699
Web site: http://www.cremonini.com

Public Company
Incorporated: 1966 as Inalca S.p.A.
Employees: 4,850
Sales: EUR 1.59 billion ($1.6 billion) (2002)
Stock Exchanges: Milan
Ticker Symbol: CRM
NAIC: 311611 Animal (Except Poultry) Slaughtering;
    424470 Meat and Meat Product Merchant
    Wholesalers; 722110 Full-Service Restaurants

Cremonini S.p.A. is Italy's largest meat products group, with vertically integrated operations spanning slaughtering, processing, packaging, and distribution, including in the catering and restaurant sectors. Cremonini is also one of the leading European meat processing specialists. The company's Production division, which accounted for 45 percent of the company's nearly EUR 1.6 billion in sales in 2002, includes its Inalca beef slaughtering and processing operations—the company's historic core, which also operates the largest slaughtering facility in Europe—and Montana Alimentaria S.p.A., which embraces the group's cured meat and snacks operations. Inalca's brands include Montana and Montana Fresco and Hamby, while Montana Alimentaria includes the Montana, Corte Buona, Hot One, Spanino, and Harry's Bar brands. At 42 percent of sales in 2002, the Distribution division operates primarily through Marr S.p.A., which is active in both the catering and door-to-door markets, and includes frozen foods and ice cream specialist Quinta Sagione. Cremonini, which had been one of the first groups to introduce fast-food dining to Italy in the early 1980s, remains present in the restaurant sector, which accounted for 12 percent of its sales in 2002. The company's restaurant operations include Agape, which operates a variety of restaurants and food services in Italy's train stations and other public facilities; Chef Express, which provides on-board dining for trains and ferries in Italy and elsewhere in Europe; and Roadhouse Grill, under a joint venture agreement that gives Cremonini the right to exploit that restaurant brand in Italy and Europe. Although most of the company's revenues come from Italy, the company has begun a push to internationalize its operations, including the establishment of new operations, through Marr, in Spain in 2002. Listed on the Milan stock exchange, Cremonini remains controlled at more than 57 percent by company founder and Chairman Luigi Cremonini, who is seconded by son and CEO Vincenzo Cremonini.

Founding Italy's Beef Leader in the 1960s

The origins of Cremonini can be traced back to the early 1960s and the Castelvetro region of Italy, where the Cremonini family operated a small cattle farm. Luigi Cremonini, born in 1939, left home to study farming in Bologna, and then began an apprenticeship at a slaughtering cooperative. Cremonini's first attempt to enter business on his own ended in disaster, when the herd of pigs he had purchased contracted swine cholera and had to be slaughtered. Instead, in 1962, Cremonini returned to the beef sector. Setting up a new company, Cremonini was joined by brother Guiseppe and family friend Luciano Brandoli, and the partners rented a shed and began processing beef.

Italy's postwar economic growth had sparked a boom in meat consumption, especially beef, which came to be equated with a higher social standing. The country's slaughterhouses remained for the most part local, small-scale operations similar to Cremonini's. Yet Cremonini and his partners quickly recognized that by adopting modern slaughtering and processing techniques found elsewhere in Europe and establishing a brand name, they would be able to expand to a national scale. In 1966, the three partners created Inalca S.p.A. and began slaughtering, processing, and marketing an expanding line of fresh and frozen beef products.

Over the next several years, Inalca added a number of new production sites, including cold-room and freezer facilities, allowing the company to launch industrialized beef slaughtering and processing. By the mid-1970s, Inalca had become Italy's foremost beef products producer, processing more than 120,000 tons of beef per year.

Inalca initially limited its production to cuts of beef; in the mid-1970s, however, the company became interested in diversifying its activities. In 1976, the company created subsidiary Corte Buona and launched its first cold-cut products, including salami and other cured meats.

The success of Corte Buona encouraged Inalca to seek further areas for diversification. In 1979, the company moved toward vertical integration with the purchase of Marr S.p.A. That company, founded as the cash-and-carry firm Magazzini Alimentari Riuniti Riminesi in 1972, had developed into the broader catering sector as a supplier of food products to restaurant and hotel markets. The company's next acquisition, of Agape in 1982, gave it its first taste of the restaurant sector. Agape specialized in the collective restaurant sector, and built up a strong business as an operator of restaurants in Italy's train stations. By then, the company had restructured under the holding company Castelvetro Finanziaria, or Cafin, but was best known as Gruppo Cremonini.

Diversified Italian Foods Leader in the 1990s

The year 1982 was to see a revolution in Italian dining—which tended to traditional, drawn-out meals—when the country's first American-style fast-food restaurant, called Burghy's, opened in Milan. The new concept, centered around hamburgers, appeared to be a natural extension for Cremonini's existing beef-based and catering operations, and in 1985, the company purchased Burghy's, which by then had grown to a chain of six restaurants, from the SME foods group, later taken over by Buitoni. Under Cremonini, the Burghy's chain grew strongly, building up a network of some 96 restaurants throughout Italy by the mid-1990s. The success of the Burghy's chain led Cremonini to launch a second fast-food chain, called Italy & Italy.

Cremonini continued to look for opportunities to diversify. In 1988, it began extending its catering division in a new direction, with a purchase of a stake in a door-to-door delivery group, Islandia, and its Quinta Stagione frozen foods delivery service. By the beginning of the 1990s, Cremonini had stepped up its interest in that group, gaining control in 1991. Cremonini had also expanded elsewhere, adding a unit producing spices and flavorings, and expanding into various other foods categories, such as mineral water, oil, and even wine.

By the mid-1990s, Cremonini had developed into one of Italy's most prominent food businesses, dominating most of its markets. The company's foodservices division, grouped under Agape, had developed a number of successful restaurants and

foodservices concepts, a branch that grew further in 1995 when the company acquired the famed Harry's Bar Roma brand. The company also had developed an on-board dining business, called Chef Express, that gained the concession to the Italian railroad system.

By the middle of the decade, Cremonini had begun to eye the public offering of at least part of its diversified empire. As part of the run-up to a public listing, the company restructured, cutting out a number of noncore operations, including its wine and oil operations. The company also decided to exit the fast-food market at this time, unloading its Italy & Italy restaurants and finding a ready buyer for its Burghy's chain in McDonald's Corporation. Long unable to crack the Italian fast-food market, McDonald's offered some $200 million to acquire the Burghy's chain. As part of the acquisition, McDonald's also agreed to give Inalca a five-year supply contract, positioning the company to become a prime supplier for McDonald's entire European operations.

The U.K. outbreak of BSE (bovine spongiform encephalopathy, more popularly known as "mad cow disease") put a damper on Cremonini's public offering plans that year. Instead, Luigi Cremonini bought up brother Guiseppe's 33 percent share in the company. The company continued to seek a public listing, now announcing its intention to list Marr on the NASDAQ. Ongoing consumer fears spurred by the BSE crisis forced the company to show losses for the first time in its history in that year. Instead, Luigi Cremonini bought out founding partner Luciano Bandolini, gaining full control of the company.

International Expansion for the New Century

Cremonini changed the company's name to Cremonini S.p.A. in October 1998. In December of that year, the company finally achieved its public offering, listing on the Milan exchange. Luigi Cremonini and his family nonetheless maintained control of the company's stock. The company also bought back the shares in Marr that had been sold on the NASDAQ.

In 1999, Cremonini moved to solidify its position in Italy, buying up its main beef processing rival, Guardamiglio Carni, in 1999. That acquisition was followed with two food distribution specialists, Discom and Adria Food, and a 76 percent stake in catering and distribution specialist Copea, all of which were acquired in 1998.

Cremonini now began to look beyond Italy for its future growth. In the late 1990s, the company began setting up a number of joint ventures in order to take it into foreign markets, including Argentina and Brazil. In Canada, the company formed a joint venture with Santamaria Foods to produce cured meats for the Canadian, Japanese, and—in a move to skirt restrictions on European meat imports—the U.S. markets as well. In October 1999, the company bought up a 25 percent stake in Stavropol, one of the largest producers of tinned meats for the Russian market. The company also formed a joint venture, Inalca Angora, taking it into Angola. By 2000, some 30 percent of Cremonini's sales were generated internationally.

That same year, Cremonini's international ambitions received a boost when the company teamed up with the United

Key Dates:

1963: Luigi Cremonini establishes a small slaughterhouse with brother Guiseppe and friend Luciano Brandolini.

1966: The business is incorporated as Inalca and begins establishing an industrialized meat processing group.

1976: The company establishes Corte Buona and begins production of cured meats.

1979: The company acquires Marr and enters the catering sector.

1982: The company acquires Agape and enters the restaurant sector.

1985: The company acquires six Burghy's fast-food restaurants and builds the chain into 96 stores nationwide.

1990: Spice and flavorings production begins.

1991: The company acquires majority control of Quinta Stagione, a frozen foods door-to-door business.

1996: Burghy's chain is sold to McDonald's Corporation.

1998: The company changes its name to Cremonini S.p.A. and goes public on the Milan Stock Exchange; the company acquires Discom, Adria, and 76 percent of Copea.

1999: The company acquires Guardamiglio Carni.

2000: In partnership with Granada, the company wins the Eurostar rail link catering concession; the company signs a joint venture agreement with Roadhouse Grill.

2001: The company opens the first Roadhouse Grill in Italy.

2002: The company sells its spice and flavorings business to Kerry Group; the company sets up a Marr subsidiary in Spain.

2003: The company acquires cold meat specialist Ibis; the company sets up a Moto joint venture with Compass to enter the roadside catering sector.

Kingdom's Granada to win the contract to supply catering services for the Eurostar rail link between France and the United Kingdom. In March of that year, Cremonini acquired a 51 percent stake in Frimo, an international meat trading group. The company also extended its catering operations in 2000 with the award of the catering contract for the Moby Vincent ferry between Olbia and Civitavecchia. Meanwhile, the company prepared to broach another frontier, setting up an e-commerce-capable web site for its frozen foods, ice cream, and ready meals.

The company also marked its return to restaurant operations in 2000, when it signed a joint venture agreement with U.S.-based Roadhouse Grill (owned by Malaysia's Berjaya Group) to introduce the Roadhouse Grill restaurant format into Italy and the rest of Europe. Cremonini began plans to introduce as

many as 40 Roadhouse Grill restaurants in Italy by 2003, and as many as 20 more in Europe by 2004. The first Italian Roadhouse Grill opened in 2001.

Cremonini was hit hard by a new BSE crisis, when the disease, initially thought to be confined to the United Kingdom, began appearing on the European continent. Cremonini's stock price slumped as a result of the new drop in consumer confidence—and the company itself came under scrutiny after shipping beef from a cow suspected of being infected with BSE to McDonald's. In response, Cremonini launched a public relations campaign to reassure the consumer public over the safety of its meat.

By 2003, Cremonini had weathered the worst of the BSE crisis, as the beef market recovered to its pre-BSE levels. By then, Cremonini had sold off its spices and flavorings unit to Ireland's Kerry Group for EUR 3 million. The company also moved to enter Spain in 2002, setting up a subsidiary of Marr on the island of Majorca in order to tap into the tourist market there.

Cremonini's expansion continued into 2003, with the acquisition of Italian cold meat specialist Ibis, for EUR 7.5 million. In that year, the company created a joint venture with the United Kingdom's Compass Group in a push to enter the highway foodservice market. The joint venture then took over Compass's existing roadside service operations in Italy and Austria, Moto S.p.A. and Autoplose Ges.mbH, and adopted the name Moto S.p.A. Cremonini appeared set to repeat its successful growth on the international food and catering markets in the new decade.

Principal Subsidiaries

Marr S.p.A.; Islandia S.p.A.; Montana Inalca S.p.A.; Montana Alimentari S.p.A.; Agape S.p.A.; Roadhouse Grill Italia S.r.l.

Principal Competitors

Orkla ASA; DANISH CROWN AmbA; Royal Cebeco Group Cooperative UA; Kerry Group PLC; Glanbia PLC; SOCOPA S.A.; Autogrill S.p.A.

Further Reading

Battaglia, Andy, ''Roadhouse Grill to Move into Europe, Inks Joint Pact with Cremonini,'' *Nation's Restaurant News,* July 24, 2000, p. 8.

''Commission Clears Motorway Foodservice JV Between Compass and Cremonini,'' *European Report,* May 10, 2003, p. 342.

Glover, John, ''Big Mac Pays Out 283m for Foothold in Pizza Land,'' *Guardian,* March 1996.

''Granada/Cremonini Replace Wagon-Lits/Sabena As Eurostar's Caterers,'' *European Report,* February 26, 2000.

—M.L. Cohen

CUNO Incorporated

400 Research Parkway
Meriden, Connecticut 06450
U.S.A.
Telephone: (203) 237-5541
Toll Free: (800) 243-6894
Fax: (203) 238-8977
Web site: http://www.cuno.com

Public Company
Incorporated: 1912 as Cuno Engineering Corporation
Employees: 1,650
Sales: $258.2 million (2002)
Stock Exchanges: NASDAQ
Ticker Symbol: CUNO
NAIC: 333319 Other Commercial and Service Industry
Machinery Manufacturing; 333999 All Other
Miscellaneous General Purpose Machinery
Manufacturing

CUNO Incorporated designs, manufactures, and markets a variety of general filtration, microfiltration, and ultra-filtration products for residential, commercial, and industrial use. A worldwide leader, CUNO has more than 300 patented technologies, including microporous membranes, depth filters, and cleanable filters and systems, which are applied to the potable water, fluid processing, and healthcare markets. Customers in the fluid processing market include chemical, gas, oil, and petrochemical processors, paints and resins manufacturers, and electronics and semi-conductor manufacturers. Healthcare customers include pharmaceutical manufacturers and biological and diagnostics specialists who require purification at the molecular level.

Water filtration and treatment systems for consumer and commercial applications are available under the Aqua-Pure, Water Factory Systems, and MacClean brands. Products include drinking water purification and whole-house water filtration under the Aqua-Pure brand, and water treatment systems, such as water softening, iron removal, acid neutralization, sulfur filtration, and microbiological control, available under both the MacClean and Aqua-Pure brands. Water Factory Systems products implement advanced technology reverse osmosis, which removes chlorine, pesticides, herbicides, radioactive particles, dissolved solids, and other contaminants. Reverse osmosis involves a pre-filtration step, purification through a reverse osmosis membrane, and a final step utilizing activated carbon to remove unpleasant tastes and odors. Water filtration products are available for the foodservice industry as well as consumers.

Engineering Diverse Industrial Products: 1912–60

Charles Cuno founded Cuno Engineering Corporation in 1912 to develop and manufacture electrical automotive equipment. The company's most enduring early product was the Cuno Electric Match, a cigarette lighter mounted on the dashboard of automobiles, promoted as a safe alternative to using matches while driving. The six models ranged in price from $6 to $15 per unit, available as standard equipment on fine cars or sold through automobile dealers and direct to the consumer. In 1926 Cuno entered the market for filtration products, applied to automotive and industrial uses. The company sold these patented products under the Micro-Klean brand name.

While Cuno Engineering became a leader in filtration technology, the company continued to produce automobile cigarette lighters. During the 1950s, however, filtration became a primary focus. Having grown to $4 million in revenues in 1954, Cuno Engineering became a public company in 1955, selling 200,000 shares at $16.50 per share. Funds from the stock offering were used to purchase Connecticut Filter as well as to pay bank debt. About this time the company began to develop filtration products for drinking water and food and beverage processing. For instance, in France Cuno filters were used to clarify fine cognacs. In 1958 Cuno Engineering expanded to European markets through a joint venture with Olin Mathieson Chemical Corporation. Olin Cuno Filter Corporation USA established a sales office and distribution center in Europe. American Machinery and Foundry, Inc. (AMF), a conglomerate of industrial and leisure and sporting goods companies, purchased Cuno

Engineering in 1960; afterward the company focused on filtration and separation technologies exclusively.

Emphasis on Filtration Technology Development: 1960–85

While AMF Cuno continued to develop, manufacture, and market filtration products for industrial use, residential water filtration became a more important part of its research and development activities. The company's engineers collaborated with other divisions at AMF, applying its expertise in water purification to development on AMF desalinization technology. As concern for water contamination grew during the 1960s, the company developed water filtration products for residential and commercial uses. Under the Aqua-Pure brand AMF Cuno sold a line of cartridges designed to fit inside the cold water pipeline to remove particles as well as unpleasant tastes and odors. The Aqua-Pure Chemical Feeder, introduced in 1967, added chlorine or bleach through the water line to kill bacteria. Adapting industrial technology to home use, AMF Cuno introduced the AP400 Lime Aid Water Conditioner for water heaters in 1975. A filter cartridge, placed in the cold water pipe that feeds into a water heater, removed dirt and sediment and minerals and prevented mineral deposits and clogs in hot water heater elements and thermostats. AMF Cuno marketed these water filtration products primarily through wholesale plumbing suppliers. Purwater brand systems provided an inexpensive home water filtration option. Sold through hardware stores and home centers, Purwater products filtered rust, dirt, and chemicals from drinking water.

AMF Cuno designed filtrations and separation technology that worked at the microscopic level for industrial, medical research, and healthcare applications. In 1973 the company patented Zeta Plus, the first nonasbestos filtration system with charged membranes capable of trapping microscopic contaminants. Zetapor brand products provided even finer filtration with microporous membranes. Both Zeta Plus and Zetapor products were used by pharmaceutical, electronics, and food and beverage manufacturing industries as well as in medical science research. After AMF acquired a biological and diagnostic products company in 1980, AMF Cuno assisted in the development of a purified cell culture serum, ZetaSera-D. The serum was used for research in the biological sciences, including genetic engineering and cancer research, and for production of vaccines and interferon. Filtration and separation technology played an integral role in producing the culture serum.

In 1982 AMF divided Cuno into two divisions to reflect patterns of existing and expected growth. General Filter Products consolidated traditional areas of business, such as industrial filters, Aqua-Pure products, Purwater systems, as well as PCP metering pumps. The Microfiltration Products division consolidated efforts to develop new products under the Zeta Plus and Zetapor brands.

In 1983 AMF added the Molecular Separations Division to design, manufacture, and market a new product. In development for two years and representing a significant advance in purification, ZetaPrep utilized an ion-exchange material to address the purification problems of biotechnology and genetic engineering. ZetaPrep separation devices were designed to be effective at the molecular level, for use in producing pure formulations of vaccines, hormones, enzymes, and antibodies. AMF expanded a research and development laboratory at its Talcottville facility to support research in chromatographic fluids separation and other fluid separation applications.

AMF Cuno continued to design filtration products for industrial use. In 1985 the company introduced a line of filters designed for coatings clarification. The Betapure product line addressed the needs of industrial filtration of extremely viscous fluid processed under high pressure. Betapure products filtered particles to create clear topcoats for automotive finishes and magnetic coatings for tapes and computer discs. AMF Cuno introduced Micro-Klean II Filter Cartridges for waterflood, disposal well, and lube oil systems.

AMF Cuno continually improved on its products with proprietary new technology. In 1985 the company introduced a new line of three Aqua-Pure Reverse Osmosis water purification systems. New to the Aqua-Pure brand was the Iron Removal System, which oxidized, then trapped iron for removal from residential, commercial, and industrial water lines.

New Ownership in 1986

New leadership at AMF narrowed the company's focus to leisure and sporting goods, leading to AMF's divestment of Cuno in 1986. Commercial Shearing, Inc. purchased Cuno for an amount estimated at more than $100 million. Commercial Shearing manufactured hydraulic power components, such as pumps, motors, valves, and cylinders, as well as a variety of metal products used in the construction, transportation, materials handling, mining, and agricultural machinery industries. At this time Cuno operated four plants in the United States, while facilities in France, Brazil, Japan, and Australia supported manufacturing and distribution for customers in 75 countries. Commercial Shearing purchased Cuno for its technological and market leadership in filtration products, particularly water purification.

Renamed Commercial Intertech Corporation (CIC), the company emphasized its interest in water filtration with the December 1988 acquisition of Water Factory Systems. Founded in Irvine, California, in 1970, Water Factory Systems sold reverse osmosis water treatment systems for consumer use and water treatment equipment for industrial applications. The acquisition included a network of retail stores serving commercial and home markets and LithoWater, a pollution control technology designed to reduce volatile organic compounds for industrial water users, such as printers.

Much of Cuno's growth at this time originated from consumer interest in water purification products. New channels of

Key Dates:

1912: Cuno Engineering Corporation is founded.

1926: Cuno Engineering develops its first industrial filters.

1955: Cuno Engineering becomes a public company.

1960: American Machinery and Foundry acquires Cuno Engineering; business is renamed AMF Cuno.

1973: Zeta Plus brand of microporous filtrations products is introduced.

1986: Commercial Shearing acquires AMF Cuno.

1988: The acquisition of Water Factory Systems strengthens Cuno in the consumer market.

1995: The Scientific Application Support Services Program adds customer focus to product research.

1996: CUNO Incorporated becomes an independent company through share dividend distribution.

1997: CUNO launches nine new products for a variety of filtration applications.

2000: *Forbes* magazine includes CUNO on its list of the 200 Best Small Companies.

2002: Sales of appliance filters account for 13.2 percent of total revenues.

distribution included hardware stores, home centers, and mass merchandisers. The company provided private label consumer water filtration products for Shaklee, Sears & Roebuck, and others.

Notable growth in industrial products involved overseas expansion and new technologies. Marketing to specific markets overseas led to increased demand for industrial filters, prompting construction of a new manufacturing facility in Japan in 1989. Sales of Microfluor filters for gases sterilization increased noticeably. A 45 percent increase in sales worldwide demanded additional production capacity for Betapure products as well as Micro-Klean products, which complemented and were often used with Betapure filters. New technology in hazardous waste control involved a combination of ion exchange and traditional filtration to remove heavy metals from wastewater at plating and printing businesses.

In 1991 CIC purchased Bioken Separations and combined it with Cuno's separations operation. Renamed Cuno Separations Division, the group manufactured proprietary crossflow membranes and devices that addressed the needs of ultra-pure filtration for applications in biopharmaceuticals, beverage, electronics, and industrial uses. Its water filtration systems were used in laboratory research and municipal water utilities, with customization available.

Cuno relocated, consolidated, and expanded its water purification systems manufacturing at one 120,000-square-foot facility in Enfield, Connecticut, purchased in late 1992. Water Factory Systems was relocated to the site from California and Aqua-Pure and other water filtration systems manufacturing was relocated from the Talcottville, Connecticut plant, which closed. In addition to housing increased manufacturing capacity, the new facility provided space for the company's major domestic distribution center.

Mid-1990s: Initiatives Positioning Cuno for Success

With fluctuating sales in the early 1990s and net losses in 1992 and 1993, Cuno established six initiatives to concentrate the company on long-term growth and continuing improvement. These included improvements in its manufacturing operations, such as more efficient use of raw materials and reduction of scrap. The company shortened its manufacturing cycles, improved inventory management, and reduced labor costs as well. Another main objective involved making select acquisitions; in 1995, however, the company divested its Cuno Separations unit because of its poor performance. The company identified the development of pre/final filter systems as essential to its success.

Three overlapping and important initiatives involved designing products for specific markets, with an emphasis on customer needs. In the past Cuno produced general products and competed on price. In 1994 the company sought to design products for specific uses and to provide quality products for markets where price was less important. Cuno formed the Scientific Application Support Services (SASS) to collaborate with customers in developing filters, often for new technological processes. The company looked at cross-functional applications of existing products as well. Cuno established direct relationships with its product users, rather than simply allow distributors to address the needs of customers. To support the SASS program, Cuno expanded the engineering staff by 28 percent between 1994 and 1996. To facilitate implementation of new products, Cuno reduced the product development cycle from four to five years to less than two years.

The SASS program succeeded in gaining new business for Cuno. A proprietary nylon membrane played a significant role in development of new products; sales related to these high margin filters increased 100 percent in 1996. Revenues increased 25 percent between fiscal 1994 and 1996, from $143 million to $179 million, respectively. Sales of Fluid Processing products rose from $69.6 million to $81.1 million, with much of the increase originating with semi-conductor manufacturers. Sales to the healthcare market rose from $32.7 million to $47.9 million as new management in Europe improved sales in the healthcare sector there. Sales to restaurants and foodservice organizations supported increases in the potable water market, from $40.9 million in 1994 to $49.3 million in 1996. The formation of a sales team dedicated to reverse osmosis products facilitated increased sales, as did improvements in countertop and under-the-sink reverse osmosis systems that allowed for competitive pricing and attracted new buyers. The company successfully introduced several existing products in overseas markets, particularly Brazil. With effective cost reductions, Cuno reported net income of $6 million in 1996.

Moving Forward As an Independent Company in the Late 1990s

During 1996 CIC deflected an attempted hostile takeover by United Dominion Industries, specifically interested in Cuno. The board rejected a tender offer as inadequate and suggested the shareholders reject it as well. CIC already planned to spin off Cuno as an independent company, seeing Cuno's leadership in the fluid purification industry as a value best left to itself. In the interests of the shareholders, CIC moved forward with the separation. After a higher offer was rejected, United Dominion attempted unsuccessfully to stop the spinoff through legal means. In September CIC distributed all Cuno shares in the form of a dividend to shareholders. The new company, CUNO Incorporated, assumed $30 million in debt and $5.3 million in spinoff costs through a dividend to CIC. To strengthen its financial position for continuing internal growth, CUNO raised $26.4 million through an equity offering in May 1997.

By May 1997 CUNO launched nine products for worldwide distribution. These included Electropor II, providing submicron level filtration for ultra-purified water necessary in semi-conductor manufacturing. The Petro Klean depth filter, used by the oil and gas industry, involved a grooved surface for more effective purification and long-lasting use. Scale Gard prevented the buildup of minerals that can block mechanisms in steam ovens and boilers used in the foodservice industry, particularly in regions with hard water. Fluid filtration products for the healthcare market included Zetaplus Biocap for laboratory and pilot project use; Zetabind II used a microporous nylon membrane for diagnostics and laboratory use.

In November 1997 the company formed the Consumer Filter Products Group to consolidate businesses worldwide in the residential, foodservice, and commercial potable water product markets, previously handled on a geographic basis. With 25 percent of revenues originating from these markets, Cuno expected continued and rapid growth in this area. In 1998 the group introduced a new Aqua-Pure reverse osmosis product that improved the quality of filtration through a thin film composite membrane. A new Water Factory reverse osmosis system incorporated performance improvements, with electronic control and thin-film membranes. A strategic alliance with NuSkin Enterprises, a health products company, prompted the introduction of Fountain Fresh, a high performance home water filtration system manufactured by Cuno and distributed in Japan under the NuSkin brand.

Continuing the business improvement program established in 1994, CUNO reorganized certain functions in late 1998. The company began to outsource metal housing manufacturing, streamlined membrane production in the United States, and consolidated distribution in the United States and Europe. Cost reductions involved the elimination of both salary and wage positions. In March 1998 CUNO acquired the Chemical Engineering Corporation (CEC). Already a supplier to CUNO for ten years, CEC designed and manufactured water conditioning equipment, including water softening, iron removal, and acid neutralization. Formerly sold under the CESCO brand, the line under CUNO was renamed MacClean.

Although sales of $220.6 million in 1999 represented an 11 percent increase over 1998, that increase occurred through a shift in markets. Sales declined slightly in the healthcare and fluid processing markets, particularly due to the oil industry in the United States and Japan. Fluid processing reported $72.3 million in sales and sales in healthcare amounted to $60.7 million. The decline was offset by increased sales in potable water markets, particularly in Australia, Brazil, and Europe. In 1999, however, sales of water purification and filtration products rose by 37.4 percent, to $87.7 million, as the introduction of a new line of water filters, primarily sold to appliance manufacturers, positively impacted North American sales.

Continuing Focus on New Product Development in the Early 2000s

Spending approximately 5 to 6 percent of net revenues on research and development, CUNO continued to design new products and improve existing filtration technologies. PolyPro XL filters provided flexible usage when a high level of purification is needed, whether for healthcare, industrial, or water filtration applications, or at the prefiltration, membrane protection, or final filtration stage. New products for the fluid processing market included PolyNet, an advanced polypropylene depth filter cartridge, and Betafine XL, an industrial polypropylene pleated filter. CUNO introduced a new line of patented carbon filters for the potable water market, providing overall superior performance with fewer service requirements.

CUNO introduced several new products for the healthcare market. Zeta Plus VR Series was produced to remove viral contaminants from blood plasma, serum, and other products of biological research. Microfluor II provided a high-flow capacity for pharmaceutical manufacturing. The LifeASSURE PB series provided a prefiltration of large particles and filtration of smaller particles in one cartridge. In collaboration with Xtrana, Inc., CUNO developed Xtra Bind Nylon-XBN membrane for nucleic-acid sample preparation. The product combined CUNO's nylon microporous membranes with Xtrana's Xtra Bind. Applications for CUNO's new Novylon membranes included test kits for pregnancy and infectious diseases. SterASSURE, introduced in late 2002, utilized a pleated, multizone membrane construction for the final step in filtration for healthcare applications.

By the end of fiscal 2002 potable water systems accounted for nearly half of revenues, $119.6 million of reported sales of $258.2 million in fiscal 2002. CUNO experienced its greatest gains in the North American market for residential water filtration systems as the company sought new outlets through home builders and upscale kitchen and bath showrooms. Appliance filters continued to sell very well, with sales to Whirlpool alone accounting for 13.2 percent of total revenues in 2002. Sales of fluid processing products continued to decline, though at a slower pace, at $68.7 million in revenues, while sales to the healthcare market increased slowly, to $70 million. With improvements to supply chain management and implementation of proprietary manufacturing technology, net income rose to $23 million in fiscal 2002.

Principal Subsidiaries

Chemical Engineering Corporation.

Principal Competitors

Millipore Corporation; Pall Corporation; United States Filter Corporation.

Further Reading

"Advanced Filtration: Hollow Fiber/Carbon MF Unit Debuts in Japan," *High Tech Separations News,* December 1998.
"AMF's Cuno Unit to Build Plant," *Wall Street Journal,* May 17, 1967, p. 14.

"Can Commercial Intertech Revamp Its Separations Unit?," *Membrane & Separation Technology News,* January 1994.

"Cuno Cuts Costs, Improves Business," *Membrane & Separation Technology News,* January 19, 1999.

"Cuno Engineering Stock Is Priced at $16.50 a Unit," *Wall Street Journal,* November 30, 1955, p. 17.

"CUNO Inc. Expands Local Operations—$2 Million in State Incentives Helps," *Fairfield County Business Journal,* September 21, 1992, p. 13.

"Cuno Separations Gets New Owner," *Membrane & Separation Technology News,* November 1994.

Gerdel, Thomas W., "Commercial Intertech Gets Higher Bid; Suitor Raises Its Hostile Offer, Attacks Target's Defensive Moves," *Plain Dealer (Cleveland),* July 16, 1996, p. 1C.

Jeffery, Noel, "The Answer Was in the Water," *Graphic Arts Monthly,* May 1992, p. 84.

"New for Home and Shop," *New York Times,* March 23, 1975, p. 146.

"Pleated Filters," *BioPharm,* July 1999, p. 33.

"Product Focus Shifts to Value-Added," *Membrane & Separation Technology News,* October 1, 1998.

"Olin Mathieson Forms Firm with Cuno Engineering Co.," *Wall Street Journal,* January 17, 1958, p. 5.

"Reverse Osmosis: Product Focus Shifts to Value-Added," *Water Technology News,* November 19, 1998.

"RO Coming Soon to Your Home!," *Water Technology News,* November 1994.

Sklarewitz, Norman, "Home Water Purifier Business Is Booming As Pollution Troubles Hit Outlying Areas," *Wall Street Journal,* March 24, 1967, p. 8.

"Stockholders of AMP Approve Acquisition of Cuno Engineering," *Wall Street Journal,* August 17, 1960, p. 12.

"Xtrana, CUNO to Develop Sample Prep Products," *Membrane & Separation Technology News,* February 2002.

—Mary Tradii

Daewoo Group

541, Namdaemunno, 5-GA
Chung-gu Seoul
Korea
Telephone: (02) 759-2114
Fax: (02) 753-9489

Defunct Company
Incorporated: 1967

Daewoo Group was founded by Kim Woo Choong in March 1967. Daewoo's emergence was inseparable from South Korea's rapid transformation from an agrarian country, racked by a long history of hostile invasions and lacking essential resources, to a land where the centrally planned "economic miracle" has become a fact of life. South Korea entered the 1960s with a crippling trade deficit and a domestic market too poor to support indigenous industries. When Korea was divided by the Allies after World War II, the territory north of the 38th parallel inherited all of the country's natural resources. With a far stronger military force than its rivals in the South, North Korea waited less than two years after the withdrawal of U.S. peace-keeping troops to invade. Peace was eventually restored in 1953, but the fear of foreign invasion has remained with the South Koreans and, indeed, has acted as a powerful incentive in the search for economic prosperity.

Daewoo means "Great Universe," and although the initial share capital of the company was a modest $18,000, Kim and his colleagues held great hopes for their business. At its peak, Daewoo was South Korea's fourth largest conglomerate, or *chaebol,* with principal operations in trading, motor vehicles, shipbuilding, heavy industry, aerospace, consumer electronics, telecommunications, and financial services. The company was comprised of 25 subsidiaries, linked together in a complicated system of cross holdings. The major company in the group was Daewoo Corporation, which was licensed as a general trading company (GTC) by the Korean government in 1975. GTCs were set up to promote exports, and license holders were required to establish offices abroad. Daewoo had a network of over 100 branches worldwide, with some 3,500 different prod-

ucts traded in over 130 countries. In exchange for promoting Korean goods abroad, the Daewoo Corporation was able to finance its expansion through preferential loan agreements, reduced foreign exchange requirements, and improved government advice on exporting and marketing abroad. However, Kim Woo Choong's global ambitions eventually overextended the company's resources, and by the late 1990s Daewoo was deep in debt, while Kim himself was being indicted on charges of corporate malfeasance. In 1999 the South Korean government issued an order to dismantle the *chaebol,* and the majority of the Daewoo Group's holdings were sold to other corporations.

Early History

Beginning in 1962 the South Korean government instigated a series of five-year plans and forced the *chaebols* to aim for a number of basic objectives. In common with their Far East competitors, Hong Kong and Taiwan, South Korea's government relied on a strategy that focused attention on the importance of exports as the method to decrease the country's balance-of-trade gap and to strengthen domestic production.

Daewoo began trading in 1967 at the start of the second five-year plan, and benefited from government-sponsored cheap loans on borrowing for exports. The company chose to concentrate on the labor-intensive clothing and textile industries, which would provide relatively high profit margins while utilizing South Korea's major asset, its large workforce. A factory was set up at Pusan and in 1990 3.6 million shirts were made there each month. Daewoo further contributed to the increases in South Korea's level of exports, which averaged 38.6 percent growth per annum during this period, by producing uncomplicated light manufacturing machines the construction of which, again, was labor intensive.

The third and fourth phases of Korea's economic recovery ran from 1973 to 1981. The country's most significant resource, labor, was then in high demand, and as wages increased, competitors from Malaysia and Thailand began to erode Korea's comparative advantage in labor-intensive production. The government responded by concentrating on mechanical and electrical engineering, shipbuilding, petrochemicals, and construction.

This change in emphasis was designed to continue Korea's export-led expansion and to provide domestic industries with parts that previously had to be imported. A home-based defense industry was also a priority as plans were announced for the total withdrawal of U.S. peacekeeping forces.

Daewoo moved into construction, serving the new village program and, in a farsighted move, the rapidly growing African and Middle Eastern markets. During this period Daewoo achieved its GTC status and received significant investment help from the South Korean government. Subsidized loans and strict import controls aroused the anger of competing nations, but the *chaebols* were in need of protectionist policies if they were to survive this period of world recession, triggered by the oil crisis of 1973.

Government policy forced Daewoo into shipbuilding, an industry to which Hyundai and Samsung were more suited because of their greater expertise in heavy engineering. Kim's reluctance to take over the world's biggest dockyard, at Okpo, in 1980 was well documented, and his comment on the Korean government indicated a growing frustration as his entrepreneurial instinct was being stifled. "They tell you it's your duty and you have to do it even if there's no profit." Displaying characteristic vigor and enthusiasm, however, Kim soon saw Daewoo Shipbuilding and Heavy Machinery earn a reputation for competitively priced ships and oil rigs that were often delivered ahead of schedule.

Established Joint Ventures in 1980s to Expand Outside Korea

The 1980s were a decade of liberalization for South Korea's economy. Small private companies were encouraged, and Daewoo was made to divest two of the textile companies that had contributed to its success. Protectionist import controls were relaxed, and the government no longer practiced positive discrimination towards the shipbuilding industry. These moves were instigated to ensure an efficient allocation of resources in a free market and to force the *chaebols* to be more aggressive in their dealings abroad.

The great change in attitude shown by the Korean government to the *chaebols* is best illustrated by the fate of one of Daewoo's competitors, the Kukje Group, which went into liquidation in 1985. At that time the government saw the *chaebols* as barriers to economic efficiency and refused to supply Kukje

with further credit. Small- and medium-sized companies were to be favored to ensure that the wealth in Korea's two industrial centers, Seoul and Pusan, eventually would be spread throughout the whole country. The only large industries to benefit from government support would be those that were internationally competitive and those that could further a more equitable distribution of income.

Daewoo responded to the challenge by establishing a number of joint ventures with U.S. and European companies. Kim's philosophy for the 1980s was that finished products would eventually lose their national identity as countries cooperated in design and manufacturing before exporting the goods to a further country. In 1986 Daewoo Heavy Industries launched a $40 million Eurobond issue in order to expand exports of machine tools, defense products, and aerospace interests. The president of Daewoo Heavy Industries, Kyung Hoon Lee, hoped that the money would enable his company to move away from simply licensing products from abroad and to enter a new phase of complementary and long-term relationships with foreign companies.

The 50/50 joint venture with Sikorsky Aerospace illustrated the benefits of operating in partnership with a U.S. company. Daewoo started by building S-76 helicopters from parts imported from the United States and gradually began to produce these parts in Korea. As the South Korean government had always regarded the defense industry as being of utmost importance, Daewoo received generous subsidies to establish new factories. By the end of 1988, Daewoo had enough confidence in the skills it had learned in the Sikorsky project to announce that it was to begin work on civilian helicopters and airplanes, which would be considerably cheaper than those produced by their U.S. counterparts.

Daewoo used other methods to capture foreign markets. It had excellent experience in turning around faltering companies in Korea and was now, increasingly, applying this knowledge abroad. In 1986 Daewoo acquired a controlling interest in the U.S. ZyMOS Corporation as a means of gaining the technical knowledge necessary to expand its interests in semiconductor manufacturing and semiconductor design. Subsidiaries that actually produced goods abroad, rather than acting solely as sales agents, were also established. Daewoo added a microwave oven assembly plant in Lorraine, France, and set up a VCR manufacturing company in Northern Ireland. Signaling that South Korea's economic recovery was reaching completion, Daewoo began considering investment in countries such as Bangladesh and Indonesia, where textiles could be produced as cheaply as in Korea during the early 1960s. Other linkups included a deal with Caterpillar to export 100,000 forklifts by 1993, a marketing contract to sell IBM-compatible personal computers, and the production of parts for the European Airbus on behalf of British Aerospace.

The mid-1980s saw an increased emphasis on the motor vehicle industry. Although the government, fearful of arousing protectionist sympathies in its foreign markets, was reticent in announcing its ambitions publicly, it was clear that South Korea was aiming to become one of the world's major car exporters before the end of the decade. In 1986 the Japanese yen appreciated 25 percent against the dollar, making Daewoo's already cheap exports even more attractive. Daewoo established a 50/50 joint venture with General Motors, called Daewoo Motor, to produce an internationally competitive small car as well as components for a number of General Motors's existing vehicles. Daewoo was not deterred by the difficulties inherent in setting up the required high-technology production lines and relied on the experience gained in other parts of the group to construct sophisticated computer systems in a relatively short period of time.

The joint venture with General Motors was initially one of Daewoo's most profitable links with a foreign company. In 1987 247,000 Pontiac LeManses were built, and the car, based on a design by the German car giant Opel, was well received in the U.S. market. Demand for the LeMans and the slightly larger Oldsmobile Royale soon faltered, however, and there were rumors of friction between the management of the two companies. The venture was not as successful as Hyundai's foray into the international car market, and it appeared that Daewoo underestimated the sophistication and technical standards required by the U.S. car buyer.

Late 1980s Crisis in Daewoo Shipbuilding

In 1989 heavy losses suffered by Daewoo Shipbuilding and Heavy Machinery made servicing the company's loans increasingly difficult. In an unprecedented demonstration against the traditional work ethic that had helped South Korea to economic prosperity, workers began an increasingly violent protest against years of long hours and low pay. The only solution available to Daewoo's management was to placate the workers with pay raises of more than 20 percent.

The reliance on shipbuilding as a way of cementing South Korea's export-led recovery looked even more dangerous as the rapidly appreciating South Korean won made exports more expensive. Demand for Daewoo's ships remained constant but the company was forced to sell ships at a loss as a way of guaranteeing a steady supply of orders. The situation was exacerbated by the bankruptcy of US Lines in 1986. A bad debt of $570 million marked the start of the crisis at the Okpo shipyard.

The Ministry of Trade and Industry, however, was no longer willing to bail out one of its most reliable *chaebols,* which was suffering as a direct result of the Daewoo Shipbuilding and Heavy Machinery acquisition forced on it by the government. Instead, the government promised a seven-year moratorium on Daewoo's debt to the Korean Development Bank and offered to provide a further W 150 billion in exchange for a number of contributions from the company. Daewoo would have to refinance the shipyards by selling off four subsidiaries, including the profitable Korea Steel Company and Daewoo Investment and Finance, as well as selling Daewoo Shipbuilding and Heavy Machinery's headquarters in Seoul. Subsidiaries were forced to raise W 85 billion on the Korean stock exchange, and Kim was ordered by the government to sell his W 150 billion investment in Daewoo Securities, the country's largest stockbroker. The government also ordered workers to curb their demands for wage increases and asked to see proof of improved management before the deal to help Daewoo was agreed to.

Kim's response was typical of his personal style. He had already moved his office to the shipyard so that he could keep direct control of the worsening situation, and had begun to take tours around the premises by bicycle to ensure that he could implement changes and cut costs where necessary. By 1990 improvements at the shipyard were already visible, and by the mid-1990s Daewoo was one of the most efficient shipbuilders in the world and, with 10 percent of the global market, was also the world's leading shipbuilder.

Aggressive Overseas Expansion in the 1990s

Daewoo entered the 1990s facing more problems than the downturn in the fortunes of its shipbuilding subsidiary. The company was highly leveraged, partly due to the ready availability of government loans, and was paying interest of W 300 million a day—about $500,000—on its debts. Daewoo had not marketed itself as well as competitors like Hyundai and, as a consequence, suffered from the lack of a strong brand image. Its heavy industries were now operating in stagnant markets and expenditure on research and development had to be increased if internationally competitive new products were to be successfully introduced. Continuing workers' demonstrations and changes in government policy further added to Daewoo's worries.

The company also had to deal with the unraveling of its relationship with General Motors. Sales of LeMans had fallen to 39,081 in 1990, a 39 percent drop from the peak of 1988. When GM and Daewoo could not agree on a plan to revive the venture, GM sold its half of Daewoo Motor to Daewoo in 1992 for $170 million. As he had done in shipbuilding, Kim decided to take direct control of Daewoo Motor and quickly turned its fortunes around. He focused the company on improving the quality of its cars; added to the production lines were detailed checks at every step along the way and, for a one-year period, every Espero and Prince car made was taken on a grueling road test to identify problems. By 1993 Daewoo had regained the number two spot in the domestic car market, still trailing Hyundai but once again ahead of Kia, and by 1995 Daewoo Motor was making a slight profit.

As he was turning Daewoo Motor around, Kim embarked on a risky strategy of overseas expansion, aggressively seeking out opportunities for both marketing and manufacturing Daewoo products in the United States, Europe, and less-developed countries. He committed more than $20 billion in numerous joint ventures and start-ups around the world.

More than half of this money—$11 billion—was slated for Daewoo Motor ventures. In 1992 Daewoo entered into a joint venture with an automaker in Uzbekistan, which led to the opening in late 1995 of an $800 million plant capable of producing 200,000 compact cars annually by 2000. Some $250 million was spent to buy a state-owned carmaker in Romania, capable—after retooling—of making another 200,000 cars each year. In 1994 Daewoo Motor committed $1 billion to a joint venture in India. The following year, the company outbid General Motors itself to buy 60 percent of Poland's state-owned FSO carmaker for $1.1 billion. Manufacturing cars in these lesser-developed countries resulted in a lower-cost product that Kim hoped would succeed even in the brand-conscious West. Early indications were positive as Daewoo, in 1995, captured more than 1 percent of the British car market in the first month that it started selling Nexia and Espero sedans, exceeding its goal. After gaining this toehold in Europe, Kim then planned to enter the U.S. market in either 1997 or 1998. But by placing manufacturing in such countries as Poland and India, Daewoo would also be well-positioned to sell the cars in these same countries, which were experiencing much higher growth in demand for new cars than Western Europe or the United States. Overall, Kim set goals of quadrupling auto output to a total of two million vehicles by 2000, and of becoming one of the world's top ten automakers.

Automobiles, however, were not the only Daewoo product Kim aggressively moved overseas; consumer electronics became another key Daewoo transplant. But first, Daewoo Electronics revamped its product line. Quality problems had hampered sales of its higher-end electronics items, so Daewoo decided to focus on such lower-tech products as televisions, VCRs, and microwave ovens. Its aggressive yet systematic approach to overseas expansion then followed; by 1996 Daewoo Electronics had 20 production subsidiaries outside South Korea, with plans for 16 more. Non-Korean production stood at 19 percent but was slated to be increased to 60 percent by 2000. Daewoo strategically chose one country within each major target region for most of its production facilities. Southeast Asia was based in Vietnam (where Daewoo was the single largest foreign investor); the Americas, Mexico; Central and Eastern Europe, Poland; and Western Europe, France. Daewoo nearly made a huge step forward in late 1996 when a deal was announced whereby Daewoo Electronics would buy Thomson Multimedia, based in France. The acquisition would have made Daewoo the world's leading maker of televisions, but the deal was quickly scuttled after protests by French workers who were angered by the prospect of Thomson Multimedia falling into foreign hands.

The importance of Daewoo's moves in Europe, as well as the importance of Daewoo Motor, were shown in late 1995 when Kim moved to Vienna to concentrate solely on the Daewoo Group's overseas auto business. Placed at least temporarily in charge of the Daewoo Group was Kim's longtime ally, Yoon Young-Suk, who had headed up Daewoo Heavy Industries. Kim's move, however, fueled speculation that he was trying to distance himself from the ongoing corruption trials involving several heads of *chaebol,* as well as two former presidents of South Korea, Chun Doo Hwan and Roh Tae Woo. The *chaebol* leaders were accused of bribing Roh in an outgrowth of the overly cozy relationship between the Korean government and the *chaebol.* In late August 1996, eight of the *chaebol* leaders— including Kim—were found guilty of bribery; Kim was sentenced to two years in prison but immediately filed an appeal.

The late 1990s and early 21st century were slated to be a critical period for Daewoo. In addition to Kim's bribery conviction and possible jail sentence, Daewoo (and other *chaebol*) faced the possibility that the Korean government would intervene to reduce the power of the *chaebol,* which were beginning to be seen as impediments to the country's economic progress. Korean reunification, which was sure to profoundly affect the entire nation's future, seemed ever more likely and Daewoo had in 1995 become the first South Korean company allowed to enter into joint ventures in the north. These prospects, combined with the company's massive commitment to overseas expansion and a continuing heavy debt load, added up to a very uncertain future for the Daewoo Group.

Pre-Millennium Collapse

By the mid-1990s Daewoo was firmly entrenched in what Kim Woo Choong dubbed the "Vision 2000" plan, his ambitious program intended to position the company to become one of the top ten car manufacturers in the world. The company's expansion into Eastern Europe seemed savvy as the region's emerging democracies could provide the car manufacturer with cheap labor, and as the market for affordable, utilitarian automobiles in the former Soviet Bloc was experiencing precipitous growth. Indeed, in Poland alone, sales of cars and commercial vehicles were projected to reach 534,000 in 1997, up from 426,000 in 1996 and 296,000 in 1995. As late as March 1999, Daewoo was poised to overtake Fiat as the leading car manufacturer in the Polish market.

By the end of the decade, however, it was becoming apparent that Mr. Kim had bitten off far more than his company could chew, as his plan to grab up market share at a loss and recuperate the investment later was not panning out. While the company was poised to meet its goal of manufacturing two million cars by 2000, the financial crisis of 1997–98 in developing countries had caused car sales to fall well short of projections, and none of Daewoo's foreign operations were actually turning a profit. Furthermore, Daewoo had accumulated colossal debt over the course of its overseas automotive expansion, which compromised the stability of its other operations, including shipbuilding. By July 1999, the company owed its creditors more than $50 billion. The company's perilous financial situation was further exacerbated by the recession that hit South Korea in 1998, the country's worst economic slump in nearly half a century. In spite of these warning signs, Mr. Kim did not desist from his aggressive acquisition strategy. While other *chaebols* had begun implementing measures to slow growth in the midst of the country's fiscal crisis, Kim Woo Choong persevered with his ill-advised program, acquiring 14 new companies and increasing the company's debt by 40 percent in 1998.

In April 1998, recently elected South Korean President Kim Dae-jung had pledged to be the first South Korean president to implement significant reform of the *chaebol* system. As the country's most financially unstable *chaebol,* the Daewoo Group soon became a prime target for these reforms. On August 16, 1999, Daewoo's creditors announced a government-mandated plan to break up the company. Faced with bankruptcy, Kim Woo Choong agreed to step down as head of the Daewoo Group in November 1999, and the South Korean banks took control of the bulk of the *chaebol*'s assets with plans to sell them off as quickly as possible. In the aftermath of the company's collapse, charges of wide-ranging accounting fraud and embezzlement began to emerge, and Kim Woo Choong became a fugitive from justice, going into hiding in numerous countries, including Morocco, France, and the Sudan. In the early years of the 21st century, however, the South Korean government remained reluctant to pursue Mr. Kim, amid insinuations that it had been complicit in the reckless expansion policies through which Kim Woo Choong overextended the Daewoo Group so flagrantly. In a 2003 interview with *Fortune* magazine, Mr. Kim lamented his unrealistic ambitions to grow the Daewoo Group so quickly, but denied all charges of corruption in his business practices.

Further Reading

Brull, Steven V., Catherine Keumhyun Lee, and Mia Trinephi, "Daewoo's Tycoon of Television," *Business Week,* September 23, 1996, pp. 142H, 142J.

Burt, Tim, "GM to Create New Carmaker from Daewoo," *Financial Times* (London), April 30, 2002, p. 19.

Burton, John, "Daewoo Motors' Downfall," *Financial Times* (London), November 9, 2000, p. 43.

——, "Disentangling Daewoo: The South Korean Government's Attitude to the Country's Second Biggest Conglomerate Will Be an Indicator of Its Commitment to Reform," *Financial Times* (London), July 20, 1999, p. 18.

——, "Global Hunt for Daewoo's Founder, *Financial Times* (London), February 6, 2001, p. 12.

Cho Dong Sung, "Government Entrepreneurs and Competition," in *Doing Business in Korea,* edited by Arthur Whitehill, Sydney: Croom Helm, 1987.

Clifford, Mark, "The Daewoo Comrade: South Korean Firm Blazes Northern Trail," *Far Eastern Economic Review,* February 20, 1992, pp. 47–48.

——, "Wheels Off the Wagon: South Korean-US Car Venture Unravels Amid Acrimony," *Far Eastern Economic Review,* January 23, 1992, pp. 44–45.

"The Death of Daewoo," *Economist,* August 21, 1999.

Glain, Steve, "Strategic Move: Daewoo Group Shifts Its Focus to Markets in the Third World," *Wall Street Journal,* October 11, 1993, p. A1.

Hoon, Shim Jae, "Going Global," *Far Eastern Economic Review,* November 2, 1995, pp. 46–50.

Kraar, Louis, "Daewoo's Daring Drive into Europe, *Fortune,* May 13, 1996, p. 145.

——, "Korea Goes for Quality," *Fortune,* April 18, 1994, p. 153.

Lee, Charles S., "Improving a Miracle," *Far Eastern Economic Review,* June 20, 1996, pp. 48–49.

Lowry, Tom, *The South Korean Motor Industry: A Rerun of Japan?,* London: Economist Intelligence Unit, 1987.

McDermott, Michael, and Stephen Young, *South Korea's Industry: New Directions in World Markets,* London: Economist Intelligence Unit, 1989.

Mi-young, Ahn, "Terrific Trio Lead Revival: Daewoo Has Pulled Itself Out of a Pit of Despair. Now Its Top Three Companies Are Flying High and Spearheading a Push Overseas," *Asian Business,* August 1994, pp. 12–13.

"Mr. Kim's Big Picture: Should Western Car Makers Be Frightened of Daewoo?," *Economist,* September 16, 1995, pp. 73–74.

"Mr. Kim's One-Man Empire," *Economist,* January 27, 1996, pp. 56–57.

Nakarmi, Laxmi, "At Daewoo, a 'Revolution' at the Top," *Business Week,* February 18, 1991, pp. 68–69.

——, "Exile of the Patriarch: Daewoo's Founder Is Off to Vienna—But Don't Count Him Out," *Business Week,* February 5, 1996, p. 58.

——, "A Flying Leap Toward the 21st Century?: Pressure from Competitors and Seoul May Transform the *Chaebol*," *Business Week,* March 20, 1995, pp. 78–80.

Schuman, Michael, "Daewoo Strains Slim Finances to Invest Fast and Hard in Overseas Expansion," *Wall Street Journal,* May 29, 1996, p. A9.

Simonian, Haig, "Daewoo Pins Its Hopes on Poland: Warsaw Is the Linchpin As the Carmaker Expands Production in the Former Eastern Bloc," *Financial Times* (London), November 4, 1997, p. 29.

Sohn, Y.J., "Another Asian Conquerer Ventures East," *Business Korea,* August 1996, pp. 34–35.

"A Tale of Two Kims: Daewoo," *Economist,* July 4, 1992, p. 61.

Thornton, Emily, "Do or Die," *Far Eastern Economic Review,* June 13, 1996, pp. 54–58.

Ward, Andrew, "Kim Tries to Mend Damaged Reputation," *Financial Times* (London), January 23, 2003, p.27.

—Andreas Loizou
—updates: David E. Salamie, Erin Brown

DNP

Dai Nippon Printing Co., Ltd.

1-1, Ichigaya Kagacho 1-chome
Skinjuku-ku, Tokyo 162-01
Japan
Telephone: +81 (03) 3266-2111
Fax: +81-3-5225-8239
Web site: http://www.dnp.co.jp

Public Company
Incorporated: 1876 as Shūeisha
Employees: 34,094
Sales: $10.6 billion (2001)
Stock Exchanges: Tokyo Osaka Nagoya Luxembourg
    Amsterdam
Ticker Symbol: DNPCY
NAIC: 323119 Other Commercial Printing; 516110
    Internet Publishing and Broadcasting; 334419 Other
    Electronic Component Manufacturing

Japan's first modern printing company, Dai Nippon Printing Co., Ltd. (DNP) eventually became the largest printing company in the world. Until World War II its only activity was the printing of publications. It now also engages in commercial printing, packaging, decorative interiors, electronics, business forms, and a range of information technology products. Dai Nippon is an industry leader in high-tech areas such as precision parts, computerized printing, and color filters for laptop computer displays. At the end of the 20th century, with demand for traditional printing materials on the decline, the company invested heavily in research and development to diversify its portfolio of high-tech products, including single-chip "smartcards." Dai Nippon remains the world's largest comprehensive printing company.

At the Forefront of Modern Japanese Printing: 1876–1900

Dai Nippon was founded as Shūeisha in Tokyo in 1876. Japan's modernization process was just beginning. As it took hold, more newspapers and documents were printed and Shūeisha grew. The only modern Japanese printing firm at the time, it was well positioned to get this business. It printed virtually all the metropolitan newspapers, its only competition being tiny printing houses which used wood blocks. Shūeisha initially printed movable type by hand, but in 1884 the company updated its equipment, installing a steam motor to run its presses, thus becoming the first private-industry user of steam power in Japan. From then on new techniques and improved equipment were added constantly as Japan's papermaking and publishing industries grew. In 1874 Japan manufactured only 35,000 pounds of paper. In 1884 it manufactured 5.3 million pounds, and in 1894, 36 million pounds. Most of that paper was used for printing, much of which was done by Shūeisha, at least until 1900 when its chief rival, Toppan Printing, was formed.

Many printing innovations were imported from the West. The Japanese government, which coordinated the modernization drive, imported foreign printing specialists to train Japanese printers. By 1887 gas and electric printing presses were in use. The rotary press appeared in 1889 for newspaper printing, and in 1899 for magazines. Research on the uses of photo copperplates was begun in 1887, and these plates were used for newspaper printing by 1903. In 1912 offset and photogravure printing equipment were imported from the West.

Early 20th-Century Printing Industry Boom

The Sino-Japanese War of 1894 created an increase in printing orders and demand for paper as more newspapers were read and more documents needed. A slump in printing and papermaking followed the end of the war in 1901, but in 1904 the outbreak of the Russo-Japanese War increased the demand for newspapers and magazines. Japan defeated China and Russia. A period of military and economic expansion began, assisted by a modern currency system, established during the 1880s. As the economy grew, so did the demand for printing.

Printing boomed during World War I. By 1927 printing and publishing were approaching Western scales; nearly 20,000 new book titles and 40 million magazines were published that year. In 1935 the company changed its name to Dai Nippon Printing Co., Ltd.

Company Perspectives:

DNP, Dai Nippon Printing, was established in 1876 as the first full-scale printing company in Japan. Always applying and developing its printing technology, the Company has expanded and diversified its operations to include packaging, decorative materials, electronic components and information media supplies. The wide variety of DNP products and services are essential to our daily lives. In addition, these products and services which enrich our lives are now taken for granted in every aspect of our society. By combining its innovative technology and expertise, DNP offers products and services that fulfill dreams, ensure a more enjoyable livelihood, and afford better communication.

During the 1930s Japan was ruled by an increasingly repressive military dictatorship that suppressed publishers and writers and banned books, making printers cautious about what they printed. Publishing, and thus printing, did not flourish in such an atmosphere. Paper shortages and the devastation of the Japanese economy during World War II further hurt the printing industry. The industry recovered fairly quickly after the war, however, growing rapidly during the 1960s and 1970s. The most important printing during the boom was encyclopedias and the complete works of authors. Periodical printing was also important. Dai Nippon was growing at about 6 percent a year by 1966.

Expanding into Other Industrial Sectors After World War II

After the war Dai Nippon expanded from printing, which accounted for all of its prewar business—into industrial areas, such as packaging, construction materials, and electronic precision devices. The broadened product range let the company expand at times when there was no growth in publications. The company invested heavily in research, setting up its own research plants, before any other Japanese printing company, in Tokyo. By 1991 Dai Nippon had eight research plants in Japan and one overseas. It soon claimed that it could print on anything but water and air.

As Japanese industry began its slow but steady postwar expansion, Dai Nippon took advantage of opportunities in new sectors of the economy. For example, Dai Nippon perfected a technology to print imitation wood grain on the dashboards of cars. Dashboards and other curved surfaces are difficult to print on, but Dai Nippon printed the grains on a water-soluble film, then immersed the dashboard and film together, causing the wood grain to transfer to the dashboard. When the Japanese auto industry began exporting heavily, orders for Dai Nippon's printed dashboards grew. Dai Nippon also moved into electronics and television, producing shadow masks for color television sets using photoprocess and etching technologies, then moving into color filters for liquid crystal display. The televised wedding of Japan's crown prince in 1959 led to a boom in color television sales in Japan and more business for Dai Nippon. Several of Japan's large publishing houses launched new, successful weeklies in 1959, bringing further business to Dai Nippon. The 1964 Tokyo Olympic Games gave the printing industry a boost.

At the same time, U.S. publishers were beginning to use Japanese printing companies because their products cost less than those of U.S. printers. In 1964 the company built a plant in Hong Kong, primarily to print for U.S. publishers, who paid only half what it cost them to print in the United States. Dai Nippon was looking for less expensive labor and equipped the Hong Kong plant with modern European presses. The plant initially confined itself to offset printing, specializing in color work. It established an apprenticeship program that sent young Chinese technicians to Japan for training. This plant, with that of rival Toppan opened in 1962, was the kernel around which the Hong Kong printing industry grew. By the late 1980s the Hong Kong printing industry rivaled that of Japan.

Overseas Expansion and Diversification: 1960s–70s

In 1968 Dai Nippon continued overseas expansion, opening offices in New York and Düsseldorf to promote its printing and binding. Dai Nippon was cautious, however, about expanding into foreign markets too rapidly because company officials believed that printing was closely related to local and community needs. Still, as business continued to expand steadily during the 1970s and 1980s, Dai Nippon launched joint ventures that included printing plants in Singapore and Jakarta, and opened offices that did not include plants in Sydney, London, Chicago, San Francisco, Los Angeles, and in Santa Clara, California.

The 1970s brought advances in rotary offset printing, particularly in color. Soon after, U.S. publishers began giving more four-color work to Japanese printers, including Dai Nippon, an industry leader in color printing. The decade also brought computerized typesetting, which changed the Japanese printing industry, making it far more efficient. In 1972 Dai Nippon established P.T. Dai Nippon Printing Indonesia, mainly to produce food packaging and decorative cartons for the Indonesian market. By the 1980s the Indonesian firm also exported to Hong Kong, Singapore, and other areas. Japanese food companies operating overseas also used its services.

By the 1980s the company had diversified into so many kinds of printing and other businesses, that it built new, more specialized research institutes to replace the general ones it had built immediately after the war. Because Dai Nippon manufactured so much food packaging, it used food sanitation experts to help research the best materials for food preservation, and often built the machinery used for packing food. The company, which put about 1 percent of sales into research and development, often developed technologies that it was not at first certain would apply to printing. These technologies, however, were often applied to the printing of non-paper materials. The non-paper sector of the printing industry grew greatly during the 1980s, increasing 20.5 percent in 1986 alone.

Assuming a Leading Role in the Information Age: 1980s–90s

In 1980 Japanese-language word processors came into use, making electronic publishing feasible in Japan. As the 1980s progressed, computers and word-processing programs became popular and less expensive, and by the end of the decade even small businesses could afford a laser printer. Businesses with laser printers had less need for commercial printers, since they could

Key Dates:

1876: Dai Nippon is founded as Shūeisha in Tokyo.

1884: The company updates its equipment, installing a steam motor to run its presses, thus becoming the first private-industry user of steam power in Japan.

1935: The Company changes its name to Dai Nippon Printing Co., Ltd.

1964: Dai Nippon Printing Company International, Ltd. is established in Hong Kong; the company builds a plant in Hong Kong, primarily to serve U.S. publishers.

1972: Dai Nippon establishes P.T. Dai Nippon Printing Indonesia, mainly to produce food packaging and decorative cartons for the Indonesian market.

1990: The company opens an information-media supplies division and founds the Information Media Supplies Research Laboratory in Saitama, Japan.

2000: The company forges an agreement with the Japanese division of Microsoft whereby Dai Nippon's smartcards will be applicable to Microsoft's Windows operating system and backed by Microsoft's technical support.

now do small, simple jobs themselves. Because these developments affected its traditional business niche, it was a logical step for Dai Nippon—and competitors like Toppan—to move into information processing. Dai Nippon believed that printing was the first information processing industry, and printing companies therefore should have a leading role in the computer age.

This view was shared by many of Dai Nippon's competitors and by the Paper and Printing Committee of the Industrial Structural Council, an advisory organ of Japan's Ministry of International Trade and Industry. In 1988 the Paper and Printing Committee released a report predicting a decline in demand for conventional printing, and urging the printing industry to use its knowledge of information processing to contribute to an information-oriented society. The shipment value of printed matter in Japan had reached ¥6.2 trillion in 1986, and the committee predicted that it would continue to grow at an annual rate of 6.5 percent, reaching ¥15 trillion by the year 2000. The committee said printing firms should aim to develop new high-tech printing techniques and information processing.

Dai Nippon had been concentrating on information-related technologies throughout the 1980s. By 1985 the company had developed the technology to manufacture a laser card the size of a credit card to hold information. The card was only 0.76 millimeters thick and used a photosensitive material to read information. While the card was suitable for mass production, there were problems recording information on it. In 1985 the company also developed a computerized printing transfer technology for textiles and a very large screen for projected television, and introduced a credit-card sized calculator developed with Casio Computer.

In 1986 Dai Nippon developed a compact-disc-based telephone directory system, a digital color printer system (together with JVC), and a special aluminum foil top for paper cartons. In 1987 Dai Nippon announced several more developments in information technology. It jointly developed a Japanese-language word processor with a spelling-check facility, introduced a foldable magnetic identification card made of a polyester resin sheet, and signed an agreement to supply American Bank Note with holographic technology and services. It also developed a smart card with 128 kilobit storage capacity and developed the technology to produce urinalysis paper at 20 percent lower than the usual cost. In 1988 Du Pont agreed to sell Dai Nippon's high-precision color printers and transfer materials in the United States, and Dai Nippon revealed that it was investing ¥70 billion a year in research and development.

In 1989 Dai Nippon announced the development of Hi-Vision Static Pictures, a method of converting data into a form used by high-definition television (HDTV). The latter was expected to be the next generation of television sets and an area of tremendous growth during the 1990s. The company also developed sophisticated printing technologies used for high-quality reproductions that were equal to those of Western printing companies. Dai Nippon printed art books in the United States with high-quality color plates using computer technology. Profits for 1989 were $222 million on sales of $6.4 million.

At the end of 1990, Dai Nippon had 20 regional offices in Japan, with 51 sales offices and 21 printing plants, and 11 overseas offices and five overseas plants. Sales and profits increased for the 41st year in a row, although the company suffered from the nationwide labor shortage and struggled to keep up with the rapid transition to an information-oriented society. To make that transition, the company opened an information-media supplies division in 1990 and founded the Information Media Supplies Research Laboratory in Saitama, Japan. One of the division's most important products was its thermal transfer ribbon, used in word processors, fax machines, and bar-code printers; and another was its dye sublimation transfer ribbon, which could print images of almost photographic quality from computer graphics with various printers.

The company also strengthened its production base, investing $486 million to expand its microproducts plant, which constructed audiovisual systems and electronic components, and its business-forms plant, which manufactured various forms for office-automation systems and cards. In the same year, Dai Nippon broke ground for a new research and production center, and bought land in Tokyo and Osaka where it planned to build highly automated manufacturing plants.

Dai Nippon also concentrated on overseas operations in 1990, marketing photomasks through a partnership with Du Pont Photomask. It increased its share in Tien Wah Press—the largest printing company in Singapore, and an important distribution center for southeast Asia—from 31 percent to 85 percent. This made Singapore Dai Nippon's largest overseas printing base. The company moved into the global market for projected-television screens, beginning production in Japan and at the Denmark plant of a new subsidiary, DNP DENMARK. The subsidiary soon bought another Danish company, Scan Screen.

Continuing its progress in the information sector, Dai Nippon began to use satellites to communicate data from its Tokyo headquarters and to distribute its business-oriented television programs, which were part of its work in audiovisual systems. It established the Multimedia Communications Center to work on HDTV, videodisks, and CD-ROMs. The company announced breakthroughs in holograms, computer graphics, and medical imaging. It also began a joint venture in smart cards, called Spom Japan, with France's Bull. The company started mass production of a smart card with one of the world's highest memory levels, aimed mainly at the Japanese market.

As electronic media grew, traditional printing slowed. Dai Nippon sought business in niche-market magazine printing. Because of growth in advertising, business forms, and precise electronic devices, book and magazine printing made up an ever-smaller portion of the company's printing sales during the 1980s. Printing Japanese magazines was good business for printers because many magazines used several kinds of paper and printing techniques in a single issue. Books for Europe and the United States also suffered from the appreciation of the yen, though this decline was partly offset by strong magazine sales in Australia and New Zealand. By 1990, books and magazines accounted for 18 percent of printing sales, commercial printing for 52 percent, and packaging and special printing for 30 percent.

The growth of commercial printing during the late 1980s was fueled by the expanding Japanese economy and its need for business forms, advertising, and credit cards. With more and more Japanese traveling, travel brochures became important. The Japanese trend for household electronics, often containing integrated circuits and other electronic components printed by Dai Nippon, also increased commercial sales. Packaging sales were hampered by changes in the Japanese lifestyle, particularly the trend toward eating out. The demand for packaged daily necessities was at a near-saturation level. Dai Nippon manufactured metal products such as mirror-finished sheets for appliances during the 1980s. The early 1990s found Dai Nippon continuing to expand into new technologies, while maintaining a sizable presence in its traditional printing market.

Entering the 21st Century

Despite signs of economic slowdown in Japan, Dai Nippon continued to report growth in all sectors in 1991. That year the company joined Fujitsu Ltd., Iwanami Shoten Publishers, Sony Corp., and Toppan Printing Co. in the formation of the Epwing group, a consortium to promote 10 to 20 percent growth in CD-ROM electronic publishing in Japan over the next several years. In one example of the lucrative possibilities afforded by CD-ROM electronic publishing, Dai Nippon launched a project in conjunction with NHK Enterprises Inc. in 1992 to compile a CD-ROM collection of still images of the world's most famous museum paintings for display on high-definition television screens. Called the World Museum Series, the project would contain 63 programs on two CD-ROM disks, and be sold for ¥3 million, with its customer base consisting primarily of Japanese museums and schools.

It was a blow to the company's reputation in late 1992, however, when top executives Norio Mizunoya and Tadashi Takehara were implicated in an illegal scheme involving four other companies, including archrival Toppan Printing Co., to fix bids on central government contracts. While historically lenient on antitrust laws, the Japanese government was now seen to be cracking down in response to complaints from foreign companies—especially American—that Japan's centuries-old insider practices presented unfair impediments to imports. Even with the arrests of numerous top executives and government raids on corporate offices, however, most analysts agreed that government antitrust measures were still largely symbolic and would have little effect on Japan's entrenched business networks. By the mid-1990s, Dai Nippon seemed to have weathered the scandal, and was reporting steady profit and sales increases, in spite of the strained Japanese business climate. Company officials said across-the-board cost-cutting measures and savvy promotional activities had contributed significantly to Dai Nippon's gains.

In 1997, *Fortune* magazine rated Dai Nippon the top Japanese company, ahead of Toyota and Sony. The company remained strongly committed to diversification through its electronics division and established itself as a frontrunner in key emerging markets, especially that for smartcards, also known as integrated-circuit, or IC, cards. Analysts believed that in the first decade of the 21st century the smartcard would become the standard, replacing magnetic strip cards altogether. Dai Nippon was part of MAOSCO, a multi-corporation consortium that announced the development in 1997 of an operating system called "Multos," that would provide smartcard user access not just to financial information and services but to personal identification, travel, media, and telecommunications applications. In an interview with the *London Financial Times* on May 16, 1997, Michael Keegan, the CEO of Mondex International, the top member of the consortium, predicted, "This will do for smart cards what Windows has done for the personal computer." Two years later, the revolution seemed to be in effect: according to projections, some one million cards based on the Multos platform would be issued worldwide by the end of fiscal 1999. Moreover, Dai Nippon's success in the smartcard arena received a giant boost in September 2000 when it forged an agreement with the Japanese division of Microsoft whereby Dai Nippon's smartcards would be applicable to Microsoft's Windows operating system and backed by Microsoft's technical support. Dai Nippon and Microsoft planned to target a range of customers, including public facilities such as schools, as well as business corporations.

In the early years of the 21st century, while demand for traditional print materials continued to decline, there appeared to be no slowdown in the race for market share in multimedia applications and digitization of content, including everything from electronic catalogues to books to maps. In addition to these avenues, Dai Nippon sought ways of strengthening its Internet-related services, with a long-term view toward Net-only broadcasting and animation distribution services. Dai Nippon remained competitive in the development of liquid-crystal display (LCD) television. With such a broadly diversified portfolio of high-tech products, Dai Nippon seemed to have laid the groundwork for continued leadership among printing companies for the foreseeable future.

Principal Subsidiaries

Hokkaido Dai Nippon Printing Co., Ltd.; Tohoku Dai Nippon Printing Co., Ltd.; Tokai Dai Nippon Printing Co., Ltd.; Shikoku Dai Nippon Printing Co., Ltd.; Kyushu Dai Nippon

Printing Co., Ltd.; DNP Media Create Co., Ltd.; DNP Media Create Kansai Co., Ltd.; Dai Nippon Art Co., Ltd.; Dai Nippon Uni Process Co., Ltd.; Dai Nippon Offset Co., Ltd.; Dai Nippon Ellio Co., Ltd.; I.M.S. Dai Nippon Co., Ltd.; Multi Print Co., Ltd.; Dai Nippon Seihon Co., Ltd.; Dai Nippon Printing Technopack Co., Ltd.; Dai Nippon Printing Technopack Kansai Co., Ltd.; Dai Nippon Printing Technopack Yokohama Co., Ltd.; Dai Nippon Printing Fine Electronics Co., Ltd.; Dai Nippon Printing Precision Device Co., Ltd; Dai Nippon Jushi Co., Ltd.; Dai Nippon Polymer Co., Ltd.; Dai Nippon Cup Co., Ltd.; Dai Nippon Hoso Co., Ltd.; Sagami Yoki Co., Ltd.; SP Dai Nippon Co., Ltd.; DNP AV Center Co., Ltd.; DNP Digitalcom Co., Ltd.; DNP Space Design Co., Ltd.; D-Square Inc.; Dai Nippon LSI Design Co., Ltd.; F.D.P. Dai Nippon Co., Ltd.; DNP Advanced Industrial Supplies Co.,Ltd.; Hokkaido Coca-Cola Bottling Co., Ltd.; The Inctec Inc.; Dai Nippon Shoji Co, Ltd.; D.N.K.Co., Ltd.; Direc Co., Ltd.; Kyoiku Shuppan Co., Ltd.; Trans Art Inc.; DNP Archives.com Co., Ltd.; MyPoint.com Japan Co., Ltd.; Dai Nippon Printing Accounting System Co., Ltd.; DNP Human Service Co., Ltd.; DNP Techno Research Co., Ltd.; Dai Nippon Kaihatsu Co., Ltd.; Uzumine Country Club Co., Ltd.; Shiobara Green Village Co., Ltd.; DNP Graphica Co., Ltd.; DNP Data Techno Co., Ltd.; Dai Nippon Printing Kenzai Co., Ltd.; DNP Information Systems Co., Ltd.; DNP Logistics Co., Ltd.; DNP Facility Service Co., Ltd.

Principal Competitors

DuPont Photomasks, Inc.; Quebecor World Inc.; Toppan Printing Co., Ltd.

Further Reading

Brown-Humes, Christopher, ''Smartcard Group Claims Global Lead,'' *Financial Times* (London), May 16, 1997, p. 07.

''Dai Nippon Printing Forms On-line Pre-Press Alliance,'' *Nikkei Weekly,* June 26, 1996, p.10.

''Dai Nippon Printing to Sell Patented Tech to Other Firms Via Internet,'' *AFX-Asia,* February 24, 2002.

''Dai Nippon's Presses Printing up Profit: Company Expects 48th Straight Record Profit Despite Nation's Sagging Business Performance,'' *Nikkei Weekly,* March 9, 1998, p.13.

Frank, Jerome P., ''Asia Printers Gearing Up for Move into U.S.,'' *Publishers Weekly,* June 29, 1984.

Harney, Alexandra, ''Dai Nippon Sees Profit Boost from US Units,'' *Financial Times* (London), September 8, 1998, p. 34.

''Japan, U.S. Firms Enter Satellite Broadcast Venture,'' *Nikkei Weekly,* September 18, 1995, p. 8.

''Motorola and Dai Nippon Printing to Bring Digital Revolution to Business Forms and Labels,'' *Business Wire,* February 22, 2000.

Okawa, Kenji, ''Use of Printing Paper Expands,'' *Business JAPAN,* March 1989.

''Printing Companies Take to Multimedia; Digitization of Contents, Downturn in Printing Prompt Up-Market Moves,'' *Nikkei Weekly,* June 28, 1999, p. 11.

''Printing Firms Involved in Bid-Rigging on Parcel Labels,'' *Japan Economic Newswire,* November 21, 1992.

''Publishing Turning to Digital Chapter; Four Major Companies Preparing to Test Network to Distribute Magazines, Comics, Books Electronically,'' *Nikkei Weekly,* October 5, 1998, p. 9.

—Scott M. Lewis
—update: Erin Brown

Daishowa Paper Manufacturing Co., Ltd.

4-1-1, Imai
Fuji City, Shizuoka 417
Japan
Telephone: (0545) 30-3000
Fax: (0545) 32-0005
Web site: http://www.daishowa.co.jp

Wholly Owned Subsidiary of Nippon Unipac Holding
Incorporated: 1938
Employees: 3,255
Sales: ¥3.18 billion (2001)
NAIC: 322122 Newsprint Mills; 322121 Paper (Except
  Newsprint) Mills; 322130 Paperboard Mills; 321219
  Reconstituted Wood Product Manufacturing

An independent public company for much of its history, Daishowa Paper Manufacturing Co., Ltd. had become the second largest paper manufacturer in Japan by 1990, when it produced about 2.5 million metric tons of paper and paperboard and generated approximately 10 percent of Japan's paper production. Known for the diversity of its operations, at its height the company's businesses included newsprint, kraft paper, and paperboard. The firm also manufactured laminated particleboard and operated forestry and related businesses. Daishowa operated five mills and a building-materials plant in Japan, and several other mills in Canada, the United States, and Australia. However, steady losses throughout the mid- to late 1990s, combined with a series of corporate scandals, shook the company to its foundation, and at the dawn of the new century Daishowa found itself in financial peril. In 2001, plagued by significant debt, rising production costs, and increased competition, Daishowa Paper became a wholly owned subsidiary of Nippon Unipac, a joint holding company formed with Nippon Paper Industries.

The Early Decades: 1921–50

Daishowa traces it origins back to Saito Ltd., a brokerage firm supplying raw materials to the paper industry, founded in 1921 by Chiichiro Saito. In 1922 the company became Saito Brothers Co. and the business expanded to include paper sales.

In March 1927 Saito Ltd. established Showa Paper Company with a capitalization of ¥100,000 and began producing paper and paperboard at Yoskinaga. Shortly thereafter, in 1933, Saito Ltd. built a mill in Suzukawa for the production of kraft paper.

War between Japan and China broke out in July 1937, and in September Japan's government approved two economic-control laws. The Temporary Capital Adjustment Act curtailed the establishment of companies, capital increases, payments, bond flotations, and long-term loans. The Temporary Export and Import Commodities Measures gave the government control of the import and export of raw materials. In 1938, nevertheless, with a capitalization of ¥5.5 million, Saito Ltd. merged with four other Shizuoka companies to form Daishowa Paper Manufacturing Company. The Saito family retained control of the new company. One year later, the Suzukawa mill became the first integrated kraft paper mill in Japan.

Japan's pulp and paper industry hit its peak wartime capacity in 1940, when its paper output was 1.7 million tons. Industry in Japan declined steadily as the war dragged on, and in 1941 Japan provoked a war in the Pacific with the attack on Pearl Harbor. By 1946 the overall production of the Japanese pulp and paper industry had shrunk to 231,190 tons, less than 20 percent of what it had been in 1940. Despite this gloomy portent, Daishowa would ride the tsunami of Japan's fierce industrial and economic recovery, landing safely on the shores of mega-prosperity with many of its fellow industrial companies. The Allied powers readily aided Japan's fast-paced growth by their postwar control of the powerful ancient Japanese business monopolies, the *zaibatsu*. In 1937 the top three *zaibatsu* controlled 65 percent of pulp and 83 percent of the paper industry; by 1950 these figures were reduced to 39 percent and 57 percent, respectively. With the democratization of industry in Japan, there erupted fierce competition in most industries, which spurred rapid technological expansion and the building of new facilities.

Rapid Growth Under Aggressive Leadership of Ryoei Saito: 1950s–60s

It was at this time that Ryoei Saito, a young businessman and Chiichiro Saito's son, assumed leadership at Daishowa. The

Company Perspectives:

Since our foundation in 1938, we have been offering the products that satisfied the stringent demands of our customer, as a comprehensive manufacturer of paper and paperboard. Also, we are proud of being a good corporate citizen maintaining good relationships with the people and areas where we have our production facilities.

On March 30, 2001, Daishowa Paper Manufacturing Co., Ltd. and Nippon Paper Industries Co., Ltd. became wholly owned subsidiaries of Nippon Unipac Holding. With a spirit of trust and respect in mind, Daishowa and Nippon are both determined to integrate two operations. We believe that the integration will improve our capability to meet our customers' diversified needs and increase our competitiveness.

In response to the many resource and environmental challenges we face, we will pursue the improvements of paper recycling and energy cost. It is our strongest desire to pursue policies that promote the harmonious coexistence of corporate activity and nature by giving special consideration to environmental conservation and cultural contributions.

Under a new management structure, Daishowa Paper will make efforts to meet the expectations of our business associates and to contribute to social and cultural roles through our corporate activities.

We would like to thank you for your continued support and cooperation.

younger Saito led his family-controlled, publicly traded company in a violent struggle against three kingpins of the Japanese paper establishment, Oji Paper Company, Jujo Paper Company, and Honshu Paper Company. This trio had been created from Oji Paper, part of the Mitsui *zaibatsu*, when Oji Paper was divided after World War II. In 1950, five years after the end of the war, construction of the Fuji mill began, and production started in 1953. In 1960 Daishowa started production of coated paper. In the same year, production was begun on a mill in Shiraoi that was to become one of Daishowa's largest integrated mills, producing pulp, paper, and paperboard. Saito's aggressive price cutting and rapidly increasing market share may have appeared uncouth to the Japanese, but by 1965 Daishowa had seized the number two spot among Japanese papermakers.

Japan's economy continued to ride high, peaking from 1965 to 1973, when production of paper and paperboard mushroomed 10 to 11 percent annually. The Iwanu mill was built in 1967. Daishowa imported its first U.S. woodchips in 1965. Daishowa Paper Trading Co., Ltd. was established as an independent sales organization in 1967, the same year that Harris Daishowa (Australia) Pty., Ltd., the corporation's Australian subsidiary, was established. In 1968 Daishowa Pulp Manufacturing Co., Ltd. was founded, followed by Daishowa-Marubeni International Ltd., in Canada in 1969, and Daishowa Uniboard Co., Ltd. in 1970.

Relentless Expansion in the 1970s and 1980s

During the late 1960s and early 1970s Japan began to pay the price for its dynamic resurgence. One particularly disturbing

cost was the pollution caused by its bustling industry. The Japanese government began to crack down on *kogai*, or pollution. In Shizouka Prefecture, there was particular trouble with toxic sludge on the bottom of Tagonoura Bay, for which the government held Daishowa responsible. Daishowa, like most industrial companies, complied with government demands for environmental protection, in particular for protecting water against pollution.

As environmental issues continued to galvanize public outcry, many businesses converted to the use of recycled paper. By the early 1990s, demand for recycled paper was growing faster than supply, and Daishowa was in tune with the trend. Daishowa had been recycling pulp since 1959, when it started producing de-inked pulp (DIP) from old newspapers at the Fuji mill. Progressive efforts to develop higher-quality recycled pulp resulted in the formation of a project in 1985 that concentrated on improving the de-inking process. In 1988 the resulting improved system was installed in a new plant at Yoshinaga that produced a superior DIP. In 1990 Daishowa had 13 de-inking facilities in four of its Japanese mills; it produced 2,000 tons a day of recycled pulp for use in making paperboard and paper. Construction of two more such facilities was planned for 1991, adding capacity for an additional 330 tons per day.

The environmental crackdown of the 1970s and the oil crisis of 1973 were followed by a severe general recession. Average annual growth in the pulp and paper market shrank to a mere 1.1 percent from 1973 through 1982. Daishowa, nevertheless, showed a striking increase in sales and profitability from 1978 to 1979, when it rose in international status from 37th to 20th place in pulp and paper companies worldwide. Daishowa ranked fifth among companies outside North America, and third among those in Japan. Its sales were $1.3 billion; earnings were $14.5 million.

Despite the oil crisis and the ensuing financial difficulties, Daishowa continued its program of unabated expansion. Having just established foreign holdings in the United States and Canada, in 1980 it upgraded its facilities at Iwanuma to lower the weight of its newsprint, in keeping with the industry trend toward lighter papers. The mill would have a capacity of 360,000 tons per day of newsprint in addition to 120,000 tons per day of coated paper. In addition, Daishowa installed a machine to produce carbonless copy paper at Yoshinaga, following the trend set by Taio Paper—now Daio Paper—earlier in the year. These expansions came at a time when imports to Japan were rising despite the weakening Japanese demand for paper. From 1977 through 1982, imports rose an average of 17 percent per year. Although imports ultimately comprised only 2 percent to 4 percent of total Japanese consumption, newsprint and kraft linerboard, two of Daishowa's specialties, represented 70 percent of total imports, accounting for 8.9 percent of the newsprint, and 14.5 percent of the kraft linerboard consumed in Japan.

If import statistics did their job to rattle the pulp and paper business, other accumulated industry-wide expenditures combined to ensure the industry's decline in the early 1980s. Excessive borrowing, expensive environmental-protection programs, and escalating energy costs took their toll. Daishowa, sporting its own portfolio of financial mistakes, became a casualty of the accelerating decline, dropping from its 1979 status as third

Key Dates:

1921: Saito Ltd., a brokerage firm supplying raw materials to the paper industry, is founded by Chiichiro Saito.

1922: The company becomes Saito Brothers Co. and the business expands to include paper sales.

1927: Saito Ltd. establishes Showa Paper Company with a capitalization of ¥100,000 and begins producing paper and paperboard at Yoskinaga.

1933: Saito Ltd. builds a mill in Suzukawa for the production of kraft paper.

1938: Saito Ltd. merges with four other Shizuoka companies to form Daishowa Paper Manufacturing.

1960: Daishowa starts production of coated paper; production begins on a mill in Shiraoi that would become one of Daishowa's largest integrated mills, producing pulp, paper, and paperboard.

1967: Daishowa Paper Trading Co., Ltd. is established as an independent sales organization; Harris Daishowa (Australia) Pty., Ltd., an Australian subsidiary, is also established.

1968: Daishowa Pulp Manufacturing Co., Ltd. is founded.

1969: Daishowa-Marubeni International Ltd. is founded in Canada in 1969.

1970: Daishowa Uniboard Co., Ltd. is founded.

1986: After a forced resignation, Ryoei Saito is able to regain control of the business, expelling his brother Kikuzo Saito from Daishowa.

1994: Shogo Nakano becomes first non-Saito family president of Daishowa.

2001: Daishowa Paper becomes a wholly owned subsidiary of Nippon Unipac Holding, a joint company formed with Nippon Paper Industries.

largest papermaker in Japan to last place among the top ten in 1982. As profits slid downward, Ryoei Saito was forced to resign and cede control of Daishowa to its principal creditor, the Sumitomo Bank, which appointed some of its own representatives to the Daishowa board. The Sumitomo Bank's rescue of Daishowa was not unique in Japan, where a firm typically cultivated a close relationship with one principal bank, relying on it for most borrowing needs. This bank maintains all financial information on the company and has substantial influence in its management. Nevertheless, Ryoei Saito did not take kindly to the management changes the Sumitiomo Bank deemed appropriate. For its part, Sumitomo found that in addition to overspending in new production facilities, Ryoei Saito had used approximately $1 billion of corporate funds to build his art collection, buy golf courses, and play the stock market. The bank compelled Saito to sell off much of the highly regarded art collection, and he begrudgingly resigned.

In 1983 Daishowa announced that it would repay the Sumitomo Bank's ¥23.5 billion in loans by June of that year and then terminate the relationship with Sumitomo. The move shocked the Japanese business community, in which bank-company relations were likely to last indefinitely. In June 1986, Ryoei Saito was able to regain control of the business, expelling his brother Kikuzo Saito from Daishowa's presidency and ousting a board

director who had close ties with Sumitomo. Kikuzo Saito later claimed that Ryoei Saito had borrowed substantially from Daishowa funds for his own personal use. The Sumitomo Bank remained one of Daishowa's major institutional shareholders, with 3.9 percent of Daishowa's stock in 1990.

Once back at Daishowa, this time as honorary chairman of the company, Ryoei Saito stayed true to his established interests and style. In May 1990, Saito caused a flurry in the international art market by purchasing the two most expensive paintings ever sold by auction: Renoir's *At the Moulin de la Galette,* which sold for $78.1 million, and Vincent van Gogh's *Portrait of Dr. Gachet,* purchased for $82.5 million. The paintings were snapped up within three days of each other, and although Saito deemed his shopping spree "no big deal" he also granted that his funds were borrowed against the collateral of Daishowa real estate.

In the early 1990s the Saito family continued to control 20 percent to 40 percent of the firm; in combination with their real estate holdings, the family's net worth was somewhere around $1 billion. In an effort to prevent dilution of the Saito family's stake, Daishowa managed to expand during the late 1980s without issuing new stock, principally by taking on additional loans. This strategy more than doubled its debt between 1987 and 1990 to $3 billion, more than five times shareholders' equity. In 1990 profits dropped 35 percent to $35 million.

Kiminori Saito, nevertheless, continued his father's aggressive expansion of Daishowa, probably fueling the growth with family resources from Ashitaka Rinsan Kogyo, the family holding company. In April 1990 that firm spent $49 million to buy Daishowa's share of a 23-year-old Australian eucalyptus-chip venture with C. Itoh. It also purchased 25 percent of the preferred shares of Daishowa's new pulp mill in Alberta, Canada. On the other hand, a Japanese corporate research firm indicated that Ashitaka's 1990 accumulated debt of $300 million was created by borrowing against the collateral of Daishowa. Whatever the stability and origins of its financial underpinnings, Daishowa's expansion showed no signs of slowing down during the early 1990s. Its domestic expansion budget was a healthy $330 million in 1991.

In addition to its development on its home turf, Daishowa aggressively expanded its overseas operations. In 1990 its major joint-venture operations included Cariboo Pulp & Paper Company, a softwood bleached kraft pulp mill, and Quesnel River Pulp Company, a chemi-thermo-mechanical pulp mill, both located in British Columbia, Canada. Foreign acquisitions made by Daishowa during 1988 included a $78 million investment for Daishowa America Port Angeles mill, in Washington state. The company upgraded the mill with another $52 million investment. In addition to producing newsprint, paperboard, pulp, lumber, and chemicals, as of 1990, the mill provided 20 percent of the paper used in U.S. telephone directories. The company spent an estimated $500 million to purchase the North American assets of Reed International, a Quebec mill chiefly generating newsprint for Canadian and U.S. newspapers such as the *Washington Post* and the *New York Post.* In 1988, Daishowa started construction of its Peace River Pulp mill, a major bleached kraft pulp mill in Alberta, Canada. In early 1990, Daishowa bought a lumber mill from Canadian Forest Products to supply the plant, which began operations in the summer of 1990.

Imperiled by Scandal, Recession, and Insolvency in the 1990s

By April 1991 it appeared that Daishowa's reckless expansion program had left the company perilously overextended. Indeed, less than a year after Ryoei Saito's sensational acquisitions of the Renoir and Van Gogh paintings, the company reported equally extravagant losses—¥14.9 billion, against revenues of ¥352 billion—in the fiscal year ending in March 1991, some of the worst figures in the history of the company. Daishowa's poor performance was due in part to crippling interest payments associated with ¥440 billion of debt. Desperate to relieve some of this burden, Daishowa had no choice but to put a freeze on future investments and begin selling off land, securities, and other assets. Further, with the entire Japanese paper industry suffering from deflated market prices resulting from overcapacity—an overcapacity that Daishowa had helped create—the company moved to suspend operations at several of its Japanese plants during the summer of 1991 in an effort to reduce its inventories.

In September 1991, the recession in the paper market was not lifting, and it was clear that Daishowa would need to take more drastic measures to regain stability. The company launched an extensive restructuring program aimed at cutting its workforce by 40 percent. To accomplish this, Daishowa planned to liquidate its Fuji plant in Shizowka Prefecture and other unprofitable domestic plants, and sell off its recently completed Peace River pulp mill in Canada. The company did not reach a deal on the Peace River plant until late in 1992, after posting losses for the second year in a row. Finally, in September of that year, Daishowa and Marubeni Corporation, already involved in other joint ventures, agreed to share 50–50 stakes in the plant, a deal that yielded ¥110 billion for Daishowa.

Daishowa's recovery efforts suffered a heavy blow in November 1993, when Ryoei Saito was arrested on bribery charges in conjunction with his land-development projects. In February 1994, with Daishowa's de facto leader continuing to jeopardize the company's welfare, the board of directors appointed Shogo Nakano president of Daishowa. Formerly Daishowa's vice-president, Nakano had been instrumental in designing the company's restructuring program. By placing the first ever non-Saito family member at the helm of the company, the move was designed to improve the transparency of corporate activity. Within six weeks of Nakano's appointment, more than ten Saito family members were purged from their executive positions at the company.

In spite of a brief return to profitability in 1996, when the company enjoyed overall sales of ¥323.2 billion, by the late 1990s Daishowa once again found itself deep in debt. In 2000, facing increased competition from imports and rising production costs, Daishowa entered into negotiations with rival paper giant Nippon Paper to form a joint holding company, with the aim of streamlining its operations and restoring itself to profitability. The new company, dubbed Nippon Unipac Holding, would be the largest paper manufacturer in Japan, with expected annual sales of ¥1.21 trillion. The merger became official on March 31, 2001. Although the formation of Nippon Unipac effectively ended Daishowa's long history as an independent entity, a number of its subsidiaries both at home and abroad continued to bear the Daishowa name, while operating under the Nippon Unipac corporate umbrella.

Principal Competitors

Hokuetsu Paper Mills, Ltd.; Mitsubishi Paper Mills Limited; Oji Paper Co., Ltd.

Further Reading

"Daishowa Paper Unit Declared Bankrupt," *Jiji Press Ticker Service*, June 22, 2002.

Hara, Nobuko, "After Van Gogh, Daishowa Set to Show £55m Loss," *Independent,* April 7, 1991, p.8.

Klamann, Edmond, "Debt-Ridden Daishowa Restructures; No. 2 Papermaker Plans to Shred Work Force, Sell Off Recently Built Canadian Pulp Plant," *Nikkei Weekly,* September 7, 1991, p. 8.

McKinnon, Ian, "Daishowa Loses Lubicon Case," *Financial Post,* April 15, 1998, p. 09.

Mizuno, Yuji, "Daishowa Appoints 'Outsider' As President: In a Bid to Promote Transparency, Paper Maker Appoints Non-Saito Family Member As President," *Nikkei Weekly,* February 14, 1994, p. 9.

——, "Daishowa Derailed by Executive's Arrest; Bribery Scandal Seen Hampering Efforts by Papermaker to Restructure, Repay Debts," *Nikkei Weekly,* November 15, 1993, p. 12.

Murayama, Mari, and Tak Kumakura, "Nippon Paper to Buy Daishowa: $1-Billion Accord," *National Post* (Canada), March 28, 2000, p. C14.

"Papermakers' Merger Runs into Some Opposition; Daio Will Try to Prevent Daishowa from Unifying with Nippon Paper," *Nikkei Weekly,* April 3, 2000, p.10.

Swoboda, Frank, "U.S. Paper Mill's Japanese Owners Win Union Allies; Daishowa Blends Two Cultures in Its Management Approach," *Washington Post*, October 27, 1991, p. H1.

Terazono, Emiko, "Daishowa Stays in Red Despite Shake-Up," *Financial Times* (London), May 31, 1995, p. 29.

Wagstyl, Stefan, "Daishowa Sells Off Assets to Cover Pre-Tax Losses," *Financial Times* (London), May 30, 1991, p. 31.

—Elaine Belsito
—update: Erin Brown

Davide Campari-Milano S.p.A.

Via Filippo Turati 27
20121 Milan
Italy
Telephone: +39-026-2251
Fax: +39-026-225312
Web site: http://www.campari.com

Public Company
Incorporated: 1860
Employees: 1,346
Sales: EUR 660.6 million ($650 million) (2002)
Stock Exchanges: Milan
Ticker Symbol: CPR
NAIC: 312140 Distilleries; 424820 Wine and Distilled Alcoholic Beverage Merchant Wholesalers

Long a single-product company, Davide Campari-Milano S.p.A. has transformed itself into one of the world's top ten spirits and beverages specialists. The company is famed for its Campari Bitters, which remains a world leader in its category after nearly 150 years. Yet, through a series of acquisitions in the 1990s and 2000s, Campari has built a strong stable of internationally recognized brands, including Cinzano, SKYY Vodka, Cynar, Ouzo 12, Gold Cup, and Gregson's. Other brands in the group's stable include winemakers Sella & Mosca and Zedda Piras, both acquired in 2002, and Biancosarti. The company also produces a line of soft drinks, including Lemonsoda, Oransoda, Pelmosoda, and the nonalcoholic aperitif Crodino. In addition to its own brands, Campari holds manufacturing and distribution licenses for a number of brands, including Glenfiddich, Grant's, Henkell Trocken, Lipton Ice Tea, and Jägermeister. Spirits represent nearly 65 percent of the company's sales, which topped EUR 660 million ($650 million) in 2002. Soft drinks contributed more than 19 percent, and wines added nearly 15 percent to sales. Campari distributes to more than 190 countries; Italy, however, remains the group's single largest market, at more than 50 percent of sales. Davide Campari-Milano has been controlled by the Garavoglia family since the 1970s; the family reduced its holding to 51 percent after listing the company on the Milan stock exchange in 2001.

Recipe for Success in the 19th Century

Born in 1828, Gaspare Campari began an apprenticeship as a "maitre licoriste" (drink master) at the Bass Bar in Turin, then an important center for Italy's liqueur market. Campari worked alongside another famed name in drinks, Alessandro Martini, who went on to lend his name not only to the famous vermouth, but to the cocktail as well.

Campari left the Bass Bar to begin developing his own drink recipes and in 1860 opened his own café in Novara called Caffé dell'Amicizia. In that year, to celebrate the unification of Italy, Campari created a new drink recipe, a bitters that contained some 60 ingredients, including herbs and spices, tree barks, and fruit peels. The resulting recipe—which remained a closely guarded family and then company secret—created a distinctive red-colored, mid-proof aperitif that quickly became known throughout Italy.

Campari decided to move to Milan two years later to tap into the expansion potential of the Lombard region capital. Then, in 1867, Campari opened a second Milan café, in the newly built Galleria Vittorio Emanuele. The café became a popular gathering point for Italy's elite, including then King Vittorio Emmanuel.

Campari was later joined by Davide Campari, a son from Campari's second marriage. Davide Campari was to prove instrumental in establishing the Campari name's international renown. The younger Campari became a fixture at the family's café, as orders for bottles of Campari Bitters poured in from throughout Italy. Meanwhile, Gaspare Campari continued adding new recipes, launching a wide variety of spirits and liqueurs. None, however, were to enjoy the same success as his bitters.

Until the end of the century, the company produced its aperitifs and other recipes at two smaller plants. The rising demand for its bitters encouraged the family to open its first large-scale production plant, in Sesto San Giovanni, in 1904. Meanwhile, Davide Campari proved an innovative marketer. As demand for the aperitif swelled, the company began requiring that bars and cafés wishing to serve the drink also display advertising bearing the Campari Bitters name. Davide Campari then began commissioning artists to create advertising posters, a move that created many classic advertisements.

Company Perspectives:

The Campari Group is one of the world's leading alcoholic beverage companies with more than 140 years of experience in the industry, producing and selling brands such as Campari, SKYY Vodka and Cynar in the spirits segment, and Cinzano and Sella & Mosca in the wines segment.

Davide Campari was also the driving force behind the company's growing international sales, after the group began exports at the dawn of the 20th century. As Campari legend has it, Davide Campari had fallen in love with Italian opera singer Lina Cavaliere, who was leaving for Nice soon after they met. Campari decided to follow her, telling his family he was leaving to set up export sales to France. Cavaliere's career led her to travel around the world, and Campari accompanied her, each time setting up imports of Campari Bitters in the new markets. In this way, it is said that the company's sales spread across Europe and to Russia and the United States.

Davide Campari took over as head of the family business at the beginning of the 1920s and led the company into a new direction. Instead of maintaining a diversified drinks portfolio, Campari decided to build the company on the basis of its popular Campari aperitif, as well as its companion cordial liqueur version. The company now turned to developing its production capacity to meet the growing international demand, opening its first foreign plant, in Nanterre, France, in 1923. Several years later, the company opened a second foreign plant, in Lugano, Switzerland.

In the 1930s, Campari hit on a new success. Campari Bitters had inspired a wide array of cocktails, including the famed Negroni and Americano cocktails. Yet by far the most popular way of drinking the bitters, at least in Italy, was mixed with soda. In 1932, the company debuted its own blend of Campari and soda, packaged in a distinctive cone-shaped bottle. The result, which was dubbed, appropriately enough, Campari Soda, became a new success for the company, and was held to be the world's first pre-mix packaged drink.

Joining the Consolidation Race in the New Century

Davide Campari died in 1936; ten years later, the company incorporated as Davide Campari-Milano S.p.A. The company remained focused on this core product for most of the rest of the century, even after Domenico Garavoglia gained control of it in the 1970s. Sales grew especially strongly during the 1960s and 1970s, as Campari became synonymous with a newly developing, "sophisticated" cocktail trend.

Although Italy remained the company's largest sales base, Campari's distribution network had brought the brand to more than 80 countries by then. To support this growth, Campari opened a new production plant in 1987, in Barueri, Brazil. At the beginning of the 1990s, the company also entered a series of production and distribution joint ventures with Veuve-Clicquot, Marnier-Lapostolle, and William Grant & Sons.

The rapid consolidation of the global drinks market, and especially the creation of a small number of dominant players,

such as Diageo and Allied Domecq, forced Campari to make a choice between joining the race for market size, or simply defending its core, but niche, product. Campari, now led by Luca Garavoglia, decided to pursue the former option.

Using the strong cash flow generated from the sales of its products—at the time limited to Campari, CampariSoda, and Cordial Campari—the company launched an aggressive acquisition campaign in the middle of the 1990s. The company's first purchase came in 1995, when it acquired the Italian drinks portfolio of The Netherlands' Koninklijke BolsWessanen. The acquisition gave Campari a strong list of soft drinks, including popular Italian brands Lemonsoda and Oransoda, and the nonalcoholic aperitif Crodino. The company also gained control of two brands, Cynar and Biancosarti, with a strong international market. In exchange, BolsWessanen acquired a 35 percent stake in the company. That year, the company also began distributing the Ricadonna brand of Asti sparkling wines, with sales especially targeted at the Australian and New Zealand markets.

The BolsWessanen agreement also led to Campari's acquisition of the Italian production and distribution rights for the German bitters brand Jägermeister in 1996. In that year, also, the company gained the distribution rights to the popular Glenfiddich and Grant's whiskey brands.

Campari's next move came in 1998, when it acquired a 10 percent stake in fast-growing U.S. vodka brand Skyy Spirits. Under the purchase agreement, Campari obtained access to Skyy's distribution network in the United States. That year, Campari gained the rights to distribute the Lipton Ice Tea brand in Italy from Unilever Italia.

In 1999, Campari took a short break from its acquisition drive to launch a new product, Pelmosoda, which, based on grapefruits, rounded out its portfolio of citrus-based soft drinks. The company then returned to the external growth trail, picking up the Ouzo 12 brand of the popular Greek anise-based drink from United Distillers and Vintners (UDV), part of Diageo, then in the process of shedding a number of its noncore "tail end" brands.

Campari returned to UDV for its next shopping spree in December 1999, when it agreed to pay EUR 106.5 million ($107 million) to acquire Cinzano and its portfolio of wines and vermouth. Cinzano, which had been in operation since 1757, had by then established itself as the world's number two vermouth brand (behind Martini).

Campari continued adding brands at the beginning of the 21st century, acquiring the distribution rights for the Swiss market from Germany's Henkell Söhnlein for its Henkell Trocken sparkling wines and its Gorbatschow Vodka. By the end of 2000, Campari began preparations for a public listing. In the meantime, the company continued building up its portfolio, returning to UDV to buy its Brazilian and Uruguay spirits and wine brands for EUR 113 million in 2001. That acquisition added such brands as Dreher, Old Eight, Liebfraumilch, Gregson's, and Druty's to Campari's impressive and well-balanced list.

Campari went public in July of that year, as Wessanen sold off the majority of its shares. The Garavoglia family nonetheless retained control of 51 percent of the group's stock. With

Key Dates:

1860: Gaspare Campari opens a café in Novara, Italy, and introduces his own aperitif recipe.
1862: Campari moves his café to Milan and begins selling Campari to other cafés.
1867: Campari opens second café in Milan's new Galleria Vittorio Emanuele.
1904: The company opens its first large-scale production plant, Sesto San Giovanni, as the company begins exports.
1923: Davide Campari takes over the company and focuses it on a single Campari recipe; the company opens its first foreign production plant, in Nanterre, France.
1932: The company introduces CampariSoda, the world's first pre-mix cocktail, which becomes a company bestseller.
1946: The company incorporates as Davide Campari-Milano S.p.A.
1970s: Domenici Garavoglia acquires control of the company, but maintains its single-product focus.
1987: The company opens a new production facility in Brazil.
1995: Campari begins an acquisition program in order to acquire scale in the rapidly consolidating global drinks industry; the first acquisition is of Bols-Wessanen's Italian soft drinks portfolio.
1996: The company acquires the Italian distribution rights to Jägermeister, Glenfiddich, and Grant's brands.
1998: The company acquires a minority stake in Skyy Spirits, giving it access to the company's U.S. distribution network.
1999: The company acquires Ouzo 12 and Cinzano.
2001: Campari goes public on the Milan stock exchange; the company acquires a portfolio of brands in Brazil and Uruguay from United Distillers & Vintners; majority control of Skyy Spirits is acquired.
2002: The company acquires Sella & Mosca and Zedda Piras.
2003: The company acquires the Ricadonna brand.

new access to capital, Campari prepared to step up its growth. In December 2001, the company agreed to purchase an additional 50 percent of Skyy Spirits, paying $207 million to take control of that group, which by then had captured one of the top spots in the U.S. vodka market. Two months later, Campari struck again, this time acquiring two Sardinia-region companies, winemaker Sella & Mosca and spirits brand Zedda Piras. The company then announced its intention to pursue more Italian wine region acquisitions.

Campari's latest flurry of acquisitions had enabled it, meanwhile, to post a revenue increase of an impressive 32 percent, as the company's sales topped EUR 660 million in 2002. The company showed no sign of slowing down in its drive to join the world's global drinks majors. By July 2003, the company had made good on its promise of pursuing more Italian wine brands when it paid EUR 11.3 million to acquire Ricadonna brand from the Bersano-Ricadonna wine group. That purchase gave Campari control of the company's Asti sparkling wines, which had grown into market leadership in Australia and New Zealand, while leaving Italian distribution of the brand under Bersano's control. Campari's thirst for brand expansion appeared certain to continue strongly into the next decade.

Principal Subsidiaries

Campari Deutschland GmbH; Campari do Brasil Ltda.; Campari France S.A.; Campari International S.A.M. (Monaco); Campari Italia S.p.A.; Campari Schweiz A.G.; Campari-Crodo S.p.A.; Francesco Cinzano & C.ia S.p.A.; Gregson's S.A. (Uruguay); N. Kaloyannis Bros. A.E.B.E. (Greece); S.A.M.O. S.p.A.; Sella & Mosca S.p.A.; Skyy Spirits, LLC (58.9%); Zedda Piras S.p.A.

Principal Competitors

Allied Domecq Netherlands BV; Diageo Plc; Seagram Company Ltd.; Fortune Brands, Inc.; Jim Beam Brands Worldwide Inc.; Brown Forman Corporation.

Further Reading

Boland, Vincent, "Campari Takes Control of Skyy Vodka Brand," *Financial Times,* December 14, 2001, p. 27.
Homer, Eric, "Salute! Campari Pours a $150 Million Round Via Deutsche Bank," *Private Placement Letter,* June 23, 2003.
Kapner, Fred, "Campari IPO Mixes Well with Italian Market," *Financial Times,* July 4, 2001, p. 24.
"A Lot of Bottle," *Economist,* June 30, 2001, p. 7.
McCann, Paul, "Cinzano and Campari Boogie Back into the Limelight," *Independent,* January 12, 1998, p. 3.
Walsh, Dominic, "Campari in Bid for Cinzano," *Times* (London), September 21, 1999, p. 29.

—M.L. Cohen

Deschutes Brewery, Inc.

901 S.W. Simpson
Bend, Oregon 97702
U.S.A.
Telephone: (541) 385-8606
Fax: (541) 383-4505
Web site: http://www.deschutesbrewery.com

Private Company
Incorporated: 1988
Employees: 55
Sales: $29.2 million (2001)
NAIC: 312120 Breweries; 722110 Full-Service Restaurants

Deschutes Brewery, Inc. has been in the business of making handcrafted, traditional style beers since 1988. Unusual for its focus on marketing the Deschutes brand name rather than its individual brews, and for featuring a porter as its flagship product, the company distributes its Black Butte Porter, Mirror Lake Pale Ale, Cascade Ale, and Obsidian Stout in nearly a dozen western states.

An Old-Style Tradition Starting Anew in 1988

The Deschutes Brewery was founded in 1988 as a "brewpub" by Gary Fish, a newcomer both to Oregon and to brewing. Fish named his business for the county in which it is located and the river that flows through it. The first brewery to open in Bend, Oregon, it met at first with an uncertain reception. "People didn't know how to take us," Fish recalled in a *Bend Bulletin* article published in 1992. "A lot of people insisted we would never last."

The new brewpub hit a low spot in December of its first year, when ten straight batches of beer went bad due to a flaw in the brewery's design and had to be dumped. The grain mill was located directly over the mash tun, and airborne bacteria on the grain dust kept infecting the beer. Once the problem was solved, Deschutes beer began selling in Portland and Fish's dark, flavorful beer caught on. The brewery sold 310 barrels of beer its first year, far exceeding Fish's expectations of a few kegs of excess capacity to nearby central Oregon resorts.

Three years later, in 1992, Deschutes sold 3,954 barrels of its traditional style ales and lagers, two-thirds of which were distributed outside the company's restaurant in downtown Bend. According to company literature, Deschutes grew because of its emphasis upon "quality first ... [u]sing the highest quality ingredients available, and taking more time and more care in the brewing process ..." and because it emphasized restoring a sense of community through locally produced and distinctive ales and lagers. "We want people to feel like this is, in a lot of ways, theirs," Fish told *Bend Bulletin* in November 1992.

Deschutes beers were distinguished from the start by their full flavor, distinctive feel, and hop character. Brewmaster John Harris used only four ingredients: water, whole hops, malt, and yeast—all selected to be fresh and pure. The brewery's beers were either unfiltered or filtered and *kraeusened* (a traditional process that occurs when beer is blended with working *wort* [rapidly fermented beer] before bottling). It results in a complex, full-bodied flavor with natural carbonation, replacing flavor that is inevitably lost during filtration.

Deschutes drew on the European tradition of beer manufacturing lost during the growth of the large American breweries and rediscovered in the mid-1970s in California with the development of microbreweries. Despite the recession in the United States in the late 1980s and early 1990s, the domestic handcrafted beer industry began expanding at a rate of about 40 percent a year, having grown in momentum and popularity as it headed north. In 1980 there were fewer than ten microbreweries nationally; by 1990, there were 178. Yet microbreweries still accounted for only 1 percent of the national beer market by 1990 as opposed to Anheuser-Busch's 43 percent. In Oregon—which became home to the largest number of microbreweries nationally—sales of all handcrafted beers combined accounted for only 4 percent of total beer sales in the state in 1993.

The philosophy and practice of the microbrewery stood in opposition to that of the U.S. food and beverage industry which favored national marketing, franchising, uniformity, and advertising. Yet this opposition seemed to be the very reason for the popularity of the trend. Microbreweries encouraged local distinction and nostalgia—a return to the time before Prohibition when locally operated breweries were as common as hardware stores

Key Dates:

1988: Gary Fish founds Deschutes Brewery.
1993: Deschutes begins production in its new facilities.
1999: Deschutes expands its warehouse, production, and administrative space.

and bakeries in the United States. The renaissance of the micro-brewery occurred at the same time that domestic big brewers and premium importers were experiencing a decline in sales. In 1989 the national sale of imported beers had dropped off 8 percent.

Growth Despite an Industry Decline in the Early 1990s

By 1992 the Deschutes Brewery & Public House could not make enough beer to keep up with demand, although the company did not do any marketing. Ready to grow from a boutique brewery to a regional brewery, the company broke ground on a new 16,000-square-foot production brewery that, when completed in 1993, dwarfed its original Bond Street home. The new brewhouse was able to produce beer in 50-barrel or 1,575-gallon batches, an increase in capacity five times that of its original facility. Newer brewery equipment and technology made for more efficient brewing.

The new building was designed to be a landmark befitting the largest brewery in central Oregon, with a glass-front, three-story brew tower. Barley grain started at the top of the tower and flowed down through the mill and into the mixer, the mash tun, and brew kettle, before being pumped into the primary fermenter. The facility also included a bottling line, allowing Deschutes to enter into package sales for the first time. The new brewery took over much of the burden of production from the company's original facility, although the brewpub continued to produce beer for on-premises customers and to be the testing ground for new products. Scaled back in size, the original pub facilities were remodeled to include a restaurant and kitchen. The move to a production brewery represented a large step forward—from a small, craft-oriented pub to a manufacturing operation. Fish was optimistic when questioned about his company's growth in the November 1992 *Bend Bulletin*. "There's still a lot of market out there we have yet to begin serving . . . [and] I think that demand is going to continue to grow. The industry as a whole is in the toddler stage now."

The new facilities began production in 1993 under the direction of the new Deschutes brewmaster, former scientist Dr. Bill Pengelly. For the next several years, Bend's first brewery continued to grow, producing beers ranging in color from amber to deep red or smoky dark brown with flavors from creamy rich to fruity or tangy. Regular Deschutes brews were complemented by seasonal or holiday ales and lagers. Interviewed in the *Oregonian* in 1996 about the state of Oregon's microbrewery industry, Fish, as president of the Oregon Brewers Guild, commented, "This industry is changing so much, growing so fast, and it's still so young. . . . Our challenge is going to be keeping the industry craft-oriented, and we do that by focusing on our common issues instead of our differences."

Continued Growth in the Late 1990s

By the late 1990s the microbrewery industry was "finally coming of age," according to Fish in an April 1998 *Bend Bulletin* article. Microbreweries had about 3 percent of the national beer market and 8 percent of the market in the Northwest. As a result, carving out additional market share became more difficult. "It's going to slow down," Fish said. "We're going to see the top of the curve." The growth rate for the craft-brewing industry had peaked in 1994 and 1995, according to David Edgar of the Institute for Brewing Studies in an April 1999 *Oregonian* article, with a growth rate of 50 percent for each of the two years. By 1997 and 1998, growth had stalled.

But as the microbrewery craze lost steam nationwide and publicly owned breweries declined in share value, Deschutes Brewery was still going strong. In 1996 Deschutes produced 45,000 barrels of beer, up from 31,000 in 1995. Among craft brewers in Oregon it was second only to Widmer Brothers Brewing Company. Although most of the company's growth came from its existing markets in Oregon and Washington, in early 1997 it began selling beer in Hawaii and planned to enter the California market in the spring.

As Deschutes tapped into the West Coast market, it made plans to expand its new facilities, doubling the size, and installing automated equipment which required more skilled, higher-wage workers. However, despite increased capacity, the company remained focused on marketing only on the West Coast. "One of the mistakes that people in this industry made, I think, was that they tried to create national brands," Fish opined in a December 1997 *Oregonian* article.

Deschutes saw its annual sales grow 18 percent from 63,500 barrels in 1997 to 76,100 barrels in 1998, with distribution in close to ten western states. Its restaurant in downtown Bend still did good business, but contributed only 15 percent of the company's revenues. The fourth largest craft brewer in the Northwest in terms of volume continued to invest very little in advertising, choosing instead to put its efforts into developing a strong network of 75 distributors.

Although there were still more than 420 small brewers in the United States (up from 200 in 1994), more microbreweries closed than opened in the United States in 1999. Deschutes, its expansion completed, had the capacity to produce 120,000 barrels a day. In 2000 it replaced Widmer as the top selling brewery in Oregon and Washington. Black Butte Porter, the brewery's flagship brew, had captured a 90 percent share of the market for porters in the Northwest.

Deschutes brewed 102,000 gallons of beer and won two medals at the prestigious Brewery International Awards in 2001—gold for its Mirror Pond Pale Ale and silver for its Black

Butte Porter. A clear leader in the field of microbreweries and remarkable for its ongoing success, Deschutes continued in its strategy—unusual for its industry—of regional sales and branding focused on the Deschutes name rather than its individual beers.

Principal Competitors

Widmer Brothers Brewing; BridgePort Brewing; Full Sail Brewing Company; Oregon Brewing Company.

Further Reading

Bolt, Greg, ''Beer-Maker Brews Up Expansion,'' *Bend Bulletin*, November 1992, p. C1.

Foyston, John, ''Brewin' in the Background,'' *Oregonian*, October 11, 1996, p. 4.

——, ''Deschutes Brewing: Good Beers Come to Those Who Wait,'' *Oregonian*, June 25, 1999, p. 8.

Francis, Mike, ''Craft Brewing Loses Its Buzz,'' *Oregonian*, December 30, 1997, p. C1.

Freeman, Mike, ''Newcomer Steps Up to Community Plate,'' *Bend Bulletin*, April 5, 1998, p. 61.

Giegerich, Andy, ''Deschutes Brewery Barreling in Now As Northwest's No. 1,'' *Business Journal-Portland*, October 20, 2000, p. 3.

Hill, Jim, ''Brewers Fight for Their Lives,'' *Oregonian*, April 20, 1999, p. C1.

Khermouch, Gerry, ''Micro Marketing,'' *Brandweek*, December 11, 2000, p. 18.

—Carrie Rothburd

Dresdner Bank

Advice you can bank on

Dresdner Bank A.G.

Jurgen-Ponto-Platz 1
60301 Frankfurt
Germany
Telephone: +49-692-630
Fax: +49-692-63-4831
Web site: http://www.dresdner-bank.com

Public Company
Incorporated: 1872 as Dresden Bankhaus
Employees: 48,455
Total Assets: $448.81 billion (2002)
Stock Exchanges: German
Ticker Symbol: DRB
NAIC: 522110 Commercial Banking; 523110 Investment
Banking and Securities Dealing; 523120 Securities
Brokerage

The third largest bank in Germany and one of the leading international banks in Europe, Dresdner Bank A.G. operates over 1,100 branch offices in 60 nations. Dresdner offers an array of products and services for private and corporate customers, including lending and deposit activities, corporate financing, equity sales, and asset management. In 2001 Dresdner was acquired by Allianz AG, a global insurance provider that saw the takeover as a way of bolstering its financial management arm. Both Dresdner and Allianz have suffered since this merger because of problems with Dresdner's investment bank business, Dresdner Kleinwort Wasserstein.

The Early Years

When Carl Freiherr von Kaskel, Felix Freiherr, and Eugene Gutman opened the doors of Dresden Bankhaus for business in Dresden on December 1, 1872, the time was ripe for new banks in Germany. Before its victory over France in 1871 organized Germany as a modern nation-state, there had not even been standardized units of currency, weight, or measurement. The opportunity for economic growth was enormous, and the management team of Dresdner Bank seized it with a vengeance.

As a universal bank, Dresdner Bank was formulated to serve all of the economic needs of its community. The role of the big banks in Germany was closely related to developing industries and expanding commercial opportunities. Accordingly, Dresdner Bank expanded rapidly in its first decade through a series of acquisitions, liquidations, and absorptions of smaller institutions. Though sometimes criticized for being unusually willing to assume risks, the management team of Dresdner Bank, led especially by Eugene Gutman, quickly made Dresdner the number two financial institution in Germany, behind only Deutsche Bank.

In 1884 Dresdner Bank moved its headquarters from Dresden to Berlin and then spent the rest of the decade expanding even more vigorously. Seeing the potential for growth in foreign markets, Dresdner began opening interests in Asia and Italy. This eye for expansion would continue to make Dresdner grow until its foreign interests were lost after World War I. Dresdner's huge credit reserve, like that of the other large German banks, also helped Germany transform itself from a capital importing to a capital exporting economy during the 1880s.

Dresdner opened new branches in Hamburg in 1892 and in Bremen and London in 1895. The London branch was especially significant for the bank because London was the financial center of the world at that time; it gave the company 19 highly profitable years before the onset of World War I.

At this time Dresdner developed close relations with the electro-technical, rail, and oil industries, which allowed it to build, with Deutsche Bank, a railroad line from Constantinople to Ankara, then an important line of transportation. The foundation of the Central Bank for Railway Securities by Dresdner in 1898 further cemented the relationship between the bank and the railroad industry.

In the early years of the 20th century Dresdner's continuous expansion made it a true giant of German industry. Dresdner achieved unprecedented success in the deposit business between 1896 and 1908 largely through innovative marketing techniques and the bold move of offering higher interest rates to deposit customers to draw a profitable volume of business.

In the first decade of this century, Dresdner formed a community of interest with Schaffhausenschor Bankverein in 1903,

Company Perspectives:

We have set ourselves a full agenda for the years to come: we want to optimize our portfolio of businesses, and to reduce those activities that fail to meet our profitability targets. This is particularly relevant in view of the rapid development of our business environment, and the continued dynamic consolidation in the European financial services sector. Dresdner Bank is impressively positioned in its core business. This is particularly true in Private Clients and Asset Management, where we will pro-actively make use of the opportunities presented through growing wealth and structural changes in retirement provisions. We see additional potential in the diminishing distinction between banks and insurance companies, and the increasing integration of the respective products into a comprehensive range of financial services. We want to seize the opportunity to play an active role in this process.

opened stock companies to start trade with Asia and South America, formed 27 branches through absorption of smaller banks, and formed an alliance with the American bank J.P. Morgan and Company to engage in international finance.

Of the four endeavors, the community of interest with Schaffhausenschor increased Dresdner's power the most. As Dresdner had always been a huge success in international business and its partner had long shown a genius for domestic banking, the alliance was a natural one, and the standings of both firms increased greatly as they shared profits and policies.

World War I and Postwar Struggles

World War I and its aftermath were a disaster for almost every company in Germany. Dresdner Bank, which had profited by financing the government's astronomical wartime expenses, found that the German economy's unpreparedness for war, coupled with the Allied blockade and the industrial might of the United States, crippled non-military industries. The war dried up all opportunities for continued expansion and placed a tremendous burden on German industry, forcing it to produce the materials necessary for war on an unprecedented scale. This stifled the basic expansionist impulse of the bank and cut off investment revenue.

The short-lived Weimar Republic (1918–23) was also difficult for Dresdner Bank. The burden of Germany's heavy war reparations stultified the entire economy. This hurt Dresdner even more than had the lack of expansion during the war years. Since one of the primary reasons for a universal bank is to back developing industry, Dresdner, as a major shareholder in many German firms, felt the pinch of the Treaty of Versailles as sharply as the rest of Germany did. On top of this was the Allies' insistence that all Allied countries be given the right to confiscate any German private property abroad. Firms with international interests as extensive as Dresdner's experienced crushing setbacks as they lost vast international securities and capital holdings.

The loss of wealth coupled with the need to pay reparations produced the legendary hyperinflation of the Weimar Republic,

further cutting into the German banking business. At the high point of economic chaos, in 1923, Dresdner held assets of 204 trillion marks. Three years later, when the banking industry was stabilized by the introduction of the Rentenmark, Dresdner's share capital and reserves totaled only 100 million Rentenmarks.

Between 1924 and 1929, Dresdner Bank was involved in a lending policy that brought economic chaos to Germany again in 1931. During those five years, Germany began to rebound economically. In 1929, the economy's volume of business was 50 percent greater than it was before the war. This was due largely to the capital loans that Dresdner and the other leading banks made to new and developing German industries. But the banks were too loyal to their customers and lent out too much money. When the effects of the American stock market crash of 1929 hit Germany in 1931, there was little cash on hand to pay investors. Also, Dresdner and the other big banks carried too much foreign credit. They needed foreign capital coming in to pay the interest. This bank crisis necessitated federal involvement: in 1931 the German government took over 90 percent of Dresdner.

Dresdner did benefit somewhat, however, from the government's plan to restructure the banks and keep credit rates down by buying up banks and giving them cash. In the year after the crash, Dresdner was able to buy another of the major Berlin banks, Darmstadter, making Dresdner for a time the largest bank in Germany.

When the Nazis assumed power in 1933, the banking crisis was far from over. The Big Three of Berlin (now Dresdner, Deutsche, and Commerzbank) had lost 1.3 billion marks in assets and capital in the previous two years. Ostensibly socialists, the Nazis were inclined to completely nationalize all the German banks under the absolute power of the Third Reich. The domination of the big banks had long fostered a populist resentment, which the Nazis carefully exploited. Dresdner Bank, as the fattest financial goose among the banks, was the chief target for total and irrevocable nationalization.

In the end, the banks were not nationalized, and Dresdner Bank prospered under state-regulated capitalism. In 1937 Dresdner was able to buy itself back from the government. Its size increased in 1939, when Länderbank, the second largest bank in Austria, merged with Dresdner after the Anschluss in Austria. The Vienna branch of a Czech bank, Zivnostenska, was also annexed.

Rehabilitation and Recovery After World War II

Dresdner's relationship with the Nazi government led to dire consequences after the conclusion of World War II. As one of the privileges of leadership, Hermann Goering was allowed to have a company of his own, Goering Werke, an iron ore processing works whose products were in heavy demand during the Nazi war buildup. A representative of Dresdner, Karl Rasche, sat on the management board of a subsidiary of Goering Werke. This was not unusual; having representatives on boards and councils, as well as controlling blocks of voting stock shares, were the chief ways that the big German banks exercised economic control. But Karl Rasche's presence on the board of a Goering Werke subsidiary during this time was later considered positive evidence by the Allies that Dresdner had not only escaped being socialized by the Nazis, but that it had maintained a close relationship with the Nazi government.

After World War II, Dresdner and the other large German banks were split up. Once again it lost branches and assets to the war's victors. With the Soviet occupation of East Germany, all of Dresdner's offices east of the Oder-Neisse line were closed permanently. Of Dresdner's total of 327 offices, only about half remained open, and most of those were badly damaged. Dresdner was at first restructured into ten separate institutions. The bank struggled to regain some of its prominence during the early postwar years but then faced another reformation from the Liquidation Commission.

The Liquidation Commission was formed by the occupation forces to study the roles that various companies and industries had played in the war economy of Nazi Germany. Citing the "silent financing" of the German war effort through loans, as well as direct links of the kind previously noted, the Liquidation Commission decided to restructure Dresdner Bank into 11 small banks, each of which could operate only within its own zone of occupation. Yet Dresdner Bank was, like Germany itself, impossible to keep down. In 1952 the 11 regional banks were turned into three successor institutions of Dresdner Bank. Each of the three derivative banks prospered so much as a part of the "economic miracle" of the 1950s that Dresdner was allowed to recombine itself again in 1957 as Dresdner Bank A.G., with its new headquarters in Frankfurt am Main.

Reunification meant more than gaining domestic strength for the new Dresdner Bank: it meant the bank could expand once again. Dresdner immediately took advantage of its situation and became the first German bank to open an office overseas after World War II when it established a representative station in Istanbul in the late 1950s.

Dresdner also expanded through technical innovation, using data processing systems to manage accounts in 1958, becoming the first West German firm to do so. Dresdner also pioneered the way for foreign stock shares to be traded on West German exchanges at about this time.

When the restrictions limiting the three major branches of Dresdner from operating outside of their zones of occupation were lifted in 1963, the domestic business needed to finance foreign expansion was finally available, and the bank started to become the international giant that it is today. Dresdner again pioneered overseas business dealings by becoming the first firm to set up a German bank outside of its own borders, opening the Company Luxemburgeoise de Banque S.A. in Luxembourg in 1967.

Dresdner continued to expand, opening branches in Singapore and New York in 1972. By developing these overseas connections, the bank was able to outgrow its involvement in various consortiums with other banks and became truly international on its own terms again. In the mid-1970s, Dresdner opened representative offices in London, Tokyo, and even Moscow.

In 1968 Dresdner established German-American Securities—now called ABD Securities Corporation—in New York. This investment-banking subsidiary was an extremely important part of Dresdner's worldwide securities expertise. As a measure of the subsidiary's, and Dresdner's, American prominence, ABD's chief, Theodor Schmidt-Scheuber, was the first foreigner to be made head of an American stock exchange, in Boston.

Dresdner earned recognition in 1974 for its adroit handling of the sale of the Quandt family's 10 percent share of Daimler-Benz to Kuwait, the largest deal of the kind at the time. Three years later, Dresdner and the entire German business community were shocked when Jürgen Ponto, Dresdner's chief executive, was killed by left-wing terrorists during a kidnapping attempt. The assassination cut short the life of the man who had headed Dresdner since 1969 and had been instrumental in turning the firm into an international business powerhouse.

Hans Friderichs, a former economics minister, was Ponto's eventual replacement. In 1978, Dresdner had officially become one of the ten largest banks in the world. But Dresdner did not prosper under Friderichs for long; his six years in charge were marked by mounting losses and turmoil among executives. Friderichs's tenure ended in February 1985, when he resigned in the wake of charges that he had accepted a bribe for a favorable tax ruling given to the Flick Industrial Group while he was economics minister.

Friderichs's replacement was Wolfgang Röller, a member of Dresdner's board whose specialty was the securities business. It was Röller who been behind the founding of ABD Securities in 1968, and who had arranged the Kuwaiti sale of Daimler-Benz. Röller's background in securities made him an especially appropriate choice as the banking industry in general, and Germany's in particular, entered an era of decreasing regulation and intensified international competition.

Under Röller, Dresdner began to prosper again. In his first year in charge, earnings rose 18 percent and assets 8 percent, to DM 189 billion. That year, Dresdner became the first German company to have its shares listed on the Tokyo stock exchange.

Re/Unification in the Late 1980s and 1990s

Beginning in the late 1980s, banks throughout Europe and the world began to gear up for the unification of the European market that was planned for 1992, which would create an integrated market for banking and financial services. "The upshot is that the German and European banking landscape will look substantially different from today," Dresdner Chairman Wolfgang Röller told the *Wall Street Journal* in 1990. The dissolution of economic barriers between European states required German banks to extend beyond their national boundaries.

Dresdner set out to bolster its international presence by concentrating on developing a global asset-management network. The company was already anchored by a strong domestic presence and its American subsidiary, ABD Securities. In May 1988, Dresdner bought a majority interest in Thornton & Company, a leading British asset-management company, to strengthen its presence in that country and also in Asia, where Thornton had a strong position. Thornton managed about $1.49 billion in mutual funds and pension accounts. Dresdner also bolstered its U.S. position by purchasing several seats on the New York Stock Exchange, and in 1993 made its first public offering there.

The reunification of East and West Germany offered Dresdner a host of new opportunities as well. In anticipation of monetary union in 1990 (which preceded political union by a year), East Germany revamped its entire banking system, spinning off its state central bank's retail operations into a new unit called Deutsche Kreditbank. Dresdner and its rival Deutsche Bank both rushed to capture this new market, forming joint ventures with Deutsche Kreditbank outlets. In 1990, Dresdner inked a deal with Deutsche Kreditbank that gave the West German firm control over 72 Kreditbank retail branches and a 49 percent stake in the outfit, which was named Dresdner Bank Kreditbank AG. Dresdner also planned to add 150 of its own branches in the former East Germany in 1991.

Dresdner also continued its pan-European development when it forged an alliance with Banque Nationale de Paris (BNP), one of the three largest banks in France, in 1991. The alliance involved a 7 percent share swap between Dresdner and BNP, which acted as a foundation for a global cooperation pact.

In 1995, Dresdner spent about $1.58 billion to acquire the British investment bank Kleinwort Benson Group PLC. With this purchase, Dresdner signaled a significant strategic switch. Long considered the most conservative of the "Big Three" German banks, Dresdner's Kleinwort acquisition showed that the company was thoroughly committed to expanding into investment banking, rather than remaining primarily focused on its lower-margin core commercial banking operations. A few months after swallowing Kleinwort, Dresdner purchased San Francisco-based RCM Capital Management from Travelers Group, which managed assets of $26 billion for institutional clients in the stock and bond markets. Dresdner then united its assets-management operations into one unit: Dresdner Kleinwort Benson, which boasted 8,000 employees and was one of Germany's largest fund managers.

The trend towards consolidation in the European banking industry continued in the late 1990s and early in the new century. European banks were eager to combine so that they could compete more effectively with American mega-financial institutions, like Citigroup Inc., which offered a panoply of services to their corporate clients and were making headway in

European markets. Dresdner and Deutsche Bank almost joined this merger frenzy. The two German banks were in the final stages of negotiating a merger in 2000, when the deal fell apart. Deutsche Bank wanted Dresdner to jettison its investment banking arm, Dresdner Kleinwort Benson; Dresdner refused, making itself "a takeover candidate more than ever," according to the April 10, 2000, *Wall Street Journal*. After the merger's failure, Dresdner's chairman, Bernhard Walter, resigned and was replaced by Bernd Fahrholz. Soon thereafter, Dresdner began merger talks with Commerzbank AG, the second largest bank in Germany, though these negotiations were also scuttled.

In September 2000, Dresdner opted to beef up its investment banking operations again, when it acquired Wasserstein Perella, a New York investment bank that had played an advisory role in the merger of Time Warner, Inc. and America Online, Inc. Wasserstein gave Dresdner a stronger presence in the United States, as well as a boost in its American mergers and acquisitions business. Dresdner renamed its investment banking operations Dresdner Kleinwort Wasserstein.

Dresdner's goal of merging with an equal was achieved at last in 2001, when it was acquired by Allianz AG, the largest insurance company in Germany, for about $20 billion. Allianz had long sought to establish itself not just as an insurance company, but as a global financial services provider along the lines of Citigroup. Allianz, which already owned 22 percent of Dresdner before the acquisition, saw Dresdner as key to this transformation. Dresdner was delighted that its investment banking arm was included as part of the package. Rather than forcing Dresdner to sell the investment bank (an obstacle in prior merger negotiations), Allianz created a new corporate and market division under the leadership of Kleinwort Wasserstein.

Soon after the Allianz merger, though, Dresdner stumbled badly. The global economic decline and the stock market drops of the early 21st century eroded Dresdner's loan business, as it was forced to write off loans to failing and insolvent companies. Particularly in the wake of the global insecurity caused by the terrorist attacks in the United States on September 11, 2001, investment banking took a beating across the globe, and Dresdner's mergers and acquisitions business dried up. In 2002 almost all of Germany's major banks reported their worst losses in the postwar era. Dresdner was not exempt. Allianz announced it would lay off 8,000 Dresdner employees that year, with another 3,000 cuts slated. In 2003 Dresdner's chief executive Bernd Fahrholz resigned and was replaced by Herbert Walter. Allianz made it clear that it would either split off or scale back Kleinwort Wasserstein. According to the *Wall Street Journal*, analysts predicted that Allianz would sell off the investment bank as soon as market conditions improved and would require Dresdner to refocus on commercial banking and pension and fund products.

Principal Subsidiaries

Dresdner Asset Management GmbH (Germany); Dresdner Asset Management Ltd. (Singapore); Dresdner Bank plc (Ireland); Dresdner International Management Services Ltd. (Ireland); Dresdner RCM Gestion; Dresdner RCM Global Advisors Asia Ltd.; Dresdner RCM Global Investors Holdings Ltd. (U.K.); Dresdner RCM Global Investors LLC; MEIJI Dresdner

Asset Management Co. Ltd.; Pension and Compensation Consulting GmbH; ALLAGO AG; Dresdner Bank Lateinamerika AG; Dresdner Bank Luxembourg SA; Dresdner Corporate Finance GmbH; Dresdner Kleinwort Wasserstein Limited (Japan); Dresdner Kleinwort Wasserstein Securities Limited; Dresdner Kleinwort Wasserstein Securities Limited (Asia); Dresdner Kleinwort Wasserstein Securities LLC (U.S.A.).

Principal Competitors

Bayerische Hypo-und Vereinsbank Aktiengesellschaft; Citigroup Inc.; Commerzbank AG; Credit Suisse Group; Deutsche Bank AG.

Further Reading

Northrop, Mildred, *Control Policies of the Reichsbank 1924–1933,* New York: AMS Press, 1968.

Riesser, Jacob, *The German Great Banks,* New York: Arno Press, 1977.

Roth, Terence, ''Deutsche Bank, Dresdner Push into East Germany,'' *Wall Street Journal,* June 27, 1990.

——, ''1992: West German Banks Rushing to Diversify in Anticipation of Barrier-Free Europe,'' *Wall Street Journal,* August 3, 1988.

Rhoads, Christopher, and Erik Portanger, ''Two Big German Banks Scramble in Wake of Aborted Megamerger,'' *Wall Street Journal,* April 10, 2000.

Schweitzer, Arthur, *Big Business in the Third Reich,* Bloomington: Indiana University Press, 1964.

Stolper, Gustav, *The German Economy: 1870 to the Present,* London: Weidenfield and Nicolson, 1967.

Vogl, Frank, *German Business After the Economic Miracle,* New York: John Wiley & Sons, 1973.

Woolston, Maxine, *The Structure of the Nazi Economy,* Cambridge: Harvard University Press, 1942.

—update: Rebecca Stanfel

Duke Realty Corporation

600 E. 96th Street, Suite 100
Indianapolis, Indiana 46240
U.S.A.
Telephone: (317) 808-6000
Toll Free: (800) 875-3366
Fax: (317) 808-6770
Web site: http://www.dukerealty.com

Public Company
Incorporated: 1985 as Duke Realty Investments
Employees: 1,001
Sales: $956.3 million (2002)
Stock Exchanges: New York
Ticker Symbol: DRE
NAIC: 525930 Real Estate Investment Trusts

Duke Realty Corporation is an Indianapolis-based real estate investment trust (REIT) that specializes in the development and management of suburban office and industrial properties located in 13 major midwestern and southern cities. The company owns interests in approximately 110 million square feet of property and also owns or controls more than 4,000 acres of undeveloped land, capable of containing an additional 62 million square feet of rentable space. Duke serves more than 4,500 tenants.

Launch of Predecessor Company in 1972

The man behind the Duke name was Phillip R. Duke, a 1959 graduate of Butler University who started out his business career as a certified public accountant. He switched to real estate development when he became a partner at C.W. Jackson Construction Co. He then struck out on his own, teaming up with attorney John Wynne to form a construction and development company. They brought in someone with a sales background, John Rosebrough, and in 1972 P.R. Duke & Associates was born. The three men pooled their money, a modest $30,000 in operating funds and another $10,000 in development funds. Despite limited capital and no reputation in development, they bought a struggling 324-acre industrial park, Park 100, from

Indianapolis businessman Howard Sams. What they may have lacked in experience they compensated for with vision. They were pioneers in the development of flex space—combining office, showroom, and warehouse space in one location. Duke transformed Park 100 into one of the country's largest industrial parks, eventually encompassing some 1,500 acres.

Phillip Duke and his partners adopted a vertically integrated approach to the real estate business, establishing five operating companies to support their development activities: P.R. Duke Co. Construction, Duke Construction Management Inc., Duke Management Inc., Duke Realty Inc., and P.R. Duke Securities. These entities were essentially designed to produce savings for development projects rather than to generate significant levels of profit. The arrangement was summarized in a 1986 *Indianapolis Business Journal* article: "The relationship between the two P.R. Duke & Associates arms allows the company to retain control of all aspects of the development of its projects from the idea to collecting rents. 'The real business we're in is creating net income streams—rents,' Duke said."

Once the business was well established in its hometown, Duke expanded into its second market, Cincinnati, in 1978. It began testing a third market in 1985 when it built an office building in Nashville, Tennessee. The timing, however, was less than fortuitous due to a number of Texas developers entering the area simultaneously, a situation that led to the area becoming overbuilt. While Duke aggressively added to its holdings in Indianapolis and Cincinnati in a bid to become the dominant developer in those cities, it was content to adopt a wait-and-see approach in Nashville. Ultimately the Texas firms abandoned the market and Duke remained to further develop the area when conditions improved.

Formation of a REIT in 1985

In 1985 Duke decided to package a number of its properties in a real estate investment trust. The REIT had been created by Congress in 1960 as a way for small investors to become involved in real estate in a manner similar to mutual funds. REITs could be taken public and their shares traded just like stock companies and they were also subject to regulation by the

Company Perspectives:

With an emphasis on using real estate to support our clients' businesses, Duke Realty Corporation has grown to become one of the most successful commercial real estate companies in the United States, serving more than 4,500 tenants.

Securities and Exchange Commission. Unlike stocks, however, REITs were required by law to pay out at least 95 percent of their taxable income to shareholders each year, a provision that severely limited the ability of REITs to raise funds internally. During the first 25 years of existence, REITs were allowed only to own real estate, a situation that hindered their growth. Third parties had to be contracted to manage the properties. REITs also fell out of favor with investors in the 1970s because of a number of heavily leveraged, poor-performing trusts. Not until the Tax Reform Act of 1986 changed the nature of real estate investment did the REIT gain widespread usage. Tax shelter schemes that had drained potential investments were shut down by the act. Interest and depreciation deductions were greatly reduced so that taxpayers could not generate paper losses in order to lower their tax liabilities. REITs also were permitted now to provide customary services for property, in effect allowing the trusts to operate and manage the properties they owned.

While the tax legislation was being passed in 1985, Duke established a REIT, Duke Realty Investments, in November of that year in preparation for the act taking effect a few months later. The trust was created to have a finite life, 10 to 12 years, which by law meant that it could not add properties to its portfolio, nor could it sell any properties for four years. The REIT completed its initial public offering of two types of shares (income and capital), netting $69 million. By buying the capital shares investors received a share of capital gains as the properties were sold off in the course of Duke Realty's existence. It proved to be an awkward structure, making the company difficult to analyze, and after two years the trust adopted a single class of stock. Regardless, the original incarnation of Duke Realty Corporation was never very popular with investors.

In 1986 Phillip Duke and Rosebrough sold their interests in the five operating companies of P.R. Duke & Associates to a partnership headed by one of the original founders, John Wynne, along with four second-level managers. The three founders, however, retained their share of ownership in the more important development arm of the organization. Duke told the press, "The truth is the younger team has been pretty much getting the job done on their own for some time now." A more dramatic change in the real estate operation would occur three months later when Duke died of a heart attack in Florida.

The Duke development arm expanded in the late 1980s, moving into new territories such as suburban Detroit and a number of markets in Ohio, Illinois, and Kentucky. Like many real estate firms it became dependent on a continually growing economy, steady rent increases, and liberal lending practices. As economic growth slowed and markets became saturated with space, many companies became trapped in a downward spiral of decreasing values. With real estate available at distressed prices

in the early 1990s REITs finally became an attractive mainstream investment option. In order to shed massive levels of debt dozens of real estate firms went public as REITs in 1993. The Duke REIT, which had been a sluggish performer, now became a means of revitalizing the fortunes of the Duke enterprises.

In October 1993 Duke Realty Investments acquired Duke Associates, then completed a public offering of stock that raised $312.7 million, of which $290 million was used to pay down debt. The reorganized company was left with approximately $243 million in debt. Duke was now in a position to raise capital to add properties to its portfolio, but management made it clear to investors that it would be circumspect. Chief Financial Officer Gene Zink told the press, "It is not our plan to gobble up properties." Serving as Duke's president and CEO was Thomas L. Hefner, who had been a managing general partner at Duke Associates since 1978 and had recently served as the firm's chief operating officer. Wynne assumed the chairmanship of the REIT.

Duke pursued a strategy of developing a regional REIT that sought to dominate the markets it entered but not become overextended. Isolated projects outside the Midwest, such as one in Florida, were the exception. In 1995 the company established a regional office in St. Louis and acquired 463,000 square feet of office properties as well as 153 acres of suburban land for the future development of industrial properties. In February 1996 Duke established a beachhead in Cleveland, acquiring Farro Enterprises Inc. Over the course of the year Duke acquired additional assets in the region so that by the end of 1996 it had nearly two million square feet of space under management. Altogether, Duke owned interests in 266 rental properties with a total of 31.2 million square feet, the vast majority located in the company's primary markets: Indianapolis, Cincinnati, Cleveland, Columbus, Detroit, St. Louis, and Nashville.

Duke continued to expand into new markets in 1997. It opened a regional office in Chicago and acquired nearly one million square feet of suburban office space and 160 acres of land for future development. In October 1997 Duke acquired Minneapolis-based R.L. Johnson Company, picking up 3.2 million square feet of industrial and office space. Moreover, in 1997 Duke added to its core markets. The company acquired 982,000 square feet of suburban office space in St. Louis, and also bought significant amounts of land and properties in Cleveland and Indianapolis. Duke began to explore the possibility of expanding further, considering such markets as Kansas City, Missouri; Memphis, Tennessee; and Pittsburgh, Pennsylvania. While it grew at a steady and cautious pace, other REITs were engaged in an acquisition binge and as a consequence took on large levels of debt. The industry average of debt-to-market capitalization was close to 50 percent; Duke maintained a level around 26 percent. Many investors believed that the industry was overbuilding again, resulting in a drop in the price of REIT shares. Reluctant to tap into the capital market at these levels, REITs were unable to complete major acquisitions.

Acquiring Weeks Corp. in 1999

Unencumbered by debt, Duke was positioned to make a major deal. Management also was convinced that its business model was manageable on a larger scale and that the time had come to expand beyond its voluntary confines. In addition, in the rapidly consolidating world of real estate, the company was virtually obligated to grow larger. Duke looked at markets to the southeast of its area of operation and discovered that Atlanta-based Weeks Corp. was a perfect complement. Only in the Nashville market was there any overlap. Weeks was formed in 1965 and went public in 1994. It owned interests in some 300 industrial properties, 34 suburban office properties, and five retail properties in ten Sunbelt cities, including Atlanta, Georgia; Miami, Florida; Raleigh-Durham-Chapel Hill, North Carolina; Dallas/Ft. Worth, Texas; Orlando, Florida; and Spartanburg, South Carolina. In March 1999 Duke and Weeks agreed to a $1.1 billion stock swap, creating a company with a market value of close to $5.4 billion. Each share of Weeks common stock was exchanged for 1.38 shares of Duke common stock. The new entity became known as Duke-Weeks Realty Corp., a name it would retain for two years before becoming Duke Realty Corporation. The company's headquarters was located in Indianapolis, and Hefner became CEO and chair. All tallied, postmerger, the company owned 846 office and industrial buildings totaling 90 million square feet.

Management was pleased with the integration of Weeks, which operated in a manner similar to Duke, but found it hard to accept the response from the investment community. In the spring of 2000 shares of its stock were selling in the $19 range, down from a 52-week high of $24.25, a situation all too common for REITs at the time. Although it was eager to strengthen its holdings in such markets as Dallas, Raleigh, Orlando, and Tampa, Duke elected in 2000 to pursue what it called a ''capital recycling'' program, with the intent of selling around $400 million in assets that year. In reality Duke disposed of $765 million in 2000 and another $541 million in 2001, followed by nearly $230 million in the first several months of 2002. None of the assets were considered to hold strategic value to the company. As a result of the selloff, at a time of economic difficulties for the country, Duke was sitting on some $2 billion in cash and

boasted a 25 percent debt-to-capital ratio, down from 38 percent when the program was launched. With such a low debt load the company held a tremendous advantage over competitors in its ability to borrow capital. Management was comfortable returning to the 38 percent level, and investors would tolerate a level as high as 45 percent. Despite its cash and ability to raise additional funds, the company simply did not see strong enough demand in the market to warrant major development projects, nor did it spot any appealing acquisition targets. Instead Duke was willing to maintain what most regarded as the cleanest balance sheet in the real estate industry and wait for economic conditions to improve.

Early in 2003 Duke began a transition in the ranks of upper management when Hefner announced his intention to retire as CEO in April 2004, and then give up the chairmanship a year later. Although his successor was not yet named, speculations in the press centered on the company's president and chief operating officer, Denny Oklak.

Principal Subsidiaries

Duke Realty Limited Partnership; Weeks Development Partnership.

Principal Competitors

Highwoods Properties, Inc.; Liberty Property Trust; Prime Group Realty Trust.

Further Reading

Andrews, Greg, ''Flush with Cash, Duke Assures Market Dominance,'' *Indianapolis Business Journal,* August 15, 1994, p. A1.

Kaufman, Leslie, and Laura M. Holson, ''Property Trusts Plan to Merge in Stock Swap,'' *New York Times,* March 1, 1999, p. 8.

Ketzenberger, John, ''How Duke Operates: A Look Inside Indianapolis' Largest Commercial Developer,'' *Indianapolis Business Journal,* October 2, 1989, p. 7.

Maurer, Katie, ''Duke Poised for Buying Spree,'' *Indianapolis Business Journal,* August 19, 2001, p. 23.

Parent, Tawn, ''Duke Offering to Raise Princely Sum,'' *Indianapolis Business Journal,* June 14, 1993, p. 1A.

Sherer, Paul M., ''Duke Realty and Weeks Plan to Merge in a Stock Swap Valued at $1.1 Billion,'' *Wall Street Journal,* March 1, 1999, p. A6.

Thompson, Cheri, ''The Little Engine That Could: Duke Thinks Small to Get Big,'' *National Real Estate Investor,* November 1998, pp. 46–47.

—Ed Dinger

Dycom Industries, Inc.

1st Union Center, 4440 PGA Boulevard
Palm Beach Gardens, Florida 33410
U.S.A.
Telephone: (561) 627-7171
Fax: (561) 627-7709
Web site: http://www.dycomind.com

Public Company
Incorporated: 1969 as Mobile Home Dynamics, Inc.
Employees: 5,700
Sales: $624.0 million (2002)
Stock Exchanges: New York
Ticker Symbol: DY
NAIC: 237110 Water and Sewer Line and Related
 Structures Construction

Dycom Industries, Inc. operates in the telecommunications infrastructure industry, providing engineering, construction, and maintenance services to telecommunications and utility companies. Dycom installs and maintains aerial, underground, and buried cable systems owned by telephone companies and cable television providers. The company installs integrated voice, data, and video networks within office buildings and similar structures. Dycom also provides locating services to map and mark underground utilities. Operating through 31 subsidiaries, Dycom served more than 100 customers in 48 states, including Qwest, Comcast, Sprint, and Verizon.

Origins

Although Dycom was founded in 1969, the company did not begin to show signs of becoming an industry leader until the mid-1980s. In part, the delay of its rise was attributable to finding its niche within the telecommunications infrastructure industry. The company did not begin to grow meaningfully until it shaped itself into a fiber-optics specialist, and it could not mount a campaign of aggressive growth until the industry it served embraced fiber optics as an alternative to copper wiring. Both of these conditions for growth, when existent, created a

fertile climate for Dycom's rise, but one crucial ingredient still remained: a leader capable of foreseeing and seizing the business opportunity. That individual arrived at Dycom in 1984. Through the vision and commitment to growth displayed by Thomas Pledger, Dycom began its assault on the telecommunications industry.

Pledger, who presided over the company during its development into an industry leader and during the most difficult period in its history, took a calculating look at the telecommunications industry when he arrived at Dycom. Telephone companies such as AT&T, MCI, and Sprint were starting the long process of replacing copper wiring with fiber-optic lines in their long-distance lines. Pledger knew he could install the lines for far less cost than could the telephone companies. Pledger's conviction was justified, based on reason more than biased hope. Telephone companies, with their unionized workforces, carried very expensive manpower, unable to compete with low-cost, non-union enterprises such as Dycom. Telephone companies realized as much and eventually outsourced nearly all of their installation and service work to other firms. Pledger saw the opportunity and acted upon it, initiating an acquisition campaign that would leave the company prepared for the transition to fiber optics.

Expansion Through Acquisitions in the 1980s

In the years following Pledger's arrival at Dycom, the company completed a series of acquisitions. The company chose to grow through acquisitions rather than through internal means for a reason. ''If the guy in the next territory is happy and the telephone company is happy,'' Pledger explained in a September 3, 1991 interview with *Financial World,* ''then he is going to be very hard to unseat.'' Consequently, growth through acquisitions was adopted as Dycom's mode of attack. The company's march, completed territory by territory, region by region, began in 1984. Typically, Pledger acquired selected companies, many of which were quite small, by purchasing them with Dycom stock. The owners of the acquired businesses became Dycom managers, creating a decentralized organizational structure. To lend accountability and drive to the company's operations, the managers were awarded bonuses when specific per-

Key Dates:

1969: Dycom's predecessor is founded.
1984: Thomas Pledger joins Dycom.
1991: A series of lawsuits leads to successive years of financial malaise.
1999: Steve Nielsen is appointed chief executive officer, replacing Pledger.
2002: Dycom acquires Arguss Communications, Inc.

formance objectives were achieved. With an acquisition procedure in place, Dycom steadily grew, insinuating itself across the nation and preparing for the future.

Being able to tout itself as a company with a genuine national presence offered Dycom the advantages of growth and stability. The greater the company's physical presence became, the greater its ability to increase revenues became. Profit margins in the telecommunications infrastructure business remained essentially constant, but sales growth could be increased as the scope of a company's geographic operation broadened. The ability to serve more territory for more customers enabled a company such as Dycom to generate more profits primarily because it generated greater revenues. Further, local installation contracts generally were too small to require competitive bidding, a sector of the telecommunications infrastructure industry known as the "local loop" business. Because competitive bidding often did not exist in the local loop business, "master contractors" were automatically given the business awarded by local installation contracts. The dynamics of the industry, consequently, demanded piecemeal expansion to ensure success. Dycom, with its decentralized organizational structure, flowered into a company consisting of a host of operating subsidiaries, each taking on the local loop business of a country divided into territories.

The conversion to fiber-optic technology fueled Dycom's growth, making the 1980s the company's signal decade of success. Between 1996 and the end of the decade, the company's role as a leader in providing the specialized services of a fiber-optic installer enabled it to post annual revenue growth of 48 percent. On the eve of an encouraging turning point in the telecommunications infrastructure industry, Dycom completed the acquisition of Ansco & Associates, LLC in 1990, marking a juncture but not the culmination of the acquisition spree touched off in 1984. Awarded its first master contract in 1981, Greensboro, North Carolina-based Ansco & Associates operated as long-distance and local loop fiber-optic cable installer in the southeastern United States.

Not long after the acquisition of Ansco & Associates, the moment Pledger had waited for arrived, promising to greatly increase the size of his $165 million-in-sales company. In 1991, Judge Harold Green decided to allow the regional Bell operating companies to enter the information business, a ruling that meant the Baby Bells—as the operating companies were commonly known—could begin to install fiber optics into offices and homes. Dycom stood to gain much from the decision, but the company appeared in the newspaper headlines for all the wrong reasons following Green's nod of consent.

Infighting in the 1990s

Judge Green's ruling caused a stir within the telecommunications infrastructure industry. In late 1991, Dycom's rival, Burnup & Sims Inc., launched an unsolicited attempt to merge with Dycom, an attempt aided in part by Pledger's fellow executive, Dycom President William Stover. In the turmoil to follow, an internal revolt ensued. Pledger fired Stover. In response, Stover sued Pledger and Robert Owens, Dycom's chief financial officer, claiming fraud and other violations. Dycom countered, filing a lawsuit of its own. Meanwhile, Dycom's stock dropped in value, shadowed by declines in the company's revenue and its net income. The company's waning strength prompted Dycom shareholders to join the fray in the form of a shareholder class-action lawsuit. The Securities and Exchange Commission (SEC) took an interest as well, launching its own investigation into the litigious battles embroiling Dycom.

The acrimony dragged on for several years, hobbling Dycom's chance to take advantage of Judge Green's ruling. In November 1992, Stover appeared at the company's shareholder meeting and tried to oust Pledger. He failed. Finally, in February 1993, both parties agreed to settle, but considerable damage already had been done. In 1993, from revenues of $136.9 million, Dycom recorded a massive loss of $31.5 million. In 1994, when revenues slipped to $122.5 million, the company lost nearly $8 million. Although Dycom ranked as one of the largest companies in the country devoted to installing fiber optics for telephone access as well as cable transmission lines, the toll incurred during the first half of the 1990s was severe. The company lost $45.6 million during a four-year period, while its stock collapsed, plummeting from $16 per share to $2 per share.

After the debacle, Pledger entered the second half of the 1990s trying to forget the sting of the preceding years. "We've got most of our problems behind us now," he said in an October 20, 1995 interview with the *South Florida Business Journal.* Pledger's words were not entirely convincing, but Dycom's actions during the second half of the 1990s unequivocally demonstrated the erasure of the problems earlier in the decade. In 1996, the company generated $145 million in sales and recorded net income of $4.6 million. By the end of the decade, the company's annual revenue volume eclipsed $600 million. Annual profits flirted with the $50 million mark. The enormous leap in the company's financial stature came in large part from the increased size of its operations geographically. By the end of the 1990s, the company was operating in 40 states providing a variety of services. Dycom installed lines for cable and telephone companies. The company installed integrated voice, data, and video networks within office buildings. Dycom installed direct broadcast satellite systems, provided locating services to map and mark underground utilities, and the company provided electrical utility power line services, including the installation and maintenance of high-voltage power grids. Dycom was bigger and broader, enabling it to record vigorous financial growth.

Pledger met with success during the 1980s and disaster during the first half of the 1990s. His third period of leadership saw Dycom exhibit the strength he foresaw in 1984, becoming the halcyon years that marked the end of his day-to-day control over the company. In 1999, he gave up his title as chief executive officer, scaling back his duties to those accorded to a chairman. His replacement was Steve Nielsen, who was appointed president and chief executive officer in March 1999. Nielsen, hired in 1993 to manage the company's Atlanta office, joined Dycom during the company's contentious struggle with Stover and shareholders. In 2000, Pledger retired, paving the way for Nielsen's appointment as Dycom's chairman of the board. The succession of a new leader and the departure of Pledger, who had directed the company's course for more than 15 years, marked the beginning of a new era.

Dycom in the 21st Century

One constant bridging the Pledger era and the Nielsen era was acquisitive activity. During the company's fiscal 2000 year, five acquisitions were completed. At the time of Nielsen's appointment as chairman, Dycom operated through 15 subsidiaries, a number that was to increase significantly during the coming years. In late 2000, Dycom announced plans to acquire Point-to-Point Communications, a provider of central office equipment, engineering, installation, testing, and maintenance services for the optical networks of telecommunication providers. At the time of the announcement, Dycom relied heavily on BellSouth Telecommunications, Inc. and Comcast Cable Communications, Inc., which together accounted for nearly 40 percent of the company's annual sales.

The first years of Nielsen's reign represented a troubled period for Dycom, as a recessive economic climate and other factors contributed to unsettling financial results. Revenues soared to $826 million in 2001, but fell nearly 25 percent the following year because of the profound financial problems experienced by two of its customers, Adelphia Communications Corp. and WorldCom Inc. In terms of profitability, the difference between the two years was far more glaring. After recording $61.4 million in net income in 2001, Dycom posted a numbing $123 million loss in 2002.

During the downturn, Nielsen and his management team prepared for the resumption of growth in the telecommunications industry. Part of the company's strategy was reflected in the February 2002 acquisition of Arguss Communications, Inc., the first large-scale merger of two publicly traded providers of telecommunications infrastructure services. The addition of Arguss significantly expanded Dycom's geographic coverage and its roster of clients, giving the company greater technical service capabilities and improved broadband offerings. The merger was expected to add to Dycom's earnings in 2003.

As Dycom prepared for the future, firm financial footing eluded the company. There were signs of improvement, however, particularly in the company's stock performance. Com-

cast's acquisition of AT&T's cable television assets in 2002 proved to be a blessing for Dycom. Comcast hired Dycom to upgrade its cable lines, an 18-month project that began in April 2003. In addition, Dycom secured a four-year maintenance contract from Sprint covering the telecommunications company's wiring and telephone equipment in the mid-South. In response to the news, the company's stock rose $2.25 per share, reaching a 52-week high of $16.21 in June 2003. In the years ahead, Nielsen and his team hoped to turn occasional highlights into consistent financial success and make Dycom the dominant company in its industry.

Principal Subsidiaries

Ansco & Associates, LLC; Apex Digital, Inc.; C-2 Utility Contractors, LLC; Cable Com, Inc.; Cable Connectors, LLC; Can-Am Communications, Inc.; Communications Construction Group, LLC; DiversiCom Site Development, LLC; Ervin Cable Construction, LLC; Fiber Cable, LLC; Globe Communications LLC; Installation Technicians, LLC; Ivy H. Smith Company, Inc.; Kohler Construction, LLC; Lamberts' Cable Splicing Co., LLC; Kitt Smith Communications, LLC; Locating, Inc.; Nichols Construction, LLC; Niels Fugal Sons Company, LLC; Point to Point Communications, LP; Stevens Communications, LLC; Star Construction, LLC; STS, LLC; TCS Communications, LLC; Tesinc, Inc.; Triple D Communications, LLC; Underground Specialties, LLC; US Communications, LLC; White Mountain Cable Construction, LLC.

Principal Competitors

MasTec, Inc.; Orius Corporation; Qunata Services, Inc.

Further Reading

Falker, John T., "Dycom Beats Estimates, Appoints Chairman, Buys Telecom Firm," *South Florida Business Journal,* December 8, 2000, p. 27A.

——, "Telecom Diggers Not Set for a Burial," *South Florida Business Journal,* July 6, 2001, p. 1A.

Madigan, Sean, "Arguss Communication Will Merge with a Florida Competitor in a Deal Worth $83.7 Million," *Washington Business Journal,* January 11, 2002, p. 27.

Montgomery, Leland, "Dycom Industries: Thanks, Judge," *Financial World,* September 3, 1991, p. 15.

Pounds, Stephen, "Familiar Names Boosting Dycom," *Palm Beach Post,* June 4, 2003, p. 5B.

Turner, Alison, "Dycom's Chairman Speaks Up," *South Florida Business Journal,* April 15, 1994, p. 17.

——, "Happy Days Are Here Again for Dycom," *South Florida Business Journal,* October 20, 1995, p. 3A.

—Jeffrey L. Covell

Editorial Television, S.A. de C.V.

Avenida Vasco de Quiroga 2000
Mexico City, D.F. 01210
Mexico
Telephone: (52) (55) 5261-2600
Fax: (52) (55) 5261-2705
Web site: http://www.esmas.com/televisa

Wholly Owned Subsidiary of Grupo Televisa, S.A. de C.V.
Incorporated: 1979 as Editorial Provenemex
Sales: 3.02 billion pesos ($288.61 million) (2002)
NAIC: 422920 Book, Periodical and Newspaper
   Wholesalers; 511120 Periodical Publishers

Editorial Television, S.A. de C.V., sometimes referred to as Edivisa, is the publishing subsidiary of Grupo Televisa, S.A. de C.V., the largest media company in Latin America. It is the leader in the publication and distribution of magazines in Mexico and world leader in the publication and distribution of magazines in the Spanish language, in terms of circulation. The Mexican magazines are edited in Mexico City; the ones destined for other Spanish-speaking countries and Hispanics in the United States are edited from Miami. Editorial Televisa plays an invaluable role for the parent company by publicizing its television, radio, and film-distribution businesses, as well as professional soccer teams.

Editorial Televisa's Predecessors to 1992

Editorial Televisa's roster of publications began with *Vanidades.* Designed as a quality monthly, it was the first to introduce—in the Spanish language—avant-garde society to French and American fashions in the 1930s. It was Cuba's most popular women's magazine until the owner and publisher, Francisco Saralegui, Jr., moved to New York in 1960, shortly after Fidel Castro came to power. Saralegui reintroduced his magazine to Latin America in 1961 and moved his company to Miami in 1966. The following year the Saralegui family sold the business to Armando de Armas, a Venezuelan who was also a leading Latin American newsstand distributor. De Armas made *Vanidades* available throughout Latin America and began adding other Spanish-language magazines to the roster of his company. Beginning in 1965 De Armas started turning out Spanish-language magazines under license from The Hearst Corporation. The first of these was *Buenhogar,* a version of *Good Housekeeping.* This was followed by Spanish-language editions of the Hearst magazines *Cosmopolitan, Harper's Bazaar, Popular Mechanics,* and *Ring. GeoMundo,* a monthly similar to *National Geographic,* was launched in 1977.

De Armas's venture became Hispanic Magazine Network, U.S.A. in 1982. Customers traditionally bought the magazines at newsstands, but in 1984 the company was experimenting for the first time with subscription sales. In all, Hispanic Magazine Network claimed 252,800 sales per issue for its combined 15 magazines. Each magazine had its own editorial staff, although about half the editorial content of the magazines published under license was being picked up from their U.S. counterparts. *Harper's Bazaar en Espanol,* for example, sent its own fashion writer and photographer to European collections to provide the Hispanic reader with the most current information.

Meanwhile, Grupo Televisa, S.A. de C.V., under the direction of Emilio Azcarraga Milmo, had come to dominate Mexican television, particularly through its wildly successful *telenovelas*— romantic dramas, often lavishly produced, aimed at female audiences and running for a period of weeks or months. Televisa established Editorial Provenemex as an editorial subsidiary to exploit its *telenovelas* by publishing *TV y Novelas,* which became Mexico's best-selling magazine. *Tele-Guia,* a weekly television guide, became the most popular in its field. Provenemex also published *Tu,* a monthly aimed at teenage girls; *Eres,* a biweekly also aimed at the adolescent market but emphasizing entertainment; *Eres Novia,* a bimonthly for young brides; and *Somos,* a biweekly aimed at young adults. All four were originated by Laura Diez Barroso (later Laura Laviada), a niece of Azcarraga.

Publishing in Miami and Mexico City: 1992–97

A Spanish publisher, Grupo Anaya, bought de Armas's operation in 1989. When (as America Publishing Group) it was sold to Grupo Televisa in 1992 for $130 million, the enterprise

Key Dates:

1960: The Cuban fashion magazine *Vanidades* moves to the United States.
1965: Armando de Armas begins publishing Spanish-language magazines under license.
1979: Televisa establishes an editorial subsidiary to exploit its television offerings.
1984: De Armas's operation is publishing 15 Spanish-language magazines in Miami.
1992: Televisa purchases the Miami business for $130 million.
1996: Editorial Televisa's magazines have been reduced from 56 to 34 in an economy drive.
2002: Editorial Televisa publishes 137 million magazine copies of more than 50 titles.

was called Editorial America and consisted of no less than 80 titles, including not only consumer magazines but also romance novels, comics, and special interest books. Grupo Televisa paid for Editorial America with funds raised from its initial public offering of stock and then paid almost as much for *Ovaciones,* a Mexican twice-daily newspaper focusing on sports and entertainment that proved unprofitable and was sold in 2000. In 1993 Televisa and Hearst created their own system of magazine distribution in a number of Latin American countries. Televisa's publishing division, which included the book publisher Clio and the magazine distributor Intermex—largest in Mexico—reached sales of $320 million that year.

With the integration of Editorial America into Grupo Televisa, many of the Miami-based magazines overlapped with the ones published by Televisa's Corporacion Editorial, as its publishing division was now called. Some of these were moved to Mexico City and, accordingly, the 400-person Miami office was pared. After the peso devaluation of late 1994, Mexico fell into recession, and Televisa's economy drive gained even more impetus. Laviada was placed in charge of Editorial Televisa in 1995 and took a 35 percent stake in Televisa's publishing division in 1996. Laviada reduced Editorial America's 56 magazines to 34 and eliminated all but one of its 35 comic book and pocketbook titles. Overall, two-thirds of the division's U.S. employees were axed.

Of the dozen or so magazines that remained in Miami, most were turned out under license from Hearst, Ziff-Davis Publishing Co. (*PC Magazine* and *PC Computing*), or the French publisher Hachette Filipacchi Medias S.A. (*Elle, Quo*). As a result of these changes, revenue dropped but profits rose. In Mexico City, the publishing division was also turning out books and magazines such as *Cantinflas* and *La Antorcha Encendida* that promoted Televisa's television programs, and cultural offerings such as the illustrated books of its book publishing arm, Clio, and the award-winning art and cultural magazine *Saber Ver.* It also introduced *Deporte Internacional,* a biweekly sports magazine for U.S. Hispanics edited in Mexico but printed in Miami. (The Mexican equivalent was *Deporte Ilustrado.*)

In 1997 the Miami office introduced an international version of *Eres,* with a 16-page U.S. section added to the Mexican

version, and of *Somos,* featuring international and Latin American entertainers as well as Mexicans. In order to tap the neglected male market, Editorial Televisa also added *Automovil Panamericano,* a car magazine introduced through a joint venture with Luke Motorpress (later Motorpress Iberica, S.A.) and *Men's Health en Espanol,* published in partnership with Rodale Press. Like *Deporte Internacional,* they appeared originally only in the United States but were soon introduced to Latin American markets in regional editions, which allowed advertisers to direct their messages to specific markets and reduced the publisher's risk in the event of an economic crisis in any particular country. (They also reduced problems arising from regional differences in the Spanish language.)

TV y Novelas was selling 1.4 million copies in its five biweekly regional editions (including *TV y Novelas USA*) at this time and helping to promote the Grupo Televisa *telenovelas* now airing from the United States to Argentina. *Vanidades,* now also a biweekly, had circulation of more than 620,000 in nine or ten regional editions. *Eres* had equivalent circulation in four editions; the Mexican edition dominated, and singers on Televisa programs often graced its covers. *Cosmopolitan en Espanol,* appearing monthly, had circulation of 448,373 in seven regional editions. The three editions of the monthly *Harper's Bazaar en Espanol* had sales of 95,517. In all, Editorial Televisa was selling about eight million issues a month and reaching an estimated 43 million readers throughout the Americas.

Like their U.S. and European counterparts, the Spanish-language women's magazines concentrated on subjects such as fashion, beauty, careers, celebrities, and relationships, but in a more conservative matter. "There's a very big double standard in Latin America," Sara Maria Castany, editor of a regional edition of *Cosmopolitan en Espanol,* told Lisa Lockwood of *WWD/Women's Wear Daily.* "We couldn't mention the word *cama* [bed] on the cover, and now we do. . . . It's opened up a lot. Still there are certain topics Latin women don't want to read about, such as abortion and lesbianism." Castany added that unlike the English-language *Cosmopolitan,* hers carried a cooking section because "Latin women still enjoy the art of cooking. They still think the way to a man's heart is through his stomach. We also deal a lot with occult subjects, such as palmistry and tarot cards." *Harper's Bazaar en Espanol* was using 70 percent original material. A former *Cosmopolitan en Espanol* editor had high praise for what she called Editorial Televisa's selling of "Anglo-European culture" to Hispanics through its magazines. "They're very art-driven, a great training ground, and they use a very beautiful, graceful Spanish," she told Andrew Paxman of *Variety.*

Editorial Televisa in 2002

By 2002 the Editorial Televisa roster of magazines produced under joint ventures included a Spanish-language version of *National Geographic* edited in Mexico City but printed in the United States, *Muy Interesante,* a Madrid-based monthly devoted to science and culture, *Autoplus* (with Motorpress Iberica), and *Golf Digest* (Advance Magazine Publishers Inc.). Joint-venture editions of *Maxim* (with Dennis Publishing), *Travel+Leisure* (with American Express Publishing Corp.), *Electronic Gambling* (with Ziff Davis), and *Disney Witch* (with

Walt Disney Co.), were introduced during the year. Editorial Televisa also launched a monthly guide for the parent company's cable-television division called *Contacto Digital* and a lifestyle magazine called *Caras.* Another popular title was the biweekly *Furia Musical* and its U.S.-printed variant *Furia Musical USA.* But Editorial Televisa had been ordered to cut its costs by about one-third and to focus on the most profitable of its titles. It was also merged with web site Es.Mas.com, the Internet platform in which Grupo Televisa had invested the equivalent of millions of dollars.

In 2002 Editorial Televisa published 137 million magazine copies of more than 50 titles distributed in 18 countries and the titles of greatest popularity of each category in its region. *TV y Novelas*—now a weekly in Mexico—had a circulation of almost two million copies a month; it and *Tele-Guia,* the company's weekly television guide, occupied first and second place, respectively, in terms of circulation in Mexico. Its Intermex subsidiary was the largest publications distributor in Latin America, accounting for about 60 percent of all magazines distributed in Mexico by means of more than 20,000 points of sale. There were more than 80,000 points of sale in other parts of Latin America and the United States, taking in more than 300 million people in 18 countries. More than 64 percent of the publications distributed by Intermex were published by Editorial Televisa. Grupo Televisa's editorial revenues came to 1.68 billion pesos ($160.55 million) and its profit to 243.6 million pesos ($23.28 million) in 2002. Distribution came to another 1.34 billion pesos ($128.06 million) in revenues.

Principal Subsidiaries

Distribuidora Intermex, S.A. de C.V.

Principal Competitors

The Condé Nast Publications Inc.; Editorial Cinco.

Further Reading

Arrate, Anne Moncreiff, ''Largest Spanish Magazine Fights to Keep Competitive Edge,'' *Miami Herald,* March 3, 1997, Business Monday, pp. 20–22.

Fernandez, Claudia, and Andrew Paxman, *El Tigre: Emilio Azcarraga y su imperio Televisa.* Mexico City: Grijalbo, 2000, pp. 225 + .

Kelly, Caitlin, ''A Spanish 'Sleeping Giant' Looking Northward,'' *Folio,* November 15, 1997, pp. 14–15.

Levine, Felicia, ''Televisa Launching Four New Magazines for U.S. Hispanics,'' *South Florida Business Journal,* December 13, 1996, pp. 3A + .

Liff, Mark, ''Spanish-Language Magazines Begin to Soar,'' *Advertising Age,* March 19, 1984, pp. M32–M33.

Lockwood, Lisa, ''The Latin Connection,'' *WWD/Women's Wear Daily,* March 21, 1997, p. 16.

Paxman, Andrew, ''Publisher Grows by Trimming Fat,'' *Variety,* December 8, 1997, pp. 74–75.

Sutter, Mary, ''Unit Hones Focus As Spanish-Lingo Pub Hub,'' *Variety,* April 1–7, 2002, p. A18.

Whitefield, Mimi, ''La Editorial Televisa vuelve con mas fuerza, *El Nuevo Herald,* March 10, 2001, p. 4B.

—Robert Halasz

ENSCO International Incorporated

500 N. Akard Street, Suite 4300
Dallas, Texas 75201-3331
U.S.A.
Telephone: (214) 397-3000
Toll Free: (800) 423-8006
Fax: (214) 397-3370
Web site: http://www.enscous.com

Public Company
Incorporated: 1975 as Blocker Energy Corporation
Employees: 4,300
Sales: $698.1 million (2002)
Stock Exchanges: New York
Ticker Symbol: ESV
NAIC: 213110 Drilling Oil and Gas Wells

ENSCO International Incorporated, based in Dallas, Texas, is one of the world's leading offshore drilling contractors, operating 56 offshore drilling rigs: 43 jackup rigs, seven barge rigs, five platform rigs, and one semisubmersible rig. The company provides its drilling services on a "day rate" contract basis, eschewing risk-based contracts that might provide great profits. ENSCO operates primarily in the Gulf of Mexico with 22 of its jackup rigs as well as its five platform rigs and lone semisubmersible rig. Of the company's remaining 21 jackup rigs, seven are operated in the North Sea, 12 in the Asia Pacific area, one offshore in West Africa, and one offshore Trinidad and Tobago. Six of the company's seven barge rigs are located in Venezuela, the other in Indonesia. Until 2003 ENSCO operated a 27-vessel transportation fleet, which management elected to sell in order to focus exclusively on its contract drilling business.

Founding the Company in 1975

ENSCO was incorporated in 1975 as Blocker Energy Corporation by longtime oilman John R. Blocker. After graduating from Texas A&M in 1948 he worked on a Gulf of Mexico oil rig for several years before establishing a South Texas drilling company with his father in 1954. When an oversupply of oil on the market crippled the contract drilling business the company

was dissolved, and in 1958 Blocker went to work for Dresser Industries as operations manager for the oil equipment division in Argentina and Venezuela, a natural fit because he had grown up in South America, learning Spanish before English. Over the next several years he learned the political and financial realities of the foreign oil business, lessons that would later serve him well with Blocker Energy. In 1965 he moved to Dresser's Houston office and ultimately rose to the level of a senior vice-president. When he left Dresser in the mid-1970s Blocker bought a small drilling company that became the core of Blocker Energy, a venture he planned to run with his son along with a ranch he purchased. His attention, however, was soon fixed on the drilling company, due to a domestic exploration boom that resulted from the 1973–74 Arab oil embargo. In recent years the major oil companies had sold off their drilling operations and were now forced to turn to contract drillers like Blocker Energy. Blocker took advantage of his South American experience to position the company in the international market, believing it was less risky than the domestic market, where he would have to contend with some 800 to 900 competitors. Not only were there only a handful of international competitors, Blocker hoped to shield his company from the volatility of the oil business, notorious for boom-or-bust cycles, by placing his drilling rigs around the globe. Blocker Energy expanded rapidly to meet the demand for its services and as a result soon found itself $44 million in debt. Blocker took the company public to pay down some of the debt and fund further expansion. By the early 1980s Blocker Energy was the world's 15th largest contract drilling company, operating in eight countries with 54 rigs. Starting in late 1978 Blocker Energy made a major commitment to exploration by investing more than $50 million. Committing further millions to the effort, however, did little more than to distract the company from its core contract drilling business. The company restructured itself in the early 1980s but was devastated by a slump in oil drilling that put it on the verge of bankruptcy by the summer of 1984.

Richard Rainwater's Investment in 1986

After Blocker Energy lost nearly $3 million in 1985, it found much needed help from multimillionaire Richard Rainwater, whose BEC Ventures made an initial investment in the company in 1986. He then commenced negotiations with Blocker

Company Perspectives:

ENSCO is focused on the offshore contract drilling business that is essential to oil companies in their worldwide exploration and development efforts.

Energy and its creditors to acquire a controlling interest in the company. Rainwater would one day become known for his relationship with George W. Bush and their ownership of the Texas Rangers, which provided the latter with his fortune and the political platform for his successful election as governor of Texas and one day the presidency of the United States. At the time he was buying into Blocker Energy, Rainwater was already well known in financial circles as the financial advisor to the wealthy Bass brothers, heirs to a Fort Worth, Texas, oil fortune. Rainwater himself had grown up in more modest circumstances in Fort Worth. After majoring in math and physics at the University of Texas he went on to the Graduate School of Business at Stanford University, where he became friends with Sid R. Bass. Rainwater served two years at Goldman, Sachs, & Co. as a trader, and then in 1970 went to work for the Basses as a financial advisor. Over the next 16 years his advice proved so beneficial that the Basses' net worth increased from $50 million to more than $5 billion. In particular, Rainwater was responsible for the Basses buying into Disney before its dramatic increase in value. Rainwater also did well for himself, so that by the time he decided to strike out on his own he had accumulated a $100 million stake. Blocker Energy was his first solo deal, followed by a string of other investments that would result in making him a billionaire.

In December 1986 Rainwater-led BEC Ventures acquired a controlling interest in Blocker Energy. In May 1987 John Blocker stepped down as chief executive officer, although he remained chairman until his retirement in November of that year. He was replaced as CEO by Carl F. Thorne, a partner in BEC Ventures. He grew up in the oil industry, born in Texas, the son of an electrical engineer who worked for Mobil Oil Corp. for 46 years, and was raised in a Mobil field camp. After receiving a degree in petroleum engineering at the University of Texas, Thorne worked briefly as a drilling and production engineer for Tenneco Inc. before continuing his education at Baylor University School of Law, earning a juris doctor degree. He returned to the oil business, serving as assistant general counsel for Sedco Drilling Co., eventually becoming president of the company. When Sedco merged with Schlumberger in 1984, Thorne became president of the resulting drilling group. Two years later, and only in his mid-40s, Thorne retired, but soon decided to join Rainwater, taking over the running of Blocker Energy, which subsequent to the acquisition by BEC changed its name to Energy Service Company Inc., its abbreviation becoming ENSCO. The company assumed the name ENSCO International Incorporated in 1992.

ENSCO, well positioned because it possessed little debt, immediately announced plans to expand its presence in the oil drilling industry, which appeared ready to rebound after one of the worst down cycles in U.S. history. It attempted to acquire Anson Drilling Co. as well as Gearhart Industries but failed. ENSCO was more successful, however, in the transportation area, in 1988 paying $22 million to acquire Golden Gulf Offshore Inc. for ten boats that supplied offshore oil rigs and another four vessels that moved the rigs' massive anchors. Finally in 1993 ENSCO completed a major acquisition, buying Penrod Holding Corporation in 1993 and adding 19 rigs to its fleet. Penrod was owned by the Hunt family, which during the 1980s had invested heavily in the fleet, but massive debt, a downturn in drilling activity, as well as an ill-fated attempt at silver speculation, forced the Hunts to seek bankruptcy protection for Penrod and eventually led to the business being sold to ENSCO.

ENSCO began to withdraw from secondary endeavors to focus solely on offshore drilling rigs. In 1993 the company sold its supply business, and then in 1994 and 1996 sold off its land-based drilling rigs. ENSCO's technical services business was divested in 1995. Anticipating increased demand for premium jackup rigs, ENSCO initiated a rig enhancement program in 1994. It also kept an eye out for attractively priced rigs that became available from other drilling companies. Rigs were purchased from J. Lauritzen in 1994, Transocean in 1995, and Smedvig in 1997. A much larger transaction took place in 1996 when ENSCO acquired Dual Drilling Company in 1996 from Mosvold Shipping A.S. of Norway, adding 15 rigs and other holdings in a stock swap transaction valued at approximately $200 million. The company now consisted of 52 drilling rigs, divided among four subsidiaries operating in the United States, the United Kingdom, the Caribbean, and Asia. In addition, ENSCO boasted a large fleet of support vessels, including tug, supply, and anchor hauling ships. The company changed the composition of its rig fleet somewhat in 1998 when it sold off four Venezuelan barge rigs.

Business Dropping Off in 1999

At the end of 1998 ENSCO had posted five consecutive years of improved earnings. The company produced record revenues of $813.2 million in 1998 and net income of $253.9 million. The following year, however, proved difficult. Economic troubles in Asia, a drop in oil prices, and cutbacks in exploration activities combined to create a major reduction in the demand for contract drilling rigs. But ENSCO, which had always taken a conservative approach to doing business, was well positioned to wait out the downturn. Although it had long-term debt of $375 million it also had $330 million in cash at the end of 1998. Management cut operating costs and essentially broke even in 1999. Matters improved significantly in 2000, when ENSCO earned $85.4 million on revenues of $533.8 million.

Even as it was retrenching during a down cycle, ENSCO was making plans for the future, becoming increasingly more committed to deep water operations, in keeping with an oil industry trend. In a 1999 interview with *Oil & Gas Investor,* Thorne explained: ''The industry's movement into the deep water is an evolution, not a revolution. In the continuous search for hydrocarbons, we've evolved from land drilling to offshore shallowwater drilling, to drilling on the continental shelf and beyond. At the same time, the cost structure of many companies has become such that they now have to look for the bigger elephants in deeper water, where their unit finding and lifting costs are much less. If one accepts that we've got to bring on large volumes of hydrocarbons to meet rising demand, then the deep water is going to play an increasingly important role.''

Key Dates:

1975: The company is formed as Blocker Energy Corporation.
1986: BEC Ventures acquires Blocker.
1987: The name is changed to Energy Service Company.
1992: The name is changed to ENSCO International Incorporated.
1993: Penrod Drilling is acquired.
1996: Dual Drilling Company is acquired.
2002: Chiles Offshore Inc. is acquired.

To support deepwater development efforts, ENSCO upgraded platform rigs acquired from Dual. All told, in the late 1990s the company invested some $500 million in rig upgrades. Moreover, it invested in the construction of a deepwater semisubmersible rig, able to drill in water depths of 8,000 feet. It was the first deepwater drilling unit ever built in the United States, a project that was completed on time and within budget. In December 2000 the rig went into service in the Gulf of Mexico. ENSCO also invested in harsh environment jackup rigs, completing the construction of a unit in 2000. It built a second harsh environment rig in partnership with Keppel FELS Limited, holding an option to purchase a 100 percent interest. In light of the company's shifting priorities in the composition of its rig fleet, ENSCO elected in 2001 to remove four less competitive rigs from operation. Two of its platform rigs were retired and two barge rigs were put up for sale.

Financial results continued to improve in 2001, with revenues growing to $817.4 million and net income soaring to $207.3 million. ENSCO added to its fleet in 2002 when it acquired Chiles Offshore Inc., paying $578 million in stock and cash, and the assumption of $140 million in debt. It was a deal that made sense for both parties. ENSCO picked up the kind of state-of-the-art jackup rigs it preferred, and in the process stifled some Wall Street critics who expressed concern that the company had not been as aggressive as its competition in making acquisitions. Chiles was simply too small to compete in the current marketplace, and as part of the deal its president and CEO, William E. Chiles, secured an executive position with ENSCO. In addition, the sale to ENSCO was profitable for Chiles's shareholders, who received close to a 20 percent premium, based on the price at which Chiles was trading before the transaction was announced.

ENSCO's balance sheet suffered somewhat in 2002, due to a weakened demand for drilling rigs in the Gulf of Mexico and a resulting drop in day rates. For the year, the company generated revenues of $698.1 million and net income of $59.3 million. Early in 2003 management announced that it was selling its 27-vessel fleet of support ships located in the Gulf of Mexico to New Orleans-based Tidewater Inc., owner and operator of more than 550 vessels used to support offshore drilling. Although the subsidiary, ENSCO Marine Company, was a profitable venture, it would require a significant investment to keep the business viable. Instead ENSCO elected to make an even greater financial commitment to its offshore rig fleet.

Principal Subsidiaries

ENSCO Drilling Company; ENSCO Holding Company; ENSCO Incorporated; ENSCO Offshore International Company.

Principal Competitors

Diamond Offshore Drilling, Inc.; GlobalSantaFe Corporation; Transocean Inc.

Further Reading

DuBois, Susan W., "The Texas Business Executive of the Year," *Texas Business Executive,* Spring/Summer 1982, p. 4.

Einhorn, Cheryl Strauss, "Gunfight," *Barron's,* December 9, 1996, pp. 31–35.

"ENSCO International Inc.," *Oil & Gas Investor,* March 1996, p. 12.

Forest, Stephanie Anderson, Kathleen Morris, Amy Barrett, Susann Rutledge, and Barbara Silverbush, "Rainwater," *Business Week,* November 30, 1998, p. 112.

Toal, Brian A., "A Driller with Drive," *Oil & Gas Investor,* July 1999, pp. 36–38.

—Ed Dinger

Erickson Retirement Communities

701 Maiden Choice Lane
Catonsville, Maryland 21228
U.S.A.
Telephone: (410) 242-2880
Fax: (410) 737-8854
Web site: http://www.ericksonretirement.com

Private Company
Founded: 1981 as Senior Campus Living
Employees: 5,541
Sales: $40 million (2002 est.)
NAIC: 623311 Continuing Care Retirement Communities

Erickson Retirement Communities (ERC) owns and operates several large-scale continuing care retirement communities that serve more than 10,000 middle-income retirees in Maryland, Virginia, New Jersey, Massachusetts, Pennsylvania, and Michigan. The company also manages Henry Ford Village for the Ford Motor Company. At each community the company offers studio, one-bedroom, and two-bedroom independent living apartments, assisted-living apartments, and skilled nursing care, providing housing for the changing needs of residents as they age. The campuses are self-contained to meet most of the daily needs of seniors. Each site provides medical facilities and an emergency ambulance service, a pharmacy, health club, pool, convenience store, banks, hair salons, and a variety of fine and casual dining options. Special purpose rooms cater to resident hobbies and interests, including wood shops, music rooms, art studios, computer labs, card and game rooms, and classrooms for college courses taught by visiting professors. Closed-circuit television provides residents with a calendar of events and classes.

ERC's pricing strategy is designed to attract middle-income retirees who own their own home and receive a monthly pension and social security. For affordability, entrance fees are set at the value of a potential resident's home value. Rather than a life contract, ERC offers services on an as-needed basis and completely refunds the entrance fee to the resident or the resident's estate. Company founder John Erickson introduced the idea of a 100 percent refundable entrance fee to the retirement community industry.

Insight and Vision Leading to Company Founding

Before founding Erickson Retirement Communities, John Erickson owned and operated several golf course mobile home parks that catered to retirees in Florida. Erickson saw that for every 100 retirees who relocated from northern states to Florida, 20 remained in their hometowns. He recognized a need for continuing care retirement communities for senior citizens who chose to remain at home, particularly for middle income retirees who owned a home and received a pension and social security; most such facilities catered to wealthy or low-income seniors.

Erickson found a site for his first retirement facility while in Washington, D.C., on a business trip in 1981. An old friend told him that St. Charles College and Seminary intended to sell the school's property in Cantonsville, Maryland. Erickson canceled his return trip to Florida and went to the 110-acre site in suburban Baltimore. Erickson decided that the campus would be a good place for a retirement community. He obtained financing and began to renovate the campus buildings, originally naming the company Senior Campus Living (SCL). In October 1982 the company began to sell one-bedroom units for independent living and 200 residents moved to Charlestown Retirement Community, named for the college, in December 1983.

Erickson developed the property through a long process that allowed the company to produce income as renovation progressed. Over the course of a decade facilities expanded to accommodate 1,313 independent living units, 134 assisted living units, and 122 beds for 24-hour nursing care. By September 30, 1992, SCL had sold 1,287 apartment units and planned to accommodate an additional 300 apartments for independent seniors. As the campus evolved, Charlestown developed "neighborhoods" and central activity areas developed as "Main Street." At this time Charlestown offered residents six dining options, two banks, three hair salons, and a medical clinic employing four full-time physicians during the regular work week. Although the community started without any social programs, resident involvement shaped the community, initiating a wide array of social activities, hobbies, crafts, and college classes and creating 150 activity-based clubs. In addition to club activity rooms, other amenities included an aquatic center, paved walking paths, a computer lab, and a library of 10,000

Company Perspectives:

Today, all the men and women of Erickson Retirement Communities continue to strive to provide the best possible programs, the best possible living spaces and facilities, and the best possible service to seniors. We are preserving the commitment that John Erickson made to seniors almost two decades ago.

books available for borrowing. A closed-circuit television studio aired a calendar of events.

The appeal of Charlestown to retirees originated with Erickson's ideas that a good retirement community rested on four pillars: independence, security, affordability, and convenient access to healthcare. In providing independence, Erickson envisioned a community that promoted an active social life for seniors while it freed them from the usual concerns of home ownership, such as maintenance and lawn care. Easy access to healthcare occurred through the presence of the onsite medical clinic, which specialized in geriatric medicine and provided visiting medical specialists. In addition to onsite nursing care and the assisted living facilities, Charlestown offered home healthcare.

In making the retirement community affordable, Erickson pioneered the 100 percent refundable entrance deposit, available at about equal to the value of a middle-class retiree's home. In 1992 an average apartment unit cost $94,430. Economies of scale provided affordability as well, with monthly fees within the means of middle-income seniors, at $890 for one person, plus an additional $350 for double occupancy. Residents paid for supplementary services, such as housekeeping, transportation, and home healthcare. As such, operating expenses, at $8,200 per resident per year, were much lower than other retirement communities.

SCL provided security by hiring a 24-hour security team and installing gates around the campus, allowing only family and friends of residents to enter the community. For health security, each bedroom and bathroom was outfitted with an emergency pull cord and each apartment door was equipped with a sentry latch. The latch would be turned up every night, if it remained up at noon the next day, because the resident had not caused the latch to fall by leaving the unit, someone would check into the well-being of the resident.

The Erickson Foundation formed in 1998 to initiate a new wellness program for preventive medicine through a health screening system. When completely developed, the portable Viva system would assess bone strength, balance, cardiac and lung function, muscle strength, driving skills, body composition and body weight, daily activity level, and psychosocial functioning.

By 2000, Charlestown was the largest continuing care retirement community in the United States, with 2,500 residents, and the waiting list grew to more than 1,300 interested retirees. Much of the growth and success of the community was due to the popularity of the 100 percent refundable entrance deposit, which prompted SCL to add more accommodations and services at Charlestown to meet demand. The large size of Charlestown became a unique facet of its success as it provided

ample possibilities for social interaction simply by housing a large number of residents.

The 1990s: Charlestown a Prototype Retirement Community

The success of the Charlestown community led, unexpectedly, to the development of another facility in 1992, when the Ford Motor Company approached SCL to be a partner in the development of a continuing care community in Dearborn, Michigan. Ford Motor had searched the country for the best facility that would provide a model for Henry Ford Village, to be located on the site of Henry Ford's birthplace and early childhood years. SCL participated in the project as a joint venture of Ford Motor Land Development Corporation and Retirement and Health Services Corporation.

Groundbreaking on the $110 million project began in September 1992 and the first phase of independent living apartments opened a year later. After completion of the five-year project, Henry Ford Village accommodated more than 1,250 residents with 862 apartments, 130 assisted living apartments, and 120 nursing beds, being the largest such facility in Michigan. The community provided amenities like those at Charlestown, with a Towne Center and residential "neighborhoods."

Charlestown provided a prototype for company-owned retirement communities opened by SCL during the late 1990s. In developing sites for new retirement facilities, SCL chose locations based on the local population of senior citizens 75 years of age and older, looking at populations within a radius of ten miles of a potential site. The company focused its expansion along the Interstate 95 corridor, near the Atlantic coast in Chesapeake and New England states. In March 1995, Oak Crest Village opened in Parkville, Maryland, on an 85-acre site only 20 miles from Charlestown. As one of the fastest growing retirement communities in the country at this time, Oak Crest accommodated more than 2,000 residents by the fall of 1998.

SCL opened the first phase of two retirement communities in 1998. The $250 million Seabrook Village project, located on a 100-acre site in Tinton Falls, New Jersey, accommodated up to 920 residents in 650 apartments when it opened. The complete project encompassed three neighborhoods of 550 apartments each in four- to seven-story buildings. A 70,000-square-foot community center housed the main dining room, the medical center, and hobby and classrooms, while enclosed, climate-controlled walkways linked all buildings on the campus. SCL applied these same site design concepts at Greenspring Village in Springfield, Virginia, which opened in November 1998. The $312 million project accommodated 1,412 independent living apartments, 125 assisted living apartments, and 20 skilled nursing beds at the 108-acre site.

The company's advertisements addressed the concerns of retirees by emphasizing the ease of the retirement community lifestyle. In the *New York Times* advertising, taglines stated, "Seniors Walk Away from Houses," while the text promoted a "worry-free, maintenance-free lifestyle" and senior women were pictured lounging in a swimming pool. The advertisement highlighted the onsite medical center, fine and casual dining, college classes, and the neighborhood center.

Key Dates:

1981: John Erickson founds Senior Campus Living.
1983: Charleston Retirement Community opens on former college campus.
1992: Ford Motor Company approaches Erickson to build and manage life care retirement community on the birthplace of Henry Ford.
1995: The second company-owned property opens in Parkville, Maryland.
1998: Seabrook Village and Greenspring Village retirement communities begin operations.
2000: Retirees begin moving into new homes at Riderwood Village and Brooksby Village; company is renamed Erickson Retirement Communities (ERC).
2003: ERC is the eighth largest senior housing developer based on number of units.

ERC Building in Underserved Markets in Early 2000s

In early 2000 the company took the name Erickson Retirement Communities (ERC), replacing Senior Campus Living with a more distinct name that honored the company's founder. Supported with $300 million in financing from several private investors and partners, ERC continued to develop new retirement communities.

Riderwood Village opened with 200 residents in May 2000. Located in Silver Spring, Maryland, Riderwood offered one-bedroom and two-bedroom units and the entrance deposit for the site averaged $73,000 with monthly fees at $1,023. As development of the site continued, Riderwood Village accommodated 850 residents. Brooksby Village opened the following June in Peabody, Massachusetts, housing 150 residents, increasing to 650 residents by early 2003. Adding variety to community facilities based on resident input, ERC opened a pub at the Riderwood Village and a bistro with exhibition cooking at Brooksby Village.

ERC renamed its assisted-living and skilled nursing centers as Renaissance Gardens, distinguishing them more clearly from regular housing accommodations. Completed at Seabrook Village in the summer of 2001, the center allowed for changeable floor functions to accommodate the changing needs of nursing the elderly. Housed in a five-story building, each floor provided a sun porch, dining room, and recreation room. Renaissance Gardens at Seabrook Village offered 96 assisted living units and 80 private nursing care rooms. The facility housed doctors' offices and physical therapy rooms in an adjacent building. Cedar Crest Village opened in Pompton Plains, New Jersey, in August 2001, with 274 residents and a community building. ERC dedicated 130 acres of the 260-acre site for open space, to provide nature trails for public and resident use. When complete, the five-year development project would house up to 2,400 residents in 1,517 apartments, ranging in price from $138,000 to $398,000, 192 assisted living units, and 320 nursing beds. In addition to the usual amenities and facilities, Cedar Crest would feature a chapel and a convention hall. ERC promoted the property by transporting groups of potential customers to nearby Seabrook Village.

During this same period, ERC began construction on a $350 million retirement community in Novi, Michigan. ERC identified the area as an underserved market, with more than a half million people over the age of 65 within a 25-mile radius. When complete, Fox Run Village would provide 1,100 apartment units for independent living as well as skilled nursing and assisted living facilities for 400 residents. The community was intended for retirees with a monthly income of $1,000 to $2,500; deposits ranged from $77,000 to $297,000 per apartment unit. The community opened in the spring of 2003 as part of a five- to seven-year development process.

In April 2001 ERC announced the development of a retirement community on the site of the former Naval Air Warfare Center in Warminster, Pennsylvania. In building Ann's Choice, ERC took advantage of the site as a Keystone Opportunity Zone for redevelopment, to receive state and local tax reductions for up to ten years. Allowing seniors age 62 years and older, the plan supported accommodations for as many as 1,500 independent living units if demand required it. The first phase of Ann's Choice opened in the late summer of 2003, upon completion of the medical center and main community facilities and 199 apartment units housing nearly 300 retirees.

Pending Plans and Projects

In 2002 ERC received approval to build Linden Ponds in Hingham, Massachusetts. The plan called for 2,000 independent and assisted living units and 324 skilled nursing beds. ERC began newspaper, television, and direct mail advertising in the fall of 2002 and opened an onsite marketing office in the summer of 2003. ERC expected construction to begin by the fall of 2003 and completion of the first phase to occur in late 2004.

In the spring of 2003 ERC sought approval to build a retirement community in Lincolnshire, Illinois. The proposal described campus housing of 1,538 independent living units in three neighborhoods of four to five structures from four to six stories high. Each neighborhood would have its own community center with health, dining, recreational, and business facilities. Renaissance Gardens would be housed in a six-story building containing 138 assisted living units and 236 skilled nursing beds. The community would accommodate up to 2,300 residents after completion of the five- to seven-year construction project.

Principal Divisions

Ann's Choice; Brooksby Village; Cedar Crest Village; Charlestown Retirement Community; Fox Run Village; Green Spring Village; Linden Ponds; Oak Crest Village; Retirement and Health Services Corporation; Riderwood Village; Seabrook Village.

Principal Competitors

Del Webb Corporation.

Further Reading

Adler, Sam, "Middle CLASS ACT: Erickson Retirement," *Contemporary Long Term Care,* March 2000, p. 28.

Ayala, Leonor, "Cedar Crest Village Gets Planners' Approval: Site Would House 2,400 Seniors," *Record (New Jersey),* August 11, 1999, p. L1.

Berton, Lee, "Waiting for Care, Continuing-Care Communities Offer Peace of Mind to Residents and Their Families; That Is, If You Can Ever Get in the Front Gate," *Wall Street Journal,* June 7, 1999, p. 10.

"Charlestown," *National Real Estate Investor,* September 1993, p. S12.

Cichowski, John, "Builder Proposes Senior Housing Route 23 Site Could Have 1,500 Units," *Record (New Jersey),* November 21, 1996, p. A1.

"CNL Retirement Properties Has Invested $35 million in Its Partnership with Erickson Retirement Communities," *Real Estate Finance and Investment,* May 5, 2003, p. 10.

Dietderich, Andrew, "$350M Community Planned; Novi Retirement Complex to Have 1,500 Units," *Crain's Detroit Business,* June 4, 2001, p. 1.

Edgar, Julie, "Developer Seeks Approval for Retirement Site in Novi, Mich.," *Detroit Free Press,* June 5, 2001.

Goodin, Michael, "Village Changes Senior Living," *Crain's Detroit Business,* October 11, 1993, p. 3.

Graham, Scott, "Erickson Eyes Pa. Property," *Baltimore Business Journal,* August 18, 2000, p. 7.

——, "A Senior Business," *Baltimore Business Journal,* August 4, 2000, p. 21.

"Industry Innovations," *Journal on Active Aging,* July-August 2002, p. 36.

"John C. Erickson," *Baltimore Business Journal,* October 6, 2000, p. 19.

Karpovich, Todd, "Encore Performance: Senior Living Outfit Lures Back Founder," *Baltimore Business Journal,* June 19, 1998, p. 1.

McCabe, Kathy, "Retirement Units Open Friday," *Boston Globe,* March 30, 2003, p. 14.

McGrath, Mary, "Clifton Gets Senior Housing Plan; Shulton Site Would Be Home to 1,800," *Record (New Jersey),* September 11, 1996, p. N1.

Oser, Alan S., "New York Area Retirees Get More Housing Choices," *New York Times,* May 10, 1998, p. RE1.

Roach, Kia, "Senior Campus Living Bound for Virginia; Company to Develop Largest Community to Date," *Daily Record,* November 12, 1996, p. 3.

Sharton, Emily, "Development Pitches Units Despite Suit; Planning Board Questions Status As 'Affordable,' " *Boston Globe,* October 24, 2002, p. 1.

Silva, Chris, "Senior Home Irked by Limits Set by State Health Agency," *Washington Business Journal,* December 14, 2001, p. 3.

"Two Hundred Residents Make Riderwood Home," *Daily Record,* May 6, 2000.

Ursery, Stephen, "Seniors Housing Beat," *National Real Estate Investor,* June 2000, p. 38.

——, "Seniors Housing Beat," *National Real Estate Investor,* September 2000, p. 40.

Werner, Ben, "SCL Changes Its Name to 'Affirm the Values,' " *Baltimore Business Journal,* February 4, 2000, p. 8.

Williams, Barbara, "Retirement Village for Up to 2,400 Under Way: Half of 260-Acre Site in Pequannock Will Remain Open Space," *Record (New Jersey),* October 20, 2000, p. L7.

—Mary Tradii

Eternal Word Television Network, Inc.

5817 Old Leeds Road
Irondale, Alabama 35210-2198
U.S.A.
Telephone: (205) 271-2900
Fax: (205) 271-2925
Web site: http://www.ewtn.com

Private Company
Incorporated: 1981
Employees: 260
Operating Revenues: $25 million (2002 est.)
NAIC: 513120 Television Broadcasting

Eternal Word Television Network, Inc. (EWTN) provides 24-hour television and radio programming for a worldwide Roman Catholic audience. The nonprofit network was founded by a Franciscan nun and has its studios in an Alabama convent, the Our Lady of the Angels Monastery. EWTN's activities are supported by private donations and sales of books, videotapes, and religious articles. One of the largest religious media networks in the world, EWTN is available to more than 70 million homes in 79 countries worldwide through cable systems, wireless cable, direct broadcast satellite, low power TV, and individual satellite systems. The network's television programming reaches audiences in North America, Europe, Africa, and Central and South America, and is also available through the Internet. In addition, EWTN offers 24-hour AM/FM shortwave radio programming.

One of EWTN's longest-running shows was *Mother Angelica Live,* an hour-long biweekly program on which the network's founder spoke directly to her viewers and took phone calls. Following a pair of strokes she suffered in 2001, Mother Angelica continued to be present to viewers through the programs *The Best of Mother Angelica Live* and *Mother Angelica Live Classics.* The original show also continued to air, under the new title *EWTN Live,* with replacement host Father Mitch Pacwa.

EWTN also produces several other regular series featuring Catholic theologians and devotional leaders and broadcasts a "Daily Mass" from the convent's chapel in Irondale. Other programming includes documentaries, music specials, a televised Rosary, and a news program with a Catholic perspective. The network makes a special effort to follow happenings at the Vatican, with live coverage of the pope's travels around the world.

Network founder Mother Angelica has been the defining personality at EWTN throughout its history. The nun is guided by a firm faith in her ministry, placing more trust in the providence of God than in practical matters such as financial planning. She has frequently set her sights on a lofty goal while having faith that the necessary means would be provided. While the network's viewers are indeed loyal supporters, others within the Catholic Church are uncomfortable with the conservative focus of Mother Angelica and EWTN. The nun has often criticized liberals and feminists in her weekly shows, and they in turn have objected to her strictly orthodox interpretation of Catholicism. Nevertheless, the network remains one of the most visible representations of the Catholic Church in the United States.

Mother Angelica's Background: 1923–81

The founder of EWTN was born Rita Francis Rizzo in 1923 in Canton, Ohio. She experienced a difficult childhood, marked by divorce and poverty, and found the nuns at her parochial school to be unsympathetic. Nevertheless, Rizzo had a profound personal faith and, when her prayers to be cured of a persistent abdominal pain were answered, she considered the healing a miracle. The experience influenced her decision in 1944 to enter a convent in Cleveland, where she became a Franciscan Nun of the Most Blessed Sacrament, also known as a Poor Clare. There "Mother Angelica" lived a life of frugality, seclusion, and prayer.

A second healing experience led Mother Angelica to found her own convent. After a back injury, doctors told her she might not walk again. She prayed to God, promising that if she regained use of her legs, she would start a convent in the Deep South, where only 2 percent of the population was Catholic. Eventually Mother Angelica was able to walk with a crutch, so she carried through on her promise. First she raised money by selling fishing lures and then, in 1961, built the Our Lady of the Angels Monastery in Irondale, Alabama. In the first year, seven sisters lived together in the new structure, among them Mother

Company Perspectives:

Eternal Word Television Network is dedicated to the advancement of truth as defined by the magisterium of the Roman Catholic Church. The mission of the Eternal Word Television Network is to serve the orthodox belief and teaching of the Church as proclaimed by the Supreme Pontiff and his predecessors.

The goal of the Eternal Word Television Network is to provide the means by which the various organizations within the Church will have a nationwide vehicle of expression. This will be provided for them without charge as long as their spirituality remains within the theological context of Mother Church. This is best evidenced by the acceptance of the Dogmas, Rules and Regulations of the Church in all matters, but especially as they relate to the topics on which their television presentation is based.

As the Eternal Word Television Network exists to provide a media for orthodox endeavors, this mission statement should be viewed as the basis of or foundation for this essential spiritual growth ministry, not as an attempt to censor any organization or individual.

Angelica's own mother. The sisters lived a secluded life, enjoying general goodwill from their neighbors and roasting peanuts to pay for their daily needs.

In 1971 Mother Angelica was invited by a local Protestant church to teach Bible study. The nun had developed her skills as a religious instructor by giving daily lessons to the sisters after breakfast. Her foray into the wider community was successful, and she soon gained a reputation as an engaging teacher. More Bible study engagements followed in both Catholic and Protestant congregations. Eventually people began requesting printed versions of Mother Angelica's talks, which led to the establishment of a printing press in the monastery. The Poor Clare sisters started shipping mini-books and leaflets around the country.

Mother Angelica made her television debut in 1978, when a video series of her talks was taped at a Birmingham station for the Christian Broadcasting Network. Shortly thereafter she set up her own studio at the monastery to tape regular shows for a series known as "Our Heritage." Mother Angelica's exposure to the world of television technology made her determined to have her own facility. After a few years she parted ways with the Christian Broadcasting Network over their airing of a film that she considered blasphemous, and moved toward the establishment of an independent Catholic network.

Early Growth in the 1980s

The Eternal Word Television Network was launched on August 15, 1981, and began transmitting four hours a day to about 60,000 homes. Preparations for the launch had filled the first half of 1981. A nonprofit company was set up under the leadership of William Steltemeier, a successful Nashville lawyer. In March a $350,000, ten-meter "dish" antenna was installed, funded by small donations from Catholics around the world. The annual cost of satellite time and operating expenses

was estimated to be around $1.5 million. Although the network's leaders were not sure where that sum would come from, they trusted that if the ministry had spiritual worth, financial support would materialize. EWTN's goal was to provide warm and personal programming, dealing more with the spiritual aspects of faith than with politics and other worldly matters.

In November 1982 Mother Angelica had her first audience with Pope John Paul II and presented him with a model of a satellite dish. By 1983 the network's subscribers had grown to one million. The first live program aired in August of that year, celebrating the network's second anniversary. In October several live shows made their debut on Tuesdays, Wednesdays, and Thursdays, featuring theologians and religious leaders such as Father Harold Cohen, Father Mitch Pacwa, and Babsie Bleasdale. By December it was apparent that the current studio was inadequate for the expanded programming activities, so Mother Angelica took a novel step to demonstrate her desire for a new studio. She directed an EWTN carpenter to tie white rags on all the trees that would have to be cut down on the new site, saying she wanted the Lord to look down and see that she needed a larger studio. The tactic, in any case, proved effective in attracting attention down on earth: a friend of the convent stopped by, asked about the rags, and ended up donating $50,000 to start construction of a new building.

A new 6,500-square-foot post-production facility was dedicated in April 1985. By that time, EWTN had more than five million subscribers and garnered nationwide attention when a profile of Mother Angelica aired a few months later on the CBS television show *60 Minutes*. As EWTN viewership grew, the network decided it was time to expand its offerings. It took a huge step forward in September 1987 when it moved to 24-hour programming. To fill the air time, the network created new series and showed documentaries and specials. EWTN also took on a commitment to broadcast internationally significant Catholic events, including happenings at the Vatican, the pope's global travels, holy day events from major shrines, and the installation of bishops. A new production vehicle was delivered in August 1988 to support location work. The "Gabriel I" was outfitted for onsite taping, production, and editing. The following month EWTN acquired an uplink truck, which made live coverage possible by beaming location programs back to Birmingham via satellite. In 1988 the network also started broadcasting live Masses of Holy Days from the Basilica of the National Shrine of the Immaculate Conception in Washington, D.C. The broadcasts were supported by a grant from the Knights of Columbus.

Mother Angelica was becoming a nationally known figure in the Catholic Church, and she used this visibility to express her convictions about her faith. For example, when the film *The Last Temptation of Christ,* directed by Martin Scorsese, was condemned by the U.S. Catholic Church, Mother Angelica was one of the voices cited against the film. The *Los Angeles Times* reported that she said anyone watching the film would be committing a "deliberate act of blasphemy." She objected to the unflattering portrayal of Christ as a figure with human weaknesses.

As EWTN's influence expanded, the network began to take the Hispanic Catholic community into consideration. In 1989

<table>
<tr><td colspan="2">

Key Dates:

</td></tr>
</table>

Key Dates:

1961: Mother Angelica founds Our Lady of the Angels Monastery in Alabama.

1971: Mother Angelica begins leading Bible study sessions in the surrounding community.

1978: Videotapes of Mother Angelica's talks air on the Christian Broadcasting Network.

1981: Eternal Word Television Network, Inc. (EWTN) is founded, broadcasting four hours a day.

1987: EWTN moves to 24-hour programming.

1992: Shortwave radio station WEWN begins broadcasting.

1995: The first international satellite service is launched.

2001: Mother Angelica suffers strokes and undergoes surgery; Fr. Mitch Pacwa takes over her show.

2003: EWTN celebrates Mother Angelica's 80th birthday; the founder is honored by the National Cable Telecommunications Association as a "Cable Television Pioneer."

three blocks of time were allotted for Spanish language programming. Hispanic viewers were particularly interested in EWTN's live coverage of the pope's visit to Mexico in May 1990. In August 1990 Mother Angelica had her second audience with the pope, during which he told her to continue her television ministry. When the Gulf War started, EWTN aired the American bishops' message of encouragement to troops and their families. During the following Lenten season, the network began broadcasting live daily Masses from its own Our Lady of the Angels Monastery. The broadcasts were initially intended to encourage the families of Gulf War soldiers, but after the war ended viewers requested that the daily masses continue. As a result, unobtrusive robotic cameras were installed in the Alabama monastery's chapel in mid-1991. The network now estimated its number of subscribers at 22 million.

An Outspoken National Presence: 1990–2002

One of the greatest challenges to EWTN's expansion consisted in persuading cable operators to carry the network. EWTN's loyal supporters initiated grass-roots campaigns to influence cable systems, meeting with mixed results. In Buffalo, New York, EWTN's backers threatened to oppose renewal of a cable operator's franchise with the city and cancel their cable service unless the Catholic network was put on the air. The cable company gave in and agreed to carry EWTN in late 1990. In the fall of 1994, EWTN was temporarily taken off the air in Raleigh, North Carolina. The network was put back on the air after its viewers prayed and marched into the offices of the local cable company singing "The Battle Hymn of the Republic." A Cincinnati campaign in the fall of 1990 was less successful. There, Warner Cablevision stuck with its decision to replace EWTN with other religious networks, despite a mail and phone campaign in opposition to the move. The Vision Interfaith Satellite Network (VISN) was one of the networks that replaced EWTN. VISN was operated by diverse Judeo-Christian faiths and had a policy against on-air solicitation of funds. That policy appealed to cable operators in the wake of the scandal involving

televangelist Jim Bakker. Because cable operators were reluctant to devote more than one channel to religious programming, there was fierce competition among religious networks for cable time.

In December 1992 the generosity of Dutch philanthropists Piet and Trude Derksen made it possible for EWTN to expand into the realm of radio. A short-wave station, WEWN, began broadcasting 24 hours a day in English and Spanish. The radio service was generated by a newly constructed complex consisting of four 500-kilowatt radio transmitters and two diesel generators for backup power. The complex was built on Alabama's third-tallest mountain beginning in April 1991. The project upset several property owners, who objected to the widening of an old logging road, the clearing of ten acres of trees, and the installation of power lines that now snaked up the mountainside. Lawsuits were filed against EWTN and the Alabama Power Co. EWTN President William Steltemeier pointed out that he could not expect to satisfy everybody. The largest subscriber increase in the network's history also occurred in 1992. Six million new homes were connected, increasing the network's audience to a total of 31 million homes.

In 1993 Mother Angelica had her third audience with the pope and presented him with photos of the new radio station. That summer EWTN provided live coverage of World Youth Day '93 in Denver, Colorado, and Mother Angelica gained attention for one of her most outspoken criticisms of liberal Catholicism yet. Specifically, she objected to the fact that a woman played the role of Jesus in an enactment of the Stations of the Cross presented by a Catholic theater troupe. Mother Angelica was one of about a dozen prominent Catholics who signed a letter to the Vatican denouncing the performance. *Time* magazine quoted her as saying, "Enough is enough. I'm tired of inclusive language that refuses to admit that the Son of God is a man. I'm tired of you, liberal church in America. You're sick." The incident solidified her reputation as an opponent of feminists, liberals, and of what she perceived as a watering-down of the church's teachings. Some Catholics were attracted to Mother Angelica's evocation of the traditional certitudes of the church as it existed before the Vatican II reforms of the 1960s. Other church figures regretted that her strident defense of orthodox Catholicism was being broadcast around the world. In an article in the *National Catholic Reporter*, for example, Jesuit priest Raymond Schroth decried what he perceived as a lack of intellectual sophistication on Mother Angelica's part, pointing to her broadcast of the traditional Latin Mass, her belief in the literal reality of miracles, and her only partial acceptance of Vatican II reforms.

Meanwhile, EWTN continued to expand its availability around the world. In August 1995 the first international satellite service was launched, providing round-the-clock broadcasts to Europe, Africa, and Central and South America. By September 1995, 40 million homes received EWTN. The network provided live coverage in both English and Spanish of the pope's visit to several American cities that fall. In December second audio programming was added to fully accommodate a Spanish-speaking audience. The network's name was also changed to EWTN Global Catholic Network. More expansion followed in 1996. That year EWTN acquired the Catholic Resource Network, which allowed it to place a large collection of Catholic documents online, and also added a daily radio and television news service through an agreement with Catholic World News. In May, a contract with PanAmSat provided for global satellite distribution. Shortly thereafter Mother Angelica gave the pope a map of the network's international satellite coverage in her fourth audience with him. Services in the Pacific Rim, including Australia, New Zealand, China, Japan, and the Philippines, were launched in December.

Several new programs were introduced in 1997. *Life on the Rock,* with host Jeff Cavins, was directed at Christian youth, while *The World Over,* with Raymond Arroyo, provided news from a Christian perspective. A third show, *The Journey Home* with host Marcus Grodi, provided an opportunity for former church leaders of other Christian faiths to discuss their personal conversion experiences and the influences that brought them home to the Roman Catholic Church. Internet broadcast of the network's worldwide AM/FM radio signal also began in 1997. Later that year another controversy arose around Mother Angelica's objection to a pastoral letter composed by Cardinal Roger Mahony, archbishop of Los Angeles. On *Mother Angelica Live,* the nun criticized the cardinal for paying insufficient attention to the doctrine of transubstantiation, and stated that he apparently did not believe in the doctrine of the real presence of Christ in the Eucharist. The topic was of particular concern to Mother Angelica, since her order was known for adoration of the Eucharist. The sisters in the Alabama convent, for example, went beyond the usual practice to prostrate themselves at Mass during the Eucharist prayer. Mother Angelica declared that she would not be obedient if she lived in the Los Angeles diocese, and Cardinal Mahony brought the case to the Vatican.

EWTN's offerings grew further in the late 1990s. In 1998 the network obtained a satellite radio service license from the Radio Authority of the United Kingdom, launched direct-to-home satellite radio service in Europe on the Astra satellite, and developed satellite television service for Africa. The first live show in Spanish, *Nuestra Fe en Vivo,* also debuted that year, hosted by Pepe Alonso. In 1999 EWTN made its television signal available on the Internet and converted its domestic playout from tape-based facilities to digital file servers. In addition, two new Spanish services were developed: La Red Global Católica for television and Radio Católica Mundial on the radio. At the end of the year, the network provided live coverage of the pope opening the door to the Jubilee of the Year 2000. Special programming was planned over the next 13 months to honor the Jubilee.

In March 2000, EWTN offered live coverage of the pope's historic visit to the Holy Land. In the summer of 2001 EWTN was finally approved to be carried by cable and satellite television in Canada. Canada had long been the only country in the western hemisphere besides Cuba that did not allow broadcast of EWTN, according to the network's spokespeople. The introduction of digitalized cable, which eliminated concerns about competition for space in the radio wave spectrum, may have influenced Canada's decision. As the network forged ahead with technological and geographic expansion, its founder was experiencing health problems. Mother Angelica had two strokes late in 2001 and underwent surgery to remove a blood clot from her brain. She was released from the hospital early in 2002 and came home to the monastery to continue her rehabilitation. Hosting duties for *Mother Angelica Live* were taken over by Father Mitch Pacwa, a Jesuit priest, prolife speaker, and Catholic apologist who had been appearing on EWTN since 1984. The show was eventually renamed *EWTN Live.*

Mother Angelica's vision and faith had built up a worldwide presence for EWTN. Despite her absence from involvement in the network's day-to-day operations, as she continued her convalescence, the network she had founded remained firmly rooted in the values she had championed. In recognition of her accomplishments within the industry, the National Cable Telecommunications Association inducted her into its hall of ''Cable Television Pioneers'' in June 2003, shortly after the celebration of her 80th birthday. EWTN, the nonprofit dynamo she had founded, appeared likely to remain a leader among Catholic media organizations.

Principal Competitors

The Christian Broadcasting Network, Inc.; Trinity Broadcasting Network.

Further Reading

Boczkiewicz, Robert, ''Religion Networks Fighting for Places on Cable Systems Television,'' *Los Angeles Times,* October 20, 1990, p. 16.

Dart, John, ''Church Declares 'Last Temptation' Morally Offensive,'' *Los Angeles Times,* August 10, 1988, p. 3.

Garrison, Greg, ''Mother Angelica's Radio Towers Rouse Static,'' *National Catholic Reporter,* January 8, 1993, p. 8.

Goolrick, Chester, ''Mother Angelica Has a Job for Heaven in a Secular World,'' *Wall Street Journal,* March 19, 1981, p. 1.

''Jesuit Priest to Fill in at EWTN for Ailing Mother Angelica,'' *America,* February 4, 2002, p. 5.

Keeler, Bob, ''Mother Angelica—Live and Riding on Faith,'' *Washington Post,* May 7, 1994, p. B07.

Martin, James, ''Cardinal Mahony and Mother Angelica,'' *America,* March 7, 1998, p. 3.

——, ''Tired of Mother Angelica?,'' *America,* October 22, 1994, p. 27.

Niebuhr, Gustav, ''Use of Actress in Jesus Role Stirs Dispute,'' *Washington Post,* September 11, 1994, p. A03.

''Nun-Launched EWTN Goes Global,'' *Satellite News,* June 18, 2001.

Ostling, Richard N., ''Mother Knows Best,'' *Time,* August 7, 1995, p. 58.

Robichaux, Mark, ''Religious Cable Networks Fight Sin—and One Another,'' *Wall Street Journal,* September 12, 1995, p. B1.

Schroth, Raymond A., ''Angelica, EWTN Push Disneyland Church,'' *National Catholic Reporter,* July 15, 1994, p. 12.

Smithson, Carla, ''Cuba of the North Relents,'' *Report Newsmagazine,* August 20, 2001.

Steltemeier, William, ''Network President Defends EWTN's Liturgies,'' *National Catholic Reporter,* September 12, 1997, p. 18.

—Sarah Ruth Lorenz

Fairfax Financial Holdings Limited

95 Wellington Street West
Suite 800
Toronto, Ontario M5J 2N7
Canada
Telephone: (416) 367-4941
Fax: (416) 367-4946
Web site: http://www.fairfax.ca

Public Company
Incorporated: 1985
Employees: 9,764
Total Assets: $22.3 billion (2002)
Stock Exchanges: Toronto New York
Ticker Symbol: FFH
NAIC: 524126 Direct Property and Casualty Insurance
    Carriers

Toronto-based Fairfax Financial Holdings Limited, a dealer in insurance and reinsurance services, has gained notoriety through its acquisition strategy and success in bringing financial gains to shareholders by means of its investments. Fairfax is led by CEO Prem Watsa. The company reported net income of $264 million in 2002, on revenues of just over $5 billion.

Acquiring Mind: 1985–95

Canada's Fairfax Financial Holdings Limited is synonymous with V. Prem Watsa. Born in India, Watsa eventually trained to be a chemical engineer. He changed his path in 1972, however, moving to London, Ontario, where his brother resided. After earning a business degree from the University of Western Ontario, Watsa worked for Confederation Life Insurance Co. in Toronto. He quickly moved from his position as an analyst to one of portfolio manager.

With ten years of experience under his belt, Watsa signed on with a start-up asset management firm. When the endeavor failed, he contacted his former boss at Confederation. The pair established Hamblin Watsa Investment Counsel in 1984. Soon after, Watsa raised the $9 million that Markel Insurance, a

trucking insurance underwriter, needed to stay afloat. Markel's holding company would later be renamed Fairfax.

When the company began trading on the market in 1985, shares went for C$3.25. Revenues for the year were C$17 million. By 1992, Fairfax subsidiaries operated in the areas of property and casualty insurance, investment management, insurance claims management, and life insurance, pulling in revenues of C$286.8 million. From 1985 to 1992 shareholder equity had grown from C$10.4 million to C$143.8 million. Return on equity exceeded 20 percent in all but one year during the period.

In November 1993, Duff & Phelps Credit Rating Co. lauded the market positioning, financial status, and management team of Fairfax property and casualty subsidiaries. But the rating agency voiced concerns as well, included among them, the issue of financial leverage. Fairfax depended on borrowed funds to grow. Its planned purchase of Houston-based specialty insurer Ranger Insurance Company, for example, would be financed by a stock offering and issuance of notes.

Buying good companies down on their luck also factored into the Fairfax acquisition strategy. A company in its fold since 1990, Vancouver-based Commonwealth Insurance Company had a strong core business but had been held back by a struggling parent company.

By 1995, a decade into operation, Fairfax consisted of six insurance companies, an investment management firm, a claims adjusting company, and a Bermuda-based reinsurer. In addition, the holding company put forth solid numbers. Profit for the year was C$87.5 million, up from C$38.1 million in 1994. Stock price closed in on C$80—a respectable showing to be sure, but it paled in comparison to what happened next.

Flying High: 1996–98

Fairfax stock began a dizzying climb when Watsa purchased Skandia America Reinsurance Corp., a major U.S. property-casualty reinsurer, in early 1996. During the years 1992 and 1993, both Skandia America and its parent Skandia Ins. Co. Ltd. were hit with significant losses. Hurricane Andrew pummeled the American operation, while the Sweden-based parent com-

---

Company Perspectives:

Fairfax Financial Holdings Limited is a financial services holding company whose corporate objective is to achieve a high rate of return on invested capital and build long-term shareholder value.

---

pany grappled with a downturn in Scandinavian real estate and corresponding investment losses. In response, Skandia America was downsized: the property business was phased out. Premium volume fell by more than half. Meanwhile, casualty insurance prices were driven down by stiff competition.

Under Fairfax, Skandia would reenter the property business and continue to operate independently, in accordance with Fairfax's decentralized operating system. Eric Simpson, vice-president in A.M. Best's property/casualty division, told *National Underwriter* in March 1996, "Generally, and almost without exception, Fairfax has taken solid properties and turned up the performance several notches."

With Skandia aboard, Fairfax's assets reached C$3.2 billion, a doubling effect. Stock price went along for the ride, reaching the C$100 level when the deal was announced. The climb continued despite the concerns of bond rating agencies. The Skandia purchase, worth approximately $230 million, was to be financed by issues of debt and stock.

Fairfax stock passed the C$200 mark in September, when the purchase of Compagnie Transcontinentale de Reassurance (CTR) from its Paris-based parent was announced. Watsa planned to finance the CTR deal with a private placement, setting the per-share price above the going rate. The C$260 offering price nudged Fairfax stock even higher.

Analysts, while surprised by the acceleration of the stock price, remained cautious, pointing to the cyclical nature of the industry, the uncertainties related to the new businesses, and the debt accumulated to bring them aboard. "And while Watsa has an excellent management team, Fairfax is mainly Watsa," observed the *Financial Post* in September 1996. What would happen to Fairfax without Watsa?

Fairfax added yet another reinsurance concern in 1997 and broadened its global reach. Business had been slipping for Sphere Drake Holdings Ltd. (Bermuda). Under Fairfax the company hoped for a more solid footing financially. In turn, Fairfax gained underwriting outlets in London and Bermuda.

Through its Odyssey Re Group, formed from Skandia and Transcontinentale, Fairfax already had reinsurance offices in the major markets of New York, Paris, and Singapore. The addition of Sphere Drake placed Odyssey Re among the world's 20 largest reinsurers, according to *Business Insurance.*

Watsa's penchant for insurance companies, his aversion to stock splits, and the company's elevated stock price begged comparisons with Warren Buffett and Berkshire Hathaway. "Like Buffett, Watsa understands how a smart investor can exploit the float. Fairfax, accordingly, owns ten property and

casualty insurers, whose huge reserves he uses to play the stock and bond markets," wrote Bruce Upbin for *Forbes.*

But there were significant differences between the two, as Upbin pointed out. "Buffett increases his book value by buying solid companies and letting them grow. Watsa does it by issuing new shares. In the last two years he has increased the number of common shares outstanding by 25%." Watsa held 15 percent of stock, valued at C$648 million.

Moreover, Fairfax had been posting underwriting losses on its insurance policies while Berkshire took in more in premiums than it paid out in claims and costs. Fairfax's underwriting problems were not over, however. Skandia and Sphere Drake, for example, came with significant asbestos and environmental claim exposure.

Fairfax picked up another company in March 1998, Crum & Forster Holdings Inc., an entity Xerox Corporation had been trying to sell for a number of years. Crum & Forster (C&F) served mid-sized companies in the U.S. commercial market and, like the others new to the Fairfax fold, came with its own set of problems.

Despite hot spots smoldering in some of its subsidiaries, Fairfax stock continued to hold the distinction of being the most expensive stock on the Toronto Exchange. It did experience volatility, ranging from C$265 in January to nearly C$500 per share in March 1998. The peak period coincided with the announcement of the C&F deal. Fairfax rounded out the year by purchasing New York-based TIG Holdings, which served specialty commercial markets. The company had been spiraling down for a number of years and had just posted a large quarterly loss.

"Clearly Fairfax is a deep-value investor looking for turnaround candidates," insurance analyst Weston Hicks told *National Underwriter.* TIG, like other struggling companies Watsa had acquired, came at a discount price, but Fairfax got more than it bargained for this time.

The Unforeseen: 1999–2003

Fairfax moved to restructure its London reinsurance business in May 1999. Business written by Sphere Drake prior to its integration with Fairfax hurt the Odyssey Re subsidiary of which it was now a part. According to a May 1999 *Business Insurance* article, the reinsurer contended that it had been used as "a dumping ground for underpriced coverages." In addition to shutting down some of its London business, Fairfax purchased $1 billion in stop-loss reinsurance coverage to mitigate the flow of any more red ink. Fairfax also had a runoff operation to handle matters related to discontinued lines of business.

Despite problems brewing in the subsidiaries, the holding company had continued to rack up return on equity in excess of 20 percent. How did Watsa do it? "When Watsa spots a cheap insurer, he moves in and buys it. Each purchase adds to Fairfax's massive $18 billion in investment assets. Watsa then uses that money to do what he does best: play the market. Fairfax's success depends on its ability to manage that huge float. Last year, the company reaped $441 million from its conservative portfolio of stocks and bonds," Jonathan Harris explained for *Canadian Business* in July 1999.

Key Dates:

1984: Hamblin Watsa Investment Counsel is founded.
1985: Now named Fairfax Financial Holdings Limited, the company begins trading on the Toronto exchange.
1996: Fairfax buys a major U.S. property-casualty reinsurer, Skandia America Reinsurance Corp.
1997: Fairfax is among the world's 20 largest reinsurers.
2001: The company loses money for the first time.
2003: Fairfax spins off its Canadian business units.

But Watsa's game plan faltered. In 1999, storms in Europe produced high catastrophic losses and the bottom dropped out of investment gains. C&F and TIG dragged the company down in 2000. Return on equity fell below the 20 percent mark for an unprecedented second year running.

Watsa's hopeful words in his letters to shareholders did not pan out. In 2001, the company lost money for the first time. The destruction of New York's World Trade Center and continuing reserve deficiencies at C&F and TIG were the culprits. Watsa also pointed to a generally troubled insurance market.

From year-end 2000 to year-end 2001, stock price fell from C$228.50 to C$164 per share. On the plus side, Fairfax took Odyssey Re public in 2001, trading on the New York Stock Exchange. The initial public offering brought in $434 million in cash and notes for Fairfax. In addition, plans were in the works to take C&F public. Watsa also set aside the Fairfax tradition of growth through acquisition. Internal growth would be the new mantra. New insurance and reinsurance business and an elevated level of retentions would have to keep the ball rolling.

Increased sales activities paid off in 2002. The Markel insurance subsidiary—Watsa's first acquisition—showed significant gains in net premiums. But the C&F public offering was scrapped. For the first time, Watsa sold Fairfax shares at a level below book value, raising suspicions, according to *Forbes,* that the company was having cash flow problems.

In December 2002, Watsa said he planned to pull the plug on the troubled TIG operation. "After setting aside sufficient cash to pay future claims on old policies, Watsa will have the right to extract from TIG its $793 million stock portfolio and deliver that to the parent in Toronto a year from now," explained Bernard Condon for *Forbes.*

Investors were not impressed and Fairfax stock slipped further. In addition, other questions lingered in the air over the solidity of some of its assets, the repeated additions to reserves, and the movement of capital through offshore subsidiaries. Debt ratings were downgraded. Analysts and regulators were on alert. Adding to the pressure, Fairfax had begun trading on the New York Stock Exchange in mid-December.

Fairfax returned to profitability in 2002, earning its highest profit in history at C$415.7 million. Watsa attributed the turn-

around to improvement in underwriting and a strong investment performance. Skeptics remained unconvinced. Fairfax's stock price continued to be depressed into early 2003, and was generally trading below $90 per share on the Toronto Stock Exchange.

In April 2003, Fairfax announced the formation of Northbridge Financial Corp., a vehicle to spin off four Canadian operating companies: Lombard, Commonwealth, Markel, and Federated. News in May included improved first quarter profit figures and improved liquidity. Watsa, long criticized for his elusiveness with not only the press but with stockholders, had opened up. Investors responded positively, driving up stock, but critics maintained a wait-and-see attitude about Fairfax's future.

Principal Subsidiaries

Crum & Forster Holdings Corporation.

Principal Competitors

American International Group, Inc.; Aviva plc; Hartford Insurance Group; State Farm Insurance Companies.

Further Reading

Bouw, Brenda, "Fairfax Powers Its Way Back to Dizzying Heights," *Financial Post,* March 21, 1998, p. 31.

Condon, Bernard, "Hoist by His Own Petard," *Forbes,* February 3, 2003, pp. 68–69.

Eavis, Peter, "Unsure Times for Insurer Fairfax Financial," *The Street.com,* January 15, 2003.

"Fairfax Extols Virtues of Spinoff," *Globe and Mail,* April 15, 2003.

"Fairfax Outpaces Expectations," *Financial Post,* September 28, 1996, p. 53.

"Fairfax Shareholders Could Use an Exit Strategy," *Globe and Mail,* May 8, 2003.

Goddard, Sarah, "Fairfax Revamps London Units," *Business Insurance,* May 31, 1999, pp. 3+.

"Good News Spurs Sale of Fairfax Shares," *Globe and Mail,* May 6, 2003.

Ha, Michael, "Reserve Concerns Impact Fairfax Shares," *National Underwriter Property & Casualty-Risk & Benefits Management,* February 10, 2003, pp. 37+.

Harris, Jonathan, "Invisible Man," *Canadian Business,* July 30, 1999, pp. 55+.

Niedzielski, Joe, "Xerox Exits Insurance with Crum & Forster Sale to Fairfax," *National Underwriter Property & Casualty,* March 16, 1998, pp. 1+.

Sclafane, Susanne, "Skandia America Re Bought by Fairfax for $230 Million," *National Underwriter Property & Casualty-Risk & Benefits Management,* March 4, 1996, pp. 2+.

——, "Fairfax Agrees to Buy TIG Holdings for $840 Million," *National Underwriter Property & Casualty,* December 14, 1998, pp. 3+.

Taylor, Fabrice, "Fairfax Unit Sale Smells of Desperation," *Globe and Mail,* April 16, 2003.

Unsworth, Edwin, "Fairfax Buys Sphere Drake," *Business Insurance,* June 30, 1997.

Upbin, Bruce, "Faux Buffett," *Forbes,* November 3, 1997, pp. 360+.

—Kathleen Peippo

First Cash Financial Services, Inc.

690 E. Lamar Boulevard, Suite 400
Arlington, Texas 76011
U.S.A.
Telephone: (817) 460-3947
Fax: (817) 461-7019
Web site: http://www.firstcash.com

Public Company
Incorporated: 1988 as First Cash Inc.
Employees: 1,257
Sales: $118.8 million (2002)
Stock Exchanges: NASDAQ
Ticker Symbol: FSFS
NAIC: 453310 Used Merchandise Stores

First Cash Financial Services, Inc. operates one of America's largest chains of pawnshops and check cashing/short-term advance stores, found in 11 states and Mexico. The Arlington, Texas company (as of March 2003) owns 137 pawnshops, located mostly in Texas and Mexico, and 62 check cashing/short-term advance stores, of which 24 are in Texas. In addition, First Cash is half-owner of a venture that operates kiosks in convenience stores to provide check cashing, money orders, wire transfers, and ''payday loans.'' Although pawnshops are well established in the United States, mom-and-pop enterprises generally suffer from a seedy reputation. First Cash and other publicly traded chains are trying to consolidate the industry as well as improve the image. For its part, First Cash pawnshops are designed very much like convenience or video stores, featuring well-lit parking and exteriors, and neatly arranged merchandise. A large share of the company's profits come from the sales of items that borrowers have forfeited, and by creating a more attractive atmosphere management hopes to attract a higher volume of bargain-hunting consumers.

Incorporation of First Cash in 1988

First Cash was founded by John R. Payne, who became involved in the pawnshop business after selling a Dallas bank he owned in 1979. He traded some Colorado property for a pawnshop in Dallas and operated it with his wife, Edith, until 1985 when they sold it and built two more modern-looking stores in Fort Worth. In July 1988 he incorporated First Cash Inc. in order to launch a chain of pawnshops. In that same month First Cash completed its first acquisition, buying two pawnshops from L.G.'s Pawn Shop, Inc. for $100,000. In January 1989 First Cash spent $500,000 to acquire more operations from L.G.'s. To run the chain Payne hired Phillip ''Rick'' Powell, the company's current chairman and chief executive officer. Like Payne, Powell had experience in the banking industry. Before coming to First Cash he had been the chairman of First Savings Bank in Arlington.

In the late 1980s pawnstore operators began to take their businesses public in order to fuel expansion; the first was Fort Worth-based Cash America, which went public in May 1987. First Cash, a six-store chain at this point, took the step in 1991. It reincorporated in Delaware and completed its initial public offering in April of that year. By the end of July, First Cash had grown by 50 percent, paying $1 million in cash for three stores in the Dallas/Fort Worth area. Later in 1991 the chain made its first out-of-state acquisitions, paying $550,000 in cash to buy Happy Hocker and Granny's Pawn in Oklahoma City. With 11 units, First Cash was now the nation's third largest public pawnshop chain.

In early 1992 First Cash made some changes in its management structure. Powell, who had held the title of president, now replaced Payne as chief executive officer and would soon take over the chairmanship as well. Payne became chairman emeritus, responsible for scouting new store sites and potential acquisitions. To help in assimilating its recent acquisitions, the chain also hired its former auditor from Price Waterhouse, Rick Wessell, to serve as chief financial officer. Moreover, First Cash took steps to beef up its computer system in order to better track loans and purchases at its stores. First Cash continued its aggressive expansion in the early months of 1992. Instead of paying cash the company now adopted a strategy of using company stock and notes payable. In this way, it added seven pawnshops in south Texas, acquired from American Pawn and Jewelry, Inc. It also signed a letter of intent to buy Regent Jewelry & Loan Co., a five-store chain, but this deal fell through when the two parties failed to come to a final understanding on payment terms, thus highlighting the difficulties of using such an acquisition financing approach. At this point First Cash owned 23 stores, some of which were new start-ups, but it remained a distant third among publicly traded pawnstore chains: Cash America owned 187 stores in the United States and another 26 in the United Kingdom, while number two EZCORP operated 93 stores. Although there was no lack of acquisition candidates, First Cash simply lacked the funds to grow as quickly as management would have liked. Nevertheless, the company was well positioned in the industry. According to a 1992 *Dallas Morning News* article quoting analysts, First Cash had "the critical mass it needs to survive in the next few years as larger chains use technology, expertise and economies of scale to nip away at the mom-and-pop shops that dominate the pawn industry today."

Change in Leadership; Resumption of Acquisition Activities: Mid-1990s

First Cash spent the balance of 1992 digesting its recent acquisitions. It was a good time for the pawnshop industry, which was prospering during a difficult period for the nation's economy. Pawnshop operators, on the other hand, maintained that the changing image of pawnshops was chiefly responsible for a wider swath of people visiting them. First Cash made no acquisitions in 1993, likely the result of differences among board members about how to grow the business. By the end of the year Payne and four other directors resigned "amicably to pursue personal and professional matters," as explained in a company statement.

First Cash resumed its acquisition activities in June 1994, when it paid nearly $4 million in cash and notes to buy Famous Pawn, a seven-store chain operating in the Baltimore/Washington, D.C. area. Famous Pawn was launched as a single store in 1988 by Mark Rothman, who agreed to stay on to run the operation for First Cash and to look for further acquisition and start-up possibilities in the area. Due to usury laws in the District and neighboring Virginia, pawnshops were permitted to charge only 5 percent interest a month. Because Maryland did not have such legislation, Famous Pawn concentrated its stores in Maryland suburbs close to the District and charged 10 percent a month. Technically, none of the stores in this market made loans. To abide by laws in all three states, the shop bought the merchandise (which in Texas would have been collateral) from the customer, who retained the right to buy back the item at a marked-up price, which in essence represented the principal of the loan plus interest.

In 1995 First Cash upgraded its computer infrastructure to improve both inventory control and loan evaluations. Employees could tap into the system to see what price an item had commanded in the past and were in this way able to make faster loan evaluations. In addition, each customer's transaction history was readily available, and the company's headquarters was now better able to track the operations of each store. First Cash also garnered

a lot of positive publicity in 1995 when it became the first pawnshop chain to stop selling handguns. Although this decision was in keeping with management's desire to improve the image of pawnshops and broaden their appeal, the main goal was to lower the company's risk of legal liability, should a handgun purchased at a First Cash store be used in a crime. Moreover, handgun sales required the completion of extensive paperwork in order to comply with both state and federal legislation. Because these sales accounted for less than 1 percent of First Cash's revenues, management opted to simply exit the business. First Cash would, however, continue to sell rifles and shotguns used for hunting and other sports, and would also continue to accept handguns as collateral. Any unredeemed weapons would then be sold to wholesale gun dealers outside of Texas.

First Cash renewed its acquisition activities in 1996 and 1997. It bought three Baltimore pawnshops in May 1996 at a cost of nearly $2.5 million in cash. A month later it bought three more pawnshops in the city at a cost of $1.6 million. Both deals were accomplished through the company's line of credit. Altogether in 1996, the First Cash chain grew by seven stores. Further, in 1996 First Cash began to manage and operate the 11-store pawnshop chain of JB Pawn, Inc., a Texas company owned by an investor group that originated in Georgia, with stores located in Texas and Maryland. First Cash then added another seven stores in 1997.

First Cash underwent a number of changes in 1998. It bought JB Pawn for $2 million, and then later in the year bought five pawnshops in El Paso and another 12 in South Carolina, both new markets for the company. Also in that year First Cash entered the Missouri market. Altogether, First Cash added 29 stores in 1998. The company also took major steps toward diversification when it acquired Miraglia Inc., involved in the check-cashing business. As part of the deal, First Cash picked up the 11-store, West Coast check-cashing chain, Cash & Go. In addition, it acquired Miraglia subsidiary Answers, etc., the country's top provider of software used in the check-cashing industry to evaluate risks associated with cashing checks and issuing payday loans. The software was also capable of storing and recalling a wide range of information, including customer photographs, signatures, and histories. It was able to handle other types of transactions, as well, such as money orders, wire transfers, and utility bill payments. First Cash then added to its slate of check-cashing stores by acquiring 11 outlets in the Chicago area, a new market for the company. In another bid to diversify, First Cash in 1998 became the first major pawnbroker to sell its merchandise on the Internet. After beefing up its technology, First Cash was able to post items from all of its stores on its web site. The company already had a real-time system and was keeping track of the necessary information, so taking the next step and making the items available online was a natural progression. The chain also began auctioning off some items: If a bid higher than a minimum price was received the item would be sold. Again, by selling online the company was attempting to appeal to customers who never thought to visit a pawnshop in person because of the stigma attached to such establishments.

Name Change in 1999: First Cash Financial Services

In 2000 First Cash continued efforts to bolster its balance sheet by signing a deal with Pawnbroker.com, making some

Key Dates:

1988:	First Cash Inc. is formed by John R. Payne.
1990:	Rick Powell is hired as president.
1991:	First Cash is taken public.
1993:	Payne and four other board members resign to pursue other interests.
1995:	Handguns are no longer sold.
1998:	Check-cashing stores are added.
1999:	First Cash enters Mexico.

250,000 items of merchandise available through its partner's web site. The venture also provided online financial and support services to the pawnshop industry. Although the online selling idea would not pan out, Pawnbroker.com expanded the type of financial services it offered to pawnshops and consumers.

As the U.S. economy soured in the early years of the new century, First Cash prospered. In 2001 it added ten new, free-standing stores, followed by 32 more outlets in 2002. In 2002 the company posted record revenues of $118.8 million and net profits just shy of $11 million. First Cash disposed of its check-cashing software business but overall was pleased with the strategy it had adopted of controlling costs while pursuing diversification, confident that the future held even greater promise.

Principal Subsidiaries

American Pawn and Jewelry, Inc.; JB Pawn, Inc.; Capital Pawnbrokers, Inc.; First Cash, S.A. De C.V.; First Cash, Inc.; Cash & Go, Inc.

Principal Competitors

Ace Cash Express, Inc.; Cash America International, Inc.; EZCORP, Inc.; PawnMart, Inc.

Further Reading

Files, Jennifer, ''First Cash on the Move in Growing Industry,'' *Dallas Morning News,* May 24, 1992, p. 3M.

McManus, Kevin, ''Consolidation Trend Hits Area Pawnshops,'' *Washington Post,* August 29, 1994, p. F5.

Mitchell, Jim, ''First Cash Pawnshops Banning Handgun Sales,'' *Dallas Morning News,* March 28, 1995, p. 1D.

''Stock Offering a Pawn in First Cash's Growth Plan,'' *Dallas Business Journal,* May 28, 1993, p. 15B.

Stringer, Kortney, ''Best of Times Is Worst of Times For Pawnshops,'' *Wall Street Journal,* August 22, 2000, p. B1.

—Ed Dinger

FKI Plc

15-19 New Fetter Lane
London EC4A 1LY
United Kingdom
Telephone: +44-20-7832-0000
Fax: +44-20-7832-0001
Web site: http://www.fki.co.uk

Public Company
Incorporated: 1920 as Fisher
Employees: 15,255
Sales: £1.45 billion ($2.3 billion) (2003)
Stock Exchanges: London
Ticker Symbol: FKI
NAIC: 541330 Engineering Services; 332510 Hardware
Manufacturing; 333298 All Other Industrial
Machinery Manufacturing; 333922 Conveyor and
Conveying Equipment Manufacturing; 333923
Overhead Traveling Crane, Hoist and Monorail
System Manufacturing; 334419 Other Electronic
Component Manufacturing; 334514 Totalizing Fluid
Meter and Counting Device Manufacturing; 334515
Instrument Manufacturing for Measuring and Testing
Electricity and Electrical Signals; 334519 Other
Measuring and Controlling Device Manufacturing;
335311 Power, Distribution, and Specialty
Transformer Manufacturing; 335999 All Other
Miscellaneous Electrical Equipment and Component
Manufacturing

FKI Plc has evolved into one of the United Kingdom's major engineering groups. The company's array of some 70 subsidiaries operates in four primary business divisions: Lifting Products and Services; Logistex; Hardware; and Energy Technology products. These operations combined for a total turnover of nearly £1.5 billion ($2.3 billion) in 2003. FKI Logistex offers automated logistics and sorting products and systems for baggage handling, freight and parcel services, warehouse and distribution facilities,

and manufacturers. This division, the company's fastest growing and most profitable, contributed 30.5 percent of FKI's revenues in 2003, and is one of the world's leading logistics systems producers. Lifting Products and Services holds the world's leading positions in lifting products and large shears, and the worldwide number two spot in chains and lifting gear, and generates more than 28 percent of company revenues. The company's Hardware division produces fittings for windows, screen and storm doors, furniture, and ergonomic hardware, holding the number one position in the United States for most of its products, and leading positions in Europe as well. That division contributed 18 percent to the company's revenues in 2003. Last, FKI, through its Energy Technology division, is the world's leading supplier of turbogenerators, and produces a range of electrical and other power generating machinery and infrastructure equipment. That division, which focuses on the North American and European markets, produced more than 23 percent of the group's sales in 2003. FKI Plc's growth has been fueled by a steady stream of acquisitions in the late 1990s and early 2000s. The company is listed on the London Stock Exchange.

From Parking Meters to Conglomerate in the 1980s

FKI's origins trace back to 1920, when the company was first registered under the Fisher name. Over the next several decades it specialized in the manufacture of parking meters, under the Karpark name. By the 1960s, the company became known as Fisher Karpark Industries. In 1973, Tony Gartland and Fred Berry took control of the company through a management buyout, ultimately changing its name to FKI Electricals. Gartland's share of the company topped 50 percent.

FKI remained a small company focused on parking meters through the 1970s. In the early 1980s, however, Gartland decided to take the company on a drive for growth. As part of that effort, the company acquired a dormant public company, Woodland Securities, which had originally operated rubber plantations in Sri Lanka. The reverse takeover enabled FKI to achieve a listing on the London Stock Exchange's Unlisted Securities Market in 1982. Joining Gartland in the quest for growth was Jeff Whalley, who had formerly worked at Babcock

International, then one of the United Kingdom's leading engineering groups.

The listing enabled the company to begin making acquisitions, such as the purchase of the money-losing English Numbering Machines, part of the Rank Organisation, for £1.3 million in 1982. FKI quickly reorganized its new operations, which became profitable by the following year. The company then applied for a listing on the London main board that year.

Other acquisitions followed, including 1984's Burndept, in a cash and share deal worth nearly £3 million that extended FKI beyond its core parking meters business and into the manufacture of radio communications equipment. The company's growth accelerated in the mid-1980s, as its revenues topped £18 million in 1985. Acquisition remained at the center of the company's growth strategy, and included the mechanical engineering and components division of Thorn EMI Plc, for which FKI paid approximately £10 million in 1986. The following year the company acquired Froude Consine, which produced dynanometers and other vehicle testing equipment, before buying up Stone International for £36.6 million in July 1987. That acquisition formed the basis of the company's new air conditioning division.

Just one month later, however, FKI launched a takeover bid that was to transform—at least temporarily—the company. In August 1987, FKI offered to acquire Babcock International, which, although its revenues were some seven times greater than FKI's, had fallen into financial difficulties by then. The deal went through for a total price of £416 million, and the newly enlarged company adopted the name FKI Babcock. Gartland and Whalley remained in control of the new company, which now took a place among the London exchange's prestigious FTSE 250 index.

Focusing for the New Century

Gartland and Whalley quickly hit a snag, as the stock market crash of October 1987 sent the company's share price reeling. The company continued to receive the cold shoulder from the investor community—which had begun to turn its back on the diversified conglomerates that had been popular in the United Kingdom in the 1970s and early 1980s. In response, FKI began a deep restructuring drive, trimming away a good deal of its Babcock side. By the beginning of 1989, FKI had shut down some 25 of Babcock's manufacturing plants.

FKI went still further in its drive to appease investors. In 1989, the company completed its restructuring by splitting the

company in two. FKI Plc took over the group's core manufacturing operations, while its large-scale engineering projects division was split off into a new Babcock, which was then floated as an independent public company. FKI also planned to sell off its U.S. industrial assets, but abandoned the plan in 1990 amid the market downturn.

Unfortunately for Gartland, FKI's profits continued to struggle amid the harsh economic climate, and after posting a fresh profit dip in 1991, Gartland stepped down from the company. Whalley took Gartland's place as chairman and, in 1992, brought in Bob Beeston as CEO. Formerly part of another British conglomerate, BTR, Beeston continued the streamlining program set in place under Gartland. In December 1991, the company sold off its Stone air conditioning business, which by then had grown to four companies operating in the United States, the United Kingdom, and Spain.

As Whalley ceded day-to-day management to Beeston in the early 1990s, FKI continued streamlining its operations in order to shed its image as a conglomerate and emerge as a focused engineering group, emphasizing its operations in lifting and handling, hardware, automotive parts, and electrical engineering. By the middle of the decade, the company had built up a war chest of some £300 million and prepared a new round of large-scale acquisitions.

In 1995, the company acquired lifting specialist Amdura, based in the United States. The following year, it paid £52.3 million to acquire Italy's Nuova Marelli Motori, which manufactured low-voltage electric motors and related components for forklifts and other lifting equipment. That year also, the company paid £182.5 million for Hawker Siddley, which had been operating as the Electric Power Group of BTR Plc, and also acquired furniture hardware producer Wright Products, based in the United States.

Not all of the company's expansion efforts were successful—in 1997, the company was forced to back down from a hostile takeover attempt for door fittings company Newman Tonks. In that year, also, the company exited the automobile parts market, selling off its holdings in that area. Instead, the company turned its attention to wire rope and engineering products manufacturer Bridon, which it bought for £131 million in 1997. Whalley retired the following year—but only after making a failed £1.1 billion bid to take FKI private.

In 1999, FKI began targeting growth in a new area, that of logistics and materials handling equipment and systems—set to boom with the growth of the e-commerce market. The company began making a series of acquisitions, including Industry General Corporation in the United States, and Crisplant Industries, in Denmark, for a total of £220 million. Soon after, FKI bundled those companies together with an existing logistics and handling company, Matthew Conveyor, and created a new division, FKI Logistex. By the end of that year, the company had made another important logistics acquisition, of Pinnacle, based in the United States, for a total cash and debt cost of $425 million.

FKI Logistex, which had cost FKI some £509 million to put into place, quickly proved to be the company's fastest growing segment, a position aided in January 2000 by the purchase of

Key Dates:

1920: Fisher, predecessor to FKI, incorporates in London and becomes a specialist in manufacturing parking meters.

1973: Tony Gartland takes over Fisher Karpark Industries, as the company is then called, in a management buyout.

1982: FKI goes public on the London secondary market through a reverse takeover.

1983: FKI switches its listing to the London main board and begins an acquisition drive.

1987: FKI acquires the larger Babcock International and becomes FKI Babcock.

1989: FKI restructures, splitting off heavy engineering assets as the publicly listed Babcock.

1996: FKI begins a new acquisition drive with the purchase of Nuovo Marelli Motori of Italy and BTR's Electric Power business.

1997: FKI sells its automotive division and acquires Bridon, a maker of cable rope and lifting equipment.

1999: The company acquires Industry General in the United States and Crisplant in Denmark to add to its logistics and handling operations.

2000: The company acquires Pinnacle in the United States and then sets up a new Logistex division to group all of its logistics and handling equipment and systems businesses.

2001: The company acquires Stearns Airport Equipment Co. (U.S.A.) and Dator (Denmark) for Logistex, and Skoda (Czech Republic), a producer of turbogenerators.

2002: The company acquires DeWind AG (Germany), a maker of wind turbines.

2003: The company is forced to slash dividends in order to make interest payments on its debt load.

U.S.-based SNE Systems, which produced integrated control systems for materials handling. By the end of that year, the company claimed the number two spot worldwide for materials handling systems, behind Germany's Siemens.

Although observers suggested that FKI, with the success of Logistex, might seek to de-merge the company again at the turn of the century, FKI remained committed to its focused, yet diversified approach, claiming that the cash flow from its hardware and turbogenerator operations enabled it to invest in gaining scale in its logistics wing. The company added to its Logistex operations, specifically materials handling, in 2001 with the purchase of Stearns Airport Equipment Co., based in the United States, and to its logistics side with the purchase of software developer Dator A/S, based in Denmark.

Not all of the company's investment went toward that division, however. In 2001, the company acquired Skoda Electrical Machines, based in the Czech Republic, for £15.2 million, which was added to its turbogenerator division. The following year, FKI acquired Germany's DeWind AG, a manufacturer of wind turbine systems, for EUR 34.5 million.

The downturn in the U.S. economy, which accounted for some 50 percent of the group's sales, exposed FKI to a drop in its market. Burdened by the heavy debt load built up during its latest acquisition drive, and further hit by the declining value of the dollar, FKI was forced to take a pause in its growth. Beeston stepped down in January 2003, replaced by Paul Heiden. By the middle of the year, FKI had been forced to shut down a number of plants, and then to slash its dividend, in order to meet short-term payments on its looming debt. Nonetheless, the company's difficulties were seen as temporary. As it waited for the economy—and business—to pick up again, FKI was able to look back on a strong record of growth, from a simple manufacturer of parking meters to an internationally operating, diversified engineering group.

Principal Subsidiaries

A Kwint Holding BV (The Netherlands; 88%); Acco Chain & Lifting Products (U.S.A.); Allen-Stevens (U.S.A.); Alvey Systems Inc. (U.S.A.); Augier SA (France); Belwith International Limited (U.S.A.); Bridon Hong Kong Limited; Bridon Inc. (U.S.A.); Bridon International Ltd; Bridon New Zealand Limited; Bridon Overseas Holdings Limited; Bridon plc; Bridon Singapore (Pte) Limited; Bridon-American Corporation (U.S.A.); Bristol Babcock Inc. (U.S.A.); Bristol Babcock Limited; Brush Electrical Machines Limited; Brush Transformers Limited; BTS Drahtseile GmbH (Germany); CERTEX Finland Oy; CERTEX France SA; CERTEX Inc. (U.S.A.); CERTEX Lifting and Service GmbH & Co. KG (Germany); CERTEX SpA (Italy); CERTEX Svenska AB (Sweden); CERTEX UK; Chautauqua Hardware Corporation (U.S.A.); CMP Corporation (U.S.A.); Crisplant Inc. (U.S.A.); Crosby Canada (Canada); Dator A/S (Denmark); Energy Technology Group; Faultless Caster (U.S.A.); FKI Engineering Limited; FKI Industrial Drives Limited; FKI Industries Canada Limited; FKI Industries Inc. (U.S.A.); FKI USA Holdings Limited; Froude Consine; Froude-Hofmann Pruftechnik GmbH (Germany); Guangzhou Bridon Ropes and Lifting (China; 60%); Hawker Siddeley Electric Africa (Proprietary) Limited (South Africa); Hawker Siddeley Power Transformers; Hawker Siddeley Switchgear Limited; Industry General Corporation; Keeler Brass Company (U.S.A.); Laurence, Scott & Electromotors Limited; FKI Logistex; Madico Inc. (Canada); Marelli Motori SpA (Italy); Mathews Conveyor; P.T. Bripindo Utama (Indonesia); Parsons Chain Company; Premier Stampings; Real Time Solutions Inc. (U.S.A.); Rhombus Continental Castors Sdn Bhd (Malaysia); Rhombus Rollen GmbH & Co. (Germany); South Wales Transformers; Stearns Airport Equipment Company (U.S.A.); Truth Hardware Corporation (U.S.A.); Weber-Knapp Company (U.S.A.); Welland Forge (Canada); West House Insurance Limited; Whipp & Bourne; Wright Products (U.S.A.).

Principal Divisions

Lifting Products and Services; Logistex; Hardware; Energy Technology.

Principal Competitors

Siemens Dematic; Daifuku Co., Ltd.; Schaefer Holding International GmbH; Columbus McKinnon Corporation; Swisslog;

Murata Machinery Ltd.; Dexion Group Ltd.; Vanderlande Industries, B.V.; Jervis B. Webb Co.

Further Reading

''Downgrade Sparks Profit Taking,'' *Financial Times,* June 25, 3003, p. 44.

Edgecliff-Johnson, Andrew, ''FKI Prepared for Acquisitions,'' *Financial Times,* June 17, 1998, p. 21.

''FKI Finds a Strategy for Tackling Problems,'' *Birmingham Post,* November 22, 2002, p. 24.

Gimbel, Florian, ''Focus on Logistics Bolsters FKI,'' *Financial Times,* June 1, 2001, p. 23.

Mathieson, Clive, ''FKI Issues Growth Plan After Investing Pounds 500m,'' *Times* (London), June 2, 2000, p. 33.

White, Dominic, ''Could Engineer a Comeback,'' *Daily Telegraph,* April 2, 3004, p. 34.

—M.L. Cohen

Freeport-McMoRan Copper & Gold, Inc.

1615 Poydras Street
New Orleans, Louisiana 70112
U.S.A.
Telephone: (504) 582-4000
Fax: (504) 582-1847
Web site: http://www.fcx.com

Public Company
Incorporated: 1912 as Freeport Sulphur Company
Employees: 10,100
Sales: $1.91 billion (2002)
Stock Exchanges: New York
Ticker Symbol: FCX
NAIC: 212234 Copper Ore and Nickel Ore Mining;
212221 Gold Ore Mining; 212222 Silver Ore Mining

Freeport-McMoRan Copper & Gold, Inc. is engaged in exploring, mining, producing, processing, and marketing metals. It is one of the world's largest and lowest-cost producers of copper, and it controls the single largest gold reserve in the world. Its principal asset is its Grasberg mine, in Papua (formerly Irian Jaya), the western half of the island of New Guinea, in Indonesia. This huge mine has proven copper and gold reserves expected to last for some 30 years. The mine is partially owned by Freeport's principal subsidiary, FT Freeport Indonesia.

Roots in the Early 20th Century

Freeport McMoRan began in 1912 under the name of Freeport Sulphur Company. It pioneered the use of the Frasch invention in the United States as an engineering method to mine sulfur. Prior to the Frasch invention, Italy monopolized the sulfur market because of its cheap labor. Herman Frasch's invention, which utilized machinery rather than manual labor, allowed U.S. companies to produce the element at competitive world prices. The process involved flushing large quantities of hot water into pipelines sunk inward toward the sulfur find. As the ore melted, it was pumped to the surface in liquid form. The process initially had been engineered on a find near Lake

Charles, Louisiana, in 1894. Frasch, along with a group of financiers, established the Union Sulphur Company in 1896 and acquired title to the Lake Charles site, as well as mineral rights and control over the Frasch patents.

Subsequently, sulfur was discovered at the Bryanmound site on the gulf coast of Texas near the Brazos River. Francis R. Pemberton, an entrepreneur, together with other investors, took an option on leases covering the Bryanmound property. Because the expiration of the patent that covered the major components of the Frasch process was imminent, Pemberton brought the find to the attention of several investors. Eric P. Swenson, vice-president of National City Bank in New York and a native Texan who retained strong financial ties throughout Texas, showed interest and visited the find in 1911. When Swenson saw the site, he realized that he could also develop a duty-free port nearby. Upon returning to New York, he formed the Vanderlip-Swenson-Tilghman Syndicate. He pooled capital of $700,000 to finance the project and purchased Bryanmound and the surrounding area.

Frasch's Union Sulphur Company sued to bar the syndicate from using the Frasch engineering method at Bryanmound on the grounds that supplementary unexpired patents were crucial to the process. After lengthy litigation, a U.S. circuit court of appeals ruled that the remaining unexpired patents did not provide needed insight to the invention. As a consequence, the syndicate founded Freeport Sulphur Company in 1912, as well as the Freeport Townsite Company to develop a city on the west bank of the Brazos River and the Freeport Terminal Company to maintain train facilities to the port. In 1913 Freeport Texas Company was chartered as a holding company for Freeport Sulphur Company; Freeport Townsite Company; Freeport Asphalt Company; Freeport Sulphur Transportation Company; Freeport Terminal Company; South Texas Stevedore Company; and La Espuela Oil Company, Ltd. Headquarters for the holding company were located in New York City and Eric Swenson served as the company's first president, remaining in that office until 1930.

New mining methods were introduced at Bryanmound during its early years of operation. Elevated pipes carrying the molten sulfur from the well to the storage vats were replaced with three-inch-wide sulfur lines encased in six-inch-thick pipes through which steam could circulate to protect the lines from

---

Key Dates:

1912: Freeport Sulphur Company is founded.
1931: Freeport purchases a controlling interest in Cuban-American Manganese Corp.
1955: Freeport establishes the National Potash Company.
1956: Freeport Oil Company is formed.
1966: Freeport Indonesia is founded.
1969: McMoRan Exploration Co. is founded.
1971: The Freeport parent company name is changed to Freeport Minerals Co.
1981: McMoRan Oil & Gas merges with Freeport Minerals to form Freeport-McMoRan Inc. (FMI).
1986: FMI forms Freeport-McMoRan Resource Partners to handle its fertilizer business.
1990: FMI spins off 27 percent of Freeport-McMoRan Copper & Gold Inc., retaining the remainder until a complete spinoff in 1994.
1997: FMI is acquired by IMC Global.
2000: Indonesian dictator Suharto leaves power; Freeport-McMoRan Copper & Gold remains principally focused on Indonesia, despite public relations battles and political uncertainty there.

---

inclement weather and reduce clogging. During World War I demand for sulfur rose sharply. Approximately 1,500 tons were generated daily at Bryanmound to cover shipments sent to U.S. factories producing combat weapons. Before its closure in 1935, the find yielded more than five million long tons of sulfur.

The company began exploration on a second mine in 1922 when it acquired sulfur rights to Hoskins Mound, 15 miles from Bryanmound. Unfavorable geological formations in the mound prompted innovative drilling methods that later were used at other sites. Company engineers checked the escape of hot water into sedimentary deposits of sand by pumping large quantities of mud into the formation, thus making the find a successful venture. They also developed a process to heat water with water boiler gases. The plant at Hoskins Mound closed in 1955 after producing more than ten million long tons of sulfur.

A growing opposition to Eric Swenson's attitude as president of FMC led to his deposal by stockholders, who felt Swenson was insensitive to their concerns. In 1930 Eugene Norton was named president and under his leadership the company became the first sulfur-producing firm in the United States to diversify its interests. In 1931 Freeport purchased controlling interest in Cuban-American Manganese Corporation and, through its Cuban subsidiary in Oriente Province, gained access to rich deposits of low-grade manganese oxide ores. Freeport's research department developed a process to refine manganese from low-grade ore for use in the manufacture of steel. As a result, between 1932 and 1946, when the find was exhausted, the company produced more than one million tons of manganese oxide. In 1936 the corporate name was changed from Freeport Texas Company to Freeport Sulphur Company.

Langbourne M. Williams was associated with Freeport Sulphur for many years. He was elected president of the company

in 1933 and chairman in 1957, and served on the board of directors until 1977. When he became president in 1933, company operations began at Grand Ecaille, a sulfur dome in the Mississippi delta region, 45 miles south of New Orleans, Louisiana. Because the dome was located beneath marshlands, engineers drove thousands of wooden pilings into the land and built reinforced concrete mats over them to provide transportation to and from the mine. Company workers also dug a ten-mile canal between the plant and a site near the Mississippi River where they shipped the product to market. The site was later named Port Sulphur. Grand Ecaille served as a model in developing engineering solutions that would be applied in the future. When the plant at Grand Ecaille closed in 1978, more than 40 million tons of sulfur had been produced. During World War II company plants at Hoskins Mound and Grand Ecaille received army and navy "E" awards from the U.S. government for outstanding wartime production. Another Freeport subsidiary, Nicaro Nickel Co., chartered in 1942, was under contract to the U.S. government and contributed more than 63 million pounds of nickel to the war effort. The plant closed in 1947 when it became unworkable to cover production costs and sell the ore at competitive peacetime prices.

Expansion After World War II

Charles Wight became a director of Freeport in 1948 and president in 1958. During the 1950s new mining discoveries allowed for continued product diversification. Discoveries of substantial finds of potash in New Mexico and Canada prompted Freeport to establish the National Potash Company in 1955, in partnership with Consolidated Coal Company. Production began in 1957, and in 1966 Freeport acquired full ownership of the successful operation.

At the same time, Freeport's research center developed several technological advances, some resulting in lower mining production costs. In 1952 the company pioneered a process substituting seawater for fresh water in sulfur mining. This process eliminated the need to transport fresh water to sites located near sources of seawater. Another process developed at Freeport's research center produced pure nickel and cobalt from nickel ore and rekindled company interest in mining Cuban ores. In 1955 Freeport chartered the Cuban American Nickel Company and a subsidiary, the Moa Bay Mining Company. The company invested $119 million in constructing plant facilities and a town at Moa Bay, Cuba, as well as a refinery at Port Nickel, Louisiana.

In 1960, however, the government of Fidel Castro confiscated the Cuban facility. In all, Freeport produced more than three million pounds of nickel, 310,000 pounds of cobalt, and more than 7,000 tons of the byproduct ammonium sulfur before the plant closed. Freeport eventually listed the Cuban facility as a tax loss.

Although Freeport began oil exploration in 1913 when it chartered La Espuela Oil Company, Ltd. to handle fuel requirements for its operation at Bryanmound, it was not until 1948 that the company began a sustained program of oil and gas exploration. In 1956 it formed Freeport Oil Company to handle ventures in Louisiana, Kansas, Texas, and New Mexico. In association with two other interests, it discovered oil and gas reserves at

Lake Washington, Louisiana, and set a record, at the time, by producing oil from the world's deepest well, which extended 22,570 feet below the ground. In 1958 Freeport Oil Company sold its interest at Lake Washington for approximately $100 million to Magnolia Petroleum Company. Throughout the 1960s and 1970s the company participated in various joint oil and gas discoveries throughout the United States.

Robert C. Hills became president of Freeport in 1961 and remained in office for six years. During his administration the company produced a record two million tons of sulfur and became the world's largest sulfur producer for 1963. At the same time, Freeport launched several new subsidiaries to meet company needs. It formed Freeport Kaolin Company in 1963 after purchasing the main assets of Southern Clays Inc. Included in the sale were white clay reserves used as filler and coating materials in the manufacture of paper. From 1964 through 1981 Freeport Kaolin Company underwent a major expansion program designed to increase mining and processing capacity and to upgrade its products.

In addition, Freeport organized Freeport of Australia in 1964 to oversee its mineral exploration, development, and production activities in Australia as well as in the surrounding Pacific Ocean region. In 1967 Freeport of Australia, in a joint venture with Metals Exploration, located large Australian nickel deposits near Greenvale, Queensland.

In 1966 Freeport established Freeport Chemical Company to embark on a phosphate chemical project, for which it constructed a plant in Uncle Sam, Louisiana. The plant produced its first shipments of phosphoric acid and sulfur acid in 1968. In the 1970s plant facilities were expanded at Uncle Sam and a plant to produce sulfuric acid was added in Port Sulphur, Louisiana. A research project undertaken at Freeport led to the recovery in 1988 of uranium oxide, commonly referred to as yellowcake, from phosphoric acid. Subsequently two uranium-recovery plants were opened: one at Uncle Sam and the second one at Agrico Chemical Company's phosphoric acid facility in Donaldsonville, Louisiana.

In 1966 Freeport founded Freeport Indonesia, Inc., to mine copper in the province of Irian Jaya. Because the find, known as Grasberg Prospect, was located in a remote, mountainous region, open-pit mining operations did not begin until late 1972. The first copper shipment was made the following year, however, and was valued at $2 million. Gold and silver also were mined at the find.

During the 1970s through 1982, significant changes occurred in the company. In 1971 the company name changed from Freeport Sulphur Company to Freeport Minerals Company (FMC) to reflect its role as a diversified mineral producer. Paul W. Douglas became president in 1975. FMC continued a policy of diversification in 1981 when it formed Freeport Gold Company to operate a gold find located in Jerrit Canyon, Nevada.

In 1980 FMC reported a record of $147.4 million in company earnings. Over the years FMC had worked in joint mining ventures with McMoRan Oil & Gas Company and acquired three million shares of its convertible preferred stock. In 1981, when the companies merged, it became one of the leading natural resources companies in the country.

McMoRan Company Background

W.K. McWilliams, Jr., and James R. (Jim Bob) Moffett, both geologists, started a private company, McMoCo, during the mid-1960s. McMoCo was the forerunner of McMoRan Oil & Gas Company. It began as a consultant for oil and gas exploration programs, but soon added personnel to enable it to handle entire projects, from locating finds to drilling and producing the product. Because the company had limited funds, outside sources provided risk capital. In return for its work, McMoCo received 25 percent interest in each find. B.M. Rankin, Jr., a specialist in land-leasing and sales operations, joined as an associate in about 1967. With his arrival, McMoCo was liquidated and the three owners formed McMoRan, the company name combining portions of their surnames. In order to secure necessary funding for its many drilling programs, the company decided to become a public company. In 1969 it merged with Horn Silver Mines Company, a public firm incorporated in 1932 and controlled by television personality Art Linkletter and several associates, that was listed on the Salt Lake City Stock Exchange. As a consequence, a new public firm, named McMoRan Exploration Company, emerged, with Linkletter as a board member. One of the firm's earliest oil explorations was on the gulf coast of Louisiana in LaFourche Parish; McMoRan owned 50 percent of the successful find.

During the 1970s, the company acquired a reputation as an aggressive petroleum explorer with cost-efficient drilling programs. It formed drilling partnerships with several organizations. In 1972 it signed an agreement with Geodynamics Oil & Gas Inc. and Comprehensive Resources Corporation and bought working interests in several oil- and gas-producing properties in Texas and Louisiana. In 1973 it formed a joint petroleum exploration program with Dow Chemical Company. In this venture, Dow Chemical Company received 50 percent interest in all exploration finds, while McMoRan Exploration Company's interest varied from 25 percent to 38 percent per find. In 1975 the company began a $36 million onshore oil and gas exploration and development program with Transco Exploration Company. During its first year of operation, McMoRan Exploration Company successfully completed five of the 17 wells drilled. As a result, budgets for the second and third year of operation were expanded from $8 million to $14 million.

While many exploration programs were in progress, administrative and operational changes took place within the organization. In 1970 stockholders voted to delist the company from the Salt Lake City Stock Exchange. In 1977 a four-member operating committee headed by Moffett was named to assume the duties of McWilliams and Rankin, who stepped down as cochairmen. Moffett became president and chief executive officer, while McWilliams and Rankin remained as consultants, directors, and stockholders. In 1978 the company was reincorporated in Delaware and was listed on the New York Stock Exchange. In 1979 the name was changed from McMoRan Exploration Company to McMoRan Oil & Gas Company.

Other operational changes included the creation of subsidiaries to separate distinct operations within the organization and provide the company with additional exploration exposure. In 1977 McMoRan Offshore Exploration Company (MOXY) began operation to manage and expand oil and gas explorations in federal waters off the Gulf of Mexico. Interests in federal offshore lease blocks were acquired through sublease arrangements. In 1980 MOXY entered a three-year program with several organizations, including Transco Exploration Company and Freeport Minerals Company. Under the agreement, MOXY provided 25 percent of exploratory expenses in exchange for 35 percent working interest in the finds.

Another subsidiary, McMoRan Exploration Company (MEC), was formed in 1979 to handle exploration and production of oil and gas properties located primarily along the gulf area of Texas and Louisiana, both onshore and in waters owned by these states. In 1980 MEC began an exploration and development program for oil and gas operations in the gulf region with several organizations. MEC provided 25 percent of total exploration funds in return for a 37.5 percent working interest in the finds.

Merged Company in the 1980s

In 1981 McMoRan Oil & Gas Company merged with Freeport Minerals Company. The new company, Freeport-McMoRan Inc. (FMI), elected Paul Douglas as president and Benno C. Schmidt as chairman of the board. James R. Moffett became vice-chairman but remained president of McMoRan Oil & Gas Company, directing all combined oil and gas activities. Freeport-McMoRan's policy put greater emphasis on domestic oil and gas exploration programs yet sustained interest in growth programs in minerals and chemical products.

In 1982 Freeport Gold Company completed its first full year of operation. It held the record as the largest gold producer for the year, reporting an output of 196,000 ounces of gold. In 1983 FMI created Freeport-McMoRan Oil and Gas Royalty Trust to afford shareholders direct participation in the income from selected U.S. offshore oil and gas properties held by McMoRan Oil & Gas Company. Although the company was unable to put a value on these properties, its annual report for 1982 listed entire oil and gas assets at $1.06 billion.

Freeport-McMoRan in 1983 purchased Stone Exploration Corporation, a company engaged in gas exploration, development, and production, primarily in south Louisiana. At the time, Stone Exploration had estimated proven reserves of 57 billion cubic feet of gas and gas equivalents.

In 1983 Paul W. Douglas resigned as president and chief executive officer. Schmidt, chairman of the company, assumed the additional position of chief executive officer but the position of president remained vacant. In 1984 Moffett succeeded Schmidt as chairman and chief executive officer. Schmidt became executive committee chairman and a director. Richard B. Stephens replaced Moffett as president of McMoRan Oil & Gas Company. Milton H. Ward assumed the duties of president and chief operating officer of Freeport-McMoRan. At the time, the company's asset base was valued at $1.4 billion.

In 1984 Freeport-McMoRan enjoyed a 133 percent increase in its oil and gas reserves when it purchased a 50 percent working interest in Voyager Petroleum Ltd. of Canada and Midlands Energy Company, operating in the midwestern and western United States. Freeport-McMoRan Oil & Gas Company, a fully owned subsidiary of Freeport-McMoRan Inc., also

became managing general partner of Freeport McMoRan Energy Partners, Ltd., which it incorporated in 1984.

In 1985 Freeport-McMoRan sold certain assets to reduce its long-term debt. It sold Freeport Kaolin Company for more than $95 million to Engelhard Corporation, a manufacturer of specialty chemical and metallurgical products and a trader in precious metals. In June 1985 it sold a 25 percent interest in Midlands Energy Company to Bristol PLC, a British energy company, for $73 million. The 25 percent interest included natural gas and oil reserves, exploration land, and a stake in three processing plants. It sold 14 percent of its domestic oil and gas business for more than $125 million on the New York Stock Exchange in the form of depository receipts representing limited partnership units in its Freeport-McMoRan Energy Partners, Ltd. In addition, it sold approximately 11 percent of its common shares in Freeport-McMoRan Gold Company, formerly known as Freeport Gold Company, to the public for more than $39 million.

Also in 1985, Freeport-McMoRan acquired two new companies and announced a program to repurchase up to ten million common shares of its stock depending on market conditions. Over the next five years, Freeport-McMoRan spent more than $1 billion to buy back common stock. Also in the mid-1980s it bought Geysers Geothermal Company (GGC), a producer of steam for electric power generation, for $216.7 million. The purchase allowed Freeport-McMoRan to extend the use of the hot-water technology it had developed while operating its sulfur reserves. It also bought most of the assets of Pel-Tex Oil Company for $74 million, thereby acquiring its oil and gas properties located in the gulf area of Louisiana and Texas.

Operational costs of the organization were significantly reduced beginning in 1985 when corporate headquarters in New York City were moved to New Orleans, Louisiana, and combined with the company's office there. Oil and gas and certain mineral functions also were moved to the new Freeport-McMoRan Building built to serve as headquarters for the organization.

In 1986 the parent company formed Freeport-McMoRan Resource Partners (FRP), whose operations included the production of phosphate, nitrogen fertilizer products, sulfur, and geothermal resources, and the recovery of uranium oxide from phosphoric acid. FRP stock was placed on the New York Stock Exchange. The same year, in partnership with Kidder, Peabody & Company, FMI reached an agreement to buy Petro-Lewis Corporation and an affiliate, American Royalty Trust Company, for $440 million. The acquisition increased Freeport-McMoRan's domestic oil and gas production.

In 1987 FRP acquired a chemical fertilizer plant located in Taft, Louisiana, from Beker Industries for $22.5 million. It also bought Agrico Chemical Company from The Williams Companies for more than $250 million. Agrico assets included phosphate rock mines, production facilities for phosphate and nitrogen fertilizers, and a large sales and distribution network.

During the year, Freeport-McMoRan changed its interests in Australia. It sold most of its holdings in the Greenvale Nickel project in Queensland in two transactions for a total of $26 million in cash and a deferred payment of $11 million. It set up Freeport McMoRan Australia Ltd. in 1987 to handle its gold and diamond projects in that country. Late in 1988 the new subsidiary merged with Poseidon Ltd., an Australian mining concern, and a new company emerged called Poseidon Exploration Ltd.

In November 1989 Moffett outlined a plan to sell between $1.2 billion to $1.5 billion in assets to reduce longstanding debts. Future company focus would be concentrated on developing two mammoth mining discoveries: the sulfur find in the Gulf of Mexico off Louisiana (Main Pass project), and the copper and gold finds in Indonesia (the Grasberg and Ertsberg projects). Moffett felt that the asset sales also would free up capital for the development of the fields, which had emerged as extremely valuable resources. The extension of the Grasberg ore body in Indonesia had transformed that operation into the largest single gold reserve in the world, and propelled it to a ranking as one of the top five copper reserves worldwide. In 1991 Freeport set up new subsidiaries to control operations in both Indonesia and the Gulf of Mexico.

The Main Pass Line was revealed as the first significant Frasch sulphur discovery on the North American continent since the 1960s, and one of the most productive oil fields in the Gulf of Mexico. Developers estimated that 67 million long tons of sulfur, 39 million barrels of oil, and seven billion cubic feet of natural gas lay beneath the Gulf near the Mississippi Delta. Extraction of these natural resources was expected to cause settling on the Gulf floor, precluding super-strong framing inside the underwater mine. Moffett liquidated $2 billion of Freeport-McMoRan's assets to finance the projects. The 1989 sales included Freeport-McMoRan Gold Company and about $85 million of its oil and gas properties; Voyager Energy; geothermal energy assets; and an interest in an Australian mining company.

Concentrating on Mining in the 1990s

In 1990 the company sold its nitrogen fertilizer business to Agricultural Minerals Corporation for $275 million. It divested itself of Freeport-McMoRan Gold Company, sold to Minorco South Africa for about $705 million, and spun off to the public Freeport-McMoRan Copper & Gold, Inc., which remained 73 percent in the parent company's hands. At the end of 1990, Freeport-McMoRan stated that it planned to auction an additional $750 million of its assets, again as part of its debt-reduction goal.

The parent company, Freeport-McMoRan Inc., was now basically a holding company for its two principal assets, Freeport-McMoRan Copper & Gold and Freeport-McMoRan Resource Partners, which ran the sulphur and fertilizer business. The main thing was to have enough cash to finance the development of the huge finds at Irian Jaya and Main Pass. Both of these assets got better the more they were studied. Main Pass was the second largest recoverable sulphur reserve known, surpassed only by a Texas deposit that was nearing the end of its usefulness. The ore reserves in Irian Jaya were huge, and by 1993 Freeport announced that after a $550 million expansion, it needed to expand again to accept the increased capacity. The company built a huge ore pass that funneled chunks of ore down the mountainside. The long drop itself crushed the ore, reducing the need for further mechanical pulverizing. This process helped make the Grasberg mine one of the world's lowest-cost producers of copper. Although world prices for Freeport's minerals were quite low in the early 1990s, the company was

nevertheless in a prime position for when prices rose again. The copper and gold affiliate's sales stood at more than $925 million in 1993, up almost 30 percent from the year previous.

But fertilizer prices remained frustratingly low, and Freeport-McMoRan entered on a series of complex deals designed to concentrate the company on its best business. With fertilizer prices hitting bottom in 1993, Freeport-McMoRan Resource Partners formed a joint venture with one of its largest competitors, IMC Global Inc. Freeport-McMoRan Inc. spent $1.06 billion in a stock swap in 1996 to acquire another fertilizer competitor, Arcadian Corp. This made a combined company with annual revenue near $2.2 billion. Yet the next year, Freeport-McMoRan Inc. agreed to be bought by joint venture partner IMC Global.

Meanwhile, in 1994 the holding company, Freeport-McMoRan Inc., spun off its majority interest in Freeport-McMoRan Copper & Gold. This company continued to be run by Jim Bob Moffett and headquartered in the Freeport-McMoRan Building in New Orleans. The subsidiary company seemed to have outlasted its parent. This company was now fully focused on its Indonesian mine. Yet the mine became a source of violent trouble and terrible publicity. In the 1960s, the company had promised the native Papuans "community development" in exchange for use of their land—as the tribes had no real concept of property rights, this was about all that could be done at first. But by the mid-1990s, many of the islanders had come to keenly resent the company. Not only were they poorly compensated, but the mine discharged tons of tailings into the forest and rivers, causing evident environmental damage. Violent incidents at the mine in 1995 and 1996 led to several deaths and scores of injuries. The company's relationship with the indigenous people was reputedly abysmal as tribal leaders sought to close the mine. The trouble at Grasberg was widely reported, and Freeport-McMoRan fought gory public relations battles. CEO Moffett stormed into the offices of the New Orleans Times-Picayune after one unfavorable story, and the company hired none other than Henry Kissinger to plead its case to the Clinton administration when it lost some government-backed insurance.

These troubles did not go away. When Indonesian dictator Suharto left power in 2000, the soundness of Freeport-McMoRan's long-term contracts was questioned. Political instability threatened all foreign investment in Indonesia, and Freeport-McMoRan Copper & Gold was probably the most visible and clearly resented foreign company in the nation. Despite the political uncertainty clouding the Indonesian mine, the company was able to make money out of it. Its costs were very low, allowing it to do well even when world metal prices were low, as they were in the early 2000s. When copper and gold prices ticked up, the company stood to make handsome profits.

Principal Subsidiaries

FT Freeport Indonesia; PT Irja Eastern Minerals; Atlantic Copper, S.A.

Principal Competitors

Newmont Mining Corporation; Phelps Dodge Corporation; Corporacion Nacional del Cobre de Chile.

Further Reading

Caney, Derek J., "Freeport Profit Drop Tied to Restructuring Charge," *American Metal Market,* February 1, 1994, p. 6.

First in Sulphur, First in Service: Freeport Sulphur Company, New York: Freeport Sulphur Company, 1961.

"A Freeport First?," *Forbes,* May 1, 1970.

Freeport-McMoRan, New Orleans: Freeport-McMoRan Inc., 1980.

"Freeport-McMoRan Is to Realign Itself, Spin Off Stake in Copper, Gold Affiliate," *Wall Street Journal,* May 4, 1994, p. B4.

"Freeport Says It with Sulfur," *Business Week,* November 4, 1967.

"Freeport's Flexible Focus," *Oil & Gas Investor,* July 1991.

Fritsch, Peter, "Freeport to Buy Arcadian for $1.06 Billion," *Wall Street Journal,* August 8, 1996, pp. A3, A5.

Haynes, Williams, *The Stone That Burns; The Story of the American Sulphur Industry,* Princeton, N.J.: Van Nostrand, 1942.

Lubove, Seth, "Trusting the CEO's Instincts," *Forbes,* January 18, 1993, p. 80.

Miller, James P., "IMC Global Agrees to $748 Million Deal to Buy Partner Freeport-McMoRan Inc.," *Wall Street Journal,* July 29, 1997, p. B6.

Moore, Gordon H., and Juan J. Campo, "Offshore Challenge," *Civil Engineering,* October 1992.

Mullener, Elizabeth, "Jim Bob Moffett: The Style of a Hot Shot, the Heart of a Wildcatter and the Soul of an Entrepreneur," *Dixie,* April 13, 1986.

"A Pit of Trouble," *Business Week,* July 31, 2000, p. 24.

Pratt, Tom, "Mining the Capital Markets," *Investment Dealers Digest,* August 12, 1991.

Press, Eyal, "Jim Bob's Indonesian Misadventure," *Progressive,* June 1996, p. 32.

Price, Robin B., "U.S. Independent Operators Step up the Pace of Non-U.S. Exploration, Development," *Oil & Gas Journal,* April 27, 1992.

"Riots in Indonesia Quelled; U.S. Mine Prepares to Reopen," *Wall Street Journal,* March 14, 1996, p. A15.

Shari, Michael, Gary McWilliams, and Stan Crock, "Gold Rush in New Guinea," *Business Week,* November 20, 1995, pp. 66–68.

"Trouble at Mine: Indonesia," *Economist,* April 20, 1996, p. 30.

Wilder, Clinton, "CIO Challenge: Managing EDS," *Computerworld,* November 11, 1991.

Yafie, Roberta C., "Back on Track in Indonesia, Freeport Sees Higher Output," *American Metal Market,* January 19, 2001, p. 1.

Zellner, Wendy, "Freeport-McMoRan, a Rare Commodity," *Business Week,* April 27, 1992.

—Beatrice Rodriguez Owsley
—updates: April Dougal Gasbarre, A. Woodward

General Atomics

3550 General Atomics Ct.
San Diego, California 92121
U.S.A.
Telephone: (858) 455-3000
Fax: (858) 455-3621
Web site: http://www.ga.com

Private Company
Incorporated: 1955 as General Atomics Division
Employees: 1,800
NAIC: 334419 Other Electronic Component
Manufacturing; 334111 Electronic Computer
Manufacturing; 334516 Analytical Laboratory
Instrument Manufacturing; 541710 Research and
Development in the Physical Sciences and
Engineering Sciences

General Atomics is involved in a number of high-tech ventures, including fusion research and gas-cooled nuclear reactors. The company's range of products in development includes Lynx high-resolution radars, magnetic levitation trains, and Ultra Wideband (UWB) wireless networking technology. General Atomics Aeronautical Systems, Inc. (GA-ASI), maker of the famous Predator unmanned aerial vehicle (UAV), is an affiliated company that was spun off in 1994.

Origins

General Atomics (GA) was established as a division of General Dynamics Corporation in mid-1955. It was the creation of General Dynamics chairman John Jay Hopkins and Frederic de Hoffmann, GA's first general manager and president. De Hoffmann was a veteran of the Manhattan Project at Los Alamos. GA's very first offices were in the General Dynamics facility on Hancock Street in San Diego.

The next summer some of the most eminent nuclear scientists and engineers of the day gathered at GA's next temporary headquarters, a schoolhouse on San Diego's Barnard Street. (GA would later ''adopt'' the school in 1994 as part of its Education Outreach program.) Their order of business was to find suitable peacetime uses for nuclear energy, and to come up with a commercial product for GA to produce.

San Diego voters approved the transfer of land to GA for permanent facilities at Torrey Pines. The John Jay Hopkins Laboratory for Pure and Applied Science was formally dedicated there on June 25, 1959, with these words from its namesake: ''We are establishing here a timeless institution, a thing of the mind and spirit, devoted to man's progress.'' GA's staff already numbered 700, and the firm was involved with several research projects.

A prototype for a small, safe research reactor, the TRIGA, had debuted on May 3, 1958. GA developed special uranium-zirconium hydride fuel elements for the reactor, which gave it a level of ''inherent safety,'' rather than the engineered safety of most reactors. Marketable within four years, the TRIGA would be one of GA's most enduring and successful projects. In the next 40 years, more than 65 TRIGA reactors would be built in two dozen countries around the world.

The company spent the next 20 years trying to make high-temperature gas-cooled reactor (HTGR) technology competitive with the light water version technology that was preferred in the 1950s, reported *Business Week.* The latter used water to cool the reactor. GA's process used helium, reducing pollution and overheating concerns and lessening the amount of fuel needed. Helium also did not become radioactive, unlike water. GA's reactor design used a graphite core, which could tolerate an increase of several thousand degrees above its 850 degrees Celsius operating temperature without damage.

GA was developing a Maritime Gas Cooled Reactor for the Atomic Energy Commission. It was also studying controlled fusion for a group of Texas utilities. A prototype gas-cooled reactor built on the system of the Philadelphia Electric Co. went online in the late 1960s.

Project Orion was an attempt to design a 4,000-ton, long-range spacecraft powered by controlled nuclear pulses, or explosions. The project progressed to the point that a small test vehicle (dubbed ''Hot Rod'') powered by conventional explosives was built. However, Orion was canceled in 1965 due to political and technical challenges.

Owned by Gulf, Royal Dutch/Shell in the 1970s

Gulf Oil acquired GA in 1967. Royal Dutch/Shell became a partner in GA in 1973 with a $200 million investment. It had added another $200 million to $300 million in another two years. GA, which had been known under the name Gulf General Atomic, then Gulf Energy & Environmental Systems, became General Atomics Company in January 1974.

Construction of GA's first commercial power plant, built for the Public Service Co. of Colorado (PSCO), was completed in 1973; however, the reactor was not online for another three years, and it would experience many equipment failures until it was shut down in 1989. Other utilities committed to buy ten more reactors in the mid-1970s; however, these commitments were canceled. GA then focused on reactor technology research. In 1977, joined by 28 utilities, it formed Gas Cooled Reactor Associates (GCRA).

Founding President Frederic de Hoffmann had left GA in 1969; he went on to head the Salk Institute. GA was led during the mid-1970s by Bill Finley. Finley's 1977 Business Plan set forth new goals of profitability and diversification. Dr. Harold Agnew, formerly director of the Los Alamos Scientific Laboratory, became president of GA in March 1979. The next month, the Three Mile Island accident dramatically affected the entire nuclear power industry. GA claimed its gas-cooled reactors were the safest in the world, and would have been capable of averting the Three Mile Island disaster. Still, the new regulatory environment raised the cost of operating any type of nuclear plant.

Agnew set GA on a course of diversification. It used its concrete structure expertise to build offshore oil tanks. The company also looked abroad, participating in a joint U.S.-Japan fusion power development project called Doublet III.

From December 1975 to June 1984, GA was embroiled in litigation by Westinghouse Electric Corp. and United Nuclear Corp. (UNC), alleging an international price-fixing conspiracy. Twenty-eight other companies were also charged in lawsuits in Illinois and New Mexico. GA ended up settling claims against it for $200 million.

Changing Hands in the 1980s

GA had revenues of $115 million in 1980, most ($85 million) of it from government nuclear-energy research contracts. The company employed about 2,200 people, down 600 from its mid-1970s peak.

Gulf Oil bought out its 50–50 partner, Royal Dutch/Shell Group's Scallop Nuclear Inc., effective January 1, 1982. Gulf became full owner of General Atomics, while Scallop received a large piece of land next to GA's San Diego headquarters.

General Atomics then became known as GA Technologies Inc. Chevron became GA's owner after its merger with Gulf Oil in mid-1984.

A systems and services group was started in 1982 as GA sought to become less dependent on government funding, specifically the Department of Energy. Among the offerings were toxic waste disposal. GA was also involved in research of particle beam weapons and a space-based nuclear reactor for the Department of Defense. Revenues reached $154.5 million in 1985.

GA joined with the University of California-San Diego (UCSD) to launch the San Diego Supercomputer Center in 1985. The center received most of its funding from the National Science Foundation, and performed research on earthquakes, the global climate, and other analytical and mathematical problems.

Two Denver-area investors, Neal and Linden Blue, acquired GA from Chevron Corporation for more than $50 million in 1986. The company was then known as GA Technologies. After the buy, Dr. Kerry Dance, who had submitted an employee buyout bid, left the company as president, a position he had held since January 1985 following the retirement of Dr. Harold Agnew. Neil Blue became CEO and board chairman, while Linden Blue became vice-chairman overseeing reactor programs.

Taking Wing in the 1990s

GA formed a 50–50 radioactive cleanup joint venture with Indiana-based hazardous waste firm Canonie Environmental Services Corp. in 1990. Nuclear Remediation Technologies Corp. was started with about six employees and $3 million in start-up capital. In the fall of 1989, the Department of Energy had identified ten military nuclear-weapon sites for remediation over the next three decades.

In 1991, GA acquired Chevron Corp.'s North American uranium assets. These holdings included the largest known uranium deposit in the United States, at Mount Taylor, New Mexico.

The break-up of the Soviet Union allowed for closer cooperation between GA and Russian nuclear researchers. In 1993, the Russian Ministry for Atomic Energy teamed with GA in designing a new prototype gas-cooled reactor. The aim was to generate commercial sales of the reactors around the world.

Former Admiral Thomas P. Cassidy and six engineers formed General Atomics Aeronautical Systems Inc. (GA-ASI) as an affiliated company of GA in 1992. The unit's mission was to develop unmanned aerial vehicles (UAVs). Drones in the past had been limited by range restrictions and the need to process film from their cameras. GA-ASI set out to develop an unmanned craft that could be controlled from greater distances, while transmitting battlefield pictures in real time.

The company's first craft was called the "Gnat." It could remain airborne for more than 40 hours. The Gnat was used in combat, but another UAV would become better known to military planners. First flown in 1994, the Predator was used over the skies of Bosnia during the NATO intervention there in the late 1990s. After the conflict, GA-ASI signed deals with several European companies to meet local requirements for UAVs.

Key Dates:

1955: General Atomics (GA) is formed as a unit of General Dynamics.
1958: TRIGA research reactor prototype is produced.
1959: John Jay Hopkins Laboratory is dedicated at Torrey Pines.
1967: Gulf Oil acquires GA.
1974: Royal Dutch/Shell becomes equal partner in GA with Gulf.
1982: Gulf Oil buys Royal Dutch/Shell's holding in GA.
1986: Denver investors Neal and Linden Blue acquire GA.
1992: General Atomics Aeronautical Systems (GA-ASI) is formed.
1994: Predator UAV makes its first flight; GA-ASI is spun off.
2002: Predator makes headlines during hunt for Taliban in Afghanistan.

GA-ASI was spun off as an independent entity in 1994. The Predator's real-time battlefield coverage capabilities made headlines over the skies of Afghanistan and Iraq after September 11, 2001.

In the mid-1990s, GA had about 1,300 employees in San Diego. GA was involved in nuclear space power systems, weapons destruction, and superconducting magnets in addition to nuclear reactors and fusion. The company had formed a short-lived bioscience division in 1991 that was closed four years later.

Promising Research: Late 1990s to Early 2000s

GA was involved in a number of unique research projects in the late 1990s and beyond. One of them was a ship using a superconducting magnet to detonate mines at sea. It was also helping market a Russian design for high-temperature batteries used to power sensors on oil rigs. In December 1999, a GA-led team was one of two to win a contract to design an electromagnetic aircraft launcher for Navy carriers. GA began selling its new high-resolution LYNX radar system to the Army in 2000.

An O-shaped magnetic field keeps plasma in place inside a chamber 15 feet in diameter, called a tokamak. The plasma is spun from 10 to 100 miles per second, creating pressure, while the temperature reaches millions of degrees. The reactions, which last only a few seconds, combine light elements such as hydrogen (deuterium, tritium) or lithium, to produce heavy elements and energy. However, scientists had been unable to produce a fusion reaction that yielded more energy than the large amount needed to sustain them in a lab.

Another GA team invented the equivalent of "lightning in a bottle." Its Rotating Tube Discharge kept a long column of plasma in place inside a spinning tube. A number of industrial applications were envisioned.

GA was also leading several Pennsylvania-based agencies in the Urban Maglev consortium to develop a rail system based on magnetic levitation. The research was sponsored by the Federal Transit Administration. In one test in early 2002, GA engineers levitated a ton of weight using a single magnet module, which could be combined with others to suspend an entire 40,000-pound train.

In 2003, GA and its affiliates were involved in a wide range of other projects at the leading edge of technology, including flexible flat panel displays (Organic Light Emitting Diodes). The Energy Products division had won a contract to produce 2,500 capacitors for Sandia National Laboratories. GA entered a joint venture with Royal Philips Electronics to develop chipsets using GA's Ultra-Wideband (UWB) wireless networking technology. The Energy Products Division had been formed in 2000 from business lines acquired from San Diego's Maxwell Technologies; it was subsequently merged with GA's Sorrento Electronics unit, a supplier of products for the petroleum and nuclear power industries.

Principal Operating Units

Advanced Technologies Group; Energy Group; Lynx Systems Group.

Principal Competitors

Northrop Grumman Corporation.

Further Reading

"American State Taxes; Gulf's War," *Economist,* June 27, 1981.
Blue, Neal, "A Nuclear Reactor That's Meltdown-Proof," *Wall Street Journal,* July 9, 1993, p. A9.
Braham, Jim, "Seagoing Superconductor Detonates Mines," *Machine Design,* November 20, 1997, pp. 33–35.
"A Court Complicates Gulf's Uranium Woes," *Business Week,* March 20, 1978, p. 38.
Dant, Jennifer, "It's No More Wait and See for GA," *San Diego Business Journal,* July 8, 1996, p. 5.
Dornheim, Michael A., "High-Altitude Drone Gets to Work on ARM-UAV Program," *Aviation Week & Space Technology,* November 11, 1996, p. 54.
"The Dwindling Orders at General Atomics," *Business Week,* October 6, 1985, p. 32.
Dyson, George, *Project Orion: The True Story of the Atomic Spaceship,* New York: Henry Holt, 2002.
Edwards, Larry M., "GA, Russians Join in Test of New Reactor Design," *San Diego Business Journal,* April 12, 1993, p. 1.
Emshwiller, John R., "General Atomics Ready for Nuclear Power Resurgence," *Wall Street Journal,* June 7, 1993, p. B2.
Fikes, Bradley J., "Two Local Companies Find Bargain of the Decade: Russian Scientists," *San Diego Business Journal,* March 30, 1992, p. 14.
Fouquet, Doug, "40th Birthday: 'The Legacy of GA's Founders'," *General Atomics Update,* August 1995, p. 3.
——, "Frederic de Hoffmann Dies at 65," *General Atomics Update,* December 1989, pp. 1, 3.
——, "GA's 25th Anniversary: That First Summer at Barnard School," *Calendar,* August 1981, pp. 4–5.
——, "GA's 30th Anniversary: Part I—The Early Years," *Calendar,* June 1985, pp. 2–5.
——, "TRIGA Reactors Celebrate Forty Years of Success," *General Atomics Update,* August 1998, pp. 1, 3.
——, "Twenty Five Years Ago at Torrey Pines," *Calendar,* June 1984, pp. 4–5.
"GA Celebrates Its 30th Anniversary," *Calendar,* July 1985, pp. 2–3.

Galvin, Cindy, "GA Technologies Officials Reviewing Potential Employee Buyout Plan," *Nucleonics Week,* October 10, 1985, p. 4.

——, "Management Reorganization Announced at GA Technologies," *Nucleonics Week,* October 30, 1986, p. 9.

Graves, Brad, "GA Makes Fusion Breakthrough," *San Diego Business Journal,* July 9, 2001, p. 8.

——, "The Right Stuff," *San Diego Business Journal,* June 25, 2001, p. 1.

"Gulf Oil to Own General Atomic," *Electric Light & Power,* February 1982, p. 6.

"Gulf to Obtain General Atomic," *New York Times,* December 22, 1981, p. D4.

Kuzela, Lad, "A Nuclear Pioneer Tries the Power of Persuasion," *Industry Week,* April 20, 1981, pp. 73+.

Morrocco, John D., "Predator Builder Teams with Europeans," *Aviation Week & Space Technology,* June 28, 1999, p. 49.

"A New Fusion Reactor," *Business Week,* June 15, 1981, p. 44.

O'Reiley, Tim, "GA Technologies on Selling Block," *San Diego Business Journal,* July 22, 1985, p. 1.

Pae, Peter, "Future Is Now for Creator of Predator; Unmanned Vehicle Made by San Diego's General Atomics Is Helping Revolutionize Warfare in Skies Over Afghanistan," *Los Angeles Times,* January 3, 2002, p. C1.

——, "Sept. 11 Proved to Be Turning Point for the Predator; San Diego Maker of the Drone Ramps Up Production and Works to Develop an Armed Version," *Los Angeles Times,* September 7, 2002, p. C1.

Penney, Stewart, "Four Tactical UAVs in U.S. Army Shoot-Out," *Flight International,* August 18, 1999, p. 17.

"Reactors Fuel GA's New Approach," *San Diego Union-Tribune,* February 22, 1988.

Salpukas, Agis, "A Negotiated Peace in Long UNC Fight," *New York Times,* June 1, 1984, p. D1.

Samuel, Eugenie, "Here Comes the Sun," *New Scientist,* July 14, 2001, p. 4.

Schena, Susan C., "Nuclear Firm Sees Profits in Radioactive Waste Disposal," *San Diego Business Journal,* January 29, 1990, p. 12.

Squeo, Anne Marie, "Small Maker of Unmanned Jets Fights Big; Goliath Competitors Scramble to Move in on General Atomic's Specialty," *Wall Street Journal,* January 29, 2003, p. B8.

"Urban Maglev Project Demonstrates Levitation," *General Atomics Update,* April 2002, pp. 1–2.

Wall, Robert, "Battle Brews Over UAV Dominance," *Aviation Week & Space Technology,* December 24, 2001, pp. 43+.

Wells, Ken R., "General Atomics Closes Division for Biosciences," *San Diego Business Journal,* March 13, 1995, p. 4.

——, "Supercomputer Operators Now Kissing, Making Up," *San Diego Business Journal,* June 10, 1996, p. 5.

—Frederick C. Ingram

General Growth Properties, Inc.

110 N. Wacker Drive
Chicago, Illinois 60606
U.S.A.
Telephone: (312) 960-5000
Fax: (312) 960-5475
Web site: http://www.generalgrowth.com

Public Company
Incorporated: 1986 as General Growth Partners, Inc.
Employees: 3,810
Sales: $1.06 billion (2002)
Stock Exchanges: New York
Ticker Symbol: GGP
NAIC: 233320 Commercial and Institutional Building
    Construction

General Growth Properties, Inc. (GGP) is the second largest shopping mall owner/operator in the United States, trailing only Simon Property Group. The Chicago-based real estate investment trust (REIT) is also the largest third-party manager of regional malls. The company has ownership stakes or management responsibility for more than 150 regional shopping malls, located in 41 states. These properties contain approximately 135 million square feet of retail space and house more than 15,000 anchor department stores, specialty retailers, as well as movie theaters, restaurants, ice skating rinks, and other family entertainment facilities. GGP is primarily owned by the founding Bucksbaum family.

Bucksbaum Family Becoming Involved in Shopping Centers in the 1950s

The Bucksbaum family was originally in the grocery business in Cedar Rapids, Iowa. In 1954, brothers Martin, Maurice, and Matthew Bucksbaum were looking for a site to locate a fourth supermarket in a chain founded by their father when they learned of a chance to finance the construction of a shopping center in Cedar Rapids. Rather than continue to be tenants in someone else's building, they borrowed $1.2 million to become landlords.

What resulted was one of the first shopping centers in the United States, the Town and Country Shopping Center, which opened in Cedar Rapids in 1956. The Bucksbaums decided that their future lay in the building of strip malls and even before Town and Country opened they had exited the supermarket business. They then built the Wakonda Shopping Center in Des Moines and another shopping strip in Bettendorf, Iowa. According to Matthew Bucksbaum's recollection some 40 years later, "There was some conversation following the completion of the third mall that we'd never have to do anything else." Instead, with Martin Bucksbaum assuming the lead role, they continued to build. By 1964 they owned five properties and formed a management company, General Management Corporation, in which the Bucksbaums were majority stockholders. With the advent of enclosed malls in the 1960s, the Bucksbaums shifted from building strip centers to the new shopping mall format.

In 1970 the Bucksbaums exchanged their interests in General Management Corporation for shares in a REIT they named General Growth Properties (GGP). Another entity, General Growth Companies, was then formed to plan, develop, and manage the REIT's assets. Ultimately, GGP spawned a management company called General Growth Management Inc. to oversee its properties on a third-party basis. The Bucksbaum brothers ran their businesses from offices located in Des Moines. REITs were a relatively new creation, established by Congress in 1960 as a way for small investors to become involved in real estate in a manner similar to mutual funds. REITs could be taken public and their shares traded just like stock. They were also subject to regulation by the Securities and Exchange Commission. Unlike companies issuing stock, however, REITs were required by law to pay out at least 95 percent of their taxable income to shareholders each year. Because REITs were allowed only to own real estate, third parties, such as General Growth Companies, had to be contracted to manage the properties. Because of a number of factors, REITs at this stage in their history did not gain much favor with the investment community.

GGP's Sale of Its Portfolio in 1984

Starting in 1979 the Bucksbaums began to believe that the market was not fairly recognizing the true value of GGP. When

Company Perspectives:

The corporate mission of General Growth Properties is to create value and profit by acquiring, developing, renovating, and managing regional malls in major and middle markets throughout the United States.

the prices for retail properties improved significantly in the early 1980s they decided to sell GGP's portfolio of 19 shopping centers. In 1984 GGP sold the centers to Equitable Life Assurance Society for $800 million, which at the time was the largest single-asset real estate transaction in history. Although GGP's shareholders, primarily the Bucksbaums, were paid off and the REIT was liquidated, the Bucksbaum family continued to manage most of the properties through General Growth Management. In 1986 Martin and Matthew Bucksbaum formed General Growth Properties, Inc. as a vehicle to purchase and own mall properties. Three years later the company acquired the assets of The Center Companies, a deal that in turn made General Growth Management the second largest manager of regional shopping malls and the leading manager for institutional owners.

Not until the Tax Reform Act of 1986 changed the nature of real estate investment did REITs begin to gain widespread usage. Tax shelter schemes that had drained potential investments were shut down. Interest and depreciation deductions were greatly reduced so that taxpayers could not generate paper losses in order to lower their tax liabilities. The act also permitted REITs to provide customary services for properties, in effect allowing the trusts to operate and manage the properties they owned. Despite these major changes in law, REITs were still not fully utilized. In the latter half of the 1980s banks, insurance companies, pension funds, and foreign investors (in particular, the Japanese) provided the lion's share of real estate investment funds. That period also witnessed overbuilding, leading to a shakeout in the marketplace. With real estate available at distressed prices in the early 1990s, REITs finally became an attractive mainstream investment option.

In 1993 the Bucksbaums packaged 55 percent of General Growth Partners' assets into a new REIT using the old GGP name in order to take the business public and look for acquisition opportunities—in particular poorly run malls whose management could be improved and facilities updated. The Bucksbaum family retained the remaining 45 percent of the General Growth Partners' holdings. An initial public offering of GGP, which owned 21 malls in 14 states, was then held, in which 19 million shares were sold at $22 per share. GGP's first acquisition came in early 1994 when it paid $182 million for a 40 percent interest in CenterMark Properties from The Prudential Insurance Company of America. CenterMark owned 16 regional malls along with three power centers, 14 freestanding department stores, a 116-unit apartment project, and other real estate assets. A year later GGP sold 25 percent of its stake to Westfield Holdings Group—an Australian mall company that had been its partner on the CenterMark deal—for $72.5 million in cash. In June 1996 GGP sold the balance of its CenterMark interests to Westfield, so that in little more than two years the REIT realized a tidy $143 million financial gain on the deal.

GGP spent much of 1995 working on a massive transaction in conjunction with four investment partners: the $1.85 billion acquisition of Homart Development Co. from Sears, Roebuck and Co., which was unloading noncore assets in order to return its focus to retailing. Of that amount, roughly $800 million was paid in cash and the balance was the assumption of $1 billion in debt. Homart owned 27 regional malls and five strip shopping centers, as well as 17 suburban office buildings. It was in the course of finalizing the deal that Martin Bucksbaum died of a heart attack at the age of 74. His brother Matthew replaced him as GGP's chairman. Following the Homart acquisition, GGP relocated its headquarters from Des Moines to Chicago.

In 1996 GGP acquired General Growth Management, which brought GGP's marketing, leasing, and marketing operations under one roof. While competitors began to buy up mall properties at a furious pace, as a consolidation wave swept the industry, GGP refused to overpay for properties and appeared content to wait for the right opportunity. In 1997 it spent just $350 million to add eight malls, including the Oaks Mall in Florida and Westroads Mall in Nebraska. The REIT's next major acquisition did not come until 1998 when it paid $871 million in cash for eight shopping malls owned by U.S. subsidiaries of MEPC plc, a London-based development company. According to one analyst quoted by the *Wall Street Journal,* "I'd be hardpressed to say there's any better pricing on this than the other deals." Regardless, GGP picked up some choice properties, including the Boulevard Mall in Las Vegas and the Cumberland Mall in Atlanta. Other transactions soon followed in 1998. GGP paid $625 million, less some $65 million in debt, to acquire U.S. Prime Property, acquiring another six malls. Also in 1998 GGP bought Northbrook Court, a suburban Chicago shopping mall. It was an important deal because it provided a flagship mall for GGP in the city where its headquarters was now located. Other acquisitions in 1998 included the Pierre Bossier Mall and Mall St. Vincent in Louisiana; Spring Hill Mall in Illinois; and Coastland Center and Altamonte Mall in Florida. Moreover, GGP was involved in the development of new malls, despite the perception that the country was overstocked with malls. In July 1998 it opened the Coral Ridge Mall in Coralville, Iowa, some 20 miles from the Bucksbaum's first strip shopping center in Cedar Rapids. Later in 1998 GGP broke ground on a new project, the Stonebriar Mall in Dallas, Texas.

Naming John Bucksbaum CEO in 1999

The year 1999 marked a significant turn in the history of GGP: Matthew Bucksbaum's son, John Bucksbaum, succeeded him as CEO of the company. (The 73-year-old Matthew Bucksbaum did stay on as chairman of the board.) John Bucksbaum was deserving of the promotion and well seasoned after being involved in the business for some 20 years. He started on the development side, after earning an economics degree from the University of Denver, Colorado, and initially worked on projects in Colorado. Following a stint in Puerto Rico he spent ten years as the head of General Growth of California, which he was responsible for creating. As GGP went public in 1993 he relocated to Chicago two years ahead of the rest of the company to help launch the offering.

A change in leadership did not affect GGP's continuing efforts to grow its holdings in 1999. In January of that year it

Key Dates:

1956: The Bucksbaum brothers open the first strip mall in Cedar Rapids, Iowa.
1964: General Management Corporation is formed.
1970: General Growth Properties is formed as a REIT.
1984: General Growth sells its holdings to Life Assurance Society for $800 million.
1993: The Bucksbaums form a new REIT using the General Growth Properties' name.
1995: Martin Bucksbaum dies.
1999: John Bucksbaum becomes CEO.

bought The Crossroads Mall in Kalamazoo, Michigan. In May 1999 GGP acquired a prized property, the Ala Moana Center, located in Honolulu, Hawaii, regarded by many as the crown jewel of Pacific Rim retailing. GGP paid $810 million to a Japanese consortium to land the 1.8 million-square-foot complex. Because of a recession in Asia, the $810 million represented a reasonable price for the property, about 12.5 times cash flow as opposed to the 15 to 17 times cash flow that GGP calculated it would have cost to purchase the property three years earlier. Later in 1999 GGP and a partner, Ivanhoe, Inc., teamed up to make a number of investments, including the acquisition of Oak View Mall in Nebraska and Eastridge Mall in California. Also in 1999 GGP acquired Baybrook Mall in Texas.

With the advent of the Internet and the rising popularity of online shopping, GGP and all mall developers and managers faced new challenges as the 20th century came to a close. For decades malls were designed to keep consumers within their confines, hopefully to induce impulse buying. As a result, planned inconvenience became the norm and malls turned into mazes, with plants and other fixtures introduced simply to create twists and turns in the customer's journey to a particular store or venue. Even directories were designed to confuse more than to help, again preventing customers from efficiently navigating through the complex. To combat the trend of shoppers opting to avoid malls in favor of big-box discounters or shopping over the Internet, GGP, after three years of testing, began to design its new malls with similar shops clustered together. In this way, for instance, someone shopping for children's clothing could confine their mall visit to a particular wing. As for the Internet, rather than fight it, GGP actually chose to embrace it. With the help of IBM GGP in 2000 launched MalibuDirect, an Internet-based kiosk system for its malls. Customers would have entry to web sites of participating retailers, although access would be hobbled to prevent users from surfing the entire Web. They would be able to purchase goods online and have them shipped to their homes. Malibu also offered job notices and other services. Not only did GGP receive a percentage of sales, it was now able to gather customer information through registration. In that way, for example, the company would be able to notify customers via email about upcoming sales that would be of interest to them. In addition to launching Malibu, GGP teamed up with Cisco Systems to install a digital broad-band cable infrastructure in its malls, which helped retailers to be more productive. Highspeed communications improved credit card verifications and inventory tracking.

Although high-tech innovations were welcome, the main focus of GGP in the new century remained growth through development and especially acquisition, as the mall sector continued to undergo consolidation. The large players were buying up the smaller operators in hopes of gaining leverage when negotiating with department store chains and national specialty retailers. In 2000 GGP opened Stonebriar Centre in Frisco, Texas, a suburb of Dallas. Early in 2001 GGP grew the management side of its business when it won the management, leasing, and marketing contracts for a 14-mall portfolio owned by an institutional investor. Acquisitions in 2001 included Houston's Willowbrook Mall and the Tucson Mall in Tucson, Arizona. In 2002 GGP paid $440 million and assumed $576 million in debt to acquire JP Realty Inc., a REIT with properties in the Intermountain region of the United States. The deal added 18 regional malls, in addition to 26 community centers and 1.3 million square feet of industrial space. Later in 2002 GGP acquired Victoria Ward, Limited, a privately held real estate company, picking up the Ward Centre, Ward Warehouse, and the new Ward Entertainment Center. The move strengthened GGP's position in Hawaii, which was already contributing a significant portion of its revenues. Although GGP was now the second largest mall operator in the United States, it would have to continue to grow to maintain that ranking. Management, in the hands of a second generation of the Bucksbaum family, was likely, however, to remain cautious and only strike deals that made long-term sense.

Principal Subsidiaries

General Growth Finance SPE, Inc.; GGP Limited Partnership.

Principal Competitors

The Rouse Company; Simon Property Group, Inc.; Westfield America Trust.

Further Reading

Coleman, Calmetta Y., ''Making Malls (Gasp!) Convenient,'' *Wall Street Journal,* February 8, 2000, p. B1.

Edgington, Denise, ''The $5.5 Billion Mall Maker,'' *Business Record,* January 11, 1999, p. 10.

Goldberger, Paul, ''Settling the Suburban Frontier,'' *New York Times Magazine,* December 31, 1995, p. 634.

Johnson, Ben, ''General Growth Lives Up to Its Name and Then Some,'' *National Real Estate Investor,* January 1996, p. 36.

Kirkpatrick, David D., ''REIT Interest: General Growth Properties: Shop 'Til They Drop,'' *Wall Street Journal,* June 4, 1997, p. B8.

Pacelle, Mitchell, ''Sears Is Close to an Agreement to Sell Shopping-Mall Assets for $800 Million,'' *Wall Street Journal,* June 13, 1995, p. A3.

Wangensteen, Betsy, ''Mall Firm's Big Stretch,'' *Crain's Chicago Business,* April 1, 1996, p. 13.

—Ed Dinger

The Gorman-Rupp Company

305 Bowman Street
P.O. Box 1217
Mansfield, Ohio 44901-1217
U.S.A.
Telephone: (419) 755-1011
Fax: (419) 755-1233
Web site: http://www.gormanrupp.com

Public Company
Incorporated: 1934
Employees: 1,033
Sales: $194.1 million (2002)
Stock Exchanges: American
Ticker Symbol: GRC
NAIC: 333911 Pump and Pumping Equipment
     Manufacturing

The Gorman-Rupp Company is one of the largest pump manufacturers in the United States, producing more than 4,000 models of pumps. The company's product line ranges from small pumps for soft drink dispensers and medical devices to massive machines capable of moving up to 500,000 gallons of fluid per minute. The larger pumps are used in such applications as boosting water pressure in municipal water systems and pumping petroleum products, as in the ground refueling of aircraft. Over the company's several decades of operation, and through both organic and acquisitive growth, the product line has expanded to include an increasingly diverse array of pumps and related equipment, including products for municipal water and sewerage systems, the construction industry, fire protection systems, a variety of industrial applications, original equipment manufacturers, government agencies such as the U.S. military, and petroleum applications. Gorman-Rupp maintains more than one million square feet of manufacturing and warehousing facilities, the bulk of which is located in the company's headquarters city of Mansfield, Ohio; other facilities are situated in Bellville, Ohio; Sand Springs, Oklahoma; Toccoa and Chamblee, Georgia; Royersford, Pennsylvania; St. Thomas, Ontario; and County Westmeath, Ireland. The plants in Canada

and Ireland support the company's efforts to penetrate international markets, and in 2002, 14 percent of sales were generated outside the United States from customers located in 75 countries. Gorman-Rupp's fairly conservative long-term strategy is codified in the corporate credo: ''It is our practice to enter a field of pumping service only when able to provide a superior product with better performance.''

Company's Founding During the Great Depression

Gorman-Rupp's roots stretch back well over half a century to 1933 when two engineers, J.C. Gorman and Herbert E. Rupp, pooled $1,500 and started a pump manufacturing business in a barn outside the small town of Mansfield, Ohio. By that time, pumps had long been integral to many businesses. In fact, pumps remained the second most common machine used in industry into the 1990s. Perceiving an opportunity to carve out a profitable niche in this highly fragmented industry, Gorman and Rupp worked diligently to design pumps with particular features for specific tasks.

They established a longstanding corporate reputation for product development early on, launching ''the first simplified self-priming centrifugal pump with no valves or orifices'' in 1933. In keeping with its name, a centrifugal pump generates drawing pressure by moving liquids (and in some applications gases) in a circular pattern. The ''self-priming'' part of the name meant that the machine did not need a consistent flow of fluids in order to maintain its pumping capacity. These relatively quiet, rugged, and inexpensive devices are most often used to remove water (known in industry parlance as ''dewatering'') at intermittently wet construction sites, sewers, and quarries. Self-priming centrifugal pumps formed the core of Gorman-Rupp's product line.

World War II and the Postwar Era

Within six years of its creation, the company was generating about $345,000 in annual sales. In the 1940s, Gorman-Rupp developed a solids handling trash pump that featured a removable endplate for easy maintenance. The company would later call it a ''bellwether'' product, one often imitated by competitors. Fueled in part by wartime contracts with the U.S. Army and Navy, for which the company was awarded an "E" for excellence, Gorman-Rupp sales multiplied to more than $2 million by 1949. Manufacturing capacity grew correspondingly, and the company moved from its rural barn to a factory in town during this decade.

Sales continued to mount rapidly in the postwar era, when Gorman-Rupp's close attention to the dewatering needs of the construction industry paid off. In 1952, the company reengineered a diaphragm pump for this market. Diaphragm pumps incorporate a flexible, but impenetrable membrane that prevents the material being pumped from coming in contact with the inner workings of the pump and vice versa. They are designed to pump abrasive or uncontaminated substances, and can also tolerate extended dry runs. Gorman-Rupp improved on the basic diaphragm pump design by decreasing the pump's weight and increasing its capacity. The pump manufacturer benefited indirectly from the residential housing boom of the 1950s. Its revenues tripled over the course of the decade, from $2.25 million in 1949 to $7 million by 1959.

Progressive Diversification: 1950s–70s

Yet company executives realized that they could not rely on a single market—especially one as cyclical as the construction industry—for consistent sales and earnings growth. The seeds of the diversification process were sown in the early 1950s, when the firm established its Gorman-Rupp Industries Division in nearby Bellville, Ohio. Created to meet the needs of original equipment manufacturers (OEMs), Gorman-Rupp Industries made small, specialized pumps used in larger machines such as photocopiers, coffee machines, kidney dialysis machines, and photo-processing equipment. This division's emphasis on research and development helped make it the parent company's highest-margin segment by the mid-1990s.

In 1960 the company went international with the construction of a plant in Ontario, Canada. Gorman-Rupp of Canada Limited mirrored the parent company's main plant in Ohio, and its product line grew accordingly.

Gorman-Rupp also began to diversify within the pump category in earnest in the 1960s. It launched new lines of submersi-

ble pumps for mining, centrifugal pumps and fiberglass pumping stations for municipal sewage systems, specialty pumps for moving home heating oil and aircraft fuel quickly and safely, as well as pumps for the consumer market (i.e., the "handy pump") and a backpack pump for firefighters. These technological developments and the new markets they opened helped triple Gorman-Rupp's sales for the second consecutive decade, from $7 million in 1959 to $21 million by 1969.

The company continued to penetrate new niches of the pump industry in the 1970s, launching a magnetic drive pump that could be used to move liquid metals. A key development of this decade was the creation of the Gorman-Rupp International Division, which marketed the entire line of pumps via overseas distributors. This segment's contribution to sales rose from 7 percent in 1980 to about 11 percent in 1995. Gorman-Rupp hoped to further increase its share of global pump sales by emphasizing the petrochemical, municipal, and industrial markets. Driven by these developments, total corporate sales doubled over the course of the 1970s, exceeding $50 million in 1978 and reaching more than $58 million by 1979. Having gone public in 1968, Gorman-Rupp common stock was listed on the American Stock Exchange in the 1970s.

Acquisitions Distinguishing the Late 1970s and Continuing in the 1980s

A fairly modest industry contraction saw manufacturers of pumps and pumping equipment shrink from 613 in 1977 to 528 in 1987. Gorman-Rupp played a role in this trend, executing three acquisitions during this period. In 1977 the company acquired Ramparts, Inc. (becoming Gorman-Rupp's Ramparts Division), which manufactured air-driven diaphragm pumps and replacement parts for the chemical industry. These specialized machines were most often used to move highly corrosive and/or viscous liquids like sulfuric acid and hydrochloric acid. Although the Ramparts Division was still only generating 1 percent of Gorman-Rupp's annual sales 20 years after its acquisition, the parent company considered its high profit margins an important contributor to long-term growth.

Like many manufacturers, U.S. pump makers faced heavy competition from foreign producers in the 1980s. To combat this problem, Gorman-Rupp acquired the IPT Pumps Division, a manufacturer of economically priced, portable, and durable pumps for the construction market, in 1986. Although this division also only contributed 1 percent of annual revenues and scant profits, it helped Gorman-Rupp maintain a presence in this competitive industry segment.

Gorman-Rupp made its largest acquisition to date in 1988, when it paid Banner Industries about $14.8 million for control of the Patterson Pump Company. Based in Toccoa, Georgia, Patterson manufactured a comprehensive line of large-volume centrifugal pumps used for flood control and irrigation as well as fire pumps for automatic sprinkler systems and fire hydrants. Patterson complemented Gorman-Rupp's existing water, sewer, and fire-fighting lines, enabling the company to offer custom-designed, large-scale fluid transport systems to these key markets.

Although Patterson added $24 million to Gorman-Rupp's sales tally, its returns were less than stellar. Treating its newest

Key Dates:

1933: J.C. Gorman and Herbert E. Rupp start a pump manufacturing business in a barn outside Mansfield, Ohio.

1934: The business is incorporated as The Gorman-Rupp Company.

1940s: The company develops a solids handling trash pump with a removable endplate.

Early 1950s: Gorman-Rupp Industries Division is formed to meet the needs of original equipment manufacturers.

1960: International expansion begins with the construction of a plant in Ontario, Canada, and the formation of the subsidiary Gorman-Rupp of Canada Limited.

1968: The company goes public.

1977: Ramparts, Inc., maker of diaphragm pumps for the chemical industry, is acquired.

1988: Gorman-Rupp acquires Patterson Pump Company, producer of large-volume centrifugal pumps used for flood control and irrigation as well as fire pumps.

1998: Patterson begins manufacturing pumps in Ireland.

2002: The company completes two acquisitions: American Machine and Tool Co., Inc. and Flo-Pak, Inc.

affiliate as a turnaround situation, Gorman-Rupp pumped an additional $20 million into plant and office renovations over the ensuing eight years.

The 1990s and Beyond

Several key factors contributed to Gorman-Rupp's seven-decade record of growth. The company long emphasized innovation and product quality. So confident were Gorman and Rupp in the capabilities of their products that they empowered their distributors "to put a Gorman-Rupp contractor's pump on any pumping job, anytime, anywhere, beside any competitor's pump of comparable size." The company guaranteed that its products would move more volume more efficiently and for a longer time. In addition, "if it wasn't the best all-around pump, our distributors would accept the return and pay the user any installation expense incurred."

Gorman-Rupp's reputation for excellent customer service was predicated on its network of knowledgeable distributors and its thorough inventory of new and replacement products. Gorman-Rupp supported its nearly 1,000 distributors in North America with in-depth product and process training. Sales representatives, distributors, engineers, and customers alike could attend corporate educational programs at one of two permanent training centers. The company also outfitted three recreational vehicles as mobile exhibitions for on-the-spot training and demonstrations. Although many industries and companies made the transition to just-in-time inventory in order to cut costs, Gorman-Rupp perceived its reserve as a key element of customer service. As James C. Gorman, CEO and son of the founder, told *Barron's* magazine in 1982, "Some 20 percent to 30 percent of our business is crisis business. They don't buy anything from us until they are up to their noses in water." A prime example of the wisdom of this strategy came in 1989, when Gorman-Rupp was able to provide

an estimated 90 percent of the pumps used to clean up after the *Exxon Valdez* oil spill. In a brief article for *Fortune* magazine in 1990, CEO Gorman crowed, "Our Alaskan distributor called us on Saturday, and at six Sunday evening we had the first DC-8 load of pumps in Anchorage." In addition to its ready supply of new pumps, Gorman-Rupp estimated its trade in replacement parts was at 20 percent to 25 percent of total revenues. This segment was doubtless another vital factor in the company's customer service equation.

Although Gorman-Rupp operated as a nonunion manufacturer, it cultivated such a good working environment that one industry observer characterized the company as "paternalistic." It launched hospitalization and profit-sharing programs in the mid-1930s and carefully avoided layoffs in the recessions of the 1970s and 1980s, a policy that possibly reflected its Depression-era origins. In return for its fair treatment of employees, Gorman-Rupp enjoyed low turnover and a strike-free history. Healthy labor-management relations also helped give Gorman-Rupp one of the industry's highest productivity rates. In 1996 the company's volume of sales per employee stood at $153,800, having risen from $120,000 in 1991.

Also in 1996, 72-year-old James C. Gorman drew the lines of corporate succession, ceding the chief executive office to President John A. Walter, 61. It was expected that Gorman's son, Jeffrey S., 44, who was named executive vice-president at that time, would eventually follow in his father's (and grandfather's) footsteps. Two years later he did just that, being named president and CEO in April 1998. Gorman remained chairman, and Walter retired but remained on the board of directors.

The period of the late 1990s and early 2000s was particularly noteworthy for the firm's aggressive pursuit of overseas revenues. In 1996 the company set up an office in Greece as a way to improve its distribution to the Middle East and Europe. Through a majority-owned subsidiary called Patterson Pump Ireland Limited, Patterson Pump Company began manufacturing pumps in Ireland in 1998 for sale in Europe. (In March 2002 Patterson purchased the minority holding in the subsidiary, making it wholly owned.) In 1999 the Mansfield Division opened a warehouse in Grindstead, Denmark, and another distribution center was opened in Singapore in 2001 to serve markets in Asia. The warehouse in Denmark was closed in 2001, however, and was replaced by one near Amsterdam. By the early 2000s, between 14 and 19 percent of overall revenues was generated outside the United States.

In 2002 Gorman-Rupp completed two significant acquisitions, the first in 14 years. In February, American Machine and Tool Co., Inc. (AMT) was purchased for $12.6 million. Based in Royersford, Pennsylvania, AMT was a producer of small centrifugal and diaphragm pumps for industrial, construction, agricultural, marine, and household use. The firm provided pumps under its own name as well as private-brand products for national distributors. In March 2002 Patterson Pump acquired Atlanta-based Flo-Pak, Inc. for about $6.5 million. Flo-Pak specialized in prepackaged pumping systems for the municipal, fire protection, industrial, plumbing, and heating, ventilating, and air conditioning (HVAC) markets.

The stellar history of Gorman-Rupp was reflected in the company's achievement of 15 consecutive years of increased revenue and earnings through the year 2001. That year, revenues surpassed the $200 million mark for the first time, hitting $202.9 million. The difficult economic climate of the early 2000s finally brought an end to this streak in 2002, however, as revenues fell 4.4 percent and earnings were down 38.7 percent. Gorman-Rupp products nevertheless continued to prove good at pumping profits for shareholders. The firm that year increased its dividend for the 30th consecutive year.

Principal Subsidiaries

American Machine and Tool Co., Inc.; Gorman-Rupp of Canada Limited; The Gorman-Rupp International Company; Patterson Pump Company; Patterson Pump Ireland Limited.

Principal Divisions

Mansfield Division; Gorman-Rupp Industries Division.

Principal Competitors

ITT Industries, Inc.; IDEX Corporation; Colfax Corporation; Roper Industries, Inc.; Haskel International, Inc.

Further Reading

Autry, Ret, ''Gorman-Rupp,'' *Fortune,* June 18, 1990, p. 93.

Brammer, Rhonda, ''Gorman-Rupp Gets No Respect,'' *Barron's,* November 22, 1999, p. 26.

Gleisser, Marcus, ''Pumping Up Profits in Mansfield,'' *Cleveland Plain Dealer,* June 28, 1998, p. 2H.

''The Gorman-Rupp Company,'' *Wall Street Transcript* (CEO Supplement), March 1999.

Rosenbaum, Michael, ''Pumping Profits: Gorman-Rupp Builds Revenues in a Harsh Climate,'' *Barron's,* January 4, 1982, pp. 44–45.

Sabath, Donald, ''Gorman-Rupp Succession in Place,'' *Cleveland Plain Dealer,* May 29, 1996, p. C1.

Talbott, Stephen, ''Gorman-Rupp Seeks OK on Egyptian Plant,'' *Cleveland Plain Dealer,* March 13, 1988, p. C6.

Winter, Ralph E., ''Gorman-Rupp Hopes to Maintain Growth Streak,'' *Wall Street Journal,* August 28, 2001.

——, ''Gorman-Rupp's Second Half to Be Slower,'' *Wall Street Journal,* August 31, 1998.

—April Dougal Gasbarre
—update: David E. Salamie

Grant Prideco, Inc.

1330 Post Oak Boulevard, Suite 2700
Houston, Texas 77056
U.S.A.
Telephone: (832) 681-8000
Fax: (832) 681-8499
Web site: http://www.grantprideco.com

Public Company
Incorporated: 1975 as Grant Corporations
Employees: 4,504
Sales: $639.7 million (2002)
Stock Exchanges: New York
Ticker Symbol: GRP
NAIC: 333132 Oil and Gas Field Machinery and
Equipment Manufacturing

Grant Prideco, Inc., based in Houston, Texas, is one of the world's largest manufacturers and distributors of piping and other drill stem products used by oil field drillers. The company also offers premium connections and tubular products, and in recent years has begun to offer products and services to offshore and deepwater drillers. Grant Prideco has three primary business units. The first, Drilling Products and Services, manufactures and sells such items as drill pipe, drill collars, heavyweight drill pipe, and accessories. This segment serves both land and offshore drilling operations. Tubular Technology and Services offers a complete line of premium connections and related premium tubular products and accessories for use in harsh conditions associated with gas wells, offshore wells, and other wells subject to high temperatures, high pressure, or difficult environmental conditions. The last Grant Prideco business segment is its newest, Marine Products and Service. It offers a line of proprietary connections and installation services for offshore operations and subsea wells. In addition, Grant Prideco sells drill bits and related items through its ReedHycalog subsidiary.

The Founding of the Company in 1960

The roots of Grant Prideco reach back to 1960 when engineer Charles Grant founded Grant Supply Company in Tulsa,

Oklahoma. Initially the company served as a distributor of pipe, valves, and fittings to oil refineries and petrochemical companies. In 1970 Grant set up a new operation, located in Houston, called Grant Oil Company Tubular Corporation, specializing in the distribution of tubular goods to oil field drilling operations. A year later Grant Supply moved into Canada, establishing a subsidiary in Calgary, Canada, called Grant Corporations Ltd. To organize his slate of businesses, in 1975 Grant established Grant Corporations, a Houston-based holding company. His next step came in 1978 with the launch of a finishing and processing plant for pipe and tube named Tubular Finishing Works Inc. (TFW), located in Navasota, Texas. Five years later TFW expanded by opening a plant in Bastrop, Texas.

Although for two decades Grant Supply had been able to succeed in the highly cyclical oil industry, in the early 1980s the company expanded too rapidly in response to strong demand for its products and took on an excessive amount of debt. By the mid-1980s Grant Supply operated six sales offices, located in Tulsa, Oklahoma; Bakersfield, California; Baton Rouge, Louisiana; and in Houston, Odessa, and Pampa, Texas. It contributed approximately 60 percent of the revenues generated by Grant Corporations. In October 1986 Grant Supply filed for Chapter 11 bankruptcy protection. According to filings, the company reported liabilities of nearly $60 million and assets of approximately $33 million.

With the demise of its original business, Grant Corporations, renamed Grant TFW, entered a new phase of its history in 1987 when Energy Ventures Inc., through a subsidiary called EVI, acquired a 32 percent stake in the company. Energy Ventures had been established as an offshore oil and gas producer. It had been in liquidation proceedings in 1985, the result of a settlement agreement that avoided a hostile takeover of the company, but because of a slump in the price of oil and gas properties, the sale was called off by the two firms that held 82 percent of the stock: Apco Oil Liquidating Trust and Appalachian Co., the firm that had launched the takeover bid. Given a reprieve, Energy Ventures began to prosper, driven in large part by acquisitions engineered by its EVI subsidiary, which was dedicated to picking up oil field equipment and service companies, such as Grant TFW, which were in need of capital as well as restructuring in order to achieve renewed growth.

EVI Gains Control in 1988

In 1988 EVI gained a 67 percent interest in Grant TFW, took control, and began to change the company's focus. Within the year Grant TFW shifted from distribution to the manufacture of two products, drill pipe and premium tubulars. By 1990 EVI brought the remaining stock to make Grant TFW a wholly owned subsidiary, which now launched an effort to strengthen its position in the energy industry. Later in the year the first step was taken: Grant TFW acquired the assets of a Baker Hughes operation, Hughes Tool Company's Tool Joints Division. In one stroke, Grant TFW became one of the world's largest manufacturers and suppliers of completed drill strings, its product lines including drill pipe, heavyweight drill pipe, and drill collars. In the deal Grant TFW picked up a number of Hughes's patented and proprietary tool joint designs, manufacturing processes, and international licensing agreements. Of particular importance was the acquisition of the Tuff-Weld process. As a result of adding the Hughes Tool Joints assets, Grant TFW launched its H-SERIES product line, creating a one-stop shopping approach to completed drill strings. Over the course of the first half of 1991, Hughes Tool Joints assets were relocated and incorporated into Grant TFW plants.

The next major acquisition occurred in 1992 when Grant TFW bought the operating assets of Atlas Bradford from Barcid Corporation and added premium threaded tubular connectors to its product mix. Included in the deal were machinery, equipment, technology, patents, sales offices, and a roster of licenses—as well as an influx of experienced personnel to spur continued growth. As had been the case with the Hughes Tool acquisition, Atlas Bradford was an excellent fit, its assets rounding out Grant TFW's premium tubular line. Moreover, in 1992 the company's plants were expanded and the distribution network broadened, making Grant TFW's products and services available worldwide. Sales offices were now found domestically in Houston and Dallas, Texas; New Orleans and Lafayette, Louisiana; and internationally in Aberdeen, Scotland; The Hague, The Netherlands; Singapore; Caracas, Venezuela; Pau, France; and Dubai, Arab Emirates. Grant TFW then bolstered its manufacturing capabilities in 1993 by acquiring a threading facility in Channelview, Texas, as well as leasing a drill pipe manufacturing plant located in Veracruz, Mexico. With a rising demand for premium tubular products, the company then acquired a tubular processing plant in Bryan, Texas, in August 1994. Six years earlier the facility, which had been built and opened in 1980, had been shut down due to a downturn in the oil industry. The plant, reactivated in the autumn of 1994, was an ideal pickup for Grant TFW because its equipment was specifically designed to manufacture the type of tubular products that the company now offered. Moreover, the equipment was relatively new, showing little wear and tear. It was also in 1994 that Grant TFW became involved in the international premium tubu-

lar market, when it introduced the TC-II line of premium casing and tubing connections under the Atlas Bradford name, a brand that to this point was sold in the United States only.

The most significant acquisition in the company's history occurred in 1995. In a stock and cash deal EVI acquired Prideco Inc., which manufactured and marketed drill pipe, heavyweight drill pipe, and drill collars. The company was 60 percent owned by Wisconsin-based Christiana Companies, Inc., which was primarily a public refrigerated warehousing and services firm that served midwestern food and consumer product companies. EVI then merged Prideco with Grant TFW, forming Grant Prideco, the largest manufacturer and supplier of drill pipe in the world, as well as one of North America's top makers of premium tubular products. With the addition of Prideco products, the company was now able to complete its H-SERIES line.

Grant Prideco's management opted to continue its growth through external means. It strengthened its position in the Asian market in 1995 by signing a manufacturing and sales agreement with Oil Country Tubular Limited (OCTL) in Hyderabad, India, in order to produce drill pipe and process premium tubulars. In 1996 Grant Prideco acquired Superior Tube Limited, an Edmonton, Canada-based company that was the only producer of drill pipe and premium tubulars in the Canadian market. Next Grant Prideco bolstered its position in the premium tubular business by acquiring Houston's Enerpro International Inc. As a result, Grant Prideco now offered the most complete line of premium threads in the industry. Further in 1996, the company added Tubular Corporation of America (TCA), an Oklahoma maker of premium tubing and casings. Because TCA's name was well known in the industry, Grant Prideco opted to run it as a semi-autonomous division using its old name. To help pay for the expansion of Grant Prideco, parent corporation EVI went public in 1996, netting close to $95 million, part of which was used to finance the TCA deal. Another 1996 acquisition also resulted in the operating of semi-autonomous divisions, that of Texas Arai, a Houston-based company that was the world's largest manufacturer of couplings. Both it and subsidiary Tube-Alloy, the world's top maker of coupling accessories, were left to do business under their old names.

Grant Prideco continued to pursue an aggressive acquisition strategy in 1997, completing four purchases. XL Systems, maker of high performance connectors for marine applications, was added first. XL Systems' products included conductors, risers, and offshore structural components. Manufacturing facilities were located in Beaumont, Texas, and Rotterdam, The Netherlands, with sales and service operations in Houston, New Orleans, Aberdeen, Dubai, and Cairo, Egypt. XL Systems would be operated as a separate division. Next in 1997 was the purchase of Houston-based Coastal Tubular Inc., a larger-diameter casing threader, whose operation meshed well with the Channelview facility. This deal was followed by the addition of RTD, a Singapore maker of drill collars and accessories, a move that helped Grant Prideco to strengthen its bid to expand into the important Asia Pacific and Australian markets. The final transaction of 1997 was a joint venture established with P.T. Citra Tubindo, an Indonesian company. The result was Citra Grant Prideco Marketing, a company that had a nonexclusive license to manufacture, market, and sell the H-SERIES drill pipe products. It also served as the exclusive marketing agent for H-tech

Key Dates:

1960: Engineer Charles Grant forms the Grant Supply Company.
1975: Holding company Grant Corporations is formed.
1987: Energy Ventures Inc. buys a stake in the company.
1990: The company becomes a wholly owned EVI subsidiary.
1995: A merger with Prideco results in Grant Prideco, Inc.
1996: Parent corporation EVI goes public.
1998: EVI merges with Weatherford Enterra, resulting in Weatherford International.
2000: Grant Prideco is spun off and becomes an independent, publicly traded company.
2002: Grant Prideco pays $350 million in cash and stock to buy Reed-Hycalog from Schlumberger Ltd.

and OCTL drill pipe products in Australia and select Asia Pacific countries.

In 1998 Grant Prideco's management made a major commitment to establishing a research and development program to create new and innovative products. The company built a laboratory on the original site of Hughes Tool Company. Also of significance in 1998 was the merger of EVI with Weatherford Enterra, resulting in Weatherford International. Despite changes with its corporate parent, Grant Prideco continued its acquisition binge. In February 1998 it bought Drill Tube International, Inc., and later in the year acquired an affiliate of Tubos de Acero de Mexico, S.A. Grant Prideco was even more active in 1999, adding Texas Pup, Inc., a controlling interest in Voest-Alpine Stahlrohr Kindberg GmbH & Co., Louisiana-based Petro-Drive, and Drill Pipe Industries, Inc.

Becoming Independent in 2000

In April 2000 Grant Prideco became an independent, publicly traded company when Weatherford decided to spin off the business through a distribution to its stockholders. The company now organized its business into three main divisions: Drilling Products and Services Premium Connections; Tubular Products; and Marine Products and Services. By the end of 2000 Grant Prideco was once again expanding by external means, in a matter of weeks acquiring Ideal Machine and Supply, Inc.; Star Iron Works, Inc.; Seam-Mac Tube, Ltd.; and Italian tool joint manufacturer CMA, Inc. In 2001 Grant Prideco acquired Intellipipe, Inc. It continued to broaden its international reach in 2002 by acquiring a controlling interest in a Chinese maker of drill pipe to the Asian markets. Also in 2002 Grant Prideco bought a controlling interest in Rotator AS, and the right to buy the remaining stock two years later. Rotator was

a leading maker of subsea control systems and valves, and greatly enhanced Grant Prideco's new Marine Services Division. In September 2002 the company closed on the acquisition of Wyoming-based Grey-Mak Pipe, Inc., but reserved its largest and most significant transaction for the end of the year. In December it paid $350 million in cash and stock to buy Reed-Hycalog from Schlumberger Ltd., the giant oil field service company. Reed-Hycalog was the third largest maker of drill bits, but it was not considered a core asset to Schlumberger, which was shedding assets in order to reduce debt load. For Grant Prideco, Reed-Hycalog offered an excellent opportunity to achieve some product diversity. Of significance was the tendency of the drill bit category to recover from drilling slumps more rapidly than drill pipe.

Grant Prideco's commitment to research and development began to be reflected in improvements in the company's product lines, especially when it came to performance in harsh environments. The company was especially optimistic about the potential of the Intellipipe telemetry product it developed in conjunction with Novatek Engineering. Going forward the company looked to concentrate further on utilizing materials that could withstand corrosive environments.

Despite diversification efforts and the establishment of a dominant position in its industry, Grant Prideco was still not immune from the cyclical nature of oil and gas drilling, which in 2001 was exacerbated by an economic slump. Starting in mid-2001 the company began to trim jobs as part of an effort to cut costs. By the end of 2002 Grant Prideco eliminated about 1,200 jobs. In 2003 the company announced that it was shutting down its Bryant, Texas plant.

Principal Subsidiaries

Texas Arai, Inc.; Tube-Alloy Corporation; XL Systems, L.P.

Principal Competitors

Lone Star Technologies, Inc.; RPC, Inc; Smith International, Inc.

Further Reading

Antosh, Nelson, "Houston-Based Maker of Oil-Field Pipe to Buy Drill-Bits Manufacturer," *Houston Chronicle,* October 29, 2002.
"From Humble Beginnings to a World Class Organization," *Oil & Gas Investor,* October 2002, pp. 2–3.
"Leading the Way," *Oil & Gas Investor,* October 2002, pp. 4–5.
"Looking Toward the Future," *Oil & Gas Investor,* October 2002, pp. 14–15.
Sapino, Brenda, "Ch. 11 Filing to Aid Grant Supply Sale," *American Metal Market,* October 15, 1986, p. 4.

—Ed Dinger

Grant Thornton International

1 Prudential Plaza, Suite 800
130 East Randolph Drive
Chicago, Illinois 60601-6050
U.S.A.
Telephone: (312) 856-0001
Fax: (312) 616-7142
Web site: http://www.gti.org

Private Company
Founded: 1924 as Alexander Grant & Co.
Employees: 21,879
Sales: $1.7 billion (2001)
NAIC: 541211 Offices of Certified Public Accountants

Grant Thornton International is an accounting and management consulting firm serving private and public middle-market companies. With 50 offices in the United States and 650 offices in 109 countries, Grant Thornton is one of the largest accounting firms in the second tier, ranking just below the Big Four (Deloitte Touche Tohmatsu, Ernst & Young International, KPMG International, and PricewaterhouseCoopers). The international firm helps its clients with accounting, audits, tax matters, and business strategies in four service areas: compliance and audit assurance; international tax; corporate finance; and PRIMA (People and Relationship Issues in Management), a 12-point framework that identifies problems in family and owner-managed businesses and recommends potential solutions.

A Chip Off the Big Blocks: 1924–85

Alexander Richardson Grant was 26 years old and a senior accountant with a Cleveland accounting firm, Ernst & Ernst (later Ernst & Young), in 1924. This was during the "golden age," after World War I and before the Great Depression, when industry and finance expanded rapidly and the nation prospered under the leadership of President Calvin Coolidge. The young accountant had a vision of becoming a business leader in public accounting by committing his services to the middle market. He thus left the security of an established firm, joined William O'Brien, and they started their own business, Alexander Grant

& Co. They built their firm in Chicago and set out to meet the accounting needs of middle market companies throughout the Midwest. Also about the same time, other large accounting firms were growing rapidly and sprouting similar offspring. A few years before, an accountant named Arthur Andersen left his Chicago employer, Price Waterhouse, to establish a new firm, Arthur Andersen & Co. Although Grant and Andersen would not live to see it, the two midwestern accounting firms were destined to join forces.

For the next three decades, Alexander Grant & Co. expanded its services to reach nationwide. The company survived the early death of 40-year-old Grant in 1938, and continued to thrive under the guidance of several new leaders. While the larger firms took on big clients, Grant stayed focus on the middle market. By 1961, the company established a national office in Chicago, enjoying revenues of more than $5 million. Meanwhile in 1959 in the United Kingdom, two regional accounting firms, Thornton & Thornton of Oxford and Baker & Co. of Leicester and Northampton, merged to form Thornton Baker. For the next 16 years, Thornton Baker attained more than 38 mergers, and as a result the firm was nicknamed "The Thundering Herd." Also during this time, other European firms were merging to form a company dedicated to the middle market. This competitive firm would later become known as Binder Dijke Otte & Co. (BDO) and would eventually surpass Grant to become the top organization serving the middle market.

Eventually the American company decided to branch out into the international market. During the 1960s the firm merged with companies in Australia, Canada, and the United Kingdom and formed an organization called Alexander Grant Tansley Witt. By the early 1970s William O'Brien had died, and Wallace E. Olson was in the driver's seat. In 1979 the accounting firm began an annual study that ranked the 50 states according to their "manufacturing climates." Based on polls of state manufacturing associations, Grant rated the states according to 18 factors such as taxes, qualified workforce, and state disbursements for highways. Although it received some controversial press, Grant continued to perform the study for the next two decades.

By 1980 Alexander Grant had joined 49 international accounting firms and formed a global network. Five years later the

Company Perspectives:

Grant Thornton focuses on the owner-managed and entrepreneurial businesses sector and continues to develop services and products tailor made to them. Research shows that these kinds of businesses require a particularly personal and commercial approach from their advisors. Grant Thornton's ambition is to be the first choice adviser for independent businesses wanting to develop internationally.

company merged with Fox & Co. and became the ninth largest accounting firm, moving one step behind the nation's "Big Eight." The firm had 80 offices and more than 3,000 employees.

Growth, Unrest, and Change: 1985–90

Many large accounting firms found themselves embroiled in lawsuits in the 1980s. One of the reasons, said Clemens Work in October 1985 for *U.S. News & World Report*, was that the growth of public accounting firms into large conglomerates created vigorous competition. In addition, because they were vying for some of the same clients, they had to reduce their audit fees, sometimes by 25 percent, to attract or keep their customers. By cutting costs, they also "cut corners on quality and put less time in the job," said attorney Stanley Grossman in Work's 1985 article. Accounting firms found themselves in the hot seat for other reasons, Work said. He explained that firms growing and diversifying their services into management consulting may create a conflict of interest because auditors could not be objective. Along with such Big Eight firms as Arthur Andersen and Price Waterhouse, Alexander Grant & Co. was scrutinized heavily for its audit practices, getting sued by the Securities and Exchange Commission (SEC) for fraud and negligence. The accountants contended that they were wrongly accused of crimes they did not commit. But whether the firms participated in shoddy practices or were caught up in misunderstandings, in a five-year period the Big Eight had paid $200 million to settle lawsuits.

Alexander Grant & Co. experienced one of its largest court cases in 1985 when one of its clients, E.S.M. Government Securities Inc., collapsed. The SEC sued a Grant managing partner for receiving $125,000 from E.S.M. officials to certify false financial statements; there were at least 11 other related lawsuits against Grant, amounting to about $1 million. The Grant partner was convicted and sent to prison. Among other lawsuits by related organizations such as shareholders of American Savings & Loan Association of Florida and a conservator of Home State Savings Bank, one was also filed by a trustee of E.S.M. who said that Grant's audit was negligent, covering up losses and creating false assets.

Following predictions that Grant would collapse from the weight of the scandals and financial instability, the firm fought hard to change its public image and institute new policies regarding auditing standards. In 1986 the company merged with U.K. accounting firm Thornton Baker, and the company changed its name to Grant Thornton. The company's efforts to rebuild and strengthen itself paid off. In 1990 the 52-office

international firm had 300 public clients and revenues of $205 million. That same year, a new executive partner, Robert E. Nason, was appointed to "help Grant consolidate gains that have been made after [the] scandal four years ago," said Lee Berton on February 14, 1990, for the *Wall Street Journal*. Nason had been an employee of the firm for 23 years and was formerly the Midwest regional partner.

Steady Growth into a New Millennium: 1990–2002

During the early 1990s, the nation suffered an economic recession. To weather the storms of adversity and financial stress, many companies sought consulting help from firms such as Grant Thornton. As the recession weakened in the mid-1990s and the economy began to flourish, so did Grant Thornton. In 1997, after international trade barriers were lowered, Grant Thornton established international business centers in four major U.S. cities. The centers helped "small to mid-sized companies to develop business relationships in emerging markets around the world," said Caitlin Kelly for *Accounting Today* in January 1998. The markets included countries in Asia, Europe, and Latin America.

As Grant Thornton grew, it continued to maintain the pace of staying just behind the multibillion-dollar firms. In 1998 Grant Thornton began offering computer consulting services and remained competitive in this quickly growing niche. A company would hire an accounting firm to help them understand and implement new accounting software packages such as Smart Stream. By the late 1990s, the Big Eight had experienced several mergers and eventually became the Big Four. Grant Thornton followed as the eighth largest firm; BDO weighed in as the fifth largest international accounting and consulting organization and the largest firm serving the middle market. In 1999, PricewaterhouseCoopers LLP approached Grant Thornton with merger talks, but eventually the two companies decided not to merge. As the 20th century drew to a close, amid public Y2K fears of computer crashes and nuclear attacks, Grant Thornton boasted revenues of $380 million and the addition of a new CEO, Domenick Esposito. The Brooklyn, New York native had worked for the company for 20 years and was committed to dodging merger trends and preserving the company's independence.

In June 2000 Grant Thornton pulled out of a different kind of merger. It had been advising London's Oryx Natural Resources, which planned to merge with Petra Diamonds Ltd. Less than 24 hours before the merged company was going to sell their stock on the London Stock Exchange, Grant Thornton threatened to resign if the two companies proceeded with the merger. Oryx, said the British government, planned to mine diamonds to finance the Zimbabwean government, which was embroiled in a civil war in Congo. Grant Thornton said the merger was too risky based on "discussions with the regulatory authorities," said Alan Crowell of the *New York Times*.

A year later the nation, again, sank into recession, and Grant Thornton faced new challenges. In March 2001 the firm's executive committee asked CEO Domenick Esposito to resign because of disagreements about the direction of the firm. During Esposito's reign, Grant Thornton experienced revenues of $416 million and helped KPMG through its initial public offering. Two months after Esposito's resignation, David

Key Dates:

1924: Alexander Richardson Grant and William O'Brien found Alexander Grant & Co. in Chicago.
1938: Alexander Grant dies.
1950s: The firm expands domestically and internationally.
1959: Thornton Baker is established in the United Kingdom.
1969: International firm Alexander Grant Tansley Witt is established.
1973: William O'Brien dies.
1986: Grant merges with U.K. accounting firm Thornton Baker to form Grant Thornton.
1990s: Grant Thornton expands into Africa, Asia, Europe, and Latin America.
2002: After the Enron scandal, Grant Thornton grows by adding former Andersen offices and employees.

McDonnell was appointed the new worldwide chief. McDonnell was a 30-year Grant Thornton employee and had been the youngest ever U.K. national managing partner when he acquired that post in 1989.

However, the executive committee could not have predicted the direction the firm would take in the coming months. After the September 11, 2001, terrorist attacks in the United States, Grant Thornton and other accounting firms found their strength in either creating or updating disaster-recovery plans for small businesses. As businesses and the nation were trying to recover from the shock of the attacks, and the recession wore on, an enormous scandal, involving accounting firm Arthur Andersen, burst onto the scene. Energy giant Enron collapsed into bankruptcy, and their accountants (Andersen) were convicted of obstructing justice because the audit team destroyed important documents. Andersen crumbled, and Grant Thornton was there to pick up some of the pieces. By July 2002 Grant Thornton had acquired from the fallen Andersen: 7 offices, 43 partners, and 396 staff.

After the Enron scandal, public confidence in the accounting profession dropped to an all-time low. In response, Grant Thornton developed a "five-point plan to restore public trust" and asked other major accounting firms to embrace it. While the SEC and the American Institute of Certified Public Accountants (AICPA) also professed changes and new policies, Grant Thornton said that was not enough. The accounting industry had to do more to dispel any conflicts of interest between the firm and its clients. Grant Thornton's plan, they hoped, would provide the leadership to make that happen and "restore public trust and confidence in the accounting profession, which has historically served so ably to make the U.S. capital markets the strongest in the world."

Principal Subsidiaries

Grant Thornton, LLP.

Principal Competitors

American Express Tax and Business Services; BDO International; Moores Rowland; Ernst & Young; KPMG International; PricewaterhouseCoopers.

Further Reading

Berton, Lee, "Grant Thornton Appoints Nason Executive Partner," *Wall Street Journal*, February 14, 1990, p. B10.
Cowell, Alan, "Diamond Miner Halts Stock Listing Plans," *New York Times*, June 13, 2000, p. C4.
"Grant Thornton," *New York Times*, January 7, 1986, p. D3.
"Grant Thornton Opens Int'l Business Centers," *Accounting Today*, January 6, 1997, p. 23.
"GT Draws Up Five-Point Plan for Major U.S. Firms," *International Accounting Bulletin*, March 28, 2002, p. 5.
Kelly, Caitlin, "Grant Thornton Combines Global Experience, Flexibility," *Accounting Today*, January 26, 1998, p. 20.
"McDonnell to Become Worldwide CEO at GT," *International Accounting Bulletin*, May 18, 2001, p. 3.
Somasundaram, Meera, "People: Insider CEO Plots Growth Course for Grant Thornton," *Crain's Chicago Business*, March 1, 1999, p. 12.
Work, Clemens P., "Accounting's Bottom Line: Big Troubles," *U.S. News & World Report*, October 21, 1985, p. 58.

—Jodi Essey-Stapleton

Grupo Posadas, S.A. de C.V.

Paseo de la Reforma 155
Mexico, D.F. 11000
Mexico
Telephone: (52) (55) 5326-6700
Toll Free: (800) FIESTA1
Fax: (52) (55) 5326-6701
Web site: http://www.posadas.com

Public Company
Incorporated: 1967 as Promotora Mexicana de Hoteles
Employees: 11,164
Sales: 3.83 billion pesos ($366.02 million) (2002)
Stock Exchanges: Mexico City; OTC (ADRs)
Ticker Symbol: POSADAS; GRPALP; GRPYP
NAIC: 721110 Hotels (Except Casino Hotels) and Motels

Grupo Posadas, S.A. de C.V., based in Mexico and owned by Mexicans, is the largest Latin American operator of hotels in Latin America and is the biggest hotel operator in Mexico. The company owns and/or operates hotels in Mexico under the Fiesta Americana, Fiesta Inn, and Explorean brand names; in Brazil and Argentina under the Caesar Park and Caesar Business names; and in Texas chiefly under the Holiday Inn name. Grupo Posadas has survived and grown despite the mid-1990s economic crisis that sent its two biggest Mexican competitors into bankruptcy and the drop in foreign tourists that followed the terrorist attacks on September 11, 2001.

Building a Hotel Chain: 1967–92

The company was founded in 1967 as Promotora Mexicana de Hoteles by Gaston Azcarraga Tomayo, a cousin of Emilio Azcarraga Milmo, who developed Grupo Televisa, S.A. de C.V. into a giant Mexican media conglomerate. Azcarraga Tomayo entered the hotel business with the construction and operation of the Fiesta Palace (now the Fiesta Americana Reforma) in Mexico City, which opened in 1970. Soon after entering the business he sold his auto-assembly factories to Chrysler Corporation and invested the funds in 1969 in a partnership with Americana

Hotels, a subsidiary of American Airlines. This partnership, Operadora Mexicana de Hoteles, began operating luxury hotels such as the Condesa del Mar (later Fiesta Americana Condesa Acapulco) and the El Presidente Acapulco. The change in operation marked a more businesslike approach to five-star lodging on the Mexican gold coast. The partnership added another tower of rooms to El Presidente, elevating its capacity by 400 rooms, but appalled one observer by soliciting group business, filling the lobby with stores, and covering the marble floor of the lobby with acrylic rugs. The luxury-class Fiesta Americana chain was founded in 1979 with the opening of a hotel by that name in Puerto Vallerta. Two more Fiesta Americana hotels opened their doors in 1982, in Cancun and Guadalajara. The partnership was now called Hoteles Fiesta Americana.

In 1982 Hoteles Fiesta Americana merged with Posadas de Mexico, which had been established in 1969 by Pratt Hotel Corp., a U.S. company that was the exclusive operator of franchised Holiday Inn hotels in Mexico. The merged enterprise, which retained the Posadas de Mexico name, became the largest Mexican hotel company, operating 13 hotels. During the 1980s Azcarraga decided to focus on building the Fiesta Americana chain. Between 1984 and 1988 Posadas de Mexico built three more Fiesta Americana hotels in Cancun and nearby Cozumel Reef in partnership with Swiss and German banks and also consolidated its position as an operator of hotels. In 1989 the Azcarraga family bought Pratt's half of the company. Gaston Azcarraga Andrade, son of the founder and a graduate of Harvard University's business school, became general manager of the company that year. Posadas de Mexico now had 30 hotels and, under Azcarraga Andrade's direction, had expanded its operations to Texas. He succeeded his father as the president of the group in 1993.

Expansion Amid Adversity: 1992–2002

Taking the name Grupo Posadas, the company went public in 1992, selling shares both in Mexico City and New York This enabled the company to open residential developments in the beach resorts of Ixtapa and Arcano and to change its focus for Fiesta Inn, a moderately priced hotel chain initially placed in four beach resorts. As revised, Fiesta Inns were placed in cities and its rooms priced at only one-quarter that of the Fiesta Americana chain because they limited services to those needed by the business traveler rather than the tourist. Fiesta Inns were laid out in such a way as to encourage guests to spend their money without leaving the hotel and featured such cost-control features as separate electric circuits for each floor so that areas unoccupied during slow periods could be cordoned off and shut down. The cities chosen as hotel sites—Aguascalientes, Chihuahua, Colima, Culiacan, Puebla, and Tepic—were seen as those most likely to benefit from the impending North American Free Trade Agreement. By this time Grupo Posadas, through Swancourt, a U.S. affiliate, also owned a Sheraton Fiesta in San Antonio, Texas; Holiday Inns in McAllen and Laredo, Texas; and a Hampton Inn in Buena Park, California.

The sudden devaluation of the peso in late 1994 was damaging to Grupo Posadas, which suffered nearly $40 million in foreign-exchange losses because most of its debt was in dollars. This left the highly leveraged group with only $140 million in equity and $260 million in debt. However, Grupo Posadas found it could make a profit in the ensuing recession because it charged foreigners in dollars while covering its costs in devalued pesos. Gross operating profits rose 60 percent in 1995 (although the company still incurred a net loss that year as well as the previous one). In addition to 17 Fiesta Americana and 14 Fiesta Inn hotels, Grupo Posadas was managing Crowne Plaza hotels in major Mexican cities and Holiday Inns in smaller ones. Sixty percent of its rooms were located in cities and 40 percent in beach resorts. Grupo Posadas' 40 hotel holdings in the summer of 1996 were a combination of company-owned units, joint ventures, and management contracts. The group was the majority shareholder in 20 hotels, a minority investor in ten more, and the operator only of the remaining ten. That year Fiesta Americana was cited by *World & Travel News* as Mexico's best hotel chain.

In 1996 Grupo Posadas and Morgan Stanley & Co. announced plans to invest about $200 million over the next 18 months to buy a number of Mexican hotels. The group failed in its effort to buy the bankrupt Camino Real chain but continued to open new hotels. It entered the South American market in 1998 by purchasing three Caesar Park hotels in Buenos Aires, Rio de Janeiro, and Sao Paulo, and taking operation of a fourth in Fortaleza, Brazil, for $122.7 million from Grupo Aoki, a Japanese investment group. "Caesar Park is the most recognized luxury brand in Brazil," Azcarraga told Megan Rowe of *Lodging Hospitality* the following year. "That's one of the

important reasons why we bought it." He hoped to expand the chain to other Latin American capitals through a combination of joint ventures and management contracts. Soon after, Grupo Posadas introduced the Caesar Business brand for the mid-level business traveler. The first two were constructed in Sao Paulo as part of a joint venture with Brazilian real estate firm Inpar Construcoes e Empreendimientos Imobiliarios. Because of economic woes in both Brazil and Argentina, the South American units were bringing in less than 10 percent of Grupo Posadas' total revenue in 2002. Occupation of hotel rooms in the Caesar chains was running at only 45 percent nightly.

Grupo Posadas launched yet another brand, Explorean, in 1998. Aimed at the adventure traveler seeking luxury as well as exoticism, the first Explorean, a 40-room hotel in a densely tropical-forested area of Yucatan near the seldom-visited Mayan ruin of Kohunlich, offered a range of activities in addition to the usual swimming, snorkeling, and scuba diving that attracted visitors to the area. Guests were able to observe native wildlife such as pumas, jaguars, toucans, and spider monkeys, explore deep wells, and take jungle walks. A second, 80-room Explorean opened at Costa Maya in 2000. Grupo Posadas hoped to expand the chain to other Central American sites with significant historic or environmental features.

In 1999 Fiesta Americana introduced a new category of service called Fiesta Americana Grand. This class of hotel was designed especially for the traveler or tourist who, according to the company, was seeking luxury, comfort, and elegance combined in perfect harmony. Another 1999 innovation was the establishment of Club Vacacional (Vacation Club), a time-sharing scheme being developed at Cancun and Los Cabos beach properties in alliance with Hilton Grand Vacation Club and Resort Condominiums International.

Immediately following the destruction of the twin towers of the World Trade Center in New York City in September 2001, the number of foreign guests in Grupo Posadas hotels fell by more than 65 percent. The company kept afloat with heavy promotions directed at the Mexican market. It closed the year with a 4 percent drop in revenues and a 38 percent fall in profits. The ensuing winter went well because, like foreigners, Mexicans were not much inclined to leave their country.

Grupo Posadas in 2002

At the end of 2002 Grupo Posadas was operating 71 hotels with 13,837 rooms, making it the fourth largest hotel operator in Latin America and the largest in Mexico, where there were 57. Thirty-four were owned by the company, either exclusively or in partnership with others; 26 were the property of others and administered by the company; and 11 were leased.

Grupo Posadas had 19 Fiesta Americana hotels (including three Grand Fiesta Americanas) and 35 Fiesta Inns in Mexico. Some Fiesta Americanas were in coastal resorts, while the remainder were urban properties. The resorts tended to draw about two-thirds of their business from the United States; the urban ones mainly served Mexican business travelers. All Fiesta Inns were of new (post-1992) construction. Competitive with such U.S.-based hotels chains as Courtyard and Hampton Inn, they were also aimed primarily at the Mexican business trav-

---

Key Dates:

1967: Gaston Azcarraga Tamayo enters the hotel business.
1969: Azcarraga's company enters a partnership with Americana Hotels.
1979: Fiesta Americana luxury chain is founded.
1982: The company merges with the operator of Holiday Inn hotels in Mexico.
1992: The Fiesta Inn chain is aimed at the Mexican business traveler.
1998: Grupo Posadas enters the South American market by purchasing Caesar Park hotels.
2002: The company opens six new hotels in Mexico and Brazil.

---

eler. Those located in large metropolitan areas were placed in the suburbs rather than the center.

The five Caesar Park and two Caesar Business hotels were in Brazil, except for the Caesar Park Buenos Aires. In addition to the two Exploreans, Grupo Posadas owned and operated the Aeropuerto Plaza in Mexico City and administered a Holiday Inn in Merida. The group owned and operated four hotels in Texas and managed two others. Four of the six were under the Holiday Inn name; another was a Sheraton Fiesta, and the sixth was a Residence Inn.

Grupo Posadas was renting rooms through a web of links that included its own online sites and call centers and also through intermediaries such as travel agencies; wholesalers of hotel rooms; event organizers; global reservation systems such as Apollo, Galileo, and Sabre; and agreements with large enterprises. The company's publicity efforts included television advertising and programs such as Fiesta Rewards for frequent guests. Intermediaries were taking some 30 percent to 40 percent of the retail cost as commissions. Dependence on wholesalers was particularly expensive, but in high season a beach-resort hotel might receive 60 to 80 percent of its guests by means of an all-expense package from Mexicana Airlines or Apple Vacations, giving them the leverage to make or break a hotel. Mexicana was flying 400,000 passengers a year—mainly Mexicans—to Grupo Posadas' hotels.

In order to avoid its dependence on intermediaries, Grupo Posadas had introduced toll-free calls at reservation centers and was offering two vacation packages: Fiesta Break for the foreign market and Days of Fiesta for the Mexican market. Fiesta Rewards was a frequent-visitor program with more than 800,000 members qualifying for such benefits as preferential prices. These efforts accounted for about 30 percent of all Fiesta Americana and Fiesta Inn rooms sold. The company's parallel effort in the United States was tied to the reservation systems of Holiday Inn and others.

Some 40 percent of the shares of Grupo Posadas were being quoted on Mexico City's stock exchange in 2002, with Banco

Nacional de Mexico (Banamex) the principal public stockholder. Banamex also had extended the company a $50 million credit line. But Grupo Posadas' major source of growth had come from the investors who had bought 47 percent of the rooms in its hotels. This kind of investment had enabled Grupo Posadas to expand without incurring major debt. Of the 31 hotels under development in 2002 at a cost of $149 million, Grupo Posadas was putting up only $4 million. The company reported revenue of 3.83 billion pesos ($366.02 million) and operating profit of 72.1 million pesos ($6.89 million) in 2002.

Principal Subsidiaries

Fondo Inmobiliario Posadas, S.A. de C.V.; Inmobililaria Hotelera Posadas, S.A. de C.V.; Operadora Mexicana de Hoteles, S.A. de C.V.; Posadas USA, Inc. (U.S.A.); Sudamerica en Fiesta, S.A. de C.V.

Principal Operating Units

Developments; Franchises; Operations.

Principal Competitors

Accor S.A.; Best Western International Inc.; Real Turismo, S.A. de C.V.; Six Continents PLC; Sol Melia, S.A.; Starwood Hotel & Resorts Worldwide Inc.

Further Reading

Alisau, Patricia, "Grupo Posadas Corners Hotel Market," *Business Mexico,* June 1992, pp. 12, 14.

Crawford, Leslie, "Posadas in Caesar Park Buy," *Financial Times,* May 5, 1998, p. 36.

Dela Cruz, Tony, "Mexican Trailblazer," *Hotels,* October 1999, p. 54.

Escudero, Francisco R., *Origen y evolucion del turismo en Acapulco,* Acapulco: Universidad Americana de Acapulco, 1977, p. 226.

Friedland, Jonathan, "Mexican Hotelier Bets Big on Latin 'Middle' Market," *Wall Street Journal,* September 17, 1998, p. A18.

Guenette, Louise, "Gaston el Conquistador," *Expansion,* October 30–November 13, 2002, pp. 36, 38, 40, 42, 44, 46.

Hernandez, Feliciano, "El grupo posadas busca socios," *Vision,* January 1997, pp. 51–52.

Luxner, Larry, "Grupo Posados Launches Explorean Alternative-Vacation Brand," *Hotel & Motel Management,* March 15, 1999, pp. 4, 40.

——. "On the Fast Track," *Travel Agent,* May 1, 2000, pp. 69–70.

"Morgan Stanley in Partnership to Acquire Hotels in Mexico," *New York Times,* January 9, 1996, p. 59.

Palmieri, Christopher, " 'More Culture, Less Beach,' " *Forbes,* June 5, 1995, pp. 47–48.

Rowe, Megan, "Grupo Posadas Plots a Course," *Lodging Hospitality,* February 2000, pp. 39–40.

Shundich, Steven, and Cherie Henedill, "Chains to Watch," *Hotels,* May 1996, pp. 40–42.

Wolff, Carlo, "Such a Deal," *Lodging Hospitality,* September 1995, pp. 43–44.

—Robert Halasz

GTSI Corp.

3902 Stonecroft Boulevard
Chantilly, Virginia 20151-1010
U.S.A.
Telephone: (703) 502-2000
Toll Free: (800) 999-4874
Fax: (703) 222-5204
Web site: http://www.gtsi.com

Public Company
Incorporated: 1983 as Government Technology Services,
　Inc.
Employees: 693
Sales: $934.7 million (2002)
Stock Exchanges: NASDAQ
Ticker Symbol: GTSI
NAIC: 423430 Computer and Computer Peripheral
　Equipment and Software Merchant Wholesalers

GTSI Corp. provides IT solutions to federal, state, and local governments. Based in the northern Virginia town of Chantilly, located just outside of Washington, D.C., the company resells computers, software, and networking products. Its most significant business comes from the Defense Department, and total contracts with the federal government, all tolled, account for approximately three-quarters of the company's sales. GTSI sells approximately 350,000 items offered by 3,400 vendors. In addition to Chantilly, the company has offices located across the United States as well as in Germany and Korea, where the Defense Department maintains a major presence.

Founding the Company in 1983

GTSI was founded in 1983 as Government Technology Services, Inc. by Kevin O'Donnell. In the beginning the company sold microcomputer software to federal agencies. In 1985 it added peripherals to its product line and also began selling to state governments. It was not until 1986 that GTSI began to sell personal computers. In addition, it now offered networking products and such services as configuring, installing, and main-

taining the PCs in local area networks. To this point GTSI primarily worked through General Services Administration (GSA) as an approved vendor for federal agencies, but in 1987 it also began to bid on large government contracts. By early 1988 GTSI had established nine field offices across the country in order to land business from state and local governments. Its vendors included top hardware manufacturers, such as NCR, Hewlett-Packard, and Unisys, as well as software publishers, most notably Microsoft and Lotus. The company employed some 350 people, maintaining a technical support staff and a burn-in center for computer equipment.

In 1988 GTSI posted revenues in the $180 million range, and a year later that number improved to $277 million, of which approximately 40 percent of sales was through the GSA schedule, a procedure that allowed federal agencies to buy individual items that cost less than $25,000. By now sales were about evenly split between hardware and software. In August 1989 GTSI made a change in management when O'Donnell stepped down as chief executive officer in favor of Ray Lunceford, who had previously headed the company's Federal Markets Division. O'Donnell continued to serve as the chairman of the board. A little more than a year later, in October 1990, Lunceford was replaced by Richard M. Rickenbach, who had previous executive experience at Control Data Corp., where he was general manager of a systems integration group for electrical utilities, and Scientific Information Services, a Minnesota company he headed. GTSI refused to discuss the reason for Lunceford's departure, merely acknowledging that he had left the company.

GTSI landed its most significant deal in its brief history in 1990 when it was awarded a $769 million, five-year contract from the Defense Department. This "Companion Contract" called for the military to purchase 350,000 personal computers and work stations in a five-year span. GTSI was contracted to supply software and peripherals to support that equipment. Due in large measure to this success, GTSI saw its sales top $300 million in 1990, 60 percent of which came from large contracts, and the balance through the GSA schedule. In the previous four years, the company enjoyed a 600 percent growth in revenues. By now the company had adopted two complementary business models: one involved the reselling of off-the-shelf products sold in large

---

Company Perspectives:

For nearly 20 years, GTSI has delivered maximum value to public sector customers by teaming with global IT leaders like HP, Panasonic, Microsoft, IBM, Sun Microsystems, and Cisco. We help our customers do their jobs more effectively through a combination of our broad range of products and services, our extensive contract portfolio, and our ISO 9000-registered logistics.

---

volumes at low margins, and the other, a value-added model, configured off-the-shelf products to meet the specific needs of customers, primarily involving workstations and networking. Taking advantage of its impressive growth, GTSI went public in the summer of 1991, with half of the money raised earmarked to pay down debt and the rest allocated to finance expansion.

Beginning to Offer Apple Products in 1993

To better meet customer needs, GTSI in January 1992 began to offer Sun Microsystems workstations using the Unix operating system, along with necessary software and peripherals. In 1992 this business accounted for $35 million of the company's $360 million in revenues posted for the year. Until this point GTSI was exclusively devoted to IBM-compatible PCs using Intel processors, then in 1993 the company began to offer a complete line of Apple Computer products. In effect, GTSI had become a one-stop shop for personal computers, offering federal agencies all major platforms. The company enjoyed a number of successes in 1994. It won a major portion of a three-year $724 million contract to supply PCs to the Air Force, a deal that had been delayed for two years because losing bidders had filed a series of appeals. GTSI was also one of a handful of companies selected to supply Unix-based products and services to NASA. In addition in 1993 GTSI had its contract with GSA renewed, allowing it to maintain its coveted spot on the GSA schedule, which in 1992 resulted in $671 million in hardware and software sales. GTSI's share of that amount was $152 million, and still represented a significant portion of its business. One GTSI official told the *Washington Post* that GSA approval was in essence a hunting license. GSA requirements were laborious, which dissuaded many companies from pursuing approval; however, for GTSI, schedule sales provided a foundation for the business.

As the federal government began to buy PCs at an increasing rate in the 1990s, a number of local companies became computer resellers. In an attempt to create a powerhouse in the field, GTSI acquired one of its biggest rivals in 1994, buying Falcon Microsystems, Inc. from its founder and sole stockholder, M. Dendy Young, at a cost of $16.5 million in cash and an option that allowed Young to buy 100,000 shares of GTSI stock, as well as additional payments based on future contingencies. With margins in the industry so low, and market conditions growing tougher, executives from both companies felt it was in their mutual interest to combine operations. In the previous year, 1993, GTSI recorded $523.6 million in revenues and Falcon had $160 million.

Falcon's founder was born in Rhodesia, since renamed Zimbabwe. Young came to the United States because of his success

in building a computer from scratch as a teenager in the early 1960s, which he entered in a science fair sponsored by the U.S. Agency for International Development. Young won a full scholarship to the university of his choice, which was the Massachusetts Institute of Technology, where he graduated with a degree in electrical engineering in 1970. After going home and working for two years with Computer Sciences Corp., he returned to Boston to further his education, this time earning an M.B.A. from Harvard. He then spent several years working at Federal Data Corp. and a short stint with a similar company before deciding to strike out on his own. In 1982 he created Falcon Systems, a systems integration company catering to the federal government. A year later the company won its first major contract, around the same time that Young became interested in the computer reselling business. In particular he saw that Apple Computer products were not being sold to the government. Recognizing an opportunity he sought a letter of supply from Apple in order to gain GSA schedule approval, only to discover that no one at the computer company appeared interested in the idea. According to *Computer Reseller News,* Young refused to give up: "Finally, after months of trying, a regional manager at Apple signed the letter. And despite the fact the manager was not officially authorized to grant Falcon permission to sell Apple's products, the General Services Administration, anxious to get Apple on its schedule, turned a blind eye." The reselling portion of Young's company grew rapidly, prompting him in 1987 to sell the integration business to Oracle Systems for $20 million, which he then plowed back into the Apple reselling operation, now renamed Falcon Microsystems. The company was the exclusive seller of Apple to the federal government until 1993, when other firms, such as GTSI, gained authorization from Apple. As a consequence, Falcon added new vendors: IBM, Compaq Computer, Silicon Graphics, and Dell Computer. Although Falcon and GTSI now began to compete against each other on contracts, they still maintained their niches in the marketplace. While GTSI was strong in Microsoft DOS and military customers, Falcon was dominant in Apple sales to civilian agencies. Merging the two operations appeared to be a wise choice for both companies, although Young called it one of the toughest decisions he ever had to make. He agreed to remain as a consultant to GTSI to help in the transition, but was not in line for a permanent post with GTSI. As part of the deal, he signed a five-year noncompete agreement. It would become a moot point, however, because less than two years later he would be called on to take the helm of GTSI, which was very much a floundering company by this time.

GTSI encountered a number of problems following the merger. First, the integration of Falcon with GTSI proved to be problematic. In a December 1994 article, *Computer Reseller News* reported, "Some former Falcon workers said corporate-culture clashes and other issues have slowed the consolidation effort, and key people have left the combined company." At this time GTSI also found itself the object of an unwanted takeover bid. Milwaukee-based Diana Corp., a distributor of meat and seafood with a small computer equipment business, offered $16 per share to purchase all of GTSI's stock in an effort to enter the federal reselling market. Although GTSI was able to fend off this attempt, it served as an unwelcomed distraction at a difficult time for the company. Its business was starting to feel the effects of cutbacks in military budgets, primarily due to the end of the Cold War. In February 1995 GTSI reported a significant decrease in

Key Dates:

1983: The company is founded by Kevin O'Donnell as a software provider.
1986: GTSI begins reselling computers.
1991: The company goes public.
1994: Falcon Microsystems is acquired.
1995: Dendy Young is named chief executive officer.
1998: BTG, Inc. is acquired.

profits for 1994, prompting the board to remove Rickenbach from the chairmanship and investors to lose confidence in the company's stock. To make matters worse, GTSI soon learned that it was the object of a Justice Department inquiry, the result of a special suit that had actually been filed in federal court against GTSI and Novell Inc. in 1992. Provisions of such suits allowed whistleblowers to sue on behalf of the government and awarded them a portion of any settlement or fine. To protect claimants the suits were sealed until the Justice Department decided to act. In this case, a former Novell employee, Mary Slutman, accused GTSI of failing to pass on rebates it received from Novell to government customers. At this stage the suit was a public relations blackeye, and it would linger in the background until the autumn of 1997 when GTSI finally agreed to pay $400,000 to settle the matter out of court while not admitting guilt. Slutman received an estimated $68,000.

Dendy Young Named CEO in 1995

The condition of GTSI deteriorated to the point that in May 1995 the management hired Atlanta-based Robinson-Humphrey Company to search for a buyer. When Rickenbach resigned several months later, GTSI called off Robinson-Humphrey and looked to focus its efforts on turning around the business. Board member Gerald Ebker, a retired IBM vice-president, assumed Rickenbach's position while a search was conducted for a permanent CEO and president. Late in 1995, just 18 months after selling Falcon to GTSI, Young was brought in to rescue the company, which had laid off a tenth of its staff and was lurching toward bankruptcy. *Forbes* in a 2003 profile of GTSI described Young's assessment of what he found when he took control: "The business was basically okay; management stank. He dismissed all six senior executives and brought in eight new ones, then paid himself $1 a year in 1996 and 1997, in part to motivate a demoralized staff." According to Young, GTSI "had all of their eggs in one basket," meaning product sales. In order to provide some diversification and improve the bottom line, he instituted technology teams to create customized bundles of hardware, software, and associated services to meet customer needs. These teams concentrated on networking, Internet functions, enterprise networks and intranets, mobile computing, and wireless communications.

GTSI had recovered enough to take advantage of a second chance to grow by external means. In late 1997 it agreed to acquire the computer reselling business of BTG, Inc., another northern Virginia company. Founded by Ed Bersoff, BTG started out as a high-end developer of complex computer pro-

grams and services, often performing highly critical, and highly profitable, work for the military. In 1992 BTG began to compete directly with GTSI on the reselling of off-the-shelf computer products, and the two companies and their employees developed an antipathy for one another. As the environment for reselling became more difficult, due to increased competition and new procurement rules imposed by the government, BTG began to experience escalating losses. In November 1997 Bersoff approached Young about selling his computer division to GTSI and the two men, over a beer at a hotel bar, quickly came to a basic understanding on a cash and stock deal. The final price was $7.3 million in cash and three million shares of GTSI stock. The news was not well received by BTG employees, many of whom, according to the *Washington Post*, regarded GTSI as "Darth Vader" and a "sweatshop." As a result GTSI was not as successful as it would have preferred in retaining BTG talent.

In 1998 GTSI integrated BTG into its operations and streamlined its information technology systems, while its new management team became better coordinated. By mid-year GTSI was able to announce its first profitable second quarter since 1994. Having turned the corner, GTSI began to implement new strategies to produce stronger results, including the realignment of its dozen technology teams. The terrorist attacks that occurred in the United States on September 11, 2001, also positioned the company for ongoing growth, as IT spending by the government became a top priority. In order to fully take advantage of this opportunity, however, GTSI needed to improve on the service side, which was the fastest growing part of GSA's technology budget, but still represented just 3 percent of GTSI revenues.

Principal Subsidiaries

Falcon Microsystems, Inc.

Principal Competitors

Anteon Corporation; Electronic Data Systems Corporation; Veridian Corporation; Science Applications International Corporation.

Further Reading

Chandrasekaran, Rajiv, "For $1 A Year, a Chance to Make a Revival," *Washington Post*, November 11, 1996, p. WBIZ9.
Hausman, Eric, "Falcon Founder Dendy Young an Old Hand at Federal Reselling," *Computer Reseller News*, October 3, 1994, p. 34.
——, "GTSI Recovery Road a Long Haul," *Computer Reseller News*, August 26, 1996, p. 39.
——, "GTSI Sees Glass As Half-Full, Fights Against Setbacks," *Computer Reseller News*, June 19, 1995, p. 37.
Leibovich, Mark, "Where a Pair Beats Two of a Kind," *Washington Post*, January 10, 1998, p. F12.
Sugawara, Sandra, "Va. Firm Acquires Rival Supplier of Federal PCs," *Washington Post*, August 17, 1994, p. F1.
Swibel, Matthew, "A Shot in the Arm," *Forbes*, May 26, 2003, pp. 168–69.
Swisher, Kara, "GTSI Names Former Chief of IBM Federal As Its CEO," *Washington Post*, November 2, 1995, p. D13.

—Ed Dinger

IMS Health, Inc.

1499 Post Road
Fairfield, Connecticut 06430
U.S.A.
Telephone: (203) 319-4700
Fax: (203) 319-4701
Web site: http://www.imshealth.com

Public Company
Incorporated: 1998
Employees: 5,900
Sales: $1.4 billion (2002)
Stock Exchanges: New York
Ticker Symbol: RX
NAIC: 541613 Marketing Consulting Services; 541910
   Marketing Research and Public Opinion Polling

IMS Health, Inc. is the leading provider of global market information to the pharmaceuticals and healthcare industries. Compiling information into more than 10,000 reports, available on a regularly updated basis, IMS Health provides a wide variety of market knowledge to support strategic decision-making in all aspects of pharmaceutical company operations. The company uses the latest information technology to provide real-time information and rapid results; data resources are available through the company's i-squared Internet portal or an online store at open.imshealth.com. The company operates in more than 100 countries around the world, collecting information from more than 29,000 data sources, including drug manufacturers, wholesalers, retailers, pharmacies, hospitals, managed care providers, and long-term care facilities. Customers include the major pharmaceutical companies, as well as government and regulatory agencies, financial analysts, researchers, and educators.

Founding in 1954 Prompted by
Need for Drug Market Information

IMS Health originated in 1954 as Intercontinental Marketing Services (IMS), the overseas extension of Frolich Intercon International, a major New York-based advertising agency established by L.W. Frolich in 1941. In conducting campaigns for pharmaceutical companies Frolich was dissatisfied with the limited market data about the new "wonder drugs." By forming IMS, Frolich and David Dubow created the first market research syndicate for the pharmaceutical industry, providing information at a level of depth and objectivity not available at the time.

With Dubow as president, IMS began its pharmaceutical research in Europe. The company's first syndicated study, published in 1957, included a sales audit of the West German pharmaceutical market. The drug audit involved tracking sales invoices and monitoring inventory at select drugstores, at chain and discount stores, as well as at drug wholesalers and physicians' offices. IMS paid participants for the opportunity of accessing this information. The study compared the market share of different drugs and brands, organizing data according to therapeutic class, package size, and form of dosage. This information enabled drug company executives to analyze product sales and make strategic marketing decisions based on this knowledge. As the syndicate developed, IMS initiated monthly and quarterly reports and translated financial data into the currency of the customer's home country.

From its London-based office IMS conducted research for pharmaceutical markets in the United Kingdom, France, Italy, Spain, and Japan. By 1969 company revenues reached $5 million and IMS was the leader in pharmaceutical market research in Europe and Asia. IMS began operations in North America through the acquisition of Davee, Koehnlein and Keating, a Chicago-based syndicate that conducted sales audits for markets in the United States and Canada. IMS entered Latin American markets through acquisition as well.

Following an initial public offering of stock in 1972, IMS reinforced its market position in the United States and Europe and augmented its research capabilities. IMS acquired Lea Associates, known for developing the first National Disease and Therapeutic Index. Through the acquisition of Armbruster, Moore and MacKerell, IMS gained the Hospital Supply Index and Laboratory Diagnostic Audits. IMS obtained important products with the acquisition of Pharmatech, which developed the precursor to online delivery systems that IMS later created, and Cambridge Computer, which developed Drug Distribution Data, providing information to pharmaceutical sales representatives across several market areas.

Company Perspectives:

Our Vision: To enable our clients to help people throughout the world live longer, happier, and healthier lives.

Our Mission: To be integral to our clients' success by delivering critical business intelligence, decision support, and services that enable them to optimize their performance and advance the quality of healthcare.

Our Values: Commitment to create continuous value for the benefit of our clients. Excellence that breeds innovation and leadership within every facet of the business. Integrity and respect for individual performance and collective success.

In 1973 IMS established the Medical Communications division and the Life Sciences division to complement its market research activities. Medical Communications published informational materials, such as professional and trade journals, directories, and audiovisual training products. The division established the IMS Pharmaceutical market letter and acquired Medicine Digest Ltd. in 1978. IMS formed the Life Sciences division by acquiring Biodynamics, Inc., which conducted toxicology testing of chemicals and pharmaceuticals. When the U.S. Toxic Substances Act passed in 1976, IMS benefited as sales exploded with increased government requirements for toxicology testing. In 1978 IMS acquired Argentan Ltd. to further capitalize on the opportunity created by the new law.

International expansion involved the 1973 acquisitions of PRSA Holding Pty of Australia and New Zealand and the Interdroma group of companies in West Germany. Interdroma was known for its *Die Gelb Liste* or "yellow list," a work similar to the *Physicians' Desk Reference.* In 1975 IMS acquired Medifrance, which published physicians' prescription pads with pharmaceutical advertising.

The pharmaceuticals industry experienced dramatic growth during the 1970s, and IMS grew with it. Between 1973 and 1979 the company's sales growth averaged 20 percent. From revenues of $113.5 million in 1978, IMS reaped $8.2 million in profit, a 36 percent increase above the previous year. Providing information services in 42 countries, international operations accounted for 69 percent of revenues. The majority of business, 66 percent, originated from Market Research, while 22 percent originated from Medical Communications and 11 percent from Life Sciences.

1980s: Personal Computers Changing Methods of Transmitting Market Data

As the use of personal desktop computers spread, IMS changed the way it distributed information. In 1979 the company introduced one of its most important products, the multinational integrated data analysis service. Known as MIDAS, the system automated access to market information as computer terminals installed in customer offices provided direct access to IMS databases via satellite. Information on MIDAS covered activities of pharmaceutical, chemical, and healthcare companies in several countries, including drug and ingredient purchases by pharmacies and hospitals and expenditure on advertising and product promotions. In the years following the introduction of MIDAS, almost every major pharmaceutical company in the world subscribed to the service.

IMS developed several online database services during the 1980s, transforming existing knowledge for ease of access. In addition to Pharmaceutical Sales Audits, services included Sales Territory Reports, based on Drug Distribution Data reports, and Call Reporting, which provided sales information for a targeted area. Doctor Profiling organized the buying habits of physicians by zip code. Sales Management Systems combined the three databases. Post Marketing Surveillance reported drug trial results. By 1988 sales for database services exceeded the company's 1990 target of $100 million.

Further product and service development at IMS was influenced by Dun & Bradstreet's (D&B) acquisition of IMS in 1988. D&B, the world's largest provider of business information, considered IMS the "jewel in its crown." Upon completion of the $1.7 billion stock transaction, D&B proceeded to create synergy between IMS and other subsidiaries. Nielsen Marketing Research and IMS began sharing data collection on the sale of over-the-counter drugs and health and beauty products. Sales Technologies, acquired by D&B in 1989, collaborated with IMS on marketing laptop-based sales management service tools for mobile sales representatives in the United States and European pharmaceuticals industries.

Another aspect of personal computer usage, which influenced IMS operations, involved improved data collection. The use of personal computers by physicians not only simplified data collection through electronic transfer, it expanded the range of information available. In 1989 IMS introduced new services based on information gathered from physicians, initially in France and West Germany.

IMS continued to introduce online versions of existing reports, including the Japan Regional Sales Report and, in seven European countries, the OTC Report on over-the-counter drugs. International expansion involved the introduction of products and services in the Soviet Union and Eastern European countries, South Africa, and Asia, including China, India, Hong Kong, Malaysia, and Indonesia.

IMS introduced many new information products and services. These included the Xponent, providing information about the activities of drug prescribers, and Plan Trak, providing information about managed care providers' handling of prescriptions. In the United States IMS introduced Xplorer to serve individual information requirements by combining data from inside the client company with IMS research resources.

In 1995, D&B made Sales Technologies an operating unit of IMS, with the intent of further developing mobile information services specifically for healthcare and pharmaceutical sales professionals. In emphasizing Pharmaceutical Relationship Management solutions, Sales Technologies developed automated sales management tools based on market information for targeting potential sales, such as Cornerstone and Premier. In collaboration with Logix, Inc., maker of handheld personal computers (HPC) used by pharmaceutical sales representatives, Sales Technologies integrated HPC applications with Cornerstone sales and marketing applications.

Key Dates:

1957: Intercontinental Marketing Services (IMS) completes its first pharmaceutical audit.
1969: The company enters the U.S. market through acquisition.
1972: IMS becomes a publicly owned company.
1973: Medical Communications and Life Sciences divisions are formed.
1979: The Multinational Integrated Data Analysis (MIDAS) system is introduced.
1988: Dun & Bradstreet (D&B) acquires IMS.
1996: Growth of healthcare industry-related businesses leads D&B to spin off IMS Health as a subsidiary of Cognizant Corporation.
1998: IMS Health becomes an independent company.
1999: IMS Health launches several new Internet-based products, including i-squared Internet portal.
2001: The acquisition of Cambridge Pharma Consultancy fortifies consulting operations.
2002: Marketing Effectiveness Suite is launched, providing sales information daily.

"Pure-Play" Global Healthcare Information Provider: 1998

In 1996 D&B began a process of separating its business operations which led to IMS becoming an independent company. During the first phase, IMS became a subsidiary of Cognizant Corporation along with Nielsen Marketing Research and the Gartner Group. In 1998 D&B spun off IMS and Nielsen from Cognizant Corporation, with Cognizant becoming a subsidiary of the newly formed IMS Health, Inc. IMS Health became an independent public company through a stock dividend distribution in June.

The main components of the company included IMS, the company's market research segment, Erisco Managed Care Technologies, which developed software applications for healthcare providers, and Cognizant, renamed Cognizant Technology Solutions, an information technology company. IMS Health subsidiaries included Enterprises, a venture capital unit investing in new healthcare businesses. IMS Health held an equity investment in Gartner Group, another information technology company. As an independent company IMS Health planned to focus solely on supplying global information solutions to high growth areas in the healthcare and pharmaceutical industries. This meant that information technology subsidiaries would be sold or spun off.

Many of the new company's activities focused on international expansion. In February IMS Europe located its worldwide headquarters in London. New research products introduced in the United Kingdom at this time included Xtrend, which tracked drug prescriptions, and PharmaTrend, which tracked sales of over-the-counter drugs. IMS developed markets in Czech and Slovak Republics, Poland, Turkey, and countries in Sub-Saharan Africa. Through acquisition or joint venture IMS Health entered markets in China, Hungary, and Switzerland. IMS Health acquired Walsh International, a Pennsylvania-

based firm whose $54 million in annual revenues came primarily from business conducted in Europe. With the acquisition of the non-U.S. assets of Pharmaceutical Marketing Services, Inc., IMS Health gained additional access to markets in Europe as well as Japan. International development also involved the introduction of new products in local languages. Sales Technologies introduced its Cornerstone automated sales management tool in local language versions in Japan and Brazil.

Among the company's new products, IMS Health introduced EarlyView for Xponent customers in mid-1998. The service provided information about product sales activity within one month of the previous month's close, compared with approximately two months for other data sources. The sales tool allowed company representatives to target drug prescribers with high sales potential by accessing early information on adoption of new products or change to competitive products.

Erisco Managed Care Technologies introduced Facets 2.7, an upgraded version of its primary software application. Facets 2.7 provided enhancements to major managed care functions, such as the Capitation/Risk Fund Management and Electronic Commerce Systems. Improvement to the Claims Processing function streamlined the release of pending claims in batches.

Late 1990s: New Technology Providing Foundation for Knowledge Products

During the late 1990s, new information technology provided a platform for creating new business decision-support tools that operated more rapidly and conveniently. As the Internet matured as a platform for information dissemination, IMS Health designed products that took advantage of its features. In collaboration with Physicians Online (POL), IMS Health created FASTview research service, to provide survey results of physician prescribing activity within 24 hours through access to POL's network of 200,000 physicians. The strength of this product included monitoring of drug prescriptions during the first eight weeks after launch, a period that was critical to the long-term success of the product.

Strategic Technologies, a merger of Sales Technologies and Walsh International, launched Insight Manager, an Internet-based tool for accessing sales information based on pharmaceutical prescribing activities. Integrated with Premier and Cornerstone applications, Insight Manager supported pharmaceutical sales representatives by providing information about potential sales opportunities.

In December 1999 IMS Health launched the i-squared Internet portal. The portal provided real-time drug market information with links to IMS Health's databases and services. The portal gave users the option of configuring their own work environment, such as merging client data with IMS resources and creating menus based on IMS Health products or by business processes, including market assessment, product launching, sales force deployment, and product portfolio management. Within the first year, more than 200 pharmaceutical corporations subscribed to the service.

As IMS Health developed market knowledge products, these products became increasingly specialized and complex. For instance, Xponent Specialty Retail monitored pharmaceutical prescriptions from specialized dealers, such as those prescribing drugs for HIV, schizophrenia, cancer, infertility, and other specific disorders. Enhanced Medical Dynamics collected and disseminated information on patient/physician consultations and treatments in 11 major markets in North America, plus Europe, Asia, Argentina, and Mexico.

New services reflected stronger attention to the way clients used information, such as specific areas of the marketing process. The new National Business Impact Assessment studied spending on direct-to-consumer advertising as it related to brand performance by measuring the incremental growth of a particular brand-name product. Another service, New Product Spectra, provided information on 265 major product introductions organized for more than 30 therapeutic classes. Analogue provided a comprehensive overview of pharmaceutical marketing in North America, Europe, and Japan, covering 1,800 major pharmaceutical new product introductions of all therapeutic classes.

As part of a movement toward qualitative information solutions, IMS Health introduced forecasting products under the new PharmaCast & Beyond service. IMS Health offered reports as a group or on an individual basis. The reports included qualitative information gathered from industry experts. Growth Analyzer, available in 40 countries, examined the causes of market growth and decline, looking at trends, differences in locality, and product promotions.

As part of its strategy to focus IMS Health activities on providing healthcare information, the company divested subsidiaries that handled technology development. IMS Health sold SSJ KK, a provider of financial application software, in March 1999, and Erisco Managed Care Technologies in October 2000. IMS Health spun off the Gartner Group in July 1999 and Sales Technologies in September 2000. In addition, IMS Health sold Source Dispensing, acquired from PMSI, as required by a British court due to a near monopoly when Whole Sale Data Services was combined with Xtrend services.

With more than 10,000 reports available, in May 2000 IMS Health introduced an online store, at open.imshealth.com, as an alternative to the i-squared portal. With a credit card, customers could download information products on an as-needed basis. The site featured the new Sales Report, on the top 20 international drugs in 189 therapeutic classes, and Pharmaceutical Company Profiles, covering product portfolios, mergers and acquisitions, and current product research and development of 100 major companies.

To accommodate the massive amount of information compiled by the company, in August IMS Health announced that it would build a global data processing center at the regional office in Plymouth Meeting, Pennsylvania. One of the largest computing centers in the world, the facility would process one billion transactions per month and store 26 terabytes of data collected from 100 countries.

Development of Consulting and Related Services in the Early 2000s

As the company streamlined operations to become purely an information resource, IMS Health sought to build on the potential of its offerings by providing consulting services. IMS Health consultants assisted clients to interpret insights garnered from market data and to translate them into business management and marketing decisions. Toward that end, in March 2002, IMS Health acquired Cambridge Pharma Consultancy, a healthcare consulting and advisory company in the United Kingdom. The acquisition supplemented IMS Health's existing consulting services and strengthened its international presence in this area.

IMS Health formed an alliance with Cognizant Technology Solutions to assist clients in building a custom infrastructure for organizing business intelligence. IMS Information Management Consulting, combined with Cognizant's capabilities in customizing information technology, would design software that catered to clients' specific needs. Consultants offered diagnostic assessments, data warehousing solutions, and integration of client data with IMS resources.

Among 20 new information services introduced in 2002, the most significant was the IMS Marketing Effectiveness Suite, a web-based tool providing detailed information on the complete lifecycle of a product, from pre-launch to patent expiration. Designed for the marketing professional, the Marketing Effectiveness Suite merged several existing databases to provide immediate response to client questions, answering with narrative or graphic displays. Services included Performance Tracker, which monitored product performance on a national, regional, and state level, following prescribing activity, sales, product inventory and withdrawal, and promotional spending. Early Insight emphasized daily prescribing activity indicative of the impact of special promotions on national sales.

Through an alliance with Harris Interactive, announced in March 2003, IMS Health planned to develop custom research and consulting services through online physicians panels. Harris Interactive's qualitative analysis on physician attitudes about prescriptions would supplement IMS Health's quantitative material to provide pharmaceutical companies worldwide with a new source of insight on market behavior.

Acquisitions in early 2003 involved specialized pharmaceutical information resources. IMS Health acquired Marketing Initiatives, Inc., which specialized in healthcare facility profile data, and Data Niche Associates (DNA), which specialized in rebate validation services for Medicaid and managed care. With managed care and Medicaid becoming a rapidly growing channel of pharmaceutical prescription activity, the DNA acquisition provided IMS Health with access to a significant information source.

IMS Health completed the transition to a pure-play global pharmaceutical information provider when the company spun off Cognizant Technology Solutions. Cognizant became an independent company in January 2003 through a stock exchange that decreased IMS Health's majority interest in the company.

Principal Subsidiaries

IMS AG (Switzerland); IMS Chinametrik Inc.; IMS Health Asia; IMS Health Australia Pty, Ltd.; IMS Health Canada; IMS Health Group Limited (U.K.).

Principal Operating Units

Marketing Effectiveness Solutions; Sales Optimization Solutions; Consulting Services.

Principal Competitors

Cegedim Group USA; NDC Health Corporation; PAREXEL International Corporation; Quintiles Transnational Corporation.

Further Reading

"Comprehensive Information That Can Be Hard to Find," *New York Times,* September 19, 1998, p. G10.

"Dun & Bradstreet to Acquire IMS International for $1.77 Billion," *IDP Report,* February 19, 1988, p. 1.

George, John, "Drug Giant Inks $347M Acquisition," *Philadelphia Business Journal,* March 27, 1998, p. 1.

Gilpin, Kenneth N., "Dun & Bradstreet to Split into 3 Public Companies," *New York Times,* January 10, 1996, p. D1.

"IMS Database Services Revenue Well Ahead of $100 Million Target for 1990," *IDP Report,* January 8, 1988, p. 1.

"IMS Health Acquires Data Niche Associates," *Fairfield County Business Journal,* March 17, 2003, p. 11.

"IMS Health Takes Over Cambridge Pharma Consultancy," *Pharmaceutical Technology Europe,* March 2002, p. 5.

"IMS International Inc. Buys Private Company for 300,000 of Common," *Wall Street Journal,* May 29, 1973, p. 22.

"IMS International Offering Is Sold Out at $25 a Share," *Wall Street Journal,* June 28, 1972, p. 15.

"IMS Launches New Information Services," *Chemical Market Reporter,* June 14, 1999, p. 49.

"IMS Told to Sell Wholesale Sales Data Service Business," *Chemist & Druggist,* March 6, 1999, p. 24.

"L.W. Frolich Led Ad Agency," *New York Times,* September 29, 1971, p. 36.

Wiggins, Phillip H., "Tracking Drug Industry Sales," *New York Times,* March 23, 1979, p. D1.

—Mary Tradii

Investcorp SA

Investcorp House
PO Box 5340
Manama
Bahrain
Telephone: (+973) 532000
Fax: (+973) 530816
Web site: http://www.investcorp.com

Public Company
Incorporated: 1982
Employees: 270
Sales: $377.3 million (2001)
Stock Exchanges: Bahrain
Ticker Symbol: INVCORP
NAIC: 551112 Offices of Other Holding Companies;
522293 International Trade Financing; 522298 All
Other Non-Depository Credit Intermediation; 523120
Securities Brokerage; 523130 Commodity Contracts
Dealing

Investcorp SA is a globally operating investment group with offices in Bahrain, London, and New York. Since its founding in 1982, Investcorp has defined itself as an investment intermediary, acting as a vehicle to channel the wealth of its Arabian Gulf clients into investments in the United States and Europe. Investcorp's three offices act in tandem, with the New York and London offices identifying investment opportunities, and the Bahrain office placing investment among a pool of clients. The company is active in four primary areas: Corporate Investments and Technology Investments, which each target the North American and Western European markets; Real Estate Investments in North America, with properties ranging from hotels to shopping malls, as well as residential and office buildings; and Global Asset Management, which, with more than $2.8 billion in assets, makes Investcorp one of the leaders in the Gulf region. Led by founder, President, and CEO Nemir A. Kirdar, Investcorp has become best known through a number of high-profile investments, including its purchase and resale of Gucci, Saks Fifth Avenue, Tiffany, and others. Investcorp typically acquires 100 percent control of a company, then works with existing management to expand the business before reselling the company at a premium. Throughout its more than 20 years in business, Investcorp has achieved an average return on investments of 26 percent per year. The company is listed on the Bahrain stock exchange. Kirdar, other employees, and a small group of founder investors retain 59 percent of the company's stock.

Targeting the Gulf in the 1980s

Nemir Kirdar was born in Iraq in 1937. His family had long held prominent positions in the country's government within the Ottoman Empire and later under the Hashemite kingdom of King Faysal. Kirdar himself had gone to study in Istanbul, receiving a B.A. from Robert College in the 1950s. In 1958, when King Faysal was deposed and executed, Kirdar fled to the United States, continuing his education at the University of the Pacific in California.

Kirdar, who had worked as a janitor in order to supplement his scholarship, returned to Iraq at the start of the 1960s to reclaim his family's properties and start his own business, Nemir Kirdar Business Enterprises. The rise of the Ba'athist party, which later propelled Saddam Hussein to power, forced Kirdar to flee Iraq again at the end of the 1960s.

Kirdar and family returned to the United States, and he enrolled in Fordham University's night school program, while working at a bank during the day. After earning his M.B.A. from Fordham, Kirdar took a job as a lending officer with Chase Manhattan Bank. In the late 1970s, as the oil-rich Persian Gulf countries, which had seen their fortunes shoot up following the Oil Embargo of 1973, launched large-scale infrastructure investment programs, Kirdar was assigned to head up Chase's operations in the region.

Kirdar quickly recognized a new business opportunity, as a whole new generation of suddenly wealthy individuals began seeking investment opportunities. Kirdar saw the potential for setting up a business that would act as an intermediary for placing Persian Gulf money in Western businesses. In 1982, Kirdar was backed by a group of investors, which included Bahrainian billionaire Ahmed Ali Kanoo and Sheikh Ahmed Zaki Yamani, then Saudi oil minister.

Company Perspectives:

Since its foundation, Investcorp's mission has been clear and consistent:

To create a working environment that demands integrity and stimulates entrepreneurial spirit, together with a deep sense of responsibility to the firm, its shareholders and its clients.

To achieve market recognition of the firm's reliability, professionalism and accountability in all the products and services it offers.

To ensure the firm's long-term growth and consistent profitability through careful yet imaginative risk and resource management.

To be global in our outlook, organization and operating structure for maximum competitive advantage.

Investcorp targeted what it considered viable companies with strong existing management that lacked only investment capital in order to pursue expansion. Unlike most investment companies, Investcorp established itself as an intermediary, purchasing a company and then approaching its client base—of some 500 to 600 individuals—with an offer to purchase a share in the investment. Investcorp and its management kept a share of the company, while individual client shares remained limited—not only to protect the client's investment, but also to make certain that no single client achieved a significant shareholding in the company.

Although Investcorp provided assistance to an acquired company's management beyond capital funding, it preferred to maintain its distance from day-to-day operations. Investcorp's acquisitions were generally made to acquire full control of a company; yet acquisitions were considered on the whole as medium-term investments. Once a company's value had increased substantially, Investcorp planned to sell it off, or take it public, usually after only four to seven years.

Investcorp's early investments reflected its diverse interests. Purchases in the early to mid-1980s included root beer maker A&W Brands; fishing boat and yacht manufacturer Bertram-Trojan, acquired in 1985; and Mueller, a manufacturer of fluid control and other plumbing equipment, and the world's leading manufacturer of fire hydrants, in 1986. Perhaps Investcorp's most publicized acquisition of the period came in 1984, when the company paid some $200 million to acquire Tiffany, the famed jeweler, from Avon Corporation. Less than three years later, after restoring Tiffany's lost luster, Investcorp spun it off in a public offering that nearly doubled its initial investment.

Investcorp also began investing in real estate, with purchases including the Manulife Building in Los Angeles in 1986. But its greatest focus remained on its corporate investments, which included the purchase of Club Car, a maker of golf carts, bought in 1986 and sold again in 1988. By then, the company also had begun adding European investments, such as its purchase of the Swiss jewelry group Chaumet, which also included luxury watchmaker Breguet.

Turning Around Gucci in the 1990s

In 1988, Investcorp bought trucking firm Burnham Service Corp., based in Columbus, Georgia. The following year, Investcorp acquired Carvel, the Connecticut-based maker of ice cream products. That acquisition, which cost the company $80 million, was to prove one of the company's least successful, however, remaining in the company's portfolio into the 2000s, with total additional investments nearing $60 million. Another unlucky purchase was that of flooring retailer Color Tile, bought in 1989 and which ultimately declared bankruptcy in 1996.

More fruitful for the company was its investment in Gucci, the famed Italian designer that had fallen on hard times amid wrangling among members of its founding family. Investcorp began building its stake in Gucci in 1987, buying up a 50 percent share, and finally gained full control of the company in 1993. Into the mid-1990s, Investcorp supported Gucci's management as it struggled to turn the company around. As Kirdar admitted to the *Financial Times:* "Those were some very hard times. We had to pour a lot of money in, and we had some sour days."

In the end, however, the Gucci purchase became one of Investcorp's most visible and most successful investments. By 1995, with the company posting strong profits and especially strong revenue gains, Investcorp cashed out, taking Gucci public. By the time Investcorp had sold off its remaining shares in Gucci in 1996, it had earned some $2.1 billion—on an initial investment of just $246 million.

Another Investcorp investment also was coming to fruition at that time. In 1990, Investcorp had acquired retail group Saks Fifth Avenue; after restoring that company's growth, it had launched Saks' public offering on the New York Stock Exchange in 1996. Two years later, Investcorp sold out its remaining stake in Saks to the Proffitt's retail group.

Investcorp had booked a number of other successful investments during the 1990s, such as its turnaround of the Simmons mattress company, bought in 1996 and sold off again to Fenway Partners in 1998, and Boston-based supermarket group Star Market, acquired in 1994 and sold to the United Kingdom's J. Sainsbury, also in 1998. Another highly successful purchase for the company involved the Circle K convenience store chain, which Investcorp had bought out of bankruptcy in 1993 and then sold a 27 percent stake on the New York Stock Exchange before leading a merger of the group with oil refiner and marketer Tosco Corporation in 1996.

By the end of the 1990s, Investcorp's track record had reached an annualized average of 30 percent on its investments. The company also had been building up a strong assets management business, in a move to produce additional, stable income flow. In 1996, it created a dedicated business unit, Investcorp Asset Management. By 1997, Investcorp's recurrent income generated through its assets management wing had topped that produced as transaction fees for its corporate investment activities.

Adapting for Expansion in the New Century

Whereas Investcorp's focus had been, in large part, North American in the 1980s and at the beginning of the 1990s, its attention turned more and more to the European market in the

Key Dates:

1982: Nemir Kirdar founds Investcorp, based in Bahrain, as an intermediary investment group to funnel Gulf States wealth into Western investments.

1984: Investcorp acquires New York jewelry firm Tiffany.

1985: Investcorp acquires fishing boat and yacht manufacturer Bertram-Trojan.

1986: Investcorp acquires Mueller, the world's leading manufacturer of fire hydrants.

1987: Investcorp acquires 50 percent of Gucci.

1990: Investcorp acquires Saks Fifth Ave.

1993: Investcorp acquires full control of Gucci; the Circle K convenience store group is acquired.

2000: The company forms the Technology Investment business unit as it begins venture capital investments.

late 1990s. As Kirdar himself pointed out to *Sunday Business:* "As far as Europe is concerned, I'm an optimist. Look at the amount of money available compared with the amount of deals there are going to be. There are a lot more deals that are coming up because of the disappearance of borders, the unification of markets and the unification of the currency, plus the conglomerates' tendency to divest."

In 1994, Investcorp boosted its position in the Swiss watchmaking industry with the acquisition of Ebel in 1994. In 1999, the company bundled Ebel with Chaumet in a sale of both companies to luxury goods group LVMH. In Germany, meanwhile, Investcorp acquired Leica Geosystems, supporting the management buyout of that well-known company, before taking it public in 2000. In that year, Investcorp returned to Germany with the purchase of Gerresheimer, a leading manufacturer of specialty glass products. Norway's Helly Hansen was acquired in 1997, in partnership with Orkla. Investcorp also spotted an opportunity in The Netherlands, acquiring Stahl, a leading maker of specialty chemicals for the leather market, in 2001.

In the United Kingdom, meanwhile, Investcorp had acquired Welcome Break, the country's second largest highway service station operator, in 1997, and, in 1998, printing specialists Watmoughs Holding and British Printing Company, which were then merged as the newly named Polestar. The breadth of Investcorp's interests was revealed again in 1999, when the company acquired the specialty chemicals business of AstraZeneca, which was renamed Avecia.

Despite its interest in the European market, Investcorp remained a patron of U.S. companies. In 1996, the company bought CSL Auto, based in Arizona, which operated more than 1,100 auto parts stores. In 1997, the company purchased Wener, the leading maker of ladders and scaffolds in the United States. Harborside Healthcare was added in 1998, followed by NationsRent in 1999, and school affinity products leader Jostens in 2000. The company's acquisitions continued into the new century, and included SI Corporation, acquired in 2000, and water-meter and related products group Neptune, based in Alabama, in 2001.

Throughout its history, Investcorp had avoided, for the most part, the volatile high-technology market. By the end of the 1990s, however, as the company faced increasing competition in the private equity market, it turned its attention to the venture capital market. In 2000, Investcorp set up its Technology Ventures business unit to guide its technology sector investment strategy, targeting primarily later-stage start-ups in the Internet, telecommunications, and IT sectors.

The Technology Ventures segment quickly built up a portfolio of more than 15 companies, including Stratus Technologies, a specialist in continuously available servers, acquired in 1999. The following year, the company acquired the U.K.'s e-business group Aspective; TelePacific, based in Los Angeles; and stakes in Germany's broadband and cable television group, Callahan's Callahan Broadband and Callahan German Cable. In 2001, Investcorp acquired ECI Conference Call Services, based in New Jersey.

Investcorp quickly turned around a number of its technology investments, such as wireless technology specialist 4thpass, which was acquired by Motorola in 2002, and Acta, a maker of enterprise software, which was sold to Business Objects that year as well. The company also merged another early tech investment, US Unwired, acquired in 1999, into Sprint PCS affiliate company Wireless One in 2002.

The difficult economic conditions, including the uncertainty in the Persian Gulf region surrounding the impending outbreak of the second Persian Gulf War, placed Investcorp under pressure. The company responded by emphasizing its real estate operations, with some 20 property acquisitions, backed by sales of 16 properties already in its portfolio during 2002.

At the end of 2002, Investcorp returned to its corporate investment activities, acquiring Aero Products, the leading maker of air-filled bedding products, based in Illinois, in November 2002; PlayPower, a maker of playground equipment in December 2002; and MW Manufacturers, based in Virginia, which manufactured window and door products, a transaction completed in 2003. Having grown into one of the world's leading private equity investment groups, Investcorp looked forward to more deals in the future.

Principal Subsidiaries

Global Strategy Limited (Cayman Islands); Investcorp A.M.P. Limited (Cayman Islands); Investcorp Capital Limited (Cayman Islands); Investcorp Capital S.A. (Luxembourg); Investcorp Financial and Investment Services S.A. (Switzerland); Investcorp Funding Limited (Cayman Islands); Investcorp International Inc. (U.S.A.); Investcorp International Limited (U.K.); Investcorp Investment Holdings Limited (Cayman Islands); Investcorp Ireland Financial Services II Limited; Investcorp Ireland Financial Services Limited; Investcorp Management Services Limited (Cayman Islands); Investcorp S.A. (Luxembourg); Investcorp Securities Limited (U.K.); Investcorp Trading Limited (Cayman Islands); Invifin S.A. (Luxembourg).

Principal Competitors

Kohlberg Kravis Roberts & Co; Forstmann Little & Co.; Sierra Ventures; Golder, Thoma, Cressey, Rauner Inc.; Warburg Pincus LLC; Hicks, Muse, Tate and Furst, Inc.

Further Reading

Forrohar, Kambiz, "Patient, But Not Too Patient," *Forbes,* March 10, 1997, p. 134.

Hancock, Jimmy, "Investcorp Buys Shopping Center in West Boca Scant Months After Selling Mall in Deerfield Beach," *Daily Business Review,* April 15, 2003, p. A3.

Lee, Peter, "Investcorp's Roving Brand Builder," *Euromoney,* November 1998.

Northedge, Richard, "Investor with Midas Touch," *Sunday Business,* November 15, 1998.

Targett, Simon, "Filling a Gulf in Investment," *Financial Times,* January 11, 2001.

Watts, Christopher, "Nemir Kirdar's New Frontiers," *Forbes,* December 27, 1999.

—M.L. Cohen

ISCOR

Iscor Limited

Roger Dyason Road
Pretoria West
Pretoria 0001
South Africa
Telephone: (+27) 12-307-3000
Fax: (+27) 12-326-4721
Web site: http://www.iscor.com

Public Company
Incorporated: 1927 as Suid Afrikaanse Yster en Staal
  Industriele Korporasie (South African Iron and Steel
  Industrial Corporation)
Employees: 13,301
Sales: R 14.18 billion ($1.37 billion) (2002)
Stock Exchanges: Johannesburg
Ticker Symbol: ISC
NAIC: 212210 Iron Ore Mining; 212111 Bituminous
  Coal and Lignite Surface Mining; 212112 Bituminous
  Coal Underground Mining; 212113 Anthracite
  Mining; 212291 Uranium-Radium-Vanadium Ore
  Mining; 213114 Support Activities for Metal Mining;
  331111 Iron and Steel Mills; 525930 Real Estate
  Investment Trusts; 551112 Offices of Other Holding
  Companies

Iscor Limited has surprised the worldwide steel industry by shedding its valuable mining assets—spun off as publicly listed Kumba Resources in 2001—and restructuring itself as one of the world's lowest cost producers of flat steel and long steel products. Iscor also has shown itself as one of the few profitable steel concerns during the industry downturn at the beginning of the new century. Formerly state-owned, Iscor remains South Africa's leading steel company, with a 68 percent market share in the country. The company's operations are conducted through four primary steel production plants: Vanderbijlpark Works and Saldanha Steel, which produce flat steel products; and Vereeniging Works and Newcastle, which both produce long steel products. Iscor's flat steel operation, which accounts for 64 percent of the group's total sales and which includes the company's 60 percent stake in Collect-a-Can, is the sub-Saharan continent's largest, supplying slabs, plates, hot-rolled, cold-rolled, galvanized, and tinplate steel. With production levels of nearly three million tons at Vanderbijlpark and nearly 900,000 tons at Saldanha—scheduled to reach 1.2 million during 2003—Iscor is capable of producing nearly 85 percent of South Africa's flat steel demand. The company is also South Africa's leading long steel producer, supplying 43 percent of that market. Total production at the Vereeniging and Newcastle sites reached 1.75 million tons, more than 90 percent of which was rolled profile products. Iscor exports 55 percent of its flat steel, although exports accounted for 47 percent of the company's total steel production. The Far East represents Iscor's primary marketplace, although the United States is the company's single largest market. As part of the unbundling of Kumba Resources, Iscor retained a guaranteed supply contract with Kumba's huge Sishen Iron Ore Mine, providing Iscor with an annual supply of 6.25 million tons for cost plus three percent. The deal enables Iscor to maintain its claim as a vertically integrated steel specialist. Iscor is listed on the Johannesburg stock exchange and is led by CEO Louis van Niekerk and Chairman Warren Clewlow.

State-Owned Beginnings in the 1920s

South Africa boasted little if any industrial development at the dawn of the 20th century. Much of the country's economic development remained agriculture-based, a sector dominated by the Afrikaner population. The country's immense mineral wealth, however, began to transform the country by the end of the 19th century. Mining—especially for gold and diamonds—quickly became the country's leading industry. Yet this mineral wealth, as well as most of its rising industry and its commercial activity, was dominated by the country's British population.

South Africa's industrial development was jump-started by the success of its mining industry, and demand for steel and steel products increased dramatically. With virtually no steel industry of its own, the country relied entirely on imported steel. The first efforts to introduce steel production in the country remained rudimentary. One of the early attempts dated back to the 1880s, with the creation of the South African Coal and Iron Company in

1882. Yet the first successful, if limited, production of pig iron occurred only in 1901, in the town of Pietermaritzburg.

The first true South African steel company appeared in 1909, when Horace Wright and Sammy Marks were granted a license to construct a furnace in Vereeniging, in the Transvaal region. Wright and Marks founded the Union Steel Corporation (USCO) and began construction of a blast furnace in 1911. By 1913, the partners had completed construction of a ten-ton open hearth furnace and launched production. The company initially relied on scrap materials from the country's railroads and mines as feedstock.

The first efforts to develop South Africa's own steel feedstock supply began in 1916, with the launch of the country's first ferrous ore mine in Pretoria West. That mine fed a newly constructed blast furnace, which produced some 4,000 tons of pig iron between 1918 and 1921. Meanwhile, USCO constructed a second blast furnace, producing some 700 tons.

Newcastle became the next site of the South African steel industry's development, with the construction of a large-scale blast furnace starting in 1919. A new company was formed to operate the furnace, called Newcastle Iron and Steel Works. That operation was to become one of the cornerstones of the later Iscor.

Throughout this early period, the country's nascent steel industry remained controlled by the wealthy British class. Despite their economic clout, however, the British were quickly losing their political clout. The Afrikaner population had begun organizing before World War I, forming the National Party in 1914. Soon after, the National Party spawned the secretive Afrikaans Broederbond, which grew into one of the most important political movements in the country, dedicated to promoting Afrikaner nationalistic interests.

The formation of the so-called ''Pact'' government between the National Party and the Labour Party in the 1920s propelled the Afrikaner community into true political power for the first time. Under the Pact government, new policies were enacted encouraging South Africa's industrial development. As part of that effort, the government commissioned a study from Germany's Gutehoffnungshütte to determine the feasibility of establishing a full-fledged steel industry in South Africa. The positive outcome of the review led to calls for a rapid expansion of the country's steel operations.

In 1927, the Pact government enacted new legislation, which led to the creation of state-owned South African Iron and Steel Industrial Corporation Limited, or, as it was known in Afrikaans,

Suid Afrikaanse Yster en Staal Industriele Korporasie. The new company, which adopted Iscor as the shortened form of its name, quickly took control of the country's nascent steel industry, including USCO's Vereeniging site and, later, the Newcastle Iron and Steel Works as well. Despite the influence of the National Party in its creation, Iscor at the outset was controlled by English-speakers and moderate Afrikaners not affiliated with the National Party. Nonetheless, as part of the legislation creating the company, Iscor was initially required to retain a whites-only workforce.

The 1929 elections, in which the National Party accused the Labour Party of promoting a mixed-race state, gave the Afrikaner community political control of the country—and led, following World War II, to the creation of the Apartheid regime. Iscor then became part of the government's effort to control much of the country's developing industries—and thereby reduce the disparity in wealth between the British and Afrikaner communities.

Iscor began building its own steelworks in Pretoria, and by 1934 had started production, becoming the chief supplier of rails for South Africa's rapidly expanding railroad network. At the same time, Iscor started its own mining operation in Thabazimbi in order to supply its own iron ore. The operation quickly proved an expensive endeavor, particularly against the group's larger and more efficient foreign competitors. To cut costs, the government relaxed the group's employment requirements, allowing Iscor to take on an unskilled black workforce paid at much lower rates.

Iscor quickly ramped up production and by 1935 was already providing for more than 17 percent of South Africa's steel needs. The company was later to benefit from a heightening degree of government protection, restricting imported steel while favoring Iscor's own later moves into the export markets.

Publicly Listed in the 1980s

Demand for Iscor's steel grew strongly into the late 1930s, prompting the company to begin construction on a new heavy plate mill in Vanderbijlpark, in 1943. By 1947, the Vanderbijlpark site had begun a major expansion to develop into an integrated steelworks and flat products mill. The first phase of that project was completed in 1953. The new production capacity brought in turn growing demand for raw materials, and in 1953, Iscor started a new mining operation, in Sishen. That mine, an open pit ore mine, was to become one of the world's largest. At the same time, the growing production from the company's coal-fired furnaces required the company to find a new fuel source, and in 1955, Iscor acquired the Durban Navigation Collieries in order to provide its own coking coal. By then, Iscor was supplying more than 70 percent of South Africa's steel needs.

By the 1960s, Iscor had become dominated by Afrikaners—many of whom were members of the Broederbond—closely associated with Afrikaner nationalist sentiment and the apartheid government. Iscor also had become an integral part of the Afrikaner community's efforts to achieve economic parity. It was also to play a critical part in maintaining the apartheid regime; the voluntary arms ban imposed against South Africa in the early 1960s had forced the government to stimulate its own

Key Dates:

1909: Horace Wright and Sammy Marks are granted rights to build a blast furnace to produce pig iron, founding Union Steel Corporation (USCO), South Africa's first active steel company.

1916: The first ferrous ore mining operation in South Africa is established.

1927: "Pact" government creates South Africa Iron and Steel Corporation (Iscor), which becomes the dominant steel producer in the country; Iscor begins construction of the Pretoria steel mill.

1934: The Pretoria mill begins steel production.

1943: Iscor begins construction of a heavy plate steel mill in Vanderbijlpark.

1947: The Vanderbijlpark site is expanded as an integrated steel mill, completed in 1953.

1971: Construction of an integrated steelworks at Newcastle begins.

1989: Iscor is privatized and listed on the Johannesburg stock exchange.

1994: Conversion of the Pretoria mill to stainless steel production begins.

1995: Iscor launches its re-engineering program.

1996: A joint venture with IDC is formed to build Saldanha Steel Mill.

1997: The Pretoria mill is shut down.

1999: The Saldanha mill begins production.

2001: Iscor splits operations, spinning off its mining interests as Kumba Resources.

2002: Iscor acquires full control of Saldanha the steel mill.

arms industry. Control of the iron and steel industry became paramount to that effort.

Through the 1960s, Iscor stepped up its production capacity, completing a major expansion to the Vanderbijlpark site between 1964 and 1968. A third expansion to the site began during the 1970s, completed in 1977. By then, Iscor had launched construction of a third integrated steelworks and long product mill, taking over the site of the earlier Newcastle works. Construction of the Newcastle plant began in 1971, and production started up in 1976. That same year saw completion of the Sishen railroad, linking the company's open pit mine to the coast. Iscor then began exporting iron ore for the first time, with initial exports topping 1.6 million tons.

Faced with increasing competition, particularly with the entry of British mining giant Anglo-American into the South African steel market, Iscor restructured at the beginning of the 1970s. The enactment of the Companies Act of 1973 led Iscor to adopt a more corporate organization that allowed it to be run in the manner of a private company. Nonetheless, Iscor remained a state-owned firm until the late 1980s, enjoying its dominant position—with up to 85 percent of the domestic steel market under its control—and protectionist trade policies. Because of this situation, Iscor's workforce grew to nearly 60,000, and the company faced little incentive to achieve operating efficiencies.

That changed with the end of apartheid and the South African government's announcement that it intended to privatize the vast array of government-held companies. Iscor was tapped as the first to undergo privatization because it already had 20 years of experience under a private-like organization. The government began a massive campaign promoting the public offering of Iscor, slated for 1989. When the company was listed on the Johannesburg exchange that year, more than 200,000 South Africans acquired stock in the company. The huge—and later unwieldy—mass of shareholders was meant to prevent any individual shareholder from gaining control of the company. By the end of the 1990s, however, the lack of growth in Iscor's stock was to lead to a vast streamlining of its shareholder base.

Streamlined for the New Century

The end of trade restrictions against South Africa buoyed the newly public company in the early 1990s, as Iscor's export markets reopened, spurring the company's growth. Mining exports became a primary growth engine during the decade to follow, especially with the rapid expansion of the Sishen open pit mine, where production reached 23 million tons per year—only seven million of which were destined for the domestic market. Instead, the fast-building Far East countries became a particularly strong market for the company, and by the end of the decade claimed more than one-third of the company's export sales. The United States became a major market for the company during the decade. The company also entered China, opening a $10 million iron ore storage site in Qianwan in 1994.

Yet the coming end of protectionist trade policies forced the company to take steps to improve its efficiency. This effort took on steam with the appointment of mining industry veteran Hans Smith as CEO in 1993. The company started its first job cuts in 1994, slashing nearly 2,000, primarily administrative, jobs. It also moved to increase its production efficiency, shutting down one of its two Johannesburg-area mills. In 1995, Iscor brought in management consultants to launch what it described as its "re-engineering" process, which resulted in the slashing of more than 30,000 jobs. The company went through its portfolio and identified six strategic markets: steel, coal, iron ore, titanium, zinc, and copper.

A part of that effort involved the conversion of the company's oldest Pretoria mill from its traditional carbon steel production to stainless steel production. The conversion cost the company R 180 million, and gave the company a production capacity of 600,000 tons per year. Yet Iscor's timing was off—soon after the conversion's completion, the bottom dropped out of the worldwide stainless steel market and the Pretoria mill quickly slipped into losses. Iscor quickly discovered the impossibility of turning a profit, other than at the top of the stainless steel price cycle. By 1997, the company was forced to retreat from the effort, shutting down the site.

More promising for the company was the launch of a 50–50 joint venture with the South African government's Industrial Development Corporation (IDC), which was also one of the company's largest shareholders with 11 percent of Iscor. The joint venture called for the construction of a new steel production plant at Saldanha. Work on the facility got underway in

1996, and production at the site began in 1999—in time to expose the company to a slump in the worldwide steel industry.

Smith faced a shareholder revolt, led by IDC and another major shareholder, Anglovaal Mining (Avmin), which had acquired a 15 percent stake in Iscor. Smith managed to hold firm to his position; by 2001, however, he was forced to give in to pressure to break up the company into its mining and steel components. The "unbundling" of Iscor was completed that year as the company spun off its various mining holdings into a new company, Kumba Resources, which was then listed on the Johannesburg exchange. Iscor nonetheless held on to a guaranteed supply of iron ore from the Sishen mine, at a highly advantageous price of cost plus 3 percent. Also as part of the unbundling, Iscor acquired IDC's 50 percent stake in Saldanha, a purchase completed in 2002. Soon after the unbundling, Hans Smith retired from the company; Louis van Niekerk was named to the CEO spot in his place. Iscor also found itself with a new major shareholder, in the form of LNM, parent company of Ispat, the world's number two steel producer.

The new Iscor now became a highly focused steel operation, with plants in Vanderbijlpark and Saldanha, focused on flat steel products, and Newcastle and Vereeniging, focused on long steel products. The company's long re-engineering process had meanwhile transformed it into one of the world's lowest-cost steel producers, enabling it to compete strongly—and profitably—on the depressed worldwide steel market. At the same time, the new Iscor had shed its past association with Afrikaner nationalism and, with a management reflecting the diversity of post-apartheid South Africa, the company prepared to claim a prominent position in the world steel market.

Principal Subsidiaries

Collect-A-Can (Pty) Ltd. (60%); Consolidated Wire Industries (50%); Dunswart Iron and Steel Works Ltd.; Dunswart Properties (Pty) Ltd.; Iscor Balaton Buildings Systems (Pty) Ltd.; Iscor Berlin (Pty) Ltd.; Iscor Investments BV; Macsteel International (50%); Newcastle and Vereeniging; Saldanha Steel (Pty) Ltd.; Steelforge (Pty) Ltd.; Suprachem (Pty) Ltd.; Vanderbijlpark; Vantin (Pty) Ltd.; Vicva Investments Nine (Pty) Ltd.; Yskor Landgoed; Yskor Landgoed (Pty) Ltd.; Yskor Newcastle Grondbesit Ltd.

Principal Competitors

Cargill, Inc.; Nippon Steel Corporation; Arcelor; Kobe Steel Ltd.; Pohang Iron and Steel Company; United States Steel Corporation; Bhuwalka Steel Industries Ltd.; Scaw Metals; Highveld Steel and Vanadium Corporation.

Further Reading

"Iscor Plans to Stay Local," *Africa News Service,* February 8, 2002.
"Iscor Shareholders Keep the Faith As Steel Giant Falters," *Business Times,* February 9, 1997.
"Iscor's Shares Surge Since Unbundling," *Africa News Service,* February 6, 2002.
McNulty, Andrew, "Now Iscor Wants to Turn Its Share into a Restructure Story," *Financial Mail,* March 9, 2001.
Schuettler, Darren, "Battle Lines Drawn at Iscor," *Mail & Guardian,* June 11, 2001.
Witherall, Raoul, "Improvement at Iscor Steel," *Steel Times International,* April 2002.

—M.L. Cohen

ISUZU

Isuzu Motors, Ltd.

26-1 Minami-Oi 6-chome
Shinagawa-ku
Tokyo 140
Japan
Telephone: +81-3-5471-1141
Fax: +81-3-5471-1043
Web site: http://www.isuzu.co.jp

Public Company
Incorporated: 1937 as Tokyo Motors, Inc.
Employees: 26,234
Sales: $12.05 billion (2002)
Stock Exchanges: Tokyo OTC
Ticker Symbol: ISUZF (ADRs)
NAIC: 333924 Industrial Trucks, Tractor, Trailer, and
    Stacker Machinery Manufacturing; 336111
    Automobile Manufacturing; 336211 Motor Vehicle
    Body Manufacturing; 336399 All Other Motor
    Vehicle Parts Manufacturing (pt)

One of the largest producers of medium- and heavy-duty trucks in the world, Isuzu Motors, Ltd. also produces sport utility vehicles, pickups, and diesel engines. Isuzu ventured into the passenger car market in the 1980s, but pulled out in 1991 after its passenger line dragged the company into heavy losses. With help from partial owner General Motors (GM), Isuzu returned to profitability in the mid-1990s, mainly by concentrating on its strong truck and diesel engine expertise. Becoming something of a manufacturing subsidiary of GM, Isuzu supplemented its strong Asian sales by building small trucks and components for distribution by General Motors. However, the Asian economic recession of the late 1990s, combined with declining truck sales in the United States, drove the company deep into debt, and in the early years of the 21st century Isuzu was forced to undertake a series of radical restructuring programs, in the hopes of reestablishing itself as a major, and profitable, truck manufacturer in the global automobile marketplace.

Early History

Isuzu Motors has its origin in a 1916 diversification plan undertaken by the Tokyo Ishikawajima Shipbuilding and Engineering Company. The company, established after the Meiji Restoration to build heavy ships on Ishikawajima Island near Tokyo, hoped to insulate itself from cyclical downturns in the shipbuilding industry. Tokyo Ishikawajima initiated the venture as a partnership with the Tokyo Gas and Electric Industrial Company, which had the engineering expertise necessary to design vehicles. In fact, Tokyo Gas produced its first vehicle, the Type A truck, in 1918, using engines from Tokyo Ishikawajima. The partnership manufactured a variety of designs under license from the English firm Wolseley, including the model A9 car, which went into production in Japan in 1922. In 1929 the enterprise was incorporated separately as Ishikawajima Automobile Manufacturing, Ltd.

The company developed an air-cooled diesel engine in 1934. Its pioneering efforts in this area established the automotive group as a leader in diesel technologies during the 1930s. Through its association with Tokyo Ishikawajima and Tokyo Gas, the company became a supplier to the military. Under a government mobilization scheme in 1937, the automotive interests of Tokyo Ishikawajima and Tokyo Gas were formally merged into a new company called Tokyo Motors. Mass production of the air-cooled diesel engine began that year.

World War II and Postwar Recovery

In 1938 Tokyo Motors began production of a truck under a new nameplate, Isuzu—Japanese for "50 bells." By this time, however, the military had gained control of the government and launched a war against China. As a result, Tokyo Motors came under government production plans and much of its output was earmarked for the military. In 1939 Tokyo Motors developed a new diesel model, the DA40, representing another advance in the company's diesel technologies. But by 1942, the United States and Britain were at war with Japan. With the war raging and the economy operating under emergency conditions, the operations of Tokyo Motors were split up to effect greater rationalization of the automotive industry. The company's truck business was spun off into a new company called Hino Heavy Industries (later Hino

Company Perspectives:

Three pillars form the foundation of the Isuzu philosophy: Environmental performance to lay the groundwork for reliability; economic advantages to make reliability cost-effective; and global quality standards to foster further development—with these three guidelines, Isuzu strives to meet the needs of the next generation. The goal is to be the first to develop and deliver excellent products that form the backbone of the distribution industry and to offer tools for efficient management based on these products. ISUZU delivers the ultimate in reliability through performance.

Motors). Tokyo Motors continued to operate as a frame manufacturer, but resumed production of engines in 1943.

A year later, Japan was exposed to bombing raids. As a military resource located in a major industrial center, Tokyo Motors was exposed to these raids. The company's production was completely disrupted until the war ended in September 1945. Yet Tokyo Motors was quick to recover from the war and resumed production before the end of the year. In 1946 the company introduced a new diesel truck called the TX80. This product helped Tokyo Motors fund major investments in its facilities and expand the scope of its product research.

The company changed its name to Isuzu Motors, Ltd. in 1949. Like many other Japanese companies that had emerged from the war, Isuzu went back into the business of supplying the military, but this time the customer was the U.S. Army. These large, stable supply agreements were instrumental in helping Isuzu recapitalize and grow. The company became an important resource for the Americans, particularly in late 1950, after hostilities erupted on the Korean Peninsula. Isuzu supplied a variety of trucks and other industrial products to the forces fighting North Korean aggression, helping to further advance the company's position in the diesel engine market. After an armistice was concluded in 1953, Isuzu reestablished licensing agreements with the British. The company signed an agreement to build automobiles designed by the Rootes Group (later named Talbot, and part of the French firm PSA). Under the terms of the agreement, Isuzu manufactured the Hillman Minx.

In 1959 Isuzu introduced a new two-ton N-series truck called the Elf. This was followed in 1961 by an attempt to equip an Isuzu automobile with a small diesel engine. While economical and reliable, the diesel Bellel car was uncomely, noisy, and, ultimately, a commercial failure. Consumers clearly favored a more cosmopolitan, if less practical, car. In 1962 Isuzu opened a new factory at Fujisawa. With expanded production capacity, the company introduced the Bellett automobile in 1963, followed by the Florian model in 1967. The next year Isuzu rolled out the sporty two-door 117 Coupe, a luxury model resembling the Ford Mustang. In 1970 Isuzu introduced two new trucks, the medium-sized Forward (named for its forward control) and a 12-ton diesel model.

Alliance with General Motors in the 1970s

Although Isuzu was a recognized leader in the truck market, its rapid development of new models had left it financially weakened. When it appeared to the company's bankers that the market would be unable to support Isuzu's new product line, they began negotiations with the company's competitors, hoping to arrange a merger of Isuzu with a more stable firm. Although companies such as Fuji Heavy Industries, Mitsubishi Corporation, and Toyota Motor Corporation were probably approached, it was General Motors that emerged with the greatest interest in Isuzu. The automotive giant was impressed with Isuzu's promise in export markets in the United States and Asia and hoped to include the company in its own global strategies. In 1971 General Motors purchased a 34.2 percent share of Isuzu. As part of its marketing tie-up with General Motors, Isuzu's KB pickup truck was sold through GM dealerships in the United States beginning in 1972. In 1974 General Motors employed Isuzu to manufacture the Kadett, a model designed by its German Opel subsidiary, under the Isuzu nameplate as the Bellett Gemini.

Isuzu introduced a fuel-efficient direct-injected diesel engine in 1974 in two new truck models, the Forward SBR and Forward JBR. Rising fuel prices made these models especially popular with inflation-weary consumers in Japan. General Motors saw the fuel efficiency of Isuzu models as a distinct competitive advantage in the American market. In 1976 it began importing the Gemini into the United States as the Buick Opel. Few consumers suspected that the German design, sold through the dealerships of an American company, was actually manufactured in Japan. But, as GM had suspected, the Gemini/Opel was an attractive alternative to gas-hungry American models, particularly as a second household car. In this role, the car displaced competitors such as Toyota, Datsun, and Volkswagen. Isuzu gained additional growth in the American market with a diesel-powered pickup sold in the United States as the Chevrolet Luv beginning in 1977. Also that year, Isuzu delved back into the diesel car market in Japan with a new Florian sedan.

The energy crisis took a rising toll on GM models in the United States, including those built by Isuzu. A consumer revolt against little, underpowered vehicles such as the Opel, Ford Pinto, and Gremlin placed Isuzu in a declining market at the wrong time. Despite a short-lived spike in fuel prices in 1979, the Isuzu product line fell increasingly out of step with American tastes. Dismayed by the poor quality of many American models, consumers were drawn to Toyota, Honda Motor Co., and Nissan in growing numbers.

Isuzu's production for General Motors declined steadily from 1979 to 1981. Responding to what it felt was a loss of synergy with GM, Isuzu established its own dealer network in the United States, American Isuzu Motors, Inc., which technically operated in competition with GM at the wholesale level. Commensurate with the formation of the new group, Isuzu undertook a complete design change of its Luv truck. General Motors' CEO Roger Smith laid a bombshell on Isuzu Chairman T. Okamoto in a landmark 1981 meeting. He announced that Isuzu had lost its favorable potential as a global partner for GM. But rather than abandon their partnership, Smith asked Okamoto to help GM buy a stake in Honda, one of Japan's fastest growing auto manufacturers.

Okamoto was stunned by the sudden change of events, but could not refuse the request of Isuzu's single largest shareholder. Ultimately, Honda expressed no interest in an alliance

Key Dates:

1937: Under a government mobilization scheme, the automotive interests of Tokyo Ishikawajima and Tokyo Gas are formally merged into a new company called Tokyo Motors, Inc.

1938: Tokyo Motors begins production of a truck under a new nameplate, Isuzu—Japanese for "50 bells."

1949: The company changes its name to Isuzu Motors, Ltd.

1971: General Motors purchases a 34.2 percent share of Isuzu.

1987: Isuzu and Subaru enter into a joint venture to build an automobile production plant in Lafayette, Indiana.

1998: Isuzu and General Motors form a joint company, DMAX-Ltd., for the production of diesel engines in the United States.

2002: Isuzu announces intention to terminate operations at Lafayette, Indiana facility by 2004.

with General Motors, seeing its own prospects for global growth as excellent even without such a partnership. General Motors settled instead for a 5 percent stake in Suzuki Motors—a small consolation. General Motors may have intended to use this new partnership to leverage Suzuki against Isuzu, hoping the two companies would compete for the right to supply GM. Whether or not that was the case, General Motors had little choice but to expand its relationship with Isuzu. The company established new contracts with GM, building a model called the Storm under an entirely new nameplate, Geo. Once again part of General Motors' international strategy, Isuzu built new joint production facilities in the United Kingdom and Australia. Isuzu also concluded a long-term marketing agreement with Suzuki and Yanase & Company, under which Isuzu provided parts for assembly by Suzuki.

In an effort to raise consciousness of the Isuzu name and boost sales of the company's trucks in the United States, Isuzu launched a revolutionary ad campaign featuring the comedian David Leisure. The performer was portrayed as a spokesman named Joe Isuzu who made outrageously false claims about Isuzu products. A series of subtitles provided factual corrections as well as punch lines to Leisure's statements. The campaign easily could have failed had it not been for the comedian's wry delivery and obviously contrived smile. In one ad, Joe Isuzu concludes by saying, "May lightning strike me if I'm lying." At this point the actor is incinerated by a blinding light, leaving only a puff of smoke. Seconds later, the irrepressible spokesman falls out of the air and into the bed of an Isuzu truck. The ads were very effective in promoting Isuzu and launching Leisure's career, but they had only a limited impact on Isuzu's sales. (The company experienced no gain in passenger car sales.) The situation was exacerbated by appreciation of the yen, in effect, artificially raising the price of Isuzu products.

Global Joint Ventures in the 1980s

To eliminate the impact of currency fluctuations and stabilize product demand forecasts, Isuzu began studying the possibility of locating a factory in the United States. Other Japanese

manufacturers, including Toyota and Honda, had already established American factories. But for Isuzu, the start-up costs were high and the company's sales volumes were too small to justify the badly needed move. Fortunately for Isuzu, Subaru, the automobile manufacturing subsidiary of Fuji Heavy Industries, suffered the same problem. The two companies operated in slightly different areas of the American market, so a joint venture between them was plausible. Isuzu and Subaru agreed to build, jointly, a factory in Lafayette, Indiana, in 1987. The facility went into operation two years later, providing Isuzu with a steady supply of American-built vehicles for distribution through its American sales organization.

Isuzu's export sales surpassed three million units in 1986, but again, much of this growth occurred in Asian markets and was accounted for in truck sales. That year, Isuzu formed a joint venture with Kawasaki Heavy Industries called IK Coach, Ltd. to manufacture coach bodies. Building on its Asian franchises, Isuzu established a subsidiary in Thailand to manufacture engines and a joint venture in Australia with General Motors the following year. These efforts helped to establish Isuzu as the world's largest truck manufacturer (on a per-unit basis) in 1987. The company marked several technological advances that year, including the development of a ceramic Adiabatic Engine and the NAVI electronically controlled transmission system, which was the first of its type.

Isuzu completed several other joint business arrangements in 1990, including an agreement with P.T. Gaya Motor of Indonesia to build pickup trucks in that country. This factory joined Isuzu plants in other developing country markets, including Thailand, Malaysia, and Egypt. The company also entered into agreements to market Isuzu's multipurpose vehicles in Japan through the Jusco Car Life Company and to handle sales of GM Opel models and Volvo trucks in Japan. These expansion efforts helped Isuzu to maintain its position as the world's largest truck maker. But the company's balance sheet indicated a high price for this leadership. The company lost $500 million in 1991 and was faltering financially.

Refocusing in the 1990s

This deeply concerned General Motors, which was unable to abandon its investment in Isuzu because of plummeting market value. Isuzu was GM's main source of imported light commercial vehicles and heavy trucks, and 37.5 percent of its shares were held by the American company. Isuzu continued to lose money into 1992, prompting the company's board to appeal to General Motors for help. As a condition, GM asked that one of its strategic planning experts, Donald T. Sullivan, be installed as executive vice-president of operations, with responsibility for revamping Isuzu's business, engineering, and manufacturing plans. This was an unprecedented move. No Japanese manufacturer had ever involved a non-Japanese speaking manager in such a high position, or given an American such wide-ranging latitude to rewrite the business plan.

Sullivan's first moves were to raise production at the company's Subaru-Isuzu Automotive facility in Indiana. He slimmed down the Isuzu's line of commercial vehicles, hoping to realize greater production efficiencies from fewer models and eliminate cannibalization within the product line. In a retrenchment strategy virtually unknown in Japan, Sullivan summarily reduced capital budgets by 12.5 percent, hoping to eliminate waste through budget-induced cost savings. Stopping short of employee layoffs, a tactic that was seen to breed only employee disloyalty in Japan, Sullivan ordered a reduction in Isuzu's temporary workforce.

Perhaps most dramatic was Sullivan's conclusion that Isuzu was not profitably competitive in the automobile market. Rather than continue to invest huge sums in an unpromising segment of the market, Sullivan recommended that Isuzu exit the automobile market and concentrate on what it did best. For Isuzu, this came down to only three products: trucks, recreational vehicles, and engines. Because GM relied on Isuzu for production of its Geo Storm model, the response back at GM was uneven. "The marketing guys at Chevrolet were disappointed," *Forbes* quoted Sullivan in 1994. "But the business people at GM looking at the financial liability at Isuzu had a different feeling."

These efforts appeared to have a positive effect on Isuzu's business, stemming losses while reversing a gradual decline in sales. By the end of Isuzu's 1993 fiscal year, the company reported a loss of only $39 million. Sullivan, however, had even higher hopes for the company. "I am proud of our success at Isuzu," he told *Forbes*. "But we are still defining success as eliminating failure." Although the 1994 fiscal year ended with even greater gains, Isuzu still carried a heavy debt burden, at $7.4 billion.

The actions taken by Isuzu under the tutelage of Donald Sullivan once again placed Isuzu thoroughly within General Motors' global strategy. Although GM lost its supplier of Geo Storms, it shifted its focus to incorporating Isuzu's expertise in other areas. For example, the General Motors European division began buying more Isuzu diesel engines. Michael Nylin, brought by Sullivan from General Motors to help lead Isuzu's strategic planning, tried to match Isuzu's product development with GM's needs. One result of that effort was a joint venture between Isuzu and General Motors to produce light trucks. Begun in 1994 in Janesville, Wisconsin, the venture called for Isuzu to supply the cab and chassis, shipping them from Japan, and General Motors to produce the gasoline engine, a technology in which GM had more expertise than Isuzu. Sullivan also hoped Isuzu would fit into GM's global strategy by providing General Motors with an entree into Asia markets. GM hoped to piggyback their passenger cars on Isuzu's strong sales of pickups in Asia by convincing Asian car dealers to sell them side by side.

The company's future had come to depend on its ties to other auto manufacturers, particularly General Motors, and on its ability to mark gains in the sales of its own products. Chief among these were the F-series (Forward) medium-duty trucks, the C-series heavy trucks, tractor trucks, and N-series (Elf) pickups. Light-duty trucks to be manufactured in China were planned in 1993 when Isuzu agreed to a joint venture with Jiangxi Automobile Factory and ITOCHU. The company expanded its relationships with other carmakers when it signed an agreement with Nissan in 1994 to cross-supply commercial vehicles, particularly Isuzu's two- and three-ton Elf trucks and Nissan's Caravan.

The company's progress in the United States, however, was hurt in 1996 when *Consumer Reports* judged the Isuzu Trooper "not acceptable." The Consumers Union (CU), publisher of *Consumer Reports,* issued a safety alert about the sport utility vehicle, claiming the Trooper "showed a pronounced propensity to roll over during our avoidance-maneuver tests." Isuzu disputed the report's findings; it pointed out that the Trooper met all applicable federal safety standards and that the company had received no reports of rollover accidents involving the Trooper. It also denounced the Consumers Union test as unreliable. The Consumers Union stood by its claims, but its petition for a defect investigation to the National Highway Traffic Safety Administration (NHTSA) was denied. The NHTSA explained: "Because of deficiencies in the CU short course testing and since none of the other information reviewed by [NHTSA] indicates that a safety-related defect exists, there is no reasonable possibility that . . . a safety-related defect in the subject vehicles would be [found]." In mid-1997 Isuzu filed a lawsuit against the Consumers Union, alleging defamation and product disparagement. Although the company sought millions of dollars in damages, Isuzu presented the suit as a means to restore the company's good name.

Entering 1998 the company's future was uncertain because of the economic crisis in Asia. In November 1997 slow sales in Japan and constricting markets in Thailand led Isuzu to close its Thai factory, which had produced 120,000 trucks in 1996. With Asian truck sales the backbone of Isuzu's business, the company was greatly threatened by the economic turmoil in the region.

Entering the 21st Century

In order to survive in this troubled economic climate, Isuzu began to seek ways to strengthen its ties with General Motors. Since the company's diesel engine manufacturing operations offered it the greatest opportunity for long-term growth, Isuzu entered into a joint venture with GM in September 1998, to begin mass-producing diesel engines in the United States. The new company, dubbed DMAX-Ltd., was formed with an overall investment of $300 million, with the aim of turning out 100,000 engines a year by 2004. The new, 650,000-square-foot manufacturing plant in Moraine, Ohio, the most state-of-the-art facility of its kind in North America, would allow Isuzu to capitalize on its award-winning 4JX1-TC direct-injection diesel engine. Although Isuzu produced more than 800,000 diesel engines worldwide in 1998, it hoped to be able to increase this figure to 1.8 million by 2005, with the aim of becoming the world's largest diesel engine manufacturer. In December 1998 GM also invested an additional $456 million in Isuzu, increasing its stake in the Japanese automaker to 49 percent.

However, in the short term the company was still in a serious slump, and significant cost-cutting measures became inevitable. To this end, the company launched a series of restructuring plans beginning in December 1998. The most comprehensive came in May 2001, when the company announced its intention to reduce its workforce by nearly 10,000 employees over a three-year period, in addition to consolidating a number of its divisions and subsidiaries. The most radical measure, however, was the company's decision to transfer its principle manufacturing operations to Thailand, where production costs were significantly lower than in Japan. At the same time, Isuzu increased its collaboration with GM even further, forging an agreement that would enable the company to begin supplying GM with diesel engines. In order to meet this goal, the company increased the production capacity of its operations in Poland, which was already responsible for the bulk of its diesel engine manufacturing, from 100,000 to 200,000 units annually.

These radical streamlining efforts were intended to reverse the company's recent poor financial performance, with the aim of achieving profits of ¥30 billion by 2004. In spite of these measures, however, Isuzu still suffered losses of ¥23.6 billion for the first half of 2001, compared to a ¥22.1 billion loss for the same period in the previous year, and in November 2001 the company was forced to slash an additional 3,300 jobs. During this difficult period Isuzu even began to contemplate shutting down its truck manufacturing operations in Lafayette, Indiana. In January 2002, with the hope of further streamlining its operations, Isuzu merged its Japanese bus-manufacturing business with Hino Motors.

In spite of a continued drop in sales during the early years of the 21st century, there were some signs of recovery. Although the company still lost ¥43 billion in fiscal 2002, this figure marked a significant improvement over the previous year's losses of ¥67 billion. At the same time, a 30 percent increase in domestic sales allowed the company to keep its Kawasaki plant operational. Still, the losses were of grave concern to General Motors, which began to reconsider its relationship with the troubled Japanese firm. Although initially reluctant to invest further in the beleaguered company, GM eventually set its sights on acquiring some of Isuzu's key businesses. In August 2002 GM announced plans to acquire a 60 percent share in Isuzu's Polish diesel engine operations, in addition to increasing its stake in the DMAX Ltd. Business from 40 to 60 percent.

Unfortunately, this fresh infusion of capital could do nothing to reverse the company's fortunes in the present, and losses for the fiscal year ending in March 2003 were in excess of $1 billion. By late 2002 Isuzu launched its fourth restructuring scheme in five years, and even began to consider dropping out of the truck business altogether. After watching its North American sales drop 36 percent in one year, the company formally announced its intention to terminate its U.S. manufacturing operations by the end of 2004. In spite of these cutbacks, Isuzu remained hopeful that it would be able to remain a player in the lucrative U.S. market by importing less expensive trucks from its Thailand plant. Although still mired in debt in the summer of 2003, Isuzu had high hopes that its revised business strategy, with a heavier emphasis on promoting its diesel technology, would soon restore the company to profitability.

Principal Subsidiaries

Isuzu Motors Asia Ltd.; Isuzu (China) Holding Co. Ltd.; Quingling Motors Co. Ltd.; Jiangling-Isuzu Motors Co. Ltd.; Guangzhou Isuzu Bus Co. Ltd.; Isuzu (Shanghai) Tradetech Co. Ltd.; Beijing Beiling Special Automobile Co. Ltd.; Isuzu Philippines Corporation; Isuzu Autoparts Manufacturing Corporation; Isuzu Vietnam Co., Ltd. (IVC); P.T. Mesin Isuzu Indonesia (MII); P.T. Pantja Motor (PM); P.T. Astra Isuzu Casting Company (AICC); Isuzu Motors Co., (Thailand) Ltd. (IMCT); Tri Petch Isuzu Sales Co., Ltd. (TIS); Isuzu Engine Manufacturing Co., (Thailand) Ltd. (IEMT); Isuzu Technical Center of Asia Co., Ltd. (ITA); Thai International Die Making Co. Ltd. (TID); IT Forging (Thailand) Co., Ltd. (ITF); Isuzu (Thailand) Co., Ltd.; Isuzu Operations (Thailand) Co., Ltd.; Malaysian Truck and Bus Sdn. Bhd.; Anadolu Isuzu Otomotiv Sanayi Ve Ticaret A.S.; Isuzu Motors Europe Ltd.; Isuzu Truck (UK) Ltd.; Isuzu Motors German GmbH (IMG); Isuzu Motors Polska Sp zo.o. (Poland); General Motors Egypt S.A.E.; American Isuzu Motors Inc. (U.S.A.); Isuzu Motors America Inc. (U.S.A.); Subaru-Isuzu Automotive Inc. (SIA); DMAX, Ltd.; General Motors Isuzu Commercial Truck, LLC (GMICT); Isuzu-General Motors Australia Ltd. (IGM); International Auto Co., Ltd.; Taiwan Isuzu Motors Co., Ltd.

Principal Competitors

Ford Motor Company; Honda Motor Co., Ltd; Toyota Motor Corporation.

Further Reading

Abrahams, Paul, "Isuzu's Restructuring Plan," *Financial Times* (London), December 28, 1998, p. 18.

Eisenstodt, Gale, "Sullivan's Travels," *Forbes,* March 28, 1994, pp. 75–76.

Evanoff, Ted, "Isuzu Desires Boost in U.S. Market," *Indianapolis Star,* January 29, 2002.

Ibison, David, "Isuzu Losses Put New Pressure on GM," *Financial Times* (London), May 27, 2002, p. 15.

"Isuzu Trooper Safety: Much Talk, Little Action," *Consumer Reports,* November 1996, pp. 6–7.

O'Dell, John, "Isuzu to Cut U.S. Vehicle Production," *Los Angeles Times,* March 11, 2003, Business, Part 3, p. 4.

Schreffler, Roger, "Interview: Takeshi Inoh, Pres. & Chief Operating Officer, Isuzu Motors Ltd: Thrusting Toward Top Spot in Diesel Engines," *Global News Wire,* July 26, 1999.

Shirouzu, Norihiko, "Japan's Firms Revamp amid Asian Crisis," *Wall Street Journal,* November 6, 1997, p. A18.

Sugawara, Sandra, "GM Boosts Its Stake in Isuzu," *Washington Post,* December 19, 1998, p. D10.

—John Simley
—updates: Susan Windisch Brown, Erin Brown

Janus Capital Group Inc.

100 Fillmore St., Ste. 300
Denver, Colorado 80206
U.S.A.
Telephone: (303) 333-3863
Fax: (303) 336-7497
Web site: http://www.janus.com

Public Company
Incorporated: 1998 as Stilwell Financial Inc.
Employees: 1,450
Total Assets: $3.32 billion (2002)
Stock Exchanges: New York
Ticker Symbol: JNS
NAIC: 523920 Portfolio Management; 525990 Other
Financial Vehicles; 551112 Offices of Other Holding
Companies

Janus Capital Group Inc. (formerly Stilwell Financial Inc.) is a holding company for businesses that offer a variety of asset management, shareowner, software, and related financial services to registered investment companies, retail investors, institutions, and individuals. The company's subsidiaries and affiliates operate in North America, Europe, and Asia. Janus's primary subsidiaries include Janus Capital Management; INTECH; Perkins, Wolf, McDonnell and Company; Bay Isle Financial; and DST Systems.

KCSI and the Mutual Funds and Financial Services Markets: 1960s–80s

The history of Janus begins in 1962 when Kansas City Southern Industries, Inc. (KCSI) entered the emerging mutual fund industry by acquiring Television Shares Management, a mutual fund management company. The company later changed its name to Supervised Investors Services and grew steadily through product expansion and diversification, then evolved into Kemper Financial Services in 1970.

KCSI's entry into the financial services industry afforded the 75-year-old railroad company the opportunity to bring its data processing resources to asset management firms needing more efficient record keeping and information technology systems. In 1968 the company created Data SysTance (later known as DST Systems, Inc.) and began marketing the data processing technology KCSI had developed for the railroad industry. DST became a leading provider of record keeping services and technology for mutual fund firms; as an anchor of KCSI's financial services division, it contributed greatly to its early growth.

KCSI's strategy as it entered the 1980s was to build its financial services division by developing an effective presence in each of the three major segments of the industry: product creation, product distribution, and product technology. In 1979, having already established a strong subsidiary in technology, it broadened its product distribution capabilities by acquiring Pioneer Western, a life insurance and mutual fund company with a nationwide sales force. Pioneer grew rapidly; within five years its earnings had increased more than 240 percent and its sales force had expanded by 50 percent. In 1984, KCSI sought to create a significant presence for itself in product creation with the purchase of a majority interest in Janus Capital Corporation for $11 million. It acquired an additional 1.6 million Janus shares a year later.

Janus Capital Corporation's history also dated back to the 1960s. Thomas Bailey had started Janus Capital Corporation in Denver, Colorado, in 1969 with a few hundred thousand dollars. Bailey's decision to locate his company in Denver rather than New York was deliberate. Bailey wanted to be free from the bounds and conventions of Wall Street—to be able to "think outside the box," according to the company's web site. From the start he emphasized a research-intensive investment approach, focusing on the merits of individual companies rather than market trends. The company engaged in its own proprietary research, building a detailed financial model for each company it followed. By the time KCSI purchased Janus, the latter had earned a reputation for its unconventional style, its preference for technology companies, and its wild success. The no-load mutual fund it advised had assets of $470 million.

Pioneer and Janus soon collaborated to introduce the IDEX series of load funds in a joint venture combining Pioneer's distribution system and the investment expertise of Janus. IDEX

Company Perspectives:

Based in Denver, Colorado, Janus Capital Group Inc. is a leading asset manager offering individual and institutional clients complementary asset management disciplines through the firm's global distribution network.

expanded into a successful family of funds, managed by Janus and distributed by Pioneer's sales force.

The 1990s: The Formation of Stilwell Financial Inc.

KCSI acquired initial ownership of a second mutual fund company, Berger Associates, in 1992. Two years later, it increased its stake in Berger to 80 percent. Mutual fund trailblazer Bill Berger had founded his company in 1974, with an emphasis on growth-oriented funds. As part of KCSI, Berger introduced additional funds, such as its Small Cap and Mid-Cap Value Funds, and its Information Technology Fund.

With the full acquisition of Berger in 1994, Landon Rowland, KCSI's chairman and chief executive officer, began taking a more active role in the company's money management business. Rowland, a wealthy Harvard-educated lawyer who had joined KCSI in 1980 as a vice-president, would soon clash with Janus's Bailey and other managers, as a result of his aspirations.

Throughout the bull market of the 1990s, Janus funds were marked by their aggressive growth style; fund managers made outsized bets on fast-growing technology companies with little regard to price. By 1997 when KCSI announced its intention to separate its financial services division (consisting of DST, Janus, Berger, and IDEX) from its transportation operations, Janus was generating 85 percent of its parent company's operating profit. It ranked in the nation's top mutual fund families, had $166 billion under management, and four million client accounts. From late 1999 to late 2000 shareholder accounts increased 62 percent from 3.7 million to 6 million, and Janus more than doubled its workforce. It was the year's top-selling mutual fund group for both 1999 and 2000.

KCSI announced its decision in 1998 to form a holding company for its financial services division, to be named Stilwell Financial after a Kansas railroad baron. The management of each of its financial subsidiaries would remain intact and day-to-day operations would remain largely unchanged. In 1998, KCSI sold its interest in IDEX and acquired Nelson Money Managers Plc, a U.K.-based firm that worked with private companies and public agencies in retirement planning. Through Nelson, Stilwell gained an opportunity to build a distribution channel in the United Kingdom.

KCSI's plan was to spin off Stilwell Financial, Inc., consisting of high performer Janus and KCSI's three smaller investment management businesses, Berger, Nelson, and DST. Yet Janus managers pressed the company to spin off Janus—which had become the nation's fifth largest mutual fund company—separately. They argued that with Janus contributing 90 percent of Stilwell's assets and 95 percent of its revenue, it would maximize shareholder value as a freestanding independent com-

pany. KCSI's executives rejected the idea and the acrimony between the two companies' chief executives intensified to the point where KCSI officials were not allowed inside Janus's Denver headquarters without prior clearance. KCSI, in turn, spelled out possible steps for firing Bailey in financial documents filed with the Securities and Exchange Commission in 1999.

Jim Craig, second in command at Janus, departed in August 1999. He had been with the company since 1983 and left to create a large foundation run by his wife amid speculation that his departure was really motivated by the forthcoming spinoff. Craig's departure was a great loss to Janus. Along with Bailey, he was responsible for the creation of a remarkable corporate culture at Janus, one based on teamwork and camaraderie.

The 2000s: The Spinoff and Market Downfall

In June 2000 federal regulators gave their approval to the tax-free spinoff and within two weeks of the initial public offering (IPO), Stilwell shares had risen 18 percent. In July, Standard & Poor's added Stilwell Financial to its S&P 500 index. Yet neither Janus nor KCSI fared well as the year wore on. KCSI's stock price dropped by half and Stilwell's by about 20 percent, both paradoxically because of their relationship to Janus. Shareholders who knew KCSI's performance to be tied to that of Janus jumped ship, not believing the company could stand on its own, while Stilwell suffered the effects of Janus's suddenly lagging fund performance.

By early December 2000 Stilwell's shares had fallen 28 percent, more than double the S&P 500's overall drop. Throughout October and November it had shed more than $1 billion a day in assets as sliding stock prices cut into the value of its holdings. For its part, Janus suffered a pounding as the technology bubble burst; it posted a dismal performance in 2000 with 14 of its 16 equity funds suffering a decline. Still, the company retained its title as the nation's best-selling mutual fund family in 2000, topping its 1999 investment inflows.

Yet from the start of 2000 through 2001, Janus became the emblem of the "tech wreck." It fared worse than many of its peers because its assets were not widely diversified and invested largely in growth equities. Further compounding its decline were its large stakes in Enron and Tyco. In 2001 Janus was forced to cut its staff in half; it laid off 15 percent more of its workforce in early 2002. The fund, which lost its four-star rating from mutual fund research firm Morningstar for the first time since 1985, also began to shift its focus from technology to the pharmaceutical, media, and financial services sectors. Janus unloaded some of its tech shares in favor of stocks such as Boeing while adding more "value" funds to its roster along with blue chips such as Citigroup, Exxon, and Pfizer. Through it all, Janus investors remained remarkably loyal.

Janus assets fell $90 billion in 2001, with most of the decline due to plunging stock prices and investors pulling their fund shares. Even founder Thomas Bailey appeared to be jumping ship; in late 2001 he arranged to sell his remaining 6.2 percent stake in the company to Stilwell under a provision negotiated in 1984 that he receive significantly more than the stock's current market value. After the sale, Stilwell owned 97.8 percent of Janus.

Key Dates:

1962: Kansas City Southern Industries (KCSI) acquires Television Shares Management.
1968: KCSI founds Data SysTance, later known as DST Systems, Inc.
1969: Thomas Bailey founds Janus Capital Corporation.
1974: Bill Berger founds Berger Financial Group LLC.
1979: KCSI acquires Pioneer Western.
1984: KCSI buys a two-thirds stake in Janus Capital Corporation and Janus Management Corporation.
1994: Berger sells Berger Financial Group to KCSI.
1998: KCSI forms Stilwell Financial Inc. as a holding company for its financial services division.
2000: KCSI completes the spinoff of Stilwell; Stilwell begins trading as an independent public company.
2001: Stilwell buys out Bailey's remaining shares in Janus.
2003: Stilwell merges into Janus and the new company is named Janus Capital Group Inc.

Berger, too, was hurt by the market freefall that began in 2000. The fund, which also specialized in growth companies, attempted to attract customers with the idea of dollar cost averaging—advising them to continue to invest steadily regardless of market swings to remain ahead of the curve. To help lower-income investors do so, it slashed its monthly minimum investment. In 1998 Berger acquired Bay Isle Financial LLC, a San Francisco-based asset manager, and in 2002 it acquired Enhanced Investment Technologies Inc. (INTECH), a company with more than a decade's experience in using a mathematical investment strategy called quantitative analysis. INTECH's innovative system capitalized on the random nature of stock price movement rather than relying on estimates of future stock performance. In mid-2002 Berger Financial Group filed with the SEC to launch three new funds managed by INTECH.

By the summer of 2002 when Bailey retired from the company he had built into the sixth largest American mutual fund house, assets for Janus—which had peaked at $330 billion in 1999—had declined to less than $200 billion. In order to retain top managers, Stilwell rewarded key Janus employees with a percentage of their company's shares and appointed Helen Young Hayes as Bailey's successor. According to KCSI executive Rowland, the markets had humbled even the most ardent backers of the New Economy. He was quoted in a July 2002 *Denver Post* article saying, "We were carried away by our confidence that we knew something our predecessors did not. For the moment, it is enough to say that we believe in these professionals and their investment strategies. We believe in their mastery of this new investment world."

By January 1, 2003, the Stilwell name had disappeared as the company merged operations with its more famous subsidiary, Janus. The new company, which was headed by new CEO and Vice-Chairman Mark Whiston, was renamed Janus Capital Group Inc. Whiston, who had worked at Janus for over a decade, had formerly served at the firm's retail and institutional services.

Principal Subsidiaries

Janus Capital Management LLC; INTECH; Perkins, Wolf, McDonnell and Company (30%); Bay Isle Financial LLC; DST Systems, Inc. (33%).

Principal Competitors

AMVESCAP; FMR Corp.; The Vanguard Group, Inc.

Further Reading

Acola, John, "Battling Egos Cloud Future at Janus," *Denver Rocky Mountain News*, September 26, 1999, p. 1G.

Davis, Mark, "Janus's Rift with Parent Company Reopened," *Denver Post*, May 2, 2000, p. C2.

Gogoi, Pallavi, "Janus Turns Over the Same Leaf," *Business Week*, September 3, 2001, p. 70.

Gonzalez, Erika, "Upstart Berger Emerges from Janus's Shadow in a Big Way," *Rocky Mountain News*, October 27, 2001, p. 1C.

Milstead, David, "Janus Founder Tom Bailey Appears to Be Unwelcome at Stilwell," *Rocky Mountain News*, March 30, 2002, p. 6C.

Svaldi, Aldo, "Investors Flee Janus Funds, but Berger Draws New Cash," *Denver Post*, July 26, 2002, p. C1.

Weiss, Miles, "Janus Shifts Focus to Spur Gains," *Washington Post*, January 20, 2002, p. H3.

—Carrie Rothburd

Karstadt Quelle AG

Theodor-Althoff-Strasse 2
D-45133
Essen
Germany
Telephone: +49-20-17271
Fax: +49-20-1727-5216
Web site: http://www.karstadtquelle.com

Public Company
Incorporated: 1920 as Rudolph Karstadt AG
Employees: 104,536
Sales: EUR 15.8 billion ($16.56 billion) (2002)
Stock Exchanges: German
Ticker Symbol: KAR
NAIC: 452110 Department Stores; 454110 Electronic
Shopping and Mail-Order Houses; 561510 Travel
Agencies; 561520 Tour Operators

Karstadt Quelle AG is the product of the 1999 merger between German retail powerhouse Karstadt Aktiengesellschaft and the Quelle Group, the largest mail-order retailer in Germany. Karstadt Quelle is the largest retail concern in Germany. Since the merger, however, Karstadt Quelle has sought to expand beyond its traditional base as a retail chain in order to withstand the vagaries of the German consumer market. It now operates in four distinct business sectors. Retail sales do remain the core of the company, as Karstadt Quelle runs 190 department stores (under the brand names Karstadt, Herties, Wetheim, Alsterhaus, and KaDeWe), as well as 280 specialty stores, such as SinnLeffers, Runners Point, WOM World of Music, and LeBuffet restaurants. But in its mail-order business, under the Quelle and Neckermann brands, Karstadt Quelle disseminates about 40 million catalogues to consumers in 17 countries. Moreover, Karstadt Quelle has emerged as a dominant force in the European travel services sector. It jointly operates Thomas Cook Group Ltd. with Deutsche Lufthansa AG. Other businesses in Karstadt Quelle's services sector provide consulting, information, and financial services. Since 2000, Karstadt Quelle has also worked to build a real estate division that manages the group's far-flung properties and develops shopping centers.

Karstadt's Mid-19th-Century Origins

Rudolph Karstadt, founder of the company and a pioneer of department store retailing in Germany, was born near Lübeck on February 16, 1856. He completed his commercial apprenticeship in Rostock and then worked in his father's textile shop in Schwerin. Rudolph soon became impatient with the business customs of the time, whereby customers generally bought items on credit, forcing merchants to set prices high as protection against nonpayment and hindering flexibility in terms of stock changes. He saw the secrets of successful retailing as low prices, cash payment, and rapid stock turnover—a revolutionary concept that caused some disagreements within the family. Finally, in 1881 Rudolph's father lent him 3,000 marks to put his ideas into practice. On May 14, 1881, Rudolph, with his brother Ernst and sister Sophie, opened a shop, Rudolph Karstadt—selling dress materials and ready-to-wear clothes—in the harbor town of Wismar. Newspaper advertisements excited local interest and ensured large crowds on the opening day. Despite the low prices, however, customers were unused to the idea of immediate payment, and monthly sales in the first year were modest. Rudolph Karstadt's brother and sister withdrew from the business at this stage, leaving him as the sole owner.

Karstadt stuck to his convictions and was soon proven right—in the second year of business monthly sales rose to 20,000 marks, and in 1884 another shop was opened in Lübeck, with a range of goods extending to household items, leather goods, and toys. Further branches were opened in Neumünster in 1888 and in Braunschweig in 1890. The business grew rapidly: the balance sheet total in 1882 was 49,000 marks, which rose to 613,000 marks in 1890, and to 1.8 million marks in 1894. Rudolph Karstadt's conception of the modern department store was perfectly in tune with the times: the increasing economic power of the middle and working classes meant that consumer goods were demanded in ever larger quantities. In founding his business, Karstadt was also in line with a broader European trend: department stores had already been successfully established in France—notably with Bon Marché, Magasins du Louvre, Sa-

---

Company Perspectives:

If you do not try to get better, you have stopped being good. That is the principle that Karstadt Quelle is committed to. Our customers, shareholders, and the public have a right to expect a great sense of responsibility and above-average service in the areas of environmental protections, social policy, and professional organizations. We are continuously trying to meet those expectations with top performances—for the benefit of all.

---

maritaine, Printemps, and Galeries Lafayette—and in England, with Whiteleys, Harrods, and Selfridges.

Karstadt's Late 19th-/Early 20th-Century Expansion

A new branch was opened in Kiel in 1893, and Karstadt, who had previously moved from Lübeck to Berlin, now moved from the capital to this rapidly growing town, a focus of imperial military expansionism. During the 1890s and the first decade of the 20th century the business continued to expand at a considerable rate: new branches were opened, established branches were extended, and in 1900 Rudolph Karstadt took over 13 stores owned by his brother Ernst, who had gotten into financial difficulties. By 1906, the 25th anniversary of the company, Rudolph Karstadt owned 24 department stores in northern Germany. In 1912 a prestigious new store was opened in Hamburg, with 10,000 square meters of sales area and a turnover of nearly seven million marks in the first year, and in 1913 Rudolph Karstadt reestablished the headquarters of the company in that city.

While Karstadt was establishing his chain of stores in northern Germany, a business run by Theodor Althoff in the western part of Germany was following a very similar course. Althoff, born in 1858, had taken over a millinery and linen shop from his mother in 1885 and had soon succeeded in expanding the business considerably, following principles similar to those espoused by Karstadt—cash payment and low prices. In 1904 Althoff opened his first department store, in Dortmund, with a sales area of 5,000 square meters, and in 1910, the 25th anniversary of the business, the enterprise consisted of 11 stores in all. The year 1912 saw the establishment of Althoff's largest store yet, in Essen, with 10,000 square meters of selling space and 53 departments.

Interwar Merger of Karstadt and Althoff

World War I put an end to the years of prosperity and expansion for both Karstadt and Althoff. People hoarded their money, and goods became increasingly scarce. The similarity of the two businesses and the need to concentrate resources during this crisis brought the two department store pioneers together for the first time in 1917. In 1919 the firms agreed on a common purchasing arrangement. In 1920 Rudolph Karstadt KG was converted into an Aktiengesellschaft—joint stock company—with founding capital of 40 million marks, based in Hamburg. Theodor Althoff was chairman of the supervisory board. A complete merger of Karstadt AG and Theodor Althoff KG followed in May of the same year, and the share capital was raised to 80 million marks; at this time Karstadt had 31 stores and Althoff 13.

The decade which followed the merger was one of rapid expansion, funded by numerous capital-raising measures. The company opened new branches and extended existing ones, as well as acquiring a number of manufacturing businesses in the furniture, textiles, and grocery sectors. EPA Einheitspreis AG, a subsidiary enterprise started by Theodor Althoff's son Heinrich, was established in 1926 following the American model of five-and-dime stores, with goods sold at four prices: 10, 25, 50, and 100 pfennigs. This business was tremendously successful, with 52 branches in Germany and a turnover of about 100 million Reichsmarks (RM) in 1932. In 1927 Karstadt acquired the 19 stores owned by M.J. Emden Söhne KG, and in 1929 a new store was opened in Berlin, one of the largest and most modern in Europe at the time, with a sales area of 37,000 square meters. Another 15 stores were added by the merger with Lindemann & Co. KG in the same year. By the time of the company's 50th anniversary, in 1931, Rudolph Karstadt AG and its subsidiaries had 89 branches and about 30,000 employees—compared with 11,500 in 1924—and a turnover of around RM 200 million.

Great Depression Threatening Karstadt's Survival

This phase of growth—conceived and carried through, it appeared, on the initiative of Hermann Schöndorff, a dominant member of the company's management board at the time—reached its climax with the construction of an impressive new headquarters in Berlin, covering 70,000 square meters. Employees in the former headquarters in Hamburg were transported to Berlin in a specially commissioned train on January 1, 1932. The plans for expansion ended in crisis, however. The national and international economic difficulties of the early 1930s, combined with debts incurred during the previous decade, brought the company into severe financial trouble. In 1931 only five of Karstadt's stores were showing any profit. Theodor Althoff died in August 1931, when the business he had helped to found was approaching collapse. In April 1933 a consortium of banks assisted in drawing up a program of reorganization in order to ensure the company's survival. All the production subsidiaries were to be divested, share capital was to be reduced from RM 80 million to RM 7.6 million, the branch network was to be reduced, and EPA Einheitspreis was to be sold. The newly built headquarters was sold in 1934, and the company's administration moved into smaller premises in Berlin.

The restructuring effected a recovery in financial terms. Karstadt then, however, had to contend with difficulties arising from the National Socialists' (Nazi) campaign against department stores, involving boycotts and restrictive legislation, as some department stores had Jewish owners and were seen as representing a threat to the specialty German retail tradition. Despite these obstacles the company reached an economic high point before World War II: in 1939 it had 67 branches, a total sales area approaching 260,000 square meters, and a workforce of 21,000. Annual sales rose from RM 190 million in 1933 to RM 300 million in 1939.

Wartime Difficulties Yield to Postwar Growth for Karstadt

Business conditions during and immediately after World War II became increasingly primitive, determined by rationing and the scarcity of goods, by changes of staff as women re-

Key Dates:

1881: Rudolph Karstadt launches eponymous store.
1904: Theodor Althoff opens his first store.
1920: Rudolph Karstadt and Theodore Althoff merge operations and form Rudolph Karstadt AG.
1926: Karstadt launches EPA Einheitspreis AG.
1927: Gustav Schickedanz founds Quelle.
1933: Restructuring of Karstadt.
1949: First Quelle department store opens.
1956: Quelle launches NORIS Bank GmbH (later Quelle Bank).
1958: Karstadt fully reacquires EPA Einheitspreis AG— now called Kepa Kaufhaus GmbH (Kepa).
1976: Karstadt purchases stake in Neckermann Versand.
1990: Quelle opens new mail-order center in Leipzig.
1994: Karstadt merges with Hertie Waren & Kaufhaus GmbH.
1997: Schickedanz purchases 20 percent stake in Karstadt.
1998: Karstadt creates C&N Touristic with Lufthansa.
1999: Karstadt purchases Quelle from Schickedanz and becomes Karstadt Quelle.
2000: Karstadt Quelle purchases Thomas Cook.

placed the men who were called for military service, and—especially in the later years—by the damage to or destruction of stores by Allied bombing. In 1944 Rudolph Karstadt died at the age of 88. The end of the war saw the expropriation of 22 stores in the Soviet occupation zones and the destruction of more than 30 of the 45 branches in the western zones.

The currency reform of 1948 marked the beginning of West Germany's economic recovery. In this year Karstadt had 6,700 employees, 55,000 square meters of sales area, and an annual turnover of DM 172 million. During the years that followed, rising incomes and consumer confidence fueled the reestablishment and renewed growth of Karstadt's retail business. In 1952 Karstadt reacquired 75 percent of the former EPA Einheitspreis AG, now called Kepa Kaufhaus GmbH (Kepa); the remaining 25 percent was acquired in 1958. In 1956, the year of the company's 75th anniversary, the turnover of Rudolph Karstadt AG exceeded DM 1 billion for the first time. By this stage Karstadt had 49 branches and Kepa 51, with a total sales area of 222,000 square meters and 31,000 employees. The company name was changed to Karstadt AG in 1963, and a new administrative headquarters was opened in Essen in 1969.

Karstadt's Diversification in 1970s

The 1970s saw another important phase of expansion for the group, accompanied, as in the 1920s, by a diversification of interests. A travel company, TransEuropa Reisen GmbH, was jointly founded by Karstadt and mail-order company Quelle Gustav Schickedanz KG in 1971. The following year the company was renamed KS-Touristik-Beteiligungs GmbH. KS-Touristik itself held 25 percent of Touristik-Union International GmbH KG. In 1976 Karstadt agreed to buy a stake in the mail-order company Neckermann Versand, which was experiencing financial difficulties. As Neckermann itself had a travel subsid-

iary, the Federal Monopolies Commission required Karstadt to sell its share in KS-Touristik. In 1977 Karstadt raised its share in Neckermann to a controlling 51.2 percent. Neckermann was converted to a joint-stock company in the same year.

As well as moving into the mail-order and travel businesses, Karstadt diversified its retailing interests during this decade. The group's first furniture and home decoration store was opened in Munich in 1972. By 1980 the group had nine such furniture outlets. Seven self-service department stores began operation with the foundation of Karstadt SB Warenhaus GmbH, a subsidiary of Kepa, in 1974. The first specialized sports equipment store was opened in 1976: nine of these outlets were in operation in 1980. Further specialty outlets for fashion, music, books, and leisure activities were opened between 1977 and 1980.

The second half of the decade also saw the rationalization of Karstadt's retailing businesses. In 1977 it was decided that the concept behind the Kepa outlets would not be successful in the long run, and 25 of Kepa's outlets were reintegrated into the Karstadt chain; the remaining 42 branches were sold or leased. The self-service department stores—by then numbering 18— were also brought into the main Karstadt network. Between 1977 and 1979, 17 of Neckermann's stores were turned into Karstadt outlets and 17 new Karstadt stores were established.

Pursuing Productivity in the 1980s

By 1981, Karstadt's department store business had 155 branches and 71,000 employees, and accounted for 77 percent of turnover. Neckermann Versand AG, the mail-order subsidiary, had a workforce of 6,600 and accounted for 13 percent of the group's annual sales. NUR Touristic GmbH, Neckermann's travel subsidiary, had 1,500 employees and a 10 percent share of sales. The restructuring at the end of the 1970s indicated a shift in strategy from expansion in store numbers to increasing the productivity of each store. This policy was pursued through the 1980s. Karstadt, in 1991, had 155 stores—the same number as in 1981. However, sales area during the decade increased from 1.3 million square meters to 1.4 million square meters. Workforce numbers tended to decline—from 79,500 in 1981 to 71,000 in 1990. Annual turnover was DM 12.7 billion in 1981; after a decline in the first half of the 1980s, this had risen to DM 16.8 billion in 1990.

Facing increasing competition from self-service and out-of-town stores, Karstadt's strategy in the 1980s was to maintain its traditional emphasis on department stores carrying a full range of goods in town centers. In the late 1980s, however, the company implemented a refurbishment and realignment program by which individual stores have been modernized and adapted to the nature of their localities. Furthermore, a distribution center was established at Unna, near Dortmund. The project was started in 1987 and was fully operational for the first time in 1990, costing DM 210 million. This center replaced regional warehouses and enabled Karstadt AG to make efficiency and cost improvements in the area of logistics, the distribution of goods between warehouses and stores. Diversification, which was at the core of Karstadt's development in the 1970s, was not part of the company's strategy during the 1980s. Although the company retained specialty outlets for sports equipment and furniture, accounting for about 9 percent of annual turnover, all other ventures into specialty areas, except Runners Point, had ceased operations by 1987.

In 1981 Karstadt raised its stake in Neckermann Versand AG to more than 94 percent, and in 1984 the group acquired all remaining shares in this subsidiary. Both Neckermann Versand AG and its travel subsidiary NUR Touristic GmbH continued to take losses during the first half of the 1980s, returning profits only since 1986 and 1987, respectively. Improvements at Neckermann were due largely to its abandonment of specialty catalogs, returning to one main catalog targeting families in the medium- to lower-income groups. Staff reductions also played a part. Neckermann, which produced around three million catalogs each season, was by the end of the decade the third largest mail-order company in Germany, behind Otto and Quelle, and had subsidiaries in the Netherlands, Belgium, France, and joint ventures in Greece and Poland. NUR Touristic, which has subsidiaries in the Netherlands and Belgium, also reduced its workforce, from 1,445 in 1981 to 937 in 1989. Despite these improvements at Neckermann and NUR, the problems were not entirely eradicated: while both businesses showed increases in turnover, their profits declined in the waning years of the decade.

Karstadt in the 1990s

The reunification of Germany, along with tax reforms that increased consumer-spending power, brought Karstadt and its subsidiaries a significant boost in sales in the early 1990s. Department stores along the border with the former German Democratic Republic benefited from visiting customers from the new federal states, while the mail-order business was able to penetrate into the eastern territories and take advantage of the rise in consumer demand without having to establish retail outlets. Karstadt had believed that its coverage of Western Germany had reached a saturation point, but the new Länder, or federal regions, presented the group with an opportunity for further expansion. In 1990, a cooperation agreement was reached with the Centrum department stores in Eastern Germany; in March 1991, Karstadt acquired seven of these stores—in Dresden, Gürlitz, Halle, Hoyerswerda, Leipzig-Lindenau, and Magdeburg—as well as leased two former Magnet stores in Brandenburg and Wismar. Conversion of these stores to Western standards required considerable investment. Neckermann and NUR also developed mail-order and tourism infrastructures in the East.

Further consolidation of Germany's retailers came in 1994, when Karstadt merged with Hertie Waren & Kaufhaus GmbH. The DM 1.5 billion deal added Hertie's 300 department and specialty stores with $4.2 billion in sales to form what *Daily News Record*'s James Fallon called "the richest retailing group in Europe." The merger also signaled Karstadt's commitment to department store business in the face of a potentially slackening business. German shoppers were increasingly looking to specialty retail stores or to the new discounters, rather than to traditional department stores such as Karstadt and Hertie, for their shopping needs

Karstadt showed off its "cyber-savvy" with the launch of "My-World," Europe's largest online shopping site, in October 1996. The electronic mall offered over 150,000 items and generated an average of $20,000 in sales every day. However, while the chain continued to seek new ways to present its wares to the buying public, it did not neglect the old ways. Thus also in 1996, Karstadt staged a grand reopening of its Berlin outlet, Kaufhaus des Westens. Known colloquially as KaDeWe ("ka-day-vay"), the store had first been built in 1907 and had long been sequestered in East Germany by the Cold War-era Berlin Wall. A renovation and expansion made it the largest department store on the European continent, with 60,000 square meters of selling space.

Karstadt was among the retailers who helped to slowly erode Germany's "blue laws" in the early 1990s. The product of lobbying efforts by the nation's powerful unions, these laws prohibited work on Sundays (known as "Feiertag" or "free day") and ended the workday at 6:30 p.m. on weekdays and 2 p.m. on Saturdays. As the German retail environment worsened in the mid-1990s, store operators were able to convince local governments and, in November 1996, the national government to ease restrictions on store hours. The national reform did not allow Sunday hours but did allow the extension of the weekday to 8 p.m. and Saturday hours to 4 p.m. Karstadt took advantage of the new selling time, but, like many of its competitors, did not see an immediate payoff.

In fact, while Karstadt's sales rose more than 60 percent in the early 1990s, from DM 16.77 billion to DM 26.98 billion, its net income declined from DM 227.8 million in 1990 to a low of DM 41.9 million in 1994 before recovering somewhat to DM 109 million in 1995.

In response to its falling income, Karstadt launched a restructuring program in 1995. Company Chairman Walter Deuss announced that Karstadt would integrate its Hertie acquisition over a five-year period by reducing the number of Hertie stores (some would be converted to the Karstadt name; others would be closed). Nevertheless, Karstadt's retail division continued to encounter difficulties, although the company's mail-order and travel arms performed well.

Karstadt also cast about for ways to insulate itself from the vicissitudes of the retail sector. Its travel business, operating chiefly through NUR Touristic, was a perpetual bright spot on earning reports, even in years when retail sales flagged. Karstadt built upon this strong base in the travel sector when in 1997 it formed a joint venture with Deutsche Lufthansa AG, Germany's flagship airline carrier. This new business, of which each company owned 50 percent, was christened C + N Condor Neckermann Touristik AG. The alliance sought to create an integrated company with a presence in all aspects of the tourist business. In particular, Karstadt and Lufthansa wanted to link charter flights and tourist packages to boost profits for both. To this end, Karstadt transferred its NUR operations to C + N.

In 1997, Karstadt sold an 18 percent stake of its operations to Schickedanz Holding AG, the parent company of Quelle, the largest mail-order retailer in Germany and the second largest in Europe. With lackluster consumer demand in Germany posing obstacles to profit, both Karstadt and Quelle sought to maximize efficiencies, particularly by synthesizing their mail-order operations. Analysts believed that this new arrangement would be advantageous, and Karstadt's share price rose immediately upon news of this transaction.

The following year, Schickedanz announced that it wanted to gain an additional 30 percent stake in Karstadt, which would raise its ownership in the company to a controlling 48 percent. In the midst of these negotiations, Karstadt and Schickedanz decided to take the bolder step of merging Karstadt with Quelle.

Early Years at Quelle

Gustav Schickedanz, Quelle's founder, was born in 1895, the son of a craft factory employee in Fürth, a small city adjacent to Nuremburg. He left school at the age of 15 to work at Speed and Son, the local branch of a sportswear firm. He soon was due to be appointed as a company representative in South America, but he decided to complete his army-service obligation first. World War I broke out and an expected service period of one year turned into seven. He was wounded and discharged in 1919. Schickedanz returned to Fürth where he worked as a salesman and married Anna Zehnder, a local master baker's daughter, in September 1919. In 1922, he opened a small haberdashery business and struggled to keep the firm going in the midst of Germany's period of hyperinflation. His employees were his father, wife, and sister.

Economic reforms led to a degree of stabilization and a short period of improvement. Schickedanz's observations of customer behavior led him to believe that he could sell to a larger market through the mail. With the resulting low overheads and greater volume, he could offer lower prices. These ideas were not new, but hyperinflation presented great difficulties to mail-order firms. The new stabilization convinced him that mail order could work. The mail-order venture opened in November 1927. The name chosen for the company, Quelle, means "source" in German. Schickedanz hired 15 new workers. One, Grete Lachner, would one day become his second wife and play an essential role in the company's future.

His first catalogs emphasized wool, thread, and materials for home sewing, rather than ready-to-wear clothes. The company enjoyed a modest success in its first 18 months of operation. Schickedanz's 33-year-old wife Anna and their five-year-old son were killed in an auto accident in July 1929; his 72-year-old father died shortly afterward. His problems were compounded by the Wall Street crash, which halted the German economy's faltering recovery and threw millions out of work. Schickedanz's sister, Liesl Kiesling, stepped into Anna's position in the company.

By the end of 1930, five million Germans were unemployed. Schickedanz's new business survived, however, and, especially by the standards of the Great Depression, prospered. Quelle was able to offer lower prices than many shops, and quickly developed a reputation for reliability and good value. Soon Schickedanz began to offer more clothes and accessories. By 1934 Quelle had 250,000 customers. By 1936 this number had grown to a million, the majority of whom were women.

Wartime and Postwar Difficulties for Quelle

This success came about despite the restrictions on trade introduced by Adolf Hitler's new Nazi regime, which came to power in January 1933. As Jews began to leave or face imprisonment, they disappeared as competitors in the clothing trade.

In 1935 Schickedanz bought VP, a paper factory, to publish catalogs and make cartons. This factory had been Jewish property. Some suspected him of having an invisible Jewish partner, but this was never proved. World War II began on September 1, 1939, and the Nazis required that the paper factory be turned over to war work. Schickedanz continued to operate under severe restrictions and clothing rationing, but the dislocations of the war meant that mail order provided an alternative source of supply to people in bombed-out cities. Schickedanz was offered several positions as an economic administrator, but he preferred to remain with the business.

In 1942 Schickedanz married Grete Lachner. One year later their only child was born in a bombproof bunker. As Allied bombers began to attack the Nuremburg-Fürth area, the Schickedanz family moved out to quarters in the nearby forest village of Hersbruck. In August 1943 Quelle was virtually put out of business when an Allied bombing raid destroyed 90 percent of the company's warehouse in Fürth. On April 19, 1945, American troops occupied the ruins of Fürth and Nuremburg. Three weeks later, Germany surrendered. Although the Schickedanzes were fortunate to find themselves in the U.S. zone of occupation, their enterprise was not initially encouraged. Schickedanz was classified as a Nazi by the occupation authorities and prohibited from reopening his business. Buildings were in ruins or requisitioned by the occupation authorities and customer records had been lost.

Grete Schickedanz opened a small clothing shop in Hersbruck to support the family. It was a success, but was closed by the military authorities. Eventually, the Schickedanzes were able to use the influence of the anti-Nazi politician and economist Ludwig Erhard, a family friend who was also from Fürth, to gain permission to reopen.

Quelle's Growth in the 1950s and 1960s

Gustav Schickedanz remained under a prohibition and, in theory, could not even discuss business with former employees. The ban was removed in 1949. Former employees were found and Quelle was off to a fresh start. It was just in time to benefit from Ludwig Erhard's currency reforms of the previous year. Following the founding of West Germany in 1949, Erhard moved as quickly as possible to remove restrictions and rationing and to encourage competition. He believed that sales of consumer goods would encourage production and jobs.

After many years of hardship, Germans responded by going on a buying spree. The Quelle name was remembered and respected by many former customers. By utilizing previous contacts, Grete Schickedanz was able to obtain superior but inexpensive goods for sale. It was on this foundation that the new Quelle was built. By the end of 1949 Quelle had a turnover of DM 12 million and mailing list of 100,000 addresses, but the couple had also opened their first department store.

Germany, especially, benefited from the economic expansion stimulated by the Korean War in the early 1950s. Between 1949 and 1952 the company's turnover rose by 900 percent. By 1952 Quelle had one million credit customers and sales of DM 103 million. The company now faced the classic problems of a successful business: how to expand without overextending and damaging a reputation for quality. The answer was to invest in new computer and data processing technology that was just appearing in the United States and barely known in Europe.

Schickedanz hired the best experts and gave them a free hand to design systems that would enable Quelle to handle millions of mail-order and credit transactions per year. Thirty-five engineers from the firm SEL in Stuttgart worked for two years to develop and set up a system appropriate for Quelle's needs. In 1955 the first phase of the company's new mail-order center was finished. By 1957 SEL had completed the building of the new system. It was one of the most sophisticated mail-order computer information systems and attracted worldwide interest. Quelle was able to rationalize its operations and achieve even greater efficiency. The company has continued to give high priority to updating its computer and data information systems. In 1990 it maintained information on some 32 million customers.

A new emphasis was placed on quality control. In 1953 Schickedanz set up an institute for testing products to be sold through Quelle. It became known as the Quelle Institute für Warenprufung and is the largest institute of its kind in German commerce. At first only textiles were tested, but gradually it began to examine other product types. In 1990 it had made more than 25,000 annual tests. The institute also attracted international interest.

Grete Schickedanz was increasingly responsible for buying. She also directed careful attention to new catalogs and added more color pages. By 1954 more than half the pages of the spring-summer catalog were in color. She carefully monitored fashion trends. Later, the company hired prominent German designers such as Heinz Oestergard as advisers.

The range of mail-order products was continually expanding. In 1954 the company bought a bicycle factory and began to sell bicycles. The next year, a favorable response to a line of small electronic appliances led to the introduction of washing machines and large appliances, which Quelle was able to offer at very competitive prices. In 1957 one of its most successful ventures was into photographic equipment, where it was able to offer large mail-order discounts. By the early 1960s it was even offering travel services.

Quelle learned how to target special interest groups and to develop special catalogs alongside its main catalog to spotlight lifestyle groups and hobbies such as gardening. A bank, NORIS Bank GmbH (later Quelle Bank) was started in 1956 and developed to help customers with credit. By 1958 Quelle had a turnover of DM 406 million. It had become the largest mail-order firm in West Germany.

From the early 1960s, Grete Schickedanz traveled to the Far East on buying trips. In 1962 Quelle opened an office in Hong Kong. Eventually, the region became one of the company's most important sources of supply. Later, Grete Schickedanz established important business contacts in the People's Republic of China and opened an office in Shanghai.

In 1964 Quelle had a turnover of DM 1.64 billion and called itself "the largest mail-order house in Europe." The 1960s and 1970s were a period of continued growth for Quelle in Germany, but unlike its competitor, Otto Versand, which made a

very successful investment in Spiegel in the United States, Quelle had been more cautious about foreign expansion. The process had been slow, mainly into neighboring countries. It began in 1959 with Austria, where results were so encouraging that the company decided in 1966 to make a much more risky move into France, opening a new mail-order facility in Orleans.

New Developments at Quelle: 1970s–80s

Gustav Schickedanz died on March 27, 1977, in the 50th anniversary year of the company. He was succeeded as chairperson by Grete Schickedanz. Because the two had worked as partners for many years, Gustav's death did not disrupt the company or bring about any major policy changes. Grete continued her worldwide buying trips. By 1981, Quelle had a turnover of DM 10 billion.

In May 1985 Grete Schickedanz broke new ground in West German–East European trade politics by signing an agreement with Hungarotex, the Hungarian foreign trade organization. The agreement allowed Quelle to sell by mail in Hungary and included plans for a new chain of jointly owned department stores. In 1990 Quelle started Intermoda, a joint-venture catalog operation in the Soviet Union. In 1987 Grete Schickedanz relinquished her position as chairperson of the board of Quelle, but she remained as head of its supervisory board. Into the 1990s she still traveled widely on behalf of the company.

The 1990s and Beyond at Quelle

The speedy German reunification process, which began with the collapse of the East German regime in November 1989 and culminated a year later, presented both new markets and challenges from Otto and other German competitors. Quelle saw opportunity in this environment, and moved quickly to capture what it viewed as a vast new market. The company distributed its catalog to nine out of ten households in the former East Germany, and opened new stores and facilities in Gera, Jena, and Erfurt.

German unification boosted Quelle's mail-order sales 40 percent by 1990, but the company struggled to handle the volume of its new business. As a result, its profits remained in the single low digits. To address this problem, Quelle began planning a huge new regional mail-order complex in Leipzig (in the former East Germany). The Leipzig facility signaled Quelle's commitment to central and eastern European markets. By the time it opened in 1995, the facility, which employed 2,500 people, could process 180,000 parcels a day.

In addition to mining the emerging consumer economies to the east, Quelle looked to diversify by entering entirely new business sectors. At the end of 1990, Quelle surprised many German financial institutions by entering into a new agreement, through its subsidiary Quelle Bank, with the Bank of Scotland to compete in the undeveloped German credit card market. (Analysts had long considered Germans to be resistant to credit cards.) According to the plan, Quelle was to offer direct banking and credit card services using its mail-order database, which contained information on more than 30 million customers in Germany, France, and Austria. Bank of Scotland would handle the processing in its facilities in Dunfermline, Fife, Scotland. Quelle hoped to issue roughly one million cards in its first five years.

During this period, Quelle also launched the first-ever home shopping television network in Germany as a joint venture with Pro-7 Television GmbH. Home Order Television GmbH (HOT), as the commercial channel was called, featured peppy German salespeople touting merchandise in a format pioneered in the United States by QVC Inc.

In 1997, Quelle found a further avenue for expansion when it purchased an 18 percent stake in Karstadt AG, Germany's largest retailer. Two years later, Quelle and Karstadt merged, creating a retail and mail-order powerhouse.

Karstadt Quelle AG: 1999–2003

The merger of Karstadt and Quelle resulted in a German retail giant with combined sales of nearly $18.1 billion. Both companies had considerable mail-order operations, as well as retail stores throughout Europe. Karstadt Quelle, as their combination was called, sought to use its newly acquired bulk to operate more efficiently, particularly in its mail-order segment.

Soon after merging, however, Karstadt Quelle encountered some significant obstacles. The German economy was in the midst of a slump, and retail sales, particularly at the higher-end Karstadt department stores, suffered accordingly. Karstadt Quelle reported a loss of nearly EUR 50 million for the first half of 2000. The market noticed. "The data [on the new company] are fundamentally bad," an analyst for Fritz Nols Global Equity Service, told the *Wall Street Journal Europe* on August 29, 2000.

In response to this dismal earnings report, Walter Deuss, the longtime chairman of Karstadt, stepped down, and was replaced by Wolfgang Urban, who had built his reputation for hard-nosed decision-making at Karstadt's chief rival, Metro AG. Urban immediately announced a ten-point plan to turn around Karstadt Quelle, and promised that the company's earnings would grow to EUR 731.2 million by 2003. As part of this process, the company would lay off 7,000 workers (mainly sales staff at Karstadt department stores) by that date.

The lynchpin of Urban's program was to move Karstadt Quelle beyond the confines of the retail sector. Sustainable profitability, Urban believed, would come only if Karstadt Quelle transformed itself into a broad-based retail and services group, diversified enough to withstand the cyclical downturns in the German retail sector. In keeping with this strategy, Karstadt Quelle announced in December 2000 that its C + N Touristic joint venture would acquire Thomas Cook Group Ltd., the second largest travel company in the United Kingdom, for EUR 890.1 million. With the merger, C + N Touristic became the second-largest travel group in Europe.

Karstadt Quelle also unveiled a series of partnerships with strategic allies that furthered its diversification efforts. In 2001, it announced its alliance with American coffee chain Starbucks to open Starbucks outlets in Karstadt department stores. In 2002, Karstadt Quelle changed the name of its in-house bank from Optimus to Karstadt Quelle Bank and broadened the range of services the institution provided. Karstadt Quelle also teamed up with Deutsche Telekom to offer customer bonus programs under the brand name "HappyDigits."

Karstadt Quelle's ongoing efforts to reinvent itself continued in 2003. Although 2002 was another difficult year for the company—retail sales in Germany were again low, as the national economies across the entire so-called "Euro-zone" struggled—Karstadt Quelle's diversification promised to develop the company in new directions.

Principal Subsidiaries

Alsterhaus; Herite; Karstadt; Runners Point and Golf House; Sinn Leffers and Wehmeyer; Neckermann; Quelle; IN-TELLIUM; Karstadt Quelle Bank; Quelle Versicherung; Karstadt Immobilien; Thomas Cook Tourism Group (50%).

Principal Competitors

American Express Company; AVA Allgemeine Handelsgesellschaft der Verbraucher AG; Douglas Holding AG; Lidl & Schwarz Stiftung & Co. KG; METRO AG; Spiegel, Inc.; TUI AG.

Further Reading

Cole, Deborah, "Berlin Reopens Beloved Symbol of Consumer Freedom," *Reuters Business Report,* September 24, 1996.

Dauer, Ulrike, and Angela Cullen, "Retailing: Karstadt Discusses Joining Forces with Schickedanz," *Wall Street Journal Europe,* April 20, 1999.

Demain, Beth, "Karstadt Quelle Unveils New Strategy, But Skeptical Investors Aren't Buying," *Wall Street Journal Europe,* October 18, 2000.

Doran, Patricia, "König Karstadt," *Sporting Goods Business,* August 1994, p. 56.

Fallon, James, "Confirm Karstadt to Acquire Hertie Department Stores; Deal Worth $1.6 Billion," *Daily News Record,* November 16, 1993, p. 10.

Fessenden, Helen, "Lufthansa-Karstadt Venture Praised But Cartel Issue Looms," *Dow Jones International News,* September 18, 1997.

Gilardi, John, "German Retail Unions Stage More Strike Actions," *Reuters,* May 30, 1995.

Grete Schickedanz: Ein Leben für die Quelle, Fürth, Quelle, 1986.

Karstadt Magazin: Jubiläumsausgabe, 1881–1981, Essen: Karstadt AG, 1981.

"Karstadt Reports Loss," *Wall Street Journal Europe,* August 29, 2000.

"A Little Online Shopping but with a European Flair," *PCWeek,* January 20, 1997, p. 115.

Pentz, Michelle, "Teleshopping Gets a Tryout in Europe," *Wall Street Journal,* September 9, 1996.

Miller, Marjorie, "Unions Seeing Red As German Blue Laws Ease," *Los Angeles Times,* October 29, 1994, p. 2A.

Prada, Paulo, "Field Thins Out After Deal by C + N for Thomas Cook," *Wall Street Journal Europe,* December 8, 2000.

Rohwedder, Cacilie, "Karstadt Agrees to Acquire Retailer Hertie," *Wall Street Journal* Europe, November 12, 1993.

Spahr, Wolfgang, "Merger Causes Alarm in Germany; Retailers Told to Sell Some Music Outlets," *Billboard,* March 19, 1994, pp. 49, 50.

"West German Shops; Geschlossen," *Economist,* March 1, 1986, pp. 67–68.

Whitney, Craig R. "Comfortable Germans, Slow to Change (Especially If It Means More Work)," *New York Times,* January 16, 1995, p. 6A.

—Clark Siewert
—update: Rebecca Stanfel

Kewpie Kabushiki Kaisha

1-4-13 Shibuya, Shibuya-ku
Tokyo 150-0002
Japan
Telephone: (+81) 33486-3331
Fax: (+81) 33498-1806
Web site: http://www.kewpie.co.jp

Public Company
Incorporated: 1919 as Shokuhin Kogyo Co., Ltd.
Employees: 8,550
Sales: ¥434.5 billion ($3.68 billion) (2002)
Stock Exchanges: Tokyo
NAIC: 311421 Fruit and Vegetable Canning; 311411
    Frozen Fruit, Juice, and Vegetable Processing; 311412
    Frozen Specialty Food Manufacturing; 311422
    Specialty Canning; 311423 Dried and Dehydrated
    Food Manufacturing; 311615 Poultry Processing

Kewpie Kabushiki Kaisha (QP Corporation is its English equivalent name), one of Japan's leading food products companies, has built an empire based on its Kewpie brand of mayonnaise products; the company is by far the dominant producer of mayonnaise and related products, including salad dressings, for the Japanese market. Mayonnaise and salad dressings account, however, for just one fourth of the company's sales of ¥434 billion ($3.7 billion) in 2002. Kewpie also produces and markets canned and retort foods through subsidiary brand Aohata, a segment that added 12 percent to the company's sales. Under the Deria brand, Kewpie sells vegetables and salads, which contributed 22 percent. As part of that operation, and in conjunction with partner Mitsubishi, Kewpie has developed a packaging system enabling a store shelf-life of four days for fresh-cut vegetable products. Meanwhile, Kewpie's intensive use of eggs for its mayonnaise operation—the company claims to use some 8 percent of Japan's total egg production—has led it to develop a variety of egg products, including liquid, frozen, and dried eggs for the institutional and restaurant and other food sectors. The company also produces a variety of other egg-based products for the cosmetics, pharmaceutical, medical, and other industries. The company's egg products

sales add 19 percent to the company's revenues. The last of the company's main food businesses is its Healthcare Products division, which produces baby food as well as special food preparations for the elderly and for the healthcare market. In addition to foods, the company is also active in the distribution and logistics market, through its control of publicly listed subsidiary KRS Corporation, which accounts for some 18 percent of sales. Kewpie, named after the famous doll, has a limited presence internationally, with subsidiaries in the United States (Q&B Foods and Henningsen Foods), The Netherlands (Henningsen), and joint ventures in Beijing, Taiwan, and Thailand. More than 90 percent of the company's sales come from Japan, however. Kewpie is listed on the Tokyo Stock Exchange; the founding Nakashima family remains the company's largest shareholder, through Nakashimato Corporation's nearly 20 percent stake.

Launching Japan's Mayonnaise Craze in the 1920s

Kewpie's origins trace back to the years following World War I, with the founding of Nakishamato Corporation by Toichiro Nakashima (alternately spelled as Nakajima) in 1918. Nakashima had served as an intern for Japan's Department of Agriculture and Commerce, and had been sent to study food production techniques in the United States and Europe. Returning to Japan, Nakashima decided to apply the canning, production, and marketing techniques he had learned to the Japanese market. In 1919, Nakashima founded a food production company, Shokuhin Kogyo Co.

The company manufactured traditional Japanese food products, including canned tangerines. In the early 1920s, however, Nakashima traveled to the United States, bringing back a jar of mayonnaise. Until then, mayonnaise had been unknown in Japan. Nakashima recognized, however, that he could adapt the spread for the Japanese market—notably by increasing the proportion of egg yolk in the recipe. The company began marketing its mayonnaise in 1925, adopting the name "Kewpie" after the popular doll created by artist and illustrator Rosie O'Neill.

Nakashima began exporting canned tangerines to England in the late 1920s. The growth of this business led to the founding of a dedicated canning company, Kidoen, in 1932. Located in

Company Perspectives:

Corporate Policy: Creating an appealing company that responds to people's trust and expectations.

The basic necessities of life are food, clothing and shelter. The Kewpie Group chooses to specialize in food. To offer delicious and wholesome products at reasonable prices we undertake rigorous testing and screening to obtain the finest ingredients available. Over the years we have devoted our utmost effort to the development and nurturing of original products, persistent improvement of quality, and enhancement of cost competitiveness. Our fundamental corporate policy is to go beyond the satisfaction of customer requirements, and further strive to ensure mutual prosperity with our business partners, to contribute to local communities, and to create an appealing company that can reward the trust and meet the expectations of our shareholders.

Hiroshima, near the heart of the Japanese citrus farming region on the Seta Inland Sea, the new company extended production beyond canned tangerines to include orange marmalade and strawberry jam—markets the company once again pioneered in Japan. For these products, Nakashima returned to the canning and production techniques learned during his days as an intern, earning the company a reputation for the quality of its products.

With the outbreak of World War II, however, Nakashima's businesses faltered. The canning facility was taken over by the government and placed under the control of Hiroshima Prefectural Consolidated Canning Company. Meanwhile, the shortage of the basic ingredients needed for the Kewpie mayonnaise recipe put an end to that operation as well.

Production resumed in 1948, and the Kewpie brands returned to grocery shelves in the country. Meanwhile, the company regained control of its canning business, renamed Aohata Canning Corporation, which soon resumed marmalade production. The Aohata business grew to include sales of canned vegetables, starting with corn in 1950, launched under a new brand name, Blue Flag. Yet the company's strongest growth came through its mayonnaise, which, with its association with the American lifestyle, became an increasingly popular condiment in the postwar period. The Kewpie brand quickly established its dominance of the Japanese mayonnaise market. In 1957, Nakashimato renamed its food production operation after its most popular brand, and the company became known as Kewpie KK (or QP Corporation).

Diversified Foods Company in the 1960s

Kewpie began experimenting with packaging in the 1950s, releasing its first squeezable mayonnaise container in 1958. That year, the company also introduced the first of a new line of mayonnaise-based products, with the launch of Kewpie French salad dressing. In 1959, the company added another line of food products, with the introduction of Kewpie Bolognese pasta sauce. Once again, Kewpie claimed the introduction of a new and popular product to a Japanese market becoming increasingly open to Western foods.

Kewpie entered another food market in 1960, when it applied its canning and production technology to the baby foods sector. The company grew to become one of Japan's leading producers of baby foods. In 1960, Kewpie added to its product list with the launch of a new subsidiary, Kewpie Jyozo Co. in 1962, dedicated to the production and distribution of vinegar products—an offshoot of the company's mayonnaise sales. (Vinegar is one of the primary ingredients of mayonnaise.) The increase in the consumption of salads in Japan in the 1960s led the company to pioneer another market segment, that of Japanese-style salad dressings, with the launch of Kewpie Oriental Salad Dressing in 1965.

Until the mid-1960s, Kewpie had concentrated in large part on the consumer market. In 1967, however, the company created a new subsidiary, Sanei Provisions, which began supplying food products, including egg-based products, to the institutional foods market. On the consumer side, meanwhile, Kewpie responded to growing health-related concerns by launching a low-sugar content marmalade, Aohata 55 Orange Marmalade.

Kewpie's growth in the postwar period was accompanied by increasingly sophisticated warehousing and distribution operations. In 1966, the company spun that division off as a separate subsidiary, originally called Kewpie Ltd. By 1968, that company had entered the transportation sector as well, developing into a full-fledged logistics company dedicated to the food industry, which took the name of KRS Corporation in 1989.

Kewpie's growth led to its public listing in 1970, with its shares placed at first on the Tokyo Stock Exchange's Second Section. Nakashimato remained the company's largest shareholder, however, and the two companies entered into a long-lasting cooperation agreement. As part of that agreement, Kewpie took over the distribution of parts of Nakashimato's own food production, including canned and frozen goods. That business was placed under a new subsidiary, Deria Foods, created in 1973. In that year, Kewpie switched its listing to the Tokyo exchange's primary board.

Kewpie continued to diversify. In 1972, the company launched a new brand, Janef, for its growing interest in the healthcare food products market, which extended beyond its original baby foods to include therapeutic and liquid diets products. Kewpie also had been developing its engineering activities to design machinery for its own food manufacturing operations. In 1975, the company created a dedicated food engineering division, which began to sell its machines to other companies. Kewpie then created a new subsidiary for another offshoot of its core businesses, placing its growing sales of eggs and egg products business under QP Egg Corporation in 1977. Kewpie's expertise in eggs led the company into the fine chemicals market, with the production of lecithin from egg yolks in 1981.

International Operations in the 1980s

The international markets attracted the company in the 1980s. In 1981, it entered Thailand, forming a production partnership with Saha Pathana Investment Company to begin producing mayonnaise. The following year, Kewpie turned to the United States, forming Q&B Foods, where it began producing its Japanese-style mayonnaise for the growing Asian commu-

Key Dates:

1918: Nakashimato Corporation is founded.

1919: Toichiro Nakashima founds a food production company called Shokuhin Kogyo Co.

1925: Production of mayonnaise begins for the Japanese market under the Kewpie brand name.

1927: The company begins exporting canned tangerines.

1932: The company begins producing marmalade for the Japanese market; the Kidoen canning company is formed in Hiroshima.

1948: Production of mayonnaise resumes; the company regains control of its canning operation, which had been confiscated during the war, and renames it Aohata.

1957: The company changes its name to Kewpie KK (QP Corporation).

1960: Production of baby foods begins.

1966: The company spins off its warehousing operation as subsidiary KRS Corporation.

1970: Kewpie goes public on the Tokyo Stock Exchange.

1981: The company begins international development with mayonnaise production in Thailand.

1982: The company forms the U.S. subsidiary Q&B and begins selling Kewpie mayonnaise in the United States.

1987: The company forms the Thai QP joint venture with Saha Pathana.

1988: The company forms the Taiwan QP joint venture with Wei Chuan and Mitsui.

1990: Henningsen Foods of Nebraska is acquired.

1993: The company enters China through a production partnership in Beijing with Mitsubishi.

1995: The company spins off KRS as a publicly listed subsidiary.

1998: The company spins off Aohata as a publicly listed subsidiary.

2000: A new medium-term strategy grouped around five core food products businesses is adopted.

2002: The company forms a new production joint venture for the Shanghai market with Mitsubishi, with production slated to begin in 2003.

nity there. That company also began adapting Kewpie's salad dressings for the American consumer market, launching the Oriental Chef line of salad dressings in 1984.

Kewpie and Saha Pathana formalized their partnership in 1987 with the creation of Thai QP Co. Ltd. The following year, Kewpie entered the Taiwan market as well, through a joint venture with Wei Chuan Foods and Mitsui & Co., called Taiwan QP Co. In the meantime, Kewpie had formed another subsidiary, Kanae Foods, which took over its egg processing activities in 1986.

Kewpie engineering operations produced another side product in the mid-1980s. The company's focus on consistent product quality led it to develop its own hydroponics system, which, using a special triangular panel (T) and spray (S) system, eliminated the need for pesticides while reducing the bacteria content of fruits and vegetables. The company put its first "TS Farm" into production in 1986, and then began marketing the system to third parties.

In 1990, Kewpie's developing operations in the United States, where its Oriental Chef line had proven popular, especially on the West Coast, led it to make its first acquisition, of Nebraska egg producer Henningsen Foods, which also had a subsidiary operation in The Netherlands. The company continued its international expansion into the 1990s, setting up a new joint venture in China, now partnering with Mitsubishi to create Beijing QP.

In the mid-1990s, the company attempted to expand its overseas production, particularly through its Asian joint ventures. Yet the economic crisis that swept through the region in the late 1990s limited Kewpie's international growth efforts. International sales remained a minor part of Kewpie's overall operations, accounting for less than 10 percent of the company's sales at the beginning of the 2000s.

Leadership Focus for the New Century

Back at home, however, Kewpie remained one of the food industry's leaders, successfully fighting off the entry of a number of competitors to its core mayonnaise business to maintain its dominance on that market—the Kewpie brand represented some 70 percent of the total Japanese mayonnaise market. In the meantime, the mayonnaise market in Japan was growing strongly during the 1990s, as a younger generation of Japanese consumers extended the product beyond its traditional role as a condiment into an actual ingredient in a growing number of recipes—including cocktails.

Kewpie also had begun to take steps to refocus itself. In 1990, the company brought its institutional food products business back under its direct control. In 1995, it spun off KRS Corporation as a public company, with a listing on the Tokyo stock exchange. The company maintained control of that company, however, with more than 50 percent of its voting rights. Three years later, Kewpie made a public offering for Aohata as well.

In 2000, Kewpie established a new medium-term strategy for the new century, one based on redefining its core markets where the company was able to establish and maintain leadership positions. As company President Gosuke Oyama said, according to *Nikkei Weekly:* "You don't know the next-highest mountain after Mount Fuji, do you? No. 2 and below cannot influence distribution or lead price trends."

The company leadership strategy led to a refocus on five core food markets: Mayonnaise and Dressings; Canned and Retort Products; Egg Products; Vegetables and Salads; and Healthcare Products, including baby foods and a rapidly growing line of food preparations for the elderly, launched in 1998. The new strategy appeared to be working, as profits rose steadily into the early years of the decade, outpacing the company's own initial medium-term goals.

In the meantime, Kewpie continued to expand both its product line and its operations. In 2002, the company joined with partner Mitsubishi to set up a new food production company in Hangzhou in order to supply jams and mayonnaise to the

Shanghai market. Kewpie took a 70 percent share of the new company, scheduled to start production in 2003. Kewpie and Mitsubishi also had been cooperating on a technical basis, resulting in the launch of a new polypropylene-based packaging that enabled fresh-cut vegetables to maintain a four-day shelf life in stores. After more than 80 years, Kewpie remained an innovative force in the Japanese food industry.

Principal Subsidiaries

Aohata Corporation; Akesaovaros Co., Ltd. (Thailand; 44%); Beijing Q.P. Foods Co., Ltd. (China; 65%); Henningsen Foods, Inc. (U.S.A.); Henningsen Nederland B.V. (Netherlands); Henningsen Van Den Burg B.V. (Netherlands; 50%); Kifuki Usa Co., Inc. (U.S.A.); K.R.S. Corporation; Q&B Foods Inc. (U.S.A.); Taiwan Q.P. Co., Ltd. (55%); Thai Q.P. Co., Ltd. (44%).

Principal Competitors

Kikkoman Corporation; Kagome Company Ltd.; Daesang Corporation; Ottogi Corporation; Kenko Mayonnaise Company Ltd.; Fujicco Company Ltd.; Kao Corporation.

Further Reading

"Food Outfit Tops Up Activity by Expanding in Asian Market," *Nikkei Weekly,* May 13, 1996, p. 20.

Itoi, Kay, "Don't Hold the Mayo!: Japanese Diners Go Crazy for the Creamy Condiment," *Newsweek International,* December 23, 2002.

"Japan's QP Corp Sees 16% Rise in FY02 Group Net Profit," *Asia Pulse,* January 10, 2003.

"Top Mayonnaise Maker Plays to Strengths: QP Prospers on Strategy of Targeting No. 1 Spot in Every Market It Enters," *Nikkei Weekly,* January 21, 2002.

—M.L. Cohen

KI

1330 Bellevue Street
Green Bay, Wisconsin 54302
U.S.A.
Telephone: (920) 468-8100
Toll Free: (800) 424-2432
Fax: (920) 468-0280
Web site: http://www.ki.com

Private Company
Founded: 1941 as Krueger Metal Products
Employees: 3,500
Sales: $600 million (2002 est.)
NAIC: 337211 Wood Office Furniture Manufacturing;
337212 Custom Architectural Woodwork and
Millwork Manufacturing; 337214 Office Furniture
(Except Wood) Manufacturing; 337215 Showcase,
Partition, Shelving, and Locker Manufacturing

KI is one of the leading designers and manufacturers of contract furnishings in the United States, producing several lines of desks, tables, workstations, chairs, filing cabinets, and wall panel systems for commercial and institutional settings. Customers include corporations, healthcare facilities, government agencies, schools, and colleges. Furniture designs combine contemporary styling and a practical attitude toward customer concerns for ergonomics, flexibility, and the requirements of electronic office tools. KI is involved with many known designers, including chair designer Giancarlo Piretti and textile designer Lori Weitzner. KI products are available through interior designers, architects, and furniture dealers, as well as the company's own sales representatives. Showrooms are located throughout the United States, and, internationally, in London and Kuala Lumpur. KI caters to the specific needs of its customers, following a philosophy that each customer is "a market of one." For maximum flexibility and responsiveness, the company is structured for decentralized responsibility and decision-making processes.

Company Origins: From Metal Folding Chairs to Office Furnishings

Al Krueger founded Krueger Metal Products in 1941 to manufacture basic metal folding chairs. The demands of war-related manufacturing created a scarcity of steel and other metals, however, forcing Krueger to be innovative in procuring and using raw materials. Based in Aurora, Illinois, he purchased excess metal from manufacturers in the Chicago area and designed a unique manufacturing system adaptable to the kinds of materials available. Krueger Metal Products became the world's largest manufacturer of metal folding chairs and operated profitably by efficiently manufacturing folding chairs and multipurpose tables and chairs for institutional and commercial customers.

In the early 1970s the company entered the market for contract office furnishings, fulfilling special orders for office furniture through interior designers, architects, and other agents. Through a licensing agreement the company manufactured and sold office furniture designed by Italian furniture maker Castelli. The company opened a factory in Treviso, Italy, producing goods for customers in Europe and the United States. Krueger Metal Products took the name Krueger International to reflect the company's new product and geographic range.

In 1977 Krueger International introduced the Vertebra office desk chair by renowned Italian chair designer Giancarlo Piretti and Emilio Ambasz of Argentina. The Vertebra chair became famous, being the first desk chair to provide passive ergonomic body support. The Vertebra was a precursor to the future of office design, which took into account the repetitive motions of office workers, especially as the desktop computer became an essential office tool.

1980s: Shift to Employee Ownership Corresponding with Changes in Business Philosophy

In 1980, 12 years after the death of Al Krueger, the Krueger family decided to sell its ownership in Krueger International. Richard Resch, then vice-president, led a management buyout of the company. Resch, who started working at the company in 1964, risked his personal financial security in order to fund the acquisition. Company managers obtained a 49 percent stake and Northwestern Mutual Life Insurance held a 51 percent stake. In 1986, management bought Northwestern Mutual's interest in Krueger International through another leveraged buyout. The company, renamed KI, became 100 percent employee owned.

By 1990 KI factory employees became eligible to purchase stock, available on a cash basis rather than through options. Later, KI extended ownership opportunities throughout the company, for some employees, through retirement and 401K plans. Resch hired a New York investment firm to determine stock value for KI's internal stock market. For Resch employee ownership was integral to his plan to initiate quality circle management practices on the factory floor as well as in company offices. In a democratic, rather than a bureaucratic, work environment, employee-owners took responsibility for quality service, productivity, and efficiency and had a stake in the success of the company beyond receiving a regular paycheck.

The management program required Resch to decertify the machinists union, which strictly limited the roles each worker could perform. In team-based management, cell (manufacturing unit) members performed whatever work was required based on where an order was in the production process. The rigid job description and financial security offered by the union was replaced with multiple tasks and pay incentives. Through the pay-for-knowledge program, factory employees obtained raises based on new knowledge and skills acquired and everyone was expected to learn how to read the company's financial statement, to use a computer, and to drive a forklift. "Gainsharing" provided monthly bonuses when workers met quality and budget standards.

In addition to greater manufacturing efficiency, the team management manufacturing process provided more flexibility in production. Resch advocated a philosophy that each customer is "a market of one," with unique requirements for organizing office space and new electronic tools. Rather than manufacture a mass of goods and then market them, KI adjusted to the changing needs of business, created by the newly computerized office operations.

Influence of Desktop Computing: 1980s

During the 1980s, office furniture designs increasingly accommodated requirements created by widespread installation of desktop computer systems for general office use. A horizontal, flexible desk arrangement provided space for computer and electronic equipment and adjusted to actual use. KI's COM System, designed in Italy, provided a system of wire manage-

ment and modules that could be clustered for collaborative work situations or an open space office, such as that common in Europe. In the United States workers tended to prefer individual spaces, so KI unveiled wall panels that offered cubicle-style privacy for individuals or small work groups. In 1989 KI introduced Systems Wall, a movable, multi-changeable, full-height panel system utilizing frames for wall panels and doors; Systems Wall allowed for office reconfiguration without having to destroy and rebuild permanent walls. KI developed the Data Board line of computer workstations, which featured slide-away and adjustable-height work surfaces for efficient body movement in the electronic work environment. For instance, keyboard drawers slid under the desktop when not in use and adjusted to the chair and body height of the computer user.

Sales at KI tripled during the 1980s, exceeding $180 million in 1990. To accommodate growth KI built a new factory in Manitowoc, Wisconsin, for the production of moveable walls and furniture systems. Opened in 1985, KI expanded the facility two years later. KI formed Pallas Textiles in 1988 to design and market upholstery, textiles, and fabrics for use in the manufacturing of chairs and wall panels, as well as for window treatments and wall coverings.

By 1990 KI had become the eighth largest manufacturer of nonresidential furniture in the United States. The company produced 50 different lines of chairs, primarily designed by Piretti, and a variety of desk workstations. KI operated three factories in Wisconsin and two in Mississippi. KI marketing involved advertising in magazines, such as *Interiors* and *Interior Design,* and displaying goods through showrooms in New York, Boston, Washington, D.C., Chicago, Dallas, Houston, Los Angeles, and San Francisco. Prominent customers included Shell Oil Company, Sun Microsystems, Northwestern Mutual Life Insurance, and J.C. Penney.

Furniture by renowned designers contributed to KI's success. In 1991 KI introduced the popular Perry chair, designed by sculptor and architect Charles Perry. The Perry chair involved a flexible, single-piece frame that supported the lower back by adjusting to the user's weight and forward and backward movements. For ease of transport and storage, the chairs were designed to be stacked up to 25 high and moved on a dolly. One of the unique features of the chair, as a stackable chair, was the option of a comfortable cushion, available in seven colors. Several publications featured short articles on the Perry chair, including *Time* and *Fortune* magazines, the *Wall Street Journal,* and the *New York Times.*

1990s Growth Through Manufacturing Expansion and Acquisitions

During the 1990s KI's internal growth created a demand for increased manufacturing capacity. On the urging of an employee, Scott Deugo, KI purchased the Storwal International factory in Pembroke, Ontario, Canada, in 1992. Storwal manufactured steel file cabinets and drawer pedestals for several years, until the factory closed in 1991. Deugo worked at Storwal as a designer, but Storwal rejected his ideas. Deugo persuaded KI to renovate the factory and to create new designs for the burgeoning home office business.

Key Dates:

1941: Al Krueger founds business to produce metal folding chairs.
1964: Sales to commercial and institutional customers near $4 million.
1977: The first passive ergonomic desk chair, the Vertebra, is introduced by KI.
1980: The Krueger family sells ownership in the company to management and investors.
1986: Senior management obtains 100 percent ownership of KI.
1990: A system of employee stock ownership is implemented.
1991: The Perry stackable chair is launched, gaining much media attention.
1998: Flexible Workspace office system wins Best of Competition at NeoCon, the contract furnishings trade show.
2002: KI products win six awards at NeoCon.

KI invested $7 million in Pembroke operations, including product design. Renovation began with the removal of comfortable offices located in the center of the factory floor, originally placed there for management oversight of production workers. KI implemented its quality management structure of self-directed teams and planned to initiate stock options five years after all debts of the facility were paid, including a $750,000 loan KI received from the city of Pembroke. In early 1993 the factory reopened with 140 employees, manufacturing nine lines of steel filing cabinets, many in attractive contemporary designs.

Investment in the Pembroke facility proved worthwhile as employees, many of whom had worked for Storwal, effectively operated the factory and won the Canada Award for Excellence in 1996. The award was based on three years of financial results, in which time Pembroke fulfilled furnishing contracts for Microsoft, Sun Microsystems, and banks in the United Kingdom; a contract with Office Depot provided office furniture for the home office market. In 1995 sales at the facility reached C$60 million. Employment peaked at 400 in 1995, declining to 320 jobs after completion of a large manufacturing contract.

KI increased its manufacturing capabilities in the United States as well. The company expanded the Manitowac plant, adding 68,000 square feet and creating 100 jobs to produce two lines of computer furniture; production began in May 1997. In 1998 the company relocated its Gillett manufacturing to a former pickling plant in Bonduel. The 220,000-square-foot plant represented a 50 percent increase in production space for new product lines.

KI pursued a strategy of acquisition to complement the company's existing product lines. In 1998 KI acquired AGI Industries of High Point, North Carolina. AGI produced tables and soft lounge seating for institutional and commercial customers, including the healthcare industry. AGI brought to KI the award-winning Gorka line of stylish desks and stackable chairs, designed by Jorge Pensi. KI further expanded into the

healthcare seating market with the acquisition of ADD Specialized Support Technology in Los Angeles. In 1999 KI acquired Period Furniture, of Henderson, Kentucky, maker of solid wood furniture for college dormitories and U.S. government housing.

KI's largest acquisition, in July 1998, involved the Spacesaver Corporation of Fort Atkinson, Wisconsin. A manufacturer of rolling shelf systems, Spacesaver products provided efficient use of storage capacity by constricting aisle space and using that space for movable shelves; at the push of a button, the electronic system activated shelf movement to create an aisle where the materials desired would be accessible. Spacesaver systems suited situations where ample storage space was required for books or files, including healthcare facilities, offices, libraries, and museums. KI expected to open new markets for Spacesaver products. With $43 million in revenues in 1997, Spacesaver would make a significant contribution to KI's revenues as well, at $450 million in 1997.

Continuing Innovation Amid Economic Downturn: Early 2000s

As the national economy expanded during the late 1990s, high technology and rapid growth companies made new demands on office furnishings. A contract with Sun Microsystems during the mid-1990s led KI to develop new systems adaptable to rapid changes in office structure prompted by mergers, downsizing, or new projects. Led by Niels Diffrient, the KI design team visited the Sun Microsystems headquarters in Mountain View, California, to assess the company's needs, primarily to eliminate cubicles in favor of open space for team collaboration. KI custom designed and manufactured modular, freestanding tables, moveable shelving, and a wall panel system that provided flexibility in reorganizing workstations.

In an open office, wire management became more of an issue in office furniture design. Wires could no longer be hidden behind desk panels, so KI designed PowerTowers, a unique overhead wire management tool. A floor-to-ceiling tower allowed power and data catalysts to be connected or disconnected easily. The towers, which managed wires and cables for up to four workstations, and wire-free panels facilitated a flexible, nonlinear process of office reconfiguration and allowed customers to easily reconfigure office space with a minimum of power disruption. KI branded the new office system Flexible Workspace. In 1998 the product won the Best of Competition award at NeoCon, the contract furnishing industry's largest annual trade show.

For the education market KI designed Einstein brand furniture, primarily for the elementary and high schools (Einstein was renamed Intellect in 2003 for copyright purposes). Introduced in 1998, the products involved tables and chairs that were lightweight, durable, flexible, and functional, to meet the needs of group and individual activities. Available in a variety of sizes, the furniture accommodated everyone from preschoolers to adults. Other products included Torsion on the Go chairs, with movable arm tablets, which were deemed good for student posture and featured a leg base design that made them difficult to tip back on. All Terrain mobile tables included larger tables for art classes. KI offered the furniture in a variety of colors, as well as in curved designs for lobby areas.

With much of the contract furnishings business dependent on high-technology companies, KI experienced a sudden drop in new orders in early 2001 as activity in the high-tech economy slowed. KI management made a strategic decision to continue developing innovative furniture to maintain a competitive edge despite economic uncertainty. At NeoCon 2002, that decision resulted in KI winning six awards. In the Architectural Products and Finishes category, KI won the Gold award for its Genius Full Height Movable Wall. Constructed with aluminum, the three-and-a-half-inch thick panel provided excellent sound absorption while being light in weight for ease of movement. The Genius walls were designed with contemporary aesthetic qualities, including rounded shapes and smooth finishes. Spacesaver's Designer Series won a Gold award in the Files & Storage category for its wide variety of design and finishing options. Spacesaver also won a Silver award for its TouchPad Release, which utilized a four-digit pin security. Pallas Textiles received a Silver award for innovation for its new Alloy panel fabric. Designer Michael Laessle looked to military technology to interlock polyester crepe with aluminum, creating a durable, textured fabric with a beautiful sheen. The Wharton Lectern, designed as a technology hub for classrooms and auditoriums, won a silver award for the Workplace Technologies category.

While economic difficulties continued in 2002 and 2003, KI endured better than some of its competitors. KI laid off few employees and temporarily cut employee hours in customer service and finance. The company experienced a sales increase of 15 to 20 percent in healthcare seating in early 2003 and maintained its number one market position in institutional furniture. New product introductions for 2003 included seating in minimalist designs. The Piretti Dance Chair, a lightweight, flexible-back, folding chair, provided easy stacking and nesting for compact storage. AGI introduced Grand Salon lounge furniture, designed by David Allan Pesso and inspired by 1930s and 1940s styles.

Principal Subsidiaries

ADD Specialized Support Technology; AGI, Inc.; Pallas Textiles; Period Furniture; Spacesaver Corporation.

Principal Competitors

Haworth, Inc.; Herman Miller Inc.; HON Industries, Inc.; Kimball Office Group; Steelcase, Inc.; Trendway Corporation.

Further Reading

Cannon, Steve, "Flexibility in Offices' Future," *News & Observer,* December 17, 2001, p. B6.
Christianson, Rich, "NeoCon Gets Totally Wired," *Wood & Wood Products,* September 1998, p. 25.
"Furniture Maker Takes Over Former Pickling Plant in Bonduel," *Wisconsin State Journal,* November 6, 1997, p. 4F.
Geran, Monica, and Elliott Martin, "KI—Best of Competition: Vignelli Associates and Eric Bartlet, Each Handling a Unified Whole, Let the Product Speak for Itself," *Interior Design,* December 1989, p. 128.
Gould, Les, "Controls Retrofit Ups Productivity at . . . This Old Plant," *Modern Materials Handling,* May 1996, p. 36.
Hill, Bert, "Pembroke Firm Wins Major Award: Cabinet Maker KI Honored for Quality," *Ottawa Citizen,* October 10, 1996, p. C7.
Joshi, Pradnya, "Not Sitting Idle KI Finds New Ways to Remodel the Workplace," *Milwaukee Journal Sentinel,* September 13, 1996, p. 1D.
Karlgaard, Rich, "Digital Rules," *Forbes,* September 2, 2002, p. 043.
Kauh, Elaine, "KI Cuts Workers' Hours Because of Slower Sales," *Green Bay Press-Gazette,* January 30, 2003, p. 10C.
"KI Buys Furniture Maker in North Carolina," *Milwaukee Journal Sentinel,* February 18, 1998, p. 2D.
"KI: Durable Einstein Furniture Saves the Day at Elementary School," *School Planning and Management,* January 2002, p. 54.
"KI Plans to Expand Its Manitowoc Plant," *Milwaukee Journal Sentinel,* December 11, 1996, p. 1D.
"Krueger to Lay Off 45 Employees," *Milwaukee Journal Sentinel,* October 17, 2001, p. 2D.
Kueny, Barbara, "Resch Cultivates Corporate Growth, Culture at Krueger International," *Business Journal-Milwaukee,* May 27, 1991, p. S16.
Newman, Judy, "New Owner Hopes to Double Spacesaver Sales: Fort Atkinson Maker of Rolling Shelves Sold to Green Bay Furniture Firm," *Wisconsin State Journal,* July 18, 1998, p. 8B.
"Polish-American Furniture Distribution Company," *Global News Wire,* September 29, 2000, p. 4.
Rodie, Janet Bealer, "Shimmer and Strength: Employing Military Technology, Pallas Textiles Bonds Polyester Crepe with Aluminum in Its Award-Winning Alloy Panel Fabric," *Textile World,* May 2003, p. 66.
Ryman, Richard, "KI President Dick Resch," *Green Bay Press-Gazette,* January 5, 2003, p. 1E.
——, "KI Takes Boredom Out of Assembly Line," *Green Bay Press-Gazette,* January 5, 2003, p. 1E.
"This Chair Stacks Up," *Time,* June 3, 1991, p. 47.
Wilton, Kelly, "KI International Can Claim Success and High Staff Morale Thanks to the Japanese Management Style of Working in Teams," *Ottawa Citizen,* August 21, 1993, p. D3.
Zelinsky, Marilyn, "A Corporate Point of View," *Interiors,* August 1994, p. 48.

—Mary Tradii

kirshenbaum bond+partners

Kirshenbaum Bond + Partners, Inc.

160 Varick Street
New York, New York 10013
U.S.A.
Telephone: (212) 633-0080
Toll Free: (877) 337-4892
Fax: (212) 463-8643
Web site: http://www.kb.com

Private Company
Founded: 1987 as Kirshenbaum & Bond Advertising Inc.
Employees: 170
Sales: $50 million (2001 est.)
NAIC: 541810 Advertising Agencies; 541860 Direct Mail
 Advertising

Kirshenbaum Bond + Partners, Inc. has quickly made its mark as one of the most original—and irreverent—advertising agencies in the United States. A healthy (or perhaps unhealthy) dose of ''New York attitude'' has helped the firm stand out in an industry homogenized by the amalgamation of other agencies into superfirms such as Interpublic Group, Omnicom Group, and WPP Group PLC. As a result of this growing concentration, Kirshenbaum Bond is one of the few independent advertising agencies of significant size remaining in New York.

Provocateurs: 1987–90

Richard Kirshenbaum was 26 and Jonathan Bond 29 when they founded their company, Kirshenbaum & Bond Advertising Inc., in 1987. Kirshenbaum was a copywriter and Bond an account executive when, on their own time, they sold shoe designer Kenneth Cole on an ad that poked fun at the enormous shoe collection of Imelda Marcos, widow of the ousted Filipino dictator.

The new kids on the block pooled $50,000 in savings, rented quarters in Manhattan's SoHo district, and hung up a giant poster, blank except for two silver balls in the lower right-hand corner and the copy, ''It takes three things to create great advertising. A great idea is one of them.'' They were quickly labeled as brats, not only for their abrasive ads but for juvenile behavior; for example, a skateboarding employee once crashed

into a visiting client. Kirshenbaum & Bond (K&B) garnered seven clients in its first month, but they were small accounts, and the partners were desperate to be noticed. Shortly after, Kenneth Cole's brother Neal paid them a visit. He owned a small jeans company named No Excuses that had earned barely $10 million in two years and needed attention as badly as K&B. The partners came up with a 15-second television spot featuring Donna Rice, a young woman recently reported to be carrying on an affair with married presidential candidate Gary Hart. As Rice modeled the jeans, she delivered the line, ''I make no excuses, I only wear them.''

Having established themselves as the bad boys of advertising, Kirshenbaum and Bond upped the ante with forays into the uncertain shoals of ethnic humor. They drew a protest from the Italian-American Defamation League for picturing bullet holes on a blank page with the headline, ''Finally, an authentic Italian restaurant where no one's been shot. Yet.'' The slogan, ''Dress British. Think Yiddish'' for a discount men's clothier inspired letters to the agency protesting the implication that Jews were cheap. A Times Square billboard for Hongson Importers' Jump sneakers that bore the legend, ''The only way to get higher is illegal'' seemed, for some, to suggest racial stereotyping. To its critics, Kirshenbaum and Bond offered no excuses—or apologies. Brashness made sense, the partners maintained, because the product had to seize the attention of prospective consumers before they would buy it. It also made sense for K&B, Bond later conceded. Speaking to Cynthia Rigg of *Advertising Age* in 1993, he explained, ''When we started the agency we didn't have a brand name, any financial backing or a big client. We decided to do outrageous advertising to get us and our clients on the map.''

Kirshenbaum & Bond certainly succeeded in this objective. Within a year from the founding of the agency it had a staff of 12 and billings of $9 million. K&B also had, in *Esquire,* a mainstream client who fancied its abrasive approach. The men's magazine wanted to drive home to advertisers the contention that its readers were upscale consumers, so Kirshenbaum & Bond introduced a print ad showing a suited man with exposed hairy chest and the headline, ''Some men will never by ready for *Esquire.*'' Another ad showed large quilted dice hanging from the rearview mirror of a car, accompanied by the headline, ''Some men will never be ready for a BMW. Or *Esquire.*''

Company Perspectives:

We tirelessly search for the "big idea" that will catapult our clients' brands to new heights and into unexplored territory.

Into the Mainstream: 1990s

K&B celebrated its second anniversary by moving into quarters four times as big as the original space; it now had 32 employees and annual billings of $25 million. The agency's clients now included such blue-chip firms as Fox Broadcasting, Bear Stearns, Austin, Nichols (makers of Wild Turkey bourbon), and New York City's Dorset and Empire hotels. Yet such was its reputation that when Randall Rothenberg of the *New York Times* visited their offices in early 1991, he feigned surprise that "nobody was swinging from the chandeliers." Rothenberg learned, however, from a liaison between marketers and ad agencies, "They've got a presentation like a big agency. They talked about strategy. They did research. They did all the things clients expect—but not from them." In 1991 the agency began requiring employees to submit weekly time sheets, a formality Kirshenbaum and Bond had sworn never to demand. The transition to professionalism also included hiring experienced account executives from larger agencies and improving graphic design by hiring Bill Oberlander, the art director of a larger agency, as creative director.

About this time Kirshenbaum told Joe Lafayette of *Advertising Age*, "I don't think we ever labeled ourselves as brats. [But] our success demonstrates that our marketing strategy works. We don't mind that certain people don't like us. We're targeting clients who want a cutting edge." Bond conceded that sometimes the agency suffered because "people always thought our work was us as people. But we're really easy to work with and get along with. Just because the ads have an edge, an attitude, doesn't mean that's the way we are when you meet us. We're rational people with big-agency backgrounds."

In the last weeks of 1990 Kirshenbaum & Bond brought its billings to around $40 million a year by garnering as new clients Chemical Bank, Savin Corp., Chase Manhattan Bank, and Guinness Import Co. Chase Manhattan hired the agency to market its credit cards to college students. Guinness was seeking a new marketing campaign for its brews and liked the work Kirshenbaum & Bond already had done for Hennessy cognac and Domain (Moet) Chandon sparkling wine. For Schieffelin & Somerset Co., K&B later publicized its "Hennessy martini" (with a lemon twist but no vermouth) by hiring young actors to ask for the drink at Manhattan nightclubs and restaurants during peak weekend hours. So successful was the stunt that Bond told Stuart Elliott of the *New York Times,* "We've heard people order Hennessy martinis in bars who were paying for them." Eventually the agency was planting shills in bars in Chicago, Miami, Los Angeles, and San Francisco as well as New York.

Another client seeking youth-oriented buzz was the dowdy Thom McAn Shoe Co. Kirshenbaum & Bond attempted to make the Thom McAn chain contemporary with television spots in which young people voiced statements such as, "I never thought I could have a B.S.A., M.B.A. and a Ph.D. and still no job" and "I never thought there could be over 80 channels and still nothing on," before concluding, "I never thought I'd find such cool-looking shoes at Thom McAn." The spots ended with a slogan also featured in print ads and on posters, "The new Thom McAn. Your feet won't believe your eyes."

By early 1993 Kirshenbaum & Bond had 95 employees, billings of $105 million a year, and a Los Angeles office (later closed). The big breakthrough came when the agency won the account for Snapple Beverage Corporation. In April 1993 Kirshenbaum & Bond launched a campaign, estimated at $30 million, that included Snapple's first ads on national television, radio, and print. The grass-roots campaign featured fan mail from real people. In one ad one of these "real people" was strapped to a lie detector and queried, "Were you lying when you wrote to Snapple?" A retired Kentucky colonel who wrote that Snapple was the "only good thing" to come out of New York was paired with former Mayor Edward Koch, who tried vainly to convince him there were other good things about the city. Wendy Kaufman, the Snapple executive in charge of answering the mail, became a celebrity herself: Wendy, the "Snapple Lady." A fan letter even inspired K&B to invent a new Snapple drink—Ralph's Cantaloupe Cocktail—named for the Yonkers, New York, letter writer.

The success of the Snapple campaign raised Kirshenbaum & Bond's credibility and transformed it into a midsized shop. By now named Kirshenbaum Bond & Partners, it had six partners, 200 employees, and annual billings of about $200 million. The 13 clients included mainstays such as Coach Leatherware and Schieffelin & Somerset (for which it was now handling six other brands besides Hennessy) and new clients such as Blimpie International, Citibank, and the cable-TV network CNBC. But as much as one-third of the agency's revenue was coming from the Snapple account, and the beverage's sales had begun to wane.

Quaker Oats Co., which now owned Snapple, dropped Kirshenbaum Bond & Partners (KB&P) on the same May 1996 day that the founding partners returned from a retreat with their employees during which they unveiled a new five-year plan. The loss of this account could have spelled doom for another agency, but KB&P was debt-free, ready to pursue new clients aggressively, and resolved to offer integrated services such as public relations, direct marketing, and media buying, like agencies many times its size. Among those who signed on were Rockport, Target, Netscape Communications, and Neuberger Berman. The agency even was able to open a San Francisco branch in 1997. By late 1998 KB&P claimed annual billings of $290 million and the addition, during the year, of 11 new clients, including Coca-Cola Co., Cablevision Systems Corp., Liberty Mutual Insurance Group, and 1-800-Flowers. The agency now employed about 245 people.

Still Independent, Full-Service Firm: 2000–02

In late 2000 Kirshenbaum Bond & Partners established an affiliate named Dotglu to focus on direct and interactive marketing services in order to help advertisers keep their existing customers. Combining two specialty KB&P units, Dotglu offered services such as customer relations marketing, database management, strategy and technology consulting, web site design, e-mail marketing, and online media planning and buying. Kirshenbaum explained to Elliott, "The ability to have a relationship with the customer brings in profits in a measurable

Key Dates:

1987: Richard Kirshenbaum and Jonathan Bond found Kirshenbaum & Bond (K&B) with $50,000 in savings; cheeky ad for No Excuses jeans garners attention for the firm.

1993: K&B makes its big breakthrough by winning the Snapple Beverage account.

1998: Despite loss of the Snapple account, K&B claims annual billings of $290 million.

2000: Dotglu, an affiliate, makes online marketing services its focus.

way. That's because persuading customers to buy again from a company they have bought from before is usually less difficult—and more profitable—than convincing consumers who have never bought from a company to do so for the first time.'' KB&P took the majority stake in Dotglu, with senior executives and an investor group holding the rest. Earlier, the agency had acquired a minority share of a start-up New York agency, Frierson Mee & Kraft. The company also had bought and sold a minority share in Mad Dogs and Englishmen, another small New York agency.

Kirshenbaum Bond & Partners ranked 24th among New York City advertising agencies in 1999 and by late 2000 was credited with annual gross income of $37 million. By this time independent midsized agencies like KB&P were practically extinct—at least in New York—swallowed by competitors or merged into bigger holding companies because of client demand for a full range of services and global marketing capacity. Advertising industry sources also cited the diversion of capital and creative talent to Hollywood and to Internet- and web-based ventures.

The year 2001 was a difficult one for the national and local economies. Kirshenbaum Bond & Partners suffered a reduction of 18 percent in estimated billings and 8 percent in revenue. The agency won Revlon Inc. as a client but lost it in January 2002, forcing a staff cut from 223 to 202. Oberlander left KB&P in December 2000 after 11 years. Agency sources, according to Ann M. Mack of *Adweek,* credited him for encouraging ''a culture open to experimentation . . . but the arty results were sometimes more misguided than innovative. In 2000, for example . . . sexually charged Tommy Hilfiger spots felt gratuitous, and a text-heavy 'Anti-Super Bowl' spot rebranding DLJdirect as CSFBdirect was confusing.'' CSFB (the financial firm Credit Suisse First Boston) departed as a client in 2001, along with the Japanese camera maker Olympus Optical Co., Ltd. Speaking to Mack, Bond conceded that the agency's work had ''lost some of that edge for some years'' and a source told her, ''If you're a client looking for something different, [they've] lost that.''

Oberlander was succeeded by Rob Feakins and Logan Wilmont, who inherited a creative department shrunk from 40 to 25. The two pushed for simple, strong ideas. For Manhattan's Downtown Alliance, which was seeking business for its members following the Twin Towers disaster, KB&P presented spots showing a construction worker getting a manicure and a bald man having a haircut, with the message, ''You may not need it, but downtown does.'' For Target, they decided to illustrate the concept: If you found a really good deal and could buy as much as you wanted, how would you use the product? and devised spots such as a driver steering through an obstacle course of Tide boxes and a guitarist using toilet paper for soundproofing. This campaign won the agency a contract to produce 16 spots in 2002 instead of the usual one or two per year.

By midsummer 2002 Kirshenbaum Bond & Partners had picked up nearly $80 million in new business billings during the year, including assignments from Clear-Blue and ClearPlan Easy, Hartz Mountain Corp., Meow Mix, USA Networks Inc., Verizon Communications' SuperPages, and VF Corp.'s Intimates. Beverage Partners Worldwide, a joint venture of Coca-Cola and Nestlé S.A., was reported to have hired the agency to introduce Tey, a bottled tea. The agency's name became Kirshenbaum Bond + Partners in 2003. That year the firm won a $95 million account from Andrew Jergens Co., manufacturer of lines of lotions, facial care products, and antiperspirants.

Principal Competitors

Arnold McGrath Worldwide; Gotham Inc.; Margeotes Fertitta + Partners.

Further Reading

Brown, Ed, ''Hold the Olives,'' *Fortune,* March 2, 1998, pp. 37, 40.

DeNitto, Emily, ''Advertising Agency Reaches Adolescence,'' *Crain's New York Business,* September 4, 1995, pp. 3, 36.

Dolce, Joe, ''Two for the Goad,'' *Advertising Age,* May 2, 1988, Creativity Supplement, pp. 14–17.

Dougherty, Philip H., ''Esquire Ads Poke Fun at Nonreaders,'' *New York Times,* April 11, 1988, p. D9.

Elliott, Stuart, ''Advertising,'' *New York Times,* August 20, 1993, p. D15.

——, ''Advertising,'' *New York Times,* December 3, 1993, p. D16.

——, ''Advertising,'' *New York Times,* January 14, 1994, p. D15.

——, ''Advertising,'' *New York Times,* November 27, 2000, p. C15.

Gault, Ylonda, ''Snapple Love Letters Sealed with a Twist,'' *Crain's New York Business,* August 16, 1993, p. 5.

Goldman, Kevin, ''Snapple Goes Big Times for New Age Drink,'' *Wall Street Journal,* April 20, 1993, p. B7.

Goldstein, Matthew, ''Forty Under Forty: New York's Rising Stars,'' *Crain's New York Business,* January 25, 1999, p. 19.

Lafayette, Joe, ''Brat Pack Grows Up,'' *Advertising Age,* January 14, 1991, p. 39.

Mack, Ann M., ''Fighting Chance,'' *Adweek ,* August 19, 2002, pp. 18–19.

McDonald, Michael, ''Adamant Agency Stays Independent,'' *Crain's New York Business,* December 11, 2000, pp. 1, 41.

McMains, Andrew, ''Kirshenbaum's Culture Shift Appears to Work,'' *Adweek,* November 23, 1998, p. 8.

Rigg, Cynthia, ''Brash Black Sheep Is Now Respectable,'' *Crain's New York Business,* March 22, 1993, p. 8.

Rothenberg, Randall, ''Advertising 'Bad Boys' Grow Up in a Downturn,'' *New York Times,* January 2, 1991, pp. D1, D3.

——, ''Outgrowing a Need to Be Outrageous,'' *New York Times,* September 26, 1989, p. D25.

Temes, Judy, ''Growing Pains for 'Bad Boys,' '' *Crain's New York Times,* June 23, 1997, p. 21.

—Robert Halasz

Kohn Pedersen Fox Associates P.C.

111 West 57th Street
New York, New York 10019
U.S.A.
Telephone: (212) 977-6500
Fax: (212) 956-2526
Web site: http://www.kpf.com

Private Company
Founded: 1976
Employees: 196
Sales: $63.2 million (2002 est.)
NAIC: 541310 Architectural Services

Kohn Pedersen Fox Associates P.C. is an architectural firm that in a relatively short period of time had achieved both commercial success and professional recognition. KPF's postmodern urban buildings have been acclaimed for evoking the spirit of the romantic office towers of the 1920s and early 1930s without copying them, employing a style of abstracted classicism. Since the end of the1980s New York City-based KPF has greatly increased its activities abroad, and its principal designer, William Pedersen, has abandoned postmodernism in favor of fragmented structures that combine a multiplicity of complex shapes.

Starting Out in the 1970s

The firm was launched on July 4, 1976—the nation's bicentennial—by A. Eugene Kohn, William Pedersen, and Sheldon Fox. Kohn had been president and a partner of John Carl Warnecke and Associates, while Pedersen and Fox were both vice-presidents in the firm. Kohn became the new firm's president and, usually, partner-in-charge of projects; Pedersen was the designer; and Fox oversaw administration and finance. Architecture was in the midst of a decade-long slump, but by the end of the year the firm had 25 employees and was expanding so rapidly that it needed new office space. Other Warnecke alumni soon joined KPF, among them Arthur May and William Louie as design partners and Robert Cioppa as a management partner.

Kohn attributed his firm's unusually successful debut to its ability to support clients in all aspects of building, not just design work. This support included financial planning, site selection, and a number of other necessary considerations, "from economics and marketing to image and esthetics," he told Paul Goldberger of the *New York Times* in 1977. "We would rather tell a client that he shouldn't build a certain building at all if it isn't going to be viable." KPF was quick to assemble a real-estate consultant, a construction manager, and other experts: personnel who usually reported directly to the client.

Interviewed many years later by Laura Heery for *Architectural Record,* Kohn observed that "Nobody called us on day one. Starting out we had a most positive and confident attitude. That is important. We were not completely new kids on the block. We had been practicing in major firms for some 20 years and had designed or managed the design and construction of major buildings and dealt with significant clients. We had no work, but we had access to people—facilities managers, developers, corporate presidents—we could call and get advice from, and that is what we did." Kohn added that "I wrote developers and marketed them aggressively. We made cold calls, wrote letters, and used the media. As articles were written about KPF, we made sure that clients and potential clients received copies." In what a staffer later called the firm's "tower an hour" days, they took on feasibility studies for anyone who would pay, even for dubious ideas like shoehorning buildings over untouchable Manhattan landmarks—designs that Goldberger later observed "the partners are probably now grateful were never built."

Among Kohn Pedersen Fox's early work were designs for an office tower in Lexington, Kentucky, an American Telephone and Telegraph Co. office complex in Oakton, Virginia, and a 36-story American Oil Co. high-rise in Denver. Of greater importance was the start of the firm's long-lasting relationship with the American Broadcasting Co. (ABC). Kohn Pedersen Fox read in the *New York Times* that ABC had just purchased an armory on Manhattan's West 66th/67th Street. According to Kohn, KPF was the only firm that contacted ABC to say it would be interested in talking about plans for the building. It was commissioned to study how to renovate the armory without any particular function in mind, such as office or studio space, and therefore it analyzed the feasibility of several uses, finally presenting to the network their choice of designs both for a studio building and for an office complex with a central atrium. Two buildings were erected in 1979 on West 67th Street from the firm's designs. By 1990 KPF had completed a dozen projects for ABC and its owner, Capital Cities/ABC Inc.

KPF's Postmodern Buildings of the 1980s and Early 1990s

One of Kohn Pedersen Fox's early, and most admired, buildings was 333 Wacker Drive in Chicago. Completed in 1983 on a triangular site at a bend in the Chicago River, this office building presented itself on the river side with a sweeping curved wall of green glass that evoked the river's own bend. The shorter two sides of the triangle faced Chicago's Loop and related to its grid pattern. Pedersen's design for a limestone extension of Procter & Gamble Co.'s headquarters in Cincinnati, completed in 1985, recalled skyscrapers of the 1920s, featuring twin octagonal towers with pyramidal roofs over an L-shaped base. KPF received national honor awards for both these buildings from the American Institute of Architects (AIA).

The building for AT&T, fashioned in trendy postmodern style, was described as a spectacular structure in a 1982 *Interior Design* article. For Philadelphia's Logan Square the firm designed a hotel on the southeast corner, with a high office building behind it. Both were clad in granite hung over the concrete structures. In a 1985 *Architectural Record* article, Darl Rastorfer cited KPF as "an innovative leader in the use of stone. . . . Rather than treating stone like flat tiles that are monotonously applied, Kohn Pedersen Fox acknowledges the sculptural character of the material." Photos displayed three examples: the Procter & Gamble building; the Wilmington, Delaware, headquarters of Hercules, Inc., a glass-walled building above a granite base; and 70 East 55th Street in New York, a brick office building with a stone facade. Other KPF-designed buildings of this period included Pedersen's Buffalo Savings Bank headquarters, topped by a Beaux-Arts dome, and Eight Penn Center in Philadelphia, by Arthur May, the design principal, essentially a concrete-and-glass box but with an assortment of curved corners.

Kohn Pedersen Fox's startling 34-story granite tower at the northwest corner of East 57th Street and Lexington Avenue in Manhattan faced the corner not in a straight line but in a great concave sweep rising to the top of the tower. A 55-story Seattle office tower—the city's most prominent downtown building—was, in Goldberger's words, "at once active and serene . . . [bespeaking] a desire to combine the formal imagery of classicism and the energizing aura of modernity." But no city

skyline seemed as transformed by KPF's presence as that of Chicago. By the fall of 1990 brand-new skyscrapers designed by the firm nuzzled the city's two tallest buildings, the Sears Tower and the John Hancock Center, joining two others by the river on South Wacker Drive. "Most of the KPF buildings," wrote Goldberger, "are visually active both on the street level and on the skyline, with multiple towers of cupolas to create a lively intersection with the sky."

Kohn Pedersen Fox also had a penchant for the ornamentation eschewed by modernist architecture but revived by postmodernism. A 1990 *Architectural Record* article cited the firm for the two painted-aluminum spires atop recently completed 225 West Wacker Drive in Chicago; the stainless-steel and bronze entrances of 101 Federal Street in Boston; the satin-finish stainless-steel and bronze railing, trim, details, and light fixtures in the lobby of One O'Hare Center, Rosemont, Illinois; and the bronze, brass, and stainless-steel ornamental details of the six-story retail mall within mixed-use 900 North Michigan Avenue in Chicago. Established in 1984, the firm's interiors subsidiary, Kohn Pedersen Fox Conway Associates, led by Patricia Conway, who joined the firm almost from the outset, also received recognition for meticulous craftsmanship and imaginative detail. Maintaining a close relationship with the parent firm, KPFC handled big jobs such as furnishing the 800,000-square-foot interior of the Procter & Gamble building, but the majority of its work was independent and ranged from an ark for a New York synagogue to apartment furnishings for muppeteer Jim Henson. Conway received the 1986 Designer of the Year award from *Interiors;* her firm had 80 employees and grossed $8.5 million the following year.

In a 1986 *New York Times Magazine* article, Goldberger credited Kohn Pedersen Fox's rise to prominence to Kohn's salesmanship as well as the firm's designers. Kohn, he wrote, was "perhaps the most persuasive salesman in the architecture business. His silver tongue could sell almost anything." What he had to sell, Goldberger added, was work that "has gotten better every year. Indeed, no body of large-scale commercial work being produced in this country right now is better or more consistent."

In 1987 Kohn attended a conference where an economist told the audience that unless their firms were working internationally by 1990, half would be out of business in five years. After designing the British headquarters of Goldman Sachs & Co. and the city's Canary Wharf Tower, Kohn Pedersen Fox opened a London office in 1988. Commissions followed in Glasgow and Hamburg, and in 1990 the firm won three Japanese commissions. By 1993 the firm was active in 19 countries but, like other architectural firms, it was still suffering the aftereffects of the 1990–91 U.S. recession. The staff had been reduced from 360 to 240, the partners had taken pay cuts, and the firm was looking for professionals who could act as entrepreneurs, managers, and marketers, as well as designers and technicians. Kohn told Yvonne Gault of *Crain's New York Business,* "We don't need caretakers. We need to be total architects in order to compete globally."

To win more commissions, KPF formed joint ventures and ad hoc partnerships. Its projects abroad included the Deutsche Genossenschaftbank in Frankfurt, Germany, the Chifley Tower in Sydney, Australia, and the $2.5 billion Nagoya Station project in Japan, which combined a department store, railroad station, and sky streets, as well as an office tower and a hotel. A Tokyo office was opened in 1995. Under construction in the United States were the Daniel Patrick Moynihan Courthouse in lower Manhattan; a Newport Harbor, California, art museum; University of Pennsylvania housing units; and the refurbishing of Philadelphia's Market Street Station. Also by this time, five new buildings had been completed and one renovated along West 66th and 67th streets in Manhattan for Capital Cities/ABC.

Beyond Postmodernism in the Late 1980s and 1990s

Designed by William Louie in 1991, Kohn Pedersen Fox's last postmodern building was the Daniel Patrick Moynihan Courthouse. During a vacation in India in 1986 Pedersen had decided that the postmodern style no longer suited his aesthetic aspirations. Buildings based on traditional European urbanism, although appropriate, he felt, for such big Eastern cities as New York, Boston, Philadelphia, and perhaps even Chicago, were unsuitable for sprawling Western cities like Los Angeles and Honolulu and also for Asian cities, where he contended that lack of compactness required a new aesthetic. Ironically, Pedersen first worked out this idea in a European city—Frankfurt—but its historical buildings had been demolished by bombing in World War II. His 1987 design for the Westendstrasse L/DG bank headquarters broke the building into parts that corresponded to the differing heights and characters of surrounding buildings. The shaft rose not from a conventional base but from a variety of low-rise structures, clad in granite and marble to contrast with the steel-and-green-glass tower. The firm won its third AIA National Honor Award for this building, in 1994.

Pedersen continued to design fragmented high-rise structures that combined a multiplicity of complex shapes, wryly conceding to Andrea Rothman of *Business Week* in 1991 that "our buildings aren't as 'nice' as they used to be." His design for Rockefeller Plaza West, a 57-story office tower in midtown Manhattan that was not realized because of the client's financial difficulties, "used the building as a 'skewer' and hung from it a variety of visually discrete layers that spiral up to a decorative

crown," wrote Carter Wiseman for *New York.* "It is certainly the fullest flowering yet of Pedersen's rapidly evolving abstract-classic aesthetic." For IBM, he designed a low-lying, Z-shaped, stainless-steel, glass, and stone headquarters on the same Armonk, New York, site as the old one. A symbol of IBM's downsizing, it was smaller than the old one and held fewer employees but gave almost everyone cubicles facing the surrounding landscape and hid from view the once prominent parking spaces. Horizontality also prevailed in Pedersen's addition to the World Bank headquarters in Washington, D.C., which placed the two new office blocks around the existing two structures. This building won the firm a fourth AIA National Honor Award in 1998. As Karrie Jacobs of *New York* observed, KPF was "designing buildings that look as if the postmodern period never happened."

By 1997 Kohn Pedersen Fox's fortunes had revived considerably, especially in the United States, where the firm completed five major buildings that year, including the IBM headquarters. The New York office was working on about 50 projects with a construction value estimated at about $7.8 billion. Among these was the Pedersen-designed huge new Vertical Campus for Baruch College, completed in 2001 to occupy almost the entire block on Lexington Avenue between East 24th and 25th streets in Manhattan. In *New York,* Joseph Giovannini hailed "The building's daring beauty. . . . The architects cleverly bypassed luxury materials in favor of the greater luxury of abundant light and open space . . . proving that a public college need not give its students bargain-basement design." KPF received its fifth National AIA Honor Award for the Baruch College Vertical Campus in 2003.

International projects included plans to build the world's tallest building in Shanghai. A vertical steel-and-glass shaft with a round hole near the top, it resembled, in drawings, nothing so much as a giant bottle opener. Ground was broken for this project, the Shanghai World Financial Center, in 1997. It was subsequently put on hold, and construction recommenced in 2003. The firm completed work in 2003 on a Tokyo complex with a central tower that was one of the highest in Japan. Paul Katz was the architect in charge of both projects. KPF was also working on a Hong Kong skyscraper that was to be almost as tall as the one in Shanghai.

Kohn Pedersen Fox provided the design for the 1997 high-rise federal courthouse in Portland, Oregon, which at more than 340 feet high and 602,000 square feet in bulk dominated the city's government district. In 2000 it designed a 34-story glass-walled hotel, said to be the largest private development underway on the East Coast, for the Mohegan Sun gaming complex in Connecticut. The London office, led by Lee Polisano, designed one of the most technically advanced office buildings in Europe for Endesa, S.A., a large Spanish electricity producer. Located near Madrid, it featured a central atrium designed without air conditioning that acted as a thermal buffer between outdoor and indoor temperatures. An array of roof solar panels was the largest of its kind in Europe.

Although Kohn and Pedersen remained the nucleus of the firm, there were numerous personnel changes in the "post-postmodern" era of the firm. May had left KPF by 1990, and Conway was gone by 1993. Fox retired in 1995 and his role was filled by Cioppa. Polisano became a partner in 1986 and senior partner of the new London office, Kohn Pedersen Fox International, in 1989. He became president of the parent firm in 2003. David Leventhal was named design partner for the London office in 1989. Kohn Pedersen Fox was employing 91 architects and a staff of 105 in 2002. It was engaged in 75 projects that year, of which 39 were overseas. The worldwide construction volume of its projects came to $2 billion.

Principal Competitors

Emery Roth & Partners LLC.; Foster and Partners Ltd.; Gwathmey Siegel & Associates Architects LLC; Hellmuth, Obata and Kassabaum Inc.; Nicholas Grimshaw & Partners; Pei Cobb Freed & Partners Architects LLP; Polshek Partnership Architects; Skidmore Owings & Merrill LLP.

Further Reading

Anderson, Grace M., "Five by KPF," *Architectural Record,* February 1987, pp. 126–35.
——, "Kohn Pedersen Fox: External Forces Shape Multiform Towers," *Architectural Record,* June 1981, pp. 81–91.
Baraban, Regina, "Kohn Pedersen Draws Blueprint for Expansion in Manhattan," *Crain's New York Business,* October 27, 1997, p. 16.
Betsky, Aaron, "Search for Justice," *Architecture,* November 1997, pp. 122–29.
Chao, Sonia R., and Trevor D. Abramson, eds., *Kohn Pedersen Fox: Buildings and Projects 1976–1986,* New York: Rizzoli, 1987.
Gault, Yvonne, "Redesigning Its House," *Crain's New York Business,* February 15, 1993, pp. 3, 23.
Giovannini, Joseph, "Open Admissions," *New York,* December 17, 2001, pp. 62–63.
Goldberger, Paul, "Architects Widen Traditional Role to Give Clients Business Service," *New York Times,* January 4, 1977, p. 25.
——, "Architecture That Pays Off Handsomely," *New York Times Magazine,* March 16, 1986, pp. 48, 51–52, 54, 74, 78.
——, "Breaking the Rules to Make a Corner an Urban Event," *New York Times,* October 9, 1988, Sec. 2, p. 32.
——, "Finding a Street," *New York Times,* January 24, 1993, Sec. 2, p. 30.
——, "A New York Firm Sets the Style in Chicago," *New York Times,* September 30, 1990, Sec. 2, pp. 34–35.
——, "Proud of Its Height, A New Tower Rules Over Seattle," *New York Times,* November 27, 1988, Sec. 2, p. 36.
"How Do They Get Their Commissions?" *Architectural Record,* January 1990, pp. 37, 39, 41.
Jacobs, Karrie, "Small Blue Thing," *New York,* November 3, 1997, pp. 24, 26–27.
James, Warren A., ed., *Kohn Pedersen Fox: Architecture and Urbanism, 1986–1992,* New York: Rizzoli, 1993.
KPF: Selected and Current Works, Australia: Images Publishing Group, 1997.
London, Donald, "An Affinity for Ornament," *Architectural Record,* May 1990, pp. 121–23.
McKee, Bradford, "Towering Ambitions," *Architecture,* November 1997, pp. 94–99.
"Onwards and Upwards," *Economist,* February 8, 2003, p. 59.
Rastorfer, Darl, "Well Tailored Stone," *Architectural Record,* June 1985, pp. 163–69.
Rothman, Andrea, "He Changed the Skyline. Now He's Changing," *Business Week,* January 28, 1991, pp. 50–51.
Sachner, Paul M., "Corporate Details," *Architectural Record,* Mid-September 1988, pp. 92–93.
Slesin, Suzanne, "Designer of the Year Points Her Firm to Office Interiors," *New York Times,* February 5, 1987, pp. C1, C8.
Wiseman, Carter, "Architecture," *New York,* September 11, 1989, p. 546.

—Robert Halasz

Kroll Inc.

900 Third Avenue
New York, New York 10022
U.S.A.
Telephone: (212) 593-1000
Toll Free: (888) 209-9526
Fax: (212) 750-5628
Web site: http://www.krollworldwide.com

Public Company
Founded: 1972 as Kroll Associates
Employees: 2,300
Sales: $289.2 million (2002)
Stock Exchanges: NASDAQ
Ticker Symbol: KROL
NAIC: 561611 Investigation Services; 514190 Other
Information Services; 541219 Other Accounting
Services; 541330 Engineering Services; 541614
Process, Physical Distribution, and Logistics
Consulting Services; 541618 Other Management
Consulting Services; 541620 Environmental
Consulting Services; 541690 Other Scientific and
Technical Consulting Services

Long considered one of the business world's best kept secrets, Kroll Inc. has been hired by multinational corporations and governments alike to investigate fraud, embezzlement, environmental compliance, even murder. Kroll's successes are world famous; they include finding millions that former president Ferdinand Marcos stole from the Philippines; tracking billions skimmed from Iraqi oil profits by Saddam Hussein; and breaking the Gambino crime family's stranglehold on the Long Island trucking industry. With former agents, police officers, prosecutors, and licensed detectives making up its ranks, Kroll has the manpower and the resources to take on even the most complicated cases.

From Lawyering to Investigating: 1970s

Jules B. Kroll was born in 1941 in Brooklyn, New York. His father owned a printing company and his mother was a homemaker. Young Jules did well in school, attended Cornell University where he earned a bachelor's degree in 1963, then went on to Georgetown University Law School. He received his law degree from Georgetown in 1966, took the New York bar exam, and worked as an assistant district attorney in Manhattan. Kroll's experiences in the D.A.'s office included prosecuting a wide range of crimes and working with up and coming politicians including Robert F. Kennedy. After a few years, however, Jules branched out on his own and founded Kroll Associates in 1972.

Kroll started off small but ended up consulting for some of New York City's largest and most powerful corporate entities. Kroll's first customer was Curtis Publishing Company, which was renamed Cadence Industries after a merger. Because of his knowledge of printing and publishing (from his father's company), Jules Kroll was hired to assist the company's purchasing department, reviewing costs and cutting waste. By 1974 Kroll took on his first white collar investigation, which had become an increasing problem in the inflationary and Watergate-tinged 1970s.

By the dawn of the 1980s Kroll Associates had proven itself adept at investigation and there was no shortage of clients as merger mania swept Wall Street and the investment world. The Kroll name became a trusted ally to many of the era's biggest newsmakers by ferreting out financial irregularities and doing so quickly and discreetly. As the firm's reputation grew, Kroll assembled an extensive network of former agents from the FBI, CIA, Mossad, and MI-5; police officers; attorneys and prosecutors; auditors and accountants; licensed private detectives; and computer experts.

High Profile Cases: 1985–94

Kroll was definitely on a roll when the firm was hired by the Foreign Affairs Committee of the U.S. House of Representatives in 1985 to confirm reports Philippines President Ferdinand Marcos and his shoe-crazed wife Imelda had embezzled upwards of $200 million. A similar request came the following year, in 1986, from the Haitian government after dictator Jean-Claude ''Baby Doc'' Duvalier fled the country with millions taken from the poverty-stricken country's treasury. In both cases, Kroll found the goods; the Marcoses owned pricey real estate in New York and elsewhere while Duvalier and his wife Michele had sizeable bank accounts in New York, London, Paris, Geneva, and elsewhere.

Kroll's ability to sniff out caches and cash led to international renown and further high profile clients. In the late 1980s the firm was on the opposite side of the fence, hired by the Reichmann family, who were under attack for allegedly collaborating with the Nazis during World War II. Instead of finding proof of wrongdoing, Kroll was able to exonerate the Reichmanns, who had not helped, but rather hindered, the Nazis in their zealous pursuit of Jews. Around the time the Reichmann case was resolved, Kroll opened another controversial investigation: New York City's Covenant House, rocked by accusations of sexual misconduct and financial irregularities. Coming under Kroll's scrutiny in 1990, charges were corroborated against Covenant's founder Father Bruce Ritter, who had been removed from his duties.

Iraqi strongman Saddam Hussein was Kroll's next target, as the firm was hired to unearth some $10 billion in missing oil profits. Believing the dictator had funneled his ill-gotten gains into Western investments, the Kuwaiti government asked Kroll to find them. Throughout 1990 and 1991, Kroll investigated and found a number of corporations and individuals fronting for Hussein, who had hidden funds in both the United States and Europe. Kroll then played Agatha Christie to prove Italian banker Roberto Calvi, nicknamed ''God's banker'' for his ties to the Vatican, had not committed suicide back in 1982. Kroll's inquiry, which began in 1991 and ended in 1994, uncovered proof that Calvi's failed Banco Ambrosiano had been laundering money for several shadowy clients. It turned out the banker had been murdered by Sicilian mobsters for mishandling some $175 million of their funds and threatening to name names in an ongoing investigation.

Kroll also went up against organized crime in the United States, investigating New York's garment and trucking industry. By this time the firm had an army of over 200 full-time sleuths and more than 500 consultants digging up dirt for clients. Hired to oversee the dismantling of the Gambino family's trucking monopoly in 1992, the case lasted five years and brought acclaim from clothiers and even the *New York Times*.

Another home-based client was the Port Authority of New York and New Jersey, which hired Kroll after the 1993 bombing of the World Trade Center. Kroll was credited with the Port Authority's ability to evacuate the majority of the towers' workers after the first plane hit on September 11, 2001, and before the buildings collapsed.

Change and Rampant Growth: 1995–99

There seemed to be no end to corporate or international intrigue, as Kroll Associates was the world's largest investigative agency by 1995, with offices in Australia, France, Hong Kong, Japan, Mexico, Russia, and the United Kingdom, with others slated to open in India, China, and Germany in 1996. Yet with Kroll's immense success came scores of competitors and the loss of executives who either defected or quit to form their own investigative agencies. While Kroll's internal turmoil never rivaled that of its clients, Jules Kroll entertained the idea of merging with a like-minded company. It was not the first time either—he had had similar thoughts back in 1991 about a merger with Nashville's Business Risk International, then changed his mind.

Kroll's next suitor was accounting firm Coopers & Lybrand in 1996, which instead lured away several of Kroll's top officials; then came Insurance Services Group (ISG), part of the Atlanta-based Equifax, in early 1997. Again, the takeover fell through and more of Kroll's management departed. The $70 million company then hooked up with O'Gara-Hess & Eisenhardt, an Ohio-based armored car manufacturer. The new firm, Kroll-O'Gara Company, traded on the NASDAQ under the ticker symbol KROG.

Unfortunately, problems seemed to crop up almost immediately for the merged companies, from two corporate headquarters to the management styles of its officers—Jules Kroll, as chairman and CEO, and the O'Gara brothers (Bill and Thomas), who were co-vice chairmen. While the O'Garas and Kroll had worked together over the years, running their companies together was something entirely different. The merger was supposed to make Kroll-O'Gara the world's premier investigative and security outfit, offering its clients a complete array of personal and corporate services—but what the executives failed to address was how different the two companies actually were. Kroll was all about esoteric, behind the scenes maneuvering; O'Gara was the world's leading manufacturer of specially outfitted Hummers, limousines, and other vehicles.

While most believed Kroll and O'Gara would be able to integrate their businesses into a working if not cohesive whole, personality clashes also kept Jules Kroll and the O'Gara brothers from seeing eye to eye. Nevertheless, Kroll-O'Gara embarked on a series of acquisitions beginning in 1998 with Lindquist Avey Macdonald Baskerville, Inc., a forensic accounting firm based in Toronto; Chicago's InPhoto Surveillance; Fact Finders Ltd., based in Hong Kong; Louisiana's Laboratory Specialists of America, Inc.; and Schiff & Associates, Inc., based in Texas.

In 1999 came two more purchases, the United Kingdom's Buchler Phillips Group in April and the Nashville-based Background America, Inc. in June. Throughout Kroll-O'Gara's spending spree the firm's problems became more pronounced and the Blackstone Group expressed an interest in acquiring the company. Although the takeover was welcomed by many, the deal fell apart by late 1999. Revenues, however, had risen to $305.2 million for 1999, up nearly $45 million from the previous year.

Kroll in the New Millennium: 2000s

Business continued as usual despite the pervading tension in 2000. Kroll-O'Gara acquired several more companies, including Minnesota-based OnTrack Data International, the country's largest information recovery firm, and Crucible, a Virginia-based protective services firm. Year-end sales figures for 2000 rose slightly to $310.6 million for the merged companies, but soon the inevitable came to pass. In August 2001 Kroll-O'Gara solved its problems with a permanent separation. The O'Gara armored car and security division was sold to Armor Holdings for around $52 million and the O'Garas went with it. The new Kroll Inc. was worth an estimated $200 million, had a network of more than 50 offices dotting the globe, and an evolving array of services including forensic accounting, background screening, travel security for high risk locations, building reinforcements, environmental compliance, and measures to combat cyber piracy and electronic infiltration.

Once the dust settled, New York-based Zolfo Cooper LLC, which specialized in corporate restructuring, joined Kroll.

Founder Steve Cooper came with the deal and his expertise landed him the highly publicized role of acting CEO at Enron after its financial meltdown. But first came a shock: the terrorist attacks of September 11, 2001. In the tragedy's aftermath Kroll received an unexpected boost in revenue, hired not only by security-conscious corporations but municipalities scrambling to protect their citizens and implement antiterrorist measures. Chicago officials and owners of the famed Sears Tower updated the skyscraper's security system through Kroll, while thousands of New Jersey Transit Corporation employees were trained by Kroll in emergency response tactics and terrorist-fighting measures after so many of their brethren had perished.

Kroll in 2003 operated with five distinct yet complementary units: Background Screening Group (BSG); Consulting Services Group (CSG); Corporate Advisory & Restructuring Group (CARG); Security Services Group (SSG); and the Technology Services Group (TSG). During the year Kroll signed on for several high profile assignments including its appointment by the U.S. Dept. of Justice and the city of Detroit to monitor the allegedly corrupt Detroit Police Department, and with the Securities and Exchange Commission (SEC) to provide security consulting services for a year.

Kroll's ongoing operations could be narrowed down to upholding one basic tenet of human behavior: ''Do unto others as you would have them do unto you.'' Back in 1994 Jules Kroll had used this Biblical adage to explain the difference between a person with ethics and one without (*Management Review*, May 1994), ''You shouldn't do unto others what you would find hateful done to you. In every society the rules are a little bit different, but basically, treat the other person the way you would like to be treated.'' If everyone followed this simple rule, there would be no need for Kroll Inc. and its thousands of full- and part-time sleuths.

Principal Subsidiaries

InPhoto Surveillance Inc; Kroll Associates Inc.; Kroll Background America Inc.; Kroll Brazil; Kroll Fact Finders Ltd.; Kroll Information Services Inc.; Kroll International Inc.; Kroll Japan; Kroll Laboratory Specialists Inc.; Kroll Lindquist Avey Company; Kroll Ltd.; Kroll Ontrack Inc.; Kroll Schiff & Associates, Inc.; Kroll Zolfo Cooper Inc.

Principal Operating Units

Background Screening Group (BSG); Consulting Services Group (CSG); Corporate Advisory & Restructuring Group (CARG); Security Services Group (SSG); Technology Services Group (TSG).

Principal Competitors

AlixPartners; Applied Discovery; ChoicePoint Inc.; Guardsmark; Securitas AB; TransNational Security.

Further Reading

Ettmore, Barbara, ''Investigation As Art and Science,'' *Management Review,* May 1994, p. 24.

Ferguson, Greg, ''Going for the Gold,'' *U.S. News and World Report,* March 16, 1992, p. 9.

Fiskenscher, Lisa, ''Diversification Makes Business a Kroll Model,'' *Crain's New York Business,* November 11, 2002.

Gubernick, Lisa, ''April Fool?'' *Forbes,* June 2, 1997, p. 58.

''Jules B. Kroll,'' *Current Biography Yearbook,* vol. 60, New York: H.W. Wilson, 1999, pp. 320–22.

Kiger, Patrick J., ''Secrets and Strategy at Kroll,'' *Workforce,* June 2001, p. 48.

Lipowicz, Alice, ''Investigating Kroll-O'Gara Merger,'' *Crain's New York Business,* August 18, 1997, p. 1.

Patey, Tony, ''Kroll Investigates Germany After Focusing on Far East,'' *European,* February 22, 1996, p. 27.

Rama, Michelle, ''Kroll Diversifies for Security of Bottom Line,'' *Wall Street Journal,* February 26, 2003.

—Nelson Rhodes

LIBERTY
PROPERTY TRUST

Liberty Property Trust

65 Valley Stream Parkway, Suite 100
Malvern, Pennsylvania 19355
U.S.A.
Telephone: (610) 648-1700
Fax: (610) 644-4129
Web site: http://www.libertyproperty.com

Public Company
Incorporated: 1994
Employees: 366
Sales: $596.7 million (2002)
Stock Exchanges: New York
Ticker Symbol: LRY
NAIC: 525930 Real Estate Investment Trusts

Liberty Property Trust is a real estate investment trust (REIT) located in Malvern, Pennsylvania, a Philadelphia suburb. Liberty owns and manages more than 50 million square feet of office and industrial properties in ten states and the United Kingdom. The company's portfolio consists of some 400 warehouses and 250 office properties. Liberty is active in acquisitions, targeting single-asset operations, as well as in development, specializing in build-to-suits. The company is best known for transforming the skyline of Philadelphia, building the first structure taller than the statue of the city's founder, William Penn, perched atop City Hall. In 2003 Liberty had a market capitalization of $4.6 billion.

Tracing the Roots of Liberty to the 1972 Founding of Rouse & Associates

Liberty grew out of the real estate business established by Willard ("Bill") Goldsmith Rouse III in 1972. Rouse was born in Baltimore, Maryland, in 1942, part of a family devoted to real estate development. His uncle, James W. Rouse, founded a Baltimore business in 1939 that originated FHA loans for single-family housing, and his father, Willard II, ultimately went to work for the company, which was then named The Rouse Company. In the 1950s it became involved in the financing of strip shopping centers, and then, believing that there was a market for a higher quality retail environment, became part of the movement that led to the development of the contemporary shopping mall. The firm also went on to build projects that revitalized urban waterfront districts, including Manhattan's South Street Seaport. Bill Rouse majored in English at the University of Virginia, graduating in 1966, his education interrupted by a two-year stint in the military. Rather than accept a permanent position with the family business, where he worked part-time while growing up, Rouse looked elsewhere for a job in real estate. He moved to Dallas to work for Texas developer Great Southwest Corporation and leased industrial buildings. He then accepted a position with Los Angeles-based Bernguil Company, charged with the task of developing and leasing a southern New Jersey industrial park, Mid-Atlantic Park, which introduced him to the greater Philadelphia market. Once his project was completed, however, he was instructed to sell the properties. As a result he received an $80,000 share of the sale, but also put himself out of a job. Deciding to stay in the Philadelphia area, he teamed up with a friend named Menard Doswell, along with two colleagues involved in the Mid-Atlantic Park project, George Congdon and Dave Hammers, to form Rouse & Associates in 1972.

At first Rouse chose to operate in the familiar South Jersey territory, building warehouses in Mid-Atlantic Park. Bill Rouse quickly displayed the same innovative spirit of his father and uncle, when he insisted on including sculpture in the landscaping, in the belief that the working environment for warehouse employees was just as important as that for office workers. The company quickly expanded its geographic range to include all of the counties surrounding the city of Philadelphia, in Pennsylvania as well as New Jersey. Rouse also became involved in the Jacksonville, Florida market when Hammers followed a tenant to the area and established a satellite operation. In 1974 the company launched one of its first major projects when it bought 650 acres in Chester County, Pennsylvania, just beyond Philadelphia's "Main Line" community, and began construction of what became the Great Valley Corporate Center, a two-million-square-foot complex of office, industrial, retail, and education facilities. Again Bill Rouse revealed a visionary approach to the development of the business park. Great Valley set a new standard for catering to the needs of the people who worked at such suburban locations. Rouse included educational facilities, for both business and general education, and the first day care center in a business park in the United States.

Also in the 1970s Rouse entered the Maryland market, opening an office in 1977 and then developing some 2.5 million square feet of office and industrial space. In 1979 the company opened an office in Philadelphia in order to develop properties in the city itself. It was also in 1979 that Rouse began to consider operating in the Lehigh Valley, following up on a suggestion from a Philadelphia real estate broker. At the time the region was a small market, but Rouse realized that with the opening of a new highway, I-78, the Lehigh Valley would be advantageously situated between Philadelphia and New York and become a thriving service and distribution area. To take advantage of this opportunity, Rouse established a Lehigh Valley office in 1980 and began to develop more than three million square feet.

Defying Philadelphia Tradition with 1980s Project

In 1981 Rouse opened its first center city Philadelphia property, the Philadelphia Stock Exchange Building, which featured a beautiful center atrium, and served notice that Bill Rouse had great plans for the city. The company's next major project in the city, Liberty Place, would prove to be controversial because it threatened to change Philadelphia's skyline. Early in the 1900s, before the advent of the modern skyscraper, the city had placed a bronze statue of William Penn atop the tower of City Hall. The top of his hat was nearly 548 feet high, some 40 stories. A tradition evolved and was maintained by way of a gentleman's agreement that city real estate developers would not build anything higher than William Penn's hat. In the early 1980s Bill Rouse was developing an office complex in center city, but in order to keep under this arbitrary height he would end up with what he considered an ugly big box complex that would significantly detract from the surrounding neighborhood. According to the *Philadelphia Inquirer,* Rouse began to think about "cutting one building in half and putting that space on top of the other two. The proposal set off a firestorm of protest for a time. Mr. Rouse would say later that he might not have even considered the idea if he had anticipated the heat of the protest. 'I was well-served by my ignorance,' he said." He finally received approval in 1985, and in 1987 One Liberty Place at 947 feet high became the first building to stand taller than the statue of William Penn. In addition, the complex proved key to the city retaining a major employer, Cigna Corporation, which had considered moving out of Philadelphia but now established its headquarters in Liberty Place.

It was also in the mid-1980s that Bill Rouse encountered difficulties of a different sort in developing projects in Philadelphia. A city councilman, Leland Beloff, and his aide, Robert Rego, had been demanding payoffs from building contractors in

order to get their plans through city council. The two men conspired with area mob boss Nicodemo "Little Nicky" Scarfo to extort $1 million from Rouse to receive city acceptance of a waterfront development project. Unlike other developers who simply paid up, Rouse immediately told the FBI. A sting operation was set up and the three men were ultimately convicted of extortion charges and sent to prison.

During the 1980s Rouse made strides in other markets. In 1985 the company started to build its first industrial facilities in New Castle, Delaware. In the Lehigh Valley area Rouse bought 107 acres from Lehigh University and two years later completed the Lehigh Valley Corporate Center, an office park. Rouse in 1988 established an office in the thriving North Carolina market and started construction of Green Point Business Park. The company also became involved overseas, developing a mixed-use business park in Kings Hill, England, the largest of its kind in Europe, which included office, light industrial, and residential space as well as a village center and golf course. Construction commenced in 1991. But the company's expansion during this period proved to be too ambitious. Baltimore's *Daily Record* in a 1994 article presented an overview of the situation Rouse faced: "Like many developers dependent on the continually growing economy of the 1980s, who assumed continual rental increases and were accustomed to liberal lending practices, Rouse & Associates eventually became trapped in a downward spiral of decreasing values. As economic growth slowed and markets became saturated with space, Rouse & Associates became saddled with debt and unable to react to lowered rental rates fueled by competition. As a result, the company lost dozens of projects to lenders."

After shedding a number of properties Rouse stabilized its financial situation in the early 1990s but still owed around $500 million in mortgages. Rouse became one of many real estate firms that now looked to escape a heavy debt burden by packaging their assets in a REIT that could then be sold in a public offering. The REIT had been created by Congress in 1960 as a way for small investors to become involved in real estate in a manner similar to mutual funds. REITs could be taken public and their shares traded just like stock, and they were also subject to regulation by the Securities and Exchange Commission. Unlike stocks, however, REITs were required by law to pay out at least 95 percent of their taxable income to shareholders each year, a provision that severely limited the ability of REITs to raise funds internally. During the first 25 years of existence, REITs were allowed only to own real estate, a situation that hindered their growth. Third parties had to be contracted to manage the properties. Not until the Tax Reform Act of 1986 changed the nature of real estate investment did REITs begin to be truly viable. Tax shelter schemes that had drained potential investments were shut down by the Act: Interest and depreciation deductions were greatly reduced so that taxpayers could not generate paper losses in order to lower their tax liabilities. The Act also permitted REITs to provide customary services for property, in effect allowing the trusts to operate and manage the properties they owned. Despite these major changes in law, the REIT was still not fully utilized. In the latter half of the 1980s the banks, insurance companies, pension funds, and foreign investors (in particular, the Japanese) provided the bulk of real estate investment funds. The resulting glutted marketplace led to a shakeout. With real estate available at distressed prices in the early 1990s REITs finally became an attractive mainstream investment option. Dozens of real estate firms went public as REITs in 1993.

Completing an Initial Public Offering in 1994

Because The Rouse Company, now headed by Bill Rouse's cousin, was also a publicly traded company, Rouse & Associates decided to call its REIT Liberty Property Trust to avoid investor confusion. Its portfolio included 77 industrial properties totaling 5.9 million square feet and 35 office properties totaling 2.2 million square feet. In June 1994 the initial public offering was completed, netting more than $600 million. As a result, Liberty was able to lower its debt to just $43.7 million. In addition, Liberty arranged a 250 million line of credit, much of which was used to purchase 44 industrial and office properties, as well as to develop several new properties.

Liberty completed a major acquisition in March 1995, paying $125 million for Richmond, Virginia-based warehouse developer Lingerfelt Development Corp. The 26-year-old company had considered converting to REIT ownership, but because of a decline in REIT prices management opted instead for a merger. Before the deal Liberty had no properties in Virginia, but now in one stroke it became a major force in the market while also increasing the REIT's commercial property base by more than 30 percent. Liberty added Lingerfelt's 35 properties and a total of 3.5 million square feet of space. Also in 1995 Liberty bought a number of other properties in New Jersey, Maryland, North Carolina, and Florida. The buying spree continued in 1996, as Liberty bought another 33 properties and completed the development of 19 new properties. By the end of the year the REIT was a $2 billion company, owning more than 20 million square feet of space. Liberty entered three new markets through acquisitions in 1997: Detroit, Michigan; South Carolina; and Minneapolis. It also continued to make purchases and develop projects in its other markets, including the largest industrial development project in its history, a 1.2-million-square-foot distribution facility located in the Lehigh Valley. Liberty's commitment to development increased in 1998, expanding to nearly $400 million.

To maintain its appetite for acquisitions and developments, Liberty arranged for more than $1 billion in financing in 2000. Rumors also were circulating that once again Bill Rouse was eyeing Philadelphia's center city. The REIT built a one-million-square-foot warehouse and distribution facility in the city, which opened in 2001, but that project was upstaged by the announcement that Liberty had commissioned architect Robert A.M. Stern to design another building that would stand taller than the statue of William Penn. The $360 million project, called One Pennsylvania Plaza, was to stand 746 feet high and include 1.23 million square feet of rentable space. It would be located across the street from the Penn Center Suburban Station and become the first Center City Class A office building to be built in more than a decade. The project was not a given, however, requiring the commitment of a major anchor tenant or a significant number of smaller tenants, but it was clearly a passion for Bill Rouse. Unfortunately, he would not be able to devote his complete energies to the project. In December 2001 Rouse, a longtime chain smoker, was diagnosed with lung cancer and began chemotherapy treatment, which he insisted be conducted at 7:30 in the morning to permit him to get to work on time.

As Rouse battled cancer in 2002 he took steps to turn over leadership in Liberty to William P. Hankowsky, the former president of the Philadelphia Industrial Development Corp., the city's economic development agency. He also turned over a great deal of responsibility for the One Pennsylvania Plaza project to executive John Gattuso. According to *Philadelphia Inquirer,* "Rouse hid in the back office while prospective tenants arrived to view the sales presentation. He did not want to upstage Gattuso." In late 2002 the transition was moved up when Rouse began a second round of chemotherapy. In January 2003 he stepped down as CEO, replaced by Hankowsky, although he retained the chairmanship and planned to remain active in the company. He continued working until he suffered a swift decline and died in May 2003. But in Liberty Property Trust he left behind a firm that was well prepared to carry on business without him.

Principal Subsidiaries

Liberty Property Limited Partnership; Liberty Lehigh Partnership; Liberty Philadelphia Trust; Liberty Property Development Corporation.

Principal Competitors

Brandywine Realty Trust; Duke Realty Corporation; Mack-Cali Realty Corporation.

Further Reading

Barkley, Meredith, "Real Estate Company Comes Knocking in Triad," *Greensboro News & Record,* July 31, 1994, p. G1.

Caliri, Lois, "Rouse Seeks to Create Publicly Held REIT," *Central Penn Business Journal,* June 13, 1994, p. 1.

Holcomb, Henry J., "Philadelphia-Area Real Estate Developer Dies," *Philadelphia Inquirer,* May 29, 2003, p. 1.

Koenig, Richard, "Philadelphia's Very Psyche May Be at Stake If William Penn Is Topped," *Wall Street Journal,* April 5, 1984.

Orenstein, Beth W., "Liberty Property Trust, REIT Makes Its Presence Felt in Valley Since 1979," *Eastern Pennsylvania Business Journal,* June 17, 2002, p. 28.

—Ed Dinger

Long John Silver's

101 Yorkshire Blvd.
Lexington, Kentucky 40509-1988
U.S.A.
Telephone: (859) 543-6000
Fax: (859) 543-6644
Web site: http://www.ljsilvers.com

Unit of YUM! Brands, Inc.
Incorporated: 1946 as Jerrico Inc.
Employees: 14,000
Sales: $300 million (2002 est.)
NAIC: 722211 Limited-Service Restaurants; 533110
　　Lessors of Nonfinancial Intangible Assets (Except
　　Copyrighted Works)

Long John Silver's is the largest quick-service seafood restaurant chain in the United States, with about one-third of the estimated $1.24 billion market. The chain's more than 1,200 units, located in 36 states, feature a nautical theme and a menu that includes, in addition to Long John Silver's trademark batter-dipped fish, chicken, and seafood, breaded fish, sandwiches, french fries, coleslaw, hush puppies, corn, and desserts. About 60 percent of the U.S. units are owned and operated by the company; the remainder, along with all of the 28 overseas outlets, are franchises. More than 120 of the U.S. units are cobranded sites also featuring an A&W All-American Food outlet.

The history of Long John Silver's is rife with ownership changes. The first Long John Silver's opened in 1969 as part of a multibrand, publicly traded restaurant group called Jerrico Inc. Jerrico was taken private in 1989 through a highly leveraged management buyout, and one year later the other restaurant concepts were divested in order to focus on Long John Silver's. After struggling for the next several years under its heavy debt load, the company was finally forced to file for bankruptcy in 1998. The following year, the owner of the A&W chain acquired Long John Silver's, creating a new restaurant firm called Yorkshire Global Restaurants, Inc. Finally in May 2002 Tricon Global Restaurants, Inc. (soon renamed YUM! Brands, Inc.), owner of the Taco Bell, Pizza Hut, and KFC chains, acquired Yorkshire and its Long John Silver's and A&W chains.

Pre-LJS History of Jerrico

The history of Long John Silver's (LJS) can be traced to 1929, when Jerome Lederer, the company founder, opened a six-seat hamburger stand he called the White Tavern Shoppe in Shelbyville, Kentucky. The concept proved popular and thrived throughout the Great Depression. Altogether, 13 White Tavern Shoppes were in existence when World War II came along and claimed ten of them because of shortages of meat, sugar, and manpower.

Lederer regrouped in 1946, establishing his company as Jerrico Inc. and introducing a new restaurant in Lexington, called Jerry's Five and Dime, reflecting the new establishment's focus on promoting 15-cent roast beef sandwiches. In 1947, realizing that people were not willing to pay that much for a roast beef sandwich, Lederer converted Jerry's menu to focus on hamburgers.

As he rebuilt his company, Lederer hired Warren W. Rosenthal to manage his restaurants in 1948. The two men reportedly met when Rosenthal rented a room from Lederer while attending the University of Kentucky. Although Rosenthal initially considered careers in retailing and in life insurance, he eventually accepted Lederer's invitation to join him in the restaurant business. Soon the two men were looking for a restaurant concept they could duplicate across the country. They tried new menu concepts at Jerry's by adapting foodservice ideas borrowed from restaurants in other locations.

The popularity of eating away from home and the growth of the restaurant business in general was just beginning; Jerrico's timing was perfect. By 1957, Jerrico was operating seven Jerry's Restaurants and was one of the first companies to use the franchise concept as a means of stimulating growth. Rosenthal, who had been made chief executive officer of Jerrico, eventually served as president and gained ownership of the company as well when Lederer died in 1963.

Jerrico's success in the foodservice industry has been credited to the company's willingness to generate ideas and take

Company Perspectives:

The first Long John Silver's Fish 'n' Chips opened in 1969 in response to growing consumer demand for quick-service seafood. This new approach gained overwhelming acceptance and has led to bold modern restaurants and a menu that meets the taste of today's consumers.

Our promise, to provide each guest great tasting, reasonably priced fish, chicken and seafood in a fast and friendly manner on every visit ensures Long John Silver's position in American Culture.

risks. Indeed, the company tested a variety of restaurant concepts during the 1960s, including: Lott's (roast beef and other sandwiches); Davy's Dock (full-service seafood); Don Q's (Spanish food); and The Governor's Table (full-service dining).

1969 Launch of Long John Silver's

Then, in 1969, Rosenthal was inspired to try out a new market for quick-service seafood as competition for the standard American favorites of hamburger, pizza, and fried chicken. Rosenthal studied the competition, particularly the menu at the H. Salt Fish and Chips chain, and then persuaded James Patterson, a Jerry's Restaurant franchisee, to join him at Jerrico to help develop the notion of an expanded version of fast food fish-and-chips. Patterson became the first president of Long John Silver's.

Shortly after taking Jerrico public in 1969, Rosenthal launched Long John Silver's Fish 'n' Chips, a name inspired by Robert Louis Stevenson's novel *Treasure Island*. Located on Southland Drive in Lexington, the first restaurant was a success; LJS developed into a chain and soon became Jerrico's most successful endeavor. By the end of 1971, there were more than 200 LJS units in operation.

Designed to provide the atmosphere of a seafood establishment along a wharf, the outlets' interiors were decked out with brass lanterns, signal flags, and boat oars. The original menu featured battered fish, chicken, french fries, and hush puppies. However, noting that competitor H. Salt had a relatively limited menu and was experiencing financial difficulties, Rosenthal quickly moved to expand LJS's offerings, implementing a more comprehensive line of seafood to augment its batter-dipped fillets. By 1973, the chain's name was changed to Long John Silver's Seafood Shoppes to reflect this expanded menu. During this time, Ernest E. Renaud, Jerrico's executive vice-president since 1971, became the second president in LJS history.

By June 1976, there were 621 LJS restaurants in operation. Of these, 262 were owned directly by Jerrico and another 359 were franchised to independent operators, who paid a fee to Jerrico for the concept and covered construction and business costs themselves. Within two years, the total number of shops had grown to 1,000, of which 464 were company-owned. In May 1978, Jerrico consolidated its operations from four buildings scattered around Lexington to a new $7 million headquarters.

Changes in LJS leadership took place in the early and mid-1980s. In 1982, Renaud was named president of parent company Jerrico in addition to his duties as LJS president, while Rosenthal retained a role as chairman of the board. In 1984, John E. Tobe, who had been LJS's chief financial officer since the early 1970s, succeeded Renaud.

Growth at LJS continued apace in the 1980s, as company-owned development increased significantly. By 1984, Jerrico owned 812 of a total 1,355 LJS restaurants, and by 1987 LJS accounted for approximately 75 percent of Jerrico's total revenues and 80 percent of its operating profits. That year, the chain boasted 1,421 outlets with reported sales of $451 million, roughly 65 percent of the "fast fish" category. Although LJS was not considered a truly national chain at the time, it was gaining enough ground to warrant an investment in regional network television advertising time. Jerrico's intent was to have stores in all areas of the country by 1990, and to have LJS become a full network television advertiser.

During this time, Jerrico's other business interests included a chain of Jerry's Restaurants and other new restaurant concepts the company was testing, including a full service Italian restaurant called Florenz, established in Ohio. Jerrico also opened its first fast-food Italian restaurant—called Gratzi's—in 1988. Such diversification was prompted in part by the continually rising prices of Icelandic cod, LJS's staple menu item; hoping not to become overly dependent on the LJS chain, with its rising operating costs, Jerrico continued to expand its holdings. Moreover, LJS was facing increasing competition from outside the industry, particularly from grocers and their suppliers, who were quick to take advantage of market demand for fast food that could be microwaved at home. In 1989, Jerrico premiered Fazoli's, a quick-service Italian pasta restaurant modeled after the Florenz establishment.

Management-Led Buyout of Jerrico: 1989

National economic recession and the high price of fish, however, brought some problems for Jerrico in the late 1980s, and the company would soon undergo dramatic changes. When the company's stock value began to waver as investors grew concerned over reduced profits, talk of taking the company private through a management-led buyout surfaced. In September 1989, Jerrico was acquired for $620 million in a leveraged buyout by a company called Pisces Inc., made up of a group of senior Jerrico executives and a joint force of Castle Harlan and DJS-Inverness, both New York-based investment firms. Warren Rosenthal, having been with the company 41 years, retired as chairman of the board at the age of 67. He was reportedly well compensated for his role in developing the company, receiving an executive severance payment of $1.275 million in addition to the $57.4 million he received from cashing in related stock interests. LJS, which reported sales of $826 million in 1989, became a subsidiary of Pisces Inc.

Clinton A. Clark, a partner at Castle Harlan, joined the board of LJS during the buyout and became the company's president in 1990. Clark was charged with bringing the company safely through the immediate post-buyout, debt-laden years. During his tenure, Clark began an effective turnaround of the company. He created an LJS mission statement centered on providing superior products, guest satisfaction, mutual respect among team members, and "a vision of excellence" for the future.

Key Dates:

1929: Jerome Lederer opens a hamburger stand called White Tavern Shoppe in Shelbyville, Kentucky.

World War II Years: Lederer is forced to close ten of his 13 White Tavern Shoppes because of shortages.

1946: Lederer regroups, establishing Jerrico Inc. and launching a new restaurant called Jerry's Five and Dime.

1947: Jerry's menu shifts from roast beef sandwiches to hamburgers.

1948: Lederer hires Warren W. Rosenthal to manage his restaurants.

1963: Rosenthal gains ownership of Jerrico when Lederer dies.

1969: Jerrico is taken public; company opens first Long John Silver's Fish 'n' Chips, located in Lexington, Kentucky.

1971: Having become Jerrico's most successful chain, Long John Silver's (LJS) has expanded to more than 200 units.

1973: With the menu expanded to include a wider line of seafood, the chain is renamed Long John Silver's Seafood Shoppes.

1989: Jerrico is taken private through a highly leveraged management-led buyout.

1990: To focus full attention on LJS, the company divests its other restaurant concepts, including Jerry's and Fazoli's; Long John Silver's Restaurants Inc. becomes the successor firm to Jerrico.

1994: Triarc Companies, owner of the Arby's chain, announces plans to acquire LJS, but the deal later falls through.

1998: Weight of huge debt load forces LJS to seek Chapter 11 bankruptcy protection.

1999: The owner of A&W Restaurants Inc. purchases LJS out of bankruptcy and creates Yorkshire Global Restaurants Inc. as the parent company of the two chains.

2000: Yorkshire begins dual-brand tests pairing Long John Silver's with A&W, KFC, and Taco Bell.

2002: Tricon Global Restaurants, Inc. acquires Yorkshire; LJS becomes an operating unit of Tricon, which soon changes its name to YUM! Brands, Inc.

As part of Clark's refocusing efforts, the new parent company decided to dedicate all of its resources to the operations of LJS in 1990. Toward that end, the company's other three restaurant concepts—Jerry's, Fazoli's, and Florenz—were put on the block. The 46 Jerry's restaurants were purchased by Atlanta-based Great American Restaurants, the country's largest franchisee of Denny's Family Restaurants. Fazoli's, a particularly promising start-up, was bought by the Japanese-owned firm Seed Restaurant Group Inc. Jerrico attempted to sell its seven Florenz restaurants as a chain, but was unsuccessful; by 1991, all seven sites were closed. Jerrico Inc., as it was, ceased to function, and the company that emerged was known by a more recognized name, Long John Silver's Restaurants Inc.

In the early 1990s, LJS began to tailor its menu to answer the growing nutrition concerns of its health-conscious customers.

Broiled and grilled items were introduced and represented the fastest-growing of the restaurant's product lines. In 1991, the company introduced three hot meals, baked rather than fried and all priced at around $4, during Lent season. According to a February 1992 article in *Restaurants and Institutions,* Mary Roseman, director of nutrition and consumer information at LJS, asserted that "the baked program provides good sales when we can support it with marketing. Unfortunately, though, when you're not on TV or not really pounding the message, it's hard to keep the interest there." Advertising on a national scale was still two years away for LJS.

Market trends were not favorable for LJS during this time. According to one Illinois-based market research firm, the share of industry traffic at fish and seafood specialty restaurants slipped from 2.8 percent in 1986 to 2.5 percent in 1991. The quick service growth area in 1991 came from other nonseafood chains, which were adding some seafood items to their menus.

This additional competition as well as increased prices of some staple menu items put seafood restaurants at a disadvantage in the quick-service industry. Value had to be improved if consumers were expected to eat a seafood dinner instead of a lower priced hamburger and fries meal. In October, LJS revealed a new value menu chainwide. The Add-a-Piece menu enabled the purchase of any basic meal with additional individual pieces of fried fish, shrimp, or chicken for 69 cents or less. With the price of a basic meal at around $1.99, the new menu allowed increased flexibility for the customer and the elimination of redundant items from the menu.

After guiding the company successfully through its move from public to private status, Clark, who had become chairman in February 1992, announced his resignation in July 1993. In October 1993, Clyde E. Culp, a member of the company's board, was named president and chief executive officer. Culp's vision for the company was to "reinvigorate the quick-service seafood category" through LJS's dominant position within the segment.

In the spring of 1993, the company's first kiosk was opened at the Louisville General Electric plant in Louisville, Kentucky. The kiosk, called Long John Silver's Express, was a smaller version of the restaurant and was franchised by Canteen Corp., a large contract foodservice provider owned by TW Services. The kiosk offered a limited menu with four meal choices. During the first three weeks of operation, Canteen's lunch participation increased by approximately 1,200 customers.

That summer, LJS reported that drive-through service, among those LJS outlets that had it, was increasing sales by almost 30 percent. Recognizing the needs of an expanded customer base, Bruce Cotton, LJS vice-president of public relations, explained in a July 1993 *Restaurants and Institutions* article that "at first, we didn't feel fish would transport very well, so we worked on better carryout containers and holding times for fish. We also changed our french fries to an extra-crispy type that holds heat really well." By early 1996, 85 percent of LJS outlets had drive-throughs.

In August 1994, in a rare advertising move, LJS unveiled its "America's Favorite Shrimp Game" tie-in with the premier of the Universal Pictures film *Little Rascals.* Jobie Dixon, LJS vice-president of marketing and creative media explained in the

August 1994 *Nation's Restaurant News* that the company was aware of movie/fast-food promotions being run by McDonald's and Burger King, and that "research shows that if you get a good, interesting tie-in, it can add some magic for the consumer that translates into extra visits." Scheduled to run through mid-September, both the movie and "America's Favorite Shrimp Game" exceeded expectations.

Because of its earlier success with kiosks, LJS continued to add these nontraditional sites, expanding primarily on university campuses. In September 1994, the company opened a storefront unit at California Polytechnic State University, its first West Coast kiosk. John Ramsey, vice-president of franchise development, stated in a September 1994 *Nation's Restaurant News* that the company believed college students would "look for branded food names that they recognize from home. . . . Students know our food will taste the same at Cal-Poly as it does in their home towns." LJS reported systemwide sales of $923 million for fiscal 1994 from its 1,456 company-owned and franchised locations in 38 states, Canada, Singapore, and Saudi Arabia; company revenues totaled $643 million.

Stumbling into Bankruptcy: Mid- to Late 1990s

Meantime, Triarc Companies, Inc., a diversified holding company and the parent of Arby's Inc., announced plans to acquire LJS for $75 million in cash and $450 million in assumed debt. Triarc's plan was to dual-brand its stores, housing its lunch-oriented Arby's restaurants under the same roofs as dinner-oriented LJS restaurants. In December, however, with rising interest rates and unfavorable capital markets looming, Triarc declared that it was canceling the debt-heavy deal. Both companies, however, said they would continue to pursue the possibility of dual-branding.

In the wake of the deal's collapse, Crédit Suisse First Boston (CSFB), LJS's principal debtholder, as well as a major shareholder, decided to transfer some of the debt into additional equity. CSFB ended up owning about 80 percent of the company. While occasionally entering negotiations on a sale of the company, most notably with CKE Restaurants, Inc., owner of the Carl's Jr. hamburger chain, CSFB focused on improving LJS's financial performance and its balance sheet in advance of a possible public offering by the year 2000. Unfortunately, missteps continued to be made during the CSFB era.

In the fall of 1994, for example, LJS made the latest change to its menu, introducing the Flavorbaked line of chicken breast and fish sandwiches, light-portion items, meals, and combination deals. LJS promoted the introduction with a $5.5 million marketing campaign, using network/cable television advertisements and couponing to support the new products. The nonfried line never caught on with customers, however, and by early 1996 it made up only 1 percent of total sales. Next came Mr. Norman Bigfish, a goofy "spokesfish" that headed up a new advertising campaign that began running prior to the 1995 Lent season. Poorly received, the campaign was quickly scuttled following complaints from franchisees that the ads were turning off customers.

Following these disasters, LJS underwent yet another change in top management. Culp resigned in June 1995, and Rolf Towe, who had been installed as chairman by CSFB, was named acting

president and CEO. After a prolonged six-month search, John M. Cranor III was hired as president and CEO in January 1996. Cranor brought with him his experience as head of KFC Corporation, the fried chicken chain, from 1989 to 1994.

In July 1996 LJS announced a streamlining that involved the elimination of 160 corporate positions and the shuttering of three divisional offices in Atlanta, Dallas, and Kansas City, Kansas. The firm also brought expansion to a near halt and placed a hold on further cobranding efforts; in regard to the latter, LJS had found some success with units that shared space with either an Arby's or a Carl's Jr., but a dual-branding experiment with Taco Time International was an outright failure and was soon abandoned.

In November 1996 new product development efforts yielded the introduction of Wraps, a line of handheld wrap sandwiches featuring shrimp, fish, or chicken fillings and five different sauces. Selling for $1.99 for a regular size and $2.99 for a large, the sandwiches represented Long John Silver's latest attempt to compete head-on with the purveyors of cheap burgers who dominated the fast-food scene as well as to offer a more healthful alternative to LJS's staple fried foods. Although the new items seemed to get off to a good start, a number of operators and franchisees were soon complaining that the new line had muddled the chain's focus and slowed service. Some operators were also critical of the attempt to woo fast-food customers to the neglect of LJS's core demographic, who tended to skew slightly older and who supported the chain's traditional emphasis on more expensive dinner platters. Late in 1997 a group of disgruntled operators formed a franchisee association in an attempt to gain more influence over the company's operation.

The additions to the menu and the other efforts of the new management team failed to halt a steady decline in sales. Systemwide sales plunged from $902 million in 1996 to about $789 million for fiscal 1998. During the same period, corporate revenues dropped from $622 million to $565 million. The company continued to be hampered by the huge debt load, some of which carried interest payments as high as 18 percent; as a result, the firm had to make debt payments rather than invest in company operations. Short on cash, LJS was finally forced to file for Chapter 11 bankruptcy protection in June 1998. At the time the company had $457.3 million in liabilities and $329.1 million in assets. LJS also announced that it would close 72 of its poorest-performing outlets and identified another 80 for possible closure.

The Yorkshire Era: 1999 to 2002

In September 1999 a new era began for Long John Silver's when the chain was bought out of bankruptcy by the owner of A&W Restaurants Inc. in a $227.5 million deal. Sidney Feltenstein had led a group of investors who purchased the A&W chain in 1994; he spearheaded a turnaround at the longtime purveyor of hamburgers, hot dogs, and other fare, best-known for its famed draft root beer. Feltenstein set up a new company called Yorkshire Global Restaurants Inc. as the parent company of both A&W and LJS. Yorkshire did not inherit any of the debt that had troubled LJS for so long, leaving the chain in its strongest financial position in years. Yorkshire was initially based in Farmington Hills, Michigan, where A&W had been based, but the headquarters of both Yorkshire and A&W were soon consolidated with those of LJS in Lexington.

Under Feltenstein's leadership, LJS embarked on a number of new initiatives. A new logo was designed for the chain, stores began to be remodeled, the quality of the food was improved, and new marketing strategies were launched. In a key decision, LJS returned to its traditional place in the restaurant industry, deemphasizing fast food and repositioning itself, according to Kevin W. Armstrong, senior vice-president of marketing, quoted in a November 1999 *Nation's Restaurant News,* as a "quick-experience restaurant that focuses on full meals and dinners and ensuring that guests are satisfied." Ad spending was increased to $40 million in 2000, compared to the little more than $22 million outlaid during 1998.

Another important action was a reemphasis on dual-branding opportunities. Feltenstein had been successful experimenting with dual A&W/KFC outlets, and one of the main reasons that LJS had interested him was the potential for dual A&W/ Long John Silver's units. The two restaurants were a good fit given that A&W was more of a lunch destination and LJS and its platters made for stronger dinner sales. Further potential came from customers eating a Long John Silver's dinner and then having an A&W root beer float for dessert. The first dual A&W/LJS outlet opened in Chattanooga, Tennessee, in early 2000; by the end of the year there were about a dozen such units. Under a license agreement between Yorkshire and Tricon Global Restaurants, Inc., Long John Silver's also began experimenting with outlets cobranded with two of Tricon's chains, KFC and Taco Bell. Sales at stores that converted from a single brand to two brands typically increased by 30 percent or more. Yorkshire soon announced plans to open about 400 dual-brand stores during the early 2000s. By March 2003 Yorkshire's two brands were involved in 121 cobranded restaurants.

Joining YUM! Brands: 2002

The success of these multibranding efforts led to another change in ownership for Long John Silver's. When Tricon Global first entered into discussions with Yorkshire about a possible acquisition, Tricon executives made it clear that they were interested only in A&W, believing LJS to be a moribund chain. Yorkshire, however, refused to break up its two brands, nearly scuttling a deal. Tricon relented after learning about the increased profits that the dual-brand LJS outlets were raking in. In March 2002 Tricon announced that it would acquire Yorkshire for about $275 million in cash and $48 million in assumed debt. The deal was completed in May 2002, and soon thereafter Tricon changed its name to YUM! Brands, Inc.

The YUM! portfolio now included five major U.S.-based restaurant chains, the fifth being Pizza Hut. Long John Silver's became an operating unit of YUM! Feltenstein continued to head up both LJS and A&W after the takeover, but in 2003 he left the company, and Aylwin Lewis took over management of the two chains. Plans were also in the works to close the Yorkshire headquarters in Lexington and transfer LJS and A&W to YUM!'s headquarters in Louisville, Kentucky. Under its new, more deeply pocketed owners, LJS was expected to accelerate its involvement in multibranded outlets. Eventually, the chain was also expected to significantly expand its rather feeble presence overseas. Given that Long John Silver's was the most popular fast-food chain among Hispanic Americans, there appeared to be great potential for the chain in predominantly Catholic countries overseas. In September 2002, meantime, a new $30 million national television advertising campaign was launched featuring a new tag line, "This Is Seafood Country."

Principal Competitors

McDonald's Corporation; Doctor's Associates Inc.; Burger King Corporation; Wendy's International, Inc.; CKE Restaurants, Inc.; Triarc Companies, Inc.; Captain D's, LLC.

Further Reading

Allen, Robin Lee, "Long John, Rascals 'Gang' Up for Shrimp Promo," *Nation's Restaurant News,* August 22, 1994, p. 12.

——, "Long John's Sails on in Wake of Clark's Exit," *Nation's Restaurant News,* July 26, 1993, p. 3.

Alva, Marilyn, "A Change in Course?," *Restaurant Business,* May 20, 1996, pp. 40, 42, 46.

Blyskal, Jeff, "Fat-Fryer Alchemy," *Forbes,* December 6, 1982, pp. 129+.

Carlino, Bill, "A&W Fishes for Growth, Hooks Long John Silver's with Merger," *Nation's Restaurant News,* March 22, 1999, pp. 1, 93.

Chaudhry, Rajan, "Fast-Food Seafood Chains Sell Health, Variety," *Restaurants and Institutions,* February 26, 1992, pp. 12–13.

Daykin, Tom, "Jerrico Will Sell Jerry's, Fazoli's," *Lexington (Ky.) Herald-Leader,* May 2, 1990, pp. A1, A5.

Dooley, Karla, "Tricon Global Restaurants Plans to Acquire A&W, Long John Silver's," *Lexington (Ky.) Herald-Leader,* March 13, 2002.

Goetz, David, "Long John Silver's Pleases Yum's Profit Palate," *Louisville Courier-Journal,* September 15, 2002, p. 1E.

——, "Tricon Global to Get New Name, Brands," *Louisville Courier-Journal,* March 13, 2002, p. 1E.

——, "Yum Hones Prototype: Fast-Food Giant Bets Its Future on Multibranding," *Louisville Courier-Journal,* June 15, 2003, p. 1E.

Hamsra, Mark, "Long John Silver's, Short on Cash Flow, Files Bankruptcy," *Nation's Restaurant News,* June 15, 1998, pp. 1, 78.

Howard, Theresa, "LJS Weighs Financial Options in Wake of Failed Triarc Deal," *Nation's Restaurant News,* January 2, 1995, pp. 7+.

"Jerrico Inc.," *Advertising Age,* November 23, 1987, p. S31.

Jordan, Jim, "From Humble Start, Jerrico Tinkered Its Way to Success," *Lexington (Ky.) Herald-Leader,* August 14, 1989, pp. D1, D8–D9.

——, "Little by Little, Jerrico Chief Maps Future," *Lexington (Ky.) Herald-Leader,* August 14, 1989, pp. D1, D9.

Kosdrosky, Terry, "Tall Order for A&W Boss: Feltenstein Formulates Plan for Long John Silver's," *Crain's Detroit Business,* September 27, 1999, pp. 1+.

——, "Turnaround Artist Casts His Lot with Long John Silver," *Crain's Detroit Business,* January 31, 2000, p. 35.

Kramer, Louise, "Cranor Named LJS Prexy, CEO," *Nation's Restaurant News,* January 15, 1996, pp. 1+.

——, "Cranor Streamlines LJS' Structure," *Nation's Restaurant News,* July 22, 1996, pp. 1, 4.

Kreisman, Richard, "Jerrico Taking Slow Approach to Fast Growth," *Advertising Age,* December 14, 1981, pp. 4+.

Lewis, Len, "Pirating Sales," *Progressive Grocer,* May 1997, pp. 95–96.

"LJS Franchisee Spawns Fast-Fish Double Drive-Thru," *Nation's Restaurant News,* August 17, 1992, p. 2.

"LJS Opens Cal-Poly Kiosk," *Nation's Restaurant News,* September 5, 1994, p. 11.

"LJS Rolls Out New Flavorbaked Line," *Nation's Restaurant News,* November 7, 1994, p. 2.

"Long John Silver's Chairman Resigns," *Nation's Restaurant News,* July 19, 1993, p. 2.

Pack, Todd, "Ex-Jerrico Restaurants: Where Are They Now?," *Lexington (Ky.) Herald-Leader,* March 26, 1995, Bus. Sec., p. 14.

"Patrons Don't Live by Fish Alone," *Restaurants and Institutions,* July 15, 1993, pp. 161, 164, 168.

Pearce, Bette, "Jerrico Is Packing Up and Heading for a New Home," *Lexington (Ky.) Herald-Leader,* January 15, 1978, p. B5.

Peters, James, "Duo Could Net Extra $5B in U.S. Sales," *Nation's Restaurant News,* March 25, 2002, pp. 1, 77.

Prather, Paul, "Rosenthal: 'Happy to Step Out'," *Lexington (Ky.) Herald-Leader,* October 8, 1990, p. A8.

Steinberg, Brian, "Long John Silver's Plans to Spread Wider Net for Fast-Fish Customers," *Wall Street Journal,* September 4, 2002, p. B5A.

"Triarc Cos. Cancels Its Plan to Acquire Long John Silver's," *Wall Street Journal,* December 13, 1994, p. B4.

Walkup, Carolyn, "Long John Silver's Teams with Canteen to Open First Kiosk," *Nation's Restaurant News,* March 22, 1993, pp. 3, 67.

Walter, Grady, "Big Fish," *Lane Report* (Lexington, Ky.), April 1995, p. 36.

"Why Jerrico Is Sailing Past the Competition," *Business Week,* January 18, 1992, pp. 84+.

Zuber, Amy, "Long John Silver's, A&W Root for Growth, Hope Co-Branding Bears Fruit," *Nation's Restaurant News,* November 27, 2000, pp. 8, 75.

——, "'Yum!' Pushes Co-Brand Binge, Eyes More Buyouts," *Nation's Restaurant News,* March 25, 2002, pp. 1, 77.

—Jennifer Voskuhl Canipe
—update: David E. Salamie

Mace Security International, Inc.

1000 Crawford Place, Suite 400
Mt. Laurel, New Jersey 08054
U.S.A.
Telephone: (856) 778-2300
Toll Free: (800) 255-2634
Fax: (856) 439-1723
Web site: http://www.mace.com

Public Company
Incorporated: 1987
Employees: 1,500
Sales: $46.7 million (2002)
Stock Exchanges: NASDAQ
Ticker Symbol: MACE
NAIC: 339999 All Other Miscellaneous Manufacturing;
    325120 Industrial Gas Manufacturing (pt); 811192
    Car Washes

Mace Security International, Inc. (MSI) first attracted attention during the early 1990s for its manufacture of the less-than-lethal defense spray Mace. Although most of the general public probably still identifies the company with its brand domination in the pepper spray industry, Mace is now a diversified company that has seen its recent growth in car washes. The company operates 55 car washes and five truck washes under several brand names. In addition to the car wash business—through which Mace has emerged as the first publicly traded car wash consolidator—the company operates retail security stores on a small scale.

1980s: Pepper Spray and Personal Safety

Mace Security International was formed in 1987. Its first product was Mace, which became so well known that it was used as the generic name for all pepper sprays. The company was founded by Jon E. Goodrich, who located its headquarters in Bennington, Vermont. Goodrich launched an entrepreneurial career after graduating from St. Lawrence University in 1967 and studying real estate law at Northwestern University. Among the firms he launched were Home Security Inc. and Smith & Wesson Chemical Company.

1990s: Going Public and Growing Secure

When the International Chiefs of Police met in St. Louis in 1993, officials identified rising fears about crime as one of the factors in the increase in the personal safety business. "Everyone is jumping on the band wagon," said Mace Training Director Tom Archmbault, according to the *St. Louis Dispatch.* "Violent crime is escalating everywhere. People want to feel safe. And it's impossible for the police to be everywhere."

This increased emphasis on safety created a good environment for Mace International's initial public offering in 1993. The first nine months of that year resulted in sales of $7 million. The fourth quarter of 1993, however, was disappointing for the company and resulted in a loss of $.03 per share. CEO Jon Goodrich attributed the loss to "internal expansion costs" and the added expenses of sales and marketing people, attending trade shows, and anticipating growth.

In 1994, Mace acquired the assets of the Federal Laboratories division of TransTechnology Corporation. Federal Laboratories was the nation's oldest producer of tear gas as well as grenades and projectiles for purchase by law enforcement and correctional facilities. Mace planned to bring Federal Laboratories back to profitability. "Under MSI's leadership, which is very familiar with Federal Laboratories and the tear gas industry, this company will again be prosperous in the near future. In addition, the synergy, primarily in the international sales and marketing area, will be very beneficial," said president and CEO Goodrich.

Kmart placed its first order for Mace pocket-sized pepper spray in 1994 and planned to carry the product in 1,300 Kmart stores nationwide. "This order is a turning point for Mace Security International because it marks the beginning of our program of selling to the country's largest mass merchandisers," said Goodrich.

Mace continued its expansion efforts in 1994 when it acquired Kindergard Corporation. Kindergard, a developer, manufacturer, and marketer of child safety products, provided another avenue for Mace's security and safety business. Kindergard's 18-item product line included cabinet latches, outlet plugs, and doorknob guards.

While Mace continued to focus on safety and security, the staple product, Mace pepper spray, occupied a lower percentage of the total sales of the company. In 1993, 90 percent of sales were attributed to the spray, but by the third quarter of 1994, only 52 percent of sales came from pepper sprays. Acquisitions and growth in other areas assisted Mace with diversification within the safety industry. The diversification led the way to record net sales in the third quarter of 1994 of more than $3.9 million, an increase of more than 100 percent over the same period in 1993.

1995–99: Growing Products and Distribution

In March 1995, Mace began distributing its products in Canada through distribution company Feelin' Secure Ltd. The first product to be distributed was Muzzle, a pepper spray dog repellent.

The American Civil Liberties Union (ACLU) questioned the use of pepper spray products in a case in southern California. The company, along with others in the defense spray industry, issued the following statement in response to the ACLU: "Pepper spray is a humane, nonlethal, and environmentally friendly alternative to lethal force and represents an effective defense for Americans and is an appropriate alternative for police officers. We believe ACLU's motives are in good faith but are based upon insufficient facts. We firmly hope the ACLU will withdraw from the position they have taken once they have become fully informed on this issue."

In October 1995, the board of directors of Mace delegated the responsibilities of CEO, which had been the position of founder Jon Goodrich, to a three-member committee: Goodrich, Robert Gould (a principal stockholder), and Robert D. Norman, the vice-chairman. While Goodrich remained in charge of daily operations, all other matters required the consent of the committee.

The legality of pepper spray in California ceased to be an issue on January 1, 1996, and Mace introduced Mace Brand Triple Action Pepper Spray in the state. The new law allowed "off the shelf" purchase of pepper spray to civilians in California.

Also in 1996, Goodrich officially resigned his positions as president and co-CEO. Robert D. Norman was named as his replacement. Goodrich remained as chairman and retained his stock in the company.

In the first quarter of 1996, the company announced three acquisitions to double Mace's annual revenues. The three com-

panies, Howard Uniform Company, Balco Uniform Cap Corp., and Gould & Goodrich Leather, Inc., provided the law enforcement industry with uniforms and accessories.

Just nine months after resigning as CEO, Goodrich as well as Gould announced that they were jointly negotiating the sale of their stock (56.2 percent collectively) to a competitor. Mace avoided the threat of competitor takeover, and Goodrich emerged again as chief executive officer of the company.

In 1997, Mace purchased MSP, Inc. to further diversify itself in the personal safety industry. MSP, Inc., based in Aurora, Colorado, marketed consumer safety products under the names of Global Security, Safetynet, and Safeguard. "The acquisition of MSP, Inc. begins to implement the future course, focus, and expansion of Mace Security International," said Goodrich. "It is the intention of Mace Security International to directly and aggressively pursue the potential available in the consumer safety and security markets." MSP operated as a subsidiary of Mace, and former principal stockholder Howard Edelman was selected to lead the subsidiary.

Despite continued acquisitions, the company announced a loss in the first quarter of 1998 and reported that continuing operations for the quarter declined 1.9 percent. The company reported a net loss of $240,341 compared with a net loss of $8,573 for the previous year in the same period. The loss information excluded reports from the company's Law Enforcement division, which was scheduled to be sold in the second quarter to Armor Holdings. The proceeds from the eventual transaction amounted to approximately $5.2 million.

The company hoped to raise profits by franchising the retail division—Mace Security Centers. "I am confident that the residual businesses of MSI are avenues of potential future growth," said Goodrich. "We have received numerous responses from individuals indicating their substantial interest to franchise Mace Security Centers. These leads currently are being qualified."

1999: A Year of Changes

The end of the first quarter of 1999 brought big changes to Mace Security International. The board reported that they had been reviewing the company's options to maximize profits. Opportunity came in the form of Louis D. Paolino, Jr., and his car wash company, American Wash Services Inc. The two companies merged, and Paolino was named as chairman and chief executive officer of the company. With the merger, Mace became the first publicly traded national car wash chain. The company's headquarters moved from Bennington, Vermont, to Mt. Laurel, New Jersey. Former CEO Jon Goodrich retained the presidency of the Mace consumer division and that portion of operations remained in Vermont.

The stock market responded favorably to the company's change in direction. Trading as low as $1.12 per share before the announcement, the stock shot up to nearly $6 per share after the merger was announced. The share price continued to rise through the year, and revenues exceeded $38 million, compared with $9.2 million in 1998. "The year 1999 was a monumental year for Mace Security International, Inc.," stated CEO and Chairman Louis Paolino in the annual report. "Mace trans-

Key Dates:

1987: Mace Security International is founded; its first product, Mace, becomes the world's best known defense spray.

1993: Company joins NASDAQ with initial public offering.

1994: Mace acquires Federal Laboratories and Kindergard Corporation.

1995: Mace expands with security products in Canada.

1996: Founder Jon E. Goodrich resigns as president and CEO; Robert D. Norman is named as replacement.

1997: Mace acquires MSP, Inc. and its diversified line of consumer safety products.

1998: Law enforcement chemical product line is sold to Armor Holdings.

1999: Mace begins diversification into car wash industry with the purchase of American Wash Services; Louis D. Paolino, Jr., founder of American Wash Services, is named president, CEO, and chairman of Mace; Mace acquires four additional car wash companies.

2000: Mace enters into licensing and marketing agreement with Goodrich, who begins selling the company's defense sprays through his venture Mark Sport.

2002: Agreement with Goodrich expires and Mace once again begins selling chemical defense sprays, in addition to operating car washes.

formed itself from a leading manufacturer of self-defense devices to an operator of one of the largest car wash chains in the United States.''

In 1999 alone, the company acquired four car wash companies: Millennia, Colonial, Eager Beaver Car Wash, and Hanna Car Wash. The acquisitions were part of the company strategy to dominate the industry. The company ended the fourth quarter of 1999 as the leader in the car wash acquisition race and still the only publicly traded player.

2000s: The Future

In March 2000, Mace announced the acquisition of Red Baron Truck Wash and Planet Truck Wash. Together the companies offered truck-washing facilities in Arizona, Indiana, Ohio, and Texas and generated more than $4 million annually. Other acquisitions in 2000 included: Beneva Car Wash in Sarasota, Florida; Blue Planet Car Wash in Dallas, Texas; and Superstar Kyrene in Phoenix, Arizona. The company considered a merger with Wash Depot Holdings, but the board of directors decided against it.

In 2000, revenues reached $48 million. That year also marked further separation of Mace from its security roots. The

company entered into an agreement with Goodrich and his company Mark Sport, whereby Goodrich would pay $20,000 per month to Mace. In exchange, Mark Sport would assume operations for all of the security products division, both risks and profits.

As Mace forged ahead in the car wash industry, it selected Super Bright Car Wash as the new brand name for the chain nationally. The transition to the new brand was slow, however, as acquired car wash businesses retained their existing names for some time.

Aggressive acquisitions and losses in 2000 led to the stock price for Mace dropping to less than a dollar in the first quarter of 2001. Because of the drop, the company was in danger of being delisted by NASDAQ. The company avoided being delisted by meeting the NASDAQ requirement of maintaining a bid price of more than one dollar for ten consecutive days.

The company started fiscal 2001 favorably, reporting increased revenue. Mace's car wash facilities were in Arizona, Delaware, Florida, New Jersey, Pennsylvania, and Texas, with truck washes located in Arizona, Indiana, Ohio, and Texas. Although by 2003 its number of car washes, as well as its revenues, had essentially remained constant, it continued to explore potential acquisitions, merger, and strategic alliances. In addition, it had returned, as of May 2002, to the direct sale of chemical defense sprays, following the expiration of the marketing agreement with Jon Goodrich, still a member of the board of directors.

Principal Subsidiaries

Global Security Products.

Principal Competitors

Armor Holdings, Inc.; Oasis Car Wash; Precision Auto.

Further Reading

Billings, Alvin, ''Industry First: Mace Takes Car Washing Public,'' *Auto Laundry News,* June 1999, p. 46.

Gormley, James, ''Mace Turns Profit, Reorganizes in Phoenix,'' *Professional Carwashing & Detailing,* May 2001.

Hart, Kevin, ''Washing Cars on Wall Street,'' *Professional Carwashing & Detailing,* May 1999, p. 54.

Librach, Phyllis Brasch, ''New Products Breed Civilian Crime Fighters; Personal Protection Business Thrives As Fear of Crime Grows,'' *St. Louis Post-Dispatch,* October 18, 1993, p. 1A.

Milbank, Dana, ''Mace Tester Takes Great Pains with His Job,'' *Wall Street Journal,* March 13, 1998, p. 3A.

Moore, Deborah, ''Interview with Louis Paolino Jr.,'' *Professional Carwashing & Detailing,* August 1999.

''Public Entity No. 1,'' *Modern Car Care,* January 2000.

—Melissa Rigney Baxter

The Macerich Company

401 Wilshire Boulevard, Suite 700
Santa Monica, California 90401
U.S.A.
Telephone: (310) 394-6000
Fax: (310) 395-2791
Web site: http://www.macerich.com

Public Company
Incorporated: 1964 as The MaceRich Real Estate
  Company
Employees: 2,065
Sales: $418.2 million (2002)
Stock Exchanges: New York
Ticker Symbol: MAC
NAIC: 525930 Real Estate Investment Trusts

The Macerich Company is a self-administered and self-managed real estate investment trust (REIT) involved in the acquisition, redevelopment, and management of regional and community shopping centers. Known as the ''Mall Doctor,'' Macerich focuses on acquiring retail properties, making improvements on the properties, and gleaning a financial return for its efforts. The company operates on a national scale, controlling 56 regional shopping centers and 21 community shopping centers. Regional shopping centers generally contain more than 400,000 square feet of gross leasable area. Community shopping centers range between 100,000 square feet of gross leasable area and 400,000 square feet of gross leasable area. Nearly one-third of the company's 60 million square feet of gross leasable area is located in California.

Origins

Mace Siegel, one of the principal founders of what would become Macerich, began his real estate career working for others. In 1952, he entered the shopping center business, working for a real estate brokerage firm that aided clients in creating shopping centers, the novel, soon-to-skyrocket retail format of the post-World War II era. Siegel spent a dozen years helping others fulfill their entrepreneurial dreams before he began pursuing his own. Siegel's desire for independence sprang from a business idea of his own: to develop strip centers whose major tenants—referred to as ''anchors'' in the retail industry—were leading discount stores. As such, Siegel envisioned founding a company that constructed its properties from the ground up, a defining characteristic later shed by his venture, as Siegel's dream evolved into a redeveloper of impressive proportions.

For help in getting his new business started, Siegel turned to a friend. He convinced an experienced builder and real estate developer named Richard Cohen to join him in business. The two friends combined their first names and, in October 1964, formed the MaceRich Real Estate Company, founded in New York City. With Cohen providing much of the fledgling company's financial muscle, the business became an operational enterprise not long after its founding date. The first real estate property acquired by the company was an athletic field in Ames, Iowa. On the site, Siegel and Cohen built a strip mall anchored by a discount store, developing a property that served as a model for expansion. In the years ahead, the pair developed 18 strip centers, each of which counted a well-known discount store as its major tenant. To a large extent, the financial success of Macerich was tied to the financial success of its anchor tenants, which served as the magnets that attracted customers to the strip centers. In this interdependent relationship between developer and retailer, Macerich maintained a close relationship with one retailer in particular. Of the 18 strip centers developed by the company, 16 were anchored by Arlan's Department Store.

The strip centers provided firm financial footing for Macerich's more ambitious projects to come, although the same could not be said for its primary tenant. The Arlan's chain began to suffer by the end of the 1960s, prompting Cohen to purchase a controlling interest in the beleaguered retailer. With control over the chain, Cohen could affect the re-tenanting of Macerich's strip centers, but his influence was not enough to stave off the chain's demise. Cohen later divested his interest in Arlan's. The chain subsequently filed for bankruptcy protection and its stores were sold to Wal-Mart, Target, and several other discount department stores. Meanwhile, Macerich had turned its focus to bigger, more profitable ventures, beginning its second era of existence just shy of its eighth anniversary.

Macerich gained one of its chief lieutenants not long after the company began building its first wave of strip centers. Dana Anderson joined the company in 1966, beginning a Macerich career that would span more than 35 years. His first great contribution to the company's development occurred during the early 1970s, when he learned of an opportunity to buy a shopping mall, a decided leap up the retail hierarchy from strip centers. Anderson's discovery led to the September 1972 acquisition of the White Lakes Mall in Topeka, Kansas, a turning point in the company's history, as Macerich evolved from a builder of strip centers into an acquirer of shopping malls. The company lacked the financial resources to complete the purchase on its own, so it sought a partner and formed a joint venture with Provident Life Accident and Assurance Company. The partnership worked well for both parties, leading to a lasting relationship that eventually saw Macerich and Provident Life acquire seven regional shopping centers in the Midwest and Southeast.

Becoming a Redeveloper in 1975

Success with strip centers encouraged Macerich to branch out into acquiring shopping malls. Success with acquiring and managing shopping malls in the Midwest and Southeast encouraged the company to extend its geographic reach. Siegel, Cohen, and Anderson began focusing on southern California as the next area for Macerich's expansion. The partners evaluated numerous properties and set their sights on a large, poorly kept shopping mall, the Lakewood Center in Lakewood, California. Macerich teamed with Provident Life and purchased the property in 1975. Because of the outdated condition of the property, Siegel and his partners embraced a new facet of their operating strategy, turning themselves into renovators and redevelopers. The company began the lengthy and costly process of transforming the derelict, open-air shopping mall into a premier regional mall, an arduous task that required Macerich to relocate its headquarters to Santa Monica, California.

Macerich's involvement with the Lakewood Center proved to be a seminal success. Once the company succeeded in thoroughly revamping the Lakewood Center, it began lending its salubrious touch to other shopping malls. The company's executives developed expertise at devising and implementing redevelopment and expansion programs, skills that would later earn the company its industry nickname as the "Mall Doctor."

For the next 20 years, Macerich patterned its activities after the success of the Lakewood Center project, assembling a stable of modern regional shopping malls through the redevelopment of older properties. Over time, project by project, Macerich's executives became more adept at turning the old into the new, at

renovating properties so that the rent charged per square foot increased significantly after the company's redevelopment and expansion programs were completed. During the 20-year period following the acquisition of the Lakewood Center, the company built a portfolio of more than a dozen regional shopping malls, enough to make its name known in the national industry but a pittance compared to the major competitors in the industry. Macerich did make a bid to join the loftier ranks of the industry, however, a charge that began in 1994, the year the company began its third era of development.

1994 IPO Fueling Aggressive Growth

Macerich achieved its greatest growth after it filed for an initial public offering (IPO) of stock, a public debut that cast the company as a real estate investment trust (REIT). The difference in the rate of growth before the IPO and after the IPO was enormous, an exponential difference in terms of the gross leased area owned by the company and in the number of properties it managed. To a great extent, the catalyst for the metamorphosis in stature was attributable to Macerich's status as a REIT. There were numerous requirements for a company to qualify as a REIT in the eyes of the Internal Revenue Service (IRS). Some of the stipulations were arcane, but essentially the conditions required a REIT to distribute nearly all of its taxable income to shareholders. In exchange for adhering to this condition— among a bevy of others—Macerich could look forward to far greater ease in raising capital, the fuel for the company's expansion. By raising capital through the sale of stock and debt as a REIT, Macerich no longer had to secure investment partners for individual projects, enabling it to acquire and to redevelop properties at a much quicker pace.

Macerich completed its IPO in March 1994, the company's 30th anniversary. At the time of the offering, the company owned 15 properties that contained roughly ten million square feet of space. Within the next few years, these two measures of its size would increase robustly, driven upward by individual acquisitions that generally ranged between $75 million and $100 million and by acquisitions of groups of properties whose aggregate value sometimes exceeded $1 billion. Concurrent with its IPO, Macerich obtained its 16th property, the Crossroads Mall in Oklahoma City, Oklahoma, followed by the July 1994 acquisition of the Chesterfield Towne Center in Richmond, Virginia. Macerich tripled its acquisition total in 1995, becoming the fifth fastest-growing acquisition company in the nation after purchasing properties in Salisbury, Maryland; Capitola, California; and New York City. In 1996, when Macerich ranked as the second fastest-growing acquisition company in the country, it added 6.1 million square feet to its portfolio through the purchase of seven properties. Revenues during this initial expansion spree increased from $86 million in 1994 to $155 million in 1996.

As Macerich entered the late 1990s, its pace of growth accelerated. The company acquired more retail projects than any other developer in 1997, adding 14.5 million square feet to its portfolio through the addition of 16 properties. In early 1998, Macerich completed the first of two massive acquisitions during the year. The company entered into a joint venture with Simon DeBartolo Group Inc. and acquired 12 regional malls from ERE Yarmouth, an institutional real estate advisor and manager that

Key Dates:

1964: The MaceRich Real Estate Company is formed; company name is later changed to The Macerich Company.
1972: Macerich acquires its first shopping mall.
1975: The acquisition of the Lakewood Center leads Macerich into the business of real estate development.
1994: Macerich completes its initial public offering of stock.
1998: In a joint venture with Simon DeBartolo Group, Macerich acquires 12 regional malls.
2002: Macerich acquires Westcor Realty in a $1.475 billion deal.

operated as a unit of Sydney, Australia-based Lend Lease Corp. The transaction, valued at a numbing $974.5 million, added 10.7 million square feet to Macerich's swelling portfolio, giving it properties located in eight states. The ERE Yarmouth acquisition bolstered Macerich's presence in the Midwest, the historical epicenter of its activities. The next big acquisition of the year extended the company's presence into uncharted territory. Late in the year the company announced it was forming a joint venture with Canada's largest pension fund, the Ontario Teachers' Pension Fund. Macerich's 51 percent interest in the joint venture gave it controlling interest over the entity's acquisition of four regional shopping malls in the Pacific Northwest, the company's first foray into the region. The deal, estimated to be worth $500 million, added 4.1 million square feet to Macerich's portfolio, making it the largest regional mall owner west of the Rocky Mountains.

By 2000, Macerich stood as a rising force in its industry, its reputation as the "Mall Doctor" known throughout the country. As it entered the 21st century, the company operated 47 regional shopping centers and five community shopping centers, controlling 42 million square feet of gross leasable area. In the six years since its IPO, Macerich had quadrupled in size, becoming a dominant owner and redeveloper of regional shopping malls. The company's achievements during the first decade of the new century suggested its committed drive toward growth was far from finished.

During the early years of the decade, Macerich strode forward, sharpening its strategic focus on acquiring the country's largest shopping centers. In 2002, the company completed the $152.5 million acquisition of The Oaks, a regional mall in Thousand Oaks, California, with 1.1 million square feet of gross leasable area. The scale of the Oaks acquisition paled in comparison with the acquisition Macerich completed in July 2002, when the company acquired Westcor Realty, an Arizona-based owner and operator of retail properties, for $1.475 billion. Included within the deal were eight regional malls in Arizona and one in Colorado. Of the eight properties in Arizona, six were located in the Phoenix market. Other assets included in the acquisition were options to more than 1,000 acres of undeveloped land and interests in 18 retail assets—referred to as

"urban villages"—that contained 5.6 million square feet of gross leasable area.

In the wake of the Westcor acquisition, there was justifiable optimism for Macerich's future. The transaction added 15.9 million square feet of gross leasable area to the company's portfolio, giving it a total of 57 million square feet, a sixfold increase in less than a decade. Further, the company reacted quickly to contend with the debt incurred from the purchase, raising $420 million in a ten million-share equity offering in November 2002. The company ended the year with $378.9 million in revenue. In the years ahead, Macerich promised to figure prominently in the commercial real estate business, its reputation as the "Mall Doctor" galvanized by nearly 40 years of operation.

Principal Subsidiaries

Macerich Property Management Company; Macerich Management Company; The Macerich Partnership, L.P.

Principal Competitors

Westfield America Inc.; Selleck Development Group; Simon Property Group, Inc.

Further Reading

"Competition Strong for Prime Centers," *Chain Store Age Executive with Shopping Center Age,* April 1985, p. 41.
"DeBartolo and Macerich Acquire 12 Regional Malls," *WWD,* December 30, 1997, p. 10.
Duell, Jennifer D., "Macerich Buys Westcor for $1.5 Billion," *Commercial Property News,* July 1, 2002, p. 3.
Garcia, Shelly, "Macerich Buys Out Its Panorama Mall Partner," *San Fernando Valley Business Journal,* September 30, 2002, p. 1.
——, "Valley Mall Operators Pursue Luxury Stores in Underserved Area," *Los Angeles Business Journal,* May 12, 2003, p. 7.
"How the West Is Being Won," *Chain Store Age Executive with Shopping Center Age,* August 2002, p. 176.
Howard, Bob, "Big Deal-Maker Macerich Acquires $92 Million Mall," *Los Angeles Business Journal,* August 18, 1997, p. 51.
Ibold, Hans, "Renovation Projects Transforming Old Malls to New," *Los Angeles Business Journal,* October 30, 2000, p. 40.
King, Danny, "Macerich Cashes Out Small Fry to Focus on Big Malls," *Los Angeles Business Journal,* January 7, 2002, p. 29.
——, "REITs Line Up As Potential Buyers for Glendale Galleria," *Los Angeles Business Journal,* October 21, 2002, p. 50.
——, "Southwest Focus Is Working to the Benefit of REIT Macerich," *Los Angeles Business Journal,* April 14, 2003, p. 28.
"Macerich Expands Presence in AZ and CO with $1.47 Billion Deal," *National Mortgage News,* June 10, 2002, p. 16.
"Maceich Masters the Art of Acquisition," *Chain Store Age Executive with Shopping Center Age,* November 1987, p. 166.
Miller, Brian K., "Safeco Corp. Set to Sell Washington Square Mall," *Business Journal-Portland,* December 11, 1998, p. 7.
Nabbefeld, Joe, "Safeco's Mall Sale: Redmond Town Center Is Part of the Deal," *Puget Sound Business Journal,* November 27, 1998, p. 1.
"New Looks for Tired Shopping Centers," *Chain Store Age Executive with Shopping Center Age,* October 2001, p. 128.
"Think Dominance," *Chain Store Age with Shopping Center Age,* May 1998, p. 80.

—Jeffrey L. Covell

Massey Energy Company

4 North 4th Street
Richmond, Virginia 23219
U.S.A.
Telephone: (804) 788-1800
Fax: (804) 788-1870
Web site: http://www.masseyenergyco.com

Public Company
Incorporated: 1924 as Fluor Construction Co.
Employees: 4,552
Sales: $1.63 billion (2002)
Stock Exchanges: New York
Ticker Symbol: MEE
NAIC: 212112 Bituminous Coal Underground Mining

Richmond, Virginia-based Massey Energy Company is one of the top coal miners in the United States. In terms of revenues it ranks as the fifth largest coal company in the country. From 19 mining complexes located in the central Appalachian region of Virginia, West Virginia, and Kentucky, Massey produces more than 40 million tons of coal each year. It serves more than 125 utility, industrial, and metallurgical customers around the world. Massey has a history of violent labor clashes and regulatory violations, and in 2002 many of its executives faced questions about insider stock trading.

Company Origins Dating Back to the Early 1900s

The founding father of Massey Energy was A.T. Massey, who in 1916 began a career as a coal broker in Richmond, Virginia. In 1920 he incorporated A.T. Massey Coal Company, Inc. (ATM) and became its first president. Sons Evan and William took over the business in 1945, with Evan succeeding his father as president of the company. It was Evan's son, E. Morgan Massey, who after graduating from the University of Virginia would be instrumental in shifting the emphasis from selling coal to mining it. According to company documents, ATM acquired its first mining operation in 1945, when Morgan was still a college student. According to the *Cincinnati En-*

quirer, ATM acquired its first mine in West Virginia in 1949. A 1985 *Business Week* profile of Massey maintains that after he graduated from college and joined the family business he "asserted his independence by pushing to move the brokerage company into the profitable but troublesome mining business. Massey's first move—a $10,000 investment in a coal venture— had to be made without his father's knowledge. And when he finally was permitted to take the company into mining, Massey was allowed to use only the profits from his own operations to expand." Despite these difficult ground rules he was able to succeed, leading to the transformation of ATM into a mining company. It was also while Massey was managing his first mining venture that he developed an antipathy for unions. According to *Business Week,* "The young manager daily shoveled coal alongside his 15 workers; when the union arrived to organize the fledgling West Virginia operation, he joined up. But six months later, Massey recalls, a UMW [United Mine Workers] official told him 'management can't be a member of the union.' "

Morgan Massey's uncle became president of ATM in 1962, as the company continued to expand its mining interests. The Peerless Eagle Coal Company was acquired in 1965, and the Martin County Coal Corporation was established in 1969. Another subsidiary, Omar Mining Company, launched in the 1950s, expanded its operations from Logan County, West Virginia, to Boone County, West Virginia. In 1972, Morgan Massey, now 46 years old, took over as president of ATM. Two years later Massey, along with his brother and uncle, sold ATM to St. Joe Minerals Corp. for 14 percent of St. Joe stock, valued at approximately $56 million.

Massey stayed on as president to run ATM for St. Joe. Due to the oil crisis of the 1970s the importance of coal in meeting the country's energy needs increased, as did the value of ATM. Companies like ATM were optimistic about the future and began to expand mining capacity and their holdings in the coal industry. In 1974 ATM bought Rawl Sales & Processing Co. It acquired the Tennessee Consolidated Coal Company in 1976. ATM launched two businesses in 1978: Massey Coal Services and Elk Run Coal Company.

Fluor Corporation's Purchase of Half of ATM in 1981

St. Joe in 1980 sold half of ATM to an oil company, Royal Dutch/Shell Group, resulting in a new entity: Massey Coal Partnership. A year later this arrangement changed when Los Angeles-based Fluor Corporation bought St. Joe, taking over its interest in ATM at a time when the price of commodities, such as coal, gold, and lead were soaring. Fluor, a major construction and engineering firm, bought St. Joe as a way to shelter it from the cyclical nature of its core business. It turned out to be a poor bet because commodity prices plunged, so that in the mid-1980s Fluor shed St. Joe's gold and lead assets. It retained ATM, however, and in 1987 bought out Shell, making ATM a wholly owned Fluor subsidiary.

During the mid-1980s the coal industry suffered from problems of excess supply, the result of overexpansion in the late 1970s and early 1980s. Because coal prices fell or remained flat, coal companies had to find ways to cut costs in order to counterbalance inflation and maintain profits. ATM made use of contract mines. Although the company directly mined the richest coal seams, it contracted out the less desirable deposits to contractors in order to squeeze what they could out of the properties. Moreover, small operators could fly under the radar screen of both regulators and the union. As explained by ATM CEO and Chairman Don Blankenship in a 2002 interview: "The general view was that small contractors could pay less because the union wouldn't focus on them. They could get by with more because the regulators wouldn't hold them to the same standards. And that was the way it was, and that was the way companies survived, particularly in the 1980s."

Another important way to contain costs was to cut back on labor costs. In the mid-1980s ATM became involved in one of the most bitter labor disputes in decades when Massey faced off against the United Mine Workers (UMW). It was Blankenship who in 1984 urged Massey to take on the UMW, which was looking to negotiate one contract that would cover all of ATM's 120 mines and subsidiaries. Blankenship and Massey wanted each mine to negotiate an individual contract, arguing that each mine was a separate profit center and operated under different conditions. For the UMW the confrontation with ATM took on greater importance because its leaders felt the need to demonstrate that the union was still a powerful force. Moreover, its fight with ATM became something of a proxy for labor in general. But there was no doubt that the UMW was not the all-powerful organization it once was. It represented about 160,000 working miners in 1978, but that number fell to 110,000 by 1985. Part of the reason the UMW was losing strength was simply because the coal industry was moving to the west where companies could engage in cheaper surface mining, and where

UMW was little represented. Because UMW mines now contributed less than 40 percent of all coal products, the union simply lacked the same economic clout should it choose to launch a massive strike. Instead, the UMW decided to strike selected mines in order to gain a uniform contract.

The ATM asset the UMW singled out for a strike beginning in the autumn of 1984 was the operation run by Blankenship: Rawls Sales & Processing Co. The mine was located in the Tug Fork Valley section of West Virginia, near the Kentucky border, where the legendary "Matewan massacre" took place some 65 years earlier, which cost nine people their lives as area miners attempted to unionize. This contemporary labor fight pitted 1,500 UMW members against ATM, and like its predecessor it became violent and drawn out. In August 1985 *Time* magazine set the scene: "Violence has become almost monotonous. In the latest incident, a midnight explosion last week rocked the three-story brick district headquarters of the U.M.W. in Pikeville, Ky., incidentally shattering a huge portrait of the late union leader John L. Lewis that hung on the wall. The strike had produced one death, hundreds of injuries and more than a thousand episodes of rock throwing, smashed windshields and punctured tires. Gunfire has been commonplace. Snipers killed a nonunion coal-truck driver, Hayes West, 35, in a convoy crossing Coeburn Mountain in late May. Gunfire wounded miner Judy Mullins, 40, in the hand in July while she was picketing in Canada, Ky." On a single day 11 bullets were fired into Blankenship's office. One smashed through a television, which became a memento for him of this turbulent period. The strike lasted for 15 months before the UMW called it off, agreeing to negotiate separate contracts with ATM's 17 major subsidiaries.

While many rival coal companies abandoned the central Appalachian area, ATM, starting in 1988, began to snap up reserves at reasonable prices. In particular, ATM bolstered its supply of metallurgical coal, which was a high-quality product suitable for steelmaking. Because an influx of cheap foreign steel crippled American steel companies, many coal companies dropped out of the metallurgical coal business, leaving ATM to pick up reserves at discount prices. The decision worked out so well for ATM that it was soon producing over a third of Fluor's operating profit despite generating just 10 percent of its revenues.

Don Blankenship Becoming President in 1990

After running two more of ATM's mining operations since his strike-breaking days at Rawls Sales, Blankenship became ATM's president in July 1990. The son of a grocer, he was raised in the coalfields of West Virginia and worked in the coal mines during college breaks. Massey now assumed the newly created posts of chairman and chief executive officer. These management changes came at a time when Fluor had retained Shearson Lehman Hutton Inc. to evaluate what it should do with its coal assets, and made it clear that it might opt to sell ATM. In the end, Fluor held on to ATM, as Blankenship took over the running of the company. He was especially interested in new federal clean air requirements, which he believed would bode well for low-sulfur coal producers such as ATM. As a consequence, he was responsible for ATM continuing to buy up reserves during the rest of the 1990s. He became ATM's chair and CEO in 1992, following Massey's retirement. His bet on

---

low-sulfur coal paid off, as demand rose and with it ATM's profits, making the company one of Fluor's crown jewels by 1997 when the engineering and construction side of the business suffered through difficult times. It was also during this period that Fluor began to search for a new chief executive and Blankenship was regarded as one of the leading candidates.

Blankenship lost out on the top slot at Fluor, but then Fluor's board decided in 2000 to split the company into two publicly traded companies, one composed of the engineering and construction assets and the other ATM, which by now was beginning to struggle. The deal was structured as a reverse spinoff, so that the construction business became a new public company while the old Fluor Corporation retained the coal operations and subsequently changed its name to Massey Energy Company. The company had $2 billion in assets and was left with some $500 million in debt.

While Massey Energy was being formed in 2000, it suffered a public relations hit when in October 2000 a wastewater reservoir collapsed above an abandoned mine and sent 230 million gallons of black sludge coursing through a tributary of the Big Sandy River. The Exxon Valdez crude oil spill, by way of comparison, leaked just 5 percent of that amount. Fish and plants were killed a full 36 miles downstream of the reservoir and the water supply of several towns was shut down for weeks. ATM ultimately paid $40 million in clean-up costs. While management maintained that the spill was an "act of God," Kentucky's Mine Safety and Health Administration as well as its Office of Surface Mining concluded that the barrier between the mine and the river was simply too thin. To make matters worse, several months later, in June 2001, a pump in another ATM mine developed a leak and before it was shut down it allowed 30,000 gallons of sludge to pour into a nearby stream. ATM failed to report the incident to authorities, who only learned of the matter when citizens called to complain that Robinson Creek had turned black. Other illegal discharges followed. According to a 2003 Forbes article, "Over the two years through 2001 Massey was cited by West Virginia officials for violating regulations 501 times. . . . These regulations can grow teeth. Regulators, citing a pattern of violations, have been slapping Massey with 'show cause' orders. They will suspend, even permanently revoke, permits to mine or process or store coal if the company doesn't show it has mended its ways. If a permit is revoked, it could prove a 'death sentence,' in the words of one Massey lawyer, because that would make it difficult for other

permits to be issued or an old one renewed. A company spokesperson says that that is an 'unlikely' scenario because it would be 'suicide' for the state."

Massey Energy faced other challenges as it became an independent company. According to Forbes, "In the winter of 2000–01 electricity demand rose and the spot price for central Appalachian coal jumped from $24 a ton to $48 a ton. Mining companies began digging furiously, hiring more workers and pushing up wages. Blankenship refused to match the increase. Miners quit in droves. The timing was awful. Blankenship had planned to increase Massey coal production for the coming year from 44 million tons to 56 million tons and so needed to add staff. He had to turn to people with little experience. By the end of 2001 half of his 5,000-person staff were new hires." As a result, productivity fell, as did operating margins.

Massey Energy endured bad news on a number of fronts in 2002 and 2003. It was found by a jury to have defrauded another coal company, Harman Mining Co., and was hit with a $50 million verdict. Blankenship and ten other current or former company officers and Massey Energy were sued by disgruntled shareholders who maintained that insiders sold shares shortly before the price of the stock dropped from $22 to $12 per share. Early in 2003 Massey lost $10 million in an arbitrated case with Duke Energy over a coal supply contract, then a few days later announced that its corporate financial filings were being reviewed by the Securities and Exchange Commission. In April 2003 the company agreed to make changes to its 2001 and 2002 filings, but according to Blankenship the impact on shareholders was minor. Instead of a loss of $30 million in fiscal 2002, it now recorded a loss of $32.6 million. Nevertheless, the news did little to improve the public image of Massey Energy.

Principal Subsidiaries

A.T. Massey Coal Company, Inc.; Massey Coal Sales Company; Massey Coal Export, Ltd.; Massey Coal Services, Inc.; Massey Consulting Services, Inc.

Principal Competitors

Arch Coal, Inc.; CONSOL Energy Inc.; Peabody Energy Corporation; Alliance Resource Partners, L.P.; NACCO Industries, Inc.; Horizon Natural Resources Company.

Further Reading

Boyer, Mike, "Massey Coal Has Had Tumultuous Past," *Cincinnati Enquirer,* October 22, 2000.

Condon, Bernard, "Not King Coal," *Forbes,* May 26, 2003, May 26, 2003, pp. 80–82.

Lubove, Seth H., "Massey Coal Strike Is Testing UMW Strategy," *Wall Street Journal,* June 3, 1985, p. 1.

Miles, Gregory, and Cynthia Green, "The Coalfield Heavyweight Who's Going the Distance," *Business Week,* October 21, 1985, p. 123.

Rundle, Rhonda L., "Fluor Board Clears Plan to Split Firm into Two Concerns," *Wall Street Journal,* June 8, 2000, p. A3.

Trippett, Frank, "Violence in the Coalfields," *Time,* August 26, 1985, p. 17.

—Ed Dinger

Memorial Sloan-Kettering Cancer Center

1275 York Avenue
New York, New York 10021
U.S.A.
Telephone: (212) 639-2000
Toll Free: (800) 525-2225
Fax: (212) 639-3576
Web site: http://www.mskcc.org

Private Company
Founded: 1884 as New York Cancer Hospital
Employees: 7,953
Operating Revenues: $1.08 billion (2002)
NAIC: 622310 Specialty (Except Psychiatric and
   Substance Abuse) Hospitals

Memorial Sloan-Kettering Cancer Center is the world's oldest and largest private nonprofit institution devoted to the prevention, treatment, and cure of cancer. It is also generally considered one of the best facilities in the United States for combating this dreaded disease. In 2001, for example, *U.S. News & World Report* rated it first in cancer care among U.S. medical institutions, a ranking it has often held. Each year Memorial Sloan-Kettering offers both inpatient and outpatient services to well over 10,000 patients.

Beginnings in the 1880s

The institution today known as Memorial Sloan-Kettering Cancer Center was founded as the New York Cancer Hospital in 1884. It was the first such hospital in the United States to devote itself solely to the study and treatment of cancer, then considered incurable and therefore shunned by many doctors. The founders were Mrs. Elizabeth Hamilton Cullum, a granddaughter of Alexander Hamilton, and financier John Jacob Astor and his wife.

The hospital, completed and opened in 1887, occupied the entire block between Central Park West and Manhattan avenues and West 105th and 106th Streets on Manhattan's Upper West Side. A stone-and-brick edifice in the French Gothic style, it resembled a chateau and featured turrets with conical roofs at each corner. These turrets allowed a good deal of natural light to enter the circular wards located within. This extra sunlight, it was then believed, would promote cleanliness and impede dust at a time when cancer was thought to be contagious. The institution was renamed the General Memorial Hospital for the Treatment of Cancer and Allied Diseases in 1899; "General" was dropped from the name in 1916. A clinical laboratory was opened in 1917 and a social service department in 1920. Among the hospital's benefactors was Edward S. Harkness, who in 1926 gave $250,000 for the purchase of radium to treat malignant tumors by radiation. Dr. James Ewing, who was director of Memorial from 1931 to 1939, later was quoted by *Time* magazine as saying that until then "the hospital had enjoyed the studied neglect of the public, while the medical profession had left us severely alone."

In 1927, John D. Rockefeller, Jr., made the first of his annual $60,000 contributions to Memorial for research and the establishment of six clinical fellowships. He also quietly began assembling parcels of land on Manhattan's East Side, between First and York avenues and 67th and 68th Streets, directly across from the Institute for Medical Research, which later became Rockefeller Institute, then Rockefeller University. In 1936, he donated this tract of land, valued at $900,000, and another $3 million for the construction of a 12-story hospital to replace the existing Upper West Side structure. When the new building opened in 1939, it was able to house 200 patients in place of the 110-bed capacity at the old one, making it the largest institution in the world for the treatment of cancer. Each arriving patient was sent to one of 11 highly specialized departments, each with its own staff.

Research Plus Treatment: 1945–89

In 1945, Alfred P. Sloan, Jr., chairman of General Motors Corporation, donated $4 million to establish, with Charles F. Kettering—another General Motors executive—the Sloan-Kettering Institute for Cancer Research. A 14-story building, erected beside Memorial Hospital, was completed in 1947 to serve as the research division of the hospital. Dr. Cornelius P. Rhoads, who had succeeded Ewing as Memorial's director, became head of Sloan-Kettering as well, but the two institutions were entirely separate in terms of budget, management, and personnel. During the 1940s, research concentrated on chemotherapy, which joined surgery and radiation as the accepted methods of treating cancer.

Also part of the Memorial Sloan-Kettering complex, and opened in 1950, was James Ewing Hospital, built by the city of New York for the treatment of city residents and staffed by Memorial. It was absorbed by Memorial in 1968, renamed the Ewing Pavilion, and later remodeled and renamed as a research facility. The Tower Building, opened in 1951, more than doubled Memorial's outpatient capacity. (It was razed for a new outpatient building in 1969.) In 1959, a research laboratory was opened in Rye, New York.

Memorial Sloan-Kettering Cancer Center (MSKCC) was established in 1960 by the consolidation of Memorial Hospital and Sloan-Kettering Institute, and John D. Rockefeller, Jr.'s son Laurance became its chairman, serving in this capacity until 1982. Additions to the complex by 1972 included the Kettering Laboratory (1964) and a radiation-therapy center. The new 19-story, 565-bed Memorial Hospital was completed on the 68th Street end of the site in 1973.

Memorial Hospital, Sloan-Kettering Institute, and Memorial Sloan-Kettering Cancer Center came under the direction of Dr. Paul A. Marks, who became president and chief executive officer of all three in 1980. Under Marks, wrote Philip M. Boffery for the *New York Times Magazine* in 1987, "once-powerful surgeons known for 'heavy cutting' are no longer the dominant faction. Marks' administration has boosted the roles of radiotherapists and doctors who treat cancer with chemical and biological agents and has made the hospital more research-oriented. At Sloan-Kettering . . . there is increased emphasis on molecular biology. . . . To accomplish this, Marks has executed a major purge of the scientific staff." Marks also embarked on a $325 million fundraising drive, of which $78 million was earmarked for a new, 13-story research laboratory. (Laurance Rockefeller donated $36.2 million for this purpose.) The new Rockefeller Research Laboratory (named for his father) consolidated laboratories from other portions of the site and from the Rye laboratory. It was completed in 1989.

According to Boffery, the shake-up was needed because many scientists, including Marks himself, considered the center's research and treatment efforts to have fallen behind the times as well as behind other institutions. (Scandal rocked Sloan-Kettering in 1974 when a staffer who was a protégé of the director was found to have faked his research.) The board of trustees was said to feel that the center was badly organized, with research and clinical activities largely independent of each other, expenditures growing out of line, and the collection of payments from patients inefficiently handled. Marks established a tenure plan for the scientists—in effect, lifetime appointments—but made all tenured professionals subject to a rigorous peer review every four years.

A Competitive Marketplace in the 1990s

By the 1990s, Memorial Sloan-Kettering, like other cancer centers, was scrambling for patients because of the rise of managed-care plans. Many health maintenance organizations (HMOs) were refusing to pay the high prices such centers traditionally charged for care and preferred to send their cancer patients to the lowest-cost hospitals available. This made it all the more vital that Memorial hold on to the more than half of its patients who were referring themselves to the hospital, without consulting their primary doctors, because of the institution's reputation. In 1992, Memorial established a freestanding breast cancer center on 64th Street. MSKCC officials said the new offsite clinic would expand its breast cancer treatment capacity by 30 percent. They then established a prostate cancer center on 65th Street and added a radiotherapy treatment center in White Plains, New York, cut costs by 10 percent (partly by closing a medical-surgical floor), and signed the center's first managed-care contract, with Travelers Insurance Co.

Like other New York hospitals, Memorial Sloan-Kettering found it would have to expand further into the suburbs in order to serve on an outpatient basis the more than 16,000 cancer patients it was discharging annually. Many of these patients lived in the metropolitan area but outside the city, sometimes beyond easy commuting distance. During 1996 and 1997, in cooperation with other medical institutions, MSKCC established treatment centers in Danville, New Jersey; Sleepy Hollow, New York; and at the Hauppauge and Rockville Centre, Long Island. By early 1998, MSKCC had begun work on a $20 million outpatient treatment center in Commack, Long Island. Meanwhile, the Rockefeller Outpatient Pavilion set up shop on 11 floors of an East 53rd Street high-rise in Manhattan, at a cost of $100 million. An outpatient center in Dover, New Jersey, a screening center in Manhattan's Greenwich Village, and a breast examination center in Harlem were in operation by 2002. To attract foreign patients who could afford to pay out of pocket, MSKCC established, in 1997, an International Center at First Avenue and 74th Street that was seeing about 200 new patients a month. In the main building, Memorial Sloan Kettering remodeled the top patient floor, transforming it into a 14-suite luxury facility with hotel-style services, including private chefs for the state-of-the-art kitchen.

Memorial Sloan-Kettering made its first major connection to managed care in 1996, when it signed a contract with Empire Blue Cross & Blue Shield, the state of New York's largest health insurer. A vital part of the agreement was MSKCC's willingness to cut its rates by as much as 30 percent. The center's chief operating officer told Lucette Lagnado of the *New York Times* that it had little choice because "Empire is 22 percent of our business—we had to protect that piece of business." Memorial was only filling about 60 percent of its beds at the time. Moreover, the state was preparing to lift regulations that had for 30 years artificially inflated the prices that hospitals could charge and that insurers would pay. Under this system, MSKCC received higher reimbursement rates than those paid other hospitals because it was one of only two specialized cancer centers in the state. In order to prepare for the new age of aggressive price-cutting, the hospital closed three patient floors—nearly a quarter of its capacity—and induced 164 nurses, doctors, and administrators to take early retirement.

Memorial Sloan-Kettering lost money throughout the 1990s, but it bolstered its finances through a combination of stepped-up fundraising, cost control, and lucrative investments in such instruments as venture-capital funds. The center's money managers had at their disposal a portfolio of assets worth $1.9 billion in early 1999. Of this sum, 36 percent was invested in equities, 25 percent in short-term fixed-income products, 21 percent in long-term fixed-income products, 11 percent in alternative investments, and 7 percent in international securities, including emerging-market stocks. In 2000, income from the center's net assets—now grown to $2.1 billion—and other sources enabled it to compensate for an operating loss of $101 million—compared to only $5 million in 1995—on its operating revenues of $876 million. Some 850,000 people contributed $124 million in funds to the center during the year. "They're very aggressive about fund-raising," a Standard & Poor's analyst told Judith Messina of *Crain's New York Business.* "They want your 10 bucks and my 10 bucks. [Their fund-raising] is much more broad-based than others'."

Memorial Sloan-Kettering's sound finances enabled it to receive by far the highest bond rating (AA) for a hospital in the state of New York from Standard & Poor's. The institution issued $450 million in variable rate bonds in January 2002 to finance a new five-story tower to a building on East 67th Street and a genito-urinary center on East 68th Street, fund a satellite clinic in Commack, pay for the construction of 265 new apartments on nearby Roosevelt Island for staff and postdoctoral students, and refinance debt. Its demonstrated fundraising ability was cited as a primary credit strength by Moody's Investors Service, which rated the new bonds—which were insured—at Aa2. MSKCC was planning to issue another $400 million in debt in 2003 to finance a 23-story Manhattan research facility on East 68th Street in the face of strong community opposition.

Memorial Sloan-Kettering's added income allowed it to pay for some cancer therapies and diagnostic techniques not fully covered by insurers and to provide more charity care. Even so, the hospital filled only an average of 79.5 percent of its 437 beds on a given day in 2000. A *Wall Street Journal* article in 2001 reported that it was considering turning away at least some of the terminally ill patients who appeared at its door but who often proved unprofitable to treat because there was little that could be done to help them. (Second-opinion cases reportedly consumed 10 percent of MSKCC physicians' time while producing less than 1 percent of its revenue.) Instead, it launched a marketing campaign aimed at recruiting more early-stage patients who not only offered a more favorable prognosis but would be much more profitable to treat. Because the decline in stock prices in 2000 reduced the value of its investment holdings, the center was also considering performing surgery on weekends and keeping its outpatient clinics open later in order to raise more revenue.

Principal Competitors

Beth Israel Medical Center; Dana Farber Cancer Institute; Johns Hopkins Hospital; Mayo Foundation; Montefiore Medical Center; Mount Sinai Hospital; New York Presbyterian Hospital; St. Luke's-Roosevelt Hospital Center; Anderson Cancer Center.

Further Reading

Becker, Cinda, "Life at the Top; Philanthropy Keeps Sloan-Kettering in the Black," *Modern Healthcare,* January 21, 2002, p. 22.

Benson, Barbara, "Changes Drive Sloan-Kettering to the Suburbs," *Crain's New York Business,* April 28, 1997, pp. 17, 20.

Boffery, Philip M., "Dr. Marks' Crusade," *New York Times Magazine,* April 26, 1987, pp. 27–30, 60, 66–7.

Burke, Christine, "Memorial Goes Abroad for a Cure," *Crain's New York Business,* October 27, 1997, p. 38.

"Cancer: Another Rockefeller Fortune to Fight the Disease," *Newsweek,* May 9, 1936, p. 53.

"Cancer Hospital," *Time,* October 7, 1940, p. 58.

A Century of Commitment: A History of Memorial Sloan-Kettering Cancer Center. New York: Memorial Sloan-Kettering Cancer Center, 1985.

"Frontal Attack," *Time,* June 27, 1949, pp. 66–8, 70–2, 75.

Goldberger, Paul, "Design Can't Heal, But It Shouldn't Make You Worse," *New York Times,* August 27, 1989, p. B30.

Kamen, Robin, "From Detection to Cure," *Crain's New York Business,* November 2, 1992, pp. 3, 60.

Kleiman, Dena, "A Hospital Celebrates 100 Years in the Battle to Vanquish Cancer," *New York Times,* May 17, 1984, pp. B1, B5.

Lagnado, Lucette, "Famed Cancer Center Gives in to Managed Care," *Wall Street Journal,* October 25, 1996, pp. B1, B6.

——, "Stock Slump Deprives Not-for-Profit Hospitals of a Seductive Crutch," *Wall Street Journal,* May 31, 2001, pp. A1, A6.

Messina, Judith, "Memorial Has Money to Make in Bonds," *Crain's New York Business,* August 27, 2001, p. 19.

——, "Stellar Reputation Gives Center Many Advantages, But Competition Grows," *Crain's New York Business,* January 8, 2001.

Nemes, Judith, "Hospitals Offer Ritzier Service to Attract the Affluent Ailing," *Crain's New York Business,* November 23, 1998, p. 32.

Polyak, Ilana, "Investment Management: Hospitals Get Creative with Investments," *Bond Buyer,* March 16, 1999, p. 5a.

Temes, Judy, "Taking the Temperature of 40 Health Care Plans," *Crain's New York Business,* January 23, 1995, p. 24.

"Toward Cancer Control," *Time,* March 19, 1973, pp. 64–9.

—Robert Halasz

Miller Publishing Group, LLC

11100 Santa Monica, Suite 600
Los Angeles, California 90025-3384
U.S.A.
Telephone: (310) 893-5400
Fax: (310) 893-5457

Private Company
Incorporated: 1997
Employees: 500
Sales: $70 million (2003 est.)
NAIC: 511120 Periodical Publishers

Miller Publishing Group, LLC owns *Tennis* magazine and nearly four dozen city-specific monthly travel guides published under the Where banner. The firm also has a stake in *Vibe* and *Spin* magazines along with several partners, including investment company Freeman Spogli & Co. and music legend Quincy Jones, who founded *Vibe* along with company head Robert Miller.

Beginnings

Miller Publishing Group was founded in Los Angeles in 1997 by Robert L. Miller, a veteran magazine industry executive who had spent 22 years at Time, Inc., most recently as head of that firm's Time, Inc. Ventures unit. Miller's accomplishments there had included helping launch *Martha Stewart Living* and assisting in the 1993 founding of *Vibe* magazine, which focused on African American rap and hip-hop performers. *Vibe* had been the brainchild of music industry giant Quincy Jones, and he, along with television producer David Salzman, also owned stakes in the magazine. When Time decided to fold the Ventures unit, Miller made a deal in early 1996 to buy its stake in *Vibe* for a reported $20 million. With Jones and Salzman he then formed a company called Vibe Ventures to run the magazine. At this time *Vibe* had a circulation of 450,000, and published ten issues per year. It had just begun to turn a profit.

In the spring of 1997 Miller added a second music magazine to his stable when, with backing from investment firm Freeman Spogli & Co., Inc., he bought *Spin* magazine, a New York-based alternative rock monthly. *Spin* had been founded in 1985 by Bob Guccione, Jr., son of the publisher of *Penthouse* magazine. The price was more than $40 million. Positioned as a young, hip alternative to what some considered the increasingly out-of-touch *Rolling Stone,* the monthly *Spin* had a circulation of about 500,000. It generated revenues estimated at $20 million and profits of approximately $1.5 million. After the sale Guccione gave up the posts of publisher and editor, and a new editor-in-chief, Michael Hirschorn, was named. Hirschorn, a former editor at *New York* magazine, would join executive editor Craig Marks in managing the publication. At this time a new holding company was formed to operate *Spin* and *Vibe,* Miller Publishing Group, LLC, which would run them through a subsidiary called Vibe/Spin Ventures.

In August, as a syndicated *Vibe* television program was being readied for launch, Miller Publishing bought 80 percent of Where Magazines International, a chain of 42 travel guide monthlies published in popular tourist cities around the world, 30 of which were located in the United States. The magazines contained entertainment calendars and maps, and were aimed at both tourists and business travelers. They were primarily distributed through hotels. Miller announced plans to expand the chain by adding several American cities and others in Asia. The Toronto, Canada-based Where Magazines International would retain full ownership of nine related Canadian travel magazines.

Fall 1997: Purchase of Six Sports Titles from New York Times

In the fall of 1997 Miller Publishing reached an agreement with New York Times Company to buy six sports-themed periodicals: *Tennis, Cruising World, Sailing World, Snow Country, Tennis Buyer's Guide,* and *Snow Country Business,* the latter two of which were sold as trade books. The deal was worth an estimated $35–$40 million. The four magazines had revenues of approximately $44 million in 1996, and boasted total subscribers of 1.5 million. After the sale Miller named Carol A. Smith, the former head of Time's Parenting publication group, to the position of group publisher for the six. Miller had by now subdivided its operations into three clusters: youth/music; travel; and sports/leisure.

In December 1997 Miller acquired *Getaways* magazine, based in Providence, Rhode Island. *Getaways,* with circulation of 150,000, had been founded in 1996 and was aimed at travelers who were taking short-duration vacations. It was published six times per year. A few months after it was acquired the magazine ceased publication.

In early 1998 Miller announced plans for the August debut of a *Vibe* spinoff, which would be called *Blaze.* The new magazine was headed by Jesse Washington, managing editor of *Vibe,* and would focus on hip-hop music for a younger audience. It was intended to go up against *The Source,* a fast-growing title with circulation of nearly 400,000. In the spring of 1998 Miller also lost out in an attempt to buy *Wired* magazine, with the firm's offer of $77.5 million failing to best Advance Magazine Publications' $80 million.

In May Miller Publishing announced that *Snow Country* would change its name to *Mountain Sports & Living* with the September issue, as the publication covered year-round mountain sports as well as winter ones. The move was accompanied by a change in design and the addition of more resort and travel coverage, along with a switch to a new distributor. *Cruising World, Tennis,* and *Spin* were also being given makeovers, with the latter's focus expanded to include more culture and fashion stories. Another new publication, *Variety Vibe Business,* was reportedly in the development stages as well.

In November *Blaze* launched a web site featuring frequent news updates and most of the print magazine's content. Produced in partnership with a firm called OnRadio, it was intended to take advantage of *The Source*'s relatively weak Internet presence, as well as a general lack of hip-hop information online. By this time the *Vibe* syndicated television show had been canceled.

1999: A Year of Many Changes

In January 1999 *Spin*'s top two editors, Michael Hirschorn and Craig Marks, were abruptly dismissed and Hirschorn replaced with former *Vibe* editor Alan Light, a move apparently caused by *Spin*'s sluggish financial performance. Light announced plans to refocus the publication on music and away

from its recent foray into fashion and culture. The titles Miller had bought from New York Times Company were also not performing up to expectations, and in March *Mountain Sports & Living* suspended publication, its advertising pages having declined some 25 percent during the previous year. At the same time, sports unit head Carol Smith left the firm.

Shortly afterwards, *Blaze* editor Jesse Washington was fired over his relationship with Montoun Hart, who had been acquitted in the murder of Jonathan Levin, the son of Time Warner chairman Gerald Levin, a friend of Robert Miller. Washington had written an unpublished editorial defending Hart and had hired him as an intern. By now Miller Publishing had begun selling discount packages for ads to run in *Spin, Vibe,* and *Blaze,* which had a combined circulation of 1.5 million.

The executive shuffle continued in May 1999, when Vibe Ventures President and CEO Keith Clinkscales quit to pursue other endeavors, reportedly because of disagreements he was having with Miller and his associate Gilbert Rogin, a former editor of *Sports Illustrated.* Clinkscales had been with *Vibe* since 1993. Associate Publisher Len Burnel also left the firm at this time, and in August *Vibe* Editor-in-Chief Danyel Smith departed to join Time, Inc.

In October Miller, Quincy Jones, and David Salzman agreed to put Vibe/Spin Ventures up for sale, seeking a reported $200 million for the triumvirate of *Vibe, Spin,* and *Blaze.* The move was reportedly made at the behest of Freeman Spogli, which was growing increasingly anxious to receive an anticipated 20 percent return on the investment. The market for media properties was hot at the time, *Vibe*'s circulation was up more than 15 percent in the first half of the year, and advertising page counts for both *Spin* and *Vibe* had been growing. The three magazines were estimated to have annual revenues of $80 million and profits of $12 million.

Though a number of potential buyers expressed interest, none could meet the steep asking price, and in March the publications were taken off the block. While they were up for sale, Robert Miller bought out Freeman Spogli's stake in Miller Publishing, though the investment firm retained its interest in the Vibe/Spin Ventures subsidiary. Miller later sold half of Miller Publishing Group to another venture capital firm, the L.A.-based Destination Group, for approximately $30 million.

Blaze *Extinguished in 2000*

In the spring of 2000 the company announced that it would suspend publication of *Blaze* after the June/July issue. Its readership had not reached projected levels, and the attempted sale had served to make advertisers skittish, resulting in reduced earnings. The publication was losing an estimated $4 million per year. Several of *Blaze*'s 20 staffers were transferred to Vibe, while others were laid off. Miller also announced the cancellation of the Vibestyle fashion trade show at this time, which the firm had co-sponsored for several years in a row.

In February 2001 Alex Mironovich, a former senior publishing executive at *Playboy,* was named CEO of Vibe/Spin Ventures. He took the place of Robert Miller, who became chairman. In August, citing the decreasing advertising revenues derived from the Internet, *Vibe* and *Spin* scaled back their online presence, reducing the staff allocated to the magazines' web sites to two. Web-only original content would no longer be added to the sites, which would continue to feature material taken from the magazines.

In early 2002 *Spin* Editor-in-Chief Alan Light stepped down, citing a desire to start a new magazine of his own. He was replaced by Executive Editor Sia Michel. July saw the sale of *Cruising World* and *Sailing World* to World Publications of Winter Park, Florida, which owned several magazines, including *Waterski* and *Garden Design.* The price was an estimated $10 million. The sale included a sports marketing event sideline, the National Offshore One Design Regattas.

The July 2002 issue of *Spin* featured another facelift as efforts were once again being stepped up to market the publication to ad buyers. Not long after this, *Spin* Publisher Jon Chalon was let go. The magazine, whose heyday had been the early 1990s "Grunge Rock" era, retained an association with that now-dated musical movement that it could not shake. Newer musical styles were also being covered by magazines devoted to them exclusively, which left *Spin* with a weaker position in the market. In the latter half of 2002 *Spin* and *Vibe* were again put up for sale, this time at a reduced asking price, but there were no takers.

In 2003 Miller's Where International unit doubled the number of cities its specialty publication *The Essential* was offered in. *The Essential,* an annual magazine targeted at high-end travelers, had debuted in 1987 in Vancouver, with London and Washington D.C. versions added in 1999 and 2001, respectively. It would now also be available in New York, Chicago, and New Orleans. *The Essential* was distributed exclusively in four- and five-star hotels, and featured articles on attractions, services, and fashions for affluent travelers. Its parent, Where, was now available in 44 markets, including 26 in the United States.

Miller Publishing Group, LLC was still struggling to develop a strong portfolio of properties, while working to improve the market position of several ailing ones. Having shed a number of underperforming publications, the firm appeared to be closer to solid ground, though its future prospects remained somewhat murky.

Principal Subsidiaries

Where International LP; Miller Sports Group, LLC; Vibe/Spin Ventures LLC (joint venture).

Principal Competitors

Time Out Group; Wenner Media, LLC; Source Publications; Harris Publications, Inc.

Further Reading

Armstrong, David, "City Tourist Magazine Sold—Where Guides Purchased By Ex-Time Publisher," *San Francisco Examiner,* August 8, 1997, p. B1.

Featherly, Kevin, "Vibe.com, Spin.com Dump Original Content, Staff," *Newsbytes News Network,* August 3, 2001.

Fine, Jon, "Magazines Lining Up for Selling Block," *Advertising Age,* July 16, 2001, p. 1.

Granatstein, Lisa, "Miller Spins Ad-Sales Web," *Brandweek,* March 30, 1999.

Huhn, Mary, "New Mag Blaze-Ing a Trail in Cyberspace," *New York Post,* November 16, 1998, p. 34.

Kelly, Keith J., "Editor's Leaving Creates Bad Vibe," *New York Post,* August 5, 1999, p. 34.

——, "Miller Feels the Pinch: The Publisher of Vibe May Be Feeling Investor Squeeze," *New York Post,* August 8, 1999, p. 56.

——, "Miller Pulls Sale—Buyers Balk at $200M Price for 3 Magazines," *New York Post,* March 23, 2000, p. 36.

Kerwin, Ann Marie, "Miller Beats Out Hachette, Meredith for NY Times Titles," *Advertising Age,* October 6, 1997, p. 3.

——, "Miller Snares 'Spin,' Looks for More Magazines, Related TV Programs Cited, 'Vibe' Show in the Works," *Advertising Age,* June 9, 1997, p. 10.

——, "Miller's 'Snow Country' Retitled 'Mountain Sports'," *Advertising Age,* May 25, 1998, p. 12.

——, "Times Prove Tougher for Smaller Publishers: Miller's Vibe/Spin, Meigher Put Up a 'For Sale' Sign," *Advertising Age,* October 11, 1999, p. 82.

"New York Times Sells Six Magazines to Miller Publishing," *Business Publisher,* October 16, 1997.

"Putting a New Spin on It," *Delaney Report,* April 21, 2003, p. 2.

Sprague, David, "Unspun," *Village Voice,* February 2, 1999, p. 127.

Steinberg, Brian, "Miller Publishing Decides to Fold 'Blaze' Magazine," *Dow Jones News Service,* May 4, 2000.

——, " 'Spin' Magazine Trades the Grunge Era for More Sophisticated Readers, Ads," *Wall Street Journal,* August 17, 1998.

Tharp, Paul, "Miller Finds Times Have Changed in Publishing," *New York Post,* March 18, 1999, p. 38.

Turner, Dan, "Former Time Exec Starting Up L.A. Magazine Empire," *Los Angeles Business Journal,* June 23, 1997, p. 12.

Wartofsky, Alona, "Turnover at the Top of 'Spin' Magazine," *Washington Post,* January 22, 1999, p. C1.

—Frank Uhle

Mitsubishi Motors Corporation

33-8 Shiba 5-chome
Minato-ku
Tokyo 108
Japan
Telephone: 81-3-3456-1111
Fax: 81-3-5232-7747
Web site: http://www.mitsubishi-motors.co.jp

Public Company
Incorporated: 1970
Employees: 63,143
Sales: ¥3.20 trillion ($24.02 billion) (2002)
Stock Exchanges: Tokyo
NAIC: 336111 Automobile Manufacturing; 336112 Light
    Truck and Utility Vehicle Manufacturing

Mitsubishi Motors Corporation is Japan's fourth largest car company, and manufactures and markets passenger cars and light commercial trucks in its domestic markets as well as in other Asian countries and North America. Its line of passenger cars includes the Diamante sedan, the Galant sedan, several mini-cars for the Japanese market, the hatchback Colt, and the Montero and Endeavor sport utility vehicles for North American consumers. Mitsubishi Motors also operates a financial services division that oversees lending and financing for its car sales. In large part to escape a crushing debt burden, though also to address declining sales, Mitsubishi Motor's parent company, the Mitsubishi Group, sold a 37 percent stake in Mitsubishi Motors to German auto giant DaimlerChrysler AG. (Mitsubishi Heavy Industries controls an additional 15 percent share of Mitsubishi Motors.) Mitsubishi Motors has embarked on a massive restructuring program instigated by DaimlerChrysler. As part of this program, Mitsubishi Motors spun off its truck business as Mitsubishi Fuso Truck and Bus Corp. in 2003.

Early History

Mitsubishi Motors was formed as a wholly owned subsidiary of Mitsubishi Heavy Industries (MHI) in 1970. MHI is the modern incarnation of Mitsubishi Shipbuilding Co. Ltd., which had begun manufacturing automobiles as early as 1917. As the sprawling network of companies under the Mitsubishi umbrella grew in the early part of the century, the Mitsubishi Internal Combustion Engine Co., Ltd. was established in 1920 to manufacture engines for airplanes. This company's name was changed to Mitsubishi Aircraft Co. in 1928. MHI was created in 1934 upon the merger of Mitsubishi Shipbuilding and Mitsubishi Aircraft. After the breakup of the Japanese conglomerates known as *zaibatsu* following World War II, use of the corporate name Mitsubishi was banned for several years. MHI was chopped into three regional sections with the names East Japan Heavy Industries, Central Japan Heavy Industries, and West Japan Heavy Industries. Eventually the forbidden name began to reappear, and in 1964 MHI was reintegrated out of its three fragments. By 1967, MHI's Motor Vehicle Division was producing about 75,000 cars a year. That division was spun off as an independent company in 1970, creating Mitsubishi Motors Corporation. Tomio Kubo, a successful engineer from MHI's aircraft operation, was placed in charge of the new company.

An important part of Kubo's early strategy was to build up the company's volume by emphasizing exports. This was to be done by making connections with well-established foreign companies. Mitsubishi's longstanding association with the Chrysler Corporation began the following year, when Chrysler purchased 15 percent of the company's stock. MHI retained the other 85 percent interest. By 1971, the company was producing 260,000 cars a year. Chrysler quickly began to market Mitsubishi-built cars in the United States. The most important of these was the subcompact sold in the United States as the Dodge Colt and Plymouth Arrow. At home in Japan, Mitsubishi concentrated on producing cars for special niche markets. Among the more successful of these models were the Lancer and the Celeste.

By 1973, annual production had reached 500,000 vehicles. That year, the Mitsubishi Motor Sale Financing Corporation was created to handle financing for the company's domestic sales. Although sales began to stall somewhat at that point due to the oil crisis, the introduction of the Galant in 1976 gave the company a welcome boost. As Mitsubishi's sales in the United States grew, friction began to arise between the company and its American

Company Perspectives:

Mitsubishi Motors Corporation intends to grow as a global player and as a strong partner within the DaimlerChrysler-Mitsubishi Motors Corporation alliance. Cross-functional alliance teams are now working together at a global level. Mitsubishi Motors Corporation boasts a proud history of technological innovation. Although automobiles have become an established part of modern life, challenges still remain to boost their safety and eco-compatibility without sacrificing any of the benefits or convenience they offer. Mitsubishi Motors Corporation is developing a variety of technologies designed to improve the safety and environmental features of its products.

affiliate Chrysler. Company officials felt that Chrysler demanded too much say in Mitsubishi decisions, and the idea of marketing its own cars in the United States gained support. By 1977, Mitsubishi had begun to set up its own collection of Colt dealerships across Europe. Tensions between Mitsubishi and Chrysler grew further around that time, as the two companies began competing head to head in the subcompact car market.

As U.S. automakers trended toward smaller cars, Chrysler unveiled the Omni hatchback, a model aimed at the same market as Mitsubishi's latest Colt model, sold in Japan as the Mirage. In spite of the disagreements, the two companies continued to cooperate, with Chrysler marketing Mitsubishi's cars in the United States and Mitsubishi contributing its advanced engineering knowhow to Chrysler. For 1978, Mitsubishi sold a total of 965,300 units, a 17 percent increase over the previous year. Of those, 534,600 were sold in Japan, a 20 percent increase.

The 1980s: Increasing Foreign Sales

Mitsubishi's annual production passed the one million mark in 1980. That year, Mitsubishi Motors teamed up with the Mitsubishi Corporation to purchase Chrysler Australia, subsequently renaming it Mitsubishi Motors Australia Ltd. By 1981, the company had captured 8 percent of the Japanese auto market, running neck and neck with Mazda behind industry leaders Toyota and Nissan. Mitsubishi entered the American automobile market under its own name for the first time in 1982. Three models were initially made available to American buyers, all of them fairly upscale: the Starion, a $12,000, turbo-charged sports car; the $7,000 Cordia sedan; and a family sedan called the Tredia, priced at around $6,500. Mitsubishi also began to sell small pickup trucks in the United States, offering vehicles under its own name identical to those already being sold by Chrysler. Under import restraints on Japanese cars, the 30,000 Mitsubishi vehicles sold in 1982 had to come out of Chrysler's annual allotment of around 120,000 cars. Seventy dealers in 22 U.S. markets sold the Mitsubishi line that year.

While the company was making its foray into the U.S. market, sales at home began to sag. In 1983 a new president, Toyoo Tate, was brought in to try to reverse this trend. Tate's early moves included personnel changes in the executive offices, along with a renewed push for more international alli-

ances. One important new connection made was with South Korea's Hyundai Motor Co., of which Mitsubishi purchased a 7.5 percent interest. By 1984 the company's revenue had reached ¥1.17 trillion. During that year, Mitsubishi Motor Sales, a separate corporation that handled domestic auto sales, was absorbed into Mitsubishi Motors.

In 1985 Mitsubishi and Chrysler launched a joint venture called Diamond-Star Motors Corp., named after the corporate logos of the two companies. The twin central Illinois towns of Bloomington and Normal were chosen as the site of the Diamond-Star plant, which was to produce a line of subcompact cars using engines and transmissions imported from Mitsubishi's Japanese facilities. For Mitsubishi, the venture provided a guaranteed source of cars to sell in the United States, the largest automobile market in the world, regardless of any restrictive trade measures that might be enacted by either country involved. By 1987, the company was selling 67,000 cars a year in the United States.

Mitsubishi Motors went public in 1988, ending its status as the only one of Japan's 11 auto manufacturers to be privately held. To pave the way for the shift to public ownership, changes had to be made in the company's stock agreements with both MHI and Chrysler. MHI agreed to reduce its share to 25 percent, retaining its position as largest single stockholder. Chrysler meanwhile increased its holding to over 20 percent. The $470 million in capital raised by the 10 percent initial offering enabled Mitsubishi to pay off part of its debt as well as to expand its investments throughout southeast Asia, where by now it was operating in the Philippines, Malaysia, and Thailand.

Toward the end of the 1980s, Mitsubishi initiated a major push to beef up its presence in the U.S. market. While Japan's quotas allowed the company to export 193,000 cars a year to the United States, two-thirds of those cars were marketed by Chrysler in 1988. In 1989 Mitsubishi pumped its U.S. sales goal up to 130,000 cars, and attacked this goal from several angles. First the company made plans to increase its U.S. dealer network by 40 percent, up to 340 dealers. Mitsubishi also aired its first national television advertising campaign. The company also began to further exploit its relationship with Hyundai, importing the Precis, a carbon copy of Hyundai's popular Excel. Diamond-Star began to pay off with the production of the Eclipse, a sporty car sold by Chrysler as the Plymouth Laser. For 1989, Mitsubishi's worldwide production, including its overseas affiliates, reached 1.5 million units.

Hirokazu Nakamura became president of Mitsubishi in 1989 and steered the company in some promising directions. Sales of the company's sport utility vehicle (SUV), the Pajero, were bucking conventional wisdom by becoming popular even in the crowded streets of Japan. Although sales of SUVs and light trucks were booming in the United States, Japan's car manufacturers dismissed the idea that such a trend could occur in their own country. Nakamura, however, increased the budget for sport utility product development at Mitsubishi. His gamble paid off; Mitsubishi's wide line of four-wheel drive vehicles, ranging from the Pajero Mini to the large Delica Space Gear, rode a wave of SUV-buying in Japan in the early to mid-1990s. Narrowly following Toyota in SUV market share in Japan, Mitsubishi saw its overall domestic share rise to 11.6 percent in 1995.

1970: Mitsubishi Motors Corporation is founded.
1980: Mitsubishi produces one million cars annually.
1982: Mitsubishi enters the U.S. market under its own brand name.
1988: Mitsubishi becomes a public company.
1991: Mitsubishi acquires Value Rent-A-Car.
2000: Mitsubishi forms partnership with DaimlerChrysler AG.
2002: Mitsubishi begins restructuring program.

U.S. and Southeast Asian Alliances in the 1990s

Nakamura also urged greater reliance on Mitsubishi's ties to southeast Asian companies and markets. Mitsubishi had entered the region in the 1970s by using the contacts of Mitsubishi Corporation, a trading company that was part of the informal Mitsubishi group of companies. By the mid-1990s, Mitsubishi Motors counted major alliances in Malaysia, South Korea, and Thailand. Proton, the joint venture between Mitsubishi and Malaysia, controlled 75 percent of the Malaysian market. Mitsubishi maintained a presence in South Korea with a 6.7 percent stake in Hyundai Motor Co. and supplied 50 percent of Taiwan's vans and trucks by sending kits to China Motor Corp. In addition, the company owned 48 percent of Thailand's MMC Sittipol, which produced Mitsubishi vehicles and exported parts to the Philippines, Malaysia, and Canada.

With almost 25 percent of the truck and car market in southeast Asia, the company soared along with the region's economy during the mid-1990s. In addition, by moving production to these countries, Mitsubishi lessened the negative effect of the rising yen. In 1995 the company moved its truck production from Japan to Thailand, which brought the percentage of its production in low-wage countries to 20 percent.

Mitsubishi's efforts in the United States continued during the early 1990s as well. In 1991 the company added a number of models to its line at a time when U.S. companies were delaying their new models and laying off workers due to sluggish sales. Among Mitsubishi's new products was the Diamante luxury sedan. The Diamante, with a price tag of $28,000, was the winner of that year's prestigious Japan's Car of the Year award. Part of Mitsubishi's strategy to increase its American market share was to target buyers who were already likely to purchase Japanese or European cars, and offer its vehicles at prices slightly lower than comparable cars in other companies' lines.

Mitsubishi gained another outlet for its cars in 1991 with the acquisition of Value Rent-A-Car. In addition, the company began producing two minivans that year, the Expo and the Expo LRV. Later in 1991, Mitsubishi bought out Chrysler's share of Diamond-Star for around $100 million, with Mitsubishi assuming all of Diamond-Star's debt. The two companies continued to split the operation's output. By this time, Chrysler's interest in Mitsubishi had fallen to about 11 percent. Of the 322,500 Mitsubishi-made vehicles sold in the United States in 1991, 187,500 were marketed under the company's own name. The year 1991 also brought the preliminary stages of a joint venture with Volvo Car Corporation and the government of the Netherlands to produce cars in that country. Mitsubishi and Volvo had equal shares in this venture.

Mitsubishi sold 176,900 vehicles in the United States in 1992, over 7 percent less than the company's 1990 peak. Although company profits declined somewhat for that year, Mitsubishi's performance was considerably better than that of its Japanese competitors, all of whom suffered dramatic drops in sales in the face of a weak global economy. Mitsubishi's results were aided by strong sales of its recreational models such as the Pajero, whose sales leaped by 52 percent in the first half of the fiscal year. With 10.7 percent of the domestic market in hand, Mitsubishi bucked another trend by spinning off a new model at a time when the other manufacturers were condensing their lines. Focusing on the lower end of the market, Mitsubishi unveiled a new two-door version of the Mirage, to be sold in Japan as the Mirage Asti. The Asti's price of about $8,500 was well below the company's previous bottom end, the $11,430 Mirage four-door sedan. For the fiscal year ending in March 1993, Mitsubishi's profits declined by 7.9 percent, a modest drop for one of the Japanese auto industry's worst years ever. Foreign exchange losses caused by a rapidly rising yen were blamed for much of the decline.

As all of the Japanese companies continued to lose market share in the United States in 1993, Mitsubishi attempted to gain a foothold in the family sedan market with the introduction of a newly redesigned Galant midsize sedan. The Galant was to be produced in the United States at the company's Normal, Illinois, plant, creating two advantages: assembling it in the United States avoided the inflated price tag the soaring yen would cause; and the Illinois plant, previously operating at only half of capacity, needed the work.

After decreasing its interest in Mitsubishi to less than 3 percent in 1992, Chrysler announced its decision in 1993 to sell off all of its remaining Mitsubishi shares on the open market. The two companies stated that they would nevertheless continue their close alliance, with Chrysler supplying engines and transmissions for Mitsubishi's Diamond-Star operation, and Mitsubishi marketing Chrysler products in Japan.

Challenges in the Late 1990s

Mitsubishi's image in North America was tarnished in the mid-1990s when two notable sexual harassment suits were brought against the company. The first suit, filed by 29 women in December 1994, accused Mitsubishi of fostering a climate of sexual harassment at its Normal, Illinois, plant. Then, in April 1996 the Equal Employment Opportunity Commission filed a class action suit on behalf of approximately 300 women who worked at the Normal plant. The company initially denied any problem at its plant but later hired former U.S. Labor Secretary Lynn Martin to recommend changes to its policies and practices. Mitsubishi settled the 1994 suit for $9.5 million in August 1997, and reached an agreement with the EEOC later that year as well.

The benefits Mitsubishi had seen because of its strong presence in southeast Asia reversed themselves in the late 1990s. The economic crisis in the region, which began in 1997, spelled big trouble for Mitsubishi. In September 1997 the company closed its Thai factory in response to a crash in the country's currency and the plummeting of consumer demand. The large truck plant, which had produced 8,700 trucks in 1996, was shut down indefinitely. In addition, Mitsubishi had little support from sales in Japan, which slowed considerably throughout 1997 and were affected by that country's own economic uncertainty into 1998. Other Japanese automakers, such as Toyota and Honda, bolstered their own slipping domestic sales with booming sales in the United States. However, with only a small percentage of the market in the United States, the impact of the turmoil in the Asian economies had a greater effect on Mitsubishi. The company reported the worst losses of its history in 1997 on plummeting sales. In addition, it lost both its rank as the third largest automaker in Japan and market share in its export markets, and its stock price fell precipitously, prompting the company to cancel its year-end dividend payment.

In November 1997, Mitsubishi tapped Katsuhiko Kawasoe to replace Takemune Kimura as company president. Kawasoe unveiled an aggressive restructuring program that aimed to cut costs by ¥350 billion in three years, reduce personnel by 1,400, and return the company to profitability in fiscal 1998. But while the program had some initial success—Mitsubishi's 1998 costs decreased ¥107 billion—the company's sales were still stagnant as the Japanese economy, like Asia's as a whole, continued to sputter. In 1999, Mitsubishi was forced once again to skip dividend payments. Its interest-bearing debt totaled ¥1.7 trillion.

New Obstacles and New Directions: 2000 and Beyond

In hopes of reversing its fortunes, Mitsubishi entered into a partnership with DaimlerChrysler in March 2000, creating the world's third largest vehicle maker, producing 6.5 million cars per year. The agreement gave DaimlerChrysler a 33.4 percent stake in Mitsubishi Motors, enough to give the German company effective control. In return, DaimlerChrysler pledged to maintain the Mitsubishi brand and preserve its workforce.

On the eve of the transaction, though, Mitsubishi faced a crisis. During a routine probe by the Japanese Transport Ministry, an official discovered in an employee's locker piles of customer complaints that should have been reported to the government. Mitsubishi asserted its innocence, but also launched a probe into the scope of the cover-up and recalled about 620,000 cars and trucks for several of the reasons identified in the concealed complaints. Additionally, it was later revealed that Mitsubishi had been hiding complaints and secretly repairing defective vehicles since 1977. Though none of these malfunctions resulted in any fatal accidents, a Tokyo court fined the company ¥4 million.

The debacle did not cause DaimlerChrysler to jettison its deal, but Mitsubishi's sales, particularly in Japan, slumped when the news became public. This loss of revenue was exacerbated by the tremendous cost of the recall, which totaled ¥5 billion—about 25 percent of the pretax profit that Mitsubishi had predicted for the year. With Mitsubishi's sales and stock price plunging, DaimlerChrysler renegotiated its deal, receiving more seats on Mitsubishi's board—including the position of chief operating officer—and paying less money for its stake.

The crisis also led to a shakeup of Mitsubishi's management. Takashi Sonobe replaced Kawasoe as company president. More dramatically, DaimlerChrysler veteran Rolf Eckrodt was named the new COO. Eckrodt had headed up the German company's Adtranz train unit, where he had presided over 3,000 job cuts and the closure of six production sites. Sonobe and Eckrodt soon applied these methods to Mitsubishi, calling for a 14 percent reduction in personnel (9,500 jobs worldwide), a 20 percent cut in auto production capacity, and a 15 percent cut in materials costs. Mitsubishi also spun off its automatic transmission unit and reacquired the 3.3 percent stake in the company that Volvo had held since 2000. Nonetheless, Mitsubishi continued to be plagued by recall issues. In February 2001, it recalled additional vehicles due to a damaged ball joint. By that time, the chaos at Mitsubishi, along with DaimlerChrysler's aggressive globalizing, had even begun eroding DaimlerChrysler's profits.

In 2002, Eckrodt took the helm of Mitsubishi and presided over additional changes. Most notable was the decision to spin off Mitsubishi's truck and bus division to create a new company in 2003. DaimlerChrysler acquired a 43 percent stake in this new entity, Mitsubishi Fuso Truck and Bus Corp. By further cementing its alliance with DaimlerChrysler—now in both passenger cars and commercial vehicles—Mitsubishi was banking on reducing material costs, leveraging common platforms, and minimizing its debt. Nevertheless, Mitsubishi continued to struggle. In July 2003, it revised its sales forecast downward for the first half of the fiscal year. Rather than seeing its anticipated ¥15 billion profit, Mitsubishi instead faced another loss. Sales in North America were sluggish and the company continued to struggle with costs and debt. In the viciously competitive global automotive industry, Mitsubishi faced the prospect of a turbulent future.

Principal Subsidiaries

Mitsubishi Motor Manufacturing of America, Inc.; Mitsubishi Motors Sales of America, Inc.; Mitsubishi Motors Credit of America, Inc.; Netherlands Car B.V.; Mitsubishi Motors Europe B.V.; Mitsubishi Motor Sales of Europe B.V.; Mitsubishi Motors Philippines Corporation; Mitsubishi Motors Australia Ltd.; Mitsubishi Automotive Techno-Metal Co., Ltd.; PABCO Co., Ltd.; Mitsubishi Automotive Techno-Service Co., Ltd.; Mitsubishi Automotive Engineering Co., Ltd.; Mitsubishi Automotive Logistics Co., Ltd.; Mitsubishi Auto Credit-Lease Corporation; Mitsubishi Fuso Bus and Truck Corp. (42%).

Principal Competitors

Honda Motor Company Limited; Nissan Motor Co., Ltd.; Toyota Motor Corporation; Ford Motor Company; General Motors Corporation; DaimlerChrysler AG.

Further Reading

Annin, Peter, and John McCormick, "More Than a Tune-Up," *Newsweek,* November 24, 1997, pp. 50–52.

Armstrong, Larry, "Mitsubishi Is Souping Up Its Image," *Business Week,* February 27, 1989, p. 56.

Cullison, A. E., "Mitsubishi Eyes Own US Sales Team," *Journal of Commerce,* April 13, 1977, p. 3.

Dodsworth, Terry, "Living with Chrysler," *Financial Times,* November 10, 1977, p. 27.

Furukawa, Tsukasa, "Mitsubishi to Retain Amiable Relationship with Chrysler, It Says," *American Metal Market,* July 5, 1993, p. 8.

Gibbs, Edwina, "Mitsubishi in Complaints Storm," *National Post*, July 19, 2000.

Holusha, John, "Mitsubishi's U.S. Car Venture," *New York Times,* October 26, 1982, p. D3.

Kanabayashi, Masayoshi, "Japan's Battered Auto Makers Adopt Mixed Outlook for the Current Year," *Wall Street Journal,* June 1, 1993, p. A9B.

Levin, Doron, "Chrysler Corp., Mitsubishi Set Site for Plant," *Wall Street Journal,* October 8, 1985, p. 2.

——, "Mitsubishi's Big Campaign in U.S.," *New York Times,* April 30, 1991, p. D1.

Maskery, Mary Ann, "Japan Niche Prompts a 2nd Mirage," *Automotive News,* May 17, 1993.

Miller, Scott, and Jeffrey Ball, "DaimlerChrysler May Report a Loss," *Wall Street Journal Europe,* February 26, 2000.

——, "Mitsubishi Sets Sights on Mazda in U.S.," *Automotive News,* September 21, 1992, p. 21.

——, "Mitsubishi to Sell Stock in Auto Firm," *Automotive News,* October 31, 1988, p. 4.

Miller, Krystal, "Mitsubishi Restyles Galant to Anchor Line," *Wall Street Journal,* June 23, 1993, p. B1.

"Mitsubishi Motors Posts 27% Decline in 1st-Half Profit," *Wall Street Journal,* November 6, 1992, p. A5A.

——, "Mitsubishi Motors' Shareholders OK Truck, Bus Spinoff," *JIJI Press English News Service,* November 26, 2002.

Morris, Kathleen, "Endgame," *Financial World,* August 1, 1995, pp. 2–33.

Ono, Yumiko, "Japanese Probe Prompts Massive Mitsubishi Recall," *Wall Street Journal,* July 19, 2000.

——, "President of Mitsubishi Motors to Resign in Wake of Recall Scandal," *Deseret News,* September 7, 2000.

Shirouzu, Norihiko, "Japan's Firms Revamp amid Asian Crisis," *Wall Street Journal,* November 6, 1997, p. A18.

Updike, Edith, and Laxmi Nakarmi, "A Movable Feast for Mitsubishi," *Business Week,* August 28, 1995, pp. 50–51.

Zaun, Todd, "Mitsubishi to Cut Japan Production and Other Costs," *Wall Street Journal Europe,* February 27, 2001.

—Robert R. Jacobson
—updates: Susan Windisch Brown, Rebecca Stanfel

Mott's Inc.

6 High Ridge Park
Stamford, Connecticut 06905
U.S.A.
Telephone: (203) 329-0911
Fax: (203) 968-5689
Web site: http://www.motts.com

Wholly Owned Subsidiary of Cadbury Schweppes PLC
Incorporated: 1914 as Duffy-Mott
Employees: 1,300
Sales: $488 million (2001 est.)
NAIC: 312100 Beverage Manufacturing; 311991
    Perishable Prepared Food Manufacturing

Mott's Inc. produces and markets a host of top-selling brands, operating as the only division within Cadbury Schweppes PLC responsible for its own processing. The company's brands include a variety of apple beverages and other fruit drinks marketed under the Mott's label. Mott's also produces and markets products under the names Clamato, Hawaiian Punch, Mr. & Mrs. T, Rose's, Holland House, ReaLemon, and ReaLime. Mott's operates ten production facilities, five of which are responsible for production of products marketed by Snapple Beverage Corp., a Cadbury Schweppes subsidiary.

19th-Century Origins

Mott's Inc.'s lengthy involvement in the beverage industry began with the decision of a Quaker to start his own cider and vinegar business. In 1842, Samuel R. Mott, a resident of Bouckville, New York, first hitched his horse to a "sweep" and began crushing apples. The production technique was centuries old, involving two large stone drums located at the center of the sweep. As Mott's horse plodded repeatedly in a circle, the apples were crushed beneath the revolving stone drums. Next, the crushed apples were shoveled into a pen with slatted sides and packed with straw. A jack screw was fitted above the apple bits and, with the weight of three men leaning on a level, the jack screw pressed downward, creating apple juice that ran off into a tank beneath the pressing pen. The cider-making tech-

nique was not innovative. Instead, Mott's drew its strength from the commitment to expansion displayed by Samuel Mott and the drive toward diversification demonstrated by his successors. The former became a hallmark of the company shortly after its inception. The latter took nearly a century before it became a defining characteristic of the Mott's enterprise.

Initially, Mott's market was restricted to Bouckville, to Mott's neighbors, who enjoyed his cider and vinegar. As word of mouth spread and demand grew, the size and reach of the company grew. Once Mott was able to rely on the help of his son, distribution of the company's cider and vinegar reached well beyond the confines of Bouckville. Along the way, the horse-powered enterprise adopted more modern production methods, using water power and steam to operate the mill's presses. With the technological advancements and a dedication to widening distribution guiding the company forward, Mott's cider, vinegar, and champagne cider—a rare diversification during the company's first century of business—appeared in markets far removed from Bouckville. Clipper ships transported the company's products to California. Mott's products appeared at Philadelphia's centennial celebration in 1876. The company's offerings were on display at the Chicago Columbian Exposition of 1893. The Bouckville-made products even graced international markets, appearing at world fairs in Paris and Brussels before the end of the century.

As the Mott Company entered the 20th century, it enjoyed widespread recognition, its reputation built upon nearly 60 years of business. The company also was set to embark on a new era, one that began with a merger completed at the start of the new century. In 1900, the Mott Company merged with the W.B. Duffy Cider Company. Based in Rochester, New York, Duffy was the first company to perfect a method for preserving apple cider in wood, an achievement registered by the company's namesake founder, who started the company in 1842, the year Samuel R. Mott made his first batch of cider and vinegar. The merger created Duffy-Mott, which was incorporated in New York in 1914. The company's first president was Harry Meinhold, who entered the cider and vinegar business as an entrepreneur at the age of 18. Eventually, Meinhold became co-manager of the New York office of the American Fruit

Product Co., the position he held before being tapped as Duffy-Mott's president.

Diversification During the Great Depression

The next notable period in the development of Mott's occurred at a time of profound despair for nearly every company in the United States. The Great Depression caused financial ruin for scores of commercial entities, having such a deleterious impact on industries of all sorts that survival represented a laudable achievement. Duffy-Mott not only survived during the 1930s, but thrived, registering perhaps the most successful decade of the company's existence. For the first time, the company diversified meaningfully beyond the cider and vinegar business, essentially the sole means of support for the first 90 years of the company's history. Duffy-Mott's decade of diversification began after the company acquired the Standard Apple Products Company and its plant in Hamlin, New York, in 1929. A slew of new product introductions followed the acquisition, beginning in 1930 when Duffy-Mott introduced apple sauce, the product most closely associated with the Mott's label at the end of the 20th century.

Next, the company sought to combat the seasonality of its business. Duffy-Mott's plants, which by this point were located in Hamlin, Holley, Voorheesville, and Rabena—all in New York—were only in operation during part of the year, remaining idle during the off-season. The solution to the problem was entering a non-apple business, a foray the company made by forging an agreement in 1933 with the California Prune and Apricot Growers Association, later to become Sunsweet Growers, Inc. California Prune, a prune growing and processing cooperative, was seeking to broaden its distribution, particularly to the East Coast, where Duffy-Mott maintained a nearly century-old presence. Under the terms of the agreement, the two organizations began producing prune juice, a product entirely new to consumers. The response from the public provided a new revenue stream to Duffy-Mott and offset the seasonality of the company's mainstay apple-processing business, as consumers embraced the new product introduction. The success of the diversification led to the perpetuation of the joint venture for more than 40 years, until Duffy-Mott eventually introduced its own product, dubbed Super Mott's Prune Juice.

Product expansion continued, as the economic climate blackened. In 1936, Duffy-Mott started making jellies, a product category that found a receptive audience during the bleak years of the decade. The company began producing pure apple jelly, orange marmalade, as well as a number of hybrid fruit flavors, including apple-raspberry, apple-strawberry, apple currant, and apple-orange. Although the line of jellies was discontinued once economic conditions improved, the initial success of the products provided a valuable source of income at a time of widespread financial crisis. In 1938, Duffy-Mott further offset the seasonality of its cider business by introducing Mott's Apple Juice, a production process that required the development of innovative filtering and pasteurizing techniques.

Duffy-Mott's diversification program resumed in the 1950s, fleshing out the company's selection of products. In 1953, the company acquired Clapp's Baby Foods, giving it an industry pioneer. Clapp's Baby Foods was founded in 1921 by Harold Clapp, who launched his business and a new U.S. industry when his wife fell ill. Clapp assumed responsibility for taking care of his young son, a duty that included the concoction of a special diet comprising beef broth, vegetables, and cereal. Clapp was impressed by the effect his formula had on his son, prompting him to produce batches of his "soup" for friends. Soon, Clapp began selling his baby food to drugstores, a business he cultivated until 1931, when he sold his company to Johnson & Johnson. Under the direction of Johnson & Johnson, the distribution of Clapp's baby food was shifted to food stores. Later, Johnson & Johnson sold the Clapp's product line to the American Home Products Company, under whose guidance the Clapp's product line was expanded to 37 items. After acquiring Clapp's Baby Foods from American Home Products, Duffy-Mott expanded the product line to include nearly 100 items. Ultimately, the Clapp's production plant in Williamson, New York, was refitted to process Duffy-Mott's apple products, and the Clapp's line was discontinued.

Duffy-Mott's consistent efforts to expand both its range of products and its geographic presence continued in the 1960s. An important step toward the company's commitment toward growth was taken in 1958, when Duffy-Mott converted to public ownership, providing it with working capital of an unprecedented amount. Before the public offering, there were slightly more than 100 owners, many of whom had held an investment in Duffy-Mott for many years. Immediately after the offering, there were roughly 3,000 shareholders. The company's new "owners" were soon gratified to see their investment make its first step west of the Rocky Mountains. In 1960, Duffy-Mott reached an agreement with a West Coast food chain named Thriftimart, Inc. to acquire the processing equipment of the Pratt-Low Preserving Corporation and to lease a 407,000-square-foot plant. Pratt-Low, founded in 1905, operated as a packer of fruit and vegetables, as well as a national distributor of a line of dietary foods. The assets included within the acquisition became the Pratt-Low Division of Duffy-Mott, which sold its products through food brokers in 49 states. The division's primary revenue earners were peaches, pears, fruit cocktail, and apricots.

During the 1970s, Mott's corporate structure, built up and spread outward during 130 years of development, was streamlined, giving the company a leaner, more efficient profile. Before the reorganization was completed, however, the late 1960s included several important additions to Mott's sizeable stable of products. In 1966, the company acquired Lord Mott Canning Co., a company engaged in the canned vegetable industry. (Despite the name "Mott" in both corporate titles, there was no connection between the two companies before the acquisition). Also in 1966, Duffy-Mott purchased the Tilghman Packaging Company, a packer of seafood products, but the single greatest acquisition of the period was the purchase of a trademark. Duffy-Mott acquired the rights for Clamato and reformulated it as a clam-and-tomato-flavored cocktail. The addition of Clamato to the company's portfolio soon led to the introduction of Beefamato and Nutramato, but the importance of the two sister products paled in importance to the lasting impact of Clamato on the fortunes of Mott's. By the end of the century, Clamato figured as a signature product, occupying much of management's attention and accounting for a sizeable portion of Mott's' annual revenue.

New Owners Spur Expansion During the 1970s and 1980s

The reorganization that occurred during the mid-1970s was precipitated by the beginning of a new era at Mott's. One outcome of the company's growing stature within its industry was the attraction it drew from larger suitors seeking to aggrandize their operations. Conglomerates coveted Mott's, and after Mott's shareholders voiced their approval, the American Tobacco Company acquired the company. Subsequent to the acquisition, Duffy-Mott became a subsidiary of the conglomerate American Brands, Inc. Duffy-Mott's new owners soon ordered the consolidation of the company's facilities, which prompted sweeping changes. Before the consolidation, Duffy-Mott operated 11 plants, facilities that were scattered throughout eight states: New York, New Jersey, Maryland, Virginia, Delaware, Pennsylvania, Michigan, and California. After the consolidation, the company's physical presence was reduced to two plants, the facility in Williamson—a vestige of the Clapp's Baby Foods acquisition—and the facility in Aspers, Pennsylvania.

Acquisition of Duffy-Mott by Cadbury Schweppes: 1982

As it happened, American Brands did not preside over its newly organized subsidiary for long. In 1982, American Brands sold Duffy-Mott to the giant candy and soft drink conglomerate Cadbury Schweppes PLC. London-based Cadbury Schweppes,

looking to broaden its own reach in the beverage industry, proved to be a perfect fit for growth-minded Duffy-Mott, providing the financial support to fuel the 140-year-old company's growth. A spate of significant acquisitions followed the arrival of Cadbury Schweppes, as well as the truncation of the company's corporate title to Mott's Inc. In 1987, the company purchased the Red Cheek apple juice brand. The year also marked the acquisition of Mr. & Mrs. T cocktail mix, a leading brand of cocktail mixers best known for the top-selling Mr. & Mrs. T Bloody Mary Mix. In 1989, the company acquired the Garden Cocktail and Zesty Garden Cocktail line from E.D. Smith, Inc., a Canadian-based concern. Once the two brands were absorbed into Mott's, the company became the largest producer of tomato-based juices in Canada.

Quickening Growth During the 1990s

During the 1990s, the roster of Mott's brands lengthened, giving the company more than a dozen well-known brands to ensure its financial stability. The Holland House and Rose's mixer brands were acquired, giving the company the greatest share of the cooking wine mixer category in the United States. The largest acquisition of the 1990s occurred at the decade's conclusion, when Cadbury Schweppes acquired the Hawaiian Punch brand. In 1999, Cadbury Schweppes paid $203 million for the brand, giving a portion of the business to Dr. Pepper/Seven Up, Inc., one of its subsidiaries, and giving Mott's responsibility for producing and marketing the shelf-stable portion of the Hawaiian Punch business.

When Mott's celebrated its 160th anniversary in 2002, the company was recording robust growth. Between 1998 and 2002, the company achieved great strides, doubling its annual sales volume. The prolific growth was attributable in part to the addition of Hawaiian Punch, but the surge in sales also was attributable to the company's marketing expertise. Roughly eight months after the purchase of Hawaiian Punch, the packaging of the brand was revamped, resulting in a more attractive product whose new design made it more efficient to manufacture and to distribute. The company also registered success in the marketing of its Clamato Tomato Cocktail product. In a December 2002 interview with *Beverage Industry*, Mott's' senior vice-president of marketing explained the cause for soaring Clamato sales. "Three years ago," he said, "we shifted our strategy 100 percent against Hispanics. Previous to that, we had been putting 90 percent of the marketing efforts against the Anglo market, and we had just been dabbling with the Hispanic market." By 2002, after pinpointing Clamato's target market, the company was deriving approximately 70 percent of its Clamato business from the Hispanic population, with more than 40 percent of sales centered in Los Angeles.

As Mott's prepared for the years ahead, the company's success in squeezing increasing revenues out of established brands boded well for the future. Further, Mott's continued to demonstrate its willingness to acquire, a corporate posture that promised to fuel growth. In 2001, for instance, the company paid $128 million for the ReaLemon and ReaLime product lines, the leading lemon and lime juices in North America. Given these traits—the ability to derive growth from the old and a penchant for adding the new—Mott's could look to the future with considerable and justifiable optimism.

Principal Subsidiaries

Mott's North America.

Principal Competitors

The Coca-Cola Company; PepsiCo, Inc.; Vitality Beverages, Inc.

Further Reading

Bruss, Jill, "Under the Apple Tree," *Beverage Industry,* December 2002, p. 30.

"Eagle Family Sells Brands to Mott's," *Food Ingredient News,* September 2001, p. 34.

Kaplan, Andrew, "En Fuego: After 30 Years, a Key Demographic Tells Mott's, 'Clamato Spoken Here,' " *Beverage World,* October 15, 2002, p. 40.

Reyes, Sonia, "Mott's $5M Clamato Creative Boosts Ties to Hispanic Consumers," *Brandweek,* June 18, 2001, p. 14.

Theodore, Sarah, "The Roots of Mott's Success," *Beverage Industry,* December 2002, p. 34.

Thompson, Stephanie, "Mott's Gets Grabby," *Advertising Age,* August 27, 2001, p. 8.

—Jeffrey L. Covell

Musgrave

G R O U P

Musgrave Group Plc

Ballycurreen, Airport Road
Cork, Ireland
Telephone: 353-21-452-2222
Fax: 353-21-452-2290
Web site: http://www.musgrave.ie

Private Company
Founded: 1876 as Musgrave Brothers
Employees: 7,360
Sales: $3.05 billion (2002)
NAIC: 422410 General Line Grocery Wholesalers;
445110 Supermarkets and Other Grocery (Except
Convenience) Stores; 445120 Convenience Stores

Musgrave Group Plc is Ireland's largest wholesale grocery distributor and the franchiser of two leading Irish grocery chains. It is one of the largest private companies in Ireland. Its SuperValu stores are large-format supermarkets with more than 170 locations in the Republic of Ireland, with additional locations in Northern Ireland and in Spain. Musgrave also franchises a chain of convenience stores or smaller markets, called Centra. Centra operates in over 300 locations. Overall, the company's franchisees hold a 24 percent share of the grocery market in the Republic of Ireland, and a 12 percent share in Northern Ireland. Musgrave Group also operates a chain of groceries in Spain under the name Dialsur. In addition, Musgrave owns the English grocery firm Budgens. Budgens runs a chain of close to 200 small and full-size groceries in the south of England. Musgrave distributes groceries through a network of nine so-called cash and carry outlets. These serve independent grocers and convenience store operators throughout Musgrave's territory. The cash and carry division also serves gas station minimarts; tobacco, sweets and newsagent stands; and sells prepared foods to bars, hotels, guesthouses, and restaurants. About 55 percent of the cash and carry business is in wholesale groceries, and 45 percent in prepared foods. Musgrave also operates a retail toy store franchise, SuperToys. Musgrave was for most of its history a family-owned and operated firm. Members of the Musgrave family

still hold about three-quarters of the firm's shares. Three Musgrave family members also sit on the firm's board, but since 1997 the chief executive position has been held by someone outside the family, and the Musgraves are no longer involved in the day-to-day running of the company.

A 19th-Century Family Business

Musgrave Group Plc got its start as a single store on North Main Street in the city of Cork. In 1876 the brothers Stuart and Thomas Musgrave opened a grocery. They were aged 25 and 18, and had moved to Cork from County Leitrim. Their father was a farmer near Drumshanbo, and before opening the store Thomas had been a draper. Little else is known about the founders, but apparently within ten years their business was doing well, and the brothers expanded to a second shop. The business incorporated in 1894 as Musgrave Brothers Limited, with a charter to retail and wholesale sugar, coffee, tea, spices, fruit, olive oil, and other foodstuffs. The company also ran a bakery and confectionary, and was listed as a mineral water manufacturer, iron and hardware merchant, druggist, fish and ice merchant, stationer, and haberdasher. The formation of the limited company in 1894 allowed the Musgrave brothers to raise funds for other ventures, too. They built the Metropole Hotel (which the company ran until 1977), as well as a candy factory and a laundry. The grocery relocated to bigger premises at No. 84 Grand Parade. By 1896 Musgrave Brothers also ran another grocery in Tralee, County Kerry.

The Musgrave main store on Grand Parade was separated into two areas, one for retail and one for wholesale. The retail store operated like other groceries of the time, with customers placing orders that were filled by clerks. Most goods were not packaged but displayed in bulk, and clerks measured out the desired amount. The back half of the Grand Parade building housed the wholesale area. This stocked a vast array of items needed by small grocers, not only food and tea, but all kinds of hardware, paint, clocks, housewares, preservatives, and medications. Musgrave Brothers grew to be a large and profitable business by the end of the 19th century. This was a time of great political instability and economic recession in Ireland. Agricultural prices dropped after 1879, as cheaper meat and grain from

Company Perspectives:

Musgrave's mission is to strive to create and share exceptional added value through: Food distribution businesses, which are different and better. Working closely with customers and suppliers. The empowerment of employees.

North and South America began to reach a global market. Irish tenant farmers agitated for land reform giving them ownership rights, and much of this turmoil was centered around Cork. Despite what seemed a poor overall business climate, Musgrave Brothers prospered, and by 1899 had sales of some £67,000.

Expansion Through the 1920s

Sales increased at Musgrave Brothers after the question of land rights was settled by the 1903 Land Act, which set up a government-sponsored program for tenants to buy their farms from their landlords. Irish farming was given a boost by the Land Act, and both the quality and quantity of goods produced increased. With more prosperous farmers, grocers too did well, and revenue grew rapidly for Musgrave during the first ten years of the new century. Thomas's son John L. Musgrave succeeded to the managing director position in 1908, and he presided over the company for the next 40 years. Sales grew steadily between 1908 and 1914, ending at £277,658. Then Ireland was swept into World War I, and the country went through difficult changes in the ensuing years. The movement for Irish independence from England came into full force immediately after the war, and much of the bitterest struggle centered around Cork. The Musgrave family was Protestant, and well-known as such, so its members were in a tricky position in the predominantly Catholic area. John L. Musgrave and his cousin Stuart Musgrave, Jr., also a director, were ready to flee Cork at any moment if they were endangered. In 1923, Ireland split into the Irish Free State (Republic of Ireland), and Northern Ireland, which remained part of the United Kingdom. Musgrave Brothers badly needed to expand its premises on Grand Parade, but the fighting and political instability had made this impossible. Finally in 1925 the company completed large new premises on Cornmarket Street. This was a huge grocery warehouse with over a million square feet of floor space. It was the most modern such business in Ireland, and gave the company some competitive advantage over other wholesale grocers in the area. By that time, the retail side of the business had dwindled, and the company was almost exclusively involved in the wholesale business.

Musgrave's customers were small grocers all over the south of Ireland. The company marketed its goods by sending out traveling salesmen, called travelers, who called on clients and took their orders. Then the traveler returned to Cornmarket Street, where the order was processed. Musgrave employees packed up each order and disbursed it by rail. This was a very labor-intensive way of doing business, though it was the standard at the time. John L. Musgrave devised several means of keeping the company competitive. Since most clients had contact with the company almost exclusively through the traveler, it was possible that the traveler could quit Musgrave for another wholesaler, and take his customers with him. John L. Musgrave

split each traveler's territory into far-flung pieces covering parts of several counties, so that they would not get too well-known in a single area. He also called on major clients personally, to enforce good relations with the company. The travelers' order books were written in a secret code, too, so that if a competitor somehow got hold of one, the valuable information in it would be safe. Musgrave Brothers did very well through the late 1920s and into the early 1930s.

Musgrave's profitability was shaken in the mid-1930s as Ireland was hit both by the Great Depression and by what was known as the Economic War with England. The Irish government elected in 1932 had stopped the payments tenant farmers had been making to their English landlords under the 1903 Land Act, and England then imposed punitive tariffs on Irish farm exports. This depressed farm sales, and also hurt Musgrave's customers. The situation was resolved in 1938, though by the next year, Ireland was affected by England's entry into World War II, and the resultant rationing of food and motor fuel. The rationing of motor fuel made it virtually impossible for the Musgrave travelers to get out to see their clients by car. The company was able to keep its fleet of delivery vans going, however, and the travelers had to hitch a ride on the vans and then go by bicycle. But Musgrave Brothers had been well-prepared for the war when it came to tea. This was a prize commodity that was rationed during the war to only half an ounce per person per week. John L. Musgrave had wisely stockpiled tea before the war, as well as sugar and spices. Musgrave helped its client groceries get an official increase in their tea allotments during the war. The company also pointedly refrained from taking anything but the government-controlled price for tea, at a time when it sold on the black market for enormous sums. This increased confidence in Musgrave, and many small groceries apparently switched their trade to the company for that reason.

Changes After World War II

Rationing continued until 1952, but sales for Musgrave picked up after the war was over. Sales in 1945 were roughly £486,000, while by the end of 1949 sales had risen to over £722,000. Though sales grew, in the 1950s the company found it increasingly difficult to make a good profit. John L. Musgrave retired in the mid-1950s, and his son Jack took over. His cousin Hugh Musgrave also became a top executive of the company at this time. The third generation of Musgraves inherited a business that was little changed from when their fathers began running it. The company still operated on the traveler system, with orders packed and shipped from the Cornmarket Street facility. Sales had doubled since 1920, but profits had stayed fairly level. Meanwhile, the grocery business was undergoing profound changes in other parts of the world. Self-service groceries on the model of today's stores, where customers picked their own goods from the shelves, had become common in the United States in the 1930s. Such stores cropped up in England and Europe later, and by the late 1950s, it was clear that Ireland would go the same way. These new stores threatened to swamp the little old-fashioned groceries that comprised Musgrave's 2,000 clients.

Jack Musgrave pushed for sweeping changes in the way Musgrave Brothers did business. In 1958 he signed the company up with a Dutch franchise called VG, or Voluntary Group, and instituted VG's trading system. Musgrave's client groceries now signed up to become part of the VG fold. This meant they pledged to buy all their stock from Musgrave, which would lower its prices based on its increased buying power and lower distribution costs. VG stores benefited from group advertising and group-wide sales. Distribution costs were lowered by another major shift in the way Musgrave did business. Instead of packing the orders for its clients, in the late 1950s Musgrave instituted the ''cash and carry'' system, where clients packed their own orders, paid cash for them, and carted them off. Initially, part of the Cornmarket Street warehouse was converted to a cash and carry area. In 1966, with business growing, Musgrave completed a new distribution center just south of Cork. The switch to the group system and to cash and carry worked well for Musgrave Brothers. Sales grew rapidly, from £1.31 million in 1961 to £3.02 million in 1969. Over that period, profits rose fourfold.

The company got a new managing director in 1971, Hugh Mackeown. Mackeown was the nephew of Jack Musgrave, and he soon instituted yet more changes. Musgrave Brothers became Musgrave Group in 1973. In the mid-1970s, the company spent approximately £5 million to build four new, gigantic cash and carry stores. The first was in Dublin, called Robinhood, which opened in 1972. In 1975 Musgrave opened a new cash and carry in Cork and another in Limerick, then in 1977 opened a second Dublin store, at Ballymun. These four stores were the biggest Ireland had ever seen. Hugh Mackeown had based them on stores he had seen in the Netherlands, and they dwarfed anything Musgrave's competitors had. Robinhood covered two and a half acres of floor space, an unprecedented size. The new cash and carries proved very profitable for Musgrave, and sales grew roughly by a factor of six in the 1970s.

Musgrave also sold off some of its non-grocery businesses during the decade. In 1972 Musgrave sold its share in a joint-venture tea company to its business partner, a company called Brooke Bond. Musgrave Tea had once had a 15 percent share of the Irish market, but in the 1960s the business had become increasingly unprofitable. The company had set up the joint venture with Brooke Bond, then got out of tea entirely as it concentrated on its grocery wholesale business. Musgrave had operated Cork's Metropole Hotel since the 1890s, and it sold this too in 1977. Musgrave had also run a candy factory in Cork since its early years. It closed the factory in 1980.

Move to Grocery Franchiser in the 1980s

The changes Musgrave instituted in the 1960s and 1970s had worked well for the company. Nevertheless, competition was increasing in the Irish grocery industry. By the late 1970s, Ireland was about evenly split between independent grocers and groceries operated by national chains. The Irish chains were Dunnes Stores, Quinnsworth, and Superquinn. In 1979 an English chain grocery, Tesco, moved into Ireland for the first time, buying up an existing chain of discount stores called 3 Guys. At this time, Hugh Mackeown and other Musgrave principals decided it was time to renovate the VG system, to allow their clients to push back against the encroaching chains. Though Musgrave's VG stores were linked by group marketing, in other ways they had little in common. Some VG stores were tiny corner stores, while others were modern, full-service supermarkets. Musgrave decided to reconfigure the VG franchise, breaking it into two brand-name stores. Large stores would go under the name SuperValu, while the smaller stores, which it considered essentially convenience stores, would be renamed Centra.

The move to the new system went slowly. Stores at first retained the old name, going by VG/SuperValu, but by the mid-1980s, SuperValu was a stand-alone title. The small convenience store owners were apparently more reluctant to sign up for Centra than the larger stores were to convert to SuperValu. Three or four years after the changeover, there were still only 50 Centras. This was again a decade of economic stagnation in Ireland, with high unemployment and emigration. Competitive pressures were only increasing in the grocery industry. Musgrave endeavored to grow its new franchises into a truly national market. Under the VG system, it had nominally owned the VG name for all of Ireland, but in practice it had dominance only in the south. In the western part of Ireland, Musgrave partnered with another grocery wholesaler called Nilands, and in the east, with a firm called J. Garvey & Sons. These firms used the VG system in their territories. In 1984 Musgrave acquired J. Garvey & Sons, which allowed SuperValu and Centra to move into the key Dublin market. In 1987 Musgrave bought another rival independent grocery franchise, H. Williams. The 15 H. Williams outlets were converted to Centras or SuperValus and sold to independent operators. Then in 1989 Musgrave bought up its other Irish partner, Nilands. After this purchase, SuperValu and Centra stores could be found in all parts of the country. By the late 1980s, the SuperValu franchise included 122 stores, and Centra had grown to over 250 outlets. Sales at Musgrave reached £320 million by 1989, and the independent sector of the Irish grocery market had recovered against the onslaught of the national chains.

International Expansion in the 1990s and After

Musgrave expanded its cash and carry business in the early 1990s by acquisition and building. It acquired a Dublin cash and carry outlet in 1992, bringing the number of Musgrave cash and carries in that city to three. That same year Musgrave built its second cash and carry outlet in Northern Ireland, on a site near Derry. The company did well in the early 1990s, with sales increasing almost 9 percent over 1993, and net income up 28 percent. At that point, the company considered taking its operation abroad. The English market at that point looked too expensive, as did the rest of northern Europe. But in 1994 the company acquired a Spanish grocery, Dialsur. Dialsur, based in Alicante, was a family-owned business with 17 cash and carry outlets and a franchise chain of 46 Dialprix retail groceries. The cost of the acquisition was estimated at £14 million. The company made another even pricier acquisition the next year, picking up an Irish chain of L&N supermarkets for an estimated £30 million from its owner, Adam F. Torrie. The L&N chain was small but lucrative, its 18 stores bringing in £95 million in 1995. The purchase also gave Musgrave the opportunity to put Super-Valus and Centras in cities such as Waterford and Kilkenny, where it had not had a foothold before.

In 1997 Seamus Scally became chief executive of Musgrave Group, the first non-Musgrave family member to hold the position since the firm's founding. Hugh Mackeown and two other Musgrave family members remained on the board of directors. Scally worked hard to bring Musgrave into new markets. One of his first goals was to penetrate Northern Ireland, where the company had a limited presence. Musgrave operated five Super-Valus in Northern Ireland in the mid-1990s, and Scally hoped to take this number to 50. In 1997 the company bought a chain of 21 Wellworth stores in Northern Ireland, rebranding them SuperValu. Musgrave also recruited independent grocers in Northern Ireland to the SuperValu name, and by the late 1990s the company had a 10 percent share of the Northern Ireland grocery market. By 2002 the firm had 60 SuperValu and Centra stores in Northern Ireland.

Sales overall continued to rise for Musgrave through the 1990s. It ended the decade with a market share of 25 percent in the Republic of Ireland, and sales at over £1 billion. The company plowed its profit back into operations, building a huge centralized distribution network for chilled, fresh, and frozen foods in the late 1990s. Musgrave had helped hold back the tide of national chain groceries in Ireland with its effective push to bind independent grocers in its SuperValu and Centra groups. Seamus Scally seemed particularly proud of this feat, exhorting a conference of Irish independent grocers in 2001 to fight back against the ''multiples,'' or national and multinational chains. ''[We] took almost 20 percent of the Irish grocery market back from under the noses of the multiples—including the UK and European multiples and discounters who . . . are now struggling in our marketplace,'' Scally told *Grocer* in April 2001. He claimed that the independent grocer's share of the market had grown from only 30 percent of the Irish market in the 1980s to almost 50 percent in the 2000s.

At that point, Scally took the fight to England itself, buying a 43 percent share of the English grocery chain Budgens in 2000. Budgens operated 167 stores in London, southern and south-eastern England, and also ran food courts at some 40 gas stations. Budgens stores, which were almost all company-owned, were primarily small markets and convenience stores, with a reputation for a large selection of fresh foods. After a year, Musgrave bought up the outstanding shares of Budgens. Budgens planned to expand, opening 15 to 20 new stores a year. These were to open under the Budgens name. Musgrave did not plan to bring Centra and SuperValu into England at this time. Budgens and Musgrave were still growing into the 2000s, despite fierce competition from chain stores. Musgrave's Spanish subsidiary Dialsur also posted strong sales gains in the early 2000s. Sales grew 10 percent for Musgrave overall in 2001, and the firm predicted that by 2005 SuperValu would be the largest grocery retailer in the Republic of Ireland.

Principal Subsidiaries

Budgens plc; Dialsur S.A.

Principal Competitors

Tesco plc; Dunnes Stores; Superquinn Supermarket Group.

Further Reading

''Ireland Signs Deal with Spain,'' *Grocer*, April 30, 1994, p. 26.

''Musgrave,'' *UK Retail Briefing*, January 2002, p. 98.

''Musgrave Group Acquires Budgens,'' *Daily Deal*, June 22, 2002.

''Musgrave Sales Booming,'' *Grocer*, May 15, 1999, p. 10.

''Scally Blasts Report's 'Sweet Damn All','' *Grocer*, November 11, 2000, p. 6.

''The SuperValu Challenge,'' *Grocer*, March 23, 2002, p. 6.

Watson, Elaine, ''Musgrave's Buying Clout Brings Boost to Budgens,'' *Grocer*, June 29, 2002, p. 12.

Wilson, Lydia, ''Musgrave Chief Welcomes Groceries Order Decision,'' *Super Marketing*, November 3, 2000, p. 2.

White, Dan, *A History of Musgrave: The First 125 Years*, Cork: Musgrave Group, 2001.

Wood, John, '' 'Draw Inspiration from Ireland and Fight Back','' *Grocer*, April 7, 2001, p. 16.

—A. Woodward

National Equipment Services, Inc.

1603 Orrington Avenue, Suite 1600
Evanston, Illinois 60201
U.S.A.
Telephone: (847) 733-1000
Fax: (847) 773-1078
Web site: http://www.n-e-s.com

Public Company
Incorporated: 1996
Employees: 2,900
Sales: $621.3 million (2002)
Stock Exchanges: OTC
Ticker Symbol: NEQSE
NAIC: 532412 Construction, Mining, and Forestry
   Machinery and Equipment Rental and Leasing

Based in Evanston, Illinois, National Equipment Services, Inc. (NES) is one of the leading equipment rental companies, offering more than 750 different types of general and specialty equipment to industrial and construction firms. NES operates through 42 companies and a total of 180 locations spread across the United States. General rental equipment includes aerial work platforms, air compressors, cranes, earth-moving equipment, and rough-terrain forklifts. NES specialty equipment includes electric and pneumatic hoists, highway safety equipment, hydraulic and truck-mounted cranes, liquid storage tanks, and pumps. As a way to save money on acquiring new equipment, NES maintains two rebuilding facilities, located in Kentucky and Pennsylvania, which completely refurbish items in the company's inventory. In addition to rental sales, NES acts as a distributor of new equipment for major original equipment manufacturers. It also sells used equipment, parts and other supplies, and merchandise, as well as provides repair and maintenance services.

Founding the Business in 1996

The two men primarily responsible for the creation of NES in 1996 were Carl Thoma and Kevin Rodgers. Thoma provided the financial backing through Golder, Thoma, Cressey, Rauner, Inc., a Chicago-based investment firm that was formed in 1980 and became instrumental in industry consolidation ventures. Thoma received an undergraduate degree from Oklahoma State University in 1970 before earning his M.B.A. from the Stanford Graduate School of Business in 1973. He became the chairman of the board of NES. Rodgers, named CEO, possessed considerable experience in the equipment business. In 1979 he went to work for Morgan Equipment Company, a construction and mining equipment firm, and in 1986 became CEO of its Australia operation, a Caterpillar dealership. Then in 1991 he became CEO of Brambles Equipment Services and Brambles Records Management, Inc., U.S. subsidiaries of a publicly traded Australian firm, Brambles Industries Limited. He helped Brambles enter the rental business through acquisitions, a roll-up approach that he would then employ with NES.

Rodgers quit Brambles in 1996, along with a senior team of management, and in June of that year joined forces with Thoma to form NES with the goal of creating a major consolidating vehicle in the rental industry, which at the time was generating some $18 billion in revenues per year and highly fragmented. More than 12,000 companies, many of them local and family-owned, operated in the industrial and construction equipment rental sector. It was also a rapidly expanding business. According to surveys conducted by the Associated Equipment Distributors, the rental industry had been growing at a compound annual rate of 24 percent. An increasing number of U.S. companies were opting to lease rather than devote precious capital to buying equipment that they were not likely to utilize as fully as a rental company. For many years these companies had few options, limited to the choice of either buying new or used equipment. Moreover, until the mid-1980s tax laws provided an incentive to purchase, due to investment tax credits. With the rise of rental companies that were able to provide equipment, and the loss of a tax incentive to buy, manufacturers and construction firms began to take advantage of the rental option, which in turn led to more rental companies cropping up to meet the growing demand. Reliance on rented equipment was much further along in such countries as Great Britain where 80 percent, and Australia where 50 percent, of such big ticket items were leased. In the United States, according to some studies, just 5 percent of equipment was leased, leaving a great deal of growth potential for rental companies. Thoma and Rodgers were not the only entrepreneurs to recognize the opportunity to create a company capable of serving as a roll-up vehicle in the industry, but the company was only one of a handful well-financed enough to be considered a true player in the consolidation game that was starting to unfold.

Thoma's venture fund controlled 86 percent of the newly created NES, with Rodgers owning a 7 percent stake. Rodgers explained the NES business strategy in a 2000 interview with *Rental Management:* "When we started in June 1996, we wanted to put together a company with a primary focus on reach equipment—aerial equipment, cranes and reach forklifts—that would earn roughly half of its revenues from industrial applications and half from non-residential construction. And other than the specialty equipment—the traffic-safety group, which represents around 15 to 17 percent of the total business—the rest of the business is split pretty evenly, in rental revenue, between industrial applications and non-residential construction. That was the plan from the beginning—to try to even out the cyclicality that you see over time when a company is focused primarily on construction applications." He further stated that "our plan was to leverage the initial equity to borrow as much as we could to grow the company as fast as we could, with a goal of trying to get the company to half a billion in revenue," a level management hoped to reach in five years.

Launching an Acquisition Spree in 1997

NES launched its acquisition program in 1997, buying six companies in separate transactions. In January it purchased Industrial Hoist Services, a national company that provided pneumatic and electric hoists. The following month NES added Aerial Platforms, an Atlanta, Georgia-based company that rented aerial work platforms. Next, in March 1997, NES added Lone Star Rentals, suppliers of general equipment to the Gulf Coast region. Another general equipment rental firm, BAT Rentals, serving Las Vegas, was acquired in April. Finally, in July 1997 NES made the last of its purchases for the year: Spintank, a Gulf Coast company that rented liquid and specialized storage tanks, and Equipco Rental & Sales, renters of general equipment to the western Virginia area. All of the acquired companies were profitable and well established in their markets. The youngest, Spintank, had been in business for nine years, while the oldest, BAT Rentals, had been in operation since 1960.

A clear acquisition strategy developed: buy profitable companies, retain the previous owners, who knew the local market and had long-term relationships with customers, and grant managers the authority to continue running the operations in a manner that helped to make the businesses successful in the first place. Further, NES provided greater access to funds, essential in the capital-intensive rental business, allowing the previous

owners to take their businesses to a higher level. In keeping with this decentralized philosophy NES maintained a lean corporate headquarters. As Rodgers explained to *Rental Management,* "If a company has a large head office, we feel that there'd be a large number of people who do not add value to the equation but rather they would be bugging the people in the field." Although NES delegated a great deal of authority to the local level, it expected a high level of results: 20 percent internal growth and 20 percent operating profit.

NES was even more aggressive in pursuing its roll-up strategy in 1998. In January it added Genpower Pump and Equipment, providers of pumps in the Gulf Coast Region, and Eagle Scaffolding, a Las Vegas scaffolding firm. A month later NES acquired Grand Hi-Reach, a Grand Rapids, Michigan, company that rented aerial work platforms, and Work Safe Supply, a Michigan company that specialized in highway safety items. In March 1998, NES made three purchases: Dragon Rentals, a Gulf Coast supplier of liquid storage tanks; Cormier Equipment Company, a general equipment provider to the East Coast; and Albany Ladder, which rented aerial work platforms in the Northeast.

There was a lull in NES's buying spree as the company prepared to make an initial public offering (IPO) of stock. The hope of management and its investment banker, Salomon Smith Barney, was to place 17.2 million shares priced between $16 and $19, which would raise approximately $300 million and establish a market capitalization in the $525 million range. Between the time the company filed its prospectus in April and the time the stock was to be sold, however, the IPO market soured, with only Internet companies and brand names attracting strong investor interest. As a result, the NES offering was postponed, and when it finally took place on July 13 it commanded a price of just $13.50.

Despite disappointment in its IPO, NES closed out 1998 with several more acquisitions. In July it bought Falconite Equipment, Inc., supplier of aerial work platforms and cranes to the mid-South and Gulf Coast markets, and R&R Rentals, which rented cranes to the Gulf Coast. In August another highway safety equipment company, Wisconsin-based Traffic Signing and Marking, was added. NES then bought Shaughnessy Crane Service, Inc., which rented aerial work platforms and cranes to the Northeast. The last acquisition in 1998 came in October when NEX picked up Rebel Studio Rentals, a California supplier of aerial work platforms.

The acquisition pace accelerated even more in 1999 when NES added 19 rental companies. In the process, NES piled on debt, but because rental companies provided consistent cash flow, it was able to service the resulting load. In March 1999 NES purchased three companies: Barricade & Light Rental, Inc., an Arizona highway safety equipment supplier; Mayer Hammant, which rented pumps and compressors in the Gulf Coast region; and Wellesley Crane Service, operating in the Northeast. The following month, NES completed two highway safety equipment acquisitions: Oklahoma-based Advanced Warnings, Inc., and the Indiana-based businesses of The Mike Madrid Company Inc., Latshaw Traffic Services, Inc., and Madrid Leasing Corp. In May 1999 NES bought the Illinois operations of S&R Equipment Co., providers of aerial work platforms and cranes to the mid-South and Gulf Coast. An earth-moving equipment firm also serving the Gulf Coast, Elite Rentals, was added in June 1999, followed the next month by Gould & Associates, Inc., which rented pumps in the Southeast. Several purchases were made in August 1999: The Plank Company, which supplied trench safety equipment to the Gulf Coast and West Coast; Interstate Traffic Control, Inc. and Rich-Lite, Inc., a southeastern highway safety equipment company; American Tool Rental Corp., an East Coast general equipment firm; and Management Technology America, a national provider of management information systems. NES then acquired a pair of highway safety equipment companies in September 1999: Alternate Construction Controls, doing business in Illinois; and L and C Flashing Barricades, serving the East Coast. Three more companies were added to NES in October 1999: highway safety equipment company, Safety Light Sales & Leasing, Inc. of Texas, serving the Gulf Coast; and two Florida general equipment renters, Tropical Ladder and Lifts and ABC Barricades. The final acquisitions in 1999 came in November when NES closed on the purchase of Cantel, Inc., a trench safety equipment company serving the Northwest, and Iowa-based Tri-State Signing, Inc., a highway safety equipment company.

Focus in 2000 on Internal Improvements

At the end of 1999 NES was ahead of schedule in reaching its goal of $500 million in annual revenues. Management eased up on external growth, opting instead to focus more attention on what had already been assembled, looking to improve operating performance and grow by internal means. Part of this equation involved the two rebuilding facilities, one that had already been opened in Paducah, Kentucky, and a second to operate in McConnellsburg, Pennsylvania. These plants were primarily intended to rebuild such high-reach equipment as booms, reach forklifts, and cranes. Each facility was capable of rebuilding about 1,000 units a year. As a result of these efforts, machinery would receive a second life at a fraction of what it would cost to buy new. On the acquisition side, management was interested in selective tuck-ins, companies that operated in existing markets, rather than to break new ground. NES made just four purchases in 2000, in March adding a pair: Cassidy & Lee, Inc., a Northeast earth-moving equipment firm, and Road Light, Inc. and Interstate Sign, Inc., providers of highway safety equipment to the East Coast. In addition in 2000, NES acquired Georgia-based trench safety equipment company Laser Products, Inc. and St. Clair Equipment Company, a Gulf Coast provider of aerial work platforms.

In 2000 Rodgers told *Rental Management,* "Even in a recession—assuming the next one is no worse than 1990–91—the cash flow is so strong in this business that you should be able to weather the storm. From 1990 to 1992, when I was traveling around the country looking for rental companies to buy at Brambles, I honestly can't recall coming across a single rental company that went out of business." As the U.S. economy slipped into recession in 2001, Rodgers' comments would assume ironic importance. A top rental company, NationsRent, with annual revenues of some $600 million, filed for Chapter 11 bankruptcy in December 2001, and the rest of the so-called recession-proof industry also showed signs of strain. Lowering business activity that resulted in declining rental rates crippled cash flow and forced NES to take several cost-cutting steps in 2002, including staff reductions and the consolidation of branch and support operations. The company also sold off its trench shoring business. Nevertheless, it still found the resources to acquire Brambles' U.S. rental business for $122 million in January 2002. The additional revenue, in excess of $150 million, was not enough, however, to offset the company's mounting difficulties. In November 2002, Rodgers stepped down as CEO, replaced by Joseph Gullion, a former aviation industry executive. Rodgers stayed on as vice-chairman, charged with focusing on acquisitions and other areas. In December 2002, the New York Stock Exchange delisted NES because it failed to meet certain financial standards.

With significant debts coming due, and the economy continuing to prove sluggish, NES faced more difficulties in 2003. In January the company defaulted on certain debt provisions, and a month later Rodgers resigned in order to "pursue other interests." With the performance of NES continuing to deteriorate the company sought to restructure its debt rather than seek bankruptcy protection, but the future of the company remained in doubt.

Principal Subsidiaries

BAT Rentals; Cormier Equipment; Equipco Rentals & Sales; Equipment Services; Shaughnessy Crane; Work Safe Supply.

Principal Competitors

NationsRent, Inc.; Rental Service Corporation; United Rentals, Inc.

Further Reading

"A Disciplined Approach to Growth," *Rental Management,* June-July 2000.

Murphy, H. Lee, "National Jumps Aboard Consolidation Bandwagon," *Crain's Chicago Business,* August 10, 1998, p. 41.

——, "Roll-up Nat'l Equipment to Grow Rental Biz," *Crain's Chicago Business,* July 12, 1999, p. 9.

Schacknow, Peter, "National Equipment Services—CEO—Interview," *CNBC/Dow Jones Business Video,* February 8, 1999.

Serwer, Andy, "Street Life: On-Again, Off-Again IPOs," *Fortune,* July 20, 1998, p. 191.

—Ed Dinger

NEC Corporation

7-1, Shiba 5-chome
Minato-ku
Tokyo 108-8001
Japan
Telephone: (03) 3454-1111
Fax: (03) 3798-1510
Web site: http://www.nec.com

Public Company
Incorporated: 1899 as Nippon Electric Company,
    Limited
Employees: 145,807
Sales: ¥4.7 trillion ($39.79 billion) (2003)
Stock Exchanges: Tokyo London NASDAQ
Ticker Symbol: NIPNY (ADRs)
NAIC: 334111 Electronic Computer Manufacturing;
    334112 Computer Storage Device Manufacturing;
    334119 Other Computer Peripheral Equipment
    Manufacturing; 334210 Telephone Apparatus
    Manufacturing; 334220 Radio and Television
    Broadcasting and Wireless Communications
    Equipment Manufacturing; 334290 Other
    Communications Equipment Manufacturing; 334413
    Semiconductor and Related Device Manufacturing;
    518111 Internet Service Providers; 541511 Custom
    Computer Programming Services; 541512 Computer
    Systems Design Services; 541519 Other Computer
    Related Services; 511210 Software Publishers

NEC Corporation is one of the world's leading makers of computers, computer peripherals, and telecommunications equipment and owns majority control of NEC Electronics Corporation, one of the leading semiconductor makers in the world. NEC is considered one of Japan's *sogo denki*, or general electric companies, a group that is typically said to also include Fujitsu Limited; Hitachi, Ltd.; Mitsubishi Electric Corporation; and Toshiba Corporation. Like the other members of the Japanese high-tech "Big Five," NEC was hit hard at the turn of the millennium by a global downturn in demand in the corporate sector for electronics products. NEC has subsequently been undertaking an ongoing and massive restructuring, including an increasing emphasis on systems integration services, software, and Internet-related services. These operations are housed within the company's IT Solutions business segment, which also includes mainframe computers, network servers, supercomputers, workstations, and computer peripherals. The Networking Solutions segment comprises optical, broadband, and wireless networking equipment and services as well as cellular phones and other communications devices. Computers, printers and other peripheral devices, Internet services, and network equipment aimed at the consumer market are handled through the Personal Solutions segment. About 17 percent of NEC's net sales originate outside of Japan.

Early History Involving Western Electric Company

The Nippon Electric Company, Limited, as NEC Corporation was originally known, was first organized in 1899 as a limited partnership between Japanese investors and the Western Electric Company. Western Electric recognized that Japan, which was undergoing an ambitious industrialization, would soon be building a telephone network. With a solid monopoly in North America as the manufacturing arm of the Bell system, Western Electric sought to establish a strong market presence in Japan, as it had done in Europe. NEC went public the following year, with Western Electric a 54 percent owner. In need of a plant, NEC took over the Miyoshi Electrical Manufacturing Company in central Tokyo.

Under the management of Kunihiko Iwadare and with substantial direction from Western Electric, NEC was at first little more than a distributor of imported telephone equipment from Western Electric and General Electric. Iwadare, however, set NEC to producing magneto-type telephone sets and secured substantial orders from the Ministry of Communications for the government-sponsored telephone-network-expansion program. With steadily increasing, and guaranteed, business from the government, NEC was able to plan further expansion. In September 1900 NEC purchased from Mitsui a site at Mita Shikokumachi, where a second NEC factory was completed in December 1902.

Company Perspectives:

"Empowered by Innovation" represents NEC's continuing contribution to the realization of society's potential through technological innovation. NEC constantly self-innovates in order to bring its customers new developments in cutting-edge IT technologies and advances in such areas as business applications. NEC also works hard to learn new applications through its customer contacts and to offer solutions that bring innovation to each customer, whether individual or corporate.

NEC strives for a relationship of creative stimulation aimed at customer innovation.

It is this determination that brings life to NEC's slogan.

In an attempt to heighten NEC's competitiveness with rival Oki Shokai, Iwadare ordered his apprentices at Western Electric to study that company's accounting and production-control systems. Takeshiro Maeda, a former Ministry of Communications official, recommended that NEC emphasize the consumer market, because he regarded the government sales as uncompetitive and limited. Still, government sales were the company's major vehicle for growth, particularly with Japan's expansion into Manchuria after the 1904–05 Russo-Japanese War.

Japan's Ministry of Communications engineered an aggressive telecommunications program, linking the islands of Japan with commercial, military, and government offices in Korea and Manchuria. As was Bell in the United States, NEC was permitted a "natural," though imperfect, monopoly over cable communications in Japan and its territories. NEC opened offices in Seoul in 1908 and Port Arthur (now Lüshun), China, in 1909.

A serious economic recession in Japan in 1913 forced the government to retrench sponsorship of its second telephone expansion program. Struggling to survive, NEC quickly turned back to importing—this time of such household appliances as the electric fan, a device never seen before in Japan. As quickly as it had fallen, the Japanese economy recovered in 1916, and the expansion program was placed back on schedule. Intelligent planning effectively insulated NEC from the effects of a second serious recession in 1922; NEC even continued to grow during that time. In the meantime, Western Electric's stake in NEC was transferred in 1918 to the company's international division, International Western Electric Company, Incorporated (IWE).

Relationship with Sumitomo Beginning in 1920s

In the early 1920s, IWE wanted to create a joint venture with NEC to produce electrical cables. NEC, however, lacked the industrial capacity to be an equal partner, and recommended the inclusion of a third party, Sumitomo Densen Seizosho, the cable-manufacturing division of the Sumitomo group. A three-way agreement was concluded, marking the beginning of an important role for Sumitomo in NEC's operations.

On September 1, 1923, a violent earthquake severely damaged Tokyo and Yokohama, killing 140,000 people and leaving 3.4 million homeless. The Great Kanto Earthquake also destroyed four NEC factories and 80,000 telephone sets. Still, the government maintained its commitment to a modern telephone network and supported NEC's development of automatic switching devices.

NEC began to work on radios and transmitting devices in 1924. As with the telephone project, the Japanese government sponsored the establishment of a radio network, the Nippon Hoso Kyokai, which began operation with Western Electric equipment from NEC. By May 1930, however, NEC had built its own transmitter, a 500-watt station at Okayama.

In 1925 American Telephone & Telegraph sold International Western Electric to International Telephone & Telegraph, which renamed the division International Standard Electric Corporation (ISE). Partially as a result, Yasujiro Niwa, a director who had joined NEC in 1924, felt NEC should lessen its dependence on technologies developed by foreign affiliates. In order to strengthen NEC's research and development, Niwa inaugurated a policy of recruiting the best graduates from top universities. By 1928 NEC engineers had completed their own wire photo device.

The Japanese economy, which had been in a slump since 1927, fell into crisis after the Wall Street crash of 1929. With a rapidly contracting economy, the government was forced year after year to scale back its telecommunications projects. While it restricted imports of electrical equipment, the government also encouraged greater competition in the domestic market. Decreased subsidization and a shrinking market share reversed many of NEC's gains during the previous decade.

The deployment of Japanese troops in Manchuria in 1931 created a strong wave of nationalism in Japan. Legislation was passed that forced ISE to transfer about 15 percent of its ownership in NEC to Sumitomo Densen. Under the directorship of Sumitomo's Takesaburo Akiyama (Iwadare had retired in 1929), NEC began to work more closely with the Japanese military. A right-wing officers corps was at the time successfully engineering a rise to power and diverting money to military and industrial projects, particularly after Japan's declaration of war against China in 1937. NEC's sales grew by seven times between 1931 and 1937, and by 1938 the company's Mita and Tamagawa plants had been placed under military control.

Under pressure from the militarists, ISE was obliged to transfer a second block of NEC shares to Sumitomo; by 1941, ISE's stake had fallen to 19.7 percent. Later that year, however, when Japan went to war against the Allied powers, ISE's remaining share of NEC was confiscated as enemy property.

During the war, NEC worked on microwave communications and radar and sonar systems for the army and navy. The company took control of its prewar Chinese affiliate, China Electric, as well as a Javanese radio-research facility belonging to the Dutch East Indies Post, Telegraph and Telephone Service. In February 1943, Sumitomo took full control of NEC and renamed it Sumitomo Communication Industries. The newly named company's production centers were removed to 15 different locations to minimize damage from American bombings. Despite this, Sumitomo Communication's major plants at Ueno, Okayama, and Tamagawa were destroyed during the spring of 1945; by the end of the war in August, the company had ceased production altogether.

Key Dates:

1899: Nippon Electric Company, Limited (NEC) is formed as a limited partnership between Japanese investors and the Western Electric Company; firm begins producing and selling telephones and switching systems.

1918: Western Electric's stake in NEC is transferred to its international division, International Western Electric (IWE).

Early 1920s: NEC, IWE, and a division of the Sumitomo group form a joint venture to produce electrical cables, marking the beginning of NEC's involvement with Sumitomo.

1924: NEC begins producing radios and transmitting devices.

1925: IWE is sold to International Telephone & Telegraph, which renames it International Standard Electric (ISE).

1932: Japanese government forces ISE to transfer about 15 percent of its ownership in NEC to Sumitomo.

1941: After the outbreak of war between Japan and the United States, ISE's remaining stake in NEC is seized as enemy property.

1943: Sumitomo takes full control of NEC and renames it Sumitomo Communication Industries.

1945: Its plants heavily damaged during World War II, Sumitomo Communication has ceased production altogether by war's end; Sumitomo and other Japanese conglomerates are ordered dissolved by the Allied occupation authority; Sumitomo Communication readopts the name Nippon Electric Company.

1950: NEC begins work on transistors.

1953: Consumer-appliance subsidiary called the New Nippon Electric Company is created.

1954: Company enters the computer field.

1960: Integrated circuit research and development begins.

1963: Marketing subsidiary is established in the United States.

1968: First overseas factories are opened in Mexico and Brazil.

1977: Company President Koji Kobayashi puts forth his prescient vision of "C&C"—the future integration of computers and communications.

1981: NEC Electronics, Inc. is formed as the company's manufacturing and marketing arm for semiconductors in the United States.

1983: Company changes its English-language name to NEC Corporation.

1996: NEC and Packard Bell merge their PC businesses outside of China and Japan into a new firm called Packard Bell NEC Inc.; Internet service provider Biglobe is launched.

1998: NEC gains majority control of Packard Bell NEC.

1999: Company reports a net loss of $1.34 billion for the fiscal year ending in March; major restructuring ensues.

2002: Bulk of NEC's semiconductor business is shifted to a newly formed subsidiary, NEC Electronics Corporation.

2003: NEC Electronics is taken public, reducing NEC's stake to 70 percent.

Struggling to Recover Following World War II

The Allied occupation authority ordered the dissolution of Japan's giant *zaibatsu* (conglomerate) enterprises such as Sumitomo in November that year. Sumitomo Communications elected to readopt the name Nippon Electric, and ownership of the company reverted to a government liquidation corporation. At the same time, the authority ordered a purge of industrialists who had cooperated with the military during the war, and Takeshi Kajii, wartime president of NEC, was removed from the company.

NEC's new president, Toshihide Watanabe, faced the nearly impossible task of rehabilitating a company paralyzed by war damage, with 27,000 employees and no demand for its products. Although it was helped by the mass resignation of 12,000 workers, NEC was soon constrained by new labor legislation sponsored by the occupation authority. This legislation resulted in the formation of a powerful labor union that frequently came into conflict with NEC management. Although NEC was able to open its major factories by January 1946, workers demanding higher wages went on strike for 45 days only 18 months later.

The Japanese government helped NEC and other companies to remain viable through the award of public works projects. Uneasy about becoming dependent on these programs, however, Watanabe ordered the reapplication of NEC's military technolo-

gies for commercial use. Submarine sonar equipment was thus converted into fish detectors, and military two-way radios were redesigned into all-band commercial radio receivers.

Still, NEC fell drastically short of its postwar recovery goals. In April 1949 the company closed its Ogaki, Seto, and Takasaki plants and its laboratory at Ikuta, and laid off 2,700 employees. The union responded by striking, yielding only after 106 days.

Next on Watanabe's agenda was the establishment of patent protection for NEC's technologies. During the war, all patented designs had become a "common national asset"—in the public domain. Eager to reestablish its link with ISE, NEC needed first to ensure that both companies' technologies would be legally protected. This accomplished, NEC and ISE signed new cooperative agreements in July 1950.

Diversifying and Expanding Internationally in the 1950s and 1960s

With Japan's new strategic importance in light of the Korean War, and with the advent of commercial radio broadcasting and subsequent telephone expansions, NEC had several new opportunities for growth. The company made great progress in television and microwave communication technologies and in 1953 created a separate consumer-appliance subsidiary called the New Nippon

Electric Company. The company had begun research and development on transistors in 1950; it entered the computer field four years later, and in 1960 began developing integrated circuits. By 1956 NEC had diversified so successfully that a major reorganization became necessary and additional plant space in Sagamihara and Fuchu was put on line. NEC also established foreign offices in Taiwan, India, and Thailand in 1961.

Watanabe, believing that NEC should more aggressively establish an international reputation, created a marketing subsidiary in the United States in 1963 called Nippon Electric New York, Inc. (which later became NEC America, Inc.). In addition, the company changed its logo, dropping the simple *igeta* diamond and "NEC" for a more distinctive script. In November of the following year, Watanabe resigned as president and became chairman of the board.

The company's new president, Koji Kobayashi, took office with the realization that because the Japanese telephone market would soon become saturated, NEC would have to diversify more aggressively into new and peripheral electronics product lines to maintain its high growth rate. In preparation for this, he introduced modern management methods, including a zero-defects quality-control policy, a concept borrowed from the Martin Aircraft Company. Over the next two years, Kobayashi split NEC's five divisions into 14, paving the way for a more decentralized management system that gave individual division heads greater autonomy and responsibility.

With the continued introduction of more advanced television-broadcasting equipment and telephone switching devices, and taking advantage of the stronger position Watanabe and Kobayashi had created, NEC opened factories in Mexico and Brazil in 1968, Australia in 1969, and Korea in 1970. Affiliates were opened in Iran in 1971 and Malaysia in 1973.

With a diminishing need for technical-assistance programs, NEC moved toward greater independence from ITT. That company's interest in NEC (held through ISE) was reduced to 9.3 percent by 1970, and eliminated completely by 1978. Similarly, NEC shares retained after the war by Sumitomo-affiliated companies were gradually sold off, an action that reduced the Sumitomo group's interest in NEC from 38 percent in 1961 to 28 percent in 1982.

NEC's competitive advantage in labor costs eroded continually from the mid-1960s, when worker scarcity became apparent, until the early 1980s. This, together with President Richard Nixon's decision to remove the U.S. dollar from the gold standard in 1971 and the effects of the Arab oil embargo of 1973, profoundly compromised NEC's competitive standing. The company was forced into a seven-month retrenchment program in 1974, losing precious momentum in its competition with European and American firms.

Pursuit of C&C Vision Beginning in Late 1970s

In an effort to promote Japanese electronics companies, the Japanese government pushed through a series of partnership agreements among the Big Six computer makers: NEC, Fujitsu, Hitachi, Mitsubishi, Oki, and Toshiba. NEC and Toshiba formed a joint venture, which gave both companies an opportunity to pool their resources and eliminate redundant research.

However, a subsequent attempt by NEC to enter the personal computer market failed miserably. Still, NEC, choosing to work with Honeywell instead of building IBM compatibles, invested heavily in its computer operations.

Later in the 1970s, NEC's computer activities suffered from the fall of Honeywell's computer fortunes. NEC recovered by relying more on its ability to develop systems in-house. The company was further spurred on by the visionary Kobayashi's concept of "C&C," his prediction of the future integration of computers and communications. This prescient vision, which was initially scoffed at, was first announced by NEC at INTELCOM 77. By 1984 NEC had sold more than one million personal computers in Japan. By 1990 the company, whose Japanese personal computers used a proprietary NEC operating system, held a commanding 56 percent share of the Japanese market, as well as a top five position in the United States, where it sold PC clones.

Kobayashi, in the meantime, was promoted to chairman and CEO, and succeeded as president first by Tadao Tanaka in 1976, and then Tadahiro Sekimoto in 1980. Under Kobayashi and Tanaka, NEC tripled its sales volume in the ten years to 1980. A greater proportion of those sales than ever before was derived from foreign markets, and between 1981 and 1983 NEC's stock was listed on several European stock exchanges. In 1982 an NEC plant in Scotland began to manufacture memory devices, then in 1987 NEC Technologies (UK) Ltd. was established in the United Kingdom to manufacture printers and other products for the European market. In 1984 NEC, Honeywell, and France's Groupe Bull entered into an agreement involving the manufacture and distribution of NEC mainframe computers; the deal also provided for cross-licensing of patents and copyrights among the three companies. One year earlier, Nippon Electric changed its English-language name to NEC Corporation.

Meanwhile, in the United States NEC formed NEC Electronics, Inc. in 1981 to be the company's manufacturing and marketing arm for semiconductors in the United States. This subsidiary in 1984 opened a $100 million plant in Roseville, California, to manufacture electron devices. In 1989 another U.S. subsidiary, NEC Technologies, Inc., was established to handle the company's computer peripheral operations in the United States.

Increased International Profile in the Early to Mid-1990s

By 1989, NEC's sales had reached ¥3.13 trillion ($21.3 billion). The company's focus on C&C had led it to top five positions in computer chips, computers, and telecommunications equipment. Like IBM, NEC was also vertically integrated, which added to its strength. Although NEC, like other Japanese electronics computers, suffered from the Japanese recession and strong yen of the early 1990s and from increased competition in Japan from U.S. companies, its aggressive pursuit of overseas opportunities helped the company maintain its leading and varied positions.

In Europe, NEC began selling its IBM-compatible PowerMate line in 1991. In late 1993 the relationship between NEC and Groupe Bull was strengthened with an additional NEC investment of ¥7 billion ($64.5 million) in the troubled state-owned computer manufacturer. By 1996 NEC had a 17 percent stake in Groupe Bull. In 1995 NEC spent $170 million to gain a 19.9 percent stake in Packard Bell Electronics, Inc., the leading U.S. marketer of home computers. In February 1996, NEC, Groupe Bull, and Packard Bell entered into a complex three-way arrangement. NEC invested an additional $283 million in Packard Bell, while Packard Bell acquired the assets of Groupe Bull's PC subsidiary, Zenith Data Systems. In June of that same year, NEC and Packard Bell merged their PC businesses outside of China and Japan into a new firm called Packard Bell NEC Inc., with NEC investing another $300 million for a larger stake in Packard Bell. Packard Bell NEC immediately became the world's fourth largest PC maker, trailing only Compaq, IBM, and Apple.

As the 1990s progressed, NEC increasingly looked to parts of Asia outside Japan for manufacturing and sales opportunities, particularly in semiconductors, transmission systems, cellular phones, and PCs. During fiscal 1996, for example, NEC entered into several joint ventures in China for the production and marketing of PBXs, PCs, and digital microwave communications systems and in Indonesia for the manufacture of semiconductors. In May 1997 NEC took a 30 percent stake in a $1 billion joint venture to construct the largest semiconductor factory in China.

In 1994 NEC announced the development of the SX-4 series of supercomputers, touted as the world's fastest. U.S.-based competitor Cray Research Inc. later filed a complaint with the U.S. Commerce Department accusing NEC of dumping the series in the U.S. market. The Commerce Department in March 1997 ruled in Cray Research's favor and imposed a 454 percent tariff on NEC's supercomputers. NEC's subsequent appeals of this ruling failed.

By 1996, Sekimoto had become chairman of NEC and Hisashi Kaneko was serving as president (Kobayashi died in 1996, when he still held the post of honorary chairman). During the 1990s, these executives had led NEC to increase the share of its sales derived outside Japan from 20 percent in 1990 to 28 percent in 1996. Nonetheless, NEC also kept its sights on its home market; NEC's share of the domestic PC market had fallen to about 50 percent by 1996, leading to a plan to sell IBM-compatible computers in Japan for the first time. In October 1997 NEC began selling PCs in Japan with Intel microprocessors and the Windows 98 operating system. The move to belatedly adopt what had become the international PC standard was made to support NEC's drive to increase its share of the global PC market.

Struggling and Restructuring: Late 1990s and Early 2000s

Through additional investments of $285 million in 1997 and $225 million in 1998 NEC gained majority control of Packard Bell NEC, which became a subsidiary of the Japanese firm. NEC and Groupe Bull had now infused more than $2 billion into Packard Bell, but the U.S. firm continued to hemorrhage, posting losses of more than $1 billion in 1997 and 1998. The company and its U.S.-based manufacturing simply could not compete with lower-cost contract manufacturers based in Asia

and elsewhere. Late in 1999, with Packard Bell NEC on its way to posting another loss, NEC pulled the plug. Packard Bell's California plant was closed, and NEC decided to abandon the retail PC market in the United States. The Packard Bell brand disappeared from the U.S. scene. NEC began focusing its U.S. PC efforts on the corporate market, where it sold computers under the NEC brand.

Meanwhile, NEC was being buffeted by a host of additional problems. The prolonged economic downturn in Japan depressed demand for high-tech products, including personal computers and consumer electronics. At the same time, fierce international competition among both electronics and chip makers was cutting drastically into profit margins on consumer electronics and semiconductors. Compounding matters was the economic crisis that erupted in Asia in mid-1997. As a result, net income for fiscal 1998 plummeted 55 percent, and the following year NEC—further battered by a sharp increase in the value of the yen—fell into the red, posting a net loss of ¥157.9 billion ($1.34 billion), its largest loss to that time. In October 1998, in the midst of the latter year, Sekimoto resigned from the chairmanship following the revelation of NEC's involvement in a defense procurement scandal. Executives of a partly owned NEC subsidiary were charged with overbilling Japan's Defense Agency and with bribing officials at the agency to gain business. The executives were later convicted.

At the end of 1999, Hajime Sasaki took over as NEC chairman, and Koji Nishigaki replaced Kaneko as president. Reflecting the profound changes that were needed to turn the company's fortunes around, Sasaki was the first chairman to have come from NEC's semiconductor side, rather than the telecommunications operations, and Nishigaki was the first president to come from the computer-systems divisions as well as the first with a background in marketing rather than engineering. The new managers recognized that they would have to make fundamental changes to the way NEC operated.

To improve profitability, they almost immediately announced that the workforce would be reduced by 10 percent, or 15,000 positions, with 6,000 workers laid off overseas and 9,000 job cuts in Japan coming through attrition (layoffs still being anathema in that society). They began a debt-reduction program to improve NEC's financial structure, which in early 1999 was weighed down by ¥2.38 trillion ($20.13 billion) in liabilities. NEC also shifted its focus from hardware to the Internet and Internet-related software and services, building on its ownership of Biglobe, one of the leading Internet service providers in Japan, boasting 2.7 million members in late 1999, three years after the service's launch. To support this shift, NEC in April 2000 reorganized its operations into three autonomous in-house companies based on customers and markets served: NEC Solutions, providing Internet solutions for corporate customers and individuals; NEC Networks, focusing on Internet solutions for network service providers; and NEC Electron Devices, supplying device solutions for manufacturers of Internet-related hardware. Like other *sogo denki* a traditionally go-it-alone company, NEC began aggressively pursuing joint ventures with its competitors to spread the costs and risks of developing new products. In one of the first such ventures, NEC joined with Hitachi to form Elpida Memory, Inc., to make the dynamic random-access memory chips (DRAMs) used in personal computers. Ventures were also formed with Mitsubishi Electric in the area of display monitors and with Toshiba in space systems. NEC's deemphasis of manufacturing also led to the closure of a number of plants located outside of Japan.

Although these and other initiatives helped NEC return to profitability in fiscal 2000 and 2001, the global downturn in the information technology sector, coupled with heightened competition from China and other low-cost countries and the economic fallout from the terrorist attacks of 9/11, sent the company deep into the red again in fiscal 2002; a net loss of ¥312 billion ($2.35 billion) was reported, reflecting ¥370.47 billion ($2.79 billion) in restructuring and other charges. The semiconductor sector suffered the deepest falloff, with the prices of certain commodity chips plunging by nearly 90 percent. In response, NEC Electron Devices closed down a number of plants and eliminated 4,000 jobs, including 2,500 in Japan. An additional 14,000 job cuts were announced in early 2002, along with additional plant closings and the elimination of certain noncore product lines.

In a further cutback of company assets and in an attempt to raise cash for other initiatives, NEC began taking some of its subsidiaries public. Both NEC Soft, Ltd., a developer of software, and NEC Machinery Corporation, a producer of semiconductor manufacturing machinery and factory automation systems, were taken public in 2000. In February 2002 NEC sold about a one-third interest in NEC Mobiling, Ltd., a distributor of mobile phones and developer of software for mobile and wireless communications network systems, to the public. Later that year, a similar one-third interest was sold to the public in NEC Fielding, Ltd., a provider of maintenance services for computers and computer peripheral products. NEC's most radical such maneuver involved its troubled semiconductor business. In November 2002 all of NEC's semiconductor operations, except for the DRAM business now residing within Elpida Memory, were placed into a separately operating subsidiary called NEC Electronics Corporation. NEC then reduced its stake in the newly formed company to 70 percent through a July 2003 IPO that raised ¥155.4 billion ($1.31 billion).

Restructuring efforts continued in 2003 under the new leadership of Akinobu Kanasugi, who took over as president from Nishigaki, named vice-chairman. Kanasugi had previously been in charge of NEC Solutions. Concurrent with the appointment of the new president, NEC replaced its in-house company structure with a business line structure, with NEC Solutions evolving into an IT Solutions segment (comprising systems integration services, software, and Internet-related services as well as computers and peripherals) and NEC Networks becoming Network Solutions (comprising network integration services as well as telecommunications and broadband Internet equipment). The eventual goal was to merge the information technology and networking groups in order to offer fully integrated ''total'' IT/ networking/telecommunications solutions encompassing software, operational and maintenance services, and equipment. NEC also established a Personal Solutions group to offer a full range of products and services, including Biglobe, to consumers.

The transformation of NEC was far from complete, and its success uncertain—the firm having posted its second straight net loss during fiscal 2003—but the company's restructuring

efforts were as aggressive as, if not more aggressive than, those of the other big Japanese electronics firms. NEC seemed determined to remain among the world's high-tech leaders.

Principal Subsidiaries

NEC Electronics Corporation (70%); NEC Personal Products, Ltd.; NEC AccessTechnica, Ltd.; NEC Kyushu, Ltd.; NEC Kansai, Ltd.; NEC Nexsolutions, Ltd.; NEC Saitama, Ltd.; NEC Systems Integration & Construction, Ltd.; NEC TOKIN Corporation; Japan Aviation Electronics Industry, Limited; NEC Infrontia Corporation; NEC Fielding, Ltd. (67.1%); Nippon Avionics Co., Ltd.; NEC Soft, Ltd. (67.4%); NEC Machinery Corporation (53.9%); NEC Mobiling, Ltd. (67.1%); NEC Electronics America, Inc. (U.S.A.); NEC America, Inc. (U.S.A.); NEC Solutions (America), Inc. (U.S.A.); NEC Computers International B.V. (Netherlands).

Principal Operating Units

IT Solutions; Network Solutions; Personal Solutions; Electron Devices.

Principal Competitors

Hitachi, Ltd.; Toshiba Corporation; Fujitsu Limited; Mitsubishi Electric Corporation.

Further Reading

Brennan, Laura, ''NEC Sets Sights on Europe,'' *PC Week,* February 25, 1991, pp. 121–22.

Bulkeley, William M., ''NEC, Cray Reach Supercomputer Deal for Sales of Japanese Machines in U.S.,'' *Wall Street Journal,* February 28, 2001, p. A3.

Fisher, Andrew, and Alexandra Harney, ''NEC Aims to Be a Fast Learner,'' *Financial Times,* July 7, 2000, p. 26.

Francis, Bob, ''Packard Bell, NEC Join Forces,'' *Computerworld,* June 10, 1996, p. 32.

Guth, Robert A., ''Electronics Giants of Japan Undergo Wrenching Change,'' *Wall Street Journal,* June 20, 2002, pp. A1+.

Hamilton, David P., ''NEC Reports Loss; Chairman Resigns,'' *Asian Wall Street Journal,* October 26, 1998, p. 3.

——, ''NEC's Nishigaki Steps Down As President,'' *Asian Wall Street Journal,* January 21, 2003, p. A1.

——, ''NEC to Boost Investment in Struggling Packard Bell,'' *Asian Wall Street Journal,* August 3, 1998, p. 6.

Hamm, Steve, ''NEC's New Face,'' *PC Week,* June 27, 1994, pp. A1, A8–A9.

Ishizawa, Masato, ''NEC to Make PCs in China,'' *Nikkei Weekly,* January 9, 1995, p. 1.

Keenan, Faith, and Peter Landers, ''Staggering Giants,'' *Far Eastern Economic Review,* April 1, 1999, pp. 10–13.

Kirkpatrick, David, ''Your Next PC May Be Japanese,'' *Fortune,* October 28, 1996, pp. 140+.

Kobayashi, Koji, *The Rise of NEC: How the World's Greatest C&C Company Is Managed,* Cambridge, Mass.: Basil Blackwell Business, 1991.

Kunii, Irene M., ''High-Tech Giants on the Ropes,'' *Business Week,* November 30, 1998, pp. 74, 78.

——, ''Under the Knife: The Global Tech Crunch Forces Chip Giants to Pare Down,'' *Business Week,* September 10, 2001, p. 62.

Landers, Peter, ''Japan's NEC Feels Crunch, but the Internet Promises Relief,'' *Wall Street Journal,* October 15, 1999, p. A10.

Landers, Peter, and Erik Guyot, ''NEC and Acer, Asian Tech Giants, Prepare to Refocus,'' *Wall Street Journal,* December 13, 2000, p. A22.

''Lay-offs with No Sign of Revival,'' *Economist,* September 1, 2001, pp. 51–52.

Mitsusada, Hisayuki, ''Bucking Industry Trend, NEC Opts for Domestic Production,'' *Nikkei Weekly,* July 24, 1995, p. 8.

Nakamoto, Michiyo, and Julia Cuthbertson, ''NEC Bows to U.S. Technology in New Generation PCs,'' *Financial Times,* September 25, 1997, p. 25.

Nakamoto, Michiyo, and William Dawkins, ''Sony and NEC Forced into Reorganizations,'' *Financial Times,* March 28, 1996, p. 30.

NEC Corporation: The First 80 Years, Tokyo: NEC Corporation, 1984.

''NEC Plans to Spin Off Chip Business,'' *Nikkei Weekly,* May 20, 2002.

Neff, Robert, et al., ''Why NEC Has U.S. Companies 'Shaking in Their Boots,' '' *Business Week,* March 26, 1990, pp. 90–92.

Nishio, Natsuo, and Hiroyuki Kachi, ''NEC Unit, Seiko Stir the Market with Big IPOs,'' *Asian Wall Street Journal,* June 17, 2003, p. M1.

Smith, Lee, ''Japan's Two-Fisted Telephone Maker,'' *Fortune,* June 25, 1984, p. 31.

''What's Japanese for 'Synergy'?,'' *Economist,* November 4, 1995, p. 72.

Wiegner, Kathleen K., ''Go Tell the Spartans,'' *Forbes,* December 30, 1985, p. 91.

Zimmerman, Michael R., ''NEC Plans New Lines and Sales Channels,'' *PC Week,* September 21, 1992, p. 173.

—update: David E. Salamie

Neuberger Berman Inc.

605 Third Avenue
New York, New York 10158
U.S.A.
Telephone: (212) 476-9000
Toll Free: (800) 877-9700
Fax: (212) 476-9890
Web site: http://www.nb.com

Public Company
Incorporated: 1939 as Neuberger & Berman
Employees: 1,247
Total Assets: $4.1 billion (2002)
Stock Exchanges: New York
Ticker Symbol: NEU
NAIC: 523120 Securities Brokerage; 522110 Commercial Banking

Neuberger Berman Inc. is the holding company for the venerable money management firm Neuberger Berman LLC. Neuberger Berman had about $56.3 billion in assets under management in 2003. About $40 billion was in individual accounts, the rest in mutual funds. Neuberger Berman also offers trust services in certain areas.

The company treasures experience in its portfolio managers; job candidates are expected to have weathered several bear markets before they will be considered. Many Neuberger Berman partners have been in the business more than 25 years. Founder Roy Neuberger once quipped, ''We don't want anyone learning to shave on our clients' faces!''

Origins

Company founder Roy Neuberger was born on July 21, 1903, in Bridgeport, Connecticut. He moved to New York City to be raised by a sister after he became an orphan at age 12. Neuberger's passion for art was in evidence by the time he was studying journalism at New York University. After taking a few art classes, he then worked in interior decorating at a department store.

Neuberger traveled to Paris in 1925 to continue his art education at the Sorbonne. While there, he became enthralled by the works of Vincent van Gogh. Touched by van Gogh's struggle with poverty and obscurity, Neuberger resolved to support living artists by collecting their works.

First, he had to make his fortune. He returned to New York and became a stockbroker at Halle & Stieglitz in 1929. It was probably not the best time to set out on Wall Street, but Neuberger's decision to short Radio Corporation of America stock before the crash earned him a reputation for uncannily good instincts.

Neuberger formed Neuberger & Berman in 1939 with partners Robert Berman and Howard Lipman. The firm's first specialty would be its most enduring, and most profitable: managing money for ''high net-worth individuals.''

Early No-Load Fund in 1950

Neuberger & Berman also launched one of the first no-load mutual funds, the Guardian Mutual Fund, in 1950. Roy Neuberger personally managed Guardian until 1978.

Roy Neuberger turned over daily management of the firm to a six-person executive committee in 1968. He would continue working at the firm for decades, however. Roy Neuberger was also a fitness enthusiast, swimming and taking long walks into his 90s.

He also remained active in his patronage of the arts. The Neuberger Museum of Art opened at the Purchase campus of the State University of New York in 1974. Its collection was based on 500 sculptures and paintings from leading contemporary artists donated by Roy Neuberger. Neuberger and his wife, Marie, would give away hundreds more art works to more than 60 other museums and universities.

Buying Manhattan Fund in 1979

Neuberger & Berman—then called the Neuberger & Berman Management Company—acquired Manhattan Fund Inc.

from CNA Financial Corporation in 1979. The Manhattan Fund, formed in the bull market of the mid-1960s, was able to replicate a measure of its early success under new ownership.

Neuberger & Berman was managing about $11 billion in assets in the mid-1980s. This more than doubled within a few years. The firm managed more than $24 billion in the early 1990s. It had about 600 employees and 49 partners. Plans for expansion consumed much of the rest of the decade.

A short-lived joint venture was formed with Banque Nationale de Paris in 1992. It ended four years later. Neuberger & Berman underwent an abortive, six-month search for a buyer in 1995. Most of the suitors were European banks, reported *Institutional Investor,* and Neuberger Berman's partners felt that the difference in cultures was insurmountable.

Late 1990s IPO

By the late 1990s, Neuberger & Berman had grown to 59 partners managing $56 billion in assets. When the firm began openly contemplating a stock offering in early 1998, the market for money management firms was hot, reported the *Wall Street Journal.* Neuberger Berman was one of the largest, and was looking to float 15 percent of its shares to raise $250 million to acquire other money management companies.

The 48-year-old Guardian Fund had grown to $9 billion in assets, and the Partners Fund was worth $7 billion. Neuberger Berman also had created a Genesis Fund, then valued at $2.5 billion, to invest in small companies. The company traditionally focused on value stocks, rather than growth stocks. It reoriented the venerable Manhattan Fund toward growth in 1997, however, and the next year launched another growth portfolio, the Millennium Fund. By 1999, the company also had one international fund and three bond portfolios in addition to its five value-oriented funds.

While 1998 was a great year for such tech stocks as Dell and Yahoo!, it was one of the worst for value-oriented investors, who saw miniscule gains. They had been slipping behind growth-oriented counterparts since the mid-1990s.

Neuberger & Berman canceled its initial public offering (IPO) plans in October 1998, citing the volatile stock market. The offering did go through a year later, in October 1999. Fifteen percent of its shares was offered, priced at $32 a share. Within a month the firm had announced a stock buyback plan due to a slide in its share price.

By this time, the company had dropped the ampersand from its name, becoming Neuberger Berman Inc. Neuberger Berman had a new chief executive, Wall Street veteran Jeffrey B. Lane. He had been brought in before the IPO from Travelers Group Inc. Lane would include real estate investment trusts (REITs) and bonds in the firm's repertoire; both areas would perform well as investors' affinity for stocks waned following the collapse of the tech bubble in the late 1990s.

New Funds for the New Millennium

High-flying Chicago fund manager Michael Fasciano sold his company to Neuberger Berman in October 2000, during a period of industry consolidation. He had started his one fund in 1987 with $1 million; a dozen years later, it peaked at assets of $420 million—too much for Fasciano to successfully invest on his own. The next month, Neuberger Berman bought Delta Capital's private asset management business, and in the first quarter of 2000 added Executive Money Management (EMM), a New York firm specializing in managing money for high net worth individuals, or those with more than $500,000 to invest. Neuberger Berman also set up a unit to cater to individually managed funds for professional athletes.

After receiving a national trust bank charter in early 2001, Neuberger Berman opened Neuberger Berman National Trust Co. in Seattle and a Los Angeles office soon after. The firm had had state charters in Delaware, Florida, and New York since the mid-1990s. The trust banks allowed Neuberger Berman to offer a much more comprehensive and intimate array of wealth management services.

In 2001, Neuberger Berman was rolling out its ''Women Partnership'' program aimed at high-net-worth businesswomen. The company had been showing impressive results with its Socially Responsive Fund, started in 1994. This fund evaluated companies on such factors as diversity in employment, and avoided connections to alcohol, tobacco, firearms, gambling, and nuclear power. Neuberger Berman's socially responsible fund focused on larger stocks than most of its peers, companies with a market capitalization of $1 billion or more.

Neuberger Berman replaced its Boston office with growth stock-oriented investment managers hired from Chicago's Northern Trust Corp. in December 2002. The Boston talent had fared poorly in the bear market of the previous three years. The Manhattan, Millennium, and Century Funds were affected; the three had combined assets of $352 million.

Neuberger Berman developed a marketing relationship with Merrill Lynch & Co. in 2002. It also had A.G. Edwards & Sons Inc. take two of its closed-end REIT funds to public offerings. Neuberger Berman had operating revenues of $650.8 million in 2002.

Key Dates:
1939: Neuberger & Berman is formed.
1950: Early no-load Guardian Mutual Fund is launched.
1979: Manhattan Fund is acquired.
1999: Neuberger Berman floats 15 percent of the firm in an initial public offering.
2000: Fasciano Fund, Delta Capital unit, and Executive Money Management are acquired.
2001: Neuberger Berman receives a national trust bank charter.

Lehman Brothers was in talks to acquire Neuberger Berman in the middle of 2003. The purchase price was estimated at $3 billion. Asset management was one of the most stable businesses in the financial services industry, and Lehman had lacked such a unit since it was spun off from American Express in 1994.

Principal Subsidiaries

Executive Money Management; Neuberger Berman National Trust Co.; Neuberger Berman LLC.

Principal Divisions

Private Asset Management; Neuberger Berman Trust Companies; Executive Money Management; Neuberger Berman Mutual Funds; Advisory Services; Institutional Separate Accounts; Broker Advised Products; Professional Investor Clearing Service; Research Sales.

Principal Operating Units

Wealth Management Services; Mutual Funds and Institutional; Professional Securities Services.

Principal Competitors

BlackRock Inc.; FMR Corporation; M.J. Whitman LLC; Old Mutual (US) Holdings, Inc.; Tweedy, Browne Company LLC; U.S. Trust Corporation.

Further Reading

Ackermann, Matt, "Northern Guarding Clients As Neuberger Hires Team," *American Banker,* December 19, 2002, p. 10.

Anderson, Amy L., "Neuberger Berman Buying N.Y. Company," *American Banker,* December 28, 2000, p. 10.

Atlas, Riva, "Neuberger's Old-Fashioned Dilemma," *Institutional Investor,* December 1998, p. 163.

Bergen, Kathy, "Fasciano to Sell Fund Company to Neuberger Berman," *Chicago Tribune,* October 18, 2000.

Bianco, Anthony, "At Neuberger & Berman the Status Quo Is Quite Enough," *Business Week,* October 6, 1986, p. 77.

——, "When the Dow Took a Dive, Roy Neuberger Didn't Even Blink," *Business Week,* October 6, 1986, p. 76.

Birger, Jon, "Tough Market Awaits Two Money Managers: Neuberger, BlackRock Eye IPOs," *Crain's New York Business,* September 20, 1999, p. 3.

——, "Value Funds Struggling to Keep Low-Ratio Faith: Humiliating Returns Prompt Neuberger to Start Diversifying; Purists See Heresy," *Crain's New York Business,* February 15, 1999, p. 17.

Boroson, Warren, "Boring Can Be Beautiful," *Record* (Bergen County, N.J.), August 7, 1996, p. B1.

Braga, Michael, "Neuberger Flexing Trust Power," *Miami Daily Business Review,* June 1, 1999, p. A2.

Brewster, Deborah, "Second Passion of a Wall Street Veteran," *Financial Times* (London), January 3, 2003, p. 15.

Brown, Ken, "Neuberger Berman Is Acquiring Fasciano," *Wall Street Journal,* October 17, 2000, p. C26.

Chu, Kathy, "Socially Responsible Fund Excels—Neuberger Berman Offering Tops Market with Returns As It Eschews Some Stocks," *Wall Street Journal,* May 15, 2003, p. D7.

Francis, David R., "One Fund's Formula: Put Stock in Women-Run Firms," *Christian Science Monitor,* February 10, 2003, p. 15.

Fredrickson, Tom, "Analyzing the Situation; Investment Chief Will Work to Hone Research Reputation at Neuberger," *Crain's New York Business,* February 10, 2003, p. 25.

Gabriel, Frederick P., Jr., "Neuberger Itching to Score with Top Athletes; Kicks Off Special Unit to Manage Pros' Bucks," *Investment News,* March 6, 2000, p. 10.

Gewirtz, Lisa, and Josh Karlen, "Neuberger Too Pricey for Lehman?," *Daily Deal,* June 27, 2003.

Gould, Carole, "Neuberger Berman Focus Fund," *New York Times,* May 14, 2000.

Healy, Beth, "Neuberger Fires Boston Fund Group; Chicago Team Replaces 3 Investment Managers," *Boston Globe,* December 18, 2002, p. C1.

Lenzner, Robert, "The Trials of a Whistle-Blower," *Boston Globe,* July 22, 1990, p. 59.

Lim, Paul J., "Neuberger & Berman Planning an IPO . . . Now?," *Los Angeles Times,* August 20, 1998, p. 4.

Loftus, Peter, "Neuberger Team Purges 3 Portfolios," *Wall Street Journal,* April 17, 2003, p. D7.

Lucchetti, Aaron, "IPO, New CEO May Make for Awkward Mix," *Wall Street Journal,* August 30, 1998, p. C1.

——, "Neuberger Sets Share Buyback Soon After IPO," *Wall Street Journal,* November 3, 1999, p. C20.

McBride, Caryn A., "Money Can Buy Happiness—Just Ask Roy Neuberger," *Westchester County Business Journal,* May 10, 1993, p. 6.

McGough, Robert, "Neuberger, After Half Century, Considers IPO," *Wall Street Journal,* April 22, 1998, p. C1.

——, "Neuberger & Berman Cancels IPO Plan," *Wall Street Journal,* October 7, 1998, p. C23.

Marcial, Gene G., "How a Go-Go Fund Is Coming Back from the Dumps," *Business Week,* October 3, 1983, p. 120.

Metz, Robert, "Fund Frenzy of Yesteryear," *New York Times,* August 18, 1980, p. D4.

"Neuberger Revives Stalled IPO Plans; Partners to Vote," *Wall Street Journal,* July 26, 1999, p. C19.

Neuberger, Roy R., and Alfred and Roma Connable, *Eighty Years in the World of Art: The Passionate Collector,* New York: John Wiley & Sons, 2002.

"Neuberger to Roll Out Women's Site," *Fund Marketing Alert,* June 4, 2001, p. 2.

O'Brian, Bridget, "Neuberger's Stock Rises, Defying a Trend," *Wall Street Journal,* November 28, 2000, p. C29.

Oppel, Richard A., Jr., "Neuberger & Berman Is Ready to Go Public, But at What Price?," *New York Times,* October 5, 1999, p. 15.

Polyak, Ilana, "It's Now or Never for Neuberger: Money Manager's IPO Won't Wait," *Investment News,* September 20, 1999, p. 1.

Rasmussen, Eric, "Neuberger & Berman Rolls Out IPO Carpet," *Investment Management Weekly,* August 24, 1998.

Ring, Niamh, "Neuberger Berman Receives National Trust Charter," *American Banker,* January 10, 2001, p. 3.

Robaton, Anna, "IPO a No-Go, It Needs a Cash Source: Neuberger May Plan Its Own (on the) Block Party," *Investment News,* November 16, 1998, p. 3.

——, "Neuberger Retools After IPO Is Nixed: Will Mutual Fund Company Have to Sell?," *Crain's New York Business,* November 23, 1998, p. 14.

Sidel, Robin, and Susanne Craig, "Lehman Talks with Neuberger About a Deal," *Wall Street Journal,* June 26, 2003, p. C1.

Southall, Brooke, "Firm Rebuilding Itself As Mutual Fund Powerhouse; Makeover Renews Neuberger," *Investment News,* June 9, 2003, p. 3.

——, "Neuberger Is on Its Feet and Walking a New Line; Revamped Leadership, Portfolio Managers Execute Turnaround Through Mutual Funds," *Crain's New York Business,* June 16, 2003, p. 17.

Steiger, Heidi L., ed., *Wealthy & Wise (Secrets About Money),* New York: John Wiley & Sons, 2002.

Ward, Sandra, "The Return of Value," *Barron's,* August 7, 2000, pp. 28–32.

Wells, David, "Lehman in Talks to Buy Neuberger Berman," *Financial Times* (London), June 26, 2003, p. 1.

—Frederick C. Ingram

Oji Paper Co., Ltd.

Ginza 4-7-5, Chuo-kuTokyo, 104-0061
Japan
Telephone: + 81-3-3563-1111
Fax: +81-3-3563-1135
Web site: http://www.ojipaper.co.jp

Public Company
Incorporated: 1949
Employees: 21,683
Sales: ¥1.09 trillion ($9.08 billion) (2002)
Stock Exchanges: Tokyo
NAIC: 322110 Pulp Mills; 322121 Paper (Except
   Newsprint) Mills (pt); 322122 Newsprint Mills (pt);
   322130 Paperboard Mills (pt); 322222 Coated and
   Laminated Paper Manufacturing (pt); 322291 Sanitary
   Paper Product Manufacturing (pt)

Oji Paper Co., Ltd., Japan's second largest paper producer, operates 16 mills in Japan that annually manufacture over seven million tons of printing and writing papers, corrugated board and boxboard, as well as packaging and wrapping papers, paper-based containers, thermal papers, plastics, and disposable diapers. Oji is also involved in the production of chemicals for papermaking and packaging. With over 120 subsidiaries and affiliates worldwide, Oji's operations extend throughout Asia, Europe, and the Americas. As Japan's paper market has become saturated, Oji, like its rival paper producers, has made expansion abroad, particularly in other parts of Asia, its key strategy.

Early Years: 1873–1933

In 1873 Eiichi Shibusawa founded Japan's first private paper manufacturer and the first Japanese company to employ Western papermaking technology. The venture, called Shoshi-Gaisha, received financial backing from the Japanese government and from two of Japan's prominent *zaibatsu*, or conglomerates, Mitsui and Shimada. Shibusawa, on the heels of a major success in which he had imported, assembled, and successfully started up Japan's first Western-style cotton-textile mill, per-

suaded his investors that he could do the same thing in the manufacture of paper. The project involved the purchase and assembly of a British paper mill. Two years later, in 1875, Shoshi-Gaisha's first mill, the Oji mill, went into production. Shoshi-Gaisha was, at first, unprofitable, but as Japanese paper consumers began to accept the first domestic paper, the company became profitable.

The 1880s showed substantial growth for Shoshi-Gaisha but little in the way of profits for the company's investors. By 1890, though still not very profitable, Shoshi-Gaisha had virtually monopolized the manufacture of Western-style paper in Japan. Shibusawa had sent his nephew, Heizaburo Okawa, abroad to study the latest foreign technology, and by 1890, a more efficient and profitable production system was developed. Shibusawa by this time needed fresh capital for Shoshi-Gaisha, and he approached the Mitsui Bank. Mitsui Bank, a leading member of the Mitsui group and one of Shoshi-Gaisha's initial backers, agreed to provide more funds to revamp Shoshi-Gaisha's production system. Hikojiro Nakamigawa, managing director of Mitsui Bank, then used the bank's equity position in the company to remove Shibusawa and Okawa, who was by then Japan's foremost papermaking expert, from Shoshi-Gaisha's management.

Nakamigawa brought in Ginjiro Fujihara from another of the huge *zaibatsu's* many operations, along with a new management and production team. In 1893 the company's name was changed to the Oji Paper Manufacturing Company. The new management team began the process of building Oji into one of Japan's largest and most successful industrial organizations.

In the years preceding and following the turn of the century Oji's growth paralleled the rapid expansion of the entire Mitsui *zaibatsu*. Abandoning many of its traditional craft-oriented and retail businesses, the Mitsui *zaibatsu* focused its growth on heavy industry. By utilizing a worldwide marketing strategy, the *zaibatsu* increased all of the group's sales and global markets. Shortages in consumer and industrial goods caused by Europe's retooling to meet the demands of World War I opened up new opportunities for Japanese business on a global scale. During World War I Japan's exports tripled, reaching more than $1 billion annually. Industrial production as a whole quadru-

Company Perspectives:

The twenty-first century will be a period of major change on a global scale, driven by advances in information technology, the trend toward globalization, and efforts to overcome urgent environmental problems. Oji Paper has set a new goal for this new and unexplored era. That goal is to become an Asian corporate citizen domiciled in Japan operating under our fundamental corporate ideals of contribution to the environment and culture, a commitment to reform and speed, and a determination to build and maintain trust throughout the world. Oji Paper is determined to achieve robust growth in the twenty-first century, while enhancing its total group strength.

pled, and during these years, Oji's sales spiraled, creating even greater opportunities in business on a level that was international in scope. The company also became one of Japan's largest employers.

The man chosen by the *zaibatsu* to guide Oji though this period of large growth was Ginjiro Fujihara. A strong proponent of all types of Japanese expansionism, Fujihara boasted in one of his books that Japan's enterprising traders would go to all points on the globe, no matter how intimidating the climate in an effort to sell Japanese goods and promote Japanese business interests. Fujihara also believed that the country's strong leanings toward military imperialism was good for Japan, in general, and Oji's business, specifically. He felt that investing in the nation's military power would result in Japan's industrial producers having more power in the international marketplace.

1930s and World War II

In 1933, in the midst of a period of rapid industrial growth, the company merged with Japan's two other paper producing giants, Fuji Paper and Karafuto Industry. The new coalition created a company that supplied Japan with 78 percent of its paper needs. Japan established a puppet government in Manchuria in 1932, and in 1937 invaded China. Despite its isolating effect, war, it seemed, was good for business. During this time, Fujihara became one of the leaders of Japan's heavily industrialized, and militarized, economy as a result of his successes in running Oji. While still in control of the company, he was appointed director of the Industrial Equipment Management Control Association, a control corporation whose sole purpose was to remove obstacles to growth in the Japanese economy and to foster the establishment of new business enterprises.

During World War II Oji participated in wartime production to the extent it was able. Fujihara bowed to government demands that production be enhanced, but as a member of the Cabinet Advisory Council Fujihara spoke out against the National Socialist goal of nationalizing industry. Fujihara became the most powerful businessman in Japan in 1943, when he was appointed to a high government post, from which he continued to defend private enterprise. In 1944 Fujihara became head of the Ministry of Munitions, a challenging post at the end of the war, with labor and materials in short supply. While Fujihara

was certainly patriotic and was equally opposed to nationalization of Japanese industry, his opinion of the war itself is less clear. Despite critical shortages of raw materials, Oji, like every other large Japanese business, contributed its share of production during the war years.

Postwar Developments

With the end of the war and the Allied occupation of Japan, Fujihara and many other business leaders were stripped of their authority. The Holding Company Liquidation Commission (HCLC) was formed by the occupation forces. The commission's job was to break up the huge *zaibatsu* that for centuries had monopolized Japanese trade and industry. The HCLC's purpose was to install the beginnings of a democratic, capitalistic system controlled by a greater number of smaller groups of Japanese businessmen and entrepreneurs, and to reestablish the Japanese economy on a self-supporting basis as quickly as possible. In all, 42 holding companies were dissolved. The Mitsui *zaibatsu's* holdings came through the process relatively intact. Oji, however, was one of Mitsui's few casualties, and, in 1949, was forced to deconcentrate. The company was broken into three separate paper manufacturing businesses, Jujo Paper Co., Ltd.; Honshu Paper Co., Ltd.; and Tomakomai Paper Co., Ltd. Tomakomai Paper was renamed Oji Paper Co., Ltd., after a brief time. The restructuring that resulted from the application of the postwar Excessive Economic Power Deconcentration Law was completed in August 1949.

Along with the forced breakup, Oji was faced with the problem of diminished supplies of imported pulp to feed the company's paper mills. The loss of forest resources in Manchuria, Korea, and Sakhalin after the war led to a boom in the domestic production of pulp. The boom in turn created a serious threat to Japan's remaining forests. The Council for the Conservation of Natural Resources, which was headed by an Oji vice-president and forestry expert, Jun'ichiro Kobayashi, put the brakes on the reckless depletion of Japan's forest.

Using his newly appointed post on the council, Kobayashi used postwar Allied competition to pressure the United States to allow the development of the Alaska Pulp Company, in 1953. The United States agreed to Kobayashi's plan, knowing that the alternative available to Oji and its sister companies was to try to exploit the Soviet Union's vast Siberian forests. U.S. leadership was wary of permitting the Soviets and Japan to develop any strong business affiliations. After a series of meetings in Washington, D.C., with the State Department and the Interior Department, tentative approval was given to form a company to import Alaskan forest products to Japan. In 1953 the Alaska Pulp Company was established with start-up capital of about $1 million. After a great deal of trans-Pacific negotiation, an additional $20 million was raised for the venture, half from U.S. investors and half from Japanese. The Alaska Pulp project was the first large postwar overseas investment made by the Japanese paper industry and helped to revitalize U.S.-Japanese business relations.

With the end of the Allied occupation in 1952, prospects for all Japanese businesses were good. Slowly those who had reigned supreme as the leaders of the prewar *zaibatsu* regained much of the control and influence they had prior to 1945.

Key Dates:

1873: Eiichi Shibusawa founds Shoshi-Gaisha.
1890: Shoshi-Gaisha changes its name to Oji Paper Manufacturing Company.
1933: Oji Paper Manufacturing Company merges with Fuji Paper and Karafuto Industry.
1953: Oji forms Alaska Pulp Company.
1970: Oji merges with Kita Nippon Paper Company.
1990: Oji forms Howe Sound Pulp and Paper Limited, a joint venture with Canfor Corporation.
1993: Oji merges with Kanzaki Paper Manufacturing Co., Ltd.
1996: Oji merges with Honshu Paper Co.
1999: Oji closes Kumano paper mill.
2001: Soichiro Suzuki takes charge of Oji.
2003: Oji announces plans for new plant in Nantong City, China.

Ginjiro Fujihara, Oji's president for many years, died in 1960 at the age of 91. His disciples were instrumental in the reorganization of the paper and pulp industry in Japan and became presidents of the four largest paper companies to emerge after the war.

Growth in the 1960s and 1970s

The new Japanese industrial sector was very different from what had existed prior to World War II. During the early 1960s Oji was one of many companies that underwent a complete modernization of its production methods and milling plants. These changes in the company's production techniques took place at a time when Japan's labor movement was also going through a new, more progressive transformation. The Japanese worker had more power than ever before; and the layoffs and firings that took place as a result of the modernization of Oji's mills caused numerous problems including strikes and, in turn, retaliatory lockouts.

Nevertheless, Oji continued its growth in the paper business with virtually no attempt at diversification. In 1970 Oji merged with Kita Nippon Paper Company, and several years later merged again, this time with Nippon Pulp Industries. A pulp mill was constructed in New Zealand in 1971 that was followed by the construction of another mill in Brazil the following year.

With so much expansion, Oji wanted to insure itself of a continuous supply of forest products to provide necessary raw materials. To this end, the company established the Institute for Forest Tree Improvement, in Kuriyama and Kameyama. One of the most important contributions made by the institute was the Biomass Conversion project. Sponsored by the Japanese government, the project developed a new variety of poplar tree capable of growing three meters in the same number of months.

Over time, Oji also became more attuned to the advantages offered by diversification. The company started to develop production methods for value-added papers, that is, photographic papers, sanitary products, and thermal and other forms of communication-equipment papers. In the 1970s and 1980s, Oji ex-panded its line of specialty and consumer-oriented paper products. In 1989, the company began producing and marketing its own line of disposable diapers. Under the guidance of Oji's president, Kazuo Chiba, the company was in the early 1990s actively involved in new product research and development to further broaden its product lines.

Rapid Growth in the 1980s

Fueled by the booming Japanese economy of the 1980s, the nation's paper industry as a whole rapidly expanded its capacity. As part of this process, in 1988 Oji participated in a $1 billion joint venture with the Canadian-based Canfor Corporation to form Howe Sound Pulp & Paper Ltd. Howe's first production mill in Vancouver was completed in 1990, and was capable of producing 585 tons of newsprint and 1,000 tons of market kraft paper per day. Oji marketed the newsprint, while the kraft pulp was sold by Canfor Pulp Sales. Howe got off to a rocky start, though. Low pulp prices and operating difficulties in the mill eroded early profits.

Undeterred, Oji further increased its size and production capabilities in 1989 as a result of another merger with Toyo Pulp Company. At that time, the company's annual output of newsprint had reached almost 900,000 tons. The company produced as many as 200 different types of newsprint to meet the specific demands of its different customers.

Consolidation in the 1990s

By the early 1990s, however, Oji and its competitors had created a supply glut that threatened to swallow the industry. Oversupply led to a collapse in paper prices, at the same time that demand for paper was flagging because of the crash of the entire Japanese economy. In response, the major players in the industry sought to retain or even increase their market share by slashing paper prices. Rather than stabilizing the industry, however, this strategy wrought further devastation. The *Wall Street Journal Europe* called the paper industry's situation the "worst of the postwar era." Like other paper companies, Oji's financial reports reflected the industry's hard times. The company's pretax profits for fiscal 1990 dropped 33 percent from the previous year. Fiscal 1991 proved no better; Oji's pretax profit plummeted another 46 percent, while sales fell 1.3 percent.

With the failure of their price-cutting strategy, Japan's leading paper manufacturers began to consolidate as a means to eliminate excess capacity. In 1992, Jujo Paper Co. (Japan's third largest producer) and Sanyo-Kokusaku Pulp Co. (Japan's fifth largest paper company) agreed to merge, setting off a nearly decade-long spree of mergers and acquisitions in the industry. The Jujo-Sanyo combination, rechristened Nippon Paper Industries Co., surpassed Oji to become the nation's largest paper company with a market share of 17.3 percent. Oji responded in 1993 when it merged with Kanzaki Paper Manufacturing Co., the seventh largest paper company in Japan. The two firms complemented each other. Oji was a dominant force in general paper products, including newsprint and printing paper (though Oji's share of Japan's printing paper market had slipped behind Nippon Paper's). Meanwhile Kanzaki (a spinoff from the pre-World War II Oji Paper) specialized in higher-end surface treated and processed paper products.

Oji further reconnected with its roots three years later, in 1996, when it merged with Honshu Paper Co. Ltd., Japan's top producer of paperboards. (Like Kanzaki, Honshu was separated from Oji during the postwar deconcentration.) The resulting company boasted Japan's largest production capacity in paper and paperboard, surpassing its chief rival, Nippon Paper Industries, and ringing up sales of ¥1 trillion. Yet Oji's eye was not squarely on the bottom line. As an analyst for SBC Warburg Securities explained to the *Asian Wall Street Journal*, ''[Oji is] thinking about winning market share more than about profitability.''

Indeed, while the Honshu merger added bulk to Oji, it did not immediately rejuvenate the company. In fact, the acquisitions of Kanzaki and Honshu presented Oji with new challenges. Oji was now faced with redundancies, overlapping subsidiaries, and unanticipated inefficiencies. By 1997, the company had sprawled to encompass 88 distinct groups, a reflection of its unwillingness to alter its cozy internal practices. As the *Nikkei Business Daily* noted, Oji was known for its ''calm corporate atmosphere,'' in which its management earned the top salaries in the industry and brutal efficiency had never been required.

Oji's traditional ways began to change in 1999, when the company reported its first postwar annual net loss. The company began consolidating its sprawling operations. In March, Oji announced it would cut its workforce by 1,500 over a three-year period. A few months later, Oji closed its Kumano paper mill in the Wakayama Prefecture. The company also began to tackle its problems with overlapping operations, particularly in the low margin paperboard products sector.

Adjustments and Renewal: 2000 and Beyond

In 2000, Oji received an additional spur to improve its profitability when its top competitor, Nippon Paper Industries, announced it was merging with the Daishowa Paper Manufacturing Co. The result of this union—Nippon Unipac Holding Co.—had sales of ¥1.22 trillion and a 32.2 percent share of the Japanese market. With this last installment in the decade-long series of acquisitions, the Japanese paper industry was largely controlled by two major powers: Oji and Nippon Unipac. Oji was falling behind.

To reverse this trend, Oji brought Shoichiro Suzuki to the helm in 2001. Suzuki immediately announced new short and long-term goals for the company, and instituted additional restructuring steps. ''To maintain profitability, the company needs to continue efforts to streamline operations and secure new earnings sources,'' Suzuki told the *Nikkei Report*. ''We intend to take a fresh look at every aspect of our operations.'' He paid special attention to the company's paperboard affiliates. Oji turned four cardboard-related affiliates into a wholly owned subsidiary and then merged the subsidiary with the newly created Oji Paperboard Co., a centralized Oji group that oversaw production and sales of cardboard material. This move was expected to save ¥10.5 billion ($87 million).

Suzuki also formally conceded what market analysts had long recognized: the Japanese paper market was saturated. Consolidating inefficient operations and bolstering domestic paper prices would only go so far. What Oji needed most was new markets, and Suzuki pinpointed Asia as the region in which his company should focus its expansion. China, in particular, was promising terrain. Spurred by its rapid economic growth, China's demand for paper was expected to grow roughly 9 percent a year. In 2001, Oji announced it would invest $1.2 billion in paper producing facilities in Asia during a five-year period. ''Japan will continue to be our home, but we need to expand our 'home' into Asia to keep the company growing,'' an Oji spokesperson told *Dow Jones Commodities Service*.

In keeping with this strategy, in 2002 Oji purchased from Procter & Gamble its P&G Suzhou operation, a paper products manufacturing plant near Shanghai. With this move, Oji gained access to the household products market in Shanghai, China's region with the largest purchasing power. Less than a year later, Oji announced an even bolder move. It would begin construction on a $1.69 billion plant in Nantong City, China. By 2006, the plant was expected to have a production capacity of 600,000 tons per year and to be the world's largest pulp/paper integrated paper works. By 2010 the company estimated that the new plant would account for 18 percent of the firm's current capacity.

Principal Subsidiaries

Oji Paperboard Co., Ltd.; Fuji Paper Co., Ltd.; Nepia Co., Ltd.; Oji Container Co., Ltd.; Chiyoda Container Corporation; Oji Packaging Co., Ltd.; Oji Tac Co., Ltd.; KS-Systems Inc.; Toyo Pack Co., Ltd.; Oji Timber Co., Ltd.; Oji Forestry & Landscaping Co., Ltd.; Oji Logistics Co., Ltd.; Yufutsu Wharf Co., Ltd.; Kokusai Pulp & Paper Co., Ltd.; Oji Trading Co., Ltd.; Oji Engineering Co., Ltd.; Oji Business Center Co., Ltd.; Honshu Toshin Co., Ltd.

Principal Competitors

Georgia-Pacific Corporation; Hokuetsu Paper Mills, Ltd.; International Paper Company; Mitsubishi Paper Mills Limited; Nippon Unipac Holding; Weyerhaeuser Company.

Further Reading

''Japan's Oji Paper to Merge with Kanzaki,'' *Asian Wall Street Journal*, February 1, 1993. ''Jujo Paper Co., Sanyo-Kokusaku Agree to Merge,'' *Wall Street Journal Europe*, July 9, 1992.

''Oji Chief Eyes Asia for New Profit Sources,'' *Nikkei Report*, September 25, 2002.

''Oji Paper Embarks on Drastic Rationalization,'' *Nikkei Business Daily*, September 24, 2002.

Roberts, John G., *Mitsui: Three Centuries of Japanese Business*, New York: Weatherhill, 1989.

Sarmiento, Prime, ''Japan's Oji Paper Plans Huge Expansion in Asia,'' *Dow Jones Commodities Service*, June 13, 2001.

A Vision of the Future, Tokyo: Oji Paper Co., Ltd., [1989].

—William R. Grossman
—update: Rebecca Stanfel

Old Dominion Freight Line, Inc.

500 Old Dominion Way
Thomasville, North Carolina 27360
U.S.A.
Telephone: (336) 889-5000
Fax: (336) 822-5229
Web site: http://www.odfl.com

Public Company
Incorporated: 1950
Employees: 6,895
Sales: $556.5 million (2002)
Stock Exchanges: NASDAQ
Ticker Symbol: ODFL
NAIC: 484122 General Freight Trucking, Long Distance,
   Less Than Truckload; 484121 General Freight
   Trucking, Long Distance, Truckload; 481112
   Scheduled Freight Air Transportation

Old Dominion Freight Line, Inc. provides less-than-load trucking (LTL) services for general commodities, such as textiles and consumer goods, and serves more than 20,000 points across North America. The company operates more than 115 local, regional, and interregional service centers in 38 states, where partial shipments are consolidated for forward transportation or are re-sorted for local distribution. Old Dominion provides full-state coverage in 24 states from New Hampshire west to Illinois and south to Florida, and including Texas and Oklahoma. Special services include Speed Service, for expedited next-day and second-day shipments, and Air Express, for airfreight forwarding. Through partnerships in Mexico and Canada, the international division provides freight transportation to several locations in those countries. Container drayage service is offered through port facilities on the Atlantic Ocean in Virginia, North and South Carolina, Georgia, and Florida; on the Gulf of Mexico at New Orleans; and on the Pacific Ocean at Long Beach, California.

Founding the Company in Virginia, the Old Dominion State

As the name suggests, Old Dominion Freight Line originated in the state of Virginia. Earl and Lillian Congdon founded the company in Richmond in 1934 and, with one truck, Earl transported general commodities between and around Norfolk and Newport News. After Congress regulated the trucking industry in 1935, Old Dominion received approval from the Interstate Commerce Commission to continue operating along that route, allowing the company to expand its fleet and driving staff.

During World War II, activities at military bases in Norfolk and Newport News increased freight traffic and Old Dominion accessed this new business for trucking service. After the war, however, traffic declined. The Teamsters Union, which had organized the truck drivers and warehouse workers during the war, led a strike at Old Dominion. The Congdons decided to close business operations, but opened 11 weeks later with nonunion labor.

Earl Congdon died in 1950, leaving Lillian and sons Earl, Jr., and Jack to manage Old Dominion Freight Line. Lillian's first action as president was to incorporate the company.

Old Dominion expanded in the late 1950s and early 1960s, adding new routes outside the state of Virginia for the first time. The acquisition of Bottoms-Fiske Truck Line, a furniture mover based in High Point, North Carolina, expanded company operations to southern Virginia and throughout North Carolina. In 1962 Old Dominion relocated to High Point to be near major furniture and textile manufacturers, but the company retained its Virginia name. Earl took the helm as president at this time, and Lillian became chairwoman.

The company continued to expand during the late 1960s and 1970s, initiating drayage service on the Atlantic coast and entering new markets through acquisition. Old Dominion acquired Barnes Truck Line, Nilson Motor Express, and White Transport in 1969, and Star Transport in 1972, extending operations to markets in the Northeast and the South. With the acquisition of New Jersey-based Deaton Trucking in 1979, Old Dominion entered the market for full-load and flat-bed trucking.

Industry Deregulation Sparking Challenges and Changes During the 1980s

Federal reform of trucking industry regulations through the Motor Carrier Act of 1980 prompted many changes at Old

Dominion. The legislation allowed Old Dominion to add service, without regulatory approval, to points in Florida, Tennessee, and California, as well as to Dallas and Chicago. Specialization in LTL freight transportation provided an opportunity to provide trucking services to more markets. Rather than shipping directly to the customer, LTL service was based on a network of terminals where freight was sorted for local distribution. Industry deregulation allowed the company to develop rapidly for flexible commodities transportation, opening service centers where freight could be resorted en route to its final destination, combining different shipments more readily for greater efficiency. Old Dominion began to build service centers for geographic concentration, opening 27 centers during the early 1980s.

Deregulation created an extremely competitive environment in the trucking industry and Old Dominion targeted customers of unionized carriers, which could not provide the flexible service of a nonunion carrier because unions limited workers to specific jobs. For instance, the new flexible scheduling of transportation services meant that a shipment could arrive at any time; without a union, anyone could handle receiving a shipment regardless of their job description if a regular worker was not available. Old Dominion workers frequently voted against unionization; the company attributed much of its success to employing nonunion workers.

The competitive atmosphere prompted the formation of many new freight transport companies that offered discount rates, frequently undercutting the rates of other carriers. In response to this difficult business environment, the Congdons hired John Ebeling, a veteran of the trucking industry, as president and chief operating officer, the first person outside the family to hold such a high-level position at Old Dominion. Ebeling was instrumental in forming quality management programs and computerizing operations for cost efficiency and improved service.

The competitive atmosphere of the 1980s, along with investment in infrastructure, led to financial losses in 1986 and 1987. Through capital investment and service improvement programs Old Dominion became profitable and entered a period of steady growth and expansion. In 1990 the company reported sales of $134.8 million, representing a 17 percent increase over 1989, and net profit of $4.7 million. A fleet of 673 tractors and 2,461 trailers transported shipments through 47 service centers in 20 states, though primarily in eight southeastern states. With greater emphasis on developing LTL services, Old Dominion discontinued its furniture shipment division and sold the general commodities truckload and flatbed freight division of its Deaton subsidiary in 1991.

1991 Public Offering of Stock Marking Decade of Expansion

Despite a recession and a decade of industry volatility, Old Dominion successfully launched an initial public offering of stock in late 1991. Selling its stock at $12.50 per share, the company grossed $15.6 million and the proceeds were applied to debt repayment and a strategy of aggressive geographic expansion. Old Dominion expanded services by increasing the density of service centers in existing markets as well by entering new markets. This was accomplished through acquisition, expansion of existing facilities, and new facility development. In 1993 the company launched new intra-regional service in the mid-Atlantic states.

In September 1995, Old Dominion acquired certain assets of Denver-based Navajo LTL, Inc., including 82 tractors, 264 trailers, and ten service centers. Six of the service centers provided Old Dominion entry into new markets, in Kansas City, Phoenix, Albuquerque, Denver, Salt Lake City, and Sacramento, while service centers in San Francisco, Los Angeles, Dallas, and Chicago were integrated into existing operations. Old Dominion purchased or opened six additional service centers, entering new markets in Minnesota, Wisconsin, Missouri, and Indiana.

By the end of 1995 the company operated a total of 67 service centers in 35 states and Washington, D.C. The availability of service culminated in a 17 percent increase in LTL tonnage transported in 1996 and an overall 12 percent increase in tonnage transported as full-load or LTL service. Revenues in 1996 reached $293 million, yielding a net profit of $6.1 million.

Although the company expanded into new territory, most expansion activity emphasized building a dense service network in the Southeast. The January 1998 acquisition of assets from Fredrickson Motor Express, based in Charlotte, involved 26 terminals in North and South Carolina, Virginia, and Georgia, though 19 terminals overlapped with Old Dominion facilities. In August Old Dominion purchased assets from Goggin Truck Line of Shelbyville, Tennessee, serving metropolitan and rural areas in the Southeast. The two acquisitions resulted in the addition of nine new service centers in 1998, while another four service centers opened in upstate New York, extending new service to that area. Old Dominion invested an unprecedented $48.7 million in tractors, trailers, and service centers in 1998, compared with an average of $30 million in the late 1990s.

Expansion continued in 1999 with the January acquisition of Skyline Transportation. Assets included 23 terminals in North and South Carolina, Georgia, Tennessee, and Alabama, with only one overlap with Old Dominion facilities. The acquisition provided Old Dominion an opportunity to improve next-day service to and from the Midwest.

Other service expansion involved new facilities in Delaware, West Virginia, and Pennsylvania, as well as the relocation and consolidation of facilities. A new $9 million facility in Rialto, California, combined and expanded operations in southern California. In November Old Dominion acquired a service center in Dallas from Nation's Way Transport Service for $3.65 million in a bankruptcy auction. Old Dominion's nearby location accommodated 63 doors, while the new facility would accommodate 164 doors within five years. Old Dominion

Key Dates:

1934: Old Dominion is founded by Earl and Lillian Congdon.
1950: Earl Congdon dies and Lillian becomes president.
1962: The company expands with the purchase of a High Point, North Carolina-based furniture mover; Earl Congdon, Jr., becomes president.
1969: New acquisitions expand Old Dominion's reach into the Northeast and the South.
1980: The Motor Carrier Act allows the company to add service to far-flung markets.
1991: An IPO follows two years of double-digit revenue growth.
1995: Acquisition provides entry into markets in the Southwest.
1998: The density of service infrastructure improves in the Southeast through acquisition and expansion; David Congdon is named COO.
1999: Old Dominion initiates international less-than-truckload (LTL) service into Mexico.
2002: Old Dominion initiates Air Express Service.

planned to develop the terminal as a hub for Texas, Louisiana, Oklahoma, Arkansas, and New Mexico. A small service center was opened in Laredo, Texas, for introduction of transportation service into Mexico.

From 2000: New Markets, New Services, New Technologies

While Old Dominion continued to pursue geographic expansion in the early 2000s, the company sought internal growth through the implementation of new services and improvements to existing services. One dimension of this concern for service involved providing full-state coverage within existing territories. In the first half of 2000, Old Dominion extended full-state service to 21 states east of the Mississippi River. This service infrastructure allowed the company to introduce the Speed Service Program, providing customized, time-sensitive delivery service.

An opportunity to improve its service network in Texas and Oklahoma came in February 2001 with the acquisition of Carter & Sons Freightways, Inc. of Carrollton, Texas. In addition to trucking and office equipment, the acquisition involved 23 service centers, which provided Old Dominion with complete service coverage of Texas and Oklahoma and complementary service to Old Dominion terminals in Louisiana, Arkansas, and New Mexico. The company merged ten service centers into existing facilities, so the acquisition provided a total of 13 new facilities. The acquisition provided infrastructure to offer next-day and second-day service in the five-state area and contributed approximately $23 million in revenue.

Old Dominion introduced two new services in 2002, OD Air Express and OD Parts Assembly and Distribution. OD Air Express, an air cargo transportation service, provided nightly schedules of service through 51 airport locations. Old Dominion

hired eight regional sale managers to promote air service through airfreight brokers, forwarders, and airlines and opened a centralized facility for air transport arrangements. Assembly and Distribution elaborated on existing service that assembled a customer's product at any Old Dominion service center and loaded it on any company's equipment for transport to a final destination. The company also received shipments from a customer's vendors or another carrier for forward distribution anywhere in the Old Dominion system.

Old Dominion supported its program of service improvements with the implementation of several new technologies. Ether wireless service for handheld devices provided mobile data synchronization, proof of delivery, real time pick-up and delivery status, and other information. Fleetwise brand dispatch and route planning software packages facilitated communication between drivers and dispatchers and determined the best delivery routes for new service orders as they were received. The Dock Yard Management System provided the status of a shipment anywhere in the Old Dominion service network using Radio Frequency Identification tags that automatically record shipment arrivals and departure. Old Dominion upgraded its web site with a new look, increased speed, and ease of navigation for customer convenience in tracing shipment status.

Lower demand for transportation services due to a weak economy in 2001 did not stop Old Dominion from continuing its strategy of expansion. Instead, the company sought to offset low demand with cost and service improvements. The company reduced transit time in more than 3,000 of 13,000 service lanes, while the transit time of coast-to-coast service was reduced by one day. Service improvements put Old Dominion in a competitively advantageous situation, attracting accolades from Wall Street, which more than doubled the company's stock value in 2002.

In 2003 Old Dominion continued to expand and upgrade its service center facilities. The company added a 22-door facility in Baton Rouge and relocated a Shreveport service center to a larger, more central location in Monroe. In May Old Dominion opened a 38-door service center in Des Moines, greatly furthering potential business opportunities in Iowa and the Midwest. In June the company announced plans to open a facility in the Reno area.

Principal Operating Units

OD Domestic; OD Expedited; OD Technology; OD Global.

Principal Competitors

Arkansas Best Corporation; Con-Way Transportation Services; Roadway Corporation; USF Corporation; Yellow Corporation.

Further Reading

Allen, Margaret, "Old Dominion to Create South-Central Hub," *Dallas Business Journal,* November 19, 1999, p. 17.
"Carrier on the Move," *Transportation & Distribution,* June 2002, p. 16.
"Delivered Data Cuts Costs," *Advanced Transportation Technology News,* December 2002, p. 6.
"Fleets Online," *Fleet Owner,* May 1, 2003.

Ludorf, Carol, "Old Dominion Freight Line and Portable Data Terminals," *Transport Technology Today,* November-December 2002, p. 26.

Martin, Edward, "The Road Not Taken," *Business North Carolina,* March 1995, p. 38.

Mildenberg, David, "Will Road-Wary Investors Pull into Truck Stocks?," *Business North Carolina,* January 1992, p. 45.

Nicholson, Gilbert, "Big Expansion for Old Dominion," *Birmingham Business Journal,* March 2, 2001, p. 1.

"Old Dominion Freight Line Rolls Out Wireless Solution," *Transport Technology Today,* August 2002, p. 33.

"Old Dominion Increases Rates," *JoC Online,* July 2, 2002.

Schulz, John D., "Adding Capacity," *Traffic World,* January 25, 1999, p. 26.

——, "What Recession? Old Dominion Freight Line Bucks Trend, Predicts 16.7 Percent Revenue Rise in '03," *Traffic World,* December 9, 2002, p. 22.

"Thomasville, NC-Based Old Dominion Freight Line Sees Revenues Grow," *Knight Ridder/Tribune Business News,* April 26, 2002.

"Thomasville, NC-Based Old Dominion Freight Line Sets Stock Price," *Knight Ridder/Tribune Business News,* November 6, 2002.

—Mary Tradii

Pei Cobb Freed & Partners Architects LLP

88 Pine Street
New York, New York 10005
U.S.A.
Telephone: (212) 751-3122
Fax: (212) 872-5443
Web site: http://www.pcf-p.com

Limited Liability Partnership
Founded: 1955 as I.M. Pei & Associates
Employees: 110
Sales: $23 million (2002 est.)
NAIC: 541310 Architectural Services

Pei Cobb Freed & Partners Architects LLP, based in New York City, is one of the world's leading architectural firms. Drawing on the work of its founder, Ieoh Ming Pei, the firm established its reputation by designing a series of prominent public and corporate buildings in a style often described as Late Modernism. Among these are the John F. Kennedy Library and John Hancock Tower in Boston; the City Hall and Morton H. Meyerson Symphony Center in Dallas; the Jacob K. Javits Convention Center in New York; and the East Building of the National Gallery of Art and the U.S. Holocaust Memorial Museum in Washington, D.C. Over a period of nearly 50 years the firm has completed more than 200 projects in over 100 cities across North America and around the world.

From Urban Development to Prestige Commissions: 1955–70

Born into a wealthy and prominent Chinese banking family, Pei studied architecture in the United States and remained there when the Japanese occupation of China, followed by World War II and subsequent rise of the Communists to power, made it unwise for him to return. Pei's education under such masters as Walter Gropius and Marcel Breuer put him firmly in the camp of the International Style of modernist architecture that derived from Gropius's famed Bauhaus design studio. Seven years in charge of architecture for real estate magnate William Zeckendorf not only enabled Pei to realize his designs but

thoroughly acquainted him with the many practical steps needed to guide a work from conception to completion.

I.M. Pei & Associates was formed in 1955, with Henry Cobb and Eason Leonard as partners. Cobb supplemented Pei on the design side, while Leonard was in charge of managing a 70-person staff—still working exclusively for Zeckendorf's Webb & Knapp Inc.—on various aspects of a dozen projects at a time. During the late 1950s the firm concentrated on such residential complexes as Kips Bay Plaza and University Plaza in New York City, University Gardens in Chicago, and Society Hill in Philadelphia. Also begun at this time was Place Ville-Marie, a seven-acre redevelopment in the heart of Montreal that included the tallest building in the British Commonwealth.

By 1960 Zeckendorf's fortunes were beginning to wane—Webb & Knapp would later go bankrupt—and Pei was increasingly conscious that his own firm would never be considered for the more artistically challenging and high visibility projects he sought as long as he was viewed as merely a house architect. Accordingly, the links between I.M. Pei & Associates and Webb & Knapp were severed that summer. Pei was in charge of recruiting clients and overseeing the design process, which was then given over to Cobb, Araldo Cossutta—who became a partner in 1963—and James Freed. Each of the three headed a team of junior architects that was dedicated to the project until completion. Administration was in the hands of Leonard, Leonard Jacobson, and Werner Wandelmaier. All of them except Cossutta, who left in 1973, would remain together until the 1990s, forming a team perhaps unprecedented in architecture for its longevity. The firm's name was changed to I.M. Pei & Partners in 1966, when it moved its headquarters northward to 600 Madison Avenue, at East 58th Street, to accommodate the growing staff, which now numbered about 150.

By this time Pei had turned away from housing and urban development, perceiving the slowdown in federal funding for projects of any size. Henceforth his firm's hallmark would be institutional buildings, some of great originality and all characterized by devotion to the materials and geometry of modernist architecture. The forerunner was Pei's own design, conceived in 1961, for the National Center of Atmospheric Research in Boulder, Colorado, and sited against a mountainous backdrop.

280

This complex of buildings was characterized by a verticality of rough concrete surfaces that evoked the walls of the mesa, and with this work, in the words of biographer Michael Cannell, Pei moved "beyond the stiff inhibitions of his Bauhaus schooling [to] explore the meditative geometry that became his trademark." About this time Pei designed the Everson Museum of Art in Syracuse, New York, the first of the many museum buildings that would become a specialty of the firm.

In 1964 Pei won the commission that brought him and his firm to national prominence for the first time—the John F. Kennedy Library to house the papers of the recently assassinated president. Pei's knack for presentation is credited for receiving the approval of Jacqueline Kennedy in the face of competition from such revered architects as Gordon Bunshaft, Philip Johnson, Louis Kahn, Ludwig Mies van der Rohe, Paul Rudolph, and John Carl Warnecke. However, his model of a truncated glass pyramid for the Cambridge site sparked a community revolt. By the time Pei's third design reached completion with the opening of the building in 1979, to tepid applause, on a swampy peninsula of Boston Harbor, the Kennedy era had lost its resonance with the public. Another prominent Boston project, the John Hancock Tower, also proved unlucky. Designed by Cobb in 1967 to be New England's tallest structure, the glass-sheathed edifice, jutting over its low-rise environs, became the building Boston loved to hate, even before its five-by-11-foot glass panels began popping out of the frame in 1973. All the more than 10,000 panes had to be replaced, and I.M. Pei & Partners lost an immeasurable amount of work because of the bad publicity, even though the building eventually received the recognition that the insurance company sought as the defining feature of the Boston skyline. According to Pei biographer Carter Wiseman, "The virtual blackballing of the firm caused by Hancock lasted for the better part of the next seven years."

I.M. Pei had better luck in Dallas, where in 1966 he designed a municipal government complex that featured an eight-story concrete-clad city hall angled over the adjacent plaza at 34 degrees. The project grew substantially in size and cost, and it was not completed until 1977, but the impact was so great that it led to five more buildings in the city designed by the firm.

Surviving the 1970s, Resurgence in the 1980s

I.M. Pei & Partners' dry spell put the firm's very existence in peril. Its founder's reputation for perfectionism, which often meant missed deadlines and cost overruns, put the firm at a competitive disadvantage amid the economic downturn of the

1970s. It struggled to meet its 150-employee payroll and fell behind in payments to consultants. There were no pay raises and no payments for overtime. "The firm was damn near bankrupt," a senior associate recalled to Cannell. "It was terrifying." Pei's Asian connections helped keep the partnership afloat during this period. Bankers in Singapore who knew his father provided the entree that gave I.M. Pei the commissions for a 52-story banking headquarters and a mixed-use project called Raffles City, plus an office building overlooking New York's South Street Seaport. Pei also built a shopping arcade in oil-rich Kuwait and, in 1974, visited China for the first time since his youth. Five years later he returned to design the Fragrant Hill hotel on the site of an old hunting preserve near Beijing.

The East Building of the National Gallery of Art was the commission that restored—and enhanced—I.M. Pei's reputation. This annex to the main building had to be constructed on an awkward trapezoidal site. Pei decided to exploit the location with a complex design featuring two triangular parts linked horizontally. They were clad in the same pink Tennessee marble as the main building. The great central space of the courtyard was spanned by a metal frame made of 25 tetrahedrons that supported hundreds of irregularly shaped panes of glass. An enormous mobile by Alexander Calder hung from the frame. The building opened to great acclaim in 1978 and in its first two months received more than a million visitors.

Pei was less interested in high-rise office buildings, leaving most of this kind of work to associates. While he gathered plaudits, Cobb operated with increasing autonomy within the firm. Among his significant designs completed in the 1970s were the Johnson & Johnson world headquarters, One Dallas Center, and the World Trade Center in Baltimore. Freed, who became a partner of the firm in 1980, along with Jacobson and Wandelmaier, was the designer, in 1984, of New York City's Jacob K. Javits Convention Center. The gigantic floor space of 1.7 million square feet was supported by a lightweight spaceframe of interlocking tubes similar to that employed for the East Building courtyard.

Pei returned to the spotlight as the designer of the 71-foot-high glass pyramid in the central courtyard of the Louvre in Paris, serving as the new entrance to France's national art museum. Three smaller glass pyramids were also built to provide light to newly added subterranean passageways leading to the three wings of the museum. When unveiled in 1984, the plan received a hostile reception; one member of the French Academy even declared that the only proper response was "insurrection." But by the time the project was completed in 1989, public opinion had swung in its favor; one writer declared that "The much-feared pyramid has become adorable."

Cobb and Freed to the Forefront: 1989–2002

The Louvre reconstruction was only one of five Pei designs completed in 1989, the others being an office building in Los Angeles for the Creative Artists Agency; the Meyerson Symphony Hall in Dallas, a rectangular limestone structure enclosed within swooping curves of glass; a science building at the Choate Rosemary Hall School in Connecticut; and a 70-story tower—the tallest in Asia—for the Bank of China in Hong Kong. Cobb was working on a planned expansion—soon aban-

Key Dates:

1955: I.M. Pei, Henry Cobb, and Eason Leonard found I.M. Pei & Associates.

1960: The firm shifts its focus from residential to institutional buildings.

1964: Pei wins commission to design the John F. Kennedy Library.

1967: Cobb designs New England's tallest building, the John Hancock Tower.

1978: Pei's East Building of the National Gallery of Art opens.

1984: Pei designs a glass pyramid for the central courtyard of the Louvre in Paris.

1989: Pei-designed Bank of China in Hong Kong is completed.

1993: Freed-designed U.S. Holocaust Memorial Museum in Washington, D.C., opens.

2001: Cobb-designed projects in Boston and Cincinnati are completed.

doned—of New York City's Kennedy Airport, an international trade center in Baltimore, and a London office complex, while Freed had begun designing the United States Holocaust Memorial Museum in Washington, D.C., and the Los Angeles Convention Center. With a staff of 229, I.M. Pei & Partners was the largest architectural firm based in New York City when, in September 1989, its name was changed to Pei Cobb Freed & Partners to reflect the ever greater role that Pei's younger designer partners inevitably were assuming.

Pei, now 73, officially retired at the end of 1990 but continued to come to his corner office every day and to design structures. These included a sculpturally shaped bell tower for a Japanese religious sect and the Rock and Roll Hall of Fame and Museum in Cleveland. When completed in 1995, the latter reminded observers of a giant record player, with an aluminum-clad auditorium (which Pei called a "glass tent") resembling a stylus and a brick round plaza resembling a turntable. Freed, who came to the United States as a German Jewish refugee, could not come up with a design for the Holocaust Museum until he had visited a number of Nazi death camps. Completed in 1993, the museum combined, within a rather bland exterior, a Hall of Witness with skewed angles and twisted roof trusses, and a hexagonal Hall of Remembrance with multiple skylights intended to throw an indirect light upon the walls and floor and encourage quiet contemplation. Freed also designed the Ronald Reagan Building and International Trade Center. Completed in 1998, on an awkward 11-acre L-shaped site in the heart of official Washington, this 3.1-million-square-foot complex was second only in size, among federal buildings, to the Pentagon.

Cobb designed the upgrade of the University of Cincinnati's conservatory of music, completed in 2001. Also completed that year was a Cobb-designed Boston courthouse, on a prime waterfront location, serving as headquarters for a federal district court and appeals court. In 2003 Freed's design was chosen for a new Air Force Memorial in Arlington, Virginia. The centerpiece consisted of three attenuated, arcing stainless-steel spires, with the tallest to be 270 feet high. Completion was scheduled for 2006.

There were a number of important personnel changes at Pei Cobb Freed during these years. George H. Miller was named a managing partner for administration and projects in 1989. Michael D. Flynn, a veteran with the firm, also was appointed a managing partner in the same year. Leonard retired in 1990, and Jacobson died in 1992. Pei's two architect sons had put about 20 years each in the firm when they resigned in 1992 to start their own partnership. Wandelmaier retired in 1995. Ian Bader and Yvonne Szeto were named partners in 1999.

Pei Cobb Freed, like other architectural firms, suffered from the 1990–91 recession, its gross billings falling from $36.7 million in 1990 to $20.5 million in 1993. Its operating revenues were estimated at $23 million in 2002, and its worldwide construction volume at $125 million. The firm was engaged in 37 projects, of which nine were overseas. In 2000 it moved its headquarters from 600 Madison Avenue to 88 Pine Street, a lower Manhattan office building designed in 1973 by Pei and Freed.

Principal Competitors

Emery Roth & Partners LLC; Gwathmey Siegel & Associates Architects LLC; Hellmuth, Obata and Kassabaum Inc.; Kohn Pedersen Fox Associates P.C.; Skidmore Owings & Merrill LLP.

Further Reading

Cannell, Michael, *I.M. Pei: Mandarin of Modernism,* New York: Carol Southern Books, 1995.

Dunlap, David W., "The Delicate Matter of Passing the Torch," *New York Times,* Sec. 11, pp. 1, 6.

Filler, Martin, "Power Pei," *Vanity Fair,* September 1989, pp. 262–63, 266–68, 270, 291–94.

"Freed, James I.," in *Current Biography Yearbook 1994,* New York: H.W. Wilson, 1995, pp. 188–92.

"Pei, I(eoh) M(ing)," in *Current Biography Yearbook 1990,* New York: H.W. Wilson, 1991, pp. 495–99.

Post, Nadine M., "The Perils and Pearls of Pei Cobb Freed," *ENR/Engineering News Record,* December 13, 1993, pp. 26–27, 30–32.

Russell, James R., "The Ronald Reagan Building," *Architectural Record,* July 1998, pp. 59–71.

Stein, Karen D., "Cleveland Rocks," *Architectural Record,* November 1995, p. 84.

Wiseman, Carter, *I.M. Pei: A Profile in American Architecture,* New York: Harry M. Abrams, 1990.

—Robert Halasz

Plains Cotton Cooperative Association

3301 E. 50th Street
Lubbock, Texas 79408
U.S.A.
Telephone: (806) 763-8011
Fax: (806) 762-7333
Web site: http://www.pcca.com

Private Company
Founded: 1953
Employees: 1,000
Sales: $800 million (2002 est.)
NAIC: 115111 Cotton Ginning; 313221 Narrow Fabric
   Mills; 422590 Other Farm Product Raw Material
   Wholesaling

The Plains Cotton Cooperative Association (PCCA) is one of the largest cotton handlers in the United States, representing 2.5 to 3 million bales annually, from 15 to 18 percent of the nation's total cotton crop. Marketing services to cooperative members include electronic marketing via TELCOT and The Seam, pool marketing, and crop contracting. The PCCA serves more than 28,000 stockholders in Texas, Oklahoma, and Kansas, with field offices, and warehouses in Oklahoma and Texas, and affiliated cotton gins and compressors throughout member territory. The PCCA operates two denim mills, the American Cotton Growers plant in Littlefield, Texas, and the Mission Valley plant in New Braunfels, Texas. The company's finished denim products are promoted through sales and marketing offices in New York and San Francisco.

1953 Formation of Cooperative Helpful to Cotton Farmers

With combined funds of $12,000, a group of cotton farmers formed the PCCA in 1953 to provide an outlet for obtaining the best price in the cotton trade. The member-owned cooperative brought together cotton farmers of the high plains of Texas, to the south, east, and north of Lubbock. The affiliation of cotton gins and compressors with PCCA streamlined the process of transforming cotton from the field, through ginning and baling, and then storage until purchased by textile mills or cotton merchants.

Formation of the cooperative provided a platform for marketing cotton, using a trading dynamic similar to that of a stock exchange. A regular offer allows buyers to bid blindly on a cotton lot offered for sale, with product going to the highest bidder, bidding occurring within a limited period of time. A firm offer provides buyers with an opportunity to evaluate the lots of cotton offered before making a selection based on a firm price; counter offers are allowed. When hedging the future price of cotton is desirable, the PCCA offers crop contracting. Under a crop contract the PCCA establishes a minimum price based on specified acreage, irrigated cotton preferred. The PCCA took responsibility for the contracts, acting as principal, marketing contracts to cotton buyers, and handling payments. Although crop contracts do not rely on margin futures or guaranteed quantity, the program has drawbacks. For instance, premiums for high-quality cotton are rare and the contract price is not guaranteed.

The PCCA's success in obtaining good prices for cotton and in providing services attracted cotton farmers, ginners, and compressors to the organization. In 1963 the cooperative extended membership to cotton producers in the rolling hills area to the west, northwest, and southwest of Lubbock. This essentially expanded PCCA territory to all of west Texas, an area referred to as "the world's biggest cotton patch."

In 1973 the PCCA assisted in the formation of the American Cotton Growers Association (ACG), a farmer-owned cooperative, also serving west Texas cotton producers. The intent of the organization was to provide pool marketing and to improve the ginning, processing, storage, and general management of the pooled cotton supply. ACG began construction on a cotton textile mill in Littlefield, Texas, north of Lubbock, in 1975. Under PCCA management, the mill went into production the following year. Applying state-of-the-art technology to produce optimum yarn strength, ACG manufactured heavyweight denim exclusively for Levi Strauss & Company; ACG shipped fabric to jean manufacturing facilities in the southwestern United States and worldwide.

Company Perspectives:

The Plains Cotton Cooperative Association mission is to add significant value to the cotton marketed for our members by being the supplier of choice to our business partners in terms of quality, service, and value.

1970s and 1980s: Development of Electronic Marketing Systems

During the 1970s and 1980s PCCA transferred its system of cotton trading, used for decades, to an electronic platform. In 1975 the PCCA introduced TELCOT, a computer-based system that allowed buyers and sellers to trade cotton in a central place. In addition to simplifying transactions, TELCOT extended the reach of PCCA marketing capabilities to additional cotton merchants and textile mills. The system incorporated all existing trading options and improved on them. The PCCA formed TELMARK, Inc. in 1985 to provide TELCOT services to independent ginning outfits and cotton producers in Texas and Oklahoma. This extension of the system increased its sales volume, thus lowering operating costs. TELCOT's effectiveness in facilitating the cotton trade earned it the title, "Window of the Marketplace."

The PCCA also introduced an Online Gin Bookkeeping (GBK) system. GBK replaced paper bookkeeping with an electronic system designed for cotton gins. In addition to regular payroll, financial statements, and tax accounting applications, the system included special features like Bale Accounting.

In February 1989 TELCOT processed the trade of 385,599 bales of cotton in a single day, a record that signaled the need for improvements to make the system more efficient. That year PCCA enhanced the TELCOT system with the Electronic Title System (ETS). ETS eliminated the need for paper warehouse receipts by recording all transactions electronically; it also facilitated shipments to textile mill customers. The system provided economic benefits as it reduced costs for gin operators and cotton buyers.

1987: Introduction of Pool Marketing

In 1987 PCCA purchased the denim cotton mill from ACG. The mill brought more than $100 million in revenue to PCCA members in west Texas and, by this time, southwestern Oklahoma. Acquisition of the mill provided security that the mill would remain in operation for the long term under regional cooperation. The acquisition furthered vertical integration of cotton processing, from cotton field to textile market, by adding the textile mill process. With new competition from overseas cotton producers, the mill provided a sure outlet for PCCA member cotton as well.

Along with the acquisition of the mill, the PCCA introduced pool marketing to its members as an alternative to regular trade and crop contracting. Pool marketing, already available to ACG members, involved combining cotton from various producers and marketing it as a group. Not only did the pool provide baling, storage, and stock management, the division employed professionals to sell the cotton for participants in the program, allowing farmers to focus on the work of cotton production. Sales occurred before, during, and after the harvest, and hedging through futures and options could be utilized to minimize risk. With the aim of obtaining a good average price, the program provided year-round income for farmers through an advance loan payment prior to harvest and a year-end dividend; general book credits provided savings to offset potential losses. Members participated through a perpetual marketing agreement, with a sign-in and sign-out period of one month offered annually. A committee of elected members provided oversight of pool marketing activities.

The PCCA introduced the Mill Option Program, allowing members to obtain earnings from the profits of the mill. Participation involved a perpetual marketing agreement, with a sign-in and sign-out period from April 1 to June 30 each year. Under the program the PCCA withheld a capital retain of $5 per bale of marketed cotton. Returns from mill earnings were shared on a per unit basis.

In 1988 the PCCA extended its services to cotton producers in south Texas. South Texas encompassed five geographic regions: the Lower Rio Grande Valley along the border with Mexico; Winter Garden south of Uvalde; the Coastal Bend at Corpus Christi; the Upper Coastal Bend at El Campa and Danevang, southwest of Houston; and the Blacklands of central Texas. Members in these areas participated in all PCCA programs.

Late 1990s: Years of Uncertainty for U.S. Cotton Producers

During the late 1990s foreign competition in cotton apparel and textiles increased, leading to market overstock and lower prices. The 1997 Asian financial crisis and the devaluation of currencies further intensified competition, as pricing of imported fabrics cut into the U.S. market share. Export buyers found the overseas markets more difficult to maneuver as well. Another concern in the cotton trade at this time involved a market oversupply, with more cotton being produced than consumed, causing a decline in mill use and high carryover stock from the previous year.

The PCCA addressed member concerns about the cotton market by implementing a "20/20 Vision Equity Plan" to improve cash payouts to cooperative members. The goals of the program were to achieve a 20 percent return on equity and a $20 per bale cash payment at the end of each fiscal year. Cash distribution occurred in January, based on the previous year's crop pools, and at the end of the June 30 fiscal year, based on total net margins. The PCCA surpassed its 20/20 Vision goals in 1997. The PCCA reported net margins of $27.4 million and the denim mill alone contributed $17.7 million from net margins. Total cash distribution of $34 million included $13.4 million in dividends, $17.1 million in stock retirements, and $3.5 million in retirement of per-unit capital retains.

Another uncertainty entered the picture when Levi Strauss informed the PCCA and other textile producers that it would no longer guarantee volume purchases of fabric. The ACG mill produced 36 million yards of heavyweight denim annually, almost exclusively for Levi Strauss. The change meant that the

Key Dates:

1953: Plains Cotton Cooperative Association (PCCA) is founded.
1963: The Association expands to include cotton farmers in the rolling hills of west Texas.
1973: ACG is formed to provide pool marketing to west Texas and Oklahoma cotton producers.
1975: The TELCOT electronic cotton marketing system is launched.
1976: ACG begins production at the denim cotton mill managed by PCCA.
1987: PCCA acquires the ACG denim mill.
1997: The Asian financial crisis lowers the price of cotton imports and intensifies competition.
1998: The PCCA acquires the Mission Valley textile mill.
2000: The Seam transfers the TELCOT system to the Internet, expanding the geographic reach of the cotton trade.
2002: Denim manufacturing rebounds, although prices remain low.

PCCA had to compete in the open market for business from Levi Strauss and find other customers.

In order to expand the ACG mill's manufacturing capabilities and attract new customers, the PCCA purchased Mission Valley Textiles, northeast of San Antonio, for $25 million in May 1998. The textile mill, renamed Mission Valley Fabrics (MVF), brought one of the leading producers of yarn-dyed woven fabric under PCCA control. With 18 million yards in annual capacity, including broad width textiles, MVF produced more than 100 different fabrics for use in making apparel, upholstery, and home textiles. MVF provided needed versatility, including the ability to produce short runs for special orders. The nature of MVF business differed from ACG in that it required a sales and marketing team to attract buyers.

The PCCA combined the capacities of the MVF and ACG mills to create a full line of denim in light-, medium-, and heavyweight fabrics. ACG wove denim with ring-spun yarn produced at MVF. The new denims were directed to the market for fashion-forward fabrics in ripstop, bleached, and rinsed looks.

To accommodate variable market demand and provide capacity for different shades of indigo and different colors of denim fabric, as well as different fabric weights, the PCCA upgraded ACG's mill equipment. The cooperative replaced 247 looms with 81 state-of-the art airjet looms, providing improved denim quality and lower production costs with speedier equipment. A second dye was added, to provide flexibility, particularly for small lots. One dye range could be prepared while another machine was in operation. Other equipment upgrades included automated mixing at the eight vats. Production expanded at ACG's Littlefield mill in June 1999.

In November the PCCA began an $11 million upgrade of equipment at the MVF mill. The cooperative replaced 202 looms with 77 state-of-the-art rapier and airjet looms; these operated at more than triple the speed of the old looms. With the new equipment and the 22 looms retained, the facility had the capacity to produce 16 million yards of fabric annually. Upgrade of the facility was completed in May 2001 with the installation of new cards, draw frames, ring-spun, and roving equipment.

By the spring of 2000 the PCCA realized the difficulty in finding customers to replace business lost from Levi Strauss. With competition from less expensive imports, denim prices were low and denim production in North America was at 15 to 20 percent overcapacity. The sales and marketing team from MVF introduced a "trend service," displaying the new denim styles at trade shows in Europe and Tokyo. Growth in the home fashions market in 1999 prompted the PCCA to place greater emphasis on home fabrics.

Pool marketing increased dramatically during the late 1990s, as farmers sought to reduce the risks involved with an uncertain market. Since it was implemented at ACG, pool marketing had proven itself a safe alternative to the open market. By 2000 pool prices averaged higher than nonpool prices for 23 out of 24 years.

As pool marketing became a more attractive marketing alternative, PCCA members used the TELCOT system less, making it less cost-effective. In May 2000 PCCA formed a joint venture to transfer TELCOT to an Internet platform for trading cotton and cotton products and services online. Participants in the joint venture were cotton merchants Allenberg Cotton Company, Dunavant Enterprises, and Hohenberg Brothers. Avondale Mills and Parkdale Mills, the nation's largest users of cotton for textile manufacturing, joined the venture in June. With 175 cotton gins with 53 U.S. cotton buyers using the TELCOT system at this time, the PCCA provided the volume of trade needed as a foundation for expansion through the Internet. The presence of large merchants and textile manufacturers in the venture was intended to attract cotton producers.

The new company, named The Seam, was formalized in November and online trading began in December. The Seam provided access to more cotton trading opportunities through a larger number of cotton buyers, providing more competitive prices for cotton and a more efficient transference of cotton from field to merchant or mill. A business-to-business site allowed for anonymous cotton trading among cotton merchants.

Worsening Situation, Followed by Improvement: Early 2000s

A slow economy in the United States exacerbated the problem of competition from imported fabrics. With Asian currencies at 40 percent below previous values, the United States experienced a dramatic increase in imported textiles in 2000. In 1999 and 2000 the textile industry cut 55,000 jobs nationwide. Congressional action on behalf of the textile industry was not sufficient to offset the PCCA's decline in sales, particularly in home fabrics. Hedging proved ineffective and low cotton prices caused farmers in west Texas and Oklahoma to abandon their crops.

In fiscal 2001 the PCCA reported its first net loss since 1985. Although the PCCA expected sales of $50 million from the MVF mill, decline in textile sales and expenses of mill conversion contributed to the loss. Loss allocation from the Textile Division was taken against book credits of members participating in the mill option since 2000; members reported the loss as a tax deduction. Other PCCA losses were allocated to a reserve fund of $7.5 million in nonpatronage income.

During the summer of 2001 the PCCA began converting the MVF facility to all denim production to meet increasing demand from Europe. The change required the cooperative to eliminate 370 positions in sales, management, and production, retaining 40 percent of the workforce. Supervisors handled the movement of equipment to reduce expenditures. The worsening U.S. economy after the attacks on the World Trade Center and Pentagon required the layoff of an additional 130 employees in November 2001. Foreign competition and a slow denim market could not sustain production.

At the MVF mill, the PCCA maintained operations that served customer needs, including production of ring spun yarn and finishing 68-inch-wide denim produced at the ACG plant. MVF closed the Creative Textiles warehouse and moved its textile inventory to vacant space at the MVF mill. The decision to retain some operations at MVF proved wise as the PCCA exceeded its product quantity sales goals in 2002. Denim prices remained low, however, and the Textile Division reported another loss at the end of fiscal 2002.

After a period for cotton producers that the PCCA likened to the Great Depression, the denim market improved. The PCCA continued to develop denim styles with new dye methods and finishes, as well as a new stretch Lycra and cotton blend fabric. In late 2002 Levi Strauss placed new orders for denim with a new flat finish for its Type One jeans. Levi Strauss also introduced a new Signature brand line of low-priced denim clothing for exclusive sale at Wal-Mart stores beginning in July 2003.

Principal Divisions

Marketing Division; Pool Division; Electronic Marketing Division; Textile Division.

Principal Competitors

Calcot, Ltd.; Cargill, Inc.; Dunavant Enterprises, Inc.; Staple Cotton Cooperative Association.

Further Reading

"Be Prepared," *(Plains Cotton Cooperative Association) Commentator,* Spring 2000, p. 1.

Chirls, Stuart, "Cotton's Future: Technology Key," *WWD,* June 16, 1998, p. 8.

——, "Texas Cotton Co-op Targets Home," *HFN The Weekly Newspaper for the Home Furnishing Network,* July 12, 1999, p. 10.

"Denim on the High Plains: Producer-Gin-Mill Co-op," *Textile World,* November 1984, p. 83.

"Designer Interest Boosts Denim Demand," *Bobbin,* April 2000, p. 36.

Duffey, Patrick, "Improving Denim Market Sparks PCCA Rebound," *Rural Cooperative,* January-February 2003, p. 36.

Flattmann, Valerie, and John Johnson, "Denim Market Surge Continues for PCCA," *(Plains Cotton Cooperative Association) Commentator,* Summer 2002, p. 3.

Hansen, Bruce, "Contenders Line Up to Computerize Cotton Receipts," *Memphis Business Journal,* August 30, 1993, p. 1.

Hughes, Kathleen A., "Cotton Industry Gains Called Transitory, China's Export-Boom Sobers U.S. Growers," *Wall Street Journal,* New York, June 4, 1984, p. 1.

Johnson, John, " 'Asian Flu' Forces Changes at Mission Valley Fabrics," *(Plains Cotton Cooperative Association) Commentator,* Summer 2001, p. 2.

——, "In the Face of More Adversity: Textile Division Continues to Adapt to Changing Marketplace," *(Plains Cotton Cooperative Association) Commentator,* Winter 2001/2002, p. 2.

——, "PCCA Develops Loss Allocation Plan," *(Plains Cotton Cooperative Association) Commentator,* Summer 2001, p. 3.

——, "Project Aims to Improve Quality, Cut Costs and Add Flexibility," *(Plains Cotton Cooperative Association) Commentator,* Winter 1999, p. 3.

——, "Two Plants Help Coop Meet Demand," *(Plains Cotton Cooperative Association) Commentator,* Spring 2002, p. 7.

Lacy, Sarah, "Cotton Exchange," *Memphis Business Journal,* July 14, 2000, p. 1.

Maycumber, S. Gray, "For the New Mission Valley, Versatility Is the Game, to Its Well-Known Yarn-Dyed Lines, Denim and Moe Have Been Added," *Daily News Record,* July 12, 1999, p. 33.

McCurry, John W., "PCCA Buys Mission Valley Textiles," *Textile World,* June 1998, p. 22.

——, "PCCA Expands Denim Operation," *Textile World,* June 1999, p. 22.

Miller, Kate, "Dot Com Fallout Aside, The Seam Has Enjoyed Success," *Memphis Business Journal,* July 20, 2001, p. 9.

"New Braunfels, Texas, Textile Factory Cuts Jobs," *Knight Ridder/ Tribune Business News,* November 28, 2001.

"New Gin Opens in Blackwell, Oklahoma, for Cooperative Members," *Knight-Ridder/Tribune Business News,* October 14, 1999.

Parker-Pope, Tara, "West Texas, Facing Its Worst Drought in 40 Years, Braces for Cotton Disaster," *Wall Street Journal,* April 20, 1994, p. T4.

Rudie, Raye, "The Many Faces of Denim," *Bobbin,* April 1999, p. 40.

"Weaving Forges New Highs in Quality," *Textile World,* January 1995, p. 38.

"Why Pooling Works," *(Plains Cotton Cooperative Association) Commentator,* Winter 1999, p. 1.

—Mary Tradii

posco

POSCO

POSCO Center
Daechi-4-dong
Kangnam-ku, Seoul
South Korea
Telephone: 82-2-3457-0114
Fax: 82-54-220-6000
Web site: http://www.posco.co.kr

Public Company
Incorporated: 1968 as Pohang Iron and Steel Company
   Ltd.
Employees: 25,000
Sales: $12.10 billion (2002)
Stock Exchanges: New York
Ticker Symbol: PKX
NAIC: 331221 Rolled Steel Shape Manufacturing (pt);
   331210 Iron and Steel Pipe and Tube Manufacturing;
   331111 Iron and Steel Mills (pt)

POSCO, formerly Pohang Iron and Steel Company Ltd., is among the world's leading steel producers. The company manufactures annually roughly 26 million tons of hot- and cold-rolled steel products, including steel coil, plate, wire rod, electrical sheets, and stainless steel. Approximately 72 percent of POSCO's steel remains in Korea, for use in that country's shipbuilding, automotive, and home appliance industries, while the rest is exported to some 60 countries. POSCO also operates numerous subsidiaries and joint ventures across the globe. Like other steel producers, POSCO struggled during the Asian economic crisis of the late 1990s. Since then, the company has focused on building partnerships with other international steel companies (including its once arch-nemesis Nippon Steel Corporation), increased its offerings of value-added steel products, and backed out of nonperforming operations and joint ventures. POSCO is also rapidly expanding in China.

Forging a Steel Industry

In the aftermath of the Korean War, it was in the interests of South Korea, as well as of the United States and its supporters in

that conflict, that the country's economy recover and develop as rapidly as possible. As the First Development Plan was elaborated, measures were included for protecting new industries with tariffs, quotas, and, in some cases, prohibition of imports of competitive products.

Steel was a crucial industry for the Koreans, domestic production capacity having been damaged severely during the war. An integrated steel mill with an annual capacity of 300,000 tons was discussed at a very early stage, and there were some hopes of including it in the First Plan. The World Bank and other international agencies considered the plan too ambitious and inappropriate because, they argued, Koreans could not master the technology, and the plant would not be large enough to operate efficiently, while anticipated domestic demand would be insufficient to justify construction of a larger mill. Ultimately they were to be proven wrong.

In place of the larger scheme, a number of small-scale steel plants based on electric furnaces and domestic scrap were built. One of the first and most important of these was the Inchon Heavy Industrial Corporation financed by the Korean government. Inchon had a 50-ton open-hearth furnace and a medium rolling mill capable of producing 10,000 tons of sheet steel per year. Further development on a similar scale led, particularly after 1963, to the establishment of some 15 firms involved in producing steel of various kinds. Initially employing old-fashioned techniques, non-continuous rolling mills produced sheet steel, bars and rods, wire, and pipe of uneven quality in quantities insufficient to meet demand. These facilities were gradually updated, though.

Birth of POSCO

With the strong support of Korean President Chung Hee Park, the chairman of Korean Tungsten Mining Company, former Major General Tae Chun Park, spearheaded a second attempt to assemble an international financial package to build an integrated steel mill. This scheme, to build a plant capable of producing 600,000 tons of crude steel per year, was elaborated by a consortium of seven Western steelmakers, known as Korea International Steel Associates (KISA). In October 1967, a contract between KISA and the Korean government stipulated that

KISA would raise an international loan by 1969, and complete the integrated mill by 1972. Costs were estimated at $100 million. The operating company, Pohang Iron and Steel, was incorporated in 1968. For most of its history, however, Pohang was commonly referred to as POSCO. Reflecting this reality, the company formally adopted that name in 2002.

Fulfillment of the plan, however, had to be postponed, in part because the consortium's structure was extremely cumbersome, making it difficult to reach rapid decisions. Koppers, the leading consultant in the group, was unable to raise the necessary capital, and the KISA was dissolved in 1969.

Advice given to the Korean government continued to oppose the building of an integrated steel capacity, primarily on the grounds of the domestic market's inability to support an efficient plant. The government remained convinced of the steel mill's importance, however, and decided to raise foreign loans to finance it rather than continuing to attempt to secure private capital.

Japanese steelmakers and the Japanese government felt they could derive worthwhile economic and political advantages from assisting the Koreans in this plan. During the annual conference between Korean and Japanese ministers in August 1969, preliminary agreement was reached for resurrecting the KISA plan. Discussions through the rest of the year led to a contract whereby Japan would arrange loans covering most of the capital required. Japan's Export-Import Bank provided $52.5 million, its Economic Cooperation Fund $46.43 million, and Japanese commercial loans $28.58 million. The remainder, some $24 million, came from other sources.

Detailed planning was carried out with the help of Mitsubishi Heavy Industries. Care at this stage was a major factor in enabling POSCO to save the large amounts of capital that would have been required to cover any delays. Construction was planned and implemented in such a way as to facilitate future expansion.

The Japanese steelmakers involved in the plans, Nippon Kokan (NK) and Nippon Steel Corporation (NSC) benefited considerably from the arrangements made in 1970 for provision of the underlying technology needed. Virtually every detail from scheduling the timing of construction to specifications, supervision, purchasing, and inspection, culminating with onsite support for start-up and operation, was in Japanese hands. The involvement of Korean engineers in this first phase was limited to the inspection of specifications, in conjunction with foreign engineers.

Building Pohang Steel Works: 1970–81

It was part of the Korean development strategy to locate the new plant as far as possible from Seoul, to create industrial centers throughout the country. Tae Chun Park and the government ministry settled on Pohang in the Kyongsangnamdo province as a location. When construction began in 1970, it was closely supervised by Tae Chun Park, who not only insisted that suppliers meet deadlines, but also, in some cases, accelerated deadlines and insisted that they be met. When the first stage of construction was completed in 1973, a month ahead of schedule, the major plant consisted of a blast furnace and two steel converters. These had capacities of 949,000 and one million tons, respectively. The plant had a foundry pig iron furnace, with production capacity of 150,000 tons, as well as a blooming and slabbing mill, billet mill, and a plate and hot rolling mill. This plant reached full production within four months rather than the minimum of 12 months the Japanese steelmakers had anticipated.

While construction of the first phase was going on, Koreans were being trained abroad, particularly in Japan, to take over some of the technological work involved in operating the mill. They labored alongside their Japanese counterparts in construction and operating work, gaining valuable experience. As a result, in subsequent expansion, the amount of operating technology that had to be brought in from outside steadily decreased.

The second phase of construction at Pohang began in 1974, and Korean engineers were still only involved in specification inspection. However, by the time the third phase had begun in 1976, Koreans had taken over material balance and facilities specification and inspection of drawings. When the fourth stage began three years later, Koreans had supplanted foreign engineers from the task of general engineering planning. The shift to domestic technological skills was also evident in the declining levels of royalties paid to outside experts from $6.2 million for the first stage, $5.8 million for the second, $4.8 million for the third, and nothing for the fourth. By the time the last stage of construction had been completed, POSCO's crude steel production capacity was 8.5 million tons.

Knowledge-Based Advances and International Growth Through the 1980s

In order to avoid some of the problems of erratic quality experienced by existing small-scale producers, POSCO's emphasis initially was on the production of plain high-carbon steels of even quality that were used for general structural purposes, rather than on the development of a wider range of specialized products. As the company expanded, and engineering skills increased, it was possible to diversify production. The development of high tensile strength steel production in 1975 laid the foundation for the first major expansion of overall production, but domestic demand for special steels remained too low to justify attempts to develop them. Only as domestic demand increased, or was expected to increase, notably as defense industries developed, were facilities to broaden production created, based once again on imported technology.

Through the period of construction and operation, machinery came primarily from Japan and Austria. As time went

Key Dates:

1968: Pohang Iron and Steel is founded.
1970: Company begins construction on first phase of Pohang plant.
1981: Last phase of Pohang plant is completed.
1985: Company begins construction on Gwangyang Works.
1992: Last phase of Gwangyang is completed.
1998: South Korean government begins privatizing POSCO.
2001: Privatization is completed.
2002: Company officially changes name to POSCO.

on, however, a larger proportion of needed equipment was produced by Korea's own heavy industry. Korean engineering skills, too, constituted a major part of the reason for POSCO's ability to produce high-quality steel at low prices. In the spheres of equipment design and operating procedures, field engineers and technicians brought about major improvements in efficiency and quality along with reductions in waste and costs.

As POSCO developed its capacity in Korea, the company began to look outward for both raw materials and new markets. Korea did not abound with the iron ore and coal that POSCO needed to produce steel, so the company sought foreign suppliers for raw materials—sometimes securing the material by direct purchase, sometimes by establishing joint ventures and partnerships abroad. In addition to early partnerships in Brazil, POSCO opened a coal mine in Pennsylvania as a joint venture with the American firm Barnes & Tucker. The joint venture, Tanoma Coal Co., sold its entire output to POSCO.

While POSCO secured from abroad the materials it needed to keep its furnaces running, the company also continued to ramp up steel manufacturing capacity in Korea. As part of its chairman's vision of regional dominance in the industry, POSCO began construction on a second integrated steel plant in Kwangyang, in South Korea's rural Chollanamdo province. Like the Pohang steel works, Kwangyang was built in four phases. By the time the facility was completed in 1992, POSCO could produce 21 million tons of steel a year. With this additional output, POSCO became the world's second largest steel maker.

Expansion and Contraction in the 1990s

The early 1990s were a period of further international expansion for POSCO. The Kwangyang facility boosted POSCO's sales, and the company used the additional revenue to fund its growth in new markets. In 1986, POSCO had established a joint venture with the American firm USX Corp. to build a steel mill in California. Although the mill soon became profitable, POSCO fell victim to its own success, as the company encountered increasing protectionism from recession-plagued Europe and the United States.

The prospect of trade wars, combined with a global slump in steel demand, prompted POSCO to eye new territory, particularly the nascent Chinese market. The Korean steel maker's expansion in the world's most populous country was breathtak-

ing. POSCO had exported only about 200,000 tons of steel to China in 1991. The following year, it shipped over one million tons, the same amount it exported to the United States. In no small part because of this success, POSCO sought to strengthen its position in China, and in 1992, announced it would invest $97 million to build a tin plate plant in Shanghai. The same year, POSCO expanded its operations in Vietnam, signing an agreement with the state-run Vietnam Steel Corp. (VCS) to construct a pipe mill and an electric arc furnace near Hanoi, as well as to expand capacity at POSCO's existing joint venture with VCS known as Posvina Co. This overseas building enabled POSCO, in the midst of a weak global steel market, to boost its net income 27 percent to W 185.1 billion ($234 million) in 1992. About 45 percent of POSCO's output was exported.

POSCO underwent internal changes, as well. After partially privatizing the company in 1988, the Korean government began in 1994 to explore the idea of privatizing POSCO completely, possibly even breaking apart the company and selling off its pieces to private investors. POSCO lobbied hard to prevent this outcome, however, and the plan was ultimately scrapped.

POSCO took another great leap forward in 1989, when the company opened itself to foreign ownership. The company began selling overseas convertible bonds the same year to fund the second phase of construction at the Kwangyang works. In 1994 POSCO went even further and made its first public stock offering, becoming the first South Korean company to be listed on the New York Stock Exchange (NYSE).

This period of growth was accompanied by new challenges for POSCO, though. In 1992, company Chairman Park suddenly resigned. A few months later, the government, under the leadership of the new South Korean President Kim Young-Sam (who had campaigned on an anti-corruption platform) launched a full-scale investigation of POSCO and Park. The following year, South Korea's National Tax Administration levied a penalty of W 79.3 billion ($99.4 million) against POSCO and W 6.3 billion against Park personally. Park left South Korea for Japan and abandoned his post of honorary chairman of the company.

As the 1990s progressed, POSCO began to seek out new markets in which to grow. POSCO launched dozens of joint ventures across the globe, including new plants in China (1995 and 1996), Indonesia (1995, 1996, and 1997), Vietnam (1996), Myanmar (1996), and Venezuela (1997). The company continued to perform well in the midst of this rapid growth. POSCO's profit surged 30 percent in 1994, while its net sales rose 12 percent in 1995. At the same time, POSCO hoped to free itself from exclusive reliance on the cyclical steel industry. To this end, it branched out into telecommunications, taking a stake in Atel Inc., a telecommunications network provider co-owned by Australia's Telstra Holdings Pty. Ltd.

While POSCO cast about for new paths (which also included electric power generation and the distribution of liquefied natural gas), the company also set a goal of boosting its production of value-added, higher-end steel. Like other Korean businesses, though, POSCO suffered during the country's massive currency devaluation of 1997 and the aftershocks that plagued the entire region. This Asian economic crisis hammered industries in Korea, Japan, Thailand, and China—the major markets for POSCO's (and its competitors') steel. Indeed, Korean steel companies Sammi Steel Co. and Hanbo went bankrupt. Steel prices plummeted worldwide, and as steel manufacturers struggled to make up the price difference in volume, they glutted the market, driving down prices even further. In 1998, POSCO announced it was cutting steel production for the first time in its history, as export prices and domestic demand continued to drop.

The crisis also buffeted the South Korean government, which ratcheted up its schedule to privatize POSCO. In order to raise foreign currency and help satisfy International Monetary Fund-imposed criteria for the release of $57 billion in much needed stabilization loans, the government sold off an additional 3.14 percent stake in POSCO in 1998. The shares were repackaged as American depository receipts and offered on the New York Stock Exchange. The following year, the government sold an additional 13 percent stake. Privatization was fully completed in 2001, when the government divested its final shares.

Despite the difficulties it encountered in its markets at home and abroad, POSCO continued to perform well in the late 1990s. In 1998, the company's net profit rose 54 percent and its sales grew 15 percent, although demand for steel dropped 35 percent in Korea during the year.

As the millennium closed, though, POSCO stumbled. In 1999 the company publicly admitted to the *Asian Wall Street Journal* that it had spent $3.83 billion on bad investments (which it defined as non-core businesses and redundant facilities) between 1994 and 1997. Another problem was posed by what had initially appeared to be a triumph. In 1994, POSCO had been selected to play the leading role in the South Korean government's consortium to build and develop the nation's second mobile phone network. POSCO had been jockeying for this position in what the *Asian Wall Street Journal* called ''the world's most lucrative telecommunications project'' for four years. POSCO recruited Air Touch—which had recently spun off from the American company, Pacific Telesis Group—as its technology partner in the project.

POSCO's competitors, including several American telecommunications firms, cried foul, though, and claimed the steel giant had corrupted the selection process. The allegations only added fuel to the movement to fully privatize POSCO, which its detractors claimed was too enmeshed in nearly every sector of South Korea's business.

Moreover, although POSCO refused publicly to classify it as such, it was clear to outsiders that its stake in Shinsegi Telecom, as the government cell phone consortium had been named, was a failure. Late in 1999, POSCO announced it would sell its entire stake in Shinsegi, thereby cutting itself loose from the new sector it had so eagerly sought to enter a few years earlier.

POSCO also continued to be plagued by corruption charges. In 1998, a South Korean government watchdog group accused POSCO executives, particularly former chairman Kim Mah Je, of embezzling more than W 7 billion ($5.8 million) in company funds for personal use. In 2003 POSCO Chairman Yoo Sang Boo also resigned, after he was indicted on embezzlement charges in 2002.

Weathering the Storm in the New Millennium

To regroup, POSCO slowed the pace of its expansion and committed to investing only in projects that were in line with its core operations. It canceled some joint ventures and suspended others. It also attempted to cut its expenses by merging subsidiaries. In 1999, for example, it united Pohang Steel Industries and Pohang Coated Steel to create Pohang Steel Co. It also merged three machinery units into one entity, POSCO Machinery Company.

Worldwide, though, steel prices remained low in the new century. According to the *Asian Wall Street Journal*, ''steel companies [could] not price their products any lower without going bankrupt.'' Industry analysts predicted that a wave of consolidation would sweep the industry. POSCO sought to stave this off by forming strategic partnerships with former rivals to secure lower prices for raw materials and share the costs of research and joint procurement. In 2001 POSCO joined with Nippon Steel and China's Baoshan Iron & Steel Works to fulfill this goal.

Despite the challenges it faced, POSCO remained optimistic. In 2003 POSCO set a mid-term goal to attain W 36 trillion ($29.8 billion) in corporate value by 2007. It also planned to redouble its export efforts in China.

Principal Subsidiaries

Dalian POSCO-CFM Coated Steel Co., Ltd. (59%); Pohang Steel America Corp. (99%); Pohang Steel Australia Pty., Ltd. (95%); POSCO Engineering & Construction Co., Ltd. (97%); POSCO International Osaka Inc. (95%); POSCO Machinery & Engineering Co., POSCO Research Institute (99%); POSCO Venezuela Caompania Anonima (59%); POSDATA Co., Ltd.; POSLILAMA Steel Structure Co., Ltd. (68%); POS-THAI Steel Service Center Co., Ltd. (67%); POS-Tianjin Coil Center Co., Ltd. (39%); Posnesia Stainless Steel industry (70%); VSC-POSCO Steel Corp. (40%); Zhangjiagang Pohang Stainless Steel CO., Ltd. (80%); Zhangjiagang POSCO Coated Steel Co., Ltd. (90%).

Principal Competitors

Arcelor S.A.; Bechtel Group, Inc.; Corus Group plc; Fluor Corporation; Kawasaki Steel Corporation; Kobe Steel, Ltd.; Nippon Steel Corporation; Shanghai Baosteel Group Corporation; Toyota Tsusho Corporation.

Further Reading

Booth, Jason, ''Heard in Asia: Asia's Steel Industry Looks More Stable, Not More Profitable,'' *Asian Wall Street Journal*, January 26, 2001.

Cho, Namju, ''Heard in Seoul: Professionals Post 'No Fishing' Signs for Korean Market,'' *Wall Street Journal Europe*, December 11, 1997.

Darlin, Damon, ''New Trade Relationship with China Is Changing South Korea's Economy,'' *Wall Street Journal*, November 17, 1992.

Enos, J. L., and W. H. Park, *The Adoption and Diffusion of Imported Technology: The Case of Korea*, London: Croom Helm, 1988.

Glain, Steve, ''Cliques and Cronies: How Korean Industrialists Carved Up a Phone License,'' *Asian Wall Street Journal*, June 30, 1994.

——, "Korea's New President Uses Old-Style Politics to Pressure Steel Magnate," *Asian Wall Street Journal*, March 12, 1993.

Glain, Steve, "Steely Nerves: Anxious POSCO Awaits Study on Privatization, Monopoly," *Asian Wall Street Journal*, March 20, 1995.

Manguno, Joseph, "Korean Steel Firm Takes on the Japanese," *Wall Street Journal*, April 29, 1988.

Mi-Hui, Kim, "Everyday Some Kind of History Is Made, Especially in a Developing Country Like Korea Where Things Change at a Lightning Pace," *Korea Herald*, July 4, 2003.

——, "POSCO Spent $3.83 Billion on Bad Investments," *Asian Wall Street Journal*, February 2, 1999.

—Simon Katzenellenbogen
—update: Rebecca Stanfel

 PPB GROUP BERHAD

PPB Group Berhad

17th Fl. Wisma Jerneh
38 Jalan Sultan Ismail
50250 Kuala Lumpur
Malaysia
Telephone: (+60) 3-214-12077
Fax: (+60) 3-214-18242
Web site: http://www.ppbgroup.com

Public Company
Incorporated: 1948 as Kuok Brothers
Employees: 15,085
Sales: M$7.86 billion ($2.07 billion) (2002)
Stock Exchanges: Kuala Lumpur
Ticker Symbol: PEPT
NAIC: 551112 Offices of Other Holding Companies;
111336 Fruit and Tree Nut Combination Farming;
212210 Iron Ore Mining; 236115 New Single-Family
Housing Construction (Except Operative Builders);
311211 Flour Milling; 311225 Fats and Oils Refining
and Blending; 311312 Cane Sugar Refining; 326299
All Other Rubber Product Manufacturing; 445110
Supermarkets and Other Grocery (Except
Convenience) Stores; 452111 Department Stores
(Except Discount Department Stores); 512110 Motion
Picture and Video Production; 512120 Motion Picture
and Video Distribution; 512131 Motion Picture
Theaters, Except Drive-In; 517212 Cellular and Other
Wireless Telecommunications; 517910 Other
Telecommunications; 541310 Architectural Services;
541330 Engineering Services; 713990 All Other
Amusement and Recreation Industries

One of Malaysia's largest companies, and one of the largest conglomerates in the ASEAN market region, PPB Group Berhad has established diversified operations ranging from food to cinemas to water and wastewater engineering. Foods remain PPB's historic and primary business, accounting for 90 percent of the company's revenues of M$7.86 billion ($2 billion) in 2002. More than 72 percent of those sales are generated through the company's vertically integrated edible oils, especially the oil palms business, through publicly listed subsidiary PPB Oil Palms (PPBOP). Sugar refining and cane plantations, the company's original business, added 9 percent to sales, while grain and feed milling, through the company's majority shareholding in FFM Bhd, another publicly listed subsidiary, added 8 percent to sales. The mature Malaysian market, coupled with strict price control on basic food items, has encouraged PPB to seek international growth for its food operations, and the company has entered Indonesia, Vietnam, Singapore, and other countries in southeast Asia and elsewhere in the world. Other operations under the PPB umbrella include businesses involved in packaging, livestock farming, and cinemas, through Golden Screen Cinemas. Despite its continued focus on foods, PPB is in the process of reinventing itself for the new century, targeting the water and wastewater engineering market for future growth. The company, through engineering subsidiary Chemquest, also publicly listed, has acquired a major share of the consortium holding the concession for the Sungei Semenyih Dam and Water Treatment Plant, and has plans to enter the Chinese market in 2003. Although PPB is itself traded on the Kuala Lumpur stock exchange, the company is controlled by the Kuok Group, one of the region's top conglomerates.

Immigrant Trading Origins in the Early 20th Century

PPB's history paralleled the rise of the Kuok family in Malaysia through the 20th century. In 1909, Kuok Keng Kang immigrated to then-British controlled Malaysia from his home in China's Fujian province. Kuok began trading rice, sugar, and flour, and formed his own company, Tong Seng & Co. Kuok's business flourished, despite his inability to speak English. Yet from the start, Kuok had taken care to build strong ties with the Malay community—which, although the majority population, were soon to be overshadowed economically by the ethnic Chinese population there.

Like most of the country's Chinese immigrants, Kuok placed a high value on education, sending his three sons, Robert, Philip, and William, to study overseas. Robert, born in

1927, was sent to Raffles, in nearby Singapore. The outbreak of World War II cut short Robert Kuok's education, however. Nonetheless, at school, Robert Kuok had become friends with Tun Abdul Razak and Tun Hussein Onn, both of whom later became Malaysian prime ministers. Another classmate was Lee Kuan Yew, who became the first prime minister of Singapore after its independence.

Returning home, Robert Kuok joined Mitsubishi, which, among other trading activities, had gained a monopoly on rice imports. The younger Kuok became fluent in Japanese and rose to become head of the rice import operation, while the elder Kuok received a license to act as a wholesaler. Following the war, the Kuoks began supplying foodstuffs to the Japanese prisoner of war camp in the province, which led in turn to the Kuok family gaining control of the wholesale market for essential foodstuffs in their South Johore region.

Kuok Keng Kang died in 1948. Robert Kuok and brother Philip, together with other members of the family, went into business together, forming Kuok Brothers Sdn Bhd. (The third brother, William Kuok, had joined the Malaysian Communist Party and was killed by the British in 1952.) After Philip Kuok turned to politics, Robert Kuok became the force behind the family business—starting the career that was to make him one of Asia's most respected and admired businessmen.

Faced with tough competition in the rice market in the early 1950s, Kuok switched the company's focus to another important commodity, sugar. As he explained to *Forbes:* "The sugar trade was conducted in English, which put me in a stronger position. I was reading Reuters." Backing his sugar business, Kuok moved to London for a time, where he learned—and mastered—the commodities trading business.

When Malaysia gained its independence in 1957, Kuok's political friendships, as well as the new Malaysian government's economic policies, which encouraged import substitution, enabled the company to grow strongly into the 1960s. The company began acquiring sugar plantations and, in 1959, established its own refinery arm, under Malayan Sugar Manufacturing Company. That company, backed by the Malaysian government, operated as a joint venture with Nissin Sugar Manufacturing and Mitsui Bussan Kaisha, both Japanese companies.

The government's import substitution-based economic policy also led Kuok into another important food commodity, flour milling, and the company founded Federal Flour Mills Berhad (FFM) in 1962. In the meantime, Kuok, who had continued to acquire sugar plantations, stepped up his sugar commodity trading activities through the 1960s. By the end of the decade, Kuok, who at times controlled more than 10 percent of the world's sugar supply, had earned the nickname "The Sugar King."

Founding a New Conglomerate in the 1970s

The Malaysian government faced increasing pressure to establish a more equitable distribution of wealth in the country, where the ethnic Chinese minority controlled most of the country's economic wealth. Kuok, who had shifted the base of his growing and increasingly international business empire to Singapore, had nonetheless maintained his family's close ties in Malaysia. Kuok also favored the distribution of wealth to the ethnic Malay population as a means of ensuring political and economic stability in the country. In 1968, Kuok took the first step toward converting part of his holdings into a "Malaysian" company, forming Perlis Plantations Bhd, which took over the company's Malaysian sugar plantations interests. Perlis Plantations then launched a 50–50 joint venture, Kilang Gula Felda Perlis Sdn (KGFP), to establish a sugar cane mill and refinery complex.

Civil unrest in 1969, accompanied by violent protests against the ethnic Chinese population, brought a new government to power, which instituted a new wave of economic reform designed to promote the emergence of a wealth base among the ethnic Malay population. In response to these reforms, Kuok took Perlis Plantations public in 1972, listing its shares on the then-joint Malaysia and Singapore stock exchange. By then, Kuok's business interests had taken him into a number of new areas, notably hotel and real estate development, under the Shangri-la Hotel group.

Perlis Plantations itself began seeking to diversify in order to reduce its initial reliance on its sugar plantations business. In 1976, the company acquired Kuok's Malayan Sugar Manufacturing Company, thereby becoming a truly vertically integrated sugar concern. That acquisition also gave Perlis a number of secondary acquisitions, with operations and shareholdings in such areas as hotels, packaging, and shipping.

Perlis Plantations continued to serve as a vehicle for much of Kuok's Malaysian business interests, as Malaysian government policies continued to emphasize ethnic Malaya priorities. At the same time, Perlis Plantations itself pursued a diversification of its activities, particularly with its absorption in 1979 of Mineral Securities Malaysia (later Minsec), which controlled the tin mining concern Rahman Hydraulic Tin, a public company since 1973. In 1980, Perlis Plantations added to its mining interests with iron ore specialist South Island Mining Company. Both companies brought Perlis rubber plantation operations, while the Minsec acquisition added property development holdings as well.

Property development took on added importance in the group in the 1980s, with the 1982 acquisition of Tai Yan Realty, which operated especially in the Cheras area of Kuala Lumpur, and the purchase of 34 percent of nationally operating Shaw Brothers in 1983. The Tai Yan acquisition was later renamed PPB Hartabina.

In 1986 the company's property development interests led it into retailing, through the Chujitsu Superstore chain. Over the next decade, the company developed its retail operations into a chain of more than 35 supermarkets. The company also built up a string of discount stores. In 1996, Perlis Plantations formed a joint venture with The Netherlands' Ahold, which sought entry into the Malaysian market, transferring its supermarkets into a new joint venture, Tops Retail (Malaysia). After several years of

Key Dates:

1909: Kuok Keng Kang emigrates from China and sets up a trade business in Malaysia.

1948: Kuok's sons, Robert Kuok and brother Philip, set up Kuok Brothers initially as rice wholesalers after their father's death.

1952: Kuok Brothers enters the less competitive sugar market and begins acquiring sugar plantations.

1959: Kuok Brothers establishes a sugar refinery operation, Malayan Sugar Manufacturing Company (MSM).

1962: Kuok Brothers founds Federal Flour Mills (FFM), entering the flour milling and refining market.

1968: Kuok Brothers forms Perlis Plantations to take over its sugar plantation operations.

1972: Perlis Plantations goes public as Robert Kuok transfers his main business group overseas.

1976: Perlis Plantations acquires MSM.

1987: Perlis Plantations acquires majority control of FFM; launches oil palm plantations operations.

1993: The company acquires 40 percent of Chemquest, and enters the environmental engineering market.

1996: The company merges its oil palm plantations into the publicly listed PPB Oil Palms (PPBOP).

2000: Chemquest, through its 25 percent stake in Konsortium Abass Sdn Bhd, wins the concession for the Sungai Semenyih Dam and Water Treatment Plant; Perlis Plantations changes its name to PPB Group.

2002: The company acquires PT Kerry Sawit Indonesia, part of the Kuok Group's Kerry Foods, to boost its international oil palms operations.

2003: The company announces a strategy to boost environmental engineering to 25 percent of sales by 2010.

losses, however, Perlis Plantations sold its 35 percent stake in Tops to Ahold in 2000. In that year, Perlis Plantations shut down its discount store operations as well, exiting the retail market.

Another offshoot of its property development business was a move into cinema operation, after the company formed the joint venture Golden Screen Cinemas (originally Golden Communications) with Hong Kong's Golden Harvest International. That entity grew into Malaysia's largest cinema operator in the 1990s, with 14 cinema complexes, including an 18-screen theater in Kuala Lumpur, the country's largest. Yet the cinema operations were to remain relatively minor for the company, reaching just 1 percent of total revenues by the end of the 20th century.

Instead, Perlis Plantations had found a new area of growth: oil palm plantations. The company's first move into this area—which was to become its major revenue center through the 1990s—came in 1986, when it established a 9,000-hectare plantation under Sarema Sdn Bhd. The following year, Perlis Plantations acquired a 60 percent stake in Sapi Plantations, which added more than 14,000 hectares of oil palm plantations under the company's control. That acquisition, which added refinery

operations as well, also enabled Perlis Plantations to move toward becoming a vertically integrated palm oil company.

From Oil Palms to Engineering in the New Century

Perlis Plantations continued to add new business areas at the end of the 1980s and the beginning of the 1990s. In 1987 the company acquired a majority stake in parent Kuok Group's flour operations, FFM. That company, which had gone public in 1982, had itself undergone a diversification, with businesses including animal feeds, livestock breeding, and a commodities brokering operation handling wheat, maize, and soybeans.

In 1987, also, Perlis Plantations took over another piece of the Kuok Group's Malaysian holdings when it acquired the Rasa Sayang Beach Hotels resort, which was later regrouped under Kuok's flagship hotel empire, Shangri-la. The Malaysian wing of that company was listed on the Kuala Lumpur stock exchange in 1992, with Perlis Plantations retaining a major shareholding until 1999, when it transferred its holding to the hotel chain's parent group Shangri-la Asia.

Perlis Plantations continued to add palm oil plantations in the 1990s, with a total of nine plantations in Malaysia by mid-decade. In 1995, the company's growing interest in that market led it to move overseas, with the acquisition of a majority stake in a 10,000-hectare plantation in Sumatra, in Indonesia. In 1997, Perlis Plantations reorganized its Malaysian oil palm plantations business, merging those operations into a single entity, PPB Oil Palms (PPBOP). The company then spun off PPBOP as a public company on the Kuala Lumpur stock exchange, keeping a majority share.

While the company built up its oil palm business—which grew to represent more than 70 percent of the company's total revenues by the end of the 20th century—it also had been investigating other business areas. In 1993, the company made one of its first moves into Indonesia, acquiring latex glove manufacturer PT Healthcare Glovindo. That investment was to prove less than successful, however, and by the beginning of the next year had slipped into losses.

A more prominent extension came with the company's purchase of a 40 percent stake in Chemquest Sdn Bhd, an environmental engineering firm focused on water and wastewater management projects and related areas. In 1998, Perlis Plantations increased its holding in Chemquest to 55 percent, while the Kuok Group took the remaining minority stake. Two years later, Chemquest, through its 25 percent stake in Konsortium Abass Sdn Bhd, won the 30-year concession to operate and manage the Sungai Semenyih Dam and Water Treatment Plant. In that year, Perlis Plantations changed its name to PPB Group.

If Chemquest remained relatively small, accounting for just 2 percent of the company's total revenues in 2002, it became PPB's spearhead for its future transformation. With the maturity of its core Malaysian foods market presenting the company with limited growth potential, PPB adopted a new, two-pronged strategy. On the one hand, PPB intended to internationalize its essential foods businesses, extending operations into new territories, such as Vietnam, Singapore, China, and other ASEAN member markets, a move begun in 1999 with the opening of a flour milling operation in Vietnam under FFM. In 2002, PPBOP boosted its Indonesian position with the purchase of PT Kerry Sawit Indonesia, part of the Kuok Group's Kerry Foods business. The purchase boosted PPB's total Indonesian oil palm plantation holdings past 100,000 hectares.

The second prong of PPB's new growth strategy involved an emphasis on its development into an important environmental engineering and wastewater management player in the region. As Chairman Ong Ie Cheong told the *Star:* "We will nurture the engineering division through acquisitions and joint ventures. We will tie up with well-known names to enter China. There is enormous growth potential for infrastructure development." The company expected its engineering division to represent as much as 25 percent of its total sales before 2010.

As part of its reorientation, PPB began shedding businesses, including its sale of its share of Tops to Ahold, and its divestment of its Shangri-la holding. The company also announced its intention to shed its money-losing Glovindo division in 2003. Instead, PPB announced a M$350 million investment program that year, with the majority of those funds earmarked for FFM and PPBOP. In 2003, also, the company's Chemquest subsidiary expected to sign a contract to build a sewage treatment plant in China. Although that contract was postponed due to the Severe Acute Respiratory Syndrome (SARS) outbreak that year, the company expected the completion of the contract to provide a springboard for its expansion into China.

Robert Kuok in the meantime remained at the head of one of Asia's largest business empires—with a publicly listed worth of more than $7.5 billion and estimates of the group's private holdings ranging to three times as much and more. PPB, which remained the historic base of Kuok's empire, had itself grown into a major regional conglomerate, with revenues of more than M$7.8 billion ($2 billion) in 2002. The company's willingness in the past to reinvent itself—from sugar to palm oil to environmental engineering concern—pointed the way to continued success in the future.

Principal Subsidiaries

Ampang Leisuremall Sdn Bhd (55%); Astakonas Sdn Bhd; FFM Bhd (54%); Kembang Developments SDN BHD; Kiland Gula Felda (50%); Malayan Sugar Manufacturing Co. BHd; Masurna Trading Co. LTd.; Malaysian Bulk Carriers Sdn Bhd; Perlis Sdn Bhd (50%); PPB Corporate Services Sdn Bhd; PPB Hartabina SDN Bhd; PPB Oil Palms Bhd (55.8%); South Island Mining Co. Sdn Bhd.

Principal Competitors

Wilmar Holdings Pte Ltd.; Goodman Fielder Ltd.; Asia Food and Properties Ltd.; COFCO International Ltd.; Sam Yang Corp.; Golden Hope Plantations Bhd.

Further Reading

"In the Palm of Its Hands," *Malaysian Business,* October 16, 2001.
Ismail, Zaidi Isham, "PPB to Spend M$275m to Streamline Operations," *Business Times (Malaysia),* March 6 2003, p. 1.
Keong, Neil Khor Jin, "Kuok—The Quintessential Asian Tycoon," *Star,* June 4, 2001.
"PPB Evolving into Global Giant," *Star (Malaysia),* May 12, 2003.
Tanxer, Andrew, "The Amazing Mr. Kuok," *Forbes,* July 28, 1997, p. 90.

—M.L. Cohen

Priceline.com Incorporated

800 Connecticut Avenue
Norwalk, Connecticut 06854-9998
U.S.A.
Telephone: (203) 299-8000
Fax: (203) 299-8948
Web site: http://www.priceline.com

Public Company
Incorporated: 1998
Employees: 359
Sales: $1.03 billion (2002)
Stock Exchanges: NASDAQ
Ticker Symbol: PCLN
NAIC: 541512 Computer Systems Design Services

Former Internet high-flyer Priceline.com Incorporated has surprised the skeptics by surviving the collapse of the tech stock market at the beginning of the 2000s. Priceline.com has pioneered a patented Internet-based ''demand collection'' pricing system that connects purchasers with sellers under the company's registered ''Name Your Own Price'' slogan. Priceline.com applies that pricing system to sales of airline tickets, hotel rooms, and car rentals, and vacation and cruise packages. The company also offers home financing services, including mortgages, mortgage refinancing, and home equity loans. In addition to its main U.S.-oriented priceline.com e-commerce web site, the company operates priceline.co.uk for the U.K. market, and licenses the Priceline system and brand to Hutchison Whampoa-backed Priceline Asia in Hong Kong. The company also offers more traditional discount travel services through Lowestfare.com. Priceline has proven that demand for its pricing system exists—revenues topped $1 billion in 2002, despite the difficult travel market. Profits, however, have proven more elusive; its share price, which peaked very early on at $165, has dropped to as low as $1.10. Richard Braddock is the company's non-executive chairman, and Jeffrey Boyd is Priceline's CEO.

Entrepreneurial Origins in the 1980s

Priceline.com was the brainchild of Jay Walker and his think tank Walker Digital. By the time he founded that company, a limited partnership, in the early 1990s, Walker had started some 20 different businesses—including launching his own newspaper at the age of nine. One of Walker's first successes came while studying as an undergraduate at Cornell University. Walker came to the conclusion that the popular board game Monopoly was, in fact, a game of skill, not chance. Putting his ideas into a book, *1000 Ways to Win Monopoly Games,* Walker sold more than 100,000 copies and earned himself a lawsuit from the game's manufacturer. (Walker won the lawsuit.) In a break from school, Walker launched a new weekly newspaper, which survived for a full year.

After receiving a bachelor's degree in industrial relations, Walker set out to blaze an entrepreneurial trail in the early 1980s. By the end of the decade, Walker had put a string of businesses behind him—ranging from a company that sought to place advertisements in catalogs, another that sought to sell catalogs in retail stores, and another that sold light sculptures, succeeding in attracting a number of prominent customers.

At the beginning of the 1990s, however, Walker hit on a new product: ideas. Walker's brainstorm came after reading about the success of the public key encryption system, which had been successfully patented by its inventors and which formed the basis of a company, RSA Data Security. Walker recognized that, like any other invention, one could successfully patent an idea, or, in Walker's case, the development of new business models. This discovery laid the basis of Walker Digital, which was incorporated as a partnership (90 percent owned by Walker himself) in 1994. In the meantime, Walker set out looking for ideas.

Walker quickly found his first successful business model. Joining with Michael Loeb, son of the *Fortune* magazine editor, Walker launched NewSub Services in 1992. Walker's idea, later patented, was simple—adapt the European model of magazine and newspaper subscriptions, which are linked to customers' bank accounts and thus automatically renewable, to the U.S. market. The concept was a success, and eventually succeeded in attracting more than 30 million customers. NewSub Services later renamed itself Synapse Group and became majority controlled by AOL TimeWarner.

Walker had moved on to new entrepreneurial frontiers, however, selling one-third of his 50 percent stake in NewSub

Services in order to raise $25 million for his next venture. In 1994, Walker founded Walker Digital as a think tank for business-oriented patents, based on the model of Thomas Edison's collaborative Menlo Park laboratory. Walker Digital's team of thinkers quickly began churning out ideas—and patent applications. By the end of the decade, the company had more than 300 patents to its name.

Pricing Revolutionary in the 1990s

By the mid-1990s, Walker Digital had developed the business model for a new style of pricing system that sought the inverse of the customer-retailer relationship. Under Walker's system, customers were to "name their own price," placing a bid at a price they were prepared to pay for a particular product. Retailers then would choose to accept or refuse the offer. Among other advantages, the system enabled retailers to unload surplus merchandise without calling attention to the discount pricing.

By 1996, Walker had targeted the first area in which to deploy the new business model. The airline industry appeared to be the perfect testing ground for the idea—on any given day, airlines were flying with some 500,000 empty seats. Walker proposed setting up a service that would allow airlines to sell off the empty seats at discounted prices—without advertising the cut-rate fares.

By 1997, Walker Digital had put into place the concept and software structure for priceline.com, an Internet-based "name your own price" ticketing service that matched customers to airlines. Customers placed bids for the round trip of their choice, and the price they were willing to pay. In return, customers accepted certain limitations—such as the choice of airline and exact travel times, while also accepting at least one connecting flight. Priceline, which reserved the right to reject unreasonably low bids, used its database software to match buyers with airlines willing to accept the price bid. Priceline was formally created in 1997, backed by the rights to part or all of some 19 Walker Digital patents, and a $500,000 investment from Walker himself. In exchange, Walker and Walker Digital took a 49 percent stake in the new company, headquartered in Connecticut.

Yet Priceline nearly did not get off the ground. Walker met with resistance from the major airlines, then in the process of developing their own Internet web sites and reluctant to assist a potential competitor. By the beginning of 1998, Walker had succeeded in attracting just two relatively small airlines, TWA and America West. Walker pressed ahead with the venture anyway and launched priceline.com in April 1998, backing the launch with a highly popular advertising campaign featuring former Star Trek star William Shatner as company spokesperson. Shatner was paid in part with shares in priceline.com.

The site was immediately successful, with more than 600,000 "hits" on its first day and more than 30,000 ticket sales in its first two months. Priceline.com, unable to meet the demand through TWA and America West alone, instead was forced to buy tickets on the retail market—subsidizing customer orders at an average of $30 per ticket. The company's losses mounted quickly. As Walker told the *Financial Times:* "I took an enormous risk launching Priceline, both personally and as a company. It took a lot of guts."

By mid-1998, the company appeared ready to collapse. At the same time, Walker faced a great deal of criticism, in part because of his boldness in patenting business models and, in part, because to many, priceline.com appeared to be simply a variant on the discount coupon—a means of identifying price-conscious consumers among the larger, brand-loyal public.

The turning point for the company came in August 1998. Walker handed over the reins of the company to Richard Braddock. "As an entrepreneur," Walker told the *Star Ledger,* "I'm good at assembling resources and starting a company and getting it up and running, but I'm certainly not the right person to be running a $100 million company." The arrival of Braddock, former president of Citicorp, gave Priceline a boost in legitimacy. It also helped overcome the airlines' resistance, and that month, Priceline signed on its first major airline, Delta. As part of that deal, the company agreed to warrant some 12 percent of its stock to Delta. With Delta onboard, the company was able to make steady gains in convincing other airlines to make their surplus seating available through Priceline.

Priceline quickly expanded its range of products to include hotel room reservation and car rental services. The company also began extending the "demand collection" system to other markets, such as car sales, launched in the New York area in July 1998. By October of that year, the company had sold more than 60,000 airline tickets and posted some $2 million in car sales.

By the beginning of 1999, the company was booking orders for more than 1,000 airline tickets and 1,000 hotel rooms per week. The company's first quarter sales that year neared 200,000 tickets, some 50 percent more than it had sold in its first nine months. In April 1999, Priceline went public, with a listing on the NASDAQ. Initially priced at just $16 per share, Priceline became one of the stars of the tech stock boom—by May 1999, Priceline's stock had shot up to its all-time high of $165 per share, valuing the company, which, like most Internet stocks of the time, had yet to turn a profit, at nearly $19 billion. Walker's own share of the company, including his holding through Walker Digital, was valued at some $9 billion.

Walker himself played down the stock's star status, telling *Forbes:* "You want to be recognized for your intellectual achievement, not for the fact that a bunch of day traders took your stock to a price that may or may not represent the real value of the firm." Nonetheless, the company's stock value encouraged the other major airlines to join the service; with promises of similar stock option packages, Priceline succeeded in signing on the rest of the major airline holdouts, including United, American Airlines, and US Airways, the first, second, and fifth largest airlines, by the end of 1999. By then, the company boasted a customer base of more than four million people. It also claimed one of the highest recognition rates among Internet-based brands. Sales, too, were gaining strongly, jumping from just $35 million in 1998 to more than $480 million in 1999. That figure more than tripled by the end of 2000.

Surviving into the New Century

Riding on its own momentum, Walker and Priceline started out the year 2000 with ambitious expansion plans. With the Priceline ticket and reservation system gaining steadily—daily revenues were topping $3 million—the company took a two-pronged approach to expanding its operations. The first of these involved exporting the priceline.com concept, signing on licensees overseas. These included the priceline.co.uk, in the United Kingdom; MyPrice in Australia and New Zealand; Priceline.com Europe, created by General Atlantic Partners and headed by former Burger King CEO Dennis Malamatinas; Hutchison Whampoa's Priceline Asia in Hong Kong; and Softbank's Priceline.com Japan. In another expansion move, the company acquired online discount travel agent Lowestfares.com, combining the Priceline model with more "traditional" online ticket sales.

At the same time, the company sought to extend the Priceline-held business model into other markets. In January 2000, the company announced its intention to launch its own national Internet service based on the Priceline model, with service to start in Atlanta. That venture never got off the ground, however; instead, the company began offering long-distance telephone services. More promising was a partnership formed with Alliance Capital Partners to create Pricelinemortgages, which began offering home mortgage, mortgage refinancing, and home equity loan products. Meanwhile, Walker Digital began developing additional concepts, launching WebHouse Club to apply the Priceline concept to grocery and gasoline

sales, and My Yardsale, which brought the concept to the used goods market. Meanwhile, Richard Braddock became company chairman, and Daniel Shulman was hired as CEO.

Yet nearly all of Priceline's expansion ventures foundered—with the only survivors remaining the Priceline UK and Priceline Asia sites, and the Pricelinemortgages services. Meanwhile, Priceline was facing increasing consumer pressure as well. In September 2000, the Connecticut Attorney General's office announced that it was investigating some 100 consumer complaints against the company. The company was already facing a groundswell of consumer dissatisfaction, in particular for the sometimes overly long layover times between connecting flights. Soon after, that state's Better Business Bureau delisted Priceline. When both WebHouse Club and My Yardsale announced that they were shutting down in October, the already fragile investor confidence in the company collapsed completely. By the end of 2000, as the Priceline ventures in Australia and Japan were abandoned, the company's shares had dropped to less than $1.50 per share—leading to a public dispute with spokesperson, and shareholder, Shatner.

After addressing consumer concerns, Priceline was readmitted to the Better Business Bureau in December 2000. At the end of that month, the company addressed shareholder concerns when Walker announced his decision to leave the company and sell off most of his holding in the company. Despite posting a revenue increase to more than $1.2 billion in 2000, Priceline's continued losses—at $25 million—and the apparent inability to apply its business model to other markets, seemed to doom the company as yet another failed tech stock in the Internet bust at the turn of the century.

Priceline began a restructuring drive at the beginning of 2001, which included the layoffs of some 150 employees. In May 2001, the company dropped CEO Shulman and Braddock instead took on a dual role as chairman and CEO. The company also stepped up its customer relations efforts.

By the summer of 2001, Priceline surprised the financial community by posting its first ever quarterly profit. While the company's cost-cutting exercise had helped, it also benefited from the slump in the U.S. economy, which drove more customers to seek its discounted service. In the second quarter of that year, the company signed on more than one million new customers; at the same time, it had built up a strong repeat business among its growing customer base. The company also received praise for quickly abandoning its expansion drive to focus on its core product. By August 2001, the company's shares had climbed back to the $9 range. Yet the company was unable to shrug off the effects of the September 11th terror attacks. By the end of 2001, its sales had slipped back to $1.16. Nonetheless, it managed to contain its losses, which reached just $7.3 million for the year.

In July 2002, Priceline hired a new CEO, Jeffrey Boyd, who shared the chief executive spot with Braddock before becoming the company's sole CEO at the end of that year. Braddock took on the role of non-executive chairman at that time. Meanwhile, Priceline struggled throughout the year, hit on one side by declines in the travel industry amid fears of terrorism and the impending war in Iraq, and on the other by the steady lowering of regular airfares as airlines struggled to fill their seats. By the end of 2002, the company's losses deepened against falling sales, which dropped to slightly more than $1 billion for the year.

Priceline's difficulties continued into the year as air traffic collapsed with the outbreak of the new war in Iraq. At the same time, the company shut down its car sales business, as well as its long-distance telecommunications operation, dropping another 65 employees from its payroll. Nonetheless, Priceline was not ready to give up the fight and began to look for new partnerships. In March 2003, Priceline agreed to buy an $8.5 million equity stake in online hotel reservation network Travelweb, owned by such hotel groups as Marriott International, Hilton Hotels, Hyatt, and others. While Priceline appeared to edge toward more traditional sales outlets, its core discount niche nonetheless seemed to have found a solid consumer market. Now Priceline needed only to find a way to turn a profit from its pricing revolution.

Principal Subsidiaries

Fastforward.com.

Principal Competitors

Cendant Corporation; Expedia, Inc.; Travelocity.com Inc.

Further Reading

Berenson, Alex, ''Priceline Losses, Sales Worse Than Predicted,'' *New York Times,* February 16, 2001, p. C2.

Collins, Amy, ''Priceline Boots CEO,'' *Business 2.0,* May 8, 2001.

Doan, Amy, ''Forbes Faces: Jay Walker,'' *Forbes,* November 30, 2000.

Gimein, Mark, ''Jay Walker's Patent Mania,'' *Salon.com,* August 27, 1999.

Hoffman, Al, ''Back to the Lab,'' *Star-Ledger,* October 12, 1998, p. 67.

Machan, Dyan, ''An Edison for a New Age?,'' *Forbes,* May 17, 1999.

Moran, John M., ''Idea Out of Fuel: Priceline Ends Sales of Groceries, Gas,'' *Hartford Courant,* October 6, 2000, p. E1.

Patsuris, Penelope, ''Priceline, a Surprising Survivor,'' *Forbes.com,* October 3, 2001.

Price, Christopher, ''Patent Approach Pays Off,'' *Financial Times,* July 25, 2000, p. 16.

Shabelman, David, ''Priceline Invests in Travelweb,'' *Daily Deal,* March 20, 2003.

Varian, Hal R., ''Priceline's Magic Show?,'' *Standard,* April 24, 2000.

—M.L. Cohen

ProLogis

14100 East 35th Place
Aurora, Colorado 80011
U.S.A.
Telephone: (303) 375-9292
Fax: (303) 375-8581
Web site: http://www.prologis.com

Public Company
Incorporated: 1991 as Security Capital Industrial Trust
Employees: 700
Sales: $679.6 million (2002)
Stock Exchanges: New York
Ticker Symbol: PLD
NAIC: 525930 Real Estate Investment Trusts

ProLogis is the world leader in leasing and managing distribution centers. It owns more industrial warehouses, and refrigerated warehouses, than anyone else. The company has kept a rather low profile, considering its rapid expansion and international reach. ProLogis (formerly ProLogis Trust) owned or managed assets worth more than $10 billion in 2002—more than 1,700 properties in North America, Europe, and Asia. Most of its U.S. facilities are concentrated in the six hubs of Atlanta, Dallas, southern California, San Francisco, Chicago, and New Jersey. ProLogis takes a customer service-driven approach, and provides management services in addition to simply building and leasing industrial and refrigerated warehouse space.

Origins

William Sanders believed in the power of leverage through size: i.e., larger companies could achieve better terms in borrowing money and charging rent. Through his Santa Fe-based Security Capital Group Inc., Sanders formed Security Capital Industrial Trust (SCI) in 1991. SCI began buying property in 1993, becoming one of the first to enter the Denver market after the real estate crash of the late 1980s.

Security Capital Industrial Trust (SCI) was a REIT—a real estate investment trust. This type of structure had been set up by Congress in 1960 to allow shareholders to invest in a range of different real estate properties at once, much like a mutual fund. What made REITs a hot prospect among investors was the fact that they were not required to pay corporate taxes as long as they disbursed 95 percent of net income to shareholders.

Security Capital Industrial Trust (SCI) began operations in 1991. According to the *Journal of Commerce,* SCI's target market was the thousand top companies with global distribution. By the end of the decade, it would have contracts with 400 of them. Leasing warehouses was attractive to these corporations because it did not tie up as much capital as owning them. Having SCI manage them allowed them to concentrate more on their core businesses.

Security Capital Industrial Trust had a successful initial public offering (IPO) in April 1994. SCI owned 16.1 million square feet of industrial property in 16 cities by the time of its IPO. It was preparing to break ground on Denver's first "spec" warehouse in ten years. Although no tenants were lined up in advance, SCI was reserving 20,000 square feet of the space for its own headquarters, where it would employ 70 people. This left 61,000 square feet of space to lease.

Cool Business, New Territory in 1997

SCI bought Christian Salvesen's U.S. refrigerated warehouse business in April 1997, paying $122.3 million (£75.2 million) for 17 warehouses. It made another cool purchase in December 1997, buying Continental Freezers of Illinois. This brought SCI up to 20 refrigerated warehouses and distribution centers, with a total of 78 million cubic feet. It was the largest U.S.-based publicly traded owner of warehouses and distribution centers. The June 1998 purchase of Hatfield, Pennsylvania-based Rosenberger Cold Storage Cos. increased SCI's cold holdings by 27 percent, reported the *Denver Post.*

SCI started its European operations with a three-person office near Amsterdam Schiphol Airport in July 1997. Within two years, it would be the market leader. A large buy in Europe in December 1997 made SCI a major player in the continent's refrigerated distribution services market. Sweden's Frigoscandia AB was acquired for $395 million from ASG, a transportation and logistics company. Frigoscandia had 90 refrigerated warehouses in eight countries; it led Europe with a 15 percent market share (SCI had a 5 percent market share in the United States). The buy tripled SCI's refrigerated distribution space, to 263 million cubic feet in the United States and Europe. It helped SCI edge out its nearest rival, Americold Corp. of Portland, Oregon, for leadership of the category, reported the *Denver Post.*

Since SCI viewed industrial property as a service business, reported the *Financial Times,* this global reach enhanced its value to such multinational clients as Nestlé, Unilever, Campbell Soup, and Pepsico. The emergence of the European Union, and the simplification of shipping between member states, was prompting many of these to consolidate their distribution operations in Europe.

New Name in 1998

Security Capital Industrial Trust got a new name in March 1998: ProLogis Trust. (The ticker symbol changed from SCN to PLD.) In March 2003, the company dropped the ''Trust'' from the name on its charter, becoming simply ''ProLogis.'' The name, an abbreviation of ''professional logistics,'' reflected the firm's dominance in logistics services around the world, and the importance of this business in light of the increasing trend toward globalization. ProLogis then owned more than 1,100 facilities in a dozen countries. It had about 4,000 employees around the world and 100 at its Aurora, Colorado headquarters.

ProLogis entered the U.K. market in August 1998 with the purchase of Kingspark Holding S.A. for $157 million (£95 million). According to the *Financial Times,* ProLogis planned to offer shorter-term leases (five to ten years) than were standard in the United Kingdom (15 to 25 years), aimed at third-party logistics providers such as NFC, which controlled a third of the United Kingdom's distribution market. (It also operated in the United States as Excel.) ProLogis's policy of building facilities ''on spec,'' before clients were lined up, made it attractive to growing international companies under pressure to find scarce space. Another factor working in the company's favor there, as one official told the *Journal of Commerce,* was the increased outsourcing of distribution in Europe compared with the United States.

Just three months later, in November 1998, ProLogis announced a massive deal that would grow its holdings by 30 percent. In a wave of mergers among REITs, the company agreed to buy Meridian Industrial Trust Inc. in a deal worth $1.47 billion in stock ($862.5 million) and assumed debt. Meridian boasted 36 million square feet of distribution space centered in Chicago, Dallas, and Los Angeles; nearly all of its assets were in core markets of ProLogis. Meridian had been

created in 1996 from the merger of four smaller companies, which had combined assets of $250 million at the time. It had grown quickly in a short time, but unlike ProLogis, had not managed its own properties. Lower stock prices and tighter credit had produced consolidation in the REIT business, reported Canada's *National Post.*

Global Expansion in the Late 1990s

Expansion continued in Europe. In December 1998, ProLogis agreed to pay $317 million for Garonor S.A., which owned five million square feet of warehouse space in France. Its holdings in Paris and Marseille would be the basis for ProLogis's presence in central Europe. Garonor's client list included Hoescht Marion Roussell Ltd. and Siemens AG.

Rapid growth in Europe was attained organically as well as by acquisition. ProLogis had built more than 600,000 square feet of warehouse space in The Netherlands, making it the country's largest developer. To fund continued development in Europe amid rising property prices, ProLogis established a $1 billion European Property Fund in September 1999. In July of the next year, it launched a much smaller North American Properties Fund to bankroll expansion on its home continent.

ProLogis also had moved into Eastern Europe, building a facility in Warsaw used by multinationals such as TDK, Eastman Kodak, and Switzerland's Novartis AG.

Continuing Expansion Beyond 2000

ProLogis survived the consolidation of William Sanders's 16 companies to five in early 2000. Sanders also controlled giant apartment developer Archstone Communities.

ProLogis debuted a new line of business in the spring of 2000, Equipment Services. This unit financed distribution equipment such as conveyor belts and storage racks. Later in the year, ProLogis acquired a 30 percent holding in GOwarehouse, a developer of supply-chain management software.

E-commerce was another important area of expansion. ProLogis developed a 750,000-square-foot warehouse in the United Kingdom for amazon.com, and developed for Barnesandnoble.com a 600,000-square-foot building near Reno, Nevada. ProLogis had a hundred e-commerce firms and related businesses on its target list.

ProLogis partnered with foreign banks and governments to fund its business at home and abroad. A June 2002 public offering with Macquarie Bank of Australia raised A$400 million to fund 55 distribution centers in the United States and Mexico (a market ProLogis had entered in 1997). Six other funds held $2.9 billion worth of property managed by ProLogis. At the same time, ProLogis was starting a $1 billion fund with the government of Singapore to develop industrial properties in Japan. Japan and Europe both had unfilled demand for industrial warehouses, a ProLogis official stated in Britain's *Financial Times.* Opportunities there helped offset a weakness in the U.S. market.

An important trend was that of consolidating warehouses. In mid-2002 ProLogis announced that it was helping Unilever PLC trim its 15 U.S. distribution centers to a $200 million network of five warehouses totaling nearly five million square feet. The deal was expected to save Unilever $20 million a year. The contract only included Unilever's household and personal products, not food products.

Annual revenues rose 15 percent from $523 million to $679 million in 2002. Net earnings more than doubled, from $91 million to $216 million. ProLogis Trust owned or managed assets worth more than $10 billion, a figure up 21 percent from the previous year.

Principal Subsidiaries

PLD International Incorporated; ProLogis BV (Luxembourg); ProLogis Developments Holdings Sarl (Luxembourg); ProLogis-France Developments Incorporated; ProLogis Japan Incorporated; ProLogis UK Holdings S.A. (Luxembourg).

Principal Operating Units

Global Development Group; Global Services Group; Market Services Group; ProLogis Solutions Group.

Principal Competitors

AMB Property Corporation; First Industrial Realty Trust.

Further Reading

Barnard, Bruce, "ProLogis Takes the Continent by Surprise," *Journal of Commerce,* July 16, 1999, p. 5.

Beard, Alison, "Real Estate Trusts Are Looking Abroad to Offset Woes at Home," *Financial Times* (London), November 5, 2002, p. 29.

Berke, Jonathan, "Prologis Closes North America Fund," *Daily Deal,* July 25, 2000.

Cohen, Norma, "ProLogis Buys UK Warehouse Chain," *Financial Times* (London), August 20, 1998, p. 21.

Couch, Mark P., "ProLogis Gets Huge Account with Unilever; Aurora Company to Provide Warehouse Network, Services," *Denver Post,* July 18, 2002, p. C1.

——, "ProLogis to Build a Third Warehouse for Coors Brewing; Distribution Facility in Golden to Be Completed by September," *Denver Post,* January 16, 2002, p. C10.

——, "Warehouse Builder Sees Growth at Home, Abroad," *Denver Post,* December 15, 2002, p. K5.

"Denver's ProLogis to Buy French Developer; Purchase Part of REIT's Global Expansion Plan," *Rocky Mountain News,* December 12, 1998, p. 1B.

Gose, Joe, "The Ground Floor: Thanks to E-Commerce, Warehouses Aren't Just for Storage Anymore," *Barron's,* March 13, 2000, p. 58.

Graham, Sandy, "ProLogis Is Quietly Successful," *Denver Rocky Mountain News,* August 27, 2000, p. 3G.

Gresser, Charis, "Christian Salvesen Makes £75m US Disposal," *Financial Times* (London), April 26, 1997, p. 19.

Harley, Robert, "Macquarie ProLogis Delivers on Acquisition Promise," *Australian Financial Review,* February 13, 2003, p. 44.

——, "Macquarie to Seek $400m for Trust," *Australian Financial Review,* May 3, 2002, p. 75.

Hijino, Ken, "Singapore Link on Japan Estates," *Financial Times* (London), June 21, 2002, p. 29.

House, Kathryn, "Flying Start for Macquarie ProLogis," *Australian Financial Review,* June 27, 2002, p. 40.

Kirkpatrick, David D., "ProLogis Agrees to Pay $940 Million to Acquire Rival Meridian Industrial," *Wall Street Journal,* November 18, 1998, p. A8.

Locke, Tom, "ProLogis Trust Sees Future in Foreign Expansion," *Wall Street Journal,* June 30, 1999.

Marcial, Gene G., "ProLogis Raises the Roof," *Business Week,* June 23, 2003, p. 130.

Martinez, Barbara, "ProLogis Raises Bet on Europe," *Wall Street Journal,* September 16, 1999, p. C1.

Narvaes, Emily, "Kings of the Warehouse; Real Estate Trust Builds, Acquires Its Way to Top," *Denver Post,* January 24, 1999, p. L1.

——, "Security Capital Adds to Cold Storage Buildings," *Denver Post,* June 17, 1998, p. C3.

——, "U.S. Realty Firms See Room for Big Growth," *Denver Post,* February 21, 1999, p. E2.

Pandya, Mukul, "A Low-Key REIT Grows Rapidly," *Business News New Jersey,* March 10, 1997, p. 8.

"ProLogis Acquires Meridian," *Denver Post,* November 18, 1998, p. C1.

"ProLogis Is Buying Developer," *Denver Post,* December 12, 1998, p. C1.

"ProLogis Purchase of Meridian Part of Real Estate Merger Trend: Slumping Stock and Tighter Credit Deter REIT Acquisitions," *National Post* (Canada), November 18, 1998, p. C13.

Raabe, Steve, " 'Cool' Deal Inked; Local Firm Buys European Outfit," *Denver Post,* December 16, 1997, p. C1.

——, " 'Spec' Industrial Warehouse to Be Built," *Denver Post,* May 25, 1994, p. C2.

"Security Capital Group," *Going Public: The IPO Reporter,* May 19, 1997, p. 9.

Thangavelu, Poonkulali, "GE Extends Reach in Commercial RE," *National Mortgage News,* December 31, 2001, p. 2.

—Frederick C. Ingram

SAN MIGUEL CORPORATION

San Miguel Corporation

40 San Miguel Avenue
Mandaluyong City
1550 Metropolitan Manila
Philippines
Telephone: (2) 632-3000
Fax: (2) 632-3099
Web site: http://www.sanmiguel.com

Public Company
Incorporated: 1913 as La Fabrica de Cerveza de San Miguel
Employees: 27,259
Sales: P 136.05 billion ($2.54 billion) (2002)
Stock Exchanges: Philippine
Ticker Symbol: SMC
NAIC: 312120 Breweries; 312140 Distilleries; 312111 Soft Drink Manufacturing; 312112 Bottled Water Manufacturing; 311421 Fruit and Vegetable Canning; 112111 Beef Cattle Ranching and Farming; 112210 Hog and Pig Farming; 112320 Broilers and Other Meat Type Chicken Production; 112340 Poultry Hatcheries; 311119 Other Animal Food Manufacturing; 311211 Flour Milling; 311223 Other Oilseed Processing; 311225 Fats and Oils Refining and Blending; 311512 Creamery Butter Manufacturing; 311513 Cheese Manufacturing; 311611 Animal (Except Poultry) Slaughtering; 311612 Meat Processed from Carcasses; 311615 Poultry Processing; 322211 Corrugated and Solid Fiber Box Manufacturing; 327213 Glass Container Manufacturing; 332115 Crown and Closure Manufacturing; 332431 Metal Can Manufacturing

Best known for its internationally distributed beer, San Miguel Corporation can only be described in superlatives. It is southeast Asia's oldest and largest brewer. It also ranks as the Philippines' largest and one of its most consistently profitable companies. San Miguel's flagship beer utterly dominates the Filipino market, with a 90 percent market share. A 1988 brief in the *Economist* noted that Filipinos order "beer" at bars and restaurants, knowing that they will receive a San Miguel. But San Miguel did not make it to the top of the regional heap on good beer alone. It also makes agricultural feeds, processed and fresh meats, dairy products, coconut products, hard liquor, nonalcoholic beverages, and packaging products such as glass containers, corrugated cartons, aluminum cans, and metal crowns and caps. Through wholly or majority-owned subsidiaries, San Miguel holds dominating market shares in several food and beverage sectors in the Philippines: 90 percent of carbonated beverages, 58 percent of powdered juice, 56 percent of hard liquor, and more than 80 percent of margarine and butter. By the early 2000s, beer and other alcoholic beverages constituted only about one-third of San Miguel's annual turnover. In fact, the conglomerate had, by 2001, grown over the course of its more than 110 years in business to generate 3.6 percent of its home country's gross domestic product and 4.5 percent of government tax revenue.

San Miguel grew to its commanding position in the southeast Asian market in spite of political upheaval, infrastructure glitches, and high taxes. It achieved its status through aggressive competitive strategies and shrewd long-range planning over the decades. Having diversified into agribusiness, foods, and packaging in the mid-20th century, the conglomerate dominated its domestic markets by the early 1980s. At that time, San Miguel undertook an aggressive program of international expansion that came to fruition in the mid-to-late 1990s.

Early History

Don Enrique Ma Barretto de Ycaza established the brewery, southeast Asia's first, in 1890 as La Fabrica de Cerveza de San Miguel. He named the company after the section of Manila in which he lived and worked. He was soon joined by Don Pedro Pablo Roxas, who brought with him a German brewmaster. San Miguel's brew won its first major award at 1895's Philippines Regional Exposition, and led its imported competitors by a five-to-one margin by the turn of the 20th century. The company was incorporated in 1913 following the death of Don Pedro Roxas.

By that time, San Miguel was exporting its namesake brew to Hong Kong, Shanghai, and Guam. Andrés Soriano y Roxas joined San Miguel in 1918, beginning a multigeneration (albeit interrupted) reign of Sorianos. In 1990, San Miguel's Beer Bulletin noted that ''Beer was the heart of San Miguel's business, and the soul from which emanated all its other businesses.'' Andrés Soriano initiated the company's diversification, which proceeded rather logically via vertical integration. The experience cultivating barley naturally evolved into other agricultural businesses, for example. San Miguel gathered steam in the 1920s, when the company expanded into nonalcoholic beverages with the creation of the Royal Soft Drinks Plant in 1922. San Miguel entered the frozen foods market in 1925 with the creation of the Magnolia Ice Cream Plant. By the early 1990s, Magnolia held four-fifths of the frozen dessert market. Soriano created the first non-U.S. national Coca-Cola bottling and distribution franchise in 1927. The Philippine company owned 70 percent of the joint venture, which grew to become Coke's sixth largest operation. By the early 1990s, San Miguel had captured over two-thirds of the domestic soft drink market.

Although World War II interrupted San Miguel's brewing business, the company got back on the growth track in the postwar era, acquiring production facilities in Hong Kong in 1948. The company also resumed its program of vertical integration, even building its own power plant so that it would not be dependent on the Philippines' notoriously poor infrastructure. San Miguel also built a liquid carbon dioxide plant, glass bottle manufacturing facilities, and a carton plant during the postwar period.

The company shortened its name to San Miguel Corporation in 1963, and Andrés Soriano, Jr., advanced to the company's presidency upon his father's 1964 death. He has been credited with instituting modern management theory, including decentralization along product lines. Soriano, Jr., continued to diversify the food business during the early 1980s, expanding into poultry production in 1982, building an ice cream plant in 1983, and adding shrimp processing and freezing in 1984.

Over the decades, San Miguel earned a formidable reputation as a fierce competitor. The company used all the tools at its disposal. When it could not beat a rival through traditional means, it acquired and intimidated upstarts into submission. The Filipino government's complicity did not hurt, either. Long protected by high tariffs, San Miguel encountered its first major competitor in the beer market in the late 1970s. That was when Asia Brewery entered the segment. The rivalry between Asia Brewery and San Miguel came to a head in 1988, when Asia

Brewery cannily introduced a bargain-priced ''brand'' called, simply, ''Beer.'' The imported product looked and tasted like its primary competitor, playing upon the fact that in the Philippines, the San Miguel brand was synonymous with ''beer.'' It was a creative counter to San Miguel's notoriously aggressive and sometimes cutthroat competitive strategy, which had reportedly included ''attempts to sabotage [Asia Brewery's] sales network and smash its empty bottles.'' Asia Brewery, whose owner was reputedly connected to Marcos sympathizers, even hired away San Miguel's brewmaster.

Although San Miguel enjoyed virtual monopolies in its markets, that status did not shield it from the political machinations of the Philippines. The dictatorial reign of Ferdinand Marcos brought this element into sharp focus in the 1980s, when an intra-familial proxy fight at San Miguel turned political. The dispute was instigated in 1983 by Enrique Zobel, a wealthy cousin of the Sorianos who owned the Ayala banking and real estate group and sided with the Marcos government. Unable to execute a takeover on his own, Zobel sold his 19.5 percent stake to Eduardo Cojuangco, Jr. (known in some circles as ''the coconut king''). Although Cojuangco was a cousin of Marcos opponent Corazon Aquino, he too sided with Marcos. Cojuangco's Coconut Industry Investment Fund (a.k.a., United Coconut Planters Bank) accumulated an additional 31 percent of San Miguel, giving him effective control of the conglomerate and leaving the Soriano family with a mere 3 percent. Cojuangco scooped up the chairmanship in 1984, when Andrés Soriano, Jr., died of cancer. However, his reign over San Miguel lasted only two years. When Marcos lost the 1986 election to Aquino amidst the ''people power'' revolution, Cojuangco and many other Marcos backers fled the country. (In fact, Marcos and Cojuangco left in the same helicopter.)

Andrés Soriano III resumed San Miguel's chairmanship and launched a campaign to reclaim the family legacy that year. But when the new chairman tried to buy back the abandoned shares, he was blocked by an unexpected agency; the Aquino administration's Presidential Commission on Good Government (PCGG) assumed control (but not legal ownership) of the 51.4 percent stake and refused to relinquish it. The government asserted that the stake had been illegally obtained. In the 1970s Marcos had imposed a tax on the production of coconuts, a major Philippine cash crop, with the proceeds supposed to fund that industry's development. It was alleged, however, that the money was funneled into the Cojuangco-controlled United Coconut Planters Bank, and that Cojuangco then used much of the funds to help him purchase his controlling stake in San Miguel. The controlling interest carried nine of San Miguel's 15 directors seats with it. The PCGG continued to tend its San Miguel stake into the early 1990s, but it acceded de facto control of the conglomerate to Andrés Soriano III via a management contract with his A. Soriano Corp.

Soriano III was characterized by *Business Week*'s Maria Shao as an ''introverted, almost reclusive'' leader. Schooled at the University of Pennsylvania's prestigious Wharton School, Soriano III had dabbled in investment banking in New York City before returning to the Philippines. Soriano tried everything from legal machinations to joint-venture buyout schemes to wrest control of San Miguel from the PCGG, but to no avail.

Key Dates:

1890: Don Enrique Ma Barretto de Ycaza establishes a brewery in Manila called La Fabrica de Cerveza de San Miguel.
1913: The brewery is incorporated.
1918: Andrés Soriano y Roxas joins San Miguel, beginning the long-term, multigenerational involvement of the Soriano family.
1922: Company expands into nonalcoholic beverages with the opening of the Royal Soft Drinks Plant.
1925: Production of ice cream begins at the Magnolia Ice Cream Plant.
1927: San Miguel becomes the first non-U.S. national Coca-Cola bottler and distributor.
1963: Company shortens its name to San Miguel Corporation.
1983: Soriano family proxy fight leads to the purchase of a 19.5 percent stake in San Miguel by Eduardo Cojuangco, Jr., a close associate of Philippine dictator Ferdinand Marcos.
1984: Cojuangco assumes the chairmanship of San Miguel.
1986: "People power" revolution forces Marcos to flee the country; Cojuangco is among those joining him in exile; the new Philippine government sequesters 51.4 percent of the company shares; Andrés Soriano III resumes the company chairmanship.
1987: San Miguel purchases majority control of La Tondeña Distillers, Inc., the leading producer of hard liquor in the Philippines.
1997: San Miguel exchanges its 70 percent stake in Coca-Cola Bottlers Philippines, Inc. for a 25 percent interest in the Australian firm Coca-Cola Amatil Limited (CCA).
1998: Cojuangco returns to the chairmanship following the election of Joseph Estrada to the Philippine presidency.
2001: Pure Foods Corporation, producer of processed meats and flour, is acquired; San Miguel joins forces with the Coca-Cola Company to reacquire Coca-Cola Bottlers Philippines, relinquishing its stake in CCA as part of the deal.
2002: The company acquires Cosmos Bottling Corporation; Kirin Brewery Company, Limited acquires a 15 percent stake in San Miguel.
2003: Litigation continues over the 47 percent of the company shares still sequestered by the government.

At the same time, Soriano III continued the company's program of expansion, acquiring majority control of La Tondeña Distillers, Inc., the leading producer of hard liquor in the Philippines, in 1987 and adding beef and pork production to the company's food operations in 1988.

In 1990 San Miguel threw a five-month party to celebrate its centenary. President Corazon Aquino called San Miguel "the best showcase of a Filipino company, a shining example of creative management and commitment to its public." The *Economist* contrastingly called San Miguel "a showcase for much that is wrong with business in the Philippines." The latter assertion was substantiated that same year, when Cojuangco returned to the Philippines (the *Journal of Commerce* noted that he "sneaked back into the country [in 1990] despite a ban on his return") to lay claim to his holdings. Notwithstanding the circumstances of his repatriation, a November 1992 article in *Asian Business* noted that "Cojuangco [was] expected to win eventually." All the same, Soriano III continued to hold the chairmanship. (Cojuangco, meantime, unsuccessfully ran for the Philippine presidency in 1992.)

International Expansion: 1980s–90s

Soriano III led the company to a new era of dramatic growth based on internationalization. This move was motivated by a number of factors. First, San Miguel had developed its core Philippine and Hong Kong markets to maturity and was faced with relatively slow growth there. Soriano hoped to expand into other countries and thereby mitigate the effects of the Philippines' unstable economy. Finally, the leader wanted to head off encroaching competition from the world's biggest breweries, namely Anheuser-Busch and Miller of the United States, Kirin of Japan, and BSN of France. In an interview with *Asian*

Business' Michael Selwyn, San Miguel President Francisco C. Eizmendi, Jr., said that "what we are aiming to do is be a David among the Goliaths of international business, without losing our grip on the local market."

Having determined that overseas growth was imperative, Soriano allocated $1 billion to a five-year strategic internationalization program that focused on shaping up domestic operations, then progressing to licensing and exporting, overseas production, and finally to distribution of non-beer products. San Miguel's plant modernization plan involved sweeping improvements, from computerization to quality circles. These efforts laid the groundwork that would enable the company to compete with the world's food and beverage multinationals. A subsequent decentralization created a holding company structure with the 18 non-beer operations positioned as subsidiaries. This corporate reorganization freed the spun-off businesses from the bureaucratic shackles of a large conglomerate. In the course of this multifaceted effort to attain optimum efficiency, San Miguel reduced its workforce by more than 16 percent, from a 1989 high of 39,138 to 32,832 by 1993. *Asian Business* noted that these programs helped increase profit per employee by 56 percent in 1991 alone.

With its domestic "ducks in a row," San Miguel turned to the next stage in its internationalization, beer licensing, and exporting initiative. Although the company had exported beer for most of its history, this effort was intensified dramatically in the late 1980s. San Miguel's beer exports grew by 150 percent from 1985 to 1989 alone, and the brand was soon exported to 24 countries, including all of Asia's key markets as well as the United States, Australia, and the Middle East. Once the core brand was established in a particular market, San Miguel would begin to create production facilities, sometimes on an independent basis and sometimes in concert with an indigenous joint-venture partner. By 1995, San Miguel had manufacturing plants in Hong Kong, China, Indonesia, Vietnam, Taiwan, and Guam.

Thus, in spite of the overarching quarrel regarding San Miguel's ownership (not to mention other problems endemic to operating in the Philippines), the company's sales quintupled from P 12.23 billion in 1986 to P 68.43 billion by 1994. Net income increased twice as fast, from P 1.11 billion to P 11.86 billion over the same period, although San Miguel's overseas operations (as a whole) were not yet profitable.

In 1996 San Miguel purchased full control of its Hong Kong arm, San Miguel Brewery Hong Kong Limited. In April of the following year, San Miguel's domestic soft-drink bottling unit, Coca-Cola Bottlers Philippines, Inc., was merged into the Australia-based Coca-Cola Amatil Limited (CCA). In effect, San Miguel exchanged its 70 percent interest in a Philippine-only operation for a 25 percent stake in CCA, which had operations in 17 countries—both in the Asia-Pacific region and in Eastern Europe. CCA soon demerged the latter operations into a U.K.-based firm called Coca-Cola Beverages plc (resulting in a reduction of San Miguel's stake in CCA to 22 percent). Seeking to maintain its focus on the Asia-Pacific region, San Miguel sold its stake in the new U.K. entity in mid-1998.

From 1995 through 1997, San Miguel suffered from a downturn in its main domestic businesses, while overseas operations were still in the red. Profits plummeted. In response, a major restructuring of the company's loss-making food businesses was undertaken. San Miguel's ice cream and pasteurized milk business was merged with operations of Nestlé to form Nestlé Philippines, Inc., and late in 1998 San Miguel's stake in this business was sold off. San Miguel also exited from the ready-to-eat meal sector and curtailed the operations of its shrimp farming business.

By late 1997 the company was also beginning to feel the effects of the exploding Asian economic crisis. In addition, the price of its stock was declining. At this point, a Hong Kong–based conglomerate, First Pacific, stepped into the picture, acquiring a 2 percent stake in San Miguel and entering into negotiations to pay as much as $1.3 billion for the two government-sequestered stakes that remained the subject of lengthy litigation. First Pacific abandoned its takeover bid early in 1998, however, when the negotiations—which required a resolution of the status of the disputed stakes—ran afoul of Philippine election-year politics.

A New Cojuangco Era: Late 1990s and Early 2000s

In April 1998 the anti-graft court handling the case of the disputed San Miguel stakes ruled that Cojuangco was entitled to vote 20 percent of the shares, although he was not given ownership of the shares. This enabled Cojuangco to install three new directors on the company board. Then in May, Joseph Estrada won the Philippine presidential election. Cojuangco had been the main financial backer of Estrada, a former movie actor who had been Cojuangco's vice-presidential running mate during their unsuccessful 1992 campaign, and Cojuangco also became chairman of Estrada's political party following Estrada's electoral victory. By early July 1998, Soriano III had resigned

from his position as chairman of San Miguel, and the board of directors, which included seven government-controlled (and hence Estrada-controlled) seats, voted to return Cojuangco to the chairmanship. This marked an amazing comeback for the once-disgraced Cojuangco, and also left many observers worried about a possible return to the crony capitalism of the Marcos era.

Cojuangco moved quickly to turn around the fortunes of the foundering company. Restructuring moves included a flattening of management layers to speed up decision-making and make the company more responsive to the marketplace. Overseas, the international headquarters were moved from high-priced Hong Kong to low-priced Manila as part of a larger cost-cutting initiative. The company also raised its domestic beer prices to make up for revenue lost from higher taxes on beverages and liquor. San Miguel increased its share of the domestic bottled water market by acquiring Metro Bottled Water Corporation, maker of Wilkins Distilled Water, in July 1999. Later in 1999 San Miguel announced that it would sell its minority stake in CCA through a stock offering, but these plans were soon abandoned when CCA's stock price declined sharply. Income from operations for San Miguel rose slightly in 1998 before surging 63 percent in 1999.

Using a huge hoard of cash built through the recent asset sales, Cojuangco completed a series of acquisitions from 2000 to early 2002. During 2000, San Miguel purchased J. Boag & Son Limited, an Australian brewer, for about P 2.4 billion ($56 million), as well as Sugarland Multi-Food Corporation, a Philippine juice maker, for P 2.9 billion. The latter firm—renamed Sugarland Beverage Corporation—was jointly acquired by San Miguel and its majority-owned subsidiary, La Tondeña Distillers. Two major acquisitions of Philippine firms were then completed in 2001. Pure Foods Corporation was acquired for P 7.02 billion. Renamed San Miguel Pure Foods Company, Inc., the acquired company was a market leader in both processed meats and flour. The deal thereby expanded San Miguel's processed meat portfolio and also marked its first foray into the flour industry. In July 2001 San Miguel joined forces with the Coca-Cola Company to reacquire Coca-Cola Bottlers Philippines, with San Miguel taking a 65 percent stake and Coca-Cola the remaining 35 percent. As part of the deal, San Miguel sold its shares in CCA back to that company. Later in 2001, San Miguel sold its bottled water and juice businesses, now amalgamated as Philippine Beverage Partners, Inc., to Coca-Cola Bottlers Philippines. Finally, in February 2002, San Miguel completed the acquisition of an 83 percent stake in Cosmos Bottling Corporation in a P 15 billion ($282 million) deal completed through Coca-Cola Bottlers Philippines. Cosmos specialized in low-priced soft drinks and held the number two position in the Philippine market. The combination of Coca-Cola Bottlers Philippines and Cosmos gave San Miguel control of more than 90 percent of the Philippine soft-drink industry.

During and following this period of acquisitiveness, the question of who owned San Miguel remained unresolved. Estrada became embroiled in a corruption scandal and was then forced from power in January 2001 in a popular uprising backed by the military. Replacing Estrada as president was Gloria Macapagal-Arroyo, who almost immediately began maneuvering to oust Cojuangco from the chairmanship of San Miguel as part of her campaign to rid the country of corruption. Arroyo sought to replace five directors appointed by Estrada, but a technicality prevented her from doing so prior to the May 2001 annual meeting. Cojuangco was thus able to retain his position as chairman. Then in December 2001 the Philippine Supreme Court ruled that Arroyo could in fact replace the five directors. Simultaneously, however, Cojuangco arranged a deal with the Japanese brewer Kirin Brewery Company, Limited whereby Kirin would invest P 27.88 billion ($544 million) for a 15 percent stake in San Miguel. Kirin finalized its investment in February 2002, gaining two board seats that Cojuangco could now count on to help him remain in power. By this time, Cojuangco had also gained popularity among investors for turning around the company and making it one of the most profitable in the country—despite a prolonged economic downswing; the government recognized this support by reaching a deal with Cojuangco in early 2002. Cojuangco could remain in control of the conglomerate until the anti-graft court determined the true ownership of the disputed shareholdings; in return the government would gain representation on important management committees and on the boards of 13 company subsidiaries.

San Miguel thus stood in the early 2000s as one of the most respected corporations in the Philippines, while at the same time facing an uncertain future because of the long-unresolved ownership dispute. In addition, there was a potential complication: Cojuangco was reportedly considering another run at the Philippine presidency for the May 2004 election.

Principal Subsidiaries

BEVERAGE BUSINESS: San Miguel Brewing International Ltd. (British Virgin Islands); San Miguel Brewery Hong Kong Limited; Guangzhou San Miguel Brewery Company Limited (China); San Miguel Bada Baoding Brewery Company Limited (China); San Miguel Shunde Brewery Company Limited (China); San Miguel Brewery Vietnam Limited; J. Boag & Son Limited (Australia); PT Delta Djakarta Tbk (Indonesia); La Tondeña Distillers, Inc. (78.81%); Coca-Cola Bottlers Philippines, Inc. (65%); Philippine Beverage Partners, Inc. (65%); Cosmos Bottling Corporation (83.2%). FOOD BUSINESS: Magnolia, Inc.; Star Dari, Inc.; San Miguel Pure Foods Company, Inc. (99.75%); San Miguel Foods, Inc. (99.75%); Monterey Foods Corporation (98%). PACKAGING BUSINESS: San Miguel Packaging International Limited (British Virgin Islands); San Miguel Yamamura Haiphong Glass Co., Ltd. (Vietnam); Zhaoqing San Miguel Glass Company Limited (China); Premium Packaging International, Inc.; Rightpak International Corporation; San Miguel Yamamura Ball Corporation (99%); San Miguel Rengo Packaging Corporation (70%); Mindanao Corrugated Fibreboard, Inc. (60%); San Miguel Yamamura Asia Corporation (60%); SMC Yamamura Fuso Molds Corporation (60%). REAL ESTATE BUSINESS: San Miguel Properties, Inc. (99%). OTHERS: ArchEn Technologies, Inc.; Beverage Packaging Specialist, Inc.; Challenger Aero Air Corp.; SMC Logistics Asia; SMC Stock Transfer Service Corporation; SMITS, Inc.; SMC Shipping & Lighterage Corporation (70%); Anchor Insurance Brokerage Corporation (58%).

Principal Divisions

Beverage; Food; Packaging.

Principal Competitors

Asia Brewery Inc.; Asahi Breweries, Ltd.; Tsingtao Brewery Company Limited; Foster's Group Limited.

Further Reading

Abueg, Jose Marte, "Soriano Adjusts to Aquino," *Asian Business,* September 1989, p. 6.

Alley, Lindsey, and Thomas Stanley, "San Miguel's Expansion into Southeast Asia," *Journal of Asian Business,* Summer 1993, pp. 71–92.

Arnold, Wayne, "Battle of San Miguel Takes an Unusual Path," *New York Times,* April 18, 2001, p. W1.

——, "Manila Decides It Can Get Along with a Marcos Ally," *New York Times,* February 27, 2002, p. W1.

Caplen, Brian, "San Miguel Brewery: Brewing Up New Business," *Asian Business,* April 1991, pp. 9–12.

Chavez, Gertrude, "Getting There," *Global Finance,* November 1997, pp. 47–49.

Frank, Robert, "Teflon Tycoon—The Crony Capitalist," *Wall Street Journal,* August 30, 1999, pp. A1+.

Friedland, Jonathan, "Not Quite the Last Rites," *Far Eastern Economic Review,* May 11, 1989, pp. 64+.

——, "Thirst for Power: Philippines' San Miguel Moves Closer to Cojuangco's Grasp," *Far Eastern Economic Review,* April 23, 1992, pp. 52+.

Furukawa, Tsukasa, "Ball Joins Philippine Can Venture," *American Metal Market,* October 20, 1994, p. 5.

Granitsas, Alkman, and Deidre Sheehan, "Manila's Strange Brew," *Far Eastern Economic Review,* May 10, 2001, pp. 46–51.

Hilsenrath, Jon E., and Rexie Reyes, "First Pacific Ends Talks to Boost San Miguel Stake," *Asian Wall Street Journal,* February 3, 1998, p. 3.

Hookway, James, "In the Philippines, San Miguel Deals a Blow to Arroyo," *Wall Street Journal,* May 4, 2001, p. A13.

Hookway, James, Cris Larano, and Helen Ubels, "San Miguel Jumps Back in As a Coca-Cola Bottler," *Wall Street Journal,* February 7, 2001, p. A21.

Jones, Arthur, "The Philippines," *Forbes,* December 19, 1983, p. 128.

Landingin, Roel, "Philippine Giant's Appeal Starts to Fall Flat," *Financial Times,* August 7, 2001, p. 31.

Martin, Neil A., "Clouds over Manila: Battle over Brewer Raises Old Issues in Philippines—Corruption and Cronyism," *Barron's,* May 10, 1999, pp. 22–23.

"Mine's a Beer (Patent Pending, All Rights Reserved)," *Economist,* October 29, 1988, p. 74.

Moore, Hannah, "Battle for San Miguel Brewing in Philippines," *Journal of Commerce,* March 6, 1991, p. 3A.

"Opéra Bouffe," *Economist,* April 28, 1990, pp. 72–73.

"The Philippines," *Asiamoney,* July/August 1995, p. 26.

"Returning the Empties," *Economist,* April 5, 1986, pp. 78–79.

Reyes, Cid, *History in the Brewing: A Centennial Celebration of San Miguel Beer,* Manila: Larawan Books, 1994, 167 p.

Reyes, Rexie, "San Miguel Puts Cojuangco Back in Driver's Seat," *Asian Wall Street Journal,* July 8, 1998, p. 1.

"San Miguel Corporation: A Tradition of Leadership," *Scientific American,* February 1996, p. P22.

Selwyn, Michael, "Honour Is the Watchword," *Asian Business,* November 1992, pp. 36–37.

——, "The Secrets of San Miguel's Sparkle," *Asian Business,* November 1992, pp. 28–30.

Shao, Maria, "Andrés Soriano's Battle for San Miguel," *Business Week,* September 28, 1987, p. 54.

"Strange Brew," *Economist,* May 16, 1998, pp. 64–65.

Tiglao, Rigoberto, "Back in Business: Philippine Tycoon Cojuangco Gears Up for a Comeback," *Far Eastern Economic Review,* July 2, 1998, pp. 56–57.

——, "Hard Sell," *Far Eastern Economic Review,* January 22, 1998, p. 60.

——, "Loss Leader," *Far Eastern Economic Review,* July 2, 1998, pp. 57–58.

——, "Storm Brewing: Philippine Beer Barons Fight Proxy Battle in Congress," *Far Eastern Economic Review,* June 20, 1996, p. 58.

——, "Sun Sets on an Empire: Strategic Errors Leave the Sorianos' San Miguel Vulnerable," *Far Eastern Economic Review,* May 11, 1989, pp. 64 + .

Williamson, Hugh, "Cronyism Crackdown Targets Estrada Associates: Head of San Miguel Feels the Heat from New President of the Philippines," *Financial Times,* March 28, 2001, p. 33.

—April Dougal Gasbarre
—update: David E. Salamie

Sarnoff Corporation

201 Washington Road
CN 5300
Princeton, New Jersey 08543
U.S.A.
Telephone: (609) 734-2000
Fax: (609) 734-2221
Web site: http://www.sarnoff.com

Wholly Owned Subsidiary of SRI International
Incorporated: 1987 as Sarnoff Laboratories
Employees: 730
Sales: $140 million (2002 est.)
NAIC: 541710 Research and Development in the
  Physical, Engineering and Life Sciences

Sarnoff Corporation is one of the leading developers of new technology in the United States. The company began as the research and development arm of RCA Corporation, and produced the first viable color television system. Sarnoff is now involved in a broad array of technological research, which it carries out under contract to client companies. The company has considerable expertise in electronic communications, and it has parlayed this into ventures in on-demand video, pharmaceutical information processing, advanced medical and genetic diagnostics, and many other fields. Sarnoff is one of the major patentholders in the United States. It collects income from licensing its technology as well as from contracting its researchers. Sarnoff also acts as an incubator for new technology companies. Since the mid-1990s Sarnoff has launched more than 20 new companies, which capitalize on specific technology markets. Some of Sarnoff's spinoffs include Orchid Biosciences Inc., Songbird Medical, and Wavexpress. Sarnoff is a subsidiary of another venerable technology research firm, SRI International.

Namesake's Rise in the 1920s

Sarnoff Corporation was originally conceived as the research and development department of RCA Corporation. RCA was established in 1919 as the Radio Corporation of America. This was a successor company to the early radio pioneer American Marconi, which had been bought by General Electric. American Marconi existed to exploit the inventions of the Italian scientist Guglielmo Marconi, the founder of wireless communications. Marconi had invented a revolutionary means of connecting people through Morse code messages traveling on radio waves, and in the early years of the 20th century, his companies in Great Britain and the United States ran a network of ship-to-shore communication stations. Radio in its early years was an effective and important means of getting news from distant points. But it took a young, poorly educated messenger boy at American Marconi to conceive of radio as mass media, which would connect an audience of thousands to music, news, and entertainment broadcast from a fixed point. This was David Sarnoff.

Sarnoff was born in a small Jewish village in Russia in 1891. He immigrated to New York when he was nine years old, and very soon became his family's breadwinner, as his father was incapacitated by tuberculosis. Sarnoff began as a newsboy, getting up before dawn to hawk newspapers on the street. Later he ran his own newsstand, employing his younger siblings. His formal education lasted only through the eighth grade. Then, at the age of 15, he went to work full time. His ambition was to be a newspaper reporter, and he duly went to the offices of the *New York Herald* to apply for an entry-level post. By mistake he applied instead to the Commercial Cable Company, located in the same building, which took him on as a messenger. Sarnoff taught himself how to operate a telegraph while working at Commercial Cable. He left that job in 1906 and next got a job as an office boy at American Marconi. The young Sarnoff made himself indispensable, doing everything from filling in for absent telegraph operators to buying flowers for Mr. Marconi's women friends. Sarnoff became something of Marconi's apprentice, and the inventor made sure that the boy had adequate opportunity to study the technical aspects of wireless. Sarnoff also enrolled in New York's Pratt Institute to take its course in electrical engineering. Sarnoff quickly moved up the ladder at American Marconi, and by 1915, he was named the company's contract manager, overseeing all of Marconi's sales and service contracts. That year Sarnoff penned a long memo to Marconi, outlining a scheme to make the radio a consumer entertainment item, a home music box that might one day be as popular as the phonograph or the piano. Apparently this memo did not make a big impression on Marconi. Yet Sarnoff was convinced he was on to something.

General Electric (GE) took over Marconi's radio empire in 1919, and Sarnoff became a mid-level executive at the new company, RCA. In 1921, Sarnoff took it upon himself to get the attention of his bosses, and the world, by masterminding the first radio broadcast of a popular sporting event. Sarnoff jerryrigged a station to broadcast the championship boxing match between the American Jack Dempsey and the French Georges Carpentier. The event was not only a technical feat (the transmitter gave out right after the match, which had luckily lasted only four rounds), but a marketing coup, as Sarnoff hooked up with a fundraising drive for French war relief headed by the daughter of financier J.P. Morgan. The broadcast coincided with Miss Morgan's fundraising parties all along the East Coast, and the radio audience for this seminal event was estimated at 300,000. The fight broadcast immediately made clear the mass entertainment possibilities of radio, and the industry began to boom.

David Sarnoff became president of RCA in 1930. The company became a leader in electronic technology, venturing beyond radio to television and motion pictures. In 1932, government antitrust litigation broke up the partnership of RCA and GE, and RCA became an independent company. RCA had a research department as of 1922, headed by an electrical engineering professor from the City College of New York. In 1924 RCA moved its research department into its own quarters in the Bronx, while corporate headquarters were in Manhattan in New York City. The research department was responsible for quality control and for making improvements to existing RCA products. Beginning in 1934, the research department began a major push to develop new product lines for the company, culminating in 1939 with RCA's introduction of television. Television had been in the works since the 1920s, with various scientists around the world contributing bits and pieces. RCA hired a Russian scientist, Vladimir Zworykin, and backed him with some $5 million in research and development money. At the same time, the company bought the Jenkins Television Company, an early television pioneer that went bankrupt in 1932. RCA also licensed the patents of the American inventor Philo T. Farnsworth. While the inventors were inventing, Sarnoff put together a broadcasting network, lining up programming and running promotional events, so that when the technology was in place, consumers would be ready for it.

Birth of RCA Laboratories in the 1940s

RCA's research and development division made several other key inventions. In 1939 RCA scientists not only unveiled television but also the electron microscope and the facsimile machine. As the United States entered World War II, RCA

researchers bent their skills to many military applications of electronics. In 1942 RCA founded a separate RCA Laboratories facility on 260 acres of land in Princeton, New Jersey. The new lab was farther from the corporate headquarters in Manhattan, but close enough for a quick commute. RCA Labs made many advances in military technology during the war, from improved radio systems for fighter planes to radar jamming devices. The labs also made significant improvements to television technology in the 1940s. In the late 1940s, RCA was manufacturing an improved black-and-white television set that retailed for an affordable $375, leading to a boom in television similar to the radio boom the company had stimulated in the 1920s.

The next step was color television. Rival CBS developed a color television system as early as 1940, but it employed a mechanical spinning disk that was incompatible with most existing television sets. By the late 1940s, RCA Laboratories scientists were working overtime to come up with a better color television system. The RCA system debuted in 1949, though the Federal Communications Commission (FCC) had already given its imprimatur to the CBS system. RCA had a huge technical advantage, however. Its color system was compatible with the millions of black-and-white televisions that were already on the market, giving minimal pain to consumers. In 1953 the FCC reversed its earlier decision, and accepted the RCA color television system as the industry standard.

In 1951 the RCA Laboratories was renamed the David Sarnoff Research Center, in honor of Sarnoff's enormous contribution to RCA and to the consumer electronics industry. The lab's physical plant expanded in the 1950s, and by 1955 the division employed 270 researchers. The lab continued to make strides in consumer electronics. A researcher at Sarnoff came up with an improved music recording technology in the late 1950s that became known as the "Dynagroove" record. Sarnoff scientists also contributed to advances in transistors and in semiconductor technology. Researchers at Sarnoff in the mid-1960s developed the liquid crystal display (LCD), which became a key component of many electronic devices. Sarnoff scientists were also responsible for the development of the CMOS (Complementary Metal Oxide Semiconductor) in the late 1960s and early 1970s. The lab also produced other advances in superconductivity, solar cells, and infrared imaging.

Corporate Changes in the 1970s and 1980s

David Sarnoff stepped down from the chief executive position at RCA in 1965. His son Robert became president, and then CEO. David Sarnoff remained chairman until 1970. He died in 1971. The company's earnings began to slide at that time, and in 1975, the RCA board refused to renew Robert Sarnoff's contract. RCA's next CEO lasted less than a year. The company then continued to flounder under its next CEO, Edgar Griffiths, as poor economic conditions socked its record division in particular. RCA also had bought up businesses unrelated to electronics, such as the Hertz car rental company and Banquet frozen foods. Meanwhile, the David Sarnoff Research Center had mushroomed. By 1980 it employed more than 1,500 scientists, engineers, and researchers. It was receiving a large number of patents, even more than its competitor Bell Labs. Yet its role at the forefront of electronics research was eroding. Another CEO, Thornton Bradshaw, took over in 1981, and he resolved

---

Key Dates:

1919: RCA is incorporated.
1942: The company founds RCA Laboratories as a separate facility.
1951: RCA Laboratories is renamed the David Sarnoff Research Center.
1986: GE buys RCA.
1987: GE gives David Sarnoff Research Center to SRI International.
1997: The company is renamed Sarnoff Corporation.

---

to get the company back to its basic business. He sold off the outlying divisions and used the cash to invest in electronics, broadcasting, and new technology research. The company turned around in the early 1980s, and seemed restored to stability. But RCA was abruptly sold to GE in 1986.

GE had divested itself of RCA more than 50 years earlier, and was now spending $6.28 billion to buy it back. It was immediately clear to GE that it did not need the David Sarnoff Research Center. GE had its own research laboratory not very far away, in Schenectady, New York, and there was no reason for the company to operate two such facilities. In 1986 the David Sarnoff Research Center employed some 1,200 people, and its annual budget was $98 million. The lab was redundant as far as GE was concerned, as its own research center was nearly twice the size of Sarnoff. Consequently, the parent company gave the David Sarnoff Research Center to another technology development firm, the nonprofit SRI International. SRI, based in Menlo Park, California, had done consulting for GE, and it had been looking for an East Coast location. The giveaway gave GE a hefty tax break. GE also agreed to support Sarnoff with $250 million in research contracts for the next five years. The lab remained in New Jersey, and operated as a for-profit subsidiary of SRI. It incorporated in 1987 as Sarnoff Laboratories.

The transition was difficult, nevertheless. The staff shrank by about one-third soon after the change in management. Sarnoff's role under SRI was quite different from what it had been as part of RCA. It was expected to pay for itself by garnering lucrative research contracts. SRI depended heavily on military contracts, while Sarnoff had only about 13 percent of its contracts with the military or government. SRI prompted Sarnoff to seek more government work, aiming to get about half its contracts from the military over the coming years. But the military market began to shrink soon after it took over Sarnoff. Sarnoff still maintained its focus on television, working with a consortium of other companies on high-definition television (HDTV), which was expected to bring theater-quality pictures to home sets. But Sarnoff's television contracts became complicated when GE sold its consumer electronics business in 1987 to the French firm Thomson. By the early 1990s, SRI was in the red, and Sarnoff, too, lost $9.3 million in 1991 on revenue of $75 million.

Technology Incubator in the 1990s

SRI got new leadership in 1993, and Sarnoff began focusing on more entrepreneurial projects. It began actively encouraging researchers to come up with viable business applications for their ideas by offering them bonuses and profit-sharing. One Sarnoff researcher who had left the company in the mid-1980s described it to a *New York Times* reporter (August 15, 1994) as having had "pretty much of an academic atmosphere" when he had worked there. But on returning to Sarnoff in 1994, the researcher said, "I didn't recognize the place. People were really plugged into the outside world." Sarnoff employees were coming up with unique high-tech projects, and the company was backing them. Some workers ran their own companies, in partnership with Sarnoff, out of their Sarnoff offices. It also spun off companies that evolved on its premises. In 1995, Sarnoff spun off Sarnoff Real Time Corporation. Real Time made a supercomputer that had first been used to simulate video circuitry. The supercomputer was next used as a flight simulator, but it soon found a consumer application as a server for video on demand. This seemed to typify the new Sarnoff trajectory. A complex electronic product with an arcane or specialized use was recast for a commercial market. Sarnoff backed the idea in development, then helped the principals launch an independent company.

In 1997, Sarnoff Laboratories renamed itself Sarnoff Corporation. Its business plan called for spinning off two new companies every year. Its offspring included Sarif Inc., a Vancouver, Washington-based company that manufactured liquid crystal optical systems. Another was Orchid Biocomputer Inc. (later Orchid Biosciences), which spun off from Sarnoff in 1995. Orchid developed a medical screening device the size of a business card, which could conduct thousands of chemical tests simultaneously. Orchid went public in 2000, the first Sarnoff spinoff to do so. By that time it had developed a new method of gene mapping. Sarnoff continued to come up with new technology in a variety of fields. Company researchers unveiled a paper-thin plastic in 2001 that could be used as a video screen. Sarnoff found a way to make television or computer monitors thinner in 2001, and was negotiating with manufacturers to license the new technology. In 2002 Sarnoff released a medical device that measured oxygen flow in the brain by shining a low-level laser at a patient's eye. By 2002 Sarnoff had spun off 20 new high-tech companies, while continuing to come up with commercial applications for its technology under its own name. The early 2000s were not the best of times for high-tech start-ups. Sarnoff's public spinoff Orchid Biosciences, for example, went through rounds of cost-cutting and a change of chief executive as its stock traded at under a dollar in 2003. Yet Sarnoff seemed to have evolved a workable way to exist as an independent company, out from under the wing of RCA. It continued to draw income from patents and licensing, as well as from research done under contract. In addition, it had fostered an entrepreneurial culture, where its workers had learned not only to invent but to market and sell the diverse products of the laboratory.

Principal Competitors

AT&T Bell Laboratories, Inc.; Battelle Memorial Institute, Inc.; Wyeth-Ayerst Research.

Further Reading

Bilby, Kenneth, *The General: David Sarnoff and the Rise of the Communications Industry,* New York: Harper & Row, 1986.

Carsey, Marcy, ''David Sarnoff,'' *Time,* December 7, 1998, p. 88.

Choi, Charles, ''Eye on the Brain,'' *Scientific American,* August 2002, p. 28.

Chunovic, Louis, ''The Long and Winding Road to Color TV,'' *Electronic Media,* November 12, 2001, p. 14.

Copeland, Ron, ''The Future's Still in Plastics,'' *InformationWeek,* July 9, 2001, p. 18.

Foremski, Tom, ''He Was the Radio Officer That Relayed the News of the Sinking of the Titanic,'' *Electronics Weekly,* April 22, 1998, p. 20.

Leopold, George, ''Sarnoff: Past Is Prologue to Future,'' *Electronic Engineering Times,* January 31, 2000, p. 68.

Port, Otis, ''GE Gift-Wraps a Landmark Lab,'' *Business Week,* February 16, 1987, p. 35.

Redburn, Tom, ''Spinoffs Giving Research Alley Industrial Base,'' *New York Times,* August 15, 1994, pp. A1, B5.

Sanders, Lisa, ''From H-Bombs to Video,'' *Forbes,* March 27, 1995, p. 120.

''Sarnoff Center Extends HDTV R&D with $100 Million Deal,'' *Satellite News,* October 1, 1990, p. 4.

Sweet, William, ''Sarnoff Center Girds Loins for Global Competition in HDTV,'' *Physics Today,* June 1989, pp. 63–65.

Taber, George M., ''Sarnoff Is Now for Hire,'' *Central New Jersey Business,* May 31, 1995, p. 35.

Yoshida, Junko, and George Leopold, ''Constant Innovation Is Par for Course,'' *Electronic Engineering Times,* June 30, 1997, p. 72.

—A. Woodward

⊞ Sealed Air

Sealed Air Corporation

Park 80 East
Saddle Brook, New Jersey 07663-5291
U.S.A.
Telephone: (201) 791-7600
Fax: (201) 703-4205
Web site: http://www.sealedair.com

Public Company
Incorporated: 1960
Employees: 17,900
Sales: $3.2 billion (2002)
Stock Exchanges: New York
Ticker Symbol: SEE
NAIC: 322221 Coated and Laminated Packaging Paper
and Plastics Film Manufacturing; 322232 Envelope
Manufacturing; 326111 Unsupported Plastics Bag
Manufacturing; 326112 Unsupported Plastics
Packaging Film and Sheet Manufacturing; 326140
Polystyrene Foam Product Manufacturing; 326150
Urethane and Other Foam Product (Except
Polystyrene) Manufacturing; 326199 All Other
Plastics Product Manufacturing

Sealed Air Corporation is one of the world's leading manufacturers of food, protective, and specialty packaging materials. The company is best-known for its protective packaging products, including AirCap and Bubble Wrap air cellular cushioning materials; inflatable packaging products under the Fill-Air and Rapid Fill brand names; Instapak, a system for injecting a protective, expanding polyurethane foam into shipping cartons and other containers; and protective mailers and bags sold under the Jiffy brand. Since its 1998 acquisition of the packaging business of W.R. Grace & Company, however, Sealed Air has derived the majority of its revenues from its line of food packaging products, mainly marketed under the Cryovac trademark. These items, which include shrink bags and films, laminated films, foam and solid plastic trays and containers, and absorbent pads, are used to package a wide variety of perishable foods, such as cheeses, produce, poultry, and fresh, smoked, and

processed meat. The company has operations in 50 countries, though its products are distributed in many more. The United States accounts for about 55 percent of net sales; Europe, the Middle East, and Africa, 26 percent; the Asia-Pacific region, 10 percent; Latin America, 7 percent; and Canada, 3 percent.

Bubble Wrap Beginnings

Sealed Air was founded by U.S. engineer Alfred W. Fielding and Swiss inventor Marc A. Chavannes, the two men who gave the world Bubble Wrap. The product, first developed in 1957, was initially created in response to a client's request for a new type of plastic wallpaper. When that idea fizzled, the pair found some success marketing the product as a greenhouse insulator. They finally stumbled onto the idea of adapting it for the packaging market. After a few years of tinkering with manufacturing methods and hustling for seed capital, Fielding and Chavannes launched Sealed Air Corporation in 1960. With $85,000 raised through an initial public stock offering, production of the AirCap material began in earnest the following year. In its earliest form AirCap packaging material suffered from slightly leaky bubbles. In spite of the problems, however, the product gained popularity throughout the 1960s, and by the middle of the decade research efforts had led to the development of a special coating that prevented the bubbles from losing air. By 1969 Bubble Wrap was beginning to catch on. For that year, Sealed Air reported sales of $4 million. This represented nearly the entire market for Bubble Wrap, because the product was still proprietary at the time.

In 1970 Sealed Air suffered a small deficit, despite continuing gains in sales. In the face of criticism from some members of the company's board, President Ted Bowers suddenly resigned. To replace him, the board turned to one of its members, T.J. Dermot Dunphy, an Irishman who had studied at Oxford and at Harvard Business School. Dunphy, who became CEO in 1971, had arrived on the Sealed Air board two years earlier after selling his own small packaging company, Custom-Made Packaging (which sold popsicle wrappers and the like), to Hammermill Paper. With cash on hand from that sale, Dunphy had asked friends at the investment firm Donaldson, Lufkin & Jenrette to find a public company for him to lead. Bowers's unexpected departure created that opportunity at Sealed Air.

Company Perspectives:

The Sealed Air Advantage is rooted in values that go back to the early days of the company. Although we are flexible enough to change over time by growth, acquisition, global expansion, societal change and new ideas, the core of the culture and philosophy remains constant, and is protected and reinforced by leadership. Sealed Air's daily operating priorities and Code of Conduct are the foundation of the company. These are woven into the fabric of everything we do at Sealed Air.

Our first priority is our customer. Throughout the life of our company, our success has been and always will be measured by our customers' success. Our second priority is cash flow. We encourage employees to spend the company's money like it is their own, because in a real sense, it is. Through our profit-sharing plan many of our employees are shareholders. The third priority is our World Class Manufacturing initiative that focuses all of us on doing our jobs a little better every day. Through employee involvement and teams, we seek to identify opportunities to create faster, simpler processes that enhance our ability to serve customers and improve cash flow. The fourth priority is innovation, and from day one, that is what Sealed Air has focused on in every aspect of our business. Our final priority is earnings per share. If we practice and successfully execute the first four fundamental priorities, growth in earnings will follow. Growth will ensure the company's long-term value and security.

Just prior to the beginning of the Dunphy era, Sealed Air had added a set of products to its line. By laminating AirCap cushioning material to kraft paper, the company developed its Mail Lite shipping envelopes, first sold in 1971. A smaller, cheaper version of Mail Lite called Bubble-Lite was introduced a few years later. The company also became international around this time, with the 1970 acquisition of Smith Packaging Ltd., later renamed Sealed Air of Canada, Ltd. Under Dunphy, the company's minor stumble of 1970 was quickly reversed, and by 1972 Sealed Air's sales had passed the $10 million mark. Another new product, PolyMask, was introduced in 1973. Poly-Mask, a pressure sensitive polyethylene film for protecting delicate surfaces against scratches, was the first Sealed Air product not based on its air bubble technology. For 1973, the company's after-tax profits topped $1 million for the first time. Of its $13.6 million in sales for that year, about 60 percent came from AirCap and about 20 percent from Mail Lite. The rest came mostly from the manufacture and distribution of a variety of packaging products by its Canadian subsidiary. The company's biggest customer was the electronics industry, which accounted for about 40 percent of sales.

Sealed Air made its first foray into Europe in 1973, acquiring 10 percent of Sibco Universal, S.A., a French manufacturing firm. Over the next few years, Sealed Air bought the rest of Sibco. During the mid-1970s Sealed Air's researchers came up with another innovative use for the company's air cell technology. The Sealed Air Solar Pool Blanket was essentially a big sheet of Bubble Wrap that was placed on swimming pools. The

Solar Pool Blanket allowed the sun's rays to heat the water and sharply reduced the evaporative loss of water and treatment chemicals. By 1977 the Solar Pool Blanket was generating 6 percent of company sales. As an offshoot of the pool blanket, the company also began making a roof-mounted solar water heater designed mainly for heating swimming pools.

Expansion Through Acquisition: Late 1970s and 1980s

The most important development of 1977 was the acquisition of Instapak Corporation, producers of a revolutionary "foam-in-place" cushioning system. The foam-in-place process, initially conceived in the 1950s by engineers at Lockheed Corporation, involves surrounding a product with urethane in a liquid form that would then quickly expand into a semirigid foam. The idea was finally made practical in 1969 by inventor Richard Sperry (whose grandfather, Elmer Sperry, invented the gyroscope). Instapak was made a division of Sealed Air, and it quickly became one of the company's most important products, generating almost as great a share of total sales as Bubble Wrap by the end of the decade. Foreign sales also increased dramatically during the second half of the 1970s, accounting for nearly a quarter of the company's total by 1977. By 1979 Sealed Air's annual sales had grown to more than $70 million.

By the beginning of the 1980s, foam-in-place was clearly a product destined for bigger things, and Sealed Air still had virtually no competition in the area. The pool blankets were also doing well, selling as fast as the company could make them. In 1981 Sealed Air added PolyCap to its product line. PolyCap was essentially a lower-cost, less durable version of AirCap, without the barrier coating, providing a less expensive option for products that required only a relatively short period of protection. Sealed Air broadened its product line further in 1983 by purchasing Cellu-Products Co., a Hickory, North Carolina, manufacturer of packaging materials, for $20 million. The Cellu-Products acquisition added thin-grade polyethylene foam, coated films, and other plastic and paper materials to the company's growing collection of packaging products. Sealed Air also gained its first presence in the food packaging segment in 1983 through the acquisition of the Dri-Loc line of absorbent pad products, which were used underneath meat, fish, and poultry sold in supermarkets. Although the recession of 1982 took a bite out of Sealed Air's revenue and earnings figures, the emergence of personal computers and other related electronic gizmos brought a new wave of business, and by 1983 the company's sales had grown to $124 million.

In an effort to diversify its product line further, and in part to prepare itself for the impending expiration of its Bubble Wrap patents, Sealed Air acquired several smaller companies during the middle part of the 1980s. In 1984 the company acquired Cortec Corporation, a small anticorrosive chemical firm. Cortec was sold off only a few years later, after being caught illegally shipping chemicals to Libya. Other acquisitions that yielded happier results included Static, Inc., in 1985; a Canadian spa manufacturer in 1987; and a Swedish packaging company in 1987. More important was the company's 1987 purchase of Jiffy Packaging Corporation, which manufactured padded mailers for items such as floppy disks and books. The addition of Jiffy solidified Sealed Air's dominant position in the protective mailer

Key Dates:

1960: Inventors of Bubble Wrap cushioning, originally called AirCap, found Sealed Air Corporation; $85,000 is raised through an initial public offering.
1961: Production of AirCap material begins in earnest.
1970: Expansion beyond the United States begins with the acquisition of Smith Packaging Ltd., later renamed Sealed Air of Canada, Ltd.
1971: Company begins selling Mail Lite cushioned shipping envelopes; T.J. Dermot Dunphy is named company CEO.
1977: Instapak Corporation, makers of a ''foam-in-place'' cushioning system, is acquired.
1983: Sealed Air purchases Cellu-Products Co., maker of thin-grade polyethylene foam, coated films, and other plastic and paper packaging products; first foray into food packaging comes via the purchase of the Dri-Loc absorbent pad product line.
1987: Jiffy Packaging Corporation, producer of padded mailers for such items as floppy disks and books, is acquired.
1989: Company effects a leveraged recapitalization to ward off takeover bids and sharpen the firm's focus.
1994: Acquisition of a French firm adds the Fill Air line of inflation-based packaging to the fold.
1995: New Zealand–based Trigon Industries Limited is acquired, nearly doubling Sealed Air's food packaging operations.
1998: Sealed Air merges with the Cryovac food-packaging business of W.R. Grace & Company.
2002: Company agrees to pay $834 million to settle all current and future asbestos-related claims connected with Grace.

market. The year 1987 also saw company cofounders Fielding and Chavannes both retire from the firm. During this period, Sealed Air also began incorporating recycled materials into a number of its air bubble and paper packaging products, at a time when few companies in the industry were doing so.

By 1988 Sealed Air had annual sales of $346 million, and it earned $42 million in profit that year. All told, $127 million of the company's sales came from Instapak, which by this time had more or less replaced Bubble Wrap as the flagship product. Meanwhile, Sealed Air's researchers, as well as freelancer Sperry (who had developed Instapak), kept busy at the drawing board. One new wrinkle was a pair of systems called Instapacker and VersaPacker, which could produce bags full of protective foam at the touch of a button.

Dunphy pulled off a remarkable financial maneuver in 1989. The company had been so profitable over the previous few years that it found itself with a huge cash surplus. Because Dunphy could not find any more companies that he felt were good acquisition candidates, he had no obvious outlets for this cash buildup. In order to avoid becoming too attractive a target for a takeover, as well as to create what he called a ''controlled crisis'' to shake his managers out of their complacency, Dunphy decided to give the money away. He announced a $40-per-share special dividend, amounting to a $328 million gift to shareholders. The move increased the company's long-term debt from $19 million to over $300 million, made up of a combination of bank loans and junk bonds.

Dunphy hoped that leveraging the company would push it to new heights of efficiency, and he was correct. The new debt situation necessitated changes in the way the company handled inventory and led to other cost-cutting measures. These changes enabled the company to begin repaying its debts ahead of schedule, creating further savings. At the same time, an unexpected reduction in the cost of raw materials resulted in yet more opportunities to work down part of the debt with extra cash. By the early 1990s it was clear that the gamble had paid off, and Sealed Air was ready to go shopping once again. In 1991 the company acquired a small company called Korrvu, which produced transparent suspension packaging—an innovative product that protects fragile items in a trampoline-like membrane. Sentinel Foam & Envelope Corporation, a packaging firm based in Philadelphia, was also acquired that year.

Significant International Expansion: Early to Mid-1990s

Sealed Air's sales figures stalled somewhat during the first part of the 1990s, advancing from $413 million in 1990 to only $452 million in 1993. Nevertheless, the company was able to generate solid profits each year. In order to boost revenue, Dunphy began concentrating heavily on worldwide expansion. Instapak was introduced in Mexico, and the company opened manufacturing facilities in Germany and Spain. Throughout, the company continued to emphasize research and development, and new products were unveiled at a steady pace. One such product was Floral, introduced in 1993. Floral was a foam that served as a base in artificial flower arrangements. Within a year of its first appearance, Floral was generating sales in the neighborhood of $5 million.

As the 1990s continued, Sealed Air made additional strategic acquisitions. In 1993 the company purchased the Shurtuff Division of Shuford Mills, Inc. Shurtuff's extremely durable plastic-based mailers meshed well with Sealed Air's existing protective mailer product line. On the product front, the company developed a new inflatable packaging system called VoidPak. The acquisition department was very active in 1994. The company reinforced its European food pad business with the purchase of Hereford Paper and Allied Products Ltd., an English food pad manufacturing firm. Packaging companies based in Norway, France, and Italy were also acquired during the year. The French acquisition added two product lines, Sup-Air-Pack and Fill Air, to the company's collection of inflation-based systems, an area considered to hold great promise for the future. Toward the end of the year the company reorganized its management structure so that its important product lines were coordinated globally rather than country by country. This move reflected an increasing focus on the international market, which was expected to continue through the rest of the century. For 1994 sales numbers at Sealed Air made their first significant jump in several years, exceeding $500 million for the first time in company history. Earnings, at $31.6 million, reached record levels as well.

Sealed Air's biggest acquisition of this period came in January 1995, when it acquired Trigon Industries Limited, a New Zealand company with operations in Australia, England, Germany, and the United States, for $54.6 million. With annual sales of $72 million, Trigon had an immediate and significant impact on Sealed Air's balance sheet as well as on its geographic reach, providing a base for expansion in the South Pacific. Trigon's lines of packaging films and systems for perishable foods almost doubled Sealed Air's food packaging operations. Other Trigon products included durable mailers and bags and specialty adhesive products.

The Trigon purchase was followed by the June 1996 acquisition of the Australian and New Zealand protective packaging business of Southcorp Holdings Limited. This further bolstered Sealed Air's position in the South Pacific, as the company saw its overseas sales grow to nearly 40 percent of overall sales. In 1985, by comparison, non-U.S. sales totaled only about 18 percent of total sales. By 1997 net sales at the company reached $843 million, while operating profits were a record $138 million.

Late 1990s Merger with Cryovac

In March 1998 Sealed Air completed the biggest deal in its history, merging with the Cryovac packaging business of W.R. Grace & Company in a complicated stock and cash transaction valued at $4.9 billion. W.R. Grace transferred Cryovac to Sealed Air in return for $1.26 billion, which was given to Grace's other subsidiaries. This group of subsidiaries was spun off to shareholders as a separate publicly owned company that assumed the W.R. Grace name. The merged Cryovac-Sealed Air entity became a subsidiary of the old W.R. Grace, which was renamed Sealed Air Corporation. The deal was undertaken in such a complex way both to ensure that it was done on a tax-free basis and to shield Sealed Air from the mounting asbestos liabilities of one of the spun-off Grace units, Grace Construction Products, which had made asbestos-containing products.

The addition of Cryovac was a ''dream'' deal for Dunphy, who had held off on discussions with Grace executives about a merger for two decades. The Cryovac operations were in fact much larger than those of the old Sealed Air, and the company saw its sales triple to more than $2.5 billion following the merger. Cryovac specialized in food packaging products, making that segment Sealed Air's largest, accounting for 60 percent of sales. The acquired lines were led by Cryovac itself, a material used to vacuum-seal food packages. The deal also significantly enhanced Sealed Air's worldwide profile, adding operations in nearly 20 more countries. Following the merger, Sealed Air remained headquartered in Saddle Brook, New Jersey, and Dunphy continued to serve as chairman and CEO.

A few months after the merger was consummated, Sealed Air announced that it would eliminate about 750 jobs from its enlarged workforce of 14,500, a reduction of more than 5 percent, as part of a restructuring program. The company combined or eliminated certain small facilities and administrative support functions, eliminated ''layers of management,'' and centralized Cryovac's U.S. research facilities. Charges associated with this restructuring totaled $111 million, reducing net earnings for 1998 to $73 million.

Sealed Air continued its history of innovation in 1999, introducing VistaFlex engineered inflatable packaging, which was designed as an alternative to corrugated inserts and other premolded shapes and die-cuts used in high-volume protective packaging applications. Also debuting that year was Instapak Quick, a simplified version of the Instapak foam-in-bag product that was targeted at smaller companies selling products over the Internet. The company also completed a number of small acquisitions from 1999 to 2001. These included manufacturers of air cellular cushioning products in Latin America, Asia, and South Africa and producers of foam and solid plastic trays used in food packaging in Latin America, Europe, and Australia. During the third quarter of 2000 a larger deal was finalized, with Sealed Air paying about $119 million for Dolphin Packaging plc, a U.K. maker of foam food trays. Another significant purchase was that of Shanklin Corporation, a U.S. manufacturer of shrink film packaging equipment, in a deal completed later in 2000. In early 2000, meantime, Dunphy retired from the CEO position, while remaining chairman. President and COO William V. Hickey, who had joined Sealed Air in 1980, was promoted to president and CEO.

Asbestos-Related and Other Travails in the Early 2000s

By the early 2000s, some analysts were beginning to question the wisdom of the Cryovac merger. The deal had greatly expanded Sealed Air's operations in Asia and Europe, meaning that the company suffered in a more pronounced way from the economic troubles in Asia that cropped up in the late 1990s and from the decline in meat consumption in Europe that followed the outbreaks of mad cow and foot-and-mouth disease. Even more ominously, the merger had left Sealed Air exposed to potential liabilities related to asbestos claims, despite both the structure of the merger, which had explicitly shielded Sealed Air from W.R. Grace's asbestos exposure, and the fact that neither Sealed Air nor Cryovac had ever produced or sold any products containing asbestos.

By 2000 Sealed Air had been named as a party in a number of lawsuits alleging that the company was responsible for possible asbestos liabilities. The asbestos claimants were suing both Sealed Air and W.R. Grace charging that Grace had fraudulently transferred Cryovac's assets in order to shelter them from Grace's asbestos liabilities. They further contended that Sealed Air was the true successor to the ''old'' W.R. Grace and that without Cryovac the ''new'' Grace was insolvent at the time of its spinoff because of the growing number of asbestos lawsuits that it faced. Weighed down by these asbestos claims, W.R. Grace filed for Chapter 11 bankruptcy protection in April 2001—a development that boded ill for Sealed Air being exonerated from the charges. Meanwhile, in response to the difficult operating environment engendered by the global economic downturn and the aforementioned decline in meat consumption, Sealed Air in 2001 conducted another restructuring, this one consisting of 470 job cuts, a $32.8 million charge, and projected annual cost savings of $23 million.

Asbestos-related events dominated 2002. Sealed Air faced a federal fraudulent-transfer lawsuit that was in its pretrial phase. In late July the company suffered a blow when the federal judge in the case issued a ruling that post-1998 asbestos claims could be considered when determining whether the new W.R. Grace was solvent when it transferred Cryovac to Sealed Air. The defendants had contended that only claims pending at the time of the merger should be considered. This news sent Sealed Air's stock plunging by 62 percent over a two-day period, although it soon recovered somewhat. With the outcome of the trial, scheduled to begin in early December 2002, in serious doubt, Sealed Air reached an agreement in late November to settle all current and future asbestos-related claims. The company agreed to pay $834 million in cash and stock into a trust that would be established as part of the bankruptcy-reorganization plan of W.R. Grace. The trust would make payments to asbestos victims on behalf of Grace and its former subsidiaries. To cover the settlement costs and associated legal fees, Sealed Air recorded an $850.1 million charge at year-end, leading to a net loss for 2002 of $309.1 million. The agreement, which appeared to represent an end to the company's asbestos nightmare, put air back into the company's stock, sending it ballooning 56 percent and returning it to where it was prior to the critical July 2002 pretrial ruling. Sealed Air could now once again focus its full attention on developing and acquiring innovative packaging products and successfully marketing them.

Principal Subsidiaries

Cryovac, Inc.; Sealed Air Corporation (US).

Principal Competitors

Pactiv Corporation; Bemis Company, Inc.; Minnesota Mining & Manufacturing Company; AEP Industries, Inc.; Reynolds Food Packaging; Interplast Group, Ltd.

Further Reading

"By the Throat," *Economist,* September 14, 1991, p. 78.

David, Gregory E., "Make My Day!" *Financial World,* January 17, 1995, pp. 38–39.

Doherty, Jacqueline, "A Package Deal?," *Barron's,* April 22, 2002, pp. 20–21.

Dunphy, T.J. Dermot, *Sealed Air Corporation: Our Products Protect Your Products,* New York: Newcomen Society in North America, 1982.

Egan, Mary Ellen, "Pop Icon," *Forbes,* January 8, 2001, p. 140.

Fadiman, Mark, "If the Bubble Bursts, Try Foam," *Forbes,* June 18, 1984, p. 104.

Gordon, Mitchell, "Sealed Air, Packaging Specialist, Headed for Eighth Straight Advance," *Barron's,* February 6, 1978, pp. 40–41.

——, "Sealed Air's Bag," *Barron's,* August 25, 1980, pp. 36–37.

"How This Bubble-Wrap Maker Boomed by Popping Its Own Bubble," *Money,* March 1994, p. 56.

"It's All in the Packaging," *Financial World,* May 1, 1980, pp. 48–49.

Kim, Queena Sook, "Sealed Air Aims to Prove Cryovac Wasn't Too Big a Bite," *Wall Street Journal,* May 23, 2001, p. B4.

"Light in the Dust," *Economist,* December 7, 2002, p. 62.

McCarthy, Michael J., "The Bubble Economy: Packaging Firm Faces Fight in Field It Began," *Wall Street Journal,* December 10, 2001, pp. A1+.

McGough, Robert, "Controlled Crisis," *Financial World,* February 6, 1990, pp. 74–75.

O'Brien, Timothy L., and Terzah Ewing, "Sealed Air to Buy Grace Packaging Unit," *Wall Street Journal,* August 15, 1997, p. A3.

"Packaging That's Light but Strong Enables Sealed Air to Keep Growing," *Barron's,* December 2, 1974, pp. 44–45.

Perone, Joseph R., "Sealed Air Agrees to Asbestos Deal," *Newark (N.J.) Star-Ledger,* December 7, 2002, p. 13.

Perone, Joseph R., and Tom Johnson, " 'Deal of a Lifetime' Weighs on Sealed Air," *Newark (N.J.) Star-Ledger,* August 4, 2002, p. 1.

Quickel, Stephen W., "How to Make a Billion," *International Business,* April 1995, p. 70.

Smith, Geoffrey, "What Turnaround?" *Forbes,* October 1, 1979, pp. 89–92.

"The Values of Sealed Air," *Leaders Magazine,* October/November/December 2002.

Welsh, Jonathan, "Sealed Air Moves Beyond Success of Its Bubble Wrap," *Wall Street Journal,* March 14, 1997, p. B3.

—Robert R. Jacobson
—update: David E. Salamie

SIEMENS

Siemens AG

Wittelsbacherplatz 2
D 80333 Munich
Germany
Telephone: +49-89-636-3300
Fax: +49-89-636-342-42
Web site: http://www.siemens.com

Public Company
Incorporated: 1966
Employees: 426,000
Sales: $82.9 billion (2002)
Stock Exchanges: New York Berlin Hamburg Dusseldorf
   Munich Brussels Paris Zurich Basel Geneva
   Amsterdam Vienna London
Ticker Symbol: SI
NAIC: 541614 Process, Physical Distribution and
   Logistics Consulting Services; 541513 Computer
   Facilities Management Services; 541330 Engineering
   Services; 333319 Other Commercial and Service
   Industry Machinery Manufacturing; 518210
   Automated Data Processing Services; 238210
   Electrical Contractors; 221121 Electric Bulk Power
   Transmission and Control; 221119 Other Electric
   Power Generation; 421690 Other Electronic Parts and
   Equipment Wholesalers; 423610 Electrical Apparatus
   and Equipment, Wiring Supplies, and Related
   Equipment Merchant Wholesalers; 334220 Radio and
   Television Broadcasting and Wireless
   Communications Equipment Manufacturing; 334510
   Electromedical and Electrotherapeutic Apparatus
   Manufacturing; 335122 Commercial, Industrial, and
   Institutional Electric Lighting Fixture Manufacturing

Founded to manufacture and install telegraphic systems, Germany-based Siemens AG has prospered and grown over 155 years to become a multifaceted electronics and electrical engineering enterprise, and one of the most international corporations in the world. With a presence in more than 190 countries, Siemens' primary business operations include information and communications networks, industrial automation and control, power generation and transmission, medical solutions, and lighting. Siemens was once viewed by analysts as a corporate dinosaur and urged to disband its conglomerate structure in favor of a more nimble and tightly focused enterprise. In the 1990s, however, under the leadership of Heinrich von Pierer, the company underwent major restructuring to minimize costs and maximize efficiencies while retaining the synergistic benefits of its broad-based structure. Siemens has entered the 21st century with a new listing on the New York Stock Exchange, and a competitive foothold in the burgeoning information technologies and communications sector.

Company Origins in Telegraph Systems: 1847–76

Siemens & Halske was founded in Berlin in 1847 by Werner Siemens and J.G. Halske to manufacture and install telegraphic systems. Siemens, a former artillery officer in the Prussian army and an engineer who already owned a profitable patent for electroplating, was the driving force behind the company and remained so for the rest of his life. The company received its first major commission in 1848, when it contracted to build a telegraph link between Berlin and Frankfurt.

Construction of telegraph systems boomed in the mid-19th century, and Siemens & Halske was well equipped to take advantage of the situation. In 1853, it received a commission to build an extensive telegraph system in Russia. Upon its completion, the company opened an office in St. Petersburg under the direction of Werner Siemens' brother Carl Siemens. In 1857 Siemens & Halske helped develop the first successful deep sea telegraphic cable. This led to the transformation of the London office into an independent company under the direction of Wilhelm Siemens, another of Werner's brothers, the next year. By 1865 the company's English operations had become substantial. Its name was changed to Siemens Brothers, still under the direction of Wilhelm, who was eventually knighted as Sir William Siemens.

In 1867 Siemens Brothers received a contract for an 11,000-kilometer telegraph line from London to Calcutta, which it completed in 1870. In 1871 it linked London and Teheran by telegraph. In 1874 Siemens Brothers launched its own cable laying ship, the Faraday, which William Siemens co-designed. The next year, it laid the first direct transatlantic cable from Ireland to the United States.

Expansion and Diversification: 1877–1929

In 1877 Alexander Graham Bell's new telephones reached Berlin for the first time. Immediately grasping their worth, Werner Siemens quickly patented an improved version of the device and began production. In the next decade, Siemens & Halske also developed and began manufacturing electrical lighting and power generating equipment after Werner Siemens discovered the dynamo electric principle in 1866.

In 1888 Werner Siemens was ennobled by the German kaiser for his achievements. Two years later he retired and his company became a limited partnership shared by his sons Arnold and Wilhelm and his brother Carl. Werner Siemens died in 1892, but the House of Siemens continued to prosper. That same year, Siemens & Halske built a power station at Erding in Bavaria and founded an American subsidiary, Siemens & Halske Electric Company, in Chicago. The latter, however, closed in 1904. In 1895 Wilhelm Conrad Roentgen discovered the X-ray, and the very next year Siemens & Halske owned the first patent for an X-ray tube. In 1897 Siemens & Halske decided to go public and reorganized with Carl Heinrich, now Carl von Siemens after being ennobled by the Russian czar in 1895, as chairman of the supervisory board. He retired after seven years in that post and was succeeded by his nephew Arnold.

Siemens & Halske remained busy as the 19th century gave way to the 20th. In 1903 it established Siemens Schuckertwerke GmbH, a subsidiary devoted to electric power engineering. In 1909 Siemens & Halske developed an automatic telephone exchange serving 2,500 customers in Munich. But when World War I broke out, orders for civilian electrical equipment slowed considerably and the company began production of communications devices for the military. Siemens & Halske also produced explosives, gun locks for rifles, and, later in the war, aircraft engines.

But perhaps the company's most successful contribution to the German war effort was the fire control system it produced for the navy's battle cruisers, which proved its worth at the Battle of Jutland in 1916. There, the battle cruiser squadron of the High Seas Fleet met its British counterpart for the only time during the war. While the main fleets fought to a draw, the German battle cruisers used their superior gunnery equipment to batter their opponents, sinking two British ships and severely damaging several others. It was a highlight for the German navy in a battle from which it otherwise won no advantage.

On the balance, however, the war hurt Siemens & Halske badly. The Bolshevik government that seized power in Russia in 1917 also seized the assets of the company's St. Petersburg subsidiary, which were worth about Ru 50 million. Siemens Brothers was taken over by the British government in 1915 and sold to British interests the next year. The company was not returned to the Siemens family after the armistice, although it retained their name for business purposes. Siemens Brothers eventually re-established links to its old parent, and its general manager, Dr. Henry Wright, even became a member of the Siemens & Halske supervisory board in 1929. But Carl Friedrich von Siemens, a son of Werner's who had headed the British subsidiary for six years and had many English friends, was shocked by these events; "they have stolen our name," he lamented.

Arnold von Siemens died in 1918, before the end of the war. He was succeeded by his brother Wilhelm, who died the next year. Carl Friedrich then became chairman. Despite the precarious state of the German economy in the 1920s and a bias among foreign customers against doing business with a German company, the company continued to make its mark in electrical manufacturing. In 1923 it started producing radio receivers for the consumer market. In the same year, recognizing the growing importance of Japan as an industrial power and not wishing to concede that market to General Electric and Westinghouse, Siemens & Halske set up a Tokyo subsidiary, Fusi Denk, later known as Fuji Electric. In 1925 Siemens began construction of a power station on the Shannon River in Ireland, and in 1927 the company began work on another hydroelectric power station for the Soviet government, near Zaporozhe. Back home in Germany, Siemens & Halske financed and produced a railway network in suburban Berlin that began operation in 1928. By the end of the decade, the company was accounting for one-third of the German electrical manufacturing industry's production and nearly the same proportion of its employees.

The Company During Wartime: 1930–45

Siemens & Halske was bloodied by the Great Depression, but it survived. It was forced to halve its dividend in the early 1930s and lay off employees in large numbers, but remained on relatively sound financial footing until the Nazi government's rearmament project helped revive its fortunes in 1935. During the remainder of the decade, Siemens & Halske manufactured a wide range of equipment for all of Germany's armed services. One of its most significant technical contributions at this time, the development of an automatic pilot system for airplanes, was the result of a project initiated for the Luftwaffe.

The company's activities during this time are difficult to evaluate. On the one hand, according to family historian Georg

Key Dates:

1847: Siemens & Halske is founded in Berlin by Werner Siemens and J.G. Halske to manufacture and install telegraphic systems.

1877: Werner Siemens quickly patents an improved version of Alexander Graham Bell's telephone and begins production.

1892: Siemens & Halske build a power station at Erding in Bavaria and establish an American subsidiary, Siemens & Halske Electric Company, in Chicago.

1897: Siemens & Halske goes public.

1903: The company establishes Siemens Schuckertwerke GmbH, a subsidiary devoted to electric power engineering.

1923: The company starts producing radio receivers for the consumer market and establishes a Tokyo subsidiary, Fusi Denk, later known as Fuji Electric.

1949: The company moves its corporate headquarters to Munich.

1966: The company undergoes a major reorganization, bringing all of its subsidiaries directly under the control of the parent company and reincorporating as Siemens A.G.

1978: *Fortune* magazine declares that Siemens has outpaced Westinghouse to become GE's primary competition.

1992: Siemens joins forces with IBM and Toshiba Corp. to develop 256M-bit chips to create microprocessors with the power of supercomputers.

1998: Company head Heinrich von Pierer introduces a ten-point excellence plan to increase earnings and crack down on underperforming businesses.

2001: Siemens makes its first listing on the New York Stock Exchange.

Siemens, Carl Friedrich von Siemens was repelled by the Nazis' anti-Semitism from the start and only grew more disgusted with their goals and methods as time went on. Just before his death in 1941, he wrote to an assistant: "My work no longer brings me satisfaction or joy. Those who were once proud that their work was devoted to the task of serving progress and humanity, can now only be sad that the results of their work merely serve the evil of destruction. Whenever I start to think, 'why,' I should prefer to creep into a corner, so as not to see or hear any more." Yet there is no question that Siemens & Halske benefited from German rearmament during the late 1930s. Certainly the company did little or nothing to hinder Nazi militarism.

Carl Friedrich went into partial retirement in 1940 and appointed Hermann von Siemens, Arnold's eldest son, to succeed him. By this time, Siemens & Halske was devoting virtually all of its manufacturing capacity to military orders and would do so for the duration of the war. In 1944 it helped develop and manufacture the V 2 rocket. Its factories also suffered substantial damage from Allied bombing raids. After the Soviet army conquered Berlin in 1945, Russian occupation authorities completely dismantled the Siemensstadt factory works and corporate headquarters.

In 1945 Hermann von Siemens, who had also been a director of Deutsche Bank, was arrested by American occupation authorities and interned for two years. There is also no question that the company employed slave labor during the war. Georg Siemens pointed out that every major German industrial concern used forced labor because of manpower shortages caused by the war, and asserted that Siemens & Halske treated its laborers better than most companies. But in 1947, allegations surfaced that three of the firm's directors had been active in importing slave laborers from occupied countries. In addition, testimony from Holocaust survivors also surfaced at this time that Siemens had supplied gas chamber equipment to the concentration camps. These allegations were never proven, however, and the company denied them both.

Rebuilding and Reorganization Through the 1950s and 1960s

Hermann von Siemens resumed the chairmanship upon his release in 1948. The company had been devastated by the war and required years of rebuilding to get back on its feet. Its corporate headquarters was relocated to Munich in 1949. By the early 1950s, Siemens & Halske was once again producing railroad, medical, telephone, and power generating equipment, as well as consumer electronics products. In 1954 it established an American subsidiary in New York, Siemens Inc. Its first product sold to the American market was an electron microscope. In the mid-1950s Siemens & Halske entered the burgeoning fields of data processing and nuclear power. It introduced its first mainframe computer in 1955, and its first nuclear reactor went into service in 1959 at Munich Garching.

Hermann von Siemens retired in 1956 and was succeeded by Ernst von Siemens, Carl Friedrich's only son. In the mid-1960s, Siemens & Halske technology went to Mars after the company developed a disc seal triode that was used in the transmitter of the American space probe Mariner IV. In 1965 it scored another coup when its 03 high-speed passenger train went into service with the German Federal Railway. Three years later, it began constructing a nuclear power station at Atucha, Argentina, the first such facility in South America.

The company underwent a major reorganization in 1966, bringing all of its subsidiaries directly under control of the parent company and reincorporating as Siemens A.G. By the end of the decade, worldwide sales had reached DM 10 billion; in 1970 they reached DM 12.6 billion. In 1971 Ernst von Siemens retired and his cousin Peter succeeded him as chairman.

Prospering in the 1970s

The 1970s were prosperous years for Siemens. Despite a slower worldwide economy that curbed customer orders in some areas and forced the company to cut its workforce, sales grew to DM 20.7 billion and net profits to DM 606 million in 1976. When the summer Olympic Games came to Munich in 1972, Siemens was its first official supplier of telecommunications and data processing equipment. In 1977 the company entered into a joint venture with the American engineering firm Allis Chalmers, called Siemens Allis Inc., to market turbine generators in the United States. In fact, Siemens' status as an electrical manufacturer rose to the point that *Fortune* wrote in

1978 that it had ''replaced Westinghouse in General Electric's demonology.'' Siemens had replaced Westinghouse as the world's number two electrical manufacturing concern, ranking ''as GE's major worldwide competitor in everything from motors and switchgear to generators and nuclear reactors.'' It also had raised its share of the West German mainframe computer market to 21 percent, cutting sharply into IBM's position as the Bundesrepublik's leading mainframe supplier.

In the late 1970s, Siemens stumbled when it initiated a research and development effort in microcircuit technology, against the advice of a consulting firm employed by the West German government to counsel the nation's industrial companies. It was thought that Siemens' slow and methodical practices would render it unable to keep up with the smaller, quicker Silicon Valley firms that were breaking ground in this area. Nonetheless, Siemens A.G., with its research and development budget of $1 billion (one-eighth of all the money spent by West German industry on research at the time), eventually entered into a joint venture with Dutch rival Philips to develop advanced microcircuits. None of the company's efforts on this front proved successful, however. Its components division lost money through 1987 and Siemens was forced to buy chips from Toshiba to meet its commitments until its own became available in early 1988.

Keeping Pace with High Technology and Globalization in the 1980s and 1990s

In 1981 Peter von Siemens retired and was succeeded by Bernhard Plettner. For the first time, the Siemens family relinquished day-to-day control over the company it had founded over a century ago. But the 67-year-old Plettner had worked for Siemens for all of his adult life, and Peter von Siemens felt that his own son, at the age of 44, was still too young and inexperienced for the top job.

Under Plettner and new CEO Karlheinz Kaske, Siemens embarked on an expensive and ambitious program of acquisitions and research and development to try to make itself into a world leader in high technology. Its effort to develop its own microchips was a part of that effort, as was the acquisition of IBM's struggling Rolm Systems subsidiary in 1988. That deal cost Siemens $844 million, but gave it control of the third largest supplier of PBX telephone switching equipment in North America. Siemens' strategy during the 1980s was designed to pay off over the long term and produced few tangible benefits in the short run. The company spent $24 billion on both research and development and acquisitions between 1983 and 1988, and the tremendous cash drain produced both a significant drop in earnings and a cut in the dividend in 1988. As one analyst told *Business Week* in 1988, ''Siemens will be an interesting story in the 1990s.''

As the company entered the new decade, globalization became a vital part of its policy—and that meant a readjustment of the company's homogeneous culture. Europe was facing a recession and the Asian and South American markets offered huge opportunities for growth. To help guide the new direction of Siemens, the company appointed Hermann Franz as chairman and Heinrich von Pierer as president and CEO. The appointment of Dr. Heinrich von Pierer as chief executive in 1992

reflected the need for a cultural change and the drive for higher profitability.

Siemens had always been dominated by engineers. When von Pierer, an economist and lawyer, was elected to head the company, it was seen as a commitment to greater commercialism for the company. Von Pierer's guidance stressed three fundamental trends: the first was that 85 percent of Siemens' business would be conducted either in global markets or in markets that showed an unmistakable trend toward globalization; second, that significant improvements in manufacturing depended on reducing manufacturing ''depth''; and third, that software was increasingly the crucial commercial factor.

Within the company, von Pierer caused a cultural revolution. He continued the reorganization begun by his predecessor, Kaske, and developed a program designed to make Siemens more competitive with Japanese companies by making it more responsive to market pressures. He replaced the hierarchical structure and engineering focus with a new emphasis on innovation and service. He gave managers in local markets free rein to cut costs and bid for projects, while also appointing a younger generation of managers in their 40s. Moreover, von Pierer cut Siemens' workforce by 7.5 percent and sold $2 billion in noncore businesses and slashed $3.6 billion in operating expenses by fiscal 1995. He continually asked if the company was flexible and changing enough, and at one point, included self-addressed postcards in the company magazine urging employees to send him their ideas.

Such measures were part of a strategy to get Siemens into new high-growth markets, especially in Asia. Von Pierer planned to invest $3.4 billion in Asia by the year 2000 and to double sales to $14.3 billion, according to *Business Week* in 1995. He set up facilities in Asia and Eastern Europe to lower costs and reach new customers, and bought telecommunications units in the United States and Italy. He also planned further acquisitions to move more production out of Germany. The strategy began to pay off. While net profits slipped 17 percent to $1.18 billion in 1994, earnings jumped 8 percent in three months and analysts saw a 20 percent increase for the year. As of 1995, sales continued to increase and the declining profits for the company began to increase.

In another move toward globalization, an international partnership brought Siemens together with the world's largest computer maker and Japan's second largest chip maker. In 1992, Siemens joined forces with IBM and Toshiba Corporation to develop 256M-bit chips to create microprocessors with the power of supercomputers. The first chip was expected to be marketed in 1998. The estimated cost for the project was a billion dollars for designing the chip and another billion for setting up the manufacturing facilities. The Siemens, IBM, and Toshiba alliance was expected to become the industry norm given rising operation costs and the focus towards a ''borderless'' world economy.

Innovation was always a part of Siemens' tradition. But new social pressures and rapidly changing technology throughout the world brought new challenges to Siemens as it faced the 21st century. To deal with this new business market, Siemens used its tradition of intelligence, resources, and systematic application to remain a strong international force. As von Pierer stated in Siemens' 1994 annual report: ''Helping set the course of change has been a vital part of our business for nearly 150 years. . . . Fifteen years ago, barely half of our worldwide sales came from products that were less than five years old. This figure has now risen to more than two-thirds—solid proof that we are not just meeting increased demands for change, but are setting the pace for innovation.''

Radical Restructuring for the 21st Century

The mid-1990s proved to be difficult years for Siemens. Coupled with sluggish conditions in Europe, the 1996 onset of the economic crisis in east Asia took a serious toll, diminishing the company's profits by two-thirds between 1996 and 1998. Analysts critiqued Siemens for being too slow to respond to the new demands of the rapidly globalizing business environment, and many called for the company to overhaul its ''old economy'' conglomerate structure, especially by unloading those businesses dependent on slow-growing markets, such as power generation.

Under the time-optimized processes, or Top, program, a three-pronged strategy promoting cost-reduction, growth, and innovation, management had effected significant restructuring and substantial productivity gains since the early 1990s. Profits were still not sufficient, however, to finance the international expansion needed to keep up with competitors. The company's earnings were particularly impaired by its semiconductor business, which, after being hard hit by a vicious price war for memory chips, lost $727 million in 1998. Other problem divisions included power generation, transportation systems, and private communication networks.

In spite of criticism, von Pierer held fast to his traditionalist belief that there were valuable synergies between the various arms of Siemens' business activities, especially as nearly all of the company's businesses were in electrics or electronics, and as the broad scope of activities helped to insulate Siemens from the inevitable ups and downs of different business cycles. By 1998, however, the CEO conceded that the company had diluted its overall strength by stretching itself in too many directions at once. Resolving to keep only the businesses in which Siemens could maintain market leadership, von Pierer moved to discontinue more than 30 of the company's minor operations, including those in military electronics and dental equipment. This also included selling its stake in the suffering telecom group GPT to the U.K.-based GEC. Still, most investors remained frustrated, contending that this streamlining constituted little more than a piecemeal restructuring and was not radical enough to restore the ailing company to solid profitability.

Finally, in late 1998 von Pierer introduced a global ten-point plan that was heralded as a revolution for the 153-year-old company. Under this sweeping shake-up, designed to bolster earnings and eliminate underperformance, Siemens would sell or spin off one-seventh of its entire domain, divisions with combined annual sales of more than $10 billion. Key to this unburdening, Siemens had resolved to spin off Infineon, its highly cyclical semiconductor business, which was forecasting huge losses again in 1998. Further, the company let go of businesses that made copper cable, electronic components, and locomotives.

The revamped Siemens consisted of four main divisions: power generation, industry, rail systems, and information and communications. To shore up power generation and achieve critical cost-cutting, Siemens purchased the electricity generation arm of Westinghouse in August 1998. With the establishment of Siemens Westinghouse Power Corporation, Siemens was well positioned to take advantage of strong demand in the United States, and to restructure its manufacturing operations worldwide. Further, the acquisition represented a major stride toward relocating the bulk of Siemens' manufacturing outside of Germany, another of von Pierer's goals. The industry division had undergone its own rigorous restructuring under the leadership of Edward Krubasik and, with a 60 percent profit increase in 1997, was beginning to thrive. Krubasik had introduced best-practice initiatives, joint account teams, and other measures to bring cohesion to the division's loosely bundled units, whose activities ranged from industrial plant building to automated machines. Rail systems, which lost $479 million in 1997, was Siemens' least vital division. With von Pierer's shake-up, it received a new management team charged with strengthening operations enough to make the division salable in the coming years.

Information and communications was Siemens' biggest division. Here, the company hoped to forge partnerships in its mobile phones and personal computers businesses, both areas in which it lacked sufficient market share to compete effectively on its own. Further, while it had a secure stake in the traditional telecoms switching market, a strategic acquisition was needed to bring the division up to speed with Internet-based network technologies, a crucial area of competence, as the world volume of data traffic was projected to surpass that of voice telephone communication in the coming years.

Success in this area depended on executing a major push into the U.S. market, where the pace of competition was being set by such companies as Nortel Networks, Lucent Technologies, and Cisco Systems. To this end, in 1999 Siemens acquired two Massachusetts-based private data networking companies, Castle Networks Inc. and Argon Networks Inc., for the establishment of a new, Boston-based subsidiary. Further, in 2001 the company made its first listing on the New York Stock Exchange, laying the groundwork for future stock-based acquisitions. Also that year, Siemens adopted more transparent U.S.-style accounting practices, and published its annual results accordingly.

Analysts applauded von Pierer's visionary restructuring, as Siemens saw its earnings double in 1999; moreover, net income increased from EUR 1.2 billion in 1999 to EUR 8.9 billion in 2000. With retirement on the horizon in 2004, von Pierer continued to laud the synergistic benefits of Siemens' conglomerate structure. As he told the *Financial Times* of London on January 21, 2002, ''Our relative strength is that we are in a range of different businesses which are subject to different economic cycles. The validity of this approach was not appreciated by everyone a few years ago.''

Still, in the ongoing quest to establish its standing as a world-class company, Siemens continued to conduct surgery on itself in the early years of the 21st century, excising fat from all divisions and honing its focus on IT & Communications and

Industry. Von Pierer was particularly intent on restoring profitability to the three IT-related divisions of telecom equipment, mobile phones, and business services, through job cuts, the closure of non-essential manufacturing sites, and a redoubled push to bring new products to market. Having used similar strategies to achieve major turnarounds in the formerly loss-plagued medical equipment and trains divisions, it seemed likely that Siemens would meet its mark.

Principal Subsidiaries

Acuson Corporation; BSH Bosch und Siemens Hausgeräte GmbH; Efficient Networks, Inc.; Fujitsu Siemens Computers (Holding) BV; Infineon Technologies AG; OSRAM GmbH; Siemens Airfield Solutions; Siemens Building Technologies AG; Siemens Corporation; Siemens Dematic AG; Siemens Energy & Automation, Inc.; Siemens Industrial Solutions and Services Group; Siemens Information and Communications; Siemens Power Generation Group; Siemens Power Transmission and Distribution Group; Siemens Solar Group; Siemens Transportation Systems Group; Siemens VDO Automotive.

Principal Competitors

ABB Ltd.; General Electric Company; Hitachi, Ltd.

Further Reading

Althaus, Sarah, "Siemens Dinosaur Learns Laws of Evolution: A Further Quantum Leap Is Needed to Turn the Industrial Blue Chip into a World-Class Company," *Financial Times* (London), November 5, 1999, p. 32.

Andrews, Edmund L., "Siemens to Sell Big Units in Bid to Shore Up Profitability," *New York Times,* November 5, 1998, p. C4.

Barber, Lionel, and Bertrand Benoit, "A Pragmatic Capitalist and Social Romantic: Interview [with] Heinrich von Pierer, Siemens," *Financial Times* (London), November 27, 2000, p. 18.

Benoit, Bertrand, "Siemens Discovers the Downside of Shareholder Capitalism: Concerns for Industrial Divisions Are Both Structural and Cyclical," *Financial Times* (London), October 18, 2001, p. 28.

Benoit, Bertrand, and Peter Marsh, "A Good Argument for Corporate Pragmatism: Interview [with] Heinrich von Pierer, Chief Executive, Siemens," *Financial Times* (London), December 4, 2002, p. 13.

Bowley, Graham, "It's Payback Time for Siemens' Industrious Unit Chief: Edward Krubasik Has Cut Back, Restructured and Boosted Productivity to Leave the Industry Division One of the German Group's Best," *Financial Times* (London), October 13, 1998, p. 27.

——, "New Lean Siemens May Still Need Toning Up," *Financial Times* (London), November 6, 1998, p. 28.

Face to Face with Technology, Berlin: Siemens Aktiengesellschaft, 1991.

Goodwin, Jack S., and Robert M. Fulmer, "Management Development at Siemens Electronics: Hitting a Moving Target," *Journal of Management Development,* September 1992, pp. 40–46.

"Half Way There: Siemens," *Economist,* July 4, 1992, p. 60.

Harrison, Michael, "Chip War Forces Siemens Shake-Up," *Independent* (London), July 17, 1998, p. 19.

Hussain, Ahrar, "Siemens—A Tradition of Excellence," *Economic Review,* August 1994, p. 109.

Kohn, Rudiger, "Siemens Plans Radical Restructuring," *Financial Times* (London), February 21, 2000, p. 28.

Lineback, J. Robert, "Siemens Braces for Rough Road Ahead," *Electronic News,* March 22, 1993, p. 18.

Marsh, Peter, "Engineering a Recovery: Management Siemens: Transforming an 'Old-Economy' Manufacturer Requires Not Only Cost-Cutting, But Also Growth and Innovation," *Financial Times* (London), August 8, 2000, p. 10.

——, "Westinghouse Buy Sets Foundation for Profitability," *Financial Times* (London), June 10, 1999, p. 6.

Miller, Karen Lowry, "Siemens Shapes Up: So Long Plodding Perfectionism. Hello, Aggressiveness," *Business Week,* May 1, 1995, pp. 52–53.

Munchau, Wolfgang, "Germany Needs Its Works Councils—The Head of Siemens Tells Wolfgang Munchau Why Consultation with Workers Is Necessary," *Financial Times* (London), December 17, 1995, p. 23.

Panni, Aziz, "Sea Change at Siemens," *Management Today,* March 1994, p. 50.

Procassini, Andrew, "Alliances and Opportunities," *Electronic News,* September 28, 1992, p. 8.

Schares, Gail E., Jonathan B. Levine, and Peter Coy, "The New Generation at Siemens," *Business Week,* March 9, 1992, p. 46.

Schiesel, Seth, "Siemens Plans U.S. Venture in Data Market," *New York Times,* March 4, 1999, p. C1.

Scott J.D., *Siemens Brothers, 1858–1958,* London: Weidenfeld and Nicolson, 1959.

Siemens, Georg, *History of the House of Siemens,* translated by A.F. Rodger and Lawrence N. Hold, Munich: Karl Alber, 1957.

Siemens, Werner von, *Inventor and Entrepreneur: Recollections of Werner von Siemens,* London: Lund Humphries, 1966.

"Technical Opportunities Beckon in Eastern Europe," *Design News,* September 20, 1993, p. 250.

Wagstyl, Stefan, and Graham Bowley, "A Strategist Who Has Everything to Play for: Profile Heinrich von Pierer, Chief Executive, Siemens," *Financial Times* (London), April 20, 1998, p. 11.

—updates: Beth Watson Highman, Erin Brown

Smith's Food & Drug Centers, Inc.

<table>
<tr><td>

1550 South Redwood Road
Salt Lake City, Utah 84104
U.S.A.
Telephone: (801) 974-1400
Fax: (801) 974-1662

Wholly Owned Subsidiary of The Kroger Company
Incorporated: 1932 as Smith and Son's Market
Employees: 1,800
NAIC: 445110 Grocery Stores

</td></tr>
</table>

Smith's Food & Drug Centers, Inc., a subsidiary of The Kroger Company, is a leading regional supermarket chain operating in the intermountain, Southwest, and Pacific Northwest regions of the United States. Smith's has realized great success by expanding its traditional supermarket model to include takeout food, photo processing, video rentals, and other services. After completing a merger with Portland-based Fred Meyer in 1997, Fred Meyer was in turn acquired by Cincinnati-based Kroger in 1999, making Kroger the largest supermarket chain in the United States.

Origins of a Family Business: 1911

The story of Smith's Food & Drug Centers, Inc., can be traced back to 1911 when Lorenzo Smith rented a space for a small grocery market stocking such staples as rice, flour, and dry beans. Smith's store was similar to other stores in Brigham City at that time, and it took Smith about ten years to accumulate enough capital to buy a larger store across the street. The family business, named Smith and Son's Market in 1932, remained afloat during the Great Depression, but growth was virtually nonexistent as many former customers were forced back into subsistence farming. Smith took most of his earnings and purchased property in the area, which was available at rock-bottom prices.

In 1942 business picked up after the U.S. Army built a hospital near the Smith market. Dee Smith returned from service in World War I and had worked in various jobs, mainly as a promoter of boxing and wrestling matches. He used these skills to promote the grocery store and also was instrumental in encouraging his father to modernize and expand the store in the late 1940s. With financial backing from his father, Dee Smith and his partner George C. Woodward opened a 10,000-square-foot grocery store, the first of its kind in Brigham City. By the end of World War II, Smith and Son's recognized that the neighborhood mom-and-pop store was becoming obsolete. Pent-up spending power from the war was being unleashed, and the dynamic expansion of production led to new demands by the average consumer.

Exponential Growth in the 1940s and 1950s

From 1946 until Lorenzo Smith's death in 1958 the company grew exponentially, with Dee Smith leading the aggressive growth campaign. The store was refurbished and expanded by 50 percent, an advanced refrigeration system was installed, and the name was changed to Smith's Super Market. Reopened in December 1952, the store posted huge sales increases; by 1954 Smith's was able to acquire American Food retail stores, a major grocery wholesaler and the primary supplier of Smith's. Soon after, another major store was opened in Brigham City with four times the space as Smith's Super Market.

These moves by Dee Smith established a firm base for expansion. Gross sales quadrupled from 1956 to 1957 and profit rates, although only 3 percent, were high by industry standards at the time. The purchase of Thiokol Chemical Corporation stock, an important business move, provided the duo with further capital for expansion. Thiokol had opened a plant north of Brigham City and was awarded a large Air Force contract. The investment reaped huge dividends, with the stock increasing in market value more than 12-fold by 1960.

With demand picking up as wages and employment grew in Brigham City, Smith and Woodward launched a growth plan, which included large ad campaigns and diversified product selection. Bolstered by increased highway construction that would provide access to residential markets, Smith's was also awarded the concession contract for Morrison-Knudsen Construction Company, which was building a causeway in the area and was housing its workforce nearby. Smith received concession rights for all services, including groceries, a restaurant, and a barber shop, to the residential construction camp. The operation was a guaranteed market and solidly profitable.

Expansion Through Strategic Acquisition in the 1960s and 1970s

By 1958 it appeared that the grocery market in Brigham City was becoming saturated, and Dee Smith was forced to look outside the area to new geographical markets. The 1960s was a time of massive expansion for Smith, but growth was uneven. For instance, its first takeover of a Safeway store in Boise, Idaho, ended in failure after the discovery that the previous owner had been doctoring the books. A major success was a contract Smith won to supply concessions to a construction camp for workers who were building Flaming Gorge Dam, a ten-year project that would provide stable demand for Smith's products. Smith also opened a new store called Food Giant.

Other successful takeovers followed as Smith expanded into wholesale trade, giving him more control over suppliers and distribution. Woodward purchased three Success Markets in Salt Lake City, and by the early 1970s Smith's had obtained more than 160 stores. The pattern was to buy failing stores at low prices, modernize them, and turn them into profitable operations. This strategy gave Dee Smith the needed funds and enabled him to build the large supermarkets that would become the standard in the industry. Although Smith was left with a high debt to assets ratio, his company was leading the industry in the southwestern United States and sat on a very profitable base of eight stores, which had sales of more than $13 million.

But like any successful business, Smith's recognized the need for continued growth to fend off competitors. In January 1968 Dee Smith announced the purchase of Mayfair Markets, a move that Howard Carlisle referred to in *The Dee Smith Story: Fulfilling a Dream*, as a "million-dollar transaction." By the end of the year Smith had acquired 16 of the Mayfair stores, expanding his empire to 23 stores in several Utah cities. Following a proven strategy, Smith and his associates had purchased the Mayfair stores at bargain prices because they were losing money and, after putting the company in a highly leveraged position (for example, Mayfair's Utah operations lost $1.5 million in 1967 while Smith's total net worth was less than $700,000), eventually turned a profit on them.

Smith achieved this task by reorganizing management, slashing wages, and intensifying workloads. He streamlined the management structure and instituted bonus incentives for managers while, at the same time, cutting salaries. An intensive labor effort also was launched to redecorate and reorganize all of the stores. Sales soared, but the company's profits were being strangled by its heavy debt service load, which limited cash flow. Nonetheless, the reorganization campaign left the company in a good position to cut prices. The discount pricing strategy helped revive sagging sales at some of the former Mayfair stores, thus expanding market share.

To further enhance its overall profit margins, Smith acquired its first nonfood business, the Utah-based Souvall Brothers, in 1969. Souvall's sold a diverse line of products—from beauty aids and housewares to yarn—and had sales of $3 million and a considerably higher profit margin than Smith's. This acquisition, according to Carlisle in *The Dee Smith Story*, kept the company afloat during the recession years of the early 1970s.

With the nonfood portion of the business growing faster than the grocery side, the company began experimenting with combination stores, gaining a jump on its competitors and momentum that lasted well into the 1980s. In addition to its many acquisitions, Smith also constructed new stores throughout the late 1960s and early 1970s, building new stores in Ogden, Roy, and Magna, Utah, as well as expanding the Souvall warehouse facilities in Salt Lake City. The biggest project was the construction of a 150,000-square-foot warehouse and distribution center in Layton, Utah. This facility, centrally located and near major highways, enabled Smith's to provide its own wholesaling and warehousing and gain greater cost and inventory control. Acquisitions had cut into profit margins, however, and coupled with the recession of 1973 and Nixon price controls, the company's cash flow problems threatened to become acute. Thus the need for external funding sources to finance the new warehousing center in Layton was vital. The public sector stepped in to foot the bill, selling $1.5 million of low interest bonds, which would be repaid over 15 years. Subsequently, Smith's realized huge cost-cutting success from its direct control over distribution and wholesaling operations.

By May 1974, however, the company was back on the acquisition trail, buying up two small chains in the populous and lucrative southern California market. Smith's had acquired 110 stores in seven years and the debt service became immense at a time of recession in the early 1970s. Competition was fierce as one-third of the retail food companies were experiencing losses. Smith's record in the decade ending in 1975 reflected this instability; sales increased 30-fold but profits only multiplied four times due to the company's cash flow problems. A severe financial crisis ensued in 1975, which led Smith to develop a new long-term competitive strategy.

After soliciting the advice of consultants and advertising experts, Smith's cut prices furiously and launched a large, general advertising campaign while operating stores under distinct names. Most important, Smith's began further experimentation with the combination superstore, sized at either 31,000 or 45,000 square feet. These changes immediately improved the bottom line of the company.

Smith's achieved further success throughout the 1970s as distribution centers were made more efficient, construction was initiated on new super combination stores, and weaker stores were sold off (notably four of the California stores). Although Dee Smith became more cautious in his acquisitions, he continued his growth through acquisition, acquiring six K-mart stores. Two of the K-mart stores were in Albuquerque, representing the

Key Dates:

1911: Lorenzo Smith opens a small dry goods grocery store in Brigham City, Utah.

1932: The family business is named Smith and Son's Market.

1952: After refurbishing and expansion, the original store is reopened as Smith's Super Market.

1969: Smith's acquires its first nonfood business, the Utah-based Souvall Brothers.

1980: Having diversified its range of products and services, the company begins using the slogan, "We're not just a food store anymore."

1989: Smith's Food & Drug Centers makes an initial public offering.

1997: Smith's is acquired by Portland, Oregon-based Fred Meyer.

1999: Smith's parent company, Fred Meyer, is acquired by Kroger Company.

company's first foray into the southwestern market. The new region was solidly profitable and, in 1978, Smith's bought 23 Foodway stores in New Mexico, the second largest acquisition in the company's history. In addition, for the first time, Smith's had to deal with a unionized workforce that went out on strike. After reaching an agreement, however, the stores quickly achieved profitable levels of operations.

Launching the Combination Outlet Concept in the 1980s

Although it continued to acquire stores, Smith's Food's main plan was to continue to expand by building more large combination outlets. The company built a total of 22 stores in 1977 and 1978 and planned an expanded production of the new outlets into the 1980s. Smith's used market research to tap new varieties of products, add more services, and merchandise new products. For instance, Smith's was one of the first retailers to market no-name, generic products—more than 200 generic items in addition to name brand items. In 1980 the company began using the slogan, "We're not just a food store anymore." The diverse mixture of departments sent sales up by 27 percent in 1978 and cash flow also improved. By 1979 the company was earning a 30 percent rate of profit on its equity.

The recession in the early 1980s only minimally affected the company's profits. During recessionary times, it became much cheaper to purchase failing businesses, and Smith's did just that. Specifically, Smith's purchased a group of eight stores in southern California. By this time about half of Smith's business had been acquisitions. Sales were slow but steady, and in 1983 the company weathered an 11-week strike by Las Vegas workers. The strike did not prevent Smith's from becoming the second largest privately held supermarket chain by the end of 1983. The California stores, operating under the name Smith's Food King, were sold in 1985 at a profit of $50 million.

In 1984 Dee Smith's five- and ten-year plans were implemented, but Smith died during the year and left the company to

the control of the third generation of Smith sons. The new management team that was assembled nearly doubled sales and profits from 1984 to 1988. Jeff Smith took over for his father as chief executive officer, and under his reign the company experienced accelerated growth. Dee Smith's plan to "phase out smaller, older conventional stores and superstores and replace them with larger combination food and drug centers" was successfully carried out by his sons despite intense competition. By 1990 76 of the company's 95 stores were combination food and drugstores ranging in size from 45,000 to 84,000 feet. New stores constructed in 1990 and 1991 averaged 72,900 square feet, continuing the modernization plan. The expansionist policy included replacing existing stores and pursuing intense cost-cutting strategies. This was supported by expanding and modernizing the company's warehouse facilities to vertically integrate the processing and distribution of perishable goods; achieve greater in-house warehousing to capitalize on economies of scale; and reorganize its transportation and distribution facilities. To this end, the company planned to build a one million-square-foot, fully integrated distribution facility to warehouse the goods for the region.

To raise the money necessary to gain a foothold in the highly competitive California market (a planned 60 stores in five years), Smith's management decided to take the company public in 1989. Management first created Smith's Management Corporation, which was merged into its wholly owned subsidiary, Smith's Food & Drug Centers. Next, in an effort to keep the company in the Smith family and also foil takeovers, certain classes of stock were designated for ownership solely by the Smith family. The value of the shares skyrocketed initially but stabilized within the year. In the early 1990s CEO Jeff Smith owned or controlled 48.2 percent of the voting stock (mainly from shares held in a trust for his mother, Ida). The next biggest block, 8.3 percent, was held by the Church of Jesus Christ of the Latter-Day Saints as part of Dee Smith's estate.

In the early 1990s Smith's ten-year plan was to invest $1.4 billion in opening 120 stores with annual sales growth targets of 20 percent. The California market would be extremely competitive and some industry analysts expected price wars. Further, the California stores would be unionized, unlike most of Smith's other stores. Yet there were more people in the southern California region than in all of Smith's other markets combined, and the store could offer competitive prices. The degree of growth realized, however, would likely depend on the state of employment in the region in the next decade and on the outcome of the battle with such chains as Von's Grocery Co., Lucky Stores Inc., and Albertson's Inc., each of which already had more than 100 stores in the region. Smith's predicted it would be able to capture about 6 percent of the region's market when its first 50 to 60 stores were opened.

Keeping Pace with Industrywide Consolidation in the 1990s

Despite the seeming promise of high population density on the West Coast, and although Smith's had fared well in competition with such formidable chains as Von's, Lucky, and Albertson's in other regions in the past, the southern California market proved particularly difficult to penetrate. By the mid-1990s, with 34 stores open in the region, Smith's resolved to pull out of southern California. Smith's incurred $84 million in restructuring charges for the closure and sale of its southern California operations, but the decision to redeploy assets back to Smith's core market in the Southwest proved propitious, as it led to a major acquisition that ultimately benefited shareholders.

Smith's broad restructuring came into full swing in 1996, when the company signed a merger agreement with Yucaipa, one of southern California's prominent grocery store operators. Under the terms of the $239 million agreement, Smith's acquired the 28-store Smitty's Supermarkets Inc., Yucaipa's Phoenix, Arizona-based chain. Yucaipa's Ronald W. Burkle became CEO of Smith's, and the company hired former Albertson's executive Allen R. Roland as president and chief operating officer. With the addition of the Smitty's stores to its ranks, Smith's became the top supermarket chain in the Phoenix area.

In the rapidly consolidating supermarket industry, Smith's further advanced its competitive position only a few months later when it agreed to merge with Portland, Oregon-based Fred Meyer, Inc., a dominant regional retailer of a broad range of products, including general merchandise, home improvement items, fine jewelry, and apparel. Under the terms of the "merger of equals," which was structured as a stock-for-stock exchange, Ron Burkle became chairman of the board, while Fred Meyer's chief executive, Robert G. Miller, became president and CEO. Together, the two companies' operations amounted to 265 stores in 11 states in the Pacific Northwest, Southwest, and intermountain regions, with an anticipated $7 billion in sales for 1997. The merger was completed by September 1997.

Little more than a year later, the Smith's-Fred Meyer merger was eclipsed when Cincinnati-based Kroger Company moved to acquire Fred Meyer. Already the biggest supermarket chain in the United States, Kroger paid $13.5 billion in stock and assumed debt to acquire Fred Meyer, boosting the parent company's projected annual sales to $43 billion. When the merger was complete in May 1999, the combined company operated 2,200 stores in 31 states. Ron Burkle lauded the deal, calling himself a "firm believer" in the benefits of consolidation, and many viewed Kroger's bulking up as a necessary step to compete effectively with the industry's reigning goliath, Wal-Mart. Indeed, Kroger received a major endorsement from the Federal Trade Commission when, despite the company's huge increase in size, it was required to sell only eight stores to meet antitrust conditions.

Kroger aimed to give its subsidiary stores as much autonomy as possible, and the merger had little effect on Smith's Utah stores. In Arizona, however, where Kroger already operated Fry's, a well-positioned chain, the majority of Smith's stores were subsumed under the Fry's name. In combining the operations of the two chains, Smith's stores received a total makeover, including new computer systems, new store decor, and new merchandise, replacing Smith's signature label products with those of Fry's. By consolidating operations to a single

chain in Arizona, Kroger aimed to cut costs significantly. Moreover, the parent company projected across-the-board cost cuts as a result of the merger with Fred Meyer, estimating annual savings of $225 million by the third year.

While major shifts occurred at the corporate level during the late 1990s, Smith's prepared to enter the 21st century by initiating numerous marketing programs at the store level that were designed to gain and retain loyal customers. In 1997 Smith's introduced its "Fresh Values Frequent Shopper Card," whereby customers received savings by using the card instead of clipping coupons and the company gained the ability to track customer spending habits in the process. In 1999, Smith's installed automated checkout systems in many of its stores in response to customer demand for greater speed and convenience at the checkout counter. In 2000, the company entered a partnership with Priceline.com that allowed customers to bargain for their groceries on the Internet before going to the grocery store to pick them up. In 2001, the company began installing fuel pumps in its parking lots and offering customers a discount on gasoline with their grocery purchase. Under the umbrella of the mighty Kroger, and with its dedication to identifying and satisfying customer needs, Smith's was poised for continued success in the 21st century.

Principal Competitors

Albertson's, Inc.; Associated Food Stores, Inc.; Safeway Inc.

Further Reading

Burnham, Rick, "Smith's Food in Deal with Arizona Grocery Chain," *Press-Enterprise,* January 30, 1996.

Carlisle, Howard M., *The Dee Smith Story: Fulfilling A Dream,* Brigham City, Utah: Ida Smith, 1992.

Creno, Glen, "Supermarket Chain Kroger Faces New Challenges in Phoenix-Area Market," *Arizona Republic,* June 20, 1999.

Lowenstein, Roger, "Smith's Food & Drug Gets Mixed Reviews As It Enters Big, Crowded Phoenix Market," *Wall Street Journal,* September 28, 1989.

Mitchell, Lesley, "Salt Lake City-Based Grocer Adds Self-Scan for Customers," *Salt Lake Tribune,* June 10, 1999.

Quick, Bob, "Rival Grocers Claim Market Leadership in Santa Fe, N.M.," *Santa Fe New Mexican,* June 16, 2002.

Sahm, Phil, "Kroger-Fred Meyer Merger Approved by Regulators," *Salt Lake Tribune,* May 28, 1999.

Silverstein, Stuart, "Heating Up the Supermarket Wars," *Los Angeles Times,* September 8, 1991.

"Smith's Scores with One-Hour Photo," *Progressive Grocer,* October, 1992.

Taylor, John H., "Mr. Smith Goes to Riverside," *Forbes,* February 17, 1992.

Tomkins, Richard, "Kroger Announces $7.2 Billion Takeover," *Financial Times* (London), October 20, 1998.

—John A. Sarich
—update: Erin Brown

Société Nationale des Chemins de Fer Français

34 rue du Commandant Mouchotte
75699 Paris Cedex 14
France
Telephone: (33) 1-53-25-60-00
Fax: (33) 1-53-25-61-08
Web site: http://www.sncf.fr

Government-Owned Company
Incorporated: 1938
Employees: 220,700
Sales: $17.8 billion (2001)
NAIC: 482111 Line-Haul Railroads; 482112 Short Line
Railroads; 485112 Commuter Rail Systems; 487110
Scenic and Sightseeing Transportation, Land;
488210 Support Activities for Rail Transportation;
561599 All Other Travel Arrangement and
Reservation Services

The Société Nationale des Chemins de Fer Français (SNCF) is the state-owned railroad of France. With a total rail network of 31,385 kilometers, SNCF provided long-distance passenger rail service to 315 million customers in 2001, in addition to hauling more than 125 million tons of freight. Also in 2001, SNCF's RATP and RER trains carried 560 million commuter passengers in Paris and throughout surrounding areas. The company manages the bulk of its operations through its principal subsidiary, SNCF Participations, which hold shares in 599 different companies involved in various aspects of the transportation, tourism, and shipping industries. SNCF incurred substantial debt throughout the 1990s, prompting French lawmakers to consider radical ways to restructure the beleaguered railroad, including privatization of some of its key operations. A significant government debt reduction, however, along with the creation in 1997 of the Reseau Ferre de France, a new company that assumed ownership and management of the country's railway infrastructure, have helped put SNCF back on the fast track at the beginning of the 21st century.

The Emergence of Rail Travel in 19th-Century France

From the earliest days of steam to the modern era of the superspeed passenger train, France has played a leading role in the development of rail transportation, and the Société Nationale des Chemins de Fer Français (SNCF) occupies an enduring place at the heart of the country's economic and social life.

The first railway line in France opened in 1827, carrying coal from Saint-Etienne to Andrezieux, a small port on the Loire. The primitive carriages were drawn by horses, but in 1831 the first steam locomotives and the first passenger service came into operation between Saint-Etienne and Lyon, initially using the former coal trucks as passenger compartments. The value of effective rail links was quickly apparent; within ten years, coal output in Saint-Etienne more than doubled, and industry boomed across the region.

Railways arrived in the capital on August 26, 1837, with a new passenger service from Paris to Le Pecq, near Saint-Germain-en-Laye. The line was inaugurated by Queen Marie-Amélie—King Louise Philippe was advised against boarding the new-fangled "steel monster"—and was an immediate success with Parisians; some 400,000 traveled the line within the first few weeks, at the then wondrous speed of 60 kilometers per hour (kmh). In 1841 a major rail link was built from Strasbourg to Basel, and by 1846 three more important routes had been laid between Paris and the provincial centers of Orléans, Rouen, and Lille.

Unlike roads or canals, the early railways were not state-owned, but built and operated by private speculators. The government, however, kept ultimate control over the expanding network by requiring each new line to seek an official license or concession, and it also assumed the right to veto or amend fares and tariffs. In 1839, for example, the fares on the Paris to Versailles line were set by the prefect of police.

Successive governments took an even closer interest in the railways. Napoleon III saw railway building as the mainspring of an ambitious program of economic and industrial expansion.

Company Perspectives:

SNCF is comprised of partner companies, which express the effectiveness of the Group through their ability to capitalize on the complementary nature of their services.

A major travel and logistics player in Europe, SNCF Group is now able to fulfill increasingly global transport service requests: intermodality, transport related services, logistics. Each Group company is active in one or more of the operating divisions making up the Group's activities: passenger transport and services; freight; infrastructure and leveraging of SNCF's assets and know-how.

His Second Empire of 1852 to 1870 encouraged a host of new lines; efficient rail links stretched from Paris to all important towns and cities, which simultaneously galvanized the regional economies and tightened the capital's hold on national life. The length of the network grew from 3,000 kilometers to 17,430 kilometers, and by the time of Napoleon III's downfall in 1870 all of the major routes that existed a century later had been laid.

Napoleon III's work was enthusiastically continued by the new republic. In 1878 the minister of public works, Charles de Freycinet, set up the first state-owned network by buying several ailing small lines in the west of the country. A year later he implemented the Freycinet Plan, which established a further 9,000 kilometers of track.

There followed a period of further expansion—between 1870 and 1914 the national network grew to a total length of 39,400 kilometers—and of increasing public and commercial popularity. The era of international prestige trains arrived in 1880, with the launch of the Orient Express, and France took its place at the center of a European rail network. Travel times improved; through the 1880s, the highly competitive Orléans line offered a Paris to Saint-Pierre-des-Corps service at slightly more than three-and-a-half hours. During this period there were further developments in the relationship between the state and the railways. Another Freycinet Plan, agreed upon between the government and railway companies in 1883, reversed the system under which the state financed new rail services. Hitherto, public funds had been used to cover estimated costs of fresh projects, with any surpluses being met by the private backers. Under the revised plan, the government would only meet the surpluses, handing responsibility for the main costs back to individual companies. The prestige of the railways was reflected in magnificent new stations across the country, including the remarkable terminus at the Quai d'Orsay in Paris, built around 1900, like a sunken cathedral at the end of a 3,100-meter tunnel beneath the left bank of the Seine. From the outset, the station used exclusively electric traction to ferry about 200 trains a day through a tunnel from the nearby Austerlitz station. In 1909 the state-owned network was considerably increased by the acquisition of a collection of lines in Normandy and Brittany previously run by the Compagnie de l'Quest. Between 1910 and 1914 the first electrified rail services in France were introduced by the Midi network, on the mountainous secondary lines of the Pyrenees.

The Move Toward State Ownership: 1900–45

Rail development was disrupted by World War I, although the French network played a major role in the conflict. As well as ferrying troops and supplies to the front and keeping the civilian population mobile, the railways proved vital to defense industries. Those in the northern and eastern sections of the country, however, suffered extensive damage, particularly in German-occupied territory. After the armistice, the railways faced a crippling backlog of repairs and improvements, made virtually impossible by spiraling costs and inflation. In 1920 all networks showed considerable losses; a 1921 agreement between individual lines to pool technology and resources was fatally undermined by world recession and mounting road competition. Against the odds there were some advances, notably in international traffic. The first nonstop express from Paris to Brussels started in 1923, traveling at 100 kmh on rebuilt track through the devastated battlefields of the recent war, and in 1932 a direct service was launched between Paris and Liège. The first 239-kilometer stretch of the Liège line, as far as Jeumont, carried trains traveling at an average speed of 106.3 kmh, much the fastest sustained run in Europe. These achievements were scored against a background of seemingly inexorable decline, however. By 1936 the railways' total deficit stood at FFr 37 billion. The network was in crisis, and turned to the state for rescue.

On August 31, 1937, the state reached an agreement with the five largest railway companies to establish a unified French railway system, the Société Nationale des Chemins de Fer Français, or SNCF. The deal was given a lifespan of 45 years, and came into effect on January 1, 1938. The SNCF embraced all of the big five rail systems—Compagnie du Nord, Compagnie de l'Est, Compagnie du Paris-Lyon-Mediterranée, Compagnie du Paris-Orléans, and Compagnie du Midi—and the two existing state services. The agreement specified that the newly integrated network be managed on a commercial basis, in that it was to increase fares and operate efficiently so as to cover its costs. The company was required, however, to recognize its public service responsibilities and undertake to uphold standards and services. These sometimes irreconcilable requirements, to operate both profitably and in the public interest, were to dog the company for four decades. The state reserved the right to block fare increases, on the understanding that it would compensate for the lost revenue. The new SNCF was under the ultimate control of the state, which owned 51 percent of capital; the remainder was held by the big five, newly formed into financial companies.

The onset of World War II predictably threw rail services into chaos. Despite German occupation from May 1940, however, some development was possible; for instance, seven large express locomotives were built to a new design and successfully introduced to the northern region. The railways in occupied France played a pivotal role in the logistics of the Nazi war effort and were put to use as a vital channel of troops, armaments, fortifications, and supplies. They quickly became priority war targets, particularly after the Normandy landings of 1944 when practically every main route in France was severely damaged by Allied bombers—and French resistance fighters—intent on disrupting enemy lines of communication.

Key Dates:

1827: The first railway line is opened in France.
1878: French Minister of Public Works Charles de Freycinet creates the first state-owned rail network.
1880: Orient Express begins operations.
1923: Express train service between Paris and Brussels is launched.
1938: Société Nationale des Chemins de Fer Français (SNCF) is formed.
1972: SNCF inaugurates a trial of its prototype gas turbine train.
1981: SNCF's Train à Grande Vitesse (TGV) begins commercial service.
1982: The French government assumes permanent ownership of SNCF.
1994: The Channel Tunnel establishes rail travel between the United Kingdom and France.
1997: Reseau Ferre de France is formed.

Postwar Recovery: 1945–70

After the war France set about rebuilding its railways for the second time in 30 years. Reconstruction was carried out with the full backing of the newly liberated state. As well as replacing and renovating damaged facilities, engineers used the opportunity to improve the network; in particular, major junctions such as those at Laroche and Melun were skillfully realigned so that trains could run through them without any loss of speed. Unfettered by government interference, the SNCF was left to embark on an aggressive period of promotion and improvement. Passenger services were improved by new rolling stock, modernized stations, and yet more new lines; the freight sector benefited from upgraded services and forceful marketing. The postwar reconstruction workforce reached a peak of 500,000 in 1947 and 1948.

Although there were detailed plans for a new generation of steam locomotives, an early decision was made to electrify the entire mainline network as soon as possible. Beginning in 1950 the SNCF made a series of technological advances in electric traction, which were subsequently exported around the globe. Instead of the 1,500-volt direct-current traction system, in use around the world and in France itself, French engineers developed a system using 20,000 volts of alternating current at the commercial frequency, adopted by all commercial Swiss traffic, of 50 cycles per second. This reduced the need for trackside substations, allowed for much lighter ancillary equipment, and brought installation costs down by a third. The scheme was successfully introduced in the French Alps, and then extended to the northern region and beyond. Furthermore, new French locomotives were designed so they could switch smoothly to differing power systems as they crossed international borders. Other innovations involved widespread automation, including luminous blocks for track spacing, and automated signal boxes and level crossings. The electrification program continued at such a pace that by 1964 France had 7,600 kilometers of powered mainline track, compared with 2,700 kilometers in Britain and 2,900 kilometers in the United States. By 1983 more than 80 percent of SNCF traffic was powered by domestically produced electricity, thus allowing the railways to claim the environmental high ground with "almost zero-level atmospheric pollution."

In 1955 two French electric engines traveled at a world record 331 kmh on the Landes line, which led to a wave of lucrative export orders and confirmed the company's resolve to remain at the forefront of high-speed technology. Railway systems throughout the developed world were suffering from the preeminence of the bus and the automobile as a means of transport over short journeys. From the 1950s the airplane posed a new threat to the railway's supremacy in the business of long-distance travel. Squeezed in this way between road and air rivals, the SNCF committed itself to meeting the dual challenge by means of speed, combined with comfort, reliability, and unrivaled safety standards. To this end French engineers studied every detail of railway design, from the locomotives to the track and signaling, to find ways of improving performance. Their achievements in this field would earn French railways a worldwide reputation for speed and efficiency.

Technological Advances, Financial Peril: 1970–90

In the 1960s the SNCF developed an aeronautical-type gas turbine to power a railway engine, thus paving the way for Europe's first turbotrains. In 1972 a prototype gas turbine train achieved speeds of 318 kmh in time trials. Turbotrains were scheduled for use on the new Paris to Lyon service, approved in 1974, but the government canceled the plan following the oil crisis.

By the late 1960s it was clear that the 1937 formation agreement had placed the SNCF in permanent financial difficulties, preventing it from responding effectively to the competition from road and air transport and new oil pipelines; the railway had to operate under the public service obligations imposed by the original agreement, while its rivals enjoyed commercial and technical freedom. To even the odds, the government revised the 1937 agreement in the codicil of January 27, 1971, which allowed a fundamental overhaul of the SNCF. In return for its new freedom, however, the railway took responsibility for balancing its books, leaving the state to make contributions to specified areas only, such as public service charges and social insurance contributions.

The SNCF entered a new period of steady development. In the early 1970s France established some 25 regional councils, with significant powers delegated by central government. The SNCF set up close dialogue with the new councils, to discuss detailed ways of improving local rail services. Although central government retained responsibility for basic transport support, the regions were given the right and resources to make local improvements. Some councils funded new rolling stock; others secured improvements or extensions to the local network, or reached agreement on fares policy. The relationship between the regions and SNCF blossomed through the 1980s and into the 1990s, and the railway company furnished the councils with regular computer bulletins on trends and developments.

By the end of the 1970s, however, the national railway company's progress was again undermined by financial imbalance. In particular, the network complained bitterly of its constant reliance on debt; since its inception, the SNCF had capital of just .03 percent of its operating budget, meaning that all investment had to be raised through loans. This placed a massive financial burden on the company. Furthermore, despite the codicil of 1971, the company still felt that it was being forced to compete on unequal terms with other haulers. These problems were tackled in another overhaul of the SNCF, introduced from December 31, 1982, the expiration date of the 1937 agreement that established the company. All assets of the SNCF passed over to the state, in accordance with the original 45-year deal, and the company became a permanently state-owned concern. The SNCF also was brought into a national program aimed at improving and integrating the various transport systems, and placing them under corporate legislative control. The new law also clarified and reconciled the SNCF's dual role as both public servant and competitive commercial enterprise. Of more immediate importance, the reorganization helped resolve the company's financial difficulties; the state reaffirmed its commitment to its national railways, the largest in Western Europe with double the traffic of, for instance, British Rail. It stepped up contributions to pension and infrastructure costs, and innovatively made capital grants toward railway projects of national value. It also continued to subsidize fares and less profitable regional services. The SNCF diversified, through a range of subsidiaries, into a wide range of transport-related fields, from hotel management to haulage and tourism.

The changes in the SNCF coincided with spectacular success in the development of the Train à Grande Vitesse (TGV), the world's fastest train. The French described the TGV, run on electric traction, as a synthesis of technological progress, combining an aerodynamic profile, stability, and cabin signaling. On February 26, 1981, the TGV set a track speed world record, clocking 380 kmh on the Paris to Lyon line. The train entered commercial service in September of the same year, with a normal operating speed limit of 270 kmh. The first TGV service followed a southeast route embracing Lyon, Saint-Etienne, Dijon, Besançon, and Geneva in Switzerland. In 1982 the service was extended to the population centers of the Rhône Valley and the south of France, and other important routes were added at the rate of more than one a year: to Lausanne and Toulon in 1984; to Lille, Lyon, and Grenoble that winter; to Rouen in 1986; and to Nice, Neuchatel, and Bern in 1987. By that time 43 cities were connected to Paris by TGV, with a further nine destinations during the winter sports season. The 300 kmh Atlantic TGV was opened in two phases during 1989 and 1990; the west branch served Le Mans, Rennes, Britanny, and Nantes, and the southwest branch took in the Bordeaux region up to the Spanish border, and Toulouse. In 1989 the pioneering Southeast service carried its 100 millionth passenger, and the line recorded a 15 percent return on its investment, 3 percent more than planned. The TGV reduced travel times dramatically, bringing Marseilles, for example, to within five hours of Paris; over medium intercity distances the railway suddenly rivaled aircraft as the fastest travel option. Moreover, the railways were cheaper and claimed clear advantages in comfort, reliability, and convenience. Trains were able to arrive in the heart of cities, rather than remote, isolated airports.

The French saw the TGV as the future of high-speed travel within a uniting Europe; in the early 1990s some airlines were investing in rail links rather than in short-haul air trips. The shift from air to rail travel for medium distances also has the backing of the European Community, which in the late 1980s commissioned an exhaustive study into the potential of a high speed, pan-European network. The SNCF was anxious for the system to use French trains and was confident its TGV would beat off fierce competition from Japan, Germany, and Scandinavia. The government was backing a FFr 210 billion scheme to more than double the size of the TGV network over 20 years. The north European TGV system was planned for 1993, to coincide with the opening of the Channel Tunnel; it would cover northern France—Paris to Lille in one hour—and extend to Brussels, Cologne, and Amsterdam. The proposed TGV East would serve the eastern edge of France and southern Germany. A TGV hub was planned for Roissy, near Paris, creating the first high-speed rail network in the world. There were domestic plans for a direct TGV link from Paris to Marseilles, to bring the travel time down from four hours and 40 minutes to just three hours. Meanwhile, the TGV continued to break records, reaching speeds of 500 kmh during 1990.

By recognizing before any of its competitors the possibility of a second rail revolution based on speed, the SNCF bucked an international trend and reversed falling passenger figures. It also adopted a leading role in transport technology that, it was hoped, had laid the foundations of a prosperous future. In the late 1980s the network focused its efforts on improving its freight business, having witnessed a 30 percent drop in goods volume over the previous 15 years. The decline was further hastened at the end of 1986 by a bitter rail strike, the longest in French history. At the end of the decade the SNCF relaunched its freight sector under the brand name Fret, and promoted it aggressively. The service claimed sweeping improvements in performance, based on the use of computers to improve customer communications and to process consignments more quickly and effectively. It also entered into partnership with road companies for intermodal traffic, using giant containers adapted for both railway and lorry haulage. The SNCF hoped that intermodal traffic would account for at least 30 percent of its goods business. Meanwhile, electrification continued apace, with many new schemes such as those on the Paris-Massif Central main line, and in Brittany.

In 1990 the SNCF announced a major reorganization of its top management structure, after consultants found the development of divisive "empires" within the company. The new structure strengthened the top-level directorate and regrouped the company into five separate businesses, each with its own budget, covering passenger, freight, Ile-de-France region, regional, and Sernam, the intermodal subsidiary.

Profit and Loss in the Era of European Unification: 1990–2003

SNCF entered the last decade of the 20th century with an aggressive growth strategy, one designed not only to increase its overall passenger transport capacity, but also to implement the technological advances the company needed to remain at the forefront of modern rail travel in Europe. To this end, the company staked the bulk of its future on the continued expansion of its high-speed train network.

In 1990 SNCF unfolded a plan to build an additional 3,400 kilometers of high-speed track for its celebrated Train à Grande Vitesse (TGV). The new system would establish links between more major French cities, thereby considerably expanding the company's domestic transportation revenues. More important, the expanded network would also forge critical connections to high-speed rail lines in neighboring countries throughout Europe, notably Germany, Belgium, and Italy. In all, SNCF planned to build 13 additional TGV lines, a notable improvement on the two TGV lines in operation in 1990. Although the TGV accounted for only 15 percent of SNCF's long distance passenger service in 1990, the company hoped that expanding the high-speed network to a total of 5,800 kilometers by 1994 would give the TGV trains closer to 50 percent of its non-commuter passenger business. During this period SNCF also saw enormous growth potential in the completion of the long-awaited Channel Tunnel, which would establish a direct rail link between Paris and London.

A series of setbacks in the early 1990s, however, soon put a damper on SNCF's ambitious growth program. The delayed opening of the Channel Tunnel, combined with a protracted legal dispute with Eurotunnel and British Rail over the issue of tariffs, took a significant bite out of SNCF's projected revenues during this period. The company's earnings were hit even harder by the dismal economic recession of the early 1990s, which caused passenger traffic between major cities to drop more than 9 percent in 1993. At the same time, a series of failed customer service initiatives, most notably an ill-conceived computerized ticketing system, undermined consumer confidence in rail travel, further reducing passenger volume. In all, the company suffered losses of FFr 7.7 billion in 1993, and FFr 7.68 billion in 1994.

Perhaps the most momentous challenge to the company's future as a state-owned enterprise came from the French government itself. In 1993, after the conservatives defeated the incumbent socialist party in the French general elections, the government's attitude toward the public sector changed considerably. By 1995, SNCF's total debt had surpassed FFr 175 billion. Although the government was willing to provide the beleaguered company with a sizable debt reduction, the latest subsidy would not come without some cost to the company's autonomy. One area where the government hoped to streamline SNCF's operations was in the separation of its railway infrastructure, which included tracks and switching stations, from the business of running trains. At the same time, France was facing pressure to privatize from the European Union, which had mandated the deregulation of Europe's national railroads in 1991. In order to comply with the EU directive, while also increasing the efficiency of SNCF service, the French government created a new entity, the Reseau Ferre de France. Formed in 1997, Reseau Ferre de France was charged with taking responsibility for managing the country's railway infrastructure. But in fact, the new company merely leased the rail system back to SNCF, who continued to take responsibility for track upkeep and maintenance, a practice that would eventually raise the ire of many of the company's rivals in other European nations.

During this period, the government also urged SNCF to make drastic cuts to its workforce. Layoffs were not a new concept for the rail company, which had watched its total number of employees drop from 246,000 in the mid-1980s to 180,000 by the end of 1995. It was the latest round of job reductions, however, that finally incurred the wrath of the nation's powerful trade unions, and in 1995 the first of a series of crippling railroad strikes hit SNCF. The strained relations between the company and the unions were exacerbated in July 1996, when newly appointed SNCF Chairman Loik Le Floch-Prigent, who was popular with labor leaders, was indicted on charges of fraud, in connection with his earlier years as chair of Elf-Aquitaine. His successor, Louis Gallois, was able to stabilize relations with the unions to some extent, although the company was still hit by several large-scale work stoppages over the next several years. The slashing of SNCF's debt from FFr 200 billion to FFr 50 billion, however, coupled with the increase in passenger traffic that accompanied the robust economy of the late 1990s, actually enabled the company to claim a profit in 2000. Although the trend toward privatization among other state-run rail carriers of Europe still threatened to introduce train competition into the French market, the company entered the new century firmly committed to its identity as a public company, with an eye toward more consistent profitability in the future.

Principal Subsidiaries

Seafrance; SCS Sernam; Sté Française de Construction Immobilière (S.F.C.I.); SNCF Participations (99.83%); Sté Hydro-Electrique du Midi (S.H.E.M.); Télécom Développement.

Principal Competitors

ARRIVA plc (U.K.); National Express Group plc (U.K.); Vivendi Environnement SA.

Further Reading

Harrison, Michael, "High-Speed Rail Plans Put France on Fast Track," *Independent* (London), April 23, 1990, p. 21.

Nock, O.S., *Railways of Western Europe,* London: Adam & Charles Black, 1977.

Owen, David, "A Fine Way to Run a Railway—and Turn a Profit: Interview with Louis Gallois, Chairman of SNCF," *Financial Times* (London), January 8, 2001, p. 12.

Rawsthorn, Alice, "State Ultimatum for Air France and SNCF," *Financial Times* (London), May 14, 1993, p. 2.

Ridding, John, "Paris Move on SNCF Fails to Derail Strike," *Financial Times* (London), November 29, 1995, p. 2.

——, "SNCF's Finances Start to Run Off the Rails," *Financial Times* (London), November 20, 1995, p. 2.

"The SNCF, Historical Background, Status, Recent Developments," Paris: SNCF, 1984.

—Linda Anderson
—update: Erin Brown

SRI International, Inc.

333 Ravenswood Avenue
Menlo Park, California 94025
U.S.A.
Telephone: (650) 859-2000
Fax: (650) 326-5512
Web site: http://www.sri.com

Nonprofit Company
Incorporated: 1946 as Stanford Research Institute
Employees: 1,400
Sales: $180 million (2001 est.)
NAIC: 541710 Research and Development in the Physical, Engineering and Life Sciences; 541720 Research and Development in the Social Sciences and Humanities; 541690 Other Scientific and Technical Consulting Services

SRI International, Inc. is a leading technology research firm. SRI is responsible for a host of innovations over the past 50 years, including some seminal contributions to computing such as magnetic core memory, the mouse, the electronic pen, and the prototype Windows operating system. SRI began as an affiliate of Stanford University, and now operates as a stand-alone nonprofit entity. Its researchers specialize in several core areas, including information science and software development, automation and robotics, chemical and material engineering, pharmaceuticals and biotechnology, and sensors and measurement systems. SRI also consults and researches in the social sciences, and contributes to new thinking in the fields of public policy, education, health, and economic development. SRI consults or carries out research under contract to scores of major corporations, including Monsanto, Hitachi, John Deere, Mattel, and Charles Schwab. It also works with various government agencies such as the Department of Defense, the Department of Energy, the National Aeronautics and Space Agency, and the U.S. Agency for International Development. Other clients include prominent foundations such as the Gates Foundation and the Ford Foundation, and industrial consortia such as the Elec-

tric Power Research Institute. SRI occupies approximately a million square feet of office space in its main campus in Menlo Park, California. The institute also maintains facilities in Washington, D.C., and 20 other U.S. locations, and has a branch in Tokyo. SRI has one major subsidiary, the for-profit Sarnoff Corporation. Sarnoff is also a technology research firm, with particular expertise in television and communications. Both Sarnoff and SRI have spun off a host of new technology firms since the late 1990s. These include Intuitive Surgical, Inc. and Nuance Communications, Inc., both listed on NASDAQ, as well as Discern Communications, Pangene Corp., PolyFuel Inc., and SRI Consulting Business Intelligence.

Under Stanford's Wing: 1940s–60s

SRI began as the Stanford Research Institute, designed as an engine of economic growth for California and the West. The idea for such an institute surfaced back in the late 1920s, when a Stanford chemistry professor, Robert E. Swain, bent the ear of Herbert Hoover, then Secretary of Commerce in the Coolidge administration. Hoover, a Stanford graduate, was enthusiastic about an industrial research center at his alma mater. He encouraged Swain and others to lay plans. The Stanford Research Institute had to be shelved because of the Great Depression, and when the idea was revived in the late 1930s, it then had to be put on hold again for World War II. Finally the Stanford Research Institute became a reality in 1946. It was chartered as a nonprofit corporation closely tied to the university, and its basic mission was to promote the educational objectives of Stanford, as well as to extend scientific knowledge in general. The relationship with the university, as well as SRI's overall aims, went through several early amendments. About six months after SRI's founding, it moved its offices off the Stanford campus into its own building in nearby Menlo Park. SRI's first director resigned after only one year, but with its second director, who took over in March 1948, the institute began mapping a strategy of growth. SRI invested not only in new facilities but in marketing its services to leading national corporations.

The postwar years were a booming time for California, which was experiencing rapid population growth. Industrial production in the United States overall rose by close to 50 percent in the ten years after the war, and total spending on research and development tripled by the end of the 1950s. Hence, SRI debuted at a propitious time. By 1950 it had revenue of $2 million, and it had already been involved in one signal invention, ENIAC, the world's first digital computer. ENIAC was installed at SRI in 1946, and the institute's researchers immediately began work scaling down the behemoth machine. SRI scientists came up with the first magnetic core computer memory, which allowed the computer to operate in a much smaller casing. SRI made many other firsts in computers, and in its early years it made key contributions to other industries as well. One of its first projects was market research that led to the development of Tide laundry detergent. SRI also did initial research on prospective sites for what became one of California's most famous tourist attractions, Disneyland. In the field of banking, SRI pioneered a way to process checks automatically. In 1955 it invented a magnetic ink process that became the standard in banking worldwide and opened the door to the automation of finance.

By 1955 the institute had become self-supporting, with its balance sheet in the black for the first time with income of some $325,000. SRI broke ground for new quarters in Menlo Park that year. By that time SRI also operated several regional offices, including one in Zurich, Switzerland. Over the next decade, SRI continued its prominence in the young field of computing. Its scientist Hew Crane invented the first all-magnetic core computer in 1961. Crane's system became the standard in the industry for the next ten years. Crane and others at SRI also were the first to make a viable desktop computer. Another famed SRI employee was Douglas Engelbart. He and his SRI team debuted the first computer mouse in 1968. Engelbart later licensed the mouse to Xerox and to Apple Computer, which developed it further. The institute was also on the ground floor of artificial intelligence. SRI researchers created the world's first robot that could demonstrate reasoning. This was a machine nicknamed Shakey, which could navigate itself across a room using various sensors.

Separating from the University in the 1970s

By the end of the 1960s, SRI had grown enormously, and its revenue in 1968 was about $65 million. It had roughly 3,000 employees by that year, and it was known the world over for its research in computers and in other fields as well. SRI researchers handled about 800 projects altogether each year, and these ranged from earthquake prediction to studies of how mosquitoes responded to repellants. Yet not all its work was clearly

benign. The institute worked increasingly for the government, and its work for the Department of Defense eventually brought a severing of relations with Stanford. By 1969, 10 percent of SRI's research was classified work for government agencies in the fields of biological and chemical warfare and in counterinsurgency techniques. SRI's work directly supported the unpopular war in Vietnam, and the institute was the subject of wrathful student demonstrations. Students occupied Stanford's applied electronics laboratory in 1969, and spoke out against SRI's chemical and biological weapons research. Almost 100 students were arrested in relation to protests at SRI that year. In 1969 a committee made up of Stanford students, faculty, and administrators began to look into ways of dissolving the ties between the university and SRI. The committee concluded that the university should not be affiliated with the kind of research SRI was engaged in, which it termed morally objectionable. Thus in 1970 Stanford gave up its control of SRI, in exchange for payments totaling $25 million. In addition, the institute was to take "Stanford" out of its name. It made this change in 1977, going by its initials, simply SRI International, Inc. The firm remained a nonprofit. It also continued to do classified work, in particular, studies of radar and other communication techniques.

SRI continued to work for government agencies in the 1970s. It carried out controversial studies in parapsychology, and in 1974 attracted much attention with its so-called "cheatproof" tests of the psychic abilities of the spoon-bending magician Uri Geller. It also developed a military technology for detecting objects at great distances using high-frequency radar. Over the 1970s SRI also was responsible for several important medical advances. Its scientists developed a medicine to treat malaria, as well as a blood clot inhibitor for heart disease. The institute had many profitable contracts, and its revenues swelled over the 1970s. By 1981 its revenues stood at $163 million. SRI had developed a strong reputation in computers and mathematics, and in behavioral sciences, biology, and pharmaceuticals. The break with Stanford did not seem to have any lasting negative effect on the institute.

A Gift of a Subsidiary in the 1980s

In the early 1980s, the federal government began watching the cost of its military research contracts more closely. As a result, SRI had to compete more vigorously for government work, and in some cases it lost out to other groups. SRI decided that it would be prudent to lessen its dependence on government contracts, and so in the early 1980s it began branching out into management consulting. SRI had expertise in a wide array of subjects, but it was up against older and better-run companies in the management consulting field. Booz, Allen & Hamilton and McKinsey & Co. were the giants of that industry, and SRI's management consulting foray did not do well against them.

SRI also looked to branch out geographically. It hoped to find a location on the East Coast near the center of the pharmaceutical industry. In the mid-1980s SRI did consulting work for General Electric (GE), which would soon become the new owner of the David Sarnoff Research Center in Princeton, New Jersey. Sarnoff functioned as the research and development arm of RCA, and its laboratories had produced color television, the fax machine, liquid crystal displays, and many other advances in electronics. GE bought RCA in 1986, and the Sarnoff lab became redundant. SRI negotiated with GE, and in the end the company donated Sarnoff to the nonprofit for a tax write-off.

The new arrangement seemed to suit both Sarnoff and SRI. The Sarnoff lab had been rumored to be closing, but with its gift to SRI, the facility stayed open, and most of its researchers kept their jobs. Sarnoff had particular strength in applied physics, an area in which SRI felt itself to be weak. Sarnoff's location was also very attractive, situated in the midst of a high-tech corridor on the East Coast, similar to the bustling Silicon Valley SRI presided over in the West. GE promised to give Sarnoff contracts worth $250 million over the five years after the giveaway. The aim was to gradually wean Sarnoff from corporate sponsorship, and within the five years it would be able to support itself. Thus SRI seemed to have little to lose by taking on the prestigious electronics lab. The transition did not go smoothly, however, and by the early 1990s both Sarnoff and SRI were losing money. GE sold its consumer electronics business to the French firm Thomson in 1987. This complicated the Sarnoff contracts with GE, though Thomson did continue to work with the lab. SRI's president, James Tietjen, wanted to shift Sarnoff's direction. Sarnoff had been doing mainly corporate work, with some 13 percent of its contracts with the government. Tietjen hoped Sarnoff could increase its proportion of government work to 50 percent over the coming years, as its work in electronics, optics, and robotics had many potential military applications. But this shift toward military work came at a time when such contracts were more difficult to procure. By 1992, Sarnoff was $9.3 million in the red.

SRI was in even worse shape than its new subsidiary. Revenues increased between 1981 and 1991 from $163 million to $300 million. Yet over the same period, a close competitor grew sixfold, and other research centers were larger and more profitable than SRI. SRI's management consulting unit was a drain on resources, losing an estimated $7 million in 1991. This contributed to an overall loss of $15.8 million that year, on revenues of $300 million. SRI's president blamed the losses on recessionary cutbacks in research spending. He stanched expenses by reducing administrative staff, and reorganized the management consulting group so it worked only in industries like computing where SRI had a strong technical background.

New Directions in the 1990s

Despite Tietjen's changes, SRI continued to lose money. A new chairman, Paul Cook, took over SRI's board in 1993, and he installed a new president, William P. Sommers. Sommers and Cook cut costs much more deeply than Tietjen had, and by

1994, SRI earned a slim surplus of $6 million on revenues of $312 million. Sarnoff took an additional year to get out of the red, but it too was financially sound by 1995. Cook's short-term goal had been to get SRI out of debt. Over the long term, he wanted SRI to find more commercial applications for its technology. SRI had a storehouse of unique inventions, particularly in technologies originally developed for the military. In 1994 SRI funded a start-up company that used speech-recognition technology SRI had developed for the Department of Defense. This was called Nuance Communications, and it soon had major clients such as United Parcel Service and Charles Schwab & Co. SRI also had a stable of biomedical technology that it could turn to consumer uses. In 1994 SRI also launched Genetrace Systems, a company that sold laboratory tools for genetic analysis. The next year it spun off Intuitive Surgical Devices, which marketed a new device for microsurgery.

The wave of spinoff companies continued through the late 1990s into the 2000s. For every company SRI launched, it estimated there were 20 more ventures waiting to go forward. SRI shared profits from these start-ups generously with its employees, so that its best researchers had an incentive to stay with the parent company. Sarnoff, too, operated in a similar manner. By 2002, SRI and Sarnoff between them had launched 20 new companies. SRI continued to do contract work for the military into the 2000s. It developed a unique material called artificial muscle for the Department of Defense. This had many military applications, including use in a flying robot, and as a generator that tucked into soldiers' boots. At the same time, SRI also licensed the technology to a consumer shoe manufacturer, and other potential commercial clients included car makers, furniture makers, and medical device companies. In the 2000s SRI also worked on strengthening the capabilities of the Internet. SRI had been one of the first four nodes on the Internet as it was developed in the 1960s. SRI's work in the 2000s focused on small wireless networks, another project that had military uses plus a host of potential commercial applications. By the early 2000s, SRI seemed to be flourishing in this new vein, where its advanced and esoteric research quickly found real-world applications.

Principal Subsidiaries

Sarnoff Corporation.

Principal Competitors

Palo Alto Research Center; Lawrence Livermore National Laboratories; Battelle Memorial Institute.

Further Reading

Copeland, Michael V., ''Tech Detective: Electric Shoes and Breadcrumbs for the Troops,'' *Venture Capital Journal,* September 1, 2002.

Davies, Lawrence E., ''Stanford Urged to Sell Institute,'' *New York Times,* April 15, 1969, p. 31.

Edwards, Owen, ''Douglas Engelbart,'' *Forbes,* October 10, 1994, p. S130.

Gibson, Weldon B., *SRI: The Founding Years,* Los Altos, Calif.: Publishing Services Center, 1980.

——, *SRI: The Take-Off Days,* Los Altos, Calif.: Publishing Services Center, 1986.

Johnson, R. Colin, "SRI: Passive Pioneer of Computer," *Electronic Engineering Times,* January 31, 2000, p. 72.

Orenstein, David, "Engineering Emporium," *Business 2.0,* November 28, 2000, p. 226.

Port, Otis, "Tales from Spin-Off City," *Business Week,* February 23, 1998, p. 112.

Rensberger, Boyce, "Physicists Test Telepathy in a 'Cheat-Proof' Setting," *New York Times,* October 22, 1974, p. 86.

"SRI CEO: The Man with His Finger on the Tech Trigger," *San Francisco Business Times,* April 27, 2001, p. 22.

Sweet, William, "Sarnoff Center Girds Loins for Global Competition in HDTV," *Physics Today,* June 1989, pp. 63–65.

Weinberg, Neil, "Back from the Brink," *Forbes,* June 19, 1995, p. 16.

—A. Woodward

STAAR Surgical Company

1911 Walker Avenue
Monrovia, California 91016
U.S.A.
Telephone: (626) 303-7902
Toll Free: (800) 292-7902
Fax: (626) 303-2962
Web site: http://www.staar.com

Public Company
Incorporated: 1986
Employees: 237
Sales: $48.3 million (2002)
Stock Exchanges: NASDAQ
Ticker Symbol: STAA
NAIC: 339115 Ophthalmic Goods Manufacturing

STAAR Surgical Company (Staar) develops and markets medical devices for use in refractive, cataract, and glaucoma surgery. Staar's principal products include foldable intraocular lenses and implantable contact lenses. The company's lenses are implanted in the eye through minimally invasive surgery, generally requiring an incision measuring less than three millimeters. Staar sells its ophthalmic products on a global basis.

Origins

Staar Surgical began as a partnership between Tom Waggoner and Dr. Thomas Mazzocco. Waggoner, in his early 30s at the time, was determined to bring Mazzocco's idea to market with his own company, a difficult route to take in the medical technology field. Generally, those who wished to bring an idea to market affiliated themselves with a larger company, a company better equipped to bear the costs and risks involved in gaining the approval of the Food & Drug Administration (FDA). For Waggoner, independence meant he faced the arduous chore of obtaining the financing to fuel Staar Surgical's research and development efforts. The fledgling company's survival depended on his success as a fund-raider. The alternative—pitching Mazzocco's idea to a well-established, well-heeled medical technology company—was dismissed by both Waggoner and Mazzocco. "We both knew that if we went to a larger company," Waggoner explained in a June 1985 interview with *Inc.,* "it would end up in research and development for eight years." Accordingly, the partners chose independence, endeavoring to bring Mazzocco's idea, a foldable intraocular lens for cataract patients, to market by themselves.

Although Staar Surgical later delved into other markets, the company initially focused its resources on entering the market for cataract surgery. Roughly 50 percent of the U.S. population between the ages of 65 and 75 suffered from cataracts, an ophthalmic condition affecting the eye's lens, turning the transparency of the lens opaque. Mazzocco's idea centered on replacing the cataractous lens with a soft intraocular lens (IOL), which was implanted in the eye through a small incision. The procedure was minimally invasive, promising to capture a bulk of the market occupied by conventional, "hard," intraocular lens products.

In early 1982, Waggoner and Mazzocco invested $250,000 to bring Staar Surgical's IOL to market, beginning the lengthy and risky process of FDA approval. As expected, the next several years were difficult, a period in which the company generated no revenues and incurred mounting overhead costs. It was the research and development phase of a new company trying to enter the medical technology market, a time of scarce capital and uncertain prospects. Waggoner, continually pressed to funnel cash into the company's operations, raised another $150,000 through a research and development partnership, but the supply of cash was soon exhausted. By early 1983, one year after starting out, Staar Surgical found itself saddled with $250,000 of debt, prompting Waggoner to seek out interest from venture capitalists. The interest was there, but far from the intensity hoped for by Waggoner—"there was a wide gulf between my want and their offer," he remembered in his June 1985 interview with *Inc.*

Waggoner's financing options were evaporating, leaving Staar Surgical in the precarious position often occupied by young, independent, medical technology concerns. With his choices dwindling, Waggoner turned to public ownership as a fund-raising option, raising $4 million from the company's

---

Company Perspectives:

STAAR Surgical is regarded as a technology leader in the industry. As STAAR continues to grow, creativity remains an important tool in technology, marketing and in building new financial strength. The company is headquartered in Monrovia, California, and has operations in various countries around the world.

---

initial public offering (IPO) of stock in July 1983. The proceeds from the IPO provided some relief, but more cash would be needed. For the first two-and-a-half years of its existence, Staar Surgical was strictly a research and development venture, unable to collect any revenues because the company did not have a product on the market. In 1983, the company lost $1.5 million. During the first six months of 1984, the company lost another $1 million, but it did enjoy the first trickle of revenue into its coffers. Staar Surgical had received approval to implant IOLs on a limited basis while investigations concerning their safety continued. Preliminary FDA approval enabled the company to collect $328,000 in sales during the first half of 1984, but the sum was meager. With full FDA approval not expected until 1987 and monthly expenses averaging $250,000, a consistent stream of revenue was needed to tide the company over until Mazzocco's IOLs completed the FDA approval process.

Research and Development Activities in the Mid-1980s

Inspiration struck Waggoner and his management team during discussions about the progress of the foldable IOLs. Waggoner and his four head managers met periodically to discuss developments on the IOL. During one of these meetings, according to Waggoner in his June 1985 interview with *Inc.*, "We looked around at our operations and realized that with all our overhead, why not produce conventional cataract lenses as well?" From this epiphany, a new way of thinking developed, evolving into what Waggoner called a "delegate" system of management. Within Waggoner's system, managers were encouraged to develop their own revenue-producing ideas, creating a decentralized and autonomous organizational structure that was intended to create subsidiary sources of revenue. Once managers developed ideas for new products, they were given the time and the space to get their side projects up and running. Managers set up the financing for their projects through research and development partnerships with outside investors or through internal sources, and shepherded the product to market. Once sales from the side venture reached a certain point, royalties were added to the manager's earnings.

The inculcation of an enterprising corporate culture spawned numerous research and development ventures within Staar Surgical, giving the company a research and development capacity that belied its small stature. By the end of 1984, the company had collected $650,000 from sales of its conventional surgical lenses, which it was able to manufacture with its existing equipment. Other successes created within the delegate system added meaningfully to the company's financial health. By delving into the manufacture of surgical equipment for ophthal-

mologists, the company grossed $650,000. Staar Tool & Die, a subsidiary created to make precision tools for optical molding, promised to broaden the company's financial footing. Within a year of its creation, the delegate system was responsible for as many as seven start-up ventures underway at one time.

Despite early indications that a multifaceted research and development strategy was working, Staar Surgical began to suffer from profound financial problems. The flurry of activity was partly to blame, as the investment in fields unrelated to minimally invasive ophthalmic surgery contributed to financial losses. The company's acquisition of Frigitronics, Inc., a manufacturer of cryosurgical equipment and diagnostic and surgical instruments, represented one such wayward move. Also to blame were delays in securing FDA approvals to fully market foldable IOLs within the United States, which severely hamstrung the company's ability to generate sufficient sales to offset research and development costs. Staar Surgical's financial condition began to sour in 1987, as losses mounted. By 1989, the company was suffering from an $8 million capital deficiency, a dire situation that demanded wholesale changes. Late in the year, new senior management took control of the company, inaugurating a new era of existence for the beleaguered Staar Surgical.

Recovery in the 1990s

The company's new management succeeded in effecting a turnaround. The executive team implemented a number of measures to give the company a sturdy foundation for the 1990s. Staar Surgical's strategic focus was sharpened, directing the company toward its original emphasis on ophthalmic products used in minimally invasive ophthalmic surgery. Capital was raised to eliminate the company's capital deficiency, and a domestic and international sales and marketing network was established. Perhaps most important, Staar Surgical received FDA approval to fully market its foldable IOLs within the United States in September 1991, at last giving the company the opportunity to achieve its potential.

In the years following the final approval by the FDA, Staar Surgical's organizational structure swelled as its annual revenue climbed upward vigorously. In a two-stage deal, Staar Surgical acquired the worldwide distribution and license rights to proprietary products owned by Intersectoral Research and Technology Complex Eye Microsurgery (IRTC), a Moscow, Russia-based concern. The transaction involved IRTC's biocompatible glaucoma devices and its biocompatible materials for IOLs. The distribution rights were acquired in March 1993, followed by the acquisition of the license rights in 1995. The first half of the 1990s also saw the company expand its operations internationally through the establishment of more than a half-dozen subsidiaries, none more important than Staar Surgical A.G. Based in Berne, Switzerland, Staar Surgical A.G. was formed in 1993 to conduct manufacturing and research and development activities, becoming the hub of the company's international business. The other subsidiaries served exclusively as sales companies, the agents through which Staar Surgical penetrated foreign markets including France, Austria, Germany, and South Africa.

With its financial position steadied and expansion occurring at a consistent rate, Staar Surgical began to record encouraging

Key Dates:

1982:	STAAR Surgical (Staar) is formed as a partnership between Tom Waggoner and Dr. Thomas Mazzocco.
1983:	Staar completes its initial public offering of stock.
1991:	Staar receives FDA approval to market its foldable intraocular lenses.
1998:	Marketing efforts begin to bring the company into the glaucoma and refractive surgery markets.
2000:	Staar receives FDA approval for its glaucoma surgery device.

growth during the first half of the 1990s. The company generated $4.2 million in sales in 1991, the year it received FDA approval to fully market foldable IOLs in the United States. Within four years, the company's sales volume increased eightfold, eclipsing $34 million by 1995. Equally as impressive, the company ended the historical pattern of losing money and emerged as a profitable enterprise. Staar Surgical lost more than $11 million in 1991 and another $5 million in 1992, but recorded a profit for the next three years, posting more than $18 million in net income during the period.

While the rousing financial figures were being posted, Staar Surgical employees were working on the next generation of the company's products, endeavoring to add significantly to the company's revenue-generating might. Research and development work was underway on several new products that would enable the company to enter the glaucoma surgery market and the refractive surgery market. The material and design assets acquired from IRTC helped propel the company's development of its own glaucoma medical devices. The IRTC deal also aided the company in the development of what promised to be its most lucrative medical device, an implantable contact lens (ICL) for the refractive surgery market. Although it would be years before any measure of the potential of ICLs could be taken, the paucity of tangible evidence did little to temper the excitement at company headquarters in Monrovia, California.

Staar Surgical's proprietary ICLs offered the hope of correcting vision in patients suffering from refractive conditions such as myopia (nearsightedness), hyperopia (farsightedness), and astigmatism (an irregularly shaped cornea)—vision problems affecting more than 50 percent of the world's population. As with the company's IOLs, the market success of ICLs and Staar Surgical's products intended for the glaucoma surgery market depended on FDA approval. Another long wait loomed, but the promise of entering the refractive surgery market in particular buoyed hopes that a period of unprecedented growth awaited the company. Staar Surgical expanded its marketing activities beyond the cataract surgery market in 1998, but the company did not receive FDA approval for either its glaucoma surgery products or its refractive surgery products until several years later.

While the company labored through the approval process for its glaucoma and refractive surgery devices, another sweeping change in management gave Staar Surgical a new leader for the future. In May 2000, the company's president and chief executive officer was fired, followed by the resignation of the company's chief operating officer, William Huddleston, in October 2000. In December 2000, David Bailey was appointed president and chief executive officer. In January 2001, when Andrew Pollet, Staar Surgical's chairman, passed away, Bailey was selected to the additional post of chairman.

Looking ahead, much of Staar Surgical's potential depended on its success in the glaucoma and refractive surgery market. In July 2000, the company received FDA approval for its glaucoma device, the AquaFlow Collagen Glaucoma Drainage Device, which was implanted in the eye to reduce intraocular pressure. As the company celebrated its 20th anniversary, however, it continued to rely heavily on its involvement in the cataract surgery market, which accounted for 95 percent of sales in 2002. In early 2003, the company's ICL device received favorable publicity in the May 2003 edition of *Cornea, The Journal of Cornea and External Disease*. The journal published findings of a study comparing the results of laser assisted in situ keratomileusis (Lasik) surgery and ICLs. According to the study, ICLs were concluded to be safer and more effective than Lasik surgery. At the time of the publication of the findings, Staar Surgical's ICLs were in the midst of clinical trials conducted by the FDA. FDA approval was expected in early 2004, at which point the true measure of Staar Surgical's strength could be measured.

Principal Subsidiaries

Staar Surgical A.G.

Principal Competitors

Alcon, Inc.; Bausch & Lomb Incorporated; Novartis AG.

Further Reading

Critser, Greg, "Optical Illusion," *Inc.,* June 1985, p. 97.

Rees, David, "Staar Bright: Intraocular Lens Firm Shines in the Over-the-Counter Market," *Los Angeles Business Journal,* February 11, 1985, p. 2.

"Study Concludes Staar's ICL Is Safer and More Effective Than Lasik," *Asia Africa Intelligence Wire,* May 15, 2003, p. 6.

White, Ronald D., "California; Staar's Stock Climbs After Lens Study," *Los Angeles Times,* May 16, 2003, p. C2.

"Why All Eyes Are on Staar Surgical," *Business Week,* May 12, 2003, p. 110.

—Jeffrey L. Covell

State Street Corporation

225 Franklin Street
Boston, Massachusetts 02110
U.S.A.
Telephone: (617) 786-3000
Fax: (617) 664-4299
Web site: http://www.statestreet.com

Public Company
Incorporated: 1792 as Union Bank
Employees: 19,753
Total Assets: $85.79 billion (2002)
Stock Exchanges: New York
Ticker Symbol: STT
NAIC: 523920 Portfolio Management; 522110
    Commercial Banking; 551111 Offices of Bank
    Holding Companies

State Street Corporation is a bank holding company conducting business principally through its subsidiary State Street Bank and Trust Co. Descended from one of the first banks in the United States—the Union Bank, which was founded in 1792—State Street is now the nation's largest custodian and trustee for mutual funds and pension funds, with $6.2 trillion under custody and $763 billion under management, as well as the sixth largest investment manager and the largest financial services specialist globally.

Since the 1970s, State Street has become one of American banking's great success stories. Beginning in that period, through a strategy of aggressive diversification and the use of the most advanced technologies, State Street rapidly evolved from a traditional, gentlemanly, old-line Massachusetts financial institution into a global banking powerhouse.

Maritime Merchant Bank Origins

State Street has deep roots in the commercial history of Boston, going back to the days when the city was a bustling shipping port and main business artery for the new republic. In the closing years of the 18th century, a group of prominent Bostonians gathered together to establish a new bank, which would be the third bank in Boston. John Hancock, Massachusetts' first governor, signed the bank's charter on June 25, 1792. The bank, named the Union Bank, was located at the corner of State and Exchange Streets and had as its first president Massachusetts Lieutenant Governor Moses Gill.

At that time State Street was the main thoroughfare in colonial Boston and a significant crossroads in the United States. Bracketed by the State House at one end and the Long Wharf at the other, State Street was a center of both commerce and politics. It was here, for instance, that the first public reading of the Declaration of Independence took place. It was also where the famous trial of Captain Kidd took place. In addition, it was on State Street that the first Boston merchant, John Coggan, had set up shop.

State Street was also known as the "Great Street to the Sea," and the economic growth of the new bank was closely tied to Boston's flourishing shipping industry. During that romantic period, sleek clippers criss-crossed Boston Harbor, escorting incoming ships, laden with cargo, to shore. Boston was by the mid-19th century in its heyday as a maritime capital. Some of the wealth from that trade would make its way into the coffers of the bank.

Meanwhile, the lore, mystique, and memorabilia of this colorful shipping past would be ardently celebrated and preserved by Union and, in its later incarnation, State Street, during the more than 200 years of its existence. For instance, ship models, prints, harpoons, and figureheads would adorn the offices of State Street Bank for years. The bank also would publish more than two dozen monographs recalling Boston's maritime history. In 1992, the bank's pride in this past would lead it to sponsor Sail Boston, an event that brought a flotilla of elegant boats from all over the world into Boston Harbor. Finally, the bank's logo, a silhouette of a clipper ship, was itself a form of homage.

Many of Boston's merchant princes and community leaders were associated with Union Bank during the first century of its operation. For instance, the bank had real estate deals with such notable local families as the Parkmans, Sargents, and Quincys,

340

and among its early officers was Oliver Wendell, the great-grandfather of Oliver Wendell Holmes.

The bank, located at 40 State Street, had its charter renewed several times, and in 1865, the directors applied for and received a National Charter. At that time, the bank was renamed the National Union Bank of Boston.

Going into the early years of the 20th century, National Union had survived to become the oldest bank in continuous operation in Boston and the second oldest bank in the United States. During all these years, despite wars and the fluctuating fortunes of the new country, the bank thrived, and it is a mark of its stability that it never failed to declare semi-annual dividends.

On July 1, 1891, National Union would have a new neighbor and banking competitor on State Street. On that day, the State Street Deposit & Trust Company was chartered and began business, with offices in the Exchange Building on State Street. The company was started by a group of directors and officers from the Third National Bank, and it opened for business with a capital of $300,000. Shortly afterward, Third National merged with Shawmut Bank, and State Street became entirely independent. In 1897, the bank's name was shortened to State Street Trust Company.

State Street Trust grew steadily during these early years. From 1900 to 1925, deposits increased from roughly $2 million to more than $40 million. In 1900, the company moved into offices in the Union Building, on the corner of Exchange and State Streets. In 1911, the main office moved again to another part of State Street. Five years later, it purchased the assets and goodwill of the Paul Revere Trust Company. The year 1924 proved an historic turning point for State Street, though it would take many years before the significance of the event would be fully appreciated. In that year, Massachusetts Investors Trust chose the bank as custodian of the country's first mutual fund.

Recognizable Identity Emerging in the Early 20th Century

A year later, National Union Bank merged with State Street and the alliance now fattened deposits at State Street to more than $57 million. That same year, State Street moved once again and the new location, 53 State Street, was, by coincidence, the site of the company's original location. The interior of this new office was an evocation of Boston history, designed to recall the old countinghouses of Boston merchants during the first part of the 18th century. Traditional oak and wood paneled rooms,

reproductions of colonial hanging lanterns, hand-forged wrought-iron grillwork, mullioned windows, and tables and chairs copied from old tavern furniture provided a living time capsule of a bygone era—and made the office something of a local landmark.

The man mostly responsible for the bank's devotion to its historic roots—and for much of its steady success during these years—was Allan Forbes. Joining State Street in 1899 shortly after graduation from Harvard, Forbes worked his way up from assistant treasurer to president in 1911, and was, from 1950 until the time of his death in 1955, chair of the board. During his 56-year career at the bank, deposits increased from less than $2 million to $187 million.

The identification of the bank with its maritime past would be one of Forbes's lasting legacies. Early in his career, he began to collect and display historical maritime artifacts in State Street's offices. The bank abounded in ship models, prints, harpoons, and figureheads, part of the Forbes collection. His own office was atmospherically steeped in his antiquarian passion; heavy ceiling beams and a great kitchen fireplace recalled the 17th century, while Forbes himself sat in a great mid-18th century, slat-backed armchair surrounded by ship models, prints, and a great sea chest that served as a drawer for papers. This office has been preserved at the bank's 53 State Street branch.

During these years, State Street's growth was fueled by mergers. One of the more significant of these mergers was with the Second National Bank in 1955. Six years later, State Street incorporated the Rockland-Atlas National Bank, which represented three banks dating from the 1800s—the Webster, Rockland, and Atlas banks—that had consolidated in 1948. In 1960, State Street incorporated as State Street Boston Financial Corp., a one-bank holding company. The title State Street Boston Corporation was adopted in May 1977.

In 1963, ground was broken for the State Street Bank building, which upon completion in 1966 was the first high-rise office building in downtown Boston. It was also the tallest bank building in New England. In 1964, State Street International opened in New York and, six years later, at the dawn of the 1970s, State Street took its first step into the global market, with the opening of an office in Munich.

Critical Change in Direction in the 1970s

The 1970s were a bruising decade for the nation's banks, and State Street was no exception. By the mid-1970s, the bank was suffering from major real estate lending problems. Fortunately, a new chief executive officer, William Edgerly, took control in 1975 and began hammering out an ambitious new strategy to turn the company around. He had already made his mark at the company as an outspoken member of the board of directors. Edgerly brought in new managers to help propel the bank into the direction that it had to go if it was to continue to hold its own in the competitive New England banking community. At that time, the bank had four major lines of business: commercial banking, financial services, investment management, and regional banking. Instead of continuing on its present path, Edgerly decided State Street should move away from its traditional commercial role and, rather than expand its

Key Dates:

1792: Union Bank becomes the third bank chartered in Boston.

1865: Union Bank receives a national charter; the bank is renamed National Union Bank of Boston.

1891: State Street Deposit & Trust Company is chartered in Boston.

1897: State Street's name is shortened to State Street Trust Company.

1924: State Street Trust becomes custodian of the nation's first mutual fund.

1925: National Union Bank and State Street merge.

1955: State Street merges with Second National Bank.

1960: State Street incorporates as State Street Boston Financial Corp., a one-bank holding company.

1961: State Street merges with Rockland-Atlas National Bank.

1964: A State Street office is opened in New York.

1972: State Street becomes international, opening an office in Munich.

1975: State Street begins changing its focus from commercial banking to investments, trusts, and securities processing.

1977: State Street becomes State Street Boston Corporation.

1991: State Street Boston is ranked as the 37th largest holding company in the United States.

1997: Company adopts the name State Street Corporation.

2003: State Street completes the acquisition of a substantial portion of Deutsche Bank's Global Securities Services.

branches, shut them down to concentrate on building up its business in investments, trusts, and securities processing. For one thing, it had an early start in the mutual funds market and was ideally situated to build upon its substantial reputation and assets in that area. State Street pushed aggressively into an area that many banks had shunned—the complex, high-technology processing of asset management, global custody, 401(k) retirement plan accounting, and trusteeship of debt securities based on securitized assets.

At the same time, Edgerly recognized that State Street needed to develop its technology if it was going to create a niche for itself with its data processing and telecommunications abilities. So the company began investing in a big way—an estimated 25 percent of its operating costs—in technology.

In 1973, the company had already made a key move in developing its technical know-how by buying 50 percent of Boston Financial Data Services and then using the software and data processing company for its shareholder-accounting and customer-service functions. The hardware backbone of State Street's numbers crunching was an IBM-mainframe-based Horizon computer system. Built from thousands of modules loaded into a mainframe, each module in Horizon was designed for a specific task and could be accessed at personal computer workstations, using a variety of software. The technological command post for the company became the bank's data-processing

headquarters, an office complex opened in Quincy, Massachusetts, a suburb of Boston, in 1974.

Edgerly, who retired as CEO in 1992, brought the stately Boston bank into the high-tech age, finding his inspiration in IBM and its emphasis on research and development. But then Edgerly himself had a degree in engineering from MIT, as well as his M.B.A. from Harvard, and had come to State Street from a petrochemical firm, Cabot Co., rather than from the banking ranks. At State Street he recruited many top-ranking executives from IBM, and by the early 1990s it was estimated that more than 100 veterans from IBM were serving in senior management positions at State Street. Beyond IBM's devotion to technical innovation, Edgerly also admired the company's aggressive approach to sales, and he designed the State Street Institute based on a sales training class at IBM. At the school, senior executives are required to teach newcomers.

The timing was right for State Street's new technology-based approach. In 1974, the Employee Retirement Income Security Act (ERISA) was passed and, as a result, companies now had new responsibilities when it came to reporting to the government on their pension plans. Recognizing a window of opportunity, State Street developed software that emphasized more advanced record-keeping abilities. Other software systems were spun off to help report on the financial ebb-and-flow of Ginnie Mae (GNMA) securities, international pension assets, and internationally indexed assets.

Typical of its services, State Street designed Pepsico Inc.'s $350 million 401(k) savings plan. In addition to providing accounting, trust, investment management, and benefit payment services for Pepsico, State Street also created a self-managed system whereby employees could transfer funds and evaluate their accounts daily by telephone.

Meanwhile, State Street moved assertively into the international market, establishing business footholds around the world. Its advanced numbers-crunching abilities and telecommunications network provided momentum for this global expansion. By the early 1990s, State Street customers could have direct, interactive computer access to their investment information from anywhere in the world, either through their mainframes or through personal computers in the office. They could design their own integrated global reports using the latest multicurrency accounting systems available.

Exploiting Unique Capabilities in the 1980s and 1990s

During the 1980s and 1990s, the company established offices throughout the globe, including Montreal, Toronto, London, Paris, Munich, the Cayman Islands, Dubai, Sydney, Melbourne, Wellington, Hong Kong, Taipei, and Tokyo. An international financial caretaker of pensions, securities, and investments, State Street had become recognized as the largest global custodian in Australia, New Zealand, and Canada and as a leading global custodian in Europe. In 1992, the company was selected as the first non-national custodian of a Swiss pension fund and the first non-Scandinavian custodian bank for a Scandinavian institutional investor. That year, the company opened a treasury center in Luxembourg, which joined the Boston, London, Hong Kong, and Tokyo facilities in providing 24-hour capital market services around the world.

While developing its portfolio of services to companies, State Street downplayed its traditional lending activity, which helped it weather the recession and the rash of loan defaults that battered many New England banks. Lending comprised an estimated 16 percent of State Street's business as compared to 60 percent at many other area banks.

At the same time, State Street's continuing financial health made it the envy of many banks. The price of State Street stock at the end of 1991 was 17 times what it was ten years earlier. Investors in State Street earned a total return of 33 percent per year for the decade of the 1980s. *Fortune* magazine ranked State Street number one in total return to investors during the period spanning 1982 to 1992, in a survey of the 100 largest banks in the United States.

State Street was also ranked by *Pensions & Investments* as the third largest manager of tax-exempt assets in the United States. By 1992, assets under management at State Street totaled $111 billion. Ranked at the end of 1991 as the 37th largest bank holding company in the United States, State Street reported $16.5 billion in assets.

Within its regional home base, State Street made loans, primarily to medium-sized businesses, and provided support for a variety of community-based organizations. These included the Metropolitan Boston Housing Partnership, which rehabilitated buildings throughout the Boston inner city, and the Boston Private Industry Council, which improved the city's public schools. The bank also awarded grants to creative partnerships in science, finance, and community development.

Marshall N. Carter, formerly of Chase Manhattan Corp.'s global custody unit, became State Street's CEO in 1991, and soon found himself at the center of converging forces in the banking industry. State Street's emphasis on technology had resulted in an organization that a February 1992 *American Banker* called "less a bank than a provider of information processing services." Most of State Street's revenue now came from fees for holding securities, settling trades, record keeping, accounting (including multicurrency accounting) and net asset value computation. A secondary stream of revenue came from fees for managed asset accounts. The result was a balance sheet in which income derived from selling fiduciary services accounted for 70 percent of overall revenues, against the background of the past decade's increasing globalization of U.S. pension fund investment. This was a highly favorable position to be in, considering that fee-based income from trading and other transactions were widely regarded as an important element for future banking profitability.

Others in the trust field found State Street a difficult competitor, as it leveraged its advantageous position to acquire new business. One such signal win was the California Public Employees Retirement System, a $67 billion custody account. State Street showed the ability to offer a sophisticated package while charging less in fees to such institutional investors, an edge that the company's leadership attributed to superior technology and economies of scale. Competition was intensified by the entry of such investment banking firms as Morgan Stanley & Company,

and veteran players in the global custody market began to fear that price wars would curtail profitability.

State Street followed Citicorp and other money center banks in the launch of a commercial paper program, formerly the preserve of investment banks. Under the program, named Clipper Receivables Corp., investors purchased asset-backed commercial paper, and the proceeds were used to fund loans by participating regional banks to investment grade companies.

By the mid-1990s, State Street found itself on the defensive. While the bank had enjoyed a pioneering position in fee-based services through the early part of the decade, other banks had ultimately followed suit. With State Street already holding some 25 percent of the mature master trust, pension fund, and mutual fund markets, bank leadership realized that it would be difficult to capture a significantly larger share. State Street knew that it would be difficult to gain a significantly larger share as well. Therefore, it channeled its energies into retaining existing business and offering new products and advanced technologies.

The mid-decade mark also brought a new direction in global markets. Whereas State Street had primarily focused on securities custody internationally, the company now began seeking to establish itself as a money manager. In 1994, it formed a new global money management division, aiming for a goal of 30 percent annual growth through the end of the 1990s. It subsequently launched an international ad campaign aimed at institutional investors. Although global custody would remain critical, the bank anticipated high profit margins in its new role as asset manager.

Looking Ahead

In December 1996, in an interview with *American Banker,* State Street CFO Ronald O'Kelley discussed the bank's long-term expectations: First, that an aging population would result in growth among privately managed investment funds; second, that relatively few banks worldwide would invest in expensive technology of their own, preferring instead to employ specialists in securities processing and custody-related services; and third, that U.S. institutional investors and pensions were increasingly looking to foreign investments, as international capital markets grew. Consequently, the company's goals were to provide advanced services not generally offered by competitors, and to continue expanding outside the United States.

A few months after this, as assets under custody passed $3 trillion, State Street changed its name from the previous State Street Boston Corporation to simply State Street Corporation. The distinctive clipper ship logo also was redesigned.

As the end of the century approached, State Street continued to produce impressive growth and innovation. The latter included the introduction of a system designed to automate the execution of fixed income trading in the U.S. Treasury, corporate, mortgage-backed, and asset-backed bond markets—a process that had remained tenaciously manual in the past. State Street's assets under custody grew to $6 trillion, and assets under management to $600 billion. State Street also divested itself of its retail and commercial banking business, selling these to Citizen's Bank, of Providence, Rhode Island; henceforth, there would be no distractions from the company's principal focus.

Since the dawn of the 21st century, David A. Spina had taken over as chairman and CEO from Marshall Carter. In 2003, State Street completed the acquisition of a substantial portion of Deutsche Bank's Global Securities Services, seemingly showing no change in the pattern of steady growth and financial performance.

Principal Subsidiaries

State Street Bank & Trust Co.; Princeton Financial Systems, Inc.

Principal Competitors

The Bank of New York Company, Inc.; Citigroup Inc.; Mellon Financial Corporation.

Further Reading

Cochran, Thomas N., "State Street Boston Corp.: It Prospers with an Alternative to Conventional Banking," *Barron's,* May 9, 1988, p. 53.

Gibson, Paul, "Getting There First with the Most," *Forbes,* January 3, 1994, p. 66.

Gullo, Karen, "State Street's Carter Plays Hardball with Trust Rivals," *American Banker,* February 24, 1992, p. 1.

Kraus, James R., "Securities Processing Still Sweet for State Street," *American Banker,* December 6, 1996, p. 4.

Leander, Tom, "State Street Bucks the New England Odds," *American Banker,* May 29, 1991, p. 1.

The Log of the State Street Trust Company, Boston: State Street Trust Company, 1926.

Merrill, Cristina, "State Street Reinventing Itself Again—As a Money Manager," *American Banker,* February 21, 1995, p. 1.

——, "State Street Thrives in Businesses Banks Didn't Want," *American Banker,* May 30, 1990, p. 8.

Quint, Michael, "Four Formulas for Avoiding the Mess in Banking," *New York Times,* Dec. 23, 1990, Sec. 3, p. 4F.

Wilke, John R., "State Street Thrives by Stressing Processing Fees," *Wall Street Journal,* June 25, 1992, p. 3B.

—Timothy Bay
—update: Shawna Brynildssen

Sun Pharmaceutical Industries Ltd.

Acme Plz.
Andheri-Kurla Rd., An
Mumbai 400 059
India
Telephone: 022 2821 1961
Fax: 022 2821 2010
Web site: http://www.sunpharma.com

Public Company
Incorporated: 1982
Sales: Rs 7.55 billion ($1.64 billion) (2002)
Stock Exchanges: OTC
Ticker Symbol: SPCE.F
NAIC: 325412 Pharmaceutical Preparation Manufacturing

Sun Pharmaceutical Industries Ltd. (Sun Pharma) is a rising star of India's fast-growing pharmaceuticals industry. In less than a decade, Sun has lifted itself into fifth position in the country's pharmaceuticals market. Sun manufactures a range of drugs for a range of medical specialties, treatments, and disorders. The company targets especially high-margin niche and specialty medications, including longtime bestseller Monotrate, as well as brands Celact (celecoxib), Oleanz (olanzapine), Rofact (rofecoxib), Nodict (naltrexone), Fexotrol (fexofenadine), Zelast (azolastine), and Ketorid (ketotifen). The company also produces a variety of specialty bulk actives and generic drugs. Sun Pharma manufactures and markets its drugs through a number of subsidiaries and divisions, including Aztec, Inca, Sun, Milmet, Synergy, TDPL, Symbiosis, and Solares. More than 70 percent of the company's sales come from within India. Sun is also present in the United States, through its control of publicly listed Caraco Pharmaceutical Laboratories, based in Detroit. The company continues to be led by founder, Chairman, and Managing Director Dilip S. Shanghvi.

Pharmaceutical Manufacturing Dream in the 1980s

While in college, Dilip Shanghvi had worked for his family's Calcutta-based wholesale drug trading business. Yet Shanghvi's own ambitions turned toward the manufacturing and development of the pharmaceuticals themselves. Shanghvi founded his company, Sun Pharmaceutical, in 1982 with just $250, and began looking for a first product.

Shanghvi soon spotted an opportunity. Lithosan, a widely used drug for the treatment of manic depressive disorders, remained unavailable in India's eastern provinces. Yet the drug was relatively easy to manufacture, and a friend of Shanghvi owned the equipment and a factory capable of producing it. In 1983, Shanghvi borrowed his friend's equipment and Rs 10,000 from his father and Sun Pharmaceutical officially opened for business.

Sun's sales were initially limited to the Calcutta market. The company quickly expanded its product line, boasting five products targeting the psychiatric segment—an area not subject to the Indian government's highly restrictive drug manufacturing laws. The psychiatric market also provided high margins on sales, a feature that was to mark much of the company's product choices over the following two decades.

By the end of its first year, Sun had moved into its own manufacturing facility—spending $50,000 to install its production into a self-described "shed" of 3,000 square feet in the town of Vapi, on the country's west coast, near the pharmaceutical center of Mumbai (Bombay). Discussing the reason behind the move with *Business World,* Shanghvi explained: "The industry was concentrated in the western region and it was easier to get permission there to launch new drugs."

The Vapi shed remained a central production plant for the company, expanding to match Sun's rapid growth. By the end of its first year, the company's sales already topped Rs 750,000. Yet Sun continued to target its production to the Calcutta region and elsewhere along India's east coast. In 1984, the company extended its marketing region to include most of the Indian eastern seaboard states.

Sun began locating and developing new drugs for its range, and began looking beyond the psychiatric segment in the mid-1980s. In the meantime, Sun moved to extend its marketing reach to India's west coast as well. In support of that effort, Sun moved its administrative offices to Mumbai in 1986. The following year, the company extended its marketing reach throughout all of India.

Sun launched a new range of cardiology products in 1987, including Angizem and, especially, Monotrate. That drug became the company's first success and remained its leading product into the next century. The success of Monotrate also helped bring the company into the scope of the ORG (Operations Research Group) audit of retail pharmacy sales for the first time, with a rating of 107 and a 0.1 percent share of the Indian drug market.

Expansion in the 1990s

Sun Pharmaceutical added another new product area in 1989 when it began marketing gastroenterology products. That year also marked the debut of the company's export operations; initial foreign markets remained in the Asian region, however.

At the start of the 1990s, Sun stepped up its research and development operations as it sought to boost its position in the Indian pharmaceutical market. In 1991, the company began construction on its own research facility in Vadodara, which opened as the Sun Pharmaceutical Advanced Research Center (Sparc) in 1993. In that year, also, Sun began to market its drugs farther afield, opening offices in Moscow and in Toronto.

The year 1994 marked a turning point for the company. Sun went public that year, listing on several of India's stock exchanges in an initial public offering (IPO) that was oversubscribed by some 55 times. The company also had placed one of its products among the top 250 pharmaceutical brands in India that year. Sun's manufacturing base grew in 1994 with the opening of a new production plant, in Panoli, supporting its entry into the bulk actives market. Sun then opened a second facility, in Silvassa, for dosage form manufacturing, while the company's main Vapi plant underwent a new and large-scale expansion program.

In 1995, the company began developing a divisional operational structure, which already included Synergy, grouping its psychiatric and neurology products, created in 1994. The company now created the Aztec division for its cardiology products, and the Inca division for its line of critical care medication.

Sun itself, backed by its IPO, embarked on its own expansion drive in the mid-1990s. Acquisitions now formed a major part of the company's growth, starting with the purchase of Knoll Pharma's bulk actives manufacturing business based in Ahmednagar in 1996. In that year, also, Sun took a step to break into the important U.S. healthcare market, with its purchase of a controlling share of Detroit-based Caraco Pharmaceutical Laboratories, which specialized in the manufacture of generic dosage form medications and gave the company its first USFDA-approved production plant.

Also in 1996, Sun purchased a shareholding in Gujarat Lyka Organics, which, in addition to adding its production of cephalexin bulk active, brought Sun a USFDA-approved manufacturing facility. The company completed its acquisition of Gujurat in 1999.

In the meantime, its acquisition drive continued, bringing it a stake in MJ Pharmaceuticals Ltd., based in Halol. With a 60,000-square-foot, UKMCA-approved plant, MJ Pharma brought Sun its strong insulin production, as well as a springboard for entry into the European market.

Sun's acquisition spurt had enabled it to boost its position to number 27 among India's pharmaceutical companies by the end of 1996. Yet the company retained its appetite for growth, adding Tamil Nadu Dadha Pharmaceuticals (TND), based in Madras, the following year. That company brought Sun such new product areas as oncology, fertility, anesthesiology, and pain management. Following the TND purchase, Sun reorganized its operations, regrouping its businesses into six operating divisions.

Indian Top Five in the New Century

Sun opened a second research and development (R&D) facility in 1997, specializing in developing dosage forms and documentation for the fast-growing U.S. and European generic drugs markets. The following year the company expanded its line with the purchase of a number of brands from Natco Pharma, adding some Rs 500 million to its sales. The Natco brands gave the company new products in the gastroenterology, orthopedics, pediatrics, and other categories, as well as access to Natco's time-release technology. In 1998, also, Sun bought Milmet Labs, enabling the company to enter the ophthalmology products market for the first time. Meanwhile, the company added a new production plant in Silvas.

By 1999, Sun had jumped into the Indian pharmaceutical industry's top ten. The company also boasted six brands in the country's top 300. Of importance, the company also had achieved leadership status in most of its specialty drug areas. By then, too, it had boosted its bulk actives business with the purchase of Madras-based Pradeep Drug Company Ltd. That company was merged into Sun itself in 2001. During that year, too, the company's Caraco subsidiary gained USFDA approval for a number of new generic drugs, as the U.S. market for generics was poised to boom in the early years of the new century.

After selling off a number of ''tail end'' brands at the end of 2001, the company merged its MJ Pharmaceuticals subsidiary into its core operation at the beginning of 2002. The company also began submitting applications as part of its plan to enter the U.K. and German pharmaceutical markets. During that year, the company commissioned a new manufacturing facility, capable

Key Dates:

1982: Dilip S. Shanghvi launches Sun Pharmaceutical in Calcutta.
1983: With a loan of Rs 10,000, Sun Pharmaceutical begins manufacturing psychiatric drugs, then opens its manufacturing "shed" in Vapi.
1986: The company moves its administrative and corporate headquarters to the West Coast and extends marketing coverage across all of India.
1987: The company unveils its cardiology products line.
1989: The company launches its gastroenterology products line and begins export operations.
1993: The SPARC research and development facility is opened; offices in Moscow and Toronto are opened.
1994: The company goes public on several Indian stock exchanges; it opens a bulk actives plant in Panoli and dosage form plant in Silvassa.
1996: The company acquires Knoll Pharma's bulk actives division; it acquires stakes in Caraco (U.S.A.) and Gujarat Lyka Organics Ltd.; a stake in MJ Pharma also is acquired.
1997: TDPL is acquired and the company reorganizes into six operating divisions.
1998: The company acquires brands from Natco Pharma, including time-release technology.
2000: The company acquires the Pradeep Drug company, based in the Madras region.
2002: A new manufacturing plant opens in Dadra; the company boosts its stake in Caraco to 65 percent.

which involved the transfer of some 25 off-patent drugs from Sun to Caraco, to boost its position in the U.S. generics market.

Meanwhile, Sun's new product launches had become the company's primary motor for growth, representing half of its turnover from products less than four years old. While acquisitions accounted for a major portion of Sun's growth since the late 1990s, in 2003 the company put its acquisition drive on hold—at least temporarily—as it turned its focus toward its R&D and exports business. In support of these, the company expected to commission a third research and development facility in Baroda in September 2003, while planning began that year for a new product development laboratory, specifically created to support the company's exports to the United States and Europe, in Mumbai. Now one of India's largest and most respected pharmaceutical companies, Sun prepared to take on the industry's global giants.

Principal Subsidiaries

Sun Pharma Global Inc.; Milmet Pharma Ltd.; Sun Pharmaceutical (Bangladesh) Ltd.; Zao Sun Pharma Ind–Russia; Sun Pharma Global Inc-BVI; Milmet Pharma; Caraco Pharmaceutical Laboratories Inc. (U.S.A.; 65%).

Principal Competitors

RPG Enterprises; GlaxoSmithKline Consumer Healthcare Ltd.; East India Pharmaceutical Works Ltd.; Dr. Reddy's Laboratories Ltd.; Cipla Ltd.; Concept Pharmaceuticals Ltd.; Khandelwal Laboratories Ltd.; Dabur India Ltd.; Claris Lifesciences Ltd.; ICI India Ltd.

Further Reading

"An Indian Chief," *Chemical Week,* December 23, 1998, p. 40.
Krishnan, Aparna, "Sun Pharma to Focus on Exports," *Hindu Businessline,* May 12, 2003.
Phansalkar, S.J., *Making Growth Happen: Learning from First-Generation Entrepreneurs,* New Delhi: Response Books, 1999.
"Prescription for Prosperity: Take the Long-Term View," *Business World,* April 7, 1999.
"Sun Pharma Buoyed by Spurt in Caraco Sales," *Hindu Businessline,* January 17, 2002.

—M. L. Cohen

of producing some three billion tabs per year, in Dadra. That company also began construction on another plant, in Jammu, that year. As its Caraco subsidiary, which had been losing money since its acquisition, finally broke even that year, Sun Pharmaceutical itself cracked the India top five.

Sun, which had withdrawn its listing from a number of Indian stock exchanges during 2002, announced a stock split at the end of that year. At the same time, the company boosted its holding of Caraco to 65 percent in a stock-for-technology deal,

✖ Swire Pacific

Swire Pacific Limited

35th Floor, Two Pacific Place
88 Queensway
Hong Kong
Telephone: +852 2840-8098
Fax: +852 2526-9365
Web site: http://www.swirepacific.com

Public Company
Incorporated: 1866 as Butterfield and Swire
Employees: 55,000
Sales: HK$15.22 billion ($1.95 billion) (2002)
Stock Exchanges: Hong Kong
Ticker Symbol: SWRAY (ADRs)
NAIC: 551112 Offices of Other Holding Companies;
    233110 Land Subdivision and Land Development;
    312111 Soft Drink Manufacturing; 481111 Scheduled
    Passenger Air Transportation; 483110 Deep Sea,
    Coastal, and Great Lakes Water Transportation

Swire Pacific Limited, which came to prominence as one of the 19th-century British-owned trading houses based in Hong Kong, is today a diversified firm with interests in real estate, aviation, and beverages, as well as the traditional marine services and trading operations. Through the wholly owned subsidiary Swire Properties Limited, Swire Pacific is one of the leading owners and developers of property in Hong Kong. The aviation holdings include significant minority stakes in two publicly traded firms—Cathay Pacific Airways Limited, a Hong Kong–based long-haul passenger airline, and Hong Kong Aircraft Engineering Company Limited, which specializes in aircraft maintenance and refurbishment—plus a 16 percent stake in Hong Kong Dragon Airlines Limited (Dragonair), a regional airline in China. Through Swire Beverages, Swire Pacific bottles products of the Coca-Cola Company, distributing them to seven provinces in mainland China, Hong Kong, Taiwan, and a large area of the western United States. Swire Pacific is part of the larger London-based Swire Group and has remained located in Hong Kong despite the handover of Hong Kong to Chinese rule in 1997. During and following the period of transition, the company in fact strengthened its ties to Hong Kong and expanded in a major way into mainland China itself.

Early History in the 19th Century

In Britain during the early 1800s a canal was built that linked the seaport of Liverpool to Halifax, a city in the northeastern county of Yorkshire. The canal introduced international trade to Halifax and in the process seriously damaged local industries that could not compete with cheaper imports. John Swire, the patriarch of the Swire family, moved from Yorkshire to Liverpool, where in 1816 he established a general trading house with primary commodities being American cotton from New Orleans and cheese, pork, and wine from Boston and New York. John Swire died in 1847, leaving the business to his two sons, John Samuel Swire and William Hudson Swire.

The John Swire & Sons, Ltd. trading company grew steadily during the next decade. It established interests in a number of Liverpool shipping companies and opened a branch office in Manchester. In 1855 John Samuel Swire traveled to the former British penal colony of Australia. He opened an office in Melbourne to handle Australian imports of his company's cotton. As soon as the business was operating successfully, he turned it over to a local agent and returned to England. His brother William was forced to retire from the company because of persistent ill health. From that time onward, John Samuel Swire was left to run the operation alone.

In 1861 the American Civil War destroyed Swire's cotton trade. Determined to reassert its position in the textile market, the company turned to the more stable markets of the Far East, where it was already engaged in the trade of tea. Swire became displeased with the performance of his agents in the Far East and decided that the company should run its own affairs there. He traveled to Shanghai in 1866 and later formed a partnership with Richard Shackleton Butterfield of the Butterfield Brothers firm in Bradford, Yorkshire. In 1867 they opened an office together in Shanghai under the name of Butterfield & Swire. The company adopted a Chinese name, *Taikoo,* meaning "great and ancient." Although the partnership was dissolved within two years, the Shanghai office continued to be called Butterfield & Swire.

The company's business in Asia benefited greatly from Japan's restoration of the Meiji leadership in 1868. Under the Meiji, Japan became a modern industrial state. Butterfield & Swire, which had opened an office near Tokyo in Yokohama the previous year, was ideally situated to take advantage of the growing strength of the Japanese economy.

By 1871 Swire's headquarters had been moved from Liverpool to London, and a third Far East office was opened in the British Colony of Hong Kong. The company expanded its interest in shipping when it became the Shanghai agent for the Blue Funnel Line. In 1872 Swire created its own shipping concern, the China Navigation Company, which served ports on the Yangtze River and along the Chinese coast. China Navigation's primary competitor on the waterways was another Hong Kong firm called Jardine Matheson & Company. In 1873 Swire established an office in New York, where the company had already been handling American imports of tea from Yokohama for several years.

Swire further diversified its business in 1883 when it created the Taikoo Sugar Refinery in Hong Kong with the intention of breaking Jardine Matheson's monopoly on sugar. The two companies competed in a fierce but gentlemanly manner for many years. According to John Samuel Swire, ''Don't fight. But if you do fight, go in sharp and win.''

In 1866 the Yokohama office, which for years had been dependent on the textile trade, began importing large quantities of sugar from Hong Kong and Taiwan in addition to soya beancake from China. Swire also handled Japanese exports of rice to Australia. In 1887 the company opened a second Japanese office in Kobe. In 1900 Butterfield & Swire founded the Taikoo Dockyard Company in Hong Kong. With expanded commercial interests in China, the company also opened a paint factory in Shanghai and a tugboat and barge company in Tianjin. The red, white, and blue Swire flag was seen flying over China Navigation ships plying waterways across China and throughout East Asia.

Early 20th Century

John Samuel Swire died in 1898. His company passed to a third generation of Swires under the direction of his son John. Despite some disruptions of business in China during the Boxer Rebellion in 1900 and the Republican Revolution in 1911, Swire's interests in China, Japan, Australia, and southeast Asia continued to prosper and expand. John Kidston Swire, grandson of John Samuel Swire, succeeded his father as director of the company in 1920.

Swire's operations were paralyzed in 1937 when Japan launched its war of expansion against China. The company's interests in northern China and Shanghai were closed. Japanese landings on either side of the Hongkong peninsula isolated the colony from the nearby Chinese city of Guangzhou (Canton), forcing Swire to curtail virtually all of its trading operations with the mainland. On December 1, 1941, six days before the attack on Pearl Harbor, Japanese troops invaded Hong Kong. During the Japanese occupation all of Swire's Far Eastern activities were suspended. By the time of the Japanese surrender in September 1945 more than half of Swire's ships, the sugar refinery, and the dockyard had been destroyed.

As soon as World War II ended a civil war erupted in China between the Communists and the Nationalists. The war was won in 1949 by the Communists, who renounced all agreements concluded by the Nationalist government. This included Swire's business arrangements with Chinese partners and the Chinese government. In addition, Swire's extensive properties in China were nationalized without compensation. In only a few short years Swire's financial empire had nearly been ruined.

Post-World War II Rebuilding and Diversification

Butterfield & Swire focused attention on rebuilding its operations in Hong Kong. The shipping facilities were rebuilt and new ships were ordered. John Kidston Swire became interested in diversifying his company's transportation interests in the Far East. In 1948 Butterfield & Swire purchased a controlling interest in Cathay Pacific Airways, a small Hong Kong-based airline company with a fleet of two DC-3s.

The company's shipping and airline activities grew rapidly during the 1950s. Shipping offices in Japan were reopened, and new connections in Papua New Guinea, Australia, and Korea were established. Cathay Pacific absorbed its local competitor, Hong Kong Airways, purchased newer aircraft, and opened new routes to Singapore, Manila, Bangkok, and Saigon. Butterfield & Swire's involvement in Cathay Pacific led it to invest in a number of other businesses related to aviation, including the Hong Kong Aircraft Engineering Company, which was formed in 1950 and which operated a virtual monopoly on aircraft maintenance in the colony. In 1959 Taikoo Dockyard & Engineering Company was floated on the Hong Kong Stock Exchange.

During the 1950s and 1960s the company's expansion was well planned and, for the most part, uneventful. On occasion, however, profits became depressed when regional or international economic recessions lowered demand for shipping services. Because the shipping business was so closely linked to the volatile economic cycles of Pacific nations, Swire Pacific began to diversify its operations. It became interested in property ownership in Hong Kong, where the supply of land was limited and demand was becoming acute. This led to the eventual formation, in 1972, of Swire Properties Limited. In 1965 Butterfield & Swire became the franchised bottler of Coca-Cola

Key Dates:

1816: John Swire establishes a general trading company in Liverpool, England.

1847: Swire dies; the company later is renamed John Swire & Sons and is under the leadership of two of Swire's sons.

1866: One of the sons, John Samuel Swire, forms a Shanghai-based partnership with Richard Shackleton Butterfield, that of Butterfield & Swire (Chinese name, Taikoo).

1872: Swire creates a shipping concern, China Navigation Company.

1883: Hong Kong–based Taikoo Sugar Refinery commences operations.

1900: Butterfield & Swire (B&S) founds the Taikoo Dockyard Company in Hong Kong.

1945: By the end of World War II, more than half of Swire's ships, the sugar refinery, and the dockyard have been destroyed.

1948: B&S purchases a controlling stake in Hong Kong–based Cathay Pacific Airways.

1949: The victory by the Communists in the Chinese civil war leads to the firm's gradual withdrawal from China.

1950: Hong Kong Aircraft Engineering Company is formed as a joint venture, with B&S as one of the partners.

1959: Taikoo Dockyard & Engineering Company is floated on the Hong Kong Stock Exchange.

1965: B&S acquires Coca-Cola bottling franchise in Hong Kong, later overseen by Swire Bottlers Limited.

1972: Swire Properties Limited is formed to oversee the firm's Hong Kong real estate interests; operations of Taikoo Dockyard are merged into Hongkong & Whampoa Dock Co. to form Hongkong United Dockyards.

1973: The Taikoo Dockyard company is renamed Taikoo Swire.

1974: Taikoo Swire is renamed Swire Pacific Limited, which becomes the publicly traded holding company for the main Hong Kong interests of the London-based Swire Group.

1986: Cathay Pacific is floated on the Hong Kong Stock Exchange.

1987: The Chinese government, through CITIC Pacific Ltd., purchases a 12.5 percent stake in Cathay Pacific.

1990: Swire Properties completes the massive Pacific Place development in Hong Kong; Swire Pacific and Cathay Pacific acquire Dragon Airlines (Dragonair) and then sell a majority stake in the regional Hong Kong airline to CITIC Pacific.

1996: Significant minority stakes in Cathay Pacific and Dragonair are sold to CITIC Pacific and China National Aviation Corporation, respectively.

1997: The firm establishes Taikoo Motors Limited.

1998: Adrian Swire retires as chairman of John Swire & Sons and is replaced by Edward Scott.

2001: Swire Properties forms a joint venture with Guangzhou Daily News Group to develop a major retail, office, and cultural complex in the Tianhe district of Guangzhou, scheduled for completion in 2007.

2002: Adrian Swire again becomes chairman of John Swire & Sons following the death of Edward Scott; Cathay Pacific acquires full ownership of Air Hong Kong and then sells a 30 percent stake to DHL Worldwide Express.

2003: The war in Iraq and the SARS outbreak lead to a 75 percent reduction in passenger traffic and Cathay Pacific cuts back its schedule.

and its allied brands in Hong Kong through the purchase of Hongkong Bottlers Federal Inc. (renamed Swire Bottlers Limited in 1974). Also in 1965, Hong Kong Aircraft Engineering gained a listing on the Hong Kong Stock Exchange.

Additional diversification occurred in the areas of shipping and warehousing services, agriculture, trucking, canning, magnetic tape, and high technology components. Cathay Pacific was continuing to grow at an annual rate of 22 percent (doubling its size every four years) and began handling air freight. As a result, Cathay Pacific became Swire's most popular subsidiary and was quickly gaining a reputation as "Hong Kong's airline."

John Kidston Swire retired as director of John Swire & Sons in 1968, leaving the company in the care of his two sons, named John and Adrian. The fifth generation of Swires oversaw most of the company's diversification and growth, especially in Hong Kong. It was during this leadership period that the Swire Pacific name emerged following a series of major organizational changes. In 1972 the Taikoo Dockyard was merged into the Hongkong & Whampoa Dock Co. to form Hongkong United Dockyards Limited, 50 percent owned by Swire. The following

year the publicly traded Taikoo Dockyard & Engineering company itself was renamed Taikoo Swire and then renamed again in 1974 Swire Pacific Limited. This firm now became the holding company for the main Hong Kong interests of the Swire Group. At the same time, the Butterfield name disappeared from company letterheads when Butterfield & Swire became John Swire & Sons (H.K.) Ltd.

There were other significant developments in the 1970s. Taikoo Sugar closed down its refinery in 1973 but remained in the food industry, concentrating on packaging and trading of food products. Swire Properties began work on its first major commercial property development, Cityplaza, the first phase of which opened in 1982. In 1976 Swire Properties entered the U.S. market with the purchase of real estate properties in Miami, Florida. Two years later, Swire Bottlers acquired its first U.S. Coca-Cola franchise in Salt Lake City, Utah.

When John Kidston Swire died in 1983, the parent company of the Swire financial empire, John Swire & Sons, Ltd., remained a privately owned family concern based in London. Meanwhile, Hong Kong, where the dynamic Swire Pacific subsidiary was located, became the subject of an international debate.

Transition to Hong Kong's 1997 Integration into China

After a series of negotiations the governments of Great Britain and the People's Republic of China agreed in 1984 to end British colonial authority over Hong Kong on July 1, 1997. This placed into doubt the future of all capitalist enterprises operating in Hong Kong, including Swire Pacific. Jardine Matheson promptly responded by relocating its legal address and much of its business to Bermuda. In an effort to forestall the exit of more companies, the Chinese promised to preserve the unique economic character of Hong Kong after taking control of the territory. After Cathay Pacific was taken public on the Hong Kong Stock Exchange in 1986, Swire Pacific announced that it was further reducing its share of ownership in the airline; and CITIC Pacific Ltd., a Chinese government investment company in Hong Kong, purchased a 12.5 percent stake. The Chinese investment in Cathay Pacific was regarded as evidence of China's sincerity in maintaining the prosperity of Hong Kong.

For its part, Swire Pacific determined early on to cast its future with China, although its vast property holdings in Hong Kong and its dependence on Cathay Pacific for most of its profits (70 percent in 1990) gave it little choice (Cathay's route rights were nontransferable, so the airline could not be moved out of Hong Kong). Even so, Swire Pacific did not have as much reason for alarm as its rivals, given that it had already established an excellent relationship with the Chinese, which promised to be advantageous when the Chinese economy developed further and selected foreign companies were invited to participate. Although the Tiananmen Square massacre of June 4, 1989, gave cause for further alarm, Swire stayed on its course, committed to Hong Kong's (and its own) future. Symbolic proof of its commitment came when Cathay Pacific painted over the Union Jack on its planes.

In fact, Swire Pacific was able to profit from others' fears in the late 1980s and early 1990s by picking up numerous additional Hong Kong real estate properties at bargain prices. Real estate subsequently recovered after the peak period of fear passed, leaving Swire with an even more lucrative portfolio.

In the early 1990s the company and Cathay Pacific strengthened their relationships and position within China itself. In 1990 Swire Pacific and Cathay bought Dragon Airlines (or Dragonair), the foreign airline with the most routes to mainland China and preferred by most business travelers over China's domestic airlines because of its superior safety record. To bolster Dragonair, Cathay transferred its routes to Shanghai and Beijing to Dragonair. Swire Pacific also tied Dragonair's future to China's by selling a majority interest in the airline to CITIC Pacific, leaving Swire Pacific with a 13 percent stake and Cathay Pacific a 30 percent holding. Cathay Pacific followed up with the 1994 purchase of a 75 percent interest in AHK Air Hong Kong Limited, an all-cargo airline. In the meantime, Peter Sutch was appointed chairman of Swire Pacific in 1992.

Further forays into China came in late 1993. In November, John Swire & Sons returned to China after a more than 30-year absence by reopening its Shanghai office. Also that month, Swire Pacific purchased a 25 percent stake in Shekou Container Terminals, located near Hong Kong in the Chinese city of Shekou, for HK$308 million ($40 million). Most important, in another alliance with CITIC Pacific, in December Swire bought 55 percent of BC Development, a major Coca-Cola bottler in China. Swire's partnerships with CITIC Pacific were seen as particularly strategic—win–win deals in which Swire gained influence in China at the same time China (through CITIC Pacific) acquired a greater and greater stake in Hong Kong's future.

Although Cathay Pacific ran into trouble in the early 1990s because of increasing competition, delays in the construction of a new Hong Kong airport, and a 1993 flight attendants strike, Swire Pacific had managed to lessen its dependence on the airline and thus weathered Cathay's difficulties. By 1993, only 51 percent of operating income was derived from aviation, with real estate coming in a close second at 41 percent. Swire had begun to leverage its vast Hong Kong real estate holdings into lucrative rental properties. The most impressive development was Pacific Place (completed in 1990), transformed by Swire from the army barracks it purchased in 1984 into a glittering complex of three fully occupied skyscrapers with 400 apartments, three first-class hotels, nearly 200 stores and restaurants, four theaters, and hundreds of thousands of square feet of office space. (Swire Pacific later relocated its headquarters to Two Pacific Place.) The company estimated that three other major projects would bring in more than $1 billion in profits annually starting in 1996.

Meanwhile, on the beverages front, Swire Bottlers and the Coca-Cola Company in 1994 entered into a new partnership arrangement that led to the formation of Swire Beverages Limited and gave Swire Pacific a larger stake in the bottling operations. That same year, the Taiwan Coca-Cola Bottling Company was acquired, further expanding Swire Pacific's bottling operations.

Swire Pacific continued its policy of dealmaking with the Chinese government in 1996. The previous year, Cathay Pacific faced a new competitive threat when China National Aviation Corporation (CNAC), the commercial arm of the China aviation authority, announced plans to start its own Hong Kong airline. CNAC agreed to drop those plans, however, following the completion of a complicated series of transactions. CITIC Pacific increased its stake in Cathay to 25 percent by purchasing newly issued shares for HK$6.3 billion ($815 million). This reduced Swire Pacific's stake in Cathay from 52.6 percent to 43.9 percent. CNAC bought a 35.9 percent interest in Dragonair for HK$1.97 billion, reducing Swire's stake in that carrier to 26 percent. Dragonair was also floated on the Hong Kong Stock Exchange in 1996. These deals secured the future of the Hong Kong–based airliners in the post-handover period. By reducing Swire's aviation interests, they also made Swire Properties the firm's largest and strongest division.

Negotiating the Uncertain Times of the Late 1990s and Early 2000s

Swire Pacific rode the good economic times of the mid-1990s to great effect: Profits increased from HK$4.4 billion in 1992 to HK$7.6 billion in 1996. But both Hong Kong and Swire were hit hard by the Asian economic crisis that erupted in mid-1997; Hong Kong property values plummeted and the demand for travel dropped significantly, seriously affecting

Swire Pacific's two biggest divisions. Profits at Swire Pacific fell precipitously in 1998, amounting to only HK$1.76 billion. In response, Swire announced an increased focus on core operations—beginning a withdrawal from the insurance business, selling a Kentucky Fried Chicken franchise, and divesting several businesses within the trading division. In January 1998 Adrian Swire retired as chairman of John Swire & Sons, with Edward Scott, a nonfamily member, replacing him. In May of the following year, Sutch relinquished his post as chairman of Swire Pacific for health reasons, and James Hughes-Hallett took over that position.

During the late 1990s, despite the economic turmoil, Swire Pacific continued to seek opportunities for expansion. The firm significantly bolstered its automotive trading interests, forming Taikoo Motors Limited, which took over the rights to distribute Volvo automobiles in Hong Kong and much of China in 1997. The following year the distributorships for Hyundai vehicles in Hong Kong and for Samsung Motors in mainland China were added, and then in 1999 Swire gained the Volkswagen and Kia dealerships in Taiwan.

The global economic downturn of the early 2000s provided further challenges for Swire Pacific, with Cathay Pacific suffering particularly from the collapse in airline traffic that followed the events of September 11, 2001. During 2001, Swire Properties formed a joint venture with Guangzhou Daily News Group to develop a major complex in the Tianhe district of Guangzhou, a major Chinese city located near Hong Kong. The four million-square-foot complex, scheduled for completion in 2007 and to be called Taikoo Hui, was slated to include a major retail center, offices, a hotel, a performing arts center, and a library.

In January 2002 Edward Scott died, and Adrian Swire once again became chairman of John Swire & Sons. That year also saw Cathay Pacific acquire full ownership of Air Hong Kong and then sell a 30 percent stake in the cargo carrier to DHL Worldwide Express. An additional 10 percent of Air Hong Kong was sold to DHL the following year. Profits for 2002 totaled HK$5.4 billion, a 31 percent increase over the preceding year, as Swire Pacific's aviation division achieved a sharp turnaround thanks to increased passenger and cargo demand.

In the spring of 2003, the war in Iraq and the outbreak of sudden acute respiratory syndrome (SARS) wreaked havoc on Cathay Pacific's passenger services. In May passenger traffic was down 75 percent from the figure in 2002. At the peak of the SARS outbreak, which hit Hong Kong particularly hard, Cathay cut back its schedule by 45 percent. The airline gradually began increasing its flight schedule as the crisis receded.

The SARS outbreak was only the latest threat that the Swire group had managed to negotiate over its long history. The group had previously survived the Boxer Rebellion, two world wars, the civil war in China, the handover of Hong Kong to Chinese rule, and the Asian economic crisis of the late 1990s. The turbulent economic situation of the early 2000s challenged all companies, but the conservatively managed Swire had proven adept at negotiating such perils. Provided that the political situation in Hong Kong and China remained relatively stable, Swire Pacific was well positioned to benefit from the growth that was expected to continue to occur in China.

Principal Subsidiaries

Swire Aviation Limited (66.7%); Swire Beverages Holdings Limited; Swire Beverages Limited (87.5%); Swire Coca-Cola HK Limited (87.5%); Swire Duro Limited; Swire Pacific Ship Management Limited; Swire Pacific Offshore Limited (Bermuda); Swire Resources Limited; Taikoo Motors Limited; Taikoo Sugar Limited; Swire Coca-Cola Taiwan Limited (78.8%); Swire Properties Limited; Swire Pacific Holdings Inc. (U.S.A.).

Principal Divisions

Property Division; Aviation Division; Beverages Division; Marine Services Division; Trading & Industries Division.

Principal Competitors

Jardine Matheson Holdings Limited; Hutchison Whampoa Limited; New World Development Company Limited; The Wharf (Holdings) Limited; Sime Darby Berhad; CITIC Pacific Ltd.

Further Reading

"Boarding for Beijing," *Economist*, May 4, 1996, p. 65.

Chan, Nichole, "Property Poses Threat to Swire," *South China Morning Post* (Hong Kong), March 13, 2002, p. 14.

Clifford, Mark, "Back to China," *Far Eastern Economic Review*, January 27, 1994, pp. 38–40.

——, "Cathay Pacific: It's Time to Buckle Up," *Business Week*, October 9, 1995, p. 146L.

Cox, Howard, Huang Biao, and Stuart Metcalfe, "Compradors, Firm Architecture, and the 'Reinvention' of British Trading Companies: John Swire & Sons' Operations in Early Twentieth-Century China," *Business History*, April 2003, pp. 15+.

"The Dragon's Embrace," *Economist*, August 26, 1989, pp. 51–52.

Edelstein, Michael, *Overseas Investment in the Age of High Imperialism: The United Kingdom 1850–1914*, New York: Columbia University Press, 1982.

Jacob, Rahul, "Cathay's China Effort Galvanises Opposition," *Financial Times*, September 24, 2002, p. 22.

Kalathil, Shanthi, "Swire Pacific Ltd. Goes Courting in China: Hong Kong Giant Aggressively Pursues New Deals," *Wall Street Journal*, October 22, 1996, p. A18.

Kennedy, Carol, "Can Two Hongs Get It Right?," *Director*, February 1996, pp. 34–40.

Lucas, Louise, "Hongs Prepare for Climate Change," *Financial Times*, April 7, 1994, p. 26.

Marriner, Sheila, and Francis E. Hyde, *The Senior John Samuel Swire, 1825–98: Management in Far Eastern Shipping Trades*, Liverpool: Liverpool University Press, 1967.

Meyer, Richard, "Hostage: Why the Taipan at Hong Kong's Biggest Public Company Is Chained to His Post," *Financial World*, September 18, 1990, pp. 22, 25–27.

Morris, Kathleen, "There's No Place Like Home: Jardine Matheson's Grip on Hong Kong Has Been Slipping, But Swire Pacific Is Doing Just Fine," *Financial World*, August 2, 1994, pp. 36–38.

"The Noble Houses Look Forward," *Economist*, October 1, 1994, pp. 77–78.

Ridding, John, "Wallflower Looks Forward to Joining the Party," *Financial Times*, May 8, 1997, p. 34.

Seidlitz, Peter, and David Murphy, "Swire Chief Refuses to Push Panic Button," *South China Morning Post* (Hong Kong), November 23, 1997, p. 4.

Sender, Henny, ''Fixed Assets: British Hongs Still Tied to the Colony,'' *Far Eastern Economic Review,* July 8, 1993, p. 22.

Silverman, Gary, ''Hong Kong: Look British, Think Chinese,'' *Far Eastern Economic Review,* December 28, 1995/January 4, 1996, pp. 64–65.

Smith, Craig S., ''Swire Pacific Deals Show Its Bets on China's Future,'' *Asian Wall Street Journal Weekly,* December 6, 1993, pp. 23 + .

''Thin Ice?,'' *Economist,* September 23, 1995, p. 58.

Wong, Yu, ''Property Drives Swire's Transformation,'' *Asian Wall Street Journal,* April 3, 1998.

Yang, Dori Jones, ''Why a Very British Family Is Creating a Somewhat Chinese Airline,'' *Business Week,* March 10, 1986, pp. 55 + .

—update: David E. Salamie

T. Marzetti Company

1105 Schrock Road, Suite 300
Columbus, Ohio 43229
U.S.A.
Telephone: (614) 846-2232
Fax: (614) 848-8330
Web site: http://www.marzetti.com

Wholly Owned Subsidiary of Lancaster Colony Corporation
Founded: 1896
Sales: $580 million (2002 est.)
NAIC: 311941 Mayonnaise, Dressing, and Other Prepared Sauce Manufacturing; 311991 Perishable Prepared Food Manufacturing

T. Marzetti Company is the Columbus, Ohio-based Specialty Foods Group of Lancaster Colony Corporation, contributing the majority of the revenues posted by its parent company, amounting to nearly $560 million in 2002. Marzctti retails a wide variety of products, packaged under some 15 labels. In the produce section of the supermarket the company sells salad dressings, croutons, vegetable dips, fruit dips, fruit glaze, and apple crisp baking mix under the T. Marzetti label, as well as a line of croutons under the Chatham Village label. On the shelves, the Marzetti name is found on salad dressings, slaw dressings, and sauces. Other shelf items include Cardini's salad dressings and marinades, Girard's salad dressings, Texas Best barbecue and grilling sauces, Inn Maid noodles, Amish Kitchen egg noodles, Jack Daniel's mustards, and Romanoff caviar. In the supermarket frozen foods section, Marzetti sells New York and Mamma Bella garlic bread, Sister Schubert's rolls, Reames egg noodles, and Mountain Top pies. In the foodservice sector, Marzetti offers both brand-name and private-label dressings and sauces; New York Frozen Foods sells frozen breads and rolls to restaurants; and the Reames subsidiary sells frozen noodles and pastas. Most of Marzetti's products are manufactured in 13 U.S. plants, with some individual items made by third parties.

From Florence to Columbus, Teresa Marzetti and the Birth of an Eatery

The person behind the T. Marzetti name was Teresa Marzetti (née Piacentini), who in 1896 at the age of 18 emigrated from Florence, Italy, to the United States, settling in Columbus, Ohio, the home of The Ohio State University. She and her husband Joseph established a small Italian restaurant that catered to the student population. According to company lore, she jotted down on a scrap of paper her goal for their endeavor: "We will start a new place and serve good food. At a profit if we can, at a loss if we must, but we will serve good food." The quality of the meals, drawn from old world recipes, assured the restaurant's popularity. After Joseph died in 1911 Teresa ran the business by herself until she was remarried to a man named Carl Schaufele. A second, larger, restaurant was opened in 1919, one that became especially known for its salad dressings, which many customers began to purchase for takeout in small buckets. While Marzetti's evolved into a four-star restaurant, known throughout the region, one of its dishes, a ground beef and pasta casserole named Johnny Marzetti after Joseph's brother, became famous across the country in the 1920s and standard fare at the family dinner table and school cafeteria.

Launching Slaw Dressing Commercially in 1947

In 1942 the older Marzetti restaurant closed and the operation consolidated in the remaining location. The demand for Marzetti's dressings grew so strong that the upstairs kitchen turned into a small-scale factory. The first product bottled for sale outside the restaurant was Marzetti's Original Slaw Dressing in 1947. The person behind the slaw recipe, however, was not Teresa Marzetti or even of Italian heritage, but a young African American woman named Katherine Hill, whose tenure with the company would last nearly 70 years.

In 1933, in the midst of the Depression, Hill was 17 years old and desperate for work. Drawn to a distant church by prayer, according to her story, she met a Marzetti's employee who told her that the restaurant was looking for someone to take over for a dishwasher who was going on a two-week vacation. She took the job at $10 a week, then stayed on for another two weeks chopping vegetables to cover for another worker on vacation. She was so hard-working that when a baker quit on her last day of employment, she was hired to take his place on a permanent basis even though she possessed no knowledge of baking and displayed no interest in cooking. Nevertheless, she soon exhibited a natural affinity for the work, so much so that she was eventually asked to develop breads, salad dressings, and sauces. Without the use of a cookbook she experimented, once explaining her method to the *Cincinnati Post:* "I taste, see, smell, feel and pour." One of Hill's greatest attributes was her insatiable desire to improve on an already delicious product. For decades she would arrive at work at 5:00 in the morning to develop new recipes for Marzetti, ultimately becoming the company's senior food scientist, despite the lack of formal training, as well as a company icon. She finally retired in 2002 at age 86 after 69 years of service.

Marzetti's dressing was followed by French and Italian, the products proving so popular that the restaurant staff simply could not keep up with the demand. As a result, in 1955 a bottling and distribution operation was established on Indianola Avenue in Columbus, a facility expanded numerous times over the years and still in operation. Moreover, the salad dressing business began to overshadow the restaurant. It attracted the attention of Lancaster Colony Corporation, which purchased the company in 1969 following the death of Schaufele. Teresa Marzetti died in 1972, at which point the restaurant was closed.

Lancaster Colony also was based in Columbus, founded in 1961 when local entrepreneur John B. Gerlach decided to create a holding company for all the businesses in which he held a controlling interest. Lancaster Colony through its subsidiaries produced a varied assortment of manufactured items, including stemware, plastic housewares, components for televisions and scientific instruments, work gloves, and kitchen and bath accessories. Gerlach took the company public in 1969, when by year's end Lancaster Colony was posting net sales of $63.9 million. The acquisition of the T. Marzetti Company for $4.6 million was completed in 1970, and the new subsidiary quickly took steps to grow. With the rising popularity of salad bars, it proved to be a good time to be in the salad dressing business. Management introduced seven new flavors and also spent $1 million to acquire the Frenchette product line from the Carter-Wallace Company. As a result of these steps, Marzetti improved its sales by 26 percent in two years.

Over the ensuing years, Lancaster Colony made further acquisitions in food products, which were folded into Marzetti, expanding the subsidiary well beyond salad dressing and ultimately transforming the former restaurant sideline into the holding company's Specialty Food Group. In 1977 Quality Bakery

Company, based in central Ohio, was acquired, which brought with it the Mountain Top Pies brand of homemade quality frozen pies, which had been successfully launched in the early 1960s and became popular throughout Ohio and surrounding states. In 1978 Lancaster Colony added New York Frozen Foods, a Cleveland family bakery, and Frozen Specialty Bakers. The holding company then bought Inn Maid Products, makers of dry egg noodles, in 1981. As had been the case with Marzetti dressings, Inn Maid noodles was a sideline that evolved into a full-fledged business. The founding Reining family operated the Smithville Inn, located in the heart of Ohio's Amish country, where egg noodles were traditional fare and served at the Inn. Guests began requesting egg noodles for home use, which eventually led to the family packaging the product under the "Inn Maid" label. By 1982 Marzetti, now offering frozen pies, partially baked frozen breads, and noodles in addition to salad dressings, contributed 11.5 percent of Lancaster Colony's profits. A year later, the salad dressing line was bolstered by the acquisition of New York-based Pfeiffer salad dressings, which had been operating as a subsidiary of Hunt-Wesson Foods. Like Marzetti's dressings, Pfeiffer products originated in a restaurant, in the Marine Grille of Buffalo New York during the 1950s.

Marzetti gradually took on greater importance for Lancaster Colony as other business segments failed to produce the same level of long-term success as Specialty Foods. In 1989 it introduced its Ranch Veggie Dip, a product that essentially refashioned the supermarket produce section. As had been the case with salad bars in the early 1970s, Marzetti successfully tapped into a popular trend. In this case, supermarkets were beginning to cut up vegetables such as celery and carrots, packaging them as convenience items. A refrigerated vegetable dip was a perfect complement, but what was even more crafty was Marzetti's decision to ignore the already crowded dairy case in favor of placing their product in the produce section, thereby inventing its own niche and avoiding competition. Until Campbell Soup Co. introduced Marie's Dip in 1993, Marzetti faced no major competition and by adding to the line with such varieties as Dill, Blue Cheese, and Spinach, the company was able to establish itself as the undisputed leader in the veggie dip category. Marzetti's hold on the business would be strengthened by an ongoing development program that eventually added a number of other flavors as well as "light" and fat-free varieties and new formats such as single-serve tubettes. Marzetti also looked beyond the produce section of supermarkets, turning to convenience stores and even airlines.

Marzetti expanded its product offerings in the early 1990s through a number of acquisitions. In 1991 Lancaster Colony acquired Girard's Fine Foods, another manufacturer of salad dressings, established in San Francisco by chef Pierre Girard, who started out with an original recipe for Original French dressing and then added other varieties. In 1993 the parent corporation paid $5.4 million for Romanoff International, which added products such as Romanoff Caviar, Texas Best Barbecue Sauce, Mr. Marinade, and Jack Daniel's Mustard. Focusing on specialty food products proved to be a wise decision by Lancaster Colony; despite a poor economy in the early 1990s, niche food products continued to prosper. In fiscal 1994, the Specialty Foods Group contributed 40 percent of the corporation's $722 million in sales, as well as 40 percent of operating

Key Dates:

1896: Teresa and Joseph Marzetti establish a restaurant in Columbus, Ohio.
1947: The restaurant's slaw dressing is sold commercially.
1955: A bottling plant is opened.
1969: The business is sold to Lancaster Colony Corporation.
1972: Teresa Marzetti dies; the restaurant is closed.
1977: Quality Bakery Company is acquired.
1978: New York Frozen Foods and Frozen Specialty Bakers are acquired.
1981: The company purchases Inn Maid Products.
1983: The salad dressing line is bolstered by the acquisition of Pfeiffer salad dressings, previously operating as a subsidiary of Hunt-Wesson foods.
1991: Lancaster Colony acquires Girard's Fine Foods, manufacturer of salad dressings.
1993: Romanoff International is acquired for $5.4 million.
1996: The company acquires the Cardini line of salad dressings.
2000: Marzetti acquires Sister Schubert's Homemade Rolls, Inc.
2001: Marzetti purchases Mamma Bella Foods, a California frozen bread manufacturer and category leader west of Denver; Marzetti surpasses leader Pepperidge Farm in the frozen bread category, capturing 27.1 percent of the market.

income. Through the first five years of the 1990s Marzetti enjoyed annual compounded sales growth of 14 percent. In 1996 the company added to its core line of salad dressings by acquiring the Cardini line. Cardini dressings bore the last name of chef Caesar Cardini. His first name will be forever linked to his 1924 culinary creation, the Caesar salad. He supposedly concocted it for guests out of necessity at his Tijuana, Mexico hotel, which was popular with Hollywood celebrities who visited the city during the Prohibition era.

Frozen Garlic Bread: A Mid-1990s Boon

Marzetti's innovative spirit was again evident in the mid-1990s when it revitalized the frozen garlic bread category, a product that had been far from convenient for consumers, requiring some 30 minutes to bake and generally resulting in a loaf that the customer squashed while attempting to slice it. In 1996 Marzetti introduced Texas Garlic Toast, which offered eight individual slices in a resealable bag, with preparation time reduced to four to five minutes. It was the first pre-sliced garlic toast product when it debuted in six states. Moreover, the bread tasted good and developed strong word-of-mouth from consumers. While the competition followed its lead, Marzetti developed new items to support its growth, in 1998 introducing

Texas Toast with Cheese, followed by a Parmesan Cheese Toast. The category as a whole enjoyed strong growth in the late 1990s, driven in large part by the success of Marzetti, which according to company officials was responsible for about half of the category's growth. In 1996 Marzetti was a distant fourth in the category, with little more than an 8 percent market share, compared to Pepperidge Farm's leading share of 40 percent. By November 2001, however, Marzetti surpassed Pepperidge Farm in a highly competitive and rapidly growing category, capturing 27.1 percent of the market.

Marzetti also added to its frozen bread business by external means. In 2000 it acquired Sister Schubert's Homemade Rolls, Inc., an Alabama producer of frozen Parker House yeast rolls. The business was established in 1989 in Troy, Alabama, by Patricia Barnes, who initially produced the rolls in her home kitchen for a small catering business. By the time Marzetti purchased the company it was generating more than $20 million in annual revenues. In 2001 Marzetti bought Mamma Bella Foods, a California frozen bread manufacturer. The 17-year-old company also produced a highly popular garlic toast and was the category leader west of Denver. As Marzetti had done with its New York brand of garlic bread, it looked to expand the Mamma Bella brand by building a reputation for quality and introducing innovative products. Shortly after the acquisition, Mamma Bella introduced Garlic Bread Sticks and Five Cheese Garlic Toast.

Acquisitions to Marzetti helped to fuel the growth of the Specialty Food Group's contribution to the Lancaster Colony's balance sheet. In 2000 the retail portion of Specialty Foods accounted for 22 percent of all revenues, and foodservice sales accounted for another 20 percent. In 2002 those numbers grew to 27 percent and 24 percent, respectively. With the group continuing to develop new branded products and expand on its existing channels of distribution, there was every reason to expect Marzetti to enjoy even stronger growth in the foreseeable future.

Principal Competitors

H.J. Heinz Company; Kraft Foods Inc.; Campbell Soup Company.

Further Reading

Bardic, Allison, "Ohio's Big Dipper," *Dairy Field*, June 2001, p. 1.
"Marzetti Toasts the Category," *Frozen Food Age*, February 2001, p. 36.
"New York Brand Is Toast of the Town," *Frozen Food Age*, February 2002, p. 52.
Rosencrans, Joyce, "Dressings Made Her Career," *Cincinnati Post*, July 31, 2002.
——, "Marzetti's Turns 100," *Cincinnati Post*, May 15, 1996, p. 12C.

—Ed Dinger

Tee Vee Toons, Inc.

23 E. 4th St., 3rd Floor
New York, New York 10003
U.S.A.
Telephone: (212) 979-6489
Fax: (212) 979-6410
Web site: http://www.tvtrecords.com

Private Company
Incorporated: 1985
Employees: 100
Sales: $100 million (2003 est.)
NAIC: 512220 Integrated Record Production/Distribution;
512230 Music Publishers

Tee Vee Toons, Inc., better known as TVT Records, is the leading independent record company in the United States. The firm's offerings range from hip-hop and heavy metal to Broadway show tunes, movie soundtracks, and television theme songs. TVT is perhaps best known for launching the career of Nine Inch Nails, but its roster also includes British pop band XTC, hip-hop acts Snoop Dogg Presents The Eastsidaz and the Ying Yang Twins, and heavy metal groups Nothingface and Sevendust, among others. TVT puts out albums under several label names, including Wax Trax!, TVT Soundtrax, and Blunt. The company is run by its founder, Steven Gottlieb.

Early Years

The story of TVT Records begins in 1984 with a recent graduate of Harvard Law School, Steven Gottlieb. When someone suggested that he compile an album of television program theme songs, the lifelong music fan decided to set aside his legal career and put one together. Determined to create a better package than several earlier, but haphazard compilations, he spent months tracking down the legal rights to 65 different songs including the classic themes from *Green Acres, Mission: Impossible,* and *Gilligan's Island.*

With the help of several friends, Gottlieb raised $125,000 and founded Tee Vee Toons, Inc. to distribute the collection,

which he initially sold out of his New York apartment. Aided by the judicious use of television advertising, the album sold well and Gottlieb's company was off and running. Over the next two years additional volumes of TV themes were also released.

In 1987 Gottlieb took the profits he had made from the television albums and formed a new label, TVT Records, which would be dedicated to signing unheralded, but promising, rock music acts. Among the early performers signed to the label were Shona Laing, The Saints, and The Connells, each of which would go on to reach the top five in *Billboard*'s alternative music chart.

The year 1988 saw Gottlieb enter another new area with the release of the soundtrack album for the hit French movie *Jean de Florette.* The following year he put together a collection of 55 classic commercial jingles, which the firm charged $7,500 per ad to appear on. Spots for Coke, Chevrolet, and Schlitz beer were among those included.

Nine Inch Nails Signed in 1989

In 1989 TVT signed an act which would go on to be one of its most successful ever, Nine Inch Nails. Fronted by charismatic vocalist/songwriter Trent Reznor, the goth/metal rock band released its debut album *Pretty Hate Machine* in 1990. With little radio or music video exposure forthcoming, the company promoted it with a series of strategically placed television advertisements, and the recording quickly sold more than 500,000 units. It would later be certified "gold" and continued to sell for years to come. TVT was also having success at this time with the groups Modern English and KLF, whose debut album *Chill Out* went on to become a classic of the electronica/ambient music genre.

In 1990 TVT began to mine the extensive archives of television's *Ed Sullivan Show,* which had been broadcast from 1948 to 1971. The label compiled the audio portion of performances by a number of major artists and released them on albums devoted to 1960s British Invasion rock bands (though Beatles and Rolling Stones cuts were omitted), Louis Armstrong, Big Bands, and Broadway performers, among others. Additional volumes in the "Sullivan Years" series appeared over the next several years.

357

Company Perspectives:

In its sixteen-year history TVT has been on the industry's cutting edge introducing to the world such impact artists as Nine Inch Nails, Underworld and Ja Rule. The label currently maintains an ever-growing staff of 100 people around the country, with field offices in Los Angeles, San Francisco, Chicago, Boston and Toronto.

TVT Records provides the credibility and focus of an indie and the marketing and distribution power of a major while priding itself on grass roots artist development.

In 1991 TVT entered into a 50/50 joint venture with Interscope Records to form Nothing Records, an independent entity run by Trent Reznor which would release new albums by Nine Inch Nails and other artists. TVT also became a minority owner of the bankrupt Chicago-based Wax Trax! records in late 1992, before buying the entire company. Wax Trax! had released 100 albums, including popular records by the groups Ministry and KMFDM.

TVT was now involved in disputes with several of its artists, including pop band The Connells, whose albums had sold more than 250,000 copies. In March the two sides agreed to settle a suit filed by the group over allegations of incomplete accounting of royalties and inadequate promotion. The band would stay on the label, with TVT pledging to improve its support for their releases.

In 1993 the company formed a new imprint, Blunt Recordings, which would feature New York-based rap and hip-hop artists. Its first release was by a performer named Mic Geronimo. TVT also signed jazz vocalist and rap precursor Gil Scott Heron during the year. In 1994 the company named Irv Gotti to head its Urban A&R department, and he soon procured the services of a new group, Cash Money Click, which included future rap star Ja Rule.

Mortal Kombat *Soundtrack a Hit in 1995*

TVT had a major success in 1995 with the soundtrack from the film *Mortal Kombat*, which hit the *Billboard* Top 10 chart and went on to sell 1.5 million copies. TVT won the rights to the album after several major labels had passed on it, partly because they had been given only a few weeks to usher it into stores before the movie's release date. The New Line film, which was based on a martial arts video game, surprised industry analysts when it became the top grossing motion picture in the United States for several weeks running. The album included material by Wax Trax! artists KMFDM and Sister Machine Gun, as well as actress Traci Lords and other non-TVT performers. The company later released a second soundtrack from the film, and in 1996 formed the TVT Soundtrax label to issue recordings from movies, television shows, and Broadway musicals.

In the fall of 1996 TVT released four more volumes of television theme music, a decade after its last such release. The new set featured 65 cuts per album, with 24-page booklets and 3-D cover graphics. To promote the series TVT created a special in-store display rack which featured television antenna-

like ''rabbit ears,'' and also sponsored radio trivia contests and sent bulk e-mails to members of Internet television discussion groups. By this time TVT had 65 employees and annual sales estimated at more than $50 million. In addition to its New York headquarters, the firm maintained satellite offices in Los Angeles, San Francisco, Boston, and Chicago. The company had established its own distribution system in the United States, and started distributing the releases of other independent labels over the next several years.

In late 1997 Gottlieb unveiled a new cassette storage case he had invented called the ''Biobox.'' Similar in appearance to a cigarette pack, the Biobox offered more space for display of graphic images and was more durable than the easily shattered plastic cases commonly used. It had taken him five years and more than $2 million to perfect the design. After it was introduced a number of major music firms switched to the Biobox for their cassette packaging. It was manufactured by SGI, Inc., a sister company to Tee Vee Toons.

June 1998 saw TVT Soundtrax release a new recording of the complete score to the Stephen Sondheim musical *Follies,* which included previously unrecorded material from the first version of the show. A retrospective of 50 years' worth of music associated with CBS television was released during the summer, and in the fall TVT put out a four CD set of music from programs on the cable television Sci Fi Channel. During the year the firm also signed veteran British pop band XTC and entered into a joint venture with United Producers, a new record label formed by ten successful record producers.

Once again seeking ways to circumvent the restrictive playlists of radio and music video programmers to break a new act, in November 1998 TVT took the unusual step of running an infomercial to promote a hard rock band called Sevendust in select markets. The program, a taped concert titled ''Live & Loud,'' was run with commercials for such companies as Epiphone Guitars and Best Buy stores, which gave Sevendust CDs prominent display space in exchange for the ads. TVT spent approximately $500,000 on the promotional campaign, which significantly boosted sales of Sevendust's albums and concert tickets.

1999: $23 Million Loan to Fund Expansion

In February 1999 TVT secured a loan for $23.5 million from CAK Universal Credit Corp., in association with Prudential Securities, to fund the creation or purchase of new record labels and to sign more artists, using revenues from the firm's record masters and music publishing as collateral. In the spring the company signed rock act Guided By Voices, and formed a distribution deal with Mushroom Records for that company to distribute TVT products in Australia and New Zealand. Later in the year the firm also reached agreements with digital streaming companies Reciprocal and Musicmaker.com to offer TVT material via the Internet. TVT would take equity stakes in both companies. In November TVT made its entire catalog available for download at tvtrecords.com for free on a timed-out basis. During the year the label also signed rap outfit Snoop Dogg Presents The Eastsidaz, in association with Dogghouse Records, and sold its stake in Reznor's Nothing operation.

Key Dates:

1985: Steven Gottlieb founds Tee Vee Toons, Inc. to release TV theme album.
1987: TVT Records is formed to record alternative rock bands.
1989: Nine Inch Nails signs with TVT.
1990: Company begins releasing musical performances from *Ed Sullivan Show*.
1992: TVT buys stake in bankrupt Wax Trax! Records; later acquires entire firm.
1993: Blunt Records is formed to release New York hip-hop recordings.
1996: TVT Soundtrax label is created after success of *Mortal Kombat* album.
1999: Firm secures $23.5 million loan to fund expansion.
2001: Lawsuits against Napster and MP3.com are settled.
2003: TVT is awarded $132 million in damages following lawsuit against Def Jam.

In the spring of 2000 TVT joined several other record companies and music publishers in suing both MP3.com and Napster, which allowed Internet users to download music for free via the Internet. The suits, which claimed copyright infringement, collectively sought hundreds of millions of dollars in damages. TVT also formed alliances with legitimate digital download providers emusic.com and Supertracks during the year.

In January 2001 TVT became the first company to officially settle its claims against Napster, which had recently agreed to start a fee-charging download operation with major label BMG. The settlement amount was not disclosed, but TVT agreed to make its recordings available on the new service. In April the company won its lawsuit against MP3.com, but due to a mistake in the jury's calculations a mistrial was declared. The jurors had told the judge they found MP3.com liable for nearly $300,000 in damages, but later revealed that they had added the numbers incorrectly and should have put the figure at $3 million. Before the case could be retried, the two firms settled out of court for an undisclosed sum. MP3.com had earlier paid $133 million to the five largest record labels.

In 2002 TVT signed well-known rap act Naughty By Nature, which had recently been dropped by Arista; made its catalog available for download via the subscription-based Rhapsody service of Listen.com; and signed a European distribution pact with Universal-Island Records UK. The company also released a new compilation called *TV Guide's 50 All-Time Favorite TV Themes* to commemorate the 50th anniversary of that publication's founding.

2003: Taking Def Jam to Court

In the spring of 2003 the firm was back in court with a lawsuit against Island Def Jam Music and its chairman, Lyor Cohen, whom TVT accused of backing out of an agreement to let it release a "reunion" album by rap trio Cash Money Click and Ja Rule, now a Def Jam artist. Some songs on the album dated to the group's original tenure with the company in the mid-1990s, while other material was to be newly recorded. In May a jury awarded $24 million in compensatory damages and $108 million in punitive damages to TVT, of which Cohen was liable for approximately half. Lawyers for Island Def Jam, a unit of Universal Music Group, declared they would appeal.

Meanwhile, the firm was in a dispute with Prudential Securities, which was trying to take over the revenues of the company's TVT Catalog Enterprises unit after payments had been missed on the $23.5 million loan. Some sources were also reporting that Gottlieb was seeking to sell TVT to a larger record company, but had found no takers. In mid-July the company's woes continued when Gottlieb's laptop computer, containing sensitive data, was stolen from the firm's New York offices in a burglary.

Tee Vee Toons, Inc., or TVT Records as it was best known, had grown from humble beginnings into the largest independent record company in the United States. Its broad range now included pop music, heavy metal and rap, as well as Broadway show tunes, movie soundtracks, and the television theme songs with which it had started. The scrappy competitor was still run by founder Steven Gottlieb.

Principal Subsidiaries

TVT Records; Wax Trax! Records; Blunt Records; TVT Soundtrax; TVT Catalog Enterprises; and Australian and Canadian distribution units.

Principal Competitors

Universal Music Group; Sony Music Entertainment, Inc.; BMG Entertainment; Warner Music Group; EMI Group plc.

Further Reading

Arango, Tim, "TVT on the Ropes—Record Co. Skips on Loan, Can't Find Buyer," *New York Post*, May 6, 2003, p. 33.

——, "Who Wants TVT? Indies' Largest Label Is Looking for a Buyer," *New York Post*, March 26, 2003, p. 35.

Bessman, Jim, "TVT Label Uses TV Concert to Market Band," *Billboard*, March 6, 1999.

Borzillo, Carrie, "Success of 'Mortal Kombat' a Surprising Kick for TVT," *Billboard*, September 30, 1995, p. 13.

Christman, Ed, "Ailing WaxTrax Label Gets Cash Flow from TVT," *Billboard*, January 9, 1993, p. 16.

Cox, James, and Stuart Elliott, "Now TV Ad Jingles Are Selling Themselves," *USA Today*, May 31, 1989, p. B5.

DiCostanzo, Frank, "TVT Taps Small-Screen Themes," *Billboard*, February 8, 1997, p. 49.

Featherly, Kevin, "Major Indie Label TVT Records Buries Napster Hatchet," *Newsbytes News Network*, January 25, 2001.

——, "TVT, MP3.com Settle Differences, End Copyright Suit," *Newsbytes News Network*, November 13, 2001.

Hadler, Pat, "TVT Lights Up 'Broadway' Campaign," *Billboard*, July 11, 1992, p. 41.

Henriques, Diana B., "Music Executive Is Still in Control of TVT Records," *New York Times*, July 14, 2003, p. 1.

Ho, Rodney, "Entrepreneur Hopes Music Lovers Flip for His Invention," *Wall Street Journal*, December 30, 1997, p. B2.

Lichtman, Irv, "TVT Makes Securitization Deal," *Billboard*, March 6, 1999.

Markon, Jerry, "We, the Jury, Find the Damages We Set Are Off by Millions," *Wall Street Journal*, April 10, 2001, p. B1.

Menconi, David, "Settling Down for a New Disc, The Connells Reach an Accord with Their Label," *News & Observer* (Raleigh, N.C.), March 12, 1993, p. W10.

Morris, Chris, "Indie Catalogs Reap Benefits of Alums' New Hits," *Billboard,* November 5, 1994, p. 14.

Neumeister, Larry, "$132 Million Awarded in Dispute Over Unreleased Ja Rule Record," *Associated Press Newswires,* May 6, 2003.

Verna, Paul, "11 Producers Form Own Label, Pact with TVT," *Billboard,* September 26, 1998, p. 8.

—Frank Uhle

TeliaSonera AB

Mårbackagatan 11
SE-123 86 Farsta
Sweden
Telephone: +46-8-713-1000
Fax: +46-8-713-3333
Web site: http://www.teliasonera.com
Public Company
Incorporated: 2003
Employees: 29,173
Sales: EUR 8.8 billion ($8.7 billion) (2002)
Stock Exchanges: Stockholm Helsinki NASDAQ
Ticker Symbol: TLSN
NAIC: 517110 Wired Telecommunications Carriers;
334210 Telephone Apparatus Manufacturing; 334220
Radio and Television Broadcasting and Wireless
Communications Equipment Manufacturing; 334290
Other Communication Equipment Manufacturing;
517212 Cellular and Other Wireless Telecommunica-
tions; 517910 Other Telecommunications

TeliaSonera AB—formed from the merger of Sweden's Telia AB and Finland's Sonera at the beginning of 2003—is the leading telecommunications provider to the Scandinavian and Baltic regions. The combined company claimed 8.6 million fixed line subscribers and nearly ten million mobile telephone subscribers, and pro forma revenues of EUR 8.8 billion ($8.7 billion) for 2002. Fixed telephony accounts for a little more than 40 percent of the group's sales; mobile telephony, at nearly 30 percent of revenues, is the company's fastest growing business segment. The company is also a leading Internet provider in both Sweden, where it is market leader with more than 1.3 million customers, and in Finland. Despite the merger, essentially a takeover of Sonera by the larger Telia, the company has maintained its two core brands—Sonera for the Finnish market and Telia for the Swedish market. Although Sweden and Finland remain the company's largest revenue markets, the company has extensive holdings throughout the Scandinavian and Baltic regions, as well as a strong share in Turkey, through its holding in that country's Turkcell mobile phone operator, and in such former Soviet Union states as Azerbaijan, Georgia, and Kazakhstan. TeliaSonera has also entered the Russian mobile telephone market, one of Europe's fastest growing. The company, which represented the first of an expected wave of cross-border European telecommunications mergers, has acknowledged its interest in future international mergers. Listed on the Helsinki, Stockholm, and NASDAQ stock exchanges, TeliaSonera has chosen Stockholm as its headquarters. The company brought in "neutral" Anders Igel, formerly head of Esselte, to lead the combined company.

19th-Century Scandinavian Telecommunications Background

Both Telia and Sonera had their roots in the 19th century. Sweden introduced its first electric telegraph line between Uppsala and Stockholm in 1853 (the company had in fact pioneered an optical telegraph network in 1794). From the start, the country's telegraph market was placed under the control of the government, which formed Kongliga Elektriska Telegraf Verket. The state body continued extending its telegraph network and, as early as 1854, had connected Sweden into a line that reached to the European mainland through central Europe. Elektriska Telegraf Verket shortened its name, to Telegrafverket, in 1860.

Finland's political situation—at the time the country existed as an autonomous Grandy Duchy under the Russian Empire—resulted in a more limited extension of the telegraph in that country. In 1855, the Russian government connected Helsinki to St. Petersburg. Traffic was initially restricted, however, to Russian governmental and military uses, and the Finnish Telegraph Office remained under imperial control until Finland's declaration of independence in 1917.

By then, however, the telegraph had given way to a new device. Telegrafverket laid Sweden's first telephone line in 1877, just one year after Bell was awarded his patent. The country's first private exchange was built in Stockholm in 1880.

Company Perspectives:

Group Strategy: TeliaSonera's overall focus is on best serving our customers in our core business and creating value for our shareholders through stronger profits and cash flows.

TeliaSonera will focus specifically on: core business in the Nordic and Baltic regions; pursuing profitable growth opportunities in the East; adopting a strong customer-oriented approach; increasing profits and cash flow.

Sweden's poor road and transport system made the company fertile ground for the new communication system. By the end of the century, Telegrafverket's own phone network had more than 60,000 customers and, by World War I, the country boasted more than 170,000 subscribers.

The Swedish government was somewhat unusual in its tolerance of private telephone networks—most other governments had moved to take control of the sector by the beginning of the century. A major contributor to developing the early Swedish phone system was H.T. Cedergrens, who founded Stockholms Allmanna Telefonaktiebolag (SAT) in 1883 in order to counter the entry of the United States' Bell, which had already achieved dominance in a number of countries. SAT itself was to gain market dominance, setting up the country's largest telephone exchange.

In 1918, with Sweden's economy under pressure, SAT was merged into telephone equipment manufacturer Ericsson. The telephone exchange was then sold to Telegrafverket, giving the state body the monopoly on the country's telephone system. Telegrafverket, which became Televerket, or Swedish Telecom, in 1953, had never been formally established as the country's telecom monopoly, however.

The evolution of Finland's telephone system continued to reflect the country's political situation. The Finnish government was eager to prevent imperial Russia from gaining control of the country's telephone system. While the Finnish government created its own telephone body, which became Telecom Finland, overseeing the installation of the country's first phone lines in 1877, private companies were encouraged to wire the country as well. By the early 1880s a number of private phone lines had been set up, linking harbors or railroad stations or warehouses. In 1882, the first private local telephone company was established. The Finnish government favored the creation of a large number of local telephone companies, rather than creating a single, statewide organism, reasoning that it would be more difficult for the czarist government to take over such a fragmented market.

Regulation of the Finnish telecommunications market began in 1886, with the passage of the Imperial Telephone Decree, which created legislation requiring telephone companies to apply for licensing. Yet these were granted only to local, Finnish-owned companies, effectively locking Russia out of the market. By 1938, there were more than 800 local telephone companies operating in Finland—very nearly one company for each village. These small companies were later brought more or less under local government control, essentially becoming owned by their subscribers.

Meanwhile, the Finnish government, following the country's independence in 1917, established the Telegraph Office as the state-owned telecommunications arm. In 1927, the Telegraph Office was merged with the country's Post Office, forming the Finnish Post and Telegraph Office, or PTT. That body was charged with hooking up the country's sparsely populated northern and eastern regions, where setting up private telephone operations would have been too costly. The PTT, which became the country's regulatory body, also began acquiring a number of local companies, yet, in the early 1930s, the PTT's share of the Finnish market amounted only to 1.2 percent. In 1935, however, the PTT bought out the country's largest long-distance provider and gained a monopoly on Finland's long-distance and international telecommunications markets.

Over the next decades, the high cost of investment in new technology led to a concentration in the Finnish telecommunications sector. By the mid-1950s, the number of telephone companies had dropped back to 550. By the beginning of the 1960s, the number had shrunk to just 200, then to 73 in 1970. By the 1990s, there were only 49 predominantly regional telephone companies in Finland.

Leading the Deregulation Movement in the 1980s

Telegrafverket remained at the forefront of the telecommunications industry, particularly through the presence of the Ericsson company, which established itself as one of the world's leading telecommunications equipment suppliers. The state-owned body had begun automating the country's telephone system as early as the 1930s; in the late 1940s, Telegrafverket debuted one of the world's first mobile telephone systems using a closed radio circuit. By then, the country's telephone market was undergoing a boom in connections, and by the 1950s Sweden boasted one of the world's highest per-capita telephone connection rates.

Televerket, as it was called after 1953, began offering data transmission services in 1965, then, forming the Ellemtel partnership with Ericsson in 1970, began developing the world's first digital switching network. The company also began offering satellite-based services that year. The company later began diversifying its operations, launching a cable television service and an early cellular telephone network. In 1978, Televerket, which had been publishing telephone directories for Sweden since 1889, began commercial telephone directory services, launching the Gula Sidorna (Yellow Pages) that year, then publishing business-to-business directories starting in 1982. The directories operation was later developed into a separate division, InfoMedia (later Eniro), which began providing directory publishing services on an international basis.

By the mid-1980s, most of the Scandinavian countries began preparing to deregulate their telecommunications industries. Sweden proved a pioneer in this development, ending government funding of Televerket in 1984. Televerket was now expected to operate on a for-profit business, although it remained owned by the Swedish government. Through the remainder of

---

Key Dates:

1794: The first optical telegraph line in Sweden is inaugurated.

1853: The first electrical telegraph line is opened between Uppsala and Stockholm; the Swedish government creates Kongliga Elektriska Telegraf Verket to oversee the telegraph network.

1855: The first electrical telegraph line is opened between Helsinki and St. Petersburg, but the telegraph network in Finland remains under the control of imperial Russia.

1877: Telegrafverket constructs the first telephone line in Sweden; the first telephone line in Finland is constructed.

1880: The first private telephone exchange in Stockholm is opened.

1882: The first private telephone exchange in Helsinki is constructed.

1883: Stockholms Allmanna Telefonaktiebolag (SAT) is founded in order to build the country's largest telephone exchange in Stockholm.

1886: Finland passes the Imperial Telephone Decree, which encourages the growth of local phone companies in order to maintain control of the telephone system under the Finnish government.

1917: The newly independent Finnish government establishes the Telegraph Office to oversee the telecommunications sector.

1918: Telegrafverket buys SAT's telephone exchange, gaining a de facto monopoly on the Swedish telecommunications market.

1927: The Finnish telegraph office is merged with the post office to create Post and Telegraph Office (PTT).

1935: PTT acquires a monopoly on Finland's long-distance and international communications market.

1947: Telegrafverket debuts a mobile, radio-based telephone system.

1953: Telegrafverket becomes Televerket.

1965: Televerket launches data transmission services.

1970: The company forms Ellemtel with Ericsson to create the first digital switching system.

1981: Post and Telegraph Office is renamed as Post and Telecommunications of Finland.

1984: Televerket is separated from the Swedish government and becomes a for-profit state-owned enterprise.

1990: Televerket forms a Unisource partnership with KPN of The Netherlands.

1993: Televerket changes its name to Telia.

1994: Post and Telecommunications is separated and Telecom Finland is created.

1998: Telecom Finland changes its name to Sonera and lists on the Helsinki stock exchanges and NASDAQ.

2000: Telia lists on the Stockholm stock exchange.

2002: Telia and Sonera announce their agreement to merge operations.

2003: TeliaSonera begins operations as a combined company.

---

the decade, the government began taking steps to liberalize the Swedish telecommunications market. As Televerket saw its monopoly positions compromised on the domestic front—the country fully liberalized the telecommunications sector in 1991—it began seeking international partners to protect it against the expected incursion of the world's largest telecommunications groups. In 1990, Televerket created Unisource in partnership with The Netherlands' KPN partnership. Later joined by Swiss Telecom, Belgacom, and others, the Unicom partnership, which intended to provide telecommunications services to large corporations, produced only limited results.

Nonetheless, the 1990s marked the start of Televerket's internationalization. If at the start of the decade, nearly all of the company's 49,000 employees were based in Sweden, by the end of the decade, a majority of the company's employees were stationed in its international operations. In 1993, Televerket, underscoring its international ambitions as well as the shift in the telecommunications market away from a focus on telephone communications, changed its name to Telia AB.

By the mid-1990s, Telia faced competition from some 30 different companies. Yet Telia remained the dominant player in the Swedish market, especially by capturing a leading share of the booming mobile telephone market. In 1995, Telia launched its own Internet access service, quickly gaining a leading share in the country.

By then, too, Finland had deregulated its telecommunications sector, a process begun in 1981 with the renaming of the Post and Telegraph Office as Posts and Telecommunications of Finland, a step toward converting the state-controlled body into a limited liability company. In 1987, the Finnish government passed a new National Telecommunications Act—replacing the original Imperial Telephone Decree of 1886—which among other things drafted new registration rules for telecommunications companies. The new legislation also removed Post and Telecommunications' regulatory powers, which were transferred to the Ministry of Transport and Communications.

In 1990, Post and Telecommunications took the next step toward private enterprise when government funding was cut off and the company was now expected to operate on a for-profit basis. In 1994, the two functions, postal services and telecommunications, were separated, and a new limited liability company was formed, Telecom Finland. In that year, Telecom Finland lost its monopoly on the country's long-distance market. By then, the Finnish telephone market had been reduced to just 49 companies, which joined together to create Telegroup of Finland in 1991 (renamed as Finnet Group in 1995).

Telecom Finland remained controlled by the Finnish government until 1998, when the company was formally privatized. Renamed Sonera, the company went public, listing on the Helsinki stock exchanges and NASDAQ. By then, Sonera was regarded as one of the most technologically advanced telecommunications companies in the world. While the group held an approximately 30 percent share of the Finnish fixed line market, it had been particularly active in the mobile telephone arena, capturing some 65 percent of a market that had already reached 60 percent of the country's population by the late 1990s—the highest penetration in the world at the time. Sonera was also the first to offer mobile Short Message Service (SMS) and to link the mobile system into the Internet through Wireless Access Protocol (WAP) services. Sonera also became the country's leading Internet service provider.

First Cross-Border Telecoms Merger in the New Century

Sonera's ambitions turned decidedly international as the Finnish market matured at the end of the 1990s. The company began buying stakes in mobile telephone operations in other countries, particularly in Latvia, Lithuania, Estonia, Russia, and Hungary. The company also bought up 41 percent of Turkey's Turkcell for $116 million—an investment that was valued at some $7.5 billion by 2000. From Turkey, Sonera turned to the former Soviet republics of Azerbaijan, Georgia, and Kazakhstan, building mobile networks in those countries. Back at home, the company, aided by fellow Finn Nokia, was building one of the world's most advanced mobile Internet networks, including its wireless Internet portal Zed. The company's developments in this area helped boost its share price—and by 2000 the company's market value had soared to some $25 billion. In that year, the Finnish government moved to cut its stake in the company, reducing its position to 54.5 percent.

Yet Sonera also had launched an ambitious attempt to enter the bidding war for Europe's next-generation UTMS high-speed mobile telephone licenses. The company spent billions of Euros, winning a 48 percent share in a German UTMS license. The purchase sank the company heavily in debt in time for a massive downturn in the global telecommunications industry. By the end of 2000 Sonera's share price had plunged by some two-thirds. By then, the company had already acknowledged its interest in being acquired by a larger telecommunications group, with Vodaphone stepping up as a potential suitor. The collapse of the telecommunications market had put an end to that effort, however.

Telia, too, had been emphasizing its international growth, particularly in the Scandinavian region, where it acquired a stake in the Norwegian and Danish mobile telephone markets. Telia also entered the mobile telephone markets in the Baltic states, where its investments found the company working alongside Sonera. After leaving Unisource in 1998, Telia began looking about for a new international partner. In 1999, the company announced that it had agreed to a merger with Telenor, of Norway. The "merger of equals" soon collapsed, however, notably because of disagreements about where to locate the new group's headquarters.

Instead Telia turned to smaller Sonera, and in 2002, the two companies announced their agreement to merge into a new entity, TeliaSonera. To avoid the mistakes of the Telenor merger attempt, the two sides agreed to maintain their existing Finnish and Swedish operations more or less intact, creating a corporate headquarters in Stockholm only for companywide decisions. Telia and Sonera also agreed to bring in a "neutral" CEO with no connection to either firm, choosing Anders Igel, former head of stationery company Esselte, for the role.

This time the merger proved a success, and in January 2003 the new company was born—marking the first of an expected wave of cross-border European telecommunications mergers. With nearly EUR 9 billion in pro-forma 2002 sales, TeliaSonera remained somewhat of a minnow in the fast-moving telecommunications sector. Nonetheless, the company held key positions in its core Scandinavian market, as well as a major role in the mobile telephone markets in the Baltic regions. As it entered its first year as a combined company, TeliaSonera looked forward to expanding its international presence, through acquisitions—or by allowing itself to be acquired.

Principal Subsidiaries

724 Solutions Inc. (Canada; 11%); AS Eesti Telefom (Estonia; 25%); Baltic Tele AB (Sweden; 50%); Business Sviaz (Russia); Datatel (Latvia); Lattelekom SIA (Latvia; 49%); Latvijas Mobilais Telefons SIA (Latvia; 25%; Sonera Corporation (Finland); Sonera Plaza Ltd.; Sonera SmartTrust Ltd.; Sonera Zed Ltd. (85%); Telia A/S (Denmark); Telia Asia Ltd.; Telia Electronic Commerce AB; Telia Foretag AB; Telia International Carrier AB; Telia Carrier Danmark (Denmark); Telia Carrier Poland Sp.zo.o; Telia France sa; Telia International Carrier Hongkong; Telia Networks Belgium S.A.; Telia Networks Italy SpA; Telia Networks Luxembourg S.A.; Telia Networks the Netherlands B.V.; Telia Networks S.A. (Switzerland); Telia Networks Spain S.A. ; Telia North America Inc.; Telia Telekommunikation GmbH (Germany); Telia UK Ltd. Network Division; Telia Internet Partner AB; Telia Latvija (Latvia); Telia Light AB; Telia Megacom AB; Telia Nara AB; Telia Promotor AB; Telia PubliCom AB; Telia Swedtel de Colombia; Telia Swedtel Inc. (U.S.A.); Telia Swedtel Philippines; Telia Swedtel Thai Ltd. (Thailand); Telia TeleCom AB; Telia UK Ltd.; Tess S.A. (Brazil; 45%); Turkcell Iletisim Hizmetleri A.S. (Turkey; 37%); UAB Omnitel (Lithuania; 28%); Xfera Móviles S.A. (Spain; 14%); ZAO North-West GSM (Russia; 24%).

Principal Competitors

Verizon Communications Inc.; Vivendi Universal S.A.; France Telecom SA; AT&T Corp.; WorldCom Inc.; Vodafone Group Plc; Bce Inc.; British Telecommunications plc; Telefonica SA; Telecom Italia SpA; Nokia Group; TRACTEBEL SA; Bouygues SA; Ericsson LM Telephone Co.; Bell Canada; Royal KPN NV; Cable and Wireless Ireland Ltd.; Lucent Technologies Inc.; Telus Communications Inc.; Scottish Power PLC; Cable and Wireless PLC; Telenor AS; Portugal Telecom SGPS SA; Union Fenosa SA; BELGACOM.

Further Reading

Brown-Humes, Christopher, "Telia and Sonera Look for New Partners After Euros 18bn Merger," *Financial Times*, March 27, 2002, p. 21.
"Crossing the Border," *Global Telecoms Business*, May-June 2002, p. 20.
Junkkari, Marko, "History of Sonera and Telia Goes Back to Telegraph Days," *Helsingin Sanomat*, March 27, 2002.

Koza, Patricia, "Sonera-Telia Back on Track," *Daily Deal,* November 8, 2002.

Morais, Richard C., "The Sonera Also Rises," *Forbes,* December 27, 1999, p. 10.

Roberts, Dan, "Sonera Surreptitiously Seeks Best Deal," *Financial Times,* August 4, 2000, p. 27.

"Telia/Sonera Promises, But Will It Deliver?," *Corporate Finance,* May 2002, p. 7.

Uimonen, Terho, "Telia Has an Eye on an Overseas Expansion As IPO Draws Closer," *InfoWorld,* March 20, 2000, p. 54.

—M.L. Cohen

The TJX Companies, Inc.

770 Cochituate Road
Framingham, Massachusetts 01701-4672
U.S.A.
Telephone: (508) 390-1000
Fax: (508) 390-2828
Web site: http://www.tjx.com

Public Company
Incorporated: 1962 as Zayre Corp.
Employees: 94,000
Sales: $11.98 billion (2002)
Stock Exchanges: New York
Ticker Symbol: TJX
NAIC: 448140 Family Clothing Stores; 442299 All Other
 Home Furnishings Stores; 454111 Electronic
 Shopping; 551112 Offices of Other Holding
 Companies

The TJX Companies, Inc. is the largest off-price apparel and home fashions retailer in both the United States and the world, with nearly 1,850 stores worldwide by the end of fiscal 2002. Six of the firm's seven divisions target middle to upper-middle income shoppers who are fashion and value conscious; the A.J. Wright chain is designed to serve more moderate-income consumers. All of the seven concepts aim to offer quality brand-name merchandise at prices 20 to 60 percent below department store and specialty store regular prices. T.J. Maxx, the largest retailer of its kind in the United States with 713 stores in 47 states, offers brand-name family apparel, accessories, fine jewelry, home fashions, women's shoes, and lingerie. Marshall's is the nation's second largest off-price apparel retailer. Acquired by TJX in 1995, Marshall's operates 629 stores in 42 states and Puerto Rico, offering a product line similar to that of T.J. Maxx but with a full line of family footwear and a wider assortment of menswear. Winners (146 units) and T.K. Maxx (123 units), each modeled after the T.J. Maxx concept, are the leading off-price family apparel chains in Canada and the United Kingdom, respectively. HomeGoods, a chain of off-price home fashion stores, operates some 140 stores offering giftware, accent furnishings, rugs,

lamps, and seasonal merchandise. A.J. Wright, a 75-unit chain launched in 1998, offers family apparel and footwear, lingerie, accessories, home fashions, and costume jewelry. Debuting in 2001 and expanded to 15 stores by the end of the following year, HomeSense is a Canadian version of the HomeGoods chain.

Company Origins

The TJX Companies, Inc. traces its history to Zayre Corp., parent of the Zayre Store chain of discount department stores incorporated in 1962. The first Zayre—Yiddish for "very good"—store opened in Hyannis, Massachusetts, in 1956. Its founders were two cousins, Stanley and Sumner Feldberg. With sales doubling every second or third year, the Feldbergs were quick to establish new Zayre stores, which numbered more than 200 by the early 1970s. By then, the company had diversified into specialty retailing.

Among Zayre's early acquisitions was the Hit or Miss chain, an off-price chain specializing in upscale women's clothing. The first store, which opened in Natick, Massachusetts, in 1965, flourished and grew into a chain so quickly that within four years it had attracted the attention of a giant by comparison, Zayre. In 1969 Zayre bought the Hit or Miss chain and began its exploration of the upscale off-price fashion market. Zayre's timing could not have been better. During the recession of the 1970s, Hit or Miss's results climbed so rapidly that Zayre began to think of expanding its off-price upscale apparel merchandising.

Zayre first attempted to buy the Marshalls chain, which had already established itself as a retailer of off-price apparel for the whole family. When that effort failed, the company hired Bernard Cammarata, who had been Marshalls' top buyer, to essentially create a Marshalls clone. In Auburn, Massachusetts, in March 1977, he opened the first T.J. Maxx.

Within six years of that opening, Zayre had found yet another avenue to the off-price fashion market. In 1983 Chadwick's of Boston began to sell selected Hit or Miss items through mail-order catalogs. Hit or Miss and Chadwick's crossover operations allowed customers to handle products before ordering, and brought the frequent buyer the convenience of home shopping.

By the mid-1980s off-price specialty retailing was becoming more important to Zayre. Hit or Miss and T.J. Maxx had brought in just 14 percent of the company's operating income in 1980; by the first half of 1983 these operations were producing nearly 45 percent of income. At the same time, however, Zayre was renovating its discount department stores and expanding its product mix. In 1984 Zayre entered the membership warehouse-club market, launching B.J.'s Wholesale Club, and also acquired Home Club, Inc., a chain of home improvement stores, the following year. While neither of these ventures was immediately profitable, Hit or Miss and T.J. Maxx continued to thrive.

By 1986 the number of Hit or Miss stores in the United States had reached 420, and sales had climbed to $300 million. Some 70 percent of its inventory was made up of nationally known brands. The remaining 30 percent consisted of standard apparel, such as turtlenecks and corduroy pants, which were produced by Hit or Miss under its own private label. With such a merchandise mix, Hit or Miss was able to sell current fashion at 20 to 50 percent less than most specialty stores.

In 1986 profits of the Zayre chain, targeting low- to middle-income customers, dropped, although T.J. Maxx, Hit or Miss, and Chadwick's of Boston, targeting mid- to higher-income customers, continued to grow. That year alone, Zayre Corp. opened 35 more T.J. Maxx stores and 31 new Hit or Miss stores. In fact, Zayre Corp.'s off-price retailing chains were so successful that by 1987 Zayre thought it prudent to organize them under one name and grant them autonomy from the decreasingly prosperous parent company.

Establishment of TJX Companies and Divestment of Zayre

In June 1987 just ten years after its flagship chain, T.J. Maxx, opened its first store, The TJX Companies, Inc. was established as a subsidiary of Zayre, with Cammarata serving as president and CEO. It sold 9.35 million shares of common stock in its initial public offering; Zayre owned 83 percent of the subsidiary.

During this time, Zayre was facing several challenges. In the first half of 1988, Zayre had operating losses of $69 million on sales of $1.4 billion. Observers blamed technological inferiority, poor maintenance, inappropriate pricing, and inventory pileups, and speculated Zayre was ripe for takeover. Throughout all this, subsidiary TJX Companies continued to yield a profit.

In October 1988 the company decided to focus on TJX. It sold the entire chain of over 400 Zayre Stores to Ames Department Stores, Inc. In exchange, the company received $431.4 million in cash, a receivable note, and what was then valued at $140 million of Ames cumulative senior convertible preferred stock.

The company continued to hone in on its profitable new core business, selling unrelated operations. In June 1989 it spun off its warehouse club division, Waban, Inc., which owned B.J.'s and Home Club. Zayre gave shareholders one share of Waban for each two shares of Zayre they owned, as well as a $3.50 per share cash payment. The same month, the company acquired an outstanding minority interest in TJX. On the day it acquired the minority interest, the company merged with TJX. Later that month, the company changed its name from Zayre Corp. to The TJX Companies, Inc. The newly named company, headed by Cammarata, began trading on the New York Stock Exchange.

The company's transition into an off-price fashion business was relatively smooth, but the Ames preferred stock it received in the Zayre transaction had been a problem. This preferred stock was not registered and had no active market. While the stock was entitled to 6 percent annual dividends, Ames had the option of paying the first four semiannual dividends with more Ames preferred stock rather than cash, an option that Ames exercised for each of the payments it had met. The value of Ames preferred stock was dubious, however, as Ames had been closing stores and experiencing losses.

In April 1990, TJX established a $185 million reserve against its Ames preferred stock and contingent lease liabilities on former Zayre stores as a result of Ames's announcement of continued poor performance. That same month, Ames filed for protection from creditors under Chapter 11 of the U.S. Bankruptcy Code.

Early to Mid-1990s: Winners and Losers, Hits and Misses

On a bright note, TJX's operations remained solid. In 1991 T.J. Maxx, by far the company's largest division, posted record results for the 15th consecutive year since it opened. At the end of 1991 T.J. Maxx had 437 stores in 46 states. It planned to open many more stores, focusing primarily on the only sparsely penetrated southwestern United States, as well as expanding several existing stores. T.J. Maxx also planned to follow its success in jewelry and shoes by opening these respective departments at locations that did not carry these items. It also planned to expand high-performance nonapparel categories, such as giftware and domestic items. In addition, T.J. Maxx embarked on an effort to enlarge a number of stores to a larger format ranging from 30,000 to 40,000 square feet. This change facilitated expansion of all departments, especially giftware and housewares, as well as other nonapparel categories. T.J. Maxx opened 21 stores during 1996 and closed 30. The chain recorded excellent sales in 1996, which increased 5 percent over the previous year.

The November 1995 purchase of Marshalls from the Melville Corporation for $606 million in cash and preferred stock brought TJX a prize to complement T.J. Maxx. The immediate plan called for closing certain underperforming T.J. Maxx and Marshalls stores. Marshalls opened 11 stores in 1996 and closed 53. Sales at Marshalls rose 10 percent in 1996. Fifteen openings and 50 closings were planned for 1997; more were not expected, because many of the existing stores had performed so well. TJX credited this success with its back-to-basics approach. The prior Marshall ownership had strayed from off-price strategies, so TJX refocused the business. It emphasized nonpromotional marketing, quality brand names at low prices, and timely markdowns—to draw customers back and strongly.

Success at T.J. Maxx and Marshalls hinged on execution of the off-price concept, which demanded rapid inventory turnover at the store level. "Opportunistic buying" was done "in season," that is, close to customer need. Merchandise moved into warehouses and out to stores through state-of-the-art distribution centers and sophisticated inventory tracking systems. In effect, each of the 1,000-plus stores received two shipments of merchandise with a total of 10,000 items. Markdowns also played a major role, adding value for customers and clearing shelves. Despite the similarities in operations, TJX was determined that T.J. Maxx and Marshalls retain distinct identities.

TJX ventured into Canada in 1990 to acquire the five-store Winners Apparel Ltd. chain. Building on the off-price concept, similar to that of T.J. Maxx, Winners opened 13 stores in 1996, bringing its total to 65. Moreover, Winners planned on opening about 13 more stores in 1997. TJX viewed Winners as a meaningful way to expand over the next several years—about 12 new stores per year. In fact, store sales posted an increase of 13 percent in 1996, plus an increase in operating income of 114 percent.

T.K. Maxx, launched in 1994 and also inspired by the T.J. Maxx concept, caught on in the United Kingdom in 1996. Comparable store sales increased by 30 percent, outperforming any predicted sales figures. This move abroad proved that further expansion was key to TJX's growth strategy.

Not all the news among TJX holdings was good. Despite concerted efforts to bolster merchandise assortment and value, sales flagged at TJX's HomeGoods chain, which had launched as an off-price home fashions retailer. Moreover, Hit or Miss had a difficult time in the early 1990s, transitioning its business in a recessionary economy. After closing many nonperforming stores and renovating others, TJX sold this women's specialty division in September 1995 to the division's management and outside investors.

In late 1996 the company also sold its Chadwick's of Boston catalog division to Brylane L.P., owner of the Lane Bryant women's fashion chain. Proceeds from the sale totaled about $300 million in cash, a note, and certain receivables. The after-tax gain enabled TJX to repay about $500 million of debt, including the debt incurred in relation to the 1995 acquisition of Marshalls. The transaction left TJX with a stronger cash position and in a position of greater flexibility. Overall, 1996 was a banner year for The TJX Companies. Sales from continuing operations hit $6.69 billion, up from $3.98 billion in 1995, fueled largely by the Marshalls acquisition and the economies of scale it allowed TJX to achieve.

A Growing Off-Price Empire into the New Century

The late 1990s saw TJX leveraging the strong performance of its main chains into the launching of experimental new hybrid formats as well as brand-new chains. Having improved the performance of HomeGoods, in part by tweaking the merchandise mix—eliminating appliances and emphasizing home decorating items—the company began testing superstore concepts that combined HomeGoods with the T.J. Maxx and Marshalls formats. By the end of 1998 there were 14 of these larger, 50,000-square-foot superstores, known as T.J. Maxx 'N More and Marshalls Mega-Stores, respectively, and these units were performing well. That year, TJX opened two T.K. Maxx stores in The Netherlands as a first tentative step onto continental Europe. These stores got off to a slower than anticipated start.

The company also launched A.J. Wright in 1998, opening six stores in New England. This marked the firm's first attempt to create an off-price family clothing store for the moderate income consumer.

As T.J. Maxx, Marshalls, and Winners continued their consistently profitable performance in the late 1990s, the HomeGoods and T.K. Maxx operations finally turned the corner into profitability in 1999. Nine more A.J. Wright outlets opened their doors in 1999, although that division remained in the red and the company still had much to learn about this new segment of the market. Overall, net sales reached $8.8 billion, with more than 88 percent attributable to T.J. Maxx and Marshalls. Cammarata took on the additional post of chairman that year, while Ted English was named president and COO. The following year, English was promoted to president and CEO, with Cammarata remaining chairman. English had joined TJX in 1983 as a buyer to T.J. Maxx, having previously worked for several years at Filene's Basement, the Boston-based off-price pioneer.

TJX maintained its growth path into the new century. During 2000 alone, the T.J. Maxx store count increased by 29, both Marshalls and HomeGoods by 30, A.J. Wright by 10, Winners by 17, and T.K. Maxx by 20. Another 172 stores were added to the overall store count during 2001, although TJX did take one step backward that year, closing its three T.K. Maxx stores in The Netherlands because of their disappointing results. That year TJX rolled out its latest new concept: a new Canadian chain called HomeSense, which was modeled after HomeGoods. Seven HomeSense stores began operating in 2001, all located in Ontario, and company officials were very pleased with their initial performance. Even in the poor economic environment of 2001 and with the post-9/11 effects on consumer spending, TJX still managed to increase revenues 12 percent, to $10.71 billion, surpassing the $10 billion mark for the first time. Net income did fall slightly, however, dropping to $500.4 million from $538.1 million. The TJX Companies were also more personally affected by the events of September 11, 2001. Seven company employees, traveling on business, died when their jetliner crashed into the World Trade Center.

During another year of economic uncertainty and worldwide geopolitical disturbance, TJX once again managed to achieve a 12 percent jump in revenues during 2002. All seven of the company's formats were expanded; overall, the firm added 178 stores, bringing the total count to 1,843. The only unprofitable operation was A.J. Wright, but the company expressed high hopes for the young chain, which was already 75 units strong. The TJX Companies had plenty of additional growth potential. The company projected that by the early 2010s, it could be operating in excess of 4,300 stores: 1,800 T.J. Maxx and Marshalls stores, 650 HomeGoods, more than 1,000 A.J. Wrights, 200 Winners, 80 HomeSense units, and 300 to 600 T.K. Maxx outlets. This was just with the current portfolio of stores. TJX was sitting on a pile of cash and had long been

expected to pursue additional acquisitions. Targets were expected to include both large chains that retained some growth potential and smaller ones needing capital to fund expansion.

Principal Divisions

T.J. Maxx; HomeGoods; Marshalls; A.J. Wright; HomeSense (Canada); Winners (Canada); T.K. Maxx (U.K.).

Principal Competitors

Federated Department Stores, Inc.; The May Department Stores Company; Target Corporation; J.C. Penney Corporation, Inc.; Sears, Roebuck and Co.; The Gap, Inc.; Kohl's Corporation; Wal-Mart Stores, Inc.; Kmart Corporation; Limited Brands, Inc.; Ross Stores, Inc.; Value City Department Stores, Inc.

Further Reading

Brady, Jennifer, "Melville to Sell Marshalls to TJX for $550 Million," *Daily News Record,* October 17, 1995, p. 3.

Chanko, Kenneth M., "Zayre Corp. Spin-off, Merger Lays Groundwork for Future Growth," *Discount Store News,* December 19, 1988, pp. 5 +.

Duff, Mike, "Resilient Record Bodes Well for Off-Price Leader," *DSN Retailing Today,* December 10, 2001, pp. 31, 32.

——, "TJX to Try New Formats, Expand Home Business," *Discount Store News,* June 22, 1998, pp. 3, 4.

——, "TJX Ups Expansion to Increase Earnings," *DSN Retailing Today,* June 18, 2001, pp. 2, 44.

——, "TJX Won't Rest on Laurels," *Discount Store News,* June 21, 1999, pp. 3, 54.

Lillo, Andrea, "TJX Maps Out Expansion Plans," *Home Textiles Today,* June 10, 2002, pp. 1, 27.

Mammarella, James, "T.J. Maxx/Marshalls Upsets Marketplace," *Discount Store News,* January 1, 1996, pp. 3, 54.

——, "TJX Diversifies, Adapts, and Survives," *Discount Store News,* February 20, 1995, pp. 19–20.

Pereira, Joseph, "TJX Tailor-Makes a Marshalls Plan to Revitalize Retailer," *Wall Street Journal,* October 8, 1996, p. B4.

Reidy, Chris, "TJX Named Company of the Year: Here, Only Profits Have Big Markups," *Boston Globe,* May 20, 1997, p. C1.

Rudnitsky, Howard, "The King of Off-Price," *Forbes,* January 31, 1994, pp. 54 +.

Smith, Geoffrey, "Can TJX Turn Off-Price On?" *Business Week,* October 30, 1995, p. 44.

"TJX Adjusting Well to Its Megachain Size," *Discount Store News,* June 17, 1996, p. 1.

"TJX Cos. Steamrolls to Front of Off-Price Pack," *Discount Store News,* July 4, 1988, p. 151.

"TJX Needs to Be Better Than Better," *Discount Store News,* March 3, 1997, pp. 6, 28.

—Maya Sahafi
—updates: Catherine Hamrick, David E. Salamie

Toys "R" Us, Inc.

461 From Road
Paramus, New Jersey 07652-3526
U.S.A.
Telephone: (201) 262-7800
Fax: (201) 262-8112
Web site: http://www.toysrusinc.com

Public Company
Incorporated: 1978
Employees: 65,000
Sales: $11.07 billion (2002)
Stock Exchanges: New York
Ticker Symbol: TOY
NAIC: 451120 Hobby, Toy, and Game Stores; 448130
   Children's and Infants' Clothing Stores; 454111
   Electronic Shopping

Toys "R" Us, Inc. is one of the world's leading retailers of toys, children's clothing, and baby products. Although Toys "R" Us stood as the only nationwide toy store chain in the United States in the early 2000s, it was no longer the nation's leading seller of toys, having lost that position to retailing behemoth Wal-Mart Stores, Inc. in 1999. Of the company's more than 1,000 U.S. locations, 681 were general toy stores under the flagship Toys "R" Us name, 183 specialized in infant and toddler products under the Babies "R" Us banner, 146 were children's clothing outlets under the Kids "R" Us brand, and 37 operated as educational specialty stores under the Imaginarium moniker. There were also four Geoffrey stores featuring products from all three of the "R" Us formats. The company operated, licensed, or franchised an additional 544 toy stores in 29 foreign countries, headed by Japan, the United Kingdom, Canada, Germany, France, Spain, and Australia. Toys "R" Us, Inc. also sold its products online through toysrus.com and other web sites, with this online retailing conducted via an alliance with Amazon.com, Inc.

Toys "R" Us Meets Interstate, 1952–79

Toys "R" Us founder Charles Lazarus was born above a Washington, D.C., shop where his father repaired and sold used bicycles. In 1948, after a stint in the Army, Lazarus began selling baby furniture in his father's shop, using as seed capital $5,000 from a combination of savings and a bank loan. This was just two years after the beginning of the baby boom, and Lazarus aimed to attract as customers the families of GIs coming home from World War II. Noting that customers often asked if he sold toys, Lazarus began adding rattles and stuffed animals to his stock within a year. The bike shop was eventually renamed Children's Supermart. In 1952 he opened the Baby Furniture and Toy Supermarket in Washington, D.C.; five years later he opened a discount toy supermarket in Rockville, Maryland, the first to bear the abbreviated Toys "R" Us name (the store's original name would not fit on its sign). By 1965 Lazarus operated four such outlets in the Washington, D.C., area, and the next year, when revenues had increased to $12 million, he sold the profitable toy supermarkets to Interstate Stores Inc. for $7.5 million but continued to run the toy business that he had created.

Founded in 1916, Interstate became publicly owned in 1927. With 46 small department stores in its fold by 1957, sales growth had dwindled to almost nothing, and profit margins were shrinking. The company sought relief for its financial woes in the burgeoning discount store arena by experimenting with a discount store in Allentown, Pennsylvania. By 1960 it had acquired two discount chains: the White Front Stores in southern California and the Topps chain, located mainly in New England.

Interstate undertook an aggressive but ill-fated expansion, overextending itself, and the 1973–74 recession aggravated its problems. In 1974 Interstate declared bankruptcy, its debt at the time the largest accumulation of liabilities in retail history. By that year Interstate had 51 Toys "R" Us stores, and it continued to open new ones during its court-ordered reorganization. Before 1974 Toys "R" Us was still ordering and counting stock manually, but that year the company streamlined its ordering and inventory system by installing its first computer mainframe. In years to come the company would upgrade its computer system many times to keep pace with its ever-growing sales volume and inventory level.

In 1978 Interstate emerged from its reorganization a vastly different company. It had closed or sold all of its discount store operations; only the 63-store toy chain and ten traditional department stores remained. To reflect its principal business, the company had changed its name to Toys "R" Us, Inc., with Lazarus serving as its president and CEO.

Toys "R" Us Taking Off: 1980–85

Lazarus's approach to pricing was vastly different from that of his competitors: he sold the items shoppers wanted most at little or no profit. Customers then automatically assumed most of the store's items were equally well-priced and did the rest of their shopping there. By 1980 Toys "R" Us had earned a solid reputation as a retailer of great efficiency, with 101 stores around the country. Since its reorganization three years earlier, sales had more than doubled to nearly $750 million in fiscal 1981, a year in which many toy sellers suffered, especially during the holiday season.

There seemed to be no serious threat to the company's growing dominance of the retail toy market—with its 120 stores—and executives were often quoted as saying they sought not so much to boost sales as to increase market share, which Toys "R" Us did from 5 percent in 1978 to 9 percent in 1981. The following year as rival Lionel Leisure, a chain of 98 toy stores, filed for bankruptcy, Toys "R" Us announced the formation of a new division to sell name-brand children's apparel at discount prices. The company had first-hand experience with the baby boom generation's willingness to spend money on their children and opened two pilot Kids "R" Us stores in the New York metropolitan area during the summer of 1983. The 15,000-square-foot exuberantly decorated stores featured electronic games and clearly marked departments. From the day the first Kids "R" Us stores opened, owners of department and specialty stores recognized them as a major threat to their survival.

All was not easy for Kids "R" Us, however. In the 1980s traditional department stores and small children's shops complained that name-brand apparel makers were selling their goods to discounters; new competition from Kids "R" Us further raised the stakes. Just a few months after Kids "R" Us opened its first two stores, Toys "R" Us filed suit in September 1983 against Federated Department Stores Inc. and General Mills, Inc., charging the companies with price-fixing. The following month, the company brought a similar suit against Absorba, which had agreed to supply the new stores, but later allegedly refused to fill the orders. Toys "R" Us later dropped the suits, noting only that circumstances had made it prudent to terminate litigation.

The Kids "R" Us concept successfully implemented many of the policies Toys "R" Us had, such as discount pricing, tight inventory control, purchasing in large volume, and opening stores in low-rent strip malls along major thoroughfares. In

1983 the company surpassed the $1 billion milestone, with sales of $1.3 billion. The following year was full of firsts for Toys "R" Us, beginning with its first foray outside the United States in 1984, with four Toys "R" Us stores in Canada and one in Singapore; two more Kids "R" Us stores (with an additional 5,000 square feet) in New Jersey; and a generous stock option plan open to all full-time employees. Lazarus later told *Dun's Business Month* that salaries alone were no longer enough to make people feel they had a stake in a company's success.

By the spring of 1985 there were ten Kids "R" Us units in New York and New Jersey with an additional 15 to be opened by year's end, while five Toys "R" Us stores opened in the United Kingdom. In early 1986 *Dun's Business Month* cited Toys "R" Us as one of the nation's best-managed companies and credited Lazarus with developing an extraordinary management team (most of whom were promoted from within). Between 1980 and 1985 the toy retailing industry grew 37 percent, while sales at Toys "R" Us surged by 185 percent, leading the company to estimate that it had 14 percent of all U.S. retail toy sales, an increase of 9 percent from its share just seven years earlier when the company had emerged from its reorganization.

A Burgeoning Empire: 1986–91

Charles Lazarus believed market share was his company's number one priority; to keep increasing market share he was even willing to cut prices—at the expense of earnings. Yet perhaps earnings did not need to suffer, because Toys "R" Us had the "ultimate marketing research tool," the company's highly computerized merchandising system. By January 1986 Toys "R" Us had 233 toy stores in the United States, 13 international stores, 23 Kids "R" Us outlets, and four traditional department stores. Moreover, as it grew into a national chain, the company aggressively fought others using an "R" in their name—Tots "R" Us, Lamps "R" Us, and Films "R" Us were among the companies successfully sued by Toys "R" Us for name infringement, a practice the company maintained for years to come.

During the summer of 1986 Toys "R" Us and Montgomery Ward announced a joint venture to begin in Gaithersburg, Maryland, that fall. Each store would operate independently, but would share an entrance and exterior sign. The arrangement was a boon to Ward, which had restructured its business and had surplus floor space in many of its locations. Toys "R" Us found the arrangement beneficial, too, because many of the Ward stores were in excellent locations and rental rates were often quite reasonable. During the 1986 Christmas season, the company's sales far exceeded many analysts' grim forecasts. Its success was attributed to its ability to consistently offer the toys shoppers were most interested in buying. By 1987 the company had 37 additional domestic Toys "R" Us stores, 11 new overseas outlets, and 14 new Kids "R" Us stores; its market share now stood at 15 percent of the $12 billion toy industry.

Even when toy sales were sluggish, Toys "R" Us managed to perform well. In another bid to further increase its market share, the company surprised the retailing industry in 1987 by announcing that it would pass on the savings it expected from lower tax rates to customers. Two additional retailers, Wal-Mart and Target, quickly followed the company's lead. This was also the year the Toys "R" Us international division moved into the

---

Key Dates:

1948: Charles Lazarus begins selling baby furniture at his father's bike shop in Washington, D.C.; toys are soon added to the stock, and the shop is renamed Children's Supermart.

1952: Lazarus opens his first Baby Furniture and Toy Supermarket.

1957: Lazarus begins operating his discount toy supermarkets under the Toys ''R'' Us name, with an outlet in Rockville, Maryland, being the first so christened.

1966: Lazarus sells his four Toys ''R'' Us stores to Interstate Stores Inc., but he continues to manage the chain.

1974: Interstate is forced to declare bankruptcy; at the time there are 51 Toys ''R'' Us outlets.

1978: Having shed most of its other retail units, Interstate emerges from bankruptcy with 63 toy stores; the company, now led by Lazarus, is renamed Toys ''R'' Us, Inc.

1983: Company opens its first Kids ''R'' Us children's apparel stores; sales surpass $1 billion.

1984: First international stores open in Canada and Singapore.

1996: The Babies ''R'' Us chain is launched.

1997: Toys ''R'' Us acquires Baby Superstore, Inc. for $376 million; its 78 stores are converted to the Babies ''R'' Us format.

1998: Company begins selling toys online and launches a huge restructuring.

1999: The Imaginarium educational toy store chain is acquired.

2000: Strategic alliance is entered into with Amazon.com to combine the two companies' toy and video-game online stores.

---

black, and the company opened four stores in as many German cities. Although there were plans to open even more stores during the year, it proved difficult to secure the required permits for a retail outlet larger than 18,000 square feet. Competing German retailers had good reason for concern; in the United Kingdom, Toys ''R'' Us had captured 9 percent of the $1.8 billion toy market in just three years. The products of two prestigious German toy manufacturers, Steiff and Maerklin, were not sold in the new German Toys ''R'' Us stores. Steiff, maker of high-quality stuffed animals and dolls, chose not to do business with the toy giant out of loyalty to smaller-scale German retailers while Maerklin's electric trains, sold without packaging, could not be offered in a toy supermarket setting.

From the very start Toys ''R'' Us overseas stores were strikingly similar to those in the United States. Most were freestanding buildings, and all bulged with many of the 18,000 items for which Toys ''R'' Us was famous. Approximately 80 percent of the items offered were the same as those found in U.S. stores, with the remaining 20 percent chosen to reflect local interests. Sales for fiscal 1987, the first year in which Kids ''R'' Us earned a profit, surpassed $3 billion. The company attributed part of its success to its upgraded universal product code (UPC) scanning system, which had been installed in all the Toys ''R'' Us stores shortly before Thanksgiving.

By January 1988 the company had 313 U.S. toy stores, 74 Kids ''R'' Us outlets, and 37 international toy stores. Plans to open stores in Italy and France were also in the offing. In August, Lazarus told the *Wall Street Journal* his goal was to sell half of all toys sold in the United States. While this may have sounded overly ambitious, signs abounded that Lazarus was well on the way to meeting his goal. Even though toy sales in 1986 and 1987 grew an average of 2 percent, sales at Toys ''R'' Us grew 27 percent during each of those years. The toy chain consistently proved itself capable of turning away all pretenders to the throne of top toy retailer. Its two nearest rivals, Child World Inc., with 152 stores and Lionel, with 78, offered similarly large toy selections in equally cavernous structures, but neither had been able to equal the success of the originator of the toy supermarket concept.

Something else Toys ''R'' Us had was a healthy sense of humor about itself and the industry, as when a Florida newspaper published a cartoon during the 1987 holiday season showing a couple burdened with many gifts leaving a Toys ''R'' Us store. The caption beneath the cartoon read ''Broke 'R' Us.'' Company executives thought it was so funny that copies were posted throughout their offices.

The company's success was attributed to many factors, including its buying clout, great selection, deep inventories, and ability to identify the latest hot items and get them on the sales floor fast. When some companies' stores were finding it difficult to get sufficient quantities of Nintendo games in early 1988, for instance, Toys ''R'' Us was able to get the number of Nintendo games it wanted. It was reported in the *Wall Street Journal* that Toys ''R'' Us sold $330.80 worth of merchandise per square foot annually, with Child World selling only $221.70, and Lionel just $193.10. Average sales for a Toys ''R'' Us store were $8.4 million; Child World, $4.9 million; and for Lionel, $4.4 million.

In the fall of 1988 Toys ''R'' Us shed the last reminder of its connection to Interstate Stores by selling the remaining department stores in Albany and Schenectady, New York, and Flint, Michigan, to that division's management. Company sales hit the $4 billion mark in fiscal 1988, and by the fall of the following year Toys ''R'' Us joined McDonald's Company (Japan) Ltd. to open several toy stores in Japan. Toys ''R'' Us would have an 80 percent interest in the venture to McDonald's 20 percent with an option to open restaurants at the store sites. During the holiday season in 1989, Toys ''R'' Us launched Geoffrey's Fun Club as a low-key, noncommercial club sending quarterly mailings featuring items such as an activity booklet with a family member's name or a storybook that presented a family child as the main character, with his or her name repeated throughout the book. The club, designed to boost the company's profile in members' homes, more than doubled original membership projections. Total sales for the year were more than $4.7 billion, with a 25 percent market share of the $13 billion U.S. retail toy market.

Lazarus told *Forbes* there would always be ''room in this tightly controlled company for innovations to further decrease operating costs." An instance of this came in 1989 when Toys "R" Us completed installation of gravity-feed-flow racks in most of its U.S. toy stores for restocking fast-moving items such as diapers and formula. Yet as every rose has its thorns, Toys "R" Us ran into some trouble in the early part of the 1990s. First came difficulties with the Consumer Product Safety Commission for importing toys it deemed dangerous. In the spring of 1990 the company recalled 38,000 "Press N Roll" toy boats with small parts that, if broken off, could choke a child. A few months later, Toys "R" Us was named as one of seven distributors sued by the Justice Department on charges of selling hazardous toys (including a xylophone painted with lead-based paint, and the aforementioned toys with unsafe, small parts). Yet Toys "R" Us successfully defended itself on the grounds that its safety record was excellent, and a federal judge dismissed the charges.

By the end of 1990 the company had a new $40 million distribution center in Rialto, California, that held 45 percent more merchandise than the company's other warehouses, but took up one-third less land. The company finished the year with sales topping $5.5 billion and net earnings reaching $326 million. An industry analyst, impressed by the company's solid sales and consistency, remarked to the *Wall Street Transcript,* "I can look at a slowing economy and still feel comfortable that Toys 'R' Us is going to grow." And grow it did, especially overseas. Although difficulties in finding store sites and circumventing the large-scale retail law still loomed before Toys "R" Us and McDonald's, the Japanese joint venture moved ahead with plans for up to 100 stores by the end of the decade. For other U.S. retailers interested in opening outlets in Japan, Toys "R" Us became a test case in how to overcome local retailers' resistance. Japanese retailers had already felt the pinch of a declining birthrate since 1973 and did not relish a further erosion of their market share. U.S. officials, however, persuaded Japanese officials to speed up their approval process on applications for large retail stores, and the first Toys "R" Us opened in Ami Town on the outskirts of Tokyo in 1991.

Overseas Growth and Debut of Babies "R" Us: 1992–97

Over the next few years, Toys "R" Us continued to expand in high gear, especially overseas. Once operating in a handful of countries worldwide, company stores now popped up all over the globe, in Hong Kong, Israel, the Netherlands, Portugal, Scandinavia, Sweden, and Turkey, while the heaviest concentrations were in Australia, Canada, France, Germany, Japan, Spain, and the United Kingdom. Consequently, Toys "R" Us's annual figures reflected this steady growth: fiscal 1992 sales reached $7.2 billion; 1993, $7.9 billion; and a big leap in 1994 to $8.7 billion. Similarly, earnings climbed from 1992's $438 million to 1994's $532 million. In early 1994, there was also a changing of the guard: Charles Lazarus, the company's longtime chairman and CEO, turned the duties of the latter over to Michael Goldstein, vice-chairman; and Robert Nakasone, formerly president of worldwide stores, was appointed president and COO.

In 1995 the company's sales once again soared to $9.4 billion (helped in part by the introduction of educational and entertaining computer software), yet earnings were heavily slashed ($148 million) due to restructuring costs and grand

plans for the near future. As Toys "R" Us looked to the new century, the company was determined to become the ultimate "one-stop kid's shop." To further this plan, the company adopted several ambitious programs to take Toys "R" Us to the end of the 1990s and beyond. First and foremost was restructuring, which included streamlining merchandise by up to 20 percent, closure of 25 underperforming stores, and the consolidation of several distribution centers and administrative facilities domestically and overseas. In addition, there would be new Kids "R" Us stores, the debut of Babies "R" Us and superstores, and the introduction of "Concept 2000," for new and renovated Toys "R" Us stores—all to provide "the ultimate kids shopping experience."

The first three Babies "R" Us stores, each measuring about 45,000 square feet, opened in 1996 with an additional seven planned before the end of the year. Like its siblings, Babies "R" Us stores were filled to the brim—with clothes, juvenile furniture, carseats, and feeding and infant care supplies. Like better department stores, Babies "R" Us also offered a computerized national gift registry. At the same time, the first Concept 2000 toy store, one of 12 announced for the year, debuted in July. The Concept 2000 facility was a megastore of 96,000 square feet, replacing the formerly successful supermarket setup with an oval format with color-coordinated departments, lower shelving, a Bike Shop, learning centers, and special sections for Barbies, Legos, and video games. Moreover, the company also introduced experimental superstores (the first one, Toys "R" Us Kids World, opened in November 1996 near company headquarters in New Jersey) combining the inventories of Kids "R" Us and Babies "R" Us with a multitude of top-of-the-line toys. Superstores were slated to include fast food, candy shops, hair salons, photo studios, party rooms, and possibly even rides such as carousels and Ferris wheels.

In February 1997 Toys "R" Us acquired Baby Superstore, Inc., a 78-store chain based in Duncan, South Carolina, for $376 million. By the end of 1997 the acquired stores had been converted to the Babies "R" Us format, and the company had instantly transformed a fledgling brand into the largest retailer of baby products in the country. With the opening of a number of brand-new Babies "R" Us outlets in time for the 1997 holiday season, the store count neared the 100-unit mark. Sales for the chain were already in excess of $600 million.

Struggling amid Heightened Competition: 1998 to Early 2000s

The successful launch of Babies "R" Us was offset by a host of problems that together had stopped the company's momentum in its tracks. Throughout the 1990s Toys "R" Us faced steadily growing competition from the discount chains, principally Wal-Mart but also Target and others. Wal-Mart had avoided the low-margin toy sector for years, but in 1990 the discount giant began stocking up on the hottest selling toys and used them as loss leaders to get customers into its stores. Target followed suit. In addition, warehouse clubs, such as Costco, began adding toys to their vast offerings and selling them at low prices. At the same time as it was facing pricing pressure from these new and burgeoning competitors, Toys "R" Us also had to contend with new competition in the form of smaller toy chains specializing in so-called edutainment products. In addition to their more specializing inventory, Zany Brainy, Noodle Kidoodle, and Imaginarium, among others, offered their customers superior customer service (as did the typical mom-and-pop toy store) and a more appealing store environment. Toys "R" Us was notorious for its poor customer service; it had been able to neglect this side of its operations for a long time because its customers could generally find any toy they were looking for and get it at a decent price. In the mid- to late 1990s, however, customers had a whole array of other options (including the growing number of online toy retailers), many of which provided better customer service and lower prices. The end result of this new competitive situation was a steady decline in Toys "R" Us's U.S. market share—from 25.4 percent in 1990 to 18.4 percent in 1997. During the same period, Wal-Mart increased its share from 9.5 percent to 16.4 percent. Furthermore, the trend toward lower prices cut Toys "R" Us's profits, and the firm saw its operating margins fall from 12 percent to 8 percent from fiscal 1993 to fiscal 1997.

The entrance of warehouse clubs into the toy sector led to another problem. An administrative law judge with the Federal Trade Commission (FTC) ruled in late 1997 that Toys "R" Us had illegally pressured manufacturers to keep certain popular toys out of the warehouse clubs. The company vigorously denied the charges and appealed the decision, eventually settling with the FTC for $40.5 million.

By early 1998, most of the recent initiatives—the exception being Babies "R" Us—had proven to be failures. By that time, only 15 percent of Toys "R" Us units had been converted to the Concept 2000 format, which had not led to the gains in sales that were expected. The Kids World superstores proved to be too large for the sales they were generating, and the format was soon abandoned. In addition, the 200-plus-unit Kids "R" Us chain was struggling in the face of stiff competition from department stores, specialty retailers, and the discount chains. At the same time that the company reported lackluster earnings for the fiscal year ending in January 1998, it also announced a management shuffle. Goldstein was bumped up to the chairman's seat, while Nakasone was named CEO; Lazarus remained on the board as chairman emeritus.

Under Nakasone's leadership, Toys "R" Us soon launched its largest revamp in history. In September 1998 the company announced a restructuring involving a huge inventory reduction; the closure of 59 underperforming Toys "R" Us stores—nine in the United States and the remainder mainly in Germany and France—as well as the shuttering of 31 Kids "R" Us units; and a workforce reduction of 3,000, or 2.6 percent. Restructuring charges for the year ending in January 1999 totaled $353 million, resulting in a net loss for the year of $132 million.

The company also began testing another new format for its flagship Toys "R" Us outlets, this one dubbed C-3 (the three C's being "customer friendly," "cost effective," and "concept with a long-term vision"). This format featured the racetrack-like style prevalent at discount chains, doing away with the aisle after aisle of ceiling-high warehouse shelving. There was colorful signage throughout the store and a number of new departments that were aimed at broadening the product range. These included deal/seasonal; baby apparel; Animal Alley, showcasing a large selection of private-label stuffed animals; the

Learning Center, which featured educational and developmental products for young children through the kindergarten age; and the "R" Zone, a glass-enclosed section with computer, electronic, and video products for children aged nine and above. The format also had 20 percent more floor space thanks to a one-third reduction in the stock room.

There were other new initiatives as well. In 1998 the company joined the online retailing boom with the launch of the toysrus.com web site, and the firm also produced its first mail-order catalog. In August 1999 the company spent $43 million to purchase Imaginarium Toy Centers, Inc., a specialty retailer focusing on educational toys with 41 stores in 13 states. The deal provided Toys "R" Us access to the higher end of the market, which carried higher profit margins and was growing at a rapid clip; it also led to the opening of Imaginarium departments within remodeled Toys "R" Us stores. Just days after this acquisition was finalized, Nakasone was forced to resign after clashing with the board of directors—particularly with his two predecessors, Goldstein and Lazarus. Further bad news came on the competition front that year as Wal-Mart surpassed Toys "R" Us as the leading U.S. toy retailer. In addition, the Christmas season was a near-disaster as the toy stores ran out of stock on some of the season's most sought-after items and toysrus.com failed to deliver a number of online orders by December 25.

Stepping in to attempt to turn around the company's flagging fortunes was John Eyler, who was named president and CEO in January 2000 (and chairman in June 2001). Eyler was hired away from specialty toy retailer F.A.O. Schwartz, where he had served as CEO and chairman for nine years. The new chief continued the rollout of the new C-3 format. By early 2001, 165 Toys "R" Us stores had been converted, and initial results showed an increase in sales. One year later, 433 of the U.S. toy stores featured the new format, now dubbed "Mission Possible." At the same time, new "combo" stores were being created—essentially Toys "R" Us outlets with a select assortment of Kids "R" Us merchandise; there were 273 of these combo stores by early 2002. Eyler also began working with toy manufacturers to secure more exclusive products for the Toys "R" Us shelves. Sales of exclusive products soon rose from 5 percent to 12 percent of overall revenues, reaching 20 percent in 2002.

Meanwhile, in April 2000, Toys "R" Us Japan was taken public through an IPO that raised $315 million for the company and took the division's large debt off the parent company's balance sheet. The transaction reduced the company's stake in the Japanese affiliate from 80 percent to 48 percent. In August 2000 Toys "R" Us entered into a ten-year strategic alliance with Amazon.com whereby the two firms united their online toy and video-game stores. Amazon.com took responsibility for web site development, customer service, order fulfillment, and warehousing of goods, while Toys "R" Us would handle purchasing and managing the inventory. The following year, babiesrus.com was shifted into the Amazon.com alliance platform, and imaginarium.com was launched.

In November 2001 Toys "R" Us opened its international flagship store in New York City's Times Square. Occupying 110,000 square feet, the three-story store featured, in addition to a huge assortment of merchandise, a 60-foot Ferris wheel, a 20-

foot-tall animatronic T-Rex dinosaur from *Jurassic Park,* and a two-story, 4,400-square-foot doll house filled with Barbie gear. The flagship store was intended to revitalize Toys "R" Us by providing a new image for what was widely considered to be a tired chain. Toward this same end, the company launched an advertising campaign featuring a new animatronic Geoffrey the Giraffe, the longtime Toys "R" Us mascot who had made his first appearance in 1960. In another 2001 initiative, the company began testing out small Toys "R" Us Toy Box sections at Giant supermarkets run by the Dutch firm Royal Ahold.

While the remodeled Mission Possible stores were generating positive results, a new Kids "R" Us format was not proving so successful. Thus as part of a broader restructuring announced in January 2002, the company closed an additional 37 Kids "R" Us outlets, bringing the unit total for that chain down to 146 at the end of fiscal 2002. Twenty-seven Toys "R" Us stores were also closed, and about 1,700 jobs, or 5 percent of the U.S. workforce, were eliminated. Restructuring charges of $213 million were recorded, resulting in anemic net earnings of $67 million for fiscal 2001 (compared to $404 million for the preceding year).

By late 2002 the conversions of the Toys "R" Us outlets had been completed, and the company launched a new type of store aimed at smaller markets where the company had not previously operated. The 42,000-square-foot stores were to be named Geoffrey, after the company mascot, and were a hybrid format offering products from Toys "R" Us, Kids "R" Us, and Babies "R" Us. Four of the new stores opened in late 2002. That same year, the company said that it wanted to add Toy Box sections to another 40 Giant supermarkets. Following a disappointing 2002 holiday season, Toys "R" Us announced that it would lay off 700 management and supervisory personnel. In June 2003 the company reached an agreement with Albertson's Inc. to set up Toy Box sections in more than 2,300 grocery and drugstores. The burgeoning Toy Box concept was giving Toys "R" Us another channel to reach customers and another way to increase its revenues in the increasingly competitive toy retailing industry.

Principal Subsidiaries

Toys "R" Us (Australia) Pty. Ltd.; Toys "R" Us (Canada) Ltd.; Toys "R" Us S.A.R.L. (France); Toys "R" Us, Iberia, S.A. (Spain); Toys "R" Us Limited (U.K.).

Principal Divisions

Toys "R" Us - United States; Toys "R" Us - International; Kids "R" Us; Babies "R" Us; Imaginarium; Toysrus.com.

Principal Competitors

Wal-Mart Stores, Inc.; KB Toys; Target Corporation; The Gap, Inc.; The Children's Place Retail Stores, Inc.; F.A.O., Inc.; Kmart Corporation; The Gymboree Corporation; Carter Holdings, Inc.; OshKosh B'Gosh, Inc.; Sears, Roebuck and Co.

Further Reading

Barmash, Isadore, "Gains in Retail Discounting: Interstate's Story of Growth," *New York Times,* July 23, 1967.
Brooker, Katrina, "Toys Were Us," *Fortune,* September 27, 1999, pp. 145–46, 148.
Byrnes, Nanette, "Old Stores, New Rivals, and Changing Trends Have Hammered Toys 'R' Us. Can CEO John Eyler Fix the Chain?," *Business Week,* December 4, 2000, pp. 128–32+.
Carmody, Dennis P., "New Jersey-Based Toys 'R' Us to Open Kids-World," *Knight-Ridder/Tribune Business News,* November 16, 1996.
Coleman-Lochner, Lauren, "Toy Turnaround: New CEO Reinventing Toys 'R' Us," *Bergen County (N.J.) Record,* February 11, 2001, p. B1.
——, "Toys 'R' Us Plans Cutbacks: 64 Stores to Close, 1,900 to Lose Jobs," *Bergen County (N.J.) Record,* January 29, 2002, p. A1.
——, "Toys 'R' Us Teams with Amazon.com," *Northern New Jersey Record,* November 22, 2000, p. B1.
Corral, Cecile B., "More Turmoil for TRU," *Discount Store News,* September 6, 1999, pp. 1, 55.
Dugan, I. Jeanne, "Can Toys 'R' Us Get on Top of Its Game?," *Business Week,* April 7, 1997, pp. 124+.
Gilman, Hank, "Retail Genius: Founder Lazarus Is a Reason Toys 'R' Us Dominates Its Industry," *Wall Street Journal,* November 21, 1985.
Halverson, Richard, "KidsWorld to Strengthen Market Position," *Discount Store News,* May 20, 1996, p. 1.
Klebnikov, Paul, "Trouble in Toyland," *Forbes,* June 1, 1998, pp. 56, 58, 60.
Liebeck, Laura, "Babies 'R' Us Rides Baby Boom and Corners a Growing Market," *Discount Store News,* September 15, 1997, pp. 25–26, 29.
——, "Toys 'R' Us Shakes It Up," *Discount Store News,* October 5, 1998, pp. 1, 51.
——, "TRU: New Leader, New Plans," *Discount Store News,* March 9, 1998, pp. 1, 83.
——, "A Venerable Concept Now Vulnerable," *Discount Store News,* December 14, 1998.
Neff, Robert, "Guess Who's Selling Barbies in Japan Now?," *Business Week,* December 9, 1991, p. 72.
Pereira, Joseph, and Joann S. Lublin, " 'Toys' Story: They Ran the Retailer As a Team for Years; Then, a Nasty Split," *Wall Street Journal,* December 2, 1999, p. A1+.
Reda, Susan, "Outlook Brightens As Toys 'R' Us Launches Major Revamp of Marketing and Operations," *Stores,* September 2000, pp. 47–48, 50, 52.
Rosen, M. Daniel, "Toys 'R' Us: Taking Toys to the Top," *Solutions,* March/April 1988.
Simon, Ellen, "Toys 'R' Us Struggling to Stay on Top," *Newark (N.J.) Star-Ledger,* November 17, 1998, p. 59.
Solomon, Goody L., "Discount Toy Stores Gladden the Hearts of Toddlers and Merchants," *Barron's,* August 11, 1969.

—Sue Mohnke
—updates: Taryn Benbow-Pfalzgraf, David E. Salamie

Tractor Supply Company

320 Plus Park Boulevard
Nashville, Tennessee 37217
U.S.A.
Telephone: (615) 366-4600
Fax: (615) 366-4744
Web site: http://www.tractorsupplyco.com

Public Company
Incorporated: 1982 as Tractor Supply Co. Industries
Employees: 6,000
Sales: $1.2 billion (2002)
Stock Exchanges: NASDAQ
Ticker Symbol: TSCO
NAIC: 422910 Farm Supplies Wholesalers

Based in Nashville, Tennessee, Tractor Supply Company (TSC) is the largest U.S. retail chain of farm and ranch stores, composed of more than 430 stores in 30 states, primarily located east of the Rocky Mountains. Although TSC stores offer daily farm and ranch maintenance supplies, a large number of the outlets are located in the suburbs of major cities, a reflection of a changing profile of TSC customers. For many years TSC served full-time farmers and ranchers, but as those numbers have declined the chain has shifted its focus to part-time farmers and, more important, to recreational farmers. Part-time farmers, often products of traditional farm families, farm on a limited basis to supplement their incomes from full-time jobs. The recreational farmer, on the other hand, typically lives on a small spread, from five to 20 acres in size, located within 20 to 50 miles of a major city. These customers do not depend financially on their farming or ranching activities. Rather, they pursue it as a lifestyle choice. According to *Kiplinger's Personal Finance* in 2001, only 8 percent of TSC customers were full-time farmers, while 31 percent were "hobby farmers." Because of this change in its customer base, TSC offers far more guidance than it once did, and each store has on staff at least one former farmer or rancher and at least one person who knows how to weld. The typical TSC store is no larger than 20,000 square feet, a far cry from the 200,000-square-foot big box affairs of Home Depot and Lowe's. TSC, however, has carved out a special niche and does not compete against the giant home improvement retailers. TSC stocks merchandise in six categories: livestock and pet products; maintenance products for agricultural and rural use; hardware and tools; seasonal products such as lawn and garden power equipment; truck, trailer, and towing gear; and work clothing for men, women, and children. Despite the wide variety of products TSC offers, the most popular item it sells harkens back to the roots of the business: the simple lynchpin.

Founding TSC in 1938

The founder of TSC was Charles E. Schmidt, who, ironically, grew up a city boy, born in Chicago in 1912. He graduated from the University of Chicago, earning a doctorate in economics at the early age of 20. Because the country was in the midst of the Great Depression, Schmidt was reduced to working as a floor sweeper in the Chicago brokerage house of Shields & Co. But six years later, in 1938, he was ready to launch his own business, a mail-order tractor parts supply business he called Tractor Supply Co. According to company lore he laid out the plans for the catalog, the Tractor Supply Co. Blue Book, at his breakfast room table. In his first year in business Schmidt posted sales of $50,000. In his second year he was able to open his first tractor parts retail store in Minot, North Dakota. Other stores followed as the company prospered under Schmidt's guidance. In 1958 he took the business public, and TSC shares began trading on the New York Stock Exchange. After he stepped away from the company, Schmidt moved to south Florida in 1964, then at the age of 63 started another career as banker, gaining control of a 27-bank chain, Gulfstream Banks, which became his second company to be listed on the New York Stock Exchange.

Management-Led 1982 Buyout

In 1969 Tractor Supply Co. was merged with National Industries, and then changed hands in 1978 when *Fortune* 500 conglomerate Fuqua Industries, Inc. bought the company. TSC struggled during this period and only four years later, in 1982, the company became independent once again when five executives of the company orchestrated a leveraged buyout of what was then called TSC Industries. One of the men was Joseph H. Scarlett, Jr., the current chairman of the board and chief executive officer. After working 15 years for a New Jersey retail chain, Two Guys Discount Stores, Scarlett came to TSC in 1979, a period of transition in the business. At the time two-thirds of the chain's customers were full-time farmers. When management bought the company in 1982 it was generating annual revenues in the $125 million range, drawn from 135 stores.

Initially serving as chairman and CEO of the company after the management buyout was Thomas J. Hennesy, III, who had a long affiliation with Fuqua. He began his business career in the radio industry, in 1947 going to work for an Augusta, Georgia, radio station owned by J.B. Fuqua. After a stint in the service during the Korean War, he returned to Fuqua, where he served in a number of executive capacities until 1968 when he left to run his own business, the Daisy Corporation. When he rejoined Fuqua in 1974 it was a much more diversified company. He served as president of Half-Gaines Co., Arizona City, and Islander Yacht before becoming president of TSC. After the buyout, under Hennesy's leadership TSC was able to turn around the business, make the adjustment to retailing in the contemporary state of agriculture, move its headquarters to the more central location of Nashville, pay off the debt incurred as a result of the leveraged buyout, and transform TSC into an industry leader.

In 1990 TSC, now with 148 stores, toyed with the idea of merging with ConAgra Inc., but in the end backed away from the deal after a letter of intent was drafted. Neither party was willing to comment on the reasons why talks broke off. Instead, TSC carried on, changing its name from TSC Industries back to Tractor Supply Company. In February 1992, Hennesy stepped down, replaced as chairman and CEO by Scarlett. At this point part-time and recreational farmers had become the target customers for the chain. Under Scarlett the company displayed strong growth, which led to the decision to take the company public once again in order to raise funds necessary to launch a major expansion of stores. The stock offering was completed in February 1994 and shares began trading on the NASDAQ.

By now TSC's present-day style of management was well entrenched. The company prided itself on taking chances, trying additions to the merchandise mix, then launching pilot programs to test how well they worked before rolling out system-wide. As much as possible the company believed in granting managers a good deal of latitude in how they ran their individual stores. Salespeople were also empowered, within a broad framework, to handle customer problems on the spot. As a way

to reward initiative, every TSC employee, even part-timers, participated in an incentive plan. If sales associates met their sales quota for the month they received a check. Store managers took part in an annual profit incentive plan that in addition to money included trips as compensation.

Following its initial public offering, TSC made a push into North Carolina in 1994, and for the year added 13 stores to the chain with plans to add more at a clip of 20 stores per year. Management looked especially to the South, with its growing population and availability of real estate. TSC was especially successful in establishing a number of stores in former Wal-Mart locations, becoming Wal-Mart's largest tenant in terms of numbers leased. Wal-Mart sites were attractive because their garden spaces were perfectly set up to accommodate TSC's outdoor merchandise. Although a TSC store would occupy only a fraction of the building, perhaps one quarter or a third, management found that the rates were still more economical than building a brand new building. In fact, only a quarter of TSC's new buildings were build-to-suits. The company was generally pleased with the size of its stores, in the range of 12,500 square feet, which took advantage of "big-box backlash," especially among the type of consumer to which TSC appealed—the executive-recreational farmer who was trying to escape the fast-paced city and preferred more of a small town feel to his shopping. Nevertheless, TSC began to consider a slightly larger format.

Between 1996 and 1999 TSC opened 90 new stores and pursued several important initiatives. It became one of the first retailers in the United States to implement the SAP Retail enterprise resource planning systems. For a few years the company had been using perpetual inventory, keeping track of individual SKUs on a real-time basis. When this tracking system was combined with SAP, TSC was able to reduce supply-chain costs and inventory levels. TSC also looked to the Internet starting in 1997, purely as a way to provide information to its customers. When it launched an e-commerce initiative two years later there was no expectation that its web site would generate a massive amount of sales from home customers. Instead, TSC looked to e-commerce to enhance its in-store business. Although it could not possibly carry every spare part for every tractor and lawnmower in the world, by using customer-service kiosks, taking advantage of the company's existing computer system, TSC associates were able to special-order these items on a vendor-direct basis. In addition, TSC took steps to attract more women into their stores, which for years had been the bastion of males, typically 50 years old. In 1997 the company launched a pilot program to address this issue. As Scarlett told *Discount Merchandiser,* "In an effort to attract more women into the store, we softened up a bit. . . . We don't want to change our image in the eyes of our target customer, but we do want to make our customer's wife a little more comfortable coming into the store. Instead of waiting in the pickup out front, we want Mrs. Farmer to hop out and take a look at what we've got and hopefully shop, too." Encouraged by initial results, TSC took the next step and began to adjust its product mix to attract more business from women. In particular it introduced brand-name lines of ladies' workwear, enlarged the pet department, and dramatically changed the equine department to appeal to women, who accounted for about 85 percent of purchases in this category. Furthermore, during the late

1990s TSC introduced its "big store format," which offered as much as 20,000 square feet of sales floor space.

2000: Aggressive Move into Florida

TSC took a major step in 2000 when it moved aggressively into the Florida market, which because of its strong agricultural and equine customer base appeared to be well suited to the TSC model. After learning that the Florida Scottie's home hardware chain might come up for sale, TSC sent a team to evaluate the market, which they concluded was fertile ground for their operation. Moreover, TSC's main competitor, Quality Stores Inc., was also looking to enter the market. Instead of buying all of the Scottie's sites, however, TSC opted to build its own. In a matter of months the company succeeded in opening a slate of 11 stores, establishing a foothold in Florida before Quality Stores, which actually purchased some of the Scottie's stores.

The price of TSC stock dipped to the $8 range in late 2000 as investors questioned the wisdom of the company's rapid move into Florida, but when it was clear that the gambit was paying off investors began to drive up the price. It rose in value 300 percent in 2001, followed by a 121 percent jump in 2002. Quality Stores in the meantime had fallen on hard times. In 1999 it had merged with Central Tractor Farm & Country of Iowa, making it the largest farm store retailer in the United States, but the debt incurred, as well as a clash in corporate cultures, led to severe repercussions. In November 2001 the company was forced into bankruptcy. Never in its history had

TSC attempted an acquisition (although it had also shown some interest in acquiring Central Tractor), but now presented with the rare opportunity to pick up the assets of its closest rival at bargain basement prices TSC came forward with an offer to the bankruptcy court in conjunction with liquidating partners Great American Group, Gordon Brothers Retail Partners, and DJM Asset Management. While the partners sold off the inventory, TSC cherry-picked the real estate for $35 million, selecting 85 of the Quality Stores it wanted. TSC then spent $12 million to redesign the stores and another $58 million to stock the shelves, part of a massive and successful effort by management to integrate the Quality Stores and their personnel into the TSC system. In one stroke TSC was able to expand its presence in key markets. The chain augmented its eight stores in New York and Pennsylvania with 25 new units. It also added five stores in West Virginia, an entirely new market. The rest of the new stores filled in markets where TSC already operated. As a result, TSC was unrivaled on the national scene in its niche operation. In 2002 it topped $1 billion in annual sales, and appeared well positioned for even greater growth in the coming years.

Principal Competitors

The Home Depot, Inc.; Sears, Roebuck and Co.; Southern States Cooperative, Incorporated.

Further Reading

Forrester, Brian, "Tractor Supply Plows Quality Row to Growth," *Nashville Business Journal,* May 10, 2002, p. 1.

Gentry, Connie Robbins, "Chain Cultivates Farming Niche," *Chain Store Age,* March 2000, pp. 67–77.

Kruger, Renee M., "Cultivating a Farmer's Market," *Discount Merchandiser,* August 1998, pp. 18–22.

McGrath, Courtney, "Harvesting a Nice Niche," *Kiplinger's Personal Finance,* October 2001, p. 68.

Pellet, Jennifer, "Tractor Supply: Filling the Farm Niche," *Discount Merchandiser,* August 1995, p. 60.

Santaniello, Neil, and Lori Crouch, "Financier Charles Schmidt Dies at 83," *Sun Sentinel,* May 3, 1996, p. 1B.

—Ed Dinger

Trader Classified Media N.V.

Parnassustoren
Locatellikade 1
1076 AZ Amsterdam
The + Netherlands
Telephone: 33 (0) 1 53 34 51 00
Fax: 33 (0) 1 53 34 50 97
Web site: http://www.trader.com

Public Company
Incorporated: 1987 as Hebdo Mag
Employees: 5,400
Sales: EUR 442.7 million (2002)
Stock Exchanges: Paris
Ticker Symbol: TRD
NAIC: 511120 Periodical Publishers; 511140 Database
   and Directory Publishers

Trader Classified Media N.V. is a leader in classified advertising, with operations in 21 countries in North and South America, Europe, Russia and the Commonwealth of Independent States (CIS), Australia, and elsewhere. It publishes classified advertising in print as well as electronic media. At the end of 2002 it claimed to connect buyers and sellers through its more than 350 publications and more than 60 web sites.

Trader Classified Media began as a small private company called Hebdo Mag in Canada in 1987. The company has gradually expanded internationally through acquisitions. It has established major offices in Paris and Amsterdam. In 2000 it went public and changed its name to Trader.com. The company became known as Trader Classified Media in September 2002. Although publicly traded, the company remains under the control of cofounder and CEO John MacBain.

Expanded Internationally As
a Private Company: 1987–2000

Hebdo Mag began operating in Canada in 1987 with three weekly publications (''Hebdo'' is a French term for ''weekly'') that sold automobiles and other goods through classified advertising. *Hebdo Mag* and *Auto Hebdo* were published in Quebec, while *Auto Trader* served western Canada. The company was founded by the husband and wife team of John MacBain and Louise Blouin MacBain, and they shared the duties of CEO until 2000.

In 1989 the company acquired *Winnipeg Buy and Sell* and *Winnipeg Auto Trader*. It made its first European acquisition in 1990, when it acquired the French publication *La Centrale*. This weekly classified publication specialized in automotive and real estate listings and was a leader in the classified automotive sector around Paris. Hebdo Mag acquired another French publication in 1992, *Les Annonces du Bateau*. This specialist monthly magazine for classified boat ads was founded in 1979. In 1993 Hebdo Mag acquired a 50 percent share of a new start-up French publication, *J'Annonce*. This weekly free classified ads paper sold a variety of merchandise, including cars and vehicles, computers and communications equipment, household equipment, and real estate, and also listed jobs and personals in its classified ads. From the start, listings in *J'Annonce* were available online through the French Minitel network, and an Internet version was launched in 1997.

During the early 1990s Hebdo Mag expanded into other European countries, purchasing *Auto Biznes* in Poland in 1992, *Gula Tidningen* in Sweden in 1993, and *Expressz* in Hungary in 1995. When it was acquired in 1993, *Gula Tidningen* was Sweden's largest classified advertising publisher. It had been in business about ten years. The paper offered a wide range of merchandise and also listed jobs, personals, and real estate, among other categories. *Expressz* was established in 1984 and offered a similar range in its classified ads. These three north and central European titles remained Hebdo's leading publications in their respective countries over the next decade. In 1995 the company also expanded its North American holdings by acquiring Canada's *Computer Paper* and the *Trader* and *Traders' Post* in the United States. *Computer Paper* specialized in selling computer equipment and had a French-language counterpart, *Québec Micro!*, while the two U.S. publications offered a variety of goods and services in their ads.

In the second half of the 1990s Hebdo Mag continued to expand geographically through acquisitions. The company's acquisition strategy was guided by its goal of achieving a dominant market position, either in national classified advertising, major metropolitan areas, or diverse markets. At the same time Hebdo began its online strategy in 1996, launching a series of online classified ad sites to serve different countries and markets. In 1996 the company acquired a leading classified advertising brand, *Via Via*, in The Netherlands, which further strengthened its position in northern Europe. Under Hebdo Mag, seven regional editions of *Via Via* provided national coverage from Amsterdam to Utrecht.

In central and southern Europe, Hebdo acquired *Cerce e Trova* in Switzerland and *Secondamano* in Italy in 1996. *Cerce e Trova* served the Italian-speaking population of Switzerland. Hebdo developed *Secondamano* into the leading classified advertising publication in northern Italy. By 2002 this free ad, paid circulation title was published in 18 regional editions throughout the major metropolitan markets of northern Italy.

In 1996 Hebdo also expanded into Russia and Taiwan. In Russia the company acquired *Pronto Moscow*, while in Taiwan it entered into a joint venture and acquired a share of Car News Publication, which published *Car Buys*, *Car Deals*, and *Car News*. Russia and the CIS proved to be a good investment for Hebdo. By 2002 the company was publishing 78 titles there, including the Russian-language edition of *Golf Digest*, and the region accounted for 18 percent of the company's global revenue.

In 1997 Hebdo acquired *Segundamano* in Argentina and Quebec's Publications d'Occasion. *Segundamano* offered a wide variety of new and used goods and services, while Publications d'Occasion published several specialized automotive weekly papers that were sold throughout Quebec and in parts of Ontario and New Brunswick.

In 1997 and 1998 Hebdo underwent a brief change in ownership before it was reacquired by its management group. In October 1997 CUC International, a consumer marketing company, acquired ownership of Hebdo for $440 million in stock and the assumption of about $200 million in debt. CUC International subsequently merged with hotel franchiser HFS Inc. in December 1997 to form Cendant Corporation. In 1998 Cendant decided to sell Hebdo back to its managers for $522 million in cash and stock. The sale was completed in December 1998. At the time of the sale Hebdo was based in Paris and known as Hebdo Mag International, Inc. It published more than 180 titles and operated in 15 countries through print and electronic media.

In 1998 Hebdo received a substantial infusion of capital when French investment firm CGIP purchased a 30 percent equity interest in the company. That year the company also expanded into Spain and Australia. In Spain, it acquired *Segundamano*, a leading free ad, paid circulation publication. Through the acquisition of the *Segundamano* brand Hebdo achieved national market leadership in Spain and developed 13 specialized, vertical publications. Hebdo also entered the Australian market with the acquisition of the *Melbourne Trading Post* and the *Personal Trading Post* of Brisbane.

In 1999 Hebdo made two acquisitions in South America. It purchased Brazil's *Jornal Balcão*, which was based in Rio de Janeiro and was the country's only paid distribution, general classified ad publication. In Colombia, it purchased a 70 percent interest in *La Guia*, a real estate catalog aimed at real estate buyers of new housing in the country's three largest cities: Bogotá, Medellin, and Cali. Hebdo extended the *La Guia* brand in September 2002 with the launch of *La Guia Clasificados*, the country's first free advertising publication. Other acquisitions in 1999 included Canada's *BC Auto Trader* and France's Garantie System.

More Acquisitions and Launching As a Public Company: 2000–03

Hebdo went public in April 2000 and changed its name to Trader.com. The parent company, Trader.com NV, had its headquarters in Amsterdam. The company also adopted a new tagline, "The International Marketplace Around the Corner." Initial public offerings were held on the NASDAQ and the Premier Marché of the Paris Bourse. For 1999, the company reported revenue of EUR 283.3 million, an operating loss of EUR 17.7 million, and a net loss of EUR 72.1 million.

During the second half of 2000 the company made several acquisitions. In Canada it acquired *Bargain Finder*, which operated in Calgary and Edmonton. *Bargain Finder* had a 25-year history of being Alberta's leading online and print classified publication. The company also acquired Vancouver's *Buy & Sell*. In Quebec it purchased Visitenet.com, a Montreal-based web site that specialized in real estate listings.

Trader.com expanded its operations in The Netherlands with the purchase of De Partikulier. De Partikulier was established in 1987 and published classified ads in print and electronic media. Following the acquisition, De Partikulier began publishing its ads under Trader.com's *Via Via* brand.

In France the company purchased an online auction site, epublik S.A., and acquired a 60 percent interest in Netclub, a leading web site for dating. Trader.com also entered the German market in 2000 with the acquisition of two leading German classified advertising companies, *Avis* and *Revier Markt*, for EUR 130 million. Both companies operated regional web sites in Germany listing Internet classified ads.

In November 2000 Louise T. Blouin, the former wife of cofounder John MacBain, announced she was resigning as co-CEO of Trader.com NV. Following her resignation the company's executive management team was led by John MacBain, president and CEO, and Didier Breton, chief operating officer. For the year the company reported revenue of EUR 372.9

million. The company's operating loss grew to EUR 138.4 million, and its net loss was EUR 172.1 million. At the end of the year the company operated 281 publications in 18 countries.

Among Trader.com's acquisitions of 2001, perhaps the most significant took place in Australia. After acquiring *Sydney Buy & Sell* in 2000, Trader.com purchased a 70 percent controlling interest in Australia's Trading Post Group, the largest classified advertising publisher in Sydney and Adelaide. In business for 33 years, the Trading Post Group published 11 periodicals. It had a web site that boasted seven million page views per month. With some 400 employees, the Trading Post Group generated revenue of EUR 25.7 million in 2000. Around the time that it acquired Trading Post Group, Trader.com relaunched Autotrader.com in Australia as a national web site. In 2002 Trader.com purchased the remaining minority interest in the Trading Post Group, thus consolidating its position in Australia and giving the company complete coverage throughout the country.

Other developments in 2001 included the acquisition of *L'Erbavoglio* in Switzerland and *Trajin* in Spain. In France *La Centrale* launched the first entirely interactive automotive classified ad service on TPS Satellite Television in conjunction with Minisat. In October 2001 Trader.com sold off four advertising papers and one web site located in California to Target Media Partners. Included in the sale were the brands Great Northern Wheels and Deals, Photo Ad, and Easy Ad.

For the year 2001 Trader.com reported consolidated revenue of EUR 419.1 million, an increase of 12 percent from EUR 372.9 million in 2000. Print media accounted for EUR 393.6 million of revenue, while online revenue reached EUR 25.5 million, a 48 percent increase over EUR 17.2 million from online sources in 2000. Despite weakening markets in North America and South America, the company was able to report overall revenue growth due to its international presence and leading local brands. At the end of the year Trader.com operated nearly 300 publications and some 60 web sites in 19 countries. It had 5,100 employees, including 2,000 sales people.

In September 2002 Trader.com changed its name to Trader Classified Media N.V. to reflect its position as a market leader

in classified advertising. In October 2003 an announcement was made that clarified future ownership of the company. Cofounder and CEO John MacBain stated his intention to purchase the remaining shares owned by his former wife, Louise T. Blouin, and increase his ownership interest in the company to about 50 percent. In addition, he would increase his holdings to 68 percent of the voting interests. French investment firm Wendel Investissement owned about 30 percent of the company. In December 2002 the company announced that it would delist its stock from NASDAQ to concentrate on the Paris Bourse Premier Marché, which had always been the primary trading market for the company's stock. Less than 3 percent of the company's total stock volume was traded on NASDAQ.

International developments in 2002 included consolidating its position in Australia and achieving full ownership of the Trading Post brand there. In France the company launched a new prestige automotive title, *Auto Première,* which featured ads for premium used vehicles. The first issues were bundled with *La Centrale.* The company also initiated a new direct marketing program in France that provided sales leads of people who had recently sold their vehicles to French manufacturers, auto dealers, and finance companies. Another direct mail initiative was introduced in North America, which involved the launch of a full-color publication featuring car dealer ads that was mailed to people who had recently sold their used vehicles.

In Italy the company launched two new publications, *il Fè* in Ferrare and *il Rò* in Rovigo, while new editions based on the *Segundamano* brand were launched in Pavia, Savona, and Como-Lecco in northern Italy. *Auto Facile,* a new direct mail publication, was introduced to deliver targeted offers from auto dealers and services directly to the homes of private vehicle sellers. In addition, a variety of new online services were introduced based on a paid access business model.

In North America the company launched 13 new print titles during 2002. Overall, North America accounted for 24 percent of Trader Classified Media's global revenue. The company published 148 print titles in North America, focusing on the categories of automotive, real estate, general merchandise, and computers. In addition, there were 12 North American Internet sites that offered the same content and categories as the print publications.

In north and central Europe the company operated in Sweden, Hungary, Poland, and The Netherlands. In Hungary the company extended its Expressz brand by launching new specialist titles in automotive, real estate, and heavy equipment categories. In October 2002 the company acquired Mai Hirdetés, a free ad, paid circulation title with national coverage that had been in business for about ten years.

In 2002 Trader Classified Media published 63 titles in Russia and the CIS. During the year the company added new editions in eight cities. The company also operated seven web sites there, the foremost being Glaza v Glaza (Eye to Eye), which was the country's leading personals site. In 2002 Russia and the CIS accounted for 18 percent of Trader Classified Media's global revenue.

Spain and Latin America accounted for 13 percent of Trader Classified Media's worldwide revenue in 2002. The company launched its paid access business model in Spain in 2001 and expanded it there and in other markets in 2002. Paid access services principally involved online and telephone access to additional classified listings for a fee. They also included ad renewals, ad placement, and voice-mail services.

Trader Classified Media became profitable in 2002, reporting net income of EUR 10.5 million on revenue of EUR 442.7 million. Print media accounted for EUR 411.5 million in revenue, while online revenue reached EUR 31.2 million. For the future the company planned to continue growing organically as well as through acquisitions. It planned to expand its classified advertising in both print and electronic media. In 2003 it acquired Webseduction.com, the leading online dating site in Canada; the leading classified advertising brands in Mexico City; and the leading local directory publisher in Hungary. The company also leveraged its content to offer paid business services, and it was developing new revenue sources through direct mail efforts tied to its classified advertising activities.

Principal Subsidiaries

Canada Trader.com; Trading Post Group Pty Ltd. (Australia); Expressz Hungary Rt.

Principal Competitors

AOL Time Warner, Inc.; Classified Ventures, LLC; eBay Inc.; Yahoo! Inc.

Further Reading

"Our Company," http://www.trader.com, August 5, 2003.
"Timeline," http://www.trader.com, August 5, 2003.
Ward, John T., "Connecticut Conglomerate Cendant Corp. to Sell Classified Ad Subsidiary," *Knight Ridder/Tribune Business News,* August 13, 1998.

—David P. Bianco

TrammellCrowCompany

Trammell Crow Company

2001 Ross Avenue, Suite 3400
Dallas, Texas 75201
U.S.A.
Telephone: (214) 863-3000
Fax: (214) 863-3138
Web site: http://www.trammellcrow.com

Public Company
Incorporated: 1948
Employees: 6,600
Sales: $653.6 million (2002)
Stock Exchanges: New York
Ticker Symbol: TCC
NAIC: 531120 Lessors of Nonresidential Property
  (Except Miniwarehouses); 531210 Offices of Real
  Estate Agents and Brokers; 531312 Nonresidential
  Property Managers; 531390 Other Activities Related
  to Real Estate

Trammell Crow Company is one of the world's largest real estate management companies. Once the nation's leading developer of real estate, the company turned increasingly in the 1990s to real estate management services. It provides a variety of management services to large corporate clients such as banks, hospitals, and energy companies. Trammell Crow's property management responsibilities run the gamut from new property development to arranging rental agreements to maintaining janitorial and landscaping services. The company operates throughout the United States and Canada, and manages properties in Europe and Asia through an alliance with a U.K. company, Savills plc. Trammell Crow also has outposts in Mexico, Chile, Brazil, and Argentina. Altogether the company services some 31,000 properties. The company is split into two main divisions. Its Global Services Group has responsibility for the real estate management aspect of the business. The Development and Investment Group develops commercial properties. Long a private company run by the family of founder Trammell Crow, the company is now publicly traded.

The Early Development of the Company: Post-World War II Years

Born in Dallas in 1914, Trammell Crow was influenced by a highly religious and disciplined household. He and his parents, along with his six brothers and sisters, struggled through the Great Depression. Despite hardship, Crow emerged from his youth with great self-confidence and what some of his colleagues called a transparent sincerity and optimism. One of Crow's favorite aphorisms was that people cannot do much about the hand that they are dealt in life, but there are a lot of different ways they can play their cards. For instance, despite little formal education, he was an avid reader and was constantly acquiring knowledge, eventually receiving three honorary doctorates.

Crow gained valuable experience in the Navy, where he managed a material procurement program during World War II. It was here that he learned accounting and financial skills that would serve him later as a businessman. He left the Navy in 1946 and served a short stint as a grain dealer. It was during this time that he got a taste of development by building a grain elevator. Crow launched his namesake company and began developing real estate full-time in 1948, at the age of 33.

Crow's first significant deal was the development of warehouse space for the Ray-O-Vac company. This opportunity launched him into a successful industrial real estate business that flourished in the fast-paced, postwar economy. While Crow continued to develop warehouse space, he started branching out into retail and office projects in the 1950s. The Hartford Insurance Building was among Crow's first office developments.

As the real estate development environment remained lucrative throughout the 1950s and 1960s, Crow also began to branch out regionally. His alliances with Frank Carter and Ewell Pope, both of Georgia, helped him to expand his warehouse development activity in Atlanta. Crow eventually became active in retail projects in Atlanta including the Peachtree Center, which transformed the downtown area. From Atlanta, Crow progressed into other southern states and also began experimenting with developments in some western states.

Company Perspectives:

Our goal is to be the very best at what we do. And our strategy to accomplish this combines a commitment to superior service for the customer with a platform of professional resources that allows us to deliver on that promise. For over half a century, this approach has allowed us to maintain a leading role in the commercial real estate industry.

Booming Business: 1960s

Although Crow built a reputation for high quality development deals and projects, one of the greatest reasons for the success of the company was his innovative approach to personnel management. Crow believed that his associates should be his partners, not his employees. In fact, Crow considered himself a partner working with the other employees of his organization. Crow envisioned himself and his associates working together, sharing the risks and rewards of the enterprise. In appraising job applicants, Crow would try to determine if the candidate was the kind of person that he would like to see walk into a room, or have a beer with. Next, Crow would determine whether or not the applicant was smart and would work hard.

Part of the partnership arrangement consisted of compensation based mostly on performance. Partners basically functioned as independent developers working under the Trammell Crow umbrella. They received a negligible base salary, but took part ownership in the projects that they developed. The organization was less of a company than it was a network of individuals. This approach, however, allowed both Crow and his partners to reap huge rewards. Many of Crow's employees became millionaires.

By the late 1960s, the Trammell Crow Company had seven national offices employing a few dozen people and representing about 100 partnership arrangements. The company was beginning to establish a significant portfolio of real estate holdings, which was another factor that distinguished Trammell Crow from many other developers. Rather than develop a property and sell it, as many other companies in the industry normally did, Trammell Crow retained ownership of many of the projects in which he was involved, enabling him to lease the development. This meant that Crow and his partners were continually increasing their revenue base and their assets.

Although most of his projects were in the Dallas area, by 1970 Crow had developed properties throughout many parts of the United States. He had also ventured, with considerable success, into residential development. At this time, however, he began looking to other parts of the world, particularly Europe, for new opportunities. Crow participated in several projects in Switzerland, Spain, Germany, Brussels, Italy, and France in the 1970s. Despite some success, the construction and development atmosphere in Europe proved too restrictive for Crow and his associates. Crow also built projects in parts of Asia, the Middle East, and Australia. As in Europe, these projects lacked the profitability available in the U.S. market. In addition to the questionable viability of foreign real estate markets, Crow began facing financial problems at home in the mid-1970s. As a result, Crow eventually abandoned most of his activities abroad so that he could concentrate on his U.S. operations.

As the development market continued to boom during much of the late 1960s and early 1970s, the Trammell Crow organization blossomed into a huge network of partnerships which developed and operated commercial real estate projects throughout much of the United States. In fact, by the mid-1970s Crow had nearly 200 employees in 15 offices representing about 600 partnership arrangements, approximately 150 of which were "in-house" partners.

Reorganization in the 1970s

Despite continued success through 1973, the petals began to fade as the American economy had begun to falter and the Crow organization became unwieldy. The energy crisis, combined with "stagflation," caused a depression in the development industry. Crow's massive decentralized network of partnerships proved inadequate to deal with the new business environment.

Oblivious to the economic problems, the Crow partners continued to borrow heavily and build as long as capital existed to develop new properties. In 1973 Crow initiated $400 million worth of projects. The Crow family fortune grew to over $110 million and Trammell Crow Company assets exceeded $1.5 billion. To finance the highly leveraged operations, Crow himself signed notes totaling more than $500 million for his approximately 650 individual companies. Crow was also expanding into other ventures, including farming. Part of the reason for the apparent mismanagement was that partners in the company were unaware of what the other partners were doing, or of the overall financial condition of the organization.

By 1974 Crow, at age 60, was facing serious financial duress and negative company cash flow. In 1975 Crow had to ask his senior partners to liquidate some of their assets to help relieve some of the massive debt that was burdening the company. Financial problems, which persisted in 1975 and 1976 and nearly caused the demise of the company, prompted Crow to begin a reorganization of the company. He relied on Don Williams, his up-and-coming protégé, to assist in the formulation of a new plan that would make the Trammell Crow enterprise more like a company. The plan called for a centralized management structure to handle strategy, financial reporting, and leadership for the partners.

Though the company struggled to survive through 1976, the following year saw a rebirth of the Trammell Crow organization. The new company was separated into Trammell Crow Residential Companies (TCRC) and Trammell Crow Company (TCC), which represented commercial development. Also in 1977 Williams was named president and CEO. In the meantime Crow again concentrated on new developments and completed one of his premier properties in 1978, The Anatole Hotel in Dallas. This project was unique for Crow because of his immersion in the details of its design and construction.

Despite a severe recession in the late 1970s and early 1980s the new Crow organization emerged unscathed. While stagflation and unemployment battered most sectors of the U.S. economy, Trammell Crow's interests grew. In 1976 the company held assets totaling about $1 billion. By 1982, near the end of the recession, the figure had ballooned to about $3 billion.

Roller-Coaster Ride in the 1980s

Contrary to the early 1980s, the middle part of the decade offered one of the most lucrative and fast-paced real estate environments in U.S. history. Deregulation of lending institutions, an influx of foreign investment dollars, and new tax laws all combined to generate a massive injection of capital into the real estate industry. Despite only moderate increases in demand for new space, development of new commercial properties boomed from less than 700 million square feet in 1982 to a peak of over 1.3 billion in 1985. In that year Crow interests initiated development of over $2.2 billion worth of new properties. The organization's assets skyrocketed to over $13 billion, and by 1986 the company had 90 offices with over 3,500 employees.

While the Crow organization enjoyed massive profits and growth during the mid-1980s, it was also trying to prepare itself for an inevitable industry slowdown like the one that almost crushed the company in the 1970s. Crow hired scores of highly educated people during the 1980s that had the skills necessary to efficiently manage the company's assets in periods of slower growth. TCC's centralized management also developed a program of identifying and selling certain properties from its portfolio in order to increase liquidity and address changing markets.

Despite efforts to prepare for a development deceleration, the company found itself ill-equipped to deal with an industry depression of a magnitude that few had anticipated. As demand for new properties plummeted in 1988, investment capital also dried up. Massively overbuilt markets resulted, causing the value of Trammell Crow's assets to fall as well. The value of new Crow developments fell from $2.2 billion in 1985 to less than $100 million in 1991, as the real estate industry plunged into a protracted depression. In addition, a recessed economy was causing a rise in vacancies which diminished revenues available from Crow's existing projects. For instance, office vacancy rates in Phoenix and Dallas, two of Crow's most active regions, leapt to nearly 30 percent by the early 1990s. Trammell Crow's personal net worth fell over 50 percent from its peak of $1 billion. Furthermore, the company's equity dropped from $1.7 billion in 1986 to $1.3 billion in 1988, while its liabilities rose from $5.9 billion to $7.7 billion.

The Crow organization had grown into a complex web of 1,500 partnerships, joint ventures, and corporations, causing the company to stagger under its heavy debt. Therefore, in 1989 Trammell Crow, under the increased influence of Williams,

reacted to the changed environment. Anticipating a metamorphosis of the entire real estate industry, rather than a cyclical change, the company took drastic measures to avoid bankruptcy and ensure long-term profitability. After compromises with more than 150 of its lenders, Crow reorganized its partnerships. Its partners were no longer active in the building process, although they still held equity interests in some 6,500 projects valued at $9 billion, down from $11.2 billion in 1989. More than half of the 170 partners involved with the company in the late 1980s left. The company eliminated eight of its 17 regional offices and reduced the number of employees to 2,650 by the end of 1989. The company also began offering market rate salaries to its employees, abandoning its old compensation system. It was at this time that founder Trammell Crow, at 75 years of age, began to distance himself from the management of the company.

Change of Focus in the 1990s

The shake-out at Trammell Crow Company resulted in several disputes over the ownership of the company assets. For instance, in 1991 TCC sued former Managing Partner Joel Peterson, who had previously been a close associate of both Crow and Don Williams. TCC claimed that Peterson had not absorbed his share of insolvent debts. Peterson filed a countersuit, accusing Crow and Williams of trying to grab control of TCC assets and the operating company for only pennies on the dollar.

Crow quickly abandoned real estate development as its primary activity and instead turned its attention to real estate management and services. The company sought to parlay its financial management talent, prominence in a large number of markets, and long experience in managing and marketing properties into a formidable service company. In addition to emphasizing the efficient management of the assets which it already controlled, Crow began offering various services to clients that owned and invested in real estate.

Williams organized the new Trammell Crow Company (TCC) into three entities—regional operating companies that leased and managed Crow holdings; national services; and national operating companies, which included Trammell Crow Ventures, Trammell Crow Asset Services, and Trammell Crow Corporate Services. *Fortune* 500 corporate customers were offered a single point of contact through Trammell Crow Corporate Services for real estate management, construction, acquisition, and tenant representation services. Trammell Crow Ventures provided real estate financing, investment, and consulting services to institutions that were active in real estate. Trammell Crow Asset Services provided asset and portfolio management services for clients that managed real estate investment properties. In marketing its services to potential clients, TCC emphasized three competencies including property management, development services, and project leasing and marketing services.

As revenue from new construction remained flat in the early 1990s, income from services rose to help the organization's bottom line. In 1988 TCC's operating income from real estate services was negative $30 million, an insignificant sum in comparison to income from development activities at the time. By 1991, however, TCC had increased its income from services to over $15 million. Crow ceded its position as the largest developer in the United States, plummeting from first place in 1991 to 15th place by 1992. At the same time, however, Crow remained the largest property manager in the nation. In 1993, TCC managed over 240 million square feet of commercial space.

Part of TCC's new philosophy in the early 1990s was the concept of "seamless quality." This entailed establishing national standards of performance and offering the most comprehensive, state-of-the-art services available. As TCC began to emphasize its management operations, occupancy rates of its properties rose from 85 percent in 1989 to over 90 percent in 1990. During the same period the average industry occupancy rate fell from 80 percent to 74 percent.

In 1991 TCC was capitalized as a privately held corporation. In 1992, the Dallas-based company developed 2.8 million square feet of new space at a value of $209 million. Its 2,400 employees served 12,000 tenants from 70 offices in the United States, Mexico, Brazil, and the Far East. Furthermore, it managed assets covering all commercial product types, including suburban and high-rise offices, warehouses, service centers, research facilities, and retail centers.

In addition to TCC, in 1993 the Crow family owned interests in several companies that were originally affiliated with Trammell Crow Company. Some of these companies included Wyndham Hotels; Trammell Crow Residential, the nation's largest multifamily developer; and Trammell Crow International, with operations in eight foreign countries.

It was Harlan Crow, the third son of founder Trammell, who came to the fore in the difficult years of retrenchment in the early 1990s. Once scorned as a mere playboy, Harlan had eventually proved his worth in the family business. He drove many of the hard bargains with former creditors and partners. When the company was forced to sell off most of its commercial property, Harlan managed to hang onto the Dallas Market Center, a huge complex for wholesalers that had been one of Trammell Crow Company's signature buildings. Harlan described himself as a highly conservative businessman, who intended to reduce risk as much as possible in order to safeguard his family's fortune. He considered real estate management a more secure business than development. Nevertheless, by the mid-1990s, he had eased the company back into new building projects. Between 1994 and 1996 Trammell Crow Company had built or begun building close to seven million square feet of warehouse or office space, mostly in the South, as well as thousands of apartments and hotel rooms.

In 1997, TCC went public on the New York Stock Exchange. Real estate stocks were back in favor, and the firm's share price quickly rose. The company forged back into markets from which it had retreated in the late 1980s. In 1997 Trammell Crow began to push into northern New Jersey. The company managed a lot of property in southern New Jersey, in the area outlying Philadelphia, and it wanted to become a force to reckon with in the rest of the state. Leasing activity in the area was on a steep rise, and that part of the country was important to many of Trammell Crow's national clients. By that time, Trammell Crow handled management contracts for major companies such as Exxon, Microsoft, OfficeMax, and IBM. It also managed property for Fleet Bank, where it oversaw, as part of its

duties, the restocking of the bank's automated teller machines. The company was willing to stretch the definition of property management in order to satisfy customers in diverse industries.

In 2000, the firm got a toe in the door in Chicago, a market it had practically abandoned in the early 1990s. Like northern New Jersey, the Chicago area was extremely important if Trammell Crow was to offer seamless service to its national accounts. But it was not always easy, even for a company of Trammell Crow's size, to make it in competitive big-city markets. The firm shut its New York City office in 2001. This market was dominated by longtime players who had extensive personal relationships with key figures throughout the city. Trammell Crow failed to do much marketing in New York, and the office was unprofitable. In this case, its nationwide reputation did not count for much. Earnings overall for 2000 were below expectations, and the company cut back in areas that were not doing well. Trammell Crow's share price fell, reflecting its disappointing results. In early 2001 the company announced an internal reorganization, simplifying its structure so that all its management services were under one leadership umbrella.

With more difficult economic conditions overall in the early 2000s, and commercial real estate in a slump, the company continued to push its real estate management services. It increased its services to existing customers in 2002, as well as added some significant new clients. It renewed its contract with ExxonMobil for another five years, and took on real estate management for another of the nation's largest banks, Bank of America. That same year it also picked up as clients the truck rental firm Ryder Systems and a San Francisco-based healthcare firm, McKesson Corp. Both these companies had offices and property throughout the United States.

The company seemed to have skillfully changed directions, coming out of the fiasco of the real estate market collapse in the late 1980s to become one of the top property management firms in the country. From a family company dominated by the personality of Trammell Crow, and then his son Harlan, the company metamorphosed into a public entity responsible to its shareholders. It increasingly did business with other firms with a national footing. The company, once dubbed a mastodon of the real estate world, showed the capacity to adapt.

Principal Subsidiaries

Trammell Crow Residential; Trammell Crow Savills plc (U.K.; 50%).

Principal Divisions

Global Services Group; Development and Investment Group.

Principal Competitors

Jones Lang Lasalle, Inc.; Insignia/ESG; Grubb & Ellis Company.

Further Reading

Croghan, Lore, "Turmoil at Trammell Crow As Retail Brokerage Closes," *Crain's New York Business*, April 16, 2001, p. 4.

Daniel, Steve, "Trammell Crow Launches New Chicago Push," *Crain's Chicago Business*, July 10, 2000, p. 9.

"Guess What Trammell Crow Is Eating," *Business Week,* March 2, 1992.

Myerson, Allen R., "More Than a Chip Off the Building Block," *New York Times*, December 1, 1996, Section 3, pp. 1, 10.

"New Game, Old Players," *Economist*, December 4, 1993, p. 80.

Rich, Motoko, "Services Firms to Unveil Deals," *Wall Street Journal*, July 3, 2002, p. B6.

Ruth, Joao-Pierre S., "Trammell Crow Looks Northward," *Business News New Jersey*, February 9, 1998, p. 30.

Sobel, Robert R., *Trammell Crow, Master Builder: The Story of America's Largest Real Estate Empire,* New York: John Wiley & Sons, 1989.

Templin, Neal, "Trammell Crow Going Back to College," *Wall Street Journal*, October 15, 1997, p. B18.

"Top Developer Survey," *National Real Estate Investor,* January 1993.

"Trammell Crow Blazes a New Trail," *National Real Estate Investor,* December 1991.

"Trammell Crow Co.," *Commercial Property News*, October 16, 2002, p. 26.

Valley, Matt, "The Discipline of Big Shoulders," *National Real Estate Investor*, July 15, 2001, p. 61.

—Dave Mote
—update: A. Woodward

Trisko Jewelry Sculptures, Ltd.

P.O. Box 674
St. Cloud, Minnesota 56320-0674
U.S.A.
Telephone: (320) 253-5346
Toll Free: (877) 874-7562
Fax: (320) 253-6413
Web site: http://www.trisko.com

Private Company
Incorporated: 1982
Sales: $3 million (2002 est.)
NAIC: 711510 Artists Independent; 541490 Jewelry
 Design Services; 339911 Jewelry (Except Costume)
 Manufacturing

Trisko Jewelry Sculptures, Ltd. is a small central Minnesota company built around the designs of founder and artist Robert C. Trisko. Trisko designs wearable sculptures out of precious metals and gems. Although Trisko's production is based in Minnesota, the artist competes in juried art shows throughout the United States. The company's sales and marketing are done though an extensive client/patron database and nationwide touring, where Trisko has made a name for himself by displaying and often winning prestigious art shows throughout the country.

Company Origins: Geometry and Jewelry in the 1970s

In the early 1970s Robert C. Trisko discovered that he possessed a unique cerebral combination. While most people work out of one hemisphere of the brain or the other, Trisko found that he could easily adapt himself to both right brain activity, generally associated with artistic, intuitive skills, and left brain reasoning, with its emphasis on logical and mathematical reasoning. It was a combination that landed him his first teaching job in the St. Cloud school district in 1970.

The St. Cloud school district had two part-time position openings when Trisko graduated from St. Cloud State University that year. The district listed a part-time opening in mathe-matics and a part-time position in art. Trisko, with his undergraduate degree in both disciplines, was hired full-time for both appointments. It was this combination of artistic sensibility and mathematical know-how that led Trisko to develop the wearable sculptures for which he has become known.

In the early 1970s Robert Trisko began experimenting artistically with horseshoe nails he salvaged from a local saddle shop. Although he originally brought the nails into the classroom for students to practice jewelry making, Trisko began molding the pieces into creations that he found worthy of the marketplace. Local art fairs and festivals presented the opportunity for the enterprising artist to sell his creations and Trisko began to supplement his teaching salary by participating in such shows.

The artist's early forms were organic and free-flowing. The designs found a following in the fashion climate of the 1970s. Ever improving on his work, Trisko found an electroplater in the Twin Cities who plated the nails in nickel and gold.

Over time Trisko's experimenting led him to produce pendants in enamel. He continued to sell the items at regional art shows for modest amounts of money. The prices for his works ranged from two or three dollars to not more than $20 for a sizable pendant.

Trisko's experimentation ultimately inspired him to strike out on his own. His work was evolving into what was to become his signature—geometric pieces, with mathematical forms and architectural characteristics. He also was beginning to work with precious metals and stones. Trisko produced his first gold band ring in 1980, and although unlike his later sculptures, it pointed to his early interest in geometric shapes. The artist shaped the ring round but played with geometric patterns on the surface of the gold. Trisko also made use of silver. Because silver was inexpensive it was the metal he used the most in the early 1980s. He preferred even then to work in gold but at $40 an ounce the metal was out of reach for a part-time artist on a teacher's income. His work in silver was short-lived, however, when he began incorporating gemstones into his pieces. Silver was too soft to allow him to set the stones in the settings he created. Trisko began using yellow gold, white gold, and platinum for the intricate geometric forms his designs were taking.

Company Perspectives:

It is the unique combination of geometry, outstanding style and craftsmanship that makes owning a piece of Trisko jewelry an investment that you will enjoy and appreciate for years to come.

While committed to form, Trisko described other elements he used in his sculptures in a June 23, 2002 *St. Cloud Times* article. The artist referred to the fundamental criteria applied to his creations as, "the elements of good design: line, texture, shape, form, balance, contrast, pattern repetition, movement."

In 1980 Trisko was an established teacher in the St. Cloud school district. He had gained a reputation as an outstanding educator and had been made chairperson of the art department. He had completed a Master's degree and additional course work toward his Ph.D. and was reluctant to turn away from the steady income that teaching provided. That all changed for the artist, however, when he won first honors at a national jewelers competition in New York the following year. Trisko realized that his work could be self-supporting and he went to the school district with a proposal for a five-year leave of absence. The school district accepted his petition and granted him a leave. In 1982 Trisko decided to resign his post and follow his artistic inclinations full-time, chasing art shows around the country and winning blue ribbons at many of them.

With a new business underway, his wife Helen took over the administrative duties of the company, freeing up Trisko to concentrate on design, manufacturing, and his participation in juried art shows. It was a combined family effort and division of labor that worked well for the company over the years.

Moving Geometrically: The 1980s Through the Dawn of the 21st Century

Throughout the 1980s Robert Trisko's work took on a more sculptural quality and he frequently found himself inspired by the work of well-known architects and their buildings. From Gothic cathedrals with their rose windows to the cascading waterfalls of Frank Lloyd Wright's Falling Water, Trisko designed wearable sculptures using precious metals in place of bricks and mortar.

Trisko's designs included rings shaped like trapezoids, ovals, and squares. At first glance the rings appeared unmatched to the round shape of a person's finger, but when fitted properly followers and patrons of the artist were amazed at the comfort and ease with which they could wear a Trisko work. Comfort had more to do with balance, according to the artist, and he maintained that so long as a ring is balanced on the hand it will not slip and slide on the finger. In fact, many of Trisko's works were made to be freestanding on a flat surface. As to the shapes of a ring, Trisko maintained that his sculptures fit more easily over the knuckle than an ordinary ring, making them an excellent shape for the human hand. The Trisko pieces would be placed on the finger sideways, moved over the knuckle, and turned into place—something conventional rings cannot do.

Robert Trisko believed that the round shape of most mass-produced rings was mostly a cost consideration, not a design one. Trisko's designs used significantly more gold than most rings. Geometric forms use gold in corners and other places that round rings do not, so it cost considerably more money to produce a ring that was not round.

Another design principle that set Trisko apart from jewelers who mass-produced their products was the selection of stones made by the company for its sculptures. Whereas most jewelers bought stones that were cut at calibrated weights, Trisko often hand-picked gems that were cut to their refractive index. The custom cuts allowed more "fire" and brilliance in the stone and a uniqueness that most jewelers could not match. The practice of cutting to a refractive index of the mineral was seen by many jewelers as wasteful because value was tied to a stone's weight. Trisko's intention was to create a sculptural statement, and a stone's value was only a small fraction of the whole.

Perhaps one of Trisko's most well-known line of designs was his "Stackables." These rings made use of several gemstone rings that could be worn independent of each other or combined to create a bolder, brighter statement of color. According to a November 2002 article in *Lapidary Journal*, Trisko created the designs with much thought given to color combinations and to his customer's wishes. He said, "Women who own a lot of my rings use a lot of 'Stackables'. It's a flexible system for women who get bored with their rings. They have different rings that they can mix and match in many ways." As to the color in his "Stackables," the artist explained, "I start with the design first, then add the stones. I'm sensitive to what color of blue topaz will go with a purple stone. I choose the right color pink. I'm playing with the intensity of the color. I don't just plop any old stone in there and put them side by side. I look within those stones and use those that really produce a statement when you put them together."

Trisko's many clients often came to him with jewelry that they wished to have remade into Trisko pieces. The artist created works from pearls formerly used in a necklace or gold refashioned into a contemporary ring.

Trisko's studio consisted of multiple rooms with several craftspeople working at casting his designs, manufacturing them, and polishing the finished product. He personally trained many of his workers, taking people with little or no experience in the trade. Trisko preferred to teach his method rather than hiring craftspeople with preconceived notions of how to execute his complex designs. His square rings were challenging for many jewelers, because as Trisko pointed out, "You can chase a square for hours on a polishing machine trying to get it perfectly balanced." Trisko admitted that perfectionism was a trait he acquired throughout his artistic career. He stated in the *Lapidary Journal,* "I'm fussy because of my math background. Everything must be perfect, perfect, perfect and neat and tidy."

Trisko's accomplishments included prizes too numerous to list. The artist took top prizes at more than 75 art shows in the past few decades. He spent a lot of his time competing and marketing his jewelry pieces in vacation destinations in Florida, Texas, and Arizona. He received national and international recognition for his work. In 1986 Trisko was selected among

---

Key Dates:

1971: Trisko begins making free-form jewelry using horseshoe nails.
1972: Trisko begins marketing his designs through local art shows and street fairs.
1981: Trisko wins the grand prize at a national jewelers competition.
1986: Trisko is selected among the top U.S. artists for a Paris exhibition.
1995: Trisko receives a trademark on ''Wearable Sculptures.''
1997: Trisko is accepted to exhibit in the Smithsonian Arts and Crafts Exhibition in Washington, D.C.

---

top U.S. artists for an international exhibition in Paris. Perhaps one of his crowning achievements domestically took place when he was selected in 1987 to be a participant in the Smithsonian Institution's Arts and Crafts Exhibit.

Trisko held memberships with many trade organizations in his field. He was a member of the Jewelers Board of Trade, The American Crafts Council, The Minnesota Jewelers of America Association, and the American Gem Traders Association.

After logging many miles, touring, and displaying his wares at shows across the country, Trisko looked toward the future of his company, his name, and his art. He had begun working with a Chicago manufacturer to develop furniture and accessories based on his sculpture. He had hoped that this effort might attract the attention of a major design house and that this would lead to a buyout of his company. An established design house could supply the necessary capital that Trisko needed to expand his business and to take the company to its next level. Trisko wanted to design his trademarked wearable sculptures, but also to expand his creative enterprises to furniture, home accessories, corporate artwork, and whatever else Trisko's mathematical and artistic mind might imagine.

Further Reading

Drazenovich, Dana, ''Jewelry Maker Robert Trisko Masters Art of Design,'' *St. Cloud Times,* June 23, 2002, pp. 1C, 5C.
Thompson, Sharon Elaine, ''Robert Trisko: Power in Architectural Designs,'' *Lapidary Journal,* November 2002, pp. 21–22.

—Susan B. Culligan

Tyndale House Publishers, Inc.

351 Executive Drive
Carol Stream, Illinois 60188-2420
U.S.A.
Telephone: (630) 668-8300
Fax: (630) 668-9092
Web site: http://www.tyndale.com

Private Company
Founded: 1962
Employees: 340
Sales: $150 million (2003 est.)
NAIC: 511130 Book Publishers; 511210 Software
Publishers; 512110 Motion Picture and Video
Production

While Tyndale House Publishers, Inc. has been known in the Christian publishing industry for decades with its popular *Living Bible*, the firm gained widespread recognition with the fictional Left Behind series first published in 1995. Located in the western suburbs of Chicago, Tyndale is a full-service Christian publisher, offering an ever-expanding line of Bibles, devotionals, fiction and nonfiction titles for adults, teens, and children, as well as videos, calendars, and stationery. With sales estimated at $150 million for 2003, Tyndale House has proven itself in both the ecumenical and mainstream publishing arenas.

In the Beginning: The 1930s to 1962

Kenneth Nathaniel Taylor was born in Portland, Oregon, on May 8, 1917. He attended local schools and met his future wife, Margaret, while in high school. The couple ventured eastward for Kenneth to attend Wheaton College, a religious establishment located in Chicago's western suburbs. After graduating from Wheaton College with a B.S. in zoology in 1938, Taylor studied at the Dallas Theological Seminary from 1940 to 1943, then enrolled in the Chicago-based Northern Baptist Theological Seminary where he earned a doctorate of theology in 1944.

In Chicago, Taylor worked as director of Moody Press, commuting via train from his Wheaton farmhouse. Moody

Press was a small part of Chicago's thriving publishing and printing industry, part of the Moody Bible Institute and one of the few Christian publishers of the day to offer a variety of inexpensive Christian literature. While at Moody in 1949, Taylor and fellow employee William Moore created a Christian bookselling organization modeled after the well known and larger American Booksellers Association. The new group, the Christian Booksellers Association (CBA), grew into a nonprofit force within the religious publishing community.

Kenneth Taylor's work at Moody proved a valuable and fertile stepping stone to his later endeavors. On his daily commute he began to rewrite passages of the New Testament in simple everyday language, since his children had trouble understanding the archaic words of the King James version of the Bible. After seven years, Taylor's *Living Letters* was finished and he approached several publishers—including Moody—but no one was interested in his updated, informal Bible. Discouraged but not defeated, the Taylors were determined to make *Living Letters* available to those who wanted it. The couple set up a small press in their Wheaton home in 1961, calling it Tyndale House Publishers, Inc.

The Tyndale name came from a 16th-century cleric and thinker named William Tyndale, who had translated the Bible from the difficult language of his times into words he reportedly said "even a plowboy could understand." The Taylors mortgaged their home and used their savings to make *Living Letters* a reality. They found a printer who produced 2,000 copies on credit and a prayer, then set about spreading the word, literally, in 1962. Using the CBA and a network of family and friends, the Taylors placed *Living Letters* in as many hands as possible.

Like Manna from Heaven: 1963–79

The Reverend Billy Graham, one of Wheaton College's most famous alumni, endorsed a copy of *Living Letters* in 1963. Graham gave copies of the book to thousands of Christians who attended his evangelical revivals, and also to audiences of his televised sermons. Correspondingly, sales of *Living Letters* soared and Tyndale earned its first profits. Whenever Kenneth Taylor was asked about the income earned from *Living Letters*,

Company Perspectives:

"Tyndale House began with a revelation from God, and it has grown and prospered as serendipities and special opportunities have poured down upon us year after year." — *Dr. Kenneth Taylor, chairman*

he replied, "The Bible is the word of God, so He should get the royalties." By the time royalties had begun to flow in earnest, the Tyndale House Foundation was created to distribute *Living Letters* around the world in as many translations as possible.

By 1965 the Taylors had moved Tyndale's operations out of their Wheaton home and into offices nearby. During the year a new Tyndale title appeared, *The Living Prophecies,* followed by *Spirit-Controlled Temperament* in 1966, and *The Living New Testament* in 1967. Also in 1967 Tyndale moved into larger offices in nearby Carol Stream, Illinois, having outgrown its Wheaton headquarters.

In 1972 Tyndale published *The Living Bible,* Taylor's revamped version of the entire Bible in colloquial language. While Tyndale had experienced success with several of its titles, the fervor over *The Living Bible* was nothing short of amazing—selling eight million copies by the end of 1972 and becoming the best-selling book in the United States by 1973. To keep up with demand Tyndale House added more than 10,000 square feet of warehouse space to its offices in Carol Stream, a move it would repeat several times in coming years as the small publisher gained nationwide acclaim.

While Tyndale House became a household word for many Christians, not all of the attention the publisher received was good. Several religious groups and scholars decried Taylor's informal language in *The Living Bible,* and others found fault with his interpretation. Tyndale and the Taylors, however, stood by the book as did millions of the faithful who bought *The Living Bible* and its message.

Growth and Change: The 1980s

After years of selling at a steady if not phenomenal rate, sales for *The Living Bible* eventually declined. Tyndale had no immediate replacement for this megaseller, though varying marketing approaches kept it selling far longer than expected. Tyndale titles were highly visible through distribution deals with such major bookselling chains as Waldenbooks, B. Dalton, and Barnes & Noble; discount stores Target, Kmart, and Wal-Mart; and major supermarkets. In addition, most Tyndale titles were available in a variety of bindings—hardcover, paperback, and deluxe editions—to fit the budget and taste of virtually everyone. The beautiful, specially bound or "deluxe" editions were designed to hold up to repeated use, with padding and fine leather covers.

Throughout the 1980s Tyndale House continued to find new ways to inspire men, women, and children to read the Bible and follow its tenets. In 1981 Margaret Taylor, cofounder of the firm, retired; three years later, in 1984, husband Kenneth followed suit by turning the company over to their son Mark D.

Taylor. Although Kenneth Taylor retained the title of chairman and was still Tyndale's "idea man," Mark Taylor became president and chief executive in charge of daily operations. The only one of the Taylors' ten children to play a role in the family business, the younger Taylor never set out to be in the executive office. He graduated from Duke University in 1973 and reluctantly became the director of the company's charitable organization. Within a few years Taylor segued into Tyndale's management, using his business skills to turn the firm into a major international publishing house.

Early in Mark Taylor's tenure came an updated version of *The Living Bible* simply called *The Book.* Unveiled in collaboration with Pat Robertson and his Christian Broadcasting Network (home to the very popular *700 Club* television show) in 1984, *The Book* was a hip, updated Bible with even less flowery language than its predecessor. For Robertson, who pitched in to the $2 million-plus advertising campaign, being involved with Tyndale and *The Book* was a business coup, since it was sold on-air to millions and became the Christian must-have of the decade. For Tyndale, it ushered in a new era of products, including videos and gift items themed to go along with *The Book,* which was marketed as though it were a snazzy bestseller rather than a staid religious text.

The Book featured a bright blue paperback cover and instead of the traditional dual columns of verse was styled like a novel. Several children's products and a series of calendars came from *The Book,* including the very popular "Verse a Day" tear-off block calendar, which had imitators in every genre. Next came another of Kenneth Taylor's ideas, *The One Year Bible,* published in 1986 to cater to increasingly harried consumers who had less time to devote to Bible reading. *The One Year Bible* was designed to get readers through the great book in 15-minute daily increments. Although many at Tyndale were reportedly less than enthused with the book, *The One Year Bible* surprised everyone but Kenneth by selling four million copies within six years.

Although Kenneth Taylor had long been considered the creative genius at Tyndale, his son Mark came up with the concept for a video series called *McGee and Me* for children in 1989. *McGee and Me* went on to sell exceedingly well, and Mark Taylor earned new respect in the Christian publishing industry. When asked about taking over for his father at Tyndale in a 1990 *Inc.* article, he said: "Was it difficult to succeed my father? Only in the sense that I had to work harder to prove myself. . . . For me, my confidence comes in recognizing that I have different strengths from my father. I know I can complement his skills."

A Coat of Many Different Colors: The 1990s

By the dawn of the 1990s Tyndale's *Living Bible* had sold more than 35 million copies worldwide. The publisher now had the clout to pursue authors with established reputations, many of whom had been with some of the nation's largest mainstream publishers. The firm bought dozens of Grace Livingston Hill's romance titles from Bantam, then signed lauded author Francine Rivers in 1991.

By 1992 the Living Books series (an imprint established in 1979) was generating upward of $30 million a year while other

Key Dates:

1954: Kenneth Taylor begins to rewrite the New Testament into simpler language.
1961: His work rejected by several publishers, Taylor decides to print *Living Letters* himself.
1962: Taylor and wife Margaret create Tyndale House Publishers, operating from their home in Wheaton, Illinois.
1963: Reverend Billy Graham endorses *Living Letters* and demand skyrockets.
1965: A new book, *Living Prophecies,* is published and Tyndale House opens its first office in Wheaton.
1971: Tyndale publishes an updated version of the New and Old Testaments called *The Living Bible.*
1972: *The Living Bible* becomes the best-selling book in the United States; Tyndale opens a warehouse to keep up with sales.
1984: Kenneth Taylor, cofounder and author, retires and son Mark D. Taylor is named chief executive.
1989: Tyndale introduces a video series called *McGee and Me* for children.
1995: *Left Behind,* a novel by Jerry Jenkins and Dr. Tim LaHaye, is published as the first in an apocalyptic literature series.
1997: Sales of *The Living Bible* reach more than 40 million copies.
2003: The 11th "Left Behind" book, *Armageddon,* is published; sales of series books and tapes reach 55 million.

Tyndale titles attracted a legion of fans. Putting out around 100 titles annually, Tyndale also maintained a healthy backlist of more than 1,000 titles and had become the biggest producer of Christian calendars in the industry. In addition to the various Bibles and religious texts, Tyndale published self-help and parenting books, and a growing number of fictional titles as well.

An adult novel by Dr. Tim LaHaye and Jerry B. Jenkins called *Left Behind* was published in 1995, as the first in a proposed series of books dealing with the end times. The book generated much attention and considerable controversy—many mainstream Christian denominations taught an eschatology far different from that outlined in the series. With the publication of succeeding titles, the series was soon crossing from religious bestseller lists to the *New York Times.* By 1998, after the fourth Left Behind title *Soul Harvest* reached booksellers, Tyndale's overall sales had reached almost $45 million and the series had a following in the millions. By the end of the decade after the fifth and sixth books (*Apollyon* and *Assassins,* 1999) were published, Tyndale rang up overall sales of more than $120 million. Each Left Behind title was so eagerly awaited that publication put them immediately on *Publishers Weekly* and *New York Times* bestseller lists.

The New Millennium: 2000–03

Tyndale House's religious empire continued to grow in the new century. In 2000 the seventh and eighth titles (*The Indwell-*

ing, The Mark) of Left Behind were released amid much fanfare and a sizable advertising campaign on radio, television, and in print. Tyndale had earned more than $23 million on the series and its merchandise alone by late 2000 and the series had taken on a life of its own, generating an entire apocalyptic or End-of-Time industry. The Left Behind web site (http://www.left behind.com), included a daily quote, newsletter, message/chat boards, branded calendars and greeting cards, graphic or comic book versions of the titles, computer screen savers, the Prophecy Club (an electronic mixed bag of political thought and revelations related to the themes expressed in the books), audio and videotapes, apparel, and collectibles, and had even led to two *Left Behind* movies starring former television star Kirk Cameron and his wife Chelsea Noble.

By the end of 2001, six years after the original *Left Behind* novel was published, some 47 million copies of the books (in adult, teen, and children's editions) had been sold, with the original novel having sold significantly more than five million copies itself. Yet Tyndale was not just about the Left Behind thrillers; it offered a multifaceted collection of bibles (*The Book, The One Year Bible, The Life Application Bible*), self-help and family-oriented titles (*The Paradox Principle of Parenting, 1001 Ways to Connect with Your Kids, Traits of a Lasting Marriage*), devotionals (*Notemaker's Bible, Men of Integrity Devotional Bible*), romance novels (*A Town Called Hope, Abounding Love, Finders Keepers, Heartquest, Northern Intrigue*), teen series (*Angel Wings, Choice Adventures, Forbidden Doors, Last Chance Detectives*), and children's books, videos, and CD-ROMs (*McGee and Me, Little Blessings, Mars Diaries, Superbook Singles, Kids' Ten Commandments*).

While the Left Behind series took Tyndale from Christian bestseller lists into the mainstream, other titles garnered attention as well. After the terrorist attacks of September 11, 2001, the widow of Todd Beamer (who died on flight 93 in Pennsylvania) chose Tyndale over all other publishers to share the story of her husband and their life together. Tyndale won the book partly because Lisa and Todd Beamer had both graduated from Wheaton College, Taylor's alma mater, and also because of the Christian ideals Tyndale set forth. Lisa Beamer's book, *Let's Roll: Ordinary People, Extraordinary Courage,* came out in August 2002 and sold more than a million hardcover copies.

Another title borne of tragedy, Gracia Burnham's *In the Presence of My Enemies,* was published by Tyndale. The 2003 book told the story of Gracia and Martin Burnham, Christian missionaries in the Philippines, who were kidnapped and held captive by terrorists. Martin died in a rescue attempt and Gracia's moving book, like Lisa Beamer's and the Left Behind titles, made it onto the *New York Times* hardcover bestsellers list.

The Future for Tyndale and Its Believers: 2004 and Beyond

Despite its phenomenal success, Tyndale House had not changed its message nor its intentions. Tyndale books, of which more than 100 million in bibles and 55 million in Left Behind titles were sold, certainly brought more entertainment into religious writing—yet every book remained full to the brim with Christian thought and devotion. Faith and profit, it appeared, could go hand in hand for Tyndale House and its growing list of admirers.

Principal Competitors

Abington Press; Moody Publishers; Thomas Nelson; Zondervan Publishing House.

Further Reading

Barnes, Shirley, ''Men with a Mission: Tyndale House Turns the Bible into an Easy Read,'' *Chicago Tribune,* October 21, 1990, p. 1.

Breu, Giovanna, ''In *The Book* Rev. Kenneth Taylor Converts King James from Holy Writ to Simple Prose,'' *People Weekly,* December 17, 1984, p. 107.

Carlozo, Lou, ''Apocalypse Soon: For Series' Authors, the Ending Justifies Their Means,'' *Chicago Tribune,* March 13, 2002, p. 5.

Cutrer, Corrie, ''Left Behind Series Puts Tyndale Ahead,'' *Christianity Today,* November 13, 2000, p. 26.

Garrett, Lynn, ''Launching *The Book,''* *Publishers Weekly,* April 12, 1999, p. 38.

Goddard, Coleen, ''New Ways to Spread the Word,'' *Publishers Weekly,* September 21, 1992, p. 44.

Mannion, Annamarie, ''Christian Readers Put Local Publishers on Map,'' *Chicago Tribune,* March 5, 2003, p. 9.

Marlyes, Daisy, ''Kudos for Tyndale,'' *Publishers Weekly,* February 22, 1999, p. 20.

——, ''No End for End Timers,'' *Publishers Weekly,* October 8, 2001, p. 22.

Wojahn, Ellen, ''Fathers and Sons,'' *Inc.,* April 1990, pp. 81 +.

—Nelson Rhodes

Vattenfall AB

Jämtlandsgatan 99
162 87 Stockholm
Sweden
Telephone: +46-8-739-50-00
Fax: +46-8-37-01-70
Web site: http://www.vattenfall.com

Government-Owned Company
Incorporated: 1992
Employees: 33,900
Sales: SKr 101 billion ($12.9 billion) (2002)
NAIC: 221122 Electric Power Distribution

Sweden's Vattenfall AB is vying for a leading role in Europe's energy generation and transmission market. The government-owned company has grown rapidly since the dawn of the 21st century, claiming the number five spot in northern Europe. Vattenfall is also the leading energy producer in the Nordic region, with a 50 percent market share, and is Europe's leading district heating company. Based in Stockholm, Vattenfall has especially targeted growth in Germany and Poland. In Germany, company subsidiary Vattenfall Europe is that country's third largest energy producer, through its holdings of Berlin's Bewag, Hamburg's Hamburgische Electricitaets-Werke AG (HEW), and VEAG, the main East German energy producer. In Poland, Vattenfall's holdings include majority control of that country's leading producer, Elektrocieplownie Warzawskie. Elsewhere, the company has entered The Netherlands, and has holdings in the Baltic states. Vattenfall (literally "Waterfall") generates much of its Nordic energy supply through hydroelectric installations along Sweden's rivers; the company also operates a small number of nuclear power plants. In other markets, such as Germany, Vattenfall relies on fossil fuels for its energy production. In 2002, the company's total electricity production topped 160 billion kilowatt hours (Twh), with additional heat production and sales of 34 Twh. These combined to produce revenues of SKr 101 billion ($12.9 billion) in 2002.

Sweden Power Producer at the Dawn of the 20th Century

The development of hydroelectric power generators in the 1880s presented a new opportunity to Sweden at the end of the 19th century. At the time, Sweden lagged behind its more industrialized European neighbors. Yet the country's vast natural resources, and particularly the many rivers and waterfalls in its mostly uncharted northern regions, offered the country the possibility to tap into an unlimited and inexpensive power supply.

By 1885, Sweden boasted one of the first cities with electric illumination. The country's industrial development took off, as the low cost of energy supplies enabled Swedish products to become highly price-competitive. The promise of an abundant supply of cheap electricity led the government to step up its hydroelectric development, in part through the leadership of its railroad system, which became the first in the world to operate electric trains.

The state-owned railroad system became the motor for Sweden's hydroelectric development at the beginning of the century. In 1901, the Swedish government acquired all water rights for the waterfalls in Tröllhattan, at the southernmost tip of Lake Vänern, in south-central Sweden. Development began on a hydroelectric dam and power plant to provide electric fuel for the rapidly expanding railroad system.

The next step toward the creation of Vattenfall came in 1905 with the establishment of Tröllhatte Kanal-och-vattenwerk (Trollhattan Canal and Waterworks Administration), which took over the development and transmission of electricity from the state's river holdings. These were expanded with the purchase by the Swedish government of additional waterfalls along the Göta river, including the Vargön, Ström, and Lilla Edet Falls, in 1908. The following year, the state body changed its name, becoming Kungliga Vattenfallsstyrelsen.

By then Vattenfall, as it came to be known, had nearly completed construction of the country's first major hydroelectric plant, at Olidan. Started in 1906, the first phase of the project was completed in 1910. Work continued at the site until

1921, when all 13 of the plant's power generators were brought online. In the meantime, Vattenfall had added two new major projects at Alvkarleby and Porjus.

The Alvkarleby site came online in 1915, featuring five power generators. Meanwhile, Sweden's vast and uncharted northern region also had become a focal point for Vattenfall's hydroelectric generation. In 1910, construction began on the first plant in the region, at the Porjus Falls on the Luleälv River. Construction of the remote site required five years and a workforce of some 1,000. Inaugurated in 1915, the Porjus plant fed the fast-growing industrial development of Sweden's northern region, and particularly the Kiruna and Gällivare iron mines.

Growth in the Late 20th Century

Vattenfall continued expanding its electricity production in order to meet the growing demand from the country's fast-growing industrial sector, which had given birth to such stars as SAAB, Volvo, and Eriksson, as well as from the swelling consumer demand for electrical power. At the Alvkarleby plant alone, power output increased more than tenfold, with total output topping 440,000 kilowatt hours by the beginning of the 1950s.

By then, Vattenfall had completed a fourth plant. Begun in 1945, the Harspranget hydroelectric plant was inaugurated in 1952 and was at the time the world's largest hydroelectric plant. The Harspranget project also led to the development of a 1,000-kilometer power line, reaching from the plant to the city of Hallsberg in the south of Sweden. Built between 1946 and 1951, the power cable itself established a record, becoming the world's first power transmission cable capable of rates up to 380 kilovolts.

Vattenfall began to look beyond Sweden for the first time in the 1960s. In 1963, the company was one of the initiators of the Nordel electricity alliance among Sweden, Denmark, Norway, and Finland. The alliance, which created a common pool of electrical power, was launched in 1965, marking Vattenfall's first sales of electricity beyond Sweden.

During the 1960s, Vattenfall began preparations for the construction of a new hydroelectric plant in Vindelälven. That project, however, was abandoned at the end of the 1960s as the country became increasingly interested in adding nuclear power production. Preparations for the launch of the first Swedish reactor began in 1965; that reactor, at Oskarshamn, came online in 1972.

Through the 1970s and 1980s, Sweden added a number of new reactors, including two more at Oskarshamn in 1974 and 1985, four at Ringhals between 1976 and 1983, three at

Forsmark between 1980 and 1985, and a sole plant at Bareseback in 1977. In the early 1980s, however, the Swedish population, through a national referendum, voted to end further nuclear plant development and dismantle the country's nuclear power capacity by 2010. Instead, Vattenfall began research and development on alternative energy sources, including wind and solar power, as well as gas turbines and fuel cells.

In the meantime, Vattenfall also had begun to prepare for its restructuring from a state-controlled government body into a full-fledged corporation. This process, initially conceived as early as the 1950s, took on steam in the late 1980s with the proposed deregulation of a number of European energy markets, including those in the Scandinavian countries.

The Swedish government announced its intention to transform Vattenfall into a corporation in 1990. Two years later, the "new" Vattenfall AB opened for business. The company's new corporate structure was expected to help it compete in the emerging deregulated and increasingly international energy market. Nonetheless, the Swedish government affirmed its commitment to maintain majority control of Vattenfall—in large part because of the government's recognition that the country's waterfalls and waterways belonged to its people and, therefore, could never become the property of a private company.

This restriction encouraged Vattenfall to begin eyeing international expansion. In 1992, the company began taking its first steps beyond its core Swedish base, with an entry into the Polish energy market. Its attention also naturally turned toward its Scandinavian neighbors, which were then in the process of deregulating their own energy sectors.

European Energy Leader in the New Century

Finland became the first of the Scandinavian countries to open its energy market to competition. Vattenfall became an early entrant, setting up a new subsidiary, Vattenfall Oy, in 1994. The following year, the company purchased two regional electricity producers in Finland. The company also began selling electricity directly to customers in Finland, including Enso-Gutzeit and mining group Outokumpu, in 1995. In that year, Vattenfall entered Norway and Denmark as well, setting up offices in those countries. The company prepared to begin direct sales of electricity to those countries upon their deregulation, which occurred in 1996. That year, the company faced competition at home as well, as the Swedish energy market joined the deregulated Scandinavian trade zone.

In the meantime, Vattenfall had begun looking farther afield for growth. The company targeted the fast-developing Asian and South American markets, setting up an investment vehicle, Nordic Power Investment (NPI). Through NPI, Vattenfall began acquiring shareholdings in a number of Asian and Latin American power plant projects, such as the 1995 purchase of a 25 percent share in Thailand's Thuen Hin-Boun hydropower station.

The economic crisis that swept through much of the Asian and Latin American markets in the mid-1990s cut short Vattenfall's expansion plans in those regions. Instead, the company decided to return its focus closer to home, where pressure had been building toward the deregulation of the entire European Community energy market. Germany, the single largest

Key Dates:

1901: The Swedish government acquires water rights for the waterfalls in Tröllhattan and begins development on a hydroelectric dam and power plant to provide electric fuel for the rapidly expanding railroad system.

1905: Tröllhatte Kanal-och-vattenwerk (Trollhattan Canal and Waterworks Administration) is created.

1906: Construction begins on the first phase of Olidan, Sweden's first hydroelectric plant.

1909: Trollhattan Canal and Waterworks Administration becomes Kuglige Vattenfallsstyrelsen.

1910: Construction begins on the Alvkarleby and Pojus hydroelectric plants, completed in 1915.

1945: Construction begins on the Harspanget hydroelectric plant, completed in 1952.

1965: The company forms Nodel electricity sharing pool with Norway, Denmark, and Finland; the decision is made to begin construction of nuclear power plants.

1972: The company inaugurates its first nuclear power plant.

1992: The company incorporates as Vattenfall AB, but remains controlled by the Swedish government; the company makes its first entry into Poland.

1994: A Finnish subsidiary is established.

1995: The company begins supplying power to Finland after that market's deregulation, and acquires two regional Finnish power companies.

1996: Sweden deregulates the energy industry; the company acquires 75 percent of the VESA Energy joint venture operating in East Germany.

1999: The company buys 25 percent of Hamburgische Electricitaets-Werke AG.

2000: The company acquires a 55 percent stake in Elektrocieplownie Warszawkskie in Poland; the company boosts its HEW holding to 37 percent, gaining majority control.

2001: The company acquires Bewag, based in Germany.

2002: The German holdings are restructured into the single Vattenfall Europe.

2003: With more than 60 percent of sales coming from beyond the Nordic Region, Vattenfall becomes one of the top five European energy groups.

European energy market, appeared a natural choice for Vattenfall's expansion, with deregulation expected to come in 1997. In 1996, Vattenfall took its first steps into the German market, setting up a joint venture, Vesa Energy, based in Hamburg, in partnership with Kommunalfinanz. Vesa's operation initially targeted East Germany, buying gas-fired plants in Neubrandenburg, Schwerin, and Cottbus. Vattenfall's share in the joint venture stood at 75 percent.

With deregulation in Germany stalled, however, Vattenfall returned its focus to the Scandinavian market. In 1998, the company launched a joint venture with Denmark's NESA, forming the company Stroem AS. Vattenfall also launched a $625 million acquisition offer for Stockholm Energi, the third largest electricity supplier in Sweden.

Germany's deregulation came in 1998, and Vattenfall soon confirmed its intention to grow into a major player on the European energy scene. In 1999, the company paid EUR 869 million to acquire a 25 percent share of Hamburgische Electricitaets-Werke AG, or HEW, owned by that city's government. Under the purchase agreement, Vattenfall also had the option of increasing its stake in HEW to majority control.

Poland became the company's next target, with the purchase of a 55 percent stake in that country's Elektrocieplownie Warszawkskie in January 2000. The acquisition, which cost Vattenfall $235 million, gave the company control of Poland's largest power generator—supplying 70 percent of the Warsaw market.

By the end of 2000, Vattenfall served more than two million customers. Yet Vattenfall's higher ambitions were revealed when newly hired CEO Lars Josefsson announced Vattenfall's plans to triple in size by 2005. The company expected to position itself as a large-scale producer in what many viewed as the coming consolidation of the European market. As Josefsson told *European Report:* "As liberalization moves across Europe, we will see a big industrial change, where I think you will be left with a handful of big players. Our vision means that we are going to be one of the survivors."

Toward that end, Vattenfall exercised its option to acquire majority control of HEW in November 2000, boosting its stake to 37.2 percent. One month later, Vattenfall stepped up its position in Germany with the purchase of VEAG, based in East Germany, from the country's top two producers RWE and E. On. The acquisition, made through HEW, was completed at a cost of some EUR 1.48 million, considered by many observers to be a hefty price. Nonetheless, the acquisition established Vattenfall as the number three electricity provider in Germany.

Vattenfall had not quite ended its march on Germany. By mid-2001, the company had added Laubag, active in lignite mining, and, especially, a 43 percent stake in Berlin's Bewag energy generating utility. The company began negotiating with the other major shareholder in Bewag, the United States' Mirant, and in December 2001 paid $1.63 billion to boost its stake in Bewag to 90 percent. In all, the company's spending spree had cost it more than $5 billion.

Following the Bewag purchase, Vattenfall regrouped its German holdings into a new subsidiary, Vattenfall Europe, in January 2002. That move was also a clear indication of the group's European intentions. Back at home, however, the company faced criticism, in part because of the seeming double-standard of its energy policies: while in Sweden, the company relied on "clean" energy sources; in its German and Polish expansion, Vattenfall had become involved in the use of high-pollution fuel sources.

Meanwhile, Vattenfall's further expansion appeared to be limited because its government-owned status restricted its access to all-important investment capital. A number of observers began calling for the company to make a public listing; however, the Swedish government maintained its commitment to ownership of the company.

Nonetheless, by 2003, Vattenfall had ceased to be a Swedish company—instead, it had become decidedly European, with the largest share of its annual sales, which topped SKr 101 billion ($13 billion) in 2002, coming from outside of its core Nordic region. Germany had become its main market, accounting for 60 percent of sales. Meanwhile, the company continued its expansion in Poland, with the purchase of GZE, an electrical distribution and sales specialist in the Upper Silesia region and the first electricity company offered for sale by the Polish government. This acquisition helped place Vattenfall in pole position for the coming race after the expected full deregulation of the Polish market in 2005.

Vattenfall expansion into Poland also was seen as a spearhead for expansion into the Baltic region. The company already held subsidiaries in Estonia and Latvia, and operated a district heating business in Estonia as well. Yet Vattenfall's major expansion focus remained in Germany, and in nearby markets, such as The Netherlands, where Vattenfall had established a presence in 1999. In 2001, Vattenfall became one of the first to sign an energy supply contract with a Dutch company, in this case, Bovag. Vattenfall's expertise in clean energy production also gave it a head start in the environmentally conscious Dutch market. After more than 100 years, Vattenfall's future appeared powerful indeed.

Principal Subsidiaries

Abonnera i Sverige AB; Arrowhead AB; Arrowhead Services AB; Elektrocieplownie Warszawskie S.A. (Poland; 38%); Energibolaget Botkyrka-Salem Försäljn. AB; Forsaströms Kraft AB; Försäkrings AB Vattenfall Insurance; Gestrikekraft AB; Gotlands Energi AB (75%); Kraftbyggarna Entreprenad AB; Kraftbyggarna Invest; Nordic Power Invest AB; Produktions-balans PBA AB; Ringhals AB (74%); Säffle Årjäng Energi AB; Vattenfall Bränsle AB; Vattenfall Bråviken AB; Vattenfall Danmark A/S; Vattenfall Data AB; Vattenfall Deutschland GmbH; Vattenfall Engineering AB; Vattenfall Estonia OÜ; Vattenfall Fastigheter AB; Vattenfall Norrnät AB; Vattenfall Östnät AB; Vattenfall Oy; Vattenfall Power Management AB; Vattenfall Regionnät AB; Vattenfall Reinsurance S.A.; Vattenfall Service Syd AB; Vattenfall Support AB; Vattenfall Sveanät AB; Vattenfall Treasury AB; Vattenfall Utveckling AB; Vattenfall Värme Uppsala AB; Vattenfall Västnät AB; VGS AB; VGS Hydro International AB.

Principal Competitors

Electricité de France; RWE AG, E.ON AG; Tractebel S.A.; Enel Distribuzione SpA; Endesa SA.

Further Reading

Brown-Humes, "Tough Decisions for Vattenfall As It Lifts German Power Stake," *Financial Times,* May 4, 2001, p. 28.
George, Nicholas, "With Every Gain Comes Some Pain," *Financial Times,* December 14, 2000, p. 30.
Hawkins, Nigel, "The Spitfire Approach," *Utility Week,* June 6, 2003, p. 24.
Newton, Paul, "Northern Light," *Utility Week,* September 13, 2002, p. 26.
Sains, Ariane, "Vattenfall: The Swedish Energy Firm's Expansion into Europe's Deregulated Market Is Raising Questions," *Europe,* April 2002, p. 22.
Shepherd, Nick, "Bewag Gives Vattenfall Clout in Germany," *Utility Week,* February 7, 2003, p. 14.

—M.L. Cohen

voestalpine

voestalpine AG

Voest-Alpine-Strasse 1
A-4020 Linz
Austria
Telephone: 43 0 732 6585 2090
Fax: 43 0 732 6980 8981
Web site: http://www.voestalpine.com

Public Company
Incorporated: 1945 as Vereinigte Österreichische Eisen-
   und Stahlwerke AG
Employees: 16,000
Sales: EUR 3.17 billion (2002)
Stock Exchanges: Vienna
Ticker Symbol: VAST
NAIC: 331111 Iron and Steel Mills; 331222 Steel Wire
   Drawing; 331513 Rolling Mill Rolls, Steel,
   Manufacturing; 331210 Iron and Steel Pipe and Tube
   Manufacturing from Purchased Steel

Formerly Voest-Alpine Stahl AG, voestalpine AG is a holding company for numerous subsidiaries, whose activities include the manufacture, processing, and sale of steel materials.
Privatized in the early 1990s and listed on the Vienna Stock
Exchange in 1995, voestalpine is among the largest industrial
enterprises in Austria, with sales of EUR 3.17 billion and a
workforce of about 16,000 in 2002. In recent years voestalpine
has sought to distance itself from its image as a steel producer
and increase its emphasis on steel processing activities, investing heavily in research and development for high-quality, high-
profit steel products. The voestalpine Group is currently comprised of four divisions: Voestalpine Stahl, a high-quality steel
producer; Voestalpine Railway Systems, which offers railway
engineering and infrastructure planning services, as well as
high-tech rail products; Voestalpine Profilform, which produces
shaped tubes and hollow sections, as well as other components;
and Voestalpine Motion Division, which develops and produces
automotive components.

Company Origins: 1938–48

Effectively, the Austrian steel industry consisted of one
company, Voest-Alpine Stahl AG, which manufactured bulk
steel and special steel products—although there were still a
few independent steel producers in Austria. The company was
founded in 1938 as the Reichswerke Hermann Göring in Linz,
Austria, as an affiliate of the state-owned Berlin Göring-
Werke. Construction of a large steelworks began in 1939 and
continued throughout World War II; the first two blast furnaces
were completed in 1941, and by 1944 the complex included
open-hearth and electric furnaces for steel conversion, and a
nitrogen plant. Allied bombing caused severe damage to the
works in 1944.

In 1945 the U.S. military government in Austria changed the
name of the company to Vereinigte Österreichische Eisen- und
Stahlwerke AG (The Austrian Iron and Steelworks), of which
"Voest" is an acronym. Reconstruction of the works commenced, and production began again in 1945. In the following
year, 1946, one million tons of crude steel were melted in the
company's electric furnace. Between 1947 and 1950 the reconstruction and expansion of the works continued apace. In 1947
the first blast furnace, the first open-hearth furnace, and the first
coke ovens started production. The company commenced production of steel for highly stressed welded structures in 1948.

Leading the World Steel Industry with a Revolutionary Innovation in 1949

In 1949 Voest decided to build the world's first steel mill
with oxygen converters; Voest led the world steel industry with
this development and by the 1970s oxygen converters dominated world steel production, replacing both open-hearth furnaces and Bessemer converters. The oxygen process is considered by many steel industry experts to be the most important
innovation in steelmaking in modern times. Voest played a
leading part in the development of the process, and this development was important in the growth of Voest. The company
gained an advantage for its own steel production and created a
downstream business supplying other steelworks with steelmaking equipment.

Company Perspectives:

Compared with other companies in the sector, voestalpine remains one of the few European companies reporting solid profits.

This is the result of a consistent strategy, to make the transition from a steel producer to a steel-processing Group. Not least, the close cooperation with customers, evident in a multitude of research and development projects with renowned automobile manufacturers, shows that voestalpine has taken advantage of the opportunity to differentiate itself from the large-volume steel producers as a comparatively small but flexible company by means of a targeted niche policy and customer orientation, and to establish itself in many different areas as the market or technology leader.

Oxygen converters, which involve the blowing of oxygen at high velocity onto the surface of molten metal in a furnace, greatly reduce the cycle time for melts and thereby increase capacity and reduce the costs per ton of the steel produced. Although the advantages of using oxygen rather than air in steelmaking furnaces had long been recognized, the development of oxygen converters had been delayed owing to the lack of cheap supplies of oxygen. The nitrogen plant that had been built at Linz during the war produced oxygen as a byproduct, and the plant engineers at Linz decided to take advantage of this oxygen production to carry out a systematic program of studies.

At first the Voest engineers arranged for oxygen to be blown into the space above the iron melt in an open-hearth furnace. Although they succeeded in accelerating the conversion of iron to steel in this way, the increased flame temperature destroyed the root of the furnace and the regenerators for preheating air became clogged with dust. In the experiments, which followed, they tried feeding oxygen into an electric furnace, but the heat again proved destructive and ruined the electrode holders. At this point the Linz engineers consulted the Swiss engineer Robert Dürrer who, with Heinrich Hellbruegge, was conducting experiments using oxygen in a two-ton Bessemer converter and in an electric furnace. They were injecting a jet of oxygen into the molten iron through a water-cooled lance placed just above the surface of the metal.

The first trials of the Dürrer system at Linz failed; the heat destroyed the lance, the stream of oxygen blown deep into the melt caused damage to the bottom and other refractories of the vessel, and the treatment failed to remove enough of the phosphorus impurity from the iron. Then the Linz engineers made their breakthrough. Abandoning the accepted practices of the time, they reduced the impact pressures of the oxygen jet by using a different nozzle and raising the lance further from the surface of the melt. The new approach worked well; steel of good quality was produced and there was no damage to the equipment.

The initial experiments in 1949 were made with a two-ton vessel, but the Linz engineers went on to make further tests with larger units, and in late 1952 they built process units on a fully commercial scale with vessels of 35-ton capacity. In 1953 a second plant with oxygen converters was installed at Donawitz in the iron making district of Styria in Austria. The oxygen converter system has since been called the LD process, from the initials of the Austrian towns Linz and Donawitz where the first two plants were installed. The development of the oxygen process by Voest was an example of a small company—in terms of the world steel industry—making a decisive technical breakthrough and leaving large U.S., German, Japanese, and U.K. companies following in its wake. By 1988 Voest and its associated companies had installed 140 oxygen converters in steelworks around the world.

Expansion and Diversification in the 1950s and 1960s

Another strategy adopted by Voest was to develop a broad range of downstream engineering businesses; in 1950 the engineering shops started production of lathes, and the development of water power plants began. The combination of electric steel-making capacity, access to cheap electricity, and the oxygen converters made Voest a leader in high-quality steel production and kept its costs highly competitive at a time when the European steel industry was expanding rapidly and was competitive in world markets. During the early 1950s a new slabbing mill and cold rolling stand were added to the works. At the same time, downstream expansion continued with the establishment of an industrial plant construction division.

The company expanded rapidly between 1955 and 1960. In 1955 a third oxygen converter was completed, and in 1959 a second LD steel mill with two 50-ton converters started production. In 1958 Voest collaborated with the German company Krupp to build an LD steel mill at Rourkela in India. Blast furnace output passed one million tons for the first time in 1955. A new 4.2-meter plate mill was added in 1958 and a new coke oven battery in 1959.

In the first half of the 1960s, several state-owned businesses were transferred to Voest, extending the company's downstream activities. Notable LD developments were the placing of a Soviet order for an LD steel mill in 1963 and the supplying of 300-ton oxygen converters to a steel mill at Taranto, Italy.

The latter half of the decade saw the spread of activities of the process plant contracting division. Examples showing the range of contracts obtained by the division were the construction of a fertilizer plant in Poland in 1965, supply of a palletizing plant for iron ore in Brazil in 1966, and of a fertilizer plant in France in 1969. In the same year an ethylene plant was completed for ÖMV, another company in the Austrian public sector. Expansion of steel production continued, and in 1969 crude steel production capacity was increased from 2.3 million tons to 3.1 million tons a year. In 1966, production of special steels began and a sixth oxygen converter started up. A first continuous casting machine started trials in the second LD steel mill in 1968, and in 1970 a multi-roll stand was added, which made possible the production of very thin steel sheets.

Reorganization and Technical Development in the 1970s and 1980s

For Voest, the 1970s began with reorganization and technical development. In 1972 Voest became part of the holding

Key Dates:

1938: Voest is originally founded as the Reichswerke Hermann Göring in Linz, Austria, as an affiliate of the state-owned Berlin Göring-Werke.

1945: The U.S. military government in Austria changes the name of the company to Vereinigte Österreichische Eisen- und Stahlwerke AG (The Austrian Iron and Steelworks), of which ''Voest'' is an acronym.

1949: Voest builds the world's first steel mill with oxygen converters, a revolutionary innovation that later became the industry standard.

1972: Voest becomes part of the holding company ÖIAG, Austria's largest industrial group.

1973: As part of a broader reorganization, Voest merges with the other leading Austrian steel producer, Alpine, which operates the Donawitz steelworks.

1975: The Austrian special steels industry is concentrated at the company VEW.

1976: Voest-Alpine Stahlhandel is formed by a merger of the separate nationalized units of the Austrian steel stockholding trade.

1988: ÖIAG is reorganized into seven separate companies, one of which is Voest-Alpine Stahl AG (VA Stahl).

1995: VA Stahl makes its initial public offering on the Vienna Stock Exchange.

2001: VA Stahl returns to its previous name, Voest-Alpine, in order to distance itself from its old image as a steelmaker; the company eventually becomes voestalpine AG.

company ÖIAG, Austria's largest industrial group. In 1973, as part of the reorganization, Voest merged with the other leading Austrian steel producer, Alpine, which operated the Donawitz steelworks. The year 1972 was a high point for investment activity. A second continuous casting machine was added to the second LD steel mill, while a third LD steel mill with a 120-ton converter and a third continuous casting machine were under construction. The wide strip mill was extended, and a cold rolling mill and a wide-strip galvanizing plant were added to the complex. Finally, a new apprentice-training shop was built. The new plants started production in 1973 and 1974.

By the time the new plants that had been started in the early 1970s were completed, the first oil shock had occurred and the European steel industry had entered a serious downturn. The cyclical fall in demand was reinforced by a switch away from steel toward other materials; greater efficiency in the use of steel, involving the substitution of thinner gauges of steel; serious recession in some European steel-using industries, such as shipbuilding; and the emergence of new low-cost steel-producing countries. The change in the industrial environment affected the Austrian steel industry. In 1975, the Austrian special steels industry was concentrated at the company VEW, followed in 1976 by a merger of the separate nationalized units of the Austrian steel stockholding trade to form Voest-Alpine Stahlhandel.

Technical rationalization followed. In 1976 the open-hearth steel mill at Linz was closed, and in 1977 the first LD steel mill

was shut. New developments were occurring at the same time, however. In 1979, the development of the harbor on the Traun River made possible the shipment of components for process plants weighing up to 750 tons. In 1979 and 1980 a wire mill and a continuous caster were built at the Donawitz works, which had been added to the group, and a seamless tube mill was added to the Kindberg works, another works that had been incorporated into the group. An electronics plant was opened at Engerwitzdorf in 1979, marking a new diversification for the group.

The industrial climate for the steel industry in the 1980s was far removed from the expansion of the early postwar period. The decade started with the second oil shock and recession. Between 1979 and 1985, the Austrian government helped the ÖIAG group with financial transfers, and the largest share of these went to the steel companies Voest-Alpine and VEW. By the end of the 1980s, a recovery had been achieved. Over the decade some updating of equipment took place. In 1981 a fourth continuous casting machine was commissioned. In 1982 a tubeworks for tubes used in oilfields was completed at Kindberg. In 1983, the world's largest plasma-melting furnace was started at the Linz works, and in 1985 an electrolytic strip coating plant was built.

The tougher industrial environment of the early 1980s exposed the weaknesses of the policy of diversification into a wide range of engineering and other industries. In 1985 the company's trading losses reached Sch 12 billion, as the result of an unsuccessful microchip venture, participation in the unsuccessful Bayon Steel Corporation in the United States, and disastrous losses at a subsidiary that was involved in speculative oil deals. This series of events led to the resignation of the chief executive and the formulation of a restructuring plan, which involved 10,000 job losses. The new management team was led by Chief Executive Dr. Herbert Lewinsky.

Changing political perceptions of the efficiency of large conglomerate corporations led to more fundamental reorganization; in 1988 ÖIAG, the holding company that had controlled Voest since the end of 1972, was reorganized into seven separate companies, of which Voest-Alpine Stahl AG was one. The Austrian government had decided to partially privatize ÖIAG. The new Voest-Alpine Stahl AG's activities included steelmaking at the Linz works, steel rolling at the Linz and Donawitz works, the manufacture of special steels—high speed and tool steels—by the Bohler companies, which were subsidiaries of Voest-Alpine Stahl at Kapfenberg and at Dusseldorf in Germany, and steel stockholding and steel scrap processing. The reorganization was designed to make the companies in the old ÖIAG group more efficient, to bring management decision-making nearer to the market, and to expand the businesses internationally. In April 1990 a tie-up between the Swedish company Uddeholm and Bohler, to form a strategic alliance between the two special steel producers, was announced.

After the reorganization, Voest-Alpine Stahl specialized in making and shaping steel; the downstream activities, which Voest developed or acquired, including the process plant activities, were split off into separate companies. In 1989 Voest produced 3.35 million tons of crude steel and 2.76 million tons of flat rolled products at Linz. The company had a wide range of steel finishing equipment; apart from rolling mills, it had equipment for making tubes, rails, and wire; drop forging facilities, which make shapes through the progressive forming of sheet metal in matched dies under repetitive blows of a hammer; and a steel foundry. The company's main investments in 1989 were designed to improve the quality of the products of the rolling mills; in addition, a second galvanizing plant was constructed.

The company then estimated that high-tech products accounted for about 10 percent of turnover, and it aimed to raise this share to 30 percent. The company's research and development program, which would play a part in achieving this target, included work on new steelmaking processes, improvements to existing processing technology, and applications. One specialty was surface-treated products, including galvanized steel and plastic-coated strip steel. Evidence of the company's commitment to training was its employment of nearly 500 apprentices, equivalent to 4 percent of its workforce.

Because of the relatively small size of Austria, Voest relied on exports to sell its output; 70 percent of its 1988 turnover came from exports. Its principal export market was the European Economic Community, followed by Comecon; only 5 percent of turnover was exported overseas, outside Europe and Comecon. Voest was well located to share in the demand for steel that would be generated by investment in the former East Germany and in Eastern European countries. In the postwar period, Voest's success was founded on electric furnaces with access to hydroelectric power and on its brilliant breakthrough with oxygen converters. It was close to markets, and had developed specialties such as coated steels. Whether these factors would be enough to ensure the company's success in the 1990s remained to be seen.

The Privatized VA Stahl Defending Its Autonomy in the 1990s

In the 1990s, as the European steel industry was being transformed by consolidation, Voest was intent on attaining sufficient girth to fend off acquisition by a larger company, and expansion into Eastern Europe offered critical opportunities for growth. To this end Voest scored a major victory in 1992 when it acquired half-ownership and managerial control of the Dunaujvaros plant in central Hungary, the country's largest cold-rolling mill. The investment gave Voest a foothold to the Hungarian market and furthered its quest to become the primary steelmaker in east-central Europe.

By 1993 Austria's ambitious program to privatize much of its industrial sector was finally underway. That year, with the breakup of the state holding company, Austrian Industries, Voest-Alpine Stahl and its sister company, Voest-Alpine Technologie, became independently established. VA Technologie AG, the engineering company, made its initial public offering on the Vienna Stock Exchange in 1994, and Voest-Alpine Stahl (VA Stahl) followed suit in 1995. VA Stahl's initial issue of 11.2 million shares—8.2 million shares offered by OIAG, the state industrial holding company, and three million new shares—at Sch 285 per share represented one of the biggest privatizations in Austrian history.

The struggle to maintain autonomy remained paramount for VA Stahl, and the company continued its strategy of interna-

tional expansion. Not all of VA Stahl's acquisition attempts were fruitful, however. In 1997, the company attempted to purchase the steel division of Germany's Preussag but was rebuffed by Gerhard Schroder—then prime minister of Lower Saxony—who refused to admit a foreign takeover. Another of VA Stahl's major expansion opportunities fell flat in 1999, when the negotiations for its acquisition of the Sendzimira steel mill in Poland reached a stalemate, and VA Stahl was compelled to withdraw its bid.

More successfully, in 1998 VA Stahl acquired the Birmingham, England-based engineering company Metsec. Together, the companies would employ 1,800 people and produce roughly 450,000 tons of steel per year, an increase of 80,000 tons to VA Stahl's own output. Further, the acquisition broadened VA Stahl's portfolio of steel products for industrial and commercial building construction. Also in 1998, VA Stahl entered a joint venture with the German company Vossloh AG to acquire more than 90 percent of the shares of VAE AG, the Austrian world leader in rail switching equipment manufacturing.

By expanding its operations into niche markets, both the Metsec and the VAE acquisitions helped to insulate VA Stahl from the dramatic cyclical downturn that hit the steel industry in the late 1990s. Indeed, in addition to the cyclical volatility of the company's core steel business, expansion opportunities in this area were seen as extremely limited, and VA Stahl was keen to broaden its activities to include higher value, more profitable products in complementary areas of business. This initiative became central to the company's forward strategy for the new century.

To this end, the VA Stahl subsidiary Voest Alpine Stahl Linz GmbH launched a concentrated effort to develop its interests in processing activities, particularly in the area of products for the automotive industry. In September 2000, it acquired Rotec Zug AG, a Swiss manufacturer of precision steel pipes. Part of Rotec's specialty involved its ability to deliver products ready for installation. As such, about 60 percent of Rotec's output went to the automotive industry. VA Stahl Linz GmbH expected to realize significant synergies with Rotec, based on the companies' similar client structures.

Effecting an Image Change for the 21st Century

In the early years of the new century, as the problem of overcapacity in the worldwide steel market persisted, VA Stahl distinguished itself as one of the few European companies in the industry to report consistently solid profits. Continuing its strategic move away from steel production and toward steel processing, the company intensified its investment in the automotive supply industry. In June 2001, the company announced a restructuring plan whereby it would operate under four main divisions: automotive, railway systems, profiles, and flat steel. Further, VA Stahl resolved to return to its previous name, Voest-Alpine, in order to distance itself from its old image as a steelmaker. The company eventually settled on the name voestalpine AG. In 2001, the company announced plans to invest EUR 2 billion for external growth and diversification over the next five years, with half of this sum set aside specifically for future acquisitions. Once again, voestalpine appeared to be keeping pace with the changing competitive landscape.

Principal Subsidiaries

Voestalpine Grobblech; Voestalpine Gießerei Linz; Voestalpine Gießerei Traisen; Voestalpine Schmiede; Voestalpine Stahl Service Center; Voestalpine Stahlhandel Logistik Service; Voestalpine Rohstoffhandel; Voestalpine Rohstoffbeschaffung Voestalpine Personalberatung und –systeme; Polynorm; Voestalpine Matzner; Voestalpine Rotec; Voestalpine Europlatinen; Turinauto (33%); Sadef N.V.; Metsec plc.; Voestalpine Krems Finaltechnik; Roll Forming Corporation; Voestalpine Profilform; Präzisionsprofil; Voestalpine Schienen; TSTG Schienentechnik; VAE AG; Voestalpine Klöckner Bahntechnik; Railpro; Voestalpine Stahl Donawitz; Voestalpine Austria Draht; Voestalpine Tubulars (50%).

Principal Competitors

USX-U.S. Steel Group; Sumitomo Metal Industries, Ltd.; Nippon Steel Corporation; Gerdau SA; Usinor SA; Thyssen Krupp AG;

Further Reading

Blum, Patrick, "Austria Launches Privatizations," *London Financial Times,* November 15, 1993, p. 23.

Cockerill, A., *The Steel Industry,* Cambridge: Cambridge University Press, 1974.

Frey, Eric, "VA Stahl Wants No Part in Mergers," *London Financial Times,* July 14, 1999, p. 30.

Hogan, W.T., *World Steel in the 1980s,* Lexington: Lexington Books, 1983.

Hudson, R., and D. Sadler, *The International Steel Industry,* London: Routledge, 1989.

Jones, K., *Politics vs. Economics in the World Steel Trade,* London: Allen & Unwin, 1986.

Marsh, Peter, "Steelmakers Aim to Beat High-Tech Path to Profit: The Theme of This Year's Industry Gathering Was the Search for Ways to Overcome Global Overcapacity," *London Financial Times,* October 16, 2002, p. 10.

McGannon, *The Making, Shaping and Treating of Steel,* Pittsburgh: United States Steel Corporation, 1971.

"Metsec Agrees to £41m Austrian Bid," *Times* (London), May 30, 1998.

Nasbeth, L., and G.F. Ray, *The Diffusion of New Industrial Processes,* Cambridge: Cambridge University Press, 1974.

Rodger, Ian, "Voest-Alpine Stahl Floated," *London Financial Times,* October 6, 1995, p. 16.

—Cliff Pratten
—update: Erin Brown

Westar Energy, Inc.

P.O. Box 889
Topeka, Kansas 66601-0889
U.S.A.
Telephone: (785) 575-6300
Fax: (785) 575-1796
Web site: http://www.wr.com

Public Company
Incorporated: 1992
Employees: 5,600
Sales: $1.77 billion (2002)
Stock Exchanges: New York
Ticker Symbol: WR
NAIC: 221112 Fossil Fuel Electric Power Generation;
    221122 Electric Power Distribution; 221210 Natural
    Gas Distribution; 486210 Pipeline Transportation of
    Natural Gas

Westar Energy, Inc.—formerly Western Resources, Inc.—was formed in 1992 as the result of a merger between the Kansas Power and Light Company (KPL) and the Kansas Gas and Electric Company (KG&E). One of the largest combination utilities in the midwestern United States, Westar Energy provides electric utility and natural gas service primarily to some 640,000 customers in Kansas via 35,000 miles of electric distribution and transmission lines.

Late 19th-Century Origins of the Utilities Industry

The history of Western Resources is a story of nearly 370 mergers and acquisitions of various utility companies. Electric lighting was first introduced in the United States in Cleveland, Ohio, on April 29, 1879. Natural gas, which was also used for lighting, had already been introduced in Fredonia, New York, in 1821. The prospect of providing lighting for businesses and homes inspired a wave of entrepreneurs to establish small companies across the country. However, many of the small companies were unable to overcome the technological and financial difficulties that accompanied the growing demand for electrical

and natural gas services. Thus the smaller companies were taken over by larger firms with professional management, more capital, and the resources to develop innovative technologies.

Founding of Kansas Power and Light Company: 1924

The Kansas Power and Light Company was incorporated on March 6, 1924, for the purpose of acquiring, financing, constructing, and equipping an electrical generator plant located in Tecumseh, Kansas. The firm was also responsible for building electrical transmission lines from Tecumseh to Topeka and Atchison in order to provide service for new customers. KPL was financed by its ultimate parent company, North American Light and Power Company. North American, which controlled a large number of utility companies throughout Kansas, Illinois, Iowa, and Missouri, was a holding company. At that time, a holding company such as North American did not directly operate utilities, but owned and directed them through outstanding voting securities. The most important function for a utility holding company was to provide the financing necessary for its subsidiaries to expand and develop technological improvements.

During the time the power plant at Tecumseh was under construction, KPL completed the Neosho facility, with 15,000 kilowatts—later 40,000 kilowatts—generated by coal. KPL also moved quickly to reach new customers by acquiring the Union Power Company, which included numerous smaller utilities in Kansas, and the entire generating facility, electrical transmission lines, and distribution system in Douglas, Wyoming. When the Tecumseh plant was finished, it started operations with a 6,000 kilowatt generator. Soon power for electricity was generated for the utilities serving Topeka and Atchison. In 1927 KPL acquired the Kansas Public Service Company, which encompassed all the utilities in Topeka and Atchison, Kansas.

Major Acquisitions for KPL: 1930s–40s

KPL's major acquisition during the 1930s was the United Power and Light Corporation. Established in 1898 by Jacob Brown in a grist mill in Abilene, United Power and Light initially used the mill machinery to produce electrical power for the city. Brown's son, C.L. Brown (who founded United Life Insurance Company and was instrumental in laying the groundwork for United Telecom and U.S. Sprint), expanded the operation to include 12 other Kansas utilities. This single acquisition brought most of central Kansas under the service of KPL.

During the 1940s, KPL made another extremely important acquisition with its purchase of the Kansas Electric Power Company. Founded in 1922, the Kansas Electric Power Company provided natural gas and electric service to a large area of Eastern Kansas. KPL extended its customer base due to Kansas Electric's involvement in Franklin D. Roosevelt's rural electrification program, and the construction of natural gas pipelines and gas-generated power plants that served the burgeoning demand for electricity. In 1949 the North American Light and Power Company, the holding company for KPL, was liquidated; KPL stock was first listed on the New York Stock Exchange that same year.

Until the 1950s, much of the area serviced by KPL was farmland. However, as the population increased the area became more urban and attractive to manufacturing companies. By 1959, KPL was providing electricity and natural gas to flour mills, chemical companies, oil refineries, iron and steel manufacturers, cement firms, and clothing stores. In 1959 the sale of electricity generated nearly two-thirds of company revenues, while the sale of natural gas generated about one-third. The number of industrial customers increased by more than 125 percent, and individual domestic customers doubled in number. Total gas revenues during the period between 1950 and 1959 increased 112 percent.

Technological Advances and Rapid Growth for KPL: 1960s–80s

During the 1960s, KPL continued to upgrade its technology and expand its customer base. In 1962 the Tecumseh plant installed a 142,000 kilowatt unit. In 1965 the company began work on the first 345 kilovolt electrical transmission line in the state of Kansas. KPL completed construction of the line, which operated from Kansas City all the way to the Oklahoma state line, one year later. Around the same time, KPL joined 16 other electrical utility companies to build the Southwest Experimental Fast Oxide Reactor (SEFOR). In 1968 one of the larger generators at the company's Lawrence Generating Station was fitted with a limestone wet scrubber system, designed to reduce the amount of sulfur emissions into the atmosphere. This system was the first of its kind in the world.

Over the next two decades, KPL grew rapidly. The company opened a number of new utility power plants with state-of-the-art technology. Coal-fired power units, combustion turbines, and nuclear reactors formed the core of KPL's utility plants. During this period the Wolf Creek Generating Station, a nuclear reactor providing electrical service to a huge number of customers in the state of Kansas, began commercial operations with a capacity of 1.15 million kilowatts. The Jeffrey Energy Center, with one of KPL's largest coal-fired units, began commercial operations at approximately the same time. When KPL merged with Kansas Gas and Electric Company in 1992, the firm was one of the largest and most successful utilities in the United States.

History of the Kansas Gas and Electric Company: 1909–92

The Kansas Gas and Electric Company was established in 1909 by the holding company American Power and Light to operate utility services in Wichita, Pittsburg, and Frontenac, Kansas. The company built a coal-burning generating station in Wichita with an 8,750 kilowatt capacity in 1912. In 1925 the company sold KG&E's natural gas service to Hutchinson, Newton, Pittsburg, and Wichita in order to concentrate exclusively on electrical power. In 1910 KG&E served only three small communities and 5,525 customers; however, by 1925 the company had extended its services to over 50 communities and a much larger number of customers.

Continuing to expand during the 1930s and 1940s, KG&E added numerous coal-fired power plants to provide a growing customer base with electricity. In 1948 American Power and Light, the holding company for KG&E, sold 150,000 shares of company stock to the public. One year later, KG&E's remaining 450,000 shares of company stock were offered to the public. In 1954 the Murray Gill Station began operations with a 124,000 kilowatt capacity; it was the company's first use of natural gas as the primary fuel for a utility plant. In 1955 KG&E was listed on the New York Stock Exchange; at the same time, the company was adding more generating power to its Murray Gill Station and other utility operations. By 1959, the Murray Gill Station alone had a capacity of 609,000 kilowatts. During the late 1960s and early 1970s, KG&E entered the field of nuclear energy and began to plan a nuclear power plant in Coffey County. In the 1980s, like most other utility companies, KG&E continued to upgrade its technology and expand its services to customers. When KG&E combined with the Kansas Power & Light Company to form Western Resources, the company was financially stable and well managed, but in need of the resources of a larger utility firm to help it weather rising costs and increasing competition.

History of Gas Service Company: 1925–83

Western Resources' third operating group, Gas Service, was established in August 1925 by Henry L. Doherty. From the turn of the century, Henry L. Doherty & Company worked as the financial agent for various utility companies operating in Kansas, Missouri, and Oklahoma. Doherty's firm also represented Cities Service Company, one of the large holding companies for both utility and non-utility businesses. Doherty was contracted by Cities Service to organize the Gas Service Company in order to develop new markets for the natural gas resources that Cities Service owned, produced, and transmitted, and also to take control of and operate Cities Service's extensive distribution systems. The Gas Service Company grew slowly but steadily. Its stock was initially traded in 1971 on the New York Stock

Key Dates:

1909: Kansas Gas and Electric Company is established in 1909 by the holding company American Power and Light.

1924: The Kansas Power and Light Company (KPL) is incorporated, with financing from its ultimate parent company, North American Light and Power Company.

1925: Western Resources' third operating group, Gas Service Company, is established by Henry L. Doherty.

1927: KPL acquires the Kansas Public Service Company, which encompassed all the utilities in Topeka and Atchison, Kansas.

1930s: KPL acquires the United Power and Light Corporation.

1940s: KPL makes another acquisition with its purchase of the Kansas Electric Power Company.

1949: The North American Light and Power Company, the holding company for KPL, is liquidated; KPL stock is first listed on the New York Stock Exchange.

1965: The company begins work on the first 345 kilovolt electrical transmission line in the state of Kansas.

1971: Gas Service Company stock is initially traded on the New York Stock Exchange.

1983: Gas Service is acquired by KPL.

1992: KPL merges with Kansas Gas and Electric Company to form Western Resources.

2001: Western Resources changes its name to Westar Energy, Inc.

2002: Kansas Corporation Commission orders a sweeping reorganization of Westar Energy.

Exchange. By the time Gas Service was acquired by KPL in 1983, the company served over one million customers in Kansas, Missouri, Oklahoma, and Nebraska. (The company's Nebraska interests were later sold.)

1990: The Birth of Western Resources, Inc.

In July 1990, Kansas City Power & Light Company (KCP&L) attempted a hostile takeover of KG&E at $27 per share. Management and the board of directors at KG&E rejected the proposal and filed a lawsuit challenging the takeover attempt. Within one month, KG&E began to search for an alternative transaction that management regarded as more beneficial for both the company and the stockholders. In October, management at KG&E announced that the company would merge with KPL at a mutually agreed upon $32 per share in stock and cash. At first, KCP&L refused to withdraw its offer; however, by December KCP&L recognized the futility of its takeover attempt and announced a halt to any further negotiations.

When the merger of KPL and KG&E became public, there was an immediate opposition to the proposal. Public hearings in Independence, Wichita, Overland Park, and various other locations served by the two utilities focused on the possibility of a rate increase to fund the costs of the merger. The Kansas House

of Representatives even introduced legislation to ''protect customers in a merger.'' With significant revisions after much debate, the Kansas House passed a bill prohibiting any rate increase that would result from the costs incurred during the merger of utility companies. On February 5, 1992, the Securities and Exchange Commission (SEC) approved the merger application. By March, KG&E had merged with KPL as a wholly owned subsidiary of the latter, and in May the shareholders approved the new name of Western Resources, Inc., for the company.

By 1993, management had fully integrated the merger between KG&E and KPL, and located its corporate office in Topeka, Kansas. Western Resources' total net generating capability amounted to 4.98 million kilowatts in 1993. Total operating revenues were reported at $1.9 billion. During that year, Western Resources produced nearly 80 percent of its electricity from low sulfur coal, 17 percent from nuclear generators, and the rest from natural gas. The company sold almost all of its natural gas properties located in Missouri to the Southern Union Company, operating out of Austin, Texas. This sale led to a decrease in the number of natural gas customers to 637,000 from a high of over one million. Nonetheless, Western Resources owned and operated an extensive natural gas transmission pipeline system throughout Kansas, and owned underground storage facilities for natural gas in south central Kansas.

Shortly after its inception, Western Resources made two significant additions to its operations. The company created a subsidiary, Astra Resources, to conduct its non-regulated business interests, searching for investment opportunities in the areas of pipeline compression services, natural gas gathering and processing, and natural gas marketing. Western Resources also established a Power Technology Center in Wichita to address the growing number of customers requiring technical assistance. Engineers from Western Resources' Power Technology Center resolved problems for customers that arose in providing electrical power for sensitive electronic equipment. The Power Technology Center also tested experimental vehicles that used electricity or natural gas; in 1993 as part of the National Consortium for Emission Reduction in Lawn Care, the company distributed 100 battery-powered lawnmowers.

Anticipating Deregulation in the Late 1990s

With utilities deregulation on the horizon, Western Resources began to take measures to shore itself up for a dramatic increase in competition. A key strategy was to expand the size of its regional platform. To this end, in 1996 Western Resources became engaged in what would be a bitter two-year contest with Utilicorp United to acquire Kansas City Power and Light (KCPL). Initially, a merger was planned between KCPL and Utilicorp, but this deal fell through when shareholders, influenced in part by the prospect of a simultaneous hostile takeover bid by Western, withheld their support.

In March 1998, in what appeared to be the final chapter of this saga, Western Resources and Kansas City Power and Light (KCPL) reached their own merger agreement. By the terms of the 1998 deal, Western and KCP&L would contribute a combined $8.2 billion in electric assets to create Westar, a new Kansas City-based utility serving Kansas City, Wichita, and

Topeka. Western Resources would control 80.1 percent of the new company's stock, which would be traded on the New York Stock Exchange. Typically, finalization of the merger was contingent upon shareholder and regulatory approval, respectively.

Though regulators seemed willing to grant their approval under certain conditions, KCPL terminated the merger agreement late in 1999. Western Resources' stock price had fallen more than 46 percent by the end of the year. On the heels of this failure, Western Chairman and CEO David Wittig spearheaded a new plan to restructure his company and revive its stock.

In March 2000, Wittig announced that Western Resources (WR) would be split into two separate, publicly traded companies: Westar Energy would own WR's utility assets, primarily KG&E of Wichita and KPL of Topeka, worth about $4.6 billion; Westar Industries would own WR's non-utility assets worth about $1.35 billion, including an 85 percent stake in Protection One Inc., a home-security company, and a 45 percent stake in Oneok Inc., the parent company of Oklahoma Natural Gas, both of which Wittig had acquired in 1997. While the Oneok investment had proved solid, Protection One had performed poorly, dragging the whole of WR down in the process. Wittig's strategy was to liberate the utility assets from this burden, while coupling the relatively attractive Oneok with Protection One. To consolidate the shift, Western was renamed Westar Energy, Inc. in 2001.

Despite the restructuring, however, the company's financial performance did not improve: by September 2002, Westar Energy's stock was trading at less than $10 a share, the lowest level since Western Resources was formed in 1992. Though the company's regulated utilities had remained strong, the company's overall financial condition was suffering from the failure of its non-regulated enterprises. Further, the company had come under intense scrutiny for continuing to pay its top executives exorbitant salaries throughout these poorly performing years. Criticism was sharply focused on David Wittig, under whose leadership, which began in 1996, the company had declined steadily.

2002: Kansas Regulators Order Restructuring

In November 2002, Wittig stepped down in the face of federal indictments charging him with bank fraud, money laundering, and conspiracy, not directly related to his leadership of Western Resources. At the same time, the Kansas Corporation Commission ordered a thorough reorganization of Westar Energy. After finding that Westar had accumulated a huge corporate debt over the course of its continued investments in Protection One, the commission directed the company to segregate its utilities from the parent company as well as the unregulated ventures, so that accountability for income and debts could be enforced. Including other sweeping measures, the thrust of the commission's order was to favor the health and solvency of the utilities business over that of the non-utilities business, thereby protecting regional utilities customers. This was a reversal of the order of priorities that Westar had followed in recent years.

Principal Subsidiaries

ONEOK, Inc.; Protection One, Inc.

Principal Competitors

Great Plains Energy Inc.; The Pittston Company; Xcel Energy Inc.

Further Reading

Cook, James, "When 2 Plus 2 Equals 5," *Forbes,* June 8, 1992, p. 128.

Lazaroff, Leon, "Western Divests Security and Gas Holdings," *Daily Deal,* March 29, 2000.

Lefler, Dion, "Kansas Regulators Order Reorganization of Westar Energy," *Wichita Eagle,* November 9, 2002.

Rosenberg, Martin, "Western Resources, KCP&L Reach Merger Agreement," *Kansas City Star,* March 19, 1998.

Rothschild, Scott, "Westar Energy's New Executive Pay Policy Raises Eyebrows Among Critics," *Journal World,* September 25, 2002.

"Western Resources: Special Merger Edition," *Stars,* May 5, 1992, pp. 1–31.

—Thomas Derdak
—update: Erin Brown

Westell Technologies, Inc.

750 N. Commons Drive
Aurora, Illinois 60504
U.S.A.
Telephone: (630) 898-2500
Fax: (630) 375-4931
Web site: http://www.westell.com

Public Company
Incorporated: 1980
Employees: 967
Sales: $210.0 million (2003)
Stock Exchanges: NASDAQ
Ticker Symbol: WSTL
NAIC: 334210 Telephone Apparatus Manufacturing;
  334290 Other Communications Equipment
  Manufacturing

Westell Technologies, Inc. is the second largest manufacturer of digital subscriber line (DSL) cable modems in the United States. Westell Technologies, Inc. is a holding company for a telecommunications equipment manufacturing company, Westell, Inc., and a provider of conference call support services, ConferencePlus, Inc. Westell is a leading provider of technology that allows telephone companies to deliver high-speed data, voice, video, and Internet access over existing copper wires. It sells its equipment directly to telecommunications companies, which then install the modems in customer homes and businesses. Westell's products allow its customers to provide enhanced communications products to their own customers, without the costly renovation or replacement of existing phone lines. Westell's principal markets are the United States and Great Britain. The company operates a manufacturing plant in Aurora, Illinois. Its ConferencePlus subsidiary operates out of Schaumburg, Illinois. Robert C. Penny, son of the company's founder, and one other investor control more than 60 percent of Westell's stock.

New Technology in the 1980s

Westell, Inc. was founded by Clint Penny in 1980 in Willowbrook, Illinois, as a company to manufacture special equipment for the telecommunications industry. Its first products were signaling and transmission equipment, which it sold directly to telephone companies. Westell's equipment allowed telephone lines equipped for voice transmission to be bumped up so they could handle bulky data transmission. At one point, Westell's equipment was considered state of the art, and revenue rose to around $15 million. The company sold its technology to the regional phone companies, including Ameritech, Bell South, and Bell Atlantic. But the company's early success did not last. Revenue dropped to $8 million as its product lines were surpassed by newer equipment from competitors. The company began losing money, and its directors searched for a new chief executive who could turn the company around.

Westell picked Gary Seamans, an electrical engineer who had spent more than a dozen years working for AT&T. After AT&T, Seamans moved to MCI Communications Corp., where he became head of marketing for the midwestern region. Seamans had a reputation as a problem solver. The customer service division he oversaw at MCI had ranked absolutely last in customer satisfaction rankings when Seamans took over. Within a year, he had moved its customer service ranking to the top of the pile. Seamans was eager to get to work at Westell, which he had been told was having difficulties. But according to *Crain's Chicago Business* (July 8, 1996), Westell was actually in very bad shape by 1987 when Seamans came in. "They told me (the company) had a few problems," he told *Crain's*. "They didn't tell me it was dead." One of Westell's bankers confirmed for *Crain's* that the company was only a year or a year-and-a-half from bankruptcy when Seamans became president and chief executive.

Seamans worked quickly to repair Westell's damaged reputation, going out to its major customers and listening to their complaints and suggestions. Seamans soon decided that what the company really needed was a new product line. In 1988 Westell came out with the T1 Network Interface Unit, or NIU. This was a diagnostic device that allowed telephone company workers to find problems on a customer's wire without having to go physically to the customer's house or office. The NIU was apparently a rapid hit with Westell's major clients, and by 1988 the company was able to move to expanded facilities in nearby Oswego, Illinois. Westell debuted another product the next year, which it sold through a subsidiary company, ConferencePlus, Inc. ConferencePlus offered a high level of service for conference calls, that is, calls that linked more than two parties. ConferencePlus offered conference call service that also supported video and data sharing. It sold this service both to telephone companies and to multinational corporations. In 1992 this subsidiary company moved to its own quarters in Schaumburg, Illinois.

Marketing DSL in the 1990s

By 1991, Westell's financial troubles seemed firmly behind it. The company was once again profitable, and revenue reached slightly more than $24 million that year. The company had at least two viable products, and it had orders from the large domestic telecommunications companies. But Gary Seamans at that point took the company in a new direction. This was a new technology called ADSL, for asymmetrical digital subscriber line. By the early 1990s it was clear that consumers were ready for more advanced communications technology. While traditional phone lines carried simple voice communications, new technologies seemed just around the corner that would allow consumers to use their phones to get pictures, video on demand, computer data, or remote access to appliances. Technologies that had been the stuff of science fiction were now plausible, though many practical considerations stood in the way. One roadblock was the expense of replacing existing telephone lines with new wire that could carry broadband (high-speed voice, data, and video) communications. Westell began developing ADSL products, which allowed copper phone wire to handle broadband. ADSL gave phone companies the same speed as fiber-optic cable over their existing networks. By 1992 Westell had completed a prototype of what became known as its Flexcap modem, and Seamans began flogging it to telecommunications companies across the United States and overseas as well. Seamans soon found almost two dozen customers, including British Telecom, Bell Atlantic, and US West. These companies initiated trials of ADSL. An initial customer group in Virginia was fitted with Westell modems to receive video on demand. Westell continued to improve its ADSL technology as the trials went on around the world.

Sales at the company doubled between 1992 and 1996, reaching $83 million. But much of this money was plowed back into research and development, and Westell lost $500,000 in

1996. Seamans remained ebullient about the possibilities of Westell and ADSL. The company held an initial public offering in November 1995, raising $33.3 million, and it raised another $62 million months later in a second offering. The company anticipated continuing to lose money, yet Seamans saw big things to come. "I honestly see this company as having the very real opportunity to become the next Microsoft," he told *Crain's Chicago Business* in an article entitled "Turning Copper to Gold." The potential sales for Westell's high bandwidth products seemed enormous. In anticipation of coming orders, the company moved into larger quarters in Aurora. But Westell was not the only company that had discovered the copper-based broadband niche. In late 1996 a number of the regional telecommunications companies that had been running Westell ADSL trials announced that they would switch to a competitor's product. The competitor was the French company Alcatel Alsthom S.A. Sales fell off slightly for Westell the next year, apparently because of the loss to Alcatel, and Westell ended up much more deeply in the red, losing $14.7 million.

Westell gained new contracts with British Telecom, Bell Atlantic, and other domestic phone companies in 1997. It introduced new products, and also formed partnerships with more established technology firms, including Texas Instruments, Fujitsu, and Lucent Technologies. In 1997 Westell also announced a merger with the San Jose, California-based firm Amati Communications Corp. Amati focused on a technology called DMT, for discreet multitone, that allowed ADSL to work over longer wire lines. The merger, which was to have been effected by a stock swap valued at $394 million, would have given Westell a boost over its competitors in the DSL world. *Electronic News* (October 6, 1997) claimed the merger would make Westell "the first supplier with the most to offer." Unfortunately, Texas Instruments stepped in at the last minute and scotched Westell's deal. It offered Amati $395 million in cash, and Amati took it, paying Westell $14.8 million to terminate their original merger plans. Westell went on to form an arrangement with Texas Instruments that still gave it access to Amati's technology.

Shortly after the Amati merger failed, the company got more bad news. CEO Seamans, who had been such a vigorous salesman for Westell, announced he was taking a leave of absence for medical reasons. The temporary leave became permanent, and the company found a new chief executive in 1998, 36-year-old Marc Zionts. Westell's stock price, meanwhile, rose and fell rapidly. In 1996, Westell had traded for as much as $56. By late 1997 it was trading around $27, and a year later it was down to less than $10. The company had developed an array of DSL products with different acronyms, including vDSL and xDSL, and it continued to sell its NIU line. In 1997 the company also incorporated a subsidiary company that specialized in customer service and product maintenance, called Westell Worldwide, Inc. Westell was holding steady with revenues in the late 1990s in the $80 million range. But increasingly, larger companies had cut in on Westell's market. Where it had had a strong early lead with ADSL, by 1998 there were nearly 100 companies marketing similar products. Some large competitors, like Alcatel, got larger in the late 1990s through acquisition. Alcatel picked up a Texas company, DSC Communications, in 1998, while Cisco Systems bought an ADSL maker called NetSpeed Inc. Westell itself made a significant acquisition in the last days of 1999, when it paid $205 million in stock for its competitor Teltrend, Inc.

Turning the Corner in the 2000s

Finally in 2000 Westell's main customers, the regional Bell telephone companies, seemed ready to deploy DSL on a large scale. For the first quarter of 2000, Westell's revenue jumped by close to 350 percent. ''We're in full-fledged ramp-up,'' Westell's CEO Zionts told *Crain's Chicago Business* (July 10, 2000), and the company was expecting sales to increase by a factor of six over the next year. The telecommunications companies that had dragged their feet through the late 1990s were now placing large orders for DSL equipment. Westell's stock, still around $10 since 1998, surged in early 2000 to more than $40. But by the end of the year, it was clear that the DSL revolution would not happen overnight. Local phone companies experienced delays and bottlenecks in getting the systems installed for their customers. Sales of Westell's DSL modems fell 20 percent over the quarter ending September 30, and the company's stock swung downward again, falling to around $5. The company also faced a lawsuit brought by stockholders, who claimed the company had misled them by not revealing that a major customer was cutting its orders. The suit also alleged that CEO Zionts and other top executives had made about $15 million between them by selling their own shares just before the bad news brought the stock price down. Of that amount, $10 million went to Zionts, who had sold some 500,000 shares when Westell's price was close to $30. (In a similar case, in 1999 two Westell sales executives and another man paid $70,000 to settle Securities and Exchange Commission charges that they had benefited from inside knowledge, selling off stock before the price fell on a customer equipment cutback in 1996.)

Zionts left the company in 2001 to become president and CEO of a small technology start-up firm called Airslide Systems. He was succeeded by E. Van Cullens. Van Cullens had worked for almost 30 years in the telecommunications industry, running Harris Corporation in Florida, and also working in a variety of positions for Siemens ICN and GTE Telephone. Over the next year, the economy slumped, and the telecommunications sector was particularly hard hit. Perversely, this seemed a good thing for Westell. Its technology had long been the cheap alternative to fiber optics and cable modems. Whereas in the early 2000s cable modem high-speed Internet access outsold DSL by a ratio of two to one, phone companies were getting more eager to push DSL, seeing it as a last chance to squeeze profits out of stagnant markets. The market for home high-speed Internet access was rising, and the phone companies needed to act quickly to prevent cable companies from sweeping up their customers. In February 2003, the Federal Communications Commission (FCC) issued a ruling indicating that telephone companies did not need to share their DSL service networks with competitors. Orders for Westell's modems picked up, and it ended fiscal 2002 with two profitable quarters. Westell's share price rose more than 600 percent over the first half of 2003. The company's sales volume for its DSL equipment was expected to go up at least 25 percent over the year. Westell had been counting on a wide rollout of DSL service since the early 1990s. Ten years later, it may finally have gotten its wish. Now its mission was to keep its position in the market, and not let newer or bigger competitors push it aside.

Principal Subsidiaries

Westell, Inc.; ConferencePlus, Inc.

Principal Competitors

Efficient Networks, Inc.; Netopia, Inc.; Alcatel Alsthom S.A.

Further Reading

Arndorfer, James B., ''Earnings Gains Lift Tech Issues in July,'' *Crain's Chicago Business,* August 14, 2000, p. 62.

Bournellis, Cynthia, ''Westell, Amati to Merge,'' *Electronic News,* October 6, 1997, p. 1.

Cahill, Joseph B., ''Turning Copper into Gold,'' *Crain's Chicago Business,* July 8, 1996, p. 15.

——, ''Westell's Rapid Link Slow to Draw Sales,'' *Crain's Chicago Business,* September 22, 1997, p. 41.

''Download: Westell Takes on Teltrend,'' *Telephony,* December 20, 1999.

Freeman, Adam L., ''Westell Soars: Advance Gain,'' *Dow Jones Business News,* March 20, 2003.

Jones, Sandra, ''DSL Static Cuts Off Westell Prospects,'' *Crain's Chicago Business,* November 6, 2000, p. 3.

Mathison, Tyler, ''Westell Technology—CFO Interview,'' *America's Intelligence Wire,* July 10, 2003.

Merrion, Paul, ''Weaving a New Net,'' *Crain's Chicago Business,* July 10, 2000, p. 15.

Mulqueen, John T., ''High Speed = Big Bucks,'' *CommunicationsWeek,* July 15, 1996, p. 69.

Murphy, H. Lee, ''Investors Wired As Westell Readies Rollout of High-Speed,'' *Crain's Chicago Business,* September 23, 1996, p. 35.

——, ''May Rally Lifts Telecom Stocks,'' *Crain's Chicago Business,* June 9, 2003, p. 7.

——, ''Telecom Prodigy Risks Becoming Just Another Takeover Casualty,'' *Crain's Chicago Business,* August 3, 1998, p. 4.

Norris, Floyd, ''Initial Public Offerings Drift Back to Earth,'' *New York Times,* July 18, 1996, p. D9.

O'Shea, Dan, ''On the Frontier,'' *Telephony,* October 31, 1997, p. 62.

''3 Men Pay $70,000 on S.E.C. Charges,'' *New York Times,* August 28, 1999, p. C14.

Van, John, ''Aurora, Ill.-Based Phone Equipment Maker CEO Resigns,'' *Knight-Ridder/Tribune Business News,* March 2, 2001.

——, ''Westell Banking on Renewal of Bells' DSL Push,'' *Chicago Tribune,* August 14, 2002.

''Westell CEO Takes Medical Leave,'' *Electronic News,* December 22, 1997, p. 10.

''Westell Lost Amati, Gains Alliance with TI,'' *Electronic News,* November 24, 1997, p. 6.

—A. Woodward

The Wolverhampton & Dudley Breweries, PLC

P.O. Box 26, Park Brewery, Bath Road
Wolverhampton
West Midlands WV1 4NY
United Kingdom
Telephone: (+44) 1902-711-811
Fax: (+44) 1902-429-136
Web site: http://www.fullpint.co.uk

Public Company
Incorporated: 1890
Employees: 12,569
Sales: £505.6 million ($789.3 million) (2002)
Stock Exchanges: London
Ticker Symbol: WOLV
NAIC: 312120 Breweries; 721110 Hotels (Except Casino
    Hotels) and Motels; 722410 Drinking Places
    (Alcoholic Beverages)

The Wolverhampton & Dudley Breweries, PLC, popularly known as Wolves, is the United Kingdom's largest integrated regional brewer and pub operator. The company operates two breweries in Wolverhampton and in Burton on Trent, with a focus on ales. Wolves' brands, grouped under its W&DB Brands unit, include the national bestseller Marstons' Pedigree, as well as Banks' Original—its historic brand—Banks' Bitter, and Mansfield Bitter. Like most of the United Kingdom's brewers, Wolves also operates its own distribution network, in the form of more than 1,600 managed and tenanted pubs. Tenanted pubs—in which the company holds the property and leases the business to an independent operator-tenant—make up the largest share of the company's estate, with 1,035 pubs in 2003. These pubs are grouped under subsidiary The Union Pub Company. The company also directly owns and operates 595 managed pubs, through its Pathfinder Pubs subsidiary. Wolves' pubs operate under several brand formats, including Bostin' Locals, as well as a small number of urban-located Pitcher & Piano pubs. Since the beginning of the 2000s, Wolves has focused its retail operations on the community pub format, selling off nearly 1,000 city center and other locations. Pathfinder generated more than 55 percent of the

company's 2002 revenues of £505 million, while W&DB Brands produced 25 percent of sales. Listed on the London Stock Exchange since 1891, Wolves is led by Chairman—and great-great-grandson of the company's founder—David Thompson, and CEO Ralph Findlay.

Midlands Brewing Start-Up in the 1890s

Wolverhampton & Dudley Breweries traced its origins back to the second half of the 19th century. In 1875, a Mr. Banks founded the Park Brewery on Wolverhampton's Chapel Ash Street on the site of an Artesian well. Said to have enjoyed living the good life, Banks built up a number of debts, in particular to his malt supplier, George Thompson, who owned a malt wholesale business as well as the Dudley & Victoria Brewery nearby in the town of Dudley. Thompson offered Banks an extended line of credit, which was secured against his business. When Banks disappeared suddenly, Thompson took over the heavily indebted brewery.

Thompson merged the Banks brewery business with his own, refinanced its debt, and then added a third brewery, owned by Charles Colonel Smith, the Fox Brewery, located in Wolverhampton. Thompson named the newly merged business Wolverhampton & Dudley Breweries, and took it public that same year. The following year, however, the business faced a major setback when fire destroyed its Dudley brewery. Nonetheless, the company rebuilt the brewery.

Taking the lead of the company was Thompson's son, Edwin John. The Thompson family was to play a prominent role within the company throughout the century to come, and by the beginning of the 21st century, the fifth generation of the Thompsons remained in the company's top management. Yet the Thompson family's shareholding of the company itself remained minor, particularly after the company began offering its stock to employees.

By the end of its first decade, Wolves, as it became popularly known, had expanded the Park and Fox site, which then became capable of brewing the entirety of the company's ale production, including its main ale brand, Banks. Wolves also had

Company Perspectives:

Our Objectives: For customers of Pathfinder Pubs: To deliver excellence in managed community pubs—with superior retailing capability in well situated pubs of a high standard offering value for money to all. Of the Union Pub Company: To stand out in the tenanted pub sector—for the quality of our pubs, our tenants, the attractiveness of our agreements—and our straightforward approach. Of W&DB Brands: To be regarded as the experts in ale—offering leading ale brands, with the best local services. For employees: To be "FIT": to operate fairly, with integrity and transparency. For shareholders: To deliver growth in cashflow and shareholder value.

begun building up its pubs estate, and by 1898 included 56 freehold sites and five tenanted sites.

In the new century, Wolves began acquiring new breweries. Between 1909 and 1928 it bought up a number of breweries, including North Worcestershire Breweries, John Robinson & Sons, Kidderminster Brewery, and the Robert Allen Brewery. The company's next brewery purchase came in 1942, when it acquired Julia Hanson & Sons and its popular Hanson's branded ale. In 1960, the company purchased the Broadway Brewery as well. These acquisitions went especially to boost the number of the company's pubs—prior to the 1990s, Britain's pubs tended to be owned by its breweries, and dedicated to their brands.

In the mid-1960s, however, Wolves joined a drive by a number of brewers, including Allied, Bass, and others, to take over the distribution of the Romanoff vodka brand, forming the partnership Vodka Romanoff Ltd. in 1965. The companies then began selling the bottled vodka product through their pubs and licensed premises. Yet brewing remained the company's core activity; in 1972, the company began a new expansion of its main Park Brewery. At the same time the company added a new line, when it began producing the popular Irish lager brand Harp under license. By then the company, under the leadership of fourth-generation Edwin Thompson, had sales of more than £15 million.

Growth Through the 1980s

Wolves stepped up its growth through the 1970s, opening a number of new pubs and starting a large-scale capital expenditures program. The company also reached a new co-partnership agreement with the then-independent Harp Lager to introduce the brand on tap to its pubs. Wolves also launched a line of canned-only beer brands, which proved a popular success. By 1975, the company's sales had shot up past £26 million.

In 1976, Wolves acquired the U.K. licensing rights to popular French lager brand Kronenbourg, which were successfully added to its pub lineup. The company also began construction of a new packaging plant, completed in 1977. The continued buildup of the company's network of managed and tenanted pubs enabled the company to book continued sales growth through the decade, as turnover topped £56 million by the end of 1979. By then, Wolves had strengthened its involvement with Harp, taking a 10 percent stake in the Harp Lager marketing and production consortium formed by Arthur Guinness and Green King.

Despite the recession of the early 1980s, Wolves' sales, backed by the company's commitment to capital expansion, continued to rise, nearing £81 million by 1982. By then, Wolves had established itself as one of the top regional brewers in the United Kingdom and a dominant force in its core Midlands region. The company's emphasis on mild ale brands—popular in its region but virtually unknown in the heavily populated south—restricted its further expansion somewhat. Nonetheless, the company had by then built up a network of more than 700 "tied" pubs for its products.

Wolves returned to the acquisition trail in 1983 when it launched a takeover bid for Birmingham-based Davenports Brewery, a move that would have given Wolves a solid base of 125 pubs in Birmingham. The company managed to acquire nearly 24 percent of the company, yet was ultimately thwarted in the attempt when a trust controlling nearly 30 percent of Davenports rejected the offer. By the following year, Wolves itself appeared to be a potential target for a takeover attempt, notably by one of the fast-growing national brewers. Yet a Monopolies & Mergers Commission's (MMC) rejection of a similar takeover attempt in 1985 effectively barred the national groups from acquiring regional leaders such as Wolves.

Instead, David Thompson, who became the company's managing director in 1986, led the company on its own expansion drive. In 1988, Wolves bought 84 pubs, including 61 tenancy pubs, from rival group Watney Mann. The purchase helped to strengthen the company's presence in the eastern and southern Midlands.

Maintaining the Regional Tradition in the New Century

In 1989, Britain's MMC struck a new blow at the market dominance of the country's national brewers by requiring brewers to choose between brewing or pub operations (of more than 2,000 pubs). The move favored the growth of regional brewers, including Wolves, in particular by signaling a vast restructuring of the industry and the sell-off of large swaths of pubs across the country. As a major regional, Wolves was especially well placed to boost its own portfolio of pubs. At the same time, the MMC ruling also included a provision that pubs open their sales to so-called "guest" beers for the first time.

Wolves stepped up to the acquisition plate again at the beginning of 1992, paying £18.7 million to acquire Hartlepool-based Cameron's Brewery, as well as its 51-pub chain, from Brent Walker. That acquisition made Wolves not only the number one brewer in the Midlands, but the top regional brewer in all of the United Kingdom. In May of that year, the company took a different tack toward growth by signing a joint distribution agreement with rival brewer and pub operator Marstons, which placed both companies' beers in each other's pubs.

Wolves had made a foray beyond its brewing and pub ownership operation, moving into hotel operations in the early 1990s. The company built up a chain of eight hotels, under the Crown & Raven name. In 1995, however, the company refo-

Key Dates:

1875: Park Brewery is founded by a Mr. Banks in Wolverhampton.

1890: George Thompson takes over Park Brewery, merges it with his own Dudley Brewery and Fox Brewery, forming Wolverhampton & Dudley Breweries (Wolves), which goes public that year.

1908: Wolves makes its first acquisition, of North Worcestershire Breweries, and then acquires John Robinson & Sons, Kidderminster, and Robert Allen by 1928.

1942: Julia Hanson & Sons and its Hanson's brand is acquired.

1960: Broadway Brewery is acquired.

1988: Wolves buys 84 pubs, including 61 tenancy pubs, from rival group Watney Mann.

1992: Wolves acquires Cameron's brewery and pub chain.

1998: Wolves launches a hostile takeover attempt of Marstons.

1999: Wolves acquires Marstons, and then acquires Mansfield Brewery later that year.

2001: Wolves fights off a hostile takeover attempt by Pubmaster, then closes two breweries.

2003: After shedding nearly 1,000 pubs, Wolves restructures as a community-focused pub operator.

cused on its core business, selling the Crown & Raven chain to the Regal Hotel Group.

Through the mid-1990s, Wolves joined an industrywide trend in building up strong branded pub chains, a move exemplified by the JD Wetherspoon group. Wolves rolled out a number of pub chains and branded concepts, such as the Fast Eddies sports bar and the Last Word café bar concepts, as well as Milestone, Taverns, Taphouses, Poacher's Pocket, and Varsity pub brands. Not all of the company's new bar concepts were a success, however, and at the end of 1997 the company dropped a number of its money-losers and scaled back its offering to just the Milestone, Varsity, and Poacher's Pocket concepts.

Instead, Wolves began stalking new takeover prey. At the end of 1998, the company found its first target, Marstons, launching a £262 million takeover bid. The takeover quickly turned hostile, and Marstons fought back, using a so-called "Pac Man" defense to launch a countertakeover bid for Wolves. In the end, Wolves won the day, and bought up Marstons for £292 million in February 1999. The acquisition gave it a new brewery in Burton on Trent, boosted its total pub holdings past 2,000, including the small but growing pub chain Pitchers & Piano, and, of importance, gave it a Marstons nationally prominent ale brand, Pedigree. The company immediately began selling off some of its new pubs, reducing its total to around 1,800.

Wolves' next target came in September of that same year, when it bid £230 million to take over Mansfield Brewery. This time the bid succeeded without a fight, for a final purchase price of £361 million—including more than £100 million in debt.

The addition of Mansfield gave Wolves its fourth brewery, and boosted its pub total back up to nearly 2,300.

Yet Wolves' aggressive expansion, coupled with a discounted pricing drive during the year, left it weakened financially. By mid-2000, David Thompson had been moved out of the managing director's position, to the more ceremonial position as chairman. Instead, the company created a new CEO position, naming former company Finance Director Ralph Findlay to the spot.

Findlay set to work integrating the company's new acquisitions, including regrouping its tenanted pub holdings under a new subsidiary, The Union Pub Company. Yet the company's financial difficulties now made it a vulnerable takeover target. The first offer came in August 2000, when Noble House made a £400 million bid for the company. Wolves rejected that bid, and instead concentrated on a review of its operations—both in its brewery and pub holdings.

A new suitor for the company turned up in May 2001, when the Pubmaster group launched its own takeover offer. Wolves fought back—and in the end beat out the Pubmaster offer with a margin of just 3 percent among shareholder votes. As part of its defense, Wolves had announced its intention to sell off some 170 pubs, including its nationally operating Pitcher & Piano pub chain.

The company made good on part of that promise, selling off 44 pubs to the Royal Bank of Scotland at the end of 2001. This sell-off was part of a larger effort by the company to refocus itself as an operator of community pubs—as opposed to urban and city center pubs. Although the company ultimately decided to keep the Pitcher & Piano chain, because it could not find an adequate purchase price, it went ahead with its pub disposals, trimming down to just 1,600 pubs by 2003. Wolves also shut down its Camerons and Mansfields breweries, shifting production back to just two core plants. The company also sought to boost its position as a premium ale specialist, suggesting that it would drop its Harp brand distribution business.

While these moves caused a drop in Wolves' turnover—which shrunk back to £505 million in 2002—the leaner company had prepared itself for a stronger, more profitable future. As Findlay told the *Birmingham Post:* "We now have one of the highest quality tenanted estates in the country." The company also continued to ply the strength of its main brand Pedigree in the fast-growing retail channel, launching a liter-sized bottle in June 2003. Meanwhile, Wolves had not entirely abandoned the prospect of new acquisitions, acknowledging that it had entered—ultimately fruitless—talks to acquire Eldridge Pope in May 2003. For the time being, Wolves appeared content to draw the rewards of being the United Kingdom's leading independent regional brewer.

Principal Subsidiaries

Pathfinder Pubs; The Union Pub Company; W&DB Brands.

Principal Competitors

Allied Domecq PLC; SABMiller PLC; Whitbread PLC; Carlsberg-Tetley Brewing Ltd.; Guinness Ltd.; Greene King

PLC; CI Traders Ltd.; Fuller Smith and Turner PLC; Daniel Thwaites PLC; Young and Co.'s Brewery PLC.

Further Reading

"Bitter?," *Independent,* June 14, 2000, p. 3.

Blackwell, David, "Tables Turned on Wolves As Hunter Becomes the Hunted," *Financial Times,* August 16, 2000, p. 24.

Murray-West, Rosie, "No Sign of a Hangover As Wolves Gets the Brew Right," *Daily Telegraph,* December 10, 2002.

Pain, Steve, "Ralph Findlay—Boss Who Leaves No Stone Unturned," *Birmingham Post,* April 12, 2003, p. 26.

Palmer, Tim, "Where We Want to Be," *Grocer,* September 8, 2001, p. 47.

"Pedigree to Be Launched in Litre Bottles," *Marketing Week,* June 12, 2003, p. 8.

"UK Drinks Its Way Out of Economic Gloom," *Caterer & Hotelkeeper,* May 29, 2003, p. 8.

Waples, John, "Brewer Embarks on Bitter Battle," *Sunday Times,* November 29, 1998, p. 6.

—M.L. Cohen

World Acceptance Corporation

108 Frederick Street
Greenville, South Carolina 29607
U.S.A.
Telephone: (864) 298-9800
Fax: (864) 298-9810

Public Company
Founded: 1962 as World Finance
Employees: 1,640
Sales: $155.7 million (2003)
Stock Exchanges: NASDAQ
Ticker Symbol: WRLD
NAIC: 522291 Consumer Lending

A provider of consumer loans, World Acceptance Corporation focuses mainly on the subprime market, comprised of individuals with limited access to credit due to low income or previous credit problems. The company offers high interest loans of less than $1,000 and maturity at less than one year. This market provides a high return on investment as the company charges the highest fees and interest rates allowable by state laws. World offers larger, lower interest loans, up to $3,000, with maturity ranging from 18 to 24 months. Related services include credit insurance in certain states and credit for the purchase of electronic goods and appliances through the World Class Buying Club. World acts as agent to sell automobile club memberships and provides tax preparation and electronic filing services as well. World operates more than 470 offices in South Carolina, Texas, Georgia, Tennessee, Oklahoma, Kentucky, Illinois, Missouri, New Mexico, Louisiana, and Alabama.

Growing Slowly But Profitably in the 1960s

World Acceptance Corporation began operations in 1962 under the name World Finance, providing small-loan consumer credit through four offices in Greenville, South Carolina. The company catered to people who had no other form of credit available due to low income or prior credit problems, but who needed cash for an unexpected expense, such as a car repair. While small-loan finance involved high-risk lending, the risk

was spread over many loans and World charged the highest fees and interest rates allowable by law; fees and interest added as much as 90 percent of the loan amount to repayment. World was managed profitably and expanded slowly and by 1973 the company operated 54 offices in South Carolina, Georgia, and Texas.

In 1973 Southern Bank, also of Greenville, acquired World. Ownership by Southern Bank enhanced World's ability to operate profitably by expanding the supply of money for loans at lower interest rates. In 1979, when interest rates reached a historical peak, Southern Bank obtained money for lending at 9.95 percent interest, lower than national rates. While return on investment was lower overall, compared with 1978 banker interest rates of approximately 7 percent, the lower rate obtained by Southern minimized the "squeeze" on investment.

In 1979 World sought to reduce costs and began a three-year process of installing an online computer system at branch offices. The system sped the pace of handling accounting functions, such as recording loans administered and loan payments. By improving operational efficiency, World freed loan officers to provide better customer service and to perform more thorough credit evaluations. As World expanded, computerized office functions played a significant role in increasing the number of loans issued at a comparatively small increase in expense.

Southern Bank continued World's expansion, opening or acquiring new loan offices. In 1980 the State of Oklahoma granted World a charter to operate and over the next two years World opened six offices in Oklahoma. In 1982 World operated 87 offices, 39 in South Carolina, 25 in Texas, 17 in Georgia, and six in Oklahoma. Loans receivable reached $26.6 million, garnering $3.3 million in earnings before taxes.

World accelerated the pace of growth, opening or acquiring 17 offices in 1983 and 14 offices in 1984. In 1985 the company opened its first office in Louisiana. When First Union Corporation of Charlotte, North Carolina, merged with Southern Bank in 1986, the company operated 143 offices in five states. First Union showed little interest in developing World's network of offices, however, and expansion at World stalled.

1989 Management Buyout Serving to Renew and Accelerate Expansion

Charles Walters, president of World and an employee since 1972, led a senior management buyout of the company from First Union. In April 1989 World became an independent company with Walters as chairman, president, and CEO. World became a public company in December 1991, raising a net of $13 million with common stock selling at $7 per share. In order to improve the company's financial situation and credit terms, World used the proceeds to redeem outstanding preferred stock and to pay junior subordinated notes.

After a hiatus of new openings between October 1987 and July 1989, World opened or acquired 30 offices between July 1989 and December 1991, ending fiscal 1992 with 176 offices. World recorded $44.6 million in loans receivable, an increase from $38.4 million in 1989 when the management buyout process began. Revenues from fees and interest increased from $32.3 million in 1989 to $39.9 million in 1992, garnering net income of just less than $2 million. Texas and South Carolina offices comprised the majority of revenues, at 39 percent and 38 percent, respectively. Georgia offices comprised 13 percent of revenues; Oklahoma, 8 percent; and Louisiana, 2 percent. The average loan issued was $368, with an average maturity of eight months.

The increasing number of offices in Texas resulted in a higher rate of charge-offs, as the state banned the sale of credit-related insurance. This not only eliminated a base of revenue, it impacted potential credit loss as well. Net charge-off as a percentage of average loan receivables increased to 8.4 percent in 1992, from 7.9 percent in 1991. The company continued to focus its expansion efforts in Texas, Louisiana, and Oklahoma (which also banned the sale of credit-related insurance), because laws in those states permitted creditors to charge higher interest and fees than in South Carolina and Georgia.

As World expanded, its strategy involved placing loan offices near other lenders, due to the tendency of customers of small-loan consumer finance to use more than one lender. Most of the company's competition came from independent offices or chains of 20 or fewer offices. The company saw its competitive advantage in terms of the volume of capital available at lower cost as well as operational cost efficiency from computerized accounting functions.

In April 1993 World purchased ParaData Financial Systems, Inc., creator of a proprietary software for administering consumer loans. After examining several software options, World chose ParaData's system as the best. The company chose to acquire ParaData in order to have an in-house system that paid for itself, saving on the costly expense of outsourcing computer systems maintenance. While World converted its computer sys-

tem to the ParaData software, a process that took a year to complete, ParaData continued to offer the software to other consumer finance companies.

Mid-1990s: Offering New Services and Continuing to Expand

First Union Corporation sold its residual interest in World Acceptance through a secondary offering of stock in May, allowing World to engage in business activities prohibited until this time. In November the company began to sell automobile club memberships, acting as agent for a third party, earning $236,000 in commissions for the remainder of the fiscal year.

In February 1995 World introduced the "World Class Buying Club" through offices in Texas. The program offered electronic goods and appliances through direct-mail catalogue and provided financing for purchases. Goods were shipped directly from the manufacturer. While World charged more than regular stores for the merchandise, they did not incur the expense of inventory, so the business proved very profitable. The program added $915,000 in new loans during the first four months. The World Class Buying Club was extended to Georgia and Tennessee in August 1995 and to South Carolina that fall.

The company's office expansion strategy involved adding 20 offices per year, through acquisition or new stores opening. World finished fiscal 1993 with 191 offices, an addition of 15 offices. This included 11 offices in Texas, primarily in south Texas, and two offices in Nashville, a new market for the company. In Tennessee, World offered involuntary unemployment insurance as well. The company closed fiscal 1994 with 217 offices. In 1995 World added 27 loan offices, only two of them acquisitions. At the close of 1996 the company operated 282 offices, including the addition of 17 new offices opened that year.

In 1996 ParaData completed its largest project to date, the conversion of Mercury Finance, one of the largest financiers for used automobiles in the United States, to ParaData's proprietary software. The sale to such a large customer resulted in an increase of revenues at ParaData to $3.4 million that year. World did not expect ParaData to maintain that level of sales; however, ParaData's software supported more than 800 consumer loan offices operated by 92 different customers.

During fiscal 1996 revenues reached $69.9 million, representing a 20 percent increase over 1995 revenues and a 15 percent annual compound growth rate since 1992. The average loan was $500 with average maturity of ten months. By maintaining tight control over costs and loan quality, World increased net income by 22.5 percent to $10.6 million.

Although loan receivables increased 11.5 percent to $99.4 million in 1996, this amount was below expectations, especially given the previous year's 23 percent increase. World attributed this slow growth to insufficient advertising during the busy Christmas shopping season. The company hired consultants to analyze the company's customer base, providing demographic and geographic profiles of potential customers. The company then purchased prospect lists that better characterized its potential market. To reduce advertising expense and improve efficiency, World Acceptance centralized advertising operations by purchasing automated mailing equipment, work previously han-

Key Dates:

1962: World Finance is founded with four offices in Greenville, South Carolina.
1973: Southern Bank acquires the company, now named World Acceptance Corporation.
1982: World issues $26.6 million in loans through 87 offices in South Carolina, Georgia, Texas, and Oklahoma.
1986: First Union Corporation merges with Southern Bank.
1989: Senior management buys World from First Union.
1991: Initial public offering prepares World for profitable expansion.
1993: World acquires ParaData Financial for its proprietary finance software.
1998: Increased competition in small-loan finance leads company to enter market for loans up to $3,000.
2001: World's ''large loan'' portfolio increases 110 percent.

dled manually at each branch office. The advertising resulted in a substantial response during the Christmas 1996 season, but many borrowers were already overextended and World Acceptance could not approve many of the applications.

The Consequences of New Competition in the Mid-1990s

During the mid-1990s, World experienced greater competition in the small-loan consumer finance industry, as credit card companies and other lenders entered the subprime lending market. Lenders were attracted by the potentially high return on investment in a large, fragmented market, with an estimated 30 percent of Americans unable to qualify for credit cards. In order to obtain a high volume of business from the outset, these lenders issued loans based on weak underwriting standards. This new competition impacted World in several ways—for instance, attracting customers from World's repeat business. The weak underwriting standards allowed borrowers to carry a higher debt load than would otherwise be possible and World's customers had a more difficult time paying debt. World experienced a rise in delinquencies and charge-offs, a trend that affected the consumer finance industry as a whole.

With customers overextended by loans granted by competitors, World's charge-off rate increased to 11.2 percent of loans outstanding during 1996 and 13.7 percent in fiscal 1997. This is in contrast to a historical norm of 9 percent of loans receivable and a charge-off rate of 7.5 percent in 1995. The charge-offs had a negative impact on profits. After World experienced a 33.9 percent compound growth in net income from 1993 to 1996, net income declined 23.4 percent during fiscal 1997, to $8.1 million garnered from $75.4 million in revenues.

In fiscal 1997 World added 54 offices through acquisitions and new locations. In December 1996 the company purchased Personal Credit Plan of San Antonio, adding $11.5 million in loans receivable to World's portfolio. The largest acquisition to

date, Personal Credit, operated 30 offices in Texas and six in New Mexico, another new market for the company. World entered the Illinois and Missouri markets as well.

Changes in the small-loan consumer finance industry prompted World to look for new business opportunities. Rather than compete for small-loan business on the basis of high-risk loan practices, the company maintained its underwriting standards and restricted guidelines for ongoing renewal business. World chose to enter the market for larger consumer loans instead and in August 1998 the company acquired two loan offices, in Georgia and Tennessee, which offered loans up to $3,000. Although the yields were lower due to lower interest rates on larger loans, the risks were lower as well.

The negative consequences of loose underwriting practices in the subprime market resulted in a devaluation of World's stock value. The company's stock price peaked at $16.25 per share during 1996 and dropped to $5.63 at the end of fiscal 1997. World's history of profitability attracted investors interested in the long-term potential of the company, however. Mills Value Advisor of Richmond acquired a 17 percent interest and Wanger Asset Management of Chicago also made a significant investment. CEO Charles Walters maintained an approximately 10 percent stake.

By 1998 profitability improved as competition abated and loan losses declined. Charge-offs declined to 9.4 percent of loans receivable. In addition, amortization of intangible assets, applied as noncash charges to earnings since the management buyout in 1989, ended in May 1997. In 1998 World reported $8.1 million in net income from $80.6 million in total revenues.

Diversification Accompanying Expansion in the Early 2000s

World continued to expand operations during the early 2000s, adding new services and expanding its large-loan portfolio. In 1999 the company tested tax return preparation and electronic filing services in 40 offices. Pleased with the results, World expanded the service to nearly all offices in 2000, collecting $1 million in fees. The service complemented World's loan business, as tax preparation occurred primarily from mid-January to late February, the slowest time of the year for issuing loans. By 2003, tax preparation revenues reached $4 million.

World expanded its network of loan offices by acquiring and opening new offices. In April 2000, World acquired four offices in Kentucky, entering a new market and adding $7.5 million in gross loans receivable. Acquisitions in 2002 included six offices in Alabama, another new market for World. During fiscal 2000 through fiscal 2002 the company acquired 77 loan offices, though several were merged into existing locations. The company opened 26 new offices over the three-year period, operating a total of 441 offices at the close of fiscal 2002.

During 2001, several acquisitions involved businesses that provided large loans of up to $3,000, and World's large-loan portfolio increased by 110 percent. In addition to diversifying its portfolio, the low-interest, large loans provided many benefits. These included lower expense and loss ratios as well as a tendency for borrowers to purchase credit insurance with the larger loans. During 2002 and 2003 large loans continued to grow, increasing by 10 percent and 24.4 percent, respectively. Large loans accounted for 27 to 28 percent of loans outstanding, with small loans accounting for approximately 70 percent. World's average loan increased accordingly, to $687, with a nine-month average maturity.

At the end of fiscal 2003, World operated 470 offices in 11 states. The company reported revenues of $155.7 million and net income of $22.9 million. While a slow national economy created a rise in delinquencies and loan charge-offs, World's charge-off rate of 14.7 percent on $266.8 million in gross loans receivable was offset by lower interest rates available to banks. During 2004 and 2005, World planned to continue its pace of expansion with 25 acquisitions or new office locations per year.

Principal Subsidiaries

ParaData Financial Systems, Inc.; World Acceptance Corporation of Alabama; World Acceptance Corporation of Missouri; World Acceptance Corporation of Oklahoma; World Finance Corporation of Georgia; World Finance Corporation of Illinois; World Finance Corporation of Kentucky; World Finance Corporation of Louisiana; World Finance Corporation of New Mexico; World Finance Corporation of South Carolina, Inc.; World Finance Corporation of Tennessee; World Finance Corporation of Texas.

Principal Competitors

Associated First Capital Corporation; Cash America International, Inc.; Citigroup, Inc.; Household International, Inc.; The Commerce Group, Inc.; Regional Finance Corporation.

Further Reading

Cline, Kenneth, "CEO Leads Lobbying Efforts to Ease Regulatory Burden on Small Loan Firms," *American Banker,* May 16, 1994, p. 5.

——, "Suits Say Lender Fudged Rates by Leaving Out an Insurance Fee," *American Banker,* May 8, 1995, p. 4.

Hansell, Saul, "A Surge in Second Chance Finance," *New York Times,* March 17, 1996, p. F1.

Jean, Sheryl, "Consumer Finance Lenders in South Carolina Report Higher Profits," *The State,* August 21, 1998.

——, "Greenville, S.C.-Based Consumer Finance Firm Settles Class-Action Suit," *The State,* November 13, 1998.

Kulkosky, Edward, "Q&A: World Acceptance Exec Warns of Risks to Novices in SubPrime," *American Banker,* August 15, 1996, p. 12.

Moore, Pamela L., "South Carolina-Based Lender World Acceptance Suffers from Competition," *Charlotte Observer,* February 19, 1998.

Veverka, Amber, "Greenville, S.C. Lender Alters Small-Loan Focus, Moves into New Areas," *Charlotte Observer,* August 15, 1998.

—Mary Tradii

INDEX TO COMPANIES

Index to Companies

Listings in this index are arranged in alphabetical order under the company name. Company names beginning with a letter or proper name such as Eli Lilly & Co. will be found under the first letter of the company name. Definite articles (The, Le, La) are ignored for alphabetical purposes as are forms of incorporation that precede the company name (AB, NV). Company names printed in bold type have full, historical essays on the page numbers appearing in bold. Updates to entries that appeared in earlier volumes are signified by the notation (**upd.**). Company names in light type are references within an essay to that company, not full historical essays. This index is cumulative with volume numbers printed in bold type.

Pacific Gas and Electric Company, I 96;
V 685–87; **11** 270; **12** 100, 106; **19** 411;
25 415. *See also* PG&E Corporation.
Pacific Glass Corp., **48** 42
Pacific Guardian Life Insurance Co., **III**
289
Pacific Health Beverage Co., **I** 292
Pacific Home Furnishings, **14** 436
Pacific Indemnity Corp., **III** 220; **14** 108,
110; **16** 204
Pacific Integrated Healthcare, **53** 7
Pacific Lighting Corp., **IV** 492; **V** 682–84;
12 477; **16** 496; **50** 496. *See also*
Sempra Energy.
Pacific Linens, **13** 81–82
Pacific Link Communication, **18** 180
Pacific Lumber Company, **III** 254; **8**
348–50
Pacific Magazines and Printing, **7** 392
Pacific Mail Steamship Company, **6** 353
Pacific Manifolding Book/Box Co., **IV** 644
Pacific Media K.K., **18** 101
Pacific Metal Bearing Co., **I** 159
Pacific Monolothics Inc., **11** 520
Pacific National Insurance Co. *See* TIG
Holdings, Inc.
Pacific Natural Gas Corp., **9** 102
Pacific Northern, **6** 66
Pacific Northwest Bell Telephone Co., **V**
341; **25** 495
Pacific Northwest Laboratories, **10** 139
Pacific Northwest Pipeline Corporation, **9**
102–104, 540; **12** 144
Pacific Northwest Power Company, **6** 597
Pacific Pearl, **I** 417
Pacific Petroleums Ltd., **IV** 494; **9** 102
Pacific Plastics, Inc., **48** 334
Pacific Platers Ltd., **IV** 100
Pacific Power & Light Company. *See*
PacifiCorp.
Pacific Pride Bakeries, **19** 192
Pacific Recycling Co. Inc., **IV** 296; **19** 226;
23 225
Pacific Refining Co., **IV** 394–95
Pacific Resources Inc., **IV** 47; **22** 107
Pacific Sentinel Gold Corp., **27** 456
Pacific-Sierra Research, **I** 155
Pacific Silver Corp., **IV** 76
Pacific/Southern Wine & Spirits, **48** 392
Pacific Southwest Airlines Inc., **I** 132; **6**
132
Pacific Steel Ltd., **IV** 279; **19** 154
Pacific Stock Exchange, **48** 226
Pacific Sunwear of California, Inc., **28**
343–45; **47** 425
Pacific Telecom, Inc., **V** 689; **6 325–28**;
25 101; **54** 62
Pacific Telesis Group, **V 318–20**; **6** 324;
9 321; **11** 10–11; **14** 345, 347; **15** 125;
25 499; **26** 520; **29** 387; **47** 318
Pacific Teletronics, Inc., **7** 15
Pacific Towboat. *See* Puget Sound Tug and
Barge Company.
Pacific Trading Co., Ltd., **IV** 442
Pacific Trail Inc., **17** 462; **29** 293, 295–96
Pacific Western Extruded Plastics
Company, **17** 441. *See also* PW Eagle
Inc.
Pacific Western Oil Co., **IV** 537
Pacific Wine Co., **18** 71; **50** 112
PacifiCare Health Systems, Inc., **III** 85;
11 378–80; **25** 318

PacifiCorp, Inc., **V 688–90**; **6** 325–26,
328; **7** 376–78; **26 357–60 (upd.)**; **27**
327, 483, 485; **32** 372; **49** 363, 366
Package Products Company, Inc., **12** 150
Packaged Ice, Inc., **21** 338; **26** 449
Packaging Corporation of America, **I**
526; **12 376–78**, 397; **16** 191; **51**
282–85 (upd.)
Packard Bell Electronics, Inc., **I** 524; **II**
86; **10** 521, 564; **11** 413; **13 387–89**,
483; **21** 391; **23** 471; **57** 263
Packard Motor Co., **I** 81; **8** 74; **9** 17
Packer's Consolidated Press, **IV** 651
Packerland Packing Company, **7** 199, 201
Pacolet Manufacturing Company, **17** 327
Pact, **50** 175
PacTel. *See* Pacific Telesis Group.
Paddington Corp., **I** 248
Paddock Publications, Inc., **53 263–65**
PAFS. *See* Pacific Alaska Fuel Services.
Page, Bacon & Co., **II** 380; **12** 533
Page Boy Inc., **9** 320
PageAhead Software, **15** 492
Pageland Coca-Cola Bottling Works, **10**
222
PageMart Wireless, Inc., **18** 164, 166
Paging Network Inc., **11 381–83**; **39**
24–25; **41** 266–67
Pagoda Trading Company, Inc., **V** 351,
353; **20** 86
Paid Prescriptions, **9** 346
Paige Publications, **18** 66
PaineWebber Group Inc., **I** 245; **II**
444–46, 449; **III** 409; **13** 449; **22** 352,
404–07 (upd.), 542; **25** 433
Painter Carpet Mills, **13** 169
Painton Co., **II** 81
PairGain Technologies, **36** 299
Paisley Products, **32** 255
La Paix, **III** 273
Pak-a-Sak, **II** 661
Pak-All Products, Inc., **IV** 345
Pak Arab Fertilizers Ltd., **IV** 364
Pak Mail Centers, **18** 316
Pak-Paino, **IV** 315
Pak Sak Industries, **17** 310; **24** 160
Pak-Well, **IV** 282; **9** 261
Pakhoed Holding, N.V., **9** 532; **26** 420; **41**
339–40
Pakistan International Airlines
Corporation, **46 323–26**
Pakkasakku Oy, **IV** 471
Paknet, **11** 548
Pakway Container Corporation, **8** 268
PAL. *See* Philippine Airlines, Inc.
Pal Plywood Co., Ltd., **IV** 327
Palace Station Hotel & Casino. *See* Station
Casinos Inc.
Paladar, **56** 116
Palais Royal, Inc., **24** 456
Palatine Insurance Co., **III** 234
Palco Industries, **19** 440
Pale Ski & Sports GmbH, **22** 461
Palestine Coca-Cola Bottling Co., **13** 163
PALIC. *See* Pan-American Life Insurance
Company.
Pall Corporation, **9 396–98**
Pallas Textiles, **57** 207, 209
Palm Beach Holdings, **9** 157
Palm Harbor Homes, Inc., **39 316–18**
Palm, Inc., **34** 441, 445; **36 355–57**; **38**
433; **49** 184; **54** 312
Palm Shipping Inc., **25** 468–70
Palmafina, **IV** 498–99

Palmax, **47** 153
Palmer Communications, **25** 418
Palmer G. Lewis Co., **8** 135
Palmolive Co. *See* Colgate-Palmolive
Company.
Palo Alto Brewing, **22** 421
Palo Alto Products International, Inc., **29** 6
Palo Alto Research Center, **10** 510
Palomar Medical Technologies, Inc., **22**
408–10; **31** 124
PAM Group, **27** 462
Pamida Holdings Corporation, **15**
341–43
Pamour Porcupine Mines, Ltd., **IV** 164
Pampa OTT, **27** 473
The Pampered Chef, Ltd., **18 406–08**
Pamplemousse, **14** 225
Pamplin Corp. *See* R.B. Pamplin Corp.
Pan-Alberta Gas Ltd., **16** 11
Pan American Banks, **II** 336
Pan-American Life Insurance Company,
48 311–13
Pan American Petroleum & Transport Co.,
IV 368–70
Pan American World Airways, Inc., **I**
20, 31, 44, 64, 67, 89–90, 92, 99,
103–04, 112–13, **115–16**, 121, 124,
126, 129, 132, 248, 452, 530, 547–48;
III 536; **6** 51, 65–66, 71, 74–76, 81–82,
103–05, 110–11, 123, 129–30; **9** 231,
417; **10** 561; **11** 266; **12** 191, **379–81**
(upd.), 419; **13** 19; **14** 73; **24** 397; **29**
189; **36** 52–53; **39** 120; **50** 523
Pan European Publishing Co., **IV** 611
Pan Geo Atlas Corporation, **18** 513
Pan Ocean, **IV** 473
Pan Pacific Fisheries, **24** 114
Panacon Corporation, **III** 766; **22** 545
Panagra, **I** 547–48; **36** 53; **50** 523
Panalpina World Transport (Holding)
Ltd., **47 286–88**; **49** 81–82
Panama Refining and Petrochemical Co.,
IV 566
Panamerican Beverages, Inc., **47 289–91**;
54 74
PanAmSat Corporation, **18** 211, 213; **46**
327–29; **54** 157
Panarctic Oils, **IV** 494
Panasonic, **9** 180; **10** 125; **12** 470; **43** 427
Panatech Research & Development Corp.,
III 160
Panavia Aircraft GmbH, **24** 84, 86–87
Panavia Consortium, **I** 74–75
Panavision Inc., **24 372–74**; **28** 249; **38**
295
PanCanadian Petroleum Ltd., **27** 217; **45**
80
Pancho's Mexican Buffet, Inc., **46**
330–32
Panda Management Company, Inc., **35**
327–29
Pandair, **13** 20
Pandel, Inc., **8** 271
Pandick Press Inc., **23** 63
PanEnergy Corporation, **27** 128, 131
Panera Bread Company, **44** 186, **327–29**
Panerai, **27** 489
Panhandle Eastern Corporation, **I** 377,
569; **IV** 425; **V 691–92**; **10** 82–84; **11**
28; **14** 135; **17** 21
Panhandle Oil Corp., **IV** 498
Panhandle Power & Light Company, **6** 580
Panificadora Bimbo, **19** 191
AB Pankakoski, **IV** 274

The Sports Authority, Inc., 15 470; **16** 457–59; **17** 453; **18** 286; **24** 173; **43** 385–88 (upd.)
The Sports Club Company, 25 448–51
Sports Experts Inc., **II** 652
Sports Holdings Corp., **34** 217
Sports Inc., **14** 8; **33** 10
Sports Plus, **44** 192
Sports-Tech Inc., **21** 300
Sports Traders, Inc., **18** 208
Sportservice Corporation, **7** 133–35
The Sportsman's Guide, Inc., 36 443–46
Sportstown, Inc., **15** 470
Sportsystems Corporation, **7** 133, 135
Sprague Devices, Inc., **11** 84
Sprague Electric Company, **6** 261
Sprague Electric Railway and Motor Co., **II** 27; **12** 193
Sprague Technologies, **21** 520
Sprague, Warner & Co., **II** 571
Spray-Rite, **I** 366
Sprayon Products, **III** 745
Spraysafe, **29** 98
Sprecher & Schub, **9** 10
Spreckels Sugar Company, Inc., **32** 274, 277
Spring Co., **21** 96, 246
Spring Forge Mill, **8** 412
Spring Group plc, **54** 191–93
Spring Grove Services, **45** 139–40
Spring Industries, Inc., V 378–79
Spring Valley Brewery. *See* Kirin Brewery Company, Limited.
Springbok Editions, **IV** 621
Springer Verlag GmbH & Co., **IV** 611, 641
Springfield Bank, **9** 474
Springfield Gas Light Company, **38** 81
Springhouse Corp., **IV** 610
Springhouse Financial Corp., **III** 204
Springmaid International, Inc., **19** 421
Springs Industries, Inc., 19 419–22 (upd.); 29 132; **31** 199
Sprint Canada Inc., **44** 49
Sprint Communications Company, L.P., 9 478–80; 10 19, 57, 97, 201–03; **11** 183, 185, 500–01; **18** 32, 164–65, 569–70; **22** 19, 162; **24** 120, 122; **25** 102; **26** 17; **27** 365; **36** 167. *See also* Sprint Corporation; US Sprint Communications.
Sprint Corporation, 46 373–76 (upd.)
Sprint PCS, **33** 34, 36–37; **38** 433
Sprocket Systems, **50** 320
Sprout Group, **37** 121
Sprout-Matador A.S., **51** 25
Spruce Falls Power and Paper Co., **III** 40; **IV** 648; **16** 302, 304; **19** 284; **43** 256
SPS Technologies, Inc., 30 428–30
Spun Yarns, Inc., **12** 503
Spur Oil Co., **7** 362
SPX Corporation, 10 492–95; 47 374–79 (upd.)
SPZ, Inc., **26** 257
SQ Software, Inc., **10** 505
SQL Solutions, Inc., **10** 505
Square D Company, **18** 473
Square Industries, **18** 103, 105
Squibb Beech-Nut. *See* Beech-Nut Nutrition Corp.
Squibb Corporation, I 380–81, 631, 651, 659, 675, **695–97; III** 17, 19, 67; **8** 166; **9** 6–7; **13** 379–80; **16** 438–39[see_aslo]Bristol-Myers Squibb Company.

Squire Fashions Inc. *See* Norton McNaughton of Squire, Inc.
SR. *See* Southern Railway.
SR Beteilgungen Aktiengesellschaft, **III** 377
SRI International, Inc., 10 139; **57** 309, 311, **333–36**
SRI Strategic Resources Inc., **6** 310
SS Cars, Ltd. *See* Jaguar Cars, Ltd.
SS Lazio. *See* Societá Sportiva Lazio SpA.
SSA. *See* Stevedoring Services of America Inc.
Ssangyong Cement Industrial Co., Ltd., III 747–50; **IV** 536–37, 539
Ssangyong Motor Company, **34** 132
SSC&B-Lintas, **I** 16–17; **14** 315
SSC Benelux & Company, **52** 310–11
SSDS, Inc., **18** 537; **43** 433
SSI Medical Services, Inc., **10** 350
SSL International plc, 49 378–81
SSMC Inc., **II** 10
SSP Company, Inc., **17** 434
St. *See under* Saint
Staal Bankiers, **13** 544
STAAR Surgical Company, 57 337–39
Stackpole Fibers, **37** 427
Stadia Colorado Corporation, **18** 140
Stadt Corporation, **26** 109
Staefa Control System Limited, **6** 490
Staff International, **40** 157
StaffAmerica, Inc., **16** 50
Stafford-Lowdon, **31** 435
Stafford Old Bank, **II** 307
Stag Cañon Fuel Co., **IV** 177
Stage Stores, Inc., 24 456–59
Stagecoach Holdings plc, 30 431–33; 55 103
Stags' Leap Winery, **22** 80
Stahl-Urban Company, **8** 287–88
Stahlwerke Peine-Salzgitter AG, **IV** 201
Stahlwerke Röchling AG, **III** 694–95
Stahlwerke Südwestfalen AG, **IV** 89
Stakis plc, **49** 193
Stal-Astra GmbH, **III** 420
Staley Continental, **II** 582
Stamford Drug Group, **9** 68
Stamford FHI Acquisition Corp., **27** 117
Stamos Associates Inc., **29** 377
Stamps.com Inc., **34** 474
Stanadyne Automotive Corporation, 37 367–70
Stanadyne, Inc., **7** 336; **12** 344
StanCorp Financial Group, Inc., 56 345–48
Standard & Poor's Corp., **IV** 29, 482, 636–37; **12** 310; **25** 542
Standard Aero, **III** 509
Standard Aircraft Equipment, **II** 16
Standard Alaska, **7** 559
Standard Bank, **17** 324
Standard Box Co., **17** 357
Standard Brands, **I** 248; **II** 542, 544; **7** 365, 367; **18** 538
Standard Car Truck, **18** 5
Standard Chartered plc, II 298, 309, 319, **357–59**, 386; **10** 170; **47** 227; **48** 371–74 (upd.)
Standard Chemical Products, **III** 33
Standard Commercial Corporation, 12 110; **13** 490–92; **27** 126
Standard Drug Co., **V** 171
Standard Electric Time Company, **13** 233
Standard Electrica, **II** 13

Standard Elektrik Lorenz A.G., **II** 13, 70; **17** 353
Standard Equities Corp., **III** 98
Standard Federal Bank, 9 481–83
Standard Fire Insurance Co., **III** 181–82
Standard Fruit and Steamship Co. of New Orleans, **II** 491; **31** 168
Standard Gauge Manufacturing Company, **13** 233
Standard General Insurance, **III** 208
Standard Gypsum Corp., **19** 77
Standard Industrial Group Ltd., **IV** 658
Standard Insert Co., **28** 350
Standard Insulation Co., **I** 321
Standard Insurance Company, **III** 385; **56** 345
Standard Investing Corp., **III** 98
Standard Kollsman Industries Inc., **13** 461
Standard Life & Accident Insurance Company, **27** 47–48
Standard Life Assurance Company, III 358–61; **IV** 696–98
Standard Life Insurance Company, **11** 481
The Standard Life Insurance Company of New York, **56** 345
Standard Magnesium & Chemical Co., **IV** 123
Standard Metals Corp., **IV** 76
Standard Microsystems Corporation, 11 462–64
Standard Milling Co., **II** 497
Standard Motor Co., **III** 651
Standard Motor Products, Inc., 40 414–17
Standard of America Life Insurance Co., **III** 324
Standard of Georgia Insurance Agency, Inc., **10** 92
Standard Oil Co., **III** 470, 513; **IV** 46, 372, 399, 426–29, 434, 463, 478, 488–89, 530–31, 540, 542, 551, 574, 577–78, 657; **V** 590, 601; **6** 455; **7** 169–72, 263, 351, 414, 551; **8** 415; **10** 110, 289; **14** 21, 491–92; **25** 230; **27** 129; **50** 350. *See also* Exxon Corporation.
Standard Oil Co. (California), **II** 448; **IV** 18–19, 385–87, 403, 429, 464, 536–37, 545, 552, 560, 578; **6** 353; **7** 172, 352, 483; **13** 448
Standard Oil Co. (Illinois), **IV** 368
Standard Oil Co. (Indiana), **II** 262; **IV** 366, 368–71, 466–67; **7** 443; **10** 86; **14** 222
Standard Oil Co. (Minnesota), **IV** 368
Standard Oil Co. (New York), **IV** 428–29, 431, 460, 463–65, 485, 504, 537, 549, 558; **7** 171, 351–52
Standard Oil Co. of Iowa, **IV** 385
Standard Oil Co. of Kentucky, **IV** 387
Standard Oil Co. of New Jersey, **I** 334, 337, 370; **II** 16, 496; **IV** 378–79, 385–86, 400, 415–16, 419, 426–29, 431–33, 438, 460, 463–64, 488, 522, 531, 537–38, 544, 558, 565, 571; **V** 658; **7** 170–72, 253, 351; **13** 124; **17** 412–13; **24** 521
Standard Oil Co. of Ohio, **IV** 373, 379, 427, 452, 463, 522, 571; **7** 57, 171, 263; **12** 309; **21** 82; **24** 521
Standard Oil Development Co., **IV** 554
Standard Oil Trust, **IV** 31, 368, 375, 385–86, 427, 463
Standard Pacific Corporation, 52 319–22
Standard Plastics, **25** 312
Standard Printing Company, **19** 333

INDEX TO INDUSTRIES

Index to Industries

AUTOMOTIVE

CONGLOMERATES

FOOD SERVICES & RETAILERS

INSURANCE

PERSONAL SERVICES

PETROLEUM

PUBLISHING & PRINTING

REAL ESTATE

RUBBER & TIRE

TELECOMMUNICATIONS

TOBACCO

TRANSPORT SERVICES

WASTE SERVICES

GEOGRAPHIC INDEX

Geographic Index

Germany

United States

A & E Television Networks, 32
A & W Brands, Inc., 25
A-dec, Inc., 53
A. Schulman, Inc., 8; 49 (upd.)
A.B. Watley Group Inc., 45
A.B.Dick Company, 28
A.C. Moore Arts & Crafts, Inc., 30
A.G. Edwards, Inc., 8; 32
A.H. Belo Corporation, 10; 30 (upd.)
A.L. Pharma Inc., 12
A.M. Castle & Co., 25
A.O. Smith Corporation, 11; 40 (upd.)
A.T. Cross Company, 17; 49 (upd.)
AAF-McQuay Incorporated, 26
AAON, Inc., 22
AAR Corp., 28
Aaron Rents, Inc., 14; 35 (upd.)
AARP, 27
Aavid Thermal Technologies, Inc., 29
Abatix Corp., 57
Abbott Laboratories, I; 11 (upd.); 40 (upd.)
ABC Appliance, Inc., 10
ABC Carpet & Home Co. Inc., 26
ABC Family Worldwide, Inc., 52
ABC Rail Products Corporation, 18
ABC Supply Co., Inc., 22
Abercrombie & Fitch Co., 15; 35 (upd.)
Abigail Adams National Bancorp, Inc., 23
Abiomed, Inc., 47
ABM Industries Incorporated, 25 (upd.)
Abrams Industries Inc., 23
Academy of Television Arts & Sciences, Inc., 55
Academy Sports & Outdoors, 27
Acadian Ambulance & Air Med Services, Inc., 39
Acclaim Entertainment Inc., 24
ACCO World Corporation, 7; 51 (upd.)
ACE Cash Express, Inc., 33
Ace Hardware Corporation, 12; 35 (upd.)
Aceto Corp., 38
Ackerley Communications, Inc., 9
Acme-Cleveland Corp., 13
ACNielsen Corporation, 13; 38 (upd.)
Acorn Products, Inc., 55
Acsys, Inc., 44
Action Performance Companies, Inc., 27
Activision, Inc., 32
Acuson Corporation, 10; 36 (upd.)
Acxiom Corporation, 35
Adams Golf, Inc., 37
Adaptec, Inc., 31
ADC Telecommunications, Inc., 10; 30 (upd.)
Adelphia Communications Corporation, 17; 52 (upd.)
Administaff, Inc., 52
Adobe Systems Inc., 10; 33 (upd.)
Adolph Coors Company, I; 13 (upd.); 36 (upd.)
ADT Security Services, Inc., 12; 44 (upd.)
Adtran Inc., 22
Advance Auto Parts, Inc., 57
Advance Publications Inc., IV; 19 (upd.)
Advanced Marketing Services, Inc., 34
Advanced Micro Devices, Inc., 6; 30 (upd.)
Advanced Technology Laboratories, Inc., 9
Advanstar Communications, Inc., 57
Advanta Corporation, 8; 38 (upd.)
Advantica Restaurant Group, Inc., 27 (upd.)
Adventist Health, 53
Advo, Inc., 6; 53 (upd.)
Advocat Inc., 46
AEI Music Network Inc., 35
AEP Industries, Inc., 36

Aeronca Inc., 46
Aeroquip Corporation, 16
AES Corporation, The, 10; 13 (upd.); 53 (upd.)
Aetna, Inc., III; 21 (upd.)
AFC Enterprises, Inc., 32
Affiliated Foods Inc., 53
Affiliated Publications, Inc., 7
Affinity Group Holding Inc., 56
AFLAC Incorporated, 10 (upd.); 38 (upd.)
Ag-Chem Equipment Company, Inc., 17
AGCO Corp., 13
Agilent Technologies Inc., 38
Agway, Inc., 7; 21 (upd.)
AHL Services, Inc., 27
Air & Water Technologies Corporation, 6
Air Express International Corporation, 13
Air Methods Corporation, 53
Air Products and Chemicals, Inc., I; 10 (upd.)
Air Wisconsin Airlines Corporation, 55
Airborne Freight Corporation, 6; 34 (upd.)
Airgas, Inc., 54
AirTouch Communications, 11
AirTran Holdings, Inc., 22
AK Steel Holding Corporation, 19; 41 (upd.)
Akin, Gump, Strauss, Hauer & Feld, L.L.P., 33
Akorn, Inc., 32
Alamo Group Inc., 32
Alamo Rent A Car, Inc., 6; 24 (upd.)
Alaska Air Group, Inc., 6; 29 (upd.)
Alba-Waldensian, Inc., 30
Albany International Corporation, 8; 51 (upd.)
Alberto-Culver Company, 8; 36 (upd.)
Albertson's Inc., II; 7 (upd.); 30 (upd.)
Alco Health Services Corporation, III
Alco Standard Corporation, I
Alcoa Inc., 56 (upd.)
Aldila, 46
Aldus Corporation, 10
Alex Lee Inc., 18; 44 (upd.)
Alexander & Alexander Services Inc., 10
Alexander & Baldwin, Inc., 10; 40 (upd.)
Alexander's, Inc., 45
All American Communications Inc., 20
Alleghany Corporation, 10
Allegheny Energy, Inc., 38 (upd.)
Allegheny Ludlum Corporation, 8
Allegheny Power System, Inc., V
Allen Organ Company, 33
Allergan, Inc., 10; 30 (upd.)
Alliance Entertainment Corp., 17
Alliant Techsystems Inc., 8; 30 (upd.)
Allied Healthcare Products, Inc., 24
Allied Products Corporation, 21
Allied Signal Engines, 9
Allied Waste Industries, Inc., 50
Allied Worldwide, Inc., 49
AlliedSignal Inc., I; 22 (upd.)
Allison Gas Turbine Division, 9
Allou Health & Beauty Care, Inc., 28
Alloy, Inc., 55
Allstate Corporation, The, 10; 27 (upd.)
ALLTEL Corporation, 6; 46 (upd.)
Alltrista Corporation, 30
Allwaste, Inc., 18
Aloha Airlines, Incorporated, 24
Alpharma Inc., 35 (upd.)
Alpine Lace Brands, Inc., 18
AltaVista Company, 43
Altera Corporation, 18; 43 (upd.)
Alterra Healthcare Corporation, 42
Altron Incorporated, 20

Aluminum Company of America, IV; 20 (upd.)
Alvin Ailey Dance Foundation, Inc., 52
ALZA Corporation, 10; 36 (upd.)
AMAX Inc., IV
Amazon.com, Inc., 25; 56 (upd.)
AMB Property Corporation, 57
Amblin Entertainment, 21
AMC Entertainment, 12; 35 (upd.)
AMCORE Financial Inc., 44
Amdahl Corporation, III; 14 (upd.); 40 (upd.)
Amdocs Ltd., 47
Amedysis, Inc., 53
Amerada Hess Corporation, IV; 21 (upd.); 55 (upd.)
Amerco, 6
America Online, Inc., 10 ; 26 (upd.)
America West Holdings Corporation, 6; 34 (upd.)
America's Favorite Chicken Company, Inc., 7
American Airlines, I; 6 (upd.)
American Banknote Corporation, 30
American Bar Association, 35
American Biltrite Inc., 16; 43 (upd.)
American Brands, Inc., V
American Building Maintenance Industries, Inc., 6
American Business Information, Inc., 18
American Business Products, Inc., 20
American Cancer Society, The, 24
American Cast Iron Pipe Company, 50
American Classic Voyages Company, 27
American Coin Merchandising, Inc., 28
American Colloid Co., 13
American Crystal Sugar Company, 9; 32 (upd.)
American Cyanamid, I; 8 (upd.)
American Eagle Outfitters, Inc., 24; 55 (upd.)
American Electric Power Company, Inc., V; 45 (upd.)
American Express Company, II; 10 (upd.); 38 (upd.)
American Family Corporation, III
American Financial Group Inc., III; 48 (upd.)
American Foods Group, 43
American Furniture Company, Inc., 21
American General Corporation, III; 10 (upd.); 46 (upd.)
American General Finance Corp., 11
American Golf Corporation, 45
American Gramaphone LLC, 52
American Greetings Corporation, 7; 22 (upd.)
American Home Mortgage Holdings, Inc., 46
American Home Products, I; 10 (upd.)
American Homestar Corporation, 18; 41 (upd.)
American Institute of Certified Public Accountants (AICPA), 44
American International Group, Inc., III; 15 (upd.); 47 (upd.)
American Italian Pasta Company, 27
American Lawyer Media Holdings, Inc., 32
American Locker Group Incorporated, 34
American Lung Association, 48
American Maize-Products Co., 14
American Management Systems, Inc., 11
American Media, Inc., 27
American Medical Association, 39
American Medical International, Inc., III
American Medical Response, Inc., 39
American Motors Corporation, I

NOTES ON CONTRIBUTORS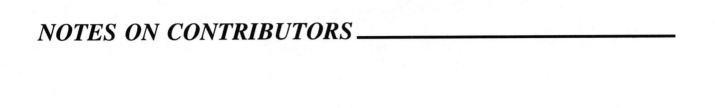

Notes on Contributors

BAXTER, Melissa Rigney. Indiana-based writer.

BIANCO, David P. Writer, editor, and publishing consultant.

BROWN, Erin. Montana-based writer and researcher.

BRYNILDSSEN, Shawna. Writer and editor based in Bloomington, Indiana.

COHEN, M. L. Novelist and researcher living in Paris.

COVELL, Jeffrey L. Seattle-based writer.

CULLIGAN, Susan B. Minnesota-based writer.

DINGER, Ed. Writer and editor based in Bronx, New York.

ESSEY-STAPLETON, Jodi. Illinois-based writer.

HALASZ, Robert. Former editor in chief of *World Progress* and *Funk & Wagnalls New Encyclopedia Yearbook*; author, *The U.S. Marines* (Millbrook Press, 1993).

INGRAM, Frederick C. Utah-based business writer who has contributed to *GSA Business, Appalachian Trailway News,* the *Encyclopedia of Business,* the *Encyclopedia of Global Industries,* the *Encyclopedia of Consumer Brands,* and other regional and trade publications.

LORENZ, Sarah Ruth. Minnesota-based writer.

PEIPPO, Kathleen. Minneapolis-based writer.

RHODES, Nelson. Editor, writer, and consultant in the Chicago area.

ROTHBURD, Carrie. Writer and editor specializing in corporate profiles, academic texts, and academic journal articles.

SALAMIE, David E. Part-owner of InfoWorks Development Group, a reference publication development and editorial services company.

STANFEL, Rebecca. Montana-based researcher and writer.

TRADII, Mary. Writer based in Denver, Colorado.

UHLE, Frank. Ann-Arbor-based writer, movie projectionist, disk jockey, and staff member of *Psychotronic Video* magazine.

WOODWARD, A. Wisconsin-based writer.